MW00610971

CORNERSTONE
B I B L I C A L
COMMENTARY

CORNERSTONE
BIBLICAL
COMMENTARY

The Gospel of Matthew

David L. Turner

The Gospel of Mark

Darrell L. Bock

GENERAL EDITOR
Philip W. Comfort

with the entire text of the
NEW LIVING TRANSLATION

TYNDALE HOUSE PUBLISHERS, INC. CAROL STREAM, ILLINOIS

Cornerstone Biblical Commentary, Volume 11

Visit Tyndale's exciting Web site at www.tyndale.com

Tyndale's quill logo is a trademark of Tyndale House Publishers, Inc.

Designed by Luke Daab and Timothy R. Botts.

Library of Congress Cataloging-in-Publication Data

Cornerstone biblical commentary.
   p. cm.
  Includes bibliographical references and index.
  ISBN-13: 978-0-8423-3437-2 (hc : alk. paper)
  ISBN-10: 0-8423-3437-8 (hc : alk. paper)
  1. Biblical—Commentaries. I. Turner, David L. II. Bock, Darrell L.
  BS491.3.C67 2006
  200.7′7 dc22   2005026928

Printed in China

12 11 10 09 08 07 06
  9   8   7   6   5   4   3   2   1

CONTENTS

CONTRIBUTORS TO VOLUME 11

Matthew: David L. Turner
BA, Cedarville University;
ThD, Grace Theological Seminary;
MPhil, PhD Candidate, Hebrew Union College—Jewish Institute of Religion;
Professor of New Testament, Grand Rapids Theological Seminary.

Mark: Darrell L. Bock
BA, University of Texas;
ThM, Dallas Theological Seminary;
PhD, University of Aberdeen; two years post-doctoral study at the University of Tübingen;
Research Professor of New Testament Studies, Dallas Theological Seminary.

GENERAL EDITOR'S PREFACE

The *Cornerstone Biblical Commentary* is based on the second edition of the New Living Translation (2004). Nearly 100 scholars from various church backgrounds and from several countries (United States, Canada, England, and Australia) participated in the creation of the NLT. Many of these same scholars are contributors to this commentary series. All the commentators, whether participants in the NLT or not, believe that the Bible is God's inspired word and have a desire to make God's word clear and accessible to his people.

This Bible commentary is the natural extension of our vision for the New Living Translation, which we believe is both exegetically accurate and idiomatically powerful. The NLT attempts to communicate God's inspired word in a lucid English translation of the original languages so that English readers can understand and appreciate the thought of the original writers. In the same way, the *Cornerstone Biblical Commentary* aims at helping teachers, pastors, students, and lay people understand every thought contained in the Bible. As such, the commentary focuses first on the words of Scripture, then on the theological truths of Scripture—inasmuch as the words express the truths.

The commentary itself has been structured in such a way as to help readers get at the meaning of Scripture, passage by passage, through the entire Bible. Each Bible book is prefaced by a substantial book introduction that gives general historical background important for understanding. Then the reader is taken through the Bible text, passage by passage, starting with the New Living Translation text printed in full. This is followed by a section called "Notes," wherein the commentator helps the reader understand the Hebrew or Greek behind the English of the NLT, interacts with other scholars on important interpretive issues, and points the reader to significant textual and contextual matters. The "Notes" are followed by the "Commentary," wherein each scholar presents a lucid interpretation of the passage, giving special attention to context and major theological themes.

The commentators represent a wide spectrum of theological positions within the evangelical community. We believe this is good because it reflects the rich variety in Christ's church. All the commentators uphold the authority of God's word and believe it is essential to heed the old adage: "Wholly apply yourself to the Scriptures and apply them wholly to you." May this commentary help you know the truths of Scripture, and may this knowledge help you "grow in your knowledge of God and Jesus our Lord" (2 Pet 1:2, NLT).

PHILIP W. COMFORT
GENERAL EDITOR

ABBREVIATIONS

GENERAL ABBREVIATIONS

b.	Babylonian Gemara	Gr.	Greek	no.	number
bar.	baraita	Heb.	Hebrew	NT	New Testament
c.	*circa*, around, approximately	ibid.	*ibidem*, in the same place	OL	Old Latin
				OS	Old Syriac
cf.	*confer*, compare	i.e.	*id est*, the same	OT	Old Testament
ch, chs	chapter, chapters	in loc.	*in loco*, in the place cited	p., pp.	page, pages
contra	in contrast to			pl.	plural
DSS	Dead Sea Scrolls	lit.	literally	Q	Quelle ("Sayings" as Gospel source)
ed.	edition, editor	LXX	Septuagint		
e.g.	*exempli gratia*, for example	𝔐	Majority Text	rev.	revision
		m.	Mishnah	sg.	singular
ET	English translation	masc.	masculine	*t.*	Tosefta
et al.	*et alli*, and others	mg	margin	v., vv.	verse, verses
fem.	feminine	MS	manuscript	vid.	*videur*, it seems
ff	following (verses, pages)	MSS	manuscripts	viz.	*videlicet*, namely
		MT	Masoretic Text	vol.	volume
fl.	flourished	n.d.	no date	*y.*	Jerusalem Gemara
		neut.	neuter		

ABBREVIATIONS FOR BIBLE TRANSLATIONS

ASV	American Standard Version	NCV	New Century Version	NKJV	New King James Version
CEV	Contemporary English Version	NEB	New English Bible	NRSV	New Revised Standard Version
ESV	English Standard Version	NIV	New International Version	NLT	New Living Translation
GW	God's Word	NIrV	New International Reader's Version	REB	Revised English Bible
HCSB	Holman Christian Standard Bible	NJB	New Jerusalem Bible	RSV	Revised Standard Version
JB	Jerusalem Bible	NJPS	The New Jewish Publication Society Translation (*Tanakh*)	TEV	Today's English Version
KJV	King James Version				
NAB	New American Bible			TLB	The Living Bible
NASB	New American Standard Bible				

ABBREVIATIONS FOR DICTIONARIES, LEXICONS, COLLECTIONS OF TEXTS, ORIGINAL LANGUAGE EDITIONS

ABD *Anchor Bible Dictionary* (6 vols., Freedman) [1992]

ANEP *The Ancient Near East in Pictures* (Pritchard) [1965]

ANET *Ancient Near Eastern Texts Relating to the Old Testament* (Pritchard) [1969]

ANF *Ante-Nicene Fathers*

BAGD *Greek-English Lexicon of the New Testament and Other Early Christian Literature*, 2nd ed. (Bauer, Arndt, Gingrich, Danker) [1979]

BDAG *Greek-English Lexicon of the New Testament and Other Early Christian Literature*, 3rd ed. (Bauer, Danker, Arndt, Gingrich) [2000]

BDB *A Hebrew and English Lexicon of the Old Testament* (Brown, Driver, Briggs) [1907]

BDF *A Greek Grammar of the New Testament and Other Early Christian Literature* (Blass, Debrunner, Funk) [1961]

BHS *Biblia Hebraica Stuttgartensia* (Elliger and Rudolph) [1983]

CAD *Assyrian Dictionary of the Oriental Institute of the University of Chicago* [1956]

COS *The Context of Scripture* (3 volumes, Hallo and Younger) [1997–2002]

DBI *Dictionary of Biblical Imagery* (Ryken, Wilhoit, Longman) [1998]

DBT *Dictionary of Biblical Theology* (2nd edition, Leon-Dufour) [1972]

DCH *Dictionary of Classical Hebrew* (5 volumes, D. Clines) [2000]

DJD *Discoveries in the Judean Desert* [1955–]

DJG *Dictionary of Jesus and the Gospels* (Green, McKnight, Marshall) [1992]

DOTP *Dictionary of the Old Testament: Pentateuch.* (T. Alexander, D.W. Baker) [2003]

DPL *Dictionary of Paul and His Letters* (Hawthorne, Martin, Reid) [1993]

EDNT *Exegetical Dictionary of the New Testament* (3 vols., H. Balz, G. Schneider. ET) [1990–1993]

HALOT *The Hebrew and Aramaic Lexicon of the Old Testament* (L. Koehler, W. Baumgartner, J. Stamm; trans. M. Richardson) [1994–1999]

IBD *Illustrated Bible Dictionary* (3 vols., Douglas, Wiseman) [1980]

IDB *The Interpreter's Dictionary of the Bible* (4 vols., Buttrick) [1962]

ISBE *International Standard Bible Encyclopedia* (4 vols., Bromiley) [1979–1988]

KBL *Lexicon in Veteris Testamenti libros* (Koehler, Baumgartner) [1958]

LCL *Loeb Classical Library*

L&N *Greek-English Lexicon of the New Testament: Based on Semantic Domains* (Louw and Nida) [1989]

LSJ *A Greek-English Lexicon* (9th edition, Liddell, Scott, Jones) [1996]

MM *The Vocabulary of the Greek New Testament* (Moulton and Milligan) [1930; 1997]

NA^{26} *Novum Testamentum Graece* (26th edition, Nestle-Aland) [1979]

NA^{27} *Novum Testamentum Graece* (27th edition, Nestle-Aland) [1993]

NBD *New Bible Dictionary* (2nd edition, Douglas, Hillyer) [1982]

NIDB *New International Dictionary of the Bible* (Douglas, Tenney) [1987]

NIDBA *New International Dictionary of Biblical Archaeology* (Blaiklock and Harrison) [1983]

NIDNTT *New International Dictionary of New Testament Theology* (4 vols., C. Brown) [1975–1985]

NIDOTTE *New International Dictionary of Old Testament Theology and Exegesis* (5 vols., W. A. VanGemeren) [1997]

PGM *Papyri Graecae magicae: Die griechischen Zauberpapyri.* (Preisendanz) [1928]

PG *Patrologia Graecae* (J. P. Migne) [1857–1886]

TBD *Tyndale Bible Dictionary* (Elwell, Comfort) [2001]

TDNT *Theological Dictionary of the New Testament* (10 vols., Kittel, Friedrich; trans. Bromiley) [1964–1976]

TDOT *Theological Dictionary of the Old Testament* (8 vols., Botterweck, Ringgren; trans. Willis, Bromiley, Green) [1974–]

TLOT *Theological Lexicon of the Old Testament* (3 vols., E. Jenni) [1997]

TWOT *Theological Wordbook of the Old Testament* (2 vols., Harris, Archer) [1980]

UBS^3 *United Bible Societies' Greek New Testament* (third edition, Metzger et al) [1975]

UBS^4 *United Bible Societies' Greek New Testament* (fourth corrected edition, Metzger et al) [1993]

WH *The New Testament in the Original Greek* (Westcott and Hort) [1882]

ABBREVIATIONS FOR BOOKS OF THE BIBLE

Old Testament

Gen	Genesis	1 Sam	1 Samuel	Esth	Esther
Exod	Exodus	2 Sam	2 Samuel	Ps, Pss	Psalm, Psalms
Lev	Leviticus	1 Kgs	1 Kings	Prov	Proverbs
Num	Numbers	2 Kgs	2 Kings	Eccl	Ecclesiastes
Deut	Deuteronomy	1 Chr	1 Chronicles	Song	Song of Songs
Josh	Joshua	2 Chr	2 Chronicles	Isa	Isaiah
Judg	Judges	Ezra	Ezra	Jer	Jeremiah
Ruth	Ruth	Neh	Nehemiah	Lam	Lamentations

Ezek	Ezekiel	Obad	Obadiah	Zeph	Zephaniah
Dan	Daniel	Jonah	Jonah	Hag	Haggai
Hos	Hosea	Mic	Micah	Zech	Zechariah
Joel	Joel	Nah	Nahum	Mal	Malachi
Amos	Amos	Hab	Habakkuk		

New Testament

Matt	Matthew	Eph	Ephesians	Heb	Hebrews
Mark	Mark	Phil	Philippians	Jas	James
Luke	Luke	Col	Colossians	1 Pet	1 Peter
John	John	1 Thess	1 Thessalonians	2 Pet	2 Peter
Acts	Acts	2 Thess	2 Thessalonians	1 John	1 John
Rom	Romans	1 Tim	1 Timothy	2 John	2 John
1 Cor	1 Corinthians	2 Tim	2 Timothy	3 John	3 John
2 Cor	2 Corinthians	Titus	Titus	Jude	Jude
Gal	Galatians	Phlm	Philemon	Rev	Revelation

Deuterocanonical

Bar	Baruch	1–2 Esdr	1–2 Esdras	Pr Man	Prayer of Manasseh
Add Dan	Additions to Daniel	Add Esth	Additions to Esther	Ps 151	Psalm 151
Pr Azar	Prayer of Azariah	Ep Jer	Epistle of Jeremiah	Sir	Sirach
Bel	Bel and the Dragon	Jdt	Judith	Tob	Tobit
Sg Three	Song of the Three Children	1–2 Macc	1–2 Maccabees	Wis	Wisdom of Solomon
Sus	Susanna	3–4 Macc	3–4 Maccabees		

MANUSCRIPTS AND LITERATURE FROM QUMRAN

Initial numerals followed by "Q" indicate particular caves at Qumran. For example, the notation 4Q267 indicates text 267 from cave 4 at Qumran. Further, 1QS 4:9-10 indicates column 4, lines 9-10 of the *Rule of the Community*; and 4Q166 1 ii 2 indicates fragment 1, column ii, line 2 of text 166 from cave 4. More examples of common abbreviations are listed below.

CD	Cairo Geniza copy of the *Damascus Document*	1QIsa[b]	Isaiah copy [b]	4QLam[a]	Lamentations
		1QM	*War Scroll*	11QPs[a]	Psalms
		1QpHab	*Pesher Habakkuk*	11QTemple[a,b]	*Temple Scroll*
1QH	*Thanksgiving Hymns*	1QS	*Rule of the Community*	11QtgJob	*Targum of Job*
1QIsa[a]	Isaiah copy [a]				

IMPORTANT NEW TESTAMENT MANUSCRIPTS

(all dates given are AD; ordinal numbers refer to centuries)

Significant Papyri (𝔓 = Papyrus)

𝔓1 Matt 1; early 3rd
𝔓4+𝔓64+𝔓67 Matt 3, 5, 26; Luke 1-6; late 2nd
𝔓5 John 1, 16, 20; early 3rd
𝔓13 Heb 2-5, 10-12; early 3rd
𝔓15+𝔓16 (probably part of same codex) 1 Cor 7-8, Phil 3-4; late 3rd

𝔓20 James 2-3; 3rd
𝔓22 John 15-16; mid 3rd
𝔓23 James 1; c. 200
𝔓27 Rom 8-9; 3rd
𝔓30 1 Thess 4-5; 2 Thess 1; early 3rd
𝔓32 Titus 1-2; late 2nd
𝔓37 Matt 26; late 3rd

𝔓39 John 8; first half of 3rd
𝔓40 Rom 1-4, 6, 9; 3rd
𝔓45 Gospels and Acts; early 3rd
𝔓46 Paul's Major Epistles (less Pastorals); late 2nd
𝔓47 Rev 9-17; 3rd

𝔓49+𝔓65 Eph 4-5; 1 Thess 1-2; 3rd
𝔓52 John 18; c. 125
𝔓53 Matt 26, Acts 9-10; middle 3rd
𝔓66 John; late 2nd
𝔓70 Matt 2-3, 11-12, 24; 3rd
𝔓72 1-2 Peter, Jude; c. 300

𝔓74 Acts, General Epistles; 7th
𝔓75 Luke and John; c. 200
𝔓77+𝔓103 (probably part of same codex) Matt 13-14, 23; late 2nd
𝔓87 Phlm; late 2nd
𝔓90 John 18-19; late 2nd
𝔓91 Acts 2-3; 3rd

𝔓92 Eph 1, 2 Thess 1; c. 300
𝔓98 Rev 1:13-20; late 2nd
𝔓100 James 3-5; c. 300
𝔓101 Matt 3-4; 3rd
𝔓104 Matt 21; 2nd
𝔓106 John 1; 3rd
𝔓115 Rev 2-3, 5-6, 8-15; 3rd

Significant Uncials

ℵ (Sinaiticus) most of NT; 4th
A (Alexandrinus) most of NT; 5th
B (Vaticanus) most of NT; 4th
C (Ephraemi Rescriptus) most of NT with many lacunae; 5th
D (Bezae) Gospels, Acts; 5th
D (Claromontanus), Paul's Epistles; 6th (different MS than Bezae)
E (Laudianus 35) Acts; 6th
F (Augensis) Paul's Epistles; 9th
G (Boernerianus) Paul's Epistles; 9th

H (Coislinianus) Paul's Epistles; 6th
I (Freerianus or Washington) Paul's Epistles; 5th
L (Regius) Gospels; 8th
Q (Guelferbytanus B) Luke, John; 5th
P (Porphyrianus) Acts—Revelation; 9th
T (Borgianus) Luke, John; 5th
W (Washingtonianus or the Freer Gospels) Gospels; 5th
Z (Dublinensis) Matthew; 6th
037 (Δ; Sangallensis) Gospels; 9th

038 (Θ; Koridethi) Gospels; 9th
040 (Ξ; Zacynthius) Luke; 6th
043 (Φ; Beratinus) Matt, Mark; 6th
044 (Ψ; Athous Laurae) Gospels, Acts, Paul's Epistles; 9th
048 Acts, Paul's Epistles, General Epistles; 5th
0171 Matt 10, Luke 22; c. 300
0189 Acts 5; c. 200

Significant Minuscules

1 Gospels, Acts, Paul's Epistles; 12th
33 All NT except Rev; 9th
81 Acts, Paul's Epistles, General Epistles; 1044
565 Gospels; 9th
700 Gospels; 11th

1424 (or Family 1424—a group of 29 manuscripts sharing nearly the same text) most of NT; 9th-10th
1739 Acts, Paul's Epistles; 10th
2053 Rev; 13th
2344 Rev; 11th

f¹ (a family of manuscripts including 1, 118, 131, 209) Gospels; 12th-14th
f¹³ (a family of manuscripts including 13, 69, 124, 174, 230, 346, 543, 788, 826, 828, 983, 1689, 1709—known as the Ferrar group) Gospels; 11th-15th

Significant Ancient Versions

SYRIAC (SYR)
syrᶜ (Syriac Curetonian) Gospels; 5th
syrˢ (Syriac Sinaiticus) Gospels; 4th
syrʰ (Syriac Harklensis) Entire NT; 616

OLD LATIN (IT)
itᵃ (Vercellenis) Gospels; 4th
itᵇ (Veronensis) Gospels; 5th
itᵈ (Cantabrigiensis—the Latin text of Bezae) Gospels, Acts, 3 John; 5th
itᵉ (Palantinus) Gospels; 5th
itᵏ (Bobiensis) Matthew, Mark; c. 400

COPTIC (COP)
copᵇᵒ (Boharic—north Egypt)
copᶠᵃʸ (Fayyumic—central Egypt)
copˢᵃ (Sahidic—southern Egypt)

OTHER VERSIONS
arm (Armenian)
eth (Ethiopic)
geo (Georgian)

TRANSLITERATION AND NUMBERING SYSTEM

Note: For words and roots from non-biblical languages (e.g., Arabic, Ugaritic), only approximate transliterations are given.

HEBREW/ARAMAIC

Consonants

א	aleph	= '	מ, ם	mem	= m
ב, בּ	beth	= b	נ, ן	nun	= n
ג, גּ	gimel	= g	ס	samekh	= s
ד, דּ	daleth	= d	ע	ayin	= '
ה	he	= h	פ, פּ, ף	pe	= p
ו	waw	= w	צ, ץ	tsadhe	= ts
ז	zayin	= z	ק	qoph	= q
ח	heth	= kh	ר	resh	= r
ט	teth	= t	שׁ	shin	= sh
י	yodh	= y	שׂ	sin	= s
כ, כּ, ך	kaph	= k	ת, תּ	taw	= t, th (spirant)
ל	lamedh	= l			

Vowels

ַ	patakh	= a	ָ	qamets khatuf	= o
ַה	furtive patakh	= a		holem	= o
ָ	qamets	= a	וֹ	full holem	= o
ָה	final qamets he	= ah	ֻ	short qibbuts	= u
ֶ	segol	= e	ֻ	long qibbuts	= u
ֵ	tsere	= e	וּ	shureq	= u
ֵי	tsere yod	= e	ֲ	khatef patakh	= a
ִ	short hireq	= i	ֳ	khatef qamets	= o
ִ	long hireq	= i	ְ	vocalic shewa	= e
ִי	hireq yod	= i	ַי	patakh yodh	= a

Greek

α	alpha	= a	ε	epsilon	= e
β	beta	= b	ζ	zeta	= z
γ	gamma	= g, n (before γ, κ, ξ, χ)	η	eta	= ē
δ	delta	= d	θ	theta	= th
			ι	iota	= i

κ	kappa	= k		τ	tau	= t
λ	lamda	= l		υ	upsilon	= u
μ	mu	= m		φ	phi	= ph
ν	nu	= n		χ	chi	= ch
ξ	ksi	= x		ψ	psi	= ps
ο	omicron	= o		ω	omega	= ō
π	pi	= p			rough	= h (with
ρ	rho	= r (ῥ = rh)			breathing	vowel or
σ, ς	sigma	= s			mark	diphthong)

THE TYNDALE-STRONG'S NUMBERING SYSTEM

The Cornerstone Biblical Commentary series uses a word-study numbering system to give both newer and more advanced Bible students alike quicker, more convenient access to helpful original-language tools (e.g., concordances, lexicons, and theological dictionaries). Those who are unfamiliar with the ancient Hebrew, Aramaic, and Greek alphabets can quickly find information on a given word by looking up the appropriate index number. Advanced students will find the system helpful because it allows them to quickly find the lexical form of obscure conjugations and inflections.

There are two main numbering systems used for biblical words today. The one familiar to most people is the Strong's numbering system (made popular by the *Strong's Exhaustive Concordance to the Bible*). Although the original Strong's system is still quite useful, the most up-to-date research has shed new light on the biblical languages and allows for more precision than is found in the original Strong's system. The Cornerstone Biblical Commentary series, therefore, features a newly revised version of the Strong's system, the Tyndale-Strong's numbering system. The Tyndale-Strong's system brings together the familiarity of the Strong's system and the best of modern scholarship. In most cases, the original Strong's numbers are preserved. In places where new research dictates, new or related numbers have been added.[1]

The second major numbering system today is the Goodrick-Kohlenberger system used in a number of study tools published by Zondervan. In order to give students broad access to a number of helpful tools, the Commentary provides index numbers for the Zondervan system as well.

The different index systems are designated as follows:

TG Tyndale-Strong's Greek number   ZH Zondervan Hebrew number
ZG Zondervan Greek number   TA Tyndale-Strong's Aramaic number
TH Tyndale-Strong's Hebrew number   ZA Zondervan Aramaic number

So in the example, "love" *agapē* [TG26, ZG27], the first number is the one to use with Greek tools keyed to the Tyndale-Strong's system, and the second applies to tools that use the Zondervan system.

---

1. Generally, one may simply use the original four-digit Strong's number to identify words in tools using Strong's system. If a Tyndale-Strong's number is followed by capital a letter (e.g., TG1692A), it generally indicates an added subdivision of meaning for the given term. Whenever a Tyndale-Strong's number has a number following a decimal point (e.g., TG2013.1), it reflects an instance where new research has yielded a separate, new classification of use for a biblical word. Forthcoming tools from Tyndale House Publishers will include these entries, which were not part of the original Strong's system.

The Gospel of
Matthew

DAVID L. TURNER

INTRODUCTION TO
Matthew

AS THE FIRST GOSPEL in the Christian canon, Matthew has received a great deal of attention through the centuries (Luz 1994). Indeed, Massuax (1990) has argued that Matthew is the New Testament book that most influenced the early church. Matthew's prominence is due to some extent to its unique structure, which focuses the reader's attention on the Sermon on the Mount and four other major discourses of Jesus. The history of the interpretation of Matthew is outside the scope of the present volume, but it is clear that through the centuries, the first Gospel has occupied the minds of many great expositors.

Nevertheless, by the twentieth century Matthean studies had become somewhat passé, due largely to the dominance of the Marcan priority view of the synoptic problem and the ensuing focus on Mark as purportedly embodying an earlier and more authentic version of the life and teaching of the historical Jesus. More recently, however, Matthew has begun to receive more attention, and several major commentaries have been written, among them those by Beare (1981), Blomberg (1992), Davies and Allison (1988, 1991, 1997), France (1985), Garland (1993), Gundry (1982, 1994), Hagner (1993, 1995), Harrington (1991), Keener (1999), Luz (1989, 2001), Meier (1978, 1980), Morris (1992), Nolland (2005), Overman (1996), and Simonetti (2001, 2002). This renewed interest in Matthew is likely due to the rise of the disciplines of redaction and narrative criticism and to the increasing awareness of Matthew's Jewish roots.

With these fine works on Matthew readily available, one may wonder why this one has been written. Many commentaries on Matthew embody a doctrinaire acceptance of the view that Matthew is rewriting and expanding Mark. Be that as it may, it is doubtful that the original readers of Matthew held it in one hand and Mark in the other, assuming that Matthew could not be understood apart from Mark. Thus, the present commentary seeks to understand Matthew in its own right, utilizing the discipline that has come to be known as narrative criticism (Powell 1990). This method of literary study attempts to relate the parts of a Gospel to the whole of it rather than operating from plausible yet unprovable hypotheses about the dependence of one Gospel upon another. Additionally, this commentary attempts to explain Matthew in the context of Second Temple Judaism, which had not yet become unified by the ascendancy of the Jabneh (Jamnia) rabbis after the AD 70 destruction of Jerusalem (cf. Lewis in Freedman 1992:3.634-37). It is written from the perspective argued in scholarly studies by Overman (1990b), Saldarini (1994), and Sim (1998) to the effect that Matthew was written to a group of Christian Jews who were still in contact with non-Christian Jews in the synagogue. This view seems to avoid the anachronistic reading of Matthew as promoting a new and distinct religion in opposition to a monolithic old religion, Judaism. In other words, Matthew and his community were part of an ongoing process in which Pharisees, Sadducees, Essenes, Jesus' followers, and others were presenting divergent and competing versions of Judaism. Matthew should not be read from a later perspective that reflects the results of this process after the "parting of the way" between Christianity and Judaism in the second century. Rather, Matthew should be read as the voice of the first "Jews for Jesus," as it were, during a time of much diversity within Judaism.

The origins of the Gospel of Matthew are not easily ascertained. Matthew is anonymous, as are the other three Gospels. One can only make educated guesses about the author, recipients, and setting of this Gospel. Such guesses amount to hypotheses that are formed by noting the book's grammar, syntax, and literary style; studying its distinctive themes; reading "between the lines"; and assessing the patristic traditions about the book.

AUTHOR

Though the Gospel of Matthew is anonymous, it seems clear that it was ascribed to Matthew the apostle by the first quarter of the second century AD. Notable ancient manuscripts have titles that ascribe the book to the apostle Matthew (Davies and Allison 1988:129). Patristic tradition univocally agrees with this ascription. Eusebius' *Ecclesiastical History* (early- to mid-fourth century AD) cites Papias (3.39; early second century), Clement of Alexandria (6.14; early third century), and Origen (6.25.4; mid third-century) to this effect. The words of Irenaeus (late second century) agree (*Against Heresies* 3.1.1; cf. Eusebius, *Ecclesiastical History* 5.8.2). Additional fourth century testimony to this effect may be found in Cyril of Jerusalem (*Catechesis* 14), Epiphanius (*Heresies* 30.3), and Jerome (*Prologue to Matthew*). The remarkable fact that some patristic tradition posits that Matthew was originally written in Hebrew will be discussed later under Canonicity and Textual History.

The patristic testimony aside, most scholars are led by the Jewish orientation of Matthew to conclude that its author was a Jewish Christian. Perhaps "Christian Jew" is a more historically accurate term. But there is a minority view that asserts that Matthew's Jewish trappings are the literary creation of a Gentile author's polemics against Judaism (Meier 1978:17-25).

DATE

It is very likely that there are allusions to Matthew in Ignatius (late first/early second century AD) and in the *Didache* (early second century AD). When these allusions are taken in conjunction with Papias' testimony (cited below), it seems clear that Matthew was well known by the early second century. Accordingly, the Gospel must have been written by the turn of the first century AD at the latest. The current scholarly consensus, based on the Marcan priority view of Gospel relationships, places

Matthew's origin in the eighties or nineties AD. In some cases, this view is buttressed by the idea that Matthew 24–25 constitutes a *vaticinium ex eventu* (prophecy after the event), written after the destruction of Jerusalem in AD 70. Additionally, it is sometimes argued that the historical situation reflected in Matthew is the conflict of the developing church with the formative rabbinic Judaism that emanated from the council of Jamnia (Jabneh) after the destruction of Jerusalem.

However, if one accepts the patristic testimony to apostolic authorship, the date will probably need to be set earlier. Additionally, if one takes Matthew 24–25 as an authentic word of Jesus, not as prophecy after the event, there is no need to date the Gospel after AD 70. And if one is not convinced of Matthew's dependence upon Mark, there is another reason for an earlier date. Noteworthy scholars who favor a pre- AD 70 Matthew include C. Blomberg, D. A. Carson, R. H. Gundry, G. Maier, B. Reicke, and J. A. T. Robinson. But these scholars are generally not dogmatic.

OCCASION OF WRITING AND AUDIENCE

Every student of Matthew is compelled to draw some conclusion about the relationship of this Gospel's recipients to Judaism. Matthew's presentation of a Jesus who came not to destroy but to fulfill the law, and his formulaic portrayal of the fulfillment of the Hebrew Scriptures in Jesus' life make the issue unavoidable. Scholars are divided, with some convinced that Matthew's community contained many Gentiles and had already separated from the synagogue (Gundry, Stanton), and others holding the opposite view that Matthew's community was largely Jewish and was still connected with the synagogue (Harrington, Overman, Saldarini, Sigal, Sim). And there are those who occupy middle ground, arguing that Matthew can be satisfactorily explained only when it is viewed against the background of an embattled minority in the process of leaving the synagogue (Hagner 1993:lxxxi). In this commentary, I maintain the view that Matthew's community was still engaged with the synagogue.

While many theories have been proposed, the location of Matthew's community will likely never be known with anything approaching certainty. Many have advocated the city of Antioch, but others suggest Tyre or Sidon (Kilpatrick), Galilee (Overman), or even Pella in Transjordan (Slingerland). It is a happy fact that grasping the message of the book does not depend on knowing the location of its original recipients.

The occasion of the Gospel's writing and its purposes are, of course, not explicitly stated anywhere in it and can only be approximated in hypotheses inferred from the text. Assuming that the audience is a Christian Jewish community, it is evidently a community that needs to understand how the life of Jesus the Messiah "fulfilled" the Hebrew Bible (see "Major Themes" later in this introduction) and how Jesus' teaching interpreted the Torah of Moses (5:17ff). The community also needed to know why the entrenched, non-Christian Jewish leaders were no longer to be emulated (ch 23). The community also evidently needed to expand its horizons toward Gentile missions. Matthew regularly portrays Gentiles in a positive light, as when the Gentile women are mentioned in Jesus' genealogy (1:3, 5, 6) and the faith of certain Gentiles is stressed (8:10; 15:28; 27:54). Such details from the narrative prepare the reader for the climactic commission that the community take Jesus' message to all the nations (28:19). The following discussion of Matthew's theological emphasis provides additional implications about the occasion and purpose of the Gospel.

CANONICITY AND TEXTUAL HISTORY

A foundational question in the textual history of Matthew is its possible origin as a Semitic text that was only later translated into our present Greek text. Patristic sources that take this position have been cited in the previous discussion of authorship. The key patristic text is found in Eusebius's *Ecclesiastical History* 33.39.16, which cites Papias to the effect that "Matthew collected the oracles [*logia*, sayings of and about Jesus] in the Hebrew language [*Hebraidi dialekto*] and each one interpreted [*hermeneusen*] them as best he could."

At first glance, Eusebius's citation of Papias seems to say that Matthew was originally composed in Hebrew and that later editions were translated from that Hebrew original. Since our present Greek Matthew does not read like a translation of a Hebrew original, some have argued that Matthew wrote both a Hebrew Gospel and a Greek Gospel. Others think that Papias's *logia* were the sayings of Jesus that modern source critics call Q, or even the discourses of Jesus found in our Greek Matthew. But there seem to be no manuscripts that exemplify the putative Hebrew Matthew mentioned by Papias (Howard 1987). For these and additional reasons, others (e.g., Gundry 1994:619-20) propose that the expression *Hebraidi dialekto* does not mean the Hebrew language but Semitic rhetorical style, and that *hermeneusen* does not refer to translation but to interpretation. If this is the case, Papias says that Matthew's style of composition was Jewish, and that subsequent individuals interpreted this Jewish style to the best of their ability. Perhaps such features as Matthew's genealogy and stress on "fulfillment" are indicative of this Jewish compositional style.

Greek Manuscripts. The textual history of Matthew is exemplified in a great number of Greek manuscripts. More than twenty uncial manuscripts contain complete or nearly complete texts of Matthew including the following: א and B (fourth century); C, D, and W (fifth century); O, Z, 042, 043 (sixth century); 0211 (seventh century); L (eighth century); K, M, U, 037, and 038 (ninth century); G and S (tenth century).

There are eighteen early and often fragmentary papyrus manuscripts containing portions of Matthew (see Comfort and Barrett 2001:6). These include the following: 𝔓104 (Matt 21; second century); 𝔓64+67 (Matt 3, 5, 26; late second century); 𝔓77 (Matt 23, late second century); 𝔓103 (Matt 13-14; second century); 𝔓1 (Matt 1, third century); 𝔓45 (Matt 20-21; 25-26, third century); 𝔓37 (Matt 26, third century); 𝔓70 (Matt 2-3, 11-12, 24, third century); 𝔓101 (Matt 3; third century); 𝔓102 (Matt 4; late third century); 𝔓110 (Matt 10; late third century); 𝔓53 (Matt 26; late third century); 𝔓86 (Matt 5, third/fourth century); 𝔓35 (Matt 25;

third/fourth century); 𝔓25 (Matt 18-19, fourth century); 𝔓62 (Matt 11, fourth century); 𝔓71 (Matt 19, fourth century); 𝔓19 (Matt 10-11, fourth century); and 𝔓21 (Matt 12, fourth century).

In addition to its presence in the above papyrus and uncial manuscripts, hundreds of minuscules testify to the text of Matthew. Of course, Matthew is also abundantly cited in patristic sources, often used in church lectionaries, and translated into other languages by the early versions.

Canonicity. As the most popular Gospel of the early church, there was no doubt about Matthew's canonicity among the orthodox in either the eastern or western regions of the church. However, the heretic Marcion (second century) and his followers held to a canon that did not include Matthew, not to mention the Old Testament, Mark, John, and the General Epistles. Marcion affirmed a sort of gnostic dualism between the Old Testament and New Testament as revelations of two different gods, so Matthew's insistence on the fulfillment of the Old Testament by Jesus was unthinkable to Marcion, who accepted only an edited version of Luke's Gospel and the Pauline Epistles as his canon. Evidently his attack upon the incipient orthodox canon was a major factor in the process which led to the formalization of the canon in ensuing days.

In addition to the patristic sources already cited, the so-called Anti-Marcionite Prologues to Luke and John (date uncertain) and the Muratorian Fragment (probably late second century) both speak of the undisputed fourfold Gospel tradition of the church (cf. Irenaeus, *Against Heresies* 3.11.8; Cyprian, *Epistle* 73:10; Clement of Alexandria, *Stromata* 3.13; Origen, cited by Eusebius, *Ecclesiastical History* 6.25.3ff; Eusebius, *Ecclesiastical History* 3.25.1; Athanasius, *Festal Letter* 39; [and many others, see Bruce 1988:134-240]).

LITERARY CONCERNS

Gospel Genre: The Question of History and Theology. Due to concerns related to affirming the historicity of the Gospel stories about Jesus, conservative evangelicals have at times been reluctant to view the composition of the Gospels as being theologically motivated. This occurs in response to "liberal" scholarship that tends to view the Gospels as imaginative documents produced to meet the church's needs rather than to transmit reliable traditions about Jesus. Such liberal scholars find in the Gospels stories they think reflect situations and controversies faced by the church after AD 70 rather than what was presented by the historical Jesus (e.g., Beare 1981:13ff). Evangelicals have rightly responded in defense of the historical reliability of the Gospels (e.g., Blomberg 1987), but in so doing, the theological import of the Gospels has sometimes been eclipsed.

Others have argued—at times from misguided dispensational views—that the Gospels simply give us history, and that we get theology from the New Testament Epistles, especially those of Paul. However, the history vs. theology dichotomy is false. The Gospels narrate what really happened but do so for theological reasons.

According to Luke's prologue, Luke did careful research in order to ascertain the reliability of oral and written traditions so that Theophilus might be taught reliable truths about Jesus. If one may extrapolate from Luke's Gospel to the Gospels in general, their procedure was to transmit the "Jesus traditions" they had received with a view to meeting the spiritual needs of their audiences.

Thus, we have in the Gospels theological interpretations of selected traditions that the authors believed to be genuine historical events from the life and ministry of Jesus. Some scholars (e.g., Shuler 1982; Talbert 1977) argue that the Gospels are examples of the ancient genre of laudatory biography or encomium, while others hold that they constitute their own genre (e.g., Guelich 1991). Be that as it may, most if not all would agree that the Gospels are not comprehensive biographies or exhaustive histories of Jesus; a perusal of any Gospel synopsis or harmony dispels that notion. But each Gospel amounts to a retelling of stories about Jesus calculated to meet the needs of each author's audience. While there is overall uniformity, at least in the three synoptic Gospels, there is a great deal of individual freedom as the authors "redact" the traditions available to them in order to meet the needs of their respective communities. If John 20:30-31 provides any sort of model, the theological purposes of the evangelists dictated how they edited the available traditions and produced Gospels that were literary narratives, not historical chronicles. Their purpose was not to satisfy intellectual curiosity by compiling historical data. Rather, they wrote to disciple their respective communities by bringing selected episodes from the life of Jesus to bear on their various needs. Thus, the Gospel narratives teach us even today by showing us the theological and existential implications of the reliable words and deeds of Jesus.

This notion that the Gospels contain theologically interpreted history is particularly important when one notes the distinctive emphases of each Gospel. For Matthew, the emphasis on Jesus' discourses and such characteristic motifs as "the Kingdom of heaven" and the "fulfillment" of the Hebrew Bible are crucial for understanding why Matthew was written to begin with. This will become increasingly evident as the discussion of the synoptic problem proceeds.

Source Criticism and the Synoptic Problem. Even a cursory reading of the Gospels reveals the fundamental difficulty known as the "Synoptic Problem"—that is, why are the first three Gospels so similar in some respects and so different in others? While evangelicals may instinctively tend toward attributing such matters solely to the Holy Spirit's leading of the Gospel authors, reflection upon Luke's prologue (Luke 1:1-4) will take us beyond naive pietistic answers. It seems clear that Luke was aware of earlier written "accounts" (Luke 1:1), which in turn were based on "reports circulating among us from the early disciples" and eyewitnesses (Luke 1:2). For this reason, it is necessary to discuss the synoptic problem further.

Theories of synoptic origins and interrelationships can be divided into two main groups: those that posit, on the one hand, the literary independence of each Gospel, and those that posit, on the other hand, some literary interdependence between the Gospels.

Literary Independence. Certain scholars point out the prevalence of oral transmission of sacred tradition in the ancient Near East and conclude that the phenomena of the Gospels may be explained solely by their individual editing of readily available oral tradition without any necessity of literary borrowing from each other (Farnell in Thomas 2002:226-309; Linneman 1992; Rist 1978). If one approaches Matthew from this perspective and with the traditional view of apostolic authorship, one would view Matthew as reflecting upon his own experiences as an eyewitness of Jesus' words and deeds and augmenting personal experience with oral traditions. Such an approach may account for the differences between the synoptic Gospels with some degree of success, but it may falter as a satisfying explanation of the synoptic agreements, which at times involve identical wording of extended passages.

Literary Interdependence. Most scholars conclude that the phenomena of the Gospels are inexplicable without some literary interrelationship. In fact, such a view was held by Augustine and many of the Church Fathers, who believed that the canonical order of the Gospels represented their order of literary dependence. In more recent times the patristic approach to Matthean priority was revised somewhat in the Griesbach hypothesis, which posited that Mark used both Matthew and Luke. While some still hold to Matthean priority, the scholarly consensus today favors Marcan priority, with Matthew and Luke composing their Gospels in dependence on Mark and another hypothetical source known as Q, which purportedly contained a collection of the sayings of Jesus. Sometimes this view is known as the "two source theory," but it has been further developed into a "four source theory" in which Mark and Q are supplemented by the additional hypothetical sources M for Matthew and L for Luke. For critiques of this consensus, see Butler (1951) and Stoldt (1980).

The Marcan priority theory tends to reduce Matthean studies to distinguishing between tradition and redaction by locating Mark, Q, and M within Matthew and looking for Matthew's editorial refinements of these sources as an indication of his unique theological interests. There is often the assumption in this endeavor that Matthew's departures from Marcan tradition are less historically reliable. Yet many evangelical scholars operate from this perspective without diminishing the historicity of Matthew (e.g., Blomberg 1992; Carson 1984). If one accepts the traditional view of apostolic authorship, however, one may wonder why an eyewitness of the words and deeds of Jesus would base his Gospel on the account of Mark, who was not an eyewitness. It is sometimes stated that Mark would not have been needed had Matthew been written first, but this overlooks the many narrative details regularly presented by Mark that are not found in Matthew. In the final analysis, whether Mark abbreviated Matthew's discourses and expanded Matthew's narratives (minority view), or whether Matthew adapted Mark's narrative to his discourses derived from Q (consensus), what matters most to the church is the meaning of the Gospels as literary and theological wholes.

Narrative Criticism. The ultimate futility of arriving at anything approaching certainty in solving the synoptic problem, coupled with the atomizing tendencies of source critical studies, has led some to adopt another approach, a literary method commonly known as narrative criticism. Narrative criticism views each Gospel as a whole and draws conclusions about meaning and theology by comparing the parts of each Gospel to the whole instead of to putative sources. Powell states that in order to read the Gospels in this way, "it is necessary to know everything that the text assumes the reader knows and to 'forget' everything that the text does not assume the reader knows" (Powell 1990:20). This approach seems fitting if the Gospels are viewed as theologically interpreted history, written for the edification of Christian communities. One would think that the Gospels functioned as wholes within those communities, not as overlays to be spread upon previous Gospels or other sources. Modern scholars have been understandably preoccupied with uncovering the history of the traditions they find in the synoptic Gospels, but such an approach was hardly that of ancient Christian communities. It seems unlikely that such communities read one Gospel as an overlay of a previous Gospel, and it is difficult even today to utilize source critical methodology for Gospel studies in the context of church ministry.

Narrative criticism seems much more appropriate than source criticism for the study of the Gospels in a church context, given the genre of the Gospels as theologically interpreted history and the canonical function of the Gospels as Holy Scripture. Therefore, this commentary is a narrative critical study, although source critical matters will occasionally be noted (See the plea for methodological eclecticism in Davies and Allison 1988:1-4). A weakness of literary criticism in general and of narrative criticism in particular is that the historical referents of the literary documents are usually ignored as being beside the point of literary studies. But when Holy Scripture is studied in an evangelical context, the historical people and events and literary sources that interpret them must be held together.

Literary Structure. Grasping the structure of Matthew is crucial in a narrative critical approach as it attempts to articulate the role of the parts in framing the whole of the Gospel. Although some scholars (e.g., Gundry, Harrington) despair of outlining Matthew, the following approaches are commonly found.

A Marcan Outline Superimposed on Matthew. Matthew has frequently been analyzed along the chronological and geographical lines that seemed to work well in analyzing Mark (e.g., Hendriksen 1973; Morris 1992). Such an approach typically yields the following analysis of Matthew:

  I. Infancy Narrative (1:1–2:23)
 II. Preparation for Ministry (3:1–4:11)
III. Public Ministry in Galilee (4:12–15:20)
 IV. Public Ministry outside Galilee (15:21–18:35)
  V. Journey to Jerusalem (19:1–20:34)
 VI. Final Days in Jerusalem (21:1–27:66)
VII. Resurrection and Great Commission (28:1-20)

In some cases an outline like the above is used but with topical themes, such as "King" or "Messiah" (e.g., Toussaint 1980). These all seem to be more or less artificially superimposed upon Matthew rather than derived from within it. Overall, this approach no doubt has some value, but it does not at all engage Matthew's distinctive pattern of alternating narrative and discourse blocks of material.

"From Then on Jesus Began." Certain scholars (e.g., Kingsbury 1988; Bauer 1989) have called attention to a phrase that occurs at two crucial junctures in Matthew's narrative. In 4:17, just after the account of the arrest of John the Baptist, Matthew announces the beginning of Jesus' public ministry with the words, "from then on Jesus began to preach." In 16:21, just after Peter's stirring confession that Jesus is the Messiah, Matthew characterizes Jesus' messianic ministry as one of suffering by commenting, "from then on Jesus began to tell his disciples plainly that it was necessary for him to go to Jerusalem . . . and be killed." With this approach, the structure of Matthew is understood as follows:

    I. The Preparation of Jesus the Messiah (1:1–4:16)

    II. The Proclamation of Jesus the Messiah (4:17–16:20)

    III. The Passion of Jesus the Messiah (16:21–28:20)

Although it is significant that Matthew uses the same phrase at two critical points in his narrative, the phrase in question seems to be more of a biographical marker than a literary device. Overall, this approach to Matthew's structure is not that different from the previous chronological-geographical approach. Neither does it handle what is perhaps the most obvious difference between Matthew and the other synoptic Gospels: the alternating narrative-discourse pattern. For this reason, the following approach is preferable, although in fairness, one should note the arguments of Bauer (1989:129-134) to the contrary.

"When Jesus Had Finished." Students of Matthew have long noticed the unique juxtapositioning of narrative and discourse materials. What is more, Matthew marks each of the five transitions from discourse back to narrative with the phrase "when Jesus had finished" (7:28; 11:1; 13:53; 19:1; 26:1; the Gr. is *kai egeneto hote etelesen ho iēsous*). Acknowledging this Matthean structural pattern does not necessitate accepting Bacon's view that Matthew sets up five books of Jesus that correspond to the five books of Moses in the Pentateuch. This approach has difficulties in that certain discourse materials in Matthew occur within narrative sections, most notably the warning to the disciples and woes upon the religious leaders found in Matthew 23. On balance, however, this approach has the most to commend it and is presented as follows:

    I. Prologue/Introduction: Origin of Jesus the Messiah (1:1–2:23)

    II. The Early Days of Kingdom Word and Deed (3:1–7:29)

        A. Narrative 1: John and Jesus and the Kingdom of God (3:1–4:25)

        B. Discourse 1: The Sermon on the Mount (5:1–7:29)

    III. The Galilean Ministry Continues (8:1–11:1)

        A. Narrative 2: Miracles and Discipleship (8:1–10:4)

        B. Discourse 2: Mission and Suffering (10:5–11:1)

IV. Growing Opposition to the Kingdom of Heaven (11:2–13:52)
   A. Narrative 3: Grace in the midst of Controversy and Rejection
      (11:2–12:50)
   B. Discourse 3: Parables of the Kingdom of Heaven (13:1-52)
V. Opposition to the Kingdom Intensifies (13:53–19:1)
   A. Narrative 4: Various Responses to the Son of God (13:53–17:27)
   B. Discourse 4: Life and Relationships in the Kingdom of Heaven
      (18:1–19:1)
VI. Opposition Comes to a Head: Ministry in Judea (19:2–26:2)
   A. Narrative 5: Ministry in Judea (19:2–23:39)
   B. Discourse 5: The Judgment of Jerusalem and the Return of Christ
      (24:1–26:2)
VII. Epilogue/Conclusion: Passion, Resurrection, and Commission
   (26:3–28:20)

For a similar outline, see Carson. Blomberg attempts a synthesis of this approach
with that of Kingsbury, explained above.

Literary Style. Scholars generally view Matthew's Greek style as aesthetically adequate if not exceptional. It is likely that the author of Matthew was relatively fluent
in Semitic languages (Hebrew and Aramaic) as well as Greek. This accounts for the
frequent "Semitisms"—i.e., Semitic ways of expressing ideas in Greek (Davies and
Allison 1988:80-85). These Semitisms emanate from Matthew's sources, the Hebrew Bible, the Septuagint, and Matthew's own personal writing style. Yet Matthew
incorporates these frequent Semitisms in a way that avoids awkwardness and harsh
expressions and retains the flow of a good Greek style.

Another matter of style relates to Matthew's purported use of sources, primarily
Mark, Q and M. Those who work with Matthew from the viewpoint of the Marcan
priority view of the synoptic problem conclude that Matthew has often abbreviated
Mark's account of a particular episode in Jesus' ministry, while at the same time
expanding Mark's version of Jesus' discourses. Whatever one's view of the synoptic
problem, it is interesting to note certain words and expressions that Matthew uses
much more frequently than Mark and Luke (Davies and Allison 1988:74-80;
Gundry 1994:674-682).

Matthew seems to be fond of various numerical patterns, such as the seven
petitions in the Lord's Prayer (6:9-13), the seven parables (13), and the fourteen (double seven) generation format of the genealogy (1:1-18). See Davies and Allison (1988:
61–72) for a discussion of Matthew's fondness for threefold structures. Bauer (1989)
and Luz (1989) have also done good work on additional features, such as repetition
of contrast and comparison, particularization and climax, *inclusio*, and chiasmus.

MAJOR THEMES
It is difficult to select and to summarize the major themes of this Gospel briefly,
but the following themes are crucial.

Matthew and the Old Testament: Fulfillment. Matthew's pervasive use of the Old Testament is one of the major reasons many interpreters note the Jewish orientation of this Gospel. In fact, the prevalence of this intertextuality calls into question the very notion of an "Old Testament" in Matthew's theology. If Matthew's Jesus came not to abolish but to fulfill the law and the prophets (5:17), it is doubtful that Matthew conceived of the Jewish Scriptures as "old," at least in the connotative senses of "antique, outmoded, quaint." Instead, Matthew viewed the ethical standards (e.g., 3:15; 5:17-20), the historical patterns (e.g., 2:15, 18) and the prophetic oracles (e.g., 2:6; 3:3) of the Hebrew Bible as filled with ultimate significance through the ministry and teaching of Jesus.

In addition to numerous informal allusions that are difficult to count, there are around 50 formal quotations. These may be categorized in various ways, such as by introductory formula ("in order that it might be fulfilled," "for it is written," etc.) or speaker (Jesus, Matthew, etc.). The commentary will deal with each of Matthew's citations of the Old Testament individually, but a convenient summary based on Aland (1994:89-99) follows. Those desiring detailed discussions should consult France (1989:166-205), Gundry (1975), and Soares-Prabhu (1976).

Matthew's Use of the Old Testament. The following list of Old Testament citations in the order they appear in Matthew uses these abbreviations: (J) = cited by Jesus; (M) = cited in a Matthean authorial comment; * = introductory formula involving fulfillment; and # = introductory formula "it is written."

1:23 (M*) Isa 7:14; 8:8, 10 *The virgin will conceive*
2:6 (M#) Mic 5:2 *The Ruler from Bethlehem*
2:15 (M*) Hos 11:1 *God's Son called from Egypt*
2:18 (M*) Jer 31:15 *Wailing for murdered children*
2:23 (M*?) Jdg 13:5, 7?; Isa 11:1? *Jesus called a "Nazarene"*
3:3 (M) Isa 40:3 *John a voice in the wilderness*
4:4 (J#) Deut 8:3 *People live by more than bread*
4:6 (M#) Ps 91:11-12 *Angelic protection*
4:7 (J#) Deut 6:16 *Do not test God*
4:10 (J#) Deut 6:13 *God alone to be worshiped*
4:15-16 (M*) Isa 9:1-2 *Galilee sees the light*
5:21 (J) Exod 20:13/Deut 5:17 *Do not murder*
5:27 (J) Exod 20:14/Deut 5:18 *Do not commit adultery*
5:31 (J) Deut 24:1 *Letter of divorce*
5:33 (J) Lev 19:12/Num 30:2 *Vows must be carried out*
5:38 (J) Exod 21:24/Lev 24:20 *Eye for an eye*
5:43 (J) Lev 19:18 *Love your neighbor*
8:17 (M*) Isa 53:4 *He took our sicknesses*
9:13 (J) Hos 6:6 *God wants mercy*
10:35-36 (J) Mic 7:6 *Enemies within the household*
11:10 (J#) Mal 3:1 *Messenger prepares the way*
12:7 (J) Hos 6:6 *God wants mercy*

12:18-21 (M*) Isa 42:1-4 *The beloved Servant*
12:40 (J) Jonah 1:17 *Jonah in the fish's belly*
13:14-15 (J*) Isa 6:9-10 *Hearing without understanding*
13:35 (M*) Ps 78:2 *Mysterious speech in parables*
15:4 (J) Exod 20:12/Deut 5:16 *Honor your parents*
15:8-9 (J) Isa 29:13 *Hypocritical worship*
18:16 (J) Deut 19:15 *Two or three witnesses*
19:4-5 (J) Gen 1:27; 2:24 *God made male and female*
19:7 (M) Deut 24:1 *Letter of divorce*
19:18-19 (M) Exod 20:12-16/Deut 5:16-20 *Do not murder*
21:5 (M*) Isa 62:11/Zech 9:9 *The king comes on a donkey*
21:9 (M) Ps 118:25-26 *Blessings for the Son of David*
21:13 (J#) Isa 56:7 *A den of thieves*
21:16 (J) Ps 8:2 *Praise from children*
21:42 (J) Ps 118:22-23 *The cornerstone*
22:24 (M) Deut 25:5 *A man dies without children*
22:32 (J) Exod 3:6, 15 *I am the God of Abraham*
22:37 (J) Deut 6:5 *Love the Lord your God*
22:39 (J) Lev 19:18 *Love your neighbor*
22:44 (J) Ps 110:1 *Sit at my right hand*
23:39 (J) Ps 118:26 *Bless the one coming*
24:30 (J) Dan 7:13 *The Son of Man arrives*
26:31 (J#) Zech 13:7 *The shepherd struck*
26:64 (J) Ps 110:1; Dan 7:13 *Son of Man returning*
27:9-10 (M*) Zech 11:12-13 *Thirty pieces of silver*
27:46 (J) Ps 22:1 *Forsaken by God*

Matthew's Understanding of Fulfillment. Matthew's distinctive use of the Old Testament is centered in his ten fulfillment formula quotations that utilize the verb *pleroō* [TG4137, ZG4444]. These are especially prominent in Matthew 1–2. It is often believed in "lay" circles that fulfillment implies a specific Old Testament prediction being "fulfilled" in a New Testament event. This is largely due to a simplistic equation of prophecy with prediction. But fulfillment in Matthew has as much to do with historical patterns as it does with prophetic predictions. Prophetic prediction involves the prophet's foresight of a future event (cf. 2:4-6), but Matthew's fulfillment quotations more often involve Christian hindsight in which an Old Testament historical event serves as a pattern for a New Testament event that it anticipated. Historical events, whether past, present, or future, are viewed as the providential outworking of God's plan. Also, Old Testament prophecy is not primarily prediction but ethical admonition that utilizes the rehearsal of past events, as well as the prediction of future events, as motivation to effect present covenant loyalty. Fulfillment in Matthew involves ethical and historical matters, as well as predictive prophecy. There are sixteen significant texts.

One passage presents the scribes and Pharisees as fulfilling the measure of the sin of their ancestors (23:32). The implication of Matthew 23:29-36 is that Jesus' enemies are the culmination of previous enmity against God's messengers, the prophets. Just as the prophets anticipate the Messiah, the prophets' enemies anticipate the Messiah's enemies. Old Testament redemptive history provides a pattern that leads up to climactic fulfillment in the New Testament. But the fulfillment is the climax of a historical pattern, not a predictive oracle.

Two passages present Jesus as fulfilling (or epitomizing) certain ideals in his person. He fulfills "all righteousness" at his baptism (3:15), and he comes not to destroy but to fulfill the law and the prophets (5:17). Strictly speaking, messianic prediction alone is not the focus of the baptism. The point is that Jesus' identification with repentant Israelites in his baptism fulfills the uprightness required of Kingdom disciples. To be sure, as the servant of Yahweh, Jesus did fulfill Old Testament prediction, but the point here is that the Messiah's uprightness will please the Father. Jesus' affirmation that he came to fulfill "the law and the prophets" should be viewed as fulfillment of the Old Testament as a whole, not merely its predictive portions. And it is clear from the ensuing context (5:18-20) that ethical concerns are preeminent, not mere predictions.

The remaining thirteen passages (ten in Matthew's narrative comments, three in the words of Jesus) speak of fulfillment of the Old Testament in some fashion. Of the ten passages in Matthew's narrative, four occur in the infancy narrative of Matthew 1–2. Matthew 1:22-23 cites Isaiah 7:14, a passage that is probably misunderstood if it is viewed as a strict prediction of a future virgin-born Messiah. Rather, Isaiah 7:14 speaks of a sign given to King Ahaz in his own lifetime, and Matthew views it as an event that anticipates the virgin birth of the Messiah, an ultimate sign to the nation of Israel. Matthew 2:15 cites Hosea 11:1, which speaks of the historical Exodus of Israel from Egypt. Matthew capitalizes on the metaphor of Israel as God's son to speak of a much greater exodus of God's unique son in recapitulation of redemptive history. Matthew 2:17 cites Jeremiah 31:15, which personifies the nation of Israel at the Babylonian exile as Rachel weeping for her children who were dead. A similar yet much more significant weeping for dead children occurred when Herod ordered the slaughter of babies from the region of Bethlehem. It is significant, though, that the sorrow in both the Old and New Testament texts occurs in the context of hope. Matthew 2:23 significantly speaks of the fulfillment of plural prophets in Jesus' move to the obscure village of Nazareth. It is argued in the commentary on Matthew 2:23 that this passage plays on the similar words Nazareth and Nazarite (Num 6; Judg 13:5-7). It is also possible that Matthew has the branch (*netser* [TH5342, ZH5342]) of Isaiah 11:1 in mind. If it is correct that Matthew 2:23 is essentially a messianic pun, it fits with the other Old Testament fulfillments cited in the infancy narratives, which are not primarily predictive in nature.

Matthew 4:14 places the return of Jesus to Galilee after his baptism in the context of Old Testament fulfillment. Isaiah 9:1-2 speaks of a deliverer who will bring salvation to Galilee after the Assyrian attack and exile. No doubt, Matthew connected this with Jesus because of the stress on sonship and the throne of David in Isaiah

9:6-7. Matthew 8:17 views Jesus' ministry of healing and exorcism as fulfillment of Isaiah 53:4, where the Servant vicariously removes the infirmities of the nation by bearing them himself. In the context of growing opposition from the Pharisees, Matthew 12:17 cites Isaiah 42:1-4 to substantiate Jesus' forbidding those whom he had healed from telling who he was. In Isaiah 42, the Spirit-empowered Servant proclaims justice to the Gentiles with mercy and gentleness. In keeping with this model, Jesus did not brashly confront his opponents with examples of spectacular healing. Instead, he chose strategic withdrawal in his mission of bringing hope to the Gentiles. Matthew 13:35 connects Jesus' use of parables to the deep sayings of the psalmist in Psalm 78:2. Though no predictions are made in the verse cited, Matthew nevertheless describes the psalmist as "the prophet." Matthew 21:4 describes Jesus' plans to ride a donkey's colt into Jerusalem as fulfilling what seems to be a composite of Isaiah 62:11 and Zechariah 9:9. Both Old Testament passages speak of the future deliverance of Jerusalem. Matthew 27:9 finds fulfillment of Zechariah 11:12-13 (with similarities to motifs in Jer 18:2-6 and 19:1-13). Apart from the obvious difficulty with a passage from Zechariah being cited as Jeremiah, the connection to the thirty pieces of silver is hermeneutically difficult as well. It seems best to view this as Matthew's application of an Old Testament situation to Jesus' betrayal due to explicit verbal parallels (thirty pieces of silver, etc.) and implicit theological parallels (Israel's apostasy and rejection of God's messengers).

Three references to the fulfillment of the Old Testament occur in the words of Jesus. In his parabolic discourse, Jesus spoke of God's sovereignty and found the unbelief of his audience to be in keeping with Israel's unbelief at an earlier stage of redemptive history (13:13-15). In answer to his disciples' question about why he spoke in parables to the crowds, Jesus first alluded to Jeremiah 5:21 (and/ or other similar Old Testament texts) and then spoke of the fulfillment of Isaiah 6:9-10. In its original context, this passage spoke of the rebellion and unbelief of Israel in the days of the prophet Isaiah, but it also suits Israel's rebellion in the days of the Messiah Jesus. The other two instances of Jesus speaking of Old Testament fulfillment occur in the same context in Matthew 26:54-56. With his arrest imminent, one of his disciples prepared to fight for him. Jesus said to this disciple that the Father could give him power to avoid arrest, but then raised the question, "How would the Scriptures be fulfilled that describe what must happen now?" Then he addressed the crowd and stated that these things had happened so that the writings of the prophets might be fulfilled. While no Old Testament text is introduced here, Jesus probably had Zechariah 13:7 in mind (introduced in 26:31). The arrest of the Shepherd led to the scattering of the sheep. But evidently Jesus saw his arrest as the beginning of fulfillment of other Old Testament passages as well, since he spoke of the prophets in the plural. Thus, the reader is sensitized to note Old Testament fulfillment in Jesus' trials, crucifixion, and resurrection.

To conclude this discussion, it has been established that Old Testament fulfillment in Matthew connotes ethical, historical, and prophetical connections. These categories are not discrete but overlapping; individual fulfillments may contain elements of all three aspects. At times, the ethical element is preeminent (3:15; 5:17). At other times, fulfillment of Old Testament prediction is primary (4:14; 8:17; 12:17; 21:4; 26:54, 56). But probably the most prevalent aspect of fulfillment in Matthew concerns historical patterns (1:22; 2:15, 17, 23; 13:14, 35; 23:32; 27:9). Events in Old Testament redemptive history anticipate events in Jesus' ministry in that Jesus fills them with new significance. Even Jesus' opponents have their precursors in the Old Testament. By recapitulating these Old Testament events, Jesus demonstrated the providence of God in fulfilling his promises to Israel. As implied in the genealogy, Old Testament redemptive history is fulfilled by Jesus the Messiah, who is Abraham's son and David's son. This is often called typology.

Christology. Matthew uses the Old Testament to demonstrate to his readers that the person, ministry, and teaching of Jesus are rooted in the history, ethics, and prophecies of Israel's Scriptures. The many titles ascribed to Jesus throughout the book of Matthew reveal Matthew's Christology. They are presented below in the order in which one encounters them in Matthew. For additional studies, see France 1989:279-317 and Kingsbury 1975:40-127.

Messiah/Christ. Jesus is called "the Messiah" in the very first verse of Matthew, at the end of the genealogy (1:16-17), and at the beginning of the description of the circumstances of his birth (1:18). This cluster of references to Jesus as the Messiah strongly links Jesus to Israel's history and hopes. It is certainly the key to the identity of Jesus in Matthew. A "messiah" is literally one anointed by God for special service or office (Exod 28:41; 1 Sam 9:15-16; 10:1; 16:3, 12-13; 1 Chr 29:22; Isa 45:1). Most significantly for Matthew, the term occurs as a royal title in some Old Testament texts (1 Sam 24:6; 2 Sam 1:14; Ps 2:2). But the Christian notion of a lowly, suffering, eventually crucified Messiah was evidently foreign to the Judaism of Jesus' day. Even John the Baptist had doubts about Jesus being the Messiah (Matt 11:2-3), but through divine revelation Peter was enabled to strongly affirm it (16:16). At that time (16:20), the disciples were told not to tell others that Jesus was the Messiah, evidently to forestall the growing opposition to Jesus' ministry.

Another cluster of references stressing Jesus as Messiah occurs in Matthew's description of the Passion Week in Jerusalem. Jesus' clashes with Israel's religious leaders culminate with an episode that stresses Jesus' Davidic messianic connections (22:41). In contrasting his own view of spirituality with that of the religious leaders, Jesus affirmed that no one except the Messiah should be called "master" (23:10). In his answer to the disciples' question about the signs of his return, Jesus warned them not to believe in counterfeit messiahs (24:23-26). At his hearing before the Jewish council, Jesus' affirmative answer to the high priest's question as to whether he was the Messiah takes the language of Daniel 7:13 (26:64), but this only leads to mockery (26:68). Later, when he offers to release Barabbas, Pilate alludes to the fact that some were calling Jesus the Messiah (27:17, 22).

Of course, in Matthew, the Messiah is crucified, but he is raised and given all authority (28:18), an allusion to Daniel 7:13-14, which recalls Jesus' use of the language of that text in 26:64. It is this exalted Messiah who sends the disciples out to disciple the nations. Perhaps the key to Matthew's distinct view of Jesus as Messiah is the linkage of "Messiah" to "Son of God" in two key passages (16:16; 26:63-64). This will be discussed below under the heading "Son of God."

Son of David. This title occurs more frequently in Matthew than in the other Gospels. Matthew identifies Jesus as the Son of David immediately after identifying him as the Messiah in 1:1 and establishes Jesus' Davidic lineage in the infancy narrative (1:20). Subsequent uses of the title occur on the lips of those who call on Jesus to heal them (9:27; 15:22; 20:30-31). On another occasion, a healing leads the crowds to wonder whether Jesus is the Son of David, the Messiah (12:23). Here the one term seems to be tantamount to the other. These texts that connect Jesus' Davidic lineage with his healing ministry demonstrate that Jesus uses his royal authority to help, not to oppress the needy. At Jesus' triumphal entry (21:9), the crowd shouts praise to God for Jesus the Son of David, echoing the language of Psalm 118:25-26. Later that day, Jesus' acceptance of this praise becomes the occasion for the indignation of the religious leaders against him (21:15). When the conflict between Jesus and the religious leaders escalates during the Passion Week, Jesus' final disputation with those leaders is put in terms of the identity of the Messiah as the Son of David. Jesus cites Psalm 110:1 to the effect that David's Son is also David's Lord (22:41-45), asserting that the Son of David is also the Son of God. Matthew's use of the Son of David motif stresses Jesus' messianic credentials to heal and to rule. This stress seems to be rooted in such Old Testament texts as 2 Samuel 7:12-16; Psalms 2 and 89; Isaiah 9:6-7 and 11:1ff; and Jeremiah 23:5-6. Jesus, as the Davidic Messiah, inherits the promises God made to David and brings God's rule to bear upon Israel.

Son of Abraham. Jesus' title Son of Abraham occurs immediately after his identification as the Messiah, the Son of David in 1:1. Evidently this title in itself does not have messianic implications. The ensuing genealogy stresses this Abrahamic lineage in 1:2, 17—not simply to show Jesus' Jewish roots but to portray Jesus as the one who culminates God's plans and promises to Abraham. One should also note John the Baptist's warning that the Pharisees and Sadducees who came to his baptism should not rely on their Abrahamic origins (3:9). For John, repentance, not descent from Abraham, was required to avoid the coming judgment (3:8-10). This theme is furthered by the response of Jesus to the remarkable faith of the Roman officer (8:10-12). Gentiles like this officer (not Jews like those leaders who came to John) would share in the great eschatological banquet with Abraham, Isaac, and Jacob. Ethics, not ethnicity, is the issue. Matthew was not excluding the Jews as a whole from God's eschatological blessings but, rather, stressing the need of all humans, Jew and Gentile alike, to believe in Jesus. Matthew's mention of Abraham reminds us of God's call of Abraham, the promise that in Abraham all nations would be blessed (Gen 12), and the near sacrifice of Abraham's only son (Gen 22). Evidently, the promise to Abraham would not be totally fulfilled in the present world because Jesus took this promise to imply that there would be a resurrection of the dead (22:32; cf. Exod 3:6).

Immanuel. The significance of Jesus as "God with us" is developed through the citation of Isaiah 7:14 in 1:23 (cf. Isa 8:8, 10). This crucial passage looms large in Christian theology of the virgin birth of Jesus. Matthew's closing portrayal of Jesus' promise to be with the disciples until the end of the age (28:20) forms a literary inclusion with 1:23 in which the presence of God in the person of Jesus is stressed at both the beginning and the end of the narrative. Another instance of this motif is 18:20.

King. The arrival of the "wise men" (*magoi* [TG3097, ZG3407]) in Matthew 2 in search of the newborn King of Israel sets in motion a story of conflict between God's true ruler and the evil pretender Herod. Matthew understood Jesus' Triumphal Entry into Jerusalem near the end of his life as the act of a king (21:5), since he cited Isaiah 62:11 to that effect. Jesus' prediction of future judgment portrays him as the enthroned Son of Man (25:31), a king who separates the blessed from the cursed (25:34, 40, 41). Later, at his hearing before Pilate, Jesus accepted Pilate's question as a true statement of his kingship (27:11). Then he endured the soldiers' mocking use of the title (27:29) and Pilate's evidently sarcastic reference to it on the signboard placed over his head on the cross (27:37). Even the Jewish religious leaders mocked Jesus' kingship (27:42), but after his resurrection, he was given all authority and sent his apostles out into the world as their exalted king (28:18; cf. 26:64; Dan 7:13-14).

Son of God. Some would argue that "Son of God" is the preeminent title of Jesus in Matthew (Kingsbury 1975:89). With such Old Testament texts as Psalm 2:7 and 89:27 as likely background, Matthew presents Jesus as the virginally conceived Son who uniquely signifies the presence of God with his people (1:23; cf. Isa 7:14). Jesus' sojourn in Egypt reenacted the history of Israel (2:15; cf. Hos 11:1). At his baptism, Jesus was endorsed as the Father's beloved Son and endowed with the Spirit for ministry (3:17; cf. Isa 42:1). Satan soon challenged this endorsement when the Spirit led Jesus to fast in the wilderness, but through reliance on the Scriptures, Jesus vanquished Satan and thereby recapitulated Israel's wilderness wanderings victoriously (4:3, 5). He did not succumb to the temptation to manifest his unique sonship by spectacular acts. Rather, he showed that divine sonship is evident in submission to the will of the Father.

Jesus' divine sonship is also shown in Matthew through his authority over evil spirits and the weather (8:29; 14:32-33). This authority is shared only by the Father and the Son, who is the sole agent through whom people may come to know the Father (11:27). This was recognized by Jesus' apostles, who through Peter acknowledged that he was "the Messiah, the Son of the living God" (16:16). This linkage of the titles Messiah and Son of God is quite significant, although Peter still had a lot to learn about divine sonship as submission to the Father (16:22-23). Soon afterward, Jesus' transfiguration demonstrated to his disciples that as God's Son, his word alone must be heeded.

Jesus' conflict with the religious leaders intensified over time; Matthew portrays this rejection through parabolic imagery (21:33ff; 22:2ff). At the end of their disputes, Jesus' allusion to Psalm 110:1 indicated (to their chagrin) that his sonship was both Davidic and divine (22:45). At his trial before the high priest, Caiaphas asked Jesus whether he was "the Messiah, the Son of God," echoing ironically the testimony of Peter (26:63; cf. 16:16). Jesus' reply ominously cited Daniel's words (Dan 7:13) about the coming of the Son of Man. The irony continues as Matthew records Jesus' crucifixion, where the mockery of the criminals and the religious leaders contrasts with the confession of the Roman soldiers—both the mockers and the confessors referred to Jesus' claim to be the Son of God (27:40, 43, 54).

Lord. Matthew's use of this title for Jesus occurs against the background of the use of the term in Graeco-Roman times, ranging from a polite greeting to a human superior (like our "sir") to a term for the Roman emperor, who was thought to be divine. The term also occurs around six thousand times in the Septuagint as a translation of the Hebrew *yhwh* (Yahweh), the sacred Tetragrammaton, the name of God. Matthew is not at all hesitant to apply the term "Lord" (*kurios* [TG2962, ZG3261]) to Jesus. Matthew 3:3 cites Isaiah 40:3, applying to Jesus a passage originally referring to Yahweh. In Matthew 7:21-22 (cf. 25:37, 44) Jesus is addressed as "Lord" in reference to his role as eschatological judge. Frequently, those desiring to be healed addressed Jesus as Lord (8:2, 6, 8; 15:22, 25, 27; 17:15; 20:30-31, 33), as did the disciples (8:21, 25; 14:28, 30; 16:22; 17:4; 18:21; 26:22).

At times Jesus called himself Lord, as when he warned his disciples that if he their Lord (NLT "master") is called prince of demons, it will be worse for them, his servants (10:24-25). Jesus expressed his authority over Sabbath law by referring to himself as Lord of the Sabbath (12:8). He described himself as Lord when he sent the disciples to get a donkey and its colt for the Triumphal Entry, instructing them to tell objectors, "the Lord needs them" (21:3). He described his return as the coming of the Lord (24:42).

The ambiguity of this term means that we must look at each of its usages carefully in context. At times it carries contextual overtones of Jesus' divinity, while at other times, it is merely a respectful way of addressing Jesus.

Teacher. In Matthew the disciples never call Jesus "teacher." Rather, this term is nearly always reserved for addresses to Jesus by those who do not follow him, such as the teachers of religious law, Pharisees, tax collectors, supporters of Herod, and Sadducees (8:19; 9:11; 12:38; 17:24; 19:16; 22:16, 24). On three occasions, Jesus called himself teacher (10:24-25; 23:8; 26:18), so it must be noted that for Matthew, there was nothing necessarily sinister in the use of the term.

Son of Man. The Gospels use this expression more than any other to refer to Jesus, and it is found with only one exception (John 12:34, in response to a saying of Jesus) in statements ascribed to Jesus. The expression is found over one hundred times in the Old Testament, more than ninety times in Ezekiel alone. It most often describes frail, finite humanity in contrast to the awesomeness of God, and often occurs in synonymous parallelism with "man" (e.g., Num 23:19; Ps 8:4, where NLT translates it as "mortals"). This term is used throughout Ezekiel when God addresses the prophet (e.g. Ezek 2:1, 3, 6; cf. Dan 8:17).

Matthew uses "son of man" thirty times, but with three primary nuances. First, Son of Man occurs in passages that stress Jesus' suffering and humility. As Son of Man, he has no place to lay his head (8:20), he is called a drunk and a glutton

(11:19), and he will be in the heart of the earth for three days and nights (12:40). While he was on earth, people thought he was merely a prophet (16:13-14), and the story of his glorious transfiguration would not be told until after his resurrection (17:9). He would be mistreated and suffer just like John the Baptist did (17:12), even to the extent of being betrayed by a close associate (17:22; 20:18; 26:2, 24, 45). Despite this treatment, he would serve others and give his life as a ransom for many (20:28). This corresponds to the Old Testament uses of this title to describe humanity in general and a prophet in particular.

Second, Son of Man occurs in certain passages that stress Jesus' present power and authority. Thus, he had authority on earth to forgive the paralytic's sins, and he healed him to demonstrate that authority (9:6). He is the Lord of the Sabbath (12:8), though his authority was so controversial that he was slandered by his enemies (12:32). His ministry planted the seed of the authoritative Kingdom message (13:37).

Third, the term occurs in passages that focus on Jesus as the glorious coming king. He will send his angels to remove sinners from his Kingdom (13:41) as he comes in the glory of his Father to judge all people (16:27-28; 24:27, 30, 37, 39; 25:31; 26:64). At the time of his glorious Kingdom, his followers will also be abundantly rewarded (19:28), but they must first be on constant alert for his unexpected return (24:44).

The background for the second and third uses of the term to stress Jesus' present authority and glorious return is no doubt Daniel 7:13, to which Jesus alludes in 26:64. The context of Daniel 7:13 involves a judgment scene in which God, pictured as the "Ancient of Days," delivers the rule of the earth to "someone like a son of man," who with his people prevails over his enemies and rules the earth. There are also overtones of Daniel 7:13-14 in the language of the great commission (28:18-20). This duality of present and future nuances, involving both the authority exercised by Jesus during his earthly ministry and the glorious authority he will exercise at his return, is crucial for one's understanding of Matthew's "Kingdom of Heaven."

Additional Titles. There are other less significant titles that Matthew applies to Jesus. Among them are bridegroom (9:15; 25:1), the Coming One (11:2; 21:9; 23:39), Servant (12:18; cf. Isa 42:1), prophet (13:57; 16:14; 21:11, 26, 46; cf. Deut 18:15), stone (21:42-44; cf. Ps 118:22-23; Dan 2:44), and rabbi (26:25, 49).

The Kingdom of Heaven. While Matthew does speak of the "Kingdom of God" occasionally (12:28; 19:24; 21:31, 43), his unique term "Kingdom of Heaven" occurs thirty-two times. Some interpreters attempt to distinguish between the expressions "Kingdom of God" and "Kingdom of Heaven," but this is untenable for at least three reasons. First, Matthew 19:23-24 uses both expressions in a synonymous fashion. Second, a comparison of parallel synoptic texts indicates that Matthew often uses the expression Kingdom of Heaven when Mark and/or Luke use the expression Kingdom of God (e.g., Matt 13:31 with Mark 4:30; Matt 19:14 with Mark 10:15 and Luke 18:17). Third, Matthew's terminology is likely due to the association of heaven as God's realm with God himself (cf. the prominence of this association in Dan 2:18-19, 28, 37, 44; 4:34-35, 37; 5:23; 12:7). This is called metonymy, and it is likely occasioned by reverence for the name of God in Matthew's Christian Jewish community (cf. Luke 16:18, 21). Matthew's four Kingdom of God texts are probably just stylistic variations for literary purposes.

Generally, the Kingdom of Heaven refers to the nearness or even presence of the rule of God in the person, works, and teaching of Jesus (3:2; 4:17; 10:7; 11:12; cf. 12:28), but there are times when it implies (5:19; 7:21; 13:24, 47; 25:1) or clearly describes (8:11; cf. 6:10; 13:38-43; 25:34; 26:29) the future reign of Jesus upon the earth. Perhaps the best way to describe the dynamic nature of God's reign is to say that it has been inaugurated at Jesus' first coming and will be consummated when he returns. Matthew characterizes the preaching of Jesus, John, and the apostles as being centered on the Kingdom (3:2; 4:17; 10:7). References to the present experience of the Kingdom (5:3, 10) frame the beatitudes, which otherwise speak of future Kingdom blessings. Jesus' Kingdom involves a radical righteousness greater than that of the Jewish teachers of the law (5:19-20); it requires disciples to seek it first, before their daily needs (6:33). Even John's greatness as a prophet of the Kingdom is eclipsed by the least one who experiences eschatological Kingdom realities (11:11-12). The preaching of the Kingdom and responses to it are presented figuratively in the parables of the Kingdom in Matthew 13, and its authority is further symbolized by the keys of Matthew 16:19. Entrance into this Kingdom requires childlike humility (18:3-4; 19:14), and the unknown time of its future arrival mandates constant alertness (25:1ff).

Conflict. The key motif in Matthew that moves the plot and portrays the struggles involved in the advance of the Kingdom is conflict (cf. 11:12). At the outset of Matthew's story, there is conflict between Herod the Great and the infant Messiah just born in Bethlehem (ch 2). Divine intervention preserves Jesus, but the male babies in Bethlehem perish. As John the Baptist announces Jesus, conflict arises between him and Israel's religious leaders over genuine righteousness (3:7ff). Later John's prophetic denunciation of Herod Antipas's illegal marriage to his brother's former wife results in his imprisonment and grisly execution (14:1-12), and Jesus likens his own treatment to that of John (17:12). Satan himself tries to tempt Jesus to gratify his human needs and accomplish his messianic mission in ways that were disobedient to the Father (4:1-11).

Once Jesus' public ministry began, his teaching about righteousness in the Sermon on the Mount clashed with that of the religious leaders (5:20–6:18), and the people were quick to pick up on the contrast (7:28-29). This led to further, more intense controversies about the forgiveness of sins (9:1-8) and Jesus' associating with sinners (9:9-13). His ministry of exorcism led to the Pharisees' charges that he was collaborating with the devil (9:34; 12:22-24). Soon he had to warn his followers that their ministries would be attended with much opposition (10:16ff; cf. 24:9). Many of the people who heard Jesus' teaching and saw his miracles did not repent and follow him, and he denounced them for their unbelief (11:16-24). The rules of

Sabbath observance occasioned a heated dispute (12:1-14); and after that, skeptical religious leaders with evil motives asked Jesus for a sign (12:38; cf. 16:1-4). Jesus' parables of the Kingdom of Heaven also spoke of conflict engendered by varying responses to the message of the Kingdom (13:19-21, 38-39). Even the people in his own synagogue in Nazareth did not believe in his message (13:53-58). Jesus' teaching about inner purity clashed with the Pharisaic tradition of ritual purity through washing hands before meals (15:1-20; cf. 16:5-12). Later, as he moved toward Jerusalem, he debated the matter of divorce with the Pharisees, contrasting their relatively liberal view of it with his own stricter view based on God's original design for marriage (19:3-9).

When Jesus entered Jerusalem, the conflict entered its most intense phase. The Jerusalem leaders were offended at the crowds who shouted Psalm 118:25-26 during the entry and at Jesus' cleansing of the Temple (21:8-17). Then Matthew's narrative presents a conflict over the source of Jesus' authority (21:23-27). This led to Jesus confronting the leaders over their unbelief in his authority (21:28-44), and they wanted to arrest him (21:45-46). Additional conflicts occur in chapter 22, leading to Jesus' indictment of the leaders (23:1-12) and his pronouncement of woes upon them (23:13-36). All that remained was for them to plan (26:3-5) and carry out his arrest (26:47-56), trials (26:57-68; 27:11-26), and crucifixion (27:32-44). Even Jesus' resurrection did not end the enmity, as the Jewish religious leaders conspired with the Roman soldiers to spread the lie that Jesus' disciples stole his body from the tomb, a lie that still circulated when Matthew wrote his Gospel (28:11-15).

Why did these controversies with the religious leaders occur? Jesus claimed that his mission was not to destroy the law and the prophets but to fulfill them, but his interpretations of the Old Testament conflicted with those of the religious leaders, who were committed to the oral traditions passed on to them from previous teachers. So it came down to who was the authoritative interpreter of Moses—Jesus or the religious leaders? For Matthew and his Christian Jewish community, Jesus' teaching about the law of Moses (halakha) was authoritative, and this brought them into conflict with the leaders of the synagogues with which they continued for a time to be associated. It is assumed in this commentary that Matthew's Gospel was written while the community was still associated with the synagogues.

Does Matthew's emphasis on the conflict between Jesus and the Jewish religious leaders involve and incite anti-Semitism? There can be no doubt that Christian anti-Semites have used Matthew to promote their agenda. But this was certainly not Matthew's purpose. Most likely Matthew was a Jew and was writing to Jews who believed that Jesus was the Jewish Messiah. These Christian Jews were evidently in a heated religious conflict with non-Christian Jews, but sectarian conflict was common during the time of Second Temple Judaism. No doubt Matthew's agenda was to refute the non-Christian Judaism of the Jewish establishment, regardless of whether that establishment was the Jerusalem leaders whom Jesus opposed or the proto-rabbinic movement that evidently came to be centered in Jabneh (Jamnia) after AD 70 (and therefore regardless of the date of Matthew's composition with

respect to the destruction of the Temple in AD 70). But the situation involved a religious dispute between Jews, not a Gentile polemic against the Jewish race. Christians must acknowledge with shame the fact that Matthew has been misused by
anti-Semites, but it is anachronistic to interpret Matthew as a (Gentile) Christian
polemic against the Jewish race. (See the commentary on Matthew 23 and the helpful essays of Russell 1986 and McKnight 1993 for additional discussion of Matthew
and anti-Semitism.)

The Church and Gentile World Mission. The Gospel of Matthew, while often and
truly described as the most Jewish of the Gospels, is also the only Gospel that uses
the word "church" (*ekklēsia* [TG1577, ZG1711]; 16:18; 18:17). As in Daniel 7, so in Matthew—the Son of Man has a community of saints who confess his identity and
maintain their own unity. The identity of this community can be gleaned by reading Matthew from the beginning and noting the hints dropped by Matthew concerning the type of people who are followers of Jesus. Or it can be ascertained by
taking note of the final triumphant commission Jesus gave his disciples (28:18-20).

From the beginning of the Gospel, Matthew begins to make it clear that the community of the Messiah is formed from unexpected sources. The mention of Tamar,
Rahab, Ruth, and Bathsheba (1:3, 5, 6), all evidently Gentiles with overtones of
scandal in their backgrounds, prepares the reader for Jesus' association with the sinners of his own day. The inexplicable arrival of the mysterious wise men (Magi)
from the east who wish to worship Jesus (2:1-2) foreshadows the power of the message of the Kingdom to summon followers in surprising ways. Jesus' amazement at
the faith of the Roman officer (8:10-12) and his acknowledgement of the faith of
the Canaanite woman (15:28) encourage the readers of this Gospel to believe that
the message of the Kingdom is able to engender faith from unlikely sources in their
own day. The Roman soldier's amazed confirmation of Jesus' true identity at the
crucifixion (27:54) has a similar effect. All of these episodes from the narrative col-
lectively encouraged Matthew's original Jewish readers to expand their vision of the
people of God. It was not that they should abandon their fellow Jews, but they were
to take the message of the Kingdom to "all the nations" (28:19).

Jesus' final commissioning of his disciples was based on his exalted, post-
resurrection status. Having received all power, he sent the eleven to all the nations
to make disciples who would obey all his commands, and he armed them with the
promise that he would constantly be with them until the end of the age (28:18-20).
The universal scope of this commission is daunting, but it can be accomplished
if the disciples remember that their Messiah, like the victorious Son of Man in
Daniel 7, has received universal authority.

There is some tension in Matthew between Jesus' exclusive ministry to Israel
(10:5-6; 15:24) and his subsequent mandate for mission to all nations. The transition from an exclusively Jewish mission to an inclusive mission encompassing all
the nations is best explained as Jesus preparing an eschatological Jewish remnant to
be a light to the Gentiles. See further the notes and commentary on 10:5-6; 15:24.

OUTLINE (see also "Literary Structure" under Literary Concerns in the Introduction)
  I. Introduction: Origin of Jesus the Messiah (1:1–2:23)
    A. Title (1:1)
    B. Genealogy of Jesus the Messiah (1:2-17; cf. Luke 3:23-38)
    C. Birth of Jesus the Messiah (1:18-25)
    D. Visit of the Magi (2:1-12)
    E. The Escape and Return of the Messiah (2:13-23)
  II. The Early Days of Jesus' Kingdom Ministry (3:1–7:29)
    A. Ministry of John the Baptist (3:1-12; cf. Mark 1:1-8; Luke 3:1-14)
    B. The Baptism of Jesus (3:13-17; cf. Mark 1:9-11; Luke 3:21-22)
    C. Testing of the Son of God (4:1-11; cf. Mark 1:12-13; Luke 4:1-13)
    D. Ministry in Galilee (4:12-25 cf. Mark 1:14-20; Luke 3:19-20;
       4:14-15, 44)
    E. The Sermon on the Mount (5:1–7:29)
       1. The Beatitudes (5:1-10; cf. Luke 6:20-26)
       2. Persecution and witness (5:11-16)
       3. Jesus' teaching about the law (5:17-20)
       4. Jesus' teaching about anger, adultery, and divorce (5:21-32)
       5. Jesus' teaching about vows, revenge, and love (5:33-48)
       6. Religious practices (6:1-18)
       7. Material possessions (6:19-34)
       8. Discernment in dealing with people (7:1-6; cf. Luke 6:37-42)
       9. God answers prayer (7:7-11; cf. Luke 11:9-13)
       10. The Golden Rule (7:12; cf. Luke 6:31)
       11. Warnings (7:13-27)
       12. Result of the Sermon (7:28-29)
  III. The Galilean Ministry Continues (8:1–10:42)
    A. Three Cycles of Miracles and Discipleship (8:1–10:4)
       1. Three healing miracles (8:1-17)
       2. Two would-be disciples (8:18-22)
       3. A storm tests the disciples' faith (8:23-27)
       4. Jesus exorcises demons (8:28-34)
       5. Jesus heals a paralyzed man (9:1-8; cf. Mark 2:1-12;
          Luke 5:17-26)
       6. Jesus calls Matthew (9:9-13; cf. Mark 2:13-17; Luke 5:27-32)
       7. A discussion about fasting (9:14-17; cf. Mark 2:18-22;
          Luke 5:33-39)
       8. Jesus raises a synagogue official's daughter and heals a woman
          (9:18-26)
       9. Jesus heals the blind and mute (9:27-34)
       10. A compassionate shepherd and a plentiful harvest (9:35-38)
       11. Jesus commissions the Twelve (10:1-4)

      10. Peter's confession and Jesus' promise (16:13-20; cf. Mark 8:27-30;
           Luke 9:18-21)

      11. Jesus' suffering and a model of discipleship (16:21-28; cf. Mark
           8:31-9:1; Luke 9:22-27)

      12. Jesus' transfiguration (17:1-13; cf. Mark 9:2-13;
           Luke 9:28-36)

      13. Jesus heals an epileptic boy (17:14-21; cf. Mark 9:14-29;
           Luke 9:37-43)

      14. Jesus predicts his death and pays his tax (17:22-27; cf.
           Mark 9:30-32; Luke 9:44-45)

   B. Life and Relationships in the Kingdom (18:1-35)

      1. Greatness in the Kingdom (18:1-14; cf. Mark 9:33-50;
        Luke 9:46-50)

      2. Correcting a sinning believer (18:15-20)

      3. Forgiving a sinning believer (18:21-35)

VII. Opposition Comes to a Head in Judea (19:1-25:46)

   A. Ministry in Judea (19:1-23:39)

      1. Teaching on marriage and divorce; blessing little children (19:1-15;
        cf. Mark 10:1-16; Luke 18:15-17)

      2. Riches or the Kingdom? (19:16-30; cf. Mark 10:17-31;
        Luke 18:18-30)

      3. The parable of the vineyard workers (20:1-16)

      4. Jesus predicts his death as a ransom for many (20:17-28;
        cf. Mark 10:32-45; Luke 18:31-33)

      5. Jesus heals two blind men (20:29-33; cf. Mark 10:46-52;
        Luke 18:35-43)

      6. The Triumphal Entry into Jerusalem (21:1-11; cf. Mark 11:1-11;
        Luke 19:29-44; John 12:12-19)

      7. Jesus clears the Temple (21:12-17; cf. Mark 11:15-18;
        Luke 19:45-48)

      8. Jesus curses the fig tree (21:18-22; cf. Mark 11:19-25)

      9. The authority of Jesus challenged (21:23-32; cf. Mark 11:27-33;
        Luke 20:1-8)

      10. The parable of the evil farmers (21:33-46; cf. Mark 12:1-12;
         Luke 20:9-19)

      11. The parable of the wedding feast (22:1-14)

      12. Paying taxes to Caesar (22:15-22; cf. Mark 12:13-17;
         Luke 20:20-26)

      13. The Sadducees' question concerning marriage in the resurrection
         (22:23-33; cf. Mark 12:18-27; Luke 20:27-40)

      14. The Pharisee lawyer's question concerning the greatest command-
         ment (22:34-40; cf. Mark 12:28-34; Luke 10:25-28)

15. Jesus questions the Pharisees concerning the Messiah's sonship
    (22:41-46; cf. Mark 12:35-37; Luke 20:41-44)
16. Jesus' teachings on leadership (23:1-12; cf. Mark 12:38-40;
    Luke 20:45-47)
17. Jesus' prophetic woes against the religious leaders (23:13-36)
18. Jesus' lament over Jerusalem (23:37-39)
B. The Judgment of Jerusalem and the Coming of Christ (24:1–25:46)
    1. The first pains of childbirth: life in the present age (24:1-14; cf.
       Mark 13:1-13; Luke 21:1-19)
    2. The desecration of the Holy Place: the Temple destroyed (24:15-28;
       cf. Mark 13:14-23; Luke 21:20-24)
    3. The coming of the Son of Man (Matt 24:29-31; cf. Mark 13:24-27;
       Luke 21:25-28)
    4. The parable of the fig tree (24:32-35; cf. Mark 13:28-31;
       Luke 21:29-33)
    5. The necessity of alertness (24:36-51; cf. Mark 13:32).
    6. The parable of the wise and foolish bridesmaids (25:1-13)
    7. The parable of the three servants (25:14-30)
    8. The final judgment (25:31-46)
VIII. Conclusion: Passion, Resurrection, and Commission (26:1–28:20)
A. The Plot to Kill Jesus (26:1-5; cf. Mark 14:1-2; Luke 21:37–22:1-2)
B. The Anointing at Bethany (26:6-13; cf. Mark 14:3-9;
   John 12:2-11)
C. Judas Agrees to Betray Jesus (26:14-16; cf. Mark 14:10-11;
   Luke 22:3-6)
D. The Last Supper (26:17-30; cf. Mark 14:12-25; Luke 22:7-20;
   John 13:21-30)
E. Prediction of the Disciples' Desertion (26:31-35; cf. Mark 14:26-31;
   Luke 22:31-34; John 13:31-38)
F. Jesus Prays in Gethsemane (26:36-46; cf. Mark 14:32-42;
   Luke 22:39-46)
G. The Arrest of Jesus (26:47-56; cf. Mark 14:43-52; Luke 22:47-53;
   John 18:1-12)
H. Jesus Appears before the Sanhedrin (26:57-68; cf. Mark 14:53-65;
   Luke 22:54-55, 63-71)
I. Peter's Three Denials (26:69-75; cf. Mark 14:66-72; Luke 22:55-62;
    John 18:25-27)
J. The Suicide of Judas (27:1-10)
K. Jesus' Trial before Pilate (27:11-26; cf. Mark 15:1-15; Luke 23:1-25;
   John 18:28–19:16)
L. The Crucifixion of Jesus (27:27-44; cf. Mark 15:16-32; Luke 23:26-43;
   John 19:17-27)

M. The Death of Jesus (27:45-56; cf. Mark 15:33-41; Luke 23:44-49; John 19:28-37)
N. The Burial of Jesus (27:57-66; cf. Mark 15:42-47; Luke 23:50-56; John 19:38-42)
O. The Resurrection of Jesus (28:1-10; cf. Mark 16:1-11; Luke 24:1-12; John 20:1-18)
P. The Report of the Guard (28:11-15)
Q. The Commission of the Risen Lord (28:16-20; cf. Mark 16:15-18)

Matthew

◆ **I. Introduction: Origin of Jesus the Messiah (1:1–2:23)**
   A. Title (1:1)

This is a record of the ancestors of Jesus
the Messiah, a descendant of David* and
of Abraham:

1:1 Greek *Jesus the Messiah, son of David.*

NOTES

1:1 *record of the ancestors.* This translates a phrase that is lit. "book of the beginning" (cf. Gen 5:1). As such, 1:1 is an introduction to the genealogy of 1:2-17 rather than a title for the infancy narrative of Matt 1–2, the narrative of Jesus' life up to the beginning of his ministry (1:1–4:11), or for the Gospel as a whole. Strictly speaking, it seems most likely that this "record of the ancestors of Jesus the Messiah" introduces the infancy narrative of Matt 1–2. However, when Matthew is read as a literary whole, the key ideas of 1:1 are found throughout this Gospel. Thus, from a literary standpoint, it is difficult to limit the title to the genealogy. Davies and Allison (1988:150) argue from the LXX usage of this expression (Gen 2:4; 5:1) that Matthew's entire book is involved in this title.

David and of Abraham. These are key persons in the genealogy that follows this verse (cf. 1:2, 6, 17).

COMMENTARY

While the word "Jesus" in 1:1 is obviously a personal name, the NLT's "the Messiah" indicates that the Greek *Christos* [TG5547, ZG5986] ("Christ," "Messiah," "anointed one"; cf. 1:16, 17, 18; 2:4; 11:2; 16:16, 20; 22:42; 23:10; 24:5, 23; 26:63, 68; 27:17, 22) should be viewed as a title that indicates Jesus' supreme role and office in God's plan. Both *Christos* and its Hebrew equivalent (*meshiakh*) are related to the ceremony of anointing a king or priest for office in recognition of God's approval (Exod 28:41; 1 Sam 9:15-16; 10:1; 16:3, 12-13; 1 Chr 29:22). In some Old Testament passages the term "the LORD's anointed" is a title for the divinely endorsed king (1 Sam 24:6; 2 Sam 1:14; Ps 2:2). During intertestamental times, messianic speculation flourished as Israel reflected on the prophetic hope of a restored Davidic monarchy. Messianic hope was tied to Israel's longing for God's final judgment of the nations and Israel's resulting freedom from Gentile domination. In Matthew *Christos* is a key title that portrays Jesus as the one who fulfills these promises.

When Matthew joins "Son of David, Son of Abraham" to "Messiah," Jesus' unique status is even more strongly stressed. "Son of David" is frequently a messianic title (1:1, 6, 17, 20; 9:27; 12:23; 15:22; 20:30, 31; 21:9, 15; 22:42, 45), drawing from such Old Testament material as 2 Samuel 7:11-16 and Psalm 91. "Son of Abraham" occurs only in 1:1, but Abraham is mentioned elsewhere (1:2, 17; 3:9; 8:11; 22:32) as the proto-typical Israelite whose eminent status in God's Kingdom is unquestionable. This close connection of Jesus with Abraham may be contrasted with John's and Jesus' severance of the Jewish religious leaders from any connection with Abraham (3:9; 8:11). Perhaps Matthew's stress on Gentiles (e.g., 2:1; 4:15; 8:5; 15:22; 27:54) implies that in Jesus, the promise that all nations would be blessed through Abraham is fulfilled (Gen 12:1-3).

It is obvious even to the casual reader that each of the four Gospels begins uniquely. Mark begins in the most concise fashion and has the reader at the outset of Jesus' ministry by 1:9. The Johannine prologue (1:1-18) concerning the "Word" who became flesh sets the tone for many of the themes of John's Gospel. Matthew and Luke alone contain material about Jesus' infancy and early years, though this material seldom overlaps. All four Gospels do, however, stress the preparatory ministry of John the Baptist before they launch into the ministry of Jesus.

Matthew's story of the origin of Jesus begins with a title and genealogy (1:1-17) that show who Jesus is. Matthew continues with the account of his miraculous birth (1:18-25), which shows how Jesus entered the world. Matthew then follows with the events surrounding the arrival of the mysterious Magi, Jesus' sojourn in Egypt, and his return to Nazareth (2:1-23), showing where Jesus lived. This unique Matthean material leads into the shared story of John's ministry (3:1-12), Jesus' baptism (3:13-17), and Jesus' temptation (4:1-11). All this paves the way for the beginning of his ministry (4:12ff) while introducing the reader to such crucial Matthean themes as the sonship of Jesus and his role in fulfilling the Old Testament.

◆   B. Genealogy of Jesus the Messiah (1:2-17; cf. Luke 3:23-38)

2 Abraham was the father of Isaac.
Isaac was the father of Jacob.
Jacob was the father of Judah and his brothers.
3 Judah was the father of Perez and Zerah (whose mother was Tamar).
Perez was the father of Hezron.
Hezron was the father of Ram.*
4 Ram was the father of Amminadab.
Amminadab was the father of Nahshon.
Nahshon was the father of Salmon.
5 Salmon was the father of Boaz (whose mother was Rahab).
Boaz was the father of Obed (whose mother was Ruth).

Obed was the father of Jesse.
6 Jesse was the father of King David.
David was the father of Solomon (whose mother was Bathsheba, the widow of Uriah).
7 Solomon was the father of Rehoboam.
Rehoboam was the father of Abijah.
Abijah was the father of Asa.*
8 Asa was the father of Jehoshaphat.
Jehoshaphat was the father of Jehoram.*
Jehoram was the father* of Uzziah.
9 Uzziah was the father of Jotham.
Jotham was the father of Ahaz.
Ahaz was the father of Hezekiah.
10 Hezekiah was the father of Manasseh.

Manasseh was the father of Amon.*
Amon was the father of Josiah.
¹¹ Josiah was the father of Jehoiachin*
and his brothers (born at the time
of the exile to Babylon).
¹² After the Babylonian exile:
Jehoiachin was the father of Shealtiel.
Shealtiel was the father of
Zerubbabel.
¹³ Zerubbabel was the father of Abiud.
Abiud was the father of Eliakim.
Eliakim was the father of Azor.
¹⁴ Azor was the father of Zadok.
Zadok was the father of Akim.

Akim was the father of Eliud.
¹⁵ Eliud was the father of Eleazar.
Eleazar was the father of Matthan.
Matthan was the father of Jacob.
¹⁶ Jacob was the father of Joseph, the
husband of Mary.
Mary gave birth to Jesus, who is called
the Messiah.

¹⁷ All those listed above include fourteen
generations from Abraham to David, fourteen from David to the Babylonian exile,
and fourteen from the Babylonian exile to
the Messiah.

1:3 Greek *Aram*, a variant spelling of Ram; also in 1:4. See 1 Chr 2:9-10.   1:7 Greek *Asaph*, a variant spelling of
Asa; also in 1:8. See 1 Chr 3:10.   1:8a Greek *Joram*, a variant spelling of Jehoram; also in 1:8b. See 1 Kgs 22:50
and note at 1 Chr 3:11.   1:8b Or *ancestor*; also in 1:11.   1:10 Greek *Amos*, a variant spelling of Amon; also in
1:10b. See 1 Chr 3:14.   1:11 Greek *Jeconiah*, a variant spelling of Jehoiachin; also in 1:12. See 2 Kgs 24:6 and
note at 1 Chr 3:16.

NOTES

1:2 With this verse, the familiar genealogical pattern "A was the father of B, B was the
father of C" begins. As the genealogy proceeds, the pattern is slightly changed in a few
places by the addition of certain details (mentioned in the notes below), until it is decisively modified in the description of Jesus' birth in 1:16. Here in 1:2 the phrase "and his
brothers" is added, perhaps as an allusion to the twelve tribes who form the nation of Israel and the pattern for the twelve apostles (Carson 1984:65; cf. 8:11; 19:28). It is important
to read 1:2 in light of 1:1. Mention of Abraham concludes 1:1 and begins 1:2, initiating an
inclusio that begins with Messiah, David, and Abraham (1:1) and concludes with Abraham,
David, and Messiah (1:17). Abraham stands at the decisive point of the origin of the nation
of Israel (Gen 12:1ff) and is also at the root of the new people of God (3:9; 8:11). In view
of the women mentioned later, it is noteworthy that the matriarchs of Israel are not
mentioned here alongside the patriarchs.

Judah. Prominent among his brothers due to the fact that his tribe bears the scepter
(Gen 49:10; cf. Matt 2:6; Heb 7:14).

1:3 Tamar. Here it is added that Tamar was the mother of Perez, and that Zerah was
Perez's brother. Tamar, the wife of Judah's son Er, is the first woman mentioned in the
genealogy. Genesis 38:6-30 relates the story of her incestuous liaison with her father-in-
law Judah after Judah did not fulfill his obligation to provide a levirate husband for her.

1:5 Rahab . . . Ruth. Here it is added that Rahab was the mother of Boaz and that Ruth
was the mother of Obed. Rahab is well known to readers of the Bible (Josh 2:1-21; 6:17,
22-25; Heb 11:31; Jas 2:25). According to Joshua 2, Rahab, the prostitute of Jericho, protected the Israelite spies due to her fear of the God of Israel. Her family was spared from
the destruction of that city and lived among the Israelites. The OT does not indicate that
Rahab married Salmon and became the mother of Boaz. The story of Ruth the Moabitess
coming to Bethlehem with her mother-in-law Naomi and marrying Boaz is told in the
book of Ruth. Ruth 4:18-22 is likely a source for Matt 1:3b-6.

1:6 King David. Here it is added that David was king, which stresses his centrality in Matthew's genealogy and theology. David is the pivotal person at the end of Matthew's first set
of fourteen generations and at the beginning of the second set. The name Bathsheba does

not occur in the verse but is added in the NLT to clarify the Gr. expression that is more lit. translated "the one who had been Uriah's wife." This is a curious way to refer to Bathsheba. Perhaps it is a euphemism, or perhaps it calls attention to David's sin in having Uriah killed in battle. More likely it hints that Solomon's mother was a Gentile (since Uriah was a Hittite). Second Samuel 11–12 relates the sad story of Bathsheba's adultery with David, the ensuing intrigue and death of her husband Uriah, the death of her son by David, and finally the birth of Solomon. With the mention of Bathsheba, Matthew has now included in Jesus' genealogy the names of four women, all of whom were evidently Gentiles with somewhat tawdry pasts.

1:11 *exile to Babylon.* Here the brothers of Jehoiachin are mentioned, along with the pivotal event of the exile to Babylon (cf. 1:12, 17). Matthew's second set of fourteen generations descends from the glories of King David to the shameful rebellion of his successors, which leads to the judgment of God in the Exile.

1:12 *Babylonian exile.* The final set of "fourteen" generations pivots on the exile to Babylon and moves from the abyss of the Exile to the apex of the Messiah.

1:13-15 *Abiud . . . Jacob.* The nine people named from Abiud to Jacob in 1:13-15 evidently span a time period of around 500 years, but none of them are mentioned in the OT.

1:16 *Joseph, the husband of Mary.* The line of Jesus from prototypical Abraham to royal David now comes down to unpretentious Joseph. In 1:18–2:23 Joseph's obedient care for his adopted son is stressed, but here in 1:16 he is described only as Mary's husband. His brief appearance in Matthew underlines his modeling of obedience and his Davidic descent, even as a humble carpenter (1:16, 18, 19, 20, 24; 2:13, 19; 13:55). His wife Mary is not mentioned frequently either (1:16, 18, 20; 2:11; 13:55; 27:56, 61; 28:1).

Mary gave birth to Jesus. After stating thirty-nine times since 1:2 that A "was the father of" B, Matthew breaks the pattern by describing the birth of Jesus only in terms of his mother. The unique circumstances of Jesus' birth, to be explained more fully as a miracle in 1:18-25, are expressed here simply by stating that Jesus was born from Mary, the wife of Joseph. The active verb *egennēsen* [TG1080, ZG1164] has occurred thirty-nine times in 1:2-16a, but in 1:16b the passive *egennēthē* occurs so that 1:16b reads "from whom (Mary—the pronoun is fem.) was born Jesus." Thus the reader is already made aware that the birth of Jesus who is called the Messiah is very different from the previous births in the genealogy and is thereby prepared for the more detailed explanation in 1:18-25.

1:17 *fourteen generations.* This verse summarizes the genealogy and clarifies its structure. The genealogy has three movements of fourteen generations: (1) from Abraham to David (1:2-6a), (2) from David to the Exile (1:6b-11), and (3) from the Exile to Jesus the Messiah (1:12-16). Careful readers will note that it is difficult to arrange the genealogy into three groups of fourteen generations, but Matthew was more interested in the symbolism of "fourteen" than in the precision of his scheme. David is the fourteenth person in the genealogy, which matches up with the symbolic number of his name when its consonants in Heb., דוד (*dalet-vav-dalet*) are added up because ד = 4 (*dalet* is the fourth letter of the Heb. alphabet), and ו = 6 (*vav* is the sixth letter). Such addition of the numerical values corresponding to letters in words is called *gematria.* By using this literary technique, Matthew underlines the importance of Jesus' Davidic roots and the providence of God through Israel's history.

COMMENTARY

After mentioning the Messiah, David, and Abraham in his title (1:1), Matthew uses a chiastic pattern in his genealogy to mention Abraham (1:2), David (1:6), and the Messiah (1:16). The structure of the genealogy is made clear by its summary in 1:17.

It traces fourteen generations from Abraham to David, fourteen generations from David to the exile in Babylon, and fourteen generations from the Exile to the Messiah. Modern readers should beware a tendency to dismiss the genealogy as a boring, irrelevant way to begin a book about Jesus. If Jesus is to be Messiah, he must be connected to David and Abraham, as 1:1 affirms, and the genealogy develops this connection. However, it is clear from 1:17 and from a comparison with Luke 3:23-38 that the genealogy does not purport to be an exhaustive or chronologically exact record of Jesus' family tree. While genuine historical information is provided, the purpose is primarily theological, not chronological.

The three sections of the genealogy pivot on King David and the exile to Babylon. David represents one of the highest points of the Old Testament narrative, and the Exile represents one of the lowest points. It is likely that in Jesus, the Son of David, Matthew saw one who would restore a new Israel from an exile even more deplorable than the one in Babylon. Matthew had evidently chosen fourteen generations to structure his genealogy because David is the fourteenth name in the genealogy and fourteen is the numerical value of David in Hebrew (see note on 1:17). Matthew's use of this *gematria* stresses the centrality of David in Jesus' background as well as the centrality of David the great's even greater son, Jesus, for Matthew's readers.

In the "fourteen" generations from Abraham to King David, Matthew demonstrates Jesus' sonship and aligns Jesus as Messiah with the historical outworking of the promise of God. In the "fourteen" generations from David to the Exile, Matthew recounts the decline of Israel under the judgment of God. And in the "fourteen" generations from the Exile to the Messiah, Matthew traces the faithful purpose of God in fulfilling his promise despite the rebellion of his people.

Three issues in the genealogy call for more extended discussion: (1) the discrepancy with the number fourteen, (2) the reason why Matthew included the women in the genealogy, and (3) the relation of Matthew's genealogy to Luke's.

The Number Fourteen. The table on the following page displays the discrepancy in the use of the number fourteen. It shows that only the second set of "fourteen" generations actually has fourteen. The first and third sets actually have thirteen generations.

Scholars have responded to this discrepancy in different fashions. One can come up with three sets of fourteen names in the following way. The first set of fourteen runs from Abraham to David (1:2-6a). The second set runs from Solomon to Jeconiah (1:6b-12). The third set runs either from Shealtiel to Jesus (including Mary) or from Jeconiah to Jesus (excluding Mary; 1:12-16). The first option for the third set is more plausible, since Jeconiah has already been counted once as the last name in the second set. Brown (1993:82) notes that there are indeed fourteen names in the first set, so perhaps Matthew intended that Abraham (1:2) be viewed as a generation. But this will not work in the third set, where the first name (Jeconiah) represents the last generation of the second set. But all this may be irrelevant, since Matthew is speaking of generations (1:17), not names.

THE THREE "FOURTEENS" OF MATTHEW'S GENEALOGY

Matthew 1:1-6a	Matthew 1:6b-11	Matthew 1:12-16
1. Abraham-Isaac	David-Solomon	Jeconiah-Shealtiel
2. Isaac-Jacob	Solomon-Rehoboam	Shealtiel-Zerubbabel
3. Jacob-Judah	Rehoboam-Abijah	Zerubbabel-Abiud
4. Judah-Perez	Abijah-Asa	Abiud-Eliakim
5. Perez-Hezron	Asa-Jehoshaphat	Eliakim-Azor
6. Hezron-Ram	Jehoshaphat-Jehoram	Azor-Zadok
7. Ram-Amminadab	Jehoram-Uzziah	Zadok-Akim
8. Amminadab-Nahshon	Uzziah-Jotham	Akim-Eliud
9. Nahshon-Salmon	Jotham-Ahaz	Eliud-Eleazar
10. Salmon-Boaz	Ahaz-Hezekiah	Eleazar-Matthan
11. Boaz-Obed	Hezekiah-Manasseh	Matthan-Jacob
12. Obed-Jesse	Manasseh-Amon	Jacob-Joseph
13. Jesse-David	Amon-Josiah	Joseph (Mary)
14.	Josiah-Jehoiachin	

Blomberg (1992:53) remarks that ancient literary convention often alternated between inclusive (first and third sets) and exclusive (second set) reckoning. If this is true, the shift between thirteen and fourteen is understandable. It has been suggested that names were omitted due to errors in the transmission of the text, but there is no manuscript evidence for any such omissions. Gundry (1994:19) solves the problem in the third set by suggesting that Matthew counts Joseph and Mary as separate generations, but this breaks the literary pattern in 1:16 and seems to count the "non-generation" of Jesus by Joseph as a generation. There are also numerous other suggestions, all of which are even less convincing.

However one handles this problem, Carson's point (1984:68) is noteworthy: "The symbolic value of the sets of fourteen is of more significance than their precise breakdown." Matthew certainly knew basic arithmetic, but Matthew's literary conventions are ancient, not modern. By modern standards, Matthew's linear genealogy is artificial because it is not exhaustive. Matthew has omitted three names found in 1 Chronicles 3:10-14 between Solomon and Josiah, and other omissions can also be noted (Brown 1993:82-84). But it is not that Matthew has erred, since he did not intend to work exhaustively and precisely. The fact that David is the fourteenth name in the genealogy, along with the symbolic significance of fourteen as the numerical value of David's name, explains the artificiality of the genealogy.

The Women in Matthew's Genealogy. A second feature of the genealogy that calls for comment is the inclusion of the women. It is generally acknowledged that women are seldom included in Jewish genealogies, which are usually patrilineal. (For some exceptions, see Gen 11:29; 22:20-24; 35:22-26; 1 Chr 2:18-21, 24, 34, 46-49; 7:24.)

Since the days of the church fathers, it has been proposed that Matthew includes the women as prototypical sinners whom Jesus came to save. Thus, the women take their place in the narrative alongside the Magi, the Roman centurion, the Canaanite woman, and others in Matthew who bear testimony to the grace of God. A similar view has it that all these women were guilty of scandalous sexual union. To be sure, Tamar and especially Rahab were guilty of heinous sins, but this does not seem to be the case with Ruth and Bathsheba. The Old Testament account of Bathsheba's adultery with David (2 Sam 11) appears to characterize her as the passive victim of his aggression. Ruth's contact with Boaz at night (Ruth 3:7-19) is not a steamy scene of seduction but involves a marriage proposal to a kinsman as enjoined in the Old Testament. Another problem here concerns Matthew's intent in listing these women alongside Mary, whose virtuous character is stressed. Unless Matthew intended these women to contrast with Mary, it makes little sense to mention them.

Another popular approach to this question asserts that all these women were Gentiles who typify Matthew's intent to stress that the gospel is for all the nations. This is repeatedly shown in the narrative and in a climactic manner at the conclusion to the book. Tamar and Rahab were Canaanites. Ruth was a Moabite, and Bathsheba was evidently a Hittite like her husband Uriah. Against this, it is argued that Jewish tradition generally viewed these women as virtuous proselytes. But their Gentile origins are not thereby denied, and this would make them even better prototypes of Matthew's stress on Gentile mission. The problem of relating these women to Mary remains, however. If this view is adopted, it must be assumed that Matthew intended for these women to neither be contrasted with Mary nor considered typical of her.

Blomberg (1991), interacting with Schaberg (1987) and Horsley (1989), argues that all these women bore illegitimate children and thus paved the way for the suspicion that Jesus was also illegitimately conceived by Mary. Thus Matthew 1–2 implies that God liberates people from the stigma of illegitimacy through the virgin birth of the Messiah. This view has the strength of tying these four women to Mary with a common thread, something lacking in the preceding views. But the view can only presume that the prostitute Rahab had an illegitimate child, since the Old Testament is silent on this. Furthermore, Ruth's union with Boaz seems to be legitimate. In these two cases, only the suspicion of illegitimacy can be implied.

It appears that Matthew's inclusion of four noteworthy or even notorious women in his genealogy has not yet been satisfactorily explained. Certain elements of all the views have merit. Perhaps all that can be said is that the presence of these women in the genealogy implies Matthew's stress on the universal world mission of the gospel and his later focus on genuine piety. God's grace in Jesus the Messiah reaches beyond Israel to Gentiles, beyond men to women, beyond the self-righteous to sinners. In saving his people from their sins, Jesus is not bound by race, gender, or even scandal.

Matthew's Genealogy and Luke's.   A third area of discussion in Matthew's genealogy concerns its relationship to Luke's genealogy (Luke 3:23-38). My discussion will first compare and contrast the genealogies and then turn to the theological issues. While Matthew's genealogy selectively and thus somewhat artificially traces Jesus' ancestors from Abraham on, Luke more comprehensively covers this ground from Jesus all the way back to Adam. There are over sixty persons mentioned by Luke who are not mentioned by Matthew. Luke has twenty-one pre-Abrahamic generations and fourteen generations between Abraham and David (one more than Matthew's "fourteen"). Between David and Shealtiel, Luke has twenty-one generations to Matthew's fifteen. From Shealtiel to Jesus, Luke has twenty generations to Matthew's twelve. The syntax of the genealogies differs in that Matthew follows the "A was the father of B" pattern, while Luke utilizes the genitive of relationship: "A was the son of B." Context differs as well: Matthew places his genealogy at the outset of his Gospel, while Luke sandwiches his between his accounts of Jesus' baptism and temptation. Matthew's 3 x 14 structure is a transparent feature of his genealogy, but there is a great deal of debate over the possibility of an 11 x 7 structure for Luke's.

A major difference occurs in Matthew 1:6 and Luke 3:31, where Matthew puts Solomon after David and Luke puts Nathan after David. From this point, the genealogies diverge totally until they converge briefly with Shealtiel and Zerubbabel in Matthew 1:12 and Luke 3:27. Then they diverge again until Joseph in Matthew 1:16 and Luke 3:23. In other words, the genealogies converge in Matthew 1:2-6 and Luke 3:32-34 (with one difference); Matthew 1:12 and Luke 3:27; and Matthew 1:16 and Luke 3:23. But they diverge much more often: in Matthew 1:3 and Luke 3:33; Matthew 1:6-16 and Luke 3:24-31 (with one agreement). Between Abraham and Jesus, Luke has 56 generations, and only 12 of these converge with Matthew's 42 generations. Convergence occurs during the premonarchial period, divergence elsewhere.

These genealogies and their relationship to each other raise some theological questions, beginning with historicity. Both genealogies have their individual historical problems, and additional problems arise when they are compared. People are mentioned in the genealogies who do not turn up in the Old Testament or anywhere else that we know of. And people in one genealogy do not match up with people in the other. At this point, one's overall theological perspective informs exegesis. Scholars who are skeptical of the historical accuracy of the Gospels tend to deprecate the historicity of the genealogies and totally despair of ever reaching anything approaching a solution to the problems. Such scholars see the genealogies as theological constructions with dubious historical moorings. There are, of course, others who prefer to remain in ignorance of the difficulties while proclaiming a faith that does not wish to be confused by facts. However, there is good reason to accept the historical reliability of the Gospels, and those who are committed to this (see Blomberg 1987) point to solutions that are plausible, though not totally satisfying. It is the faith commitment of the individual scholar that is decisive. The problem is that there is simply insufficient information for convincing conclusions to be reached.

Another line of theological discussion is the question of the differences in the genealogies and their respective purposes. It has been argued by many older commentators (e.g., Broadus 1886:6; though disputed by Barnes 1868:2 and Calvin 1972:54-55) that Matthew gives Joseph's genealogy, while Luke gives Mary's. While it is possible that Mary was a descendant of David (Luke 1:32), she is not mentioned in the genealogy. Rather Joseph is (Luke 3:23). This theory arises not from reading Luke but as an expedient to relieve a difficulty (Carson 1984:64).

Another approach sees both genealogies as Joseph's, but with the nuance that Matthew provides Joseph's royal succession to the throne and Luke provides his real genealogy. In this approach, Joseph's real father was Heli (Luke 3:23), and Jacob (Matt 1:16) was Heli's full brother, who died without an heir. Heli carried out a levirate marriage (Deut 25:5-10) with Jacob's widow. But this theory raises many other questions too numerous to be discussed here.

When all is said and done, it is clear that the overall theological perspective of the interpreter is decisive. Evangelicals must admit that there are insuperable difficulties in fully resolving all the problems in the genealogies. But this does not amount to rejecting biblical authority and accuracy. While there is not sufficient evidence to solve the difficulties, there is likewise insufficient evidence to falsify the biblical record. No doubt, both genealogies are based on traditions available to Matthew and Luke, which they passed on in good faith (Albright and Mann 1971:5-6). Matthew and Luke had distinct purposes in composing their genealogies, and neither of their intentions was to exhaustively summarize the biological lineage of Jesus (Brown 1993:85). With this in mind, many of the difficulties are more understandable. Difficulties aside, both Matthew and Luke affirm Jesus' Abrahamic and Davidic ancestry, as well as his miraculous conception by the virgin Mary.

Another area of theological concern is the respective purposes of the genealogies in their literary contexts. Matthew used his genealogy primarily for Christological purposes, to demonstrate the Abrahamic and Davidic ancestry of Jesus the Messiah while showing him to be the fulfillment of God's promises. Additionally, the presence of the women (who are probably all Gentiles) hints at Matthew's agenda for universal mission to all the nations.

The situation is quite different for Luke's genealogy, which occurs not at the beginning of his gospel but between his accounts of Jesus' baptism and temptation. It seems significant that both the preceding baptism pericope and following temptation pericope stress the divine sonship of Jesus. At the baptism, the Father affirmed this unique sonship (3:22), and at the temptation the devil unsuccessfully tested it (4:3, 9). The genealogy, tracing Jesus back to Adam and to God himself (3:38), leads one to the same conclusion: Jesus is the Son of God. The first Adam was also a son of God, but he failed under satanic testing. Endued with the Spirit (3:22; 4:1, 14, 18), the second Adam is victorious over Satan. Thus at the beginning of his ministry Jesus is viewed as the representative person for all human beings

(Marshall 1978:161). Luke mentions Abraham and David, just as Matthew does, but Luke's purpose is not to relate Jesus to Abraham and David. Rather, it is to relate all mankind to the God of Abraham, of David, and, preeminently, of Jesus.

◆   ## C. Birth of Jesus the Messiah (1:18-25)

[18]This is how Jesus the Messiah was born. His mother, Mary, was engaged to be married to Joseph. But before the marriage took place, while she was still a virgin, she became pregnant through the power of the Holy Spirit. [19]Joseph, her fiancé, was a good man and did not want to disgrace her publicly, so he decided to break the engagement* quietly.

[20]As he considered this, an angel of the Lord appeared to him in a dream. "Joseph, son of David," the angel said, "do not be afraid to take Mary as your wife. For the child within her was conceived by the Holy Spirit. [21]And she will have a son, and you are to name him Jesus,* for he will save his people from their sins."

[22]All of this occurred to fulfill the Lord's message through his prophet:

[23]"Look! The virgin will conceive
    a child!
She will give birth to a son,
and they will call him Immanuel,*
    which means 'God is with us.'"

[24]When Joseph woke up, he did as the angel of the Lord commanded and took Mary as his wife. [25]But he did not have sexual relations with her until her son was born. And Joseph named him Jesus.

1:19 Greek *to divorce her.*   1:21 *Jesus* means "The LORD saves."   1:23 Isa 7:14; 8:8, 10 (Greek version).

NOTES

1:18 *This is how Jesus the Messiah was born.* The verb in this rendering is based on the word *genesis* [TG1078, ZG1161], which occurred previously in 1:1.

Mary, was engaged . . . she became pregnant. Two details provided in 1:18 are crucial for understanding Joseph's dilemma in 1:19. Mary was engaged to Joseph, but before their marriage was consummated she was discovered to be pregnant. Engagement or betrothal frequently occurred when girls were twelve years old. When the groom had completed his obligations to the bride's father according to the marriage contract, the bride came under the authority of her husband, though she did not necessarily move to her husband's house at that time. Evidently, the situation in 1:18 involved all but the final stage of the process (cf. 25:1-12 and Brown 1993:123-124). Joseph had become engaged to Mary and had assumed authority over her. He was already her husband, but planned to divorce Mary because of the apparent unfaithfulness (1:21; cf. Deut 22:23-24).

while she was still a virgin. Lit., before she and Joseph "came together" sexually, she became pregnant from the work of the Holy Spirit (cf. Luke 1:34-35).

through the power of the Holy Spirit. The Holy Spirit is mentioned here for the first time in Matthew. The Spirit is involved in Jesus' conception (cf. 1:20), empowerment (3:16; 12:18, 28), and leading (4:1). In Jesus' view, the OT Scriptures came from the Spirit (22:43). John spoke of the day when Jesus would baptize in the Spirit (3:11), and Jesus promised his disciples that the Spirit would supply their testimony during persecution (10:20). They were mandated to baptize in the name of the Father, the Son, and the Holy Spirit (28:19).

1:19 *decided to break the engagement.* Joseph's plan to quietly divorce Mary (see NLT mg) is explained here. The plan emanated from Joseph's character as a just man who did not want to publicly disgrace Mary. This seems to mean that though Joseph was a law-abiding man, he did not want to use the law in all its rigor against Mary. Instead, he planned a quiet divorce. If this interpretation is correct, Joseph becomes something of a model of one whose high standards were balanced with compassion. (For Matthew's approach to righteousness as obedience to the law, see 3:15; 5:6, 10, 20, 45; 6:1, 33; 9:13; 10:41; 12:37; 13:17, 43, 49; 20:4; 21:32; 23:28, 29, 35, 37; 25:46; 27:19. For general discussion of righteousness in Matthew see Przybylski 1980.)

1:20 *an angel of the Lord appeared to him.* Joseph's plans were suddenly changed by the angelic visitation and revelation. Revelation in dreams was not uncommon in the OT (Gen 37:5-7; Job 33:15-17; Dan 2; 7) or in Matthew (1:25; 2:12, 13, 19, 22; 27:19). Since Joseph was called a son of David by the angel, the story of Jesus' birth is thereby tied to the genealogy and Jesus' Davidic roots. This is the only time in Matthew that "son of David" does not refer to Jesus. Joseph was commanded not to fear taking Mary as his wife because her pregnancy was induced by the Holy Spirit. Joseph finally knew what the narrator told the reader in 1:18. What follows shows how well Joseph heeded this command.

1:21 *she will have a son, and you are to name him Jesus.* The angel's annunciation to Joseph continues. Mary will bear a son whom Joseph will name Jesus, because of the son's mission to save his people from their sins. This angelic annunciation has a form common to other biblical birth announcements (Gen 16:11; 17:19; Luke 1:13, 30). The name "Jesus" fits the predicted mission of this son. It is a Gr. form of the OT name Joshua, and was a common name among Jews. It was popularly related to the Heb. verb "to save" and understood to mean "Yahweh saves." By naming Mary's son, Joseph was accepting legal paternity. By naming him Jesus, Joseph was making a statement about Jesus' redemptive mission: "he will save his people from their sins." A similar play on words (paronomasia) with a personal name occurs with Simon Peter in 16:18 (cf. 1 Sam 25:25).

"Jesus" is the appropriate name for Mary's son because as Messiah he will fulfill the eschatological hopes of the OT by "saving his people from their sins" (cf. Ps 130:8). Salvation in Matthew can refer to deliverance from physical danger, illness, and death (8:25; 9:21-22; 24:22). But salvation from sins is the focus of the angel's announcement. In Matthew, sins are confessed by those whom John baptizes and forgiven by Jesus (3:6; 9:2, 5, 6; 12:31; 26:28). Forgiveness is accomplished by Jesus' gift of himself as a ransom for sinners in sacrificial death, as exemplified in the elements of the Last Supper (20:28; 26:26-30). It is perhaps significant that the allusion to Psalm 130:8 substitutes "his people" for "Israel." Jesus' saving ministry creates a division within Israel. Those who admit they are sick come to Jesus as their physician, but most Israelites will not admit their sickness (9:9-12). Thus Jesus begins to build his church (16:18-19), "a nation that will produce [the Kingdom's] fruit" (21:43). Israel as a nation is not abandoned, but only those Jews who will repent and turn to Jesus the Messiah will receive the forgiveness of their sins and experience all of the OT eschatological blessings (19:28-30).

1:22 *fulfill the Lord's message.* There is some question as to whether the angel's announcement to Joseph continues in 1:22 or whether it concludes in 1:21, with 1:22 beginning Matthew's explanation of the prophetic significance of the situation. Most likely the latter is the case. Whoever the speaker is, it is crucial to grasp the meaning of the fulfillment concept mentioned in 1:22. Note the discussions of this concept in the Introduction (pp. 13–17) and in the following commentary on 1:18-25.

1:23 *The virgin will conceive a child!* Through the centuries there has been a great deal of discussion concerning the Gr. and Heb. words for "virgin" in Isa 7:14 and Matt 1:23. The Gr. word in Matt 1:23 is *parthenos* [TG3933, ZG4221], while the Heb. word in Isa 7:14 is *'almah* [TH5959, ZH5959], which refers to a young woman who is old enough to be married. The reference in Isaiah is not to a virgin birth in its immediate historical setting, as the context makes clear. However, the LXX uses the term *parthenos* (virgin) to translate the Heb.

word. Matthew followed this. There has never been any debate about what Matthew intended; his wording makes it absolutely clear that he was describing a female with no sexual experience. The debate has been over the term Isaiah used, as to whether it means "virgin" or "young woman" (see Walker 2005:45).

Isaiah 7:14 is cited as the text "fulfilled" by Mary's virginal conception of Jesus. The nature of the fulfillment of Isa 7:14 has produced a great deal of discussion. Some take the view that Isa 7:14 is a direct prediction of the virgin birth of Jesus. Others believe that Matthew saw in the historical circumstances of Isa 7:14 a type of the virgin birth of Jesus. An extended discussion of this passage with an argument for the latter view will be found in the following commentary section.

Immanuel. See Isa 7:14; 8:8, 10.

1:24 he did as the angel of the Lord commanded. Joseph is a model of quiet obedience (Bruner 1987:35-36) to three angelic revelations in Matt 1-2 (cf. 2:13-15, 19-21). He got up and did exactly as he was told without hesitation or question. Given his previous plan (1:19), this is nothing less than remarkable and compares with Mary's humble obedience in Luke 1:38.

1:25 he did not have sexual relations with her. Joseph took Mary to his house as his wife, yet (Matthew adds another detail to underline Jesus' miraculous birth) Joseph had no sexual relations with Mary (lit., "he was not knowing Mary") before Jesus was born. This statement does not affirm the perpetual virginity of Mary, because she had other children (cf. 12:46; 13:55, 56; Mark 3:31-32; 6:3; Luke 8:19-20; John 2:12; 7:3, 5, 10; Acts 1:14). Mary is best honored as a model believer if she is given the normal role of wife and mother (Bruner 1987:36-40).

COMMENTARY

Matthew announced that he was giving a record of the birth of the Messiah (1:1), and he provided an overview of the Messiah's Abrahamic and Davidic ancestry (1:1-17). Now that the Messiah has been firmly rooted in the context of redemptive history, Matthew goes on to provide the specifics of his birth. The miraculous birth of Jesus, hinted at in 1:16, is now explained. Matthew 1:18-25 is a commentary on 1:16. In the following commentary, two major matters will be discussed: Matthew's use of Isaiah 7:14 and Matthew's understanding of fulfillment.

Matthew's Use of Isaiah 7:14. At the heart of this passage on the miraculous birth of Jesus is the citation of Isaiah 7:14 in Matthew 1:23. According to Isaiah 7, King Ahaz of Judah was under threat of attack by the kings of Aram and Israel. But God promised Ahaz that the threatened attack would not take place, and invited him to ask for a sign to that effect. Ahaz refused, but God supplied a sign anyway: "the virgin will give birth to a child." Matthew's citation of this passage has given rise to three major interpretive approaches, which may be categorized as typological, predictive, and multiple fulfillment.

The typological view stresses the immediacy of the sign to Ahaz (Isa 7:14a, 16) and the possible fulfillments of Isaiah 7:14 in the near future of the Old Testament context (Isa 8:3-4, 8, 10, 18). Thus, Isaiah 7:14 is viewed as a sign to Ahaz that was fulfilled during his days, and Matthew sees in the passage a historical pattern that comes to fulfillment with the birth of Jesus. A young woman in Isaiah's day conceived a significant son who served as a sign of deliverance from Syria to Ahaz and the house of David (Isa 7:2, 13). But much more significantly, a young woman in Matthew's day who was literally a virgin conceived, by the Spirit, a Son of ultimate significance to the house of David, the nation of Israel, and to all the nations of the earth. In Isaiah's day, the son was a token of divine presence and deliverance. In Matthew's day, the Son was himself "God with us," the deliverer of his people (Barnes 1868:7-8; Broadus 1886:12).

The predictive view takes Isaiah 7:14 as foreseeing the eventual miraculous birth of the Messiah from a woman who was literally a virgin. Matthew interpreted this predictive prophecy literally and viewed it as predicting the birth of Jesus alone. Thus, the prophecy transcends the contemporary difficulties facing King Ahaz and points to a sign in the future. Nevertheless, the overwhelming significance of the sign transcends its temporal distance. Proponents of this view (e.g., Barbieri 1983:20; Calvin 1972:65-69; Carson 1984:78-79; Fowler 1968:38-42; Hendriksen 1973:134-141) argue that the normal birth of a son from a young woman (as required in the typological view) would have little or no force as a sign to King Ahaz. Additionally, they believe that only the predictive view does justice to the son's name being "Immanuel" (meaning "God with us").

The strength of the typological view is its focus on the historical context of the original prophecy, and the strength of the predictive view is its focus on the New Testament fulfillment. The third view, multiple fulfillment, attempts to draw from both of these strengths. In this approach, the prophecy foresees not only a partial fulfillment in the days of Ahaz but also a climactic fulfillment in New Testament times (Blomberg 1992:59-60; Gundry 1982:24-25; Toussaint 1980:44-46). The human prophet Isaiah may not have fully grasped this, but after all, the prophecy is the Lord's, and Isaiah is merely the messenger. Such a *sensus plenior* (fuller meaning) was intended by the divine author if not fully understood by the human author.

One should hesitate to be dogmatic on this matter since each position has its credible advocates and arguments. However, the typological view seems best for several reasons. First, there are the weaknesses of the other views. The multiple fulfillment view introduces an unwarranted distinction between what the prophet predicted and what God intended to reveal by the text. Additionally, the double fulfillment view assumes that the esoteric connection between the near and far fulfillments of the prophecy is available only to one who is divinely inspired. But if the Christological significance of the Old Testament is accessible only from such a revelatory stance, the organic unity of the Bible is compromised and made inaccessible to ordinary believers (cf. Luke 24:27, 44-45; John 5:39). Instead of this view, which posits enigmatic double entendre and subsequent divine inspiration to recognize it, it is much better to assert a typological connection in which the Old Testament historical events contain theological motifs that anticipate the Christ-event when seen with Christian hindsight. Such hindsight is not limited to those who wrote the New Testament but is available to all who will search the historical events and theological motifs of the Old Testament. The dynamic that connects Isaiah 7:14

to Matthew 1:23 is not two levels of foresight, one on the surface of the text and the other beneath it. Rather, Matthew read the events of the Old Testament from a Christian perspective and from a belief in divine providence. Thus, he discovered events and motifs that come to climactic fulfillment in Jesus the Messiah, who is David's son, a descendant of Abraham.

The predictive view has its problems with relevance to the immediate historical context, and the original context must be primary in any sound exegesis. It seems clear from Isaiah 7:15-17 that the son to be born signals the demise of Ahaz's enemies, for they will be forsaken before the son comes to the age of moral discretion. It is difficult, if not impossible, to relate this to the birth of Jesus several hundred years later. It is sometimes argued that only a miraculous event such as Jesus' virgin birth could have value as a "sign," but a study of Isaiah's use of this word elsewhere (Isa 7:11, 14; 8:18; 19:20; 20:3; 37:30; 38:7, 22; 55:13; 66:19) shows that this is not always the case. Additionally, such a study shows that signs in Isaiah are contemporaneous with the time frame of the prophecy, not distantly removed from it. This would indicate that signs in Isaiah are "present persuaders," not "future confirmation" (contra Carson 1984:79). Even more problematic to the predictive view, it is doubtful that Isaiah 7:14 should even be translated as a prediction of the future, since it is a verbless clause, and such clauses are normally translated as present or past tense, depending on the context (Walton 1987:290-291). Thus, the translation should likely be "a young woman is pregnant, and is about to bear a son."

Though some believe that Isaiah 7:14 describes the birth of Maher-shalal-hash-baz (Isa 8:3-4, 10, 18), Walton (1987:289-297; cf. Willis 1978:1-18 for a similar approach) has argued plausibly that Isaiah 7:14 originally described the coming birth of a son to a nameless young woman in Ahaz' harem. Perhaps this son was Hezekiah himself, a common Jewish view, but this is conjecture. The issue is not *who* the child was but *what* the child signified. The point is that even though times were bad at the moment, judgment would soon fall on the enemies Pekah and Rezin. Thus, the young woman should give her son the name Immanuel, since God was still with his people and would deliver them.

When Matthew, as a disciple of Jesus the Messiah, read Isaiah 7, Isaiah's prophecy came to new significance. Matthew did not create the virgin birth narrative as an imaginative midrash on Isaiah 7. Neither did he view Isaiah 7 as an intended prediction of Jesus' virgin birth. Rather, he saw the motifs of the oracle of Isaiah 7, particularly its stress upon the house of David (Isa 7:2, 13; 9:7), a young girl giving birth to a son (Isa 7:14-16; 8:3-4), and the presence of God with his people (Isa 7:14; 8:8, 10), in light of the miraculous birth of the Messiah. Matthew was obviously aware of these Isaianic motifs, as well as Isaiah's specific future predictions of the Messiah in the following context (Isa 9:1-7, cf. Matt 4:15-16. Isa 11:1-5, cf. Matt 2:23?; 3:16. Isa 42:1-4, cf. Matt 12:18-21). The motifs of Isaiah 7–8 anticipated and thus supported the message of Jesus the Messiah as Matthew understood it and wished to communicate it. In Jesus the Messiah, the house of David was culminated. Mary's virginal conception of Jesus the Messiah amounted to an infinitely greater sign to Israel. And Jesus the Messiah was himself God with the nation of Israel.

Though the preceding extended discussion is necessary for this *crux interpretum*, it runs the risk of causing the reader to "miss the forest for the trees." Whatever position one takes on the matter of Matthew's characteristic understanding of the Old Testament, one must not miss the most crucial matter, that Mary's son Jesus is Immanuel, God-with-us. This was Matthew's main concern here, and there is a risk of missing it if attention is given only to the preceding controversy. Matthew's Christian Jewish community would evidently already know the Hebrew name *Immanuel* (Gr. *Emmanouēl* [TG1694, ZG1842]), but for added emphasis Matthew also translated the meaning into Greek: "God is with us." This "name" is more of a title signifying the character and mission of Jesus as God with his people to save them from their sins. It is not just that God is present in Jesus to help his people (Hill 1972:80). Judging from the implications of his previous material (1:1, 16, 18, 20) and his overall high Christology (e.g., 3:17; 11:27; 28:18-20), it is likely that Matthew intended this in the fullest sense: Jesus as God's Son is also God himself with his people, effecting their deliverance. This is the ultimate manifestation of God's presence, and the significance of Isaiah's Immanuel, though great in itself, pales in comparison to it.

That Jesus is God with his people is a recurring theme in Matthew. Jesus was with his disciples when the storm struck and he saved them from it (8:23-27). He was with them as they were received or rejected while preaching his Kingdom (10:25, 40; 17:17). He would be with them as they solemnly handled intractable offenders in his new community (18:15-20). He is so identified with their experiences that he views them as his own (25:40, 45). In fact, the final reference to the Immanuel theme concludes the gospel and creates an *inclusio* enveloping the entire Gospel with this motif. As the church obeys its mandate to disciple all the nations, Jesus promises to continue his presence with the church all the days until the end of the age (28:18-20).

Summary. Matthew 1 has two major sections: the genealogy and the virginal conception story. This chapter reveals who Jesus is and what he has come to do. He is the Messiah, son of David and son of Abraham. In fulfillment of God's plan for redemptive history, he has come as the "with-us God" (Bruner 1987:28) who will save his people from their sins. In Matthew 1, then, we have in seed form the two doctrines that are widely acknowledged to be Matthew's chief concerns, Christology and ecclesiology.

◆ D. Visit of the Magi (2:1-12)

Jesus was born in Bethlehem in Judea, during the reign of King Herod. About that time some wise men* from eastern lands arrived in Jerusalem, asking, 2"Where is the newborn king of the Jews? We saw his star as it rose,* and we have come to worship him."

3King Herod was deeply disturbed when

he heard this, as was everyone in Jerusalem. [4]He called a meeting of the leading priests and teachers of religious law and asked, "Where is the Messiah supposed to be born?"

[5]"In Bethlehem in Judea," they said, "for this is what the prophet wrote:

[6]'And you, O Bethlehem in the land of Judah,
are not least among the ruling cities* of Judah,
for a ruler will come from you
who will be the shepherd for my people Israel.'*"

[7]Then Herod called for a private meeting with the wise men, and he learned from them the time when the star first appeared. [8]Then he told them, "Go to Bethlehem and search carefully for the child. And when you find him, come back and tell me so that I can go and worship him, too!"

[9]After this interview the wise men went their way. And the star they had seen in the east guided them to Bethlehem. It went ahead of them and stopped over the place where the child was. [10]When they saw the star, they were filled with joy! [11]They entered the house and saw the child with his mother, Mary, and they bowed down and worshiped him. Then they opened their treasure chests and gave him gifts of gold, frankincense, and myrrh.

[12]When it was time to leave, they returned to their own country by another route, for God had warned them in a dream not to return to Herod.

2:1 Or *royal astrologers;* Greek reads *magi;* also in 2:7, 16.   2:2 Or *star in the east.*   2:6a Greek *the rulers.*
2:6b Mic 5:2; 2 Sam 5:2.

NOTES

2:1 *Jesus was born in Bethlehem.* A comparison of 2:1 with 2:7 and 16 indicates that the wise men evidently arrived around two years after the birth of Jesus. Luke 1:26; 2:1-7 mentions Joseph and Mary's origins in Nazareth and trip to Bethlehem in response to the decree of Caesar Augustus. Matthew says nothing of this background, simply mentioning that Jesus was born in Bethlehem and connecting this in 2:5ff with Mic 5:2. Readers of Matthew who were familiar with the OT would recognize Bethlehem as David's city and connect it with Matthew's earlier stress on David (1:1, 6, 17, 20).

during the reign of King Herod. Jesus was born near the end of the reign of Herod the Great. Modern scholars often date his birth around 6-4 BC. The puzzling BC dating of Christ's birth is due to mistakes made when the Christian calendar was instituted in the sixth century AD. Herod the Great ruled from 37-4 BC. Half Jewish and half Idumean, he was known for his shrewd diplomacy and his many public works programs, including his expansion of the Second Temple. But Herod's personal life was in shambles, and palace intrigue was rampant. The Bethlehem atrocity (2:16) kept with Herod's usual manner of guarding his throne from any potential usurpers. Josephus (*Antiquities* 14-18) describes many of Herod's atrocities, including the murder of one of his wives and three of his sons.

wise men from eastern lands. The "wise men" (Gr. *magoi* [TG3097, ZG3407]; see NLT mg) were not kings but more likely prominent priestly professionals involved in studying the stars and discerning the signs of the times. They may have come from Arabia, Babylon, or Persia. Perhaps there are historical connections between them and the "Chaldeans" mentioned in Dan 1:20; 2:2; 4:7; 5:7, who were adept in the interpretation of dreams. How these men came to interpret the star as an indication of the birth of the Messiah is a mystery, though some speculate that they were somehow aware of the prophecy of Balaam in Num 24:17. Matthew includes this incident to contrast the mysterious insight of the wise men with the incredible obtuseness of Herod and the religious leaders.

2:2 *as it rose.* The Gr. means "in the east." "Star in the east" (NLT mg) is preferable because the wise men came from the east (2:1), not from the west toward an eastern star. Modern readers wonder whether the rising of the star may be explained scientifically as a comet, a planetary conjunction, or a supernova providentially arranged by God. Whether these modern explanations have merit or not, Matthew would evidently view it as a miracle. In some mysterious manner, the rising star led the wise men to Jerusalem to worship the one born king of the Jews. This contrasted with Herod's kingship, which was merely the result of shrewd political manipulation.

we have come to worship him. It is remarkable that the wise men came to worship Jesus. This word (cf. 2:8, 11; 8:2; 9:18; 14:33; 15:25; 18:26; 20:20; 28:9, 17) is not limited to religious contexts and may simply signify bowing or kneeling to pay homage or respect to a superior, such as a king. But given Matthew's high Christology and the stricture of 4:10, one wonders whether religious worship is indicated in every passage referring to Jesus.

2:3 *King Herod was deeply disturbed.* When King Herod heard that the wise men had come to worship the newborn king he became quite disturbed at this threat to his own rule.

as was everyone in Jerusalem. It is not clear whether all of Jerusalem was disturbed due to the prevalence of messianic speculation in those days or whether the residents of the city feared that Herod would be provoked to further cruelty by the wise men's arrival (Carson 1984:86). As Matthew's story proceeds, the Jerusalem "establishment" will unite in diametrical opposition to the newly born king of the Jews (see 15:1; 16:21; 20:17-18; 21:1, 10; 23:37).

2:4 *He called a meeting of the leading priests and teachers of religious law.* Because he feared the news brought by the wise men, Herod gathered the religious experts to find the answer to their question about the place of Jesus' birth. This reveals Herod's ignorance of the OT, as well as his quick response to a potential rival. The mention of the leading priests and the teachers of religious law at Jesus' birth tends to anticipate their active involvement in his death (16:21; 20:18; 21:15; 26:57). Matthew mentions the high priests in 2:4; 16:21; 20:18; 21:15, 23, 45; 26:3, 14, 47, 59; 27:1, 3, 6, 12, 20, 41, 62; 28:11. The high priest himself is mentioned in 26:51, 57, 62, 63, 65 and the teachers of the law in 2:4; 5:20; 7:29; 8:19; 9:3; 12:38; 13:52; 15:1; 16:21; 17:10; 20:18; 21:15; 23:2, 13, 15, 23, 25, 27, 29, 34; 26:57; 27:41. The two groups are mentioned together in 2:4; 16:21; 20:18; 21:15; 26:57. Another group connected at times to the high priests and teachers of the law is the elders (usually "leaders" in the NLT; 15:2; 16:21; 21:23; 26:3, 47, 57; 27:1, 3, 12, 20, 41; 28:12). The three groups are portrayed together as plotting against Jesus in 16:21; 26:57; 27:41. Evidently these three groups made up the high court or Sanhedrin. Herod would soon die (2:19), but the religious leaders remained and came to violently oppose Jesus. Herod's question equates the wise men's "king of the Jews" with "the Messiah." The linkage of Messiah with king also appears in the passion narrative (26:63, 68; 27:11, 17, 22, 29, 37).

2:5 *Bethlehem in Judea.* The Jewish religious leaders univocally answered Herod's question and cited Mic 5:2 (combined with 2 Sam 5:2) in support. They believed that the Messiah would be born in Bethlehem of Judea because it was so written by the prophet. This introductory formula differs from the others in Matt 1–2 in that "fulfillment" is not mentioned. The leaders cite the OT here as a text that proves their answer to Herod. This would make little sense unless they understood Mic 5:2 as a direct prediction of the Messiah's birth place.

what the prophet wrote. This introductory formula (lit., "it is written") generally occurs on the lips of Jesus in Matthew, with the exception of its use here by the leaders and Satan's use of it in 4:6. Its nine uses in Matthew are as follows: the leaders (2:5; cites Mic 5:2/ 2 Sam 5:2), Satan (4:6; cites Ps 91:11-12), Jesus (4:4, 7, 10; 11:10; 21:13; 26:24; 26:31; cite [in order] Deut 8:3; 6:16; 6:13; 11:10; Exod 23:20/Mal 3:1; Isa 56:7/Jer 7:11; no specific text; Zech 13:7).

2:6 The form of the text of Mic 5:2 appearing in Matthew differs from both the Hebrew Bible and the LXX. The key difference between Matthew and MT/LXX is his addition of a Gr. word (*oudamōs* [TG3760, ZG4027], "by no means;" rendered "not just" in the NLT) to the second line of the quote. Where MT and LXX make a simple assertion to the effect that Bethlehem is insignificant among the clans of Judah, Matthew's addition asserts the contrary: "by no means are you least among the rulers of Judah." But this contradiction is only superficial. In the MT and LXX, the geographical insignificance of Bethlehem is implicitly contrasted with its theological significance. Micah foresaw that the Messiah would rise from a geographically insignificant town. As Matthew looked back to Micah's prophecy, he noted in hindsight that the birth of Jesus had transformed the significance of Bethlehem.

The OT quotation is actually a combination of Mic 5:2 and 2 Sam 5:2. Matthew omits the end of Mic 5:2, "whose origins are from the distant past" and appends a line from 2 Sam 5:2 to the effect that Jesus will shepherd God's people Israel. While the last line of Mic 5:2 is certainly compatible with Matthew's high Christology, the material from 2 Sam fits Matthew's Davidic emphasis. The image of Jesus as shepherd fits into Matthew quite well (9:35-36; 14:14; 15:32; 25:31-46; 26:31) and is based on the OT (cf. Ps 23; Jer 23; Ezek 34; Mic 2:12-3:3). There is also an implicit contrast between Jesus as the genuine Davidic shepherd of Israel and Herod with his religious leaders, who are false shepherds, counterfeit successors of David.

2:7-8 *he learned from them the time.* By the time Herod had secretly summoned the wise men, he had already concocted his scheme to murder Jesus. He needed to ascertain from them the time when the star that marked the birth of Jesus had first appeared (cf. 2:16). In their naiveté, the wise men unwittingly gave Herod the information he needed. He also surreptitiously asked them to report the child's exact whereabouts under the pretense of wanting to go and worship him. Then he sent them off to Bethlehem, only five miles or so to the south. So Herod already knew when the helpless baby had been born and where he was living. As the unknowing wise men eagerly completed their long journey, Herod anticipated that their report would confirm the child's exact identity, making his plot quite easy to accomplish.

From a literary standpoint this situation is interesting. Matthew the narrator knew all about Herod's duplicity, but the wise men as characters in the story have not yet even a clue of it. The perceptive reader might gradually pick up on this, perhaps with previous knowledge of Herod's character (2:1), with possible suspicion of Herod's ignorance of the Messiah's birth place (2:4), and with probable suspicion of Herod's conspiratorial, if not sinister, secret meeting with the wise men (2:7-8). The perceptive reader's suspicions are confirmed as the story unfolds in 2:12-20.

2:9-10 *the wise men went their way.* After learning from the king where to go and becoming unwitting accomplices in his plot to murder Jesus, the wise men set out on the short trip to Bethlehem. As they went, the star they originally saw unexpectedly reappeared and miraculously led them to the vicinity of Jesus, perhaps to his exact location. This astral guarantee of God's guidance exhilarated the wise men. Whatever the merit of positing an explanation from known astronomical phenomenon for what the wise men saw earlier (2:1), no comet, supernova, or planetary conjunction would exhibit the characteristics observed here by the wise men.

2:11 *They entered the house.* Led by the miraculous star, the wise men arrived at the house where Jesus resided. The house is not a contradiction to the "manger" of Luke 2:7 (contra

Davies and Allison 1988:248), since perhaps as much as two years had passed since Jesus was born (2:16). The focus of the wise men was on the child Jesus, not on his mother Mary (who is mentioned) or on his adoptive father Joseph (who is not).

they bowed down and worshiped him. The wise men's worship has already been mentioned in 2:2, and here is reason to see in their worship a high Christology: If "worshiped" implies only a kneeling down before a superior, "bowed down" is redundant. Their worship was followed by opening their "treasures" (cf. 6:19-21; 19:21) and giving to Jesus gifts appropriate for a king: gold, frankincense (Exod 30:34-38; Lev 2:1-2, 14-16; 6:14-18; 24:7; Neh 13:5, 9; Isa 60:6; Jer 6:20), and myrrh (Gen 37:25; Exod 30:23; Esth 2:12; Ps 45:8; Song 1:13; 3:6; Mark 15:23; John 19:39). Frankincense and myrrh were both aromatic gum resins derived from trees and bushes and imported from the east. Commentators from Origen to Hendriksen (1973:171-176) have found symbolic significance in these gifts, gold for a king, frankincense for deity, and myrrh for death (Davies and Allison 1988:249-250). More likely, 2:11 alludes to such OT passages as Pss 72:10-12; 110:3; and Isa 60:6. Solomon received gifts from Gentile visitors and the prophets foresaw glorious days when Gentile tribute would be brought to Zion.

2:12 *they returned to their own country by another route.* Before they could unwittingly participate in Herod's monstrous scheme, the wise men were warned by God in a dream not to go back to Herod. Dreams occur frequently in Matthew's infancy material (1:20; 2:12, 13, 19, 22), but angelic visitation is not mentioned here or in 2:22. The wise men returned by another route, evidently bypassing Jerusalem entirely and following trade routes through the wilderness of Judah to the east. They could have traveled either north or south of the Dead Sea, but the southern route might have promised more secrecy. The departure of the wise men is expressed by the verb *anachōreō* [TG402, ZG432], which often expresses what might be called "strategic withdrawal" from those who oppose Jesus and the message of the Kingdom. Thus the wise men, along with Joseph, Mary, and Jesus, withdraw at crucial times to places of safety (2:12, 13, 14, 22; 4:12; 12:15; 14:13; 15:21).

COMMENTARY

The RSV and Fenton (1963:44ff), among others, divide Matthew 2 into five sections, each concluding with an Old Testament allusion. This scheme places a break between 2:6 and 2:7, due to an unwarranted stress on minor Old Testament allusions in 2:11. It is better to stress the four major Old Testament quotations and have four sections (1-12, 13-15, 16-18, 19-23). This chapter can also be profitably viewed as a drama in two acts comprising 2:1-12 and 2:13-23 respectively (Brown 1993:178-179). This is the approach followed here. The worship of the wise men in the first act contrasts with the treachery of Herod in the second. There is also the strange indifference of the chief priests and scribes (2:4-6), who quickly displayed knowledge of the Old Testament but did not act in obedience to that knowledge. Through it all, God protected the nascent Messiah by angelic appearances in dreams to the wise men and especially to Joseph, who obeyed at each juncture. These events hint at two motifs that are stressed as Matthew's story of Jesus develops further. First, the worship of the wise men implies that God's redemptive purposes extend beyond the nation of Israel. Second, the treachery of Herod and the indifference of the religious leaders shows that many within Israel will not believe in Jesus. Herod's unbelief is particularly blatant and also instructive. He used his newly acquired knowledge of Jesus the Messiah to plot against him. Ironically, as the chapter comes to a close, we see that Herod is dead (2:19), while Jesus is alive, still fulfilling the patterns and predictions of the Old Testament. Further occurrences of these motifs may be found in 8:10; 15:28; 21:31; 22:8-10.

Matthew 2:1-12 can also be displayed chiastically. This helps to place the focus of the pericope on the citation of Micah 5:2 (see note on 2:6) and thus on Matthew's characteristic emphasis on Jesus' continuity with Old Testament patterns and predictions:

2:1 Wise men arrive from the east.

    2:2 Wise men have seen a special star and seek to worship Jesus.

        2:3 Herod is terrified of the one born king of the Jews.

            2:4 Herod questions the religious leaders.

            2:5-6 Religious leaders answer Herod.

        2:7-8 Herod plots against the one born king of the Jews.

    2:11 Wise men see the star again and are enabled to worship Jesus.

2:12 Wise men depart to their own country.

It is significant in view of later developments that Matthew referred to Herod as king and then specified that the wise men arrived in Jerusalem. Herod's kingship was merely a political office and he would guard it against any potential rival. By contrast, Jesus' kingship, like David's (1:6), is genuine and legitimate, given him by God at birth (2:2). As such, it is appropriate that the wise men arrived in Jerusalem, David's capital city, the city of the great king (5:35; Ps 48:2), to worship the newly born king. It is the city of Solomon's Temple, but Jesus is greater than Solomon and his Temple (12:6, 42). He would cleanse the Temple when he entered the city as its rightful king (ch 21), only to be crucified there a few days later (ch 27).

It is ironic that the birth of Jesus produced only anxious fear in the leaders of Israel (2:3), while it was an occasion of overwhelming joy for the mysterious Gentile wise men. The devotion of the wise men is in stark contrast to Herod's treachery and the seeming apathy of the chief priests and teachers of the law. Why were these wise men the only ones who traveled to Bethlehem?

How the wise men originally understood that an astral phenomenon signaled prophetic fulfillment and the birth of the Messiah is shrouded in mystery. Numbers 24:17 was evidently understood as messianic by the Jews, but how the wise men might have come to associate a particular star with that prophecy is unclear. Dispersed Jews in the east may have influenced the wise men, but in the final analysis their worship of the Messiah was nothing less than a miracle of divine grace. Matthew 11:25-27 explains the divine initiative involved when anyone comes to faith in Jesus the Messiah, and 11:28-29 supplies Jesus' invitation for others to emulate the example of the wise men. This incident illustrates a truth that has become something of a cliche: God works in mysterious ways, his wonders to perform. The religious leaders, replete with scriptural knowledge, reacted with apathy here and with antipathy later. The wise men, whose knowledge was quite limited, nevertheless offered genuine worship to the newly born king of the Jews.

◆   E. The Escape and Return of the Messiah (2:13-23)

¹³After the wise men were gone, an angel of the LORD appeared to Joseph in a dream. "Get up! Flee to Egypt with the child and his mother," the angel said. "Stay there until I tell you to return, because Herod is going to search for the child to kill him."

¹⁴That night Joseph left for Egypt with the child and Mary, his mother, ¹⁵and they stayed there until Herod's death. This fulfilled what the Lord had spoken through the prophet: "I called my Son out of Egypt."*

¹⁶Herod was furious when he realized that the wise men had outwitted him. He sent soldiers to kill all the boys in and around Bethlehem who were two years old and under, based on the wise men's report of the star's first appearance. ¹⁷Herod's brutal action fulfilled what God had spoken through the prophet Jeremiah:

¹⁸ "A cry was heard in Ramah—
    weeping and great mourning.
Rachel weeps for her children,
    refusing to be comforted,
    for they are dead."*

¹⁹When Herod died, an angel of the Lord appeared in a dream to Joseph in Egypt. ²⁰"Get up!" the angel said. "Take the child and his mother back to the land of Israel, because those who were trying to kill the child are dead."

²¹So Joseph got up and returned to the land of Israel with Jesus and his mother. ²²But when he learned that the new ruler of Judea was Herod's son Archelaus, he was afraid to go there. Then, after being warned in a dream, he left for the region of Galilee. ²³So the family went and lived in a town called Nazareth. This fulfilled what the prophets had said: "He will be called a Nazarene."

2:15 Hos 11:1.   2:18 Jer 31:15.

NOTES

2:13 *After the wise men were gone, an angel of the Lord appeared to Joseph.* After they left, the divine intervention to thwart Herod's plot took another step. For the second time (cf. 1:20), Joseph unexpectedly received a revelation from an angel in a dream. He was to take Jesus and Mary to Egypt and stay there until he received further notice, because Herod was going to try to murder Jesus.

2:14 *That night Joseph left for Egypt.* Joseph again responded to the angel with prompt, unquestioning obedience (cf. 1:24). Under cover of darkness, Joseph, Mary, and Jesus withdrew to Egypt and remained there until Herod died and they received another angelic revelation (2:19). Egypt was a natural place to flee from Herod. He had no jurisdiction there and many Jews lived there. Perhaps Matthew wanted his readers to remember the family of Jacob sojourning in Egypt to avoid famine in Palestine (Gen 46–50). On the level of the infancy story, the withdrawal to Egypt preserved Jesus from Herod's plot, but Matthew had a deeper purpose in mind in presenting this event.

2:15 *This fulfilled.* God in his sovereignty achieved not only the immediate welfare of the infant Jesus but also the ultimate fulfillment of a well-known OT pattern. Matthew's second fulfillment formula quotation (see the discussion in the commentary on Matt 1) alludes to the new significance of the event described in Hos 11:1, "I called my son out of Egypt." The introductory formula is identical to the one that occurs in 1:22 and denotes the accomplishment of God's purpose in his word through the prophetic channel. Matthew cited only the last clause of Hos 11:1. No doubt, the concept of sonship was the reason Matthew was attracted to Hos 11:1 in the first place. The initial words of Hos 11:1, though not cited by Matthew, are also crucial for the sonship theme. The verse as a whole affirms that God loved Israel and called him from Egypt when he was a child. (See commentary below for further discussion.)

2:16 *he realized that the wise men had outwitted him.* With 2:16-18, Matthew returns to the story of Herod and the wise men. Since Bethlehem is only five or six miles from Jerusalem, Herod would soon realize that the wise men were not coming back. So he used the information he had previously received from the religious leaders and the wise men. He knew from the religious leaders where Jesus was born (2:5-6), and he knew from the wise men when Jesus was born (2:7). With this information, he launched the atrocity of murdering all the male children in the Bethlehem area who were under two years of age. Since Bethlehem was a small village, the loss of life was relatively low, but the innocence of the victims underscores the outrageous nature of this heinous act. While there is no other record of this atrocity, it fits well into what is known from Josephus about the ruthless nature of Herod's rule.

While Herod believed that the wise men had tricked him, their lack of complicity in his plot was due to divine intervention. Herod's rage was not in reality directed against the wise men; it was against God, who directed them not to return to Herod. Thus his fury is pathetic and futile, like that of the kings whom God warned in Ps 2 (cf. Acts 4:24-28).

2:17-18 *fulfilled what God had spoken through the prophet Jeremiah.* Herod's heinous act fulfills his own rage and paranoid fear, but Matthew was more interested in how it fulfilled Scripture. He introduced Jer 31:15 with a fulfillment formula similar to those used earlier in 1:22 and 2:15. For the first time, he named the prophet he was citing. Jeremiah was named only by Matthew in all of the NT writings (2:17; 27:9). See the commentary below for discussion on the significance of Jeremiah's words as used by Matthew.

2:19 *an angel of the Lord appeared in a dream to Joseph.* This is the fourth dream and third appearance of an angel of the Lord in the infancy narratives. The death of Herod allowed for the safe return of Jesus to Israel, but Joseph thought it wise to live in Nazareth of Galilee, not in Judea, where Herod's son Archelaus ruled in the place of his father. This unit picks up again the narrative of 2:13-15, which was briefly interrupted by the story of the murder of Bethlehem's male infants. Herod was the antagonist of Jesus up to this point and attempted to annihilate any potential rivals to his throne. But due to divine intervention, Jesus was still alive when Herod died. Herod's final illness and death is described in gruesome detail in Josephus's *Antiquities* 17.6.5.

2:20 *those who were trying to kill the child are dead.* The words of the angel commanding Joseph to take Mary and Jesus and return to Israel repeat the instructions given in 2:13 that they should leave Israel. There is also a similar clause explaining why the instructions must be followed in both 2:13 and 2:20. The plural "those who were trying to kill the child are dead" is curious since it was Herod alone who died.

2:21-22 *Joseph got up and returned.* By now Joseph's pattern of immediate response to angelic instructions is expected (cf. 1:24; 2:14). Joseph evidently planned to settle in Bethlehem, perhaps because he assumed Herod's son Antipas would succeed his father as ruler there. But he changed his plans when he learned that Herod's son Archelaus ruled Judea. Archelaus had a reputation for ruthlessness and cruelty (Josephus *Antiquities* 17.9.3). Herod had made a late change in his will, dividing his kingdom into three parts. Archelaus received Judea, Samaria, and Idumea. Antipas was to rule Galilee and Perea, and Philip received Iturea and Trachonitis. Joseph's fear of Archelaus was confirmed by yet another angelic dream revelation that warned him to avoid Judah and Archelaus. The interplay here between Joseph's responsible decision making and God's leading is intriguing. The warning of the angel underlined the fear Joseph already felt and evidently left it up to him where to settle. The withdrawal to Egypt was due to specific angelic revelation, and similarly the decision to withdraw to Galilee was influenced by a more general angelic warning.

Galilee is very important in Matthew's portrayal of Jesus as the one who fulfills Isa 9:1-2 (see Matt 4:12-16). After John's imprisonment, Jesus withdrew there and began his Kingdom ministry in "Galilee where so many Gentiles live" (4:15). Other important events also occurred there, but it is important to note that it is from this same Galilee that Jesus sent his successors to disciple all the nations (28:7, 16). Some have found a contradiction between Matthew and Luke regarding Galilee. It is clear from Luke 1:26-27; 2:1-7 that Mary and Joseph originally lived in Nazareth. While one would not gather this from Matthew, nothing said by Matthew contradicts it. Matthew simply picks up the story after Joseph and Mary have arrived in Bethlehem to register for Augustus's census. Another supposed discrepancy is the sojourn in Egypt, mentioned by Matthew but not by Luke. But Luke's account does not contradict Matthew's Egyptian visit, which may be placed in Luke 2 at some time prior to the return to Nazareth described in 2:29. Evidently, the presentation of Jesus in the Temple (Luke 2:21-38; cf. Lev. 12:2-8) should be viewed as historical background for the arrival of the wise men some time later. Certainly popular messianic speculation would be stirred by both events. At any rate, both of these difficulties are examples of the selectivity of the Gospel authors in omitting material that did not fit their individual theological interests or literary structure.

2:23 the family went and lived in a town called Nazareth. Due to political danger, common sense, and the angelic warning, Joseph decided to settle in Nazareth. One does not learn from Matthew what readers of Luke would know; it was only natural for Joseph and Mary to return to their hometown. Nazareth was an obscure village, not mentioned anywhere in pre-Christian literature. Fifteen miles west of the southern tip of the Sea of Galilee, it sat on the northern rim of the Megiddo valley just south of the thriving city of Sepphoris.

This fulfilled what the prophets had said, "He will be called a Nazarene." Joseph's decision to settle in this unremarkable hamlet had one consequence that was remarkable to Matthew: the fulfillment of the prophetic word. The introductory formula is like those used earlier in 1:22; 2:15, 17. It indicates that Joseph's decision to settle in Nazareth was a matter of God's purpose. It may be noteworthy that Matthew used the plural "the prophets" (cf. 26:54, 56), since this may help to explain which text (or texts) Matthew had in mind as being fulfilled by Jesus' settling in Nazareth. This is discussed further in the commentary.

COMMENTARY

Matthew 2:13-23 concludes Matthew's infancy narrative, which has explained the origins of Jesus the Messiah and his early movements. It contains three sections: the flight to Egypt (2:13-15), the massacre of the infants in Bethlehem (2:16-18), and the return to Israel (2:19-23). Each of these sections ends with an Old Testament citation introduced with Matthew's characteristic language of fulfillment. Each of these is worthy of detailed comment.

The Flight to Egypt: Fulfillment of Hosea 1:11. There are essentially three approaches to understanding Matthew's use of Hosea 11:1. Some believe that Matthew saw in the passage a prediction of Jesus' sojourn in Egypt and departure from there. But most would agree that in its original context Hosea 11:1 is not a prediction of the future but a reference to the Exodus, God's past redemptive act of bringing the nation of Israel out of Egypt. Thus, those who think that Matthew saw a prediction of Jesus in Hosea 11:1 must either disparage Matthew's hermeneutic or attribute to Matthew a revelatory insight into the *sensus plenior* (fuller meaning) of Hosea. Neither of these views is satisfactory. In its original context, Hosea 11:1 is not a prediction of Jesus but a reminiscence of the Exodus. That was at least as clear to Matthew as it is to modern interpreters. But Hosea 11:1 alludes to a theological motif that was dear to Matthew—namely, divine sonship. The Exodus demonstrated Israel's unique status as God's firstborn son. What was true of Israel on a metaphorical level is more profoundly true of Jesus the Messiah. Matthew has already shown the uniqueness of Jesus' sonship from the perspective of his Davidic genealogy and miraculous conception. He will go on to show how his baptism and temptation demonstrate his divine sonship even more fully. In Hosea 11:1, the Exodus provides a historical pattern of God's loving preservation of his son Israel from Pharaoh's wrath. From a Christian perspective, this past event is recapitulated by God's loving preservation of his son Jesus from Herod's wrath. In the Old Testament the nation is the son of God (Exod 4:22-23; Jer 31:9, 20; Hos 1:10), and the Davidic kings are sons of God (2 Sam 7:14-15; Ps 2:6-7, 12; 72:1; 89:26-37). God's special love and covenant loyalty were promised to both the nation and the kings. For Matthew, these themes are consummated in Jesus, whose life is an antitypical microcosm of the typical journey of the historical people of Israel.

The Mothers Mourning in Bethlehem: Fulfillment of Jeremiah 31:15. Jeremiah 31:15 occurs in an oracle of hope to those who were about to be exiled, probably to Babylon due to Nebuchadnezzar's conquest of Judah in 587 BC. The captivity was unavoidable. The captives had to wait seventy years before God would restore them to the land God promised to their forefathers (Jer 29:4-14). God punished Israel and Judah for their apostasy, but he would restore them to himself and to the Davidic dynasty (Jer 30:8-9; 33:14-15, 17). Israel was viewed as a virgin (Jer 31:4, 21) whom God loved as his special people (Jer 30:3, 22; 31:1, 2, 7, 33) and would save as a remnant (Jer 31:7). God yearned for Israel because he was Israel's father and Israel was his firstborn (Jer 31:9, 20). Thus, there was hope that Israel's children would return (Jer 31:17) because God would make a new covenant with the nation and forgive their sins (Jer 31:31, 34). Nevertheless, there was great mourning by Rachel (who personified the mothers of Israel) for her children who had died in the ravages of war.

In light of this background, it seems that "fulfillment" here should not be viewed simplistically as the eventuation of a prediction. Jeremiah 31:15 is not a prediction but a lament in the context of hope for future blessing. This context of hope is probably Matthew's main theological interest (Carson 1984:95; Tasker 1961:44). In Jeremiah's view of the eschaton, Rachel's mourning for her children would be consoled by Israel's return to the land and the beginning of a new covenant. The similar mourning of the mothers of Bethlehem also occurs in the context of hope, but the hope there was about to be actualized through the sacrificial death and resurrection of the Messiah (26:27-28). God comforted the exiles with the hope of restoration and the new covenant, and this hope was about to be actualized through the Messiah. Thus, the mourning mothers of Bethlehem were anticipated by the mothers who lost children at the time of the Exile.

"He Will Be Called a Nazarene": Fulfillment of the Prophets. The difficulty involved here is very simple—there are no Old Testament texts that refer to Jesus as a

Nazarene, let alone explicitly say "he shall be called a Nazarene." Gundry (1975:97-104) has a very thorough discussion of this matter. There are two major approaches to solving the difficulty. The one posits a pun or paronomasia where Matthew is associating the place name "Nazareth" and the word for a resident of Nazareth, "Nazarene," with either the Hebrew word for "branch" (*netser* [TH5342, ZH5342]; Isa 11:1; cf. synonyms in Isa 4:2; 53:2) or the Old Testament "Nazirite" [TH5139B, ZH5687], one especially dedicated to God (Num 6; Judg 13:5, 7; 16:17; 1 Sam 1:11; Lam 4:7; Amos 2:11-12; cf. Luke 1:15; Acts 18:18; 21:23-24). In light of Matthew's emphasis on Jesus' Davidic roots, the "branch" pun is plausible. But the Nazirite pun seems unlikely, given the insistence of Matthew 11:18-19 that Jesus did not live an ascetic lifestyle.

Another approach views the pun theories as overly subtle and posits instead that Matthew was drawing together the obscure geographical origins of the Messiah and the theological thrust of the Old Testament that the Messiah would be humble and despised. This view notes the obscurity and humility of the Messiah in Matthew and connects this with the general tenor of the Old Testament that the Messiah would be despised and rejected (Ps 22:6-8, 13; 69:8, 20-21; Isa 49:7; 53:2-3, 7-8; Dan 9:26). Matthew's mention of the transformation of obscure Bethlehem by Jesus' birth (2:6), along with his stress on Jesus' humility (11:29; 12:19; 21:5) and rejection (8:20; 11:16-19; 15:7-8), are cited by advocates of this position (Carson 1984:97; Gundry 1975:103-104; Morris 1992:49; Tasker 1961:45; Toussaint 1980:56-57). Other references to Nazareth in Matthew also imply its unsavory Gentile connections and obscurity—that is, from the perspective of urban Jerusalem (4:13; 21:11; 26:71). Additional support is found in the evidence elsewhere in the New Testament that Nazareth was a despised place (John 1:46-47; 7:41-42; 52) and that "Nazarene" was a term of derision for the early disciples of Jesus (Acts 24:5).

Though it is difficult to rule out the first approach as a possible secondary allusion, the second approach is preferable. Matthew's introductory formula cites the prophets in general, so it seems that he was alluding to the general teaching of the prophets, not to a word play on a specific word in a single passage. The general tenor of the prophets that the Messiah would be lowly and despised is echoed repeatedly in Matthew, though it evidently cut against the grain of first-century messianic speculation.

The Significance of the Infancy Narratives. In retrospect it is clear that the message of the narratives in Matthew 1–2 has little to do with Jesus' infancy. Rather, it traces his ancestry, miraculous conception, early worship and opposition, and residence in Nazareth. All this is interwoven with Old Testament historical pattern and prophetic prediction. Jesus is the Messiah, the son of David, the son of Abraham. He is the culmination of Old Testament history and prophecy. As the son of David, he is the genuine king of Israel, contrasted with the wicked usurper Herod. As the son of Abraham, he brings the blessings of God to the Gentile wise men. Davies and Allison (1988:282) put all this deftly: "Jesus culminates Israel's history in chapter 1; in chapter 2 he repeats it." As Matthew's story of Jesus continues, both of these themes are developed. The contrast between Jesus and the false leaders of Israel erupts into full fledged hostility leading to his death. But his outreach to the Gentiles culminates with his resurrection and mandate to the disciples to take the gospel to all the nations (28:19-20).

Jesus' genuine kingship is tied to his Davidic sonship, as is shown in the genealogy. Yet Jesus is also the Son of God, as implied in 1:18-25; this is made more explicit as the narrative proceeds in chapter two. As the king of the Jews, Jesus could resist Satan's test in offering him all the world's kingdoms (4:8). He could affirm his superiority to king Solomon (12:42) and promise a glorious future return to the earth (16:28; 19:28; 20:21; 25:34). Yet he could enter Jerusalem humbly (21:5) and endure the unspeakable mockery leading to his crucifixion (27:11, 29, 37, 42). The resurrection would vindicate his claims and validate him as the king of the Jews, to whom all power had been given (28:18).

◆ II. The Early Days of Jesus' Kingdom Ministry (3:1–7:29)
   A. Ministry of John the Baptist (3:1–12; cf. Mark 1:1-8; Luke 3:1-14)

In those days John the Baptist came to the Judean wilderness and began preaching. His message was, 2"Repent of your sins and turn to God, for the Kingdom of Heaven is near.*" 3The prophet Isaiah was speaking about John when he said,

"He is a voice shouting in the
   wilderness,
'Prepare the way for the LORD's
   coming!
Clear the road for him!'"*

4John's clothes were woven from coarse camel hair, and he wore a leather belt around his waist. For food he ate locusts and wild honey. 5People from Jerusalem and from all of Judea and all over the Jordan Valley went out to see and hear John. 6And when they confessed their sins, he baptized them in the Jordan River.

7But when he saw many Pharisees and Sadducees coming to watch him baptize,* he denounced them. "You brood of snakes!" he exclaimed. "Who warned you to flee God's coming wrath? 8Prove by the way you live that you have repented of your sins and turned to God. 9Don't just say to each other, 'We're safe, for we are descendants of Abraham.' That means nothing, for I tell you, God can create children of Abraham from these very stones. 10Even now the ax of God's judgment is poised, ready to sever the roots of the trees. Yes, every tree that does not produce good fruit will be chopped down and thrown into the fire.

11"I baptize with* water those who repent of their sins and turn to God. But someone is coming soon who is greater than I am—so much greater that I'm not worthy even to be his slave and carry his sandals. He will baptize you with the Holy Spirit and with fire.* 12He is ready to separate the chaff from the wheat with his winnowing fork. Then he will clean up the threshing area, gathering the wheat into his barn but burning the chaff with never-ending fire."

3:2 Or has come, or is coming soon.   3:3 Isa 40:3 (Greek version).   3:7 Or coming to be baptized.   3:11a Or in.   3:11b Or in the Holy Spirit and in fire.

NOTES
3:1 In those days. This is intentionally somewhat vague (cf. 13:1; 24:22, 29, 36; 26:29). Unlike Luke, Matthew did not mention the circumstances surrounding the birth of John the Baptist.

Judean wilderness. John's ministry was carried out in the desert (cf. 3:3; 4:1; 11:7; 15:33) of Judea, the barren area just west of the Dead Sea. This largely uninhabited area is characterized by a dry climate and a topography featuring valleys (wadis) running from the hills in the west to the geological Rift Valley of the Jordan River and Dead Sea in the east. During the rainy season, these wadis become swift streams, but they are largely dry the rest of the year (cf. 7:26-27). Therefore, the NLT's translation "wilderness" should not be understood as a forest or jungle. The role of the wilderness in redemptive history as the place of refuge, testing, the Exodus, and the giving of the law may be significant here.

began preaching. Though he is known as "the baptizer," John commenced his ministry with preaching (cf. 4:17; 10:7; 24:14).

3:2 Repent . . . the Kingdom of Heaven is near. John's message is characterized as having two aspects, (1) an ethical imperative ("Repent"), based on (2) an eschatological reality ("the Kingdom of Heaven is near"). This is the first occurrence of the message that echoes throughout Matthew's gospel (cf. 4:17, 23; 9:35; 10:7; 13:19; 16:19; 21:43; 24:14). Repentance is the turning of the whole person from sin to God in obedience to the message of the Kingdom. This involves cognition of need, sorrow for sin, a decision to turn from sin to God, and subsequent obedient lifestyle. The "Kingdom of Heaven" is a distinctively Matthean expression for the Kingdom of God. Matthew probably used it in order to avoid mentioning the name of God, which was held in awe by pious Jews. "Heaven" stands for "God" by metonymy (cf. Dan 4:26; Matt 21:25; Luke 15:18, 21), which is the substitution of one word for another with which it is readily associated. Instead of thinking of the Kingdom as a concrete entity, which is either present or future, one should view it as gradually and dynamically exerting its power through the words and works of God's messengers. God's reign has drawn near in redemptive history; it is imminent. Matthew portrays John, Jesus, the first disciples, and subsequent Christians as proclaiming this message. (3:2; 4:17; 10:7; 24:14). For a more extended discussion of Matthew's use of the phrase "Kingdom of Heaven," see the discussion of Major Themes in the Introduction.

3:3 The prophet Isaiah. Having summarized John's message (3:1-2), Matthew now turns to his characteristic motif of OT support. John's origins in the obscurity of the desert as well as Jesus' origins in the small village of Bethlehem are both grounded in the OT. Although the characteristic fulfillment formula is not present here, Matthew's "the prophet Isaiah was speaking about John when he said, . . ." clearly points to John as the eschatological fulfillment of Isa 40:3.

Prepare the way . . . Clear the road. The topographical changes mentioned here allude to the ancient custom of building or repairing roads to honor the visit of a king. John used them to picture the need for moral change. In its immediate context, Isa 40:3 comforted the exiles in Babylon with the hope of return to the land. But in the larger context of Isa 40–66 the prophecy of Isaiah describes the eschatological restoration of Israel with worldwide consequences experienced by all mankind (Isa 40:5). The overall perspective of Isa 40–66 involves the Spirit-endowed Messiah (Isa 42:1-4; see Matt 12:18-21), who is the suffering servant (Isa 52:15; see Matt 28:19; Isa 53:4; see Matt 8:17; Isa 53:7; see Matt 26:63; 27:14), envisioning nothing less than a new heavens and new earth (Isa 65:17; 66:22; see Matt 19:28).

3:4 clothes were woven from coarse camel hair . . . he ate locusts. According to Davies and Allison (1988:295-296), modern Bedouin still wear camel hair garments and eat locusts (grasshoppers). A camel hair garment bound with a leather belt might suggest poverty in another context, but here it is suggestive of John's prophetic role and stern message of repentance. In fact, John was much like Elijah in this respect (2 Kgs 1:8; Zech 13:4; cf. Mal 4:5; Matt 11:7-9, 14; 17:10-13). Eating locusts was permitted by the OT (Lev. 11:20-23), and wild honey is mentioned several times there (Gen 43:11; Exod 3:8; Deut 32:13; Judg 14:8; 1 Sam 14:25; Ps 81:16; Ezek 27:17). All in all, John's clothing and diet modeled the message he preached. He was unconcerned with the niceties of wardrobe and food (11:8, 18), and he called Israel away from preoccupation with such things and toward the Kingdom.

3:5 *People from Jerusalem and from all of Judea and all over the Jordan valley went out.* Actually, the tense of the Gr. verb (imperfect) implies that there was a steady stream of people regularly going out to John. The three place names and the words "all" and "all over" add to the impression that the response to John was truly sensational. This is corroborated by Josephus (*Antiquities* 18.5.2).

3:6 *when they confessed their sins, he baptized them.* The meaning of the word "baptize" (to immerse), along with the fact that the baptisms were being done in the Jordan River, probably indicates that John immersed those who had repented. Their confession of sins probably occurred at the same time as their baptism. In light of 3:7-8, there is the additional implication that John did not baptize those whom he deemed unrepentant. Thus, Matthew evidently did not mean to imply that baptism itself effected repentance. Rather, baptism was a confirmation of repentance and a seal of forgiveness. Perhaps the custom was for repentant baptismal candidates to confess their sins publicly as they were being baptized. The implications of 3:6 for a theology of John's baptism must be compared with the similar statements of 3:11. John's baptism evidently had some connections with OT ritual cleansings, Jewish proselyte baptism, and the cleansing rituals of the Qumran community (see Taylor 1997).

3:7 *many Pharisees and Sadducees coming to watch him baptize.* Though the popular response to John's ministry was sensational, Matthew here indicates the contrasting response of the religious establishment. But it is difficult to know exactly why the Pharisees and Sadducees came to John's baptism. The Gr. phrase translated by the NLT as "coming to watch him baptize" is ambiguous. It is doubtful that it was simply a matter of curiosity. Possibly they had come to be baptized (see NLT mg), or they were there in an official capacity to investigate the furor in the desert. At any rate, John did not view their motivation as genuine.

brood of snakes! His vivid accusatory description of the Pharisees and Sadducees as an evil "brood of snakes" is twice echoed by Jesus (12:34; 23:33, cf. Gen 3:1; Ps 58:4). They viewed themselves as children of Abraham (3:9), but John had a very different idea of their spiritual ancestry.

Who warned you to flee God's coming wrath? John's sarcastic question indicates that he did not believe that the Pharisees and Sadducees were genuine converts. If the emphasis is placed on "who," John was disclaiming any connection with their pilgrimage to the Jordan. He certainly hadn't warned them to flee the coming judgment. If the emphasis is placed on "you," the implication is that they were unrepentant and thus were not fit candidates for baptism. Those who do not repent when they hear the message of God's eschatological rule will face imminent judgment, "the coming wrath."

3:8-9 *Prove by the way you live.* Lit., "produce fruit." John's observation of the Pharisees and Sadducees led him to believe they were unrepentant, so he demanded that they produce fruit (3:8) and then responded to an anticipated objection (3:9). Producing fruit as a metaphor for a repentant lifestyle occurs elsewhere in Matthew (3:10; 7:16-20; 12:33; 13:8, 23, 26; 21:19) and is common in the OT (Ps 1:3; Isa 3:10; 5:1-7; Hos 10:1). John now and Jesus later both affirm that the lifestyle of converts must fit or correspond to their profession of repentance. Such a change in lifestyle will never occur if confidence is placed in descent from Abraham.

3:10 *chopped down and thrown into the fire.* John's demand for proof of repentance (3:8) is underlined with a vivid picture of judgment. Unrepentant hearers of the Kingdom message are likened to trees that do not bear fruit—they are cut down and thrown into the fire.

A similar picture of false prophets as unfruitful trees is found in 7:19 (cf. Isa 10:15-19; Jer 11:16), and 13:24-30 pictures the weeds among the wheat being thrown into the fire at the harvest (cf. the chaff in 3:12). Jesus' cursing the unfruitful fig tree in 21:19 is another simi-lar image. The burning of unfruitful trees is also related to the punishment of evildoers in the fires of hell (5:22; 13:42, 50; 18:8-9; 25:41). The vividness of the picture is heightened by the words "even now," which depict the chopping down of unfruitful trees as a process that is presently occurring. As the Kingdom message is preached, those who reject it are already being marked out for judgment, even though the full force of that awful judgment has not yet been felt.

3:11 *I baptize with water . . . He will baptize you with the Holy Spirit and with fire.*
John contrasts his ministry with that of the one who is coming after him. John's water bap-tism for repentance prepares Israel for the more powerful "Spirit and fire" baptism of Jesus. John is not even fit to perform the menial task of carrying Jesus' shoes. Jesus' powerful min-istry is likened to a harvest in which the grain is gathered (cf. 6:26; 13:30) and the chaff is burnt. Jesus, the mighty one who comes after John, is the eschatological harvester who saves and judges. The imagery of 3:12 is similar to that of such OT texts as Ps 1:4; Isa 5:24; Dan 2:35; and Hos 13:3.

There is no little controversy over the relationship of John's baptism to repentance. The NLT's "I baptize with water those who repent . . ." interpretively translates a clause that is more lit. rendered "I baptize you with water for repentance" (see NASB, NIV, NJB, and NRSV). But this might be taken to mean that baptism in water somehow accomplishes repentance, which seems contrary to the contextual call for repentance, evidently as a pre-requisite for baptism (3:7-9). Perhaps the meaning is simply that the baptism is in refer-ence or connection to repentance. This connection is twofold in that baptism both assumes and expresses repentance.

John's baptism uses water, but Jesus' baptism will involve the Holy Spirit and fire. Though some (e.g., Bruner 1987:79-80; Luz 1989:171; Ridderbos 1987:55) see two baptisms here, one in the Spirit indicating salvation and the other in fire indicating judgment, it is prefer-able to see only one purifying baptism (Davies and Allison 1988:317). In this under-standing the phrase, "Spirit and fire," is understood as a hendiadys, a figure of speech in which one idea is expressed by two words. This seems to be indicated also by OT texts that associate the eschatological outpouring of the Spirit with both cleansing water (Isa 32:15; 44:3; Ezek 36:25-27; Joel 2:28-29; cf. 1QS 4:20-22) and refining fire (Isa 1:25; 4:4; 30:27-30; Zech 13:9; Mal 3:1-3; 4:1; cf. Acts 2:3; 4 Ezra 13:8-11). So it is best to conclude that the one eschatological outpouring of the Spirit through Jesus will purify and judge. The Holy Spirit has been mentioned as the miraculous agent behind Jesus' conception (1:18, 20). Now as John speaks of the future, he asserts that Jesus will baptize in the Holy Spirit. Though he would eventually dispense the Spirit to others (3:11), Jesus presently needs the empowerment of the Spirit for his own mission (4:1; 12:18, 28). For a perceptive study of the ministry of the Spirit to Jesus see Hawthorne 1991.

3:12 *separate the chaff from the wheat.* The purifying judgment of Jesus is pictured here as a harvest in which the threshing process separates the wheat from the chaff (cf. Ps 1:4; Prov 20:26; Isa 41:14-16; Jer 15:7; 51:33; Dan 2:35; Hos 6:11; 13:3; Joel 3:13; Mic 4:12-13; Rev 14:14-20). The fork or shovel was used to toss the harvested and threshed grain in the air, and the wind dispersed the chaff while the heavier grain fell to the floor. The grain was gathered, but the chaff was swept up and burnt. Matthew's capsulized portrayal of John's Kingdom message stresses the judgment of God upon the unrepentant.

never-ending fire. The image of "never-ending" (lit. "unquenchable") fire underlines the severity of the punishment in a way that is tantamount to the Christian doctrine of eternal punishment.

COMMENTARY

Matthew 3 is the first section in Matthew with synoptic parallels (Mark 1:1-11; Luke 3:1-14, 21-22). The chapter naturally divides into three sections: (1) John's ministry in the desert (3:1-6), (2) John's conflict with the Pharisees and Sadducees (3:7-12), and (3) John's baptism of Jesus (3:13-17). Nearly thirty years (Luke 3:23) had evidently transpired between the events of Matthew 2:23 and 3:1. Though the apocryphal Gospels contain many fanciful stories about Jesus' childhood, the New Testament is largely silent. What little scriptural knowledge that is available for this period is found in the Gospel of Luke. According to Luke, Joseph and Mary returned to Nazareth amazed at the revelations given about Jesus in the Temple (2:25-38). Jesus' childhood and early adolescence are described in Luke 2:40, 52. But Matthew says nothing directly about the years between Jesus' coming to live in Nazareth as a small child and his coming to John for baptism as an adult (2:22; 3:13). One can draw a few inferences from Matthew 13:54-58 about Jesus' upbringing in Nazareth, but the fact is that Matthew's theological purposes are not furthered by biographical details of this period. Matthew is interested in telling the story of Jesus' origins (chs 1–2) and his preparation for ministry (3:1–4:16).

The story of Jesus' preparation for ministry begins with the ministry of John the Baptist and ends with John's imprisonment. John's ministry in the desert of Judea, predicted in Isaiah 40:3, results in many Judeans coming to him for baptism (3:1-6). It seems best to see John's baptism against a broad background of similar activities in Second Temple Judaism rather than to attempt an explanation that draws from only one of the possible backgrounds, such as the Dead Sea Scrolls. The Old Testament itself frequently alludes to water cleansing as a picture of forgiveness, spiritual purity, and eschatological blessing (Ps 51:6-9; Isa 4:4; 44:3; Jer 4:11-14; Ezek 36:24-27; Zech 13:1). But there are three important contrasts between John's baptism and these possible backgrounds. First, John insisted on repentance and baptism for Jews, not Gentile proselytes. This would counter the current view that Israel's problems were due only to Gentile oppression, and that the Messiah's mission was merely to set Israel free from this oppression. Descent from Abraham was no guarantee of God's favor (3:9). Second, John's baptism was a single act of confession, not a repeated ritual as in the Old Testament and in the Qumran community. Third, John's ministry and baptism were directed toward the nation of Israel as a whole, not toward a sectarian monastic community as at Qumran. Therefore, Davies and Allison (1988:299) seem to be correct in viewing John's baptism as a creative reapplication of biblical and cultural motifs.

When John's ministry attracted Pharisees and Sadducees, he rebuffed them and warned them of judgment (3:7-12). Matthew speaks of the Pharisees often—nearly 30 times. On eleven occasions, they are mentioned alone (9:11, 14, 34; 12:2, 14, 24; 15:12; 19:3; 22:15, 41; 23:36). They are linked with the teachers of the law (scribes) ten times (5:20; 12:38; 15:1; 23:2, 13, 15, 23, 25, 27, 29). Five times they appear (as here) with the Sadducees, although the other four times occur in one pericope (3:7; 16:1, 6, 11, 12). The Pharisees also appear with the chief priests, who were Sadducees, in 21:45 and 27:62. In 22:34-35 one of the Pharisees is described as a lawyer. According to Josephus (*Antiquities* 17.2.4) there were over 6,000 Pharisees. Their roots are most likely traced to the *Hasidim* who rebelled against the Seleucid king Antiochus IV (Epiphanes) in the 160s BC. The name "Pharisee" may be derived from a word meaning "separatist." Their chief characteristic was rigorous adherence to the law, which in their view encompassed both the written Old Testament and the oral traditions that had grown up as a "fence around the law" (*Pirke Avoth* 1:1). In Matthew their preoccupation with the "traditions of the elders" as rules of conduct put them at loggerheads with Jesus. Their views of such matters as Sabbath observance and ritual washings were determined by the oral law. But these were viewed by Jesus as pedantic and burdensome additions to the genuine (written) law of God (cf., e.g., 15:1-20; 23). Blomberg (1992: 77) rightly points out that not all Pharisees were hypocrites.

The Sadducees are mentioned much less frequently in Matthew, seven times in three pericopes. They appear with the Pharisees in the context of John's ministry (3:7) and later join with them in an attempt to put Jesus to the test by asking for a heavenly sign (16:1, 6, 11, 12). Once Jesus entered Jerusalem, they unsuccessfully attempted to question him on the resurrection (22:23, 34). Less is known about the Sadducees. Josephus spent some time describing them in *Wars* 2.8.14, *Antiquities* 13.5.9; 13.10.6; and 18.1.1, 4. A smaller group than the Pharisees, they evidently were made up of wealthy priests who had no use for the oral law of the Pharisees. They were evidently more pro-Roman than the Pharisees, and they stressed human freedom more than the Pharisees did. Their denial of the resurrection and the afterlife is well known (cf. 22:23-33). Perhaps this was due to preoccupation with the five books of Moses and neglect of the rest of the Old Testament, though Davies and Allison (1988:302-303) doubt this. Pharisaic Judaism lived on after the AD 70 destruction of the Temple in Jerusalem, but this event evidently marked the end of the Sadducees.

Just as Matthew 2 presents Herod and the Jewish teachers as a foil to the wise men, so here John's baptism of the repentant masses is contrasted with his denunciation of the religious leaders who have come only to watch the baptisms. The linkage of the Pharisees and Sadducees, two entrenched groups that were theologically and socially disparate, shows that both "establishment" movements were unified in opposition to the mass appeal of the charismatic prophet John. This anticipates their later unified opposition to Jesus (cf. 16:1, 6, 11, 12).

John pronounced judgment on them in no uncertain terms. His message of repentance and fruitbearing, winnowing and eternal fire are poignant. The images of 3:7-12 present a very different picture of God and his rule than is often presented in pulpits today, where the stress is on God's provision of goods and services to meet people's felt needs. One wonders whether John would even recognize this "gospel" of self-actualization as an authentic interpretation of the message of God's Kingdom.

◆   B. The Baptism of Jesus (3:13-17; cf. Mark 1:9-11; Luke 3:21-22)

¹³Then Jesus went from Galilee to the Jordan River to be baptized by John. ¹⁴But John tried to talk him out of it. "I am the one who needs to be baptized by you," he said, "so why are you coming to me?"

¹⁵But Jesus said, "It should be done, for we must carry out all that God requires.*" So John agreed to baptize him.

¹⁶After his baptism, as Jesus came up out of the water, the heavens were opened* and he saw the Spirit of God descending like a dove and settling on him. ¹⁷And a voice from heaven said, "This is my dearly loved Son, who brings me great joy."

3:15 Or *for we must fulfill all righteousness.*   3:16 Some manuscripts read *opened to him.*

NOTES

3:13 *to be baptized by John.* Jesus' arrival at the Jordan (cf. 3:6) to be baptized by John led to a brief discussion between John and Jesus before John acquiesced (3:14-15). The statement that Jesus had come from Galilee connects with 2:22-23 and resumes the narrative of Jesus' preparation for ministry. According to Luke 3:23, Jesus was about 30 years old at this time.

3:14 *I am the one who needs to be baptized by you.* The paradoxical character of Jesus' baptism has always challenged interpreters. John was baptizing those who repented and confessed their sins (3:6). John refused to baptize those who bore no fruit of repentance (3:8). In contrast, Jesus was initially refused baptism because he evidently did not need to repent and bring forth fruit (3:14). John did not view his baptism as worthy of Jesus (Carson 1984:107). In historical perspective, if John's baptism only prepared people for Jesus' ultimate baptism in Spirit and fire, why should Jesus submit to John's authority (Davies and Allison 1988:324)? John expressed his incredulity at Jesus' request by noting that their roles should be reversed: Jesus should baptize John. It is unclear how John came to his convictions about Jesus, but it seems plausible that John would have learned from his mother Elizabeth about the remarkable circumstances of Jesus' birth and his own role as Jesus' forerunner (Luke 1).

3:15 *It should be done.* Jesus commanded John to perform the baptism immediately because it was appropriate for them in this way to fulfill all righteousness. It is anachronistic to take this statement as pertaining to Christian baptism (as does Bruner 1987:84-85). This statement features two key Matthean themes, fulfillment (see the discussion in the commentary on 1:25) and righteousness. It has been argued that fulfilling all righteousness means that Jesus was taking upon himself the obligation to obey the law, which had been stressed by John (Harrington 1991:62; Hill 1972:96; cf. 21:33). This fits Matthew's theology but still does not adequately handle the fulfillment theme in Matthew. It seems best to conclude with others (Carson 1984:105-108; Davies and Allison 1988:325-327) that Jesus fulfilled all righteousness by fulfilling the OT pattern and prediction about the Messiah. In Jesus' baptism, he and John fulfilled the OT by introducing the Messiah to Israel. This baptism, an inauguration of Jesus' ministry to Israel, led immediately to OT fulfillment in that the Spirit, as a dove, came upon the Messiah (Isa 11:1-2; 42:1; cf. Matt 12:18, 28) and the Father endorsed his Son in the voice from heaven (Ps 2:7; Isa 42:1; cf. Matt 17:5). In baptism, Jesus as the servant proclaimed and exemplified the righteousness envisioned by the prophets. Additionally he identified in baptism with the repentant righteous remnant within the nation of Israel (cf. 3:5-6). Though he had no sin to confess, his baptism nevertheless demonstrated his humility and anticipated his ministry to lowly but repentant people (cf. 2:23; 11:19; 12:20; 21:5).

3:16 *After his baptism.* Matthew passed over the baptism of Jesus quickly in order to stress two attesting events that pertain to OT fulfillment: the heavenly vision (3:16) and the heavenly voice (3:17). The former relates to the coming of the Spirit upon Jesus (cf. Isa 11:1; 42:1; 61:1), and the latter relates to the Father's endorsement of Jesus (cf. Ps 2:7; Isa 42:1). Taken together, the two events foreshadow two key interrelated features of Jesus' ministry. He is empowered by the Spirit (cf. 12:18, 28) and he is approved by the Father (cf. 17:5). Theologians often look at this text as an anticipation of the Christian doctrine of the Trinity (cf. 28:19). In 3:16 Matthew stresses the immediacy of the dramatic attesting events that followed the baptism. Jesus left the water, received the vision of the heavens standing open, and saw the Spirit descending as a dove upon him (cf. Gen 1:2; 8:8-12; Hos 7:11). The opening of heaven is a regular feature of biblical apocalyptic visions (cf., e.g., Isa 64:1; Ezek 1:1; John 1:51; Acts 7:56; Rev 4:1). It is likely that the dove's descent recalls Gen 1:2 and hints that Jesus is the agent of God's eschatological new creation (19:28).

3:17 This is my dearly loved Son. The heavenly voice confirms and interprets the import of the heavenly vision of the Spirit's descent. The words of the heavenly voice express the Father's approval of the Son (cf. 17:5) in words blending the suffering servant motif from Isa 42:1 with the sonship motif of Ps 2:7. The servant motif interprets the baptism by which Jesus identified with the righteous remnant of Israel. The sonship motif recalls the unique circumstances of Jesus' conception and infancy (1:16, 18-25; 2:15) and sets the scene for Satan's tests (4:3, 6). The sonship motif also implies Jesus' Davidic connections (1:1; cf. 2 Sam 7:13-14; Ps 89:27). Although it is true, as a matter of Christian theology, that the Father is eternally pleased with the Son, it is more likely here that the baptism of Jesus is the specific event that pleased the Father (Gundry 1982:53).

COMMENTARY

The story of Jesus in Matthew 3:1–4:16 centers on John's ministry. John prepared the way for Jesus, and his baptism of Jesus was the occasion for the coming of the Spirit and the Father's approval of his beloved son. This sonship, affirmed by the Father at John's baptism of Jesus, was immediately tested by Satan. After this testing, the imprisonment of John led to the beginning of Jesus' ministry in Galilee. With the presentation of the ministry of John, Matthew's Gospel for the first time parallels Mark (1:1-11), Luke (3:1-23), and John (1:19-34).

When compared to Mark and Luke, Matthew's account presents two very noticeable unique features. He alone presents the dialogue between Jesus and John in which John hesitates and Jesus ties the necessity of his baptism to the fulfilling of all righteousness (3:14-15). This unique section highlights distinctive Matthean themes of fulfillment and righteousness.

Another unique feature of Matthew is his account of the Father's endorsement of the Son (3:17). Here Matthew couches the Father's words in the third person ("*this* is my son . . . with *him* I am pleased"), instead of the second person ("*you* are my son . . . with *you* I am pleased"). As frequently noted by interpreters, this has the effect of making the endorsement more public in Matthew, though Matthew may intend the endorsement to be only for John's benefit. Also this form of the endorsement brings it into conformity with the Father's words at the transfiguration (17:5). Perhaps the third person language is also intended to confront Matthew's audience more directly with the truth of Jesus' sonship.

The concluding pericope of Matthew 3 on Jesus' baptism (3:13-17) has profound

Christological implications. Several trajectories should be mentioned. In 3:17 Jesus is described in terms that clearly represent Isaiah's suffering servant whom God has chosen (cf. especially Isa 42:1). Related to this is the sonship typology metaphorically applied to Israel as a nation (Exod 4:22; Jer 3:19; 31:9, 20; Hos 11:1) and to David as the ideal king who serves God (2 Sam 7:5-16; Ps 2:7; 89:3, 20, 26-27). The fulfillment of Old Testament covenantal promises to the nation and to the king is found in Jesus, who recapitulated Israel's history as he sojourned in Egypt and passed through the waters before being tested in the wilderness. Additionally, it is possible that the emphasis on Jesus as the Father's *beloved* son is intended to recall Isaac's relationship to Abraham (Gen 22:2). More likely are the creation overtones found in the dove-like Spirit, who descends upon Jesus in a manner that calls Genesis 1:2 to mind. Thus, in Jesus God has begun nothing less than the renewal of all of creation (cf. 19:28). It remains for the rest of Matthew's narrative to develop the distinctive understanding of Jesus and the new people of God that has been begun here.

Matthew 3 has an important role in the Gospel narrative. Gardner (1991:68) is correct in pointing out that two main purposes are served by the story of John and Jesus' baptism. This account provides the basis for the transition between John and Jesus, and it attests Jesus' unique identity as the Servant-Son of God. John as the forerunner now passes from center stage so that the spotlight may shine on Jesus. While John will appear again in the story, there can be no doubt about his subservience to Jesus in redemptive history. Jesus will proclaim the same message as John (3:2; 4:17) and eventually suffer a similar fate as John's (17:12), but John's great redemptive historical significance pales in comparison with that of Jesus' (11:11). Davies and Allison (1988:343) also point out how John's ministry serves to initiate Matthew's definition of the genuine people of God and Matthew's dualism regarding those who respond correctly and incorrectly to the message of God's rule. The genuine people of God are not merely Abraham's descendants but those who show their repentance by their changed lifestyles. Those who show no repentance are in danger of imminent judgment.

In concluding the discussion of Matthew 3, first a brief word needs to be said on synoptic relationships. After his unique material on Jesus' genealogy and infancy in the first two chapters, Matthew's narrative of John's ministry and the baptism of Jesus in chapter 3 parallels the other Gospels to some extent. All three of the synoptics cite Isaiah 40:3 as speaking of John's ministry. Mark's account is briefest, though Mark 1:2 alludes to Malachi 3:1, along with Isaiah 40:3, as the basis of John's ministry. Luke's account is the most lengthy, detailing the rulers who were on the scene when John arrived (Luke 3:1-2), citing a lengthier section of Isaiah 40 than Matthew does (Luke 3:5-6) and giving a brief summary of dialogue between John and his audience (Luke 3:10-15). Luke and Matthew both speak of Jesus baptizing in the Spirit and fire (Matt 3:11; Luke 3:16), whereas Mark mentions only the Spirit (Mark 1:8).

◆   ## C. Testing of the Son of God (4:1-11; cf. Mark 1:12-13; Luke 4:1-13)

Then Jesus was led by the Spirit into the wilderness to be tempted there by the devil. ²For forty days and forty nights he fasted and became very hungry.

³During that time the devil* came and said to him, "If you are the Son of God, tell these stones to become loaves of bread."

⁴But Jesus told him, "No! The Scriptures say,

'People do not live by bread alone,
   but by every word that comes from
      the mouth of God.'*"

⁵Then the devil took him to the holy city, Jerusalem, to the highest point of the Temple, ⁶and said, "If you are the Son of God, jump off! For the Scriptures say,

'He will order his angels to protect
   you.

And they will hold you up with their
      hands
   so you won't even hurt your foot on
      a stone.'*"

⁷Jesus responded, "The Scriptures also say, 'You must not test the LORD your God.'*"

⁸Next the devil took him to the peak of a very high mountain and showed him all the kingdoms of the world and their glory. ⁹"I will give it all to you," he said, "if you will kneel down and worship me."

¹⁰"Get out of here, Satan," Jesus told him. "For the Scriptures say,

'You must worship the LORD your God
   and serve only him.'*"

¹¹Then the devil went away, and angels came and took care of Jesus.

4:3 Greek *the tempter*.   4:4 Deut 8:3.   4:6 Ps 91:11-12.   4:7 Deut 6:16.   4:10 Deut 6:13.

NOTES

4:1 *Jesus was led by the Spirit into the wilderness.* The testing of Jesus occurred immediately after he was endowed with the Spirit and heard the Father's words of approval as his beloved son (3:16-17). The same Spirit who equipped Jesus for his messianic vocation led Jesus to the wilderness, where his unique sonship and vocation would be challenged by Satan. Jesus' wilderness experience recapitulated the wilderness wandering of Israel. This seems clear from the similarities between the OT and NT accounts and from the repeated citations of Deut 6-8. Yet there is a crucial difference; unlike Israel, Jesus obeyed the Father, passed the test, and vanquished Satan.

to be tempted there by the devil. The devil or Satan appears several times in Matthew. Seven times he is described as "the devil" (4:1, 3, 5, 8, 11; 13:39; 25:41). He is also referred to as Satan in 4:10; 12:26 (cf. 16:23), as Beelzeboul (NLT "prince of demons") in 10:25; 12:24, parabolically as "the enemy" in 13:39, and probably as "the evil one" in 6:13.

4:2 *forty days and forty nights.* As a concordance study will show, the number forty is pregnant with theological implications throughout Scripture. Especially pertinent here are the forty-year wanderings of Israel in the wilderness (Deut 8:2-4) and the forty-day fast of Moses (Exod 34:28; cf. Elijah in 1 Kgs 19:8). As Israel hungered (Deut 8:3), so did Jesus. How would this need be met?

4:3 *the devil.* Gr., "the tempter" (so NLT mg). Perhaps the use of "tempter" here anticipates the similar activity of the unbelieving Jewish religious leaders as Matthew's story develops (Gundry 1994:55; cf. 12:38; 16:1; 19:3; 22:15, 18, 35). While the word "tempt" does not occur in 16:21ff, it is clear from 16:23 that Peter's unwitting attempt to deter Jesus from the cross was also a temptation. As the tempter, Satan referred to Jesus' divine sonship as the pretext to solicit Jesus to perform an act that would sever his filial relationship to the Father. It was not so much that Satan doubted Jesus' sonship but that he utilized it to deceive Jesus into exercising his filial prerogatives in a selfish manner. Jesus was not tempted to doubt his sonship but to exercise it in a manner that would not be approved by the Father. Jesus' baptism (3:17) evoked the Father's approving words concerning his sonship; now those approving words evoke Satan's command for Jesus to relieve his hunger by turning stones into loaves of bread. At issue here is the type of son Jesus will be. Will he utilize his endowment with the Spirit in a selfish fashion, or will he humbly depend on his Father to meet his needs? As God's servant, how will he fulfill his mission? It is noteworthy here that Satan's mention of rocks echoes John's words in 3:9. If God is able to make disciples out of stones, shouldn't God's Son have the right to make bread out of stones?

4:4 *The Scriptures say.* Lit., "it is written." Jesus' response simply cites the second half of Deut 8:3 with an introductory formula that stresses the abiding authority of the OT. This passage in context rehearses God's care for Israel during its forty-year wilderness experience. It is interesting to note that the first half of Deut 8:3 alludes to God's purpose in permitting Israel's hunger in the wilderness—it was so that they might learn that they needed not only bread but also God's word to survive. This purpose of God in Deut 8:3 is similar to the statement of purpose in Matt 4:1. Deut 8:5 likens the wilderness wandering to a father's discipline, and this terminology finds its full implications in the testing of Jesus. He was aware of the daily need to depend on the Father for bread (7:9), and he would not use his power as some sort of magician.

4:5 Matthew and Luke present the second and third temptations in opposite orders. The scene now shifts from the isolation of the desert to the political and religious center of Israel.

the devil took him. This most likely describes a visionary experience rather than physical movement, as does 4:8-9.

the holy city, Jerusalem. Jerusalem is also described as "the holy city" in 27:53.

the highest point of the Temple. Satan showed Jesus the perspective from "the highest point" (Gr., *pterugion* [TG4419, ZG4762]) of the Temple. This word, related to the word for "wing," has a range of meanings including tip, end, peak, or turret. It could plausibly refer to the southeastern corner of the Temple complex, overlooking the Kidron Valley (cf. Josephus *Antiquities* 15.411-412; Eusebius *Ecclesiastical History* 2.23.11), but any elevated location could be in view.

4:6 *If you are the Son of God, jump off!* The second temptation again questoned Jesus' sonship but with a new twist: biblical support! Satan cited Ps 91:11-12 with the same introductory formula ("for the Scriptures say") Jesus had just uttered. Satan tempted Jesus to jump off a high pinnacle of the Temple and assured him that Scripture says that God would protect him. In the previous temptation, Jesus proclaimed his dependence on the Word of God, citing Deut 8:3, so Satan cited a word from God, Ps 91, which speaks beautifully of the security of those who depend on the Lord.

4:7 *You must not test the LORD your God.* Jesus countered Satan's use of Ps 91:11-12 with Deut 6:16, which refers to Israel's doubting God's provision of water in Exod 17:7 (cf. Ps 95:7-11; 1 Cor 10:9; Heb 3:7ff). It is not that Deut 6:16 contradicts the Psalm but that Satan misapplied it. Satan tempted Jesus to capitalize on his unique messianic status as a way out of self-induced mortal peril, perhaps as a stunt to appeal to the masses. But since Jesus received the Father's approval by serving as an obedient son, the proposed leap from the pinnacle of the Temple would have amounted not to trusting God but to testing God. Once again Jesus recapitulated an event from Israel's history but with better results. He would not use his status as the beloved son to satisfy his hunger, and he would not put God to the test as Israel did.

4:8-9 It is possible that this scene is intended to recall God's promise to Abraham (Gen 13:14-15) or Moses looking at the Promised Land from Mt. Pisgah (Deut 3:27; 34:1-4).

The third temptation, like the second, probably involved a visionary experience. Jesus was taken to a high mountain, presented with the glory of all the world's kingdoms, and promised that he would receive it all if he would only worship Satan. This temptation was unlike the first two in at least two ways. First, it did not address Jesus as the Son of God because it did not involve a misuse of his messianic prerogatives. Second, it blatantly asked Jesus to break the first commandment. In keeping with the recapitulation theme in Matthew, Jesus' being asked to bow down and worship Satan recalled Israel's idolatrous worship in the desert (Exod 32).

4:10 Get out of here, Satan. Satan's opposition to the Father's first commandment received a blunt rejection by the beloved Son.

You must worship the LORD your God and serve only him. Jesus based his outright rejection of Satan on Deut 6:13, which is only three verses before the verse cited in the previous test. Deut 6, perhaps the greatest chapter in the Torah, proclaims the exclusivity of Israel's God and Israel's responsibility to love him exclusively (Deut 6:4-5). Israel is warned not to forget God when they come into their land, but to fear him and not to fear false gods (Deut 6:12-14). By not worshipping Satan, Jesus avoided repeating the sin of Israel when they worshipped the golden calf. If he was to rule the world, it would be by the path of obedience to the Father. Later in Matthew, it becomes clear that this path led to the cross, a difficult fact for Peter to grasp (16:21-26).

4:11 the devil went away. Satan had to depart in response to Jesus' authoritative rebuke. But Matthew does not imply by this that Satan's evil activity was finished (cf. 5:37; 6:13; 12:28-29; 13:19, 38). Luke 4:13 makes this clear—"he left him until the next opportunity came."

angels came and took care of Jesus. The ministry of angels to Jesus is referred to again in 26:53. Jesus mentioned other angelic ministries in 13:39, 41, 49; 16:27; 18:10; 22:30; 24:31, 36; 25:31. This mention of angelic ministry recalls Satan's previous use of Ps 91:11-12 in 4:6 to the effect that if Jesus were to jump off the pinnacle of the Temple, angels would protect him. Ironically, Jesus did receive angelic ministry, but only after he obeyed the Father.

COMMENTARY

Matthew 4 leads from the final preparatory episode (the temptation; 4:1-11) to the beginning of Jesus' ministry in Galilee (4:12-25). Thus, the chapter amounts to a transition from preparatory events to public ministry. The testing narrative itself (4:1-11) consists of three incidents wrapped in an introduction, where Satan arrives (4:1-2), and a conclusion, where Satan departs (4:11). Here Jesus authenticates the Father's baptismal endorsement in his victory over Satan's triple test. The things Satan offered him—physical sustenance, spectacular protection, and authority to rule the world—were already his by virtue of his unique status as the Father's beloved Son. But his testing recapitulates that of Israel in the wilderness and becomes a positive example for his people.

Matthew's account of the temptation differs significantly from both Mark's and Luke's. Mark's short summary of the temptation (Mark 1:12-13) does not mention Jesus' fasting or that there were three distinct episodes of temptation. Neither Mark nor Luke indicates that the Spirit's leading was for the express purpose of Jesus' temptation, as Matthew does in 4:1. Mark alone mentions the presence of wild animals in the wilderness, and his description of the angels' ministry does not specify, as Matthew's does, that this ministry began at Satan's departure. Luke does not mention the angels at all. Luke 4:1-13 agrees with Matthew in describing Jesus' fast and the three distinct episodes of temptation, but Luke's order differs. Matthew and Luke agree in placing the turning of stones into bread as the first temptation but differ in the order of the next two. Matthew puts jumping from the temple pinnacle second and worshipping the devil third, but Luke reverses this order. Luke alone ominously remarks that Satan's departure at the end of the pericope was only temporary.

Jesus, the Spirit, and Temptation.   It is not surprising to read in 4:1 that the Spirit led Jesus, since the reader already knows that the Spirit is the agency behind Jesus' virginal conception (1:18, 20) and empowerment for ministry (3:16-17; cf. 12:18-28). Furthermore, John's prediction that Jesus would baptize in the Spirit (3:16) anticipated his exaltation following his death in Jerusalem (cf. 28:18-20). But it is striking that Jesus was led by the Spirit to the desert in order to be tempted by the devil. Matthew 4 clearly indicates that while the Spirit is the agent who led Jesus, the devil is the agent who tested Jesus. How should we understand this convergence of God's benevolent purpose with Satan's evil designs? The verb used here (*peirazō* [TG3985, ZG4279]) may express both the positive nuance of testing, which develops character and achieves approval (cf. John 6:6; LXX Gen 22:1; Exod 20:20), and the negative nuance of tempting, which solicits evil and achieves disapproval (cf. 1 Cor 7:5; 1 Thess 3:5). The positive or negative nuance depends upon the motive in each context. Here both nuances are pertinent, since the Father, through the Spirit, led Jesus to be tested in order to confirm him in his role as the messianic son and servant, yet the devil tempted Jesus to achieve messianic status by using his prerogatives selfishly in disobedience to the son/servant paradigm. The Father's aim was to accredit Jesus, the devil's to discredit Jesus (Calvin 1972:1.136). The convergence of the benevolent plan of God and the malevolent schemes of Satan may be difficult to explain fully, but it is found elsewhere in Scripture (Job 1:6-12; 2:1-6; Acts 2:23).

Jesus as a Model for Christians.   In Matthew 4:1-11, Satan appears in a role that ought to be familiar to those who read the Scriptures. In challenging Jesus' unique sonship, so recently announced by the approving Father, it is as if Satan were saying again, "'Did God really say 'you are the Son of God?'" (cf. Gen 3:1). It is clear from the narrative parallels and from the Scriptures Jesus cites that his temptation recapitulates that of Israel in the wilderness. But from the widest scriptural perspective Jesus' temptation recapitulates that of Adam and Eve in the garden (so the theme of John Milton's epic poem, "Paradise Regained"). Through Jesus, God is calling into existence a new humanity (16:18), which will be characterized by the obedience modeled by Jesus, not the rebellion of its first parents. What can be learned from the example of the beloved son?

Concerning the avenues of temptation, it is clear that Satan tempted Jesus (and continues to tempt Jesus' people) in the area of daily sustenance. But instead of succumbing to the temptation to acquire one's "bread" by sinful means, Christians must remind themselves of the biblical truth that true life comes from hearing and obeying the word of God (Deut 8:3), and that the God of the word knows all about their daily needs (6:11). Another avenue of temptation could be a desire for spectacular manifestations of God's power or protection, but Christians must never leap disobediently away from the path God has revealed and ask God to catch them while in mid-air. This amounts to a selfish testing of God (Deut 6:16), not a serene reliance on his love and providence. Yet another avenue of temptation is the desire for glory and power. Satan continues to promote idolatrous ways of achieving status, but the Christian must rely on God for advancement and seek only that glory which is consistent with the way of the cross (Deut 6:13; cf. Matt 6:24, 33).

How did Jesus withstand temptation? His spontaneous citation of appropriate Scriptures when under temptation showed that he was conscious of the past failure of God's people and aware of the reasons for their failure. In short, he knew the Bible. But he also was conscious of the endowment and leading of the Spirit of God (3:16; 4:1; 12:18-21). Therefore, Christians today must likewise withstand temptation by knowing the Scripture and by being strengthened in the Spirit. Obedience and victory in the face of temptation come from knowing what God commands and having the capacity to perform it. Christians who regularly study the Bible and humbly depend on the Spirit for the strength to obey it can successfully resist the devil today.

Conclusion. This section of Matthew cannot be left without a reiteration of how Jesus is presented as the personification of Israel in Matthew 3–4. Jesus passed through the waters and entered the desert to be tested, just as Israel did. Remarkably, Scriptures from Deuteronomy 6–8, which remind Israel of its past failures in the wilderness and present obligations in the Promised Land, were on the tip of Jesus' tongue when Satan tested him. Once Satan was vanquished, Jesus moved on to begin his own ministry and to call his first disciples (4:12ff). Davies and Allison (1988:402-403) are certainly right when they say "this means that the baptism and temptation of Jesus inaugurated the renewal of the people of God." We should also note here that Matthew's Gospel uses the literary technique of inclusion—the mount of temptation (4:8) ultimately leads to the mount of commission (28:16). Jesus' obedience to the Father eventually led to his crucifixion, but he was raised from the dead and received all authority, not only on earth but also in heaven. Thus, by obedience to the way of the cross, he received infinitely more than Satan promised.

◆   ## D. Ministry in Galilee (4:12-25; cf. Mark 1:14-20; Luke 3:19-20; 4:14-15, 44)

[12]When Jesus heard that John had been arrested, he left Judea and returned to Galilee. [13]He went first to Nazareth, then left there and moved to Capernaum, beside the Sea of Galilee, in the region of Zebulun and Naphtali. [14]This fulfilled what God said through the prophet Isaiah:

15 "In the land of Zebulun and of
   Naphtali,
   beside the sea, beyond the Jordan
   River,
   in Galilee where so many Gentiles
   live,
16 the people who sat in darkness
   have seen a great light.
   And for those who lived in the land
   where death casts its shadow,
   a light has shined."*

17 From then on Jesus began to preach, "Repent of your sins and turn to God, for the Kingdom of Heaven is near.*"

18 One day as Jesus was walking along the shore of the Sea of Galilee, he saw two brothers—Simon, also called Peter, and Andrew—throwing a net into the water, for they fished for a living. 19 Jesus called out to them, "Come, follow me, and I will show you how to fish for people!" 20 And they left their nets at once and followed him.

21 A little farther up the shore he saw two other brothers, James and John, sitting in a boat with their father, Zebedee, repairing their nets. And he called them to come, too. 22 They immediately followed him, leaving the boat and their father behind.

23 Jesus traveled throughout the region of Galilee, teaching in the synagogues and announcing the Good News about the Kingdom. And he healed every kind of disease and illness. 24 News about him spread as far as Syria, and people soon began bringing to him all who were sick. And whatever their sickness or disease, or if they were demon-possessed or epileptic or paralyzed—he healed them all. 25 Large crowds followed him wherever he went—people from Galilee, the Ten Towns,* Jerusalem, from all over Judea, and from east of the Jordan River.

4:15-16 Isa 9:1-2 (Greek version).   4:17 Or has come, or is coming soon.   4:25 Greek Decapolis.

NOTES

4:12-13 *he left Judea and returned to Galilee.* Jesus made this journey when he learned that John had been imprisoned. The NLT's "left and returned" translates a word (*anachōreō* [TG402, ZG432]) used several times in Matthew to describe a strategic withdrawal in the face of danger (2:12-14, 22; 10:23; 12:15; 14:13; 15:21). The arrest and imprisonment of John led to his grisly execution (14:1-12), which in turn led to another strategic withdrawal by Jesus (14:13). Perhaps these two withdrawals by Jesus anticipate the close connection made later between the fate of John and the fate of Jesus (17:12).

He went first to Nazareth . . . and moved to Capernaum. Jesus' first stop in Galilee was Nazareth, the village where he grew up (2:23). At the Triumphal Entry, Nazareth was still known as his hometown (21:11). But Matthew does not dwell on Nazareth (but cf. Luke 4:16-30), preferring to stress Capernaum because its location has prophetic significance. Capernaum (cf. 8:5; 11:23; 17:24) is on the northwest shore of the Sea of Galilee, roughly two miles west of the Jordan River. Because Capernaum is not mentioned in the OT, Matthew stressed its location in the territory of Zebulun and Naphtali (cf. Josh 19:32-39); these two are mentioned in Isaiah 9:1-2.

4:14-16 For Matthew, Jesus' residence in Capernaum, located in the territory of Zebulun and Naphtali, has prophetic implications. With his characteristic fulfillment formula (see the notes on 1:23; 2:15, 17, 23 and the commentary on 1:18-25), Matthew introduces a quote from Isa 9:1-2. In its original context, Isaiah 7–9 promises deliverance from the threat of Assyria. Matthew has already connected the birth of Jesus with the sign promised to Ahaz (1:23; cf. Isa 7:14; 8:8, 10). Here he connects the political darkness facing Israel in the days of Isaiah to the spiritual problem that caused it. Israel's defection from the Mosaic covenant had led to her oppression by other kingdoms. But for Matthew, Israel's dark political prospects were symptomatic of her need for the redemption from sin that was now coming through Jesus the Messiah.

in Galilee where so many Gentiles live. This is the key to the use of the Isaiah passage. It stood out to Matthew since it resonated with his theme of mission to the Gentiles (see the discussion of this in the Major Themes section of the Introduction). Galilee was evidently looked down upon by the "enlightened" Jerusalem establishment and those who supported it. Its population was evidently a mixture of Jews and Gentiles (2 Kgs 15:29; 17:24-27; 1 Macc 5). It was to this darkened place (cf. Ps 107:10; Luke 1:79) that Jesus brought the light of the Kingdom of God. His mission was not to the Gentiles during these early days of the Galilean ministry (9:35; 10:5-6; 15:24), although he did occasionally minister to Gentiles (8:5-13; 15:21-28). Evidently, the Gentiles to whom Jesus ministered took the initiative to come to him, suggesting the applicability of Jesus' message for all the nations (24:14). The beginnings of Jesus' ministry in a remote, despised place, largely populated by Gentiles, foreshadows the expansion of mission to all the nations at the end of Jesus' ministry (28:19).

4:17 *From then on.* Many interpreters of Matthew think this phrase signals a transition to the second major section of Matthew. One may grant the role this phrase plays in Matthew's presentation of the stages of the life and ministry of Jesus. But this phrase is not nearly as prominent as Matthew's unique literary structure, which alternates discourse and narrative material by inserting the phrase "when Jesus had finished" (7:28; 11:1; 13:53; 19:1; 26:1) at the end of each major discourse. Therefore a different view is favored in the discussion and outline found in the Literary Structure section of the Introduction.

Jesus began to preach. Jesus' early message is portrayed here with the same language used to portray John's message in 3:2. In this verse, an ethical imperative (*repent of your sins and turn to God*) is grounded in an eschatological reality (*the Kingdom of Heaven is near*). For discussion of repentance and the "Kingdom of Heaven," see the note on 3:2 and the Major Themes section of the Introduction. This linkage of the messages of John and Jesus seems to lay a foundation for the similar fates of the two messengers (14:2; 17:12-13).

4:18 *Simon, also called Peter, and Andrew.* The name Simon (cf. 10:2; 16:16-17; 17:25) appears much less often than the popular nickname Peter (23 times), which Jesus gave Simon in 16:17-18. In view of the prominence of Peter in Matthew, especially Matt 16:13ff, it is not merely coincidental that Peter is the first disciple who responds to the call of Jesus. Andrew, by contrast, is mentioned only once after this (10:2; but cf. John 1:35-42).

4:19 *Come, follow me.* The call to discipleship was an unconditional, unexplained demand, not a polite, reasoned invitation. Following Jesus involved both traveling with him and ethically obeying his teaching and modeling of God's will. It could and did lead to hardship and peril (8:19, 22; 10:38; 16:24; 19:21).

fish for people. This is an expression found elsewhere in the NT only in Mark 1:17. It is just possible that fishing here is an allusion to Jer 16:16, or that fishing for people implies eschatological judgment (13:47-50). In any event, this new "fishing" results in life for those "caught" by the message of Jesus.

4:20 *they left their nets at once and followed him.* In response to Jesus' call, Peter and Andrew—with immediate sacrificial obedience—walked away from their livelihood as commercial fishermen and followed Jesus in a life of homelessness (8:20). For the similar story of the call of Matthew, see 9:9.

4:21-22 *James and John.* The call of James and John follows the pattern just discussed. These brothers are mentioned later in the narrative, sometimes by name (10:2; 17:1) and sometimes as "the sons of Zebedee" (20:20; 26:37; 27:56). They too were commercial fishermen. They were mending their nets in preparation for another voyage on the lake. At the summons of Jesus, they too immediately walked away from their maritime career, but in this case it is added that they also left their father behind (cf. 8:21-22!). Their sacrifice entailed not only the loss of finances but also of family.

4:23 Matthew 4:23-25 encapsulates the ministry of Jesus (Hagner 1993:78). It may be viewed as a concluding summary of Jesus' early ministry in Galilee (so here), or as the introduction to the Sermon on the Mount (so Davies and Allison 1988:410). It is note-worthy that 4:23 is repeated almost verbatim in 9:35. Both 4:23 and 9:35 are located just before major discourses of Jesus, and they serve to summarize his deeds as the context for his words. But there is likely more to the repetition than that. Taken together, 4:23 and 9:35 form an *inclusio*, a set of literary bookends, which summarize Jesus' words and deeds at the beginning and end of two sections that present his words (Matt 5–7) and deeds (Matt 8–9) in detail. Significantly, both the words (7:29) and deeds (8:9; 9:6) demonstrate Jesus' Kingdom authority, an authority he passed on to his disciples in 10:1. As his words and deeds proclaim and demonstrate the Kingdom, so will the words and deeds of his disciples (10:7-8; 24:14).

4:24-25 *News about him spread as far as Syria.* These verses describe the far-reaching results of Jesus' ministry. His reputation spread north from Galilee into Syria, and soon people from all over were coming to Jesus for healing. Matthew 4:24 describes the diseases healed in more detail than 4:23 and adds that Jesus also dealt with demonic possession (cf. 8:16, 28; 9:32-34; 10:8; 12:22, 24, 27-28; 15:22-28; 17:18). All who were brought to Jesus were healed, and this led to crowds of people following him. People not only from Galilee, but also from the regions surrounding Galilee, were "following" Jesus, which here does not have the strict ethical sense of 4:19, 21.

Large crowds. Matthew's use of the term "crowds" is noteworthy, since it often portrays those who are attracted to Jesus because of his sensational deeds (cf. 8:1, 18; 11:7; 12:46; 15:30; 17:14; 19:2). The crowds occupied a middle ground between Jesus' committed dis-ciples on the one hand, and the hostile religious leaders on the other. At times, the crowd seemed favorable to Jesus (9:8; 12:23; 15:31), and he to the crowd (9:36; 14:14; 15:32). But as time went on, under the influence of the leaders, the crowd ultimately called for Jesus' death (26:47, 55; 27:20, 24). In this context, the presence of the crowds led Jesus away to the mountain where he delivered his first discourse (5:1).

the Ten Towns. Lit., "the Decapolis," a league of Hellenistic cities southeast of Galilee. Nearly all of them were east of the Jordan River (cf. Mark 5:20; 7:31).

east of the Jordan River. Lit., "beyond the Jordan." This refers to the region farther south, east of Jerusalem and the Jordan River. Matthew's geographical language covers the whole land of Israel, moving from northwest (Galilee) to northeast (Decapolis) to Jerusalem (probably to be understood as the center of the land) to southwest (Judea) to southeast ("beyond the Jordan").

COMMENTARY

In the second part of the chapter (4:12-25), John's ministry ends, and Jesus with-draws from Judea to Galilee to begin his own ministry in fulfillment of Old Testa-ment prophecy (4:14-16; cf. Isa 9:1-2). The theme of his preaching is the Kingdom of Heaven, which is mentioned in a "hinge" verse (4:17), linking Jesus' message to that of his predecessor John (3:2). He began to call his core disciples (4:18-22), and his message was authenticated by powerful works (4:23-25). Geographically, Jesus moved from the wilderness of Judea (4:1) to Galilee (4:12), where he went first to

Nazareth (4:13) and then lived in Capernaum, where he called his disciples (4:18-22). Then his ministry expanded into all Galilee, where he was followed by multitudes from all over the land (4:23-25). This Galilean ministry, which is the setting for the Sermon on the Mount, also features themes that are important throughout this Gospel, such as the Kingdom of Heaven, the fulfillment of Scripture, and the salvation of Gentiles.

The Mission of Jesus.   Matthew 4:15-16 is a citation of Isaiah 9:1-2, a passage that presented a promise of hope to Israel in the midst of a time of judgment. The stress of Isaiah 9:6-7 upon a son who will rule David's kingdom fits nicely with the Matthean theme that Jesus is the son of David. But the mention in Isaiah 9:1-2 of the scorned area of Galilee and its association with despised Gentiles repeats the idea that God rejects the proud and receives the most unlikely sinners into fellowship with himself. Matthew repeatedly stresses mission to the Gentiles, either by implicit details (1:3, 5-6; 2:1; 15:22-28; 22:9) or by explicit teaching of Jesus (8:10-12; 21:43; 24:14). Jesus' Galilean ministry prepares the reader for his Galilean commission that his disciples should disciple all the nations (28:16-20).

It is also clear from Matthew 4:12-25 that Jesus' ministry was, to use a popular contemporary term, "holistic." He dealt with the people's physical needs as well as their spiritual needs—the former sometimes evidently preceding the latter. While he demanded repentance, he did not make repentance the prerequisite for healing. Jesus had compassion on the needy crowds and helped them, evidently in many cases before they heard him preach. Davies and Allison put it well: "The first act of the Messiah is not the imposition of his commandments but the giving of himself" (1988:427). In narrating the gracious ministry of Jesus, Matthew surely intended it to be a model for the ministry of the disciples. They, too, were not only to preach the Kingdom (4:17; 10:7), but also were to do works of compassion that demonstrated its power and grace (4:24; 10:1).

It was also Jesus' mission to defeat the devil. As soon as Jesus emerges victorious from his testing (4:1-11), he is presented at the outset of his ministry as one who heals not only physical diseases but also demonic possession. Jesus' power over the forces of darkness is made more clear after the Sermon on the Mount, when Matthew narrates Jesus' Galilean ministry (8:16, 28-34; 9:32-34; 12:22ff; 15:22-31; 17:18). One incident in particular (8:29) shows that the demons intuitively recognized Jesus' messianic identity and his ultimate eschatological authority over them. In another (12:22ff), Jesus countered the false accusation that he was in league with the devil (cf. 9:34) with the affirmation that his Spirit-empowered exorcism ministry amounts to the binding of a strong man and the removal of his property. Thus, in Matthew it is clear that the Kingdom had already encroached upon Satan's territory, and that Satan would ultimately be defeated. Additional New Testament teaching makes this even more clear (John 12:31; 16:11; Heb 2:14; 1 John 3:8; Rev 5:5; 12:7-10; 20:1-10).

Jesus' ministry is presented in a threefold fashion in 4:23-25, involving synagogue teaching, public preaching of the Kingdom, and powerful healings. Synagogues (cf. 9:35; 12:9; 13:54; 23:6, 34) evidently began to develop after the exile to Babylon. They were gatherings where prayer and the study of Scripture, primarily the Torah, took place (cf. Luke 4:16ff). They evidently also functioned as community courts, especially with the rise of the Rabbinic movement after the destruction of the Temple in AD 70. The central theme of the proclamation of the nearness of God's Kingdom rule through the Messiah was already stressed in 3:2 and 4:17 and continues to be featured in Matthew's narrative (cf. 9:35; 10:7, 27; 11:1; 13:19; 24:14; 26:13). In addition to the verbal aspect of Jesus' ministry, Matthew also shows that Jesus' powerful acts of mercy demonstrated the reality of the rule of God (cf. 8:7, 16; 9:35; 10:1, 8; 12:13, 15, 22; 14:14; 15:30; 17:18; 19:2; 21:14). Matthew's comment that Jesus healed every kind of sickness and disease stresses the extent of Jesus' kingly power.

The Call to Discipleship.   Matthew 4:18-22 narrates for us the obedient response of Jesus' first disciples, who immediately left family and livelihood to follow him. The story of the call of Simon Peter and Andrew is very similar to the following story about the call of James and John. Both stories, perhaps in dependence on the story of Elijah's call of Elisha (1 Kgs 19:19-21), involve a fourfold structure (Davies and Allison 1988:392-393): (1) the appearance of Jesus (4:18, 21); (2) the comment on the work of the prospective disciples (4:18, 21); (3) the call to discipleship (4:19, 21); and (4) obedience to the call (4:20, 22). It should also be noted that in both narratives it is Jesus who sees the prospective disciples and takes the initiative in calling them to follow him. This is an important factor in distinguishing Jesus as a charismatic or prophetic figure, after the model of Elijah, from the late Rabbinic model in which the disciples took the initiative in attaching themselves to the Rabbi (cf. *m. Avot* 1:6).

We should come away from this text understanding that Jesus' ministry is a model for our own ministries. Furthermore, we should view the obedience of the first disciples as examples that challenge us to similar obedience. The immediate, unquestioning, sacrificial response of the first disciples to Jesus' absolutely authoritative call to discipleship is a model for radical discipleship today. Discipleship is still incumbent upon Christians, whether or not they are called to "vocational" ministry. The unquestioning obedience of Peter and Andrew, James and John, condemns any delay or ambivalence in responding to Jesus. Their complete break with former loyalties shames any half-hearted attempt to serve two masters. This obedience of Jesus' first disciples is contrasted later in the narrative to the excuses of would-be disciples who will not make the requisite sacrifice (8:18-22; cf. 19:16-22). Even true disciples who have responded to the call need to have their faith strengthened (8:23-27). Their task is daunting (10:5-42), but their reward is great (19:27-30).

Conclusion.   Matthew 4:12-25 has set the scene for Jesus' first discourse, the Sermon on the Mount (Matt 5–7), where we will find the values and ethics that should characterize those who answer the call of the Kingdom. Following this discourse, Matthew provides us with a narrative of Jesus' powerful deeds (8:1–9:34) before the summary statement of 9:35 closes the circle begun in 4:23. Thus, Matthew 4:23–9:35 provides a clearly structured look at Jesus' proclamation and demonstration of the Kingdom of Heaven. Matthew 9:35-38 stresses the need for Jesus' disciples to take up this ministry, which is realistically portrayed in the next discourse, 10:5-42.

◆   E. The Sermon on the Mount (5:1–7:29)
   1. The Beatitudes (5:1–10; cf. Luke 6:20–26)

One day as he saw the crowds gathering, Jesus went up on the mountainside and sat down. His disciples gathered around him, ²and he began to teach them.

³"God blesses those who are poor and realize their need for him,*
   for the Kingdom of Heaven is theirs.
⁴God blesses those who mourn,
   for they will be comforted.
⁵God blesses those who are humble,
   for they will inherit the whole earth.
⁶God blesses those who hunger and thirst for justice,*
   for they will be satisfied.
⁷God blesses those who are merciful,
   for they will be shown mercy.
⁸God blesses those whose hearts are pure,
   for they will see God.
⁹God blesses those who work for peace,
   for they will be called the children of God.
¹⁰God blesses those who are persecuted for doing right,
   for the Kingdom of Heaven is theirs.

5:3 Greek *poor in spirit.*   5:6 Or *for righteousness.*

NOTES
5:1-2 These verses provide the narrative setting for the Sermon (cf. 7:28–8:1).

Jesus went up on the mountainside. Once again Matthew presents Jesus doing something significant on a mountain, which may reflect an intended typological relationship between Jesus and Moses (cf. 4:8 and note; 14:23; 15:29; 17:1; 24:3; 28:16 with Exod 19–20; 34; and Donaldson 1985).

His disciples gathered around him. Jesus evidently retired to the mountainside to teach his disciples more privately, but it is doubtful that we are to view the crowd as entirely absent from this discourse. More likely, Matthew presents the disciples as the inner circle closely listening to Jesus, while a throng of people gathered around the periphery of the scene, exhibiting varied levels of interest and comprehension.

sat down. Teaching while sitting was evidently customary (cf. 13:1-2; 24:3), but in other contexts, sitting is the posture of judgment (19:28; 20:21, 23; 22:44; 25:31; 26:64). Matthew often speaks of various people "gathering around" Jesus to hear him teach or to ask him for something.

5:3 The word "beatitude" is related to the Latin *beatus,* which means "blessed." There is considerable similarity between 5:3-12 and Luke 6:20-26.

God blesses those who . . This makes the implicit divine agency of "blessed" explicit. Beatitudes are found elsewhere in the Bible (e.g., Ps 1:1; 32:1; Dan 12:12; Rom 14:22; Rev 1:3). To be blessed is to receive God's approval, favor, endorsement, congratulations. "Blessed" should not be understood merely in the sense of "happy," since happiness is a vague idea, often with a shallow, emotional ring to it. God initiates blessing by graciously condescending to save people. They respond to God's initiative by blessing God in thanks and praise for that grace and by living obediently. Structurally, each of the beatitudes is composed of a statement of *who* is blessed ("blessed are the poor in spirit," etc.) followed by a statement of *why* the person is blessed ("for theirs is the Kingdom of Heaven"). First the character of the blessed person is highlighted, and then the promise of God to that person is explained.

those who are poor and realize their need for him. The first beatitude concerns authentic spirituality (5:3). Matthew's phrase is lit. "poor in spirit" (cf. Isa 57:15), but Luke's version of this beatitude has only "blesses you who are poor" (Luke 6:20). God's approval does not come to those who boast of their spiritual riches. Rather, his endorsement is for those who admit their spiritual poverty. In the OT there is repeated reference to the *'ani* [TH6041, ZH6714], people whose economic distress left them with nothing to rely upon except God (Lev 19:9-15, 32-33; Deut 15:4, 7, 11; Ps 37:10-19; Prov 16:18-19; Isa 66:1-2; Jer 22:15-17; Amos 2:6-8; cf. Jas 2:5). Their distress was due to such problems as death in the family, physical handicap, advancing age, military defeat, social injustice, or alien status. This seems to be the OT background of Jesus' words, but spiritual poverty should be acknowledged by everyone, not just those who have adverse circumstances. Material prosperity should not deaden our sensitivity to our spiritual poverty. Those who realize they have nothing spiritually are the only ones who really have anything.

the Kingdom of Heaven is theirs. It is noteworthy that 5:3 and 5:10 have identical promise statements ("for the Kingdom of Heaven is theirs"), and thus frame the entire section. Also the promise statements of 5:3 and 5:10 both use the present tense, while the promise statements of the intervening verses (5:4-9) use the future tense. There is debate over the significance of the present tense in 5:3, 10. Some opt for the futuristic use of the present (e.g., Gundry 1994:68), and others stress the present realization of Kingdom blessing (e.g., Carson 1984:132). The latter view—that a presently inaugurated Kingdom will be consummated in the future—is highly preferable. The oppressed poor presently experience Kingdom blessing only partially.

5:4 God blesses those who mourn, for they will be comforted. Here Jesus indicates that those who mourn will receive God's approval. People mourn over many different misfortunes, but the most likely reason for mourning here is sin or persecution. Some interpreters argue that mourning over sinfulness, not merely one's own but also that of the world in general, is in view here (Bruner 1987:138-39; Carson 1984:133; Hendriksen 1973:270-271). This fits the Matthean theme of the necessity of repentance (3:2; 4:17) and the testimony of such great saints as Isaiah (Isa 6) and Job (Job 42). But perhaps the focus here is more on those who mourn over afflictions and persecution that arise due to their allegiance to the Kingdom (Hagner 1993:92; cf. 5:10-12, 38-48; 10:16-22; 23:34; 24:9). Matt 5:3-4 seems to be alluding to the themes of affliction and mourning found in Isa 61:1-2 (cf. Matt 11:5b). In reality, it is impossible to separate mourning over sin from mourning over affliction, since only those who mourn over sin turn away from it, and only those who turn away from sin face affliction from sinners. It is noteworthy that the grammar of 5:4 is mirrored by 5:9. See the commentary below for discussion.

5:5 God blesses those who are humble, for they will inherit the whole earth. Humble disciples, not arrogant tyrants, will inherit the earth. The language here clearly alludes to Ps 37:11, where the context stresses the oppression of the godly by the wicked. Such oppression is also implicit in Matthew's thought, so Hagner is likely correct that this beatitude does not speak of those who are humble in an abstract sense but of those who have been humbled, "bent over by the injustice of the ungodly" (1993:92). "Meekness is not weakness"— so goes the evangelical cliche. But true meekness is an unassuming humility that rests in God (Ps 37:7) and renounces self-effort to relieve oneself from oppression and to achieve one's wants and needs. This kind of person will inherit the earth (see also 19:28-29; 25:34). Once again Jesus went against the grain of human culture and experience by asserting that the meek, not the yuppies, the militarists, the financial tycoons, or the super-pious types, will inherit the earth. Matthew often mentions the earth, highlighting its theological significance (5:13, 18, 35; 6:10, 19; 9:6; 10:34; 11:25; 16:19; 18:18-19; 23:9; 24:30, 35; 28:18). Instead of longing for removal from earth to heaven, as some Christians do, Jesus' disciples are to be the salt of the earth, as they long for earth to be transformed by the values of the Kingdom—even as they long for God's will to be done on earth as it is in heaven.

5:6 *God blesses those who hunger and thirst for justice, for they will be satisfied.* Those who are famished for righteousness will be satisfied. There is a probable allusion here to Ps 107:5, 9. The NLT's "justice" tends to reflect only the social nuance of righteousness, that of being treated justly by others. But in Matthew the term more often implies right behavior before God. The vocabulary of righteousness is often found in Matthew, including the noun "righteousness" (*dikaiosune* [TG1343, ZG1466]; 3:15; 5:10, 20; 6:1, 33; 21:32), the verb "to justify" (*dikaioō* [TG1344, ZG1467]; 11:19; 12:37), and the adjective "righteous" (*dikaios* [TG1342, ZG1465]; 1:19; 5:45; 9:13; 10:41; 13:17, 43, 49; 23:28, 35; 25:37, 46). See Przybylski 1980 for a full discussion of this language. Protestant Christians who are used to reading Paul may think that Matthew is speaking of the imputed righteousness of Christ (cf., e.g., Rom 5:1-2), but this forensic sense is not a Matthean nuance. Here the emphasis is on the practical side, the upright lifestyle (see also 1:19; 3:15; 5:10, 20, 45; 6:1, 33). Those who realize their lack in attaining right behavior before God, rather than those who boast of their righteous accomplishments, will receive what they long for. Those who repent in view of the nearness of the Kingdom long not only for personal righteousness but also for righteous living to permeate society as a whole. Only then will social justice be achieved. The grammar of 5:6 is mirrored by that of 5:7. See the commentary below for discussion.

5:7 This verse begins the second set of beatitudes, which describe the pattern of divine approval in relating to people (5:7-10).

God blesses those who are merciful, for they will be shown mercy. It is first stated that God's approval comes to those who relate to others with mercy, which involves pity plus action. An allusion here to the language of Prov 14:21 and/or Prov 17:5 LXX seems likely. That the theme of mercy is important for the disciple of Jesus may be seen in 6:2; 9:27, 36; 15:22; 17:15; 20:30. In contrast, mercy is not present where Pharisaic isolationism (9:13), legalism (12:7), and trivialism (23:23) are the rule of life (see also Hos 6:6; Mic 6:8). Even if an oppressed disciple has not received mercy, that disciple must still extend mercy to others. Those who have experienced God's mercy will show it to others (see 18:21-35), and thus demonstrate their destiny as those who will receive mercy at the last day.

5:8 *God blesses those whose hearts are pure, for they will see God.* The promise that the pure in heart will see God is perhaps an echo of Ps 24:3-4 (cf. Ps 51:10; 73:1). Purity of heart amounts to internal integrity that transparently manifests itself in outward behavior. Matthew presents certain Pharisees as models of an external, rule-oriented purity that Jesus rejected and condemned because it masked inner corruption (cf. 15:1-20; 23:25-28). His disciples must possess an inner piety and purity that surpasses mere externally acceptable behavior (5:20-22, 27-28). They have experienced the power of the Kingdom, which purifies from the inside out. Thus, they must cultivate integrity in their private intellectual, emotional, and volitional lives (cf. 5:28; 6:21; 9:4; 12:34; 15:8, 18, 19; 18:35; 22:37). Seeing God is impossible in this life (Exod 33:20), but prophetic visions describe seeing God as a part of the blessings of the world to come (1 John 3:2; Rev 22:4).

5:9 *those who work for peace.* This correctly stresses that this beatitude is not about being a passively peaceful person but an active reconciler of people (cf. Luke 2:14; 19:38; Acts 10:36; Eph 2:14-18; Jas 3:18; *m. Avot* 1:12). Those who would be called God's children will bear a filial likeness to their heavenly Father who treats enemies well (5:43-48). The experience of peace with God enables Jesus' disciples to seek the cessation of their hostilities with people. While the gospel itself may offend some people and lead to hostility (10:34), Jesus' disciples actively seek harmonious relationships with others. In this age of individual, ethnic, and national aggression, Jesus' reminder that peacemakers, not warmongers, have God's approval, is sorely needed. Ultimately, peacemakers will be recognized as members of God's family.

5:10 *the Kingdom of Heaven is theirs*. With the repetition of this phrase (see 5:3), the beatitudes have come full circle. The chief marks of those who already live under God's rule are humility toward God and mercy toward people. One might expect such humble, merciful people to be valued highly by their fellow humans, but such is not the case. Jesus preeminently displayed these righteous characteristics, and he was persecuted to the point of death (23:31-32). He warned his disciples that their upright behavior would receive similar treatment (cf. esp. 21:42; also 10:16-42; 24:9-14). Their persecution is analogous to that of the OT prophets. (See also 5:44; 10:23; 1 Pet 3:14; and Hare 1967.) This beatitude is expanded in 5:11-12.

COMMENTARY

Introduction to the Sermon on the Mount. The Sermon on the Mount does not appear as such in Mark and appears only partially in Luke (6:17–7:1). Several theories exist to explain this variation among the synoptic Gospels. Some think Matthew created the sermon from traditions, documentary sources, and his own ingenuity, so that the sermon should not be attributed to the historical Jesus. This view is not accepted by evangelical Christians, since it tends to take the Gospels as unhistorical fabrications, concocted for strictly theological reasons. A second view is that Matthew created the structure of the sermon by collating various teachings of the historical Jesus that were originally uttered at different times in different locations. There are many evangelicals who hold this view (e.g., Hagner 1993:83), but it will not be followed here because Matthew's narrative plainly brackets the sermon with indicators of a specific time and place in which the sermon occurred (5:1-2; 7:28–8:1). These historical markers must be ignored or viewed as fictional for the second view to be adopted. The third view is that Matthew accurately records "the very voice" of Jesus (*ipsissima vox*), giving the gist of a historical sermon that Jesus actually uttered. The last view is that Matthew gives an exact and complete word for word (*ipsissima verba*, "the very words") transcription of the sermon Jesus uttered. These last two views are both held by conservative evangelicals, but the third view is highly preferable for reasons pertaining to the genre of the Gospels and the historical transmission of the teachings of Jesus. An authentic report of a historical event need not involve a word-for-word transcription, and it is difficult to conceive how such a transcription could have been compiled in the first place, let alone transmitted to the likely author, Matthew, who was not yet a disciple of Jesus (9:9). Rather, in the sermon we have a reliable summary of what Jesus said, an account that bears the marks of an editor. The fact that certain sayings of Matthew's Sermon occur in other contexts in Mark and Luke is evidently due to Jesus' repeating key themes in his itinerant ministry.

Literary Structure. After his unique story of Jesus' infancy (chs 1-2), Matthew develops the body of his gospel as five blocks of narrative material (chs 3-7, 8-10, 11-13, 14-18, 19-25), and concludes with Jesus' death, resurrection, and mission mandate (26-28). The body's five sections of Jesus' works and words are divided by the key phrase "when Jesus had finished" (7:28; 11:1; 13:53; 19:1; 26:1). This has been discussed more fully in the Introduction. The discourse we call the Sermon on the Mount (chs 5-7) should be seen as the representative ethical teachings of Jesus, developing the summary statement of 4:23, which presents a word/deed complex. Thus 4:23 and the similar summary in 9:35 provide a "frame" or "bookends" for Jesus' ministry of teaching and doing miracles. His teaching is represented in chapters 5-7 and his miracles in chapters 8-9. Both the words and the works demonstrate the authority of the Kingdom of Heaven (7:28-29; 9:6-8).

Major Interpretive Approaches. For the plethora of interpretive approaches to the Sermon, see Kissinger 1975. Here only a few approaches can be mentioned. Dispensational interpreters traditionally view the Sermon as Jewish law for the Kingdom, not gracious teaching that is directly relevant for the church. This Kingdom teaching may relate to the time of Jesus' earthly ministry, or to the future tribulation or millennium. This view mistakenly assumes that Matthew was written to Jews. Lutheran interpreters similarly view the Sermon as law, not gospel, but think that its high legal standards will show people their sinfulness and draw them to the cross for forgiveness. Schweitzer viewed the Sermon as an ethic for the supposedly short interim Matthew conceived between the advents of Jesus. Other interpreters, across the spectrum of denominations and views of eschatology, take the Sermon as an ethic for today, but differ on whether the Sermon is merely personal ethics or an agenda to be implemented through political processes. The view I take is that the Sermon amounts to personal ethics for followers of Jesus. This does not amount to privatism inasmuch as followers of Jesus are to be salt and light in this world.

The Sermon on the Mount is Jesus' authoritative teaching about the way believers should live today. Those who repented when they heard the gospel preached by John and Jesus (3:2; 4:17) needed to know how to live under God's saving rule, "the Kingdom of Heaven." As Jewish Christians, they especially needed to know how Jesus' teaching related to the Old Testament, and that their righteousness must exceed that of the scribes and Pharisees. They needed to practice their religion for God's reward, not for human approval. They needed to put physical needs and material possessions into proper perspective. Spiritual discernment and prayer were also priority matters. In case anyone was listening carelessly without a desire for obedience, they were warned to enter the narrow gate, to avoid fruitless trees, and to build on the rock. In all this, they would realize that full obedience to these high standards would be attained at the future coming of the Kingdom (6:10).

The Structure of the Beatitudes: Divine Approval in Relating to God and People.

Altogether there are nine beatitudes in 5:3-12, but the ninth (5:11-12) is really an expansion of the eighth (5:10). Although some (e.g., Davies and Allison 1988:430-431) opt for a structure with three sets of three, the first eight exhibit such a tightly knit parallel structure that it is more likely that we should understand them as two sets of four (Gundry 1994:73; Turner 1992b). The first set emphasizes the disciple's vertical relationship to God; the second emphasizes the disciple's horizontal relationship to people. Both relationships occur in the midst of oppression. The flow of these verses may be shown as follows:

5:3 Poor in spirit blessed because theirs is the Kingdom of Heaven (Present tense in promise identical to 5:10)

   5:4 Mourners blessed because they will be comforted (Future passive promise as in 5:9)

      5:5 Meek blessed because they will inherit the earth (Future transitive verb with direct object as in 5:8)

         5:6 Hungry blessed because they will be filled (Future passive promise as in 5:7)

         5:7 Merciful blessed because they will receive mercy (Future passive promise as in 5:6)

      5:8 Pure blessed because they will see God (Future transitive verb with direct object as in 5:5)

   5:9 Peacemakers blessed because they will be called sons of God (Future passive promise as in 5:4)

5:10 Persecuted blessed because theirs is the Kingdom of Heaven (Present tense in promise identical to 5:3)

The Meaning of the Beatitudes. There are two contrasting views of the meaning of the beatitudes, centering on whether they should be understood as gracious Kingdom blessings or as ethical entrance requirements (Guelich 1976). If the latter, one should try to work up the characteristics mentioned here so that one might earn God's approval. If the former, one should thankfully acknowledge these characteristics as evidence of God's gracious work in his or her life and cultivate them as one lives as a disciple of Christ. Certainly this second view is correct. Those who repent at the message of the Kingdom (3:2; 4:17) acknowledge their own spiritual bankruptcy and rejoice in God's blessings of salvation. The NLT translation ("God blesses those who . . .") could be taken to imply the entrance requirement view. It would be better to say "God *has* blessed those who . . ." since these are unmerited blessings.

The beatitudes reveal key character traits that God approves in his people. These traits are gracious gifts indicating God's approval, not requirements for works that merit God's approval. However, those who have repented should cultivate these characteristics. Each beatitude contains a pronouncement (who are blessed) backed up by a promise (why they are blessed). God does not necessarily endorse popularity, keeping the rules, possessions, spectacular displays, or knowledge. The qualities God approves are explained in two sets of four, describing respectively one's relationship to God and one's relationship to other people (see also

22:37-40). He approves those who relate to him by admitting their spiritual poverty and mourning over their sin, humbly seeking spiritual fullness (5:3-6). He approves those who relate to others mercifully and purely as peacemakers, even though such people may be persecuted for their righteous behavior (5:7-12). At first, this may sound like some sort of cruel, sadistic joke, appealing only to masochistic types. It is as if Jesus was saying that those who are unhappy are happy. But in reality Jesus was showing the error of superficial, self-centered living. Genuine realism, not false optimism, is true bliss for the followers of Jesus, for it will lead to ultimate comfort.

The radical spirituality of the beatitudes directly confronts several cultural views of God's approval. One of these is that popularity with one's peers indicates divine approval, but this is plainly contradicted by the statement that those who are persecuted by their peers on account of Jesus have God's approval (5:10-12; 7:13-14). Another mistaken viewpoint is that one may have divine approval if one simply keeps a prescribed set of rules, but Jesus states that only a righteousness that surpasses mere rule-keeping will suffice for his Kingdom (5:20). Some would say that an abundance of material possessions is an indication of divine favor, but according to Jesus, preoccupation with such possessions is antithetical to the values of the Kingdom (6:19-21, 33). Ability to perform miraculous displays is commonly associated with divine approval, but some miracle workers will learn on the last day that Jesus will not acknowledge them as his people (7:22-23). In the civilized world, there is a premium on education, and this has influenced Christianity in many ways, including its view of its clergy. But according to Jesus, one must obey his words, not simply know what they are (7:26).

Conclusion. The first four beatitudes show that divine approval means that one has been humbled under God's mighty hand through the preaching of the Kingdom so that one admits one's spiritual poverty, mourns over sin and the oppression of God's people, rests in God's care in the face of oppression, and hungers for greater righteousness on earth (5:3-6). Thus humility is the basic trait of authentic spirituality (see also Mic 6:6-8; Matt 11:25-30; 18:1-5; 19:13-15). A humble person who acknowledges sin, not a smug one who congratulates himself on his goodness, receives God's endorsement (see also 9:12-13).

The character traits of Kingdom rule are chiefly humility toward God and mercy toward people. By God's grace, these traits are present in principle in the lives of his people. Yet God's people must cultivate these traits so they are present in reality. In a world that values pride over humility and aggression over mercy, Jesus' disciples are, in the words of J.R.W. Stott (1978), "Christian Counter-Culture." As disciples cultivate the counter-cultural graces of the beatitudes, they are in reality cultivating likeness to their master, who perfectly exemplified the character traits of the beatitudes. Jesus was meek (11:29). He mourned (26:36-46). He "fulfilled all righteousness" (3:15; 27:4, 19). He was merciful (9:27; 15:22; 17:15; 20:30-31). And above all, he was oppressed and persecuted for doing what was right.

◆   ## 2. Persecution and witness (5:11-16)

¹¹"God blesses you when people mock you and persecute you and lie about you* and say all sorts of evil things against you because you are my followers. ¹²Be happy about it! Be very glad! For a great reward awaits you in heaven. And remember, the ancient prophets were persecuted in the same way.

¹³"You are the salt of the earth. But what good is salt if it has lost its flavor? Can you make it salty again? It will be thrown out and trampled underfoot as worthless.

¹⁴"You are the light of the world—like a city on a hilltop that cannot be hidden. ¹⁵No one lights a lamp and then puts it under a basket. Instead, a lamp is placed on a stand, where it gives light to everyone in the house. ¹⁶In the same way, let your good deeds shine out for all to see, so that everyone will praise your heavenly Father."

5:11 Some manuscripts omit *and lie about you.*

NOTES

5:11-12 Davies and Allison (1988:430) make a strong case against the approach followed here, which construes 5:11-12 with 5:13-16 instead of with 5:3-10. It is clear that 5:11-12 is related to 5:3-10, since 5:11-12 contains another beatitude and relates to persecution (cf. 5:10). But there are differences that justify viewing 5:11-12 as literarily distinct from 5:3-10. These differences chiefly relate to the departure from the tightly knit pattern of 5:3-10 (explained in the commentary on 5:3-10). The beatitude of 5:11-12 uses the second person, while those in 5:3-10 all use the third person. Also, the beatitude of 5:11-12 is considerably longer than those in 5:3-10, with a lengthened description of the oppression (*when people mock you and persecute you and lie about you and say all sorts of evil things against you*), its reason (*because you are my followers*), and commands on dealing with it (*Be happy about it! Be very glad!*), all of which intervene before the promise of reward occurs. And an additional command occurs after the promise (*remember, the ancient prophets were persecuted in the same way*). Thus, there is reason to take this expanded beatitude with 5:13-16 as a distinct description of the life of a disciple in the world.

In 5:11-12 followers of Jesus are told that they must not simply endure persecution with a stoic disposition. Rather, they are to endure it with deep joy, since in it they are identified with their Messiah Jesus (cf. 10:22, 25; 24:9) and continue in the train of the prophets who have been previously persecuted (cf. 23:29-36 in light of 2 Chr 36:16, along with Acts 7:52; 1 Thess 2:15; Jas 5:10). What is more, they will experience great future reward (cf. 6:1-18; 10:41-42; 19:29).

5:13 *You are the salt of the earth.* The image of salt (cf. Mark 9:50; Luke 14:35) is not an easy one to interpret because of its several uses in the ancient world. In the OT, salt was added to sacrifices (Lev 2:13), connected with purity (Exod 30:35; 2 Kgs 2:19-22), symbolic of loyalty (Num 18:19 NLT mg; Ezra 4:14 NLT mg), and used as a seasoning for food (Job 6:6). In the Mishnah salt is associated with wisdom (*m. Sotah* 9:15). The Roman historian Pliny described uses for salt in his *Natural History* (31.73-92). One would think that the purifying use of salt could be intended here, given 5:8, but perhaps the multiple ways in which salt benefits the world is the point of the metaphor. In context, salt is viewed as a metaphor of beneficial influence upon the world, in a manner analogous to the way light (5:14) is beneficial in illumining darkness. However, salt that has lost its saltiness is good for nothing. The presence of other minerals in it—impurities—could result in the loss of its distinctive flavor and its preservative effects.

5:14 *You are the light of the world.* Light is a much more prominent and univocal image in the Bible than salt. Matthew 4:16 (citing Isa 9:2) has already associated light with Jesus and the Kingdom ministry in dark Galilee. Isaiah 42:6 speaks of Israel's role in the world as a "light to the Gentiles" (cf. Isa 49:6; 51:4-5; Dan 12:3; Rom 2:19).

city on a hilltop. The image of the city on the hill makes sense even if no particular city is in mind, but it is plausible, in view of OT prophecy, that Jerusalem is intended (Isa 2:2-5; 49:8-26; 54; 60; cf. Heb 11:16; 12:22; Rev 3:12; 21:2ff; Campbell 1978; Turner 1992a). Jesus' statement that it is his disciples who illumine the world for God is implicitly polemical since it assumes that the nation of Israel is not living up to this lofty role. The polemic is stronger if the city is an allusion to Jerusalem, since it would imply that God's illumining presence in the world flows from Jesus' disciples, not a place. The image of Jesus and the church as light in a dark world is prominent elsewhere in the NT, especially in the Johannine and Pauline writings.

5:15-16 *a lamp is placed on a stand.* The second image that develops the metaphor of light is an oil lamp, which would obviously be placed up high on a stand, not covered up with a basket. Jesus argues from common sense to show that it would be ridiculous for his disciples to hide their good deeds from the world. Matthew frequently stresses that good deeds are the mark of discipleship. The grace-induced character traits just highlighted in the beatitudes are good deeds. Previously, John had demanded "fruit" (NLT: "the way you live") in connection with his baptism (3:8, 10), and Jesus returns to this metaphor for good deeds later in the Sermon (7:16-20). Indeed, without good works one simply is not a disciple of Jesus (7:24-27; 13:23, 38). A so-called "disciple" without good works is of no more value than flavorless salt or a concealed lamp, but a true disciple impacts people and thereby brings glory to the heavenly Father (cf. 1 Pet 2:12).

COMMENTARY

The structure of this short section is relatively simple. Its first part (5:11-12) is a beatitude that expands the implications of the beatitude on persecution in 5:10. Four aspects of the expansion may be noted: (1) the beatitude is made more personal by the switch to the second person; (2) the beatitude is made more challenging by the commands to rejoice during persecution; (3) the beatitude is made more rationally satisfying by the mention of the reason for persecution and of others who have been persecuted; and (4) the beatitude is made more specific in terms of its promised reward.

The second part of this section (5:13-16) speaks to the matter of Kingdom testimony in the midst of an oppressive world. This testimony is described metaphorically as salt (5:13) and light (5:14-16). The metaphor of light is further pictured as a prominent hilltop city (5:14) and an oil lamp set upon a high stand, not under a basket (5:15). These pictures aid the disciples in their task of illuminating the world (5:16).

Those who repent and submit to God's rule in Christ are approved by him as humble, merciful people as they relate to God (5:3-6) and to other people (5:7-10). Now Jesus explains, in 5:11-16, that such people will influence the world in tangible ways. This should put to rest any notion that discipleship is merely a private matter between a person and God. First, in 5:11-12, Jesus expands his beatitude on persecution (5:10) by pointing out that insults and slander may occur because of his disciples' connection with him. When this occurs, the disciples are in good company with the prophets and may expect a great reward. Thus the disciples' influence on the world will often be unappreciated and opposed. Second, in 5:13-16 Jesus uses two vivid pictures to speak of his disciples' influence. They are salt (5:13) and light (5:14-16). As salt, they will purify and preserve their society if only they retain their saltiness. As light, their good deeds will result in praise going to their Father if only they display that light prominently for all to see.

Jesus' disciples are to be influential for the Kingdom even in the midst of an oppressive world. Salt and light can be understood to imply two aspects of witness in the world. Disciples, like salt, must mingle with the world in order to give it good flavor, or to purify or preserve it. But disciples, like lamps, must remain distinct from the world in order to illumine it. Salt is of no value if it loses its flavor, but its flavor is not meant to be kept in a salt shaker. There is a tension here that each disciple must reckon with.

The terminology of 5:13-16 underlines Matthew's stress on the church's universal mission. Jesus' disciples have a role to perform in the world, and they have been graciously equipped to perform that role (5:3-10). The church Jesus will build (16:18) is the agency by which the Kingdom influences mankind. The entire earth (cf. 6:10; 16:19; 18:18-19; 28:18) must be salted, and the whole world (13:38; 24:14; 26:13) must be illumined. The disciples' light must shine upon people. This means that the isolationism of some Christians and local churches, even though it may ostensibly spring from sincere motives related to maintaining the church's purity or orthodoxy, cannot be sustained. Matthew tells us that Jesus was not an ascetic, that he associated with "disreputable sinners" (9:10), and "feasted and drank" (11:19). Yet in these relationships Jesus did not lose his saltiness or conceal his light. No doubt disciples must not take lightly the wiles of "the world, the flesh, and the devil," but the answer to this danger is not isolation. It is active engagement that leads to the conversion of individuals and the transformation of culture. Anything less is an inexcusable truncation of the gospel of the Kingdom.

◆   ## 3. Jesus' teachings about the law (5:17-20)

17"Don't misunderstand why I have come. I did not come to abolish the law of Moses or the writings of the prophets. No, I came to accomplish their purpose. 18I tell you the truth, until heaven and earth disappear, not even the smallest detail of God's law will disappear until its purpose is achieved. 19So if you ignore the least commandment and teach others to do the same, you will be called the least in the Kingdom of Heaven. But anyone who obeys God's laws and teaches them will be called great in the Kingdom of Heaven.

20"But I warn you—unless your righteousness is better than the righteousness of the teachers of religious law and the Pharisees, you will never enter the Kingdom of Heaven!"

NOTES

5:17 *I did not come to abolish the law of Moses or the writings of the prophets. No, I came to accomplish their purpose.* To Matthew's Christian Jewish audience, "good deeds" (5:16) would imply performance of the commands (*mitswoth* [TH4687, ZH5184]) enjoined by the law and the prophets. But this is not a full picture of Jesus' ethics or relationship to the

Hebrew Bible, so he elaborates. The relationship of Jesus' coming to the law and to the prophets is a watershed issue for the interpretation of Matthew and for biblical theology. The contrasting terms "abolish" and "accomplish their purpose" (lit. "fulfill") set the agenda for a general statement (5:17-20) that is expanded in the six so-called "antitheses" (5:21-48) that take up the rest of the chapter. The mention of the law and the prophets here and in the summary statement of 7:12 is an *inclusio*, which brings the main body of the Sermon full circle. The metaphorical use of "abolish" (lit. "destroy") may be illustrated by its literal use in 24:2; 26:61; 27:40. The meaning of "accomplish" (lit. "fulfill") must be examined in light of its frequent usage in OT introductory formulas: 1:22; 2:15, 17, 23; 4:14; 8:17; 12:17; 13:35; 21:4; 26:54, 56; 27:9. Other significant uses are 3:15 and 23:32. Jesus does not contradict or abrogate the law and the prophets, but neither does he merely reaffirm them. He fulfills them or brings them to their divinely intended goal because they point to him. See the previous discussion of this topic in the commentary on 1:18-25. Additional discussion of this text occurs in the commentary below. Davies and Allison (1988:485-487) have a convenient summary and discussion of the several views of this matter.

5:18-19 *until heaven and earth disappear.* Matthew 5:18 serves to explain 5:17. Jesus, far from abolishing the law, brings it to its desired goal because not the slightest detail of it will go unaccomplished. The phrases "until heaven and earth disappear" and "until its purpose is achieved" (cf. 24:34-35) refer to the end of the present world and the beginning of the eschaton. Until that time the law is valid. Matthew 5:19 goes on to infer from 5:18's statement of the perpetual authority of the law that it had better be obeyed and taught by disciples of the Kingdom. It would be hard to make a stronger statement of the ongoing authority of the Torah than is made in 5:18.

the smallest detail. Jesus claims that not even the "smallest detail" of the Torah would disappear from it before its purpose was accomplished. The NLT's "smallest detail" translates a phrase that refers to the smallest letter of the Heb. alphabet (*yod;* translated in Gr. as *iōta* [TG2503, ZG2740]) and the smallest stroke of the pen (cf. Luke 16:17). In other words, in an implicit argument from lesser to greater, Jesus affirms that God will bring to pass even the most trivial parts of the law, implying that its weightier matters are absolutely certain to be accomplished. Therefore, Jesus' disciples must not make the mistake of ignoring any part of the law, however trivial it may seem.

5:20 The inference of 5:19 on the necessity of obeying and teaching the law is followed here by a further inference—if Jesus fulfills the law and declares it to be perpetually authoritative for his disciples, then he, as its only fully authoritative interpreter, demands a higher righteousness than that taught and followed by his contemporary religious leaders. Their understanding and practice of the law is deficient because it does not reckon with him as its fulfillment. Here Christology is the foundation of ethics. Jesus, the one to whom the law points, identifies the true ethical intent of the law. The higher righteousness spoken of here is developed in the following "antitheses" of 5:21-28. As these verses are examined, it is crucial to determine whether Jesus is primarily replacing, intensifying, or simply expounding the OT.

COMMENTARY

Matthew 5:17-48 involves a general introduction (vv. 17-20) followed by two sets (vv. 21-32 and 33-48) of three specific contrasts between traditional understandings of the Old Testament and Jesus' understanding of the Old Testament. Both sets of contrasts confront those who would aggressively dominate others by anger, lust, divorce, oaths, retaliation, or hatred.

The basic point of 5:17-20 is that if Jesus has come not to destroy but to fulfill the law (5:17), then the entire law is eternally valid (5:18), and the disciples must obey him as its ultimate interpreter and teach his interpretations of it (5:19) in order to have a moral uprightness that exceeds that of the scribes and Pharisees and that is fitting for the Kingdom (5:20).

Jesus and the Law: Continuity and Discontinuity. What does it mean when Jesus affirms that he has come to fulfill the law and the prophets? The NLT's "I came to accomplish their purpose" is an interpretive translation that stresses the continuity of the mission of Jesus with the ethical intent of the Hebrew Bible. But accomplishing the purpose of the law (lit. "fulfilling" it) should not be taken to mean that Jesus came only to reaffirm, establish, or confirm the law. Such a viewpoint overstates the continuity of Jesus' teaching and that of the law and would render the six specific examples of 5:21-48 superfluous. Jesus was not simply saying "Ditto, what Moses said, I say." On the other hand, the discontinuity of Jesus and Moses should not be taken too far because Jesus said that he did not come to abolish the law and the prophets. His teaching is therefore not contradictory to anything in the Hebrew Bible, although it must in some sense transcend it. So two extremes must be ruled out—to say that Jesus came to abolish the law drastically overstates the discontinuity between Jesus and Moses, and to say that Jesus came only to reaffirm Moses understates the discontinuity between Jesus and Moses.

So how do we avoid saying too much or saying too little about the relationship of Jesus to the law? First we must allow Matthew himself to define the term "fulfill" by paying close attention to how he uses the term throughout his Gospel and by carefully noting the relationship between Jesus' teaching and the law of Moses in the six specific examples that occur in 5:21-48. For Matthew, Jesus is the ultimate goal of the law and the prophets, the one to whom they point. His mission of Kingdom words and deeds fulfills the ethical standards and eschatological promises of the law and prophets. Thus he becomes the sole authoritative teacher of the law, and his interpretations take on the character of new law for his disciples. His teachings are not new in the sense of having no root in the Hebrew Bible but in the sense of transcending the traditional understanding of the law promulgated by the religious leaders. It is not Moses, much less the religious leaders, who authoritatively teach Jesus' disciples. Jesus alone fills that role. The six examples of 5:21-48 do not amount to Jesus contradicting Moses but to Jesus unfolding implications that were in Moses all along, although undetected by the contemporary religious leaders of Israel. In this respect, Jesus' "fulfillment" of the Hebrew Bible is not unlike the interpretations of the Bible found in the later rabbinic literature. Those rabbis maintained that their seemingly innovative rulings were all along implied in the Torah revealed to Moses at Sinai. But Jesus claims far more than this, as we shall see in the next section of this commentary.

Law and Grace. Jesus' statements in 5:19-20 about his disciples' obligation to the law may be nothing less than astonishing to Christians who believe themselves to be under grace, not law. Those who are accustomed to reading certain sections of Paul's epistles in which the law seems to be deprecated may be amazed to read of its perpetual, binding authority on Jesus' disciples (Overman 1996:77). After all, didn't Paul say that Jesus was the end of the law and that his followers are not under law but under grace (e.g., Rom 6:14; 7:1-6; 10:4)? But Paul's situations, audiences, and problems were very different from Matthew's. Paul labored to extend the gospel from Christian Jewish communities like Matthew's to Gentiles. In so doing, Paul taught that the Gentiles who believed in Jesus were not obligated to follow the law. This of course resulted in no little tension with Christian Jews (Acts 15:1-5; 21:20-21), not to mention non-Christian Jews (Acts 21:27-28).

According to the narrative in Acts, Paul himself continued in synagogue worship and other Jewish practices throughout the span of his ministry (Acts 18:18; 20:17-26; 22:3, 17; 23:1-6; 24:11-21; 25:8; 26:20-23). As an evangelist to Gentiles, however, his strategy involved flexibility in areas he deemed expedient (1 Cor 9:19-23). Much of his seemingly negative teaching on the law was not directed against the law per se, but against teachers who erroneously wished to bring his Gentile converts under the law. While insisting that such converts were not obligated to the law as a rule of life, he also stated that their obedience to Jesus through the Spirit would "fulfill" the law's righteous requirements (Rom 8:1-4). Paul's identification of the "weightier matters" of the law with love (Rom 13:8-10; Gal 3:14) seems to follow Jesus' teaching (Matt 22:34-40).

Conclusion. Matthew's Christian Jewish community must not think that Jesus has come to abolish Mosaic law. Rather Jesus fulfills it by upholding its perpetual authority and interpreting it in an ultimately definitive manner, which leads his disciples to a righteousness surpassing that of the religious leaders. This general notion of a surpassing righteousness will now be explained by six concrete examples in which Jesus' teaching brings out the true meaning of the law of Moses and transcends the way it has been traditionally understood. As his disciples live by this teaching, their righteousness will surpass that of the Jewish religious leaders, and their good deeds will be like a shining light that causes people to glorify their heavenly Father (5:16).

◆   4. Jesus' teaching about anger, adultery, and divorce (5:21-32)

21"You have heard that our ancestors were told, 'You must not murder. If you commit murder, you are subject to judgment.'* 22But I say, if you are even angry with someone,* you are subject to judgment! If you call someone an idiot,* you are in danger of being brought before the court. And if you curse someone,* you are in danger of the fires of hell.*

23"So if you are presenting a sacrifice* at the altar in the Temple and you suddenly remember that someone has something against you, 24leave your sacrifice there at the altar. Go and be reconciled to that person. Then come and offer your sacrifice to God.

25"When you are on the way to court with your adversary, settle your differences quickly. Otherwise, your accuser may hand you over to the judge, who will hand you over to an officer, and you will be thrown into prison. 26And if that happens, you surely won't be free again until you have paid the last penny.*

27"You have heard the commandment that says, 'You must not commit adultery.'* 28But I say, anyone who even looks at a woman with lust has already committed adultery with her in his heart. 29So if your eye—even your good eye*—causes you to lust, gouge it out and throw it away. It is better for you to lose one part of your body than for your whole body to be thrown into hell. 30And if your hand—

even your stronger hand*—causes you to sin, cut it off and throw it away. It is better for you to lose one part of your body than for your whole body to be thrown into hell.

31"You have heard the law that says, 'A man can divorce his wife by merely giving her a written notice of divorce.'* 32But I say that a man who divorces his wife, unless she has been unfaithful, causes her to commit adultery. And anyone who marries a divorced woman also commits adultery."

5:21 Exod 20:13; Deut 5:17. **5:22a** Some manuscripts add *without cause.* **5:22b** Greek uses an Aramaic term of contempt: *If you say to your brother, 'Raca.'* **5:22c** Greek *if you say, 'You fool.'* **5:22d** Greek *Gehenna;* also in 5:29, 30. **5:23** Greek *gift;* also in 5:24. **5:26** Greek *the last kodrantes* [i.e., quadrans]. **5:27** Exod 20:14; Deut 5:18. **5:29** Greek *your right eye.* **5:30** Greek *your right hand.* **5:31** Deut 24:1.

NOTES

5:21-22 *You have heard that our ancestors were told.* This appears again in the fourth example (5:33) with the added word "also" (lit. "again"). This implies that the six examples are intended to be viewed as two groups of three. This first example of how Jesus definitively interprets the law (5:21-26) develops the OT teaching on murder. Matt 5:21 refers to Exod 20:13 and Deut 5:17, but only the words "you must not murder" are taken verbatim from the OT.

If you commit murder, you are subject to judgment. This is probably a summary of texts like Exod 21:12 and Deut 17:8-13. In contrast, Jesus lists three hypothetical instances in 5:22 in which anger or angry speech will lead to judgment just as surely as murder will. It is likely that the three descriptions of judgment (judgment, court, hell) are not ascending in severity but are progressively more vivid descriptions of the consequences of anger and abusive speech.

if you are even angry with someone. This calls attention to Jesus' shocking elevation of anger to a capital crime. "Someone" is lit. "brother," which likely means another person in one's religious community rather than another human being in general (5:47; 7:3-5; 18:15; 25:40). The second and third instances both move from a furious attitude to abusive speech, calling a brother an idiot or a fool (see NLT mg).

5:23-24 *be reconciled to that person.* In keeping with the teaching of 5:22 on the consequences of anger and abusive speech within the community, Jesus poses a concrete situation in which personal reconciliation takes precedence over religious duty. Significantly the situation here does not pertain to one's own anger but to the anger or grudge of another. Disciples are thus responsible not only to reign in their own anger but to take steps to reconcile with others who are angry at them. It is not a question of arguing about who offended whom but of both offender and injured party taking responsibility for reconciliation. Such reconciliation to a fellow disciple (NLT's "someone" and "that person" both translate the word "brother") must be addressed before one offers a sacrifice in the Temple. Jesus' stress on the priority of reconciliation and justice over sacrificial worship is in keeping with such OT texts as 1 Sam 15:22; Isa 1:10-18; Hos 6:6, and Mic 6:6-8. As in the model prayer (6:12, 14-15; cf. 18:15-17), divine forgiveness is linked with human forgiveness. The Temple imagery is interesting in light of the likelihood that Matthew is addressing a Christian Jewish community. According to Acts, the Christian Jews in Jerusalem continued to observe the Temple rituals (2:46; 3:1; 5:12, 42; 21:26; 22:17; 24:12, 18; 25:8; 26:21).

5:25-26 *settle your differences quickly.* Here another concrete situation is posed. The obligation to seek reconciliation applies not only to relations within the community of disciples (5:23-24) but also to relationships outside that community. Adversarial legal situations should be settled out of court, or else serious judicial consequences will result. Debtors were evidently incarcerated until payment was made in the judicial system assumed here. Perhaps these verses are primarily metaphorical and speak to the matter of averting the wrath of God, but this is not so obvious as some think (e.g., Blomberg 1992:108). Compare the last contrast in 5:38-48, where disciples are enjoined to love their enemies. See also Luke 12:57-59 for this saying in a different context. Evangelical Protestant commentators frequently point out that these verses do not support the Roman Catholic doctrine of purgatory.

5:27-28 *anyone who looks at a woman with lust has already committed adultery.* The second example of how Jesus definitively interprets the law moves from the sixth to the seventh commandment, developing the OT teaching on adultery (Exod 20:14; Deut 5:18; cf. Matt 5:32; 19:9, 18). By way of contrast to this command against adulterous behavior, Matt 5:28 likewise condemns adulterous thoughts, viewing them as tantamount to the act. By condemning the internal seed of the outward sin, Jesus obviously condemns the act itself. While the OT certainly does not condone lust, Jesus' direct linkage of lust to adultery is a more stringent standard of sexual ethics. By stressing the lustful intention over the act itself, Jesus seems to be interpreting the seventh commandment by the tenth commandment (Exod 20:17; "You must not covet your neighbor's wife"). But Matt 5:28 is speaking of women in general, not just married women. And it is possible that 5:28 is not simply about looking with lust at a woman but about looking at a woman in such a way as to entice her to lust (Carson 1984:151).

5:29-30 Both of these verses speak hyperbolically in parallel fashion to underline the gravity of Jesus' teaching on lust in 5:28 (cf. 18:7-9 for similar language). Sin must be avoided even if radical sacrifice is required. Lust must be treated with the utmost seriousness because it can cause a person to be thrown into hell. The "good" (lit. "right") eye (5:29; cf. 1 Sam 11:2; Zech 11:17; 2 Pet 2:14) and the "stronger" (lit. "right") hand (5:30; cf. Gen 48:14; Ps 137:5) are respectively the means by which lustful thoughts are initially engendered and subsequently carried out (Josh 7:21; 2 Sam 11:2; Ezek 6:9). If these bring one into an occasion of sin, they must be dealt with by radical surgery (cf. Col 3:5). The mention of the right eye reminds the reader of the verb of seeing in 5:28. It should go without saying that the two commands here are hyperbolic. Since evil arises in the heart (15:19), amputation cannot cure it. But the hyperbole shocks the reader with the real point: it is better to deal decisively with lust than to be thrown into hell because of it.

5:31-32 The third example of how Jesus definitively interprets the law develops the OT teaching on divorce. Matt 5:31 (cf. Mark 10:11-12; Luke 16:18) refers to Deut 24:1-4 (cf. 19:7), which in its original context prohibits a man from remarrying a woman he has previously married and divorced if she has in the interim been married to and divorced by another man. The part of the Deuteronomy passage most relevant to Matthew 5 is the mention of the written divorce document in 24:1, 3. Evidently many teachers of Jesus' day had taken this passage as *carte blanche* for divorce. Hillel is cited by the Mishnah (compiled from earlier oral tradition around AD 200) as permitting divorce for *any* indecency (Deut 24:1; *m. Gittin* 9:10).

Jesus' strict view of divorce is evidently much like that of Rabbi Shammai, who is also cited by the above text from the Mishnah. According to Jesus, a man who divorces his wife (*unless she has been unfaithful*) causes her and her potential future spouse to commit adultery. If there has been no sexual infidelity, there can be no real divorce. If there has been no real divorce, there can be no remarriage, and any additional sexual unions are adulterous. There is much debate on the word *porneia* [TG4202, ZG4518], (the Gr. word represented by the NLT's "unless she has been unfaithful") but it seems most likely that Jesus has in mind any sort of sexual activity not involving one's spouse (Davies and Allison 1988:529ff). It is plausible that the phrase "unless she has been unfaithful" is an allusion to the phrase "something about her that is shameful" in Deut 24:1 (lit. "something indecent" or "a matter of indecency").

Jesus prohibits what the OT was understood to permit regarding divorce. As the definitive eschatological teacher of the law, his interpretation is evidently (cf. 19:3-9) based on the original divine intent for marriage, not the expediency of the moment. The Pharisaic misinterpretation of the OT capitalized on a concession to human sinfulness (cf. 19:8). See further discussion at 19:3-9.

COMMENTARY

In 5:21-32 Jesus begins to unpack what he meant when he said that he had come not to destroy but to fulfill the law and the prophets, and that his disciples' uprightness must exceed that of the scribes and Pharisees. He gives three concrete interpretations: (1) anger is tantamount to murder (5:21-26), (2) lust is tantamount to adultery (5:27-30), and (3) divorce and remarriage are tantamount to adultery (except when infidelity has occurred; 5:31-32). In each of the three examples the traditional understanding of the Torah is contrasted with Jesus' understanding of it, and in the first two interpretations, there are examples that apply the teaching to concrete situations. The structure of each interpretation is very similar:

1. Traditional teaching (5:21, 27, 31)
2. Jesus' contrasting teaching (5:22, 28, 32)
3. Concrete applications of Jesus' teaching (5:23-26, 29-30)

The Question of Antithesis or Contrast. Although it is common for commentators to speak of Jesus' six teachings in Matthew 5:21-48 as antitheses (see Harrington 1991:90), this is certainly a mistake. An antithesis is not merely a contrasting statement, it is a contradictory statement. If Jesus had intended to teach antithetically to the law and the prophets, he would have needed to say what amounts to an antithesis to Matthew 5:17 because he would have come to abolish the law and the prophets. If Jesus had been speaking antithetically, he would have said, "You have heard that it has been said, 'you shall not murder,' but I say unto you, 'you shall murder.'" This is, of course, unthinkable. No doubt the transcendent teaching of Jesus here is in contrast to that of the traditional teachers of the law, but it does not formally contradict the law.

In all six of the contrasts there are two crucial matters to keep in mind. First there is the contrasting parallel in audiences: the ancestors (national Israel) versus "you" (Jesus' disciples), implying that the disciples, not the Jews as a nation, are the locus of Jesus' revelatory ministry. Second and even more noteworthy is the contrast between the agency of what has been said and what is now being said. The Greek text emphasizes that Jesus himself was speaking with an authority transcending that of the previous divine revelation through Moses. Jesus did not deny that God had spoken through Moses (cf. 15:4), but he affirmed his own transcendent revelatory agency in strong language. This authoritative way of speaking was not lost on those who heard him (7:29; 8:8-9; 9:8; 10:1; 28:18).

The Greater Righteousness Taught by Jesus. It is clear in each of the first three examples of Jesus' teaching that his standards were higher than those of the traditional interpreters of the law. In the first two examples, Jesus goes to the heart of the matters of murder and adultery—anger and lust. It is not that the Old Testament does not condemn anger and lust, but that Jesus' definitive teaching connects the outward behavioral symptoms with the inner attitudinal causes. Jesus means to nip the buds of anger and lust in order to avoid the blooms of murder and adultery. On the matter of divorce, Jesus seems to stand with Shammai over Hillel on the interpretation of the "indecency" of Deuteronomy 24:1 (see note on 5:31-32). Only infidelity is a permissible reason for divorce. In all other cases, adultery results. Jesus' standard was much higher than was customary as can be seen from Matthew 19:9 and from the Mishnah passage cited in the notes.

◆   ## 5. Jesus' teaching about vows, revenge, and love (5:33-48)

³³"You have also heard that our ancestors were told, 'You must not break your vows; you must carry out the vows you make to the LORD.'* ³⁴But I say, do not make any vows! Do not say, 'By heaven!' because heaven is God's throne. ³⁵And do not say, 'By the earth!' because the earth is his footstool. And do not say, 'By Jerusalem!' for Jerusalem is the city of the great King. ³⁶Do not even say, 'By my head!' for you can't turn one hair white or black. ³⁷Just say a simple, 'Yes, I will,' or 'No, I won't.' Anything beyond this is from the evil one.

³⁸"You have heard the law that says the punishment must match the injury: 'An eye for an eye, and a tooth for a tooth.'* ³⁹But I say, do not resist an evil person! If someone slaps you on the right cheek, offer the other cheek also. ⁴⁰If you are sued in court and your shirt is taken from you, give your coat, too. ⁴¹If a soldier demands that you carry his gear for a mile,* carry it two miles. ⁴²Give to those who ask, and don't turn away from those who want to borrow.

⁴³"You have heard the law that says, 'Love your neighbor'* and hate your enemy. ⁴⁴But I say, love your enemies!* Pray for those who persecute you! ⁴⁵In that way, you will be acting as true children of your Father in heaven. For he gives his sunlight to both the evil and the good, and he sends rain on the just and the unjust alike. ⁴⁶If you love only those who love you, what reward is there for that? Even corrupt tax collectors do that much. ⁴⁷If you are kind only to your friends,* how are you different from anyone else? Even pagans do that. ⁴⁸But you are to be perfect, even as your Father in heaven is perfect."

5:33 Num 30:2. **5:38** Greek *the law that says: 'An eye for an eye and a tooth for a tooth.'* Exod 21:24; Lev 24:20; Deut 19:21. **5:41** Greek *milion* [4,854 feet or 1,478 meters]. **5:43** Lev 19:18. **5:44** Some manuscripts add *Bless those who curse you. Do good to those who hate you.* Compare Luke 6:27-28. **5:47** Greek *your brothers.*

NOTES

5:33-34a *do not make any vows!* Matthew 5:33-48 comprises the second set of three examples of Jesus' definitive interpretation of the OT. The matter of vows or oaths is addressed in 5:33-37, which begins in the familiar pattern of first alluding to the OT (5:33; cf. Lev 19:12; Num 30:3-16; Deut 23:21-23; Ps 50:14; see also Jas 5:12) and then giving the contrasting teaching of Jesus (5:34a). Jesus forbids four specific vows, because the one who takes them assumes prerogatives that belong solely to God (5:34b-36). One's word ought to be trustworthy apart from a vow (5:37). This section on vows has no synoptic parallels, although 23:16-22 takes up oaths from a negative perspective again.

Matthew 5:33 is not a direct quote of an OT passage but a summary of the gist of relevant passages, much like the statement about murderers being liable to judgment in 5:21. In the OT one was permitted to take a vow or an oath as long as irreverence and falsehood were not involved. Vows were intended to ensure one's resolve to follow through on an obligation. But ironically, vows resulted in there being two classes of utterances, the one with the vow committing the speaker to veracity, and the one without the vow implying no such commitment. By Jesus' time, certain Pharisees had perverted the practice of vows by subtle casuistic distinctions (cf. 23:16-22). Jesus' response is to forbid what the OT permits, but truth is the goal of both the OT permission and Jesus' prohibition. So while Jesus may be said to have contradicted the letter of the law here, he did so in order to uphold its spirit, and he thereby upheld the commandment against false witness (Exod 20:7). Vows are superfluous if truth invariably characterizes one's speech (Eccl 5:4-5). Josephus (*War* 2.135) indicates that the Essenes, the group likely behind the Dead Sea Scrolls, were reluctant to make vows. Jesus did not take a vow when he was charged to do so by the high priest (26:63).

5:34b-36 *Do not say.* Here Jesus develops the general prohibition of oaths in 5:34a by forbidding four specific oaths and explaining why each is forbidden. The first two prohibited oaths call respectively upon heaven and earth, and both are inappropriate because heaven and earth are under the control of God, not humans (cf. Isa 66:1) The third oath calls upon Jerusalem, which is also inappropriate because it is the city of the great King (cf. Ps 48:2), the place where the Creator chooses to make his presence visible on earth. The fourth oath, swearing by one's head, is similarly out of place because it ascribes to a human power that belongs only to God. According to Deut 6:13; 10:20, vows were to be taken in the name of God, but by Jesus' time, pious Jews would not utter that name. This implies that heaven, earth, and Jerusalem were metonymies, circumlocutions associated with God. Such vows are mentioned in the Mishnah (e.g., *m. Shevu'ot* 4:13; *m. Nedarim* 1:3; *m. Sanhedrin* 3:2).

5:37 *"Yes, I will" . . . "No, I won't."* Lit., "yes, yes" and "no, no." A positive command concludes the section previously characterized by negatives: Jesus teaches that one's word should be reliable at all times, rendering oaths unnecessary. If one's heart is right with God, uprightness will characterize one's speech because one's speech will transparently represent what is in one's heart. There will be no such thing as perjury or false witness. Taking oaths tends to be a concession to potential prevarication, and is therefore from the evil one (cf. 6:13; 13:19, 38), Satan, the originator of deception (John 8:12).

Again Jesus prohibits what the OT permits in the area of oaths. Here he comes the closest to actual contradiction of the OT because he views the traditional interpretation as thoroughly abusing the spirit of the law. According to Deut 23:21-23 one may or may not vow, but one must perform what one vows. If Paul was familiar with this word from Jesus, it did not keep him from taking a vow (Acts 18:18; cf. 21:23-26.)

5:38-39a *An eye for an eye, and a tooth for a tooth.* The fifth example (5:38-42; cf. Isa 50:4-9; Luke 6:29-30) refers to Exod 21:24; Lev 24:20; and Deut 19:21. Jesus qualifies the application of the OT principle of retribution in kind (*lex talionis*). Matthew 5:38 contains the allusion to the "eye for an eye, tooth for a tooth" legislation and 5:39a contrasts Jesus' own teaching. The NLT's words "the punishment must match the injury" have no basis in the Gr. text, although they are a correct description of the relevant legal principle. Jesus' own contrasting teaching in 5:39 is that disciples should forsake the idea of retribution altogether by not resisting an evil person. The OT insistence on punishment matching the crime might seem harsh at first glance, but as it mandates matching punishment, it thereby forbids excessive punishment. Granted, an eye must be taken for an eye, but two eyes or a life may not be taken for an eye. The OT concern for justice leads to this prohibition of overly severe retribution. Personal revenge is contrary to Lev 19:18, but Jesus goes further and teaches that godly kindness should transcend retaliation in personal disputes. As in the case of divorce (5:31-32; 19:3-12), Jesus' teaching transcends an OT regulation that arose as a concession to the hardness of the human heart. Yet Jesus' teaching is not altogether unanticipated in the OT (cf. Deut 32:35-36; Prov 20:22; 25:21-22; Isa 50:6; Lam 3:30).

This teaching would obviously be at odds with the cause of the Jewish zealots who favored armed rebellion against Rome, but it is primarily a personal ethic that does not contradict the legitimate role of the state in protecting its citizens from lawlessness and aggression.

5:39b-42 These verses list four concrete situations in which Jesus' general teaching on non-retaliation applies (cf. Luke 6:29; *Didache* 1:4-5). The first (5:39b) seems to picture a personal dispute that leads to an insulting back-hand slap by a right-handed person to the right cheek of another person (cf. Ps 3:7; Isa 50:6; Lam 3:30; Matt 26:67; Acts 23:2-3; *m. Bava Qamma* 8:6). The second (5:40) speaks of a legal dispute in which one is ordered to forfeit one's shirt to supply collateral for a debt or satisfy a claim for damages. The third situation (5:41) envisions an occupying Roman soldier conscripting a Jewish person to carry his equipment (cf. 27:32). In each situation Jesus commands his disciples to go beyond the expected response. Instead of angrily slapping the aggressor back, the disciple is to allow himself to be slapped again on the other cheek. Instead of standing up for his rights with further litigation, the disciple is to give up his coat (cf. the reverse in Luke 6:29), which, according to the OT, may not be legally required (Exod 22:25-27; Deut 24:12-13), as well as his shirt. Instead of resisting occupying military forces, the disciple is to help them by carrying their equipment two miles instead of one. The point of the first three situations is that the disciple is not to be a part of furthering the usual chain of evil action and reaction in this fallen world (Blomberg 1992:113).

The fourth example (5:42) takes the teaching of Jesus one step further. Not only is a disciple to be non-retaliatory when injured, he or she is to be generous to those who are in need (cf. Luke 6:34-35). Not only must disciples not further evil by retaliation, they must further good in the world by benevolence. This teaching is in keeping with OT law (cf. esp. Deut 15:7-11; also Lev 25:35-55). At his own arrest and trials Jesus exemplified the essence of what is taught here (26:67; 27:11-13, 35; cf. Mark 14:65; John 18:22-23; 19:3; 1 Pet 2:23). But these four examples should not be taken in a pedantic fashion that would limit their intended application. One may never need to physically turn the other cheek, give up one's coat, or go an extra mile, but one must be willing to unselfishly suffer personal loss with faith that the heavenly Father will meet one's needs and deal with the injustice in his own time. Paul was evidently familiar with this tradition (Rom 12:14-21, which cites Deut 32:35-36 and Prov 25:21-22; 1 Cor 6:7-8; 1 Thess 5:15).

5:43-44 But I say, love your enemies! The sixth and final example of Jesus' transcendent teaching refers to Lev 19:18. Jesus states that one should love and pray for even one's enemies and persecutors (cf. Luke 6:27-28). Such behavior will emulate the actions of the heavenly Father (5:45) and go beyond the typical human practice (5:46-47). A concluding word commands that the disciple compare his or her behavior not to cultural norms but Kingdom norms—he or she is to be perfect, like the heavenly Father is perfect (5:48). Evidently, the traditional view of the OT mistakenly restricted the scope of the word "neighbor" in order to legitimize hatred of enemies. Jesus rejected this approach and insisted that disciples of the Kingdom emulate the King.

As a careful reading shows, Lev 19:18 commands love for neighbors, not hatred for enemies. Perhaps hating enemies was taken as a logical corollary of loving neighbors, or as a legitimate conclusion from such texts as Deut 7:2; 23:3-6; Ps 26:4-5; 137:7-9; 139:19-22 (cf. *Mekilta Exodus* 21:35; *Sifra* on Lev 19:18; 1QS 1:10-11; Josephus *War* 2.139). In Lev 19:18, one's neighbor is evidently a fellow-Jew, and perhaps the traditional teaching in Jesus' day read the text restrictively as applying only to Jews. But certain OT texts also speak of humane treatment for non-Israelites (esp. Lev 19:33-34; Deut 10:18-19; cf. Exod 22:21-22; 23:9; Deut 1:16; 27:19; Ps 146:9; Jer 7:5-6; 22:3; Ezek 22:7, 29; 47:22-23; Zech 7:9-10; Mal 3:5). And some of these texts include non-Israelites under the general heading of "neighbor" (Jer 7:5-6; Zech 7:9-10). As the parable of the good Samaritan shows (Luke 10:25-37), Jesus would not have accepted a restrictive reading of the word "neighbor."

Pray for those who persecute you! Praying for one's persecutors is a striking demonstration of one's love for them (cf. Luke 23:34; Acts 7:59-60). This, too, is anticipated in the OT (Gen 20:17-18; Exod 23:4-5; Num 12:13; 21:7; 1 Sam 24:17-19; Job 31:29; Ps 7:3-5; Prov 24:17-18; 25:21-22; Jer 29:7; Jonah 4:10-11).

5:45-47 These verses develop the idea of loving one's enemies by first comparing such love to God's love for people (5:45) and then by asking two rhetorical questions that call on disciples to practice a higher righteousness than tax collectors and pagans do (5:46-47).

corrupt tax collectors. "Corrupt" refers to the practices of "tax farmers," who paid the Romans for the right to collect taxes and then collected more than was due, keeping the overage for themselves. When Jews sometimes became "tax farmers," they were regarded as thieves and traitors, which may explain Jesus' pairing of tax collectors (5:46) with pagans (5:47; cf. 18:17). For Jesus' association with tax collectors, see 9:9-11; 11:19; 21:31-32; Luke 18:9-14; 19:1-10.

It is clear that action, not emotion, is called for here, since disciples are not only to pray for enemies (5:44) but also to do them good, as God does (5:45; cf. Ps 145:9; Luke 6:35; Acts 14:17), and to greet them respectfully (5:47). This last action may imply a wish for their welfare (Gen 43:27; Exod 18:7 LXX).

Once again Jesus' words contradict a zealot mentality, since the "enemies" of Jewish disciples would certainly include the Romans. Matthew 5:9 has already spoken of how the disciples' role as reconcilers in the world manifests their filial resemblance to the heavenly Father. Other NT texts stress how a Christian's love for people, especially enemies, marks him or her as a member of God's family (Eph 4:31-5:2; 1 Pet 1:14-25; 1 John 4:7-12). Loving one's enemies is imitating God.

5:48 *But you are to be perfect, even as your Father in heaven is perfect.* The NLT begins this verse with "but," highlighting the contrast between the practice of the pagans and that of the disciples. However, it would be more accurate to translate the Gr. conjunction *oun* [TG3767, ZG4036] as "therefore," and understand the verse as drawing a conclusion based on 5:45-47. Disciples are to model their lives after the universal benevolence of their heavenly Father, not after the mutual-admiration-society piety of the tax collectors and pagans. The language of this verse seems to be modeled on that of Lev 19:2, "You must be holy because I, the LORD your God, am holy." But the language and emphasis of Deut 18:13 on blamelessness is probably echoed here as well. To be "perfect" is to be complete, mature, grown up in one's likeness to God's benevolence (cf. 19:21 and the word *tamim* [TH8549, ZH9459] "blameless," in the OT, e.g., Gen 6:9; 17:1; Job 1:1, 8; 2:3). What is involved in becoming perfect is uprightness and blamelessness in consistently obeying God's laws. The idea of perfection as sinlessness, held by relatively few Christians, would not be acceptable to the one who taught his disciples to pray for forgiveness (6:12; cf. 1 John 1:8). The surpassing righteousness of which Jesus speaks is summarized as mirroring the Father's characteristic of universal benevolence, not sinlessness.

Matthew 5:48 forms the conclusion of the sixth and final example of Jesus' teaching and of 5:21-48 as a whole. All six of the areas addressed by Jesus call for perfection or modeling of the Father's benevolence. One can do no better than to imitate the Father. This is the surpassing righteousness of which Jesus spoke in 5:20.

COMMENTARY

In this section of Matthew 5, the second set of three examples (5:33-48), much like the first set (5:21-32), follows a clear pattern:

1. Traditional teaching (5:33, 38, 43)
2. Jesus' contrasting teaching (5:34a, 39a, 44)
3. Concrete application or further explanation (5:34b-37, 39b-42, 45-47)

In the application sections (#3 above), there is frequent use of parallel statements and repeated sentence structure. Overall, the second set of contrasting teachings is a bit longer than the first set, mainly due to the lack of any concrete applications in the third example (5:31-32). The final verse, 5:48, serves just as much as the conclusion to the whole (5:21-48) as it does to the sixth contrasting teaching (5:43-47).

The Contrast: Jesus versus Moses or Jesus versus the Pharisees? It must be asked whether, in 5:21-48, Matthew intends to set Jesus against Moses or against the ostensible contemporary experts on Moses, the Pharisees. Is Jesus presented as contesting Moses or as officially speaking for Moses (cf. 23:2ff)? The question is perhaps impossible to answer because the issue is too complex to be put in such reductionistic terms. It seems that in some instances, Jesus dealt with contemporary paraphrases of the implications of the law and in others more directly with the law itself. In the former category would be contrasts one, three, four, and six (5:21, 31, 33, 43), in which the Old Testament text is cited with additional material appended (5:21, 43) or in a modified manner (5:31), or in which a summary of several texts is given (5:33). In the latter category, contrasts two and five, the Old Testament is quoted directly without any additions (5:27, 38). Thus, in most of the contrasts, there is evidence that contemporary construals of Moses were involved in the contrast. This is natural since by the time of Christ the ancient text of Moses had been subject to hundreds of years of interpretation and developing oral tradition.

Since Matthew presents Jesus as coming to accomplish the purpose of the law and the prophets and not to abolish them (5:17), one would expect Jesus' teaching to transcend the Old Testament in a manner that does not violate its ethical authority. Because Jesus warned his disciples that their righteousness must exceed that of the Jewish teachers (5:20), one would also expect his teaching to expose the errors of those teachers. In other texts (e.g., 9:10-13; 15:1-9; 19:1-9), Jesus explicitly re-bukes the Jewish religious leaders for their mistaken views of the law and prophets, so it is not surprising to find a similar confrontation occurring implicitly here. This model of exposition plus exposure is most clear in examples three and six (5:31, 43), but it is present to some extent in each contrast. For example, in 5:33-37, Jesus first alludes to Old Testament texts on vows as revealed to the ancestors and then proceeds to refute accepted abuses of vows. As he illumines the ultimate goal of Moses and the prophets, Jesus shows that the religious leaders are in the dark re-garding these issues.

The Hermeneutic of Jesus.   The relationship of Jesus to the Old Testament is a theological watershed. Jesus' general statement about accomplishing the Old Testa-ment's purpose, not abolishing it, and the six contrasting teachings he presents have been variously understood. Some have held that this means that Jesus' life and teaching established or confirmed the law. But this understates the legitimate dis-continuity between Jesus and the Old Testament. Others have stressed that Jesus' own obedience to the law completed its role in redemptive history. This idea is valid in its understanding of Jesus' obedience to the law but dubious in its estima-tion of the implications of that obedience. Others have argued that Jesus, as a new Moses, brought a new law that superseded the Old Testament, but this errs on the side of excessive discontinuity. Certain systematic theologians have thought that Jesus stressed the "moral law," not the law's civil or ceremonial aspects. But what-ever the relation of Jesus to the law, it is a relation to the whole law—one cannot partition the law into anachronistic categories that suit only its modern readers. Others conclude that Jesus revealed or intensified the true inner meaning of the law. This has some merit, but at best it is only a partial answer.

It is most likely that we should think Jesus is the end or goal of the law, and thus he is its ultimate, definitive interpreter. He alone is the authoritative eschatological teacher of the law and the prophets. The life and teaching of Jesus fulfill the law just as New Testament events fulfill Old Testament predictions and patterns. On the one hand, Jesus did not contradict the law, but on the other hand he did not preserve it unchanged. He revealed the ultimate meaning of the law of God for those whose righteousness must exceed that of the scribes and the Pharisees (5:20; cf. 22:34-40; 23:23-24). He brought the law to its intended goal by:

1. Teaching that the prohibition of murder implicitly prohibits the anger and abusive speech which lead to murder. While the Old Testament does not con-done anger, Jesus' transcendent teaching links it to a capital crime. Anger and angry words are tantamount to murder (5:21-26).
2. Teaching that the prohibition of adultery implicitly prohibits the lust that leads to adultery. While the Old Testament does not condone lust, Jesus' direct linkage of lust to adultery is a more stringent standard of sexual ethics, which interprets the seventh commandment by the tenth commandment (Exod 20:17). Lust is tantamount to adultery (5:27-30).

3. Teaching that marriage is a sacred union, inviolable except when infidelity occurs. While the Old Testament does not condone divorce (Mal 2:14-16), there is reason to believe that it was condoned by many of Jesus' contemporaries. But he taught that divorce and remarriage (except in the case of infidelity) are tantamount to adultery (5:31-32). Divorce is merely a temporal concession to human sinfulness, but permanent marriage is the original model for humans (19:8).

4. Teaching that the use of vows would be unnecessary if disciples consistently took to heart the biblical admonitions to tell the truth. While the Old Testament does not condone the misuse of vows, Jesus criticized their use. He forbade (although the prohibition may not be absolute; cf. Blomberg 1992:112; Davies and Allison 1988:536; Hagner 1993:129) what the letter of the Old Testament permits, but he did so to uphold the spirit of the Old Testament against the bearing of false witness. For Jesus, casuistry in the taking of vows is tantamount to bearing false witness (5:33-37; cf. 23:16-22).

5. Teaching that the law on retaliation was designed primarily to limit conflict, and only secondarily to endorse it. The Old Testament does not condone unjust punishment for crimes and damages, but Jesus teaches that instead of responding to wrongdoing in kind, his disciples should respond with grace. Insistence on taking one's own vengeance is tantamount to denying that God will avenge his people (5:38-42).

6. Teaching that all humans, not only one's friends, are to be loved. While the Old Testament does not condone hatred of one's enemies, Jesus makes love of enemies the preeminent evidence of one's filial relationship to the heavenly Father. Hating one's enemies is tantamount to paganism (5:43-48).

Contemporary Application.   It has been argued here that Matthew 5:21-48 is in continuity with the law and the prophets to an extent greater than is commonly held. Be that as it may, there is no doubt that there is much in Matthew 5:21-48 that is antithetical to the individualism of American culture. Jesus' ethic contradicts the anger and aggression that seek to dominate other people. However, his words against the misuse of women by adultery and divorce sound a note that resonates with contemporary sensibilities. The stress on integrity in speech is much needed in the Christian community, where it is not uncommon for prominent believers to be caught in lies. The words against retaliation are important but difficult to apply in a society where Christians have religious liberty. Finally, there is no doubt that evangelicals have a lot to learn about loving their enemies.

The six examples that contrast Jesus' transcendent teaching of the Old Testament with the traditional understandings of it amount to pointers in the direction of the righteousness that is greater than that of the religious leaders (5:20). Now Jesus will turn from relationships with people to religious activities (6:1-18) and attitudes toward material things (6:19-34). The message of the Kingdom dynamically transforms the disciple's conduct in this area also.

◆   6. Religious practices (6:1-18)

"Watch out! Don't do your good deeds publicly, to be admired by others, for you will lose the reward from your Father in heaven. ²When you give to someone in need, don't do as the hypocrites do—blowing trumpets in the synagogues and streets to call attention to their acts of charity! I tell you the truth, they have received all the reward they will ever get. ³But when you give to someone in need, don't let your left hand know what your right hand is doing. ⁴Give your gifts in private, and your Father, who sees everything, will reward you.

⁵"When you pray, don't be like the hypocrites who love to pray publicly on street corners and in the synagogues where everyone can see them. I tell you the truth, that is all the reward they will ever get. ⁶But when you pray, go away by yourself, shut the door behind you, and pray to your Father in private. Then your Father, who sees everything, will reward you.

⁷"When you pray, don't babble on and on as people of other religions do. They think their prayers are answered merely by repeating their words again and again. ⁸Don't be like them, for your Father knows exactly what you need even before you ask him! ⁹Pray like this:

Our Father in heaven,
    may your name be kept holy.
¹⁰May your Kingdom come soon.
May your will be done on earth,
    as it is in heaven.
¹¹Give us today the food we need,*
¹²and forgive us our sins,
    as we have forgiven those who sin
    against us.
¹³And don't let us yield to temptation,*
    but rescue us from the evil one.*

¹⁴"If you forgive those who sin against you, your heavenly Father will forgive you. ¹⁵But if you refuse to forgive others, your Father will not forgive your sins.

¹⁶"And when you fast, don't make it obvious, as the hypocrites do, for they try to look miserable and disheveled so people will admire them for their fasting. I tell you the truth, that is the only reward they will ever get. ¹⁷But when you fast, comb your hair and wash your face. ¹⁸Then no one will notice that you are fasting, except your Father, who knows what you do in private. And your Father, who sees everything, will reward you."

6:11 Or Give us today our food for the day; or Give us today our food for tomorrow.   6:13a Or And keep us from being tested.   6:13b Or from evil. Some manuscripts add For yours is the kingdom and the power and the glory forever. Amen.

NOTES

6:1 *Don't do your good deeds publicly.* This verse enunciates the general principle that is unpacked in the three specific areas treated by Jesus in this section: giving (6:2-4), praying (6:5-15), and fasting (6:16-18). This principle relates to the disciple's intention in prayer—disciples must watch out for a perverse tendency to do good deeds in order to receive human admiration. When this occurs, the disciple forfeits divine reward (cf. 10:41-42; 19:27-29). The NLT's "good deeds" is lit. "righteousness," which refers to practical or functional godliness—that is, obedience to God's laws. Jesus had just taught that his standard of righteousness was higher than that of the religious leaders (5:20; cf. 1:19; 3:15; 5:6, 10; 6:33; 25:37-39). All in all, this verse constitutes a sort of "flip side" to 5:16. There disciples are enjoined to do good deeds to the Father's glory; here they are enjoined not to do them for their own glory.

6:2 The first concrete application of the principle enunciated in 6:1 is giving to the needy. See the commentary below for discussion of the literary pattern that begins here and is followed in the sections on prayer (6:5-15) and fasting (6:16-18).

hypocrites. This word occurs here for the first time in Matthew (see also 6:5, 16; 7:5; 15:7; 22:18; 23:13-15, 27; 24:51.).

blowing trumpets in the synagogues. This may be metaphorical (like the modern expression "blowing your own horn") or a hyperbolic reference to drawing attention to oneself. Or it might refer to a trumpet-shaped collection box that resounded when coins were thrown into it.

to call attention to their acts of charity! This refers to the sinful motive of seeking the praise and glory of humans rather than the reward of the heavenly Father. Instead of giving in a flashy public manner to attain self-aggrandizement, disciples are to give secretly so that the Father, who is aware of secret actions, will reward them (cf. 16:27).

6:3 *don't let your left hand know what your right hand is doing.* The emphasis on secrecy is underlined by this hyperbole. Disciples are seek eternal reward from God rather than present human fleeting praise.

6:5-6 *When you pray, don't be like the hypocrites . . . [but] pray to your Father in private.* The section on prayer (6:5-15) is more extensive than the sections on giving and fasting. It consists of two warnings on how not to pray, each balanced by positive teaching (6:5-6; 6:7-8), followed by the model prayer (6:9-13). Jesus first forbids his disciples to pray hypocritically on the street or in the synagogue (cf. 23:5-7), commanding them instead to pray privately in an inner room (6:5-6). There is an allusion here to Isa 26:20, which in its original context speaks of Israel's hiding from temporary judgment in anticipation of blessing. Jesus forbids hypocrisy here, not sincere prayer in public or in religious services. This critique addresses hypocritical Jewish practice, and may have in mind hypocrisy in the praying of the *'Amidah* or Eighteen Benedictions (to be uttered three times a day), the recitation of the *Shema* (to be done twice daily), and various other blessings.

6:7-8 *don't babble on and on as people of other religions do.* In 6:7-8 Jesus critiques the prayers of "people of other religions" (lit. "Gentiles" or "pagans"). These prayers of the Gentiles evidently involved long-winded babbling in order to get the attention of a god, or the utterance of repeated magical incantations. But Jesus reminded his disciples that their Father already knows what they need before they ask (cf. 6:32).

6:9-10 As form-critical scholars note, the model prayer of 6:9-13 (cf. a shorter version in Luke 11:1-4) seems to interrupt the repeated pattern of 6:2-4, 6:5-8, and 6:16-18. But this does not necessarily bring the prayer's authenticity or the literary unity of 6:1-18 into doubt. The model prayer gives a positive example that nicely balances the preceding critique of hypocritical prayer, and it exemplifies the Kingdom values Jesus has inculcated since the beatitudes. If one takes the two requests of 6:13 as two aspects of one petition, the model prayer is composed of six requests. Assuming this, the six seem to be arranged in two sets of three.

The first set is directed toward the glory and praise of God (6:9-10), the second toward the daily needs of the disciples (6:11-13). The similarity of this prayer to the Kaddish, a synagogue prayer, is noted by many (e.g., Davies and Allison, 1988:595-597; Hagner 1993:147). It also appears in *Didache* 8, where it is to be said three times a day. More on the structure, theology, and practical implications of the prayer will be found in the commentary below.

Pray like this. It is important to note (with respect to *Didache* 8 and much later Christian tradition) that Jesus did not enjoin his disciples to pray this prayer by rote. He says, "Pray *like* this," not "pray this." The prayer puts the interests of the Father and his Kingdom ahead of the daily needs of the disciple. This is the kind of prayer one should pray, one in which doxology (exemplified by the first three "your" requests) precedes and permeates requests for human needs (exemplified by the last three "us" requests).

Our Father in heaven. Prayer is to be addressed to "our Father in heaven" (cf. 3:17; 5:9, 16, 45, 48; 6:1, 4, 6, 8, 14-15, 18, 26; 7:11, 21). The family imagery speaks of the intimacy of the disciples' relationship to God, but the qualifier "in heaven" reminds one that God is not a chum or a pal. Rather, one is to remember that the awesome God of heaven has come near in the person of his beloved Son and counts disciples of the Kingdom as his dear family (cf. Isa 57:15). The view of Jeremias (1967:29, 57), that Jesus' injunction to address God as Father (Aramaic, *abba*) is unique, is overstated if not mistaken. God was understood as Father by the Jews in Jesus' day (Isa 63:16; 64:8; Tob 13:4; *m. Berachot* 5:1; *Sota* 9:15; *Yoma* 8:9). Yet Jesus' model prayer is remarkably simple and intimate in the way it addresses God (cf. Rom. 8:15-16; Gal. 4:6-7).

may your name be kept holy. May your kingdom come soon. May your will be done on earth, as it is in heaven. The three "your" requests should be seen as three ways of asking for essentially the same thing. That God's name (his character or reputation) be "kept holy" or revered, that his Kingdom would come, and that his will would be done are the requests of one who is famished for righteousness on earth (5:6). The final phrase of 6:10, "on earth as it is in heaven," describes all three requests, not just the third one. Disciples long for the realities of heaven to be realized on earth. All three requests imply that certain aspects of the Kingdom are yet future, involving the progressive actualization of God's character, reign, and will on earth, that is, universally. The Father is the Lord of heaven and earth (11:25), and after the resurrection he gave Jesus universal authority in heaven and on earth (28:18). In the meantime, as disciples are involved in the gradual extension of the Kingdom by their words and deeds, their utmost desire is for the ultimate realization of God's reign on earth.

6:11-13a Three petitions for the needs of the disciple now balance the three previous theocentric petitions. Whatever else people may want, the deepest human needs are found in these requests: daily sustenance (6:11), forgiveness (6:12), and avoidance of sin (6:13).

Give us today the food we need. The word translated "today" is the obscure Gr. word *epiousios* [TG1967, ZG2157], whose etymology is translated in various ways, including "daily," "necessary," and "for tomorrow" (sometimes taken as a reference to the eschatological "tomorrow" that follows this age, which is "today")—see NLT mg. The point seems to be that the disciple prays for immediate day-to-day necessities rather than for long-term luxuries.

forgive us our sins. Prayer for ongoing forgiveness (6:12) assumes that the disciple has made the decisive turn from sin to God demanded by the message of the Kingdom (3:2; 4:17). This request shows that authentic disciples still have their faults, which need to be dealt with on a daily basis.

don't let us yield to temptation, but rescue us from the evil one. The third request (6:13) is stated in two contrasting ways, negatively ("don't let us yield to temptation") and positively ("but rescue us from the evil one"). Since the Spirit led Jesus into a time of testing (4:1), this petition should be understood not so much as one for God not to lead the disciple into temptation, but for the disciple to be delivered from Satan so as not to yield to temptation.

6:13b The doxology printed in the NLT mg ("For yours is the kingdom and the power and the glory forever. Amen.") is not found in the most ancient manuscripts (‌א B D Z 0170) and is very likely not a part of the original version of this Gospel. It seems to have been added for liturgical purposes and is based on 1 Chr 29:11-13 (for a further explanation, see Comfort 2007:[Matt 6:13]).

6:14-15 *If you forgive those who sin against you.* Just as the phrase "on earth as it is in heaven" (6:10) relates to all three of the previous petitions, so also here the words of

6:14-15 on the necessity of a forgiving spirit relate not just to 6:12, the fifth petition, but to all three requests for human needs. The disciple will not ask for his or her needs to be met with an unforgiving spirit, but will realize that his experience of God's forgiveness enables him to forgive others (cf. 5:23-24, 38-48; 18:21-35).

your Father will not forgive your sins. The relationship of God's forgiving humans to humans' forgiving others is much debated. This is not "legal ground," where our act of forgiving others merits God's act of forgiving us, as some classic dispensationalists implied. Rather the point is that God's initiative in graciously forgiving one should motivate one to forgive others. Forgiving others demonstrates that one has been forgiven by God. Forgiven, we are freed to forgive (cf. 9:2, 5, 6; 12:31-32; 18:32; Eph 4:31-5:2; Col 3:13).

6:16-18 *when you fast, don't make it obvious.* The section on fasting addresses this religious act with the same pattern found in the previous teaching on giving and praying.

comb your hair and wash your face. One should not neglect one's appearance while fasting so as to draw attention to oneself. Rather, one should groom oneself as usual so that God alone notices and rewards. Of the three activities treated in 6:1-18, fasting is certainly the least important to most Christians. It is not commanded in any of the NT Epistles. Fasting was a prescribed part of various OT community activities involving repentance (Joel 1:14); in addition, pious Jews fasted voluntarily (1 Sam 7:5-6; Neh 1:4; Dan 9:3; Jonah 3:5; Luke 2:37; 18:12). Here, the voluntary fasting is primarily in view. Jesus himself fasted (4:2; cf. Moses and Elijah, Exod 34:28; 1 Kgs 19:8) and spoke metaphorically of the appropriateness of fasting for his disciples after his departure from earth (9:14-15). The Pharisees fasted (9:14; cf. Luke 18:12), and Jesus did not criticize them for the practice. In Acts, the disciples fasted before the important decision of selecting church leaders (13:2-3; 14:23). Isaiah's critique of fasting that was not accompanied by just behavior (Isa 58:1-9; cf. Zech 7:4-14) is not unlike Jesus' condemnation of hypocritical fasting here.

COMMENTARY

Matthew 6:1-18 presents the teaching of Jesus on three religious duties that would be basic for Matthew's Christian Jewish community. After enunciating the general principle (6:1), Jesus addresses the practice of alms (6:2-4), prayer (6:5-15), and fasting (6:16-18). This material is closely related thematically and literarily to the preceding section, 5:21-48. Thematically, 6:1-18 presents another area of life in which Jesus, the ultimate teacher of the law and prophets, explains the greater righteousness (5:20) by which disciples emulate the righteous character of the Father (5:48). Literarily, 6:1-18 resembles the structure of 5:21-48 by its logical movement from a general principle of righteousness (6:1; cf. 5:20) to specific examples (three examples in 6:2-18; cf. six examples in 5:21-48). Another literary similarity is the use of a repeated phrase that clearly demarcates the structure of the material (6:2, 5, 16; cf. 5:21, 27, 31, 33, 38, 43). Throughout the text, contrasting statements are used to show the difference between the greater righteousness of Jesus' Kingdom and the traditional teaching of the religious leaders.

The general principle enunciated by 6:1 connects righteousness with the disciples' intention. The disciples must watch out for religious acts done in order to impress people, since such acts will not be rewarded by the heavenly Father. Each time Jesus applies this to a specific practice, a similar pattern occurs:

	Hypocritical Religion Prohibited	Genuine Religion Commanded
1. The occasion	"when you . . . give . . . pray . . . pray . . . fast" (6:2, 5, 7, 16)	"but when you . . . give . . . pray . . . pray . . . fast" (6:3, 6, 9, 17)
2. The activity	ostentatious action (6:2, 5, 7, 16)	secret action (6:3, 6, 9-13, 17)
3. The motivation	to be admired by others (6:1, 2, 5, 16)	to be seen only by the Father (6:4, 6, 18)
4. The solemn affirmation	they have received all the reward they will ever get (6:2, 5, 16)	"your Father, who sees everything, will reward you" (6:4, 6, 18)

Matthew 6:5-15, Jesus' teaching on prayer, is the centerpiece of 6:1-18. It contains more detailed teaching than the sections on alms and fasting. In 6:5-8 Jesus contrasts publicity and privacy (5-6), and verbosity and simplicity (7-8) in prayer. The Pharisees sought publicity, and the pagans were known for verbosity, but the disciples were to pray privately and simply. These two contrasts lead naturally into the model prayer, which balances three petitions for the Father's glory (6:9-10) with three petitions for the disciple's needs (6:11-13). The phrase "on earth as it is in heaven" (6:10) characterizes the first set of three petitions, and the attitude of forgiveness (6:14-15) characterizes the second set of three petitions.

Religious Performance and Its Proper Audience. The disciple of Jesus strives to be perfect as the heavenly Father is perfect (5:48). This means that holiness comes from the inside out. The disciple's *character* is to be modeled on the Father's character, and the disciple's *performance* is to be done for the Father's approval. This certainly cuts against the grain of Western culture, which is often characterized by exhibitionism and ostentation. The world's "if you've got it, flaunt it" principle has infiltrated the modern church as surely as it had the synagogues of Jesus' day. But Jesus would have his disciples not only do the right thing, he would also have them do it the right way.

When it comes to giving, trumpets should not be blown, but the names of those who give the most are often publicized in modern churches. Surely this violates the central principle of this passage and forgets the lesson of the widow's mite (Mark 12:41-44). In the matter of praying, eloquence and length are confused with effectiveness. This makes it seem that God is ignorant of the disciples' needs and reluctant to meet them. As for fasting, the tendency is to ignore it altogether, but similar religious endeavors we think are "above and beyond the call of duty" are often given much publicity. In all three areas mentioned in Matthew 6:1-18, we are reminded that to gain the fleeting applause of today's crowd is to forfeit the approval of our heavenly Father tomorrow and forever. We must learn the lesson that disciples are content to be noticed by the Father, realizing that the crowd's approval does not matter in light of eternity. Giving to the needy in order to receive publicity is not giving at all—it is paying for human approval, and it forfeits divine approval (Plummer 1915:91).

The Model Prayer. The "Lord's Prayer" is in fact the model prayer for his disciples. It provides for them not a mantra to be mindlessly and superstitiously repeated but an example of godly Kingdom priorities in prayer. It is helpful to think of 6:9-10 as indicating the *person* to whom prayer is addressed (6:9b) and the *priorities* by which prayers are formed (6:9c-10). Concerning the *person* to whom prayer is addressed, he is characterized as "Father." One's relationship to one's human father inevitably colors one's view of the heavenly Father. In this day of awareness of dysfunctional families, it can be helpful to acknowledge that one's relationship to one's human father may help or hinder one's perception of God as heavenly Father.

God is "our Father in heaven" because he has come near to his children by his grace. Yet he is at the same time "our Father in heaven" because he remains distant from his children due to his glory. The fact that he is "our" Father leads disciples to intimacy and community. He is not someone else's Father—he is *ours*. And he is not *my* Father in individualistic isolation from others who know him; he belongs to all disciples. The fact that he is in heaven leads his disciples to approach him with awe and reverence. God deserves the utmost respect as the one who perfectly blends goodness and greatness, grace and power, immanence and transcendence. When prayer is made, one's view of God must balance his goodness and his greatness to avoid a syrupy sentimentality on the one hand and an austere apathy on the other.

Concerning the *priorities* by which prayers are formed (6:9c-10), one must keep foremost in one's mind that one's motive should not be to receive goods and services from God but to render service to God. Prayer is not primarily to vindicate the disciple's causes, meet the disciple's needs, fulfill the disciple's desires, or solve the disciple's problems. Therefore, one must not rush into God's presence with one's spiritual grocery list and demand instant gratification. Rather, the disciple's priorities are to be the promotion of God's reputation, the advancement of his rule, and the performance of his will. These three petitions are essentially one, as each is characterized by a burning desire to see the Father honored on earth as he is already honored in heaven (cf. Rev 4-5). As believers become partners with God's purposes, they begin to realize these priorities, but they also increasingly long for the day when God's priorities will be fully realized on earth.

The Kingdom of God encroaches on Satan's domain whenever people come to faith in Jesus Christ. The Kingdom comes when Jesus' disciples grow in their relationships to God and neighbor. The Kingdom is not merely future, and the disciples' hope is not escapism—they do not look to leave the earth for an ethereal heavenly existence. Rather, they look for a concrete existence in which heaven comes to earth, and they seek heaven's interests on earth today.

It is helpful to think of Matthew 6:11-15 as concerning the *problems* about which disciples pray (6:11-13) and the *principle* that governs their prayers (6:14-15). They pray for problems relating to provision (6:11), pardon (6:12), and protection

(6:13). As they pray, they remind themselves that if God had not forgiven them, they would not be praying at all. And they respond to God by forgiving others (6:14-15).

When disciples pray for provisions, they pray for daily bread, which represents the necessities rather than the luxuries of life. In biblical times, workers were paid on a daily basis (20:8). When one prays for daily bread, one asks God for immediate necessities. In Matthew 6:25, disciples are told not to worry about such necessities, and in 6:34 they are told not to worry about tomorrow. Rather, they are to trust their Father implicitly for everything.

When disciples pray for pardon, they recognize that by God's grace they are now better than they were but not as good as they ought to be. Disciples are not yet perfect and must realize that their attitudes and activities fall short of Kingdom standards. As they admit spiritual poverty, and hunger and thirst for righteousness (5:3, 6), they pray for God to forgive their ethical lapses. Receiving his pardon is an unspeakable privilege, but it comes with a corresponding responsibility—extending pardon to others. A forgiven person is a forgiving person.

When disciples pray for protection from temptation to sin, they are praying for God to break the cycle that so often plagues them (cf. Josh 7:20-21; Jas 1:13-15). Disciples are tempted by the world, the flesh, and the devil. Temptation leads to sin, and sin leads to the necessity of praying for forgiveness. And the cycle goes on and on. That is why they pray for protection from temptation and deliverance from the evil one's strategies (cf. 4:1-11).

As disciples pray about their problems, their petitions are governed by a principle. Just as petitions for the Father's glory are based on the principle "on earth, as it is in heaven" (6:10), so their petitions for their own needs are based on the principle "as we have forgiven those who sin against us" (6:12, 14-15). Disciples may not presume to ask God to forgive them if they have not forgiven others. Reconciliation with God will not happen apart from reconciliation with neighbors (cf. 5:23-24). One has no right to pray for divine reconciliation if one has not practiced human reconciliation. It is not that disciples merit God's forgiveness by forgiving others, but that they demonstrate that God has forgiven them when they forgive others (cf. 18:21-35).

Conclusion. Disciples today must reflect on how their prayers compare to the Lord's model prayer. They must first consider whether they are truly exercised by the vision that God's will must be done on earth as it is in heaven. They also must be reconciled with neighbors, as they depend on reconciliation with God when they pray for their own needs. As prayer for personal needs is considered, anxiety over material things inevitably surfaces. Matthew 6:19-34 presents Jesus' teaching on this topic.

◆   7. Material possessions (6:19-34)

[19]"Don't store up treasures here on earth, where moths eat them and rust destroys them, and where thieves break in and steal. [20]Store your treasures in heaven, where moths and rust cannot destroy, and thieves do not break in and steal. [21]Wherever your treasure is, there the desires of your heart will also be.

²²"Your eye is a lamp that provides light for your body. When your eye is good, your whole body is filled with light. ²³But when your eye is bad, your whole body is filled with darkness. And if the light you think you have is actually darkness, how deep that darkness is!

²⁴"No one can serve two masters. For you will hate one and love the other; you will be devoted to one and despise the other. You cannot serve both God and money.

²⁵"That is why I tell you not to worry about everyday life—whether you have enough food and drink, or enough clothes to wear. Isn't life more than food, and your body more than clothing? ²⁶Look at the birds. They don't plant or harvest or store food in barns, for your heavenly Father feeds them. And aren't you far more valuable to him than they are? ²⁷Can all your worries add a single moment to your life?

²⁸"And why worry about your clothing? Look at the lilies of the field and how they grow. They don't work or make their clothing, ²⁹yet Solomon in all his glory was not dressed as beautifully as they are. ³⁰And if God cares so wonderfully for wildflowers that are here today and thrown into the fire tomorrow, he will certainly care for you. Why do you have so little faith?

³¹"So don't worry about these things, saying, 'What will we eat? What will we drink? What will we wear?' ³²These things dominate the thoughts of unbelievers, but your heavenly Father already knows all your needs. ³³Seek the Kingdom of God* above all else, and live righteously, and he will give you everything you need.

³⁴"So don't worry about tomorrow, for tomorrow will bring its own worries. Today's trouble is enough for today."

6:33 Some manuscripts do not include *of God.*

NOTES

6:19-21 *Don't store up treasures here on earth.* These verses (cf. Luke 12:33-34) contain a prohibition against the hoarding of earthly treasures (6:19), followed by a symmetrical command enjoining the accumulation of heavenly treasure (6:20), followed by an explanation that one's heart will inevitably be devoted to what one treasures (6:21).

where moths eat them and rust destroys them. Heavenly treasure (cf. 13:44) is not susceptible to decay from moths (cf. Isa 50:9; Jas 5:2-3) and "eating" (NLT, "rust"; *brōsis* [TG1035, ZG1111], cf. Isa 51:8 LXX) or to theft (cf. 24:43) like earthly treasure is. The "eating" spoken of here could be from rust, other insects, dry rot, or some other type of decay. Heavenly treasure alone can provide genuine security (Matt 19:21; cf. Luke 12:16-21; 1 Tim 6:18-19), and it should be the focus of one's heart.

Wherever your treasure is, there the desires of your heart will also be. Here the heart (cf. 5:8, 28) stands for the person's intellectual and volitional core, the source of one's deeds (cf. 15:17-20). Human finiteness alone, even without the exacerbating effects of sin, makes it very difficult to focus the heart solely on God and not on possessions (cf. 6:24). The heart is inevitably drawn to what one values most. If one's life is focused on the values of the Kingdom, as expressed succinctly in the beatitudes of 5:3-10, one is indeed laying up treasure in heaven.

6:22-23 *Your eye is a lamp that provides light for your body.* The metaphor of the eye found here (cf. Luke 11:34-36) is difficult to understand. This verse begins with a proverbial statement about the eye being the body's lamp, which is followed by two opposite scenarios that emanate from good and bad eyesight respectively.

When your eye is good, your whole body is filled with light. Good eyesight illumines one's whole life, while poor eyesight is a great hindrance. But Jesus is speaking metaphorically.

your eye is bad, your whole body is filled with darkness. There may be an allusion in 6:23 to the "evil eye," which in ancient eastern culture was viewed as a source of greed and avarice (Hagner 1993:158; cf. Matt 20:15; *m. Avot* 2:12, 15; 5:16, 22). Given what precedes (the heart is where the treasure is) and what follows (the dilemma of two masters), it seems that Jesus was saying that a proper view of possessions is basic to Kingdom values. An evil and covetous eye will hoard earthly possessions only to see them decay. A good and generous eye will store up treasures in heaven that will never decay.

light you think you have. It is a perversely ironic situation when one's eye, which should provide light (metaphorically, generosity), provides only darkness (metaphorically, avarice). This last comment is a call to self-examination (Davies and Allison 1988:640).

6:24 No one can serve two masters. Structurally, this verse is a perfect example of chiastic or introverted parallelism. The practice of slavery is the background for the statement (cf. Luke 16:13); a slave cannot successfully and wholeheartedly serve two masters, since slavery demands the total, undivided attention of the slave to the master. If there are two masters, their demands will be incompatible. Similarly, Jesus' disciples cannot divide their loyalties between the heavenly Kingdom and earthly treasures.

you will hate one and love the other. The use of the polar opposites "hate" and "love" reflects a Semitic idiom that should not be pressed unduly (cf. Luke 14:26). The point is that the slave will inevitably love and be devoted to one master more than the other one (cf. 10:37).

You cannot serve both God and money. This metaphor on the impossibility of divided loyalty is meant to show that a disciple cannot be the loyal slave of both God (resulting in heavenly treasure) and money (resulting in earthly treasure). God's Kingdom demands an exclusive, transcendent loyalty. One's devotion to it must be single-minded.

6:25-27 If a person serves God rather than money (6:24), he should not be anxious about the material things money can buy. These verses contain a general prohibition against worrying about "everyday life," followed by applications to two areas of day-to-day life: what one eats and what one wears (6:25). God's provision of food and clothing is then stressed in 6:26-27 and 6:28-30 respectively, before the general prohibition against worry is restated in 6:31 and again in 6:34 (cf. Luke 12:22-31).

not to worry about everyday life. The first occurrence of the triple prohibition sets the agenda for the entire paragraph of 6:25-34—the disciple must not be anxious over "everyday life." This general term stands for the material goods that support life: food, drink, and clothing. Food and drink appear separately in 6:25a and 6:31, but in 6:25b-26 food alone is mentioned.

Isn't life more than food, and your body more than clothing? The prohibition against worrying is underlined by three rhetorical questions, the first (6:25d) on whether life is more than food and clothing. The implication is that the God who gives life itself can easily supply the means to sustain life (cf. 4:4).

aren't you far more valuable to him? The second question (6:26) is based on God's providential care for birds (cf. 8:20; 13:32), who do not work to grow their food, let alone worry about it. The argument is from the lesser to the greater, a common pattern in rabbinic texts, where it is called *qal vahomer* (light and heavy). Evidently reasoning from the fact that humans are created in the image of God, Jesus asked whether humans are not of more value than birds (cf. 10:31; 12:12).

Can all your worries add a single moment to your life? The third question (6:27) is asked bluntly without an accompanying illustration. It alludes to the impotence of worry to lengthen one's life. This question's power lies in its absurdity—of course worry cannot add "a single moment" to one's life. In fact, worrying may actually shorten a person's life. The

Gr. wording here seems to speak of adding a cubit (*pēchus*— approximately 18 inches; cf. Luke 12:25; John 21:8; Rev 21:17) to one's height (*hēlikia*; cf. Luke 12:25; Eph 4:13), but this does not make the best sense in the context. Since *hēlikia* can arguably refer to length of life, and *pēchus* can be used metaphorically to describe a short period or span of time (Sir 30:24; *Psalms of Solomon* 5:6; cf. Ps 39:5), the NLT and many modern translations render the idea accordingly (cf. BDAG 435-436; 812).

6:28-30 *why worry about your clothing?* These verses turn from worry about sustenance back to worry about clothing (cf. 6:25).

Look at the lilies of the field. The lesser to greater argument is very similar to that of 6:26. The illustration is drawn from God's providential care for lilies (though the word may refer to flowers in general), which without a moment of work are more beautiful than King Solomon in all his royal splendor (6:29; cf. 1 Kgs 4:20-34; 10:14-29).

Why do you have so little faith? The rhetorical question of 6:30 causes disciples to reflect on the nature of God's wonderful providence. If God cares so much for flowers, which have such a short life span (cf. Pss 37:2; 103:15-16; Isa 40:6-8; Jas 1:10-11; 1 Pet 1:24-25), will he not care much more for the disciples of his beloved Son? If the disciples hesitated for a moment in giving a positive response to this question, it is because they had "little faith." This expression occurs in other challenges to the disciples in Matthew (8:26; 14:31; 16:8; 17:20). It points to the need for Jesus' disciples to strengthen their genuine although insufficient commitment to the values of the Kingdom.

6:31-32 These verses form an *inclusio* by repeating the prohibition of 6:25 and summarizing the reasons of 6:26-30.

What will we eat . . . drink . . . wear? Disciples must not ask what they will eat, drink, or wear, since these questions are like those of "unbelievers" (lit. "Gentiles," meaning non-Jewish pagans; cf. 6:7) who do not realize that they have a heavenly Father (cf. 5:45, 48; 6:1, 4, 6, 8, 9, 15, 18, 26) who knows their needs (cf. 6:8; 7:11). The Greco-Roman deities were notorious for their capricious, arbitrary actions. Devotees of these gods had to wonder whether their gifts and offerings had sufficiently appeased the gods and rendered them benevolent. Not so with the disciples' heavenly Father, whose love and concern were trustworthy and unchanging. Previously, Jesus stated that the practice of loving only one's friends was unacceptable for his disciples since it was acceptable pagan conduct (5:47). Now he points out similarly that worry over food and clothing is similarly unacceptable. As Mounce (1985:58) states, "Worry is practical atheism and an affront to God." The heavenly Father who loves his enemies also cares for his disciples. In response, they must love their enemies and trust their Father to meet their needs.

6:33 *Seek the Kingdom of God above all else.* The positive command of 6:33 balances the prohibition of 6:31. The disciples must not be anxious but must have as their primary concern God's Kingdom and the upright lifestyle that accompanies it. Putting God first in this way will result in God giving them all the food and clothing they need. By contrast, worrying does nothing except marginalize God and his Kingdom. The present seeking of Kingdom values is equivalent to living righteously in this world. Prayer for the progressive realization of God's Kingdom and will on earth (6:10) must be linked to the disciple's own efforts to realize its greater righteousness (5:20). While the disciples' needs may be met only partially during the present life (5:3-10; 6:11), they will receive an abundant reward when the Kingdom comes in its fullness (19:28-29).

6:34 *don't worry about tomorrow.* The conclusion of all this returns to the initial prohibition of anxiety (6:25)—tomorrow's food and clothing is not the disciple's concern. Disciples must address themselves to today's concerns while believing that tomorrow is in the hands of the loving heavenly Father (cf. Prov 27:1; Jas 4:13-15). This passage does not teach that the disciple will receive food and clothing automatically without planning and work but that such planning and work must not lead to anxiety that distracts from the first things—God's Kingdom and righteous standards. When his disciples put first things first, God will meet their needs for sustenance and clothing.

COMMENTARY

Matthew 6:19-34 can be understood as an interweaving of commands against anxiety and materialism with commands to believe that God will meet one's material needs. Some divide the passage into two units, the first on materialism (6:19-24) and the second on anxiety (6:25-34). Others agree that 6:25-34 is a unit but divide 6:19-24 into three units, 6:19-21, 6:22-23, and 6:24. The most difficult part of this passage is 6:22-23, which is not only hard to understand in itself but is also hard to relate to its context. Overall, Matthew 6:19-34 does not seem to be structured as clearly as preceding parts of the Sermon, but Davies and Allison (1988:625-627) attempt to diagram it and point out its strong structural resemblance to 7:1-12.

Matthew 6:19-34 is closely tied to the human needs portion of the disciples' prayer, especially the request for daily sustenance (6:8b, 11, 25, 31). It would also seem to be related to the ostensible state of persecution in which the disciples will often find themselves. Anxiety over material needs would be exacerbated by persecution. The passage revolves around three kinds of statements:

1. Prohibitions against materialistic activities and anxious thoughts (6:19, 25, 31, 34a).
2. Exhortations enjoining Kingdom priorities in activities and attitudes (6:20, 33).
3. Motivations (statements, proverbs, illustrations, and rhetorical questions) that move disciples toward obedience (6:21-24, 26-30, 32, 34b).

These three types of statements are woven together in a repetitive manner that reinforces Jesus' teaching. Instead of materialistic pursuits, Jesus' disciples are to pursue Kingdom priorities, while being assured of the Father's care.

In Matthew 6, Jesus addresses two matters, religious hypocrisy (6:1-18) and anxious materialism (6:19-34). The first part of the chapter enjoins the proper practice of religious duties, and the second part stresses the proper priority in meeting one's worldly needs. Both parts of the chapter call upon disciples to put God first. Davies and Allison (1988:648) comment, "Having prayed the prayer of Jesus, how could one remain anxious?" Disciples are taught in 6:1-18 to live for the Father's reward, not the crowd's applause. Their prayers are first to express zeal for God's glory and only second to express concern for their own needs. Disciples are taught in 6:19-34 that their heavenly Father's care for them is much greater than his care for birds and flowers. Ironically, if disciples seek the Father's Kingdom first, their needs will be met (cf. Lev 25:18-22; Ps 127:2; Phil 4:6-7; 1 Tim 6:6-10; Heb 13:5; 1 Pet 5:7). They will receive that for which they did not seek. But if they seek first to meet their own needs, they will be no different than the pagans who do not have a God who knows what they need.

The Father expects his children to put him first, but he delights to meet their needs. Disciples must not permit their needs to dominate their prayers, their thoughts, and their activities. That is immaturity. However, disciples must not think that God doesn't care about their needs. That is unbelief. Disciples must prioritize their allegiance to God, his rule, and his righteous standards. In so doing they will receive all they need to eat and wear, as it were, as fringe benefits. But if they insist on prioritizing their own needs in their prayers and activities, they will never experience the joy of resting in the Father's care and provision. As the hymn by Carolina Berg puts it, "Children of the Heavenly Father safely to his bosom gather; Nestling bird nor star in heaven such a refuge e'er was given."

This section of Matthew provides Christians with great insight about how to live and how to teach. Concerning how to teach, one should note how Jesus balances the positive and negative elements of his teaching and in the process blends in clear motivation and vivid illustration. Concerning how to live, this passage has much to say to materialistic cultures. God's care for his own does not necessarily guarantee an easy life filled with luxuries (see 5:10-12; 10:16-39; 24:9-13). God's care for his own may involve poverty for some and wealth for others. Contrary to human stereotypes, wealthy people are not necessarily materialistic, and poor people are not necessarily living by Kingdom priorities. The issues are one's priorities and one's stewardship of whatever resources one has for God's glory. This passage does not prohibit planning and work, as if food and clothing will come floating down out of the sky. The passage prohibits making one's plans and work the center of one's life and living as if God and his Kingdom did not exist.

◆   ## 8. Discernment in dealing with people (7:1-6; cf. Luke 6:37-42)

"Do not judge others, and you will not be judged. ²For you will be treated as you treat others.* The standard you use in judging is the standard by which you will be judged.*

³"And why worry about a speck in your friend's eye* when you have a log in your own? ⁴How can you think of saying to your friend,* 'Let me help you get rid of that speck in your eye,' when you can't see past the log in your own eye? ⁵Hypocrite! First get rid of the log in your own eye; then you will see well enough to deal with the speck in your friend's eye.

⁶"Don't waste what is holy on people who are unholy.* Don't throw your pearls to pigs! They will trample the pearls, then turn and attack you."

7:2a Or For God will judge you as you judge others.   7:2b Or The measure you give will be the measure you get back.   7:3 Greek your brother's eye; also in 7:5.   7:4 Greek your brother.   7:6 Greek Don't give the sacred to dogs.

NOTES

7:1 *Do not judge others.* The prohibition relates to previous commands about reconciliation (5:21-26), love, loving one's enemies (5:43-48), and forgiveness (6:12, 14-15; cf. 18:21-22). It is an instance of practicing the "golden rule" (7:12), and it does not rule out the need for spiritual discernment (7:6). Jesus prohibits judgmentalism and warns of divine judgment.

It may be, as Davies and Allison (1988:668) suggest, that this teaching is intended to warn the disciples against being like certain Pharisees, who are presented as being judgmental (9:10-13; 12:1-8; cf. Luke 15:1-2; 18:9-14).

and you will not be judged. This is a "divine passive," referring to God's judgment on the last day. God alone can make ultimate judgments about people (cf. 13:36-43, 47-50). The motivation for stopping such judgmental activity (7:2) is the principle of *lex talionis,* punishment in kind (cf. 5:38; Jas 2:13). God will judge people by the same standards they use to judge other people. If people don't want to be judged and punished harshly by God, they will not judge and punish fellow humans harshly. This prohibition is closely related to previous commands that the disciples must seek reconciliation (5:21-26), love their enemies (5:43-48), and forgive those who injure them (6:12, 14-15; cf. 18:21-22). It amounts to a specific instance of the practice of the "golden rule" (7:12). But this prohibition of judgmentalism does not rule out the need for spiritual discernment (7:6).

7:3-5 *How can you think of saying to your friend . . ?* In these verses, this translates the Gr. word *adelphos* [TG80, ZG81], which is more commonly translated as "brother." It evidently refers to one's fellow member of the community of disciples. The motivation provided by the warning of harsh divine judgment is here augmented by two rhetorical questions (7:3-4) that stress the perverse tendency of humans to criticize in others what they excuse in themselves (cf. Luke 6:41-42).

Hypocrite! These questions are followed by a charge of hypocrisy and a command to look honestly at oneself before one looks judgmentally at another (7:5, which forms a chiasmus with 7:4).

log in your own eye . . . speck in your friend's eye. Jesus' hyperbolic metaphors of the log and the speck refer respectively to blatant sins and minor shortcomings. Picturing one's sin as a log in one's eye stresses the inability of fallen human beings to render just judgment. How can someone whose vision is totally obscured by a log in his eye render a just assessment of another person's minor vision problems that are due to a speck or splinter (7:3)? And how can the person with the log in his eye think that he is capable of rendering assistance in removing the speck from his brother's eye (7:4)? Jesus labels this absurd situation as hypocrisy and plainly states that judgment of others can be rendered justly only when one has first judged oneself (7:5; cf. 18:15-17; 1 Cor 11:31; Gal 6:1; Jas 4:11-12).

7:6 *Don't give the sacred to dogs* [NLT mg]. *Don't throw your pearls to pigs!* This unique Matthean verse guards against an attitude that is the very opposite of the one addressed in 7:1-5. Jesus' disciples must not be censorious, but neither must they be oblivious to genuinely evil people. It appears that the setting of this warning is not so much the Eucharist service (*Didache* 9:5) as mission activity. It is quite unlikely that this verse concerns secret teachings that should be held back from outsiders. Rather, disciples should realize that the sacred message of the Kingdom must be handled with discernment, since there are malicious people who will respond to the message with violence against the messengers. In first-century Palestine, dogs were generally wild scavengers (15:26-27; cf. 1 Kgs 21:19; Ps 22:16; Phil 3:2; 2 Pet 2:22; Rev 22:15), and pigs were viewed as unclean beasts (8:32; cf. Lev 11:26; Deut 14:4, 8; Acts 10:12-14). Their use as metaphors of those who contemptuously and viciously reject the message of the Kingdom is striking. This teaching did not forbid the evangelization of Gentiles, although the Gentile mission had not yet been mandated (10:5; 15:24). In fact, Matthew repeatedly drops hints into his narrative about Gentile receptivity to the Kingdom (e.g., 1:3, 5-6; 2:2; 8:10; 15:28; 27:54), and concludes his Gospel with a statement that leaves little doubt about the extent of the disciples' mission (28:19-20). But disciples are to be wary while preaching the message of the Kingdom, since it is volatile truth and will often polarize those who hear it (10:14-15; 24:9; cf. Acts 5:33-40; 6:8–8:3; 13:44-51; 16:19-22; 18:12-17; 19:23-41; 21:27-32; Titus 3:10-11; Heb 10:32-34).

COMMENTARY

The flow of Matthew 7:1-11 is difficult to understand. Judgmentalism is the topic of 7:1-5. Keener (1999:240) aptly points out that this prohibition of judgmentalism is related to the previous command for forgiveness (6:12-15). With due respect to some scholars (e.g., Hagner 1993:171), 7:6 should be understood not as a detached unrelated saying but a warning against gullibility, the opposite of judgmentalism (Carson 1984:185; Gundry 1994:122). The difficulties in understanding the connection of 7:7-11 to 7:1-6 and 7:12 will be discussed in the next section of the commentary.

Jesus' teaching on how to deal with people in 7:1-6 presents two opposite extremes. First there is a warning against judgmentalism in 7:1-5, which may be analyzed as an initial prohibition (7:1) supported by a theological motivation (7:2) and a humorous hyperbolic illustration (7:3-5). Then there is a brief warning against the opposite of judgmentalism—namely, gullibility (7:6). This warning takes the literary form of chiasmus or introverted parallelism in the Greek text:

"Don't waste what is holy on dogs,

and don't throw your pearls to pigs!

They [the pigs] will trample the pearls,

then [the dogs will] turn and attack you."

Hypocritical Judgmentalism versus Genuine Discernment. Matthew 7:1 has the dubious distinction of being one of the most misquoted verses in the New Testament. Some postmoderns use this verse in particular to supply a sophisticated philosophical basis for those before them who have stressed relativism and subjectivity and denied that there were moral absolutes on which one could make absolute statements about right and wrong, good and evil. But depending on the context, the words "judge" and "judgment" can connote either analysis and evaluation or condemnation and punishment. Discipleship inevitably requires discerning "judgments" about individuals and their teachings (e.g., 3:7; 5:20; 6:24; 7:6, 16, 20; 10:13-17). Jesus himself made such judgments (see 4:10; 6:2, 5, 16; 7:21-23; 8:10-12; 13:10-13; 15:14). Therefore, Jesus did not forbid here what he has commanded and exemplified elsewhere.

What is forbidden is a rigid, censorious judgmentalism that scrutinizes others without even a glance at oneself (7:3; cf. Rom 2:1; 14:10; 1 Cor 4:5; 5:12; Jas 4:11-12; 5:9). Such a rigorous standard will return to haunt the one who condemns others by it (7:2; cf. 5:43-47; 18:15-20; Luke 6:37-42). King David learned this lesson the hard way (2 Sam 12:1-15). Jesus taught that genuine, honest introspection is an indispensable prerequisite for clear discernment and just moral judgments. Such judgments will be ultimately constructive, not retributive, since Jesus' disciples will not demand an eye for an eye and will love their enemies (5:33-48; 18:15-20; cf. Gal 6:1).

Jesus' disciples should be neither censorious inquisitors (7:1-5) nor naive simpletons (7:6). Those who viciously reject and continue to scorn the gospel must be regarded as dangerous enemies of the Kingdom whose evil actions can do great damage (cf. 2:16; 4:10; 5:11-12; 10:14-31; 12:14). Disciples must be wary of such people (cf. Prov 9:7; Col 4:5; 2 Tim 3:5; Titus 3:10). But unless one has removed the log from one's own eye, as it were, one will not be able to discern the difference between a fellow disciple with a relatively minor problem and an enemy who will do great harm to the Kingdom (cf. 11:12; 13:28-39). If genuine introspection does not occur, a disciple may blunder on the side of judgmental hypocrisy or naive gullibility. Ignorance of oneself is often mixed with arrogance toward others (Davies and Allison 1988:673), with disastrous results.

◆ ## 9. God answers prayer (7:7-11; cf. Luke 11:9-13)

⁷"Keep on asking, and you will receive what you ask for. Keep on seeking, and you will find. Keep on knocking, and the door will be opened to you. ⁸For everyone who asks, receives. Everyone who seeks, finds. And to everyone who knocks, the door will be opened.

⁹"You parents—if your children ask for a loaf of bread, do you give them a stone instead? ¹⁰Or if they ask for a fish, do you give them a snake? Of course not! ¹¹So if you sinful people know how to give good gifts to your children, how much more will your heavenly Father give good gifts to those who ask him."

NOTES

7:7-8 The instructions about prayer in 7:7-11 (cf. Luke 11:9-13) are not easily related to the preceding and following contexts. See the commentary below for discussion. The three commands of 7:7 correspond exactly to the three promises of 7:8. The paired triple constructions emphasize the reality of answered prayer.

Keep on asking . . . Keep on seeking . . . Keep on knocking. The NLT interprets the three Gr. present imperatives as enjoining habitual prayer. The three corresponding promises of 7:8 stress the readiness of the heavenly Father to meet the needs of the disciples, who will receive what they need, find what they are looking for, and have the opportunities they desire.

7:9-11 The triple command/promise structure of 7:7-8 is now supported by two rhetorical questions (7:9-10; cf. Luke 11:11-12), which lead to a lesser-to-greater argument (7:11). Both rhetorical techniques have been used previously in the Sermon, questions in 5:13, 46, 47; 6:25-27; 7:3-4 and lesser-to-greater arguments in 6:26-30. Family imagery is the key to 7:9-11.

You parents—if your children ask for a loaf of bread, do you give them a stone instead? Or if they ask for a fish, do you give them a snake? The questions of 7:9-10 forcefully make the point that human parents (lit. "man," referring to a father) would not give their children (lit. "his son," although "children" is the literal translation in 7:11) a stone (cf. 4:3) and a snake when they are hungry and ask for bread and fish. The argument of 7:11 builds on the normal human situation; even though human parents are sinful, they generally know how to meet their children's basic needs and act accordingly.

how much more will your heavenly Father give good gifts to those who ask him. Prayer is thus encouraged all the more by the force of Jesus' lesser-to-greater logic, which augments the threefold promise of 7:8.

Careful readers of this passage will note that the positive, gracious tone of 7:7-11 provides a welcome change from the many prohibitions that have preceded it. Commands have led to reassurance. Kingdom standards are high, but disciples should not be discouraged or anxious in pursuing them. God is infinitely better than the best of human parents, and he promises to supply the needs of his family. A similar argument with feminine imagery is found in Isa 49:15.

C O M M E N T A R Y

These verses are in the form of an *inclusio*, with "your heavenly Father [will] give good gifts to those who ask" in 7:11 corresponding to "Keep on asking and you will receive" in 7:7 (cf. John 16:23-24). Hagner (1993:173) is right that on the surface, 7:7-11 is about prayer and has no obvious connection to the preceding or following topics. However, other scholars (e.g., Gundry 1994:119, 123) attempt to find a connection in the common theme of how to treat people. If this is the case, the passage teaches that one must treat people with discernment, not being judgmental (7:1-5) or gullible (7:6), but displaying the same generosity exhibited by the heavenly Father in answering prayers (7:7-11). In so doing, they must remember the "golden rule" and treat others as they would like to be treated (7:12). Carson (1984:186) finds a connection by relating 7:7-11 as the disciples' resource, as they aspire to the greater righteousness taught by Jesus from 5:21–7:6. But it must be admitted that neither of these options shows a really convincing connection. Davies and Allison (1988:626-627) present an interesting comparison of the structure of 7:1-12 to that of 6:19-34, though their discussion of the connection of 7:1-12 to the preceding and following contexts is not as helpful (1988:677-678).

Jesus on Prayer. Matthew 7:7-11 may be regarded as a sort of postscript to the model prayer of 6:9-13 (cf. Luke 11:1-13). That prayer builds on the truth that religious duties are to be performed for God's eyes only (6:4, 6, 18). He sees what is done in private and will reward his disciples. Additionally, Jesus assured the disciples that their heavenly Father knew what they needed even before they could ask him (6:8, 32). So it has already been taught that God is aware of his disciples and their needs. Accordingly, 7:7-11 goes even further by stressing that the God who knows his disciples' needs will certainly answer their prayers (7:7-8) from the depths of his goodness (7:11).

In the midst of their trials, disciples of the Kingdom are often tempted to think that God is unaware of their problems and needs. That understandable but absolutely mistaken notion is put to rest by Matthew 6:8, 32—"your Father knows." Even when they are assured that God knows their needs, disciples still wonder at times whether God is able to answer their prayers, but 7:7-8 makes it abundantly clear that an answer is certain to come—"you will receive." And even when disciples believe that God knows and will answer, they may doubt that the answer is good. But they are comforted by the affirmation of God's benevolence provided by 7:9-11—"how much more will your heavenly Father give good gifts." God is not ignorant. God is not impotent. God is not malevolent. These truths must be learned and relearned daily in the crucible of Christian experience.

◆   10. The Golden Rule (7:12; cf. Luke 6:31)

¹²"Do to others whatever you would like them to do to you. This is the essence of all that is taught in the law and the prophets."

NOTES

7:12 *Do to others whatever you would like them to do to you.* Because it is connected to the preceding verses by the Gr. conjunction *oun* [TG3767, ZG4036] ("therefore"; not translated in NLT), this verse (cf. Luke 6:31) should be understood as a conclusion to everything said since 5:20. In one sense, 7:12 can be understood as concluding from God's benevolent response to the wishes of his disciples that his disciples should likewise do for others whatever they would like to be done for them. But in a wider and much more profound sense, 7:12 concludes the entire body of the Sermon that began in 5:17 with Jesus' statement of his mission. Just as he did not come to cancel but to accomplish the purpose of the law and the prophets, so his disciples must live according to Scripture.

The essence of the law and the prophets is that one should treat other humans just like one would like to be treated by them (cf. 19:19; 22:34-40). All of Jesus' teaching since 5:21 about the greater righteousness necessary for his Kingdom (5:20) is summarized here by the "golden rule." It may be argued that Jesus sets this "rule" in the unique context of his own words and deeds, which manifest the nearness of the Kingdom, but it is well known that similar "rules" may be found in Jewish and Greco-Roman literature of the period. See Davies and Allison (1988:686-688) for examples. The wellspring for Jesus' teaching was, of course, the Hebrew Bible (Lev. 19:18, 34; Exod 23:4-5). Jesus brought the law and prophets to their intended goal, setting their teaching in the context of his own definitive eschatological message.

COMMENTARY

Inspired by the beneficence of their heavenly Father, disciples of the Kingdom must be like him. As their Lord had come not to abolish but to accomplish the purpose of the law and the prophets, they too should live by a transcendent ethic. These themes meet in 7:12, where doing good to others (as the heavenly Father does; cf. 5:45-48) is identified as the quintessence of biblical ethics. The general statement of 7:12 condenses the 39 books of the Hebrew Bible into 12 words in the NLT. In 5:21-7:11, Matthew has summarized the definitive teaching of Jesus on several key areas of ethical and religious life. Matthew presents this definitive teaching as climactic in nature (5:17-20)—a more profound ethical standard could not be conceived in his view. The ethic is explained in the concrete contexts of obeying the Torah (5:21-48), practicing religious duties (6:1-18), dealing with material possessions (6:19-34), relating to people (7:1-6), and praying (7:7-11).

The Father's character and standards as incarnated in the Son's ministry of word and deed is the basis for this sublime ethic. "Do to others whatever you would like them to do to you" could be construed as a sort of "ten commandments" of Jesus:

1. You will not commit "verbal murder" (5:21-26). You will make reconciliation with fellow disciples your first religious priority.
2. You will not commit "mental adultery" (5:27-30). You will deal decisively with your sinful thoughts.

3. You will not divorce, except when infidelity has occurred (5:31-32). You will make every effort to remain with your spouse.

4. You will not make vows (5:33-37). You will always tell the truth.

5. You will not seek personal retribution (5:38-42). You will be generous even to those who injure you.

6. You will not hate your enemies (5:43-48). You will love and pray for your persecutors.

7. You will not perform religious duties to gain temporary human approval (6:1-18). You will perform religious duties only to gain eternal divine reward.

8. You will not be anxious over things (6:19-34). You will be exclusively loyal to God's Kingdom and righteous standards.

9. You will not be judgmental or naive in your estimate of fellow humans (7:1-6). You will examine your own life before making judgments about others.

10. You will not avoid prayer because you doubt God's goodness (7:7-11). You will believe that God is good and rest in his answers to prayer.

Conclusion. With the summarizing statement of the "golden rule" in 7:12, the Sermon's main body has concluded. Jesus came not to abolish but to fulfill the law and the prophets (5:17), and he requires that his disciples do no less. The summation of the law as loving one's neighbor or doing for others whatever one would like them to do to him is therefore not a higher law that replaces the Torah but the true goal of the law. (Paul's view is similar on this point; cf. Rom 13:8-9; Gal 5:14). The Sermon will now conclude with solemn warnings on the necessity of obedience to his teaching (7:13-27).

◆   ## 11. Warnings (7:13-27)

[13]"You can enter God's Kingdom only through the narrow gate. The highway to hell* is broad, and its gate is wide for the many who choose that way. [14]But the gateway to life is very narrow and the road is difficult, and only a few ever find it.

[15]"Beware of false prophets who come disguised as harmless sheep but are really vicious wolves. [16]You can identify them by their fruit, that is, by the way they act. Can you pick grapes from thornbushes, or figs from thistles? [17]A good tree produces good fruit, and a bad tree produces bad fruit. [18]A good tree can't produce bad fruit, and a bad tree can't produce good fruit. [19]So every tree that does not produce good fruit is chopped down and thrown into the fire. [20]Yes, just as you can identify a tree by its fruit, so you can identify people by their actions.

[21]"Not everyone who calls out to me, 'Lord! Lord!' will enter the Kingdom of Heaven. Only those who actually do the will of my Father in heaven will enter. [22]On judgment day many will say to me, 'Lord! Lord! We prophesied in your name and cast out demons in your name and performed many miracles in your name.' [23]But I will reply, 'I never knew you. Get away from me, you who break God's laws.'

[24]"Anyone who listens to my teaching and follows it is wise, like a person who builds a house on solid rock. [25]Though the rain comes in torrents and the flood-waters rise and the winds beat against that house, it won't collapse because it is

built on bedrock. ²⁶But anyone who hears my teaching and doesn't obey it is foolish, like a person who builds a house on sand.

²⁷When the rains and floods come and the winds beat against that house, it will collapse with a mighty crash."

7:13 Greek *The road that leads to destruction.*

NOTES

7:13-14 *The highway to hell is broad . . . the gateway to life is very narrow.* This image (cf. Jer 21:8; Luke 13:23-24) contrasts the narrow gate and the difficult road that lead to life with the wide gate and broad highway to "hell" (lit. "destruction" or "ruin").

7:15-16 The second and most complex picture of contrasting responses to the Kingdom is found in 7:15-23. The vivid imagery of this section is drawn from both animal (7:15) and plant (7:16-20) life and is meant to portray the false prophets who endanger the journey of the disciples (cf. Luke 6:43-44). The section begins with the general warning of 7:15, which compares the deceptiveness of the false prophets (cf. 24:11, 24) to vicious wolves (cf. John 10:12; Acts:20:29) that somehow appear as sheep (10:16; 25:33; cf. Ps 78:52).

harmless sheep. The word "harmless," though clearly implied by the metaphor, is not in the Gr. text. This warning is followed by the basic instruction on how to detect the marauding wolves (7:16a).

identify them by their fruit. The notion of identifying the false prophets by their fruit (lit. "fruits" here and throughout the section except for 7:19; cf. 3:8, 10; 12:33; 13:8, 26; 21:19; John 15:2-8; Gal 5:22) involves an abrupt shift of metaphor from the animal kingdom to that of plants.

Can you pick grapes from thornbushes, or figs from thistles? The plant metaphor continues in 7:16b with a rhetorical question that highlights the folly of expecting harmful weeds to produce beneficial fruit. These false prophets are in some sense part of the community of the disciples, since they call Jesus "Lord" and minister in his name (7:21-22; cf. 10:16; 24:11, 24).

7:17-18 *A good tree produces good fruit, and a bad tree produces bad fruit.* The imagery of the rhetorical question of 7:16 is the basis for the developed imagery of 7:17-19, where "good fruit" answers to the grapes and figs, and the "bad tree" corresponds to the thornbushes and thistles. The same idea is stated first positively and then negatively in the parallel clauses of 7:17-18. Both good and bad trees produce corresponding fruit (7:17); it is impossible for them to do otherwise (7:18; cf. Jas. 3:12).

7:19 *every tree that does not produce good fruit is chopped down and thrown into the fire.* Here the imagery reminds the reader of John the Baptist's stern words, which speak of eschatological judgment (3:8-10; cf. 13:40, 42, 50; 18:8-9; 25:41). Disciples (good trees) repent and obey Jesus (good fruit). Others (worthless trees) turn away from God and his Kingdom and live accordingly (bad fruit).

7:20 Here Jesus draws a conclusion that repeats verbatim the words of 7:16a. Thus the *inclusio* structure of 7:16-20 involves the initial statement of a thesis (7:16a) followed by supporting argument (7:16b-19), which brings one full circle back to the initial statement, restated as a conclusion (7:20). The conclusion of the matter is that the false prophets' sheep-like appearance need not deceive the disciples because their true identity can be perceived by examining their deeds or works, metaphorically described as "fruits." For Matthew, one's spiritual identity is determined not by what one says but by what one does, because what one does inexorably reveals one's heart. In this situation as in many others, the truism holds—actions speak louder than words. The latter are empty and hypocritical when the former are missing. For Matthew, "faith and works never part company" (Davies and Allison 1988:705).

7:21-23 Jesus now turns from the works of the false prophets to their words (cf. Luke 6:46; 13:25-27). It is noteworthy that Jesus refers to the Father as "my Father" in 7:21 (cf. 6:9, 15). This is evidently due to his unique sonship (cf. 3:17) and his unique role as the Father's appointed eschatological judge.

On judgment day. Lit., "that day" (cf. 10:15; 11:22, 24; 24:19, 22, 29, 36, 38; Isa 10:20).

many will say to me, "Lord! Lord!" We prophesied . . . cast out demons . . . and performed many miracles in your name. These people claim they have prophesied, exorcised demons, and done many miracles in Jesus' name (cf. 4:24; 8:3, 13, 16; 9:6, 22; 10:1, 8; 12:24-29). The problem is not that there is no fruit, but that the fruit is counterfeit, though the false prophets claim it is genuine (cf. 13:24-30, 36-43, 47-50; 24:23-28). Only those who do the Father's will (6:10; 12:50; 21:28-32; 26:42) will enter the Kingdom.

7:23 *I never knew you.* Jesus' reply is chilling: he affirms that despite their claims he never "knew" (cf. 25:12) the false prophets. He does not accept their addressing him as Lord, and he utterly renounces them as his followers. This expression is akin to OT passages in which God's knowledge of his people implies a personal relationship, not merely an awareness of facts (Heb. *yada'* [TH3045, ZH3359]; Gen 18:19; Ps 1:6; Jer 1:5; Amos 3:2; cf. John 10:14; 1 Cor 8:3; Gal 4:9; 2 Tim 2:19).

Get away from me, you who break God's laws. An allusion to Ps 6:8 (cf. 25:41), this statement seems to be a key to the identity of the false prophets (though see the cautions of Davies and Allison 1988:718-719). It describes them literally as those "who do lawlessness" (cf. 24:12 where lawlessness is probably connected with the false prophets in 24:11, as well as 13:41; 23:28), which means that they take a lax view of the law and the need of obedience to it. Jesus came to fulfill the law (5:20), so antinomians, those who disregard the law, are not genuine disciples no matter how many spectacular deeds they perform. Jesus' disciples must be on guard against these counterfeit prophets who will lead them away from the narrow road of repentance and down the wide boulevard of lawlessness.

7:24-27 These verses (cf. Luke 6:47-49) present a third picture of contrasting responses to the Kingdom. The form of the language used in 7:24, 26 ("anyone who . . .") amounts to an implied invitation to obey and an implied warning to those who refuse to obey. Again Matthew employs parallel contrasting statements.

Anyone who listens to my teaching and follows it is wise, like a person who builds a house on solid rock. The wise (cf. 10:16; 24:45; 25:2, 4, 9) response to the message of the Kingdom is pictured as building one's house on bedrock.

anyone who hears my teaching and doesn't obey it is foolish. The foolish (cf. 5:22; 23:17; 25:2, 3, 8) response is pictured as building one's house on sand. When the trials of life, pictured as rains, floods, and winds, beat upon it, the house built on sand falls with a crash— but the house wisely built on bedrock does not collapse. Evidently, the houses are pictured as being built along a "wadi," which is a dry gulch in the summer but becomes a raging torrent during the winter rains.

It is important to note that both the wise and foolish builders hear the teaching of Jesus. It is his teaching, no longer that of Moses, that is the standard of judgment. But it is not enough to have heard the teaching of Jesus. Hearing and knowing the teaching of Jesus are worthwhile activities only when they result in application. The false prophets, whatever their appearance and words, are lawless. The wide gate, though attractive, leads to destruction. Eschatological judgment utterly destroys houses built on sand, but houses built on rock withstand it. (See 16:18 for the use of the building metaphor in a different context.)

COMMENTARY

The statement of the epitome of Kingdom ethics in 7:12 ends the body of the Sermon. There are no more commands to be obeyed, except for those that warn against disobedience. Matthew 7:13-27 is a warning that features three pictures of contrasting responses to the message of the Kingdom.

Matthew 7:13-27, the conclusion to the Sermon, is divided by the NLT into four paragraphs: 13-14, 15-20, 21-23, and 24-27. But the judgment scene in 7:21-23 is clearly tied to the parabolic language of 7:15-20, since both paragraphs speak of false prophets (7:15, 22; cf. 24:5, 11, 24) whose evil deeds (7:17-19, 22) are known (7:16, 20, 23) and judged (7:19, 22-23). Therefore, 7:15-20 (actions of the false prophets) is linked to 7:21-23 (words of the false prophets), and there are really only three sections in 7:13-27. These verses constitute a stern warning that presents two contrasting responses to the Sermon in the form of three metaphors: (1) two gates (7:13-14; cf. Luke 13:24); (2) two trees (7:15-23; cf. Luke 6:43-46); and (3) two builders (7:24-27; cf. Luke 6:47-49).

The chart below portrays the ethical dualism of 7:13-27, which vividly and repeatedly contrasts discipleship with antinomianism. Such dualism has roots in the Hebrew Bible (e.g., Deut 30:15, 19; Jer 21:8; Ps 1). It is found in intertestamental literature (e.g., *4 Ezra* 7:6-14), Qumran texts (e.g., 1QS 3:20-21), early Christian literature (*Didache* 1–6, *Barnabas* 18–20), and rabbinic literature (*m. Avot* 2:12-13; *Sifre* 86a).

	DISCIPLESHIP	ANTINOMIANISM
Two gates *(7:13-14)*	Narrow gate	Wide gate
	Difficult way	Broad way
	Life	Destruction
	Few	Many
Two trees *(7:15-23)*	True Prophets (implied)	False prophets
	Sheep	Wolves
	Good trees	Bad trees (thorns, thistles)
	Good fruit (grapes, figs)	Bad fruit
	Life (implied)	Judgment (fire)
	Doing the Father's will	Saying "Lord, lord . . ."
Two builders *(7:24-27)*	Wise person	Foolish person
	Hears/obeys Jesus	Hears/does not obey Jesus
	House built on rock	House built on sand
	House stands during flood	House falls during flood

Two Roads. This section begins with a command to enter by the narrow gate (7:13a). Then there are two symmetrical contrasting statements supporting the command. The first (7:13b) explains that many (those who are spiritually complacent) take the gate and road to destruction, evidently because this looks like the easy way. The second (7:14) speaks, in contrast, of the few (those who are spiritually committed) who opt for the difficult path to life (cf. 19:24). The narrow gate and the difficult road are metaphors for repentance and Kingdom ethics, and the relatively few who find this route are the disciples. The description of the road as difficult may allude to trials caused by persecution (cf. 5:10-12; 10:16-23; 13:21; 24:9, 21, 29). "Finding" the gateway to life implicitly pictures the activity of discipleship as a search for the Kingdom, the opposite of the passive complacency that takes the easy way. "Life" is the full experience of eternal fellowship with God, the polar opposite of the destruction of hell. It is roughly synonymous with the future manifestation of the Kingdom (19:23-24; cf. 18:8-9; 19:29; 25:46).

It is difficult to know exactly how to imagine the gates and roads of Matthew 7:13-14. Some take it that one travels the road and then comes to the gate, but this reverses the order of the terms as they occur in the text. Although it is not necessary to answer this question to "get the picture," it is helpful to picture a wall with a narrow gate and a wide gate. One can easily enter the wide gate, and once inside, the path of antinomianism is smooth. But suddenly, as if a bridge has collapsed without warning, one arrives in hell. The wide path that seemed to promise freedom has ended in destruction—separation from God. By contrast, when one takes the difficult step of entering the narrow gate, the path of discipleship can be very arduous. But suddenly one is ushered into eternal life. The rugged path that threatened to destroy has ended in freedom, sharing in the life of God. These two gates and roads vividly indicate that those who do not turn from sin to God take an easy road, but it leads to the most difficult destination imaginable. But those who take the difficult way of the Kingdom arrive at the best possible destination, where they experience the ultimate in the life of the Father.

The contrast of the many and the few in 7:13-14 is sobering. While in one sense there will be many who opt for the rigorous way to life (cf. 8:11; 20:28), the many who become disciples are relatively few when compared with all of humanity (cf. 22:14). Instead of speculating on the number of the elect (Luke 13:23-24), disciples should strive first to enter the narrow gate themselves. Then they should focus on their master's universal authority and his command to make disciples from all the nations of the earth (24:14; 28:18-20).

Two Trees. Jesus' plain words in 7:15-23, which clearly distinguish between two kinds of fruit and two kinds of trees, seem to be regularly blurred in some circles. At times, evangelical Christians tend to exchange Jesus' stark soteriological dualism for the "cheap grace" thinking that says that many who luxuriate on the broad path will somehow after all end up in the Kingdom with those who have made the rigorous trek of discipleship. That there should be anything controversial about Christ's Lordship in salvation is amazing when one considers a text such as Matthew 7:15-29.

Elsewhere in Matthew, the metaphor of fruit has been used to show that only an upright lifestyle is compatible with discipleship (3:10; 12:33; 13:18-23, 37-42; cf. 10:22; 19:16-30; 24:13). Matthew would agree with James 2:26 that "faith without works is dead." While this teaching must not be made even more rigorous by legalistic and perfectionistic accretions, neither must it be diluted by antinomianism. Even Paul, to whom antinomians regularly appeal, frequently stressed the necessity (not the option) of perseverance and good works (e.g., Rom 2:13; 3:8; 11:22; 13:14; Gal 5:6; Eph 2:10; Col 1:23; Titus 2:7, 14; 3:8, 14).

But the focus of the good and bad trees in Matthew 7:15-23 is on false prophets, who are likened not only to bad trees that produce worthless fruit but also to wolves that masquerade as sheep. This disguise is extremely deceptive—the wolves are even able to perform the "sheep-like" activities of prophecy, exorcism, and miracles, and they do not hesitate to mouth the Lordship of Jesus. Though the situation is grim, there is a solution. These wolves masquerading as sheep can be unmasked when their works, pictured as fruit, are inspected by the standards of the Sermon. If their ethical activities are incompatible with the values of the Kingdom expounded here, they are to be identified and exposed as false prophets. Their spectacular charismatic achievements aside (24:23-28; cf. Deut 13:1-5), their ministries will only detour would-be disciples from the repentance road to life onto the antinomian highway to hell. Beware!

It would be wrong to conclude from this warning against antinomian prophets that Matthew takes a consistently dim view of prophets and their charismatic activities. Jesus himself is the prophet *par excellence*, and he commissioned his disciples to do powerful deeds (10:1, 8) and to preach, which to some extent is related to prophesying (10:6). Such ministry is to be supported by the disciples, whose reception of prophets will bring them a reward equivalent to that of the prophets themselves (10:41). Indeed, Jesus promised to send future prophets (23:34), but their destiny is to share in the persecution that their master and his other disciples would experience. Thus, Matthew opposes antinomianism, not prophets per se.

Two Builders. The comparison of discipleship to the construction of a house in 7:24-27 is very effective. This picture is found elsewhere in Scripture (Deut 28:15, 30; Prov 10:25; 14:11), especially in Ezekiel 13:8-16, which denounces false prophets as those who build a defective wall that falls down during a storm. This metaphor also rings true today, since one regularly hears of housing problems, caused by shoddy craftsmanship and inferior materials, which come to light during times of extreme weather. But what is the difference between a wise builder who constructs a solid house and a foolish cobbler who throws up a shoddy house? In Jesus' metaphor, the difference is the obedient deeds of wise disciples who act on what they hear from their master, contrasted with the inactivity of the complacent hearers who do nothing. The former build an enduring house on rock, the latter a doomed edifice on sand.

For the third time, the clear warning has been given. Neither the ancient crowds who originally heard the Sermon from Jesus on the mount nor the modern readers who encounter the gist of it today in Matthew 5–7 can dare to walk away unchanged, complacent. To do so is ultimately to not weather the storm, to be eternally separated from Jesus, to arrive in hell. So let us heed the warnings, weather the storm, enter the Kingdom, and find life! We have been warned.

◆ 12. Result of the Sermon (7:28-29)

²⁸When Jesus had finished saying these things, the crowds were amazed at his teaching, ²⁹for he taught with real authority—quite unlike their teachers of religious law.

NOTES

7:28-29 Just as 4:25–5:2 led the reader from the narrative into the discourse, so 7:28–8:1 leads the reader out of the discourse back into the narrative. Both passages mention large crowds following Jesus and his respective ascent or descent of the mountain.

the crowds were amazed at his teaching. The response of the crowd (cf. 4:25; 5:1) was amazement (7:28; cf. 13:54; 22:33).

he taught with real authority. They were overwhelmed, not by the novelty or clever presentation of the teaching, but by Jesus' uniquely authoritative way of teaching, which was so different from what they were used to hearing from their "teachers of religious law" (7:29; cf. the discussion in the notes on 2:4). Jesus' teaching assumed a transcendent authority that their teachers rightly did not claim to possess.

quite unlike their teachers of religious law. The pronoun "their" evidently distinguishes Jewish scribes in general from those Jewish scribes who believed in Jesus (13:52; 23:34). Matthew as narrator did not mention whether the crowd engaged Jesus with questions or disputed any his teaching. Thus, the crowd's amazement further underlines the unique authority of Jesus as the definitive teacher of the law (cf. 17:5) who expects a righteousness greater than that of the religious leaders (5:20).

COMMENTARY

The alternation of narrative and discourse blocks throughout Matthew, signaled at the end of each discourse by the recurring words, "When Jesus had finished saying . . . ," is probably the most distinctive element of Matthew's approach to telling the story of Jesus. The crowd's amazed response to Jesus' authoritative words contained in the discourse (Matt 5–7) anticipates their amazed response to his authoritative works contained in the narrative (8:1–9:34; esp. 8:9; 9:6-8). The effect of this alternating narrative and discourse structure is heightened by the matching "bookends" of 4:23 and 9:35.

The crowd's amazement at the authority of Jesus was evidently derived not so much from the clarity and bluntness of what he said but more from his daring juxtaposition of his own views with statements from the Torah in the contrasts of 5:21-48. Jesus' teaching included exegesis of Torah, but it was not primarily exegesis of Torah. Jesus did not cite human authorities who might support his views. This authoritarian mode of communication put Jesus above even Moses, who received the Torah from the finger of God on Mount Sinai. As astonishing as that revelation to

Moses was, God's revelation of his ultimate law through the definitive teachings of Jesus the Messiah was even more so.

This authority of Jesus that amazed the crowds has only begun to impact the reader of Matthew. Matthew has yet to show that the deeds of Jesus are also authoritative (Matt 8–9), that the disciples will soon receive like authority for their early ministries (10:1), and that even fuller authority will ultimately be given to the exalted Jesus, who will use it to commission his disciples for worldwide ministry to all the nations (28:18-20).

Conclusion. Jesus' Sermon on the Mount gets to the heart of authentic discipleship. Various camps within evangelicalism push pop theologies to the effect that Jesus' disciples are popular with people, keep a list of human rules, have many possessions, perform spectacular works, or have deep knowledge. But the Sermon explicitly denies that any of these is at the heart of authentic discipleship. Instead, the Beatitudes summarize the character traits that, by God's grace, become the norms for disciples of the Kingdom. Jesus' Kingdom fulfills the Old Testament; the disciples of this Kingdom obey the ethical norms of the Old Testament in a manner transcending that of the Pharisees. The disciples' religious devotions are done privately, and their public careers put the righteousness of the Kingdom first. They also avoid judgmentalism and gullibility in their dealings with people. In loving God wholeheartedly and in loving their neighbors as themselves, they take the narrow way, they produce good fruit, and they build their lives on bedrock.

Those of us who hear the Sermon on the Mount's emphasis on *doing* risk misunderstanding it when we compare it with the apostle Paul's emphasis on *believing*. All this stress in the Sermon on works may sound like the type of religion Paul condemned in Galatians. But any "contradiction" is only apparent. Paul was writing to correct the error that made salvation a result of works, while Jesus' Sermon speaks of the works that result from repentance. According to Matthew, only those who repent when they hear the Kingdom message are inclined by God's grace to obey the norms of the Kingdom by loving God and neighbor (5:17; 7:12). And according to Paul, authentic religion is essentially a matter of "faith expressing itself in love" (Gal 5:6). All who seek to grasp the Sermon must ask themselves whether *they* have been grasped by it. If they have, they will express their repentance in love to God and neighbor.

◆ III. The Galilean Ministry Continues (8:1–10:42)
A. Three Cycles of Miracles and Discipleship (8:1–10:4)
1. Three healing miracles (8:1-17)

Large crowds followed Jesus as he came down the mountainside. ²Suddenly, a man with leprosy approached him and knelt before him. "Lord," the man said, "if you are willing, you can heal me and make me clean."

³Jesus reached out and touched him. "I am willing," he said. "Be healed!" And

instantly the leprosy disappeared. ⁴Then Jesus said to him, "Don't tell anyone about this. Instead, go to the priest and let him examine you. Take along the offering required in the law of Moses for those who have been healed of leprosy.* This will be a public testimony that you have been cleansed."

⁵When Jesus returned to Capernaum, a Roman officer* came and pleaded with him, ⁶"Lord, my young servant* lies in bed, paralyzed and in terrible pain."

⁷Jesus said, "I will come and heal him."

⁸But the officer said, "Lord, I am not worthy to have you come into my home. Just say the word from where you are, and my servant will be healed. ⁹I know this because I am under the authority of my superior officers, and I have authority over my soldiers. I only need to say, 'Go,' and they go, or 'Come,' and they come. And if I say to my slaves, 'Do this,' they do it."

¹⁰When Jesus heard this, he was amazed. Turning to those who were following him, he said, "I tell you the truth, I haven't seen faith like this in all Israel! ¹¹And I tell you this, that many Gentiles will come from all over the world—from east and west—and sit down with Abraham, Isaac, and Jacob at the feast in the Kingdom of Heaven. ¹²But many Israelites—those for whom the Kingdom was prepared—will be thrown into outer darkness, where there will be weeping and gnashing of teeth."

¹³Then Jesus said to the Roman officer, "Go back home. Because you believed, it has happened." And the young servant was healed that same hour.

¹⁴When Jesus arrived at Peter's house, Peter's mother-in-law was sick in bed with a high fever. ¹⁵But when Jesus touched her hand, the fever left her. Then she got up and prepared a meal for him.

¹⁶That evening many demon-possessed people were brought to Jesus. He cast out the evil spirits with a simple command, and he healed all the sick. ¹⁷This fulfilled the word of the Lord through the prophet Isaiah, who said,

"He took our sicknesses
and removed our diseases."*

8:4 See Lev 14:2-32.   8:5 Greek *a centurion;* similarly in 8:8, 13.   8:6 Or *child;* also in 8:13.   8:17 Isa 53:4.

NOTES

8:1 *mountainside.* This recalls 5:1 and frames the intervening discourse. A mountain is repeatedly mentioned in Matthew at theologically significant junctures (4:8; 5:1; 8:1; 14:23; 15:29; 17:1, 9, 20; 21:21; 24:3, 16; 26:30; 28:16). Some argue that this implies a comparison between Jesus and Moses. The "crowds" are also frequently mentioned in Matthew (4:25; 5:1; 8:1, 18; 9:8, 33, 36, 37; 11:7; 12:15; 13:2; 14:22-23; 15:30; 19:2; 21:9; 26:55).

8:2 Here the first of three sets of three miracle stories begins (see the analysis in the following commentary). The first set involves individuals who were at the margins of Israelite society.

a man with leprosy. Matthew's first story is about a leper who was healed by Jesus (cf. Mark 1:40-44; Luke 5:12-14). Lepers were social and religious outcasts in biblical times. Leprosy in the Bible can refer to a variety of skin problems and should not be equated with the dreaded modern malady known as leprosy (Hansen's disease). Even garments could become "leprous" (Lev 13:47-59). In all these cases, the priests were responsible to make official rulings on the ritual status of the questionable individual, impurity or uncleanness versus purity or cleanness. They were to quarantine questionable individuals until their status became clear. Lepers were not permitted any social contact with other Israelites but were to shout warnings of their impurity to those who might come near them (Lev 13:45-46). As such, this leper was rather audacious even to approach Jesus (contrast Luke 17:12) and to request cleansing, although his posture, his calling Jesus "Lord" (See the discussion under Christology in the Major Themes section of the Introduction.), and his confidence in Jesus' power indicate his great respect for Jesus (8:2). Although this leper's faith is striking, the next story involves even greater faith. (For the OT background on leprosy see Lev 13-14; Num 12:10-15; 2 Kgs 5 [cf. Luke 4:27]; 2 Chr 26. In the Gospels see Matt 8:2-3; 10:8; 11:5; 26:6; Mark 1:40-42; 14:3; Luke 4:27; 5:12-13; 7:22; 17:12. See also *m. Negai'm*.)

8:3-4 *I am willing.* Jesus' willingness, not his touch, was all that was necessary for the healing (cf. 8:8), but the touch was probably the first human contact the leper had experienced throughout the duration of his illness. Touching the leper was even more audacious than the leper's approaching Jesus, since Jesus would also became ritually unclean when he touched the leper (Lev 5:3). But the touch, instead of defiling Jesus, immediately cleansed the leper.

Don't tell anyone about this. Instead, go to the priest. Jesus' instructions (8:4) for the cleansed leper were twofold. First, he was to tell no one about his cleansing. This surprising command may be due simply to the necessary priority of the second instruction, to go to a priest to certify the cleansing and to offer a sacrifice (cf. Luke 17:14), which was in keeping with Lev 13–14, especially 14:2ff. The instructions were also intended to make the cleansing of the leper a testimony to the religious leaders (cf. 10:18; 24:14). This is not simply a testimony of the cleansed leper's fitness to rejoin society, as Hagner maintains (1993:200). Jesus commissioned his disciples to cleanse lepers (10:8), and he mentioned the cleansing of lepers as a messianic sign when he was asked by John's messengers whether he was the Messiah (11:5).

Why did Jesus command silence about the healing (cf. 9:30; 12:16; 16:20; 17:9)? W. Wrede's "messianic secret" theory (cf. Tuckett 1983) took texts like this one, which are more prominent in Mark, as non-historical interpolations by the early church, designed to explain why so few people believed in Jesus during his lifetime. But such a theory is not only dubious on historical grounds, it is also unnecessary given the nature of Jesus' mission. At times, Jesus found it necessary to withdraw from the scene when his popularity due to his miracles reached near-riot proportions (e.g., 4:23–5:1; 8:18; 13:2; 21:11). At other times, he seemed simply to need solitude, a respite from the press of the multitudes (14:23). Also, there was the looming presence of the religious leaders, whose hostility seemed to grow in direct proportion to Jesus' popularity with the masses (9:32-34; 12:22-24; 15:21; 16:4, 20). But it was not only prudent for Jesus to avoid inflaming the messianic speculations of the crowds and to keep a low profile at times (9:30; 14:13; 17:9), it was also in keeping with messianic prophecy (12:15-21; cf. Isa 42:1-4).

8:5-9 Matthew's second story is about the healing of a Roman officer's servant at Capernaum (cf. Luke 7:1-10).

Roman officer. This is often translated "centurion" since the Gr. word's etymology contains the word "one hundred" (cf. Cornelius in Acts 10).

young servant. Or "child" (NLT mg). This reflects the semantic range of the Gr. word *pais* [TG3816, ZG4090], which can connote a child (cf. 2:16; 17:18; 21:15; Luke 2:43) or a servant (14:2; Luke 7:7; 12:45; 15:26). Some think the term should be translated "boy" or "son" (e.g., Hagner 1993:204). Capernaum has already been mentioned as Jesus' hometown in 4:13 (cf. 9:1; 17:24). It will later be excoriated by Jesus for its unbelief (11:23), a marked contrast to the officer's faith.

8:8 *Lord.* As in the previous case of the leper, the officer sought out Jesus and called him "Lord." He pled for his servant because he had severe pain and paralysis (8:6; cf. 4:24). Jesus immediately agreed to go to the servant and heal him but the officer then displayed his amazing faith. He acknowledged he was unworthy (cf. 3:11) for Jesus to come to his house, which may imply both a degree of perception of Jesus' Lordship and an awareness that coming to the house of a Gentile was not an acceptable Jewish practice (cf. Acts 10:28; 11:3). Having already addressed Jesus as "Lord" twice (8:6, 8), the officer compared Jesus' authority (cf. 7:29; 9:6-8) to his own position in the military chain of command.

Just say the word. He realized that only a word from Jesus was necessary (8:8; cf. 8:16). Such healing from a distance is unprecedented in Matthew at this point and was quite unusual in the ancient world.

8:10-12 *he was amazed.* Since the officer was a Gentile, his astonishing faith (cf. 9:2, 22, 29; 15:28; 21:21 and contrast "little faith" in 6:30; 8:26; 14:31; 16:8) became the occasion of an even more astonishing teaching. Matthew 15:21-28 contains a very similar story.

those who were following him. This phrase implies discipleship at some level, and it likely includes both the inner circle and the crowd that was less committed to Jesus (cf. 8:1).

many Gentiles will come from all over the world. After contrasting the Gentile officer's faith with the lack of faith shown by many Jews, Jesus spoke of the future Kingdom as a time when "many Gentiles" ("Gentiles" is not in the Gr. text but is a correct interpretation) from all over the world (cf. Ps 107:3; Isa 2:2-3) would sit with Abraham and the patriarchs, enjoying the great eschatological feast (cf. Isa 25:6-9; Matt 22:1-14; 25:10; Luke 14:15-16; Rev 19:9), while many Israelites would be excluded. Thus, the officer became a forerunner or harbinger of future Gentile salvation, a theme related to Matthew's stress on the universal mission of the church (28:20).

The presence of many Gentiles at the feast signals a reversal in which many Israelites, "those for whom the Kingdom was prepared" (NLT; lit. "the sons of the Kingdom"; cf. the metaphor in 9:15; 23:15), will not experience its glories. Instead of being the privileged companions of the patriarchs at a banquet where they would sink their teeth into a sumptuous meal, they will be thrown into a horrible place of darkness (the opposite of Christ's light in 4:16; cf. 22:13; 25:30), where they will grind their teeth in pain (cf. 13:42, 50; 22:13; 24:51; 25:30). This frightening imagery achieves for the reader one of the most sobering moments of Matthew's story of Jesus and his teaching. Yet one must note that Matthew's reversal and "universalism" must be qualified by the word "many," which describes both the included Gentiles and the excluded Jews. The reversal is not as "absolute" as some indicate (e.g., Hagner 1993:206). For the inclusion of Gentiles in God's plan, see also 1:1, 3-5; 2:1-12; 3:9-10; 4:15-16; 15:21-28. For the exclusion of unbelieving Jews, see 3:9-10; 21:43.

8:13 *Jesus said to the Roman officer.* Jesus turned from addressing his evidently stunned followers to the officer whose shocking faith led to the shocking teaching of 8:10-12. He told the man to go home since, lit., "Because you believed, it has happened" (cf. 9:29; 15:28). At that time his servant was healed, not by touch as in the case of the leper, but from a distance. The precise timing and the distance are noted to underline the supernatural authority of Jesus.

8:14-15 The third and final healing story in Matthew's first set is the shortest. It involves Peter's mother-in-law (cf. 1 Cor 9:5), who was *sick in bed with a high fever* at Peter's house (cf. Mark 1:29-31; Luke 4:38-39). It is possible that excavations in Capernaum have uncovered the foundations of this very house (Davies and Allison 1991:33-34). The leper took the initiative for his own cleansing, the centurion took the initiative for his servant's healing, but here the initiative is solely that of Jesus.

Jesus touched her hand. As in the case of the leper, this healing involved touch (cf. 9:29; 20:34). Again, the authority of Jesus is underlined, this time by the immediacy and totality of the healing. As soon as Jesus touched her, the woman got up and started serving Jesus. The NLT's "prepared a meal" is plausible, but the Gr. text is not that specific. This brief story is clearly chiastic in structure (Hagner 1993:209), with the touch of Jesus transforming the situation from one in which he served her to one in which she served him:

Jesus sees Peter's mother-in-law
  She is sick in bed
    with a fever
      Jesus touches her
    The fever stops
  She gets up
She serves Jesus

8:16-17 The leper was healed somewhere on the journey between the mountain and Capernaum, the officer's servant upon arrival in Capernaum, and Peter's mother-in-law in Peter's house. Evidently this string of healings encouraged the residents of the area to bring many other sick and demon-possessed people to Jesus later that evening (cf. Mark 1:32-34; Luke 4:40-41).

with a simple command. The exorcism of the evil spirits was lit. "by a word" (cf. 8:8), which again shows the authority of Jesus.

he healed all the sick. Jesus' authority is further stressed by the statement that he healed "all" who were ill. This summary statement (cf. 4:23-24; 9:35) leads into another OT fulfillment formula in 8:17, which cites Isa 53:4.

He took our sicknesses and removed our diseases. Isaiah 53, a passage rich in messianic significance, describes the servant (Isa 52:13; 53:11) as a despised person who bears the sins (Isa 53:4-6, 8, 11-12) of others without complaint (Isa 53:7). The words used by Matthew in 8:17 are evidently his own translation of Isa 53:4 (he also alludes to Isa 53 in 26:28; 27:12, 38). The words usually refer to literal illness and pain but can also serve as metaphors for sin. Matthew obviously took them in the physical sense here. See the commentary below for further discussion of the matter of healing in the atonement.

COMMENTARY

As previously discussed (see the commentary on 7:28-29), Matthew presents the authoritative words of Jesus in chapters 5-7 and the authoritative works of Jesus in chapters 8-9. This prepares the reader for the mission of the disciples, who are commissioned in chapter 10 for a similar ministry of word and works. Thus, in chapter 8, Matthew begins a selected and representative list of Jesus' miracles in order to demonstrate his authority (8:9; 9:6-8). Jesus' miracles have already been generally noted (4:23-24) and will be summarized again (8:16; 9:35). Matthew's tendency toward topical arrangement and the location of the parallel passages in Mark and Luke make it likely that some of these events actually occurred before the Sermon on the Mount.

The stories included in Matthew 8-9 are not presented in a random fashion but in a clear pattern. It appears that Matthew in 8:2-9:17 has interwoven three sets of three miracle stories with two sets of two discipleship stories. This is followed by a pericope stressing the need for messengers of the Kingdom (9:35-38). All in all, the emphasis is on faith, following Jesus in discipleship, and mission to the Gentiles. As Davies and Allison explain (1991:1-2), some have stressed that there are actually ten miracles in this section (8:18-26 contains two miracles), and have concluded that Matthew intended a comparison between Jesus' miracles and Moses' ten plagues on Egypt. But the arguments for this are unconvincing. Yet the structure of three cycles, each containing alternating stories about miracles and discipleship, remains, as the following analysis shows:

1a. Miracles (8:1-17): Three healing miracles

1b. Discipleship (8:18-22): Two would-be disciples confronted

2a. Miracles (8:23-9:8): Three miracles (storm, demons, paralytic)

2b. Discipleship (9:9-17): Association with sinners, newness

3a. Miracles (9:18-34): Three miracles (daughter/woman, blind men, demons)

3b. Summary/transition (9:35-38): Plentiful harvest yet few workers

The three miracle stories that comprise Matthew's first set are about a leper (8:1-4), a Roman centurion (8:5-13), and a woman (8:14-17). It is interesting that the first and third stories are both about Jewish people and both conclude with Scripture citations (Lev 13:49; 14:2 in 8:4 and Isa 53:4 in 8:17). Although the second story does not contain a Scripture citation, it is nevertheless the featured story in this set because (1) it is given more space than the other two; (2) it stresses the key theme of Matthew 5-9, the authority of Jesus (8:9); and (3) it emphasizes the faith of a Gentile (8:10-12), another key Matthean motif.

Jesus and the Outsiders. Why did Matthew select—from the many stories about healing evidently available to him—these three stories about a leper, a Gentile, and a woman? It is very likely that the selection was made to show Jesus as a friend to those who were powerless in Jewish society. The leper was ceremonially impure and would thus have been an outcast from all Jewish social and religious functions. The Roman officer would have had military power over the Jews, whose land his empire occupied, but due to his ethnicity, he would have had no religious clout whatsoever in Judaism. Peter's mother-in-law would have no ceremonial or ethnic handicaps, but her sex would preclude her from many privileges available only to males. None of the three would have been able to be admitted to the "court of Israel" in the Temple, where Jewish males presented their offerings to the priests (Bruner 1987:307-308). Nevertheless, it is these people, who for various reasons were at the margins of society, whose healing stories Matthew tells. Matthew does not feature stories about the social elite of his day but stories about those who lacked status. Why is that?

Matthew was consistently interested in those who were "down and out" because he knew they had been surprisingly open to the message of the Kingdom. From the tawdry women in Jesus' genealogy (ch 1), to the appearance of the bizarre astrologers (ch 2), to those healed in Matthew 8, and on and on throughout this Gospel, Matthew frequently shows his readers not only that Jesus will save his people from their sins but also that his people are amazingly diverse. Matthew's community was most likely made up of Christian Jews (See "Occasion of Writing and Audience" in the Introduction), and it was crucial for them to acknowledge their mission to disciple not only their own nation (10:5-6), but all the nations (24:14;

28:19). Matthew therefore presented Jesus not only as the Messiah of all nations but also as the model for ministry that brings the Messiah to all the nations. Jesus' disciples in Matthew's community must go beyond their understandable but mistaken scruples in the areas of ritual purity, ethnic exclusivity, and sexual stereotypes. And so must any Christian community today examine its own myopia in comparable areas. Whatever one's culturally driven views of illnesses, ethnicity, and sex, one must submit to the Master's model and love outsiders as he did (Bruner 1987:308; Keener 2000:364).

Healing and the Atonement. The use of Isaiah 53:4 in Matthew 8:17 has occasioned much debate over the relationship of Jesus' ministry and death to physical healing. It is helpful to note that pain, illness, and death are rooted in sin (Gen 3), and that redemption from sin will ultimately result in the redemption of the body (Rom 8:23) and the end of pain (Rev 21:4). Matthew saw the healings and exorcisms performed by Jesus as indications of the presence of the Kingdom, the first few raindrops before the full outpouring of that future reality (11:2-6; 12:28-29). Therefore, Matthew connected Jesus' healing of physical illnesses to his substitutionary death, as well as to his ministry of healing (20:28; 26:28). In connection with the Kingdom message, the healings are tokens of the ultimate eschatological results of Jesus' redemption. While some have made far too much of this, taking it as supporting the notion that Christians need never be sick, the answer to the perennial question about whether there is healing in the atonement is "yes." But this must be qualified by pointing out that such healing is guaranteed for all only in the future aspect of the Kingdom. There are individual experiences of healing in the present age, but these do not warrant the notion that Christians can simply "name and claim" their healing on the basis that it has already been guaranteed by the atonement. Matthew 8:17 applies Isaiah 53:4 to Jesus' earthly ministry, not to his atoning death. The point of the miracles is to stress Jesus' unique authority, not the blessings he brings to his people. This is Christology, not therapy.

The role of faith in these three healings is not uniform. Faith was obviously involved in the first two healings, that of the leper and the officer's servant, though in the latter case it was not the faith of the servant but of the officer. In the third case, that of Peter's mother-in-law, there is no indication of anyone's faith precipitating the healing. Perhaps it is the leper whose words best imply an appropriate view of healing. The leper knew that Jesus *could* heal him if he *wished* to heal him. This puts omnipotence and providence side by side. There is no doubt about the former—Jesus is able. But the leper did not presume upon Jesus' sovereignty—that would be putting the Lord to the test (cf. Matt 4:7). The disciple cannot dictate that God is willing to heal but must rest in a sovereign providence that makes no mistakes (Bruner 1987:299-300). The leper was not deficient in faith and was amazingly proficient in spiritual wisdom.

◆ 2. Two would-be disciples (8:18-22)

¹⁸When Jesus saw the crowd around him, he instructed his disciples to cross to the other side of the lake.

¹⁹Then one of the teachers of religious law said to him, "Teacher, I will follow you wherever you go."

²⁰But Jesus replied, "Foxes have dens to live in, and birds have nests, but the Son of Man* has no place even to lay his head."

²¹Another of his disciples said, "Lord, first let me return home and bury my father."

²²But Jesus told him, "Follow me now. Let the spiritually dead bury their own dead.*"

8:20 "Son of Man" is a title Jesus used for himself.   8:22 Greek *Let the dead bury their own dead.*

NOTES

8:18-20 Two interviews with would-be disciples (8:18-20 and 8:21-22; cf. Luke 9:57-62) now occur between the first (8:1-17) and second (8:23–9:8) sets of three miracle stories. These two interviews illustrate the nature of Jesus' ministry and show by contrast what type of disciples he was seeking (see 6:33).

the other side of the lake. In view of the ever-increasing press of the crowd at Capernaum, Jesus commanded the disciples to go to the other side of the Sea of Galilee (8:18), which required a boat trip. This command is important in the ensuing narrative, since it places the interviews with the would-be disciples in the context of the account of the stilling of the storm, which encourages the reader to view the historical storm also as a metaphor of discipleship (Bornkamm 1963:52-57). Matthew's narrative itself implies the reader should understand 8:18 as a call to discipleship, not just as a command to get away from the crowd by taking a boat across the lake.

one of the teachers of religious law. Lit., "one of the scribes." He addressed Jesus as teacher and promised to follow him wherever he might go (8:19). Thus far in Matthew, the scribes have not been presented positively (2:4; 5:20; 23:13, 15, 23, 25, 27, 29; but see 13:52; 23:2-3, 36), and in Matthew those who call Jesus "teacher" are not disciples (12:38; 19:16; 22:16, 24, 36). The scribe's promise was evidently made solely on his own initiative, and Jesus took a dim view of it.

the Son of Man has no place even to lay his head. Jesus starkly alluded to his itinerant form of ministry, which left him with not even a place to sleep. Even the animals have that (cf. 6:26). Matthew's readers can only conclude that the scribe's enthusiasm was superficial and that he had not counted the cost of discipleship. Perhaps his enthusiasm was due to witnessing the many miracles Jesus was performing. Be that as it may, his promise was hasty and unreliable.

It is important to note that 8:20 is the first time the Christological title "Son of Man" occurs in Matthew. Here it stands in place of the pronoun "I." This much debated title, derived from Dan 7:13-14, stresses the exaltation of Jesus (cf. 9:6; 19:28; 25:31; 26:64). Here it describes a strange situation: even though Jesus is the exalted miracle-working Messiah, he is a homeless itinerant preacher, deprived of basic creature comforts. When he stays in a house, it is someone else's, like Peter's in this context. (For additional discussion of the "Son of Man," see "Christology" in the Major Features section of the Introduction, and the convenient summaries in Davies and Allison 1991:43-53; Hagner 1993:214-215.)

8:21-22 *Lord, first let me return home and bury my father.* A second individual made an excuse for not immediately following Jesus (cf. 1 Kgs 19:19-21). Matthew's use of the phrase "another of his disciples" in 8:21 shows that both the scribe in 8:20 and the person who was concerned about his father here were followers of Jesus in some sense of the word. Matthew used the term "disciple" approximately 75 times and the precise nuance of the term must be picked up in each context (cf. Wilkins 1988). This second individual purported to have a family situation that took priority over following Jesus—namely, his father's funeral. Some scholars think that such Jewish customs as extended mourning or eventual secondary burial of the deceased's bones in an ossuary are implied here (cf. the possibilities in Davies and Allison 1991:56-58). But such conjectures must not be allowed to soften the harshness of Jesus' words. Jesus will have none of the excuse.

Let the dead bury their own dead (NLT mg). Though there may be hyperbole here (cf. 5:29-30), Jesus demanded immediate loyalty to the Kingdom ministry and stated that those who were not loyal to the Kingdom could care for the burial. The NLT's "spiritually dead" attempts to clarify Jesus' pun that the dead can bury their own dead. These "dead" people who would bury the would-be disciple's father were dead to the Kingdom, not alive to its unique eschatological demands that supersede even one's duty to one's parents. This would-be disciple seems to have had the opposite problem of the scribe in 8:18-20. That scribe's superficial enthusiasm is a foil to this would-be disciple's excessive caution.

COMMENTARY

The two individuals who spoke to Jesus about discipleship in 8:18-22 illustrate opposite problems. The first (8:18-20) was carried away with emotional enthusiasm but had not fully considered the sacrifice involved in an itinerant ministry. Perhaps his mind was on all the miracles Jesus had been performing and he wanted to continue to experience these glorious events. But there will be miracle workers who are not acknowledged by Jesus as his own at the final judgment (7:21-23), and true disciples must be willing to be deprived of life's basic necessities.

The second individual evidently had a more realistic understanding of the sacrifice entailed in Jesus' ministry. He wanted to postpone following Jesus until he could bury his father, an excuse that seems legitimate in view of Genesis 50:5, Exodus 20:12, and Deuteronomy 5:16. Jesus himself, in the context of debunking the traditions of the Pharisees, reaffirmed the Torah on the necessity of honoring one's parents (15:4-6). But, harsh as it may seem, Jesus taught that the demands of his Kingdom revise one's notions of family (cf. 10:37; 12:46-50).

Neither individual was the stuff of which a faithful disciple is made. The first's enthusiasm was due to his ignorance of the cost of discipleship, and the second's timidity was due to his awareness of that cost. Jesus needs people who have counted the cost of discipleship, people whose faith is tempered with a realistic understanding of the deprivations that may come to the one who follows Jesus (cf. 10:34-39; 16:24-25; 19:29; 20:26-27). We hope that both these individuals were prompted by these rebukes to examine themselves and later to follow Jesus. But the silence of Matthew's narrative is sobering.

◆   3. A storm tests the disciples' faith (8:23-27)

23Then Jesus got into the boat and started across the lake with his disciples. 24Suddenly, a fierce storm struck the lake, with waves breaking into the boat. But Jesus was sleeping. 25The disciples went and woke him up, shouting, "Lord, save us! We're going to drown!"

26Jesus responded, "Why are you afraid?

You have so little faith!" Then he got up
and rebuked the wind and waves, and
suddenly there was a great calm.

²⁷The disciples were amazed. "Who is
this man?" they asked. "Even the winds
and waves obey him!"

NOTES

8:23 into the boat . . . with his disciples. Lit. "his disciples followed him." The NLT does
not translate the word "follow," which obscures a theologically significant detail—the
disciples followed Jesus' initiative in getting into the boat. This is another indication that
this nature miracle is also a test of discipleship.

8:24-25 a fierce storm. Matthew uses the Gr. word *seismos* [TG4578, ZG4939] to describe the
storm. This is an unusual nuance for a word that generally refers to the shaking of earthquakes (cf. 24:7; 27:51).

Jesus was sleeping. Perhaps his sleep has implications of trusting in God's protection (Ps
3:5-6; Prov 3:24-26), or perhaps the reader is to recall OT texts in which it seemed that during trials God had gone to sleep and forgotten Israel (Pss 35:23; 44:23-24; 59:5; Isa 51:9).

The disciples went and woke him up, shouting. The disciples frantically went to him and
pled for deliverance from imminent death by drowning (cf. 14:30). The force of this storm
must have been significantly strong since it terrified even the four disciples who were commercial fishermen, used to the weather on the Sea of Galilee (cf. 4:18-22).

8:26 You have so little faith! Instead of immediately responding to their plea for deliverance from the storm, as would be expected, Jesus first rebuked them for their lack of faith
(cf. 14:31).

rebuked the wind and waves. The sudden squall was over as quickly as it began. This calming of the storm by Jesus is reminiscent of God's actions in the OT (Pss 65:7; 89:8-9;
107:23-32; Isa 51:9-10; Jonah 1:1-16). Jesus' "rebuke" of the wind and waves is striking in
that these supposedly "natural" forces were personified and spoken to in language used at
times in exorcisms (cf. 17:18). This may imply that this "nature" miracle was actually a victory over evil supernatural forces.

8:27 The disciples were amazed. The theme of amazement recalls 7:28 and anticipates
9:8, 33; 12:23 (cf. 21:20). Jesus' authority over nature produced the same result with the
disciples as his authoritative teaching had with the crowd.

Who is this man? More lit., "what sort of man is this?" This causes the attentive reader's
mind to wander back to Matthew 1–4, where Jesus' unique birth, early experiences, baptism, and temptation all imply his uniqueness among human beings. Due to the work of
the narrator, the reader knows more about this than the disciples do.

COMMENTARY

The story of the calming of the storm (cf. Mark 4:35-41; Luke 8:22-25) begins the
second set of three miracle stories (8:23-27, 28-34; 9:1-6). Matthew's previous
narrative has shown Jesus' authority over sin, disease, and demons, but here he
demonstrates Jesus' authority over nature. It also appears, from the way Matthew
tells the story, that the nature miracle is intended to teach about discipleship.
Davies and Allison (1991:68) point out a chiastic structure that places the key
interaction between Jesus and the disciples in 8:25-26 at the center of the
pericope. Jesus planned to go to the other side of the Sea of Galilee (8:18). Two
would-be disciples apparently delayed the voyage, but their interviews with Jesus

teach the reader important lessons about following Jesus. As soon as the voyage commences, the storm erupts and the disciples' "little faith" (cf. 6:30; 14:31; 16:8) is tested. It is genuine faith, but it is limited in its awareness of the power of Jesus. After the challenge of the storm, and the rebuke of Jesus, their faith was ostensibly strengthened. The most critical concern of Jesus' disciples is not the potential persecutions or disasters they might face. Rather, it is the quality of their faith, which is directly proportionate to the accuracy of their perception of Jesus, the object of their faith. On this point, it is instructive to recall 8:26, where in the middle of a disaster in process, as the boat is about to go under, Jesus addresses the disciples' weak faith before he rebukes the storm. This indicates that the first priority of both ancient and modern disciples must be to focus on the power of Jesus, not the power of life's "storms," which sometimes threaten to overcome them. It may seem that Jesus is "asleep," unaware of their difficulties, but he is able to handle the difficulties easily, as his disciples maintain their faith in him. They must realize that Jesus, the object of their faith, is able to get them to "the other side of the lake."

Blomberg (1992:150) makes the valid point that this pericope is more about Christology than discipleship, but Matthew would not bifurcate the two. The inter-relationship between Christology and discipleship is especially apparent in 8:25, where the disciples do indeed call Jesus "Lord" in the face of imminent death by drowning, but evidently do not have a strong grasp on the authority implied by that title. The Old Testament texts cited in the note on 8:26 show that Matthew is not the first to use storms on the sea as metaphors for life's perils. Matthew's teaching is that disciples must trust in the potency of Jesus in order to overcome anemic faith. Unless they are saved from little faith, they will indeed perish. One need not go so far as to allegorize the boat as symbolizing the Church (as did Tertullian in *On Baptism 12*) *to come to this conclusion.*

◆   ## 4. Jesus exorcises demons (8:28-34)

28When Jesus arrived on the other side of the lake, in the region of the Gadarenes,* two men who were possessed by demons met him. They lived in a cemetery and were so violent that no one could go through that area.

29They began screaming at him, "Why are you interfering with us, Son of God? Have you come here to torture us before God's appointed time?"

30There happened to be a large herd of pigs feeding in the distance. 31So the demons begged, "If you cast us out, send us into that herd of pigs."

32"All right, go!" Jesus commanded them. So the demons came out of the men and entered the pigs, and the whole herd plunged down the steep hillside into the lake and drowned in the water.

33The herdsmen fled to the nearby town, telling everyone what happened to the demon-possessed men. 34Then the entire town came out to meet Jesus, but they begged him to go away and leave them alone.

8:28 Other manuscripts read *Gerasenes;* still others read *Gergesenes.* Compare Mark 5:1; Luke 8:26.

NOTES

8:28-29 *arrived on the other side of the lake, in the region of the Gadarenes.* The group evidently crossed the Sea of Galilee from Capernaum on the northwest to some locale on the eastern shore. The town of Gadara was five or six miles from the Sea of Galilee, but according to Josephus (*Life* 9.42), the region of Gadara was adjacent to the sea. See Blomberg (1987:149-50) for discussion of the geographical and textual questions (some manuscripts read "Gerasenes" [TG1046A, ZG1170] and others read "Gergesenes" [TG1086, ZG1171]), which arise from a comparison of Matt 8:28 with Mark 5:1 and Luke 8:26.

Have you come here to torture us before God's appointed time? The demons wondered whether Jesus had come to torture (cf. Rev 14:10; 20:10) them prematurely, before the appointed time of judgment (cf. 13:30; 16:3). Their awareness of Jesus' identity as the Son of God, a key Matthean theme (1:23; 2:15; 3:17; 4:3, 6; 14:33; 16:16; 17:5; 27:54; cf. Jas 2:19), and of the future judgment of demons (25:41; cf. 1 Cor 4:5) is striking. Their question points up Matthew's "inaugurated" eschatology, in which the future reign of God is already encroaching on Satan's domain, even now (cf. 12:28).

8:30-32 *the demons came out of the men and entered the pigs.* The presence of a large herd of pigs nearby provided a way for the demons to escape Jesus' presence. The demons themselves spoke, requesting to be sent into the pigs if Jesus cast them out of the men (cf. 12:43-45). It may be that the reader is to think of the pigs and the previous cemetery residence as ritually unclean for Jews. It is striking that the demoniacs have thus far done all the talking in this pericope, and that Jesus' reply is only one word, "Go!" (NLT's "all right" is based on the contextual notion of permission). Jesus granted them this wish, and they entered the pigs, precipitating a stampede of the entire herd down a steep hillside into the lake, where all the pigs were drowned. This dramatic result from a single word of Jesus underscores his authority. This authority, although genuine, is not yet exercised as universal, since Jesus freed the two men but permitted the demons to destroy the pigs and presumably to continue their devious activities elsewhere before their ultimate judgment. The herding of pigs (cf. Luke 15:15) and the eating of pork were of course forbidden to Jews (Lev 11:7; Deut 14:8; Isa 65:4; 66:3, 17; 1 Macc 1:47; 2 Macc 6:18-23; *m. Bava Qamma* 7:7). Evidently the reader is to think of Gadara as Gentile or mixed race territory, since it is east of the Sea of Galilee and supports pig herding. One wonders whether the demoniacs were Gentiles, since the mission to the Gentiles had not yet begun (10:5-6, 18), but this was a chance encounter, not a sustained mission.

8:33-34 *the entire town came out to meet Jesus.* The result of the exorcism was that those who herded the pigs observed their watery demise and spread the news to the people of the nearby town, who came to Jesus en masse to ask him to go away. Their reasoning is not made clear, but it is plausible that this region was populated by Gentiles whose livelihood depended upon the drowned pigs. If so, economics was more important to these people than the freeing of the demoniacs from Satan's dominion. Matthew's Christian Jewish readers would probably take the opposite view, that the destruction of a herd of unclean pigs was appropriate and even humorous. At any rate, this negative response to a miracle is quite a contrast to the responses to Jesus' miracles preciously narrated by Matthew.

COMMENTARY

The story of the exorcism in the land of the Gadarenes (8:28-34; cf. Mark 5:1-20; Luke 8:26-39) is the second miracle story in the second set of three such stories in Matthew 8–9 (see the commentary on 8:1-17. Matthew 9 will conclude the second set with the story of the healing of the paralytic (9:1-8).

Demon possession appears frequently in Matthew (4:24; 7:22; 8:16, 28, 31, 33;

9:32-34; 10:8; 11:18; 12:22, 24, 27, 28; 15:22; 17:18), but the details of this particular incident are remarkable. Previously, Jesus had cast out demons, and he had just calmed a storm, but here his single word, "go," demonstrates his authority over demons, animals, and the Sea of Galilee. The authority of Jesus' words (7:28-29) and deeds (8:9; 9:6) is thus a key point of this story, as it is in all of Matthew 8-9. But this episode shows that the authority of Jesus operates alongside his mercy (Davies and Allison 1991:116). Jesus treated these dangerous demoniacs with the same compassion that has been implicit in his ministry since 4:23 and that will become explicit in 9:36 as a model for his disciples' own mission in chapter 10.

Evidently, the country of the Gadarenes was Gentile country. The rejection of Jesus by the inhabitants may parallel 10:13-15, in which the disciples are warned that their mission trip will also result in rejection in some households and villages. The rejection of Jesus is exemplary for his disciples, who should not view themselves as above their Master. Rather, they must face rejection and persecution realistically, with faith instead of fear (10:24-33). All who minister for Jesus need to be reminded that, at times, their best intentions for unbelievers will be received in a negative way (cf. 7:6). Those who do not know Jesus often make it clear that they do not want to know about Jesus. But people who reject his authority exclude themselves from his mercy. Carson's wry comment (1984:219) about the Gadarenes puts it well: "They preferred pigs to persons, swine to the Savior." But the grace of God can still turn those who reject Jesus into his followers when the gospel is faithfully proclaimed in the words and deeds of Christians.

◆   ## 5. Jesus heals a paralyzed man (9:1-8; cf. Mark 2:1-12; Luke 5:17-26)

Jesus climbed into a boat and went back across the lake to his own town. ²Some people brought to him a paralyzed man on a mat. Seeing their faith, Jesus said to the paralyzed man, "Be encouraged, my child! Your sins are forgiven."

³But some of the teachers of religious law said to themselves, "That's blasphemy! Does he think he's God?"

⁴Jesus knew* what they were thinking, so he asked them, "Why do you have such evil thoughts in your hearts? ⁵Is it easier to say 'Your sins are forgiven,' or 'Stand up and walk'? ⁶So I will prove to you that the Son of Man* has the authority on earth to forgive sins." Then Jesus turned to the paralyzed man and said, "Stand up, pick up your mat, and go home!"

⁷And the man jumped up and went home! ⁸Fear swept through the crowd as they saw this happen. And they praised God for sending a man with such great authority.*

9:4 Some manuscripts read *saw.* 9:6 "Son of Man" is a title Jesus used for himself. 9:8 Greek *for giving such authority to human beings.*

NOTES

9:2 *Be encouraged, my child. Your sins are forgiven!* His encouraging words to the paralyzed man and his tender reference to him as "my child" (cf. 9:22) again show that Jesus' authority was exercised with compassion. The forgiveness of sins reminds the attentive reader of the prediction of 1:21 that Jesus would save his people from their sins (cf. 3:6; 6:12; 9:13; 11:19; 12:31; 26:28).

9:3 *blasphemy! Does he think he's God?* The teachers of religious law thought Jesus had blasphemed (cf. 26:65; John 10:33). Ironically, it was not Jesus who was blaspheming, but the scribes themselves, who ascribed his miracles to Satan (cf. 9:34; 12:24, 31; 26:65). The NLT's "Does he think he's God?" is not in the Gr. text but brings out the implications of Jesus' forgiving the man's sins. Blasphemy amounts to the slander of God by reviling his name or by pretending to do what he alone can do. The forgiveness Jesus granted the paralyzed man was not pretend, but the teachers' words slandered the Son of God.

9:4-5 *Jesus knew what they were thinking.* Jesus' knowledge of the teachers' thoughts (cf. 12:25; 22:18) should be attributed to the ministry of the Holy Spirit in his life, not simply to his divinity (3:16; 4:1; 12:28; cf. 10:20).

Why do you have such evil thoughts? In light of this knowledge, Jesus asked them why they thought evil of him and then posed a second question, aimed at the root of their evil thoughts (9:4-5). Evidently the teachers thought Jesus spoke of sin being forgiven because it was easier to pronounce forgiveness than to heal paralysis. Indeed, it is easier, so Jesus told them that the imminent healing would demonstrate his authority to forgive sins.

9:6 *So I will prove.* Lit., "in order that you may know." The man's immediate healing and departure (9:7) underlines the central point of Matt 9–10: Jesus' works confirm Jesus' authority as the Son of Man (cf. 8:20; Dan 7:13-14) to forgive sins. Both his teaching and his miracles demonstrate the authority of God's rule on earth.

9:7-8 From 9:3 the reader knows that one result of this incident is the opposition of the teachers of religious law. But here two additional results are explained: the paralytic's healing and the crowd's reaction. First we see the paralyzed man get up, pick up the mat he was lying on, and go home (9:7). Then, though there is no comment on Jesus' emotions in this account, the crowd's emotions are described. The miracle caused a reverential fear in them (cf. 14:30; 17:6; 27:54), and they praised God for giving such authority to humans.

for sending a man with such great authority. The reading in the NLT mg is more helpful—"for giving such authority to human beings." The use of the plural here is either a reference to the idea that the authority given to Jesus benefits mankind or that the authority has been given to Jesus and his disciples (cf. 16:19; 18:19).

COMMENTARY

Matthew 9:1-8 completes the second set of three miracle stories with the account of the healing of a paralyzed man. Thus, the three miracle stories of Matthew 8:23-9:8 correspond to 8:1-17, and the second pair of discipleship stories in Matthew 9:9-17 answers to 8:18-22. Rejected in a Gentile area (Gadara), Jesus traveled "back across the lake to his own town" (Capernaum, not Nazareth; cf. 4:13; 8:14), where he healed a paralyzed man (cf. 4:24; 8:6). Comparison of this account with the synoptic parallels (cf. Mark 2:1-12; Luke 5:17-26) shows that Matthew probably placed this story here for topical rather than chronological reasons.

The pericope on the healing of the paralytic (9:1-8) occurs after a return to Capernaum (9:1), where Jesus intentionally stressed his authority to forgive sins (9:2). This occasioned the charge of blasphemy from the scribes who were present (9:3). Jesus read their thoughts—they were thinking he vainly pronounced forgiveness because he was unable to heal (9:4-5). In response, Jesus healed the man to demonstrate his authority to forgive (9:6-7), and the crowd marveled at his authority and glorified God (9:8).

The healing of the paralyzed man extends the authority of Jesus to its most crucial aspect, the forgiveness of sins. Readers of Matthew have already seen how Jesus taught with authority in the Sermon on the Mount (7:28-29) and have become aware of his authoritative acts of healing, even from a distance (8:9). But authority over the forgiveness of sins is much greater than authoritative words and actions. Authority to forgive sins gets to the root of the problems and illnesses that are the symptoms of sin. One can teach against sin, but this does not cause the sin to stop, let alone secure its forgiveness. One can heal sick people, but sooner or later they will get sick again, and ultimately they will die. Jesus' authority in these domains, as great as it is, pales in comparison to his authority to forgive the sins that are the root of all the other problems. Such authority is at the heart of Jesus' mission to save his people from their sins (1:21) by giving his life as a ransom for them (20:28), thereby inaugurating the new covenant (26:28; cf. Jer 31:31). As God's beloved Son, Jesus acts with divine prerogative. He does not blaspheme; he saves.

The relation of sin and sickness is a complex matter. Humans do not have the requisite insight to diagnose whether sin is the cause of sickness in individual cases (Job; Luke 13:1-5; John 9:2-3; Jas 5:15; but cf. Paul's apostolic insight in 1 Cor 11:30). Yet it is possible that Jesus, through the Spirit, knew that this man's illness was due to sin (Bruner 1987:329-330). And it is also possible that his illness was psychosomatic, and that the forgiveness of his sins freed his mind of guilt and thereby healed him (Barclay 1975:1.327-328). However, Matthew does not focus on the reason for the man's paralysis but on the authority of Jesus to forgive his sins. In the present age, the righteous may suffer many physical maladies. But in redemptive history, human sickness and death are ultimately the results of human sin (Gen 3). Human beings find themselves caught in the maelstrom of sickness and death because of the rebellion of the first Adam. But through the obedience of the second Adam, the new humanity can find immediate release from sin's bondage and ultimate physical healing as well (cf. Ps 103:3 and the comments on 8:17). Jesus' healings are a sign that the ultimate defeat of sin and Satan has begun.

It is significant that Matthew's portrayal of Jesus' response to the Jewish teachers here is not conciliatory but confrontational. The accusation of blasphemy contradicts Jesus' unique standing as the Son of God, and no gentle compromise is possible in this case. This confrontation signals that Matthew has begun to touch on the theme of opposition, which escalates as his story continues.

◆   ## 6. Jesus calls Matthew (9:9-13; cf. Mark 2:13-17; Luke 5:27-32)

[9]As Jesus was walking along, he saw a man named Matthew sitting at his tax collector's booth. "Follow me and be my disciple," Jesus said to him. So Matthew got up and followed him.

[10]Later, Matthew invited Jesus and his disciples to his home as dinner guests, along with many tax collectors and other disreputable sinners. [11]But when the Pharisees saw this, they asked his disciples, "Why does your teacher eat with such scum?*"

[12]When Jesus heard this, he said, "Healthy people don't need a doctor—sick

people do." ¹³Then he added, "Now go and
learn the meaning of this Scripture: 'I
want you to show mercy, not offer sacri-

fices.'* For I have come to call not those
who think they are righteous, but those
who know they are sinners."

9:11 Greek *with tax collectors and sinners?*   9:13 Hos 6:6 (Greek version).

NOTES

9:9 *a man named Matthew sitting at his tax collector's booth.* Somewhere near Capernaum Jesus encountered Matthew working at a tax collector's booth (cf. 5:46; 10:3). Matthew
was called Levi in Mark and Luke. The collector's booth may have been near the Sea of Galilee, where Matthew would have collected taxes on fishermen or duties on goods brought
into Antipas's domain by boat. The call of Matthew to follow Jesus recalls the previous call
of four other disciples in 4:18-22 and anticipates the list of the Twelve in 10:1-4. One
wonders whether there was any contact between Matthew and Jesus before the call, but as
in 4:18-22, Jesus took the initiative, and Matthew responded immediately, without question.

Follow me and be my disciple. Although the words "and be my disciple" are not in the Gr.
text, it makes explicit what is entailed in following Jesus. (Following Jesus is mentioned in
4:19-25; 8:1, 10, 19, 22; 9:9, 27; 12:15; 14:13; 16:24; 19:2, 21, 27-28; 20:29, 34; 21:9;
26:58; 27:55.)

9:10-11 *Later, Matthew invited Jesus and his disciples to his home as dinner guests.* The
length of time between Matthew's call and the dinner mentioned here is not specified in
the text, but it was likely a short time span. The NLT's translation of 9:10 expresses the
likely view that Matthew invited Jesus and the disciples to a dinner at his house (cf. Luke
5:29), but the Gr. text is not explicit on this matter.

many tax collectors and other disreputable sinners. The NLT's somewhat redundant "disreputable" is not in the Gr. text, though it gives the right connotation. Undoubtedly, these
were Matthew's friends and colleagues, who were invited to the dinner along with Jesus
and his disciples (cf. 11:19; 21:31-32). Tax collectors would likely be unacceptable to the
Pharisees due not only to their deserved reputation for extortion (cf. Luke 3:12-13) but also
to their frequent associations with Gentiles. The term "sinners" (9:11, 13; 11:19; 26:45; cf.
Mark 2:14-22; Luke 5:27-32) designates those whose behavior was egregiously ungodly,
but from the Pharisaic perspective it may also include those who did not observe the traditional interpretations of the Bible (15:2) on such matters as ritual purity, food laws, and
Sabbath observance. The Pharisees would not attend such a dinner as this, and they were
offended that Jesus and his disciples did attend. Fellowship around a table was taken seriously in Jesus' time, as being an act that implies deeper unity than is currently attributed to
it in the West. His participation in table fellowship probably should be viewed as a fore-
taste of eschatological festivities (8:11; 22:1-14; 25:1-13; 26:29).

Why does your teacher eat with such scum? The phrase "such scum" interprets the tone of
the question, which lit. repeats the same terms used in 9:10, "tax collectors and sinners."

9:12-13 *Healthy people don't need a doctor—sick people do.* Jesus' answer depends upon
a cultural association of sin with disease, which is involved in some way in 8:16-17; 9:1-8.
Metaphorically and proverbially speaking, the sinners with whom he associated were "ill"
and needed a "physician."

I want you to show mercy, not offer sacrifices. This is an allusion to Hos 6:6, a prophetic
critique of the mentality that prioritized the performance of religious ritual over the maintenance of personal integrity (cf. 5:7; 12:7; 1 Sam 15:22; Jer 7:22-23; Ps 40:6-8; Heb 10:4-
9). Jesus bluntly put the two as "either-or" alternatives, but it is likely this is an idiomatic
way of saying that God desires ethical loyalty more than participation in the sacrificial

system (cf. Isa 1:10-17; Jer 7). The prophets did not want to abolish the sacrificial system but to reform it by stressing inner purity over ritual purity. Jesus' final words apply the metaphorical language to the reality of his mission—the "healthy" are those who think they are righteous, like the Pharisees (whose question was really an accusation), and the "sick" are those who realize that they need Jesus' "medicine." It is to this second group that Jesus was sent, and he called them to repentance (3:2; 4:17).

COMMENTARY

The second set of three miracle stories is now complete, so once again the narrative turns to a discipleship story (9:9-13; cf. Mark 2:13-17; Luke 5:27-32). This pericope clarifies the mission of Jesus by recounting events that transpired after the call of Matthew (9:9). After being called, Matthew had a dinner party for his associates, both old and new (9:10). Certain Pharisees accusingly asked Jesus' disciples about their social companions (9:11; cf. the similar story about Zacchaeus in Luke 19:1-10). The teaching about Jesus' mission flows from this controversy (9:12-13; cf. Hos 6:6).

As the ultimate and definitive teacher of the law (5:17), Jesus exemplified the ideals of Hosea 6:6 in calling Matthew the tax collector to be his disciple and in associating with tax collectors and sinners. While the Pharisees no doubt knew this text, they did not grasp its applicability to the matter of associating with outcasts. Jesus had previously exemplified such ideals in his ministry to the leper, the Roman officer, and Peter's mother (8:1-17). His Kingdom ministry is not circumscribed by ritual impurity, ethnicity, or gender, and neither will social stigmas limit its outreach. God's primary attribute in relating to sinful humans is mercy. Thus, God's primary desire for his people is for them to show mercy, not to offer sacrifices. Matthew portrays Jesus' ministry to outcasts as epitomizing this ideal. It is not that Jesus downplays adherence to the law or the sacrificial system, but that for him, adherence to the law starts with a compassionate heart. Davies and Allison (1991:105) put it well: "cultic observance without inner faith and heart-felt covenant loyalty is vain." Certain Pharisees opposed this kind of ministry.

Matthew skillfully presented the opposition to Jesus from the religious leaders as becoming more and more pronounced. Here the Pharisees questioned Jesus indirectly through his disciples, but later (excepting 17:24) the questions of the various Jewish religious leaders will be addressed to him directly (cf. 15:1-2; 16:1; 19:3; 21:16, 23; 22:16, 23, 35). Ultimately, Jesus "turns the tables" and asks them a question they either cannot or will not answer, and this effectively ends the pattern of interrogation (22:41-46). Jesus' social interaction with notorious sinners scandalized the Pharisees of his own day, and it likewise tends to embarrass those in our day whose views of separation from worldliness stress externals rather than personal integrity. Jesus and his disciples had no qualms about associating with sinners, and Christians today dare not hide their light under a basket due to legalistic scruples. Associations with unbelievers must be handled with wisdom, so that ethical compromise is avoided, but fear of such compromise cannot become an excuse for isolation from those who most need the message of the Kingdom (5:13-16). Associating with unbelievers is the way to summon them into the Kingdom of God.

◆ ### 7. A discussion about fasting (9:14-17; cf. Mark 2:18-22; Luke 5:33-39)

¹⁴One day the disciples of John the Baptist came to Jesus and asked him, "Why don't your disciples fast* like we do and the Pharisees do?"

¹⁵Jesus replied, "Do wedding guests mourn while celebrating with the groom? Of course not. But someday the groom will be taken away from them, and then they will fast.

¹⁶"Besides, who would patch old clothing with new cloth? For the new patch would shrink and rip away from the old cloth, leaving an even bigger tear than before.

¹⁷"And no one puts new wine into old wineskins. For the old skins would burst from the pressure, spilling the wine and ruining the skins. New wine is stored in new wineskins so that both are preserved."

9:14 Some manuscripts read *fast often.*

NOTES

9:14 *Why don't your disciples fast like we do and the Pharisees do?* The question of John's disciples regarding fasting (cf. 6:16, 18; Mark 2:18-22; Luke 5:33-39) indicates that they and the Pharisees regularly fasted but that Jesus' disciples did not. The phrase "like we do" should not be interpreted as meaning that Jesus' disciples fasted in a different manner than John's disciples and the Pharisees. John's ascetic lifestyle is mentioned elsewhere in Matthew (3:4; 11:18). His disciples evidently felt that the absence of fasting was inconsistent with Jesus' avowal of loyalty to God and the law of Moses. The fasting in question here was most likely the voluntary twice-weekly fast favored by the Pharisees (cf. Luke 18:12), not the obligatory fast commanded in connection with the Day of Atonement (Num 29:7-11), which Jesus and his disciples evidently kept. *Didache* 8:1 says the Pharisees fasted specifically on Monday and Thursday and encourages Christians to fast on Wednesday and Friday (cf. 1QpHab 11:7; *Psalms of Solomon* 3:8).

9:15 *Do wedding guests mourn while celebrating with the groom?* Jesus' answer employs images from weddings (9:15; cf. 22:1-14; 25:1-13), garment mending, and wine making (9:16-17) in a metaphorical fashion. Just as it would be inappropriate for "wedding guests" (lit., "sons of the wedding hall") to fast while they are with the bridegroom, so it was inappropriate for Jesus' disciples to fast while he was with them. The arrival of the long-awaited Messiah is hardly the time to mourn or fast. Note also that in the OT (e.g., Isa 54:5-6; 62:4-5; Hos 2:16-23), God is sometimes pictured as a bridegroom, and that John the Baptist used this image to describe Jesus accordingly (John 3:29).

someday the groom will be taken away from them, and then they will fast. The mention of the groom being taken away (cf. Isa 53:8) is probably a veiled prediction of Jesus' arrest and crucifixion (cf. 12:38-40; 16:21; 17:9-13, 22-23; 20:28; 26:11).

9:16-17 *who would patch old clothing with new cloth? . . . And no one puts new wine into old wineskins.* The second part of Jesus' answer to the question of John's disciples contains two metaphors about the incompatibility of the new with the old, the first concerning patching garments (9:16) and the second concerning wine and wineskins (9:17). No one would patch an old garment with new cloth, since the new cloth would shrink when washed and the old garment would be ripped worse than before. Similarly, no one would put new wine in old wineskins, since the pressure from the fermentation process would burst the old, brittle skins (cf. Job 32:19). Rather, new wine would be put into new, flexible skins.

How do these two metaphors connect with the bridegroom metaphor of 9:15, and what is the answer to the question of John's disciples? Commentators (e.g., Blomberg 1992:159; Hagner 1993:244-245) take the point of the three metaphors to be the incompatibility of the old age, exemplified by the traditional piety of the Pharisees, with the new age, exemplified by the definitive climactic teaching of Jesus. The rule of God in Jesus' life, words, and works cannot coexist with the old ways (e.g., fasting) of Pharisaic Judaism. The weakness with this interpretation is that Jesus was answering John's disciples, not the Pharisees. The disciples were taught how to fast in 6:16-18. Also, Jesus indicates that his disciples would fast after he had gone. A different interpretive approach will be articulated in the commentary that follows.

COMMENTARY

This pericope concerning the question of John's disciples about fasting is similar to the previous pericope on associating with sinners in that in both stories Jesus' disciples did not follow the traditional practices of the Pharisees. They enjoyed table fellowship with undesirable persons and did not fast. So again the basic issue is the relationship of Jesus, his teaching, and his disciples, to Moses, his law, and his disciples (the Pharisees saw themselves in this role). While many interpreters argue that this pericope shows the fundamental incompatibility of Jesus and Moses, Israel and the Church, law and grace, this view cannot be sustained in light of Matthew 5:17-20. A more nuanced approach is needed, one that takes due note of the temporary presence of the bridegroom with the wedding guests. A wedding celebration obviously calls for a feast, not a fast. During the short time of messianic jubilation, while Jesus was with his disciples, fasting was inappropriate. But Jesus would not always be with the disciples (26:18), so the time while he was with them should be characterized by extraordinary joy and devotion. After Jesus was taken away, his disciples would fast once again.

Matthew 9:14-17 is a key text on the matter of continuity and discontinuity in biblical theology. While it has been argued above that the text does not teach a blunt supersessionism in which Jesus replaces Moses, it is clear that when the disciples fast after Jesus has been taken away, they will not go back to fasting as if he had never come. Jesus did not endorse the Pharisaic fasting traditions, but he did teach his followers how to fast (6:16-18). What did Jesus imply with the final clause of the pericope, "so that both are preserved"? Did he mean to say that the new wineskins and new wine are both preserved (Hagner 1993:244), or that the old wineskins and new wine are both preserved (Davies and Allison 1991:112, 115)? It appears, in light of 5:17-20 and Matthew's overall teaching, that the second option is best.

Jesus, as the ultimate teacher of Israel, preserved the law and prophets by fulfilling them, not by merely reiterating past teaching (which overstates continuity) or by bluntly jettisoning past teaching (which overstates discontinuity). Fasting is preserved, but in the new context of the righteousness of the inaugurated Kingdom, not in the old context of Pharisaic tradition.

◆ 8. Jesus raises a synagogue official's daughter and heals a woman (9:18-26)

[18]As Jesus was saying this, the leader of a synagogue came and knelt before him. "My daughter has just died," he said, "but you can bring her back to life again if you just come and lay your hand on her."

[19]So Jesus and his disciples got up and

went with him. ²⁰Just then a woman who had suffered for twelve years with constant bleeding came up behind him. She touched the fringe of his robe, ²¹for she thought, "If I can just touch his robe, I will be healed."

²²Jesus turned around, and when he saw her he said, "Daughter, be encouraged! Your faith has made you well." And the woman was healed at that moment.

²³When Jesus arrived at the official's home, he saw the noisy crowd and heard the funeral music. ²⁴"Get out!" he told them. "The girl isn't dead; she's only asleep." But the crowd laughed at him. ²⁵After the crowd was put outside, however, Jesus went in and took the girl by the hand, and she stood up! ²⁶The report of this miracle swept through the entire countryside.

NOTES

9:18-19 *the leader of a synagogue came and knelt before him. "My daughter has just died," he said, "but you can bring her back to life again."* As the encompassing story of the official's daughter begins, the official expresses the hope that although his daughter has just died, Jesus can nevertheless revive her. Synagogue officials are also mentioned in Mark 5:22; Luke 13:14; Acts 18:8. According to a later passage from the Talmud (*b. Pesachim* 49b), such officials were highly respected.

if you just come and lay your hand on her. This is the only healing by the laying on of hands in Matthew (but cf. 8:15). The ruler's exceptional faith in Jesus is shown not only by these words but by his worshipful posture before Jesus (cf. 2:11; 8:2; 15:25). In response, Jesus said nothing but acted by rising and following the official, accompanied by his disciples (9:19). At this point (9:20) the story of the healing of the hemorrhaging woman begins.

9:20-22 Now the encompassed story of the healing of the woman is told.

a woman who had suffered for twelve years with constant bleeding. Her problem, a twelve-year chronic hemorrhage (evidently due to a uterine disorder), led her to touch the fringe of Jesus' cloak (9:20; cf. 14:36; 23:5; the required tassels of Num 15:38-39; Deut 22:12). The thoughts that caused her action are mentioned in 9:21.

Daughter, be encouraged! Your faith has made you well. In 9:22 Jesus encouraged her (cf. 9:2; 14:27) and pointed to her faith as the means of her healing. As in the healing of the leper (8:2-4), Jesus would technically contract ritual impurity by touching this woman (Lev 15:25-27; *m. Zavim* 5:6; *Negaim* 3:1; 13:9). However, her hemorrhage immediately vanished at his touch. Possibly, she approached Jesus from behind due to her condition of ritual impurity. The Gr. word that expresses her healing in these verses is *sōzō* [TG4982, ZG5392], which may describe deliverance from physical problems (see 8:25; 14:30; 24:22; 27:40, 42, 49) as well as spiritual ones (1:21; 10:22; 16:25; 19:25). This is the most direct statement of the agency of faith in healing in Matthew. It was the power of the woman's faith, not some quasi-magical power of touching Jesus' garment, that accomplished her healing.

9:23-24 Here the encompassing story of the official's daughter resumes.

he saw the noisy crowd and heard the funeral music. Jesus arrived at the official's house to find a disorderly crowd and flute (or perhaps clarinet) players, indicating that it was believed that the girl had died. The NLT's "heard the funeral music" is a rendering of "flute players"—this renders explicit what is implicit in the text. Hired musicians were customarily included in wakes (cf. 11:17; 2 Chr 35:25; Jer 9:17; Ezek 24:17; Amos 5:16; Rev 18:22; Josephus *War* 3.437; *m. Ketubbot* 4:4; *m. Shabbat* 23:4).

9:24 *Get out! . . . The girl isn't dead; she's only asleep.* Jesus told this unruly group to leave, since the girl was merely sleeping, not dead (cf. John 11:11-14; Acts 20:9-12). Most likely Jesus' words "the girl isn't dead" did not so much deny the fact of her death as its finality; they affirmed that she would be raised from death (Davies and Allison

1991:131-132; Hagner 1993:250). In any event, biblical language cannot be pressed into the mold of modern medical precision.

the crowd laughed at him. The skeptical laughter of the crowd underlines the greatness of the miracle that Jesus was about to accomplish.

9:26 *The report of this miracle swept through the entire countryside.* The news of this miracle immediately spread throughout the area (cf. 4:24; 9:31). The simplicity and compactness of this story should not take away from the fact that raising the dead is probably the most spectacular of all Jesus' miracles (cf. 10:8; Luke 7:11-17; John 11:43-44). Jesus' raising the dead reminds the reader of similar miracles done by Elijah and Elisha (1 Kgs 17:17-24; 2 Kgs 4:17-37). Davies and Allison (1991:125) raise the intriguing question of the placement of the most spectacular miracle here instead of at the end of this section (9:34). They answer it by noting that an exorcism appears at the end in order to further the theme of the Jewish religious leaders' increasing rejection of Jesus and their attribution of his miracles to the prince of the demons (9:32-34; cf. 12:24).

COMMENTARY

The miracle of raising the synagogue official's daughter from the dead (9:18-19, 23-26) encompasses the miracle of the healing of the hemorrhaging woman (9:20-22; cf. Mark 5:21-43; Luke 8:40-56). This complex or double pericope marks the first of the third set of three miracle stories in Matthew 8-9. Both stories stress the activity of faith in initiating touch as the means of healing. In comparison with Mark and Luke, Matthew's version of the double story is highly condensed. The placement of the story of the healing of the woman in the middle of the story of the raising of the official's daughter delays the outcome of the initial story and heightens the suspense for the reader.

The two miracles in this double story address two basic issues of human existence, the depths of parental love and the pain of chronic disease (in this case resulting in social ostracism due to ritual impurity). The synagogue ruler's love for his little girl confronted the power of death when he took the initiative to plead for Jesus to touch and heal her. The power of Jesus defeated the power of death, and a family was spared the shattering effects of the loss of a child. When one keeps in mind the already/not yet conception of the Kingdom in Matthew, the raising of the little girl hints at the ultimate resurrection of the dead by the power of Jesus (cf. 27:52).

The hemorrhaging woman took the initiative to touch Jesus' garment so that she could be rid of her chronic disease and thus free of its ritual impurity and able to experience normal human social relationships again. Her condition may not have been as hopeless as that of the official's daughter, but her despair must have been deep after twelve years in which she had found no relief. The Greek verb used for her "deliverance" (*sōzō* [TG4982, ZG5392]) implies an even greater deliverance from the sin that was the root cause of the physical infirmity. (See the notes and commentary on 8:17; 9:2, 6 for further reflection on this theme.)

As touching as these human needs are, the major thrust of Matthew's narrative is Christological. Jesus is presented once again as the One whose authority on earth to forgive sins is demonstrated by his powerful deeds of compassion (9:36). This presentation continues in the next two incidents, in which Jesus heals blind and mute men.

◆   9. Jesus heals the blind and mute (9:27-34)

²⁷After Jesus left the girl's home, two blind men followed along behind him, shouting, "Son of David, have mercy on us!"

²⁸They went right into the house where he was staying, and Jesus asked them, "Do you believe I can make you see?"

"Yes, Lord," they told him, "we do."

²⁹Then he touched their eyes and said, "Because of your faith, it will happen." ³⁰Then their eyes were opened, and they could see! Jesus sternly warned them, "Don't tell anyone about this." ³¹But instead, they went out and spread his fame all over the region.

³²When they left, a demon-possessed man who couldn't speak was brought to Jesus. ³³So Jesus cast out the demon, and then the man began to speak. The crowds were amazed. "Nothing like this has ever happened in Israel!" they exclaimed.

³⁴But the Pharisees said, "He can cast out demons because he is empowered by the prince of demons."

NOTES

9:27 *Son of David.* This title implies that Jesus possesses messianic authority to heal (1:1; 12:22-23; 15:22; 20:30; cf. Mark 10:47-48; Luke 18:38-39). As Jesus moved onward toward Jerusalem, his Davidic origins become an occasion for controversy (12:3; 21:9, 15; 22:42, 45).

9:28 *They went right into the house.* The initiative of these two men was remarkable, since they followed Jesus right into a house.

Do you believe I can make you see? Although their initiative had already demonstrated their faith, Jesus asked them if they believed he could heal them, and they readily affirmed their faith in him. Jesus, as God's Son, thereby became the specific object of the blind men's general faith in God.

9:29-31 *he touched their eyes.* The declaration of the blind men's faith led directly to Jesus' touching and healing them. This healing, like that of Peter's mother-in-law (8:14-15) and the official's daughter (9:25), occurred in the relative privacy of a house.

Don't tell anyone about this. Jesus' command for silence brings up the vexed question of the "messianic secret" (cf. 8:4; 12:16; 17:9). As the citation of Isa 42:1-4 in Matt 12:15-21 shows, Jesus did not want his spectacular works to result in a mob scene that would eclipse his authoritative words, not to mention incite the Jewish religious leaders and the Romans to view him as politically subversive.

spread his fame all over the region. The two men did not follow Jesus' orders (cf. 4:24; 9:26).

9:32 *a demon-possessed man who couldn't speak.* Matthew makes a distinction here between the physical malady of muteness (cf. 12:22, 24; Isa 35:5-6) and its supernatural cause, demon possession (cf. 4:24; 8:16, 28, 33; 9:32; 12:22; 15:22). The story of this healing is without parallel in Mark and Luke

COMMENTARY

With these two miracle stories, the third set of three miracle stories (9:18-34) comes to an end. Matthew began this pattern in 8:1, and the narrative block containing this material is now complete except for a concluding summary in 9:35-38, which answers to 4:22-25. (See the analysis of this structure in the commentary on 8:1-17.) Although the story of the healing of the two blind men (cf. 20:29-34; Isa 35:5-6) is without parallel in Mark and Luke, one need not conclude, with Davies and Allison (1991:133-134), that its historicity is thereby compromised.

Since 8:1, Jesus has been portrayed as a healer of leprosy, paralysis, fever, demon-possession, blindness, and muteness. He has even raised a little girl from the dead. It must be remembered that these acts not only demonstrate his compassion, which is highlighted next in 9:35-38, but also demonstrate his authority on earth to forgive sin (9:6). For Matthew, the miracles are not so much about human needs as they are about God's grace through his Son, the Messiah.

In the concluding verses of this pericope, a seemingly unremarkable exorcism has two antithetical results. The multitudes were amazed at Jesus' unique power, but the Pharisees attributed the exorcism to Jesus' being empowered by the devil. This latter theme, mentioned again in the mission discourse in 10:25, comes to its ugly climax in 12:22-37 and is discussed further in the commentary on that passage.

◆   ## 10. A compassionate shepherd and a plentiful harvest (9:35-38)

35Jesus traveled through all the towns and villages of that area, teaching in the synagogues and announcing the Good News about the Kingdom. And he healed every kind of disease and illness. 36When he saw the crowds, he had compassion on them because they were confused and helpless, like sheep without a shepherd. 37He said to his disciples, "The harvest is great, but the workers are few. 38So pray to the Lord who is in charge of the harvest; ask him to send more workers into his fields."

NOTES

9:35 The summary of Jesus' ministry in this verse repeats verbatim the summary statement of 4:23 except for its replacement of "the region of Galilee" with "all the towns and villages of that area" and its omission of the final phrase of 4:23, "among the people," though this Gr. phrase is not reflected in the NLT. With this verse Matthew begins to close the narrative of Jesus' miracles that began in 8:1. (See the note on 4:23 for further comments.)

9:36 *he had compassion on them because they were confused and helpless, like sheep without a shepherd.* As Jesus healed the multitudes of all their diseases, taught in the synagogues, and preached the rule of God, there were many occasions for his compassion to be manifested (cf. 14:14; 15:32; 20:34). But the needs of the multitudes were not the only reason for the compassion of Jesus—his pity for the crowds was heightened because their state of distress and helplessness was similar to that of sheep without a shepherd (cf. Mark 6:34). The language pictures a predator mangling the sheep and throwing them to the ground. This metaphor recalls many passages in the Heb. Bible that speak of Israel as God's flock and Israel's leaders as shepherds (e.g., Num 27:17; 2 Sam 5:2; 1 Kgs 22:17; Jer 3:15; 10:21; 23:1; Ezek 34:5; Zech 10:2-3; 11:16; Jdt 11:19). Matthew himself used this imagery elsewhere (2:6; 25:32; 26:31). Thus, the comparison of Israel to sheep without a shepherd implies that the religious leaders of Israel were not faithful shepherds of Israel but vicious predators. On this point, Matthew echoes the prophetic critique of the Jerusalem establishment and prepares the reader for the sustained polemics against the leaders yet to come.

9:37-38 *The harvest is great, but the workers are few.* Jesus' compassion for needy Israel, which is beset with many problems and lacks godly leaders, brings him to another metaphor, that of the harvest. He points out to his disciples that the situation is like a bountiful harvest without sufficient workers. This saying is also found in Luke 10:2.

pray to the Lord who is in charge of the harvest; ask him to send more workers into his fields. They should pray that God would send even more workers into the field. Harvest imagery is found elsewhere in Matthew (3:8-10, 12; 6:26; 13:30, 39; 21:34; 25:24, 26; cf. Mark 4:29; John 4:35-38). These words about the paucity of laborers for the abundant harvest provide a transition into the next chapter (Blomberg 1992:165-167), where Jesus commissions his disciples for their own mission to Israel (10:1-4) and instructs them on the rigors they will endure (10:5-42).

COMMENTARY

Matthew 9:35-38 concludes a narrative of selected miracle stories that began in 8:1; at the same time, it introduces the mission discourse of chapter 10. For the structure of Matthew 8-9, see the commentary on 8:1-17. It is important to note how the stress in Matthew 8-9 on the authoritative deeds of Jesus (8:8-9; 9:6) answers to the stress in Matthew 5-7 on the authoritative teaching of Jesus (7:28-29). Thus, Matthew 5-9 presents Jesus as the authoritative Messiah of Israel, whose words and deeds proclaim the rule of God. The nearly identical summaries in Matthew 4:23 and 9:35 serve as bookends bracketing the two "books" of Jesus' words and deeds respectively. At the same time, 4:23-5:2 and 9:35-10:4 provide narrative contexts for the discourses in Matthew 5-7 and Matthew 10 respectively (Davies and Allison 1991:143).

When one considers Matthew 9:35-38 as a "bookend" with 4:22-25, it becomes apparent that Matthew 5-9 amounts to a sampling of Jesus' authoritative words and deeds. Both his teachings and his actions demonstrate the authority of God's rule, and his actions demonstrate his authority as Son of Man to forgive sins. Thus, the most important theme of Matthew 5-9 in general and 9:35-38 in particular is Christological. As Immanuel ("God with us"), Jesus' words and deeds epitomize the character and compassion of his Father in heaven. His ethical teaching and his compassionate acts exemplify the values and power of the Kingdom of Heaven

Matthew 9:35-38 serves two functions. It not only looks back to 4:22, it also looks ahead to the mission discourse of chapter 10. Matthew 8-9 presents three sets of three miracle stories, and interspersed before and after the second set are stories emphasizing discipleship (8:18-22; 9:9-17). These discipleship stories prepare the reader for the need for mission workers, expressed through the dual metaphor of shepherds for Israel who work in the harvest fields (9:36-38). Such workers count the cost of serving Jesus (8:18-22). They could perhaps come from the undesirable elements of the culture (9:9-13), and they understand the newness of Jesus' Kingdom message (9:14-17). Such are the kind of workers for whom the disciples were told to pray in 9:38. Judging from the sobering instructions in the mission discourse just ahead in the narrative, these workers will endure much opposition.

The opposition ahead for the disciples as shepherd-harvesters is also hinted at in Matthew 5-9. Jesus had taught that his disciples' righteousness must surpass that of the current religious leaders (5:20); his authoritative teachings had a powerful impact upon the crowds that transcended the influence of their current leaders (7:28-29). Many of those leaders would evidently be displaced at the eschatological banquet by people who acknowledged Jesus' authority (8:11-12). Certain of these leaders believed Jesus was blaspheming when he forgave sin and accused him of being in league with Beelzebub when he cast out demons (9:3, 34). Thus, it is no wonder that Jesus pictured Israel as sheep without a shepherd (9:36) and called for more harvesters (9:37-38). And it is not surprising that the current leaders would oppose the disciples' mission (10:14-25). In the next chapter, Matthew narrates how Jesus prepares his disciples to encounter the growing opposition already engendered by his own ministry.

◆　　## 10. Jesus commissions the Twelve (10:1-4)

Jesus called his twelve disciples together and gave them authority to cast out evil* spirits and to heal every kind of disease and illness. ²Here are the names of the twelve apostles:

first, Simon (also called Peter),
then Andrew (Peter's brother),
James (son of Zebedee),
John (James's brother),
³Philip,
Bartholomew,
Thomas,
Matthew (the tax collector),
James (son of Alphaeus),
Thaddaeus,*
⁴Simon (the zealot*),
Judas Iscariot (who later betrayed him).

10:1 Greek *unclean*.　10:3 Other manuscripts read *Lebbaeus;* still others read *Lebbaeus who is called Thaddaeus*.　10:4 Greek *the Cananean*, an Aramaic term for Jewish nationalists.

NOTES

10:1 *Jesus called his twelve disciples*. Jesus now commissions his twelve disciples to extend his ministry of the Kingdom through word and deeds (cf. Mark 3:13-19; Luke 6:12-16). The inner core of Jesus' disciples are first called "the twelve" here (cf. 10:2, 5; 11:1; 20:17; 26:14, 20, 47), and the number twelve also occurs in several other contexts in Matthew (9:20; 14:20; 19:28; 26:53 NLT mg). It is clear that Jesus' choice of twelve disciples was intended to correspond to the twelve tribes of Israel (19:28), who were lacking godly leaders (9:36). The disciples were presented by Matthew as Israel's new leaders (Turner 2002) to advance the Kingdom.

***gave them authority*.** The authority of the Kingdom is a crucial theme in Matthew (7:28-29; 8:9; 9:6-8; 21:23-27; 28:18; cf. 12:22-29).

***to cast out evil spirits and to heal every kind of disease and illness*.** This reminds the reader of Jesus' authority over evil spirits and every disease (4:23-24; 9:35). Jesus took the initiative in calling (4:18-22) and commissioning his disciples; he extended to them his authority.

10:2-4 *the twelve apostles*. Here is the only time in Matthew when the Twelve are described more technically as apostles, not disciples—as in 10:1 (cf. 11:1; 20:17; 26:20). Other lists of the Twelve are found in Mark 3:16-19; Luke 6:12-16; Acts 1:13. Of the Twelve, Simon (Peter), Andrew, James, and John have been mentioned previously (4:18, 21), so it is appropriate that they are the first four mentioned here. Matthew has already been mentioned in 9:9.

Simon Peter is mentioned many times in Matthew (Turner 1991), but Andrew is not mentioned again. In view of 4:18 and 16:16-19, it is fitting that Peter is mentioned at the head of the list with the description "first." The brothers James and John, the sons of Zebedee, are mentioned later (along with Peter) in the experience of Jesus' transfiguration (17:1). They are also mentioned as those who wanted to sit at Jesus' side in the Kingdom (20:20).

Of the apostles listed in 10:3-4, Philip, Bartholomew, Thomas, Thaddaeus, and Simon the zealot are not mentioned elsewhere in Matthew. James the son of Alphaeus may be the James mentioned in 27:56. Judas Iscariot, the betrayer, looms large toward the end of the Gospel (26:14, 25, 47; 27:3), and it is fitting that he is mentioned at the end of the list.

COMMENTARY

Matthew 10 comprises the second discourse of Jesus featured by Matthew. The discourse proper begins after 10:1-5a, which summarizes the commissioning of the apostles and lists them individually. It concludes with Matthew's characteristic transitional formula at 11:1 (cf. 7:28; 13:53; 19:1; 26:1). The Twelve had seen Jesus' words and works; now it was their turn to go out on their own itinerant ministries as he continued his own ministry (11:1). Up to this point in the narrative, Jesus had demonstrated Kingdom authority through word and work, message and miracle, and now he delegated this Kingdom ministry to the Twelve for their mission to Israel (10:1, 5-8). They were to extend Jesus' ministry by announcing the Kingdom and demonstrating its power to Israel through mighty works. The chapter includes the setting of the discourse (10:1-5a), followed by instructions on (1) the audience and message of the mission (10:5b-8); (2) support for the mission (10:9-15); and (3) dealing with persecution and suffering (10:16-42).

As there are many different views of the structure of this discourse, it is probably safe to say that its structure is not as clear as that of the first discourse, the Sermon on the Mount. Davies and Allison's chiastic approach (1991:160-162) is not totally convincing, but there is a certain symmetry in that, after the initial instructions (10:5-10), the emphasis falls upon Kingdom reception or rejection:

A. Reception (10:11-13): Blessings for worthy houses and towns

B. Rejection (10:14-15): General warning for unworthy houses and towns

B'. Rejection (10:16-39): Specific warnings for synagogues, governors, kings, families

A'. Reception (10:40-42): Rewards for receiving Jesus' followers

The mission discourse is related primarily to the ministry of Jesus' original disciples to the cities of Israel, but there are indications that it speaks to the ongoing world mission of the church at large. There are references to appearing before Gentile rulers and to the necessity of perseverance until the day of judgment (10:18, 22, 26, 28). Thus, the discourse is very relevant to the church today. The fact that the modern Western church has not experienced widespread persecution of the sort mentioned in the discourse should not blind Western Christians to the profound truths presented here.

Jesus Chooses the Twelve. Jesus had just emphasized to his disciples the need for his mission and commanded them to pray for workers for the harvest (9:37-38). Now his commission amounts to their "putting feet to their prayers." Since the needy multitudes of Israel must be reached with the redeeming power of God's rule, the disciples were given authority to minister as Jesus had ministered in words and deeds. In the discourse to come, the disciples are repeatedly reminded that their fortunes will be inescapably linked to their allegiance to Jesus. As they continue his ministry of Kingdom, they will experience a mixed response to their message, which centers on his identity. If they are rejected and persecuted, he is rejected and persecuted (10:14, 18, 22, 24-25). If they are received, he is received (10:40). So it is today.

It is instructive to note that those of the apostles who are mentioned elsewhere in Matthew are not necessarily portrayed in a positive light. Judas is the best example of this. The sons of Zebedee are complicit in their mother's selfish petition that they be the greatest in the coming Kingdom (20:20-22). Peter's foibles are famous, yet when he confesses Jesus' identity, he becomes foundational for the church. It is humbling to acknowledge that the earliest leaders of the church were redeemed though flawed individuals, but at the same time this attributes the credit where it belongs, to Jesus (cf. 2 Cor 4:7). Yet the Twelve are the human agents upon whom Jesus will build the church. They are crucial for the continuity between the pre- and post-resurrection ministries of Jesus (Davies and Allison 1991:151), and they will be the eschatological rulers of Israel (19:28).

◆ B. Mission and Suffering (10:5-42)
   1. The apostles' commission (10:5-15; cf. Mark 6:8-11; Luke 9:3-5)

[5]Jesus sent out the twelve apostles with these instructions: "Don't go to the Gentiles or the Samaritans, [6]but only to the people of Israel—God's lost sheep. [7]Go and announce to them that the Kingdom of Heaven is near.* [8]Heal the sick, raise the dead, cure those with leprosy, and cast out demons. Give as freely as you have received!

[9]"Don't take any money in your money belts—no gold, silver, or even copper coins. [10]Don't carry a traveler's bag with a change of clothes and sandals or even a walking stick. Don't hesitate to accept hospitality, because those who work deserve to be fed.

[11]"Whenever you enter a city or village, search for a worthy person and stay in his home until you leave town. [12]When you enter the home, give it your blessing. [13]If it turns out to be a worthy home, let your blessing stand; if it is not, take back the blessing. [14]If any household or town refuses to welcome you or listen to your message, shake its dust from your feet as you leave. [15]I tell you the truth, the wicked cities of Sodom and Gomorrah will be better off than such a town on the judgment day."

10:7 Or *has come,* or *is coming soon.*

NOTES

10:5-6 After listing the twelve apostles, Matthew narrated the instructions Jesus gave them just before he sent them out.

Don't go to the Gentiles or the Samaritans, but only to the people of Israel. The discourse begins abruptly with a striking prohibition: the disciples must not go to Gentiles or Samaritans (cf. 15:24). Thus, the destination of the mission is to be limited to the people of Israel, who are again likened to lost sheep needing a shepherd (cf. 9:36; 10:16; 12:11-12; 15:24; 18:12; 25:32-33; 26:31; Jer 50:6; Ezek 34:11, 16, 30). Gentiles and Samaritans are to be excluded at this point, yet before his death Jesus anticipated the mission to all nations (8:11; 10:18; 21:43; 22:9; 24:14), and after his resurrection he commanded it (28:19). Despite this, mission to Gentiles was controversial in the early church, as noted in the book of Acts (e.g., Acts 11:1-18). The priority of Israel in redemptive history is underlined by this stress in Jesus' ministry (Levine 1988). This is the only time the Samaritans, who occupied territory between Judah and Galilee, are mentioned in Matthew.

10:7-8 *the Kingdom of Heaven is near.* The central message of the disciples is to be that which John and Jesus have already preached: "the Kingdom of Heaven is near" (cf. 3:2; 4:17; 9:35; 13:19). The anticipated church, which will be built by Jesus, is also to preach this message of the rule of God (24:14). The authority of the ministry of word is to be demonstrated by the ministry of deed: the disciples are to heal, cast out demons, and even raise the dead. They have already seen Jesus do each of these deeds. Since they have freely received the gracious blessings of the Kingdom, they are to extend those blessings freely to others.

10:9 *Don't take any money.* The Twelve are told not to take money or extra clothes with them on the mission. Rather, their needs are to be met by the anticipated hospitality and support of those who receive their message (cf. 10:11-13; 40-42). The message of the Kingdom is not for sale (cf. Acts 8:20), but those who receive it should also receive its messengers.

10:10 *or even a walking stick.* The instructions of 10:9-10, especially regarding the walking stick, are difficult to reconcile with Mark 6:8-9 (cf. Luke 9:3), but see Blomberg (1987:145-146) for suggestions.

Don't hesitate to accept hospitality. Though not based on the Gr. text, this phrase was evidently added in view of the implications of the following context and to help explain the proverbial words "those who work deserve to be fed." This saying probably distills OT principles regarding day laborers and priests (Num 18:31; Deut 24:15; cf. Luke 10:7; 1 Cor 9:9-10, 14). In this culture, hospitality to God's messengers was viewed as a sacred duty (cf. *Didache* 11–13).

10:11-13 In this passage contrasting responses to the Kingdom message are anticipated (cf. Mark 6:10-12; Luke 10:5-6).

search for a worthy person. The disciples were to seek out those purported to be "worthy" people and to stay with them. Their acceptance of the Kingdom message would show their genuine worthiness. Jesus' disciples were to accept offers of hospitality and give their blessing to worthy households who received the message of the Kingdom. But those who rejected the message of God's reign were unworthy of his messengers.

let your blessing stand . . . take back the blessing. If the disciples were staying in an unworthy home, they were to retract their blessing, evidently as they departed from the home. The word "blessing" is more lit. a "greeting" (cf. 5:47), which wishes peace for the house (cf. Luke 10:5). In 10:13 the words "let your blessing stand" and "take back the blessing" can be respectively translated "let your [greeting of] peace come upon it" and "let your [greeting of] peace return to you."

10:14 Reception of the disciples was linked to the response to their message (cf. Mark 6:11; Luke 9:5; 10:10-11). Refusal to heed the message was tantamount to rejection of the messenger. The disciples were to demonstrate the gravity of such rejection by a symbolic act of renunciation, shaking the dust of such houses or towns off their feet as they left. Some commentators understand this as shaking from one's outer garment the dust stirred up by one's feet (Gundry 1994:190; cf. Neh 5:13; Acts 13:51; 18:6), but it seems more naturally taken to be the dust on one's feet (cf. Luke 10:11). Either way, the action symbolizes the severance of fellowship—the disciples are to reject those who have rejected the Kingdom message and leave them to their inevitable judgment.

10:15 *the wicked cities of Sodom and Gomorrah will be better off.* Jesus assured the disciples that those who reject them make a mistake even more serious than Sodom and Gomorrah's outrageously shameful treatment of God's angels (Gen 18–19). Rejection of God's rule in Christ renders one liable to a judgment more severe than the judgment of notorious Sodom and Gomorrah, which had attained proverbial status (11:24; 2 Pet 2:6; Jude 1:7; cf. Gen 18:20–19:26; Deut 29:22-23; Isa 1:9-10; 3:9; 13:19; Jer 23:14; 50:40; Lam 4:6; and esp. Ezek 16:46-56).

COMMENTARY

The instructions in this section deal with the destination (10:5-6), message (10:7), miracles (10:8), outfit (10:9-10), and reception (10:11-15) of the disciples' mission. The reader is impressed by the continuity of the disciples' mission with that of Jesus and John, as well as by the relative lack of funds and equipment the disciples are to take. This last feature reminds believers today that their ultimate resource in ministry is the Lord's power and promises, not their own provisions. Similarly, the simplicity of the disciples' provisions tends to reflect negatively upon the fund-raising techniques and lavish accoutrements that are in vogue with certain ministries today.

The prohibition of ministry to non-Jews (10:5) is perhaps the most noteworthy aspect of 10:5-15. This prohibition is obviously quite different from the concluding commission of this Gospel, which mandates mission to all the nations (28:18). How should this major difference be understood? The priority of Israel in God's covenant plan cannot be minimized. Matthew presents Jesus as the son of Abraham, through whom all the nations will be blessed (1:1; cf. Gen 12:2-3). Although mere physical descent from Abraham does not merit God's favor (3:9; 8:12), the Jews remain the foundational covenant people of God, and eschatological blessing amounts to sharing in the promises made to the patriarchs (8:11; 19:28). Thus, the Gentile world mission does not replace the foundational mission to Israel but supplements and broadens it. Christianity must not be separated from its roots in the Hebrew Bible. It is not a religion primarily, let alone exclusively, for Gentiles. The particularism of 10:5 is necessary for Jesus to be the fulfillment of Israel's history and prophetic hope. His disciples would become the nucleus and foundational leaders of the nascent church (cf. 16:28; 19:28; 21:43). In God's mysterious plan, most Jews—then and now—do not accept Jesus as their promised Messiah, but a messianic remnant of Christian Jews remains to this day. Therefore, Gentile Christians must always acknowledge the priority of Israel in redemptive history. This was taught by Jesus and Paul alike (John 4:22; 10:16; Rom 11:16-24; 15:7-12; Eph 2:11-13). Thus, there is a sense even today in which "to the Jew first" still rings true (Rom 1:16).

◆   **2. Jesus warns of persecution (10:16-23)**

¹⁶"Look, I am sending you out as sheep among wolves. So be as shrewd as snakes and harmless as doves. ¹⁷But beware! For you will be handed over to the courts and will be flogged with whips in the syna-gogues. ¹⁸You will stand trial before governors and kings because you are my followers. But this will be your opportunity to tell the rulers and other unbelievers about me.* ¹⁹When you are arrested, don't

worry about how to respond or what to say. God will give you the right words at the right time. ²⁰For it is not you who will be speaking—it will be the Spirit of your Father speaking through you.

²¹"A brother will betray his brother to death, a father will betray his own child, and children will rebel against their par-ents and cause them to be killed. ²²And all nations will hate you because you are my followers.* But everyone who endures to the end will be saved. ²³When you are persecuted in one town, flee to the next. I tell you the truth, the Son of Man* will re-turn before you have reached all the towns of Israel."

10:18 Or *But this will be your testimony against the rulers and other unbelievers.* **10:22** Greek *on account of my name.* **10:23** "Son of Man" is a title Jesus used for himself.

NOTES

10:16 *I am sending you out as sheep among wolves.* In this passage, the disciples were warned that those who rejected the Kingdom message would not leave it at passive unbe-lief. They would take active steps to oppress the messengers of the Kingdom. Metaphors from the animal world abound in this verse. The disciples are likened to sheep among wolves (cf. 7:15; John 10:12; Acts 20:29; Ezek 22:27)

as shrewd as snakes and harmless as doves. The disciples were encouraged to be as shrewd as snakes (cf. Gen 3:1) and harmless (cf. Rom 16:19; Phil 2:15) as doves. This command inculcates wisdom accompanied by integrity, a combination of intellectual and ethical char-acteristics. It is striking that the disciples will be among wolves as they minister only in Isra-el—their fellow countrymen, not Gentiles, will pose significant danger for them. The wolves of 10:16 are the religious leaders whose opposition to Jesus mounts as the narrative unfolds.

10:17-18 The persecution from the "wolves" is described in detail in the following verses (cf. Mark 13:9-13). Both Jews and Gentile rulers will be involved, with 10:17 probably alluding to religious persecution from Jewish courts (cf. Acts 5:27; 6:12) and 10:18 to negative treat-ment at the hands of provincial rulers and kings, usually Gentiles (cf. Acts 25:23; 27:24).

will be flogged with whips in the synagogues. Punishment in the synagogues would involve painful flogging (cf. 23:34; 2 Cor 11:23-25), but persecution for the sake of Jesus and his Kingdom was ironically an opportunity for further testimony. Jesus himself would be brought before both Jewish and Gentile authorities (cf. 26:57, 59; 27:2, 11), but the lan-guage of these verses looks beyond the immediate ministry of the disciples to their work after the resurrection of Jesus (cf. Acts 4:1-22; 5:17-41; 6:12; 12:1-3; 16:19-21; 21:27; Phil 1:12-18).

10:19-20 *don't worry.* Disciples need not worry (cf. 6:25, 31, 34) about what they will say during these coming times of duress because God will give them the appropriate words through the Spirit (cf. Mark 13:11-13; Luke 21:12-15).

the Spirit of your Father. This continues the frequent references in Matthew to God as the father of Jesus' disciples (5:16, 45, 48; 6:1, 4, 6, 8, 9, 14, 15, 18, 26, 32; 7:11; 10:20, 29; 13:43; 23:9). But God is the father of Jesus' disciples because he is first the father of Jesus (7:21; 10:32, 33; 11:25-27; 12:50; 15:13; 16:17, 27; 18:10, 14, 19, 35; 20:23; 25:34; 26:29, 39, 42, 53). Up to this point in Matthew, the Spirit has been mentioned solely in connection with Jesus and his Kingdom ministry (1:18, 20; 3:11, 16; 4:1; cf. 12:18, 28, 31-32). As the disciples extended the message of Jesus and the Kingdom, they too would experience the work of the Spirit in their lives (cf. John 14:15-17; 15:26;). Eventually, the post-resurrection church would experience Jesus' baptism with the Spirit (3:11) and be led by the Spirit in responding to persecutors (Acts 4:8, 31; 5:32; 6:5, 10; 7:55; 13:9).

10:21 *A brother will betray his brother to death.* In this most poignant verse of the dis-course, it is predicted that even one's own family members will further this persecution (cf. 10:35-37), to the point of Jesus' disciples being killed because of the betrayal of their own siblings, parents, and children (cf. Mic 7:6, to which this verse alludes). Such betrayal is extremely distressing, but it is mollified somewhat by the existence of a new Kingdom family of disciples, with God as the father (10:20; 12:46-50; 23:8-9). It is a difficult teaching, but the primary allegiance of disciples must be to Jesus and to their new family of Kingdom disciples, not to their natural families (10:34-39). See the commentary on 10:24-33 for additional discussion.

10:22 *everyone who endures to the end will be saved.* During such a horrible scenario, in which disciples are universally despised, endurance is the mark of the true disciple (cf. 7:21, 24; 13:21). When disciples face persecution, only those whose perseverance demonstrates the authenticity of their faith will be saved.

10:23 *the Son of Man will return before you have reached all the towns of Israel.* As the disciples encountered persecution on their mission in one town, they were to flee to the next town (cf. 23:34) with the assurance that Jesus would come before they had finished going through the towns of Israel. Various views of this extremely difficult verse are discussed in the following commentary. It seems best to conclude that the "coming" of Jesus mentioned here is his return to earth. Therefore, this verse anticipates a continuing mission to Israel until the second coming of Christ.

COMMENTARY

This section contains two cycles of warning and encouragement. The first warns of persecution from religious courts and civil rulers (10:16-18) but encourages the disciples with the promise of the Spirit, who will speak through them in these dire circumstances (10:19-20). The second cycle warns of what is almost unthinkable—betrayal by one's own family (10:21)—and encourages by stressing the coming of Jesus, who will save those who remain faithful to the end (10:23).

The reference to the coming of the Son of Man in 10:23 is one of the more difficult passages in Matthew. There are several plausible explanations:

1. Jesus will soon "follow up" the ministry of the disciples. In this view the "coming" is not eschatological but simply refers to Jesus rejoining the disciples before they complete their immediate ministries.
2. Jesus' resurrection amounts to a "coming," since by it the new era of the church is inaugurated (Albright and Mann 1971:125; Stonehouse 1979:240).
3. The coming of Jesus is a process beginning with the resurrection, continuing through Pentecost, and culminating in his return to earth (Hendriksen 1973:467-468).
4. The destruction of Jerusalem in AD 70 amounts to a coming in judgment upon Israel (Carson 1984:252-253; Hagner 1993:279-280).
5. Jesus will return to the earth before the disciples complete their mission to Israel (Davies and Allison 1991:192; Blomberg 1992:176; Gundry 1994:194-195; Harrington 1991:147-148).

Choosing between the various views is not easy. One's decision must be made with three matters in mind. First, one's view of other Matthean "coming" texts (16:28; 24:30, 44; 25:31; 26:64) must be considered. Presumably, a consistent picture should emerge when these texts are interpreted. Second, at least some of these "coming" texts depend on Daniel 7:13, and one must look carefully at it also. Third, one must decide whether Jesus' mission discourse in Matthew 10 describes solely the original mission of the Twelve, or in some places anticipates the later mission of the post-resurrection church. It seems best when all these things are considered to opt for view 5, but certainty is not possible.

Jesus' mission discourse does anticipate the mission of the church throughout the period between his first and second comings (Davies and Allison 1991:179-180), and that mission includes ongoing mission to Israel during the outreach to all the nations.

◆   ### 3. Jesus forbids fear (10:24-33)

24"Students* are not greater than their teacher, and slaves are not greater than their master. 25Students are to be like their teacher, and slaves are to be like their master. And since I, the master of the household, have been called the prince of demons,* the members of my household will be called by even worse names!

26"But don't be afraid of those who threaten you. For the time is coming when everything that is covered will be revealed, and all that is secret will be made known to all. 27What I tell you now in the darkness, shout abroad when daybreak comes. What I whisper in your ear, shout from the housetops for all to hear!

28"Don't be afraid of those who want to kill your body; they cannot touch your soul. Fear only God, who can destroy both soul and body in hell.* 29What is the price of two sparrows—one copper coin*? But not a single sparrow can fall to the ground without your Father knowing it. 30And the very hairs on your head are all numbered. 31So don't be afraid; you are more valuable to God than a whole flock of sparrows.

32"Everyone who acknowledges me publicly here on earth, I will also acknowledge before my Father in heaven. 33But everyone who denies me here on earth, I will also deny before my Father in heaven."

10:24 Or Disciples.   10:25 Greek Beelzeboul; other manuscripts read Beezeboul; Latin version reads Beelzebub.
10:28 Greek Gehenna.   10:29 Greek one assarion [i.e., one "as," a Roman coin equal to $\frac{1}{16}$ of a denarius].

NOTES

10:24 *Students are not greater than their teacher, and slaves are not greater than their master.* In case the disciples were surprised at the bleak prospects of their mission, Jesus reminded them of their place as his servants. The students or disciples should not expect better treatment than their teacher or master had received (cf. 23:8; Luke 6:40; John 15:20). Their identity was inextricably linked to his, and they would be treated as he had been treated.

10:25 *the prince of demons.* Gr., "Beelzeboul," which is evidently derived from Heb. words meaning "lord of the house" or "lord of the heights"; cf. 9:34; 12:24, 27. The term probably portrays Satan as exalted head of the demons. If Jesus had been called this, why should his disciples expect to be praised? The argument is from the greater to the lesser— if the persecutors are bold enough to call the master Beelzeboul, much more certainly they will call his servants Beelzeboul.

will be called by even worse names! The disciples' identification with their Teacher means not only that they will be called worse names than Jesus but also that they will share his fate. The malfeasance directed against Jesus will also fall upon them.

10:26 *don't be afraid.* Although fear of persecutors seems only natural, it is forbidden in 10:26-33 three times (cf. Luke 12:4-5; 1 Pet 3:14; Rev 2:10; 14:7). Both 10:26 and 10:27 are structured in the poetic fashion of Heb. "synonymous parallelism." Matthew 10:26 is not so much in contrast with the preceding (NLT "but"), as it is a conclusion drawn from the preceding. Recognizing that they share their master's fate should release disciples from fear (cf. 5:11-12). They should be emboldened by the realization that they are following in the footsteps of Jesus.

everything that is covered will be revealed. Additional motivation is found in the realization that the future will reverse the present. Secrets, evidently the hidden sins of the persecutors, will be revealed on judgment day.

10:27 *shout from the housetops for all to hear!* The truth of Jesus' message will win out on the last day. Therefore, the disciples must not fear but must openly proclaim what Jesus taught them privately, in spite of persecutors.

10:28 *Fear only God, who can destroy both soul and body.* The disciples are here told whom they should fear, not the ones whose powers are merely temporal and physical but the One whose power is eternal (cf. Ps 33:18-19; 4 Macc 13:13-15). The language of this verse seems to assume a sort of dualism of body and soul. The "destruction" of body and soul in hell (*geenna* [TG1067, ZG1147]) does not support annihilationism (cf. 25:41, 46). See the commentary at the end of this section for further discussion of this. The persecutors are able only to cause physical death, but God is able to punish eternally in hell. Thus, God is viewed by Jesus as not only a loving father but also as the eternal judge. The disciples were encouraged to draw near to God as Father (cf., e.g., 10:20, 29), but as they do so, they are also reminded that they must be in awe of his authority as judge to determine their eternal destinies. The temporary peril of persecution should not be taken lightly, but it pales in comparison with the eternal punishment of God in hell.

hell. The word *Gehenna* is used in a number of NT texts to designate the fiery place for punishment of sinners and is often translated "hell" or "the fires of hell" (5:22, 29-30; 10:28; 18:9; 23:15, 33; Mark 9:43, 45, 47). It is usually used in connection with the final judgment and often has the suggestion that the punishment spoken of is eternal. *Gehenna* is derived by transliteration from the Heb. of the OT, "valley of Hinnom," a ravine on the south side of Jerusalem. This valley was the center of idolatrous worship in which children were burned by fire as an offering to the heathen god Molech (2 Chr 28:3; 33:6). In the time of Josiah it became a place of abomination, polluted by dead men's bones and the filth of Jerusalem (2 Kgs 23:10) and by garbage and rubbish dumped there. A fire burned continuously in this valley. It thus became a symbol of the unending fires of hell where the lost are consumed in torment (TBD 592). The term *geenna* is not the same as *hadēs* [TG86, ZG87], which is the place where the dead wait for the final judgment (NLT renders it "the place of the dead"; see 11:23; 16:18; Acts 2:27, 31; Rev 1:18).

10:29 *one copper coin?* Gr. *assarion* [TG787, ZG837], which was worth one sixteenth of a denarius—the denarius being the normal wage for day laborers (cf. 20:2ff). Yet God's awareness of a comparatively worthless sparrow's fall to the ground provides much incentive for trusting that he is aware of the persecution of his people.

10:30 *the very hairs on your head are all numbered.* God's awareness extends even to the trivial matter of the number of hairs on their heads (cf. Luke 21:18; Acts 27:34), so they are of more value than a whole flock of sparrows (cf. 6:26; 12:12).

10:31 *you are more valuable to God than a whole flock of sparrows.* This reassuring section begins with a lesser-to-greater argument to the effect that disciples are of more value to God than sparrows (10:29-30). The rhetorical question that begins the section invites the disciples to reflect on the matter themselves (10:29). Such reflection should lead them to conclude that they need not fear persecutors. Disciples may never know fully why God permits persecution, but they can be sure that he knows their difficulties and will deal justly with their persecutors (10:26, 28, 33). Hagner 1993:286 puts it well: "God has the knowledge, the power, and the concern to protect the disciples from any ultimate harm or injury."

10:32-33 *Everyone who acknowledges me publicly here on earth, I will also acknowledge before my Father in heaven.* Persecutors will call upon disciples to join them in denying Jesus, so there will always be the temptation to deny Jesus and the Kingdom in order to avoid persecution. Confessing Christ before persecutors is a specific instance of the endurance called for earlier (10:22). These verses put the matter of facing up to persecutors as a stark antithesis, with the confession of 10:32 contrasting with the denial of 10:33 (cf. Luke 12:8-9; 2 Tim 2:12). Denial is rejecting or disowning Jesus. If a person confesses Jesus before persecutors, Jesus will confess that person before his Father on judgment day (cf. 7:21). But if a person joins the persecutors in denying Jesus, that person will be denied by Jesus. This language seems to imply a setting on judgment day in which a person's public recognition or denial of Jesus in this life anticipates Jesus' recognition or denial of that person at the judgment. Loyalty to Jesus may result in persecution in this life, but it results in the loyalty of Jesus on judgment day.

COMMENTARY

This section provides three reasons why disciples should not fear the prospect of persecution. First, the disciples are reminded that as servants of their master, Jesus, they are not above him, and that they are to be like him. As his servants, they will share in his treatment by the persecutors (10:24-25). As the narrative proceeds and the opposition to Jesus intensifies, culminating in the disputes with the Jerusalem leaders during the passion week, the disciples presumably grasped this teaching more fully. Second, since they would share in Jesus' treatment, they need not fear because they would also share in Jesus' vindication (10:26-27). Later they could look back from a post-resurrection perspective, as Matthew the author does, and realize that the resurrection vindicated Jesus and that his return would vindicate them. Then the hidden things would be revealed. Third, the disciples should not fear persecutors but the One to whom both they and the persecutors will answer on judgment day (10:28-33). The ordeal inflicted by the persecutors is only temporary, but the persecutors will suffer eternal punishment. Disciples who acknowledge Jesus will be acknowledged by him before the Father, but persecutors who deny Jesus will be denied by him before the Father. Thus, the disciples can deal with fear by recalling their shared identity with Jesus, by focusing on his return, and by maintaining their awe of God.

Matthew 10:28 is frequently cited in support of the notion of annihilationism (sometimes called conditional immortality), the belief that those who reject God and Jesus cease to exist at the final judgment. In this view eternal punishment amounts to eternal nonexistence rather than conscious punishment, which is the traditional Christian teaching on the destiny of unbelievers. This was not a matter with which Matthew was concerned, but it is a common question today. The issue hinges on 10:28b, in which God is described as the One "who can destroy both body and soul in hell."

Annihilationists take the word "destroy" (*apollumi* [TG622, ZG660]) quite literally and posit a final judgment in which unbelievers are destroyed—that is, they cease to exist. But it is clear from other texts that this "destruction" is a state of punishment for the whole person (Matt 5:22, 29-30; 18:9; 23:15, 33), which is as eternal in duration as the bliss of eternal life in God's Kingdom (25:41, 46; cf. Dan 12:2; 2 Thess 1:9; Rev 14:10-11; 20:10). The matter of eternal punishment is, to say the least, a fearful doctrine. But it is precisely the motivation given in Matthew 10 for fidelity in discipleship during days of persecution (10:22, 28, 33). To put it bluntly, if there were no hell to avoid, there would be one less reason to be faithful to Jesus, and there would be one more reason to deny him.

◆   ### 4. Jesus promises reward after suffering (10:34-42)

³⁴"Don't imagine that I came to bring peace to the earth! I came not to bring peace, but a sword.

³⁵'I have come to set a man against his father,

a daughter against her mother,

and a daughter-in-law against her mother-in-law.

³⁶   Your enemies will be right in your own household!'*

³⁷"If you love your father or mother more than you love me, you are not worthy of being mine; or if you love your son or daughter more than me, you are not worthy of being mine. ³⁸If you refuse to take up your cross and follow me, you are not worthy of being mine. ³⁹If you cling to your life, you will lose it; but if you give up your life for me, you will find it.

⁴⁰"Anyone who receives you receives me, and anyone who receives me receives the Father who sent me. ⁴¹If you receive a prophet as one who speaks for God,* you will be given the same reward as a prophet. And if you receive righteous people because of their righteousness, you will be given a reward like theirs. ⁴²And if you give even a cup of cold water to one of the least of my followers, you will surely be rewarded."

10:35-36 Mic 7:6.   10:41 Greek *receive a prophet in the name of a prophet.*

NOTES

10:34 *I came not to bring peace, but a sword.* The opening verses concern the relationship of Jesus' Kingdom to peace. The presence of the Kingdom does not mean the absence of hostility. Jesus forbade the disciples from entertaining idealistic thoughts about the immediate results of his mission. His ministry would not bring unconditional serendipity to the world. Peace on earth (cf. Luke 2:14) cannot be attained apart from Jesus' work of reconciling people to God. Then people have the capacity to be reconciled to each other and are equipped to work for peace themselves (cf. 5:9; 10:13). But for those who refuse to acknowledge Jesus as God's agent of peace, the message of the Kingdom is another reason for division and alienation, even from one's own family members (cf. Luke 12:51-53).

10:36 *Your enemies will be right in your own household!* The division of families was mentioned earlier in 10:21, and Mic 7:6, the OT text cited here in 10:35-36, was also alluded to there. The alternative to peace is a sword, a symbol of conflict and warfare. The Kingdom message of repentance is indeed confrontational, and conflicting responses to this message can fracture even the dearest human relationships. The point of these sobering words is that family loyalties must not supersede loyalty to Christ.

10:37 *If you love your father or mother more than you love me.* In the setting of potential family strife due to opposite responses to the Kingdom message, disciples are warned not to misplace their loyalties. To love one's parents or children more than Jesus is to be unworthy of him.

10:38 *take up your cross and follow me.* Only when one is willing to sacrifice one's life and relationship to one's family for the sake of Jesus does one begin to live. Taking up the cross may allude to the Roman custom of the condemned man carrying his cross to his own crucifixion (cf. 27:32). The paradox here is similar to that found in Jesus' warning of Peter and the disciples in 16:24-25—if the prospect of martyrdom or alienation from family leads one to renounce Jesus, one loses one's life even while trying to save it.

10:40-42 *you will be given a reward like theirs.* The solemn words of 10:37-39 about one's deepest loyalties in the face of persecution are now balanced somewhat by these concluding words of the discourse, which stress reward. Those who receive the messengers of the Kingdom will be rewarded because reception of the Messiah's messengers amounts to receiving the Messiah, and reception of the Messiah amounts to receiving the Father. More specifically (10:41), those who receive a prophet (cf. 5:12) or a righteous person will receive a reward equivalent to the prophet or righteous person's reward. The words "prophets and righteous people" occur together again in 13:17. These are to receive hospitality due to what they stand for, prophets for the message and righteous people for the character of God.

if you give even a cup of cold water to one of the least of my followers. Even the seemingly insignificant gift of a cup of cold water to a disciple will bring a future reward to the hospitable person (10:42). Jesus' disciples are characterized en masse as "little ones" here (cf. 18:6, 10, 14; 25:40, 45). Thus, the NLT's "to one of the least of my followers" implies a gradation among disciples not present in the text.

COMMENTARY

Jesus' second discourse moves to its conclusion with a warning that he and his Kingdom message will not automatically bring peace to the earth. Indeed, the most sacred human relationships could be severed by his message. Thus, even one's family cannot take precedence over one's allegiance to Jesus. This difficult teaching is made even more so when one considers the importance of the family in the Hebrew Bible (Exod 20:12; Lev 20:9; Deut 5:16) and in the teaching of Jesus elsewhere (cf. 15:4-6; 19:8-9, 19). But one's allegiance to Jesus can cause such dissension in a family that one's family relationships must be severed. This loss would certainly bring deep anguish, but that temporary pain must be compared with the horror of eternal separation from Jesus. Jesus' own example shows that one's loyalties must lie with the new family of his followers (12:46-50). He promises that the pain of lost relationships in the present life will somehow be offset by the blessings of the future Kingdom (19:29).

The discourse ends on a positive note in 10:40-42, with the prospect of reward for those who show hospitality to Jesus' disciples. It is important to remember that it takes more than missionaries to accomplish Jesus' mission; the whole community must be involved. Those who support the missionaries will receive an equivalent reward. After the sobering words about the inevitability of persecution, even from one's own family, the conclusion provides a note of balance that encourages the disciples for their mission. Despite the difficulties of the coming days, they will find hospitable people who will respond positively to the message of Jesus and the

Kingdom. But the conclusion of this discourse is not unlike that of the Sermon on the Mount. Both discourses present loyalty to Jesus and his Kingdom in blunt either-or language. One's "house" is built either on rock or on sand (7:24-27). One's life will be either lost or found (10:39). No doubt, some try to find ways of compromise so that one may have both family and Jesus, both "self-actualization" and discipleship, but there is no such middle ground in Jesus' teaching.

◆ IV. Increased Opposition to the Kingdom of Heaven (11:1–12:50)
A. John the Baptist's Question (11:1-6; cf. Luke 7:18-23)

When Jesus had finished giving these instructions to his twelve disciples, he went out to teach and preach in towns throughout the region.

²John the Baptist, who was in prison, heard about all the things the Messiah was doing. So he sent his disciples to ask Jesus, ³"Are you the Messiah we've been expecting,* or should we keep looking for someone else?"

⁴Jesus told them, "Go back to John and tell him what you have heard and seen— ⁵the blind see, the lame walk, the lepers are cured, the deaf hear, the dead are raised to life, and the Good News is being preached to the poor. ⁶And tell him, 'God blesses those who do not turn away because of me.*'"

11:3 Greek *Are you the one who is coming?*   11:6 Or *who are not offended by me.*

NOTES
11:1 *When Jesus had finished.* With a characteristic transitional formula (cf. 7:28; 13:53; 19:1; 26:1), Matthew turned from Jesus' discourse on mission to another block of narrative material. Having commissioned and instructed his disciples, Jesus embarked once again on his own itinerant ministry. The disciples were to carry out their ministry to the cities of Israel until Jesus returned (10:23), but in the meantime, he continued his own ministry of teaching and preaching (4:23; 9:35)

11:2 *John the Baptist, who was in prison.* Though his disciples were mentioned in 8:14, John has not been mentioned since his imprisonment at the beginning of Jesus' ministry in Galilee (4:12). Here another "beginning" of the ministry of Jesus is tied to John, which is significant for redemptive history. Although John had become aware of Jesus' identity (3:13-17), his question was evidently due to the limited outward effects of Jesus' ministry. He had heard about what Jesus was doing (lit., "Messiah's works"), but he probably expected a more immediate judgment of the religious and political *status quo* (cf. Matt 3:7-12; Luke 7:18-23). For more on John the Baptist in Matthew, see 14:1-12; 17:9-13.

11:3 *the Messiah we've been expecting.* Lit., "the coming one," an expression that also occurs in 3:11; 21:9; 23:39.

11:4-6 *tell him about what you have heard and seen.* Jesus' answer calls John's messengers' attention to what is heard (words) as well as to what is seen (works). Six specifics are enumerated: the healing of blindness (cf. 9:27-28; 12:22; 20:30; 21:14), lameness (cf. 15:30-31; 21:14), leprosy (cf. 8:20), and deafness (cf. 9:32-33; 12:22; 15:30-31); the raising of the dead (cf. 9:18; 10:8); and evangelism to the poor (cf. 4:14-17, 23; 5:3; Luke 4:18). This description of Jesus' ministry is drawn from the OT (Isa 26:19; 29:18; 35:5-6; 42:7, 18; 61:1).

God blesses those who do not turn away because of me. If John focused on these words and works of Jesus, he would be blessed because he would not "turn away" from Jesus.

Turning away is lit. "stumbling," which refers to spiritual defeat or apostasy (cf. 5:29-30; 13:21, 41, 57; 15:12; 16:23; 17:27; 18:6-9; 24:10; 26:31, 33). Thus, John was encouraged that he was on the right track and that he should stay on it despite the delay in the judgment he predicted.

COMMENTARY

Just as Matthew's first discourse, the Sermon on the Mount (chs 5-7), is followed by the narrative of Matthew 8-9, so the discourse on mission (ch 10) is followed by another narrative section (chs 11-12). And just as the structure of Matthew 8-9 is significant (see the commentary on 8:1-4), so is the structure of Matthew 11:12 (Verseput 1986). Overall, these two chapters stress Israel's unbelief (esp. 11:16-24; 12:41-42) and the escalating opposition to Jesus from the leaders of Israel (esp. 12:2, 10, 14, 24, 38). But there are more positive sections that respond to the unbelief and opposition with trust in God's sovereignty (11:25-30), fulfillment of prophecy (12:17-21), and commendation of discipleship (12:46-50).

Blomberg (1992:183) lays out an analysis of Matthew 11-12 that takes chapter 11 as implicit opposition and chapter 12 as explicit opposition. Although Matthew 11:1-16 might be rightly viewed as implicit opposition, Matthew 11:12, 18-24 is best understood as explicit animosity. A preferable analysis is suggested in general terms by Hagner (1993:298) and addressed in specifics by Davies and Allison (1991:233-234). This approach identifies three sets or collections of passages, each of which contains three elements, the first two stressing unbelief and the third belief:

I. First collection (11:2-30)
   1. Unbelief: John the Baptist (11:2-19)
   2. Unbelief: the towns of Galilee (11:20-24)
   3. Belief: "Come unto me" (11:25-30)
II. Second collection (12:1-21)
   1. Unbelief: Sabbath controversy (12:1-8)
   2. Unbelief: Sabbath controversy (12:9-14)
   3. Belief: "the hope of the Gentiles" (12:15-21)
III. Third collection (12:22-50)
   1. Unbelief: the unforgivable sin (12:22-37)
   2. Unbelief: an evil generation (12:38-45)
   3. Belief: Jesus' true family (12:46-50)

It is interesting that Matthew 11:1 mentions only that Jesus had instructed the disciples before setting out on his own ministry. Matthew does not mention either that Jesus sent the disciples or that they later returned to follow Jesus, although they appear with him again in 12:1. Evidently, Matthew did not narrate the mission of the disciples or their return to Jesus because his literary purpose was centered on Jesus and the teaching of Jesus for the disciples and the church, which is built on them.

John's question (11:2-3) was essentially about what kind of Messiah Jesus was.

It focused on Jesus' works, which Matthew has highlighted since 4:23. Matthew has shown that the response to these works was mixed, with popular acclaim (4:25; 7:28; 8:1, 18; 9:8, 33) balanced by increasing opposition from the religious leaders (5:20; 7:29; 9:3, 11, 34). So John's question as to whether Jesus was the expected Messiah is crucial for the reader of Matthew. Although John's doubts are often downplayed, they should be given full force. Although John had ample reason to believe in Jesus (3:13-17), his imprisonment (4:12) and the seeming delay in the coming of the Kingdom inevitably took a toll on his confidence. Jesus' answer to John served to refocus him on the fulfillment of the Old Testament promises of salvation, not the promises of judgment. Not only John, but all those who focus on the messianic works of Jesus will be blessed because they will not lose faith (11:6). John's doubts and the way Jesus dealt with them are exemplary for all of Jesus' disciples.

Matthew 11:1-6 interprets all of Matthew 4–10 (Davies and Allison 1991:242). Jesus was indeed the coming one whom John announced. His words and works bring the saving rule of God to bear on human sin and suffering, fulfilling the prophecies of Isaiah. But if one as great as John could doubt this, what of Jesus' other followers, both ancient and modern? They, too, must focus on Jesus' messianic words and works, for the opposition will only get worse as Matthew's narrative unfolds. If the followers of Jesus focus on the delay in God's judgment of sin, doubts will arise. Their focus must be instead on the presence of salvation (cf. 2 Pet 3:8-9, 15a).

◆ B. Jesus' Testimony to John the Baptist (11:7-19)

[7]As John's disciples were leaving, Jesus began talking about him to the crowds. "What kind of man did you go into the wilderness to see? Was he a weak reed, swayed by every breath of wind? [8]Or were you expecting to see a man dressed in expensive clothes? No, people with expensive clothes live in palaces. [9]Were you looking for a prophet? Yes, and he is more than a prophet. [10]John is the man to whom the Scriptures refer when they say,

'Look, I am sending my messenger
   ahead of you,
and he will prepare your way before
   you.'*

[11]"I tell you the truth, of all who have ever lived, none is greater than John the Baptist. Yet even the least person in the Kingdom of Heaven is greater than he is!

[12]And from the time John the Baptist began preaching until now, the Kingdom of Heaven has been forcefully advancing,* and violent people are attacking it. [13]For before John came, all the prophets and the law of Moses looked forward to this present time. [14]And if you are willing to accept what I say, he is Elijah, the one the prophets said would come.* [15]Anyone with ears to hear should listen and understand!

[16]"To what can I compare this generation? It is like children playing a game in the public square. They complain to their friends,

[17]'We played wedding songs,
   and you didn't dance,
so we played funeral songs,
   and you didn't mourn.'

¹⁸For John didn't spend his time eating and drinking, and you say, 'He's possessed by a demon.' ¹⁹The Son of Man,* on the other hand, feasts and drinks, and you say, 'He's a glutton and a drunkard, and a friend of tax collectors and other sinners!' But wisdom is shown to be right by its results."

11:10 Mal 3:1.   11:12 Or *the Kingdom of Heaven has suffered from violence.*   11:14 See Mal 4:5.
11:19 "Son of Man" is a title Jesus used for himself.

NOTES

11:7-8 The inquiry of John's disciples occasioned a mini-discourse to the crowd on John's significance in redemptive history (cf. Luke 7:24-35). As John's disciples departed to tell him of Jesus' answer, Jesus seized the moment to teach about John's epochal significance. His teaching first took the form of rhetorical questions: "What kind of man did you go out into the wilderness to see?" Then Jesus' words become a bit sarcastic and expect a negative answer—John was not "a weak reed," which evidently portays a feeble, wavering person. Nor was John "dressed in expensive clothes" (cf. 3:4; 2 Kgs 1:8) fitting the delicate luxury of a king's palace.

11:9-10 *Were you looking for a prophet? Yes, and he is more than a prophet.* The next rhetorical question (11:9) gets to the heart of the matter and expects a positive answer— John was neither a vacillating weakling nor a dapper gentleman but a prophet (cf. 14:5; 21:25; Luke 1:76), even the "superprophet."

I am sending my messenger ahead of you. The prophet's crucial role involved preparing the way for Jesus in fulfillment of Mal 3:1 (cf. Matt 3:3; Isa 40:3). This one who prepared the way is identified as Elijah in Mal 4:5-6, which is alluded to in Matt 11:14 in reference to John.

11:11 *none is greater than John the Baptist. Yet even the least person in the Kingdom of Heaven is greater than he is!* Jesus' testimony to John's greatness continued with a striking contrast. No one greater than John had ever lived. But surprisingly, John's greatness pales in significance when compared with that of the least person who experiences the inauguration of the Kingdom of Heaven (cf. 13:17).

11:12 *from the time John the Baptist began preaching until now, the Kingdom of Heaven has been forcefully advancing, and violent people are attacking it.* John was an epochal messenger of God, one whose ministry marked the apex of the old era and the outset of the new. Matthew 11:12 (cf. Luke 16:16) speaks of the Kingdom as inaugurated since the days of John, but the exact meaning of this verse is difficult to ascertain due to the ambiguity of the Gr. word *biazō* [TG971, ZG1041]. The word speaks of forceful, even violent advance, and it can have a positive or negative nuance, depending on the context. It is possible that the first half of 11:12 describes the forceful attack of enemies upon the Kingdom. In that case both statements in 11:12 make the same point. But it is more likely 11:12 should be understood (as in the NLT) as contrasting the forceful advance of the Kingdom with the violent attack upon it. John's ministry marks the beginning of both these trends, growth and opposition, and thus he culminates the era of the law and the prophets and inaugurates the era of the Kingdom. See Carson (1984:265-268) and BDAG (175-176) for discussion of various views of this difficult passage.

11:13-14 *before John came, all the prophets and the law of Moses looked forward to this present time.* John's epochal role as the climax of the law and the prophets, an expression referring to the entire OT, is repeated here.

he is Elijah, the one the prophets said would come. In this role, John functions as Elijah, whose return is prophesied in Mal 4:5-6 (cf. 17:9-13). This reference to the coming of Elijah is anticipated by the reference to Mal 3:1 in Matt 11:10. Some believe this prophecy requires the literal return of Elijah, but most interpret it in the sense of Luke 1:17, that

John's ministry in the "spirit and power of Elijah" fulfills Mal 4:5-6. Either way, the citation of Mal 3:1 in Matt 11:10 and the allusion to Mal 4:5-6 here make it clear that John's preparatory ministry was anticipated in the OT. For further discussion of the relationship of John and Elijah, see Kaiser 1982 and the commentary below.

11:15 *Anyone with ears to hear should listen and understand!* This formula (cf. 13:9, 43) underlines the urgency of John's ministry and prepares for the tragic rebellion involved in rejecting it in 11:16ff.

11:16-19 *To what can I compare this generation?* Jesus then turned from explaining John's significance to confronting the unbelief of "this generation" (cf. 12:39, 41-42, 45; 16:4; 17:17; 23:36; 24:34). Jesus' words in 11:17-19 amount to a parable, which he applied to the contemporary situation (cf. Luke 7:32-35). Jesus compared John's rejection and his own to the behavior of childish brats who would not play either the wedding game or the funeral game. Neither John's ascetic abstinence (compared to mourning or singing a dirge at a funeral) nor Jesus' enjoyment of food and drink (likened to dancing at a wedding feast) was satisfactory. John was slandered with the charge of demon possession, and Jesus was smeared as a glutton and drunkard because he associated with tax collectors and sinners. No doubt Jesus did associate with such folk (cf. 9:10), but the charges of drunkenness and gluttony were unsubstantiated lies, evidently circulated by the Pharisees, who objected to table fellowship with sinners.

wisdom is shown to be right by its results. This probably refers to the righteous activities of both John and Jesus. Their deeds proved their wisdom.

COMMENTARY

Despite John's doubts (11:2-6), he should not be viewed as a weak, vacillating person. To the contrary, no greater human being ever lived, and there could be no prophet greater than the one spoken of in Malachi 3:1, who would prepare the way for the Messiah (11:7-10). John also lived at a great time, the crucial juncture of the end of the prophetic era, but he was martyred just before the death, burial, and resurrection of Jesus inaugurated the new covenant (cf. 26:28). John's ministry heralded the forceful advance of the Kingdom, but he became a victim of the violent people who were attacking it. His role was that of Elijah. (11:11-15). Neither John nor Jesus, whose lifestyles were quite opposite, were acceptable to their evil contemporaries (11:16-19). "John is too holy; Jesus is not holy enough" (Hagner 1993:311). But ultimately Jesus, perhaps personified as wisdom, will be vindicated by his deeds (11:19). Matthew 11:7-19 sets the scene for the blatant slander raised against Jesus in Matthew 12.

John and Elijah. Jesus' solemn words, "anyone with ears to hear should listen and understand," underline the importance of grasping his identification of John the Baptist with Elijah (11:14-15). These words have been the occasion of a great deal of discussion. A first reading of Malachi 4:5-6 seems to indicate a future return of Elijah the prophet to the earth to herald the day of the Lord. That Malachi 4:5-6 was taken at face value may be seen from John 1:21 and Matthew 16:14; 17:10; 27:47, 49 (cf. Sir 48:10). Jesus himself seems to affirm a future role for Elijah in Matthew 17:11, and some believe that Malachi 4:5-6 will yet be literally fulfilled (see Toussaint 1980:211). But in what sense was John said to be Elijah? In other passages John denied that he was Elijah (John 1:21), but he was said to minister in Elijah's spirit and power (Luke 1:17), which may remind the reader of the manner in which Elisha succeeded Elijah (2 Kgs 2:9-15). John was not Elijah reborn, but he fulfilled a role similar to that of Elijah. Sadly, his contemporaries were, for the most part, not willing to accept this (11:14; 21:32), and his martyrdom (14:1-12) ominously hinted at a similar end for Jesus (17:12). Whether there is yet to be a literal return of Elijah to fulfill Malachi 4:5-6 must be left as an open question.

◆ C. Jesus Pronounces Woe to Unbelievers (11:20-24)

[20]Then Jesus began to denounce the towns where he had done so many of his miracles, because they hadn't repented of their sins and turned to God. [21]"What sorrow awaits you, Korazin and Bethsaida! For if the miracles I did in you had been done in wicked Tyre and Sidon, their people would have repented of their sins long ago, clothing themselves in burlap and throwing ashes on their heads to show their remorse. [22]I tell you, Tyre and Sidon will be better off on judgment day than you.

[23]"And you people of Capernaum, will you be honored in heaven? No, you will go down to the place of the dead.* For if the miracles I did for you had been done in wicked Sodom, it would still be here today. [24]I tell you, even Sodom will be better off on judgment day than you."

11:23 Greek *to Hades.*

N O T E S

11:20 *Jesus began to denounce the towns where he had done so many of his miracles.* The denunciation of Jesus' contemporaries begun in 11:16-19 is sharpened by two similar reproaches in 11:20-24. The reproaches are introduced by the general statement of 11:20, which highlights the guilt of those who saw Jesus' miracles but refused to repent (cf. John 12:37).

What sorrow awaits. This translates the word "woe." The pronouncement of woe here balances the beatitude spoken to John's followers in 11:11. Additional pronouncements of woe upon unbelief occur in the OT (see Num 21:29; Isa 3:9-11; Ezek 24:6-9) and in Matt 18:7; 23:13-16, 23-29; 24:19; 26:24.

11:21-22 *Korazin and Bethsaida!* These were towns near Capernaum at the north end of the Sea of Galilee. Jesus charged them with unbelief even worse than that of Tyre and Sidon, important coastal cities that were ancient enemies of Israel.

Tyre and Sidon would have shown their repentance with burlap and ashes (cf. Esth 4:1-4; Ps 69:11; Jonah 3:5) had they seen Jesus' miracles, so the verdict was rendered that Korazin and Bethsaida will fare worse than Tyre and Sidon on judgment day (cf. 15:21-28). Korazin and Bethsaida are not mentioned elsewhere in Matthew, but evidently were involved in the ministry of Jesus summarized in 4:23; 9:35; 11:1. (For Tyre and Sidon see 2 Sam 5:11; 1 Kgs 9:11-12; 2 Chron 2:10-11; Pss 45:12; 87:4; Isa 23:1-9; Jer 25:15, 22; 47:4; Joel 3:4-8; Amos 1:9-10; Zech 9:2-4.)

11:23 *Capernaum.* The second reproach follows the same pattern of charge (11:23) and verdict (11:24). Sodom will fare better on judgment day than will Jesus' own city of Capernaum (4:13; 9:1).

you will go down to the place of the dead. In describing Capernaum's unbelief, Jesus alluded to the OT (Isa 14:13-15; Ezek 26:20; 31:14; 32:18, 24) to compare Capernaum's arrogance to that of the pagan king of Babylon. Far from being exalted to heaven, Capernaum would be punished in hades, the place of the dead. And that punishment would be worse than that of Sodom, the most notoriously wicked city in the entire Bible. Jesus had already spoken in a similar way about Sodom in 10:15 (cf. among many texts Gen 18:20-19:28; Deut 29:23; 32:32; Isa 1:9-10; Ezek 16:46-56; 2 Pet 2:6; Jude 1:7). These three Galilean towns would face such severe judgment because they had received such clear and sustained revelation. With greater access to truth comes greater accountability to believe it.

COMMENTARY

The reproaches of 11:20-24 are the most severe words of Jesus to this point in Matthew (but see 23:13-36). If there are any questions on the part of the reader as to how Jesus' ministry was being received, they are put to rest here. Although Matthew has stressed how the multitudes followed Jesus due to his healing miracles, here he shows that the majority of these crowds did not grasp the point of the miracles—Jesus' authority on earth to forgive sins (9:6). Many had personally experienced the blessings of the miracles, and evidently many more had observed the miracles taking place. But sadly, relatively few had grasped the significance of the miracles as authenticating the Kingdom message of repentance (cf. John 6:14-15; 26-27). The eschatological blessings of the Kingdom were enthusiastically received, but the ethical imperative of repentance was rejected.

Jesus' woes against Korazin, Bethsaida, and Capernaum assume an important principle of divine judgment, that of proportional accountability, which results in degrees of reward and punishment (cf. Luke 12:47-48). Tyre and Sidon, along with Sodom, were wicked cities that had rejected God's revelation. But the revelation they had received was not nearly so clear or sustained as the revelation of Jesus to Korazin, Bethsaida, and especially Capernaum, Jesus' adopted hometown (4:13; 9:1). Thus, the judgment of Tyre, Sidon, and even Sodom would be more tolerable than that of Korazin, Bethsaida, and Capernaum.

Korazin, Bethsaida, and Capernaum also serve as a warning to all those today whose familiarity with Christianity seems to have bred contempt. Being born into a Christian family, being a member of a church where the gospel is faithfully proclaimed, or even being a citizen of a country where Christianity is prominent are choice blessings from God, but none of them is a substitute for personal repentance. It is one thing to know about the gospel due to one's environment; it is another thing entirely to have personally acknowledged one's own need of the gospel. Judas Iscariot's life bears sad testimony to the fact that those who are nearest to the means of grace are sometimes the farthest from its end. Bruner (1987:424-429) makes some pointed and appropriate remarks about how this passage ought to impact those who have become nonchalant about the gospel.

◆ **D. Jesus' Thanksgiving and Invitation (11:25-30)**

25At that time Jesus prayed this prayer: "O Father, Lord of heaven and earth, thank you for hiding these things from those who think themselves wise and clever, and for revealing them to the childlike. 26Yes, Father, it pleased you to do it this way!

27"My Father has entrusted everything

to me. No one truly knows the Son except the Father, and no one truly knows the Father except the Son and those to whom the Son chooses to reveal him." [28]Then Jesus said, "Come to me, all of you who are weary and carry heavy burdens, and I will give you rest. [29]Take my yoke upon you. Let me teach you, because I am humble and gentle at heart, and you will find rest for your souls. [30]For my yoke is easy to bear, and the burden I give you is light."

NOTES

11:25-26 *Jesus prayed.* At 11:25 things take a striking turn from rebuke to a prayer, not of lament but of thanksgiving. The prayer is evidently public.

hiding these things from those who think themselves wise and clever, and for revealing them to the childlike. In the midst of increasing conflict and rejection, Jesus rested in the Father's sovereignty in hiding "these things" (perhaps the eschatological significance of the miracles) from those who "think themselves wise and clever" and revealing himself to the "childlike" (cf. 13:10-17; Luke 10:21-22). A similar contrast was made previously between those who thought themselves to be healthy and those who were ill (9:12-13). Here the contrast is not between the brilliant and the stupid but between the proud and the humble. The former refuse to humble themselves under God's authority and to repent when they are confronted with the gospel of the Kingdom. The latter respond to the Kingdom message by repenting, humbly acknowledging their childlike dependence upon the heavenly Father. Matthew speaks rather frequently of the followers of Jesus as poor, little, or childlike (cf. 5:3; 10:42; 18:6; 21:16; 25:40; Luke 10:21-22).

11:27 *no one truly knows the Father except the Son and those to whom the Son chooses to reveal him.* Jesus affirmed his unique messianic status as sole revealer of the Father. The Father has delegated all things to the Son (cf. 28:18), with whom he shares a unique reciprocal intimate knowledge. Only through the Son can humans receive the knowledge of the Father. The high Christology of these words reminds one of the Gospel of John (1:14, 18; 3:35; 14:6-9; 17:1-8).

11:28-30 *I will give you rest.* Jesus turns from taking solace in God's sovereignty to an invitation for people to come to him. It is only through Jesus that people come to know the Father, so it is fitting for Jesus to invite them to come to *him* and to promise that *he* will give them rest as they take *his* yoke upon them. Here Jesus takes on the role of God in fulfilling the OT promises of rest (Exod 33:14; cf. Deut 12:10; 25:19; Josh 1:13; 22:4; 2 Sam 7:11; Isa 14:3; 28:12; Heb 3:11, 18; 4:1-11). This broader concept of rest is based on God's rest after creation as the model for Israel's rest on the Sabbath (Gen 2:2; Exod 35:2). The invitation is stated in a twofold manner: Jesus invites people (1) to come to him (cf. 4:19; 22:4) and (2) to take his yoke upon them and learn from him. Both invitations are followed by promises of rest (an allusion to Jer 6:16), and there is additional incentive provided in the description of Jesus' yoke and burden in 11:30. But in reality there is only one invitation, and it is to a life of discipleship, one of following Jesus' teaching and example of humility and gentleness (cf. 5:5), symbolized by the yoke.

Jesus promised rest to those who were weary because his yoke was easy to bear and his burden was light. This language echoes the way wisdom (cf. 11:19; 23:34) was characterized in the intertestamental book of Sirach (Sir 6:23-31; 24:19; 51:23-27), which seems to develop the personification of wisdom in Prov 8:1–9:6. It is likely that there is an implied contrast to the yoke (cf. Acts 15:10; Gal 5:1) and burden (cf. 23:4; Luke 11:46) of Pharisaism here. It is not that the Torah is a heavy burden that Jesus will remove but that the Pharisaic traditions have encumbered those who wish to obey the Torah. Jesus, as the definitive interpreter of Torah (5:17-20), fulfilled the role of wisdom and was the sole agent who could provide rest for the people of God. (See Laansma 1997 for a penetrating analysis of this passage.)

COMMENTARY

In this passage Jesus responds in two ways to growing opposition. First, he finds comfort and strength in the sovereignty of God, his Father (11:25-27). Second, he continues to invite people to follow him (11:28-30). It is striking that both of these responses follow the announcement of doom upon the towns that rejected Jesus' Kingdom message. We can find no better response to opposition than that modeled by Jesus. When people reject the gospel of Christ, we can only rest in God's sovereignty and continue to offer God's grace. People come to faith in Christ for two reasons, ultimately because of God's purpose in election and immediately because they have heard the gospel. We can continue today to rest in the sovereignty of God and the sufficiency of the gospel to bring people to faith.

With the end of Matthew 11 we have come to the end of the first of three sets of two passages on unbelief (11:2-19; 11:20-24) followed by a passage on belief (11:25-30; see the analysis of chs 11–12 in the commentary on 11:1-6 above). Opposition to the Messiah and his messengers has been increasingly alluded to as Matthew's story continues (2:16; 3:7; 4:1; 5:10-12; 7:6; 8:20, 34; 9:3, 11, 34; 10:14-39). But as Matthew 11 unfolds, the situation is unmistakably grim. The Messiah's forerunner was in prison, and even he was beginning to have doubts about Jesus' ministry (11:1-3). Jesus pointed to the unmistakable signs of the Kingdom's presence in word and work (11:4-6) and extolled John's unsurpassed greatness. However, the Kingdom was being violently attacked by people who arrogantly and obstinately refused its authority (11:12, 16-24). Nevertheless, the Father was revealed (and continued to be revealed) by the Son to certain "childlike" people whose weariness compelled them to find the rest Jesus offered in Kingdom discipleship (11:25-30; cf. 10:42; 18:1-10; 25:40). Those who are wise in their own eyes increasingly reject this humbling message as Matthew's narrative unfolds the second (12:1-21) and third (12:22-50) sets of unbelief and belief passages (cf. 9:11; 12:2, 10, 24; 18:6; 25:45).

The Father and Son. The unique relationship of the Father and the Son in the redemption of God's people is described with unparalleled clarity in 11:25-27. Matthew has prepared the reader for this quintessential statement by means of previous declarations about the Son. Immanuel, the Son miraculously born to Mary, signifies the unique saving presence of God with his people (1:23). Matthew's narrative of Jesus' baptism mentions the pleasure the Father takes in the Son in words echoing Isaiah 42:1 (3:17; cf. 17:5). Satan was unable to shake the Son from his resolve not to test the Father (4:1-11). Jesus did miracles to show that the Father had given the Son of Man authority to forgive sins on the earth (9:6). In times of persecution, the disciples must confess the Son if they wish the Son to confess them to the Father (10:32-33, 40). Further comments on the grandeur of the Son will occur, culminating in the "great commission" being predicated on the Son's unique authority

(28:18-20). But one would be hard pressed to speak of the Son in terms more exalted than those used in 11:27, which bluntly yet elegantly says that saving knowledge of God the Father comes only through the selective revelation of Jesus, the exclusive mediator of salvation.

The reader of Matthew 11:25-30 may be surprised at the way in which the sovereignty of God (11:25-27) is joined to the appeal for human decision (11:28-30) in this passage. The history of the church has often witnessed polarization on these two areas of its doctrine, with some emphasizing the sovereignty of God and others human responsibility. But since biblical texts often speak of these matters side by side (see Gen 50:20; Acts 2:23; 13:48; 2 Tim 2:10), it seems foolish to attempt to separate them. It is only due to the sovereign grace of God that sinners repent and believe in Jesus. And that sovereign grace operates only through the message of the gospel of Jesus. The church must rest in the sovereignty of God if it is to gain strength for its labor of inviting people all over the world to believe in Jesus.

It is also important to note how Jesus spoke of discipleship here. The mention of a yoke is in keeping with Jewish metaphors of discipleship, but in what sense was Jesus' yoke easy and his burden light? It was light because Jesus did not endorse the oral traditions of the Pharisees, which threatened to obscure the weightier matters of the law (cf. 15:3-9; 23:16-24). But Jesus' yoke should not be viewed as less rigorous than that of the Pharisees, since he stated that the righteousness he required surpassed that of the Pharisees (5:20). Jesus' yoke of discipleship is light compared to that of the Pharisees, but it is still a yoke. Jesus is the sole revealer of the Father and he, not the Pharisees, is the definitive teacher of the Torah (5:17-48). He is gentle and humble, while they are proud and ostentatious (6:1-18; 23:1-7). Their traditions obscure and even transgress the obligations demanded by the Torah (15:3, 6), but Jesus goes to the heart of the Torah by stressing its weightier matters. Paradoxically, his focus on weightier matters leads to a lighter yoke (cf. 1 John 5:3).

◆   ## E. Controversy about the Sabbath (12:1-8; cf. Mark 2:23-28; Luke 6:1-5)

At about that time Jesus was walking through some grainfields on the Sabbath. His disciples were hungry, so they began breaking off some heads of grain and eating them. [2]But some Pharisees saw them do it and protested, "Look, your disciples are breaking the law by harvesting grain on the Sabbath."

[3]Jesus said to them, "Haven't you read in the Scriptures what David did when he and his companions were hungry? [4]He went into the house of God, and he and his companions broke the law by eating the sacred loaves of bread that only the priests are allowed to eat. [5]And haven't you read in the law of Moses that the priests on duty in the Temple may work on the Sabbath? [6]I tell you, there is one here who is even greater than the Temple! [7]But you would not have condemned my innocent disciples if you knew the meaning of this Scripture: 'I want you to show mercy, not offer sacrifices.'* [8]For the Son of Man* is Lord, even over the Sabbath!"

12:7 Hos 6:6 (Greek version).   12:8 "Son of Man" is a title Jesus used for himself.

NOTES

12:1-2 *At about that time.* Matthew places the events of 12:1-8 during the days of opposition narrated in ch 11 (cf. Mark 2:23-28; Luke 6:1-5).

they began breaking off some heads of grain and eating them. It was not against the law of Moses to pick a few heads of grain as one walked through a field, but one was not allowed to use a sickle (Deut 23:25).

some Pharisees saw them do it and protested. The Pharisees objected because in their view this amounted to work (harvesting grain) on the Sabbath (cf. Exod 20:10; 34:21; Deut 5:12-15; Isa 56:2, 4, 6). Perhaps their oral traditions spoke to this matter (cf. *m. Shabbat* 7:2).

12:3-4 *Haven't you read in the Scriptures?* Jesus' two questions (12:3, 5) imply that he was surprised at the Pharisees' ignorance of the law. Both questions "turn the tables" and put the burden on the Pharisees. They had read, but they had not understood and obeyed. Jesus' first question alludes to 1 Sam 21:1-6 (cf. Lev 24:8), the account of the sorry incident in which David was famished while fleeing from Saul and lied to the priest Ahimelech, which resulted in Saul's executing all the priests at Nob. The argument is from lesser to greater, as is explicitly stated in 12:6. Evidently, the Pharisees did not object to David's technically illegal behavior of eating the sacred bread (cf. Lev 24:5-9) with the permission of the priest Ahimelech, but they objected to Jesus' hungry disciples doing what was permitted by Deut 23:25. It is implied that Jesus is greater than David (cf. 12:6, 8, 41, 42; 22:41-46).

12:5-6 *Haven't you read in the law of Moses that the priests on duty in the Temple may work on the Sabbath?* Jesus' second question relates to the priests' "work" in the Temple on the Sabbath. Technically their work broke the law, but the priests were guiltless in that they were instructed to do this work on the Sabbath, evidently because this obligation overrode the normal Sabbath law (Lev 24:8; Num 28:9-10; cf. John 7:23). Thus, the "work" of the Temple took precedence over the "rest" of the Sabbath. The Pharisees did not object to this "work" by the priests, but they objected to Jesus, who is greater than the Temple and its sacrificial ministry. As with the previous question, the point is that there are legitimate exceptions to the general rules of Sabbath observance.

12:7-8 The remaining verses of this section bring it to a conclusion and get to the heart of Jesus' differences with the Pharisees. Two major problems surface here: the Pharisees did not interpret the OT as Jesus did and they did not recognize his position as Lord of the Sabbath.

I want you to show mercy, not offer sacrifices. For the second time (cf. 9:13), Jesus cited Hos 6:6 to the effect that the Pharisees' harsh approach to the Sabbath contradicted God's compassionate purposes for his people.

the Son of Man is Lord, even over the Sabbath! This is the third such superiority statement. Already he had stated that he is greater than David (implicitly in 12:3; cf. 22:41-45) and the Temple (12:6).

COMMENTARY

This passage describes a controversy that occurred when the Pharisees objected to Jesus' disciples' innocently (12:7; Deut 23:25) picking and eating grain as they walked through a field (12:1-2). In response, Jesus referred to King David, the Temple, and the Sabbath, with the upshot that he is greater than each of them (12:3-8). The argument from David's activities (12:3-4) was problematic enough for the Pharisees, but the clear affirmation of Jesus as greater than the Temple and as Lord of the Sabbath was viewed as outrageous, even blasphemous.

Key to understanding Jesus' differences with the Pharisees is seeing their contrasting ways of interpreting the OT. The Pharisees began with the institution of the Sabbath and viewed it as all important—it overrode the humanitarian concerns behind the legislation of Deuteronomy 23:25, which permitted the picking and eating of grain as one walked through a field. By contrast, Jesus began with God's concern for his people, which overrides the institution of the Sabbath on certain occasions. "The Sabbath was made to meet the needs of people, and not people to meet the requirements of the Sabbath" (Mark 2:27). As Hagner (1993:328) points out, Jesus' argument is both *haggadic* (analogy drawn from a narrative passage about David) and *halakhic* (precept drawn from a legal passage about the priests). As Lord of the Sabbath (12:8), he provides the ultimate authoritative interpretation of its role in the life of God's people (cf. 5:17-48). Jesus promised his disciples rest, an easy yoke, and a light burden (11:29-30). His approach to the Sabbath is a clear example of how his promise is fulfilled. But far more than mere interpretive skill distinguishes Jesus from the Pharisees. His interpretive prowess is due to his supreme position as one greater than David, the Temple, and the Sabbath. Davidic promises, priestly activities, and Sabbath rest all find fulfillment in him.

◆ **F. Healing on the Sabbath in the Synagogue (12:9-14; cf. Mark 3:1-6; Luke 6:6-11)**

⁹Then Jesus went over to their synagogue, ¹⁰where he noticed a man with a deformed hand. The Pharisees asked Jesus, "Does the law permit a person to work by healing on the Sabbath?" (They were hoping he would say yes, so they could bring charges against him.)

¹¹And he answered, "If you had a sheep that fell into a well on the Sabbath, wouldn't you work to pull it out? Of course you would. ¹²And how much more valuable is a person than a sheep! Yes, the law permits a person to do good on the Sabbath."

¹³Then he said to the man, "Hold out your hand." So the man held out his hand, and it was restored, just like the other one! ¹⁴Then the Pharisees called a meeting to plot how to kill Jesus.

NOTES

12:9-12 *Does the law permit a person to work by healing on the Sabbath?* The Sabbath conflict intensified when Jesus healed a deformed (lit., "withered" or paralyzed) hand in the synagogue in response to the Pharisees' question about its legality (cf. Mark 3:1-6; Luke 6:6-11).

so they could bring charges against him. The Pharisees wanted to have an accusation against Jesus, so they asked him whether it was lawful to heal on the Sabbath (12:10; cf. Luke 13:14; John 5:7-10). The NLT's translation expands this somewhat to bring out the Pharisees' assumption that the healing would amount to work and would break the Sabbath. If the tradition later codified in the Mishnah around AD 200 was current in Jesus' day, the Pharisees themselves would have evidently permitted healing when life was in danger (*m. Yoma* 8:6).

the law permits a person to do good on the Sabbath. Jesus responded (12:11-12) that it is lawful to do good on the Sabbath, even when an emergency constitutes a technical violation. He referred to a practice the Pharisees would evidently permit—removing a sheep from a "well" (more likely a cistern or pit; cf. Deut 22:4; Prov 12:10). Again the argument is from lesser to greater, since healing a needy person is more necessary than getting a sheep out of a cistern (cf. 6:26-30; 10:31).

12:13-14 The theological argument of the previous verses was concluded by Jesus doing what the Pharisees considered to be unlawful—he commanded the man to stretch out his hand, and as he did so, it was restored to normal function.

to plot how to kill Jesus. That the Pharisees would decide to kill Jesus is not a surprise to the attentive reader of Matthew (cf. 3:7; 9:11, 34; 12:24; 15:7, 12; 16:6, 21; 17:10, 12, 22; 20:18; 21:45-46; 22:15, 34; 23:29-32; 26:2-5, 14-16).

C O M M E N T A R Y

This passage reinforces the basic impasse between Jesus and the Pharisees, which is evident in 12:1-8. They were at loggerheads over the relation of Sabbath law to deeds of compassion. The Pharisees evidently interpreted the Sabbath law strictly and made no exceptions for instances of compassion like those involved in Jesus' healings, but Jesus pointed out an inconsistency in their approach. They had no problem with a sheep being rescued from a cistern on the Sabbath, yet they condemned him for healing a person, who is much more valuable to God than a sheep. Theoretically, they might have responded to Jesus that the healing of the man's hand was not a matter of life or death, and could have waited until the next day, but Matthew's narrative ends with this rejoinder of Jesus. Jesus showed that the written Torah was not violated by such healing.

The legal dispute is one thing, but it led the Pharisees to take steps to end the dispute by eliminating Jesus. At first glance, this seems to be a rather draconian solution to a religious dispute. Perhaps the Pharisees were simply planning to enforce Exodus 31:14, but baser motives were probably at work. Evidently, Jesus was perceived as a threat to the status quo, so jealousy could also be involved, since an increase in Jesus' popularity and influence would inevitably mean a decrease in that of the Pharisees (cf. 27:18). Additionally, the Pharisees may have feared that Jesus' followers would become a riotous mob, which the Roman authorities would view as a threat to their rule over Judea (cf. 26:4). At any rate, it is not a little ironic that a dispute over the finer points of Sabbath law led the Pharisees to plan to break the sixth commandment, "you shall not murder."

◆   **G. Jesus, the Servant of the Lord (12:15-21)**

¹⁵But Jesus knew what they were planning. So he left that area, and many people followed him. He healed all the sick among them, ¹⁶but he warned them not to reveal who he was. ¹⁷This fulfilled the prophecy of Isaiah concerning him:

¹⁸"Look at my Servant, whom I have chosen.
He is my Beloved, who pleases me.
I will put my Spirit upon him,

and he will proclaim justice to the nations.
¹⁹He will not fight or shout or raise his voice in public.
²⁰He will not crush the weakest reed or put out a flickering candle.
Finally he will cause justice to be victorious.
²¹And his name will be the hope of all the world."*

12:18-21 Isa 42:1-4 (Greek version for 42:4).

NOTES

12:15-16 *Jesus knew what they were planning. So he left that area.* By some means, Jesus became aware of the Pharisees' conspiracy and made a strategic withdrawal to another area (cf. 2:12-14, 22; 4:12; 14:13; 15:21).

many people followed him. As usual, crowds followed Jesus, and there were many healings.

he warned them not to reveal who he was. Jesus' warnings that those healed should not make him known (cf. 8:4; 9:30; 17:9) seem to be due to his desire not to pander to the crowd's thirst for the spectacular. Any wave of popular enthusiasm for Jesus would clearly precipitate intensified Pharisaic opposition.

12:17-18 *my Servant, whom I have chosen.* Jesus' desire to keep a low profile in the face of Pharisaic opposition and popular enthusiasm was in keeping with Isa 42:1-4, which, as cited here, is the longest OT passage in Matthew. This text, already alluded to in the Father's endorsement at Jesus' baptism (3:17; cf. 17:5), speaks of the Lord's beloved servant as one who is enabled by the Spirit to proclaim justice to the nations (12:18). This reference to the Gentiles ("nations") is significant, given the opposition Jesus was receiving from the Jews. It anticipates the positive responses from Gentiles to Jesus and the Kingdom that follow (cf. 15:28; 27:54).

12:19-21 *He will not fight or shout.* The Spirit led the Servant away from the type of ministry that might please the carnal desires of the crowd. The Servant's ministry is not characterized by fighting, shouting, or rhetoric calculated to incite the crowd.

He will not crush the weakest reed or put out a flickering candle. He will handle weak people, pictured as bruised reeds and flickering candles, with gentleness and compassion.

his name will be the hope of all the world. Lit., "the Gentiles will hope in his name." Thus, his proclamation of justice to the Gentiles (12:18), characterized by compassionate deeds rather than inflammatory words (12:19-20), will be successful (12:21).

COMMENTARY

Matthew 11–12 comprises a block of narrative material stressing the increasing opposition to Jesus and the Kingdom. The threefold structure of this narrative block has been discussed previously in the commentary on 11:1-6. This structure involves three sets of passages, each containing two passages stressing unbelief followed by a passage stressing belief. With Matthew 12:21 we have come to the end of the second of these three sets, with 12:1-8 and 12:9-14 stressing unbelief and 12:15-21 stressing belief.

The citation of Isaiah 42:1-4 here serves three purposes. First, it explains why Jesus withdrew from conflict with the Pharisees and why he urged the people whom he had healed not to reveal who he was. Jesus' ministry would not be characterized by conflict and by loud words spoken to incite the masses. Instead, he would prove to be gentle and merciful in his ministry to the weak (cf. 5:5, 7; 11:29). Second, Isaiah 42:1-4 indicates that the Servant would have a ministry to the Gentiles. Although Jesus was being increasingly rejected by many of "the sons of the Kingdom" (cf. 8:12), Matthew has gradually been making it clear that certain Gentiles were receptive to the Kingdom (cf. 1:3, 5-6; 2:1-2, 11; 4:15-16; 8:10-12; 15:28; 27:54) and that the followers of Jesus must widen their horizons for a worldwide ministry to all the nations (22:9; 24:14; 25:32; 28:18-20). Third, Isaiah 42:1 stressed that the Servant's ministry would be Spirit-empowered. This lays the background for Jesus' response to the slander that his powers of exorcism were demonic. Thus, the Pharisees' charge in 12:24 is found to be anti-Scriptural, and amounts to an unforgivable slander of the Spirit of God (12:31-32).

It is paradoxical that the power of Jesus and the Kingdom is found in service born out of humility and compassion (cf. 11:29). The Messiah used his power not to gain control over people but to serve them. Jesus did not attempt to extend the Kingdom by selfish quarrels involving inflammatory rhetoric. His ministry would eventually bring justice to victory (12:20), but even John the Baptist had doubts about the way in which this was being accomplished. Certainly Christians today have a great deal to learn from their Lord on this matter. Their course of life is likewise to be that of sacrificial service (cf. 16:21-25; 20:25-28).

◆   H. Jesus and the Prince of Demons (12:22-37; cf. Mark 3:20-30)

²²Then a demon-possessed man, who was blind and couldn't speak, was brought to Jesus. He healed the man so that he could both speak and see. ²³The crowd was amazed and asked, "Could it be that Jesus is the Son of David, the Messiah?"

²⁴But when the Pharisees heard about the miracle, they said, "No wonder he can cast out demons. He gets his power from Satan,* the prince of demons."

²⁵Jesus knew their thoughts and replied, "Any kingdom divided by civil war is doomed. A town or family splintered by feuding will fall apart. ²⁶And if Satan is casting out Satan, he is divided and fighting against himself. His own kingdom will not survive. ²⁷And if I am empowered by Satan, what about your own exorcists? They cast out demons, too, so they will condemn you for what you have said. ²⁸But if I am casting out demons by the Spirit of God, then the Kingdom of God has arrived among you. ²⁹For who is powerful enough to enter the house of a strong man like Satan and plunder his goods? Only someone even stronger—someone who could tie him up and then plunder his house.

³⁰"Anyone who isn't with me opposes me, and anyone who isn't working with me is actually working against me.

³¹"So I tell you, every sin and blasphemy can be forgiven—except blasphemy against the Holy Spirit, which will never be forgiven. ³²Anyone who speaks against the Son of Man can be forgiven, but anyone who speaks against the Holy Spirit will never be forgiven, either in this world or in the world to come.

³³"A tree is identified by its fruit. If a tree is good, its fruit will be good. If a tree is bad, its fruit will be bad. ³⁴You brood of snakes! How could evil men like you speak what is good and right? For whatever is in your heart determines what you say. ³⁵A good person produces good things from the treasury of a good heart, and an evil person produces evil things from the treasury of an evil heart. ³⁶And I tell you this, you must give an account on judgment day for every idle word you speak. ³⁷The words you say will either acquit you or condemn you."

12:24 Greek Beelzeboul; also in 12:27. Other manuscripts read Beezeboul; Latin version reads Beelzebub.

NOTES

12:22-23 The healing of a demon-possessed, blind, and mute man produced opposing reactions from onlookers (cf. Mark 3:20-30; Luke 11:14-23; 12:10). The healing is mentioned only briefly; the focus is on the following controversy. Jesus had previously healed blind people and mute people, but this is the only place in the Gospels where Jesus is said to have healed a person who had both maladies. The reaction of the crowd is in stark contrast to that of the Pharisees.

Could it be that Jesus is the Son of David, the Messiah? The crowds were amazed and wondered whether Jesus was the Son of David. The NLT adds "the Messiah" to bring out the messianic significance of the expression "son of David" (cf. the discussion in the Christology section of "Major Themes" in the Introduction and 1:1, 20; 9:27; 12:23; 15:22; 20:30-31; 21:9, 15; 22:41-45).

12:24 *no wonder he can cast out demons. He gets his power from Satan, the prince of demons.* The Pharisees viewed Jesus not as messianic but as demonic, essentially repeating a charge originally made in 9:34. The NLT handles the charge of the Pharisees in 12:24 rather freely. The Gr. text does not have the expressions "no wonder" or "power" and the word translated as "Satan" is lit. "Beelzeboul" (see NLT mg), as in 10:25. Taken lit., the Pharisees counter the popular interpretation of Jesus' miracle with the idea that "he does not cast out demons except by Beelzeboul, prince of the demons." Beelzeboul probably means "lord of the house" or "lord of the heights." The Pharisees did not deny the reality of Jesus' miracles but attributed them to Satan, not to God.

12:25-28 *if Satan is casting out Satan, he is divided and fighting against himself.* Jesus' answer to the Pharisees contains two rhetorical questions that address their false interpretation of his exorcism, followed by a statement of its true interpretation. He first asked whether Satan would work against himself (12:25-26), then asked whether the Pharisees' own exorcists were empowered by Satan (12:27).

I am casting out demons by the Spirit of God. Jesus stated the real power behind his works: the Spirit of God empowers the words and works of the Kingdom (12:28).

The first question is based on common sense observations about the need for unity in any kingdom, city, or household. It shows that the Pharisees' view of Jesus is untenable because it is illogical and contrary to experience. Jesus reduced the Pharisees' charge to absurdity. The second question is *ad hominem*, based on the fact that evidently there were Pharisees who practiced exorcisms (cf. Acts 19:13-14). It shows that the Pharisees' view of Jesus was untenable because it was inconsistent—the Pharisees themselves practiced exorcism but slandered Jesus for doing the same thing. After showing that the Pharisees' charge of collaboration with demons was nonsensical and false, Jesus affirmed the real power behind his miracles. Far from being demonic, it was divine. The same Holy Spirit of God who was active in Jesus' conception (1:18, 20) had been empowering him for ministry since his baptism in fulfillment of Isa 42:1 (3:16-4:1; 12:18). Thus, there is only one conclusion that can be drawn from the Spirit-empowered miracles of Jesus—the saving power of God's Kingdom has arrived among Jesus' contemporaries (cf. 3:2; 4:17; 10:7; 24:14). This is probably the strongest statement of the presence of the Kingdom in Matthew.

12:29 *who is powerful enough to enter the house of a strong man like Satan and plunder his goods? Only someone even stronger.* This pictures the presence and advance of the Kingdom upon Satan's domain as the tying up of a strong man and the looting of his house. So Jesus' preaching, teaching, and miraculous deeds were encroaching upon Satan's territory (see 11:1, 5, 21-23; 12:13, 18, 22; cf. 1 John 3:8).

12:30 *Anyone who isn't with me opposes me.* In light of this, opposition to Jesus (9:3, 11, 34; 10:25; 12:2, 10, 24) is unthinkable, and neutrality is impossible, since the one who does not actively support Jesus and the Kingdom opposes him. Perhaps these words were intended to warn the wondering crowd more than the Pharisees, whose minds were made up.

12:31-32 *blasphemy against the Holy Spirit, which will never be forgiven.* Here Jesus moves from defense to offense, from explanation to warning (Davies and Allison

1991:344). In these verses Jesus tells the Pharisees in no uncertain terms that their slanderous charges (cf. 9:34; 10:25; 12:24) are unforgivable. The two verses are roughly parallel, with 32a and 32b expanding the positive and negative statements of 31a and 31b.
If the Pharisees had merely spoken against Jesus, their sin might have been forgiven. But
they spoke against the Spirit and attributed the work of the Spirit to the prince of the
demons. Since the power of the Spirit was the source of Jesus' works (12:28), it is really
the Spirit who was being slandered, not Jesus. For similar sins, see Isa 63:10 and Acts
7:52. The consequences of such sin are eternal; it will not be forgiven in the present or
the world to come (cf 13:22, 39, 40; 24:3). One may slander Jesus without slandering
the Spirit, since one can slander Jesus without being aware of the Spirit's empowerment
of Jesus. This may be forgiven. But to slander the Spirit is to look at the miraculous works
of the Spirit present in Jesus' ministry and ascribe these works to Satan. This will not
be forgiven.

12:33 *If a tree is good, its fruit will be good.* The rejoinder to the Pharisees continues
with a new metaphor, that of a tree and its fruit (cf. 3:7-10; 7:16-20). The Pharisees must
make a consistent decision. They must either view Jesus (the tree) and its fruit (his words
and deeds) as worthless, or they must view them as good. Jesus' good fruit demonstrates
that he is good, but the Pharisees attribute the good deeds to a demonic source. When the
Pharisees speak, their words are like the worthless fruit of a worthless tree because they
speak from an evil heart (12:34-35; cf. 15:11, 19).

12:34 *brood of snakes!* Jesus' depiction of the Pharisees as a brood of snakes recalls 3:7
and anticipates 23:33. The words of the Pharisees are therefore suggestive of their ultimate
destiny. Evil words spoken from the treasury of an evil heart portend eschatological doom.
These words spoken against the Spirit will ultimately condemn the Pharisees. On the other
hand, good people will speak good words that will ultimately acquit them.

COMMENTARY

The Pharisaic opposition to Jesus comes to a head in this section. The healing of a
blind, mute, demon-possessed man results in antithetical responses. The crowd
wondered whether Jesus was the Messiah, but the Pharisees, perhaps in response to
both the miracle and the crowd's openness to Jesus, slandered Jesus (and, more
importantly, the Spirit) with the charge of collaborating with the prince of the
demons (12:22-24). Jesus' response comprises the rest of the passage (12:25-37). In
it he argues convincingly against the Pharisees' view of his ministry and affirms that
his ministry must be understood as nothing less that the arrival of the Kingdom by
the power of God's Spirit (12:25-28). Then he likens the advance of the Kingdom
into Satan's domain to the binding of a strong man and the looting of his household and warns his listeners that neutrality is impossible when it comes to the work
of the Kingdom (12:29-30). The Pharisees' slander amounts to an unforgivable
blasphemy—not merely of Jesus but of the Spirit of God who empowers him
(12:31-32). Further, their slanderous words betray their evil hearts and portend
their eschatological doom, just as worthless fruit proves that a tree is worthless
(12:33-37).

The Coming(s) of Jesus and the Binding of Satan. Most expositors (Toussaint
1980:163-164 is an exception) acknowledge that Matthew 12:28-29 teaches the
presence of the Kingdom, and that God's saving power began to encroach upon the

domain of Satan during the life and ministry of Jesus. Generally, this encroach-
ment or binding is linked in some way to the description of the binding of Satan in
the abyss in Revelation 20:1-10. Theologians who hold an amillennial view generally argue that Satan has been bound by the first coming of Christ so that he can no
longer deceive the nations (cf. Rev 20:3). Those who hold to premillennialism, especially dispensational premillennialism, take an opposite view, stressing that the
binding of Satan in Revelation 20 is a yet future event that will happen only at the
second coming of Christ to the earth. It appears that one must find some truth in
both of these views. Dispensationalists must make room for the decisive defeat of
Satan at Jesus' first coming, and amillennialists must not underestimate the extent
to which Satan's limited power can still injure the church. Satan's power to claim
any true victory has been shattered in Christ's first coming, yet he remains a sinister
enemy who must be resisted by all the means of grace (Eph 6:11-18; Jas 4:7; 1 Pet
5:8-9). Only in the future will he be totally incapacitated (Rev 20:1-10). Believers
can rejoice that the power of the gospel of Jesus already overcomes the enemy
(John 12:31; 16:11; Acts 26:18; Eph 2:1-6; Col 1:13), and that God will eventually
fully destroy Satan's evil work so that in the new earth only righteousness will
dwell (Rev 21-22).

The Unforgivable Slander of the Holy Spirit.   The solemn words of 12:31-32 ought
to be taken to heart by all readers of Matthew. But the question remains as to the
precise nature of "the unpardonable sin." Well-meaning but over-zealous preachers
have at times used this verse to threaten their listeners that to disbelieve the gospel
message is to commit the unpardonable sin. In ministry, one may encounter individuals who are under the impression that there is no hope for them because they
have "sinned away their day of grace." Theologians tend to interpret the unpardonable sin as the generic sin of unbelief, linking this Matthean passage to such texts as
John 3:18; 16:9; 1 John 5:16. But as serious as general disbelief in Jesus is, those
who take this passage as a reference to it are mistaken.

   The specific situation in Matthew 12 involves the Spirit-empowered miracles of
Jesus, which ought to have been viewed as evidence of his messianic status (12:23)
and his authority to forgive sins on earth (9:6). Far from simply disbelieving this,
the Pharisees slandered the ministry of the Spirit through the Messiah by accusing
Jesus of collaborating with the very forces his ministry was overpowering (12:29).
Therefore, it would be wise for expositors to exercise caution in the broad application of this text to unbelief in general. To be sure, ultimate unbelief in Jesus is unforgivable, but the point of this text is to underline not only unbelief in the face of
clear evidence that Jesus is the Messiah, but also the slanderous perversion of this
messianic evidence into demonic evidence. Today people are accountable to believe the gospel when they hear it, but this hardly warrants the notion that those
who do not immediately accept Jesus have entered an unalterable state of unforgivable doom.

◆ **I. The Sign of Jonah (12:38-45)**

38One day some teachers of religious law and Pharisees came to Jesus and said, "Teacher, we want you to show us a miraculous sign to prove your authority." 39But Jesus replied, "Only an evil, adulterous generation would demand a miraculous sign; but the only sign I will give them is the sign of the prophet Jonah. 40For as Jonah was in the belly of the great fish for three days and three nights, so will the Son of Man be in the heart of the earth for three days and three nights. 41"The people of Nineveh will stand up against this generation on judgment day and condemn it, for they repented of their sins at the preaching of Jonah. Now someone greater than Jonah is here—but you refuse to repent. 42The queen of Sheba* will also stand up against this generation on judgment day and condemn it, for she came from a distant land to hear the wisdom of Solomon. Now someone greater than Solomon is here—but you refuse to listen.

43"When an evil* spirit leaves a person, it goes into the desert, seeking rest but finding none. 44Then it says, 'I will return to the person I came from.' So it returns and finds its former home empty, swept, and in order. 45Then the spirit finds seven other spirits more evil than itself, and they all enter the person and live there. And so that person is worse off than before. That will be the experience of this evil generation."

12:42 Greek *The queen of the south.* **12:43** Greek *unclean.*

NOTES

12:38 *One day.* In the Gr. this is lit. "then"; it need not imply the beginning of a separate event. It is best to understand 12:38 as a response by the Pharisees to Jesus' previous rejoinder (12:25-37) to their accusation that he had cast out demons by the power of the prince of the demons (12:22-24).

Teacher, we want you to show us a miraculous sign. Those who call Jesus "teacher" in Matthew are not believers in him (cf. 8:19; 9:11; 17:24; 22:16, 36). Jesus' solemn words about the Pharisees' accountability for their accusation led them to ask him to prove himself with a sign (16:1, 4; 24:3, 30; cf. Mark 8:11-12; Luke 11:16, 29-32). But Jesus had performed many miracles before the Pharisees, and his last miracle led them to slander the Holy Spirit. So why should he perform an especially significant miracle, a "sign" (*semeion* [TG4592, ZG4956]; cf. John 6:30)? Although there was precedence for Israel's leaders to perform signs (Exod 4:30-31), Jesus simply answered that this evil and adulterous generation (cf. 11:16-19; 16:4; 17:17; 23:29-36; 24:34) would see no more signs except that of the prophet Jonah (cf. 16:4).

12:39 *an evil, adulterous generation.* Jesus' description of his contemporaries as adulterous uses a common biblical metaphor for sin (Deut 32:5; Jer 2:23; Ezek 16; Jas 4:4). This incident is similar to that of 16:1-4.

12:40 *Jonah was in the belly of the great fish for three days and three nights.* The reference to Jonah 1:17 provides a cryptic prophecy of the death of Jesus. Jonah himself is the sign—his three days and nights in the belly of the great fish are to be compared to Jesus' three days and nights in the earth. This language need not mean that Jesus would be in the grave for seventy-two hours, since in Jewish reckoning any part of a day could count as a day (cf. Gen 42:17-18; 1 Kgs 20:29; Esth 4:16-5:1). Thus, the traditional passion week chronology of Jesus' death on Friday and resurrection on Sunday is not necessarily challenged. This appears to be the first time Jesus hints at his upcoming death in Matthew (cf. 16:21; 17:9, 22-23).

12:41 *The people of Nineveh will stand up against this generation.* The allusion to Jonah continues with Jesus' unfavorable comparison of his contemporaries to Jonah's audience.

In language reminiscent of 11:21-24, Jesus underlines the severity of their sin—the Ninevites repented when Jonah preached (Jonah 3:2), but Jesus' contemporaries would not repent when one greater than Jonah preached (cf. 12:6).

12:42 *The queen of Sheba.* Lit., "the queen of the south." She came from a distant land to hear Solomon's wisdom (1 Kgs 10:1-10; 2 Chr 9:1-9), but Jesus' contemporaries would not accept the wisdom of one greater than Solomon. Compare the implicit comparison with David in 12:3. Thus, both the Ninevites and the queen of Sheba will condemn Jesus' contemporaries on the day of judgment.

12:43-45 *When an evil spirit leaves a person.* This parabolic passage about the activities of an unclean spirit (cf. Matt 10:1 and several texts in Mark and Luke) returns to the matter of exorcism with which Jesus' debate with the Pharisees began (12:22). The spirit leaves its human abode for the desert and later returns with seven other spirits to the man, who has become a more attractive abode (cf. Isa 13:21; 34:14 concerning spirits inhabiting the desert). Now inhabited by the original spirit and seven others, the man becomes thoroughly dominated by them, much worse off than he was before the first spirit left. Evidently, nothing good came into the man to fill the vacuum left when the first spirit left. For various views of this enigmatic passage, see Davies and Allison (1991:359-362).

COMMENTARY

Matthew 12:38-45 contains two parts, both of which stress the gravity of the unbelief of Jesus' contemporaries. In fact, Jesus' words in this section begin and end by mentioning "this evil generation," and there are two additional references to it (12:39, 41-42, 45). The first part contrasts the Pharisees' unbelief with notable and surprising cases of belief in the OT (12:38-42). The second part portrays this unbelief parabolically, evidently to point out that Israel would be worse off after not believing in Jesus than it was before he came. It seems to be a cryptic warning against superficial repentance and a veiled prophecy of the eschatological doom of Jesus' contemporaries (cf. Luke 11:24-26).

This passage underlines the evils of hardened unbelief as do few others. After the Pharisees had seen Jesus do many miracles, instead of believing, they outrageously attributed the miracles to Satan. When they were shown the untenability of that position, they responded not with belief but with an evidently insincere request for another miracle. Their unbelief in the face of overwhelming evidence is contrasted with the belief of the Ninevites and the queen of the south in the face of relatively little evidence. Thus, they provide a grim illustration of what Jesus spoke of in 11:25—that God had hidden the message of the Kingdom from those who were wise and clever in their own estimation and had revealed it to those who were childlike. No amount of further signs would avail for such people, not even the resurrection of Jesus from the dead (12:40; cf. 28:11-15; Luke 16:27-31; 1 Cor 1:22). This passage also illustrates why Jesus did miracles. Miracles were deeds of power done with compassion for those in need, not spectacular feats designed to convince those already hardened in skepticism. For hearts not hardened in rebellion, comparatively little evidence was needed, as in the case of Nineveh and the queen of Sheba.

The parable of 12:43-45 is enigmatic. The mere absence of evil spirits does not accomplish redemption. The house has been cleaned, but a good tenant has not taken up residence. Perhaps this refers to the response of Jesus' contemporaries to John's and Jesus' ministries. Some repented, but many did not, with the result that there was no genuine national repentance, and bleak prospects for the future (23:36).

◆ J. The True Family of Jesus (12:46-50; cf. Mark 3:31-35; Luke 8:19-21)

⁴⁶As Jesus was speaking to the crowd, his mother and brothers stood outside, asking to speak to him. ⁴⁷Someone told Jesus, "Your mother and your brothers are outside, and they want to speak to you."* ⁴⁸Jesus asked, "Who is my mother? Who are my brothers?" ⁴⁹Then he pointed to his disciples and said, "Look, these are my mother and brothers. ⁵⁰Anyone who does the will of my Father in heaven is my brother and sister and mother!"

12:47 Some manuscripts do not include verse 47. Compare Mark 3:32 and Luke 8:20.

NOTES

12:46-50 *these are my mother and brothers.* As Jesus continued to speak to the crowd, his mother and brothers (cf. 1:16, 18; 13:55-56) appeared outside and wanted to speak with him (cf. Mark 3:31-35; Luke 8:19-21). Perhaps they were concerned over the intensifying conflict between Jesus and the Pharisees. The absence of Joseph is generally taken to indicate that he had died by this time. When Jesus is told of their presence and desire to speak with him, he finds a "teachable moment" and speaks of his true family, those who do the will of his Father in heaven. Jesus teaches by means of a question (12:48), an answer (12:49), and an explanation (12:50). Other NT passages make it clear that Jesus' family was not always in complete sympathy with his messianic mission (Mark 3:21; John 7:1-5). It is perhaps significant that Matthew says that Jesus' mother and brothers were "outside." If so, Jesus' disciples, who do the will of his Father in heaven, are "inside," and are his true family. His disciples are his brothers (cf. 28:10). The mention of Jesus' brothers in this passage (and sisters in 13:56) makes the notion of Mary's perpetual virginity difficult to maintain.

COMMENTARY

Matthew 11-12 comprises a block of narrative material stressing the increasing opposition to Jesus and the Kingdom. The threefold structure of this narrative block has been discussed already in the commentary on Matthew 11:1-6. This structure involves three sets of passages, each containing two passages stressing unbelief followed by a passage stressing belief. With Matthew 12:50 we have come to the end of the second of these three sets, with 12:22-37 and 12:38-45 stressing unbelief and 12:46-50 stressing belief.

In this passage the mood turns from unbelief to belief, from a negative to a positive perspective. Jesus' own family becomes a warning against superficial discipleship. Elsewhere Jesus affirms the family (15:1-9; 19:19; John 19:27), so the point here is not disrespect for them but allegiance to those whose lives are ordered by the values of the Kingdom. Davies and Allison (1991:364) put it well: "The words do not dissolve family bonds but rather relativize them." Jesus' disciples may have to leave their families behind (19:29), and they may even face betrayal by the members of their own families (10:21; 12:35-37). When confronted by the urgent demands of discipleship, they cannot make excuses. Everyday family duties (cf. 4:22; 8:22) cannot take precedence over one's loyalty to the Messiah and his Kingdom. Christians today must follow Jesus' example in the area of family loyalties. It is not at all unusual for Christians to treat their brothers and sisters in Christ in a harsh manner, which is totally inconsistent with Kingdom values and their relationship in the family of God (cf. 23:8). There is great need for a renewed appreciation of the truth portrayed in Matthew 12:46-50.

Summary of Matthew 11–12 and Transition to Matthew 13. In chapters 11–12 Matthew gradually makes his readers aware of the rising opposition and rejection that Jesus experienced. He has previously alluded to the issue that erupts into unforgivable blasphemy in this chapter (12:24-32; cf 9:34), but chapter 12 amounts to a total rift between Jesus and the religious leaders. The chapter records increasing conflict as Jesus confronted the Pharisees over two Sabbath issues (12:1-8, 9-14). Aware of their murder plot, Jesus withdrew (cf. 4:12; 14:13; 15:21; 16:4) to an unnamed location where he healed many (12:15-21). His counsel that those who were healed should remain silent was disregarded, but it served to fulfill Isaiah 42:1-4. The healing of a demonized deaf and mute man precipitates the climactic conflict (12:22-37), which was followed by Jesus' condemnation of that evil generation (12:38-46). The chapter concludes with an incident that shows that even the members of Jesus' own family were not necessarily his real family. Overall, the chapter makes it clear that Jesus' approach to the OT law (cf. 5:17-32) was totally at variance with that of the Pharisees, who ominously planned to murder the one who was greater than David, the Temple, the Sabbath, Jonah, and Solomon (12:3, 6, 8, 41-42). As this opposition by the evil and adulterous generation escalated, Jesus delivered more of his speeches in the form of parables, by which he communicated with his disciples and at the same time obscured the truth from his enemies, who refused to acknowledge the coming of the Kingdom.

◆ **V. Parables of the Kingdom of Heaven (13:1-53)**
   A. The Parable of the Sower (13:1-9; cf. Mark 4:1-9; Luke 8:4-8)

Later that same day Jesus left the house and sat beside the lake. ²A large crowd soon gathered around him, so he got into a boat. Then he sat there and taught as the people stood on the shore. ³He told many stories in the form of parables, such as this one:

"Listen! A farmer went out to plant some seeds. ⁴As he scattered them across his field, some seeds fell on a footpath, and the birds came and ate them. ⁵Other seeds fell on shallow soil with underlying rock. The seeds sprouted quickly because the soil was shallow. ⁶But the plants soon wilted under the hot sun, and since they didn't have deep roots, they died. ⁷Other seeds fell among thorns that grew up and choked out the tender plants. ⁸Still other seeds fell on fertile soil, and they produced a crop that was thirty, sixty, and even a hundred times as much as had been planted! ⁹Anyone with ears to hear should listen and understand."

NOTES

13:1-2 *A large crowd soon gathered.* The setting of the third discourse is similar to that of the first (cf. 5:1); in both cases Jesus was surrounded by crowds. Jesus apparently paid little attention to his mother and brothers who wanted to speak with him (12:46; 13:1) and shortly left the house where he had been teaching for the nearby Sea of Galilee, where he spoke to the crowd standing by the shore (cf. Mark 4:1-9; Luke 8:4-8) while seated in a boat (cf. 5:1; 24:3). In 13:36, Matthew reports Jesus' move from the seashore back to the house.

13:3 *parables.* Though Matthew's narrative of Jesus' teaching has already included occasional parabolic elements (7:24-27; 9:15-17; 11:16-19; 12:29, 33, 43-45), the word "parable" (*parabolē* [TG3850, ZG4130]) occurs here for the first time as Jesus speaks to the multitudes (13:3, 10, 13, 18, 24, 33-36, 53; 15:15; 21:33, 45; 22:1; 24:32). The word "parable" in the NT is related semantically to the word *mashal* [TH4912, ZH5442] in the OT (see Num 23:7, 18; 1 Sam 10:12; Ezek 17:2; 24:3), and both may be used to describe a proverb, an enigma, a riddle, a taunt, a simile, or an allegorical story. In all of these nuanced meanings, the common denominator is the use of analogy to illumine or obscure. From 13:3 one would assume that Jesus told many parables, and that Matthew selects representative stories that reflect the main themes of Jesus' teaching that Matthew viewed as most relevant for his community.

A farmer went out to plant some seeds. The picture is of a farmer scattering seed by hand (cf. Ps 126:5-6; Isa 55:10-11; 2 Esdr 4:26-32; 8:41; 9:31-37; 1 Cor 3:6-9).

13:4-8 Jesus spoke of four places where the scattered seed fell. It is not clear whether the practice was to plow the ground before or after the seed was sown. In the first three cases, the seed did not produce a crop because it was eaten by birds, fell on shallow soil, or was choked by thorns (cf. Job 31:40). In the fourth case, however, the seed fell on fertile ground and produced various levels of crops, the least of which would be quite remarkable by ancient standards (13:8; cf. Gen 26:12). In 13:4, the seed should probably be understood as falling on the packed soil beside the path, not the packed soil of the path itself (cf. "on a footpath," NLT). In 13:5-6 the problem is an underlying shelf of bedrock, not multiple rocks in the soil. Such soil warms rapidly, and the seed sprouts quickly, but the plant wilts as the soil soon loses moisture (cf. Jas 1:11).

13:9 *Anyone with ears to hear should listen and understand.* Jesus' affirmation in 13:9 (cf. 11:15; 13:43; cf. Mark 4:23; Luke 14:35; Rev 2:7; 13:9) underlines the importance of the crowd's grasping the meaning of the parable. His interpretation of the parable (13:18-23) shows its relevance to the crowd's relationship to the message of the Kingdom.

COMMENTARY

After briefly mentioning the setting (13:1-2), Matthew narrates Jesus' third major discourse (13:3-52; cf. the first discourse in Matt 5–7 and the second in Matt 10). The discourse can be seen as having two sections of four parables each if 13:51-52 is interpreted (correctly) as a parable. The first section is addressed to the crowds (13:3-33) and the second to the disciples (13:36-52). In both of these sections, Jesus answers a question from the disciples about parables (13:10-17, 36-43). Between the two sections is Matthew's comment on the parables as prophetic fulfillment (13:34-35). It is also interesting to note that a pair of similar short parables concludes the first section and begins the second section (13:31-33, 44-46). Though some (see Hagner 1993:362-364) doubt that there is any symmetrical structure in the discourse, at least two proposals have some merit.

Wenham 1979 presents a structure involving chiasmus or introverted parallelism:

A. Parable of the Sower: Hearing the word of the Kingdom (13:1-9)

B. Disciples' Question and Jesus' Answer with Interpretation of the Sower (13:10-23)

C. Parable of the Tares: Good and evil (13:24-30)

D. Parables of the Mustard Seed and Leaven: Growth (13:31-33)

E. Explanation of parables and Interpretation of the Tares (13:34-43)

D'. Parables of Treasure and Pearl: Sacrifice (13:44-46)

C'. Parable of the Net: Good and evil (13:47-50)

B'. Jesus' Question and Disciples' Answer about Understanding Parables (13:51)

A'. Parable of the Homeowner: Trained for the Kingdom (13:52)

Wenham's analysis notes the two halves of the discourse well. It also is correct in seeing the symmetry or the short paired parables of mustard seed/leaven and treasure/pearl. But it is not as convincing in its non-symmetrical placement of Jesus' two interpretations of parables (13:10-17, 34-43).

Davies and Allison (1991:370-371) suggest a three part structure with each part beginning with a parable and containing both an interpretation of a parable and discussion of the parables:

1a. Parable of the Sower (13:1-9)

1b. Discussion of Parables with Scriptural Citation (13:10-17)

1c. Interpretation of the Sower (13:18-23)

2a. Parables of Tares, Mustard Seed, and Leaven (13:24-33)

2b. Discussion of Parables with Scriptural Citation (13:34-35)

2c. Interpretation of the Tares (13:36-43)

3a. Parables of the Treasure, Pearl, and Net (13:44-48)

3b. Interpretation of the Net (13:49-50)

3c. Discussion of Parables (13:51-52)

This approach has obvious strengths, but it tends to break down in section 3, where the order of discussion and interpretation is reversed.

The Interpretation of Parables. Davies and Allison (1991:378-382) present a brief, very helpful excursus on this matter. The history of the church and the experience of many Christians both testify to the prevalence of imaginative interpretations of Jesus' parables. If a parable is "an earthly story with a heavenly meaning," multitudes of such "heavenly" meanings have been superimposed upon the parables. The patristic transformation of the parable of the Good Samaritan into the story of Adam's fall and redemption is probably the most notorious example of this allegorizing approach, which tends to atomize the parables and ignore their literary contexts. In recent years, a very different approach, reader-response criticism, yields results that frequently have only a tangential relationship to the historical and literary context of the parables. Over a hundred years ago, in reaction to the excesses of the allegorizers, A. Jülicher (*Die Gleichnisreden Jesu*, 1899) and many others since him have argued that Jesus' parables, unlike allegories, have only one main point. But this narrow approach seems contrary to Jesus' own interpretations of his parables (13:18-23, 37-43), let alone the polyvalence or flexibility of meaning inherent in the use of stories by skilled speakers and authors.

Therefore, it seems best to look at each parable in its own context in order to determine the degree to which its "earthly" details convey a "heavenly" meaning (Blomberg 1990:68-69; Ryken 1984:145-153, 199-203). Parables are indeed allegories, but they must not be allegorized. Their imagery must be understood in terms of their own ancient historical and literary conventions, not in terms of extraneous categories superimposed upon them by allegorizers. Since the imagery of Jesus' parables is drawn from first-century Palestine, an understanding of the historical context is crucial. It is also important to note the literary context. At times, the preceding context provides the key since the parabolic imagery corresponds to key characters and issues in the narrative. Also, at times there is a concluding general comment that applies the parabolic imagery to a contextual matter.

The Interpretation of Matthew 13. Reading Matthew 13 in its context seems to indicate that Jesus intended his parables to reveal truths of the Kingdom to his disciples and to conceal those truths from the enemies of the Kingdom (13:10-15). The primary focus of the parables is reflection upon the varied responses to the Kingdom message (13:19). Thus, the primary background for the parables of Matthew 13 is the increasing opposition to Jesus and his message, which has been narrated in Matthew 11-12. The parables help the disciples understand this opposition. Classical dispensationalism is mistaken in its attempt to understand the parables as primarily referring to the future millennial kingdom, or as teaching the "mystery" of the offered, rejected, and postponed kingdom (Toussaint 1980:170-176; Walvoord 1974:96-97). The Kingdom was already inaugurated, according to Matthew 3:2; 4:17; 10:7; 12:28 (cf. the discussion of the Kingdom in the Major Themes section of the Introduction), and the parables are about its present progress in the ministry of Jesus and his disciples, as well as its future glories (13:43). Of course, application may be drawn from this historical context to modern contexts in which the message of the Kingdom is still being proclaimed. Ultimately, the disciples continue the mission of Jesus (24:14; 28:19), and their ministry continues until the end of the age (13:39, 43, 49; 24:14; 28:18-20).

Exposition of Matthew 13:1-9. Since the conclusion of the second discourse (11:1), Matthew has stressed the repeated rejection and opposition that Jesus experienced. The disciples would continue to experience the same trials in their mission as well (10:18, 24-25). Even John, whose doubts begin this section of the narrative (11:1-6), and Jesus' own family, who occupy a position "outside" that of Jesus' disciples as the narrative closes (12:46-50), were not fully in step with the proclamation of the gospel of the Kingdom. The Pharisees' murder plot (12:14) indicates the implacable opposition of the religious leaders to Jesus' ministry.

Thus, the third discourse heavily stresses the mixed response to the Kingdom message and indicates that this will continue until the end of the age (13:23, 30, 40-43, 49-50), when God will punish those who reject the Kingdom and reward those who receive it.

Jesus spoke to the crowd in 13:2-33, and his parables directly addressed this crowd as a "mixed multitude" representing different responses to the message of the Kingdom. The parable of the sower becomes the predominant parable of this discourse, as it occasions the disciples' question about the purpose of parables (13:10) and is given a detailed interpretation by Jesus (13:18-23). Many will not genuinely receive the message (13:19-23), and some who seem to receive it will ultimately turn out to be satanic counterfeits (13:24-30, 36-43). The parables will conceal the Kingdom from such unbelievers (13:10-17), but they will also reveal the glorious destiny of those who believe the message (13:43). Although this parable is usually called the parable of the sower, its interpretation by Jesus indicates that it is really about the soil, which pictures the varying responses to the message of the Kingdom. The parable amounts to an explanation of the opposition to the Kingdom proclaimed in the words of Jesus and exemplified by his deeds.

◆   ## B. The Reason for Parables (13:10-17)

¹⁰His disciples came and asked him, "Why do you use parables when you talk to the people?"

¹¹He replied, "You are permitted to understand the secrets* of the Kingdom of Heaven, but others are not. ¹²To those who listen to my teaching, more understanding will be given, and they will have an abundance of knowledge. But for those who are not listening, even what little understanding they have will be taken away from them. ¹³That is why I use these parables,

For they look, but they don't
    really see.
They hear, but they don't really
    listen or understand.

¹⁴This fulfills the prophecy of Isaiah that says,

'When you hear what I say,
    you will not understand.
When you see what I do,
    you will not comprehend.
¹⁵For the hearts of these people are
    hardened,
and their ears cannot hear,
and they have closed their eyes—
    so their eyes cannot see,
and their ears cannot hear,
    and their hearts cannot understand,
and they cannot turn to me
    and let me heal them.'*

¹⁶"But blessed are your eyes, because they see; and your ears, because they hear. ¹⁷I tell you the truth, many prophets and righteous people longed to see what you see, but they didn't see it. And they longed to hear what you hear, but they didn't hear it."

13:11 Greek *the mysteries.*   13:14-15 Isa 6:9-10 (Greek version).

NOTES

13:10 *Why do you use parables when you talk to the people?* As Jesus spoke to the crowd, his disciples asked him why he was speaking to them in parables (cf. Mark 4:10-12; Luke 8:9-10).

13:11 *You are permitted to understand the secrets of the Kingdom.* Jesus' answer to the question implies that this manner of speaking was due to the rejection of his message by many of his listeners. But this was ultimately due to God's sovereign purpose in revealing the secrets of the Kingdom (lit. "mysteries"; cf. Dan 2:28; Mark 4:11; Luke 8:10) to whom he chooses (cf. 11:25-27). These secrets evidently amount to the Kingdom truths signified in the parables of this chapter. God permits (lit. "gives") some to understand these secrets, but he does not give this understanding to others.

13:12 *To those who listen to my teaching, more understanding will be given. . . . But for those who are not listening, even what little understanding they have will be taken away from them.* These solemn words confront Jesus' disciples with God's sovereignty in graciously revealing himself to some and in justly withholding that revelation from others.

13:13-15 Jesus' language in 13:13 echoes Isa 6:9-10, and in 13:14-15 he goes on to directly cite those verses from Isaiah as an OT pattern now fulfilled in his own ministry (cf. John 12:39-40; Acts 28:26-27). Isaiah 6 describes a well-known vision of God in all his holiness that led Isaiah to confess the sinfulness of his people and himself. God cleansed Isaiah of his sin and called him to ministry to his sinful people. But the commission involved the awesome and awful responsibility of confronting the people with their rebellious unbelief of God's message. They had revelatory opportunities, but they did not understand what they heard or perceive what they saw. Due to their hardened hearts, they were unable to respond with believing ears and eyes in turning to God so that he might heal them (cf. Jer 5:21-23). By analogy, the rebellious response to Jesus' announcement of God's rule led to judicial hardening through further enigmatic teaching, which those on the outside were not able to grasp. But God is sovereign over the initial rebellious response, as well as over the further hardening. Mark 4:11 makes an even stronger statement about the use of parables to conceal truth.

13:16-17 *many prophets and righteous people longed to see what you see.* The disciples not only see what the crowds do not, but their blessedness also exceeds that of many OT worthies, both prophets and righteous people, who longed to hear and see what the disciples heard and saw. They were privileged by God's grace to experience the climactic eschatological words and deeds of Jesus that inaugurated the Kingdom. The OT luminaries could only anticipate these things (cf. 11:11-13; Heb 11:39-40; 1 Pet 1:10-12), but Jesus' disciples witnessed them and received Jesus' private explanations of their significance (13:18-23, 36-43).

COMMENTARY

The fact that the disciples asked Jesus why he was speaking in parables implies that this was something relatively new in his ministry. Yet some commentators take this too far, holding the view that the Jews had decisively rejected the offer of the Kingdom and that in response, Jesus would now speak of the postponed Kingdom exclusively in mysterious language (Toussaint 1980:168; Walvoord 1974:96). In fact, Jesus had previously used some parabolic imagery (7:24-27; 9:15-17; 11:16-19; 12:29, 33, 43-45), and he would continue to speak plainly (without parables) to unbelievers as the narrative proceeds (see 15:3-7; 16:2-4; 19:4-9, 17-22; and most of chs 21–23). There is a sense in which Matthew 13 marks a transition in Jesus' ministry. Opposition has indeed come to a head in Matthew 12, but the parabolic discourse of Matthew 13 is neither an entirely novel method of teaching or a new teaching about a postponed Kingdom. Jesus' parables describe the present response of Israel to his Kingdom message. When his disciples take up that message after Jesus' death and resurrection, the parables will just as accurately describe the response of the nations to the preaching of the church until the end of the age. My disagreement with Toussaint's and Walvoord's views on this is not so much over the decisive nature of Matthew 13 as it is over the presence of the Kingdom.

The Sovereignty of God. Finite creatures will never, even after their glorification, fully understand the interplay of God's sovereignty and human responsibility. Matthew 13:11-15, with its citation of Isaiah 6:9-10, is one of the most abrupt affirmations in the Bible of God's prerogative to reveal himself to whomever he wishes. Yet this statement is not as striking as the previous one in 11:25-27, which speaks even more bluntly of God's "hiding" the Kingdom message from those who reject it. Matthew 11:27 also goes further than 13:11-15 in affirming that Jesus shares the divine prerogative of revealing the Father to whomever he wills. Be that as it may, one can only respond to these affirmations of divine sovereignty with a spirit of awe and worship. One must remember that in the Bible, if not in every Christian theology, the sovereignty of God and the responsibility of God's creatures go hand in hand. This is clear when Matthew 11:25-27 is compared with 11:28-30, and when Peter willingly makes a true confession of Jesus, but God has revealed this truth to him (16:15-17). It is also clear that those whom God sovereignly rejects are those who willfully reject God. God does not throw his pearls before pigs (7:6). The doctrine of God's sovereign election, as the saying goes, comforts those afflicted by sin and afflicts those comfortable with sin. It also provides assurance that the preaching of the Kingdom message will be attended with God's blessing in bringing people to faith. God will bring his people to himself.

♦   ## C. Jesus Explains the Parable of the Sower (13:18-23)

¹⁸"Now listen to the explanation of the parable about the farmer planting seeds: ¹⁹The seed that fell on the footpath represents those who hear the message about the Kingdom and don't understand it. Then the evil one comes and snatches away the seed that was planted in their hearts. ²⁰The seed on the rocky soil represents those who hear the message and immediately receive it with joy. ²¹But since they don't have deep roots, they don't last long. They fall away as soon as they have problems or are persecuted for believing God's word. ²²The seed that fell among the thorns represents those who hear God's word, but all too quickly the message is crowded out by the worries of this life and the lure of wealth, so no fruit is produced. ²³The seed that fell on good soil represents those who truly hear and understand God's word and produce a harvest of thirty, sixty, or even a hundred times as much as had been planted!"

NOTES

13:18 *listen to the explanation.* This section (13:18-23) is an example of the disciples' getting more understanding of the Kingdom, as Jesus promised in 13:11-12. After speaking of the blessedness of those who heard what the disciples heard, Jesus began to explain the parable of the sower by telling them to "hear" it (cf. Mark 4:13-20; Luke 8:11-15). The NLT's "listen" tends to obscure this play on words. The following verses simply lay out the four types of soil in order and explain their spiritual significance as portraying four responses to the message about the Kingdom.

13:19 *The seed that fell on the footpath.* This is the seed beside the path that was eaten by birds; it represents a superficial hearing of the Kingdom message that is thwarted by the evil one, Satan (cf. *Jubilees* 11:11-12).

13:20-21 *The seed on the rocky soil.* The seed that sprouted in shallow soil and withered in the sun represents a fickle hearing of the message, where initial enthusiasm turns to apostasy (24:10) due to problems or persecution (cf. 5:11-12; 10:16-25; 23:34-36; 24:9-13).

13:22 *The seed that fell among the thorns.* The seed that sprouted and grew but was choked by thorns represents a promising hearing of the message that ends due to competition from secular concerns, especially greed (cf. 6:19-34). Each of the first three types of soil successively represents more growth, from the seed snatched before it sprouts to the wilted sprouts to the choked plants, but in none of them is there any fruit.

13:23 *The seed that fell on good soil.* Only the fourth soil produces fruit, which in Matthew signifies genuine discipleship (3:8-10; 7:16-20; 12:33; 21:19, 34, 41, 43). It is significant that fruit is borne only when there is understanding of the message (21:19, 23). As pointed out in 13:13-15, such understanding (or the lack of it) is a matter of both God's sovereignty and human responsibility.

COMMENTARY

As noted above in the introduction to Matthew 13, Jesus' detailed interpretation of the parable of the sower invalidates the popular idea that a parable has only a single point of reference to reality. Although the central point is clearly the reception of the Kingdom message, several signifying details add depth and detail to this central point. Apparently Jesus himself is the sower, but the parable has immediate application to the disciples' ministry and further application to the church's proclamation.

The first three types of soil successively outline three factors that hinder the reception of the Kingdom message: Satan, persecution, and greed. Satanic opposition is pictured as effective when the seed falls on the hard ground beside the path, which probably represents hearts hardened by both human sin and divine abandonment (13:15; cf. 9:4; 12:34; 15:8, 18, 19; 24:48). Persecution is effective when there is an immediate joyful reception of the message, evidently a solely emotional response, lacking the "root" of intellectual understanding (13:21). Greed and secular concerns are also effective in thwarting the reception of the Kingdom message, evidently when the demands of discipleship confront a materialistic lifestyle (13:22; cf. 6:19-34; 16:24-26; 19:23). In light of this, preachers of the gospel will do well to warn their listeners of the eternal danger of having a heart hardened to God and pliable to Satan. Similarly, a heart open to shallow, emotional influences but closed to deep understanding of the Kingdom easily turns from God when troubles arise. Finally, a heart that is easily attracted to worldly concerns and wealth is a heart that is soon distracted from the message of the Kingdom.

Another crucial question here is whether only the good ground (13:23) represents a genuine disciple of the Kingdom or whether others who bear no fruit should be viewed as genuine, though unproductive, disciples. This is the so called "Lordship salvation" debate. There are those whose belief in "eternal security" leads them to conclude that any reception of the gospel, even that eventually thwarted by Satan, persecution, or worldliness, amounts to a genuine reception that infallibly leads to eternity with God. But this will not do for Matthew, who teaches consistently that "fruit" is a test of genuine discipleship (3:8-10; 7:16-20; 12:33; 21:19, 34, 41, 43). However, it is also important to note that there are degrees of fruitbearing (13:23), a factor that should lead those who stress discipleship to avoid legalism and perfectionism. One cannot set up human standards for discipleship and authoritatively condemn would-be disciples as unbelievers. Neither can one expect mature discipleship overnight, as it were, since godliness, like fruitbearing, involves a growing season before there can be a harvest.

In the flow of Matthew's narrative, 13:1-23 provides an explanation for the rejection experienced by Jesus in Matthew 11-12 (Davies and Allison 1991:402-403). The message has come to many, but relatively few have received it and borne fruit. The very next parable and its interpretation (13:24-33, 36-43) make it clear that this mixed response to the Kingdom will continue until the end of the age. This is explained in part by the wickedness and unbelief of humans but is still ultimately attributed to God's mysterious and sovereign purpose.

◆   ## D. Jesus Tells Three More Parables (13:24-33; cf. Mark 4:30-34)

[24]Here is another story Jesus told: "The Kingdom of Heaven is like a farmer who planted good seed in his field. [25]But that night as the workers slept, his enemy came and planted weeds among the wheat, then slipped away. [26]When the crop began to grow and produce grain, the weeds also grew.

[27]"The farmer's workers went to him and said, 'Sir, the field where you planted that good seed is full of weeds! Where did they come from?'

[28]"'An enemy has done this!' the farmer exclaimed.

"'Should we pull out the weeds?' they asked.

[29]"'No,' he replied, 'you'll uproot the wheat if you do. [30]Let both grow together until the harvest. Then I will tell the harvesters to sort out the weeds, tie them into bundles, and burn them, and to put the wheat in the barn.'"

[31]Here is another illustration Jesus used: "The Kingdom of Heaven is like a mustard seed planted in a field. [32]It is the smallest of all seeds, but it becomes the largest of garden plants; it grows into a tree, and birds come and make nests in its branches."

[33]Jesus also used this illustration: "The Kingdom of Heaven is like the yeast a woman used in making bread. Even though she put only a little yeast in three measures of flour, it permeated every part of the dough."

NOTES

13:24-26 *the Kingdom of Heaven is like.* This or a similar formula appears many times in Matthew (13:31, 33, 44, 45, 47, 52; 18:23; 20:1; 22:2; 25:1). This parable, like the first, leads to the disciples' request for interpretation (13:36-43). The basic imagery of the second parable is the same as the first—a farmer plants good seed. But here the resemblance ends since this story involves the nefarious act of an enemy (cf. 22:44) who plants weeds among the wheat one night while everyone is asleep. So, as the wheat grows, so do the weeds. But evidently the weeds are indistinguishable from the wheat until the point in the growing season when the wheat plants form heads of grain. This may be a picture of false disciples as opposed to unbelievers in general (Gundry 1994:261-262), although nothing is made of it in Jesus' later interpretation (Davies and Allison 1991:408-409).

13:27-30 *farmer's workers.* Lit., "landowner's slaves." They notice the weeds growing together with the wheat, so they inform the landowner of this problem, and ask him how his good seed has produced weeds. He correctly surmises that an enemy was responsible. He tells his slaves not to attempt to root out the weeds at this point since this would also damage the wheat. Instead, the weeds will be gathered and burnt at harvest time, when the wheat is gathered into the barn or granary (cf. 3:12). This portrayal of final judgment will be explained in 13:36-43.

13:31-32 *illustration.* The parables of the mustard seed (13:31-32) and yeast (13:33) are much shorter than the previous parables of the sower and the weeds (cf. Mark 4:30-32; Luke 13:18-21). The NLT calls both of these "illustrations" because they are too short to be called "stories," as in 13:3, 18, 24. But the Gr. word throughout this chapter is *parabolē* [TG3850, ZG4130] "parable," (13:3, 10, 18, 24, 31, 33, 34, 35, 36, 53). Both parables are introduced with the formula first noted in 13:24, and both seem to have a similar point—the growth of the Kingdom.

the smallest of all seeds. Some quibble with the scientific accuracy of Jesus' statement that the mustard seed is the smallest seed, but it must be taken in its context as affirming only that the mustard seed was the smallest herb seed commonly planted in Palestine. The mustard seed emphasizes how the Kingdom grows from an insignificant beginning ("the smallest of all seeds") into the largest of garden shrubs, suitable for nesting birds (cf. Ps 104:12; Ezek 17:23; 31:6; Dan 4:12).

13:33 *yeast in three measures of flour, it permeated every part of the dough.* The yeast pictures the tangible but subtle influence of the Kingdom as it permeates the world. The amount of flour leavened by the yeast is three *satas* [TG4568, ZG4929]. This is surprisingly large, amounting to 21.6 pints, 35 liters, or nearly a bushel of flour, enough to feed around 150 people (BDAG 917; Hagner 1993:390). These two parables, unlike the first two, are not interpreted by Jesus, so there is less agreement among scholars as to their meaning. The major question is whether the symbolism portrays the spread of evil within Christendom, or the spread of the rule of God in the world through the words and works of Jesus and his disciples. For reasons given in the commentary below, I favor the second view.

COMMENTARY

The Parable of the Wheat and Weeds.

The parable of the weeds (13:24-30) is yet to be interpreted (cf. 13:36, but the attentive reader is already drawing tentative conclusions about it from its similarities to the parable of the sower, which Jesus had interpreted already. These similar motifs include sowing, seed, and mixed results. We will see in 13:37-43 that one would be mistaken to identify the significance of the respective sowers and seeds in the two parables. The parable of the weeds has a different thrust and contains new elements: the enemy, the weeds (but see the thorns in 13:7, 22), the landowner, the workers, the harvest and harvesters, the fire, and the barn. Nonetheless, the developing dualism between the landowner and his enemy, the good seed/wheat and the weeds, the barn and the fire, can already be seen as portraying an ominous battle between the cosmic forces of good and evil.

The Parables of the Mustard Seed and Yeast. There is much debate over the meaning of these two short parables. Most classical dispensationalists believe that the imagery of the parables is meant to portray the presence of evil within professing Christendom. This is due primarily to an understanding of the Kingdom of Heaven as a "mystery" encompassing Christendom, understood as organized or nominal Christianity. Christendom as a whole contains evil elements mixed with the good, so both parables are usually viewed as picturing that evil. The birds nesting in the mustard tree are unbelievers (Walvoord 1974:101); Toussaint (1980:181) disagrees, viewing the mustard tree as portraying the Kingdom positively. It is also pointed out that yeast is often a symbol of evil (Exod 12:15, 19; Matt 16:6, 11-12; 1 Cor 5:6-8; Gal 5:9; but see Lev 7:13-14; 23:17) and asserted that the parable of the yeast portrays the growth of evil within Christendom (Walvoord 1974:103-104; Toussaint 1980:182). This view of the parables is often held in conscious opposition to postmillennialism, which understands the images of the growth of the Kingdom in the two parables as indicating the ultimate conversion of the world to Christianity before Christ returns.

There is good reason to disagree with the classic dispensational position. First, its understanding of the Kingdom of Heaven as the mystery of evil within Christendom between the two advents of Jesus is doubtful. Rather, the Kingdom in Matthew is the rule of God, inaugurated through the words and works of Jesus and consummated at his return. Second, it is very doubtful that straightforward statements that compare the Kingdom of God to leaven or to mustard seed should be understood as a portrayal of evil. After all, it is the growth of God's rule, not Satan's, which is being portrayed. One need not assume that birds or yeast must always be viewed as biblical symbols for evil—consider that the imagery of a lion portrays Satan in one context and Jesus in another (1 Pet 5:8; Rev 5:5). The parables of the mustard seed and the yeast speak of the deceptively subtle yet dramatically significant growth of God's Kingdom. Despite frequent fruitless responses to the Kingdom message, it does bear much fruit in many cases (13:23). Even John the Baptist may doubt its advance, but it is advancing just the same (11:1-6). The strong man is being bound, and his goods are being plundered (12:29).

While postmillennialists may view this advance of the Kingdom over-optimistically, classic dispensationalists view the present age too pessimistically because they do not acknowledge that the Kingdom was inaugurated and began its advance during the earthly ministry of Jesus. It may presently seem as insignificant as a mustard seed, but it will eventually be the largest tree in the garden. Its growth may be as imperceptible as the influence of yeast in a loaf of bread, but in the end it will be pervasive throughout the earth. The use of humble symbols like mustard seeds and yeast is appropriate for God's humble servant who does not cry out in the streets (12:19) and who rides into Jerusalem on a donkey, not a stallion (21:1-5). Davies and Allison (1991:415) are correct that these parables portray a contrast between the present reality and the ultimate destiny of the Kingdom. That which is now humble will be glorious. The realization that God is already at work and that there is a unity of the ultimate with the present should give all believers hope.

◆   E. Matthew Explains Why Jesus Told Parables (13:34-35)

³⁴Jesus always used stories and illustrations like these when speaking to the
crowds. In fact, he never spoke to them
without using such parables. ³⁵This fulfilled what God had spoken through the
prophet:

"I will speak to you in parables.
    I will explain things hidden
    since the creation of the
    world.*"

13:35 Some manuscripts do not include *of the world.* Ps 78:2.

NOTES

13:34-35 *I will speak to you in parables.* These verses provide a transition from Jesus'
parables to the crowd, spoken from the boat (13:2-33), to his parables to his disciples,
spoken in the house (13:36-50). By moving into the more private setting, Jesus turned
from those who for the most part did not understand to those who did (13:11-12). Matthew's editorial insertion states that Jesus' customary way of speaking to the crowds at this
time was through parables. Furthermore, Matthew asserted that Jesus' parabolic speech
fulfilled what the prophet said in Ps 78:2 (cf. Mark 4:33-34; John 6:31). In this lengthy
Psalm, Asaph the seer (1 Chr 25:2; 2 Chr 29:30) recounted the history of Israel for the next
generation (Ps 78:4), stressing Israel's unbelief (Ps 78:8, 11, 17-22, 32-33, 36-37, 39-42,
56-58), which led to God's punishment (Ps 78:21, 31-34, 59-64). In spite of Israel's rebellion and God's judgment, the continuing faithfulness of God to his people was manifested
in mighty works of power (Ps 78:4-7, 12-16, 23-29, 38-39, 42-55) and in choosing David
to shepherd them (Ps 78:65-72). In Matthew's view, Jesus is the Son of David who fulfills
the role of Israel's ultimate shepherd (1:1; 9:36). His parables, like those of Asaph, portray
Israel's unbelief and God's judgment, but more importantly, they stress God's ongoing
faithfulness to Israel through the words and deeds of the Kingdom.

COMMENTARY

These verses contain the second fulfillment citation of the Old Testament in the
discourse. According to Jesus, the unbelief of most of the Jews who saw his deeds
and heard his words was not unprecedented. The pattern of unbelief that occurred
in the days of Isaiah was recurring in the days of Jesus. Israel as a whole did not
believe Isaiah's warnings of impending invasion, and neither did they believe
Jesus' Kingdom message (13:14-15; Isa 6:9-10). Now Matthew inserts his own
commentary on the discourse he was narrating, citing Psalm 78:2 as the pattern
being fulfilled by Jesus. Asaph characterizes Psalm 78 at its opening as parabolic
and hidden, but as the psalm unfolds, one reads a narrative of God's faithfulness to
a rebellious people under his discipline, not a mysterious discourse full of enigmatic sayings.

Two key questions need to be answered. The first concerns why Asaph described
his historical narrative as parabolic and enigmatic in Psalm 78:2. He did this first
because matters well known to his own generation were as yet ancient secrets to the
coming generation. Thus, he employs a bit of poetic hyperbole: To coming generations (Ps 78:4) this recounting of God's mighty acts might seem like secrets hidden
since ancient times (78:2), but in reality these were matters known by Asaph's generation because they were told them by their ancestors, and Asaph, in turn, passed

on these ancient secrets to the next generation. Asaph's psalm is also parabolic in the sense that his recounting of the past reveals the profound pattern that may be discerned from the bare historical events (Carson 1984:321). Asaph did not merely recount but also interpreted Israel's story as the story of God's faithfulness to his people in spite of their sin and deserved punishment. This faithfulness is manifested in his mighty acts of redemption (Ps 78:4, 7, 11-12, 32, 42-43). By his interpretation of Israel's history in this manner, Asaph revealed to a new generation the profound truth of God's redeeming grace.

The second question concerns why Matthew cited Asaph's words in Psalm 78. On the surface, we have the connection of the key word "parable," but Matthew appears to be taking the psalm out of context. While it may be granted that the psalm is not a prediction of Jesus, we observe that Matthew often finds patterns in the literature and history of the Old Testament and points to their ultimate significance in Jesus. That his view of the Old Testament is frequently typological was seen earlier in the infancy narrative of Matthew 1-2. Here, Matthew finds in Asaph's words a precedent for a pattern that Jesus fulfilled. As Asaph uttered profundities for a new generation, so Jesus revealed the ultimate secrets of the Kingdom of Heaven to his own generation (13:11; cf. 12:39, 41-42). As Asaph discerned the pattern of God's faithfulness to his people overarching their disobedience and his consequent discipline, so Jesus' parables presented the pattern of the reception and rejection of the growing Kingdom until the day of ultimate judgment and reward (13:19, 39-43). As Asaph's reflection on the "old days" brought out truth for a new generation, so Jesus' parables equip his disciples to bring out of their treasure things new and old in their own teaching (13:51-52). What was new in Asaph's day is now a part of what is old in the disciples' treasury, but what they have learned from Jesus will remain new as they teach all nations, accompanied by Jesus' presence until the end of the age (28:19-20; cf. Carson 1984:322-323).

◆   F. Jesus Explains the Parable of the Weeds and Wheat (13:36-43)

36Then, leaving the crowds outside, Jesus went into the house. His disciples said, "Please explain to us the story of the weeds in the field."

37Jesus replied, "The Son of Man* is the farmer who plants the good seed. 38The field is the world, and the good seed represents the people of the Kingdom. The weeds are the people who belong to the evil one. 39The enemy who planted the weeds among the wheat is the devil. The harvest is the end of the world,* and the harvesters are the angels.

40"Just as the weeds are sorted out and burned in the fire, so it will be at the end of the world. 41The Son of Man will send his angels, and they will remove from his Kingdom everything that causes sin and all who do evil. 42And the angels will throw them into the fiery furnace, where there will be weeping and gnashing of teeth. 43Then the righteous will shine like the sun in their Father's Kingdom. Anyone with ears to hear should listen and understand!"

13:37 "Son of Man" is a title Jesus used for himself.   13:39 Or the age; also in 13:40, 49.

NOTES

13:36-39 *explain to us the story of the weeds in the field.* Following Matthew's editorial comment on Jesus' parables as fulfillment of Psalm 78:2, the narrative picks up again. After telling the parable of the weeds, Jesus left the boat and returned to the house, reversing the movement of 13:1-2. He was no longer speaking to the crowds, where there would be many to whom the secrets of the Kingdom would not be revealed, but to the disciples, to whom these mysteries were revealed (13:10-13). In response to the disciples' question, Jesus explained the parable of the weeds. His explanation of this parable is just as detailed as his earlier explanation of the parable of the sower (13:18-23), with seven key details interpreted. Put briefly, Jesus (the sower) is responsible for the people (lit. "sons"; cf. 8:12) of the Kingdom (the good seed) who are in the world (the field), and the devil (the enemy) is responsible for the people who belong to him (the weeds). This expression is lit. "the sons of the evil one" (cf. 5:37; 6:13; John 8:44; Acts 13:10; 1 John 3:10). At the end of the world (the harvest), the angels (the harvesters; cf. 24:31; 25:31-33) separate Satan's people from Jesus' people (the wheat grown from the good seed), throwing the former into the fiery furnace or hell (the fire; cf. 3:12; 5:22; 18:8-9; 2 Esdr 7:36) and gathering the latter into the Kingdom (the barn; cf. 3:12).

13:40 *they will remove from his Kingdom everything that causes sin and all who do evil.* The judgment at the end of the world is portrayed as the removal of sinners from God's Kingdom, not the removal of saints from the world, which is then destroyed (13:41). The people of Satan are further characterized as lawless ones who cause sin (cf. Zeph 1:3), and the pain of their judgment is vividly described (13:41-42, 50; cf. 8:12; 22:13; 24:51; 25:30). Matthew frequently stresses lawlessness as at the heart of sin (7:23; 23:28; 24:12).

13:43 *the righteous will shine like the sun in their Father's Kingdom.* In an allusion to Dan 12:3, the glorious bliss of Jesus' disciples, the righteous ones (10:41; 13:49; 25:37, 46), is portrayed as the shining of the sun (cf. 17:2). The importance of this explanation is underlined by the solemn encouragement to listeners found at the end (cf. 11:15; 13:9).

COMMENTARY

Jesus' interpretation of his parable of the weeds has a more dualistic and eschatological tone than that of the sower. Instead of speaking in general terms about people (soils) who do and do not bear fruit, this second parable stresses in vivid terms the destinies of the two groups. The contrasting ethical qualities (lawlessness versus righteousness) that lead to these opposite destinies are also brought out (13:41-43). There is also the contrast between the role of Jesus (13:37) and that of the devil (13:39; but see 13:19), the two ultimate figures behind the cosmic struggle and the contrasting people, ethics, and destinies found in the parable. The imagery of Jesus as the sower of the good seed—the people of the Kingdom (13:38)—is specially noteworthy, since it is a picturesque way of putting something that Jesus had stated previously: he is the sole revealer of the Father (11:27). The enemy, Satan, like the wolves who wear sheep's clothing (7:15), also sows seed, and the resulting weeds are difficult to distinguish from the wheat. Satan is the great imitator.

Matthew's narrative frequently stresses the end of the age and the judgment to follow. John the Baptist spoke of this in vivid language, which anticipates Jesus' words in this passage (3:12). Jesus spoke of himself as the eschatological judge in the Sermon on the Mount (7:22-23), and there he stressed the bliss of the future Kingdom on earth as the reward for faithful discipleship (5:3, 5, 10; 6:10; 7:21).

Unexpectedly, many Gentiles will share in the eschatological banquet with the patriarchs (8:11-12). Confessing Jesus and aiding his messengers will result in reward (10:32-33, 41-42). The peril of the towns that did not believe Jesus will be worse than the notorious towns of the Old Testament when the judgment comes (11:22, 24; 12:41). Those who slander the Holy Spirit will never be forgiven, even in the world to come (12:32). With this background, the reader of Matthew is not surprised at the vivid portrayal of the end of the age in this parable. Of course, much additional teaching on this matter is yet to come (13:49; 16:27; 17:10-11; 18:8-9; 19:27-30; 22:1-13, 30-32; 24-25; 26:29, 64; 28:20).

It is also worth mentioning here that this parable should not be cited as supporting a casual attitude on the part of Christians toward the matter of church discipline (Gundry 1994:262). No doubt, there are false disciples in the church, but Jesus stated that the field is the world, not the church (13:38; Davies and Allison 1991:428). This again points to the eventual global mission of the church (24:14; 28:19). Other texts in Matthew make it clear that God does not take the sin of professing Christians lightly (7:21-23; 18:15-17, 21-35; 22:11-14). It is not an easy task to maintain a pure church, but it is a mandatory task for those who take Jesus' call to discipleship seriously.

◆   G. Jesus Tells the Parables of the Hidden Treasure, the Pearl, and the Fishing Net (13:44-50)

44"The Kingdom of Heaven is like a treasure that a man discovered hidden in a field. In his excitement, he hid it again and sold everything he owned to get enough money to buy the field.

45"Again, the Kingdom of Heaven is like a merchant on the lookout for choice pearls. 46When he discovered a pearl of great value, he sold everything he owned and bought it!

47"Again, the Kingdom of Heaven is like a fishing net that was thrown into the water and caught fish of every kind. 48When the net was full, they dragged it up onto the shore, sat down, and sorted the good fish into crates, but threw the bad ones away. 49That is the way it will be at the end of the world. The angels will come and separate the wicked people from the righteous, 50throwing the wicked into the fiery furnace, where there will be weeping and gnashing of teeth."

NOTES

13:44 *the Kingdom of Heaven is like a treasure that a man discovered hidden in a field.* The first parable speaks of a man who sells all that he has so that he may buy a field in which he has discovered a hidden treasure (cf. Prov 2:4; Sir 20:30).

13:45 *the Kingdom of Heaven is like a merchant on the lookout for choice pearls.* The second describes a merchant who similarly sells all he has so that he might purchase a pearl of great value (cf. 7:6; Job 28:18; Prov 3:13-15). In Jesus' day pearls were evidently regarded much like diamonds are regarded today. Pearls were often associated with gold (1 Tim 2:9; Rev 17:4; 18:12, 16; cf. Origen *Commentary on Matthew* 10:7).

13:47-50 *the Kingdom of Heaven is like a fishing net.* The parable of the dragnet is immediately explained as a picture of eschatological judgment. It uses the imagery of fishing to convey a message similar to that of the parable of the weeds (13:24-30, 36-43). The net here is not the small one used by modern anglers to bring individual fish into a boat, but a large net or seine with weights on the bottom and floats on the top that encircles many fish. Such a net could contain hundreds of fish and require a great deal of effort to haul in (cf. Luke 5:4-11; John 21:5-7, although a different Gr. word for net is used in these passages). In view of the parabolic formula found in 13:52, this parable should not be viewed as the last one in Matthew 13 (contra Hagner 1993:398).

COMMENTARY

The Parables of the Hidden Treasure and the Pearl. In both of these parables, a person sacrifices everything to acquire one highly valuable, intensely desired object. Although some interpret both parables as pictures of the redemption of the church by God through Jesus, this tends to neglect the context and read Pauline theology into Matthew. Although Matthew did speak of Jesus as a ransom for many (20:28; cf. 26:28), another approach better fits the context. Throughout Matthew 13, Jesus is speaking parabolically of the mixed response to his Kingdom teachings and deeds. One may trace positive responses to the Kingdom as well as negative responses. As to positive responses, in the parable of the sower there was good soil that produced fruit (13:8, 23). The secrets of the Kingdom were revealed to the disciples (13:11). The parable of the wheat and weeds speaks of the glorious future of the righteous as good seed gathered into a barn (13:43), and this is reinforced by the parable of the fishing net (13:48). The parables of the mustard seed and yeast speak of the almost imperceptible growth of the Kingdom from insignificance to greatness (13:31-33).

It seems very likely that the parables under consideration here fit into this pattern of positive response to the Kingdom. The Kingdom is portrayed as a hidden treasure and a valuable pearl, and it is pursued by men who sell all they have in order to gain it. Surely this fits the picture of discipleship one finds throughout Matthew. Jesus' first disciples left their families and fishing gear to follow Jesus (4:20, 22; cf. 9:9). Following Jesus entails the sacrifice of losing one's life for Jesus and thereby finding it (16:25-26). The rich young ruler would not sell all he had to follow Jesus (19:21-22), but all who do make such a sacrifice will be richly rewarded (19:27-29). Thus, these parables present both the sacrifice required in following Jesus and the disciples' joy (13:44; cf. 2:10; 28:8; for temporary joy see 13:20) in the present possession of the Kingdom as well as its future rewards. Despite the lure of wealth (13:22) and the many distractions of life in this world, millions continue to follow Jesus at great cost in the present life but with greater prospects for the future.

The Parable of the Fishing Net. The message of the parable of the fishing net is obviously similar to that of the parable of the weeds. Among the differences between the two is the presence of "fish of every kind" in this parable, as opposed to only two kinds of plants, wheat and weeds, in the previous parable. Perhaps this is a subtle reminder of the universality of the Kingdom mission, which is mandated to "all the nations" (28:19). The net does not discriminate as it gathers the fish, and neither should disciples of the Kingdom as they fish for people (cf. 4:19; 22:9-10).

According to this parable, the angels (fishermen) separate (sort the contents of the net) the wicked people (bad fish) from the righteous people (good fish). They throw the bad fish away into the fiery furnace (or hell). In this parable, unlike the parable of the weeds, there is no emphasis on the glory and bliss of the righteous disciples, but there is a similar description of the punishment of the wicked (13:49-50).

◆ H. Jesus Tells the Parable of the Homeowner (13:51-52)

⁵¹"Do you understand all these things?" "Yes," they said, "we do." ⁵²Then he added, "Every teacher of religious law who becomes a disciple in the Kingdom of Heaven is like a homeowner who brings from his storeroom new gems of truth as well as old."

NOTES

13:51 *Do you understand all these things?* Previously, the disciples implicitly acknowledged a lack of understanding when they asked Jesus twice about his parables (13:10, 36), so it is not surprising that Jesus now asks them whether they have finally grasped his parabolic teaching. Evidently "all these things" refers to the growth of the Kingdom despite the mixed reception of its message.

13:52 *is like a homeowner.* When the disciples affirmed that they had indeed understood, Jesus responded with what should be understood as the eighth and final parable of Matthew 13, since it is introduced with the characteristic formula "is like" (cf. 13:24, 31, 33, 44, 45, 47).

The parable likens disciples of the Kingdom to a homeowner (cf. 20:1; 21:33) who brings both new and old things from his storeroom (cf. 12:35). Jesus surprisingly uses the term "teacher of religious law" (lit. "scribe"; cf. 2:4; 5:20; 7:29; 8:19; 9:3; 12:38; 15:1; 16:21; 17:10; 20:18; 21:15; 23:2, 13-15, 34; 26:57; 27:41; cf. Sir 39:2-3). He calls the disciples he has trained "scribes of the Kingdom" because their ministries will entail teaching the Kingdom message as they draw upon what Jesus has taught them and teach their own disciples new truths tied to old truths (cf. 5:17-20; 9:16-17; 11:11-13).

COMMENTARY

Many of Jesus' hearers in the "crowds" of Matthew 11–13 did not understand the Kingdom message (13:13), and the animosity of the Jewish religious leaders toward Jesus and his message was becoming potentially lethal (12:14). Even Jesus' disciples were slow to grasp what his parables meant (13:10, 36). Jesus was teaching that the Kingdom would have a mixed reception all the way to the end of the age. The Kingdom's growth would be real, though imperceptible, and its humble beginnings would eventually lead to a substantial entity. The sacrifice required to enter it is great, but those who abandon everything else to follow Jesus will be greatly rewarded. All this was stated parabolically and mysteriously, however, and even though three of the parables had been interpreted, it was not certain that the disciples had understood. So Jesus put that question to them, and they answered it in the affirmative. Thus, the parables were (and are) an effective means of communication to those to whom it has been given to understand the secrets of the Kingdom (13:11).

Since the disciples affirmed that they understood Jesus' parabolic teaching (but see 15:15), Jesus concluded the third discourse with yet another parable. It is a short one, more of a simile than a story, and like the two previous pairs of short parables it was not interpreted (cf. 13:31-33, 44-46). It is a bit surprising that Jesus spoke of his disciples as being "scribes" (NLT, "teacher of religious law") since the scribes were consistently among Jesus' enemies, according to Matthew. But in their teaching capacity, the disciples will function in Matthew's Christian Jewish community like the scribes functioned in the larger Jewish community (cf. 23:34; Cope 1976; Orton 1989). Their role is compared to that of a homeowner who uses both new and old resources in managing his household. (NLT's "new gems of truth" is a bit expansive but probably right on track.) It would seem that the reference to new and old things should be understood in light of Jesus' teaching that he had come not to cancel but to fulfill the law and the prophets (5:17ff). Thus, Israel's pre-Christian Scriptures were not old in the sense of being decrepit, outdated, or obsolete, since they are still part of the Kingdom scribe's resources, but the new things, the ultimately definitive teachings of Jesus about the Kingdom, are to be used first as the scribe's primary resources. Matthew makes much of the teachings of Jesus, featuring them in five major discourses (Matt 5-7; 10; 13:1-52; 18; and 24-25). This Gospel concludes with Jesus' mandate that all nations be discipled and that new disciples be taught all that Jesus had commanded. Kingdom scribes must now manage God's household with the resources Jesus provided, his new definitive teachings about the eschatological inauguration of God's reign, which fulfill the old Scriptures of Israel. Hagner is correct that Christians "must represent a Christianity encompassing both Testaments" (1993:402).

◆ **VI. Opposition to the Kingdom Continues (13:53–18:35)**
  A. Various Responses to the Son of God (13:53–17:27)
    1. Jesus rejected at Nazareth (13:53–58; cf. Mark 6:1-6; Luke 4:16-30)

53When Jesus had finished telling these stories and illustrations, he left that part of the country. 54He returned to Nazareth, his hometown. When he taught there in the synagogue, everyone was amazed and said, "Where does he get this wisdom and the power to do miracles?" 55Then they scoffed, "He's just the carpenter's son, and we know Mary, his mother, and his brothers—James, Joseph,* Simon, and Judas. 56All his sisters live right here among us. Where did he learn all these things?" 57And they were deeply offended and refused to believe in him.

Then Jesus told them, "A prophet is honored everywhere except in his own hometown and among his own family." 58And so he did only a few miracles there because of their unbelief.

13:55 Other manuscripts read *Joses;* still others read *John.*

NOTES

13:53 When Jesus had finished telling. With his characteristic transitional statement (cf. 7:28; 11:1; 19:1; 26:1), Matthew's story of Jesus moves from the third discourse to a new narrative block (13:53–17:27). Jesus departed the house (evidently in Capernaum; 13:1, 36) and came back to his hometown, Nazareth (4:13; cf. Mark 6:1-6; Luke 4:16-30).

13:55 He's just the carpenter's son. Since the people of Nazareth were aware of Jesus' humble family origins, they did not understand how he had become so formidable. The problem is a matter of frame of reference, such that the extraordinary words and deeds of Jesus were explained away by associating them with Jesus' familiar past (Davies and Allison 1991:455). Joseph is traditionally viewed as a carpenter, but the word commonly translated "carpenter" can also refer to a stonemason.

his mother, and his brothers . . . his sisters. His brothers and mother are mentioned in 12:46, but in this passage the brothers are named and sisters are also mentioned.

13:56 Where did he learn all these things? Perhaps they were referring to Jesus' lack of a rabbinical education (cf. John 7:15).

13:57 they were deeply offended and refused to believe. This translates one Gr. word, *skandalizoomai* [TG4624A, ZG4997], which is variously translated "to stumble," "to take offense," "to fall into sin," or "to cause to sin." The word occurs rather frequently in Matthew to describe serious sin, unbelief, and even apostasy (cf. 5:29, 30; 11:6; 13:21; 18:6, 8, 9; 24:10; 26:31, 33). So the residents of Nazareth sadly fell into the same sin as did the residents of Chorazin, Bethsaida, and Capernaum (cf. 11:20-24), and the recently told parable of the sower sadly fits yet another situation.

A prophet is honored everywhere except in his own hometown. Jesus' response to their unbelief is proverbial, reflecting on the common human experience that well-known people are often not highly regarded by those who knew them before they achieved fame.

13:58 only a few miracles. In such circumstances where unbelief reigned supreme, Jesus did not do many miracles.

COMMENTARY

Matthew 13:53–17:27, the narrative block between the third (ch 13) and fourth (ch 18) discourses, may be the most difficult section of this Gospel to analyze as to structure. The conventional wisdom among scholars who believe that Matthew was depending on Mark (cf. the discussion of the synoptic problem in the "Literary Style" section of the Introduction) is that at this point Matthew ceases his distinctive topical or thematic arrangement of Jesus' traditions and begins to follow the order of Mark (Davies and Allison 1991:451; Hagner 1995:410). Although Matthew's structuring of the material in this narrative block may not be as meticulous as it was previously, it is clear that he wanted his story of Jesus to convey the ever-increasing polarization of the responses to Jesus and the Kingdom. In what is perhaps the crucial text in this section, 16:13-28, the contrast between the false and true views of Jesus (16:13-16) and of discipleship (16:21-26) is made clear, and Jesus' fate at the hands of the religious leaders in Jerusalem is foretold (16:21; cf. 17:9, 12, 22-23; 20:17-19; 21:39).

There are approximately sixteen episodes in the narrative block of Matthew 13:53–17:27 (cf. the outline of Matthew at the end of the Introduction). Of these, at least six emphasize a negative, unbelieving response to Jesus and the Kingdom

(13:53-58; 14:1-12; 15:1-20; 16:1-12, 21-28; 7:22-23). Four clearly stress a positive, believing response (15:21-28, 29-31; 16:13-20; 17:1-13), and the remainder are mildly positive yet ambiguous since they contain no clear affirmation of faith (14:13-21, 22-33, 34-36; 15:32-39; 17:14-20, 24-27). These episodes generally highlight a miracle or teaching of Jesus but do not clearly portray an ethical response to it.

Another clear theme of this material, which is not often highlighted, is the development of the "little faith" of the disciples. This theme occurs in negative, positive, and ambiguous episodes, as Jesus uses every opportunity to strengthen his disciples (often with Peter at the forefront) for their future ministries in his absence. Examples of Jesus strengthening the disciples' faith in negative passages include 15:12-20; 16:5-12, 22; and 17:23. Examples of this in positive texts include 15:28; 17:4-6; and 17:10-13. Examples in ambiguous texts include 14:15, 31; 15:33; 17:16, 19-20; and 17:25. Although deficiencies in the disciples' faith have already been noted (8:26), it is fair to say that this theme comes into its own in this narrative block. Therefore, despite the relative absence of triadic patterns and other structural devices that mark his other sections, Matthew's crucial concerns emerge once again as he narrates the continuing polarization in the responses to Jesus and the Kingdom.

Jesus Rejected at Nazareth. Although a naive reader might expect otherwise, Jesus' reception at Nazareth was not a warm one. His ministry in the synagogue produced astonishment and skepticism as to the source of his wisdom and power instead of praise to God for its blessings.

Unbelief is always a sad thing, but in this case it was especially pathetic. It does not take a great deal of imagination to think that Jesus, like most people who return home, arrived with fond memories and wishes to renew old acquaintances. But in this case it was not to be, for Jesus' former associates refused to accept his messianic status and mission because they remembered his humble beginnings. Perhaps there was an element of jealousy here—the townspeople could not accept a small town boy who made good. All that aside, they were not merely quibbling over the anomaly of Jesus' humble, ordinary pedigree and his special, powerful ministry; they were rejecting the Kingdom of God. The saying "familiarity breeds contempt" is applicable here, and the consequences were devastating. In a sense, the unbelief of Nazareth typifies that of Israel as a whole. Jesus was dishonored by the Jews, but he would be held in high esteem by the Gentiles. Yet this must not be pressed, since some among Israel—and some from Nazareth, eventually including Jesus' family— believed in Jesus and became the Kingdom's messengers to the Gentiles.

Jesus' lack of miracles in Nazareth should not be viewed as a matter of inability but as a matter of choice. It is not that Jesus' power was hindered by unbelief but that he did not resort to loud tactics and perform miracles simply to please skeptics (cf. 12:19, 38-39). The sower is parabolic but also prophetic. As soon as Jesus told this parable and the others, he saw its truth in his own hometown. People before whom and with whom he'd grown up simply could not grasp his Kingdom mission, even though they acknowledged his wisdom and power (13:54, 56). They simply did not understand—as such, they are to be identified with the case of the seed sown on the packed soil beside the path, devoured by birds (Satan) before it can even sprout (13:4, 19).

◆ ## 2. The death of John the Baptist (14:1-12; cf. Mark 6:14-29; Luke 9:7-9)

When Herod Antipas, the ruler of Galilee,* heard about Jesus, [2]he said to his advisers, "This must be John the Baptist raised from the dead! That is why he can do such miracles."

[3]For Herod had arrested and imprisoned John as a favor to his wife Herodias (the former wife of Herod's brother Philip). [4]John had been telling Herod, "It is against God's law for you to marry her." [5]Herod wanted to kill John, but he was afraid of a riot, because all the people believed John was a prophet.

[6]But at a birthday party for Herod, Herodias's daughter performed a dance that greatly pleased him, [7]so he promised with a vow to give her anything she wanted. [8]At her mother's urging, the girl said, "I want the head of John the Baptist on a tray!" [9]Then the king regretted what he had said; but because of the vow he had made in front of his guests, he issued the necessary orders. [10]So John was beheaded in the prison, [11]and his head was brought on a tray and given to the girl, who took it to her mother. [12]Later, John's disciples came for his body and buried it. Then they went and told Jesus what had happened.

14:1 Greek *Herod the tetrarch.* Herod Antipas was a son of King Herod and was ruler over Galilee.

NOTES

14:1 *Herod Antipas, the ruler of Galilee.* Lit., "Herod the tetrarch" (cf. NLT mg). "Tetrarch" describes a ruler of one fourth of Herod the Great's former kingdom. Antipas ruled over Galilee and Perea, the area east of the Jordan, from 4 BC to AD 39 (cf. Luke 3:1). He was a minor figure of history compared to his father Herod the Great (2:1). For details see Hoehner (1972:110-171). At about the time when Jesus was rejected in Nazareth, his ministry came to the attention of Herod the Tetrarch (cf. Mark 6:14-29; Luke 9:7-9).

14:2 *This must be John the Baptist raised from the dead!* Antipas's superstitious explanation for Jesus' miraculous powers (cf. 13:54) evidently stemmed from a guilty conscience, given the story recorded in 14:3-12. But his erroneous theory for Jesus' powerful works served Matthew's literary purpose to link John's mission and destiny to that of Jesus (11:18-19; 17:12). As 14:3-12 makes clear, it must have been terrifying for Antipas to think that John had been raised from the dead. Antipas was evidently not the only one to think that Jesus was John the Baptist (see 16:14).

14:3-4 *Herod had arrested and imprisoned John.* Matthew 14:3-12 is a flashback that fills in the grisly details of the death of John the Baptist, mentioned in 14:2.

his wife Herodias (the former wife of Herod's brother Philip). Antipas had divorced his first wife in order to marry Herodias, who was formerly married to his half brother, Philip. This was illegal according to Lev 18:16; 20:21, which forbids sexual intercourse with one's brother's wife. For additional details see Josephus *Antiquities* 18.116-119, 136-137.

14:5 *he was afraid of a riot.* This interprets a clause that lit. reads, "he was afraid of the crowd." Antipas was afraid of the crowd's response to the execution of a man they believed to be a prophet (cf. 11:9; 21:26). However, as 14:6-9 explains, political expedience eventually gave way to something more powerful.

all the people believed John was a prophet. The mention of John's status as a prophet and his maltreatment by Antipas links him to the previous context and Jesus' saying about his own rejection at Nazareth (13:57). Further, Antipas's fear of the crowd anticipates the fear of the religious leaders to arrest Jesus later in Jerusalem (21:46).

14:6-7 Antipas's concern for political expedience was trumped by the greater concern of trying to appease his second wife. No doubt, Herodias held a grudge against John for denouncing her marriage to Antipas, and she found a way to be rid of John when her daughter's dance at Antipas's birthday party led to his rash promise. This unnamed daughter may have been Salome, Herodias' daughter by her former husband Philip (Antipas's half brother). Or, according to some manuscripts of Mark 6:22, she could have had the same name as her mother, Herodias. The girl's dance so enthralled Antipas that he foolishly vowed to give her anything she wanted.

14:8-10 *I want the head of John the Baptist on a tray!* Herodias prompted her daughter to ask for a grotesque present, John's head on a platter (cf. Mark 6:19).

because of the vow he had made in front of his guests. Antipas regretted his rash promise but granted the request because he did not want to lose face with his palace guests. So John was executed without a trial, and the macabre scene at the birthday party played out. Herodias avenged herself of John, but Antipas's guilty conscience led him to fear that Jesus was John brought back to life. See Hoehner (1972:124-165) for a detailed discussion of Josephus and the Gospels on this matter.

14:11 *his head was brought on a tray and given to the girl.* The word describing Herodias' daughter in this verse is *korasion* [TG2877, ZG3166], which indicates a young girl, perhaps around twelve years of age. This word and the silence of the text otherwise make it unlikely that the dance that so enthralled Antipas was erotic.

14:12 *John's disciples came for his body and buried it.* John's ignominious end was a terrible atrocity, yet his disciples maintained their loyalty to him to the bitter end, caring for his body and properly burying it. Devout Jews were extremely concerned for proper burial of corpses, as the intertestamental book of Tobit shows. After the burial, John's disciples informed Jesus of John's horrific demise (cf. 9:14; 11:2). This links Jesus' withdrawal of 14:13-21 to 14:1-12. Since Jesus' ministry began when John was imprisoned (4:12), John's death was also significant for Jesus (17:12).

COMMENTARY

The violent history of the Herodian dynasty continues. Herod the Great's evil deeds are well chronicled in ancient history and in Matthew 2. Here Antipas proved to be his father's son, although he was smitten in conscience for the evil that his rash promise had caused him to do. Antipas was a weak, pathetic, despicable figure, whose evil caprice was prompted by his vengeful wife's suggestion to her daughter. Plumptre's (1957) oft-cited remark deserves repeating: "Like most weak men, Herod feared to be thought weak." Instead of humbly acknowledging the error of his rash promise, he saved his own face by destroying God's prophet. His palace guests were shown a blatant example of corrupt power in action, and Herod took his place in the list of evil rulers who have rejected and destroyed God's messengers.

In Matthew's narrative, the execution of John by Antipas follows the rejection of Jesus by the people at Nazareth. The two consecutive episodes stress unbelief in two different situations, but the unifying theme is the rejection of God's messengers (11:18-19). This motif of the rejection of the prophets had been mentioned previously (5:12) and will be greatly stressed in Jesus' woes against the religious leaders in Matthew 23. Israel's rejection of her own prophets was well known from the Old Testament (see 2 Chr 36:16; Dan 9:6, 10), but for Matthew the rejection of the prophets culminates in the rejection of Jesus, the ultimate prophet (23:32).

As Jesus said, there was no greater human than John the Baptist (Matt 11:11). John fearlessly and faithfully fulfilled his role as the one who prepared the way for Jesus. Antipas may have been "king" at his birthday party when he ordered John's execution, but one day he will stand before the King of kings and give account for his atrocious treatment of the King's forerunner. Since this section of Matthew intentionally stresses how Jesus develops the faith of his disciples (this is explained in the commentary on 13:53-58), the action of John's disciples in properly burying their master should be read as a lesson for Jesus' disciples. John's death anticipates the death of Jesus (17:12), and the action of John's disciples here is exemplary for disciples of Jesus (27:57-61). Even Antipas's reluctance to behead John may anticipate Pilate's reluctance to crucify Jesus (14:9; 27:18-24). The similarities between John and Jesus are almost uncanny, leading Davies and Allison (1991:476) to remark that Matthew 14:1-12 is a Christological parable.

◆   **3. Jesus feeds five thousand (14:13-21; cf. Mark 6:31-44; Luke 9:10-17; John 6:1-15)**

¹³As soon as Jesus heard the news, he left in a boat to a remote area to be alone. But the crowds heard where he was headed and followed on foot from many towns. ¹⁴Jesus saw the huge crowd as he stepped from the boat, and he had compassion on them and healed their sick.

¹⁵That evening the disciples came to him and said, "This is a remote place, and it's already getting late. Send the crowds away so they can go to the villages and buy food for themselves."

¹⁶But Jesus said, "That isn't necessary—you feed them."

¹⁷"But we have only five loaves of bread and two fish!" they answered.

¹⁸"Bring them here," he said. ¹⁹Then he told the people to sit down on the grass. Jesus took the five loaves and two fish, looked up toward heaven, and blessed them. Then, breaking the loaves into pieces, he gave the bread to the disciples, who distributed it to the people. ²⁰They all ate as much as they wanted, and afterward, the disciples picked up twelve baskets of leftovers. ²¹About 5,000 men were fed that day, in addition to all the women and children!

NOTES

14:13-14 *he left in a boat to a remote area.* As John's imprisonment marked the beginning of Jesus' ministry (4:12), so John's death prompted Jesus to withdraw to a remote place. John's demise hinted at the demise of Jesus (17:12), and at this strategic time Jesus withdrew by boat to the less inhabited region east of the Sea of Galilee. Why Jesus left is not stated, but perhaps it was to grieve and pray (14:23), to avoid Antipas's interest and hostility (14:1-2), or to teach his disciples privately.

the crowds heard where he was headed and followed . . . he had compassion on them and healed their sick. When the press of the needy crowds did not permit private reflection, Jesus responded with compassion and healed the sick. The description of Jesus as a compassionate healer recalls 4:23-24; 9:35-36 and anticipates 15:30-32. It contrasts with the less concerned, more pragmatic view of the disciples in 14:15; 15:33.

14:15 The feeding of the five thousand is found in all four Gospels (cf. Mark 6:32-44; Luke 9:10-17; John 6:1-13), though the later, similar feeding of the four thousand is found only in 15:32-39 and Mark 8:1-9.

Send the crowds away. The disciples wanted to be rid of the hungry crowd, and maintained that their food resources were inadequate when Jesus told them to feed the people.

14:18 Jesus took the five loaves and two fish, looked up toward heaven, and blessed them. Jesus took what little food the disciples had, five loaves of bread and two fish (evidently dried), looked up to heaven (cf. 1 Esdr 4:58), blessed the bread, and broke it into pieces. The "blessing" of the bread involved praise to God for supplying it. The blessing used by Jesus may have been similar to the traditional Jewish prayer dating back to the Mishnah (*m. Berakhot* 6:1), "Blessed art thou, O Lord our God, King of the world, who brings forth bread from the earth." Bread and fish were evidently staples of the diet of Jews in Galilee (cf. 7:9-10; John 21:9-10).

14:19-21 distributed it. Jesus gave the pieces to the disciples, who then gave the pieces to the crowd. Amazingly, there was enough to go around, with much more left over (twelve full baskets) than the little there had been to begin with. Five thousand men were fed, not to mention the women and children who accompanied them.

COMMENTARY

One might naturally conclude from Matthew 4:13-21 that Jesus fed the five thousand out of compassion for hungry people. The miracle also demonstrated Jesus' Kingdom authority and challenged people to believe in him. But in addition to this straightforward interpretation of the miracle, a number of approaches have been suggested. Barclay (1975:102-103) suggests that the "miracle" should be understood as a spontaneous sharing of the food that had been brought by individuals, due to the power of Jesus' example. Jesus takes the meager stores that the disciples have brought and begins to distribute them, others follow suit, and there is more than enough to go around. Thus, the miracle is a matter of selfishness being overcome by generosity as everyone follows Jesus' example. Despite the wholesome lesson derived by this interpretation, it cannot be sustained exegetically. It is clear from the passage that the meager stores of the disciples, five loaves and two fish, were somehow miraculously multiplied to feed a crowd of perhaps twenty-thousand people. There is no mention of others bringing out additional food, or any comment about selfishness being turned into generosity. This is a miracle story, not a fable about generosity.

Another interpretation stresses the Eucharistic overtones in the passage, viewing it as "an allegory of the Eucharist" (Davies and Allison 1991:481). Indeed, there are so many clear verbal parallels between Matthew 14:13-21 and 26:20-29 that some connection between the two seems inevitable. But it seems to be a stretch to read the story of the Last Supper and subsequent Christian sacramental practice back into this story of hungry people being miraculously fed. It is more likely that Matthew intended his readers to view this story as reminiscent of the miraculous feeding of the Israelites with manna in the wilderness (Exod 16; Deut 8:3; Neh 9:20;

Ps 78:24; John 6:30-59) and as anticipatory of the eschatological messianic banquet alluded to in 8:11 and 26:29 (cf. Rev 2:17). Matthew may have also intended the reader to hear echoes of the ministries of Elijah (1 Kgs 17:9-16) and Elisha (2 Kgs 4:42-44). Just as God had miraculously met the needs of his people in former days through Moses, Elijah, and Elisha, so he met their needs ultimately through his beloved Son, the definitive prophet and teacher of Israel, Jesus (cf. Ps 132:13-18). While the number of loaves and fishes seem intended only to show the inadequacy of the disciples' resources, the detail that there were twelve baskets of leftover food is probably significant (16:9-10; 19:28). In Jesus there is *shalom* [TH7965, ZH8934] (peace, wholeness), an abundance of messianic blessings for Israel.

In this passage, Jesus continues to strengthen and develop the faith of his disciples. They learn two lessons from Jesus: compassion and faith. When they coldly wanted to dismiss the multitudes, Jesus compassionately chose to feed them. When they viewed their meager resources as inadequate for the need, Jesus nevertheless commanded them to meet the need. They learned to model their ministries after the compassionate model of Jesus and to believe in his power to multiply their resources.

◆   ## 4. Jesus walks on water (14:22-36; cf. Mark 6:45-56; John 6:16-21)

22Immediately after this, Jesus insisted that his disciples get back into the boat and cross to the other side of the lake, while he sent the people home. 23After sending them home, he went up into the hills by himself to pray. Night fell while he was there alone.

24Meanwhile, the disciples were in trouble far away from land, for a strong wind had risen, and they were fighting heavy waves. 25About three o'clock in the morning* Jesus came toward them, walking on the water. 26When the disciples saw him walking on the water, they were terrified. In their fear, they cried out, "It's a ghost!"

27But Jesus spoke to them at once. "Don't be afraid," he said. "Take courage. I am here!*"

28Then Peter called to him, "Lord, if it's really you, tell me to come to you, walking on the water."

29"Yes, come," Jesus said.

So Peter went over the side of the boat and walked on the water toward Jesus. 30But when he saw the strong* wind and the waves, he was terrified and began to sink. "Save me, Lord!" he shouted.

31Jesus immediately reached out and grabbed him. "You have so little faith," Jesus said. "Why did you doubt me?"

32When they climbed back into the boat, the wind stopped. 33Then the disciples worshiped him. "You really are the Son of God!" they exclaimed.

34After they had crossed the lake, they landed at Gennesaret. 35When the people recognized Jesus, the news of his arrival spread quickly throughout the whole area, and soon people were bringing all their sick to be healed. 36They begged him to let the sick touch at least the fringe of his robe, and all who touched him were healed.

14:25 Greek *In the fourth watch of the night.*   14:27 Or *The 'I AM' is here;* Greek reads *I am.* See Exod 3:14.
14:30 Some manuscripts do not include *strong.*

NOTES

14:22 *Jesus insisted that his disciples get back into the boat.* As soon as the miraculous meal was over, Jesus sent the crowd away and had the disciples take the boat back to the other side of the lake, evidently retracing the voyage mentioned in 14:13 (cf. Mark 6:45-51; John 6:15-21).

14:23 *he went up into the hills by himself to pray.* He stayed on the east side of the Sea of Galilee and found a place in the hills for prayer. Matthew only recounts Jesus praying here, in 11:25-26, and in the garden of Gethsemane (26:36-45; but see Luke 5:16; 9:18, 28-29; 11:1). One would assume that this was his original goal in 14:13, but that it was hindered by the crowds. Now alone in the hills, he prays on into the night, evidently for several hours.

14:24 *the disciples were in trouble far away from land.* As Jesus prayed alone, the disciples were also alone, away from him, struggling with the wind-blown waves on the lake (cf. 8:23-27 for a similar story). The NLT's "far away from land" renders an expression lit. translated "many stadia." A *stadion* [™G4712A, ᶻG5084] was around 192 meters or just over 600 feet in length, and the Sea of Galilee is up to 5 miles wide, so the disciples were evidently miles from shore (cf. John 6:19).

14:25 *About three o'clock in the morning.* Lit., "in the fourth watch of the night." This apparently reflects the custom of dividing the night, from 6 p.m. to 6 a.m., into four watches of three hours each (cf. the Gr. of 24:43).

Jesus came toward them. At this point, after the disciples had rowed for several hours (14:13, 22) under terrifying conditions in the dark, Jesus suddenly appeared, miraculously walking on the water.

14:26 *It's a ghost.* But the disciples did not recognize him and cried out that a ghost or disembodied spirit had appeared to them.

14:27 *Take courage.* Jesus' words evidently identified him to the disciples. He told them not to fear (cf. 17:7; 28:5, 10) but to take courage (cf. 9:2, 22), since he was there.

I am here. Lit., "I am." This may be an allusion to Exod 3:14 (cf. 22:32)—as in NLT mg: "The 'I AM' is here."

14:28 *Lord, if it's really you, tell me to come to you, walking on the water.* Peter proposed a sort of test—if it was really Jesus, would he command Peter to come to him on the water? Blomberg (1992:235) views Peter's words as a request to imitate Jesus' miracle in terms of the commission to ministry in 10:1, 8.

14:29-30 *Peter . . . walked on the water.* When Jesus agreed, Peter indeed walked on the water toward Jesus, but only briefly. He was distracted and terrified by the wind and waves, so as he began to sink he cried out for Jesus to rescue him (cf. the disciples' cry in 8:25). In view of the discipleship context of the previous storm miracle (8:23-27), it is not mistaken to view Peter's faith and doubt in the face of danger as exemplary of the trials of discipleship.

14:31 *You have so little faith.* Jesus rescued Peter by grasping him with his hand, but his words were aimed at rescue on another level. He pointed out Peter's weak faith and asked why Peter doubted him (cf. 6:30; 8:26; 16:8).

14:32 *the wind stopped.* When Peter and Jesus climbed into the boat, the storm ceased. There was no command as in 8:26 for the storm to stop; this time all that was needed was the presence of Jesus.

14:33 *You really are the Son of God!* When they realized that Jesus had walked on the storm-tossed sea and stopped the storm, the disciples worshiped him and uttered a ringing confession of his unique, divine sonship.

14:34-36 *they landed at Gennesaret.* This was about three miles southwest of Capernaum on the west shore of the Sea of Galilee (cf. Mark 6:53-56). Perhaps the boat was blown off its probable course to Capernaum by the storm. Once again Jesus is beset by crowds of needy people when news of his arrival spreads, and once again many are healed (cf. 14:13-14).

all who touched him were healed. An added detail this time was that people who merely touched the fringe of Jesus' robe were healed (cf. 9:20-21). These verses provide the kind of summary that is by now familiar to the reader of Matthew (cf. 4:23-24; 8:16; 9:35; 14:14; 15:30-31).

C O M M E N T A R Y

Jesus' appearance to the disciples during the storm in the middle of the Sea of Galilee follows on the heels of the feeding of the five thousand. These two consecutive stories focusing on Jesus' messianic powers provide a welcome contrast to the two previous episodes, which stress unbelief (13:53-58; 14:1-12). Jesus' messianic powers must be seen against the background of the Old Testament. To walk on the sea and to still a storm are prerogatives that belong only to God (Job 26:11-12; Pss 65:7; 89:9-10; 107:29; Jonah 1:15; Sir 43:23). These actions of Jesus should be understood as evidence of a status equal to that of which Jesus spoke in 11:25. The worship and testimony of the disciples to Jesus' divine sonship in 14:33 is a direct response to the divine acts he performed.

According to Matthew, Jesus was "worshiped" several times, by such people as the Magi, a leper, a synagogue official, a Canaanite woman, the mother of Zebedee's sons, and the disciples (2:2, 8, 11; 8:2; 9:18; 15:25; 20:20; 28:9, 17). The Greek word *proskuneō* [TG4351, ZG4685] may describe only a respectful bow to a superior, not the religious worship of deity (18:26), but in the overall Christological context of Matthew, the translation "worship" is frequently warranted. According to 14:33, the disciples worshiped Jesus and confessed that he is really the Son of God. This confession of Jesus' divine sonship should also be viewed in the highest sense, given other passages on the matter (2:15; 3:17; 4:3, 6; 8:29; 16:16; 17:5; 22:45; 26:63; 27:40, 43, 54; 28:19), and it should be noted as anticipating 16:16; 26:63-64; 27:54; 28:19. One who has made claims such as those in 11:25 and who has done such deeds as those narrated in Matthew 14 must be worshiped as the Son of God. (See the discussion of Jesus as Son of God in the "Major Themes" section of the Introduction.)

Although the disciples' faith was implicitly challenged in the feeding miracle (14:15, 17), the storm miracle directly challenged them, reinforced their need for stronger faith, and provided the occasion for their stirring confession (14:33). Davies and Allison (1991:512-513) state it well: "So often the First Evangelist, while addressing Christological themes with his right hand, is at the same time delivering teaching on discipleship with his left." This second storm miracle, just like the first (8:23-27), should be read as a picture of discipleship in the midst of the trials of life. This miracle also portrays Peter as the model disciple, the first among equals (14:28-30). Peter's actions led to the disciples' confession (14:33), which anticipates 16:16, where Peter alone confesses that Jesus is the Christ, the Son of the living God. Blomberg (1992:235) is correct to note Matthew's distinctive position-ing of Peter in this section (cf. 15:15; 16:16-19; 17:24-27; 18:21). Peter's failure due to lack of faith—even more than his success due to faith—is exemplary for growing disciples of Jesus, both then and now. See Turner 1991 for a detailed discussion.

Summary of Matthew 14.   Matthew 13:53 marks the transition from Jesus' third discourse to a narrative of the next stage of Jesus' ministry. He arrived in Nazareth where his ministry was not honored (13:57). News of Jesus came to Herod, who mistakenly took Jesus as John *redivivus* (14:2). When Jesus heard of John's martyr-dom, he withdrew to a lonely place but was followed by multitudes whom he mi-raculously fed (14:19). This is followed by the second storm incident (14:22-33) and many healings in Gennesaret (14:36).

One theme that continues to characterize Matthew's narrative is Jesus' rejection, which now occurs even in Nazareth (13:54-58). Another blow comes from John's grisly martyrdom, which caused Jesus to withdraw from the public eye. Yet he could not avoid the multitudes who were clamoring for healing. Jesus' disciples contin-ued to exercise "little faith" when they were tested by another storm (14:22-32), but they repeated the affirmation that Jesus is God's Son (14:33). In general, one can conclude that in the midst of growing opposition, the Kingdom was still growing through Jesus' miracles and through the weak but genuine and maturing faith of the disciples.

◆   ## 5. Conflict over the tradition of the elders (15:1-20; cf. Mark 7:1-23)

Some Pharisees and teachers of religious law now arrived from Jerusalem to see Jesus. They asked him, [2]"Why do your disciples disobey our age-old tradition? For they ignore our tradition of ceremo-nial hand washing before they eat."

[3]Jesus replied, "And why do you, by your traditions, violate the direct command-ments of God? [4]For instance, God says, 'Honor your father and mother,'* and 'Anyone who speaks disrespectfully of father or mother must be put to death.'* [5]But you say it is all right for people to say to their parents, 'Sorry, I can't help you. For I have vowed to give to God what I would have given to you.' [6]In this way, you say they don't need to honor their par-ents.* And so you cancel the word of God for the sake of your own tradition. [7]You hypocrites! Isaiah was right when he prophesied about you, for he wrote,

[8]'These people honor me with their lips,
    but their hearts are far from me.
[9]Their worship is a farce,
    for they teach man-made ideas as
        commands from God.'*"

[10]Then Jesus called to the crowd to come and hear. "Listen," he said, "and try to understand. [11]It's not what goes into your mouth that defiles you; you are de-filed by the words that come out of your mouth."

[12]Then the disciples came to him and asked, "Do you realize you offended the Pharisees by what you just said?"

[13]Jesus replied, "Every plant not planted by my heavenly Father will be uprooted, [14]so ignore them. They are blind guides leading the blind, and if one blind person guides another, they will both fall into a ditch."

¹⁵Then Peter said to Jesus, "Explain to us the parable that says people aren't defiled by what they eat."

¹⁶"Don't you understand yet?" Jesus asked. ¹⁷"Anything you eat passes through the stomach and then goes into the sewer. ¹⁸But the words you speak come from the heart—that's what defiles you. ¹⁹For from the heart come evil thoughts, murder, adultery, all sexual immorality, theft, lying, and slander. ²⁰These are what defile you. Eating with unwashed hands will never defile you."

15:4a Exod 20:12; Deut 5:16. 15:4b Exod 21:17 (Greek version); Lev 20:9 (Greek version). 15:6 Greek *their father*; other manuscripts read *their father or their mother*. 15:8-9 Isa 29:13 (Greek version).

NOTES

15:1 *Pharisees and teachers of religious law.* The last mention of these groups was in 12:38; here they accuse Jesus' disciples of ignoring traditional teaching about washing hands before a meal (cf. Mark 7:1-23).

15:2 *Why do your disciples disobey our age-old tradition?* Lit., "traditions of the elders." It is significant that the Pharisees and scribes come all the way to Galilee from Jerusalem, perhaps as part of an official inquiry stemming from earlier conflicts (cf. Mark 3:22; John 1:19). It is not clear why they accused the disciples instead of Jesus. Evidently, if the disciples did not practice this tradition, neither did Jesus (cf. Luke 11:38).

they ignore our tradition of ceremonial hand washing. The complaint does not directly concern the violation of OT ritual purity (Exod 30:17-21), since this was prescribed for the priests, not the common folk. But the Pharisees had evidently extrapolated the laws of priestly purity to themselves and—theoretically—to all Jews (Neusner 1973:83). Jesus' disciples were accused of transgressing the oral "law" which had grown up to protect the OT (*m. Avot* 1:1-3; *m. Yadayim*; Josephus *Antiquities* 13.297; 17.41; Gal 1:14). The Pharisees believed that God had revealed to Moses not only the written law but also the oral law, which further expounded and applied the written law. The oral law was transmitted from generation to generation and could be deduced from the written law with proper interpretive methodology. This oral law was eventually edited in written form as the Mishnah by Rabbi Judah haNasi (the Patriarch) around AD 200. The massive rabbinic commentary (*Gemara*) that grew around the Mishnah for the next three or four centuries became the Babylonian Talmud.

15:3 *why do you, by your traditions, violate the direct commandments of God?* Jesus' answer directly confronts the Pharisees with a parody of their own question to him. The term used in both questions has to do with willful transgression or violation of known standards of conduct. Jesus brushed aside the specific matter of violation of the tradition on hand washing with the general charge that by such traditions the Pharisees violated God's command.

15:4-5 *Honor your father and mother.* Jesus cited the fifth commandment on the respect due one's parents (Exod 20:12; 21:17; Lev 20:9; Deut 5:16) and asserted that the tradition of the elders on gifts to God (15:5) had invalidated the true intent of the law.

I have vowed to give to God what I would have given to you. This refers to the practice of *qorban* [ᵀᴴ7133, ᶻᴴ7933] (cf. *korban* [ᵀᴳ2878A, ᶻᴳ3168]), which involved the pledging of funds to the Temple (Num 30:3-5; Deut 23:21-23; Mark 7:11; *m. Nedarim* 1:2-4; 3:11; 5:6; 9:1, 7). Evidently, such funds were not transferable to others, such as one's parents, but were still accessible to the one who pledged them. A person could claim that he was unable to meet a charitable obligation because he had already given his money to God, when in fact no money had yet changed hands.

15:6 *you cancel the word of God for the sake of your own tradition.* Jesus juxtaposed God's word and human traditions, and concluded that the scribes and Pharisees had allowed human traditions to nullify God's word. It is significant that Jesus twice refers to the tradition as "your" tradition (15:3, 6). It is clear that he did not view these traditions as coming from God.

15:7-9 *Isaiah was right when he prophesied about you.* Here Jesus' accusation went beyond the matter of behavioral violation of the law to the more serious matter of the heart: the religious leaders from Jerusalem were hypocrites whose seeming obedience to the law was mere pretense, a mask for disobedience (6:1-2, 5, 16; 23:13-36) Isaiah had prophesied about them (Isa 29:13; cf. Ps 78:36-37). Isaiah's critique of the hypocritical situation in his own day also fit the situation in Jesus' day.

they teach man-made ideas as commands from God. Isaiah and Jesus both dealt with the hypocritical human traditions that set aside the authority of God's word and resulted in empty worship. The *korban* [TG2878A, ZG3168] practice amounted to a false piety that excused the genuine impiety of neglecting one's parents. Human traditions could engage the lips in religious activities, but only the word of God could engage the heart (cf. Col 2:22; Titus 1:14). Jesus made a similar point about futile worship in 9:13 and 12:7, where he cited Hos 6:6. Portions of Isa 29:13-16 are also cited in Rom 9:20; 11:8; 1 Cor 1:19.

15:10-11 The conflict with the Pharisees provided an opportunity for Jesus to teach the crowd and then the disciples (15:12-20).

It's not what goes into your mouth that defiles you; you are defiled by the words that come out of your mouth. True purity is not a matter of a ritual that protects one from unclean things outside one's body but a matter of the things inside one's heart that are expressed in one's words. Jesus changed the subject from a specific oral tradition about ritual hand washing to a general ethical maxim about true defilement. Many think that Jesus was revoking the OT dietary laws here. This is spelled out explicitly in the parallel passage, Mark 7:19.

It is clear from 15:15 (cf. the note on that passage) that the teaching of Jesus to the crowd in 15:11 was viewed as difficult or enigmatic. In keeping with the principle Jesus enunciated in 13:11-12, this confusing public teaching was augmented by private explanation to the disciples. It should be noted that Jesus' stress on inner purity was not novel; similar teaching is found in the OT and in other Jewish literature (Exod 20:17; 2 Chron 30:18-20; Pss 24:3-4; 51:2-3, 6, 10, 16-17; 1QS 3:6-9; 5:13-14; Josephus *Antiquities* 18.117).

15:12 *you offended the Pharisees.* The opposition of the Pharisees could only be fueled by Jesus' scathing words, and the disciples were concerned about it. Jesus did not share the disciples' concern that the Pharisees were offended (cf. 11:6; 13:57).

15:13 *Every plant not planted by my heavenly Father will be uprooted.* His negative description of the Pharisees as uprooted plants alludes to Isa 60:21; 61:3, which speak positively of plants God has planted (cf. Jer 32:41). This imagery also recalls the parable of the weeds (13:24-30, 37-43). The Pharisees had not been planted by God, so they would be uprooted in judgment. This seems to contrast with the mentality of the Mishnah, which seems to assume that all Israelites are God's "planting" and will have a part in the world to come (*m. Sanhedrin* 10:1).

15:14 *blind guides leading the blind.* Jesus' bitingly sarcastic language about blind guides anticipates 23:16, 24 (cf. Luke 6:39). The mention of falling into a ditch or pit might hearken back to the disagreement with the Pharisees in 12:11 (cf. Ps 7:15; Prov 26:7;). It was Jesus' counsel that the disciples ignore the Pharisees or leave them alone. Jesus either regarded their opposition as so hardened that he could not spend time being concerned with it (cf. 7:6), or he was subtly alluding to the parable of the weeds, in which the weeds are to be left alone until harvest.

15:15 *Peter said to Jesus, "Explain to us the parable."* Peter characteristically spoke up for the group (cf. 16:16) and asked what Jesus had meant by the statement in 15:11.

15:16 *Don't you understand yet?* This recalls 13:51 but casts the disciples' degree of understanding in a negative light (cf. 13:13-15; 15:10). The question implies a rebuke— by now they should have understood the teaching.

15:17-18 *Anything you eat passes through the stomach.* Whatever goes into the mouth, whether it is "clean" or "unclean," passes from the body as waste and is disposed of. *the words you speak come from the heart—that's what defiles you.* What one says origi- nates in the heart, the source of ethical defilement (5:8, 28; 18:35). Jesus' teaching was not new. That the heart is central to ethics is taught in the OT (e.g., Gen 8:21; Deut 6:5; 10:16; 30:6; 1 Sam 16:7; Ps 51:10, 17; Prov 4:23; Joel 2:13).

15:19 This enumeration of seven sins that come from the heart begins with a general state- ment about evil thoughts and goes on to list behavioral sins. These sins, for the most part, are drawn from the second table of the Ten Commandments. Jesus' "inside-out" ethic clashes primarily with the Pharisees' externalism, not the OT. Nevertheless, Jesus seems to treat the OT ritual purity laws in the same way he previously treated the laws on vows and vengeance (5:33-42). The editorial comment in Mark 7:19 makes this explicit.

COMMENTARY

The structure of Matthew 15:1-20 develops from the Pharisees' question (15:1-2), which is answered by Jesus in 15:3-9. Then Jesus turns to the crowd and addresses them parabolically, evidently in the presence of the Pharisees (15:10-11). Finally, in response to two questions from the disciples, Jesus first denounces the Pharisees (15:12-14) and then explains the enigmatic saying of 15:11 to the crowd (15:15- 20). The movement is from (1) Jesus' enemies, the Pharisees, to (2) the crowd, which views Jesus in a very superficial manner, to (3) the disciples, whose under- standing of Jesus is genuine though flawed. The passage is an example of *inclusio* as it begins and ends with the matter of eating with unwashed hands (15:2, 20).

Jesus' Response to the Oral Traditions and Written Torah. This passage is crucial in understanding Jesus' view of the oral and written law and the relationship of his teaching to the traditions of the Pharisees and the law of Moses. Jesus clearly set aside the "traditions of the elders" as at cross purposes with God's Word (15:3-6), but did he do the same with the dietary laws of the OT (Lev 11; Deut 14)? Those who answer this question in the affirmative (see Beare 1981:338; Blomberg 1992:239; Meier 1978:100-104) stress 15:11, 17 to the effect that Jesus categorically denied that food can defile a person. They also note that whatever is left in doubt in Matthew is made clear by the editorial comment "he declared all foods clean" in the parallel text, Mark 7:19. But in view of Matthew 5:17, it seems a bit simplistic and presumptuous to think that Matthew would present Jesus as dismissing a key OT law in such an abrupt and facile manner.

Others argue that Matthew does not present Jesus as annulling the OT dietary laws (see Davies and Allison 1991:528-531; Overman 1996:226-227). Such schol- ars, assuming the priority of Mark, argue that Matthew toned down Mark's version of this incident, mainly by omitting Mark 7:19b, "he declared all foods clean."

Another argument is that Matthew 15:11 is hortatory and its antithesis is a rhetorical strategy, not a prosaic proposition. It is also pointed out that Matthew's stress is on Jesus' disagreement with the Pharisees, not the law itself. This is shown by the *inclusio* of 15:2, 20, which denies the validity of the Pharisaic tradition on washing hands, not the dietary laws themselves. Another noteworthy factor is that the enigmatic saying of 15:11, often taken as annulling the dietary laws, is not interpreted by Jesus in terms of dietary law but in terms of the Pharisaic traditions. Granted, Jesus did say that whatever food (clean or unclean) enters the mouth is eliminated and that what comes out of the mouth is the real problem (5:17-18). But in his final comment, he contrasts the sins that defile with eating with unwashed hands (15:20)—not with eating unclean foods. Thus, there is reason to doubt that Matthew intended for his readers to conclude that Jesus was simply annulling the dietary laws.

Carson (1984:352) is correct in pointing to Matthew 5:17-48 as the key to the interpretation of 15:1-20. Jesus had come not to destroy but to fulfill the law and prophets. In so doing, he definitively taught the law and thus accomplished its purpose. Jesus fulfilled the Old Testament dietary laws by pointing out that ultimately, defilement is a matter of the heart. It is helpful to frame the issue here in terms of the six contrasting structures found in 5:21-48. Davies and Allison (1991:530) take this tack and compare Matthew 15:11 to Matthew 5:27-28 on adultery. If this is analogous, Jesus was not permitting adultery/eating unclean food (5:27; 15:17) so much as forbidding lust/evil thoughts (5:28; 15:19). But it might be a closer analogy to make the comparison to 5:33-34 on vows or 5:38-39 on vengeance. If Jesus' teaching on vows is analogous, Jesus would be saying that vows/dietary restrictions (5:33-34; 15:17) are unnecessary when one puts the priority on integrity/the heart (5:37; 15:19). In this case, the continuing role of vows or dietary laws might be as a cultural preference, not a revelatory duty. Or dietary laws might be viewed as the tithing of garden herbs—as lighter matters that should still be done but should not eclipse the weightier matters of the law (23:23).

Eventually the apostolic church will deal with the implications of Matthew 15:11 for the Old Testament dietary laws (cf. Acts 10:10-16, 28; Rom 14:2-3, 6, 14-15; Col 2:16-17). But at this point, Matthew narrates the teaching of Jesus for his Christian Jewish community in an implicit, cryptic manner (rather than drawing a full conclusion as Mark 7:19 does). The principle of putting the priority on internal ethical matters rather than on Pharisaic hand washing traditions is clear. Nonetheless, Matthew's community would probably go on practicing the OT dietary laws as reminders of the deeper ethical concerns voiced by Jesus, the ultimate teacher of Torah.

A larger issue raised by this passage concerns the relationship of later ecclesiastical traditions to the express teaching of the original canonical Scriptures. The root of the problem in this passage is identified by Jesus in the words of Isaiah 29:13 ("they replace God's commands with their own man-made teachings"). Protestants may be quick to think of this only as a problem with Roman Catholic and Eastern Orthodox Christianity, but Protestant groups are also prone to elevating their various traditions to a position of functional authority over Scripture. The church must always remember that the Scriptures possess authority over all ideas and practices developed by the church in the exercise of its ministry.

◆ 6. Faith of a Gentile woman (15:21-28; cf. Mark 7:24-30)

²¹Then Jesus left Galilee and went north to the region of Tyre and Sidon. ²²A Gentile* woman who lived there came to him, pleading, "Have mercy on me, O Lord, Son of David! For my daughter is possessed by a demon that torments her severely."

²³But Jesus gave her no reply, not even a word. Then his disciples urged him to send her away. "Tell her to go away," they said. "She is bothering us with all her begging."

²⁴Then Jesus said to the woman, "I was sent only to help God's lost sheep—the people of Israel."

²⁵But she came and worshiped him, pleading again, "Lord, help me!"

²⁶Jesus responded, "It isn't right to take food from the children and throw it to the dogs."

²⁷She replied, "That's true, Lord, but even dogs are allowed to eat the scraps that fall beneath their masters' table."

²⁸"Dear woman," Jesus said to her, "your faith is great. Your request is granted." And her daughter was instantly healed.

15:22 Greek *Canaanite.*

NOTES

15:21 *Jesus left Galilee.* Blomberg's view (1991:242) that Jesus withdrew from Israel ideologically in 15:1-20 and geographically in 15:21-28 is debatable. Certainly Jesus had withdrawn from Pharisaic traditionalism, but one could argue that it was the Pharisees, not Jesus, who had withdrawn from Israel. This was Jesus' fourth strategic withdrawal from conflict (cf. 2:12-14, 22; 4:12; 12:15; 14:13).

the region of Tyre and Sidon. Cf. 11:22; a journey of perhaps fifty miles to the north (cf. Mark 7:24-30). Jesus' previous statements about true purity (15:10-20) were immediately put into practice in ministry to unclean Gentiles.

15:22-24 *Jesus gave her no reply.* At first, Jesus uncharacteristically ignored the Gentile (lit. "Canaanite") woman's request that he have mercy on her and help her demon-possessed daughter (cf. 4:24; 9:32; 12:22). But the woman's surprising reference to Jesus as "Lord" (3:3; 7:21-22; 8:2, 6, 8, 25; 9:28; 12:8; 14:28, 30; etc.) and "Son of David" (1:1, 20; 9:27; 12:23; 20:30-31; 21:9, 15; 22:42) implies that she had genuine insight into his identity and mission.

tell her to go away. The disciples urged Jesus to send the woman away, once again showing insensitivity about ministry to needy people (cf. 14:15; 15:32-33).

I was sent only to help God's lost sheep—the people of Israel. Jesus told the woman that the lost sheep of Israel were his sole mission priority (cf. 9:36; 10:6). It is possible that 15:23-24 should be understood a bit differently, with the disciples implying that Jesus should heal the woman in 15:23 and him answering them, not her, in 15:24.

15:25 *she came and worshiped him.* Undaunted, the woman persisted, this time bowing before Jesus. It is likely that Matthew intended the reader to view this as worship in the strongest sense of the word (cf. 14:33).

15:26 *It isn't right to take food from the children and throw it to the dogs.* Jesus' reply metaphorically reflects the Jews' special covenant relationship with God (the children's food) and the Gentiles' lack of such a relationship (dogs under the master's table). The "children" of 15:26 are "God's lost sheep—the people of Israel" in 15:24. Such language is offensive to modern sensibilities even when one notes that the word "dogs" (*kunarion* [TG2952, ZG3249]) is a word which might be understood as house dogs or pets and might imply affection, not the more common word that often implies wild scavengers (*kuōn* [TG2965, ZG3264]; cf. Matthew 7:6; Luke 16:21; Phil 3:2; 2 Pet 2:22; Rev 22:15).

15:27 even dogs are allowed to eat the scraps that fall beneath their masters' table. Despite the pejorative nature of Jesus' response, the woman amazingly persisted in yet a third plea for her daughter. This time she even adapted Jesus' metaphor to her own needs and extended it, accepting her place as a dog but requesting his mercy nevertheless as a dog might beg for table scraps.

15:28 your faith is great. Jesus commended the woman for her great faith and immediately healed her daughter. Thus, the woman's faith truly was great (cf. 9:22, 29). She had persisted through three rebuffs from Jesus, and her remarks manifest an amazing understanding of Jesus' identity, power, and mission.

COMMENTARY

In this dialogue, Jesus responds three times to the pleas of the Canaanite woman, and once to his disciples. The request of the disciples comes after Jesus' first response to the woman, when he ignores her (15:22-23). His second response may be to the disciples more than to the woman, and in it he flatly denies that his mission concerns her (15:24). His third response to the woman, whose pleas this time are underlined by her bowing before him, uses blunt, even harsh language to compare the woman to a dog that cannot have the children's bread (15:25-26). The woman's final plea exhibits amazing humility and insight, asking Jesus to permit her a scrap from the children's bread. He responds by commending her great faith and granting her request (15:27-28). The repeated requests and responses induce a dramatic anticipation in the reader, as each time Jesus places an additional obstacle in front of the woman. Seen in this light, the woman's faith is all the more remarkable.

Jesus and the Gentiles. It is already clear in Matthew that Jesus and his disciples ministered only to the lost sheep of Israel (9:35-36; 10:5-6). However, there has already been at least one notable exception to this rule, the healing of the Roman officer's servant (8:5-13). It is noteworthy that both the previous and the present cases of ministry to Gentiles center around exceptional faith (8:10; 15:28). Both cases involve a request for another person, the Roman officer's servant and the Canaanite woman's daughter (8:6, 8; 15:22). Both cases also speak of blessing in terms of table fellowship (8:11; 15:26-27), which is then applied to the primacy of Israel. The Roman official may look forward to sitting down at a table with the Jewish patriarchs, and the woman may have scraps of the children's bread. The language of the table is clearly eschatological in 8:11 and is implicitly so here in Matthew 15, since the woman received blessings flowing from the presence of the Kingdom (12:28). Jesus' language at the Last Supper also has an eschatological context (26:29). Thus, every meal among Christians and, even more so, every Christian Eucharist service anticipates the eschatological feast with Jesus (cf. 1 Cor 11:26). Seen in this light, the miracle meals of Jesus are also powerful anticipations of the *shalom* [TH7965, ZH8934] that will one day come to his disciples from Israel and all the nations. "What a blessing it will be to attend a banquet in the Kingdom of God" (Luke 14:15).

Davies and Allison (1991:557) are correct when they say that this passage "makes it abundantly plain that the biblical doctrine of Israel's election must be taken seriously." As Jesus said to the Samaritan woman, "salvation comes through the Jews" (John 4:22). The world mission of the church that concludes Matthew (28:18-20) is couched in language that echoes Daniel 7:13-14. This world mission does not contradict the earlier mission to Israel but expands it. Matthew would agree with Paul that through Jesus the Gentiles have been brought near to Israel's covenant promises (Eph 2:11-19; Rom 11:17; 15:7-12). The covenantal language from which both Matthew's and Paul's views arise is evidently Genesis 12:3—"All the families on earth will be blessed through you [Abraham]." (For further discussion, see the commentary on Matthew 10:5-6 and Levine 1988.)

◆   ## 7. Miracles by the Sea of Galilee (15:29-39; cf. Mark 7:31-8:10)

²⁹Jesus returned to the Sea of Galilee and climbed a hill and sat down. ³⁰A vast crowd brought to him people who were lame, blind, crippled, those who couldn't speak, and many others. They laid them before Jesus, and he healed them all. ³¹The crowd was amazed! Those who hadn't been able to speak were talking, the crippled were made well, the lame were walking, and the blind could see again! And they praised the God of Israel.

³²Then Jesus called his disciples and told them, "I feel sorry for these people. They have been here with me for three days, and they have nothing left to eat. I don't want to send them away hungry, or they will faint along the way."

³³The disciples replied, "Where would we get enough food here in the wilderness for such a huge crowd?"

³⁴Jesus asked, "How much bread do you have?"

They replied, "Seven loaves, and a few small fish."

³⁵So Jesus told all the people to sit down on the ground. ³⁶Then he took the seven loaves and the fish, thanked God for them, and broke them into pieces. He gave them to the disciples, who distributed the food to the crowd.

³⁷They all ate as much as they wanted. Afterward, the disciples picked up seven large baskets of leftover food. ³⁸There were 4,000 men who were fed that day, in addition to all the women and children. ³⁹Then Jesus sent the people home, and he got into a boat and crossed over to the region of Magadan.

NOTES

15:29 *Jesus returned to the Sea of Galilee.* Jesus left the region of Tyre and Sidon. He climbed a hill in Galilee (cf. 5:1) overlooking the Sea of Galilee (cf. Mark 7:31-37). It is impossible to track this movement precisely because the language is vague. (The town of Magadan mentioned in 15:39 is also obscure and cannot be located with confidence.) However, many expositors (Blomberg 1992:245; Carson 1984:356-357) believe it is most likely that the area intended here is northeast of the Sea of Galilee in Gentile territory (Mark 7:31; cf. Matthew 8:28-34). It is argued that seeing the feeding of the four thousand as a miracle meal for Gentiles better fits the parallel passage in Mark 7, as well as the praise of "the God of Israel" and the description of the place as a "wilderness" (15:31, 33). This view will be evaluated in the commentary that follows.

15:30-31 *he healed them all.* The general statement about many miracles in 15:30-31 is similar to those found elsewhere in Matthew (4:23-24; 9:35; 14:34-36). Once again, Jesus healed all who were afflicted with a plethora of diseases. If this occurred in a Gentile region, as many argue, the receptivity of the Canaanite woman and these Gentiles to Jesus' works contrasts with his rejection by the residents of Nazareth and the Pharisees (13:54-58; 15:1-9).

15:32-33 Jesus' second miracle meal (cf. Mark 8:1-9) resembles the first in many details (cf. 14:13-21). The resemblance has led some scholars to view it as an unhistorical "doublet" or a second version of the same event (Hagner 1995:449-450), but see Blomberg (1987:146-148) for a response.

They have been here with me for three days. Jesus was surrounded by needy people who had been with him for three days, so he told the disciples that he felt compassion for their hunger and did not want to send the crowd away hungry (cf. 9:36; 14:14; 20:34).

15:33-34 *Where would we get enough food?* The disciples' response indicates that they thought Jesus wanted them to feed the multitudes; they stated that their resources were inadequate. But Jesus used these resources: "seven loaves, and a few small fish."

15:37-38 *There were 4,000 men who were fed that day, in addition to all the women and children.* If this miracle is to be understood as occurring in Gentile territory, Matthew's purpose in including a second miracle meal story is evidently to demonstrate Jesus' concern for the Gentiles and to underline the theme of Gentile world mission with which the Gospel concludes.

15:39 *crossed over to the region of Magadan.* After the miracle, Jesus crossed over the Sea in a boat and arrived at Magadan. This is an obscure town, perhaps to be identified with Magdala on the west side of the Sea of Galilee. At any rate, Jesus was clearly now in Jewish territory and thus available for the Pharisees' official inquisition (16:1).

COMMENTARY

Davies and Allison (1991:563-564) lay out a convenient summary of the reasons many scholars view the feeding of the four thousand as a miracle meal for Gentiles, which balances the previous feeding of five thousand Jews. This is quite convenient theologically but cannot be proven. The geographical language is too vague and obscure to prove that Jesus was in Gentile territory. The statement that the crowd that witnessed the healing "praised the God of Israel" (15:31) is fitting in the mouths of Gentiles, but it also is a common phrase in the Old Testament for Israel's worship (1 Kgs 1:48; 1 Chr 16:36; Pss 41:13; 59:5; 68:35; 69:6; 72:18; 106:48; Luke 1:68). Therefore, neither the geography nor this key phrase prove that the meal was for Gentiles, and one must make the case for this from the context in which the meal occurs. Jesus had recently gone to an area bordering Israel and had healed a Canaanite woman's daughter. It would fit this emphasis on ministry to believing Gentiles if the healings and miracle meal narrated in Matthew 15:32-39 were done for Gentiles. Similarly, one might even view the four thousand people as symbolic of Gentiles from the four corners of the earth and the seven baskets of leftover food as symbolic of the completeness or universality of Jesus' Kingdom ministry, but this is mere speculation that fits a preconceived theory. In fact, the context probably speaks against the view that four thousand Gentiles were fed because it indicates that Jesus' ministry to the Canaanite woman was exceptional (15:24; Hagner 1995:446). Up to this point in Matthew, the Gentiles to whom Jesus ministered have exercised unusually great faith. There is no indication of such exceptional faith on the part of the four thousand. Thus, it is quite unlikely that this was a miracle for Gentiles.

If the feeding of the four thousand should not be regarded as a miracle for Gentiles, why did Matthew include it? For one thing, if Matthew was following Mark, he would have encountered this second story (Mark 8:1-10). But Matthew likely has a theological motive, not just a historical one. Donaldson (1985:122-135) argues that several elements of the passage combine to fit "Zion eschatology," which portrays the gathering of scattered Israel to Mount Zion for healing, a great feast, and many other blessings (cf. Isa 35:5-6). In other words, Matthew has crafted his narrative of this miracle to connect it with Old Testament prophetic images of God's eschatological blessing upon his people. Davies and Allison (1991:238-242) add to this imagery the likelihood of linkage with Moses, finding in the "mountain" and the miraculous meal echoes of Sinai and manna from heaven.

Matthew's story reminds those who are familiar with the Old Testament of God blessing his people, both in the past blessings through Moses and the future blessings foreseen by the prophets. This is to be expected in a Gospel that stresses the role of Jesus as the ultimate fulfillment of the law and the prophets. But one would also expect to find a reason for the second miracle meal in the narrative of Matthew itself. It seems probable that Matthew included a second miracle meal to emphasize the lessons his readers should learn from it (such as the compassion of Jesus and his power to do great things with meager resources) and to foreshadow the eschatological feast with Jesus. Yet another lesson will soon be taught based on the two meal miracle stories—see 16:5-11, in which the disciples' "little faith" will once again be confronted with their preoccupation with physical needs instead of Kingdom truths.

Lessons for the Disciples.   In each of the main sections of Matthew 15, Jesus addresses the genuine but flawed faith of the disciples. In 15:1-20, the story of the controversy over purity, the disciples were evidently slow to perceive that the rift between Jesus and the Jewish religious leaders was irreversible. They were overly concerned that the Pharisees were offended by Jesus' teaching, but Jesus' response to their concern makes it quite plain that these leaders were blind to the Kingdom because they were not God's "plants" (15:12-14). The disciples were also slow to understand Jesus' teaching that genuine purity comes from within. Jesus' reply to their question makes it clear that the disciples should have understood what he meant (15:15-16). This passage shows that the disciples' response in 13:51 should not be taken totally at face value. No doubt they thought they understood the Kingdom well, but their genuine knowledge needed considerable deepening.

In the other two sections of Matthew 15, the disciples appear to be impatient with the needs of people. They asked Jesus to dismiss the Canaanite woman because her repeated pleas bothered them (15:23), and they were incredulous that

Jesus wanted to feed the four thousand because they had inadequate provisions (15:33). The disciples had forgotten Jesus' merciful response to a previous request from another Gentile (8:5-13), and his ability to feed a previous crowd even larger than this one (14:13-21). From the lack of compassion and short memories of the disciples, Matthew's readers learn that they must have Christ-like compassion on the needy as they trust Jesus to use their meager resources to meet the needs of others. In the very next section of Matthew, the "little faith" of the disciples is once again exposed (16:8), and Matthew's readers are once again reminded of the power of the Kingdom.

Summary of Matthew 15. The events of 13:53-14:36 serve to illustrate the mixed response to the gospel that Jesus stressed in the parables of 13:1-52. However, opposition in this section (13:57; 14:1-12) does not come from the Pharisees, whose ultimate slander was stressed in 12:1-45. Even though the murder of John anticipates that of Jesus (12:14; 17:12), the absence of the Pharisees in chapters 13–14 reduces the tension to just below the level it reached in chapter 12. With chapter 15, the Pharisees return to criticize Jesus' disciples for not obeying their "age-old tradition." After answering their charge (15:3-20), Jesus withdraws to Gentile territory and heals the daughter of a remarkable Canaanite woman (15:21-28). He then moves into territory near the Sea of Galilee, performing additional miracles of healing (15:29-31) and another miraculous feeding (15:32-39).

The events of this chapter not only portray the continuing obduracy of the Pharisees but also further our understanding of Jesus as the fulfiller of the law (cf. 5:17-20). As he confronted the Pharisees (15:1-9), taught the multitudes (15:10-11), and explained the teaching to the disciples (15:12-20), Jesus was, in effect, repeating the formula of 5:21ff—emphasizing a righteousness exceeding that of the scribes and Pharisees. Though this righteousness was not appreciated by the Pharisees, it was welcomed by the Canaanite woman, who hungrily took the crumbs from the meal the Pharisees refused to eat. Her great faith (15:28) reminds us of that of the centurion (8:10), who would participate in the Kingdom meal. The ensuing miracles and meal continue the story of Jesus as compassionate miracle worker and patient teacher. The Kingdom was forcefully advancing, but violent people were attacking it (11:12).

◆   **8. The demand for a sign (16:1-4; cf. Mark 8:11-13)**

One day the Pharisees and Sadducees came to test Jesus, demanding that he show them a miraculous sign from heaven to prove his authority.

²He replied, "You know the saying, 'Red sky at night means fair weather tomorrow; ³red sky in the morning means foul weather all day.' You know how to interpret the weather signs in the sky, but you don't know how to interpret the signs of the times!* ⁴Only an evil, adulterous generation would demand a miraculous sign, but the only sign I will give them is the sign of the prophet Jonah.*" Then Jesus left them and went away.

16:2-3 Several manuscripts do not include any of the words in 16:2-3 after *He replied.* 16:4 Greek *the sign of Jonah.*

NOTES

16:1 *One day the Pharisees and Sadducees came to test Jesus, demanding that he show them a miraculous sign from heaven to prove his authority.* For the second time, the religious leaders ask Jesus for a sign (cf. 12:38; Mark 8:10-12; 1 Cor 1:22). The NLT's "one day" tends to obscure the close connection between this episode and the previous chapter. The leaders' demand that Jesus prove his authority amounts to "testing" him with the assumption that he will fail (cf. 4:1, 7; 22:18, 35).

16:2-3 The words of Jesus in verses 2b and 3 are textually dubious (see NLT mg) because they are not found in many early manuscripts, such as ℵ B syr℮·ˢ copˢᵃ and manuscripts known to Jerome. The verses were likely borrowed from Luke 12:54-56 (for further discussion see Metzger 1994:33; Comfort 2007:[Matt 16:2].

16:4 *Then Jesus left them and went away.* At this point Jesus walked away from the Pharisees and Sadducees. Perhaps this physical act demonstrates Jesus' rejection of the leaders of Israel.

COMMENTARY

The Pharisees were associated with the Sadducees here and in other places in Matthew, evidently because these two normally disparate groups had found a common enemy in Jesus (3:7; 16:1, 6, 11, 12). Their request for a sign was motivated by a desire to test Jesus, which put them in the company of Satan (4:1, 7). That they asked for a sign "from heaven" perhaps refers to something so spectacular that it could not be denied. But again, Jesus had just fed more than four thousand people with seven loaves of bread and a few small fish. What more could be done? Jesus did signs to help the needy, not to soften hardened hearts. Seeing does not necessarily cause believing (Luke 16:31; Davies and Allison 1991:583-584).

In these verses, Jesus contrasted the Pharisees' ability to discern meteorological signs with their culpable inability to discern that his miracles demonstrated the messianic significance of his ministry (cf. 9:6-8; 12:28). They could discern the signs of clear and stormy weather depending on the color of the sky in the morning or the evening, but they were unable to discern the signs of the times—that is, the significance of Jesus' epiphany as the Son of God on earth.

The second request for a sign was met with the same enigmatic answer here as in the first request, "Only an evil, adulterous generation would demand a miraculous sign, but the only sign I will give them is the sign of the prophet Jonah." However, the answer here is not explained, as it was in 12:40ff (see comments there).

◆   **9. The leaven of the Pharisees and Sadducees (16:5-12; cf. Mark 8:14-21)**

⁵Later, after they crossed to the other side of the lake, the disciples discovered they had forgotten to bring any bread. ⁶"Watch out!" Jesus warned them. "Beware of the yeast of the Pharisees and Sadducees."

⁷At this they began to argue with each other because they hadn't brought any bread. ⁸Jesus knew what they were saying, so he said, "You have so little faith! Why are you arguing with each other about having no bread? ⁹Don't you understand even yet? Don't you remember the

5,000 I fed with five loaves, and the bas- "Beware of the yeast of the Pharisees and
kets of leftovers you picked up? [10]Or the Sadducees.'"
4,000 I fed with seven loaves, and the [12]Then at last they understood that he
large baskets of leftovers you picked up? wasn't speaking about the yeast in bread,
[11]Why can't you understand that I'm but about the deceptive teaching of the
not talking about bread? So again I say, Pharisees and Sadducees.

NOTES

16:5-6 *Later, after they crossed to the other side of the lake.* The movements of Jesus
and the disciples are not easy to follow. If 15:39 implies that Jesus left the disciples behind
when he took the boat trip to Magadan, then the disciples evidently rejoin him at this
point. This approach is implied by the NASB and NLT, and seems most likely overall
(Hagner 1994:454-459). Another approach would be to take 15:39 as indicating a trip
of Jesus and the disciples to Magadan and 16:5 as a return trip, as implied by the NIV
(Blomberg 1992:248).

Watch out! The disciples' memory lapse in forgetting to bring bread serves as a spring-
board for Jesus' warning about the "yeast of the Pharisees and Sadducees" (cf. Mark 8:13-
21). In view of the many disagreements between the Pharisees and Sadducees, this yeast
(cf. 13:33) must represent their shared opposition to Jesus and the Kingdom (see note on
16:12).

16:7 *they began to argue with each other because they hadn't brought any bread.* It is
difficult to know exactly how 16:7 relates to 16:6, but in light of 16:8-12, it seems that the
disciples thought Jesus was angry with them because they had forgotten to bring bread, or
that he was warning them not to buy bread from Pharisees and Sadducees.

16:8-11 *Don't you understand even yet?* The disciples' preoccupation with their material
needs rendered them insensitive to the more vital issue of the conflict between Jesus and
the religious leaders. Their misunderstanding of Jesus' yeast metaphor showed their dull-
ness to spiritual things.

Don't you remember the 5,000 I fed. . . . Or the 4,000? The disciples lacked faith in
Jesus' ability to provide bread for their needs. This lack of faith is all the more amazing in
view of the two miraculous feedings in which the disciples had recently participated. Five
loaves had fed more than five thousand people, with much left over, and seven loaves fed
more than four thousand, again with leftovers. But somehow the disciples obtusely concluded that Jesus had a problem with their lack of food. (For the theme of the disciples'
"little faith," see also 6:30; 8:26; 14:31; 17:20.)

16:12 *the deceptive teaching of the Pharisees and Sadducees.* Finally the disciples understood that Jesus' concern was the anti-Kingdom teaching of the Pharisees and Sadducees,
not their literal yeast. In view of their obvious differences on such matters as the validity of
the oral law and the existence of an afterlife (cf. 15:1-2; 22:23-32), it is surprising that the
Pharisees and Sadducees were lumped together here. Their common opposition to Jesus,
his Kingdom, and his definitive teaching of the Torah must be in view.

COMMENTARY

This passage does not present the disciples at one of their better moments.
Although they had affirmed that they understood Jesus' parabolic teaching about
the Kingdom (13:51-52), their thinking did not manifest Kingdom values. They forgot Jesus' recent warning about the blindness of the Pharisees (15:13-14), not to
mention the two astounding examples of his ability to provide food in a miraculous

fashion (14:13-21; 15:32-38). Their first memory lapse desensitized them to the danger posed by the Pharisees and Sadducees, so they did not pick up on Jesus' metaphor about yeast. Since the spiritual conflict between Jesus' Kingdom and the religious leaders did not occupy their thinking at this time, they were primarily occupied with temporal matters like bread. Since they had somehow forgotten to bring bread, they freely yet mistakenly associated Jesus' yeast metaphor with their empty stomachs rather than the growing controversy with the religious leaders (15:1-14) and the mortal danger the leaders posed to Jesus (12:14).

Once again Jesus patiently but firmly dealt with the "little faith" of the disciples. When he realized that they had misunderstood his yeast metaphor, he improved their understanding by prodding their memory. If they could recall how he twice miraculously fed thousands of people with more leftover than he had to start with, they would realize that food was not the problem. Rather, they must be occupied with the message of the Kingdom, which was being increasingly and intensively opposed. They needed to watch out for the teaching of the religious leaders. If they did that, the food problem would take care of itself. Jesus' rebuke of the disciples is appropriate for his disciples today whose preoccupation with temporal and material concerns renders them dull and forgetful of eternal Kingdom values. Today, as then, disciples need to have their memories of God's faithful, even miraculous, provision for their needs refreshed. Such a reminder, coupled with a renewed awareness of the spiritual battle being waged against the Kingdom (cf. 11:12), should sharpen the mental and spiritual focus of God's people.

◆   ## 10. Peter's confession and Jesus' promise (16:13-20; cf. Mark 8:27-30; Luke 9:18-21)

[13]When Jesus came to the region of Caesarea Philippi, he asked his disciples, "Who do people say that the Son of Man is?"* [14]"Well," they replied, "some say John the Baptist, some say Elijah, and others say Jeremiah or one of the other prophets." [15]Then he asked them, "But who do you say I am?" [16]Simon Peter answered, "You are the Messiah,* the Son of the living God." [17]Jesus replied, "You are blessed, Simon son of John,* because my Father in heaven has revealed this to you. You did not learn this from any human being. [18]Now I say to you that you are Peter (which means 'rock'),* and upon this rock I will build my church, and all the powers of hell* will not conquer it. [19]And I will give you the keys of the Kingdom of Heaven. Whatever you forbid* on earth will be forbidden in heaven, and whatever you permit* on earth will be permitted in heaven." [20]Then he sternly warned the disciples not to tell anyone that he was the Messiah.

16:13 "Son of Man" is a title Jesus used for himself. 16:16 Or the Christ. Messiah (a Hebrew term) and Christ (a Greek term) both mean "the anointed one." 16:17 Greek Simon bar-Jonah; see John 1:42; 21:15-17. 16:18a Greek that you are Peter. 16:18b Greek and the gates of Hades. 16:19a Or bind, or lock. 16:19b Or loose, or open.

NOTES

16:13-14 Caesarea Philippi. This was located at the headwaters of the Jordan River about twenty-five miles north of the Sea of Galilee. As noted previously, it is unclear exactly where Jesus was when he began this trip (15:39; 16:5).

Who do people say that the Son of Man is? Jesus' first query of the disciples concerned the popular consensus about his identity (cf. Mark 8:27-30; Luke 9:18-21).

some say John the Baptist, some say Elijah, and others say Jeremiah or one of the other prophets. These answers reveal something of the messianic speculation that existed in the first century. Herod Antipas had already superstitiously identified Jesus as John the Baptist, raised from the dead (14:2). The view that Jesus was Elijah was evidently based on Mal 4:5, which speaks of God sending Elijah before the eschatological day of the Lord (cf. 27:45-49). The speculation that Jesus was Jeremiah or another of the prophets is harder to explain (cf. 21:11). Perhaps the association of Jesus with Jeremiah is due to Jeremiah's preaching of judgment and opposition to the Temple leaders of his day (cf. 2 Esdr 2:16-18; 2 Macc 15:12-16). There is also indication that Deut 18:15-18 was understood messianically by some Jews in Jesus' day (cf. John 1:21, 25; 6:14-15; 7:40). These views of Jesus were positive, but they proved to be inadequate. The crowd may have viewed Jesus as a prophetic messenger of God, but as the ensuing narrative shows, their understanding was extremely superficial and fickle (27:15-26).

16:15-17 But who do you say I am? Jesus' second query probes the disciples' understanding of his identity.

Peter answered, "You are the Messiah, the Son of the living God." This implies that Peter answered for the group in 16:16 and that Jesus spoke to Peter as spokesman for the group in 16:17-19 (cf. 15:15; 19:27). Peter's remarkable answer links Jesus' messiahship (see 1:1, 16-18; 2:4; 11:2; 16:20; 22:42; 23:10; 24:5, 23; 26:63, 68; 27:17, 22) to his divine sonship (see 2:15; 3:17; 4:3, 6; 8:29; 11:27; 14:33; 16:16; 26:63; 27:40, 43, 54; 28:19). The likely OT background for the linkage of the terms Messiah and Son of God is found in 2 Sam 7:14; 1 Chr 17:13; Pss 2:6-8, 12; 89:27). At this answer Jesus pronounces Peter's blessedness (cf. 5:3).

You are blessed, Simon son of John, because my Father in heaven has revealed this to you. Peter's awareness of Jesus' true identity in the context of confusion among many Jews (16:14) was not due to any special brilliance on Peter's part but to God's special revelation to him (cf. 11:25-27; 13:10-17). It is ironic that Peter described Jesus as the Son of the living God, since later, in Jerusalem, the high priest demanded in the name of the living God that Jesus tell whether he was the Messiah, the Son of God. The high priest's question thus reprises the main themes of Peter's confession. If Peter's faithful confession is the Christological high point of the Gospel, the high priest's angry question is certainly the low point. The expression "the living God" implicitly distances the true God of Israel from the false gods of the nations (cf. Deut 5:26; 2 Kgs 19:4; 1 Sam 19:26; Ps 42:2; 84:2).

16:18 you are Peter (which means "rock"), and upon this rock I will build my church. Jesus' response to Peter's resounding confession continued with a pronouncement of Peter's foundational authority in the church that Jesus would build. The word "church" occurs only twice in the Gospels, here and in Matthew 18:17. Though many Protestants think otherwise, Jesus played on the name of Peter in order to speak of him (as spokesman for the disciples) as the foundation of the nascent church (cf. Eph 2:20; Rev 21:14). This is the more natural understanding of Jesus' words, much to be preferred over reactionary views that take the rock to be Jesus himself or Peter's confession of Jesus. (The NLT's parenthetical "which means 'rock'" supports this interpretation, although the Gr. text does not contain the clause as noted in NLT mg.)

all the powers of hell. Lit., "the gates of Hades" (NLT mg), which probably refers to the domain of Satan and death (cf. the "gates of Sheol" in Isa 38:10; Wis 16:13; 3 Macc 5:51; *Psalms of Solomon* 16:2; and "the gates of death" in Job 38:17; 1QH^a 14:24; 4Q184 1:10). Jesus promises that the church he will build on the foundation of the apostles will not be destroyed by the evil powers arrayed against it.

16:19 *I will give you the keys of the Kingdom of Heaven.* Jesus' linkage of the church and the keys of the Kingdom in 16:18-19 indicates that the church is the agency of Kingdom authority on the earth.

forbid . . . permit. Keys seem to symbolize authority (cf. Isa 22:22; Luke 11:52; Rev 1:18), and the authority concerns forbidding and permitting. This language of "forbidding" and "permitting" (lit. "binding" and "loosing") is highly unique and controversial. It is debated whether this language refers to evangelism, exegetical and doctrinal pronouncements, or church discipline. It is also hard to determine whether Jesus promised that the church's decisions would be ratified in heaven, or that heaven's decisions would be ratified by the church (cf. 18:18; John 20:23).

16:20 *not to tell anyone that he was the Messiah.* After this remarkable revelatory moment, it is striking that Jesus forbade the disciples to make him known as the Messiah (cf. 8:4; 9:30; 12:16; 17:9). Jesus evidently did this in order to reduce the excitement of the crowds who tended to view the Messiah as a merely political figure. This may also be due to the increasing opposition of the religious leaders and the principle of God's sovereignty (11:25-27; 13:10-17). The commentary below discusses the difficulties of 16:18-20 more fully (cf. Burgess 1966).

COMMENTARY

The Rock of the Church. Through the centuries, there has been a great deal of discussion of Matthew 16:18. In response to Roman Catholic teaching about Peter as first pope and apostolic succession, Protestants have often argued that Jesus did not mean that Peter was the rock. Instead, it has been suggested that Jesus was speaking of himself (Lenski 1961:626) or of Peter's confession (McNeile 1949:241) as the foundation of the church. Gundry (1994:334-335) argues that 16:18 alludes to 7:24, and that Jesus meant he would build his church on his own words. But 7:24 is so far removed from 16:18 that such an allusion is overly subtle. It is sometimes argued that Peter cannot be in view since the Greek word for Peter (*Petros* [TG4074, ZG4377]) is masculine, and the Greek word for rock (*petra* [TG4073, ZG4376]) is feminine. But this is a metaphor, and grammatical precision is not necessary. It is also argued that since *petra* means bedrock and *petros* means an individual stone, Peter is not the foundation of the church. But again, this is overly subtle and would render metaphorical speech impossible. Jesus was speaking of Peter in 16:18 just as clearly as Peter was speaking of Jesus in 16:16 (France 1985:254).

The metaphor of a foundation may refer in various contexts to such entities as Jesus' teaching (7:24), Jesus himself (1 Cor 3:10-11), and repentance (Heb 6:1). The individual context is decisive about the entity to which the metaphor points. In this context, Jesus' reply to Peter's confession is a pun (the technical term is paronomasia) on the nickname he had just given Peter (4:18; 10:2). The pun concerns Peter's unique role as the model disciple whose words and deeds frequently represent the disciples as a whole in Matthew. Peter's future role as preacher to Jews and Gentiles (Acts 2; 10) is also projected here. Jesus was not speaking of himself as the foundation of the church, since his own metaphor describes him as the builder. Neither is Peter's apostolic confession the foundation of the church—he as the confessing apostle is that foundation. Yet, Christ does not address Peter as a lone individual here but as the first among equals, since the context makes it clear that Peter was speaking for the apostles as a whole in 16:16 (Turner 1991). This best fits the Matthean context, and it also coheres with other New Testament texts that speak of the apostles (plural) as the foundation of the church (Eph 2:20; Rev 21:14). The Baptist teacher Broadus (1886:355-358) recognized this over a hundred years ago, and recent evangelical commentaries concur (see Blomberg 1994:251-253; Carson 1984:368; France 1985:254-256; Hagner 1995:469-471).

The real difficulty Protestants have with the Roman Catholic teaching concerning Peter is the notion of sole apostolic succession emanating from Peter as the first bishop of Rome. This notion clearly injects anachronistic political concerns into the text of Matthew, which says nothing about Peter being the first pope or about the primacy of Rome over other Christian churches. Certainly Matthew would not have endorsed the idea of Peter's infallibility or sole authority in the church, since it is quite clear in Matthew that Peter speaks as a representative of the other apostles and often makes mistakes (15:15; 16:16; 17:4, 25; 18:21; 19:27; 26:33-35; cf. Acts 11:1-18; Gal 2:11-14). In Peter's own words, Jesus himself is the chief shepherd, senior pastor, or *pontifex maximus* of the church (1 Pet 5:4). For further discussion of Peter, see Brown, Donfried et al. (1973); Cullmann (1962), Davies and Allison (1991: 647-652); Kingsbury (1979); and Turner (1991).

The Keys and Binding and Loosing.   As noted above, Jesus spoke of Peter as both foundation of the church and holder of the keys of the Kingdom. The linkage of the foundation and key metaphors makes it clear that one cannot divorce the church and the Kingdom because the former is the agency by which the latter is extended on earth. The foundational ecclesiastical role of Peter and the other apostles is carried out through their handling of the keys, which is their exercise of Kingdom authority (cf. Isa 22:15, 22; Rev 1:18; 3:7; 9:1-4; 20:1-3). This authority is exercised through binding and loosing (NLT "forbidding" and "permitting"). Scholars differ in their explanations of binding and loosing. Some stress the idea that keys are a metaphor of authority over who enters the church; thus, the apostles, through their confession of Jesus, control who is permitted and who is forbidden to enter (cf. 10:7; 28:18-20). Others compare 16:19 to 18:18 and posit discipline within the church as the area of the authority described as binding and loosing. In rabbinic Judaism the motif of binding and loosing was often applied to careful interpretation of biblical law in areas of personal conduct, or halakha; the rabbis rendered authoritative opinions on what was permitted and what was forbidden.

It is not easy to decide which of the above interpretations is correct. Interpreting 16:19 along the lines of 18:18 is problematic because the context of Matthew 18 concerns maintenance of the community, not entrance into it. Further, the binding and loosing in 18:18 is a function of the community, not the apostles. The problem with interpreting the binding and loosing in terms of the rabbinic usage is that such usage is later than Matthew and occurs in a different religious context. Matthew's imagery in 16:16-19 concerns the building of the church and entrance into it by those who, with Peter and the apostles, confess Jesus as Messiah, Son of God. The apostles, therefore, were in a real sense the gatekeepers of the Kingdom, since they were the foundational leaders of the church, the agency that extends the Kingdom on earth. Their role was to continue the authoritative proclamation of the truth of Matthew 16:16, and in doing so, they permitted those who confessed Jesus to enter the church and through it the Kingdom. Those who refuse to confess Jesus find the door closed and locked; they are forbidden entrance. (See Hagner 1995:472-474; Hiers 1985 for further discussion of the possibilities.)

◆   **11. Jesus' suffering as a model of discipleship (16:21-28; cf. Mark 8:31-9:1; Luke 9:22-27)**

21From then on Jesus* began to tell his disciples plainly that it was necessary for him to go to Jerusalem, and that he would suffer many terrible things at the hands of the elders, the leading priests, and the teachers of religious law. He would be killed, but on the third day he would be raised from the dead.

22But Peter took him aside and began to reprimand him* for saying such things. "Heaven forbid, Lord," he said. "This will never happen to you!"

23Jesus turned to Peter and said, "Get away from me, Satan! You are a dangerous trap to me. You are seeing things merely from a human point of view, not from God's."

24Then Jesus said to his disciples, "If any of you wants to be my follower, you must turn from your selfish ways, take up your cross, and follow me. 25If you try to hang on to your life, you will lose it. But if you give up your life for my sake, you will save it. 26And what do you benefit if you gain the whole world but lose your own soul?* Is anything worth more than your soul? 27For the Son of Man will come with his angels in the glory of his Father and will judge all people according to their deeds. 28And I tell you the truth, some standing here right now will not die before they see the Son of Man coming in his Kingdom."

16:21 Some manuscripts read *Jesus the Messiah.* 16:22 Or *began to correct him.* 16:26 Or *your self?* also in 16:26b.

NOTES

16:21 *From then on.* At this crucial point in Matthew's narrative (cf. the same phrase "from then on" in 4:17), Jesus begins to make his death and resurrection explicit.

it was necessary for him to go to Jerusalem. . . . He would be killed, but on the third day he would be raised from the dead. Jesus predicted that he would be killed but raised up later (cf. 17:9, 22-23; 20:17-19, 28; 26:2, 12, 20-32). Up to this point, this has only been implied (1:21; 10:38; 12:14, 40; 16:4). His suffering, death, and resurrection, are "necessary" in the plan of God and will fulfill Scripture (17:10; 24:6; 26:54; cf. Luke 24:26-27).

elders, the leading priests, and the teachers of religious law. The Pharisees and Sadducees are omitted from the list of Jewish religious leaders who will make Jesus suffer in Jerusalem, perhaps because the chief priests were for the most part Sadducees, and the scribes were for the most part Pharisees. The "elders" mentioned here are venerable leaders, perhaps members of the Sanhedrin or supreme court (cf. 21:23; 26:3, 47, 57; 27:1, 3, 12, 20, 41; 28:12). The elders mentioned in 15:2 were probably the ancient worthies to whom the Pharisaic traditions were traced.

16:22 Peter . . . began to reprimand him. Peter showed his own lack of understanding of Jesus' mission (cf. Mark 8:31-9:1; Luke 9:22-27).

Heaven forbid. Lit., "may God be merciful to you!" This is an extremely strong protest against what Jesus had just said about his death and resurrection. The death of Jesus was incompatible with Peter's notion of what the Messiah ought to be, and so it should never happen. Peter could accept the notion of a glorious Messiah (16:27-28), but not one who suffers. Peter erred here, but one should note that even the OT prophets had difficulty reconciling the sufferings and glory of the Messiah (1 Pet 1:10-12).

16:23 Get away from me, Satan! You are a dangerous trap to me. It is striking that Peter went, in so short a time, from being the rock solid foundation on which Jesus would build the church (16:18) to being a dangerous trap or even a stone over which Jesus might stumble (cf. Isa 8:14). This is due to Peter's mental fixation on human priorities, not divine revelation. Matthew 16:23 is the polar opposite of 16:17—Peter confessed Jesus as Messiah when he thought in line with divine revelation, but when his thinking was in keeping with human intuition, he grievously erred and functioned just as Satan had previously. The words "Get way from me, Satan" do not mean that Jesus identified Peter with the devil but that Peter's opposition to the cross put him and Jesus in an adversarial relationship. Peter's attempt to keep Jesus from doing the Father's will is reminiscent of Satan's similar attempt (4:8-10). Satan had attempted to keep Jesus from doing the Father's will, and he would do the same with the disciples.

16:24 If any of you wants to be my follower, you must . . . take up your cross, and follow me. Jesus' strong and stinging rebuke of Peter (compare 16:23 with 4:10) became a teachable moment for the rest of the disciples, in which Jesus explained that the cross would define not only his own future but theirs as well (cf. 10:38). Jesus could not reign as the glorious Messiah until he went to the cross as suffering servant, and his disciples, likewise, could not reign with him until they deny themselves and suffer with him. The cross is paradigmatic for Jesus and his followers alike (cf. 20:26-28).

16:25-27 The way of the cross is for the present; glory and reward will come only in the future when Jesus comes again. Jesus presents three reasons that Christ-like self-denial is the path his disciples must pursue.

If you try to hang on to your life, you will lose it. But if you give up your life for my sake, you will save it. The first reason states the double paradox that self-preservation leads to self-destruction and self-denial leads to self-fulfillment (cf. 10:39).

Is anything worth more than your soul? The second reason for self-denial speaks of the folly of gaining material wealth while losing one's own soul (cf. 4:8; 6:19-21). It is likely that the word "soul" here refers to one's selfhood. The implication is that true humanity is found not in the acquisition of goods but in humble service to others.

the Son of Man will come with his angels. The third reason for taking up one's cross is the prospect of future reward at the glorious return of Jesus with his angels (13:40-41; 24:30-31; 25:31; 26:64; cf. Zech 14:5). The language of 16:27b echoes several OT passages (Ps 28:4; 62:12; Prov 24:12; cf. Sir 35:19; Rom 2:6; Rev 22:12).

16:28 some standing here right now will not die before they see the Son of Man coming in his Kingdom. This difficult statement most likely refers to the transfiguration, which occurs next in the narrative. This is discussed in more detail in the following commentary.

COMMENTARY

Matthew 16:21 is widely recognized as a crucial text in Matthew's narrative. In one view of the structure of Matthew, 16:21 begins the third major section of Matthew with its phrase "from then on" (cf. 4:17; Bauer 1989). That threefold view of Matthew's structure has not been followed in this commentary, but nonetheless Matthew 16:21 is the first time in Matthew that Jesus unambiguously announces his death and resurrection to his disciples. The rest of Matthew's narrative from chapters 16–28 is encapsulated here. This announcement immediately elicited strong disagreement from Peter, who, despite his previous stirring confession (16:16), could not be more wrong in 16:22. Peter was rebuked in 16:23 just as strongly as he was blessed in 16:17; his words in 16:16 were revealed to him by God, and his words in 16:22 were strictly human in origin. In 16:24-27, Jesus turned from Peter, always the model disciple, to address the disciples as a whole with the message of cross before crown, suffering before glory, service before reign. Peter had given voice to a way of thinking that was apparently pervasive among the disciples, and all of them needed to be shown their fundamental error.

Peter's shockingly swift decline from blessed confessor to rebuked adversary ought to speak loudly to every disciple of Jesus. For just a moment, Peter's mindset became positively satanic, since he sought to dissuade Jesus from following the Father's will to the cross (cf. 4:8-9). Peter heard only that Jesus would be killed—the words about resurrection did not register at all. And so it is with disciples today who all too often do not grasp that their present sufferings are not worthy to be compared to the glory that is to come at Jesus' return (16:27; cf. Rom 8:18; 2 Tim 2:11-13). The desire for a comfortable lifestyle and the avoidance of suffering is a hindrance to Kingdom work that can be overcome only by divine grace (19:23-26). Even those who have seemingly overcome the lure of self-aggrandizement and who have followed Jesus still need periodic reorientation to the values of the Kingdom, as did the sons of Zebedee and their mother (20:20-28). The values and example of "the rulers in this world" always threaten to infiltrate the Kingdom, and Jesus' disciples need to constantly reflect on his counsel that "among you it will be different" (20:25-26). The lesson is not that glory and reward do not await faithful disciples (19:27-29), but that such are attained only after a life of self-denying service that follows in the steps of Jesus to the cross.

The Coming of Jesus in His Kingdom. According to Matthew 16:27, Jesus promised his disciples that their lives of self-denial would be rewarded at his return—in his Father's glory with his angels. This is a clear reference to the coming of Jesus to the earth at the final judgment (13:40-41; 24:30-31; 25:31; 26:64). But 16:28 is more perplexing because it seems to emphasize the certainty of that glorious coming by stating that some of Jesus' contemporaries would live to see "the Son of Man coming in his Kingdom." All of Jesus' disciples died long ago, so either Jesus and Matthew were wrong (Beare 1981:360, 472-473), or the "coming" spoken of here is something other than that which ushers in the final judgment. Evangelical scholars understandably take the second option and suggest that Jesus was speaking of his transfiguration (Blomberg 1992:261; Toussaint 1980:209), his resurrection, his sending the Spirit at Pentecost, or the judgment of Jerusalem in AD 70. Some attempt to see 16:28 as a general prediction of Christ's future glory up to his return to earth, encompassing the resurrection, ascension, Pentecost, and present heavenly session (Carson 1984:380-382; France 1985:261; Hendriksen 1973:659-660; Morris 1992:434-435).

Although the last view mentioned above has merit, the view associating this "coming" with the transfiguration seems most likely. Seen in the light of 16:28, the transfiguration, which occurred only six days later (17:1), amounts to a foreshadowing of the future glorious coming. Perhaps Keener (1999:436) is correct in saying "probably the transfiguration proleptically introduces the whole eschatological sphere." The transfiguration was a glorious experience (17:2, 5), and though it was only temporary, it could serve as a preview of what was to come with permanence at Jesus' future return to the earth. Some of those who heard Jesus make the prediction in 16:28—namely Peter, James and John—did witness the transfiguration (17:1). Peter himself seems to reflect on his participation in the temporary glory of the transfiguration as a confirming anticipation of the truth of Christ's powerful future coming to the earth (2 Pet 1:16-18). For further discussion of 16:28, see Beasley-Murray (1986:187-193). A previous text that presents similar difficulties is 10:23. In the commentary on 10:23, I argued that this passage states that the mission of the church to Israel will continue until Jesus' glorious return to the earth.

Summary of Matthew 16. Earlier in Matthew, confrontations with the Pharisees (and other religious leaders) occurred as the religious leaders responded to the words and works of Jesus (3:7; 9:3, 11, 34; 12:2, 10, 14, 24, 38). As things proceeded, however, the Pharisees began to seek Jesus out in order to initiate confrontation (15:1; 16:1; 19:3; 21:23; 22:23, 34). Their second request for a sign (16:1-4; cf. 12:38) necessitated Jesus' warning that the disciples beware their teaching (16:5-12). This leads to what is perhaps the most crucial pericope in this Gospel, in which Jesus receives Peter's representative confession of his messiahship and promises to build and empower his church (16:13-20). At this crucial juncture, Jesus clearly announces his death and resurrection for the first time, and then points his disciples to a self-denying lifestyle, which will be rewarded when he comes again (16:21-28).

This chapter continues to underline the theme of opposition from the Pharisees and goes a step further in that Jesus clearly tells the disciples that the opposition will lead to his death (16:21). Once again, the "little faith" of the disciples is confronted as Jesus prepares them to carry on the Kingdom mission in his absence (16:8). In spite of their weakness, they received the Father's revelation that Jesus is the Messiah and they would become the foundation of the messianic community that Jesus would build (16:16-19). Their futures would be tied to that of Jesus; each would, like him, bear a cross on his way to future glorious reward (16:24-28).

◆   12. Jesus' transfiguration (17:1-13; cf. Mark 9:2-13; Luke 9:28-36)

Six days later Jesus took Peter and the two brothers, James and John, and led them up a high mountain to be alone. ²As the men watched, Jesus' appearance was transformed so that his face shone like the sun, and his clothes became as white as light. ³Suddenly, Moses and Elijah appeared and began talking with Jesus.

⁴Peter exclaimed, "Lord, it's wonderful for us to be here! If you want, I'll make three shelters as memorials*—one for you, one for Moses, and one for Elijah."

⁵But even as he spoke, a bright cloud overshadowed them, and a voice from the cloud said, "This is my dearly loved Son, who brings me great joy. Listen to him." ⁶The disciples were terrified and fell face down on the ground.

⁷Then Jesus came over and touched them. "Get up," he said. "Don't be afraid." ⁸And when they looked up, Moses and Elijah were gone, and they saw only Jesus.

⁹As they went back down the mountain, Jesus commanded them, "Don't tell anyone what you have seen until the Son of Man* has been raised from the dead."

¹⁰Then his disciples asked him, "Why do the teachers of religious law insist that Elijah must return before the Messiah comes?*"

¹¹Jesus replied, "Elijah is indeed coming first to get everything ready. ¹²But I tell you, Elijah has already come, but he wasn't recognized, and they chose to abuse him. And in the same way they will also make the Son of Man suffer." ¹³Then the disciples realized he was talking about John the Baptist.

17:4 Greek *three tabernacles.*   **17:9** "Son of Man" is a title Jesus used for himself.   **17:10** Greek *that Elijah must come first?*

NOTES

17:1 *Six days later Jesus took Peter and the two brothers, James and John, and led them up a high mountain to be alone.* If the interpretation of 16:28 suggested above is correct, Jesus' prediction there that some of his disciples would see a royal "coming" before they died was fulfilled only six days afterward (Mark 9:2-13; Luke 9:28-36). Exod 24:16, which mentions that a cloud rested on Mt. Sinai for six days, is the first of many OT allusions in this passage. Only Peter, James, and John observed the miracle (cf. 26:37). These are three of the first four disciples Jesus called (4:18-22); Peter's brother Andrew was left behind. Jesus' being accompanied by these three may be intended to remind the reader of Moses' being accompanied by Aaron, Nadab, and Abihu, but the seventy elders were also present with Moses (Exod 24:1, 9). The event, which occurred on an unnamed, high mountain, reminds the reader of Moses' experience at the giving of the law from Sinai (cf. 5:1; 15:29; Exod 24:12-18; 31:18).

17:2 *Jesus' appearance was transformed so that his face shone like the sun.* The traditional though opaque term "transfiguration" underlines the difficulty in describing the transformation that happened to Jesus. The word used in the Gr. text eventually gave rise to the English "metamorphosis" (cf. Rom 12:2; 2 Cor 3:18). Matthew relies on two similes to describe this event, describing its glory as something that dazzles like bright sunlight. The detail that Jesus' face shone recalls Exod 34:29-35.

17:3 *Moses and Elijah appeared and began talking with Jesus.* Allison (1993) argues that Moses typology occurs throughout Matthew, and it is clear that Matthew presents Jesus' teaching as fulfilling the law of Moses. It is clear from Matt 17:5 that Deut 18:15-19 is also implied here. Elijah's presence is undoubtedly connected to Mal 4:5-6, to which Jesus alluded concerning John the Baptist in 11:14. It is sometimes held that Moses and Elijah represent respectively the OT law and prophets (cf. 5:17; 7:12). Others point out that both had mountaintop experiences with God—Moses at Sinai and Elijah at Horeb (1 Kgs

19:8). In any event, Moses and Elijah were both key prophetic figures in the OT, so their presence with Jesus is fitting. If the presence of the two individuals is understood typologically, Jesus was the "prophet like Moses" spoken of in Deut 18:15, and John was Elijah (17:10-13). Matthew's comment that Jesus conversed with Moses and Elijah is tantalizingly brief. Luke 9:31 indicates ominously that the conversation concerned Jesus' upcoming departure (lit. "exodus") from the world, which would be fulfilled in Jerusalem. For a detailed study of the transfiguration, see McGuckin (1986).

17:4-5 *I'll make three shelters as memorials.* Peter's knee-jerk response to this glorious manifestation was perhaps to suggest a reenactment of the feast of tabernacles (*sukkoth* [TH5521, ZH6109] "booths," cf. Lev 23:42-43; Zech 14:16ff). Or maybe Peter was thinking in terms of the "tent of meeting" where God spoke with Moses outside the camp (Exod 33:7). His plan was to put up three tents or huts as temporary quarters or memorials for the three prominent persons there. This idea was well-intentioned, and Peter did acknowledge Jesus' lordship and prerogatives in the way he put the question, but it nevertheless threatened to blur the uniqueness of Jesus as God's Son.

a bright cloud overshadowed them, and a voice from the cloud said. The voice coming from the bright cloud reminds the reader of significant revelations to Israel from clouds in the days of Moses (Exod 40:34-38; cf. 2 Macc 2:8). The brightness of the cloud is a bit oxymoronic and suggests the "shekinah" or visible manifestation of God's glory (Exod 24:16-17; cf. Ezek 1:4; 10:4). The cloud also anticipates the clouds that will accompany Jesus at his return (24:30; 26:64).

This is my dearly loved Son, who brings me great joy. Listen to him. The heavenly voice reiterates the words spoken at Jesus' baptism (3:17; cf. Ps 2:7) and adds "listen to him." This command that the disciples attend exclusively to Jesus quashes Peter's idea for three tents in language that alludes to Deut 18:15. Jesus and Jesus alone must be heard and obeyed. It is significant that this endorsement occurred not long after Jesus' clear announcement of his upcoming suffering in Jerusalem and Peter's negative response to it (16:21-22). The disciples were still likely perplexed at the notion of a suffering Messiah, and they needed this renewed divine endorsement of Jesus.

17:6-7 *The disciples were terrified.* Peter's enthusiasm at being present for this occasion must have rapidly changed to terror when the voice rang out from the cloud (Deut 4:33).

Then Jesus came over and touched them. He and the other disciples fell on their faces in fear and did not get up until Jesus touched them and told them to do so (cf. 8:25-26; 14:26-27; cf. Dan 8:17; 10:8-10; Rev 1:17).

17:8 *they saw only Jesus.* When the disciples got up and looked around, Moses and Elijah had vanished and only Jesus was with them. This underlines the word from heaven that Jesus alone is to be heard and obeyed. As Jesus moved toward Jerusalem and the suffering he would endure there, the disciples must not lose their focus on him.

17:9 *don't tell anyone what you have seen until the Son of Man has been raised from the dead.* This is the last time in Matthew that Jesus enjoins silence concerning miraculous events (cf. 16:20 for the most recent time). This and other commands for silence aimed to avoid "superficial political messianism" (Carson 1984:388), which would have further exacerbated the enmity of the religious leaders. After Jesus had been vindicated by his resurrection, the true nature of his messianic ministry would become clearer, and the story of his miracles could be told in a proper context.

17:10 *Elijah must return before the Messiah comes.* Jesus had already spoken of the complex relationship of John the Baptist to Elijah in Matt 11:10-14, but the disciples' question shows that they still did not understand how the coming of Elijah related to the Messiah's death and resurrection. Evidently the appearance of Elijah with Jesus reminded them of Mal 4:4-5, which predicted the coming of Elijah as a forerunner of the Messiah and the day of the Lord. Since Elijah had indeed appeared, they might have wondered what hindered the coming of the day of the Lord and the restoration spoken by Malachi, and why Jesus must suffer in Jerusalem.

17:11-13 *Elijah has already come, but he wasn't recognized.* Jesus replied in effect that the disciples should focus on John the Baptist's Elijah-like ministry (not the recent appearance of Elijah at the transfiguration). If they did so, they would understand that John's death foreshadowed the death of Jesus.

COMMENTARY

The description of the transfiguration proper is brief—just the first three verses of Matthew 17. But the incident becomes the backdrop for two significant incidents for the disciples. In the first, Peter's hasty response to the glory of the Lord is corrected by the same heavenly voice heard at Jesus' baptism (17:4-8; cf. 3:17). In the second, Jesus once again forbids the disciples to make him known (cf. 16:20), which leads to their question about the future coming of Elijah (17:9-13). Jesus answers their question cryptically in terms of a past coming of "Elijah," and when he compares his own future suffering to what has happened to this "Elijah," the disciples finally grasp that he is speaking of John the Baptist. Thus, the passage contains the transfiguration proper (17:1-3), a lesson on the preeminence of Jesus (17:4-8), and a lesson on the continuity of John the Baptist with Elijah of old and with Jesus himself (17:9-13).

This passage presents two lessons, one relating to the disciples' deepest spiritual needs and one relating to a perplexing intellectual question. The first lesson concerns Jesus' preeminence in the disciples' lives. Confronted with the amazing scene of Moses and Elijah speaking with a gloriously transformed Jesus, Peter proposed the construction of temporary shelters for all three of them. We will never know exactly what Peter had in mind for these three shelters, since his proposal was interrupted by the voice from heaven. But we can be sure that Peter was on the wrong track, since his proposal did not reflect the sole sufficiency of Jesus for his disciples. Setting up three tents for Moses, Elijah, and Jesus would have had two erroneous effects: it would have belittled Jesus with faint praise, and arrogated Moses and Elijah to a status that belongs only to Jesus. As great as Moses and Elijah were, each was only God's servant, not his Son (3:17). Moses was the prototypical prophet, but he spoke of Jesus as the definitive eschatological prophet whose words must be heeded (Deut 18:15-19). Elijah's ministry courageously stood for the law of Moses, but Jesus as the definitive teacher of that law brings it to its ultimate goal (5:17-19). Therefore, however well-meaning Peter's proposal was, it suggested the unthinkable notion that Moses and Elijah were on the same level as Jesus. This would not do, for Jesus alone is the beloved Son who pleases the Father, and Jesus alone must be heard and obeyed.

The second lesson has to do with the disciples' understanding of the mysteries of biblical prophecy. In the plan of God, the ministries of Elijah, John, and Jesus are intricately interwoven. In his own right, John was not Elijah but came to minister in the spirit of Elijah (Luke 1:17; John 1:21). John's ministry as the forerunner of Jesus was in line with that spoken of by Isaiah concerning the one who would prepare the Lord's way (3:3; Isa 40:3).

According to Matthew 17:13, it seems that the disciples did understand that John's ministry was a fulfillment of Malachi's prophecy (Mal 4:4-5) and that John's suffering and death anticipated what was about to happen to Jesus. Matthew 17:11 remains perplexing, however, since it seems to leave the future coming of Elijah as an open question. Perhaps Revelation 11:3-6, another perplexing text, has something to do with this.

The Transfiguration and Theology. The transfiguration of Jesus is an amazing event but not totally unexpected for Matthew's readers. After all, Jesus had a miraculous birth, and his ministry began with the ringing endorsement of the heavenly Father (3:17). He had done mighty works of compassion and had definitively taught the Torah with nothing less than heavenly authority (7:29). He had even demonstrated supernatural control of natural processes by calming storms and feeding thousands of people with a few loaves of bread. He had promised a glorious return, a judgment of all people, and a righteous Kingdom on the earth. After his resurrection, he would receive total authority in heaven and on earth, and his presence would accompany his disciples in their communication of his Kingdom message to all the nations until the end of the present age before his return (28:18-20).

Thus, from the standpoint of Matthew as a whole, Jesus' glorious transfiguration is in keeping with his status as the Son of God, his fulfillment of Old Testament patterns and predictions, and his promise of a future Kingdom. The transfiguration is an integral part of Matthew's high Christology and his apocalyptic eschatology. It authenticates both Jesus' divine identity and God's plan to invade this world and rule it forever. By the transfiguration, the disciples were given a glimpse of who Jesus is and what he will one day bring to this world (see 2 Pet 1:16-18). Moses and Elijah are worthy figures, but they are only supporting actors in the redemptive drama the disciples witness. As the scene ends, Moses and Elijah have exited, and only Jesus remains in the center of the stage. The "listen to him" of the transfiguration becomes the "teaching them to observe all things I have commanded you" of the Great Commission.

In light of other New Testament texts, the transfiguration should probably be viewed not as the illumination of the man Jesus with an extrinsic glory but as the momentary uncovering of the Son of God's own intrinsic glory, which has been temporarily veiled and will be reassumed at the resurrection and ascension (John 17:4-5, 24; Phil 2:5-11; Col 1:16-19; Heb 1:1-4). Orthodox systematic theologians are challenged by the transfiguration to attempt an explanation of what must be ultimately inexplicable to mere humans. God alone knows how the eternal Son of God came to earth as a genuinely human child, and how the divine and human natures of Jesus were implicated in his transfiguration.

◆   13. Jesus heals an epileptic boy (17:14–21; cf. Mark 9:14–29; Luke 9:37–43)

[14]At the foot of the mountain, a large crowd was waiting for them. A man came and knelt before Jesus and said, [15]"Lord, have mercy on my son. He has seizures and suffers terribly. He often falls into the fire or into the water. [16]So I brought him to your disciples, but they couldn't heal him."

[17]Jesus said, "You faithless and corrupt people! How long must I be with you? How long must I put up with you? Bring the boy here to me." [18]Then Jesus rebuked the demon in the boy, and it left him. From that moment the boy was well.

[19]Afterward the disciples asked Jesus privately, "Why couldn't we cast out that demon?"

[20]"You don't have enough faith," Jesus told them. "I tell you the truth, if you had faith even as small as a mustard seed, you could say to this mountain, 'Move from here to there,' and it would move. Nothing would be impossible.*"

17:20 Some manuscripts add verse 21, *But this kind of demon won't leave except by prayer and fasting.* Compare Mark 9:29.

NOTES

17:14-15 *He often falls into the fire or into the water.* The man's son was an epileptic whose seizures were life-threatening. Still worse, the timing of the seizures when he was near water or fire pointed to something that was not accidental but sinister: he was demon-possessed (17:18).

17:16-17 *your disciples . . . couldn't heal him.* The inability of Jesus' disciples' to heal the boy is puzzling in view of their commission in 10:8, but it is explained by a familiar theme in 17:20.

You faithless and corrupt people. Jesus spoke of his contemporaries in very negative terms (cf. 11:16; 12:39, 45; Deut 32:5, 20). They were not only faithless but also morally crooked or depraved. It is not clear whether Jesus directed this rebuke only to the crowd, including the man whose epileptic son was demon-possessed, or to the crowd and his own disciples. Blomberg (1992:267) and Davies and Allison (1991:724) take it that Jesus lumped the disciples in with the crowd here, but this is unlikely because the disciples' "little faith" hardly characterizes them as a faithless and perverse generation. They received their own rebuke in 17:20, so it is better to take 17:17 as Jesus' exasperation with the crowd, which continued to hound him for miracles while not grasping his unique identity and mission (16:13-14).

How long must I be with you? How long must I put up with you? These are very striking questions in light of Jesus' previous compassion for the crowd (cf. most recently 15:29-32). The questions may remind the reader of God's complaint against Israel in Num 14:27 or Isaiah's question in Isa 6:11 (cf. John 14:9). Nevertheless, Jesus shows compassion in casting out the demon and healing the boy. On balance, Jesus was growing impatient with Israel's unbelief and was expressing "prophetic exasperation" (Hill 1972:270).

17:19 *Why couldn't we cast out that demon?* Privately the disciples came to Jesus to unravel the mystery of their inability to heal the boy. Their question reminds the reader of previous private questions (13:36; 15:12).

17:20 *You don't have enough faith.* Jesus explained that the disciples' inability was due to their all too familiar "little faith" (6:30; 8:26; 14:31; 16:8). The weakness of the disciples is repeatedly stressed in the narrative section between chapters 13 and 18 (see 14:16-17, 26-31; 15:16, 23, 33; 16:5-12, 22; 17:4, 10-11).

I tell you the truth. This underlines the importance and authority of what follows. This phrase occurs on Jesus' lips over thirty times in Matthew.

if you had faith even as small as a mustard seed you could say to this mountain, "Move." The disciples' ability to do miraculous works (10:8) was evidently conditioned upon their faith in the power of God, so Jesus challenged them in that area by using hyperboles for both the minuscule size ("as small as a mustard seed;" cf. 13:31) and the huge potential (moving mountains; 21:21; 1 Cor 13:2) of their faith (cf. 17:1, 9).

17:21 This verse, noted in the NLT mg, is textually suspect because it is absent from the earliest manuscripts (including ℵ B Θ 0281 it syrᶜ copˢᵃ). It was likely borrowed from Mark 9:29 (cf. Metzger 1994:35, 85). The idea of this disputed verse is that true faith will manifest itself in prayer and fasting in difficult situations (cf. 6:16-18).

COMMENTARY

The story of the exorcism and healing of the epileptic boy has two main parts, the first dealing with the healing itself (17:14-18), and the second with the question raised by Jesus' disciples. In both parts there is a request (17:14-16, 19) and a response from Jesus (17:17-18, 20-21). In both parts the inability of the disciples (17:16, 19) is contrasted with the power of Jesus (17:18, 20). The problem throughout the episode is lack of faith, on the part of both Jesus' contemporaries (17:17) and his own disciples (17:20). The attentive reader is not surprised at either.

The pericope about the healing of the epileptic boy (cf. Mark 9:14-29; Luke 9:37-43) underlines two themes previously seen in Matthew. The "little faith" of the disciples was pointed out by Jesus as recently as 16:8, and the wickedness of Jesus' generation is underlined in 3:7; 11:16; 12:34-45; 16:4; 17:17; 23:33, 36; 24:34. Both themes are striking in contrast to the glory of Jesus' transfiguration, and both figure into Jesus' rebuke in 17:17, which alludes to Deuteronomy 32:5, 20.

The lesson of this passage is that disciples are vulnerable to taking on the moral and spiritual values of their contemporaries. Jesus' disciples had "little faith" as they lived among a faithless and depraved generation. This faithlessness was true even of those in the crowd who, like the man with the epileptic son, believed that Jesus could heal their illnesses. This sort of "faith" operated only in the material realm and did not recognize Jesus for who he was as the Messiah, the Son of the living God. Rather, he was acknowledged only as some sort of prophetic figure (16:14; 21:11). In contrast, Jesus' disciples had "little faith," but it was genuine faith that confessed the true identity of their Lord (14:33; 16:16). The issue is not the intensity or amount of faith but the degree to which that faith perceives its object. The power of faith is in the person in whom it is placed. Jesus' disciples were unable to heal the epileptic boy because they had taken their eyes off of Jesus and looked at the obstacles, just as Peter did during the storm when he began to sink (14:31). Faith is not believing in faith but in the heavenly Father. It is not believing that the Father will do whatever we demand but believing that the Father can, and will, do whatever is best for us. We cannot assume that God will endorse and perform our selfish biddings, but we must believe he will empower us to do great things to extend his Kingdom through word and deed.

◆ 14. Jesus predicts his death and pays his tax (17:22-27; cf. Mark 9:30-32; Luke 9:43-45)

²²After they gathered again in Galilee, Jesus told them, "The Son of Man is going to be betrayed into the hands of his enemies. ²³He will be killed, but on the third day he will be raised from the dead." And the disciples were filled with grief.

²⁴On their arrival in Capernaum, the collectors of the Temple tax* came to Peter and asked him, "Doesn't your teacher pay the Temple tax?"

²⁵"Yes, he does," Peter replied. Then he went into the house.

But before he had a chance to speak, Jesus asked him, "What do you think, Peter?* Do kings tax their own people or the people they have conquered?*"

²⁶"They tax the people they have conquered," Peter replied.

"Well, then," Jesus said, "the citizens are free! ²⁷However, we don't want to offend them, so go down to the lake and throw in a line. Open the mouth of the first fish you catch, and you will find a large silver coin.* Take it and pay the tax for both of us."

17:24 Greek *the two-drachma [tax]*; also in 17:24b. See Exod 30:13-16; Neh 10:32-33.   17:25a Greek *Simon?*
17:25b Greek *their sons or others?*   17:27 Greek *a stater* [a Greek coin equivalent to four drachmas].

NOTES

17:22-23 *After they had gathered again in Galilee.* Geographical movement south from Caesarea Philippi back into Galilee occurs here.

The Son of Man is going to be betrayed. . . . He will be killed, but on the third day he will be raised from the dead. The second of three passion predictions occurs here (cf. the first in 16:21 and the third in 20:18-19). There were previous "hints" also (9:15; 10:38; 12:40; 16:4; 17:12). This second prediction adds the detail that Jesus will be delivered or betrayed, hinting at the sordid role of Judas (cf. 10:4; 20:18-19; 26:2, 15, 16, 21, 23-25, 45, 46, 48; 27:3-5). In this prediction Jesus spoke of himself as the Son of Man and of his enemies with the generic phrase "into the hands of men."

the disciples were filled with grief. The disciples finally grasped the stark reality of the impending events in Jerusalem, and this anticipates their grief at the Last Supper and Jesus' grief at Gethsemane (26:22, 37). They did not speak against this reality as Peter did in 16:22, but their severe grief implies that they had not yet begun to grasp the reality of Jesus' resurrection.

17:24-25 Doesn't your teacher pay the Temple tax? A reference to the annual Temple tax of two drachmas (Exod 30:11-16; 38:25-26; Neh 10:32-33; Josephus *Antiquities* 18.312; *War* 7.218; *m. Sheqalim* 1-2). See Davies and Allison (1991:738-741) for a discussion and dismissal of the view that a Roman civil tax is in view here. A drachma was roughly equivalent to a denarius, a day's wage for a laborer (20:2, 9, 10, 13). Evidently, Peter was approached with the question because he was perceived as the leader of the disciples. The question is phrased in a manner which expects an affirmative answer, and Peter so replied before checking with Jesus about it.

Do kings tax their own people or people they have conquered? Jesus speaks first, asking Peter a metaphorical question. The upshot of the question is clear: Kings do not tax their sons but their subjects. By analogy, Jesus as the unique Son of God, is greater than the Temple and is exempt from paying this tax to his father's house (cf. 12:6; 21:12-13). Unfortunately, the NLT's translation tends to obscure the key analogy of sonship by rendering the Gr. word "sons" as "their own people" and "the citizens" in 17:25-26 (but see NLT mg). If anything, the plural "sons" includes the disciples with Jesus since they too are the sons of God, their heavenly Father (5:9, 45; 6:9, 26).

17:27 Open the mouth of the first fish you catch, and you will find a large silver coin. Despite the fact that Jesus was exempt from the Temple tax, he decided to pay it in order to avoid offense (cf. 12:19; 22:15-22). Jesus provided the money for the tax in an amazing, even bizarre fashion that prompts Blomberg's (1992:271) comment, "this verse is perhaps the strangest in Matthew's Gospel." The "large silver coin" Peter would find in the fish's mouth is lit. a "stater," which was worth four drachmas (see NLT mg) and would pay the tax for both Peter and Jesus. It is noteworthy that Jesus commanded Peter to fish with a hook. Peter did not need a net this time since only one fish would be needed (4:18, 20, 21; 13:47).

COMMENTARY

This passage contains two elements, another prediction of Jesus' suffering and death (17:22-23) and an incident concerning the payment of the Temple tax (17:24-27). The narrative of the Temple tax incident has Peter answering two questions, the first from the Temple tax collectors (17:24-25a) and the second from Jesus (17:25b-26a). The rest of the passage (17:26b-27) contains Jesus' teaching on the matter, both in principle (17:26b) and in practice (17:27). For the record, Peter answered the tax collectors' question wrongly and Jesus' question rightly.

One cannot help but recall that Jesus did not mind offending the Pharisees on the matter of ritual hand washing (15:12), but in the spirit of 12:19 (cf. Isa 42:2) he would not protest the Temple tax (cf. 22:15-22; Rom 13:6-7; 1 Pet 2:13-14). Jesus had previously had cordial relations with the tax collectors at Capernaum, and this only exacerbated his tension with the Pharisees (cf. 9:9-11). Jesus' disciples today often get this backwards, treating religious hypocrites with much deference while making loud protests against perceived injustices by sinners. The lesson of 12:19-20/Isaiah 42:2-3 still is needed. Jesus treated non-religious sinners gently and religious hypocrites harshly, and his disciples should do the same. Foregoing one's liberties for the sake of avoiding offense and furthering the testimony of the Kingdom is also a Pauline teaching (Rom 14:13-23; 1 Cor 8:9-9:1; 9:19).

There is a striking blend of humility and power in this passage. Jesus worked a miracle in order to submit to the tax collectors and avoid causing them offense. Once again, Peter learned a lesson about the danger of speaking too quickly.

Summary of Matthew 17. It is important to note that since 16:5, Matthew has been stressing Jesus' private interaction with the disciples. He has taught them to beware the Pharisees' teaching (16:5-11) and revealed to them his identity (16:13-17), his program for the church (16:18-20), and his future, along with theirs (16:21-28). Peter's confession of Jesus as Messiah and Son of God was confirmed miraculously by the transfiguration. The last mention of John's Elijah-like ministry turned into a passion prediction (17:12). The healing pericope recalls two familiar themes, the lack of faith of Jesus' generation (17:17) and the little faith of Jesus' disciples (17:20). The final mention of Capernaum in Matthew also implies the unbelief of Jesus' adopted hometown (cf. 11:23-24). Capernaum, after all the miracles Jesus did there, should have recognized that Jesus' unique sonship would preclude his paying the Temple tax. Nevertheless, he would pay it to avoid causing them to sin (17:27).

Matthew 17 is interwoven with a wide array of theological themes prevalent in Matthew. It also is full of themes that have been preeminent throughout the narrative block that begins in 13:53. Jesus had done many miracles, but his evil contemporaries—for the most part—still did not believe in him. The conflict with the Jewish religious leaders continued and intensified, but Jesus was faithfully teaching his disciples, and their little faith was growing. They had accepted with great sadness his clear prediction that he would suffer, die, and rise again in Jerusalem, but they were still preoccupied with carnal concerns, such as who would be the greatest (18:1; cf. 16:23). There was still much for them to learn about the Kingdom before they made the fateful trip to Jerusalem with Jesus.

◆ B. Life and Relationships in the Kingdom (18:1-35)
  1. Greatness in the Kingdom (18:1-14; cf. Mark 9:33-50;
     Luke 9:46-50)

About that time the disciples came to Jesus and asked, "Who is greatest in the Kingdom of Heaven?"

²Jesus called a little child to him and put the child among them. ³Then he said, "I tell you the truth, unless you turn from your sins and become like little children, you will never get into the Kingdom of Heaven. ⁴So anyone who becomes as humble as this little child is the greatest in the Kingdom of Heaven.

⁵"And anyone who welcomes a little child like this on my behalf* is welcoming me. ⁶But if you cause one of these little ones who trusts in me to fall into sin, it would be better for you to have a large millstone tied around your neck and be drowned in the depths of the sea.

⁷"What sorrow awaits the world, because it tempts people to sin. Temptations are inevitable, but what sorrow awaits the person who does the tempting. ⁸So if your hand or foot causes you to sin, cut it off and throw it away. It's better to enter eternal life with only one hand or one foot than to be thrown into eternal fire with both of your hands and feet. ⁹And if your eye causes you to sin, gouge it out and throw it away. It's better to enter eternal life with only one eye than to have two eyes and be thrown into the fire of hell.*

¹⁰"Beware that you don't look down on any of these little ones. For I tell you that in heaven their angels are always in the presence of my heavenly Father.*

¹²"If a man has a hundred sheep and one of them wanders away, what will he do? Won't he leave the ninety-nine others on the hills and go out to search for the one that is lost? ¹³And if he finds it, I tell you the truth, he will rejoice over it more than over the ninety-nine that didn't wander away! ¹⁴In the same way, it is not my heavenly Father's will that even one of these little ones should perish."

18:5 Greek *in my name.* 18:9 Greek *the Gehenna of fire.* 18:10 Some manuscripts add verse 11, *And the Son of Man came to save those who are lost.* Compare Luke 19:10.

NOTES

18:1 *Who is the greatest in the Kingdom of Heaven?* Evidently while Jesus was still at Capernaum, the disciples came to him with a question (cf. Mark 9:33-37; Luke 9:46-48). The disciples questioned Jesus several times in Matthew (13:10; 15:12; 17:19; 21:20; 24:3). What led to this question about greatness (cf. 5:19; 11:11) in the Kingdom is unclear in Matthew, but see Mark 9:34. Perhaps some of the other disciples were concerned about the prominence of Peter (16:17-19; 17:24) or of James and John (17:1). The desire for greatness is part and parcel of fallen human existence, and it runs counter to what Jesus taught in 16:21-28. Two matters are unclear: whether the disciples were concerned about greatness in an abstract sense or about which *of them* was the greatest; and whether they were concerned about greatness in the present or in the future manifestation of the Kingdom. If this story should be understood in light of the later story of the sons of Zebedee and their mother (20:20-28), it seems likely that the disciples were concerned about which of them would be the greatest in the future (19:27-20:16).

18:2 *Jesus called a little child to him and put the child among them.* Jesus answered the question with a visual display, a sort of acted parable (18:2), before he explained greatness verbally (18:3-4). The NLT describes the child whom Jesus placed in the midst of the disciples as a "little child." It is difficult to know the exact age of the child. The Gr. word *paidion* [TG3813, ZG4086] can refer to a child of any age from infancy to puberty (BDAG 749; cf. 2:8ff; 11:16; 14:21; 15:38; 19:13-14), and all that can be determined from the context is that the child was old enough to respond to Jesus' calling him/her into the midst of the disciples.

18:3-4 *unless you turn from your sins and become like little children, you will never get into the Kingdom.* Matthew contains many statements about entering into the Kingdom (See 5:20; 7:21; 19:23-24; 23:13; cf. 19:17; 25:21, 23).

as humble as this little child. The character trait that appears to be foremost in the simile of becoming like a child is humility (11:29; 23:12; Luke 1:52; 3:5; Eph 4:2; Phil 2:3; Jas 1:9; 4:6, 10; 1 Pet 5:5-6; cf. "meekness" in 5:5; 21:5). In this sense conversion amounts to a renunciation of all one's human prestige or status and an acceptance of the values of the Kingdom. It is not that children are innocent of selfishness or that they consistently model humility, but that children have no status in society. As they are at the mercy of adults, so disciples acknowledge in repentance that they have no status before God and that they depend solely on the love and mercy of the heavenly Father. (It is not at all clear that John 3:3 is another version of this saying of Jesus, as advocated by Davies and Allison 1991:758.)

18:5-6 Since those who exercise childlike faith exhibit the essence of the Kingdom (cf. 21:15-16), the Father will severely judge those who cause such "children" to sin (cf. Mark 9:38-50; Luke 17:1-2). Here the use of the metaphor shifts from a child as the model of humility (18:1-4) to a child as the object of godly or sinful behavior. Causing Jesus' little ones to sin is contrasted with receiving them hospitably.

a large millstone tied around your neck. If receiving them hospitably is tantamount to receiving Jesus himself (10:40-41; John 13:20), causing them to sin is tantamount to rejecting Jesus himself, which brings consequences immeasurably more severe than drowning with a large millstone around one's neck (cf. Josephus *Antiquities* 14.450). "Heavy millstone" is more literally "millstone for a donkey," a large millstone turned by a donkey. This detail along with the stress on the depth of the sea vividly portrays the horrible consequences of causing a believer to fall into sin. To cause someone to fall into sin is to corrupt that person morally and spiritually and, as 18:7-9 points out, to render him or her liable to eternal punishment (5:29-30; 17:27). The transition from the child as metaphor to the reality of discipleship probably occurs in 18:5 (Hagner 1995:520), not in 18:6 (Davies and Allison 1991:754, 761). The point of the metaphor is that disciples should be humble and demonstrate this humility by welcoming other disciples, not causing them to sin.

18:7-9 *What sorrow awaits the world.* Jesus' pronouncements of woe upon those who cause his disciples to fall into sin recalls 11:21 and anticipates 23:13-16, 23-29; 24:19; 26:24. Evidently, the offense spoken of here is somewhat different from that of 17:27, which speaks of offending those who do not believe. In 18:7 God's sovereignty and human responsibility are combined in the idea that incidents of causing believers to stumble are inevitable (24:10-11) yet culpable (13:41; cf. 26:24).

Temptations are inevitable, but what sorrow awaits the person who does the tempting. Offense inevitably will come from the outsiders, but it may even come from the disciples themselves! Therefore, any potential offense must be dealt with promptly and decisively. Failure to deal radically with sinful proclivities indicates that the "disciple" is in danger of punishment in hell.

cut it off and throw it away. Jesus used the amputation of a hand or foot and of the gouging out of an eye as hyperboles here as he had previously in 5:29-30. As awful as these images are, the prospect of eternal punishment is worse. It should go without saying that this language is hypothetical as well as hyperbolical. One's hands, feet, and eyes do not cause one to sin, and ridding oneself of them would not get at the root of sin, the heart (15:18-20). The point is that one must deal radically with one's sinful tendencies (cf. Prov 4:23). For eschatological judgment as "fire," see also 3:10-12; 5:22; 25:41.

18:10-11 *don't look down on any of these little ones.* Disciples must not only deal radically with sin in their own lives, they must also studiously avoid looking down on their brothers and sisters (cf. Rom 14:3, 10, 15). One's fellow believers are styled here as "little ones," as in 18:6 (cf. 10:42; 25:40, 45).

their angels are always in the presence of my heavenly Father. This implies that there are angels with access to God who care in some way for believers (Heb 1:14). This should probably not be pressed so far as to insist that every believer has an individual guardian angel, but it is clear that angelic ministry to believers is real, albeit mysterious (cf. Pss 34:7; 91:11-12; Dan 10:10-14; Acts 12:15; Rev 2:1, 8, 12, 18; 3:1, 7, 14).

Verse 11 is not included in the most ancient manuscripts ($\aleph$ B L* $f^{1.13}$ 33 it^e syr^s cop^{sa}) and seems to break the continuity of the passage. Its authenticity is doubtful here. It probably has been interpolated from Luke 19:10 (Metzger 1994:36). All in all, the tone of 18:1-10 alternates between warnings of eschatological judgment (18:3, 6-10) and promises of eschatological blessing (18:4-5), depending on the course of action chosen.

18:12-13 NLT omits the question "what do you think?" (cf. 17:25; 21:28; 22:17, 42; 26:66), with which Jesus introduces a parable involving a lost sheep that is of great value to the shepherd (cf. Luke 15:3-7).

search for the one that is lost. The effort taken by a shepherd to retrieve one lost sheep has been illustrated in modern times by the story of the discovery of the Dead Sea Scrolls by a shepherd looking in a Qumran cave for a lost sheep. The analogy of believers and sheep is from the OT (e.g., Ps 23; Jer 23; Ezek 34) and is found elsewhere in Matthew (9:36; 10:6, 16; 12:11-12; 15:24; 18:12; 25:32-33; 26:31; cf. John 10). Based on Matthew's other uses of this imagery, we can see that Jesus is the shepherd who rescues the lost sheep and rejoices over it. Although the shepherd leaves the ninety-nine sheep "on the hills," one would assume that they are not in imminent danger as he seeks the single lost sheep. When the lost sheep is found, the shepherd greatly rejoices that he has rescued it.

18:14 *In the same way, it is not my heavenly Father's will that even one of these little ones should perish.* By analogy, the Father is concerned for his little ones (disciples) and does not wish that any of them should go astray and perish (cf. 5:29-30; 10:28). The implication is that disciples should model their own lives after the concern of the Father as expressed by the parable of the shepherd. Disciples must receive one another, not cause one another to go astray (18:5-8).

COMMENTARY

Introduction to the Fourth Discourse: The Values of the Kingdom. Matthew 18:1-35 comprises the fourth discourse of Jesus in Matthew. Like the first three discourses, it has a narrative setting (18:1) and is concluded with the characteristic "when Jesus had finished" (19:1). The setting is somewhat vague in that "about that time" seems to refer only to the general time frame when Jesus began to tell his disciples about his death and resurrection. Though the disciples grieved at this announcement (17:23), their grief sadly turned to speculation over who was or would be the greatest in the Kingdom of Heaven (18:1; cf. 20:20-28). The fourth discourse is Jesus' answer to this question and a subsequent question by Peter about forgiveness (18:21). A unique feature of this discourse is Jesus' use of a child as a visual aid (18:2) prior to his verbal response to the disciples' question.

The fourth discourse concerns genuine spiritual greatness. Jesus used a child as the ultimate object lesson of humility and the duty of hospitality to fellow disciples (18:3-5). Then he turned to the opposite of hospitality, giving offense, and spoke in vivid language about the horrible end of anyone who causes a disciple to fall into sin (18:6-14). Next come instructions on handling brothers who sin (18:15-20), and the answer to Peter's question about longsuffering in forgiveness, which leads to the parable of the unmerciful servant (18:21-35). The discourse holds together along the lines of God's concern for the "little ones" who believe. Their humble status is zealously guarded by the heavenly Father (18:7). His little ones must deal promptly with sin in their midst, yet the solemnity of the process of discipline underlines once again the Father's concern for his children (18:15-20). Peter's question with Jesus' answer underlines the absolute necessity of the rule of forgiveness in the Kingdom community (18:35).

The fourth discourse is not highly structured. One could divide it into two parts, each beginning with a question (18:1-20, 21-35) or each ending in a parable (18:1-14, 15-35). The latter of these two approaches seems better. In any event, the discourse holds together through its use of key terms such as "children" (18:2-5), who are the little ones (18:6, 10, 14). These children must be mimicked (18:4) and received (18:5), not caused to fall into sin or despised (18:6, 10). The use of family imagery for the community of disciples is perhaps the most noticeable motif. Disciples are children, and even those who sin against them are their brothers (18:15, cf. NLT mg), fellow children of the heavenly Father (18:10, 14, 19, 35). The language of 18:8-9 exhibits a clause-by-clause parallelism. The repetition of "two or three" and the juxtaposition of heaven and earth are key aspects of 18:15-20.

The Humble Enter God's Kingdom. Once again Jesus proved himself to be the master teacher as he spontaneously chose just the right object lesson to answer a question. He did not choose a child out of a sentimental notion of the innocence or subjective humility of children, since children may already exhibit in seed form the traits which Jesus spoke against here. He chose the metaphor or acted-out parable to stress that a child is at the mercy of adults and lacks social status. A child depends entirely on adults, particularly its parents, for its welfare. Thus, turning to God as a disciple of Jesus involves humbling oneself as a child before the heavenly Father. Such humility in total dependence upon the Father's mercy renounces any power, position, or status one might claim from human resources (cf. 5:3, 5). This perspective is nothing less than a total renunciation and reversal of the ways and values of the world, where the drive to get ahead leads to all sorts of sinful strategies to achieve greatness (20:26-27; 23:11-12). The opposite of humility is pride, which by implication would make one least in the Kingdom of Heaven.

Humility or genuine greatness leads to treating Kingdom disciples well, since it is tantamount to treating Jesus himself well (18:5; cf. 10:40). Mistreating disciples also has eternal consequences (18:7). No sacrifice is too great, even the spiritual equivalent of a hand, a foot, or an eye, if it gets one into the Kingdom (18:8-9; cf. 13:44). In light of this polarity of reward and punishment, disciples must carefully scrutinize themselves and make very sure that they do not despise one another (18:10). Instead of holding one another in contempt, they must have the same concern for one another that motivates the shepherd to rescue a straying sheep (18:12-14). Regarding oneself as a child before God continues to demand deep humility, and treating children/disciples well is not likely to win the world's applause. But such behavior is only walking in the steps of Jesus, who epitomizes humility and concern for children/disciples (11:25; 12:18-21; 20:28; 21:5). Walking in his steps in this fashion is counter-cultural behavior; it can be used by the Spirit to convict a world obsessed with power and status due to the sin of pride (5:13-16). Also, humility and concern for fellow disciples will insure that when church discipline is necessary (18:15-20), it will be carried out with proper motives (cf. Gal 6:1).

It is clear that the disciples still have many lessons to learn. Jesus had already made it clear that his destiny was suffering, death, and resurrection, and that they would share in his destiny. Suffering comes before reward (16:21-28). Thus, it is highly ironic that they were preoccupied with greatness so soon after Jesus' clear teaching on his destiny and theirs (Hagner 1995:517). This preoccupation simply will not go away (20:20-28). The disciples of Jesus must constantly remind themselves that their Lord's experience must be the paradigm of their own (10:38; 11:29; 16:24; 20:28; Phil 2:5; Col 1:24; Heb 10:32-38; 1 Pet 2:21; Rev 1:9)

◆   ## 2. Correcting a sinning believer (18:15-20)

15"If another believer* sins against you,* go privately and point out the offense. If the other person listens and confesses it, you have won that person back. 16But if you are unsuccessful, take one or two others with you and go back again, so that everything you say may be confirmed by two or three witnesses. 17If the person still refuses to listen, take your case to the church. Then if he or she won't accept the church's decision, treat that person as a pagan or a corrupt tax collector.

18"I tell you the truth, whatever you forbid* on earth will be forbidden in heaven, and whatever you permit* on earth will be permitted in heaven.

19"I also tell you this: If two of you agree here on earth concerning anything you ask, my Father in heaven will do it for you. 20For where two or three gather together as my followers,* I am there among them."

18:15a Greek If your brother. 18:15b Some manuscripts do not include against you. 18:18a Or bind, or lock. 18:18b Or loose, or open. 18:20 Greek gather together in my name.

NOTES

18:15-17 *If another believer sins against you.* The warnings against despising a fellow disciple or causing him or her to fall into sin inform the procedure laid out here (cf. 18:6, 10). In view of this background and Peter's question in 18:21, it is possible that the disputed words "against you" in 18:15 are authentic, despite their absence in many early manuscripts of the NT (cf. Davies and Allison 1991:782; Metzger 1971:45). The NLT's "another believer" is lit. "your brother" (so NLT mg).

go privately . . . take one or two others with you . . . take your case to the church. Three stages of confrontation are clear here, involving successively more members of the community of disciples. Ideally, the sin of one against another can be reconciled between the two of them (cf. Lev 19:17-18; Prov 3:12; 25:9-10; 27:5-6), but if this is unsuccessful, the next step is to secure peace by bringing in one or two others, evidently to underline the gravity of the problem and to add their wisdom to its solution. Verse 16 supports this practice by citing Deut 19:15 (cf. 26:60; Num 35:30; John 8:17; 2 Cor 13:1; 1 Tim 5:19; Heb 6:18; 10:28; Rev 11:3). Regrettably, if these two steps cannot resolve the matter, it must be taken before the whole local community, the "church" (cf. 16:18).

if he or she won't accept the church's decision, treat that person as a pagan or a corrupt tax collector. At this point, after three opportunities for reconciliation, the gravity of the situation ought to be clear, and the offender ought to acknowledge his or her error. But if the offender will not heed the church, there is no higher earthly authority. The only remaining alternative is withdrawal of fellowship from the offender, who is regarded no longer as a disciple but as a notorious sinner, like a "pagan or a corrupt tax collector" (lit. "Gentile or a tax collector"). This sort of treatment would mean that the offender would be regarded as an outsider and could not participate in the community's activities. But in view of Jesus' own compassionate treatment of notorious sinners (5:46-47; 9:10-13; 10:3), it would not necessarily mean a "shunning," or total withdrawal from personal contact. The Community Rule from Qumran lays out a similar procedure for dealing with interpersonal problems (1QS 5:25-6:1; CD 9:2-8).

18:18-20 These verses supply a theological foundation for the process of discipline outlined in 18:15-17. The consequences of the community's decision are ominous, since the community on earth acts in conjunction with the God of heaven.

whatever you forbid on earth will be forbidden in heaven, and whatever you permit on earth will be permitted in heaven. The forbidding and permitting (lit. "binding and loosing") mentioned here recalls 16:19 and is tied to the exercise of the keys of the Kingdom (cf. John 20:23). Here the authority is clearly the community's, not just Peter's or the apostles'. This involves authoritative proclamation of entrance or exclusion, forgiveness of sins or retention, and eventual punishment for sins. In 18:18 the matter of discipline is in view, showing that the process of 18:15-17 is an extremely serious one involving the eternal destiny of the offending party (see notes on 16:19).

If two of you agree here on earth concerning anything you ask, my Father in heaven will do it for you. The promises in 18:19-20 of answered prayer and God's presence also refer to the solemn matter of the sinning brother. It is possible that the two who agree in 18:19 are two members of a three-member court that represents the community (*m. Sanhedrin* 1:1; Hagner 1995:533). During the discipline process, the church may be assured that their deliberations on earth will be confirmed by their Father in heaven and that Jesus is present with them throughout the difficulties.

I am there among them. The presence of Jesus with the church during the process of discipline is similar to the rabbinic notion that God's presence (the Shekinah) is with a group as small as two people who are studying the Torah (*m. Avot* 3:2, 3, 6). Jesus' promise that he is with his church speaks of nothing less than divine activity (Joel 2:27; Zech

2:10-11). It recalls 1:23 and anticipates 28:20. The high Christology of Matthew is once again obvious.

COMMENTARY

Matthew 18:15-20 contains a procedure for discipline (18:15-17) followed by its theological basis. There are three steps in the procedure, and the basis involves three truths: the authority of the church, the promise of answered prayer, and the presence of Jesus. The procedure spelled out here will be a necessary one since Jesus has just taught that offenses are inevitable. The Father's total dedication to his little ones dictates that offenses within the community be dealt with promptly and fairly. After the model of the rescue of the straying sheep, the offended person must take the initiative to bring the offender back into the fold (18:12, 15). There is no place for the offended person to become bitter or gossip about the offender to a third person (cf. Prov 25:9-10). The three stages of confrontation assure the fair treatment of both the offender and the injured party with as little fanfare as possible. Though "church discipline" (cf. 1 Cor 5:1–6:11; 2 Cor 2:5-11; Gal 6:1-5; 2 Thess 3:6, 14-15; 1 Tim 5:19-20; 2 Tim 4:2; Titus 2:15; 3:10; 1 John 5:16; 3 John 1:10; Jude 1:20-23) is often taken lightly in evangelical circles, it is an ominous matter, an aspect of letting God's will be done on earth as it is in heaven (cf. 6:10). Successively rejecting the overtures of a brother, two or three witnesses, and the church is tantamount to rejecting Jesus and the Father.

Yet the severity of 18:15-20 is cushioned by its context, since it is "embedded in a section filled with kindness" (Davies and Allison 1991:804). Jesus has been speaking of his disciples as humble children (18:5), little ones (18:6), and lost sheep (18:12-13). He will go on to stress the necessity of forgiveness in his community (18:21-35). The sinner is described as a brother, a fellow child of the heavenly Father (18:15). Even the discipline process allows the sinner three chances to repent, and those who are involved in it are to view themselves as agents of the Father, who is like a shepherd seeking straying sheep. The goal is reconciliation and return to the flock, not severance of relationship.

The flippant way in which 18:19 is often cited to assure small meetings of Christians that God is with them is disturbing because it twists a solemn passage into a cliche. No doubt God is present with any legitimate meeting of his people, whatever its size, and there is no need to mishandle Scripture to prove it. Taking this solemn passage out of context cheapens it and profanes the sacred duty of the church to maintain the harmony of its interpersonal relationships.

◆   ## 3. Forgiving a sinning believer (18:21-35)

[21]Then Peter came to him and asked, "Lord, how often should I forgive someone* who sins against me? Seven times?"
[22]"No, not seven times," Jesus replied, "but seventy times seven!*

[23]"Therefore, the Kingdom of Heaven can be compared to a king who decided to bring his accounts up to date with servants who had borrowed money from him. [24]In the process, one of his debtors

was brought in who owed him millions of dollars.* 25He couldn't pay, so his master ordered that he be sold—along with his wife, his children, and everything he owned—to pay the debt.

26"But the man fell down before his master and begged him, 'Please, be patient with me, and I will pay it all.' 27Then his master was filled with pity for him, and he released him and forgave his debt.

28"But when the man left the king, he went to a fellow servant who owed him a few thousand dollars.* He grabbed him by the throat and demanded instant payment.

29"His fellow servant fell down before him and begged for a little more time. 'Be patient with me, and I will pay it,' he pleaded. 30But his creditor wouldn't wait.

He had the man arrested and put in prison until the debt could be paid in full.

31"When some of the other servants saw this, they were very upset. They went to the king and told him everything that had happened. 32Then the king called in the man he had forgiven and said, 'You evil servant! I forgave you that tremendous debt because you pleaded with me. 33Shouldn't you have mercy on your fellow servant, just as I had mercy on you?' 34Then the angry king sent the man to prison to be tortured until he had paid his entire debt.

35"That's what my heavenly Father will do to you if you refuse to forgive your brothers and sisters* from your heart."

18:21 Greek *my brother.* **18:22** Or *seventy-seven times.* **18:24** Greek *10,000 talents* [375 tons or 340 metric tons of silver]. **18:28** Greek *100 denarii.* A denarius was equivalent to a laborer's full day's wage. **18:35** Greek *your brother.*

NOTES

18:21-22 *how often should I forgive someone who sins against me? Seven times?* Peter once again spoke up, evidently for the rest of the disciples, and asked a question about forgiveness. Perhaps his question was asked impulsively and interrupted Jesus' discourse. Peter already knew that Jesus taught forgiveness (6:12, 14-15), but he was concerned here with the extent of the longsuffering that should be shown to a brother who repeatedly sinned against another disciple. It is not clear whether this hypothetical sinner has repeatedly responded to the process outlined in 18:15-20. Even if he has not, it would seem that there is no contradiction between corporate exclusion (18:15-20) and personal forgiveness (18:21-35).

seventy times seven! Peter seemed to think that forgiving seven times was quite adequate, but Jesus' hyperbolic answer indicates that forgiveness must be unending (cf. 5:21-26; 6:12, 14-15; *m. Yoma* 8:9). Whether 18:22 is translated "seventy-seven times" (NIV; BDAG 269) or "seventy times seven" (NLT), the following parable of the unforgiving servant (18:23-35) demonstrates that disciples have been forgiven by their heavenly Father of much more than they could ever forgive their fellow disciples. Thus, to be forgiven is to be freed to forgive. The response to offense mandated by Jesus is the opposite of Lamech's vengeful boast that he would be avenged seventy-seven times upon anyone who injured him (Gen 4:24).

18:23-27 Jesus' answer to Peter continues with a parable of the Kingdom, introduced by the common similarity formula (cf. 13:24, 31, 33, 45, 47; 20:1; 22:2; 25:1). The king's servants are likely to be understood as his governors or officials, since it seems unlikely that slaves would be entrusted with so much money or would owe money to a king (BDAG 260).

owed him millions of dollars. The first scene of the story tells the reader that a servant was forgiven an amazingly large debt by a king who wished to settle his financial affairs. The servant owed the king an extremely large amount of money (NLT "millions of dollars"), lit. "10,000 talents" (cf. NLT mg). A talent was probably worth around 6,000 drachmas (17:24) or denarii (20:2ff; BDAG 988). A laborer was paid a denarius a day (20:2), so if this is taken lit. a laborer would have to work 60,000,000 days or roughly 193,000 years (60,000,000 days divided by 310 work days a year) to earn this much money! But the figure ("10,000"; Gr. *mupioi*) here is hyperbolic; Danker (BDAG 661) suggests the English slang "zillions" to translate it (cf. the large amounts found in 1 Chr 29:3-7 and Josephus *Antiquities* 17.320). What is meant is an incalculably large amount in contrast to the amount owed this servant by his fellow servant in 18:28.

ordered that he be sold . . . to pay the debt. The king's plan to sell the servant and his family into slavery in order to obtain a modicum of satisfaction was evidently a legal solution (cf. 2 Kgs 4:1; Isa 50:1; Amos 2:6; 8:6), but the pleas of the prostrate servant for more time to pay touched the king's heart and changed his mind. His compassion reminds the reader of Jesus' compassion (9:36; 14:14; 15:32; 20:34).

forgave his debt. Instead of merely allowing his servant time to repay the enormous debt, with astonishing mercy he forgives it entirely.

18:28-30 In the second scene of the story the forgiven servant does not respond in kind to the king's compassion (18:28-30). The language of the second scene is quite similar to that of the first.

owed him a few thousand dollars. After being forgiven an enormous debt by the king, he refused to forgive his fellow servant a comparatively small debt, lit. "100 denarii" (NLT mg), roughly four months' work for a laborer. If our calculation in 18:24 is contrasted with the amount here, the servant was forgiven nearly 600,000 times the amount he refuses to forgive, but this is hyperbole.

put in prison until the debt could be paid in full. Despite the pleas of his fellow servant for more time, the unforgiving servant choked him and had him thrown in jail until he could repay (cf. 5:25-26; 24:49). This violent behavior is in stark contrast to the previous compassion of the king. The unforgiving servant did not do for the other as he would have had the other do for him (7:12), let alone do for the other as the king had already done for him.

18:31-34 In the third scene, other servants saw how the forgiven servant treated his fellow servants. There was a monstrous inconsistency. Should not this servant have imitated the mercy he received from the king? The servants were so horrified they told the king, who reversed his previous compassionate treatment and angrily punished the servant whom he had previously forgiven.

tortured until he had paid his entire debt. The evil servant (25:26) was to be tortured until he made arrangements for the king to be repaid. There is clear irony here in that the unforgiving servant was treated in the end as he treated his fellow servant (18:30, 34). In this way, the third scene resolves the incongruity between the first and second scenes.

18:35 *That's what my heavenly Father will do to you if you refuse to forgive your brothers and sisters from your heart.* The moral or application of the story comes at its conclusion: the heavenly Father's actions toward unforgiving disciples will be like those of the unforgiving servant's master. This was made clear in the parable when the king asked the evil servant why he did not treat his fellow servant as he had been treated by the king (18:32). If one presses the details, it will be impossible for the evil unforgiving servant ever to repay all that he owes to the king. Perhaps there is a hint here of the horror of eternal punishment (cf. 18:6-9). The connection with 6:14 is clear. Disciples dare not presume that God will forgive them if they are unwilling to forgive their fellow disciples. And this forgiveness must be genuine, from the heart, which touches on Matthew's recurrent theme of the heart or motivation as integral to true righteousness (cf. 5:8, 28; 6:21; 12:34; 13:15, 19; 15:8, 18, 19; 22:37). Peter's question (18:21) has been answered vividly.

COMMENTARY

Jesus answered Peter's question about forgiveness prosaically (18:22) and poetically (18:23-35). Both answers contain striking hyperboles. Peter thought it was remarkable that he was willing to forgive someone seven times, but Jesus said that seventy-seven times is more appropriate. Then he told a story containing the striking contrast of a servant who had been forgiven a vast amount (it would have taken the earnings of several lifetimes to repay it) but refused to forgive a paltry amount that could be repaid in a few months. The forgiven servant proved to be unforgiving and was severely judged by his master. The point is that those who have genuinely received forgiveness are forgiving to others (6:14-15; cf. Luke 6:36; Eph 4:31–5:2; Jas 2:13; 1 John 4:11). But the unforgiving character of this servant indicates that his entreaty to his master was a hoax (18:26). This contrast clearly portrays the infinite grace of God in forgiving humans their many trespasses against him over against the refusal of a disciple to forgive a minor offense against him. The incompatibility of the two situations could not be clearer, and the resulting teaching is that those who have been forgiven by God can and must forgive their fellow humans. To be forgiven is to be empowered to forgive. No matter how offensively one has been treated by a fellow human, there is no comparison to the heinous rebellion of wicked humans against a holy and loving God. Anyone who has truly experienced the compassion of the heavenly Father should have little problem showing genuine compassion to a fellow human.

Perhaps it is difficult to reconcile the process of discipline laid out in 18:15-20 with the duty of unlimited forgiveness taught in 18:21-35. But both can be tied back to the controlling motif of the chapter: disciples as the little ones, brothers (and sisters) of one another, together children of the heavenly Father. Disciples dare not allow this family to be disrupted by offenses, yet they cannot resolve offenses without a forgiving spirit. In terms of another metaphor found in this chapter, a straying sheep cannot be left alone in the wilderness, but those who seek it must be willing to receive it back into the flock. When this delicate balance between discipline and forgiveness is faithfully maintained, excommunication from the church is in reality a self-imposed exile (Davies and Allison 1991:804).

Summary and Transition. In one key sense, the journey to Jerusalem has already begun with Jesus' announcement of his suffering, death, and resurrection in 16:21, and the disciples must realistically face the grim prospects awaiting them. This will be impossible if there is a selfish preoccupation with greatness and an accompanying devaluation of others. Instead, disciples must receive each other as they would a child (18:5-10), shepherd each other as they would a lost sheep (18:12-14), deal patiently but decisively with unrepentant sinners in their midst (18:15-20), and genuinely forgive those who sin against them as many times as necessary (18:21-35). These values will strengthen the community's relationships and enable it to withstand the rigors that lie ahead in Jerusalem and beyond.

With 19:1, Jesus begins his journey to Jerusalem. He would continue to model the values he inculcated in Matthew 18 (e.g., 19:14), and the disciples would continue to struggle with a worldly notion of greatness (e.g., 20:20-28).

◆ VII. Opposition Comes to a Head in Judea (19:1–25:46)
  A. Ministry in Judea (19:1–23:39)
    1. Teaching on marriage and divorce; blessing little children
       (19:1–15; cf. Mark 10:1–16; Luke 18:15–17)

When Jesus had finished saying these things, he left Galilee and went down to the region of Judea east of the Jordan River. [2]Large crowds followed him there, and he healed their sick.

[3]Some Pharisees came and tried to trap him with this question: "Should a man be allowed to divorce his wife for just any reason?"

[4]"Haven't you read the Scriptures?" Jesus replied. "They record that from the beginning 'God made them male and female.'* [5]And he said, 'This explains why a man leaves his father and mother and is joined to his wife, and the two are united into one.'* [6]Since they are no longer two but one, let no one split apart what God has joined together."

[7]"Then why did Moses say in the law that a man could give his wife a written notice of divorce and send her away?"* they asked.

[8]Jesus replied, "Moses permitted divorce only as a concession to your hard hearts, but it was not what God had originally intended. [9]And I tell you this, whoever divorces his wife and marries someone else commits adultery—unless his wife has been unfaithful.*"

[10]Jesus' disciples then said to him, "If this is the case, it is better not to marry!"

[11]"Not everyone can accept this statement," Jesus said. "Only those whom God helps. [12]Some are born as eunuchs, some have been made eunuchs by others, and some choose not to marry* for the sake of the Kingdom of Heaven. Let anyone accept this who can."

[13]One day some parents brought their children to Jesus so he could lay his hands on them and pray for them. But the disciples scolded the parents for bothering him.

[14]But Jesus said, "Let the children come to me. Don't stop them! For the Kingdom of Heaven belongs to those who are like these children." [15]And he placed his hands on their heads and blessed them before he left.

19:4 Gen 1:27; 5:2.   19:5 Gen 2:24.   19:7 See Deut 24:1.   19:9 Some manuscripts add *And anyone who marries a divorced woman commits adultery.* Compare Matt 5:32.   19:12 Greek *and some make themselves eunuchs.*

NOTES

19:1 *When Jesus had finished saying these things, he left Galilee and went down to the region of Judea east of the Jordan River.* Following the characteristic formula that concludes each of Jesus' five discourses (cf. 7:28; 11:1; 13:53; 26:1), Matt 19 begins with the fateful geographical note that Jesus departed Galilee for the area of Judea east of the Jordan River (cf. 4:15, 25). He would not return to Galilee until after the resurrection (28:7, 16). The journey south to Jerusalem (over fifty miles) would customarily be made on the east side of the Jordan in order to avoid Samaria (10:5; cf. Luke 9:51-53; John 4:3-4, 9). The reference in 20:29 to Jericho as the point of departure for the journey to Jerusalem could imply that Jesus had already crossed the Jordan from east to west at Jericho. The journey would bring him nearer to those who would soon arrest, try, and crucify him, as he himself had predicted (16:21; 17:22-23).

19:2 *Large crowds followed him there, and he healed their sick.* Jesus characteristically continued to heal those who were sick in the large crowd following him (cf. 12:15; 14:14; 15:30-31).

19:3-6 From here to 20:28 the focus is on Jesus the teacher. In Matthew's literary structure, the fourth discourse ends with 18:35-19:1, but Jesus continued to teach and discourse.

Should a man be allowed to divorce his wife for just any reason? While Jesus was still east of the Jordan, he was drawn into a discussion of divorce by some Pharisees who wanted to test his understanding of divorce law (cf. Mark 10:1-12). Perhaps they wanted to make it seem that Jesus contradicted Moses (19:7). This renews the important Matthean theme of opposition from the religious leaders (cf. 12:14, 24, 38; 15:1, 12; 16:1; 22:15, 35). The discussion here reprises Jesus' teaching in the Sermon on the Mount (5:31-32). The background of the Pharisees' question appears to be the rabbinic dispute over divorce and Deut 24:1-4 between Hillel and Shammai. Hillel took a rather loose view of what the shameful or indecent matter mentioned in Deut 24:1 entails, so he permitted divorce for any reason. But Shammai interpreted Deut 24:1 strictly as a reference to sexual impropriety. Later, around AD 200, the Mishnah would codify this oral tradition (*m. Gittin* 9:10; cf. Josephus *Antiquities* 4.244-259).

God made them male and female. . . . This explains why a man leaves his father and mother and is joined to his wife, and the two are united into one. Jesus did not enter into the specifics of the exegesis of Deut 24 but instead cited Gen 1:27 (cf. Gen 5:2) and 2:24 in succession, stressing the original divine purpose for marriage in the creation account. Genesis 2:24 was also cited by Paul in 1 Cor 6:16 and Eph 5:31, and in the Damascus Document (CD) 4:21. The gist of Jesus' approach is that the original divine plan for monogamy should be more normative than subsequent concessions to human sinfulness. The clause rendered "the two are united into one" by the NLT is lit. "the two shall become one flesh." It is this "one-flesh" relationship that makes divorce wrong. When God has so united two people, humans may not split them apart. The marital union is a basic, intimate relationship that demands one's total allegiance. When two people are married, their identity as their parents' children is permanently altered. Their new identity as husband and wife is forever.

19:7-9 why did Moses say in the law that a man could give his wife a written notice of divorce and send her away? Given the apparent prevalence of divorce in that day, Jesus' argument for the permanence of marriage understandably concerned the Pharisees. Their response to Jesus pits Deut 24:1 against Gen 1-2, evidently still with the motive of trapping Jesus (19:3). Their understanding of Deut 24:1 appears to have been similar to the liberal view of the school of Hillel. Rather than the NLT's "could give," their response is more lit. "Why did Moses command to . . . send her away?" and shows that they understood Moses as commanding divorce. Jesus would not accept this view. His citation of Gen 1-2 places the creation narrative in Genesis over the legislation of Deut 24. God's original purpose for marriage overrides the Mosaic concession for human sin.

Moses permitted divorce. He did not command it. Sexual infidelity is the only permissible grounds for the dissolution of a marriage (cf. 5:32). On this point, Jesus seems to share the strict perspective of Shammai, but his appeal to the creation ordinance rather than Deut 24 might not be accepted by either Shammai or Hillel. The original divine ordinance of marriage trumps the subsequent human expedient of divorce. This is quite different from the Mishnaic view that unfaithful wives had to be divorced by their husbands (*m. Nedarim* 11:12; *m. Sotah* 5:1; *m. Yevamot* 2:8). But divorce is not a matter of course even in the OT (Mal 2:16).

19:10-12 If this is the case, it is better not to marry! The disciples were amazed at the strictness of Jesus' approach and considered a life of celibacy to be better than marriage under such tight constraints (cf. Sir 25:16-26).

Not everyone can accept this statement. Jesus noted that celibacy is only for certain people who are divinely gifted to accept it (cf. 1 Cor 7:1-2, 7-9). The words "this statement" in 19:11 refer to the disciples' comment about celibacy in 19:10, not back to Jesus' comments on divorce in 19:9. The disciples were already aware of (1) eunuchs (Lev 21:20; Isa 39:7;

56:4; Dan 1:3-8; Acts 8:27; cf. *m. Zavim* 2:1; *m. Yevamot* 8:4), and (2) those who cannot marry and have children due to birth defects in their genitals or castration, but Jesus added a third category: (3) those who "choose not to marry" (NLT) due to their commitment to the Kingdom. The choice not to marry is literally to "make a eunuch of oneself" (cf. NLT mg), but this is not to be taken literally. It refers to those who choose celibacy for the sake of the Kingdom over marriage and parenting. Among those who fit this category are probably John the Baptist, Jesus, and Paul (cf. 1 Cor 7:32-38; 9:5). The eschatological urgency of the Kingdom makes it a priority even over normal family relationships (cf. 8:21; 12:46-50). On the other hand, the Mishnah's reflection on Gen 1:31 leads to the conclusion that no man is exempt from the duty to have children (*m. Yevamot* 6:6).

It should be noted here that there is not even a hint in this passage that celibates are more spiritual than married people, or that their lifestyle is a morally superior model to which others should aspire. Rather, only those who are specially gifted should choose celibacy as their role for the sake of the Kingdom. There is no basis here for the promotion of an ascetic lifestyle as the ideal for human existence. For further discussion of celibacy, see Davies and Allison (1997:26-27); Trautman (1966).

19:13-15 Let the children come to me. This incident recalls and reinforces 18:1-14 (cf. Mark 10:13-16; Luke 18:15-17). It is fitting here since Jesus had been discussing divorce, marriage, and singleness. With this background Jesus was asked to bless some children by laying his hands on them and praying for them (cf. Gen 48:14-15). The disciples rebuked those who asked for the blessing as unwelcome intruders. But Jesus turned the rebuke back on the disciples; they were not to hinder children from coming to him because the Kingdom belongs to such as them.

COMMENTARY

Introduction to the Narrative Section of Matthew 19:1-23:39. The narrative block between Matthew's fourth (Matt 18) and fifth (Matt 24-25) discourses begins with Jesus' journey south from Galilee to Judea beyond (east of) the Jordan (19:1). After a time, he crossed the river to Jericho (20:29) and then moved further westward up into the hills toward Jerusalem as far as Bethphage and the Mount of Olives (20:17; 21:1). When proper arrangements were made, Jesus entered the city (21:10), had a confrontation with the Temple leaders, and left to spend the night in Bethany (21:17). The next morning he returned to the city (21:18), entered the Temple again (21:23), and became embroiled in a series of heated disputes with various Jewish religious leaders. These disputes culminated in the seven woe oracles of Matthew 23, after which Jesus left the Temple for the Mount of Olives (24:1-3), the setting for the fifth and final discourse. In all of this, Matthew's story is very similar to that found in Mark, with few significant differences (Davies and Allison 1997:1).

The material in Matthew 19-23 continues such basic themes as Jesus the healer, the opposition of the religious leaders, the teaching of the disciples, and the movement of Jesus ever closer to his suffering in Jerusalem. But while the themes are familiar, the content is more topically arranged than in the last narrative block. There is comparatively less stress on healing (19:2; 20:34; 21:14) and passion predictions (20:17-19; cf. the cryptic language in 21:37-39; 23:32). The bulk of the material is devoted to Jesus teaching his disciples (19:10-20:28) and confronting the

Jerusalem religious establishment (21:12–23:39). The disciple-oriented material in Matthew 19–20 is, in effect, a continuation of themes from the fourth discourse in Matthew 18 on the values of the Kingdom community. In the material covering Jesus' Temple confrontations with the religious leaders, a bad situation goes from worse (Matt 21–22) to worst (Matt 23).

Davies and Allison (1997:1-3) present the material in this fourth narrative block as falling into four major sections. First, in 19:1–20:28, Jesus teaches the disciples on family obligations. Second, in 20:29–21:22, Jesus speaks and acts prophetically in healing, cleansing the Temple, and disputing with the chief priests. Third, deeds are left behind as Jesus engages in controversial dialogues with various Jewish religious leaders in 21:23–22:46. Fourth, in Matthew 23, Jesus turns back to the disciples to warn them against Pharisaic practices before he announces seven woes on the Pharisees and laments the fate of Jerusalem.

The Structure of Matthew 19:1-15. Matthew 19:1-15 begins with a transition and introduction that sets off this new narrative block here from the discourse of Matthew 18. The narrative block begins with a controversy initiated by the Pharisees concerning the legality of divorce (19:3-9). Jesus' strictures against divorce were the occasion for his disciples' jaded remark on the superiority of singleness; Jesus responded to this as well (19:10-12). At this point children entered the picture, and against the wishes of the disciples, Jesus affirmed and blessed them. So there are three units in this section, with the initial debate with the Pharisees leading to two discussions in which Jesus corrects the disciples' views of marriage and children respectively. The key motif in the section is the four answers of Jesus, the first pair given to the Pharisees (19:4, 8) and the second pair to the disciples (19:11, 14). Jesus' dispute with the Pharisees on the permanence of marriage and the undesirability of divorce leads naturally into the discussions of singleness and children with his disciples.

Jesus' Teachings on Marriage. The permanence and normative nature of marriage is the major point of this passage. Jesus' citation of Genesis 1–2 makes this point explicitly, and his deprecation of divorce as due to sin further supports it. His explanation of celibate singleness as a lifestyle appropriate only for relatively few specially gifted people implicitly honors marriage as the norm for most people. Similarly, his affirmation of the children who result from marriage lends implicit support to the institution of marriage itself. In our day, just as in Jesus' day, divorce occurs all too frequently; singleness is often exalted over marriage as the more fulfilling lifestyle (although seldom is singleness celibate today!); and children are deprecated as a time-consuming drag on one's career. But Jesus speaks strongly for marriage as the divine pattern for people, a pattern to which all except a relative few should aspire. This pattern can be abandoned by legal divorce only after it has been broken by sexual infidelity. The obligations of this pattern are preferable to the seeming freedom of singleness, except in cases of special divine endowment. The offspring of this pattern are to be affirmed and blessed. In a sense, marriage can be viewed in terms of Jesus' teaching on taking up one's cross and denying oneself (16:25). Divorce, singleness, and childlessness may seem to be the way of success and fulfillment ("saving one's life"), but in the end the seemingly carefree life will be a lonely, lost life. Marriage and parenting may appear to lead to a burdensome life ("losing one's life"), but in the end "married with children" will prove to be the richest possible life for most because it is life according to the Creator's pattern for his creatures.

In the present fallen world, the ideal relationships intended in the created pattern are not easy to attain. Yet the inauguration of the power of the Kingdom enables disciples to live to a great extent according to the created pattern. Many genuine followers of Jesus have failed as spouses, parents, or singles, and the church must reach out to restore them to obedience and fellowship. Nevertheless, it is better to avoid sin than to be forgiven of it. Prevention is superior to cure. For a superb discussion of the passage and ministry in light of it, see the pastorally oriented discussion in Bruner (1990:675-687).

Jesus' Teaching on Divorce and Remarriage. It is likely that the Pharisees' question in 19:3 was directed toward Jesus' understanding of Deuteronomy 24:1ff. In its original context, this passage prohibits a woman who has been remarried and divorced from two different men to remarry her first husband. Deuteronomy 24 is not a divine mandate to divorce but only a concession due to the hardness of hearts. Jesus interprets the original "one-flesh" implications of marriage (Gen 2:24) as requiring the permanence. He will *permit* divorce only in the instance of sexual immorality, which breaks the one-flesh character of the union. Except in cases of infidelity, divorce leads to adultery. The language here assumes, as did the Old Testament, that a man could divorce his wife but a wife could not divorce her husband (cf. 19:3). However, a wife could appeal to the community elders for redress of grievances (*m. Ketubbot*).

Matthew 19:9 (cf. 5:32) has been understood in a variety of ways, and its exegetical difficulties are compounded by textual difficulties (Metzger 1994:38-39). One difficulty is the meaning of the word *porneia* [TG4202, ZG4518], which has been understood variously as marital infidelity (NLT), premarital infidelity (as in Matt 1:19), or incest (as in Lev 18:6; 1 Cor 5:1; cf. BDAG 854). All in all, the approach of NLT seems best because the context does not restrict the general sense of *porneia* in any specific way. Another major difficulty is the scope of the exception clause, "unless his wife has been unfaithful." The question is whether this clause permits both divorce and remarriage when infidelity has occurred or only divorce and not remarriage. Most protestant scholars take the former view (Davies and Allison 1997:17), but there are notable exceptions (e.g., Hagner 1995:549; Heth and Wenham 1984). Those who take the second view tend to view 19:11-12 as spoken specifically to the celibacy required of those who have been divorced.

It appears that this issue cannot be resolved by grammatical arguments, but the view that both divorce and remarriage are permitted in the case of infidelity seems best: Freedom to remarry is the essence of divorce; it is meaningless otherwise (*m. Gittin* 9:3). Further, it seems arbitrary to think that divorced people are universally given the gift of celibacy. Rather, repentant individuals who have been divorced due to infidelity should have the freedom to get it right the second time. For a helpful discussion of the many exegetical difficulties here and reference to scholarly literature, see Carson (1984:412-418). For a superb pastoral discussion of the passage, see Bruner (1995:675-687).

The disciples of Jesus are a "new creation" in Christ (2 Cor 5:17; Eph 2:11-14). Participation in Christ's Kingdom amounts to being a new people, whose identity and relationships are drawn from humanity as defined before the Fall. Similarly, when Jesus says that divorce "was not what God originally intended," he implicitly tells his disciples that their identity is to recapitulate the human identity and relationships from before the Fall—before hard hearts began to pervert God's intention. Jesus' disciples look forward to the time "when the world is made new" (19:28), but they also long for God's will to be done on earth as it is in heaven (6:10). In this light, the permanence of marriage ought to be a matter of course in the Christian community, an aspect of its present life that mirrors and anticipates the righteousness that will come with God's Kingdom to the earth (Hagner 1995:549-551). If Moses did not command divorce, then certainly Jesus did not. Even in cases of marital infidelity, divorce should not be the first—let alone the only—option. Are not the deep wounds caused by marital infidelity susceptible to healing by the love of God? Should not couples contemplating divorce, even in cases of infidelity, be made to consider the implications of Matthew 18:21-35? Forgiveness must be rendered in every situation, including this one, and such forgiveness can often lead to a restored relationship and renewed testimony to the power of Jesus' Kingdom message. If God hated divorce under the old covenant (Mal 2:14-16), how much more so now that the Kingdom has dawned.

Jesus Blesses the Children. Here, as in 18:3-10, children represent those to whom the Kingdom belongs—i.e., Jesus' disciples. Because of their spiritual significance, Jesus welcomed them, laid his hands on them, and prayed for them. This passage indicates that Jesus affirmed and cared for children and that his disciples should too. After this incident, he left that area, perhaps to avoid further arguments with the Pharisees (cf. 19:3).

It is doubtful whether this passage should be pressed into the service of later theological concerns. Whatever the merits of the practice of infant baptism, it is extremely doubtful that it is implied here (Davies and Allison 1997:34-35). As in 18:5, where "a little child like this" refers to believers (18:6), here "children" (19:13) represents Jesus' disciples. The use of little children as an illustration of the humility of the Kingdom is consistent with Matthew's teaching elsewhere (10:42; 11:25; 18:14; 21:15-16; 25:40, 45). Infant baptism is not explicitly mentioned in patristic literature until Tertullian (*On Baptism* 18; c. AD 175), who opposed it. But for a well-stated evangelical view to the contrary, see Bruner (1990:695-698).

◆ ## 2. Riches or the Kingdom? (19:16-30; cf. Mark 10:17-31; Luke 18:18-30)

[16]Someone came to Jesus with this question: "Teacher,* what good deed must I do to have eternal life?"

[17]"Why ask me about what is good?" Jesus replied. "There is only One who is good. But to answer your question—if you want to receive eternal life, keep* the commandments."

[18]"Which ones?" the man asked.

And Jesus replied: "'You must not murder. You must not commit adultery. You must not steal. You must not testify falsely. [19]Honor your father and mother. Love your neighbor as yourself.'*"

[20]"I've obeyed all these commandments," the young man replied. "What else must I do?"

[21]Jesus told him, "If you want to be perfect, go and sell all your possessions and give the money to the poor, and you will have treasure in heaven. Then come, follow me."

[22]But when the young man heard this, he went away sad, for he had many possessions.

[23]Then Jesus said to his disciples, "I tell you the truth, it is very hard for a rich person to enter the Kingdom of Heaven. [24]I'll say it again—it is easier for a camel to go through the eye of a needle than for a rich person to enter the Kingdom of God!"

[25]The disciples were astounded. "Then who in the world can be saved?" they asked.

[26]Jesus looked at them intently and said, "Humanly speaking, it is impossible. But with God everything is possible."

[27]Then Peter said to him, "We've given up everything to follow you. What will we get?"

[28]Jesus replied, "I assure you that when the world is made new* and the Son of Man* sits upon his glorious throne, you who have been my followers will also sit on twelve thrones, judging the twelve tribes of Israel. [29]And everyone who has given up houses or brothers or sisters or father or mother or children or property, for my sake, will receive a hundred times as much in return and will inherit eternal life. [30]But many who are the greatest now will be least important then, and those who seem least important now will be the greatest then.*

19:16 Some manuscripts read *Good Teacher.* 19:17 Some manuscripts read *continue to keep.* 19:18-19 Exod 20:12-16; Deut 5:16-20; Lev 19:18. 19:28a Or *in the regeneration.* 19:28b "Son of Man" is a title Jesus used for himself. 19:30 Greek *But many who are first will be last; and the last, first.*

NOTES

19:16-17 *Teacher, what good deed must I do to have eternal life?* The second half of Matthew 19 begins with a question just like the first half did (19:3). After his teaching on family matters, Jesus was approached by a man who wanted to know what good deeds he must do to inherit eternal life (7:14; 18:8-9; 19:29; 25:46; cf. Mark 10:17-22; Luke 18:18-23). The Marcan and Lukan versions of this episode contain important differences from Matthew's account. The man addresses Jesus as "teacher," which implies that he did not adequately grasp Jesus' identity (cf. 8:19; 12:38). But there is no indication in the passage that the man approached Jesus with insincere motives.

Why ask me about what is good? . . . There is only One who is good. This puzzling question may imply that the man should focus not on his own good deeds, but on the goodness of the one true God (perhaps an allusion to Deut 6:4). Or it may mean that since God is good, his commandments provide a detailed definition of goodness. At any rate, Jesus' eventual reply that the man should keep the commandments is not novel, but restates the gist of Lev 18:5.

19:18-20 Which ones? Although the man knew that all the commandments in the Torah are binding, he asked Jesus to be more specific. Perhaps his question is similar to that of 22:36, where a Pharisee asks Jesus to identify the greatest commandment in the law. Or perhaps he wanted Jesus to assign him one remarkable act of righteousness that would assure him of eternal life. In reply, Jesus rapidly cited five of the ten commandments, from the sixth through the ninth followed by the fifth (Exod 20:12-16; Deut 5:16-20). To these he added the "golden rule" from Lev 19:18 (cf. 5:43; 7:12; 22:39; Rom 12:9; 13:9; Gal 5:14; Jas 2:8; *Didache* 1:2). The sixth through ninth commandments prohibit specific sinful behaviors, while the fifth commandment and the golden rule enjoin godly behavior toward one's parents and toward one's neighbors in general terms.

I've obeyed all these commandments. The man responded to Jesus by baldly affirming that he had kept all these (cf. Paul in Phil 3:6), but acknowledging that he needed something more.

19:21 If you want to be perfect. Jesus had just reaffirmed the central social tenets of the Torah, but as its definitive teacher he added his own authoritative directives (cf. 5:17ff). Jesus told the man that in order to be perfect he must sell his possessions and give them to the poor (cf. 1 Cor 13:3). The word "perfect" refers to spiritual maturity or development in godliness, in contrast to the man's admitted inadequacies (5:48; BDAG 996).

come, follow me. In addition to exchanging his earthly treasures for heavenly treasure (6:20), he should follow Jesus as an itinerant disciple (4:22; 8:22; 9:9), laying up treasure in heaven (6:19-21; 13:44-46). Jesus demanded that the ruler forsake the wealth to which he was devoted, since that wealth was preventing him from loving God and neighbor (6:24). It is striking that Jesus appended his own commands to those of Moses, but this should not be surprising in light of 5:17-19. Genuine obedience to the Torah is determined by Jesus alone. This radical demand for total commitment to the Kingdom is in reality an offer of the gospel of grace, calling the ruler to renounce his reliance on wealth and to commit himself to the Kingdom. This passage serves as further commentary on previous texts in Matthew that juxtapose serving materialism and serving God (6:21, 24; 13:22).

19:22 he went away sad. Jesus had identified the inadequacy haunting this young man, but the man was not yet willing to obey Jesus, become perfect, and obtain eternal life.

19:23 it is very hard for a rich person to enter the Kingdom of Heaven. Jesus took the incident with the ruler as an opportunity to teach his disciples about the deceitfulness of riches (cf. Mark 10:23-31; Luke 18:24-30). Wealth can desensitize people regarding their deepest needs, just as poverty can alert them to the Kingdom (5:3).

19:24 it is easier for a camel to go through the eye of a needle. This restates 19:23 with an absurd hyperbolic metaphor, utilizing the largest animal and the smallest opening commonly considered by the disciples. Just as it is humanly impossible for a camel to pass through the eye of a needle, so it is impossible, apart from the power of God's grace, for a rich person to enter God's Kingdom. Despite sermonic lore, there is no historical evidence for the existence of a small gate in Jerusalem, supposedly called the "Needle's Eye," through which a camel on his knees could barely squeeze. Such an illustration weakens Jesus' hyperbolic statement that it is impossible for rich people to enter the Kingdom.

19:25-26 who in the world can be saved? The disciples' incredulous question may be based on the idea that riches are proof of God's approval. If so, then the rich of all people would be most likely to enter the Kingdom (Prov 22:4). Jesus was not condemning riches but the idolatrous manner of coveting riches (6:24; cf. 27:57). Only by the sovereign grace of God can such idolatry be overcome.

19:27-28 We've given up everything to follow you. What will we get? Recalling Jesus' words (19:21), Peter asserted that the disciples had done what the young man would not do and inquired about their reward (cf. 10:41-42; 16:27). Evidently, Peter was speaking for the disciples once again (as in 15:15; 16:16; 17:4). That Jesus did not rebuke Peter for asking this question may surprise those who think that one serves God strictly out of love, not for rewards. Jesus first speaks of the reward of the twelve (19:28) and then expands his perspective to include all who have sacrificed to follow him (19:29).

when the world is made new . . . you . . . will also sit on twelve thrones, judging the twelve tribes of Israel. The terminology focusing on the twelve tribes of Israel is remarkable (cf. Luke 22:30; Rev 21:12). So is the description of the eschaton as a time "when the world is made new" (lit. "the regeneration;" cf. Isa 65:17; 66:22; John 3:5; Acts 3:21; Rom 8:18-23; 2 Pet 3:13; Rev 21-22; *1 Enoch* 45:3-5). Renewal of the present world is necessary because it is passing away (5:18; 24:35). The idea of eschatological renewal stresses the cosmic effects of Christ's redemptive work.

In this context, "judging" Israel probably implies both sharing in final judgment and ruling in the world to come. The striking teaching that the disciples will share the rule of the coming Kingdom with Jesus may be based on Dan 7:9, 13-14, 18, 22, 27 (cf. Luke 22:30; 1 Cor 6:2; Rev 2:26-27; 3:21; 20:6; Wis 3:8).

19:29 *property.* Lit., "field" or "farm."

hundred times. This is the reading of some manuscripts (א C W 𝔐); other manuscripts (B L) read "manifold." The former may be the result of harmonization to Mark 10:30; the latter, to Luke 18:30. Whichever is the original reading, the idea is that the eschatological blessing that will come to all who follow Jesus will far outweigh their present sacrifices. Such compensation adds to the motivation to suffer with Jesus in the present (16:24-28; Rom 8:18)

19:30 *many who are the greatest now will be least important then, and those who seem least important now will be the greatest then.* This enigmatic saying, which is repeated in 20:16, brackets the parable of 20:1-15. The Gr. speaks of the "first" and the "last," not the "greatest" and the "least." The saying warns the rich young man, currently among the first/greatest of the world, against leveraging his present wealth against his eternal destiny. The disciples may be encouraged, on the one hand, that their sacrifice will be rewarded. On the other hand, they also are warned against presuming on the grace of God. The chapter division at 20:1 is unfortunate, since the parable of the landowner in 20:1-16 continues the answer to Peter's question just as did the parable of the unforgiving servant in 18:21-35.

COMMENTARY

The "rich young ruler" episode is a Gospel text that is frequently viewed as instructive for those who do personal evangelism (cf. John 4), but this passage can be misunderstood. By his stress on the second table of the law, Jesus was not teaching a way of salvation by mechanical observation of the commandments. Jesus' use of the term "perfect" in 19:21 does not imply a notion of two levels of discipleship (Thomas 1961:292). Jesus was simply answering the young man's question by gradually showing him his root problem, which was covetousness. Jesus began by shifting the focus from preoccupation with self to preoccupation with God. Instead of being preoccupied with good deeds, the man should have been occupied with God's goodness (19:16-17). Perhaps the man was asking Jesus to assign him one good deed that would bring him the eternal life he wanted. When Jesus directed him to the commandments, he seemed confused as to which commandments were relevant. When Jesus cited commandments 5-9, the man affirmed he had kept the commandments but still lacked something.

At this point Jesus got to the heart of the problem by commanding the man to give his wealth to the poor and become a disciple, which would bring heavenly treasure. In a sense, Jesus asked the man to reprise a role previously scripted in two parables (13:44-46). "Jesus demands not alms but everything" (Davies and Allison 1997:46). The man would lose everything material but gain Jesus and the Kingdom. This is what he lacked all along. But his sorrowful departure makes it clear that he had not kept all the commandments, since he had not truly loved his neighbor as himself and was unwilling to give his possessions to the poor (19:19). Jesus did not cite the tenth commandment, "you must not covet" (Exod 20:17), but the man's response clearly shows he had broken this commandment also. Jesus brought the man to the point where he acknowledged what he lacked by his decision not to follow Jesus. His wealth had become a god that took priority over the true God, which violates the first commandment (Exod 20:2-3). The ruler's refusal to do a good thing—to divest himself of his wealth and follow Jesus—shows that he did not acknowledge the goodness of God in his life. He served money, so he could not serve God (6:24). His materialism prevented him from seeking the Kingdom first (6:33). But his sorrow indicates not only that he was not ready to follow Jesus but that he also realized what he lacked.

Jesus' commands to the rich young man are directed specifically toward his individual spiritual need. All of Jesus' disciples need to help the poor (e.g., Acts 4:34-37; Gal 2:10; 6:10; Jas 2:1), but not all need to totally divest themselves of their wealth to do so (see 27:57; Luke 8:3; 19:2, 8-9; Acts 5:4). Greed for material gain bars one from the Kingdom (1 Tim 6:9-10), but the sin of greed is not limited to the rich. There are those within the Kingdom who are rich by God's providence (1 Cor 1:26), and they are accountable for the use of their resources to further God's work (1 Tim 6:17-19).

Jesus and the Kingdom. It is noteworthy that in this context five terms are used in a very similar way. In 19:24 Jesus speaks of the "Kingdom of God" in tandem with his more characteristic term "Kingdom of Heaven" (19:23)—this in response to the young man's question about inheriting "eternal life" (19:16, 29). Jesus further described the same concept as being "perfect" (19:21), and the disciples refer to it as being "saved" (19:25; cf. 1:21; 10:22; 16:25). Two conclusions can be drawn from this semantic interplay. First, as is already evident from comparisons with the synoptic Gospels (Matt 13:31-32; Mark 4:30-32; Luke 13:18-19 and Matt 19:14; Mark 10:14; Luke 18:16), there is no real difference between the Kingdom of God and the Kingdom of Heaven in Matthew. Rather, the term "Kingdom of God" is occasionally used for subtle literary and contextual reasons to describe the same referent as the more common Kingdom of Heaven. Second, while the language here about inheriting eternal life and entering the Kingdom may imply that the Kingdom is future, the language of being "perfect" and "saved" implies that the Kingdom may be truly—if not totally—experienced in the present life. The Kingdom of God is both present and future, and those who do not recognize both its aspects truncate the riches of scriptural truth and spiritual blessing.

The description of the future Kingdom in terms of the twelve tribes of Israel appears to justify a belief in the eschatological conversion of the nation of Israel to faith in Jesus as Messiah. This would be in keeping with Matthew's overall emphasis on the preeminent fulfillment of Scripture through the words and deeds of Jesus the Messiah. The followers of Jesus, the ultimate teacher of the Torah, constitute Israel within Israel, the eschatological remnant. In the end they will judge or govern the nation as a whole (Gundry 1994:393-394; Overman 1996:285). Yet somehow certain commentators view this language as indicating that the Gentile church, which replaces Israel, will rule over the nations as a whole (Blomberg 1992:301; Hendriksen 1973:730). Among the problems with this view is its dissolution of the distinction made by Jesus between the rule of the disciples over Israel (19:28) and the reward of all who sacrifice to follow Jesus (19:29). If the church supersedes Israel, this distinction is rendered meaningless.

Summary and Transition. The flow of Matthew 19 actually carries over to 20:16, since the parable of the workers is the conclusion of Jesus' answer to Peter's question in 19:27 about rewards. It is significant that immediately after this answer comes Jesus' third passion prediction (20:17-19). Following another answer to another question about rewards (20:20-28), the Triumphal Entry into Jerusalem occurs, and the passion week begins. In this way the geographical movement of Matthew 19:1 (toward Jerusalem) signifies the beginning of the end of Jesus' earthly ministry.

Matthew 19 begins with an extended discussion of the divorce question (19:3-12; cf. 5:31-32). A brief incident of blessing children (19:13-15; cf. 18:1-14) leads to the well-known "rich young ruler" pericope (19:16-22), which precipitates Jesus' teaching the disciples about the deceitfulness of riches (19:23-26; cf. 6:19-24; 13:22). Then Peter questions Jesus about rewards, and Jesus answers with a parable (19:27–20:16).

Matthew 19 continues several themes already prominent in Matthew. Jesus continues to heal multitudes of people (19:2; cf. 20:29). The Pharisees appear once again with questions designed to trip Jesus up (19:3; cf. 21:23; 22:15, 34). The theme of reward, stressed by Jesus after his initial passion prediction (16:21), is amplified in this chapter as well (19:27–20:15; 20:20-28). It is also interesting to note how the disciples seem to be amazed at Jesus' radical teachings on divorce and riches (19:10, 25). Their remarks continue to show that Jesus was working with men of little faith whose messianic understanding was limited. Connected to this is Peter's continuing role as the model disciple, who as *primus inter pares* (first among equals) verbalized the questions that were in the minds of all the apostles (19:27; cf. 14:28;16:16, 22; 17:4, 24; 18:21; 26:33-35, 40).

◆   ### 3. The parable of the vineyard workers (20:1-16)

"For the Kingdom of Heaven is like the landowner who went out early one morning to hire workers for his vineyard. ²He agreed to pay the normal daily wage* and sent them out to work.

³"At nine o'clock in the morning he was passing through the marketplace and saw some people standing around doing nothing. ⁴So he hired them, telling them he would pay them whatever was right at

the end of the day. ⁵So they went to work in the vineyard. At noon and again at three o'clock he did the same thing.

⁶"At five o'clock that afternoon he was in town again and saw some more people standing around. He asked them, 'Why haven't you been working today?'

⁷"They replied, 'Because no one hired us.'

"The landowner told them, 'Then go out and join the others in my vineyard.'

⁸"That evening he told the foreman to call the workers in and pay them, beginning with the last workers first. ⁹When those hired at five o'clock were paid, each received a full day's wage. ¹⁰When those hired first came to get their pay, they assumed they would receive more. But they, too, were paid a day's wage. ¹¹When they received their pay, they protested to the owner, ¹²'Those people worked only one hour, and yet you've paid them just as much as you paid us who worked all day in the scorching heat.'

¹³"He answered one of them, 'Friend, I haven't been unfair! Didn't you agree to work all day for the usual wage? ¹⁴Take your money and go. I wanted to pay this last worker the same as you. ¹⁵Is it against the law for me to do what I want with my money? Should you be jealous because I am kind to others?'

¹⁶"So those who are last now will be first then, and those who are first will be last."

20:2 Greek *a denarius*, the payment for a full day's labor; similarly in 20:9, 10, 13.

NOTES

20:1 The chapter division here is misleading, since the parable of the vineyard workers occurs as an explanation for the cryptic saying of 19:30 about the reversal of those who are first (NLT "the greatest") and those who are last (NLT "least important"). The saying is repeated in 20:16 as the conclusion of the parable, so it is doubly clear that the parable completes Jesus' answer to Peter's question about reward in 19:27. Jesus' answer has two stages, the first a prosaic promise (19:28-30) and the second a poetic warning (20:1-16).

the Kingdom of Heaven is like. This is the usual way a parable is introduced (13:24, 31 etc.).

the landowner who went out early one morning to hire workers for his vineyard. The parable is about a landowner (13:27; 21:33) who hires, at different times during the day, five groups of workers to harvest his vineyard. The situation is one of socioeconomic extremes. A wealthy landowner hires poor men who must subsist on what they earn from day to day.

20:2 *the normal daily wage.* A denarius was the "normal daily wage" (so NLT mg; see 18:28; 22:19), and those hired at dawn are promised this amount.

20:3-7 The first "act" of the parable continues, as four additional groups of workers are hired throughout the day at successive intervals, 9 a.m. (20:3), noon (20:5), 3 p.m. (20:5), and 5 p.m. (20:6). The literal terms for the times of day were counted from 6 a.m., so 9 a.m. is lit. "the third hour," noon is "the sixth hour," 3 p.m. is "the ninth hour," and 5 p.m. is "the eleventh hour." It seems a bit unrealistic that workers would be hired throughout the day, but this may imply some urgency to complete the harvest.

marketplace. The workers are hired in the "marketplace," which in ancient towns was the center of activities (23:7).

he would pay them whatever was right. Those hired at 9 a.m., noon, and 3 p.m. were promised "whatever was right," and in their cases a fair wage would be progressively less than a denarius. Those hired at 5 p.m. would work a very short time and could expect only a small wage. One should note that the narrative of the hiring of the workers at 9 a.m., noon, and 3 p.m. is quite brief (20:3-5), contrasting with the more extended descriptions of the hiring of the first and last workers (20:1-2, 6-7). The stress is clearly on the first and last groups of workers. Hagner (1995:571) may be correct in stressing the detail that no one had hired the last group of workers all day long. For him, this signifies that no one had considered outcasts such as the tax collectors and sinners worthy of the Kingdom until Jesus called them to repentance.

20:8-9 *call the workers in and pay them.* The second "act" of the parable occurs after sundown (Lev 19:13; Deut 24:15; Josephus *Antiquities* 20.220), when the owner of the vineyard instructed his foreman to pay the workers.

each received a full day's wage. Those who were hired last would have been astonished to receive twelve times what they might expect.

20:10-11 *they assumed they would receive more.* Those who were hired first, who toiled all day in the heat, observed that those who worked only one hour were paid the amount for a full day's work. So they excitedly expected to receive much more.

they protested. When they were paid the same amount as those who only worked one hour, they protested (lit. "grumbled") to the vineyard owner.

20:13-14 *Friend, I haven't been unfair!"* The landowner addressed them as friends (22:12; 26:50) and told them they were treated fairly since they were paid what they had agreed to (20:2).

I wanted to pay this last worker the same as you. For unspecified reasons the owner of the vineyard wanted to be especially generous to the last group of workers. The other workers had no right to complain, since they received a normal wage.

20:15 The parable concludes with two rhetorical questions (20:15) that affirm that the owner of the vineyard acted legally and accuse the first workers of jealousy.

Should you be jealous because I am kind to others? Lit., "Is your eye evil because I am good?" The goodness of the landowner is probably intended to remind the reader of God, who alone is good (19:17). The expression "evil eye" reflects the deep envy of the first workers and possibly their intent to do harm to the owner of the vineyard (6:33; Mark 7:22; cf. Deut 15:9; Prov 23:6; 28:22; Tob 4:7; Sir 14:8-10). The landowner had been fair to those who worked all day (20:13) and generous to those who worked only a short time (20:14), since he wanted to treat all his workers equally (20:16; Blomberg 1990:224).

20:16 *So those who are last now will be first then, and those who are first will be last.* The parable, once concluded, is here framed with the same cryptic pronouncement that occurred just before it. The order of 20:16 reverses that of 19:30—there the first are mentioned before the last, but here the last are mentioned before the first. The idea of reversal is clear, but the identities of "the first" and "the last" are not. The NLT interprets correctly the reversal as the result of eschatological judgment with its adverbs "now" and "then," which are not in the Gr. text. The parable comes immediately after the promise of reward to the disciples that concludes Matthew 19. The first occurrence of the reversal pronounce-ment in 19:30 begins with "but," which implies that it is a warning against the simplistic assumption that reward is an automatic entitlement of the original disciples.

COMMENTARY

If a parable is "an earthly story with a heavenly meaning," one wonders about the heavenly counterparts of the earthlings described here. Most would agree that the vineyard stands for Israel (Isa 5:1-7; Jer 12:10; Matt 21:28, 33-39), and that the landowner represents God, who sovereignly and graciously bestows rewards upon his servants. The harvest speaks of eschatological judgment (see 13:39). Beyond this the identification of the first/greatest and last/least is more controversial. Perhaps "those who are first" represent Peter and the disciples, given Peter's question in 19:27. If so, Peter and the disciples are warned not to presume upon God's grace just because they sacrificed to serve his Kingdom. They will be fairly rewarded for their rigorous service, but they must not grumble if others who seem to have sacrificed less receive as great a reward as they do. In every case, God's generosity far outstrips human expectations, and we should not side with those who asked the question of 20:12. The servants may not complain if they receive a reward appropriate for their work. In the Kingdom, human standards of merit are replaced by divine generosity. This seems to be a true accounting for the details of the parable in its immediate context, but there are other interpretations of this imagery. See the discussion in Davies and Allison (1997:67-68).

Several approaches to the reversal described in this crucial saying (19:30; 20:16) are particularly noteworthy:

1. Social reversal. At the final judgment the poor will be enriched, and the rich will be impoverished. This Gospel has spoken of such a reversal in the Beatitudes (cf. 5:3), though this is a much stronger theme in Luke.
2. Religious reversal. The tax collectors and sinners who enter the Kingdom last are preferred by God to the Jewish religious leaders (Hagner 1995:573; Hill 1972:285). This is undoubtedly a key Matthean theme (9:11-13; 11:19; 21:31).
3. Redemptive-historical reversal. In God's plan, Gentiles instead of Jews will come into prominence (Gundry 1994:399). Matthew indicates in many places that surprisingly many Jews reject the Kingdom and many Gentiles receive it (8:10-12; 15:22-28). This may well be the most prominent view throughout the history of the church.
4. Ecclesiastical reversal. Those among the disciples who want to be prominent will be humbled, but those who are humble will be considered truly great. At least two important texts underline this point (18:1-4; 20:25-28).
5. Anthropological reversal. At the consummation of the age, God's sovereign grace will humble proud people and exalt humble people. While this is true, Matthew seems more concerned about the community of disciples than humanity at large.

The problem with all the above approaches is that they are not supported by the immediate context, which addresses the parable as a warning to Peter and the disciples that they should not presume on God's grace and rewards. They are the ones who are in danger of grumbling against God (cf. Exod 16:7-12; Num 14:27; Deut 1:27) when others who come into the Kingdom later are rewarded. They must accept whatever reward God graciously gives them, and they must not compare themselves with others. Thus, the parable of the landowner anticipates the problem of Zebedee's sons—ambitiously seeking the greatest rewards in the future Kingdom (20:20-28).

◆   4. Jesus predicts his death as a ransom for many (20:17-28;
         cf. Mark 10:32-45; Luke 18:31-33)

¹⁷As Jesus was going up to Jerusalem, he took the twelve disciples aside privately and told them what was going to happen to him. ¹⁸"Listen," he said, "we're going up to Jerusalem, where the Son of Man* will be betrayed to the leading priests and the teachers of religious law. They will sentence him to die. ¹⁹Then they will hand him over to the Romans* to be mocked, flogged with a whip, and crucified. But on the third day he will be raised from the dead."

²⁰Then the mother of James and John, the sons of Zebedee, came to Jesus with her sons. She knelt respectfully to ask a favor. ²¹"What is your request?" he asked.

She replied, "In your Kingdom, please let my two sons sit in places of honor next to you, one on your right and the other on your left."

²²But Jesus answered by saying to them, "You don't know what you are asking! Are you able to drink from the bitter cup of suffering I am about to drink?"

"Oh yes," they replied, "we are able!"

²³Jesus told them, "You will indeed drink from my bitter cup. But I have no right to say who will sit on my right or my left. My Father has prepared those places for the ones he has chosen."

²⁴When the ten other disciples heard what James and John had asked, they were indignant. ²⁵But Jesus called them together and said, "You know that the rulers in this world lord it over their people, and officials flaunt their authority over those under them. ²⁶But among you it will be different. Whoever wants to be a leader among you must be your servant, ²⁷and whoever wants to be first among you must become your slave. ²⁸For even the Son of Man came not to be served but to serve others and to give his life as a ransom for many."

20:18 "Son of Man" is a title Jesus used for himself.   20:19 Greek *the Gentiles.*

N O T E S

20:17-19 *Jesus was going up to Jerusalem.* The mention that Jesus had begun the ominous journey to Jerusalem lends drama and urgency to the third passion prediction (cf. Mark 10:32-34; Luke 18:31-34).

he took the twelve disciples aside privately. Matthew notes that this was a private announcement (cf. 17:1; 26:37), which probably was difficult since crowds constantly followed Jesus (19:2; 20:29).

hand him over to the Romans to be mocked, flogged with a whip, and crucified. This third passion prediction is more explicit than the first two in that it states that the Jewish authorities will condemn Jesus to death (26:66), but that the Gentile authorities will actually carry out the execution (27:2; cf. John 18:31). This is the first time crucifixion has been mentioned in the passion predictions (cf. 16:21; 17:22-23;). Crucifixion was a Roman form of execution, not a Jewish one (*m. Sanhedrin* 7:1-4), but it could be viewed in terms of Deut 21:23 as an indication of being cursed by God (cf. Gal 3:13). The mention of the leading priests and teachers of religious law recalls 2:4. The predicted details of Jesus' sufferings anticipate the occurrence of those sufferings: he was mocked (27:29-41; cf. Ps 22:7), flogged (27:26), and crucified (27:35), just as predicted here. The additional details of this third prediction serve to stress the exactness of Jesus' knowledge of what would happen. The involvement of both Jews and Romans stresses the universality of Jesus' rejection (Davies and Allison 1997:80-81). All three of the passion predictions conclude with the resurrection of Jesus, which becomes the central focus of the preaching of the early church (26:32; 27:63; 28:6; Acts 2:24; 3:15; 4:10; 5:30; 10:40-41; 1 Cor 15:4-8).

20:20 *the mother of James and John.* In obvious contrast to Jesus' projected sufferings, the mother of Zebedee's sons ironically sought their future glory (cf. Mark 10:35-45; Luke 22:24-30). The two sons of Zebedee were indeed James and John, but their names do not occur in the Gr. text of this verse (cf. 4:21; 10:2; 17:1; 26:37; 27:56).

knelt respectfully. This translates the same Gr. word (*proskuneō* [TG4352, ZG4686]) that in other contexts is translated "worship" (2:2, 11).

20:21 *in places of honor.* This does not occur in the Gr. text but brings out the implication of sitting at Jesus' right or left hand. These seats probably connote proximity to the king's prestige and authority in ruling the future Kingdom (19:28), rather than simply sitting next to him at the eschatological banquet (8:11) or at the final judgment (25:31-33). The fact that the mother made the request for her sons probably reflects negatively on them, not her (see next note). James, John, and their mother had not even begun to understand the significance of Jesus' repeated passion predictions or the meaning of such statements as found in 19:30, 20:16.

20:22 *You don't know what you are asking!* Jesus had asked the mother what she wanted from him, but at this point he addressed the mother and her sons. This implies that the sons had instigated their mother's original question. None of them understood the gravity of their request, or its monstrous inappropriateness at this point.

bitter cup of suffering. This translates one Gr. word (*potērion* [TG4221, ZG4539] "cup"). To be sure, drinking the cup is a metaphor for experiencing suffering (26:39; cf. Ps 75:8; Isa 51:17, 22; Jer 25:17; Ezek 23:31; John 18:11).

we are able! Their answer to Jesus' question was sincere, though brash, since they did not know what they were talking about. Similarly, they all promised Jesus at the Last Supper that they would not desert him in his sufferings (26:35).

20:23 *You will indeed drink from my bitter cup.* The disciples would share in drinking the cup—that is, in suffering with Jesus. James was later martyred by Herod Agrippa I, but John was evidently spared such a fate (John 21:20-23; Acts 12:1-2).

I have no right to say who will sit on my right or my left. My Father has prepared those places for the ones he has chosen. Jesus could not promise them the best seats in his future Kingdom. In accord with the mysterious reality of the incarnation, Jesus acknowledged his human limitations, much as he does in 24:36.

20:24 *when the ten other disciples heard what James and John had asked, they were indignant.* The NLT's "James and John" is lit. "the two brothers." The ambition of James and John angered the remaining disciples, probably because they were jealous.

20:25 This quest for status became an opportune time for teaching Kingdom values to all the disciples, similar to a previous occasion (18:1-4).

rulers in this world. Lit., "rulers of the Gentiles." Jesus once again explained the norms of the Kingdom for spiritual greatness (18:1-14; cf. 10:39; 16:25; 19:30; 23:11-12). He did this first by contrasting the values of the world (20:25) with the values of the Kingdom (20:26-27). Then he pointed to his own life and death as the model for their aspirations.

20:28 *the Son of Man came not to be served but to serve others and to give his life as a ransom for many.* While worldly rulers tend to flaunt their power and status with ostentatious displays of "pomp and circumstance," Jesus is the epitome of greatness because he has served and ransomed his people (see commentary below). On the authenticity of 20:28 as a saying of the historical Jesus, see Blomberg (1987:243-244); Carson (1984:432-433); Hagner (1995:579-580).

COMMENTARY

Matthew 20:17-28 narrates the third and fullest prediction of Jesus' passion, followed by an episode stressing the disciples' ambition. In this passage, Matthew contrasts Jesus' humility and suffering (20:17-19, 28) with the disciples' pride and desire for glory. The verses 20:17-19 contain the main elements of the two previous passion predictions: betrayal, death, and resurrection, but they also contain unique elements (discussed below). The structure of the second part of the passage involves a dialogue (20:20-23), which turns into an occasion of teaching (20:24-28). First, Jesus responded to a request from the mother of Zebedee's children (20:20-23). When the rest of the disciples learned of this, their anger became another opportunity for Jesus to teach his disciples about genuine greatness in his Kingdom (20:24-28). This teaching takes the form of two parallel statements about worldly greatness (20:25) in antithesis to two parallel statements about Kingdom greatness (20:26-27). True greatness involves following in Jesus' steps along the path of sacrificial service (20:28; cf. 10:38-39; 16:24-26; 19:21). In this passage the reader is influenced to respond in sympathy to Jesus and antipathy to the disciples. Their ignorance, pride, and false confidence contrast with Jesus' knowledge, humility, and acceptance of the Father's will.

Jesus' Passion Predictions. As noted previously, Matthew 20:17-19 is the third of three explicit predictions of Jesus' sufferings, death, and resurrection in Jerusalem. There are, of course, several implicit references to the Passion that prepare the reader for these explicit predictions (10:21, 24-25, 28, 38; 12:14, 38-40; 16:4). It is helpful to lay the three out side-by-side to note similarities and differences. When this is done, it is clear that the third prediction is the most detailed of the three. It stresses the imminence of Jesus' sufferings in Jerusalem, as well as the dual agency of his death by a Jewish sentence carried out by Roman authorities. There is also a detailed description of his horrible sufferings. Only the third prediction mentions that Jesus' death will be by crucifixion. The second prediction is the briefest. It alone omits mention of Jerusalem, but it alone mentions the grieving response of the disciples. Only the first prediction is presented as a summary of what Jesus said rather than as a direct quotation.

Jesus' Passion and the Disciples' Ambition. Matthew 20:20-28 is a remarkable study in the definition of authentic greatness. Ever since the fall of humanity, greatness has been defined in terms of prestige, power, and glory. Jesus alluded to this state of affairs in 20:25 and immediately repudiated it in 20:26. His definition of greatness in terms of service turns the world's model on its head. His disciples are to follow his example of sacrificial, suffering servanthood even to the point of death. Paul clearly grasped this radically altered definition of greatness (2 Cor 4:5; 10:1; 12:9-10; Phil 2:3-11), which McNeile (1949:290) defines as *servire est regnare* (to serve is to reign). One can do no better than to reflect on these words of Jesus from Luke's account of the Last Supper: "Who is more important, the one who sits at the table or the one who serves? . . . I am among you as one who serves." (Luke 22:27). John's account of Jesus' explanation of his washing the disciples' feet is also highly relevant here (John 13:12-17).

JESUS' THREE PASSION PREDICTIONS

Matthew 16:21	Matthew 17:22-23	Matthew 20:18-19
From then on Jesus began to tell his disciples plainly that it was necessary for him to go to Jerusalem, and that he would suffer many terrible things at the hands of the elders, the leading priests, and the teachers of religious law. He would be killed, but on the third day he would be raised from the dead.	After they had gathered together again in Galilee, Jesus told them, "The Son of Man is going to be betrayed. He will be killed, but on the third day he will be raised from the dead." And the disciples' hearts were filled with grief.	As Jesus was going up to Jerusalem, he took the twelve disciples aside privately and told them what was going to happen to him. "Listen," he said, "we're going up to Jerusalem, where the Son of Man will be betrayed to the leading priests and the teachers of religious law. They will sentence him to die. Then they will hand him over to the Romans to be mocked, flogged with a whip, and crucified. But on the third day he will be raised from the dead."

Words similar in the first and second predictions
Words similar in the first and third predictions
Words similar in the second and third predictions
Words similar in all three predictions

In this passage, the reader's emotions are torn between positive feelings for Jesus and negative feelings toward Jesus' disciples. Jesus has now spoken of his coming sufferings in Jerusalem three times, but, inexplicably, his disciples have forgotten their previous grief over this prospect. It is instructive to compare the selfish request of the mother of Zebedee's sons with the selfless request of the Canaanite woman for her daughter (15:21-28). One would have thought that the mother of two of Jesus' disciples would have had more spiritual insight than the Canaanite woman, but such was not the case. The disciples were preoccupied with thoughts of their own glory instead of concern for their Lord's sufferings. Davies and Allison (1997:82) put it well: "The loneliness of the Passion narrative begins here." Later, Peter and the very disciples who wanted to sit at Jesus' right and left in the Kingdom would sleep as Jesus agonized in the garden of Gethsemane (26:36-46). As Jesus predicted, he did not sit on a throne in Jerusalem but was crucified, with thieves on his right and left hand (27:38). How shocking it is to contemplate the disciples' insensitivity to Jesus' priorities! But it is all the more shocking to realize that many professed followers of Jesus still do not seem to grasp the nature of greatness in his Kingdom.

Jesus, a Ransom for Many. In giving himself as a "ransom" (*lutron* [TG3083, ZG3389]) for many, Jesus paid a price that frees them from slavery to sin (cf. Mark 10:45; Luke 1:68; 1 Tim 2:6; Titus 2:14; Heb 9:12; 1 Pet 1:18). The concept of ransom probably draws on such OT texts as Exodus 30:12, Psalm 49:7-9, and especially Isaiah 53:10-12, since

Matthew had previously viewed Jesus as the suffering servant in 8:17 (citing Isa 53:4) and 12:18-21 (citing Isa 42:1-4).

Matthew 20:28 recalls 1:21 and anticipates 26:28. In 1:21 it is stated that Jesus will save his people from their sins. This affirmation, a play on the meaning of the name "Jesus," indicates that the problem of Israel is not its occupation by Rome but its sin against God. But *how* would Jesus deliver his people from their sins? By paying a ransom that would free them from the bondage of alienation from God, according to 20:28. In view of the background in Isaiah 53:10-12, the haunting question of 16:26 (lit., "What can a man give in exchange for his soul?"), and the use of the preposition "for" (*anti* [TG473, ZG505], "instead of," "in behalf of") in 20:28, we should understand Matthew as teaching that redemption is vicarious; it comes when Jesus substitutes his own life for the lives of his people. But *when* will Jesus pay this ransom? According to 26:28, the wine of the Last Supper was intended as a sacred sign of Jesus' blood, shed for the remission of his people's sins. His blood was shed at his crucifixion, and clearly this was when the ransom was paid (cf. 1 Pet 1:18-19). The tearing of the Temple veil when Jesus died probably symbolizes the completion of this redemption (27:51). In summary, Jesus saved his people by shedding his blood as a ransom that frees them from the bondage of their sins. While this falls short of a comprehensive "doctrine" of the atonement, Davies and Allison (1997:100) are overly pessimistic when they say that "it is impossible to construct a Matthean theory of the atonement." While there are some unanswered questions, the general thrust is clear.

◆   ## 5. Jesus heals two blind men (20:29-34; cf. Mark 10:46-52; Luke 18:35-43)

²⁹As Jesus and the disciples left the town of Jericho, a large crowd followed behind. ³⁰Two blind men were sitting beside the road. When they heard that Jesus was coming that way, they began shouting, "Lord, Son of David, have mercy on us!"

³¹"Be quiet!" the crowd yelled at them. But they only shouted louder, "Lord, Son of David, have mercy on us!"

³²When Jesus heard them, he stopped and called, "What do you want me to do for you?"

³³"Lord," they said, "we want to see!" ³⁴Jesus felt sorry for them and touched their eyes. Instantly they could see! Then they followed him.

NOTES

20:29-30 The details of this pericope present several difficulties when compared with the accounts in Mark and Luke (cf. Mark 10:46-52; Luke 18:35-43; and Blomberg 1987:128-130).

As Jesus and the disciples left the town of Jericho. Since Jericho was about 10 miles northwest of the Dead Sea, they would need to walk about 15 miles southwest to reach Jerusalem. It would be an uphill climb of almost 3500 feet, since Jericho (846 feet below sea level) is in the Jordan rift valley, near the lowest spot on earth, the Dead Sea, and Jerusalem (2625 feet above sea level) is in the central hills of Judea.

Two blind men. Matthew has previously included another story of the healing of two blind men (9:27-31), but this is a different event. Perhaps Matthew intended that the two stories provide two witnesses to Jesus' power (Deut 19:15).

Lord, Son of David, have mercy on us! Jesus' reputation had evidently preceded him, since the blind men called out to him as soon as they heard he was coming. The blind men called Jesus "Lord" (7:21-22; 8:2; 9:28; 12:8; 14:28; 15:22) and "Son of David" (1:1, 20; 9:27; 12:23; 15:22; 21:9, 15; 22:42). These terms are often associated with healings in Matthew. The men asked Jesus to have mercy on them (cf. 5:7; 9:27; 15:22; 17:15; 18:33).

20:31 "Be quiet!" the crowd yelled. The crowd tried to silence the blind men, perhaps because they did not want Jesus to be delayed from his trip to Jerusalem. But the men cried out all the more when they were opposed.

20:32-34 What do you want me to do for you? Jesus stopped to help them, asking them what they wanted. This seemed obvious, but Jesus probably asked the question to draw out the men's faith.

we want to see! In response to their request that their eyes be opened, Jesus touched them (8:3, 15; 9:29), and instantly they saw (cf. 8:3). Jesus stood above the crowd in showing compassion to the blind men (cf. 9:36; 14:14; 15:32).

they followed him. It is significant that the men followed Jesus, evidently joining the throng making its way up to Jerusalem with him (21:8-9). Thus, the episode is framed as an *inclusio* by the references at its beginning and end to following Jesus (20:29, 34). The trip that began in 19:1 is nearly complete. At this point, Jesus' entry into Jerusalem might indeed seem triumphal, but the note of triumph will soon turn to tragedy.

COMMENTARY

Jesus had told his disciples that they were on their way to Jerusalem, and that he would be betrayed and crucified there (20:17-19). When they left Jericho, Jerusalem was only 15 miles away, and it was inevitable that the ominous events Jesus had predicted would occur soon. But Jesus could not focus on his own concerns since, as usual, he and the disciples were accompanied by a large crowd. On their journey, Jesus exercised compassion and healed two blind men. At their first cry for help, the crowd disdained them. But their faith was strong and they called out to Jesus again and again. Jesus had just told his disciples that greatness in his Kingdom is calculated on the scale of service, not power. He used his power to serve the blind men, who responded by following him on the way to Jerusalem. There was no need to command the blind men to be silent (contrast 8:4; 9:30), for Jesus' hour had come. Their cries to the Son of David would soon be echoed by others on the approach to Jerusalem, but the religious leaders there would not join the chorus (21:9, 15-16).

Summary and Transition. Matthew 20 begins with the parable of the landowner and workers (20:1-16). As noted in the last chapter, this parable is actually the conclusion of Jesus' answer to Peter's question in 19:27. The saying, "those who are last now will be first then, and those who are first will be last," brackets the parable (19:30; 20:16). Following the parable, there is a significant mention of Jerusalem in connection with Jesus' third Passion prediction (20:17-19). Then, the mother of Zebedee's children voices her ambitions for her sons (20:20-28). The chapter concludes with the healing of two blind men at Jericho, as Jesus drew ever closer to Jerusalem (20:29-34).

It is important to note that Matthew 20 revolves around Jesus' proximity to Jerusalem and plan to go there (20:17, 18, 29; cf. 16:21; 21:1, 10; 23:37). His passion prediction is made all the more dramatic by this nearness to Jerusalem. The mother of Zebedee's sons makes her request at a late hour in Jesus' earthly career, and Jesus' response stresses that his humble service to mankind involves his sacrificial death (20:28). The healing of the blind men features their messianic confession that Jesus is the Son of David, a confession soon echoed in Jerusalem at the Triumphal Entry (20:30-31; 21:9, 15). All these things tend to pique the reader's anticipation of the epochal events about to be accomplished in Jerusalem.

◆ 6. The Triumphal Entry into Jerusalem (21:1-11; cf. Mark 11:1-11; Luke 19:29-44; John 12:12-19)

As Jesus and the disciples approached Jerusalem, they came to the town of Bethphage on the Mount of Olives. Jesus sent two of them on ahead. 2"Go into the village over there," he said. "As soon as you enter it, you will see a donkey tied there, with its colt beside it. Untie them and bring them to me. 3If anyone asks what you are doing, just say, 'The Lord needs them,' and he will immediately let you take them."

4This took place to fulfill the prophecy that said,

5"Tell the people of Israel,*
   'Look, your King is coming to you.
   He is humble, riding on a donkey—
   riding on a donkey's colt.'"*

6The two disciples did as Jesus commanded. 7They brought the donkey and the colt to him and threw their garments over the colt, and he sat on it.*

8Most of the crowd spread their garments on the road ahead of him, and others cut branches from the trees and spread them on the road. 9Jesus was in the center of the procession, and the people all around him were shouting,

"Praise God* for the Son of David!
   Blessings on the one who comes in
      the name of the LORD!
   Praise God in highest heaven!"*

10The entire city of Jerusalem was in an uproar as he entered. "Who is this?" they asked.

11And the crowds replied, "It's Jesus, the prophet from Nazareth in Galilee."

21:5a Greek *Tell the daughter of Zion.* Isa 62:11. 21:5b Zech 9:9. 21:7 Greek *over them, and he sat on them.* 21:9a Greek *Hosanna,* an exclamation of praise that literally means "save now"; also in 21:9b, 15. 21:9b Pss 118:25-26; 148:1.

NOTES

21:1 *Jesus and the disciples approached Jerusalem.* Jesus finally approached the ultimate destination of his trip from Galilee, the city where he had predicted he would be crucified (16:21; 19:1; 20:18-19; cf. Mark 11:1-11; Luke 19:29-44; John 12:12-19). Getting to Jerusalem from Jericho involved an arduous uphill hike of about 15 miles in distance and about 3500 feet in altitude.

they came to the town of Bethphage on the Mount of Olives. The Mount of Olives is a ridge, about two and a half miles long, lying just east of Jerusalem and running roughly north and south (cf. 24:3; Zech 14:4). Bethphage is mentioned only here and in the Synoptic parallels (Mark 11:1; Luke 19:29). It was evidently located on the east slope of the

Mount of Olives near Bethany. When one comes from the east to the top of the Mount of Olives, the panorama of Jerusalem just across the Kidron Valley to the west is magnificent.

21:2-3 *a donkey tied there, with its colt beside it.* For his entrance into Jerusalem, Jesus told two disciples to acquire a donkey and its colt from a village near Bethphage. Perhaps this nearby village was Bethany (Mark 11:1). The disciples only needed to tell anyone who asked about their use of the donkeys that the Lord needed them. Jesus' plan to ride into Jerusalem on a donkey is hardly the picture of a conquering general mounted on a stallion.

21:4-5 Matthew cited Zech 9:9, with introductory words from Isa 62:11, to underline Jesus' humility (cf. John 12:14-15).

the people of Israel. Lit., "the daughter of Zion" (NLT mg), a common OT expression that refers to Jerusalem and its inhabitants (cf. 2 Kgs 19:21; Isa 37:22; Jer 4:31; Lam 1:6; Mic 4:8; Zeph 3:14).

Look, your King is coming to you. He is humble. Zechariah 9:9 mentions that the coming King will be just, have salvation, and be humble, but Matthew includes only the last characteristic, humility. The prophecies of Zechariah frequently concern the troubles of Jerusalem and God's concern for it (Zech 1:12-17; 2:2-5; 3:2; 8:3-8; 12:3,10; 13:1; 14:4-9). Particularly noteworthy are texts that speak of God's coming or return to Zion (Zech 1:16; 8:3; 14:4, 16), the joining of Gentiles to the people of God (Zech 2:11; 8:22-23; 9:9), and the eschatological worship of the King (Zech 14:9, 16-17).

riding on a donkey—riding on a donkey's colt. In Zech 9:9 the words "donkey" and "donkey's colt" are arranged in synonymous parallelism and do not refer to two animals.

21:6 *The two disciples did as Jesus commanded.* In some unknown way, God's providence had prepared those in charge of the donkeys to permit Jesus to use them (Luke 19:32-34).

21:7 *They . . . threw their garments over the colt and he sat on it.* The Gr. text says the disciples put their garments on *both* donkeys and that Jesus sat on *them*. Grammatically the pronoun "them" may refer either to the donkeys or to the garments thrown on the donkeys. It seems doubtful that Matthew is affirming that Jesus somehow straddled both animals, although some scholars argue that Matthew did intend this due to a misunderstanding of the Heb. parallelism in Zech 9:9 (Meier 1978:21-22, 144). Hagner (1995:594) thinks Matthew understood the parallelism but maximized the details of the correspondence with Zech 9:9 with a typically rabbinic hermeneutic. Instead, the idea is probably that Jesus rode on the garments spread on the colt (cf. Mark 11:2; Luke 19:35; John 12:14). Only Matthew mentions two donkeys; Mark and Luke state that Jesus rode a colt that had never been previously ridden. Matthew's mention of the colt's mother highlights its youth and the fact that it had not been ridden before. For further discussion see Davies and Allison (1997:120-123).

21:8 *spread their garments on the road . . . others cut branches.* The crowd's spreading garments and palm branches on the road is a festive acknowledgement of Jesus' kingship (cf. 1 Kgs 1:32-40; 2 Kgs 9:13; 1 Macc 5:45-54; 13:51; 2 Macc 10:7).

21:9 *praise God for the Son of David!* Lit., "Hosanna to the Son of David" (see NLT mg). Hosanna is a cry for help ("Save!"), but was used idiomatically as an expression of jubilant praise. Jesus is frequently called "the Son of David" in Matthew (1:1; 9:27; 12:23; 15:22; 20:30-31; cf. 12:3; 22:41-46; 2 Sam 7:8, 12-16). Another messianic title is "the one who comes" (3:11; 11:3; 23:39; Ps 118:26). "Praise God in highest heaven" probably echoes Ps 148:1 (cf. Luke 2:14; 19:38). Psalms 113–118 were known as the Hallel and were frequently sung during Israel's major feasts. Sadly, the excitement of the crowd was not in the end matched by faithful commitment to Jesus (27:20). Their confession that Jesus was a prophet turned out to be inadequate (21:11).

21:10-11 *It's Jesus, the prophet from Nazareth in Galilee.* Even though Jerusalem was accustomed to large crowds of pilgrims during major festivals, Jesus' entrance into the city resulted in a major uproar. All over the city, people were asking about the identity of the one who had clamorously entered the city (cf. 2:3). The answer of the exultant crowds here did not echo the messianic terms used in 21:9. Instead, Jesus was described merely as the prophet from Nazareth in Galilee (2:23; 13:54; see also 16:13-14). This was accurate but fell short of fully describing Jesus. Hagner's suggestion (1995:596) that the crowds in 21:11 were Jerusalem residents, not the crowd of pilgrims as in 20:29; 21:8, 9, is doubtful.

COMMENTARY

The scene played out at Jesus' entry into Jerusalem is a familiar one. A conquering king parades triumphantly into a city with all the trappings of glory and power (Davies and Allison 1997:112-113). But there is something very strange about this Triumphal Entry. The king was clothed plainly, not in royal robes or in full military splendor. He rode an unpretentious young donkey, not a dashing war horse. He was meek, not militaristic. His entry sent mixed signals, and it is no wonder that all Jerusalem was perplexed about his identity. Paradoxically, Jesus' entry combined the trappings of power and glory with the imagery of humility. Throughout his ministry, his teaching and example had exalted humility and downplayed pride (5:5; 8:20; 11:25; 12:18-21; 16:24-25; 18:4; 19:14; 20:26-28; 21:5; 23:12). The "Triumphal" Entry epitomizes the upside-down values of the Kingdom. Jesus radically shifted the world's paradigm of greatness, showing greatness to be found in humble service, not arrogant rule. For a very different picture, one of Jesus' return in judgment, see Revelation 19:11-16.

There is much irony in the shouts of the crowd. They were at the same time correct and incorrect. They were correct in ascribing messianic language to Jesus, but incorrect in their understanding of the meaning of that language. They rightly quoted messianic texts, but they wrongly thought of their Messiah as a conquering military hero. And this is not surprising, since even the disciples still struggled to grasp Jesus' words, "among you it will be different" (20:26). For this reason the Triumphal Entry was also a tragic entry.

◆ ## 7. Jesus clears the Temple (21:12-17; cf. Mark 11:15-18; Luke 19:45-48)

[12]Jesus entered the Temple and began to drive out all the people buying and selling animals for sacrifice. He knocked over the tables of the money changers and the chairs of those selling doves. [13]He said to them, "The Scriptures declare, 'My Temple will be called a house of prayer,' but you have turned it into a den of thieves!"*

[14]The blind and the lame came to him in the Temple, and he healed them. [15]The leading priests and the teachers of religious law saw these wonderful miracles and heard even the children in the Temple shouting, "Praise God for the Son of David."

But the leaders were indignant. [16]They asked Jesus, "Do you hear what these children are saying?"

"Yes," Jesus replied. "Haven't you ever read the Scriptures? For they say, 'You have taught children and infants to give you praise.'*" [17]Then he returned to Bethany, where he stayed overnight.

21:13 Isa 56:7; Jer 7:11.   21:16 Ps 8:2.

NOTES

21:12 Jesus entered the Temple and began to drive out all the people buying and selling animals. Having entered the city proper, Jesus proceeded to the Temple area and disrupted the financial transactions going on there (cf. Mark 11:15-18; Luke 19:45-48). While his entry to the city was royal, his action in the Temple was prophetic (Davies and Allison 1997:133-134). Previous "cleansings" of the Temple were accomplished by Josiah, Hezekiah, and Judah Maccabaeus (2 Kgs 23:1-7; 2 Chr 29:3-11; 1 Macc 4; 2 Macc 10). This episode reinforces the previous episode's stress on Jesus as the messianic Son of David. In distinction from the Synoptic accounts that Jesus cleared the Temple at the end of his ministry, John's Gospel describes a similar scene at the beginning of Jesus' ministry (John 2:14-22). It is possible that John adapted the Synoptic account for literary purposes, but it is more likely that there were two clearings of the Temple by Jesus.

It is important to realize that the word "Temple" (*hieron* [TG2411, ZG2639]) refers to the entire walled complex, which was roughly rectangular, with the area of thirty-five football fields. The outer Court of the Gentiles was probably where Jesus drove out the merchants, healed the blind and lame, and received the children's praise (21:12, 14-15). The first inner court was the Court of the Women, where all Jews could enter (evidently the case in Mark 12:44; Luke 2:37; John 8:2-3). Only ritually pure Jewish males could go further, into the Court of the Israelites, where the sacrificial altar stood (as may be the case in Mark 11:11; Luke 18:11; 24:53). Beyond this area was the Temple proper, or Court of the Priests, where only priests could go (Herzog in Green and McKnight 1992:812).

the tables of the money changers. Money changers were necessary because many pilgrims holding foreign coins were present at the major festivals, such as Passover. Presumably, the pilgrims would exchange their currency to pay the half-shekel Temple tax (17:24; Exod 30:11-16; *m. Sheqalim*). Doves were a permissible sacrifice for those who could not afford a lamb for a sin offering, a firstborn offering, or an offering for the ritual purity of a recent mother (Luke 2:22-24; Lev 5:7, 11; 12:6, 8). Jesus' disgust was probably not due merely to mercantile activities, since those were required by the Law itself. He was likely angry because those transactions were taking place within the Temple itself or because the merchants were dealing dishonestly with the pilgrims—or both. Perhaps money was not being changed equitably, and the pilgrims were being charged exorbitant prices for their sacrificial animals (21:13; *m. Keritot* 1:7).

21:13 'My Temple will be called a house of prayer,' but you have turned it into a den of thieves. Jesus' disruptive acts are based on his biblical citations, which highlight monstrous incongruity of turning a house of prayer into a den of thieves (Isa 56:7; Jer 7:11). The word translated "thieves" (*lēstēs*) can have overtones of insurrection or guerilla warfare (26:55; 27:38, 44; BDAG 594). If this is the case, Jesus' action is not simply against dishonesty but also against revolutionary extremism. Possibly Jesus' actions should be viewed as a portent of the Temple's destruction by the Romans in AD 70 (Evans 1989).

21:14 The blind and the lame came to him in the Temple. In addition to acting against dishonest practices in the Temple, Jesus acted on behalf of the physically needy there. This account of the healing of blind and lame people in the Temple (evidently in the outer court of the Gentiles; cf. Lev 21:17-23; *m. Hagigah* 1:1) is the last record of healing miracles in Matthew (cf. 11:5; 15:30-31).

21:15-16 As Blomberg (1992:315) points out, Jesus' activities in the Temple model the values of Hos 6:6—God prefers mercy over sacrifice (cf. 9:12-13; 12:7).

leading priests and the teachers of religious law. These were the ones consulted by Herod as to the place of Jesus' birth, and they appear in two of Jesus' Passion predictions (2:4; 16:21; 20:18). Given their earlier opposition, the indignation of the religious leaders is not

at all surprising. They were evidently incensed at Jesus' miracles and at the messianic over-tones of the cries of the children, which echo the citation of Ps 118:26 in Matt 21:9.
Haven't you ever read the Scriptures? For they say, "You have taught children and infants to give you praise." Jesus cited Ps 8:2 to vindicate the cries of the children. His introductory formula stresses their ignorance, or rather their obstinacy (cf. 12:3, 5; 19:4; 21:42). They had read but would not believe that Jesus was the Messiah. In contrast, the "children and infants" praise Jesus in messianic language, and once again the theme of the "little ones" receiving the Kingdom is stressed by Jesus, this time as endorsed by the Psalm (cf. 10:42; 11:25; 18:6). Psalm 8 is understood messianically elsewhere in the NT (1 Cor 15:27; Eph 1:22; Phil 3:21; Heb 2:6-9; 1 Pet 3:22).
21:17 *he returned to Bethany.* After this confrontation with the leaders, Jesus left the reli-gious leaders in the Temple and returned to Bethany (26:6; cf. Mark 11:1, 11-12; 14:3; Luke 19:29; 24:50; John 11:1, 18; 12:1) to spend the night there.

COMMENTARY

Unexpectedly, Jesus' first action upon entering Jerusalem was not to deliver it from the oppressive Roman occupying forces but to deliver it from its own hypocrisy. Instead of directly threatening the political status quo, he confronted the Temple, the religious center of Israel, and its established leadership. Instead of being a house of prayer, it had been perverted into a center of commercial activity. It is not com-pletely clear whether Jesus objected to commerce in the outer Temple courts as a matter of principle, or whether his actions were directed against unscrupulous greed that capitalized on the sincere religious motives of the pilgrims. At any rate, it is sig-nificant that his major activities in the Temple were directed against hypocrisy and on behalf of the needy. Like the prophets before him, Jesus spoke and acted against the corruption of Israel's established worship and for those who were without sta-tus. Therefore, Jesus' acts in the Temple augur the eschatological reversal in which the meek "will inherit the earth," while corrupt leaders will be brought low.

The Christology implicit in this episode is impressive. Jesus' acts of healing in the Temple and of clearing it both demonstrate what he said earlier in 12:6: "there is one here who is even greater than the Temple" (cf. Mal 3:1). When Jesus cited Ps 8:2 to vindicate the children's praise, he implicitly claimed to be worthy of the praise and worship that the psalm directs to God the Creator. For Matthew such insight is due to divine revelation, not human intellect or intuition (11:25). It is altogether fitting that mere children have a better grasp of Jesus' identity than the established hierarchy of Israel.

Renewal or Destruction?   It has been common to view Jesus' action in the Temple as an act of correction or purification. But some argue that Jesus was not so much re-forming the Temple as announcing its doom. Jesus did, in fact, predict the destruc-tion of the Temple (24:2), but the activities portrayed in the Gospels do not confront the sacrificial ministry of the Temple. Instead they confront the commer-cial enterprises that were parasitic to it. Jesus did not interfere with the priests but with those engaged in financial transactions. In the OT, the prophets commonly denounced the corruption of the Temple and its priests, but such oracles oppose abuses of the sacrificial system rather than the system itself (Jer 6:13; Ezek 7-10;

Hos 4:4-6; Mic 3:11; Zeph 3:4). The corruption of Jerusalem and the Temple is also cited in later Jewish texts (*Jubilees* 23:21; *1 Enoch* 83–90; *4 Ezra* 3:25-27; *2 Baruch* 1:1-5; 13:4; *Apocalypse of Abraham* 27:1-7; *4 Baruch* 4:3-8; Josephus *Antiquities* 20:179-181, 204-207, 213).

Davies and Allison (1997:135-137) rightly conclude that the cleansing of the Temple was an act that symbolized both the reformation of abuses and the judgment to come if the abuses continued. Protest against present corruption and prediction of future destruction are not mutually exclusive, especially when there is hope for repentance (23:39) and the rise of an eschatological Temple (Ezek 40–48). Genuine prophetic activity in the Old Testament not only predicted judgment and hope but also confronted Israel's abandonment of covenant obligations. It may be that Matthew saw in Jesus' acts a fulfillment of the Lord's coming suddenly into his Temple (Mal 3:1). Another possibility is stated by the most likely translation of Zechariah 14:21, which envisions a day in which there will be no more merchants in the house of the Lord.

◆   ## 8. Jesus curses the fig tree (21:18-22; cf. Mark 11:19-25)

18In the morning, as Jesus was returning to Jerusalem, he was hungry, 19and he noticed a fig tree beside the road. He went over to see if there were any figs, but there were only leaves. Then he said to it, "May you never bear fruit again!" And immediately the fig tree withered up.

20The disciples were amazed when they saw this and asked, "How did the fig tree wither so quickly?"

21Then Jesus told them, "I tell you the truth, if you have faith and don't doubt, you can do things like this and much more. You can even say to this mountain, 'May you be lifted up and thrown into the sea,' and it will happen. 22You can pray for anything, and if you have faith, you will receive it."

NOTES

21:18-19 *he was hungry.* Jesus looked for figs on a roadside tree and found the tree had leaves but no fruit (cf. 21:34).

May you never bear fruit again! Jesus pronounced a curse upon the tree, and it immediately withered, showing that it indeed would never bear fruit again. The cursing of the fig tree amounts to a prophetic parable in action (cf. Isa 8:1-4; Jer 13:1-9; Ezek 5:1-4; Hos 1:2-9). The tree probably should be understood as a symbol, not of Israel as a whole (Blomberg 1992:318; Hagner 1995:603-04), but of Jerusalem and the leaders of Israel, particularly the Temple leaders (Davies and Allison 1997:148, 151-52; Overman 1995: 295-96). Fruitless fig trees are used in OT prophetic texts as symbols of judgment (Isa 34:4; Jer 8:13; 24:1-10; Hos 2:12; Joel 1:7).

21:20-22 *How did the fig tree wither so quickly?* The object lesson of the fig tree received a new twist when Jesus responded to his disciples' question. (In Mark's account this happens on the next day; Matthew's account has evidently telescoped events that originally took place over two days into a single narrative; cf. Mark 11:12-14, 20-24). The disciples' amazement at how rapidly the tree withered overrides their perception of why the tree has withered and what it signifies. Again they lacked understanding of what Jesus was doing, and their question was beside the point. But Jesus used the occasion to teach them about faith and answers to prayer.

if you have faith and don't doubt, you can do things like this and much more. If the disciples pray in faith (6:8; 7:7-11; 18:19), they will see even greater things than a tree wither, such as a mountain being thrown into the sea (cf. 17:19-20; Luke 17:6; Rom 4:20; 1 Cor 13:2; Jas 1:6). This emphasis on believing prayer for the power of God to do what is humanly impossible must be correlated with the emphasis on asking for God's will to be de done, as found in the Lord's Prayer (6:9-13).

this mountain. If Jesus was speaking of the Temple mount when he referred to "this mountain" being thrown into the sea, the cursing of the fig tree portends the destruction of the Temple in AD 70 by the Romans (Telford 1980).

COMMENTARY

The cursing of the fig tree is the third symbolic act of Jesus in this context. Jesus had ridden a donkey's colt into the city and cleared its Temple of commercial activity. These acts respectively convey Jesus' kingly and prophetic roles. The prophetic role continues in the cursing of the fig tree, which, by all accounts, appears to be one of the strangest things Jesus ever did. But if one consults the Old Testament passages cited above (in the notes on 21:18-19), one will recognize that the symbolic acts of the prophets (living parables) were often strange. The rebuke or cursing of the fig tree conveys two theological lessons.

First, the barren tree pictures the fruitless religious leaders, whose Temple was recently cleared. The leaders did not appreciate Jesus, while the children did (21:15-16). They responded to Jesus' undeniable miracles by questioning Jesus' authority instead of praising God for his blessings. The fruitlessness of the leaders has been stressed all along in Matthew. It is pointed out very strongly again here, but Jesus' full and final denunciation will come in Matthew 23. The rejection of God's messengers will have consequences. Second, the weak disciples still need to develop faith in the power of God to answer their prayers. Their "little faith" was rebuked by Jesus before (6:30; 8:26; 14:31; 16:8; 17:20), and once again they were challenged to grow in it. It is appropriate that this lesson occurs in a context connected with the Temple, since it is "called a house of prayer" (21:13; Isa 56:7). Perhaps the reason these two seemingly unrelated lessons are put together here is to contrast the fruitlessness of the unbelieving religious leaders with the potential fruitfulness of Jesus' believing disciples (Hagner 1995:606-607).

◆   ## 9. The authority of Jesus challenged (21:23-32; cf. Mark 11:27-33; Luke 20:1-8)

23When Jesus returned to the Temple and began teaching, the leading priests and elders came up to him. They demanded, "By what authority are you doing all these things? Who gave you the right?"

24"I'll tell you by what authority I do

these things if you answer one question," Jesus replied. 25"Did John's authority to baptize come from heaven, or was it merely human?"

They talked it over among themselves. "If we say it was from heaven, he will ask us why we didn't believe John. ²⁶But if we say it was merely human, we'll be mobbed because the people believe John was a prophet." ²⁷So they finally replied, "We don't know."

And Jesus responded, "Then I won't tell you by what authority I do these things.

²⁸"But what do you think about this? A man with two sons told the older boy, 'Son, go out and work in the vineyard today.' ²⁹The son answered, 'No, I won't go,' but later he changed his mind and went anyway. ³⁰Then the father told the other son, 'You go,' and he said, 'Yes, sir, I will.' But he didn't go.

³¹"Which of the two obeyed his father?" They replied, "The first."*

Then Jesus explained his meaning: "I tell you the truth, corrupt tax collectors and prostitutes will get into the Kingdom of God before you do. ³²For John the Baptist came and showed you the right way to live, but you didn't believe him, while tax collectors and prostitutes did. And even when you saw this happening, you refused to believe him and repent of your sins."

21:29-31 Other manuscripts read *"The second."* In still other manuscripts the first son says "Yes" but does nothing, the second son says "No" but then repents and goes, and the answer to Jesus' question is that the second son obeyed his father.

NOTES

21:23-26 By what authority are you doing all these things? When Jesus returned to the Temple, the question of the religious leaders about his authority (cf. Mark 11:27-33) renewed the controversy that began in 21:12-16. This running controversy grew more and more heated as it led up to the prophetic woes of Matt 23. The leading priests and elders (26:3, 47; 27:1, 3, 12, 20) were in charge of the Temple, so it is not surprising that they questioned Jesus' presumption in acting as he had (cf. Acts 4:7).

I'll tell you . . . if you answer one question. Jesus did not answer their question directly but struck a sort of bargain with them. If they would answer his question, he would answer theirs. His question about whether John the Baptist's authority was human or divine (cf. Acts 5:38-39) put them in a quandary. If they said John's authority was merely human, they would anger the crowds who believed John and Jesus to be true prophets. (For the leaders' fear of the crowds, cf. 14:5; 21:46. The Jewish historian Josephus also speaks of the wide popularity of John the Baptist in *Antiquities* 18.118). But if the leaders affirmed that John's authority was divine (cf. 11:7-15), their unbelief in John and Jesus and rejection of divine authority would be exposed. Jesus' response to their question with one of his own is typical in all of his encounters with the religious leaders in this section of Matthew. The leaders were repeatedly tripped up in their attempts to trip up Jesus (21:25-27; 22:21-22, 42-46). Jesus' authority is already a familiar theme in Matthew (7:29; 8:9; 9:6; 10:1; 28:19; cf. Acts 4:7-10).

21:27 We don't know. The only way out of the quandary for the religious leaders was to feign ignorance. In reality, this was a refusal to answer, and it betrays their negative estimate of John.

Then I won't tell you. Jesus responded in kind to their feigned ignorance by refusing to answer their question about his authority. But "his refusal is in fact veiled affirmation" of John (Davies and Allison 1997:162).

21:28-30 A man with two sons. Jesus' response to their question does not end in this stalemate. It continues with a parable about two sons who respond oppositely to their father's request to work in his vineyard (cf. 20:1; 21:33). The father's two commands and the responses of the two sons are exactly parallel in terms of literary structure but exactly opposite in terms of ethics. The first son initially agrees to work but eventually does not. The second initially refuses but eventually does work. This is the first of a set of three parables that rebuke the religious leaders for their unbelief (21:28-32, 33-44; 22:1-14). For a discussion of the textual difficulties referred to in the NLT mg on 21:29-31, see Metzger (1994:44-46).

21:31-32 *Which of the two obeyed his father?* Jesus applies the parable by asking the leaders another question, and this time they do answer.

The first. This answer condemned them. Since they did not believe John, they are like the first son who did not work in the vineyard even though he said he would. In contrast, since the tax collectors and prostitutes (cf. 9:10-11; 11:19) did believe John, they were like the second son who did work in the vineyard even though he said he would not.

tax collectors and prostitutes will get into the Kingdom of God before you do. These notorious sinners who repent will enter the Kingdom before the leaders who do not believe the Kingdom message.

even when you saw this happening, you refused to believe him. The leaders were still unrepentant, even after they saw the repentance of the notorious sinners. Their righteousness was like a tree with leaves but no fruit (21:19). The dregs of society who believed the gospel would enter the Kingdom of God (cf. 21:43), but these leaders would not (cf. 5:20). Jesus' statement that John showed the right way to live amounts to a statement that John's authority came from heaven. With that heavenly authority John pointed to Jesus.

COMMENTARY

The question put to Jesus about the source of his authority was not an innocent one (Blomberg 1992:319; Davies and Allison 1997:159). Matthew's narrative shows that Jesus' powerful words and works repeatedly made it plain to the religious leaders that Jesus' authority was from heaven (9:1-8; 12:6, 8, 28, 41-42; 15:1-12). But they were less perceptive than the crowd they presumed to lead, since even the crowd regarded John and Jesus as prophets. The leaders' question was motivated by animosity and probably by the desire to trap Jesus into saying something that could be construed as blasphemous (9:3; 22:15; 26:63-65). But Jesus turned the tables on this line of questioning by asking the leaders a question they dared not answer—the question about the source of John's authority (21:25). Then he asked them to respond to a parable about two sons, and this time they did answer, with devastating consequences (21:28-31). Their sin was not only refusing to perform what they promised, like the second son, but it was also refusing to follow the example of the first son, who symbolizes the tax collectors and prostitutes, whose repentance ought to have influenced the leaders to repent (21:32).

It is clear from this passage that being a disciple of the Kingdom involves deeds, not mere words (cf. 7:21-27). One's initial words may be reversed by one's subsequent deeds, and it is one's deeds that matter. It is astonishing to think that the Temple officials, despite their knowledge of the law and religious occupation, did not perform the will of the Father. Even more so, they did not contemplate the grace of God in drawing notorious sinners to repentance and into the Kingdom (cf. 9:10-13). This passage warns Christians today not to presume upon their own supposed righteous standing before God and not to assume that the unrighteous status of notorious sinners cannot change. One dare not be complacent about one's own supposed righteousness any more than the supposed unrighteousness of another. The call of the Father into the Kingdom is still powerful today, but entrance into the Kingdom is promised not to those who merely say "Lord, Lord," but to those who actually do the will of the Father (7:21).

Israel and the Church. It has been common for Christian exegetes to view the parable of the two sons in terms of salvation history, with the first son, who initially refused but later obeyed, representing the Gentiles, and the second son, who initially promised but later refused, representing Israel (Chrysostom, *Homily on Matthew*, 67.2; Meier 1978:149-150). However, this interpretation posits something not found in the context—namely, the relationship of Jews and Gentiles in God's overall plan. The contextual focus is on the response of the Jews to John, so it is much preferable to see the parties contrasted in this parable as groups within Israel, not as Jews versus Gentiles. The messages of both John and Jesus confront the Jews with an eschatological reversal in which the unrepentant establishment is replaced by repentant people of no status. But the enfranchised replacements are just as Jewish as the disenfranchised former leaders. And the lesson to today's predominantly Gentile church is to avoid repeating the error of the Jewish establishment, just as Paul taught in Romans 11:19-22. (For further discussion on this theme, see the notes and commentary on 21:43.)

◆   **10. The parable of the evil farmers (21:33-46; cf. Mark 12:1-12; Luke 20:9-19)**

³³"Now listen to another story. A certain landowner planted a vineyard, built a wall around it, dug a pit for pressing out the grape juice, and built a lookout tower. Then he leased the vineyard to tenant farmers and moved to another country. ³⁴At the time of the grape harvest, he sent his servants to collect his share of the crop. ³⁵But the farmers grabbed his servants, beat one, killed one, and stoned another. ³⁶So the landowner sent a larger group of his servants to collect for him, but the results were the same.

³⁷"Finally, the owner sent his son, thinking, 'Surely they will respect my son.' ³⁸But when the tenant farmers saw his son coming, they said to one another, 'Here comes the heir to this estate. Come on, let's kill him and get the estate for ourselves!' ³⁹So they grabbed him, dragged him out of the vineyard, and murdered him.

⁴⁰"When the owner of the vineyard returns," Jesus asked, "what do you think he will do to those farmers?"

⁴¹The religious leaders replied, "He will put the wicked men to a horrible death and lease the vineyard to others who will give him his share of the crop after each harvest."

⁴²Then Jesus asked them, "Didn't you ever read this in the Scriptures?

'The stone that the builders rejected
   has now become the cornerstone.
This is the LORD's doing,
   and it is wonderful to see.'*

⁴³I tell you, the Kingdom of God will be taken away from you and given to a nation that will produce the proper fruit. ⁴⁴Anyone who stumbles over that stone will be broken to pieces, and it will crush anyone it falls on.*"

⁴⁵When the leading priests and Pharisees heard this parable, they realized he was telling the story against them—they were the wicked farmers. ⁴⁶They wanted to arrest him, but they were afraid of the crowds, who considered Jesus to be a prophet.

21:42 Ps 118:22-23.   **21:44** This verse is omitted in some early manuscripts. Compare Luke 20:18.

NOTES

21:33 listen to another story. This second confronting parable (cf. Mark 12:1-12; Luke 20:9-19) is based on the familiar OT image of a vineyard (21:28; cf. Ps 80:8-12; Isa 27:2-6; Jer 2:21; 12:10; Ezek 19:10-14; Hos 10:1; *1 Enoch* 10:16; 84:6; *Jubilees* 1:16; *Psalms of Solomon* 14:3-4; Elliott 2000:329-344). But this time the vineyard workers are tenant farmers, not the owner's sons.

he leased the vineyard to tenant farmers. The song of the vineyard in Isa 5:1-7 is specifically alluded to here, but Matthew adds the crucial new element of the tenant farmers who leased the vineyard while the owner went on a journey. The vineyard is Israel, the receptor of God's Kingdom blessings (21:43; Isa 5:7); the tenant farmers are Israel's leaders (21:43, 45).

moved to another country. This translates a word (*apedēmēsen* [TG589, ZG623]) that simply means to go away on a journey. Unlike the wealthy landowner of 20:1 who oversees his own harvest, this absentee owner hires tenants to work his land. For a detailed study of the parable see Snodgrass (1983).

21:34 to collect his share of the crop. As the parable proceeds, the crucial matter is the owner's receiving his share of the crop. Lit., this crop is "fruit," a key Matthean metaphor for right living or obedience to God's law (3:10; 7:16-20; 12:33; 13:8; 21:19, 34, 41, 43). Israel's covenant relationship with God obligated her leaders to righteousness, just as the tenant farmers were obligated by contract to produce fruit for the owner of the vineyard.

21:35-36 the farmers grabbed his servants, beat one, killed one, and stoned another. Another group of servants (lit. "slaves") is mistreated in the same way.

21:37-39 sent his son. The third time the owner sends his son (10:40; 15:24), thinking the son will be respected by the farmers. But the farmers also kill the son, thinking they will get the vineyard for themselves if they murder the heir. It is clear from both the OT and from Matthew itself that the maltreatment of the slaves and son sent by the landowner is meant to picture Israel's ongoing rejection of her prophets (1 Kgs 18:4; 2 Chr 24:19-21; 36:16; Neh 9:26-30; Jer 7:25-26; 20:1-2; 26:20-24; Dan 9:6, 10; Matt 5:12; 22:6; 23:29-37; cf. Acts 7:52; 1 Thess 2:15; Heb 11:33–12:1; Rev 11:3-7).

dragged him out of the vineyard, and murdered him. The detail that the son was thrown out of the vineyard before being killed may be intended as a veiled reference to Jesus' crucifixion outside the city walls in keeping with OT law (Lev 24:14; Num 15:36; Deut 17:5; 21:9; Heb 13:12). This parable clearly sets the scene for Jesus' accusation in Matt 23:29-36 that the leaders of Israel have frequently rejected God's prophets and are now about to reject him. At this point in the story, one is impressed not only by the unprovoked violence of the evil farmers but also by the extreme patience, if not foolhardiness, of the owner. But the story is not over. How will the owner respond to the atrocity of his son's murder?

21:40-41 He will put the wicked men to a horrible death. At this point Jesus applied the story by drawing his listeners into it and asking them how it would end. They knew all too well that the remarkable patience of the owner had reached its end, and they told Jesus that the owner would bring the farmers to an end fitting their wicked deeds.

lease the vineyard to others. The owner would then replace the wicked farmers with new farmers, who would render to the owner his share of the produce. Again, the religious leaders were condemned by their own words (21:31).

21:42-43 Jesus' gives his interpretation of the landowner's replacement of the tenants. The reference to the owner's getting his share of the crop after each harvest (lit. "the fruits in their seasons") may allude to Ps 1:3 (cf. 21:34, 43).

Didn't you ever read this in the Scriptures? Jesus' incredulous question reproves the religious leaders and recalls 12:3; 19:4; 21:16. The leaders are again portrayed as ignorant of the Scriptures, and of Ps 118:22 in particular.

The stone that the builders rejected has now become the cornerstone. Parts of Psalm 118 have already been cited in 21:9, 15, and Ps 118:22 also appears in Acts 4:11 and 1 Pet 2:7 (cf. Isa 8:14; 28:16). In light of the Psalms Targum, an ancient translation of the original Heb. into Aramaic, the citation of this verse probably involves a play on words "son" (*ben* [TH1121, ZH1202]) and "stone" (*'eben* [TH68, ZH74]). The rejection of the son (*ben*) in the parable (21:37-39) answers to the rejection of the stone (*'eben*) in Ps 118:22. It is also noteworthy that the Isaiah Targum interprets the "fertile hill" of Isa 5:1 as the Temple mount (Evans 1995:397-405; Snodgrass 1983:95-118). The architectural function of the stone that becomes the cornerstone (lit. "the head of the corner") is unclear. It may be a typical foundational cornerstone, the keystone of an arch, or the capstone at the top of a corner.

the Kingdom of God will be taken away from you and given to a nation that will produce the proper fruit. See 1 Sam 15:28 LXX; Dan 2:44; 7:27. Although it is common to take "you" as a reference to the Jewish people as a whole and "nation" as a reference to the predominantly Gentile church (Blomberg 1992:325; Hendriksen 1973:786), there is good reason to take the view that "you" refers to the unbelieving Jewish leaders and "nation" to the twelve disciples of Jesus who will lead his church (16:18-19; 19:28; Overman 1996:302-304). It is clear from numerous OT passages that the word "nation" does not only refer to Gentiles and Gentile nations (Gen 12:2; Exod 19:6, cited in 1 Pet 2:9; 2 Sam 7:23; Ps 33:12; Isa 1:4; 26:2; Jer 31:36; Ezek 37:22). Matthew did not think of the church as a Gentile entity that supersedes Israel but as the eschatological Jewish remnant that spreads the Kingdom message to all the nations, including Israel. For further discussion, see the commentary below and Turner (2002).

21:44 *Anyone who stumbles over that stone will be broken to pieces, and it will crush anyone it falls on.* The stone metaphor is continued in the language of 21:44, which echoes Isa 8:14-15 and Dan 2:34-35, 44-45. Those who reject the cornerstone will, as it were, stumble and fall on it, while at the same time their judgment will be like the stone falling on them. The destruction of the Temple in AD 70 was at least part of the judgment Jesus spoke of here (cf. 24:2; Luke 21:20). There is some doubt over the authenticity of 21:44, which may be interpolated from Luke 20:18 (see Metzger 1994:47; Comfort 2007:[Matt 21:44]). It is not included in several ancient witnesses (𝔓104^vid D 33 it syr^s Origen Eusebius).

21:45 *they realized he was telling the story against them.* This verse erases any doubt that the tenant farmers picture Israel's leaders, not Israel as a whole—the leaders themselves recognize this. The "leading priests and Pharisees" are joined together elsewhere only in 27:62. Tragically, the Jewish religious leaders understood what Jesus was saying but refused to give assent to it. When they were told that they would reject God's cornerstone and be crushed by it, they set out undaunted to crush that cornerstone. Their rejection of God fulfills God's prophecy through Jesus.

21:46 *They wanted to arrest him, but they were afraid of the crowds, who considered Jesus to be a prophet.* The leaders' fear of the crowd of festival pilgrims who believed that Jesus was a prophet (21:11, 26) was the only factor that slowed their murder plot (12:14; 26:3-5). If the leaders openly arrested Jesus, the volatile crowd of pilgrims might riot, bringing Roman soldiers onto the Temple grounds. Eventually, their plot would be aided by Judas' betrayal. The Jewish religious leaders would manipulate the Romans and persuade the fickle crowd to see things their way (26:3-5, 14-16, 47; 27:2, 20-26).

COMMENTARY

As Davies and Allison (1997:176-177) point out, this parable joins two Old Testament themes—Israel as God's vineyard and its rejection of the prophets—with the new themes of Jesus as the culmination of God's revelation and Israel's rejection of him as the culmination of their rebellion. This parable continues Jesus' answer to the religious leaders' question as to the source of Jesus' authority (21:23). It comes from God, the owner of the vineyard, Israel. God had been amazingly patient with the leaders of his people, who had regularly rejected his messengers throughout Israel's history. These leaders had not produced fruit, or right living according to the law. Now they were about to destroy the owner's son, Jesus, thinking that this would clear the way for their ongoing authority over the people. But the owner of the vineyard would have the last word, destroying these leaders and replacing them with new ones, the disciples of Jesus. Ultimately, God will have fruit from his people. Thus, the parable of the evil farmers is a miniature history of redemption. It is just as much a prediction of Jesus' death and resurrection as the passion predictions Jesus has been making (16:21; 17:22-23; 20:18-19).

Matthew and Isaiah's Song of the Vineyard. Isaiah 5:1-7 poignantly decries the unfaithfulness of Israel with the imagery of a well-cultivated vineyard that inexplicably fails to produce good fruit. The Beloved's transformation of a fertile hill into a promising vineyard is described in six steps in Isaiah 5:1b-2a. These steps bear much resemblance to the six steps of Matthew 21:33-34, although Matthew 21 does not put the steps in the same order. Also, Matthew omits mention of digging and removing stones, but adds a wall to the description. Despite the obvious similarities, there remain some crucial differences between Isaiah 5:1-7 and Matthew 21:33-46. Perhaps the most obvious is that the crucial figures in Matthew, the tenant farmers, are not mentioned in Isaiah. The problem in Isaiah is the lack of good fruit, but the problem in Matthew is the farmers who will not render the fruit to the owner. This necessitates the process of sending servants, and ultimately the son, to appeal to the farmers to pay the owner his share of the harvest. The resolution of the problem of the lack of good fruit in Isaiah is the destruction of the vineyard (but see Isa 27:2-6), while in Matthew the problem of the recalcitrant farmers is solved by replacing them with farmers who will render the harvest to the owner.

The Kingdom Taken and Given. From whom will the Kingdom of God be taken? Christian exegesis has often viewed Matthew 21:43 as predicting the demise of national Israel as the people of God and its replacement by the predominantly Gentile church. But what group is represented by the recalcitrant farmers from whom authority over the vineyard is to be taken? In terms of the parable proper, Israel is represented by the vineyard, not by the farmers, who ostensibly stand for the leaders of Israel. This is made clear in the response of Israel's leaders to the parable and its application by Jesus; they recognized that he had been talking about them (21:45). They were the recalcitrant farmers (21:35-39), the builders who rejected the stone (21:42), and those broken to pieces and ground into powder by the stone (21:44). The identification of the recalcitrant farmers of the parable with the Jewish religious leaders of Jesus' day seems clear (Carson 1984:454; Davies and Allison 1997:189-190; Keener 1999:510-511, 515-516).

But if 21:43 speaks of Kingdom authority being taken away from these religious leaders, to whom does the text say this Kingdom authority will be given? Some scholars take this phrase as conclusive evidence that a new "nation," the church, has replaced the nation of Israel in God's plan (Bruner 1990:770; Hagner 1995:623; Hare 1967:153; Morris 1992:544). But this view is unconvincing in view of the previous discussion of the entity from whom the Kingdom is taken. The pronoun "you" in 21:43 has as its parabolic antecedent the recalcitrant farmers, not the fruitful vineyard. In the following context it is clear that the religious leaders believed Jesus was talking about them, not Israel as a whole (21:46). Thus it is reading far too much into this verse to view it as indicating the replacement of Israel by the Gentile church. Nor does Matthew's use of the word "nation" (*ethnos* [TG1484, ZG1620]; 21:43) clearly support this view (Levine 1988:187-189, 207-211). If the Gentiles were in view here, one would expect the plural, "nations" (cf. Gr. of 4:15; 6:32; 10:5, 18; 12:18, 21; 20:19, 25; 24:9, 14; 25:32; 28:19). In Matthew 21:43 the entity to which the Kingdom will be given is an ethical, not ethnic, entity. Those who produce fruit—that is, those who practice Kingdom ethics—will replace the recalcitrant farmers who have refused to render the harvest to the landowner. In Matthew's view, his Christian Jewish community and others like it, who view Jesus as the ultimate teacher of the Torah (5:17-48), practice Kingdom ethics. It is they who replace the Jerusalem religious establishment as the leaders of Israel.

Israel and the Church.   Matthew 21:33-46 is part of Matthew's indictment of the Jerusalem religious establishment, whose franchise to lead Israel will be forfeited to Matthew's Christian Jewish community. The "nation" of Matthew 21:43 speaks of the Matthean community as an eschatological messianic remnant whose leaders will replace the current Jerusalem religious establishment and lead Israel in bearing the fruit of righteousness to God. Thus, the parable of the recalcitrant farmers is about ethics, not ethnicity, and a Jewish remnant, not a Gentile replacement. This remnant is pictured as a repentant son (21:29), responsible farmers (21:41), and responsive guests (22:9-10). None of these parabolic details need be interpreted as speaking in ethnic terms (Levine 1988:193-239). To read this passage as Israel's rejection and replacement by the Gentile church is to read into it a later theology of supersession (Hultgren 2000:372-374). Such a view is dubious exegetically and has contributed, perhaps unwittingly in some cases, to anti-Semitism. The theology of supersession may not lead inexorably to the practice of anti-Semitism, but the connections are there in all too many cases in the history of the church. Hence, it is high time to seriously reconsider such an exegesis (Farmer 1999:30-31, 40, 48).

Matthew 21:33-46 should rather be interpreted as an intramural transferal of leadership in the Kingdom from the fruitless Jerusalem religious establishment to the fruitful Matthean Christian Jewish community, led by Jesus' apostles. This community amounts to the eschatological remnant of Israel that continues its mission to Israel while expanding its horizons to all the nations. In the larger scheme of New Testament biblical theology, this eschatological Jewish remnant becomes the nucleus of the nascent church. Although the church expands primarily by winning Gentiles to Messiah Jesus, its roots in the promises of God to the seed of Abraham must not be forgotten. Jesus' words to the Samaritan woman warrant repeating: "Salvation comes through the Jews" (John 4:22; cf. John 10:16; Acts 24:14; 28:20; Rom 11:16-24; Eph 2:11-22; Rev 21:12).

Summary and Transition. After earlier predictions of Jesus' death in Jerusalem (16:21; 20:18), and after Matthew has set the scene geographically (19:1; 20:17, 29), we observe the Triumphal Entry into Jerusalem (21:1-11). Matthew next describes Jesus' activities in the Temple, including casting out the money changers, healing the blind and the lame, and confronting the chief priests and scribes (21:12-17). Next, the cursing of the fig tree becomes an object lesson for prayer (21:18-22). Reentering the Temple, Jesus answered the chief priests' and elders' question regarding his authority (21:23-44). This answer comes in three stages: (1) Jesus posed a question to the religious leaders, which they refused to answer (21:24-27); (2) Jesus told a brief story about a man who had two sons (21:28-32); and (3) Jesus told another story about a landowner and his vineyard (21:33-44). The chapter concludes with the Pharisees understanding that Jesus' stories condemned them; they seek to seize him but are held in check by their fear of the multitudes (21:45-46). Chapter 22 continues in the same vein, with Jesus continuing his parables to the Pharisees, who escalate their plot against him (22:1, 15).

◆   ## 11. The parable of the wedding feast (22:1-14)

Jesus also told them other parables. He said, 2"The Kingdom of Heaven can be illustrated by the story of a king who prepared a great wedding feast for his son. 3When the banquet was ready, he sent his servants to notify those who were invited. But they all refused to come!

4"So he sent other servants to tell them, 'The feast has been prepared. The bulls and fattened cattle have been killed, and everything is ready. Come to the banquet!' 5But the guests he had invited ignored them and went their own way, one to his farm, another to his business. 6Others seized his messengers and insulted them and killed them.

7"The king was furious, and he sent out his army to destroy the murderers and burn their town. 8And he said to his servants, 'The wedding feast is ready, and the guests I invited aren't worthy of the honor. 9Now go out to the street corners and invite everyone you see.' 10So the servants brought in everyone they could find, good and bad alike, and the banquet hall was filled with guests.

11"But when the king came in to meet the guests, he noticed a man who wasn't wearing the proper clothes for a wedding. 12'Friend,' he asked, 'how is it that you are here without wedding clothes?' But the man had no reply. 13Then the king said to his aides, 'Bind his hands and feet and throw him into the outer darkness, where there will be weeping and gnashing of teeth.'

14"For many are called, but few are chosen."

NOTES

22:1-3 Here Jesus again speaks in parables, uttering the third in a set of three parables that put forth an authority figure's problems with his subordinates (cf. 21:28, 33). The parable in Luke 14:15-24 is similar but probably reflects a different event in the life of Jesus.

The Kingdom of Heaven can be illustrated by. This is a standard introductory formula (13:24, 31, 33, 44, 45, 47; 18:23). In the previous two parables, the main character was a vineyard owner who dealt with his sons and tenant farmers respectively. This time the main character is a king who sent his slaves to summon those he had already invited to his son's wedding feast. Amazingly, those whom the king invited were not willing to come (cf. 23:37). Given the preceding context, there can be little doubt that this is intended to portray the recalcitrant religious leaders, who did not believe the prophets sent by God and who ultimately rejected the Kingdom announced by Jesus, God's Son. Elsewhere in Matthew the Kingdom is spoken of as a great banquet at the end of the ages (8:11-12; cf. 26:26-29; Luke 13:29; Rev 19:9).

22:4-6 *The feast has been prepared.* The king patiently sent out other slaves to reaffirm the invitation. This time the slaves were instructed to point out in detail the nature of the preparations that had been made. Surely this would entice the invited guests to come.

bulls and fattened cattle. The second term is more lit. "fattened animals" (*sitista* [TG4619A, ZG4990]) and occurs only here in the NT; BDAG (925) posits that the fattened animals were cattle. The slaves announced that all preparations were complete and repeated the invitation, but those who had been invited paid no heed. Some were too busy with everyday concerns, such as their farms and their businesses. Others were subversive and revolted against the king by apprehending his slaves, mocking them, and killing them (cf. 2 Sam 10:4; Josephus *Antiquities*, 9.263-266). This horrible turn of events could not have been anticipated. The second group of slaves here answers to the second group in 21:36. The nearness of the Kingdom is portrayed by the servants' repeated statement that the feast was prepared (cf. 3:2; 4:17:10:7). The recalcitrance of the religious leaders is habitual; they had regularly killed God's messengers (cf. 5:12; 23:29-36).

22:7 *he sent out his army to destroy the murderers.* His army put their city to the torch (Judg 1:8; Isa 5:24-25; 1 Macc 5:28). The king's angry treatment of his treacherous subjects portrays the judgment of the Jerusalem establishment (cf. 21:41-45). The burning of the Temple in AD 70 is at least a partial fulfillment of this veiled prophecy (Blomberg 1992:328).

22:8-10 *go out to the street corners and invite everyone you see.* He told his slaves for the third time that the feast was ready but notes that those previously invited were not worthy (on being "worthy," see 3:8; 10:10-11, 13, 37-38). He sent the slaves out into the byways to invite everyone they could find. The term NLT renders "street corners" (Gr. *diexodous* [TG1327, ZG1447]) more likely refers to the places where the streets leave town and go into the surrounding countryside (BDAG 244).

22:11-12 *he noticed a man who wasn't wearing the proper clothes.* When the king greeted his guests, he discovered a man who was not wearing the proper clothes for a wedding. He called him "friend," which, in view of 26:50, may be ominous. It is possible that it was the custom in that day for kings to provide suitable clothing for such feasts (Gen 45:22; Judg 14:12; 2 Kgs 25:29; Esth 6:8-9; Luke 15:22; Rev 19:8; Josephus *War*, 2.128-133; Gundry 1994:439), but some scholars deny this (Carson 1984:457; Hagner 1995:631).

the man had no reply. The man was at fault for insulting the king because he could not explain his inappropriate attire.

22:13-14 *throw him into the outer darkness.* The man was arrested and severely punished (8:12; 13:40-42; 24:51; 25:30). This horrible outcome pictures eternal punishment. The parable was told to prepare the listeners for the conclusion: "many are called, but few are chosen." The point of this parable is similar to that of the two sons. The established leaders of Israel had rejected Jesus and the Kingdom, but some from the dregs of society had repented (9:10-13; 21:31-32). But even among these who overtly respond to the Kingdom message, there are both good and bad (cf. 13:19-23, 38, 48). God calls many, good and bad alike, into his Kingdom, but relatively few of them are truly obedient to the call (7:13-14).

COMMENTARY

Matthew 22:1-14 comprises a narrative introduction (22:1), the parable itself (22:2-13), and a general conclusion (22:14). The parable itself contains four cycles of activity by a king (22:2, 4, 7, 11). As noted above, the parable of the wedding feast is the third in a set of three parables that share many themes and together make a case against the leaders of Israel. All three parables are about failure, whether that of the second son, the tenant farmers, those originally invited to the wedding feast, or the man without wedding clothes (Davies and Allison 1997:188-189).

According to a common interpretation of this parable, the king (God) sends his servants (prophets) to invite his subjects (Israel) to a wedding feast for his son (Jesus, cf. 8:11). The subjects refuse to come, and they kill the king's servants. The king sends his armies (Rome) and destroys the city (Jerusalem). Then the guests are secured from the main highways (Gentiles). A wedding guest without wedding garments (a hypocrite) is punished. There is truth here, but it is doubtful that the parable is intended to portray a redemptive-historical transition from Jews to Gentiles (as, e.g., Hagner 1995:632). Those who seized, mocked, and killed God's messengers are not Israel as a whole but the leaders of Israel (Overman 1996:300-302). "The exegete must be careful not to assume that the allegorical destruction of Jerusalem terminates Israel's role in God's story" (Davies and Allison 1997:202, cf. 207 n. 76).

Theological Significance. The conclusion of the parable is that "many are called but few are chosen." This must be understood as summarizing the point of the whole parable, not just 22:13. The parable stresses the contempt with which the religious leaders treated God's rule in Jesus the Messiah. Some had merely been indifferent (22:5), but others were growing more and more hostile (22:6). The invitation had gone out to many, but only relatively few responded. However, this "surprising" turn of events was not unexpected to God; he has his elect (cf. 11:25-30; 24:22, 24, 31). The biblical concept implied by 22:14 is that of the remnant (e.g., Isa 1:9; 10:20-22; Elliott 2000). Such a concept seems to be contrary to that of the Mishnah in *m. Sanhedrin* 10:1, where it says, "All Israel has a place in the world to come."

The disastrous end of the man without a wedding garment adds a dimension not found in the previous two parables (Davies and Allison 1997:207-208). The fate of this man vividly pictures the horrific end of those who finally reject Jesus and the Kingdom, whether they appear to be righteous or not. In this respect, 22:11-13 portrays the final judgment. This man had evidently responded to the invitation to the wedding feast and had assembled in the banquet hall, but his garment showed that he did not truly belong there. His fate reminds the reader of the false prophets in 7:15-23 and of the lawless ones in 13:42. Through this part of the parable, Jesus warned his disciples that their troubles will not come merely from outside opponents. They cannot become complacent and assume a notion of divine approval that overrides the necessity of obedience to all that Jesus had commanded. Later, the betrayal of Jesus will make this point crystal clear—Judas Iscariot is another who was called but not chosen. The future will bring many troubles to the disciples from the outside, but they must also beware of defectors within the church. Only those who endure to the end will be saved (24:10-13).

◆   **12. Paying taxes to Caesar (22:15-22; cf. Mark 12:13-17; Luke 20:20-26)**

¹⁵Then the Pharisees met together to plot how to trap Jesus into saying something for which he could be arrested. ¹⁶They sent some of their disciples, along with the supporters of Herod, to meet with him. "Teacher," they said, "we know how honest you are. You teach the way of God truthfully. You are impartial and don't play favorites. ¹⁷Now tell us what you think about this: Is it right to pay taxes to Caesar or not?"
¹⁸But Jesus knew their evil motives.

"You hypocrites!" he said. "Why are you trying to trap me? ¹⁹Here, show me the coin used for the tax." When they handed him a Roman coin,* ²⁰he asked, "Whose picture and title are stamped on it?"
²¹"Caesar's," they replied.
"Well, then," he said, "give to Caesar what belongs to Caesar, and give to God what belongs to God."
²²His reply amazed them, and they went away.

22:19 Greek *a denarius.*

N O T E S
22:15-17 Following Jesus' three parables on the failure of the Jewish religious leaders (21:23–22:14), the Pharisees regrouped and conferred about how to trap Jesus in his speech (cf. Mark 12:13-17; Luke 20:20-26). Their desire to test and destroy Jesus was noted previously (12:14; 16:1; 19:3; cf. 22:35).

supporters of Herod. It was unusual for the Herodians (cf. Mark 3:6) to join in a common cause with the Pharisees, since the Pharisees did not support the pro-Roman Herodian dynasty and did not favor a tax that was not based on the Torah. Little is known of the Herodians, who were evidently a relatively small but well entrenched group that stood to profit from the status quo. This mixed group first speaks flattering words to Jesus about his integrity and impartiality, evidently to set up their trap (22:16). Their question about paying taxes to the Roman emperor is evidently about the "head tax," which was based on a census of Israel's population by the Romans (Josephus *Antiquities*, 18.1, 3; *War* 1.154; 2.118, 403-405, 433; Tacitus *Annals* 2.42). This is a different tax than the OT-mandated tax to support the Temple, which Jesus did pay (17:24-27). It seems that the religious leaders wanted to catch Jesus in a dilemma. He would be sure to anger one group or the other either way he answered their question. To support the tax would be to alienate the Pharisees, and to reject the tax would be treasonous to Rome.

Is it right to pay taxes to Caesar or not? Better rendered as "Is it lawful . . . ?" Jesus was being asked to interpret the Torah. Cf. 12:2, 4, 10; 14:4; 19:3; 27:6 for the use of *exestin* [ᵀᴳ1832, ᶻᴳ2003], which simply means "it is permitted."

22:18-20 *hypocrites.* "Jesus recognizes the daggers in the men's smiles" (Davies and Allison 1997:215). He saw through their flattery to their evil motives and called them on it (cf. 6:2, 5, 16; 7:5; 15:7; 23:13-15; 24:51).

show me the coin. . . . Whose picture and title are stamped on it? He answered their question by dramatically requiring them to produce the coin used to pay the tax (a denarius, cf. 18:28; 20:2, 9-10, 13), and asking them whose image and inscription are on it.

22:21 give to Caesar what belongs to Caesar, and give to God what belongs to God. Jesus' answer when they replied that it was Caesar's image assumes God's control over Rome's temporal power (Dan 1:1-2; 2:20-21, 37-38), and on the surface it seems to support the Herodians. The image of the emperor on the coin would indicate that it would be appropriate to pay it back to him. However, a Jew who was obedient to the second commandment would not be comfortable holding the coin anyway (Exod 20:4). Also, the inscription on the denarius referred to Tiberius Caesar as divine and as high priest. The image of Tiberius and both of these titles would be offensive to Jews. Jesus' distinction between duty to state and duty to God indicates that Tiberius was neither divine nor high priest.

22:22 His reply amazed them. Jesus' reply stunned his interrogators, and they left without further disputation. According to Matthew, Jesus words and deeds often astonished people (see 8:27; 9:33; 15:31; 21:20).

COMMENTARY

Jesus had been speaking from 21:24-22:14 in answer to the religious leaders' question about the source of his authority. Here in 22:15 begins a series of three confrontations where the religious leaders attempt to challenge Jesus' wisdom. However, Jesus proved that his teaching far surpassed that of the Pharisees (22:15, 34), Sadducees (22:23), and Herodians (22:16). In the end, he answered all their questions, but they could not answer one of his (22:46).

Jesus' masterful answer to the question about the propriety of paying taxes to the emperor confounded both the Herodians and the Pharisees. A simple positive answer might have been expected from someone who befriended tax collectors, but it would have alienated the Pharisees and those who were even more nationalistic. A simple negative answer might have been expected from one who had recently been praised in messianic terms (21:1-11), but it would have left Jesus open to the charge of sedition (Davies and Allison 1997:212). Most likely, the Pharisees were looking for a negative answer, but they were astounded by what they heard. The anti-Herod Pharisees were told that they should pay taxes to the Roman government because, evidently, the providence of God had placed the Romans over the Jews (cf. Rom 13:1-7; 1 Pet 2:13-17). The Herodians were reminded that their allegiance to the emperor could not supersede their allegiance to God. The inscription on the emperor's coin was wrong—he was neither God nor high priest, but Jesus' hypocritical questioners had brought the blasphemous coin into the Temple complex (Davies and Allison 1997:215). Jesus did not comfort the Pharisees by denying the validity of the head tax, but neither did he comfort the Herodians by affirming blind loyalty to the Romans. Ironically, Jesus had indeed taught the way of God truthfully despite the insincere flattery of his questioners (22:16). This passage has clear implications on submission to governing authorities. (For additional study of this passage, see Kennard 1950 and Loewe 1940.)

◆   **13. The Sadducees' question concerning marriage in the resurrection (22:23-33; cf. Mark 12:18-27; Luke 20:27-40)**

²³That same day Jesus was approached by some Sadducees—religious leaders who say there is no resurrection from the dead.

They posed this question: ²⁴"Teacher, Moses said, 'If a man dies without children, his brother should marry the widow and have a child who will carry on the brother's name.'* ²⁵Well, suppose there were seven brothers. The oldest one married and then died without children, so his brother married the widow. ²⁶But the second brother also died, and the third brother married her. This continued with all seven of them. ²⁷Last of all, the woman also died. ²⁸So tell us, whose wife will she be in the resurrection? For all seven were married to her."

²⁹Jesus replied, "Your mistake is that you don't know the Scriptures, and you don't know the power of God. ³⁰For when the dead rise, they will neither marry nor be given in marriage. In this respect they will be like the angels in heaven.

³¹"But now, as to whether there will be a resurrection of the dead—haven't you ever read about this in the Scriptures? Long after Abraham, Isaac, and Jacob had died, God said,* ³²'I am the God of Abraham, the God of Isaac, and the God of Jacob.'* So he is the God of the living, not the dead."

³³When the crowds heard him, they were astounded at his teaching.

22:24 Deut 25:5-6.   22:31 Greek *read about this? God said.*   22:32 Exod 3:6.

NOTES

22:23-24 Jesus had been telling parables, so the Sadducees approached him later that same day with a sort of parable of their own (cf. Mark 12:18-27; Luke 20:27-40).

who say there is no resurrection from the dead. A major feature of the Sadducees' beliefs was the denial of an afterlife (Acts 23:8; Josephus *Antiquities* 18.12-17; *War* 2.162-166). This seems to have been due to their rejection of the Pharisees' oral tradition and their prioritization of the Torah, which does not explicitly address the afterlife.

Teacher. Like others who were not Jesus' disciples, they addressed Jesus as "teacher" (cf. 8:19; 9:11; 12:38; 17:24; 19:16; 22:16, 36). They came to Jesus with a hypothetical case based on Deut 25:5-10, the law of levirate marriage in which a brother was responsible to have a child with his childless, deceased brother's widow so that the deceased brother would have an heir (cf. Gen 38:6-11; Ruth 4:1-10; *m. Yevamot*). But as the extreme circumstances of the story develop in the following verses, it is clear that the story was meant to ridicule the idea of life after death. The Pharisees and Jesus both agreed that there is life after death, so this is a rare case of agreement between them. (Their shared belief could be based on Dan 12:2; Job 19:25-27; Isa 26:19.) But in asking the question, the Sadducees were not sincerely inquiring about religious truth. Rather, they too were looking to trap Jesus and discredit his teaching.

22:25-28 *suppose there were seven brothers.* Having set up the topic from Deut 25:5, the Sadducees posed the highly unlikely scenario in which a woman was successively married to seven brothers, each of whom died childless (cf. Tob 3:7-8). Finally, the woman herself died, and the question was raised as to which of the brothers she would be married to in the resurrection. (For the "resurrection" as the beginning of the afterlife, see Luke 14:14; John 5:29; 11:24-25; Acts 23:6; 24:15, 21; 1 Cor 15:12-24; Heb 11:35; Rev 20:5-6).

22:29 *you don't know the Scriptures, and you don't know the power of God.* As usual, Jesus did not directly answer the Sadducees' question. Instead, he told them that their ignorance of Scripture and of God's power had caused them to err. This was a strong rebuke.

22:30 *when the dead rise, they will neither marry nor be given in marriage.* Jesus first responded to their anti-resurrection argument from Deut 25:5. He affirmed that people do not exist as married couples in the afterlife.

In this respect, they will be like the angels. The Sadducees' error assumed that the afterlife would be just like the present life. Their extrapolation from the present to the future is mistaken (Hagner 1995:641). They did not take into account the power of God to transform human existence. Since the Sadducees did not believe in angels (Acts 23:8), Blomberg (1992:333) may be correct that Jesus' reference to angels in 22:30 was meant to irritate the Sadducees, but see Davies and Allison (1997:227) for a contrary view.

22:31-32 *I am the God of Abraham, the God of Isaac, and the God of Jacob.* Second, Jesus proved the resurrection from the Scriptures, specifically from the Torah favored by the Sadducees. He cited Exod 3:6, where God speaks from the burning bush to identify himself as the God of the patriarchs Abraham, Isaac, and Jacob. Jesus reasoned that God's loyalty to his covenant with the patriarchs did not end at their death because death was not their end. Hundreds of years after the patriarchs, during the time of Moses, God told Moses that he "is" still their God (cf. 4 Macc 7:19; 16:25). This description of God's ongoing covenantal relationship with the patriarchs implies their eventual resurrection. God's claim to be the God of the patriarchs during their "intermediate state" between death and resurrection is tantamount to (and guarantees) his relationship with them in their final resurrected state (cf. *1 Enoch* 20:8; 22:1-14; 60:8; 62:15; 2 Macc 7:9; 36; *4 Ezra* 7; Josephus *War* 3.374).

22:33 *they were astounded at his teaching.* The Sadducees had not a word to say by way of rejoinder to this argument (22:34), and the watching crowd was amazed (cf. 7:28; 13:54).

COMMENTARY

This encounter with the Sadducees is similar to the previous episode with the Pharisees. In both instances, Jesus was asked a difficult question by people who wanted to trap or discredit him, but his answer discredited them and resulted in amazement. In this case, however, the question revolved not around a hot political issue, taxation, but around the interpretation of Scripture. The Sadducees asked Jesus to deal with the notion of an afterlife in view of the command for levirate marriage in Deuteronomy 25:5. They apparently believed that Torah-based levirate marriage could not be squared with the Pharisees' notion of an afterlife. Perhaps they wanted to get Jesus to come over to their side against the Pharisees (Hagner 1995:640). Whatever their agenda, Jesus told them that their denial of the resurrection was an error caused by ignorance. Their view of resurrection and the afterlife was evidently one of mere reanimation to life as before. They were ignorant of the power of God to transform people at their resurrection so that they are no longer sexually active beings (cf. 1 Cor 15:35-40). Sexuality is part of the goodness of the initial creation but life in the "regeneration" (19:28) or "resurrection" (22:30) will transcend this aspect of the original creation. This transformation renders the Sadducees' citation of the levirate law irrelevant. The Sadducees were also ignorant of the Scriptures, specifically Exodus 3:6. Jesus argued from this verse that God's covenantal loyalty to the patriarchs implies their eventual resurrection, along with that of all God's people. In sum, "Jesus treats his opponents' cunning objection as the product of culpable ignorance and bad theology" (Davies and Allison 1997:226).

Those with a modernist, rationalistic mind-set also deny the power of God to miraculously resurrect and transform humanity, albeit for very different reasons. The fact of the resurrection of Jesus, predicted several times by Jesus and narrated afterward by Matthew, confronts this skepticism. Those with a postmodern, relativistic mindset also have a way of denying the power of the resurrection. They do not necessarily deny that the resurrection happened but deny its universal significance as taught in the New Testament (Craig in Wilkins and Moreland 1995:141-176). For Paul, the resurrection of Jesus guarantees the resurrection of the followers of Jesus. Belief in the future resurrection, with the judgment and reward that follow it, is therefore a strong motivation for faithful discipleship in the present (5:3-12; 8:11; 13:40-43; 16:27; 19:28; John 5:28-29; Acts 17:30-31; 1 Cor 15:51-58; Heb 11:35).

◆ ### 14. The Pharisee lawyer's question concerning the greatest commandment (22:34-40; cf. Mark 12:28-34; Luke 10:25-28)

³⁴But when the Pharisees heard that he had silenced the Sadducees with his reply, they met together to question him again. ³⁵One of them, an expert in religious law, tried to trap him with this question: ³⁶"Teacher, which is the most important commandment in the law of Moses?"

³⁷Jesus replied, " 'You must love the LORD your God with all your heart, all your soul, and all your mind.'* ³⁸This is the first and greatest commandment. ³⁹A second is equally important: 'Love your neighbor as yourself.'* ⁴⁰The entire law and all the demands of the prophets are based on these two commandments."

22:37 Deut 6:5.   22:39 Lev 19:18.

NOTES

22:34-36 *they met together.* When the Pharisees learned that Jesus had silenced the Sadducees, they got together for yet another attempt to trap him (cf. Mark 12:28-34). There may be an allusion to the gathering of the nations against the Lord's anointed in Ps 2:2 here. It will be their last. Ironically, the Pharisees would have agreed with Jesus' response to the Sadducees, but this was a small matter in comparison to their many problems with Jesus.

an expert in religious law. This was a Pharisaic legal expert, not merely a disciple of the Pharisees (22:16).

the most important commandment. The request that Jesus identify the greatest commandment in the law may reflect a debate within Judaism at that time (Blomberg 1995:334), but its purpose was to trap Jesus, not to gain insight into the law (cf. 16:1; 19:3; 22:15). The OT itself at times presents summaries of the crucial demands of the law (e.g., Mic 6:8). A different view is found in the Mishnah, where the idea is expressed that the more commandments, the better, since there is more potential for merit for Israel (*m. Makkot* 3:16; *m. Avot* 6:11). On the other hand, Montefiore and Loewe (1974:199-201) cite several passages from the Talmud and Midrashim where certain key commandments are prioritized. Of these, *b. Makkot* 23b-24a in the Babylonian Talmud is most noteworthy, since it progressively reduces the 613 commandments of the Torah, 365 negative and 248 positive commandments, to one commandment: "the just will live by faith" (Hab 2:4).

22:37-39 *You must love the LORD your God with all your heart, all your soul, and all your mind.* This is the most straightforward of all Jesus' answers to questions in this section of Matthew. Jesus immediately replied by citing Deut 6:5 as the greatest commandment. The words "with all your heart, . . . soul, and . . . mind" stand for the whole person; they do not distinguish aspects of one's being which are responsible to love God from those which are not. Jesus' description of Deut 6:5 as the "first and greatest commandment" is similar to the phrase "the more important aspects of the law" in 23:23.

Love your neighbor as yourself. Jesus followed the greatest commandment with another of similar import, Lev 19:18. The former text enjoins love for God with one's entire being, and the latter love for one's neighbor (cf. 5:43; 19:19; Josh 22:5; Luke 10:25-28). The description of Lev 19:18 alongside Deut 6:5 is striking because the second text echoes the obligation of love from the first but changes the object from God the Creator to humans as God's creatures (cf. Lev 19:34). Both of these passages were crucial to the Judaism of Jesus' day. Pious Jews recited the Shema, a prayer named for the first word of Deut 6:4, twice daily (*m. Berakhot* 1:1-2). Rabbinic sources allude to Lev 19:18 as the fundamental principle of the law (*Sifra* Lev 19:18; *b. Shabbat* 31a; cf. Philo, *On the Special Laws* 2.15, 63).

22:40 *The entire law and all the demands of the prophets are based on these two commandments.* After citing these two texts, Jesus stated that all of the law and prophets depend (lit. "hang") on them. In other words, the entire OT may be viewed as an exposition of the ideals expressed in these two verses. There is no mention here of the lawyer's response (but see Mark 12:32-34), or even of his departure. In contrast to the two preceding interviews, the lawyer probably found no fault with Jesus and had no rejoinder to him. Perhaps 22:46 describes this interchange as well as that of 22:41-45. At any rate, the episode closes with the words of Jesus still ringing in the reader's ears.

COMMENTARY

This third story concerning Jesus' interaction with the religious leaders is the least controversial. In this exchange, reminiscent of the teaching of 7:12, Jesus succinctly synthesized the ethical teaching of the Old Testament. A prominent part of Jesus' teaching has been his relationship to the law (5:17-48). The legal expert's question indicates how Jesus' view of the law compares with that of his contemporaries (Hagner 1995:644). Jesus did not set love over against the law but, as always, got to the heart of obedience to the law, which is love for God and for those who are created in God's image. If one truly loves God, one will love those created in his image (cf. Jas 3:9-10). When one loves human beings, one indirectly expresses love to their Creator. This basic principle is the basis of the specific stipulations of the Mosaic code, and of the message of the prophets who sought to call Israel back into obedience to Moses (9:13; 12:7; 23:23). Other New Testament texts echo this one in affirming that love is the root obligation of the law (Rom 13:9-10; Gal 5:14; Col 3:14; Jas 2:8; cf. Furnish 1972).

The Theological Significance of These Commandments. The NLT's description of Leviticus 19:18 as "equally important" to Deuteronomy 6:5 may be a bit overstated, although it has strong scholarly support (cf. *omoios*, BDAG 706; Davies and Allison 1997:243). Literally, the expression is "similar to" or "of the same nature as." One could argue that by labeling Deuteronomy 6:5 as the "first and greatest commandment" Jesus intended it to be viewed as foundational for Leviticus 19:18. Can fallen humans begin to love their neighbors as themselves if they have not first acknowledged God's grace to them and their prior obligation to love God? Divine love to humans enables them to respond in love to God and their fellow humans. It would appear, then, that the theocentric or vertical obligation is the basis of the anthropocentric or horizontal obligation. This is the reason why the statement "I am the Lord your God" appears at the beginning of the ten commandments (Exod 20:2; Deut

5:6). While Leviticus 19:18 may be equally important as Deuteronomy 6:5, it cannot stand apart from the foundation of Deuteronomy 6:5. And without Leviticus 19:18, one cannot practice Deuteronomy 6:5, since one expresses love to God by obeying his commandments, many of which concern relationships with people. Hagner (1995:648) correctly notes that loving God involves reverence and obedience, while loving humans involves serving them and seeking their well-being.

Leviticus 19:18 and its New Testament echoes assume that one will instinctively love oneself. The modern psychological jargon about the necessity of learning to love oneself as a prerequisite for loving God and one's neighbor seems to turn the biblical pattern on its head (cf. Eph 5:28-29). No doubt one must have a biblical view of oneself as a flawed yet redeemed individual, but this hardly amounts to uncritical self-affirmation. For Paul, it is crucial to view oneself as a new creation "in Christ" (e.g., Rom 6:1-4; 2 Cor 5:17; Col 3:1-4), but this amounts to self-crucifixion, which is not far from the counsel of Jesus to take up one's cross (Gal 2:20; 6:14). For Jesus, self-love is death, and self-denial is life (10:38-39; 16:24-25).

◆   ## 15. Jesus questions the Pharisees concerning the Messiah's sonship (22:41-46; cf. Mark 12:35-37; Luke 20:41-44)

[41]Then, surrounded by the Pharisees, Jesus asked them a question: [42]"What do you think about the Messiah? Whose son is he?"

They replied, "He is the son of David."

[43]Jesus responded, "Then why does David, speaking under the inspiration of the Spirit, call the Messiah 'my Lord'? For David said,

22:44 Ps 110:1.

[44]'The LORD said to my Lord,
Sit in the place of honor at my right hand
until I humble your enemies beneath your feet.'*

[45]Since David called the Messiah 'my Lord,' how can the Messiah be his son?"

[46]No one could answer him. And after that, no one dared to ask him any more questions.

NOTES

22:41-42 *What do you think about the Messiah? Whose son is he?* After enduring three insincere questions from his enemies and silencing them with his wise answers, Jesus took the initiative and reciprocated with three questions of his own (cf. Mark 12:35-37; Luke 20:41-44). Jesus' first question regarding the sonship of the Messiah was an easy question and is answered correctly by the Pharisees. The Messiah is "the son of David" (2 Sam 7:8, 13-14; Ps 89:3-4; Isa 11:1, 10; Jer 23:5; Matt 1:1; 9:27-28; 20:30; 21:9, 15; John 7:42; Rom 15:12; Rev 5:5; 22:16). However, this is not the whole truth of the matter, as the next question shows. Evidently, the Pharisees viewed Davidic messianic sonship in nationalistic, militaristic terms. They looked for a powerful human being to liberate them from their Roman oppressors. In so doing they looked past Jesus, whose Kingdom promised no such thing.

22:43-44 *why does David . . . call the Messiah 'my Lord'?* Jesus' second question focuses on the more profound truth that David called his son (the Messiah) "my Lord." Normally, sons speak in such terms of their fathers, not fathers of their sons. How can David's son be his Lord? How can someone possess higher authority than the king of Israel?

For David said, 'The LORD said to my Lord.' This reference to Ps 110 is theologically significant in that it affirms and depends upon the Davidic authorship of the psalm and the Spirit's moving David to write it (cf. Acts 1:16; 2:25-31; 4:25; Josephus *Antiquities* 6.166). If David did not write the Psalm, Jesus' argument evaporates, since a third party is speaking about what God said to David (or another king), described as "my Lord." There are two different Heb. words for "Lord" in Ps 110:1, cited in 22:44—"The LORD (*yhwh* [TH3068, ZH3378]) said to my Lord (*'adonay* [TH136, ZH151])."

Sit in the place of honor at my right hand. The reference to David's Lord (*'adonay*) sitting at the LORD's (Yahweh's) right hand speaks of messianic authority in terms reminiscent of Ps 2:7-9 and Dan 7:13-14. This reference foreshadows 26:64, where Jesus' application of Dan 7:13-14 to himself is taken by the high priest as blasphemous. For further discussion of the messianic interpretation of Ps 110, see Fitzmeyer (1997:113-126) and Hay (1973). For other NT citations and allusions to this psalm, see Acts 2:34-35; 1 Cor 15:25; Eph 1:20; Col 3:1; Heb 1:3, 13; 5:6, 10; 7:17, 21; 8:1; 10:12-13; Rev 3:21.

22:45-46 Since David called the Messiah 'my Lord,' how can the Messiah be his son? Jesus' third and final question reverses the second question: how can David's Lord be his son? The answer to the enigma is found in Jesus' dual "paternity." He is David's son because he is humanly descended from David, but he is David's Lord because he is God's Son. Jesus' transcendent sonship is prominently featured in Matthew (1:23; 2:15; 3:17; 4:3, 6; 7:21; 8:29; 11:25-27; 16:16; 17:5; 21:37-39; 22:2; 24:36; 26:29, 39, 42, 53, 63-64; 27:40, 43, 46, 54; 28:19). It is also found in OT texts other than Ps 110, featuring a Messiah who transcends human limitations (Ps 45:6-7; Isa 9:6; Jer 23:5-6; 33:15-16; Zech 12:10), especially Isa 11:1, 10, where the Messiah is both David's offshoot and David's root. The Pharisees and other religious leaders cease interrogating Jesus at this point. They cannot refute the truth of his interpretation of the OT, yet they are unwilling to accept his divine sonship. Their plot against him continues (cf. 26:3-5, 14-16; 27:62). Jesus had been temporarily vindicated, but in view of his repeated predictions about what would happen in Jerusalem, there is no reason for celebration.

COMMENTARY

Jesus took the initiative to question the Pharisees, but he was not merely attempting to trap them, as they were him. He was not involved in trying to win a debate, but in trying to win their hearts with his teaching of the Old Testament (23:37). The issues they raised, the validity of Rome's taxes, eschatological speculation, and even fundamental ethical obligations, were not of paramount importance at this decisive point in Israel's history. The paramount issue was that they were in the process of rejecting the true Messiah—Jesus himself. His relationship to King David was worthy of their consideration at this critical moment. The religious leaders and Jesus agreed in affirming that the Messiah is David's son (22:42), but the real question is what this affirmation of messianic identity means. Jesus' second and third questions unpack the matter.

Jesus' second and third questions address the same issue from opposite directions. The second question in 22:43 seems to assume the humanity of the Messiah as David's descendant. Assuming the Messiah is the human descendant of David, how does David call him Lord in Psalm 110:1? The third question puts it the opposite way, if the Messiah is David's Lord, how can he be David's descendant? In

Matthew's theology, Jesus' humble family and Davidic roots (1:1, 16-17, 20; cf. Luke 1:27, 32, 69; 2:4, 11) are not the whole story. Jesus is also the miraculously-born, divinely-attested Son of God (1:23; 3:17; 16:16; 17:5). Matthew had previously implied that Jesus is greater than David (Matt 12:1-4; cf. 12:6, 8, 41), and now he explains why. The son of David is also the Son of God. But the Pharisees would not accept a Davidic Messiah who was greater than David—who is David's Lord. On this sad note, Matthew's story of Jesus' conflicts with the religious leaders ends. Nothing more could be said. Even today this is the basic difference between Judaism's and Christianity's respective messiahs.

Summary and Transition.   Matthew 22 continues to describe the heated controversies between Jesus and the religious leaders in Jerusalem that began soon after the Triumphal Entry. The parable of the wedding feast (22:1-14) is the third in a series begun in 21:28. All three parables stress the fact that the leaders rejected the rule of God in Messiah Jesus, using the images of a disobedient son, wicked tenant farmers, and rebellious subjects who refuse their king's invitation.

Following the parable sequence, there are three controversy stories. The Pharisees plotted to trap Jesus in his words and sent their disciples to ask him about the payment of the poll tax (22:15-22). Then the Sadducees attempted to confound Jesus with their question about a woman who had seven husbands (22:23-33). A Pharisaic legal expert then came to ask Jesus about the greatest commandment in the law (22:34-40). Finally, the chapter concludes as Jesus "turns the tables" with three questions of his own on the paternity of the Messiah and the interpretation of Psalm 110. The Pharisees were unable to answer, and from then on they did not ask Jesus any more questions (22:41-46). This final confrontation left Jesus and the religious leaders in a hopeless impasse, thereby leading to Jesus' pronouncement of woes against them in the next chapter (23).

All in all, Matthew 22 takes the verbal hostilities between Jesus and the religious leaders to its sorry end. Jesus' parables magnify Israel's rebellion and guilt in not submitting to the rule of God in Christ. The religious leaders attempted to trap Jesus and to discredit his teaching. If there was ever any doubt, it is now abundantly clear that there can be no rapprochement between Jesus and the leaders of Israel. His final question to them was unanswerable; the only way that David can call his messiah-son "Lord" is if his son is divine. The Pharisees who wanted to trap Jesus by challenging his identity were now themselves trapped by Jesus who had identified himself as David's descendant and his exalted Lord. At this point, all dialogue ceased, with ominous implications.

◆   ## 16. Jesus' teachings on leadership (23:1-12; cf. Mark 12:38-40; Luke 20:45-47)

Then Jesus said to the crowds and to his disciples, 2"The teachers of religious law and the Pharisees are the official inter-preters of the law of Moses.* 3So practice and obey whatever they tell you, but don't follow their example. For they don't practice what they teach. ⁴They crush people with unbearable religious demands and never lift a finger to ease the burden. ⁵"Everything they do is for show. On their arms they wear extra wide prayer boxes with Scripture verses inside, and they wear robes with extra long tassels.* ⁶And they love to sit at the head table at banquets and in the seats of honor in the synagogues. ⁷They love to receive respectful greetings as they walk in the marketplaces, and to be called 'Rabbi.'*

⁸"Don't let anyone call you 'Rabbi,' for you have only one teacher, and all of you are equal as brothers and sisters.* ⁹And don't address anyone here on earth as 'Father,' for only God in heaven is your spiritual Father. ¹⁰And don't let anyone call you 'Teacher,' for you have only one teacher, the Messiah. ¹¹The greatest among you must be a servant. ¹²But those who exalt themselves will be humbled, and those who humble themselves will be exalted."

23:2 Greek *and the Pharisees sit in the seat of Moses.* **23:5** Greek *They enlarge their phylacteries and lengthen their tassels.* **23:7** *Rabbi,* from Aramaic, means "master" or "teacher." **23:8** Greek *brothers.*

NOTES

23:1-2 *The teachers of religious law and the Pharisees are the official interpreters of the law of Moses.* The various religious leaders with whom Jesus had been in conflict since 21:12 are no longer in view, evidently because they were incorrigible (cf. Mark 12:38-40; Luke 20:45-47). Jesus' words to the crowds and his disciples surprisingly seem to authenticate the role of his opponents, the scribes (NLT "teachers of religious law") and Pharisees. The scribes were teachers of the law who frequently espoused the Pharisaic oral traditions. The two groups were previously associated in Matthew (5:20; 12:38; 15:1) and in chapter 23 they receive the brunt of Jesus' denunciation (23:2, 13-15, 23, 25, 27, 29). But here, Jesus acknowledges their capacity as "the official interpreters of the law of Moses" (lit. "they have seated themselves in the seat of Moses"). The seat of Moses may refer to an actual seat in the synagogues where authoritative teaching occurred, but the evidence for this comes from times later than the first century (Davies and Allison 1997:268). In any event, occupying the "chair" signified continuity with Moses and the ongoing exercise of the authority which came from Sinai (*m. Avot* 1:1, 3-4, 6, 8, 10, 12; 2:8).

23:3 *practice and obey whatever they tell you.* Jesus' counsel that his disciples obey the teachings of the scribes and Pharisees echoes Deut 17:10 (23:3, cf. 23:23), but it is truly surprising in light of his earlier confrontations with them. Therefore, interpreters tend to downplay the words by adding implied qualifications to them. France (1985:324) views this language as tongue in cheek, and Carson (1984:473-474) views 23:2-3a as irony or sarcasm, followed by Jesus' true intent in 23:3b-4, but these interpretatations are not convincing.

but don't follow their example. Jesus enjoins total obedience to the leaders' teachings in spite of their hypocritical example. What they teach should be followed because of their authoritative position, but their example was inconsistent with this teaching and should not be imitated (cf. Rom 2:21-24).

23:4 *unbearable religious demands.* This interprets Jesus' metaphor, which lit. speaks of heavy burdens being loaded on people's shoulders (cf. Luke 11:46). The heavy burden of the Pharisaic system contrasts with the light load of Jesus, expressed in 11:30 (cf. Acts 15:10, 28; 1 John 5:3).

23:5 *Everything they do is for show.* Jesus exposes Pharisaic externalism with its shallow purpose of garnering human applause. The disciples must not imitate the motives of the scribes and Pharisees any more than their example. The general statement of 23:5a is illustrated by six examples arranged in three pairs in 23:5b-7. Compare this passage to 6:1-18, where Jesus contrasts such externalism with the norms of the Kingdom for genuine religious practice.

prayer boxes . . . tassels. The prayer boxes and tassels were public displays of piety. "Prayer boxes" (lit. "phylacteries"; so NLT mg), are small leather boxes containing Torah portions and are worn due to a literal interpretation of the law (Exod 13:9; Deut 6:8; 11:18). "Tassels" or fringes on robes or prayer shawls have been mentioned previously in Matthew and are based on the OT laws (Num 15:37-39; Deut 22:12; Matt 9:20; 14:36).

23:6 *head table . . . seats of honor.* Seeking prominence in public gatherings was another indication of these leaders' desire for prestige (Luke 11:43; 14:7-11; 20:46; cf. Jas 2:1-4).

23:7 *respectful greetings . . . 'Rabbi.'* The third pair of examples concerns the love of being addressed with prestigious titles in public. At that time "Rabbi" was a respectful greeting which lit. meant "my great one" (cf. 26:25, 49; Mark 9:5; 11:21; John 1:38, 49; 3:2). After the events of AD 70, it would come to describe someone who occupied an ordained position of religious and civil leadership.

23:8-10 *Don't let anyone call you 'Rabbi.'* At this point Jesus turns from denouncing the religious leaders' false piety to commanding true piety among his disciples (23:8 is lit. "But don't let . . ."). Responding to the final Pharisaic practice mentioned in 23:7, Jesus forbade disciples of the Kingdom to use ostentatious greetings involving lofty titles. Each verse in this section consists of a prohibition followed by a reason. The disciples are forbidden the use of respectful titles such as "Rabbi," "Father" (Acts 7:2; 22:1), and "Teacher," (or "leader"), because no human being is worthy of such honor. Rather, such titles should be reserved for the heavenly Father and Jesus the Messiah.

23:11-12 *must be a servant.* Lit., "will be your servant." Here the contrasting norms of the Kingdom are explained in words reminiscent of Jesus' answer to the request of the mother of James and John (20:25-28; cf. 18:4). True greatness is a matter of service, not title. Those, like the scribes and Pharisees, who seek to exalt themselves will be humbled, but Jesus' disciples who seek humble service will be exalted. This is the language of the eschaton—those who respond to God's rule in Jesus the Messiah have humbled themselves now and will be exalted in the last days. The Pharisees' vain attempt to exalt themselves over God's rule in Christ will result in their being humbled.

COMMENTARY

Introduction to Matthew 23.   Matthew 23 is difficult to place in the flow of argument in Matthew. Since it is discourse, it is tempting to connect it with chapters 24–25 (e.g., Blomberg 1992:25, 49, 339). If this is done, the discourse follows the pattern of Matthew 13 (cf. 13:34-36), with initial public teaching (ch 23) followed by private instruction for the disciples (chs 24–25). However, the public and private portions of Matthew 13 are united in theme, genre, and literary structure, whereas there are obvious differences between chapters 23 and 24–25 in terms of audience (compare 23:1, 13 with 24:1-3), content, and tone. Therefore, it is probably better to view chapter 23 as the climax of Jesus' confrontations with the religious leaders in Jerusalem, which began in 21:15 (Hagner 1995:654). At the same time, one must note that there are clear connections between chapters 23 and 24–25, primarily the references to persecution of Jesus' disciples (23:29-36; cf. 24:9-13, 21-22; 25:34-40), the desolation of the Temple (23:38; cf. 24:1-3, 15) and the return of Jesus (23:39; cf. 24:3, 30, 37, 39, 42, 44; 25:6, 13, 19, 31).

Matthew 23 seems to involve three major sections. First, Jesus warns the crowds and his disciples against the errors of the scribes and Pharisees (23:1-12). Then he denounces the scribes and Pharisees with prophetic woe—oracles against their sin that tie their rebellion to that of their ancestors (23:13-36). Finally, he poignantly speaks to rebellious Jerusalem in words of lament that depict his longings for her people, as well as their deserved judgment (23:37-39).

Beginning in 21:12, Jesus has argued successively with the following: (1) the chief priests and scribes (21:12-17); (2) the chief priests and elders of the people (21:23-22:14; according to 21:45, this included Pharisees); (3) certain Pharisees (specifically, their disciples, 22:15-22); (4) certain Sadducees (22:23-33); (5) certain Pharisees (specifically, a lawyer; 22:34-46). These arguments take the form of questions by the various religious leaders (21:16, 23; 22:17, 28, 36), and responses by Jesus, which include scriptural quotations (21:16, 42; 22:32, 37, 39, 44), parables (21:28-30, 33-39; 22:1-14), and questions directed back at the leaders (21:16, 24-25, 28, 31, 40, 42; 22:18, 20, 42-45). Finally, the disputes come to the point where no further dialogue is possible, and the indictments of Matthew 23 ensue.

Matthew 23 also serves as a sort of introduction to the eschatological discourse of Matthew 24–25. Jesus' disputes with the religious leaders in Jerusalem end in an impasse (22:46). Jesus then warns his followers against being like those leaders (23:1-12) and pronounces woes upon them (23:13-36). He laments Jerusalem's fate, yet he holds out hope for its future (23:37-39). As he departs the Temple, perhaps reenacting the departure of the Shekinah, his disciples nervously point out to him the glorious architecture (24:1). At this point he speaks bluntly about the coming destruction of the Temple, and the disciples respond with the question that gives rise to the discourse, "when will all this happen? What sign will signal your return and the end of the world?" (24:3). Thus the judgment of Jerusalem, primarily its leaders and its Temple, is justified in Matthew 23 before it is predicted in Matthew 24–25. (For further study of Matt 23, see Davies and Allison 1997:257-263; Garland 1979 and Newport 1995.)

Matthew 23 and Anti-Semitism. It is a fact that Matthew 23 looms large in discussions of the New Testament and anti-Semitism. Matthew 23 has been called "a unique, unparalleled specimen of invective" (Sandmel 1978:68; cf. Beare 1981: 461). Matthew presents Jesus' disputes with the Jewish religious leaders in bold relief, and those disputes come to a head with Jesus' prophetic pronouncements of woe against them in Matthew 23. These strident denunciations disturb many people today, but heated rhetoric in the service of religious disputes was quite the norm in ancient times (Johnson 1989; Saldarini 1992a). In fact, it can be argued that such rhetoric was used in Jewish circles since the days of the biblical prophets, and that it continued to be used in the days of the Second Temple as various Jewish groups critiqued the religious establishment in Jerusalem. It has been argued in the Introduction to this commentary that Matthew wrote his Gospel before the "parting of the ways" between the Christian church and Judaism. At the time of his writing, "Christianity" (viewed today as a separate religion from Judaism) was still a sect of the diverse Judaism(s) of the period before the destruction of the Temple in AD 70. Therefore, Matthew must not be viewed anachronistically as a Christian

critic of the Jewish people but as a Christian Jew who was engaged in a vigorous in-
tramural dispute with other Jews over the identity of the Jew, Jesus (Davies and
Allison 1997:260-261; Harrington 1991:303-305; Overman 1990; 1996:302-304;
Saldarini 1994:59-63; Sim 1999:148-149).

Matthew was not attacking Jews or Judaism as an Gentile outsider claiming that
his new religion has superseded the outdated religion of the Jews. This mistaken approach may be traced to the polemical writings of some of the early church fathers,
but it is anachronistic to find it in Matthew on the lips of Jesus. On the contrary,
Matthew presents the dispute of Jesus with the religious leaders as a thoroughly *Jewish* prophetic critique of the Jerusalem religious establishment. This must not be
misconstrued as an attack on the Jewish people of all times or even of Jesus' day.
Rather, Jesus' stringent critique was directed against certain scribes and Pharisees
who were prominent in the religious establishment of Jerusalem. Davies and
Allison (1997:260-261) explain this perspective very well:

> The ferocity of rhetoric in Jewish texts, and especially the volatile language of
> the Dead Sea Scrolls, shows that Matthew's polemic need not signal a break
> with Judaism. So far from that being the case, we indeed deny that Matthew
> is a Christian critique of Judaism. It is rather a Jewish-Christian critique of
> Jewish opponents—and therefore no more "anti-Semitic" than the Dead Sea
> Scrolls.

Exposition of Matthew 23:1-12. Matthew 23:1-12 is directed to the crowds and
disciples, not to the religious leaders with whom Jesus had been in conflict. But the
leaders were still very much in the picture, as Jesus commanded his disciples not to
imitate their hypocrisy (23:3b), oppressive demands (23:4), and love of prestige
and power (23:5-7). In contrast, Jesus' disciples are to reverence only the Father and
the Messiah (23:8-10). Their community must imitate the egalitarian model of the
family, not the hierarchical model of the Jewish religious leaders (cf. 20:25). That
Jesus himself as their teacher or leader humbly practiced what he preached is not
stated here, but it is clear from 20:28.

In contrast, the scribes and Pharisees did not practice what they preached. This
inconsistency is the reason why Jesus warned his disciples against them. Jesus did
not attack the legitimacy of their authority, but he told his disciples to follow their
exposition of the Torah and the halakha (23:3a, 23). Many expositors have great
difficulty with this point because they assume that Matthew's community had already broken from Judaism. But 23:3a makes good sense if Matthew's community
was still engaged in an intramural dispute with the leaders of formative Judaism.

◆   **17. Jesus' prophetic woes against the religious leaders (23:13-36)**

[13]"What sorrow awaits you teachers of re-
ligious law and you Pharisees. Hypocrites!
For you shut the door of the Kingdom of
Heaven in people's faces. You won't go in

yourselves, and you don't let others enter
either.*

[15]"What sorrow awaits you teachers of
religious law and you Pharisees. Hypo-

crites! For you cross land and sea to make one convert, and then you turn that person into twice the child of hell* you yourselves are!

¹⁶"Blind guides! What sorrow awaits you! For you say that it means nothing to swear 'by God's Temple,' but that it is binding to swear 'by the gold in the Temple.' ¹⁷Blind fools! Which is more important—the gold or the Temple that makes the gold sacred? ¹⁸And you say that to swear 'by the altar' is not binding, but to swear 'by the gifts on the altar' is binding. ¹⁹How blind! For which is more important—the gift on the altar or the altar that makes the gift sacred? ²⁰When you swear 'by the altar,' you are swearing by it and by everything on it. ²¹And when you swear 'by the Temple,' you are swearing by it and by God, who lives in it. ²²And when you swear 'by heaven,' you are swearing by the throne of God and by God, who sits on the throne.

²³"What sorrow awaits you teachers of religious law and you Pharisees. Hypocrites! For you are careful to tithe even the tiniest income from your herb gardens,* but you ignore the more important aspects of the law—justice, mercy, and faith. You should tithe, yes, but do not neglect the more important things. ²⁴Blind guides! You strain your water so you won't accidentally swallow a gnat, but you swallow a camel!*

²⁵"What sorrow awaits you teachers of religious law and you Pharisees. Hypocrites! For you are so careful to clean the outside of the cup and the dish, but inside you are filthy—full of greed and self-

indulgence! ²⁶You blind Pharisee! First wash the inside of the cup and the dish,* and then the outside will become clean, too.

²⁷"What sorrow awaits you teachers of religious law and you Pharisees. Hypocrites! For you are like whitewashed tombs—beautiful on the outside but filled on the inside with dead people's bones and all sorts of impurity. ²⁸Outwardly you look like righteous people, but inwardly your hearts are filled with hypocrisy and lawlessness.

²⁹"What sorrow awaits you teachers of religious law and you Pharisees. Hypocrites! For you build tombs for the prophets your ancestors killed, and you decorate the monuments of the godly people your ancestors destroyed. ³⁰Then you say, 'If we had lived in the days of our ancestors, we would never have joined them in killing the prophets.'

³¹"But in saying that, you testify against yourselves that you are indeed the descendants of those who murdered the prophets. ³²Go ahead and finish what your ancestors started. ³³Snakes! Sons of vipers! How will you escape the judgment of hell?

³⁴"Therefore, I am sending you prophets and wise men and teachers of religious law. But you will kill some by crucifixion, and you will flog others with whips in your synagogues, chasing them from city to city. ³⁵As a result, you will be held responsible for the murder of all godly people of all time—from the murder of righteous Abel to the murder of Zechariah son of Barachiah, whom you killed in the Temple between the sanctuary and the altar. ³⁶I tell you the truth, this judgment will fall on this very generation."

23:13 Some manuscripts add verse 14, *What sorrow awaits you teachers of religious law and you Pharisees. Hypocrites! You shamelessly cheat widows out of their property and then pretend to be pious by making long prayers in public. Because of this, you will be severely punished.* Compare Mark 12:40 and Luke 20:47.
23:15 Greek *of Gehenna;* also in 23:33. 23:23 Greek *tithe the mint, the dill, and the cumin.* 23:24 See Lev 11:4, 23, where gnats and camels are both forbidden as food. 23:26 Some manuscripts do not include *and the dish.*

NOTES

23:13-14 These verses are the first of seven prophetic denunciations against the Pharisees (23:13, 15, 16, 23, 25, 27, 29; cf. 11:21; 18:7; 24:19; 26:24). Each woe, except that of 23:16 which refers to the "blind guides," is spoken to the "teachers of religious laws and you Pharisees. Hypocrites!" The general pattern seems to be (1) pronouncement of woe, (2) reason for pronouncement, and (3) explanation of the reason for the pronouncement. The stark contrast between Pharisaic "righteousness" and Kingdom norms is reminiscent of the antitheses of the Sermon on the Mount in 5:21–6:33.

What sorrow awaits you. This renders the words "woe to you," a phrase that reminds the reader of prophetic oracles in the OT. See the commentary below for discussion of this motif.

you shut the door of the Kingdom of Heaven in people's faces. The first woe goes right to the heart of the matter with the ironic charge that the scribes and Pharisees who claim to open the door actually keep people out of the Kingdom. The scribes and Pharisees "are not leaders but misleaders" (Davies and Allison 1997:285). Not only do they not enter the Kingdom, they prevent others from doing so. This language is similar to that of Jer 23:2 and Ezek 34:2-8, which likens the wicked leaders of Israel to shepherds which feed themselves and scatter the flock rather than feed them.

The textual authenticity of 23:14 is extremely doubtful; thus, it is not included in the NLT text (see mg). Many early and diverse manuscripts (‭א‬ B D L Z 33 it* syr* cop**) do not include it, and those manuscripts that do include it have disparity in placement (some place it after 23:12). The verse was likely interpolated from Mark 12:40 and/or Luke 20:47 (Metzger 1994:50). Whatever its textual authenticity, 23:14 resonates with the prevalent prophetic theme of justice for widows (cf., e.g., Isa 1:23).

23:15 *cross land and sea to make one convert.* The second woe builds on the theme of the first. The efforts of the scribes and Pharisees to convert others (lit. "to make proselytes," cf. Acts 2:10-11; 6:5; 13:43) are tragically ironic. It is not certain whether this refers to efforts to convert Gentiles to Judaism or efforts to convert Jews to Pharisaism. Possibly both are in view. McKnight (1991:106-108) concludes that the Pharisees did not actively pursue new converts from among the Gentiles, but that they urged that "God-fearing" Gentiles (cf. Acts 10:22; 13:16, 43; 16:14; 17:17; 18:7) become full converts to Judaism and observe the Pharisaic halakha. The description of the extent of their efforts ("land and sea") recalls Jonah 1:9; Hag 2:6, 21.

then you turn that person into twice the child of hell you yourselves are. Since they themselves were not entering the Kingdom, their efforts only result in others not entering it. Far from their converts becoming children of the Kingdom (18:3), they become children of hell (8:12).

23:16-24 While the first two woes deal with the general matter of preventing access to the Kingdom, the next two (23:16, 23) speak of specific legal rulings or *halakhot* (Heb. plural of halakha). This woe regarding oaths (cf. 5:33-37) is the most extensively developed of the seven oracles. It takes the form of pronouncement of woe (23:16a), description of the two acts that occasion the woe (23:16b, 18), two rhetorical questions underlining the falseness of the Pharisaic distinctions (23:17, 19), and three concluding statements on oaths (23:20-22).

23:16-19 *Blind guides.* The bitingly sarcastic reference to the Pharisees as "blind guides" is repeated in 23:24 (cf. 15:14).

you say that it means nothing to swear 'by God's Temple' but that it is binding to swear 'by the gold in the Temple.' This casuistry of the Pharisees amounted to an evasion of duty before God and was roundly condemned. Two different loopholes involving empty distinctions are exposed, one in 23:16-17 concerning the Temple and gold within it, and another in 23:18-19, involving the altar and what is sacrificed on it. Although the scribes and Pharisees viewed some oaths as binding and others as non-binding, Jesus taught that this distinction was meaningless and that all oaths are valid (23:20-22). He totally rejected their halakhic distinctions on valid and invalid oaths. Previously in this Gospel, Jesus flatly denied the need for any oaths at all (5:33-37). It is well known that the halakha on oaths and vows was very important in Second Temple Judaism (*m. Nedarim* and CD 15).

23:20-22 These verses draw three conclusions from the preceding two examples. When it comes to oath-taking, there is no valid distinction between the altar and what is offered on it (23:20, against 23:18). There is also no difference between the Temple and him who dwells in it (23:21; against 23:16). Finally, there is no difference between heaven and the throne of God and the One who sits on it (23:22; cf. 5:34). A person may not reduce his obligation to be true to an oath by constructing facile distinctions between the objects mentioned in that oath. Personal integrity means that one does what one says one will do (cf. 5:33-37).

23:23 *you are careful to tithe even the tiniest income from your herb gardens.* Lit., "you tithe the mint, the dill, and the cumin" (so NLT mg). For the Pharisees, only food that had been tithed was ritually pure and lawful to eat. Cf. *m. Avot* 1:16; *Demai* 2:1.

but you ignore the more important aspects of the law—justice, mercy, and faith. Here the Pharisees were condemned not for tithing herbs, understood as a crop (Lev 27:30; Deut 14:22-23), but for tithing herbs without attending to the weightier matters of the law (cf. Luke 11:42). *M. Shevi'it* 9:1 exempts certain herbs from the tithing requirement. NLT's "important aspects" might be taken to imply that tithing herbs is not important. But Jesus did not say this—he said justice, mercy, and faith are more important than tithing herbs. Jesus did not support a hierarchical ethic but cut through the external observance to the central value or ethic which supports that observance: justice, mercy, and faithfulness (cf. Hos 6:6, cited in Matt 9:13; 12:7, and also Mic 6:8; Zech 7:9-10).

23:24 *You strain your water so you won't accidentally swallow a gnat, but you swallow a camel!* In terms of hyperbolic metaphor, the Pharisees were scrupulous in straining out gnats (tithing herbs), but they should have been more concerned to guard against swallowing camels (omitting the weightier matters). It is interesting to note that the Aramaic words for "gnat" (*qalma*) and "camel" (*gamla*) are quite similar, so Jesus' hyperbole was also a pun. Additionally, this language speaks to the inconsistency of the Pharisees, since both gnats and camels were unclean and could not be eaten (Lev 11:4, 23).

23:25-26 The fifth and sixth woes together address the Pharisees' neglect of heart piety in favor of mere outward piety.

you are so careful to clean the outside . . . but inside you are filthy. In the fifth woe, the scribes and Pharisees are described metaphorically as those who clean the outside of tableware but neglect the inside (cf. Luke 11:39-41). Despite their zeal for the Torah and their traditions, they were people characterized by extortion and self-indulgence. Davies and Allison (1997:296-299) are probably correct in saying that Jesus was not disputing existing Pharisaic tradition here but was simply using the washing of tableware metaphorically (cf. Blomberg 1992:347). Pharisaic fastidiousness about such matters renders the metaphor fitting, but Jesus was not attacking that fastidiousness per se.

23:27-28 *you are like whitewashed tombs—beautiful on the outside but filled on the inside with dead people's bones.* Jesus turned from the metaphor of cups and dishes to the macabre simile of tombs (cf. Luke 11:44). Tombs are made beautiful on the outside, but on the inside there are only bones and decaying corpses (which, by the way, ritually defile the Pharisees). It is not clear whether the whitewash on the tombs was intended to further beautify their architecture or to indicate that the bones inside were a cause of ritual impurity (Davies and Allison 1997:300-302; Garland 1979:152-157).

Outwardly you look like righteous people, but inwardly your hearts are filled with hypocrisy and lawlessness. The scribes and Pharisees appeared to men as righteous, but their hearts were full of hypocrisy and lawlessness. For Jesus the law must be obeyed from the heart. Outwardly lawful behavior may conceal a lawless heart (5:20, 22, 28; 6:1; 7:22-23; 12:34; 13:41; 15:7-9, 19; 18:35; 24:12, 48).

23:29-30 *you build tombs for the prophets.* The simile of tombs from the sixth woe becomes the transitional motif which links the sixth to the seventh. But here the tombs are those of the prophets, which the Pharisees adorn while claiming that they would never have taken part with their ancestors in killing the prophets. This seventh woe is climactic in that it addresses the root problem of all the others. If Israel had listened to the prophets whom God sent to them, they would not have faced the consequences of God's judgment announced by the prophets. This theme is developed in the commentary below. For references to well-known tombs in ancient sources, see Acts 2:29; 1 Macc 13:27-30; Josephus *Antiquities* 7.392; 13.249; 18.108; 20.95; *War* 4.531-532.

23:31 *you are indeed the descendants of those who murdered the prophets.* Jesus pointed out that their disavowal of complicity in the murder of the prophets unwittingly implicated them in the guilt of their ancestors (cf. Luke 11:47-48). Jesus was using the word "descendants" to imply inherited character traits, not just physical descent. Modern sayings such as "a chip off the old block" or "an apple does not fall from the tree" speak to the same point.

23:32 *finish what your ancestors started.* Jesus' ironic imperative (cf. Amos 4:4-5 in light of Amos 5:5) is lit. "fill up the measure of your ancestors," and should be viewed in the context of Matthew's characteristic motif of OT fulfillment. (See the discussion in the Major Themes section of the Introduction.) Jesus was speaking of his impending crucifixion as the culmination of Israel's historical pattern of rejecting its own prophets. The motif of sin coming to its full measure is found elsewhere (Gen 15:16; 1 Thess 2:16). Stephen, Paul, and the author of Hebrews also reflect on Israel's sad history of rejecting its own prophets (Acts 7:52; 1 Thess 2:14-16; Heb 11:32-38).

23:33 *Snakes! Sons of vipers! How will you escape the judgment of hell?* Jesus' epithets recall 3:7; 12:34. The sobering "judgment of hell" recalls 5:22, 29, 30; 10:28; 18:9; 23:15.

23:34-35 This section takes Israel's rejection of God's messengers one step further to the persecution of Jesus' disciples after his death. This continues the seventh woe but also forms a sort of summary of all seven woes. Just as the murder of Jesus was anticipated by that of the prophets, so the murder of Jesus augurs the persecution and death of his followers, who succeed him in the ministry of the ?ingdom (cf. 10:16-33; 20:23; Acts 7:52; 12:1-3). The murder of Jesus will bring horrible judgment because it is the ultimate atrocity in an atrocious sequence which began when Cain murdered his brother Abel (Gen 4:8ff).

righteous Abel to . . . Zechariah son of Barachiah. The final woe and its development concerning Zechariah assumes that Jesus is the climactic prophet of God. Abel and Zechariah were the first and last martyrs of the Heb. Bible, which ends not with Malachi but with 2 Chronicles. The mention of the martyrdom of Zechariah son of Berekiah (cf. Zech 1:1) causes some problems in identification, but clearly Matthew has in mind the murder of Zechariah the son of Jehoida, whose martyrdom is recorded in 2 Chr 24:21. (For discussions of this problem see Blomberg 1987:193-195; Gundry 1967:86-88; Hagner 1995:676-677.)

23:36 *this judgment will fall on this very generation.* Jesus solemnly reaffirmed that the wicked generation which rebelled against his words and works will bear the brunt of the woes he has just uttered (11:16; 12:39, 41, 42, 45; 16:4; 17:17; 24:34). Since they are in solidarity with those who murdered Zechariah, it is as though they did it themselves. Though the woes are directed against the leaders, the entire generation that followed the leaders gave tacit approval to the leaders and became implicated in their guilt.

COMMENTARY

Prophetic Oracles of Woe. The Old Testament prophets frequently cried woe against Israel's sins. For example, see Isaiah 5:8, 11, 18, 20, 21, 22 (a series of six woes); Amos 5:18; 6:1, 4; Habakkuk 2:6, 9, 12, 15, 19 (a series of five woes); Zechariah 11:17. These oracles spoke with a blend of anger, grief, and alarm about the excruciating consequences that would come upon Israel due to her sin. After the pronouncement of woe, such oracles contain a description of the persons upon whom the woe will come. This description amounts to the reason why the woe is merited. Thus, a woe oracle states the conclusion before the premises on which it is based. Woe oracles may have developed from covenant curses (Deut 27:15) or even from funeral lamentations (Jer 22:18). The New Testament contains oracles of woe in other places besides Matthew 23 (Luke 6:24-26; Rev 18:10, 16, 19). Woe oracles are also found in Second Temple Jewish literature. The Qumran literature has notable woe oracles, including some against Jerusalem and its leaders (2Q23 1:2; 4Q179 1 i 4, 1 ii 1; 4Q511 63 iii 4-5). *1 Enoch* contains four series of woes (*1 Enoch* 94:6-95:7; 96:4-8; 98:9-99:2; 100:7-9). *2 Enoch* 52 contains a series of alternating blessings and cursings (cf. Luke 6:20-26). The Talmud also contains exclamations of woe.

It is important to note that the prophet's attitude in oracles of woe is not simply one of anger. Clearly the prophet's anger at Israel's sin is tempered at times by his grief and alarm at the horrible price Israel will pay for that sin. The prophet speaks for God against sin and this explains his anger. But that anger is directed toward his own people, and this explains the grief. The palpable pathos of woe oracles was due to the prophet's dual solidarities. Isaiah, for example, pronounced woe upon himself, not only because he himself was a person of unclean lips but also because he lived among a people of unclean lips. The prophet must speak for God, but in announcing oracles of judgment, he knew that he was announcing the doom of his own people.

Two important conclusions flow from this brief sketch of prophetic woe oracles. First, Jesus' pronouncements of woe upon the religious leaders were not innovative. His severe language must have sounded familiar to the religious leaders, given their ostensible acquaintance with the Old Testament. To the extent that these leaders were aware of Second Temple sectarian literature, Jesus' woes would have sounded rather contemporary. Second, Jesus' pronouncement of woe oracles was not merely an exercise in spiting his enemies. Rather, as is made clear in 23:37, his words come from at least as much grief as anger.

The Charge of Hypocrisy. Matthew spoke explicitly of hypocrites thirteen times in his Gospel (6:2, 5, 16; 7:5; 15:7; 22:18; 23:13, 15, 23, 25, 27, 29; 24:51). All but one

(23:16) of the seven pronouncements of woe in Matthew 23 speak of the scribes and Pharisees as hypocrites, and even 23:16 portrays the scribes and Pharisees as hypocrites—"blind guides." The various words related to "hypocrite" come not from the Hebrew Bible but from the Graeco-Roman world, describing someone who gave an answer, interpreted an oracle, mimicked another person, or acted a part in a drama. At times, the idea of pretending in order to deceive is present, but the word itself does not have a negative connotation (BDAG 1038). In Matthew hypocrites are more specifically those who live for fleeting human applause rather than for eternal divine approval (6:2, 5, 16). Hypocrites honor God outwardly, while their hearts are far from God (15:7-8). A hypocrite pretends to have sincere religious interest while questioning Jesus with evil intent. Further, such a person says one thing but does another (23:3; cf. Rom 2:21-24). Thus, in Matthew, hypocrisy involves religious fraud, a basic discrepancy or inconsistency between one's outwardly godly behavior and one's inner evil thoughts or motives.

Isaiah 29:13 may be the most important prophetic text condemning religious fraud. This passage, cited by Jesus in 15:7-9, concerns the religious leaders (Isa 29:1, 10, 14, 20-21) of Jerusalem ("Ariel"; Isa 29:1, 2, 7). The fraud described there involves seemingly pious words and traditional rulings which in reality disguise hearts that are far from God and plans that are thought to be hidden from God's sight (Isa 29:15). Israel's charismatic leaders, the prophets, were mute (Isa 29:10-12) and its judges were corrupt (Isa 29:20-21). But in spite of this, Israel's outward religious observances went on (Isa 29:1). Jesus applied this passage to certain Pharisees and scribes, who insisted on the ritual washing of hands before meals but dishonored their parents by the fraudulent claim that what might have been given to the parents had already been promised to God (15:5). For Jesus, this "corban" practice, evidently sanctioned by the "tradition of the elders," violated and set aside God's law (15:6). Additionally, the practice of ritual washing of hands made the fundamental error of viewing defilement as coming to humans from external sources rather than coming from humans due to an internal problem, an evil heart (15:11-20).

Jesus' rebuke of hypocrisy is not only deeply rooted in the Old Testament (cf. Ps 50:16-23, 78:36-37; Isa 48:1-2; 58:1-9; Jer 3:10; 7:4-11; 12:2; Ezek 33:30-33; Mic 3:11; Mal 1:6-10), it is also similar to rebukes found in Second Temple Jewish literature. For example, *Psalms of Solomon* presents a withering critique of hypocritical religious and political leaders, including the wish that crows would peck out their eyes and that their corpses would not be buried (4:19-20). *Assumption of Moses* 7 predicts the demise of hypocrites who behave unjustly and sensuously while at the same time being concerned for ritual purity. *Rule of the Community*, from Qumran, divides humanity into the righteous who will be eternally rewarded and the deceitful who will be eternally punished, and includes hypocrisy in a list of the vices of the deceitful (1QS 4:10). The later Rabbinic literature was also sensitive to the problem of hypocrisy, even among the Pharisees. The Talmudic discussions of seven types of Pharisees, of whom only the one who acted out of love was approved, is illuminating (*y. Berakhot* 14b; *y. Sotah* 20c; *b. Sotah* 22b). The "shoulder" Pharisee, who conspicuously carries his good deeds on his shoulder so that people can see them, is particularly relevant to the charge of hypocrisy in Matthew 23. See also *b. Sotah* 41b and 42a which affirm respectively that hypocrites will go to hell and never see the Shekinah.

The Charge of Rejecting the Prophets. The charge that Israel had rejected its own prophets (23:29-31) is perhaps the most serious accusation found in Matthew 23, since it addresses the root cause of the other problems confronted there. If Israel had listened to its prophets, the Pharisees would not have prevented people from entering the Kingdom. If Israel had listened to its prophets, casuistry in oaths and the elevation of trivial duties over basic duties would not have become commonplace. If Israel had listened to its prophets, matters of the heart would have remained primary, not the external appearance of righteousness. But Israel had rejected its prophets throughout its history, and that rejection would reach its horrible culmination in the rejection of its Messiah (23:32) and his messengers (23:34). This would bring all the guilt of the innocent blood shed from the first to the last book of the Old Testament upon Jerusalem (23:35-36).

This is not the first time Matthew pointed out that Israel had rejected its prophets. The genealogy of Jesus stressed the exile to Babylon, which of course was due to rejection of the prophets (1:11-12, 17). The ministry of John the Baptist is presented in terms of prophetic rebuke (3:7-12), and Israel's rejection of John is explained as the rejection of an Elijah-like figure who is more than a prophet (11:7-18; 17:12; 21:32). When Jesus' disciples are persecuted, they are to be encouraged because the prophets were similarly persecuted (5:12). Rejection or reception of the ministry of Jesus' disciples is described as that of a prophet (10:41-42; 25:35-45). Jesus also repeatedly cited prophetic literature, sometimes with an introduction that stressed his incredulity at the religious leaders' ignorance of the prophets' message (9:13;12:7; 13:14-15; 15:7-9; 21:13, 16, 42). All these factors combine to make it clear to the reader of Matthew that Israel had rejected its prophets.

Jesus' charge that Israel has rejected its prophets clearly echoes many similar charges in the Old Testament itself. The Chronicler's sad commentary on the end of the southern kingdom stresses Israel's obstinacy in not only ignoring but even mocking God's messengers. It had come to the place where there was no remedy, and the exile to Babylon ensued (2 Chr 36:15-16). Daniel's great prayer of confession is centered on the admission that "we have refused to listen to your servants the prophets" (Dan 9:6, 10; cf. Neh 9:26, 30; Jer 25:4; 26:5). Israel abandoned the Torah and rejected the prophets whom God sent to remind her of her obligations (Deut 28:15-68; 1 Kgs 8:46-51). Notable examples of the rejection of the prophets include Ahab and Jezebel's rejection of Elijah and Micaiah (1 Kgs 19:1-3; 22:7-38), Amaziah's rejection of Amos (Amos 7:10-17), Pashhur's persecution of Jeremiah (Jer 20:1-6), Jehoiakim's murder of Uriah son of Shemaiah (Jer 26:20-23), and Zedekiah's imprisonment of Jeremiah (Jer 37:11-38:28). Even Jesus' "ironic imperative" telling the religious leaders to fill up the measure of their ancestors' guilt by killing him (23:32) has a prophetic ring to it (Jer 7:21; Amos 4:4-5; Nah 3:14-15). His allusion to the murders of Abel and Zechariah effectively sums up the entire history of the murder of God's prophets in the Old Testament, which in its Hebrew text ends with 2 Chronicles (23:35; cf. Gen 4:8ff; 2 Chr 24:21).

Israel's rejection of the prophets is also mentioned in Second Temple literature. The book of *Jubilees*, probably to be dated around 150 BC, predicts the judgment which will come to Israel when they refuse to listen to the prophets (here called "witnesses") and instead kill them (*Jubilees* 1:12-14). *4 Baruch* (a.k.a. *Paraleipomena of Jeremiah*), which is probably a Jewish work with Christian interpolations or a Jewish-Christian work, mentions at the outset that the prophet Jeremiah must leave Jerusalem before God can allow the Babylonians to destroy it due to its sins. This is because Jeremiah's prayers buttress the city against its enemies (*4 Baruch* 1:1-8). This same work ends with a note about the desire of the people to kill Jeremiah as they had previously killed Isaiah (*4 Baruch* 9:19-31). The Jewish work of the first century AD, *Lives of the Prophets*, recounts how 23 prophets died. Most are reported to have died peacefully, but seven are reported to have been martyred (chs 1-3, 6-7, 15, 23). The composite Jewish-Christian book, *Martyrdom and Ascension of Isaiah*, is relevant here also. The deuterocanonical book of Tobit describes Tobit's belief in the words of the prophets, and his conviction that the Second Temple would be destroyed and Israel scattered, and then finally that Israel would be restored, the Temple rebuilt, and the nations converted (Tob 14:3-7).

Materials from Qumran also refer to Israel's rejection of the prophets. 4Q166 2:1-6, commenting on Hosea 2:10, states that Israel forgot the God who gave them commandments through his servants the prophets and blindly revered false prophets as gods. 4Q266 3 iii 18-19 states that Israel despised the words of the prophets (cf. CD 7:17-18). 4Q390 2 i 5 predicts a coming time of evil when Israel will violate the statutes given to them by God's servants the prophets.

The mention of the martyrdom of Zechariah son of Berekiah in Matthew 23:35 causes some problems in identification, but clearly Matthew had in mind the murder of Zechariah the son of Jehoida in 2 Chronicles 24:21. This murder is recounted in *Lamentations Rabbah* (Proems 5, 23; cf. 1.16.51; 2.2.4; 2.20.23; 4.13.16) and in other Rabbinic works (*Midrash Tanhuma Yelamdenu* on Lev 4:1; *Ecclesiastes Rabbah* 3:16; 10:4; *Targum Lamentations* 2:20; *y. Ta'anit* 69a; *b. Gittin* 57b; *b. Sanhedrin* 96b). Matthew's use of this story is not unlike that of the Rabbinic materials in that the murder of Zechariah is a particularly egregious sin, one for which the victim implored God's retribution. For Matthew, as well as for the rabbis, that retribution was put into the context of lament over the destruction of Jerusalem.

◆   **18. Jesus' lament over Jerusalem (23:37-39)**

[37]"O Jerusalem, Jerusalem, the city that kills the prophets and stones God's messengers! How often I have wanted to gather your children together as a hen protects her chicks beneath her wings, but you wouldn't let me. [38]And now, look,

your house is abandoned and desolate.*
³⁹For I tell you this, you will never see me

again until you say, 'Blessings on the one
who comes in the name of the LORD!'*"

23:38 Some manuscripts do not include *and desolate.* 23:39 Ps 118:26.

NOTES

23:37-39 These verses constitute "the climax of Jesus' public ministry to Israel" (Garland 1993:232). The tone of 23:37-39 changes from accusation to lament, but the element of lament is not lacking entirely from the woe oracles.

I have wanted to gather your children together as a hen protects her chicks beneath her wings, but you wouldn't let me. These final public words of Jesus to his contemporaries strike a note of unspeakable sadness at their unwillingness to respond to his motherly concern (cf. Luke 13:34-35). The feminine image is striking (cf. Deut 32:11; Ruth 2:12; Ps 17:8; 36:7; 91:1-4; Isa 31:5).

your house is abandoned and desolate. The prediction of the desolation of "your house" in 23:38 probably refers to the Temple itself (21:13; 24:1-2; cf. 1 Kgs 9:7-8), although this language may be a metaphor for Jerusalem or the nation itself (Jer 12:7; *1 Enoch* 89:56). Although some take 23:39 as only stressing the certainty of judgment (e.g., Meier 1980:274-275), the image of the mother hen gathering her chicks (23:37) speaks of compassion, not rejection (Davies and Allison 1997:323-324; Garland 1993:232-233).

you will never see me again until you say, 'Blessings on the one who comes in the name of the LORD!' There is a glimmer of hope for salvation if only Israel will acknowledge Jesus to be her Messiah. Israel sinned in rejecting Jesus, and there will be punishment for that sin. But here, as throughout biblical history, repentance after sin and judgment brings grace and redemption (cf. Rom 11:1-2, 11-12, 15, 23-27). Jesus will return only when Israel in true repentance utters the words which were uttered without adequate understanding in 21:9. (See the balanced discussion in Bruner 1990:835-837.)

COMMENTARY

Jesus' lament over Jerusalem is a remarkably sympathetic conclusion to his antipathetic denunciation of the scribes and Pharisees. In this lament the compassion of Jesus for his people and his city is palpable (cf. 9:36; 11:28). Other touching biblical laments (e.g., 2 Sam 1:17-27; 18:33; 19:4; Rom 9:1-3; Rev 18:10, 16-19) pale in comparison with it. Jesus was deeply moved for his people and for his city in spite of the shameful manner in which its leaders had treated him and in spite of the horrible sufferings that he knew still lie ahead. Christians today must ponder their Lord's compassion for the Jewish people and reflect on their own level of concern for the people of the Messiah (Rom 10:1). An arrogant attitude toward those who are lost is always despicable, but it is especially so when it concerns the Jewish people (Rom 11:16-24).

This passage also illustrates the mysterious relationship between divine sovereignty and human responsibility. The same Greek word (*thelō* [ᵀᴳ2309, ᶻᴳ2527]) is used in 23:37 for Jesus' desire to gather the people of Jerusalem ("I have *wanted* to gather") and for their refusal to be gathered ("you *wouldn't* let me"). Yet, in 11:27 Jesus appears to accomplish his purpose in revealing the Father to whomever he wills (cf. 16:17). Despite the judgment announced in 23:38, according to 23:39 the tension continues into the future. Unless and until the people of Jerusalem utter in faith the words of Psalm 118:26, they will not see Jesus again. But the implication is that if they do bless the one who comes in the name of the Lord, they will ultimately receive the Kingdom blessings they have rejected up to this point.

Matthew 23 and Jewish-Christian Relations. No one can doubt that the language of Matthew 23 is severe, and that it castigates certain Jewish religious leaders of Jesus' day in terms that make genteel modern folks extremely uncomfortable. And no one should deny that through the centuries misguided Christians have used this language as a justification of anti-Semitic attitudes and, worse yet, inquisitions, pogroms, and even the holocaust of World War II. But all this is due to a misunderstanding of Matthew 23 by the early Gentile Church, a misunderstanding borne out of an arrogance against which Paul warned in Romans 11:18-21. Ironically, this has become the (mis)understanding of modern Jews as well as modern Christians. Perhaps this history of a "Gentilized" misunderstanding of Matthew 23 can be alleviated somewhat by a "Judaized" understanding, stressing the Jewishness of the woe oracles and the concerns about hypocrisy and the rejection of the prophets.

But the intellectual understanding which has been outlined above will fall on deaf ears unless it is conveyed with a sensitive and loving spirit. Unless Christians today are willing to love Jewish people and grieve for the sad state of Jewish-Christian relations, as did Jesus (23:37) and Paul (Rom 9:1-3), there is little reason to think that intellectual arguments will make any difference at all. In light of the sad history of Jewish-Christian relations, Christians have much to live down. Matthew 23 itself, especially 23:8-12, would be a good place to start a much needed check of Christian character. Christians must not read Matthew 23 as only a critique of Jerusalem's ancient leaders. It is also clearly intended to warn Jesus' disciples, both ancient and modern, not to follow the example of the scribes and Pharisees (cf. 1 Pet 2:1). "All of the vices here attributed to the scribes and Pharisees have attached themselves to Christians, and that in abundance" (Davies and Allison 1997:262). Those who want be salt and light in this world will get nowhere if their testimony is ruined by hypocrisy and vanity. But the integrity and humility of Christians, modeled on that of the Jewish Messiah, can alleviate the damage done by the attitudes and atrocities which mar Jewish-Christian relations today.

Summary and Transition. At Jesus' entry into Jerusalem, the crowds shouted Psalm 118:25-26: "Blessings on the one who comes in the name of the Lord" (21:9) and the leaders looked on angrily. According to 23:39, Jesus pronounced judgment on those same leaders and used the same words that the crowds shouted a few days earlier. The sinful rebellion of the leaders outlined in 23 is made all the more monstrous by their official capacity: they "are the official interpreters of the law of Moses." This is the context in which Jesus spoke his final discourse about the end of the ages. The impressive Temple precinct, where the spiritless leadership officiated, would be totally destroyed by a desolating sacrilege before Jesus would come again and the nation would genuinely turn to him with the words "blessings on the one who comes in the name of the Lord."

◆   B. The Judgment of Jerusalem and the Coming of Christ (24:1–25:46)
    1. The first pains of childbirth: life in the present age (24:1-14; cf.
    Mark 13:1-13; Luke 21:1-19)

As Jesus was leaving the Temple grounds, his disciples pointed out to him the various Temple buildings. ²But he responded, "Do you see all these buildings? I tell you the truth, they will be completely demolished. Not one stone will be left on top of another!"

³Later, Jesus sat on the Mount of Olives. His disciples came to him privately and said, "Tell us, when will all this happen? What sign will signal your return and the end of the world?*"

⁴Jesus told them, "Don't let anyone mislead you, ⁵for many will come in my name, claiming, 'I am the Messiah.' They will deceive many. ⁶And you will hear of wars and threats of wars, but don't panic. Yes, these things must take place, but the end won't follow immediately. ⁷Nation will go to war against nation, and kingdom against kingdom. There will be famines and earthquakes in many parts of the world. ⁸But all this is only the first of the birth pains, with more to come.

⁹"Then you will be arrested, persecuted, and killed. You will be hated all over the world because you are my followers.* ¹⁰And many will turn away from me and betray and hate each other. ¹¹And many false prophets will appear and will deceive many people. ¹²Sin will be rampant everywhere, and the love of many will grow cold. ¹³But the one who endures to the end will be saved. ¹⁴And the Good News about the Kingdom will be preached throughout the whole world, so that all nations* will hear it; and then the end will come."

24:3 Or *the age?* 24:9 Greek *on account of my name.* 24:14 Or *all peoples.*

NOTES

24:1 *Jesus was leaving the Temple grounds.* After summarily denouncing the scribes and Pharisees, Jesus left the Temple (cf. Mark 13:1-4; Luke 21:5-7). This departure takes on symbolic overtones of divine abandonment. Jesus had just announced the desolation of the Temple, and now he acted it out (Ezek 11:22-23).

his disciples pointed out to him the various Temple buildings. As they walked away east toward the Mount of Olives, the disciples pointed out the magnificence of the Temple to Jesus, perhaps to break the tension or even because they found his prediction of its judgment incredible (Davies and Allison 1997:334). The beauty of Herod's extensive renovation was well known (Mark 13:1; John 2:20; Josephus *War* 5.184-226; *Antiquities* 15.391-402; Tacitus *Histories*, 5.8; *b. Sukkah* 51b).

24:2 *they will be completely demolished. Not one stone will be left.* Any doubts as to the Temple's destruction were dispelled by Jesus' graphic statement in 24:2b that not one stone would be left standing (cf. 26:61; 27:40; Acts 6:14; Josephus *War* 6.300ff; 7.1).

24:3 *Jesus sat on the Mount of Olives.* When the walk to the Mount of Olives had been completed, Jesus sat down (cf. 5:1; 13:1; 15:29; 19:28; 22:44; 23:2; 25:31). From the Mount of Olives, Jesus could look westward right at the entrance to the Temple's holiest place (*m. Berakhot* 9:5; *m. Middot* 2:4). This mountain is prophetically significant (Zech 14:4). Here the disciples approached Jesus privately (cf. 17:19) and asked him what is best understood as a two part question (not three parts as in Walvoord 1974:182), concerning the destruction of Jerusalem and his coming to end the age.

when will all this happen? Lit., "When will these things occur?" A reference to what Jesus had just said about the total destruction of the Temple.

What sign will signal your return and the end of the world? In the disciples' thinking the end of the Temple would have epochal significance and could only augur the end of the present world (cf. 13:39-40, 49; 28:20; Hagner 1995:688). Modern readers of Matthew should not artificially superimpose their chronological hindsight on this text. Although such hindsight reveals the historical distance between the past destruction of the Temple in AD 70 and the yet future coming of Jesus, at the same time it obscures the conceptual link-age between the two events. (See the commentary below and Turner 1989.) Jesus' answer to this two-part question does not stress chronology (24:36-44), but ethics (24:45ff). The signs are imprecise to the extent that they cannot be used to determine the date, so disci-ples must always be alert.

24:4-5 Jesus' prophetic words in 24:4ff are in character with what he had already spoken— he had already repeatedly spoken of the future (5:3-12; 7:21-23; 8:11-12; 10:23; 11:22-24; 13:36-43, 47-50; 16:27-28; 19:28-30; 22:29-32; 23:39; cf. 26:13, 21, 29, 64).

Don't let anyone mislead you, for many will come in my name, claiming, 'I am the Mes-siah.' Jesus' answer to the disciples' twofold question begins with a warning against decep-tion by false messiahs (cf. Mark 13:5-13; Luke 21:8-19; 2 Thess 2:3). Future deceivers who come "in my name" need not claim to be Jesus himself but only to be the Messiah. This warning is expanded later in the discourse (24:23-27).

They will deceive many. The double use of the word "many" is sobering—not only will there be many false messiahs, there will also be many who are deceived by them (cf. 24:24; 1 John 2:18, 22; 4:3; 2 John 1:7). The well-known Jewish messianic pretender Bar Kochba led a second Jewish revolt against Rome that ended in AD 135 with the total banishing of all Jews from Jerusalem (Josephus *Antiquities,* 20:97-99, 160-172, 188). Other pretenders were Theudas, Judas of Galilee (Acts 5:36-37), and one known as "the Egyptian" (Acts 21:38). There have also been numerous nominal Christians who have claimed in Jesus' name to be the Messiah.

24:6-7 *you will hear of wars and threats of wars.* Religious error will coincide with political upheavals.

these things must take place. Because God has predestined them (cf. 26:54; Dan 2:28-29, 45; Rev 1:1; 4:1).

Nation will go to war against nation, and kingdom against kingdom. International aggression, real and rumored (cf. Jer 51:46; Dan 9:26; 11:44), should not frighten the disciples, since such disturbances do not signify the end. The Jewish War of rebellion against Rome in AD 66-70 looms large here. Rather, these are merely the first stages of the messianic woes to come upon the world.

famines and earthquakes. Famine is mentioned elsewhere in the NT and would inevitably result from war in ancient times (Acts 11:27-30; Rev 6:8; 18:8; 2 Esdr 9:3-4). Earthquakes are an additional ominous matter, as chaos extends to nature itself (cf. 8:24; 27:54; 28:2; Joel 2:10; Hag 2:6; Zech 14:4-5; Acts 16:26; Rev 6:12; 8:5; 11:13, 19; 16:18; *1 Enoch* 1:6-7; 102:2; 1QH^a 11:12-15).

24:8 *the first of the birth pains.* The use of the pains of a woman in labor as a metaphor for eschatological troubles and/or the woe of God's judgment is found elsewhere in Jewish literature and the NT (Isa 13:8; 26:17; 66:7-8; Jer 4:31; 6:24; 22:23; 30:5-6; 48:41; Hos 13:13; Mic 4:9-13; Mark 13:8; 1 Thess 5:3; Rev 12:2; cf. John 16:20-22; Gal 4:19; 1QH^a 11:7-11; *1 Enoch* 62:4; 2 Esdr 4:42; *Targum Psalms* 18:14).

24:9 *persecuted.* The dangers from false messiahs and wars will be accompanied by per-secution (cf. 10:17ff; 23:34). The disciples will be universally hated because of their affil-iation with Jesus (cf. 5:11; 10:18, 22, 25, 32-33, 38). The hatred and persecution will even result in murder (cf. 10:28; 21:35; 22:6). The Gr. word underlying "persecution" is *thlipsis* [TG2347, ZG2568], usually translated "tribulation." A perusal of the use of this word in the NT indicates that it sometimes describes the typical generic troubles which Christians have often faced, but other times describes severe, unparalleled eschatological troubles (e.g., 13:21; 24:21, 29; John 16:33; Acts 14:22; 20:23; Rom 2:9; 8:35; 12:12; 2 Thess 1:6; Heb 10:33; Rev 1:9; 2:9-10, 22; 7:14; cf. Dan 12:1; Joel 2:2; Zeph 1:15).

24:10 *many will turn away from me and betray and hate each other.* The external pressure will have devastating internal consequences as some disciples fall away (lit. "to be offended" or "caused to stumble;" cf. 5:29-30; 13:21; 18:6, 8-9) from their commitment to Jesus and hatefully betray genuine disciples.

24:11 *many false prophets will appear.* The false prophets here (cf. 7:15; 24:24; Acts 13:6; 20:29-30; 2 Pet 2:1ff; 1 John 4:1; Rev 16:13; 19:20; 20:10) are evidently promoters of the false messiahs with whom they are associated in this passage (cf. 24:5, 23-26).

24:12 *Sin will be rampant.* Lit., "the increase of lawlessness." The false religious teachings result in the increase of lawlessness (7:23; 13:41; 23:28; cf. 2 Thess 2:8).

the love of many will grow cold. True love for God and truth will decline (2 Thess 2:10; 2 Tim 3:4; Rev 2:4). If loving God and neighbor is the quintessence of the law and prophets (22:34-40), its decline amounts to lawlessness and is devastating for God's people.

24:13 *the one who endures to the end will be saved.* The response of Jesus' disciples to all these horrifying circumstances—false messiahs and prophets, wars, famines, earthquakes, apostasy, betrayal—is fidelity to the bitter end. Perseverance in obedience to Jesus contrasts with lawlessness and is the true test of discipleship. The salvation promised to those who endure is not merely physical deliverance from persecution (Walvoord 1974:184) but the future salvific reward for those whose endurance demonstrates their genuine faith, in contrast to those in 24:10-12 who fall away or promote false teaching (Blomberg 1992:356; Carson 1984:498-499). This verse contains a verbatim echo of 10:22 (cf. 12:32; 13:21, 41; Rom 12:12; 2 Tim 2:3, 10, 12; Jas 1:12; 5:11; 1 Pet 2:20; Rev 1:9; 3:10; 13:10; 14:12).

24:14 *the Good News about the Kingdom will be preached throughout the whole world.* The perseverance of the believers will result in the Kingdom message (3:2; 4:17, 23; 9:35; 10:7; 13:19; 26:13) being preached to all the nations before the end comes. Note the similarities of this passage with 10:22-23 and 28:18-20.

the end will come. This statement should be compared with statements about the end in 24:6, 8.

COMMENTARY

Introduction to the Olivet Discourse: Various Interpretations. The crucial question in interpreting the discourse concerns the relationship between the destruction of the Temple in AD 70 and the eschatological judgment of God at Christ's second coming. There are essentially three views, although there are shades of difference within each of them. According to the *preterist* (past) view, most or all of the predictions of the discourse were all fulfilled in AD 70, when the Romans destroyed the Temple (France 1985:333ff, Kik 1948; Sproul 1998; Tasker 1961:223ff). In the view of partial preterists, 24:1-35 describes the AD 70 destruction of Jerusalem, and only 24:36ff refers to the return of Jesus. However, full or comprehensive preterists attempt to explain the entire discourse as fulfilled in AD 70.

According to an opposite approach, the *futurist* view, the discourse concerns only the return of Christ to the earth (Barbieri 1983:76ff; Toussaint 1980:266ff;

Walvoord 1974:179ff). According to this view, Christ does not answer the first part of the disciples' question in 24:3, which concerns the destruction of the Temple. For several reasons which are mentioned in the notes on Matthew 24 (cf. Turner 1989), it seems best to conclude that both of the above views are one-sided and inadequate to handle the complexities of the passage. After all, the disciples asked not only about the destruction of Jerusalem but also about the end of the world. Only an approach which deals carefully with both of these matters is acceptable.

According to the *preterist-futurist* view, the predictions of the discourse intertwine both the historical destruction of Jerusalem and the yet future return of Jesus. Some advocates of this view distinguish between portions of the discourse having to do with AD 70 from other portions having to do with the end times, and others view ·the events of AD 70 as a partial or anticipatory fulfillment of that which will be consummated at Christ's return (Blomberg 1992:352; Carson 1984:495; Hagner 1995:685). Involved in this view is the prophetic perspective of foreshortening or double (near and far) fulfillment (Broadus 1886:479-480; Hendriksen 1973:846ff; Ladd 1974:309ff). This is the approach I follow. Jesus' eschatological discourse answers both parts of the disciples' question. His words about the fall of the Temple provide the reader with a preliminary picture which anticipates and forecasts the eventual end of the world.

According to 24:1, Jesus left the Temple after an extended conflict with various groups of Jewish religious leaders (cf. 21:17). His authority had been clearly demonstrated in the Temple in numerous confrontations with them; however, as he put it in 23:38, they would not believe in him. The disciples' preoccupation with the grandeur of the Temple stands in contrast to Jesus' words of judgment upon Israel. They called Jesus' attention to the glorious Temple precinct, but Jesus spoke only of its demolition. The disciples' question about the time of this demolition and (they assumed) Jesus' return (24:1-3) leads into the body of the discourse.

Jesus' Olivet Discourse begins with an initial section which is didactic in nature (24:4-31). It seems best to view the "first pains of childbirth" in 24:4-14 as preliminaries that characterize the entire period between the comings of Jesus (Blomberg 1992:353ff; Carson 1984:495; Hagner 1995:684-685). In 24:15-28, the language is more ominous, with descriptions of the desecration of the Temple (24:15), as well as unparalleled great tribulation (24:21). It seems best to see this section as envisioning the destruction of the Temple in AD 70, which becomes a token of the ultimate judgment which ends the present world. The coming of Jesus to judge humankind after that tribulation is described with standard Old Testament apocalyptic imagery in 24:29-31. At 24:32 the tone becomes more paraenetic (or hortatory) as the stress shifts from the "what" to the "so what." Jesus speaks in parabolic imagery to stress the urgency and unknown time of his coming (24:32-36). This leads to an emphasis upon alertness in the reference to Noah (24:37-44) and in the parables of the wise servant (24:45-51) and the wise and foolish virgins (25:1-13). The parable of the talents emphasizes faithful use of God's gifts (25:14-30), and the picture of the last judgment (25:31-46) indicates that Jesus is still concerned for the "little ones."

The Olivet Discourse makes it clear that biblical prophecy includes more than mere prediction. The knowledge of what God will do in the future (24:1-31) must have a profound effect upon God's people in the present (24:32-25:46). In other words, if we have properly understood this prophetic Scripture, we will avoid date-setting and will be characterized by alertness, faithfulness, fruitfulness, and service to the little brothers of Christ. As Davies and Allison (1997:337) put it, "the question 'when' does not elicit a date but help to maintain the disciples' faith."

The Synoptic Problem. In seeking any solution to the synoptic problem (see the discussion of this matter in the Introduction to the commentary), it must be acknowledged that Matthew's version of the discourse is much longer than that of Mark and Luke (see the table below). The three treatments of the setting (#1 in the table below) and the beginning of birth pains (#2 below) are rather similar. Matthew's version of the abomination of desolation (#3 below) is slightly longer than Mark's, and Luke's section on armies surrounding Jerusalem is much shorter than either Matthew or Mark. Matthew's treatment of the coming of the Son of Man (#4 below) is slightly longer than Mark's or Luke's. The three versions of the lesson of the fig tree (#5 below) are similar, but Matthew also has material at this point on the days of Noah. The versions of #6, "Necessity of alertness," are rather different, although of similar length. Matthew 24:45-25:46 (comprising 7–10 below) has no parallel in the other Gospels. (For further study of the discourse, see Beasley-Murray 1993, Burnett 1981, Carson 1984:488-495; Gaston 1970, Hartman 1966, Turner 1989, and Wenham 1984b.)

Brief Synopsis of the Olivet Discourse
Content: Matthew/Mark/Luke

1. Setting: 24:1-3/13:1-4/21:5-7
2. Beginning of birth pains: 24:4-14/13:5-13/21:8-19
3. Abomination of desolation: 24:15-28/13:14-23/21:20-24
4. Coming of the Son of Man: 24:29-31/13:24-27/21:25-28
5. Lesson of the fig tree: 24:32-41/13:28-32/21:29-33
6. Necessity of alertness: 24:42-44/13:33-37/21:34-36
7. Parable of the servant: 24:45-51
8. Parable of ten virgins: 25:1-13
9. Parable of the talents: 25:14-30
10. Judgment of the nations: 25:31-46

Exposition of Matthew 24:1-14. After Jesus' blunt comments on the coming destruction of the Temple (24:2), Jesus' disciples asked him when it would happen (24:3). They linked the destruction of the Temple with the return of Jesus and the end of the age, so they wanted to know about the sign that would indicate that these things were about to happen.

Of course, one might wonder whether the disciples had comprehended enough of Jesus' previous teaching in order to ask a question that reflected a grasp of his departure and return. Matthew makes it clear that their grasp of certain matters was weak at best, but by now they knew enough to realize that Jesus was about to go. They had heard Jesus' three passion predictions (16:21; 17:22-23; 20:18-19), and their comprehension is indicated by their indignation (16:22) and grief (17:23). So, whatever their subjective lack of perception at various points, Matthew has shown that they knew enough to ask a question about Jesus' coming.

Their question was primarily concerned with timing, since they wanted to know "when" and they wanted to know how to know "when" by discerning a preliminary sign. But Jesus did not answer their question in a precise way (24:4-14). He mentioned several matters—false messiahs and prophets, wars, famines, earthquakes, persecution, apostasy, betrayal, and lawlessness—but all these are so general that they are of no help in calculating when the Temple will be destroyed. Jesus also warned them against assuming that the turmoil he mentioned is an indicator that the end is imminent. He stated that such matters do not signify the end (24:6). They are but the first pains of childbirth, which intimates that there may be an extended time of labor before the end (24:8; cf. 25:5). There will be enough time for the Kingdom message to be preached throughout the world before the end comes (24:14). Therefore, the disciples needed to ponder not the chronology of the end times but their own ethical responsibility to persevere in faithful discipleship and Kingdom ministry (24:13). They have asked the wrong question, but Jesus has given them the right answer. Paul also warned about the danger of coming to the premature, false conclusion that the church's present woes are to be identified with the onset of the end of the world (2 Thess 2:2-3).

Matthew 24:4-14 should be viewed as a summation of the difficulties the church will face in its early days before AD 70—and indeed throughout its existence until Jesus returns (Blomberg 1992:356-357; Hagner 1995:693-694). Expositors frequently note the similarities between Matthew 24:4-14 and Rev 6:1ff, which speaks in terms of the breaking of seals, of which the first four are the famed four horsemen of the Apocalypse. If the view presented here is correct, these horsemen also portray events that typify the church's present experience in the world, not the final days of tribulation at the end of the age.

◆   ## 2. The desecration of the Holy Place: the Temple destroyed (24:15-28; cf. Mark 13:14-23; Luke 21:20-24)

15"The day is coming when you will see what Daniel the prophet spoke about—the sacrilegious object that causes desecration* standing in the Holy Place." (Reader, pay attention!) 16"Then those in Judea must flee to the hills. 17A person out on the deck of a roof must not go down into the house to pack. 18A person out in the field must not return even to get a coat. 19How terrible it will be for pregnant women and for nursing mothers in those days. 20And pray that your flight will not be in winter or on the Sabbath. 21For there will be greater anguish than at any time since the world began. And it will never be so great again. 22In fact, unless that time of calamity is shortened, not a single person will survive. But it will be shortened for the sake of God's chosen ones. ²³"Then if anyone tells you, 'Look, here is the Messiah,' or 'There he is,' don't believe it. ²⁴For false messiahs and false prophets will rise up and perform great signs and wonders so as to deceive, if possible, even God's chosen ones. ²⁵See, I have warned you about this ahead of time.

²⁶"So if someone tells you, 'Look, the Messiah is out in the desert,' don't bother to go and look. Or, 'Look, he is hiding here,' don't believe it! ²⁷For as the lightning flashes in the east and shines to the west, so it will be when the Son of Man* comes. ²⁸Just as the gathering of vultures shows there is a carcass nearby, so these signs indicate that the end is near.*

24:15 Greek *the abomination of desolation.* See Dan 9:27; 11:31; 12:11.   24:27 "Son of Man" is a title Jesus used for himself.   24:28 Greek *Wherever the carcass is, the vultures gather.*

NOTES

24:15 *The day is coming when you will see what Daniel the prophet spoke about.* This is the closest Jesus comes to answering the disciples' question about the Temple (24:3; cf. Mark 13:14-23; Luke 21:20-24).

the sacrilegious object that causes desecration. This is an allusion to Dan 8:13; 9:27; 11:31; 12:11 (cf. *Testament of Levi* 15:1; *Apocalypse of Elijah* 2:41; 4:21). Perhaps 23:38 also hints at this. Daniel's prophecy of the desecration of the Temple is often tied to the pagan altar set up in the holy place by the Seleucid King Antiochus IV Epiphanes in 167 BC (1 Macc 1:54, 59; 6:7; 2 Macc 6:1-5), but a desecration of the Temple had occurred long before Antiochus IV when in 597 BC Nebuchadnezzar, king of Babylon, conquered the city, destroyed the first Temple, and carried off its treasures (Dan 1:1-2; 5:2-4, 22-23; cf. 2 Kgs 24:10-15). Jesus envisioned a future desecration here (cf. 2 Thess 2:4).

Reader, pay attention. This may be Jesus encouraging his hearers to read Daniel, or it could be Matthew's editorial words to his own readers. In either view, these words underline the gravity of the desecration of the holy place as a signal of the horrible events described in the following verses.

24:16-18 *those in Judea must flee to the hills.* When the Temple is desecrated, the only course of action for Jesus' disciples is flight to the Judean hill country (24:16, 20). Evidently the situation envisioned is the siege of Jerusalem (Luke 21:20-24; cf. Deut 28:53-57). Verse 16 is a general command, and the specific commands of 24:17-18 enforce its urgency (cf. Luke 17:31). The urgency of the hour would preclude packing or even getting a coat. Whether one is on a flat clay rooftop (Josh 2:6; 1 Sam 9:25; 2 Sam 11:2; Mark 2:4; Acts 10:9, 20) or in a field, there is no time to return to one's house for supplies (cf. 1 Macc 2:28).

24:19-20 *pregnant women and for nursing mothers . . . on the Sabbath.* Fleeing would be especially difficult for women with young or unborn children and for everyone if it occured on the Sabbath. The rigors of the time will be even more horrible for pregnant women and nursing mothers (cf. Luke 23:28-31; 1 Cor 7:26; 2 *Baruch* 10:13-14). With winter came colder weather and the rainy season, and muddy roads would mean slower, more laborious travel. It is uncertain why flight on the Sabbath is especially difficult; most likely, Matthew's Christian Jewish community would have scruples against breaking the traditional Sabbath travel restrictions (cf. Exod 16:29; Acts 1:12; *m. Eruvin*). Or perhaps it would be difficult to get out of walled cities or to obtain supplies on the Sabbath. In any event, movement on the Sabbath would be more noticeable than on other days. According to Eusebius's *Ecclesiastical History* (3.5.3), the Christians in Jerusalem fled to Pella, just east of the Jordan River about 65 miles northeast of Jerusalem, prior to the destruction of Jerusalem in AD 70.

24:21-22 there will be greater anguish than at any time since the world began. Here it is made clear that the unparalleled severity of these times is the reason for the urgent warnings of the previous verses. Unlike the generic troubles mentioned previously, which do not augur the end (24:9), such anguish (lit. "great tribulation") has never been seen before and will never be seen again (cf. 24:29; Dan 12:1; Joel 2:2; Rev 7:14; 16:18; 1QM 1:9-14; 1 Macc 9:27; *Testament of Moses* 8:1; Josephus *War* 1.12). But God's care for his chosen ones (22:14; 24:24, 31; cf. 13:38) will result in the shortening of this most horrible of times so that they might be saved (Dan 12:1; 4Q385 3 i 1-7; *Barnabas* 4:3; cf. *2 Baruch* 20:1-2; 54:1; 83:1). It is difficult to accept the preterist view that this language was totally fulfilled by the events of AD 70. Hagner (1995:702-703) is probably correct in viewing the language as a hyperbolic reference to the catastrophe of AD 70 that will be literally true of the eschatological horrors.

24:23-25 false messiahs and false prophets will rise up. The topic of false messiahs and false prophets has been mentioned previously (24:4-5, 11), and it is developed at length in 24:23-28.

so as to deceive, if possible, even God's chosen ones. Their miraculous signs and wonders would deceive God's chosen ones if that were possible (cf. Exod 7:11; Deut 13:1-5; 2 Thess 2:9; 2 Pet 2:1; 1 John 2:18, 4:1; Rev 13:3; 19:20; *Didache* 16:4). Jesus had been reticent to perform and publicize miracles merely to gain a following (4:1-11; 12:15-21, 39; 16:1-4; 27:40), but the false messiahs will not be. Jesus' warning the disciples about this danger ahead of time is evidently one of the means God uses to preserve his chosen ones.

24:26-27 don't believe it! The general warning mentioned in 24:25 is spelled out in detail here. The disciples are not to believe claims that the Messiah is in some obscure place, like the desert or a hidden chamber in a building (cf. Luke 17:23-24). Messianic pretenders frequently hid out in the desert, away from the threat of Roman soldiers (Acts 21:38; Josephus *War* 2.258-263; *Antiquities* 20.97-99, 167-172, 188).

as the lightning flashes in the east and shines to the west, so it will be when the Son of Man comes. In contrast to false claims, the genuine coming of Jesus (cf. 1 Cor 15:23; 1 Thess 2:19; 3:13; 4:15-17; Jas 5:7; 2 Pet 3:4; 1 John 2:28) will be unmistakably clear, like lightning which flashes across the sky from east to west (cf. Zech 9:14). There will be no doubt as to the identity of the Messiah when this happens.

24:28 as the gathering of vultures shows there is a carcass nearby, so these signs indicate that the end is near. The meaning of the proverb about the vultures and the carcass in 24:28 is difficult (cf. Luke 17:37). The NLT spells out the most common interpretation with its rendering "so these signs indicate that the end is near" (France 1985:343), but this comparative clause is not in the Gr. text. It is doubtful that this is intended as a picture of moral corruption (Hendriksen 1973:861; Walvoord 1974:190), or the consumption of lifeless Israel by false prophets (Lenski 1961:946; Toussaint 1980:276). Perhaps Jesus simply intended his hearers to envision the grisly picture of vultures hovering over the bodies of those who rebel against God in the final eschatological battle (Rev 19:17-18).

COMMENTARY

Matthew 24:15-29 is a warning of intense, unparalleled persecution and false prophecy that will arise in connection with the desecration of the Jerusalem Temple (24:15). This warning involves instructions for flight (24:16-20), a promise that God will shorten those days for the sake of his elect (24:21-22), and a renewed warning against false messiahs and false prophets (24:23-28). In the view taken here, this warning primarily relates to the destruction of the Temple in AD 70, but there is good reason (esp. 24:21-22) to see it as ultimately intended for God's people in the end times who will face the ultimate Antichrist. Certainly, the disciples of Jesus throughout history have realized the constant relevance of his warning against false prophets and false messiahs. The suffering which confronts disciples inevitably causes them to long for the Messiah's appearance, but they must not allow that longing to lead them to be deceived by messianic pretenders.

Despite the space often given to discussing it, the most profound question in this section is not the chronological referents of the prophecy according to the various preterist and futurist views. The real question here is an existential one, and it concerns the need for wisdom in grasping the providence of God. Somehow, one must reconcile God's permitting his elect to suffer with his concern that their suffering not result in their spiritual ruin. Suffering is a way of life for Jesus' disciples throughout this age (5:10; 10:16ff; John 16:33; Acts 14:22; 2 Tim 3:12), and it will intensify as that age comes to an end. But God, for the sake of his elect, will somehow wisely permit that suffering to accomplish his own goals, rather than those of the persecutors (Acts 4:27-28; Rom 8:28-39). Although the disciples of Jesus may never fully grasp why their suffering is necessary, they may be assured from the example of Jesus himself that God will enable them to endure it and that in the end they will reign victoriously with Jesus (4:1-11; 10:24-33; 1 Cor 10:13; 2 Pet 2:9; Rev 2:26-28; 3:21-22; 17:17).

The Sacrilegious Desecration.   Jesus' reference to the sacrilegious desecration of the Temple in 24:15 calls up a complex typology of prophecy and fulfillment, stretching all the way from Nebuchadnezzar to the ultimate eschatological antichrist. Several historical events comprise a sort of continuum of fulfillment, including (1) Nebuchadnezzar's conquest in 605 BC (Dan 1:1-2; 5:1-4, 22-23), (2) Antiochus IV Epiphanes' outrageous sacrilege which led to the Hasmonean revolt (167 BC), (3) the Roman conquest of the Hasmonean Kingdom in 63 BC, (4) the planned but unaccomplished setting up of a bust of Caligula in the Temple (AD 40–41), (5) the zealots' misuse of the Temple precincts in the days preceding the Roman destruction of AD 70, (6) the Roman destruction of AD 70 itself, (7) the further desolation of Jerusalem by the Romans in AD 135 due to the Bar Kochba revolt (Dio Cassius 69.12.1-2), and (8) the ultimate sacrilege of the Antichrist (Matt 24:15; 2 Thess 2:3-4; Rev 13:8; *Didache* 16).

In light of these things, there is no warrant for supposing that the desecration of 24:15, echoing Daniel, is a narrow prediction that is fulfilled solely by either the past AD 70 destruction of Jerusalem or by the future antichrist. Rather, there is good reason to believe that the various historical desolations of Jerusalem and the Temple all provide anticipatory fulfillments which lead up to the ultimate desolation in the end times. If it be objected that this scenario involves an implausible future rebuilding of the Temple, such a rebuilding was envisioned in ancient sources, both Jewish (*m. Pesahim* 10:6; *b. Sukkah* 41a; *b. Shabbat* 12b) and Christian (*Barnabas* 16:3-4; Irenaeus *Against Heresies* 5.30.4; *Apocalypse of Elijah* 4:1-6). Second Thessalonians 2:4 and Revelation 11 also imply that the Temple will be rebuilt.

◆   3. The coming of the Son of Man (24:29-31; cf. Mark 13:24-27;
      Luke 21:25-28)

²⁹"Immediately after the anguish of those days,

the sun will be darkened,
the moon will give no light,
the stars will fall from the sky,
and the powers in the heavens will
be shaken.*

³⁰And then at last, the sign that the Son of Man is coming will appear in the heavens, and there will be deep mourning among all the peoples of the earth. And they will see the Son of Man coming on the clouds of heaven with power and great glory.* ³¹And he will send out his angels with the mighty blast of a trumpet, and they will gather his chosen ones from all over the world*—from the farthest ends of the earth and heaven."

24:29 See Isa 13:10; 34:4; Joel 2:10.   24:30 See Dan 7:13.   24:31 Greek *from the four winds.*

NOTES

24:29 *Immediately after the anguish of those days.* This is the period of ultimate, unparalleled anguish (lit. "tribulation") described in 24:15ff (cf. Dan 12:1).

the sun will be darkened, the moon will give no light, the stars will fall from the sky. Significant heavenly disturbances will occur after the great tribulation (cf. Mark 13:24-27; Luke 21:25-28). This cosmic upheaval is expressed through apocalyptic imagery. The heavenly signs delineated here develop the statement of 24:27 that Jesus' coming will be like a flash of lightning from the east to the west. The sun and moon will be darkened, and the stars will fall from the sky. See the chart in the commentary below for the OT passages alluded to here (cf. Acts 2:20; Rev 6:12-13; 8:12). It is commonly believed that 24:15-28 speaks of events accompanying the destruction of Jerusalem in AD 70, although some, including myself, see an additional eschatological fulfillment. In 24:29ff, despite the prevalence of apocalyptic imagery, it seems that the coming of Jesus to the earth is in view. Preterist scholars disagree and take this language as speaking of Jesus' enthronement in heaven and/or the destruction of Jerusalem on earth, but their arguments are not convincing (Davies and Allison 1997:329). Hagner (1995:711-713) takes the "anguish" spoken of here as a reference to the events of AD 70 and thus concludes that Matthew believed that Jesus would return immediately after the destruction of Jerusalem. But this is doubtful in view of the preceding argument that 24:15-28 describes both the AD 70 destruction of Jerusalem and the ultimate eschatological persecution of God's people.

24:30 Here begins the description of the event to which all the signs point, the coming of Jesus. This verse is a conflation of Jer 4:13; Dan 7:13-14; and Zech 12:10, 14.

the sign that the Son of Man is coming. Lit., "the sign of the Son of man." This may mean that the appearance of Jesus is itself the sign. Taken with the blowing of the trumpet in 24:31, the "sign" may refer to a military ensign or insignia, possibly the cross, which musters troops for the eschatological battle (Isa 11:10-12; 18:3; 62:10; Jer 4:21; 51:27). Or the "sign" may be a reference back to the disciples' question in 24:3.

will appear in the heavens. After the description of the heavenly disturbances, it is not surprising that this sign appears in the heavens.

mourning among all the peoples of the earth. It is not clear whether the mourning of the nations (Zech 12:10; Rev 1:7) is an indication of true repentance or of despair because they are not prepared to meet Jesus.

the Son of Man coming on the clouds of heaven with power and great glory. This is familiar from other passages, and may allude to the presence of God in terms of "the cloud" signaling a theophany (16:27; 25:31; Acts 1:9-11; Rev 1:7; cf. Exod 13:21-22; 40:35-38).

24:31 his angels . . . will gather his chosen ones from all over the world. The purpose of the coming of the Son of Man is the gathering of his chosen ones. It is noteworthy that Jesus, as Son of Man, exercises divine prerogatives in sending *his* angels (cf. Dan 7:10) for *his* elect.

The mighty blast of a trumpet. In the OT a trumpet was sounded for religious and military purposes (Exod 19:16; Josh 6:5; Ps 81:3; Isa 27:13; Ezek 33:3-6; Joel 2:1; Zeph 1:16; cf. 1 Cor 15:52; 1 Thess 4:16; *Didache* 16:6; *Shemoneh Esreh* 10).

gather his chosen ones. The people who comprise God's elect are from all the nations, judging from the two ways they are described here. They are literally "from the four winds" (cf. Isa 43:6; Dan 7:2; Zech 2:6; Rev 7:1) and "from one end of the sky to another." The gathering of the elect here is similar to John's words about the gathering of the wheat into the barn (3:12), and may imply a sort of "rapture," as in 1 Thess 4:17. It is a bit different from Jesus' parabolic language about the tares or wicked people being gathered out of his Kingdom (13:40-41; cf. 25:46). The description of one being taken and another being left is similar (24:40-41). Whatever the specific imagery, the point of all these passages is the separation that will be effected at Christ's return.

COMMENTARY

Matthew 24:29-31 describes the climactic heavenly signs immediately preceding the coming of Jesus, the glorious coming itself, and the purpose of the coming—to gather God's elect for their reward. The glorious coming of Jesus has been mentioned several times in Matthew (10:23; 16:27-28; 23:39; 24:3, 27, 37, 39, 42, 44, 46, 48, 50; 25:6, 13, 19, 31; 26:64), but here it is placed most clearly in its eschatological context. While the date of this coming is unknown, Jesus' disciples must not assume that it is in the distant future. Rather, they must alertly expect Jesus' return and faithfully serve him until that day. This coming is placed after the tribulation (24:29), which may give advocates of the pre-tribulational rapture theory some pause (but see notes and commentary on 24:40-41). Jesus' coming creates reversal: there will be mourning among all the nations who caused the disciples to mourn, but joy among all the formerly mourning disciples (cf. 2 Thess 1:6-10). At this time, the reign of heaven will come to earth more fully (6:9-10; 25:34). All nations will be judged, and the disciples of Jesus will be rewarded (5:5; 5:6-9; 13:40-43; 16:27-28; 19:27-30; 25:46).

A very different scenario is presented by the preterist understanding of 24:29-31. Preterists interpret these verses as speaking symbolically of the theological significance of the destruction of the Temple (France 1985:345; cf. Lightfoot 1997:2.319-320; Tasker 1961:225-228). The coming of Jesus is viewed as his coming to heaven to be exalted after the resurrection (Dan 7:13-14). The significance of this exaltation is played out in the judgment on Israel demonstrated by the destruction of the Temple by the Romans in AD 70. The tribulation or anguish mentioned in the passage is taken to be the horrific conditions experienced by the zealots in Jerusalem during the days prior to the Roman attack. The heavenly disturbances are interpreted as symbolically fulfilled by phenomena observed during those days. The sending of the angels to gather the elect is viewed as the mission of the church in discipling all the nations (24:14; 28:19).

Preterists are motivated by their understanding of 24:34, which they take as Jesus' promise that everything he has spoken of will be accomplished during the lives of his contemporaries. Since he did not literally return during their lifetimes, a different solution is sought, and the entire passage is viewed as a prediction of the destruction of the Temple in AD 70, which did occur during the lifetime of Jesus' contemporaries. (See the notes and commentary on 24:34 for a different interpretation of this crucial matter.) Additional difficulties with preterism are due to its truncation of Christ's eschatological program, which is to bring the reign of heaven to earth. Since that program is viewed by preterists as already fulfilled, one is tempted to ask, "Is that all there is?" It also seems very doubtful that the global language of Matthew 24 (e.g., 24:3, 7, 14, 21-22, 27, 30-31; 25:31-32) can be explained satisfactorily by a local event that occurred in AD 70, as significant as that event was (Blomberg 1992:363).

Old Testament Allusions. Matthew 24:29-31 is permeated with imagery drawn from the Old Testament. The chart below lays out some of the significant citations and allusions. Although several Old Testament passages are clearly alluded to here, it seems that Daniel 7 is the crucial text. In this passage, God is pictured as an awesome judge, "the Ancient One" (Dan 7:9), who passes sentence in favor of the Son of Man, giving universal dominion to him and his people (Dan 7:14, 22, 27). All this is in the context of reversal, in which the eschatological enemy of God and Israel, the "little horn" (Dan 7:8, 20, 24-25) is judged and defeated. As in Daniel 7, in Matthew 24 the coming of the Son of Man ends the persecution and suffering of God's saints, who then begin their glorious rule with Jesus.

MATTHEW 24:29-31 AND THE OLD TESTAMENT

Matthew	Content	Old Testament Passage(s)
24:29a	Tribulation	Dan 12:1
24:29b	Sun and moon darkened	Isa 13:10; 24:23; Ezek 32:7; Joel 2:10, 31; 3:15; Amos 5:20; 8:9; Zeph1:5a
24:29c	Stars fallen, shaken	Isa 34:4; Hag 2:6
24:30a, c	Son of Man coming on the clouds	Dan 7:13-14
24:30b	Tribes mourn	Zech 12:10, 14
24:31a	Trumpet	Isa 27:13
24:31b	Elect gathered	Deut 30:4; Zech 2:6
24:31b	Four winds	Dan 7:2; Zech 2:6
24:31b	Ends of the sky	Deut 4:32

◆   **4. The parable of the fig tree (24:32-35; cf. Mark 13:28-31; Luke 21:29-33)**

³²"Now learn a lesson from the fig tree. When its branches bud and its leaves begin to sprout, you know that summer is near. ³³In the same way, when you see all these things, you can know his return is very near, right at the door. ³⁴I tell you the truth, this generation* will not pass from the scene until all these things take place. ³⁵Heaven and earth will disappear, but my words will never disappear."

24:34 Or *this age,* or *this nation.*

NOTES

24:32 *lesson from the fig tree.* "Lesson" here is lit. "parable." This is more like the short parables of 13:31-33, 44-46 than the longer narrative parables in that chapter. The parable proper is stated in 24:32, and it is applied in 24:33 ("in the same way . . .").

when its branches bud and its leaves begin to sprout, you know that summer is near. The budding of the fig tree in the spring is a sure sign of the nearness of summer. Similarly, the matters of which Jesus had been speaking are reliable indicators that he is near (cf. Isa 13:6; Ezek 30:3; Joel 1:15; 2:1; Zeph 1:7, 14; Jas 5:8), ready to walk through the door, so to speak (cf. Jas 5:9; Rev 3:20).

24:33 *when you see all these things.* A crucial matter here is the referent of the expression "all these things." In the commentary to follow, it will be argued that "all these things" refers to the signs about which the disciples asked and of which Jesus spoke in 24:4ff. For another parabolic statement on the signs of the times, see 16:1-4.

24:34-35 *this generation will not pass from the scene until all these things take place. Heaven and earth will disappear, but my words will never disappear.* These verses contain two statements that stress the reliability of Jesus' promise about the signs of his coming in 24:32-33. The promise is so reliable that Jesus' contemporaries ("this generation") will not pass away until it is fulfilled. Secondly, heaven and earth will pass away, but his promise will not. This statement places the words of Jesus, the ultimate and definitive interpreter of the Torah, on a par with the Torah itself (cf. 5:18). Jesus' words are equivalent to the very words of God, which are as eternal and authoritative as God himself (Ps 119:89; Isa 40:8). There are two major issues in the interpretation of 24:34—the meaning of "this generation" and of "all these things." In the commentary to follow, it will be argued that Jesus promises his contemporaries that they will still be living when the signs he has mentioned, including the destruction of the Temple, occur (Turner 1989; Blomberg 1992:364). Thus, Jesus did not mistakenly predict his return during his lifetime (McNeile 1949:355), nor is this a piece of mistaken early church tradition (Beare 1981:473; Davies and Allison 1997:367-368).

COMMENTARY

At this point, Jesus moved from speaking predictively to speaking paraenetically or hortatively. From this point on, his goal was not to provide additional information to answer the disciples' question (24:3) but to exhort them on the proper response to that information. This may not be what the disciples wanted to know, but it is what they needed to know. Matthew 24:32-35 parabolically expresses the nearness of the coming of Christ. Jesus' contemporaries were familiar with the process by which the fig tree in the spring buds, blossoms, and eventually in the summer bears fruit (24:32), so he compared his coming to that process (24:33). The signs about which the disciples asked in 24:3 are signified by the budding of the tree in the spring, and his coming by the summer, when fruit was borne. When the disciples see the signs (of spring), they know the coming (summer) is near. The certainty of these things is underlined by 24:34-35, which affirm that Jesus' contemporaries will observe the signs, and that Jesus' words are eternally trustworthy. In days of relative peace and prosperity, it is difficult to take these words of Jesus to heart. One may become so occupied with the details of everyday living and enjoying the fruits of one's labors that one forgets that it all may end abruptly (24:37-42). The skepticism of unbelievers compounds the problem by influencing disciples of Jesus to doubt his words (2 Pet 3:3-9). But genuine followers of Jesus dare not become too comfortable with the status quo because it will surely—if not speedily—give way to the Kingdom of Heaven's coming to earth.

Two crucial terms in these verses must be explained. First, what did Jesus mean by the expression "all these things" in 24:33-34? This expression refers to the preliminary signs that anticipate the coming of Jesus, not that coming itself. This is clear from the parabolic imagery used by Jesus. If "all these things" included the coming of Jesus, 24:33 would be saying, "when you see the coming of Jesus, you will know that he is near." This would be a tautology, a statement which belabors the obvious and goes without saying. If "all these things" refers merely to all the preliminary signs, the statement makes sense since viewing the signs confirms that the coming is near.

The second crucial term in these verses is "this generation." Although some futurist scholars argue that the word refers either to the nation of Israel as a whole or to the eschatological generation which is alive at Jesus' return (e.g., Toussaint 1980:279-280; Walvoord 1974:192-193), Matthew's use of the term clearly shows that Jesus was talking about his contemporaries (11:16; 12:39, 41-42, 45; 16:4; 17:17; 23:36). Scholars who argue otherwise opt for an understanding of "this generation" which is contrary to Matthew's clear usage because they want to protect Jesus from affirming that his coming will occur during the lifetime of his contemporaries, when, in fact, it didn't. If Jesus was speaking only of the preliminary signs which augur his coming, however, he did not err. As argued in the previous paragraph, "all these things" refers to the signs, not the coming itself, and Jesus predicted that his contemporaries would see those signs, including the destruction of the Temple by the Romans in AD 70.

◆   ## 5. The necessity of alertness (24:36-51; cf. Mark 13:32)

36"However, no one knows the day or hour when these things will happen, not even the angels in heaven or the Son himself.* Only the Father knows.

37"When the Son of Man returns, it will be like it was in Noah's day. 38In those days before the flood, the people were enjoying banquets and parties and weddings right up to the time Noah entered his boat. 39People didn't realize what was going to happen until the flood came and swept them all away. That is the way it will be when the Son of Man comes.

40"Two men will be working together in

the field; one will be taken, the other left. ⁴¹Two women will be grinding flour at the mill; one will be taken, the other left.

⁴²"So you, too, must keep watch! For you don't know what day your Lord is coming. ⁴³Understand this: If a homeowner knew exactly when a burglar was coming, he would keep watch and not permit his house to be broken into. ⁴⁴You also must be ready all the time, for the Son of Man will come when least expected.

⁴⁵"A faithful, sensible servant is one to whom the master can give the responsibility of managing his other household

servants and feeding them. ⁴⁶If the master returns and finds that the servant has done a good job, there will be a reward. ⁴⁷I tell you the truth, the master will put that servant in charge of all he owns. ⁴⁸But what if the servant is evil and thinks, 'My master won't be back for a while,' ⁴⁹and he begins beating the other servants, partying, and getting drunk? ⁵⁰The master will return unannounced and unexpected, ⁵¹and he will cut the servant to pieces and assign him a place with the hypocrites. In that place there will be weeping and gnashing of teeth."

24:36 Some manuscripts do not include *or the Son himself.*

NOTES

24:36 In 24:32-35, Jesus stressed the nearness of his coming, but in 24:36ff he begins to stress that the time of his coming is unknowable (cf. Mark 13:32). Thus, 24:36 is a "declaration of eschatological ignorance" (Davies and Allison 1997:374).

no one knows the day or hour. This expression is a general time indicator, not a precise expression (7:22; 10:19; 24:42, 44, 50; 25:13; 26:45). The word "day" (*hēmera* [TG2250, ZG2465]) may imply the eschatological significance of the OT "day of the Lord" (e.g., Isa 2:11-12; 61:2; Jer 30:7-8; 46:10; Ezek 7:10-19; 30:3; Joel 1:15; 2:1-2; 3:14; Amos 5:18-20; Zeph 1:7, 14; Zech 14:1; Mal 3:2; 2 Thess 2:2; 2 Pet 3:10). How the time can be near and yet unknowable is difficult to articulate, but both are taught here.

not even the angels in heaven or the Son himself. In stating that no one knows the time of his coming, Jesus went so far as to state that not even the angels or even he himself have this information. Various scribes eliminated the words "or the Son himself" (ℵ¹ L W f 𝔐 syr cop and MSS known to Jerome) in order to eliminate the notion that the Son did not know when he would return. The words, included in early and diverse manuscripts (ℵ* B D f³ it and MSS known to Jerome), are certain (for further discussion, see Comfort 2007:[Matt 24:36]).

Only the Father knows. He alone is the one who controls the vicissitudes of human life. He alone can shorten the days of eschatological anguish (24:22), and he alone will bring Jesus back to earth in his own time.

24:37 *it will be like it was in Noah's day.* Humans living in the days preceding Jesus' return will be as unaware of it as Noah's contemporaries were of the flood (Gen 6:5ff; Isa 54:9; cf. 2 Pet 2:5; 3:6). The timing of God's judgment in both instances is totally unanticipated.

24:38-39 *right up to the time Noah entered his boat.* This clause comes from Gen 7:7. Jewish literature of the Second Temple period often portrayed Noah's generation as notorious sinners (Sir 16:7; Jubilees 20:5-6; 1 Enoch 67:10; 2 Macc 2:4; Josephus *Antiquities* 1.72-76).

People didn't realize what was going to happen until the flood came. In Noah's time, humanity was going about its business as usual (cf. Luke 17:26-30). People were caring for their daily needs and planning for what they perceived to be the future. But despite the preaching of Noah (2 Pet 2:5), they were oblivious to the imminent judgment which threatened them, and they were unexpectedly overtaken by the flood. At that point, their concern for matters such as food and drink and marriage became pathetically superfluous.

24:40-42 *one will be taken, the other left.* The illustration from the days of Noah is now applied to the days of Jesus' return (cf. Luke 17:34-35). The twin scenarios of 24:40-41 are expressed as exact parallels. Two men will be in the field, cultivating crops for food and drink, and the return of Jesus will suddenly overtake them, taking one and leaving the other. The same experience will overtake two women grinding grain at home. The prospect of such unexpected events underlines the absolute necessity of alert expectancy of the return of Jesus. Ignorance as to the time of his return must not lead to ambivalence as to the fact of his return, which will cause a sudden separation between those who alertly expect it and those who do not (25:31-46). The NT as a whole makes much of the necessity of watchful preparation for Christ's return (1 Cor 16:13; 1 Thess 5:6; 1 Pet 5:8; Rev 3:2-3; 16:15). There will be no leisure for repentance.

24:43-44 *be ready all the time.* The matter of alertness in the face of danger whose timing is unknown is further illustrated with a story (24:43) and its application (24:44). The story is about a thief unexpectedly robbing a house (cf. 6:19-20; 12:29; 1 Thess 5:2; 2 Pet 3:10; Rev 3:3; 16:15). If the head of the house (10:25; 13:27, 52; 20:1, 11; 21:33) had been warned as to the time of the burglary, it could have been prevented (cf. Luke 12:39-40).

the Son of Man will come when least expected. Similarly, Jesus' disciples do not know when he will return so they must be alert and prepared to meet him. He is coming at an unexpected time.

24:45 *A faithful, sensible servant.* Another household illustration underlines the necessity of alertness with the positive example of a faithful slave (24:45-47) and the negative example of a wicked slave (24:48-51). This time the unexpected factor is not a burglary but the return of a master who puts his slave in charge of feeding his household while he is away (cf. Luke 12:42-48). The disciples must be like that faithful and sensible slave (cf. 7:24; 10:16; 25:21, 23; 1 Cor 4:2), who is promoted to even greater responsibilities.

24:46 *If the master returns and finds that the servant has done a good job, there will be a reward.* This rendering obscures the literary form of the verse, which is a beatitude extolling the blessedness of the dependable slave who is found doing his master's will when the master returns (cf. 5:3-11; 11:6; 13:16; 16:17; Luke 12:38).

24:48-51 An opposite scenario is now described. This time the slave put in charge of the household assumes that his master's return is a long way off (cf. 25:5). This speaks to the problem of delay in the fulfillment of prophecy (cf. Ezek 12:22; Hab 2:3; 2 Pet 3:4). Instead of faithfully discharging the duties assigned him by the master, the slave treats his fellow slaves violently (cf. 18:28-33) and over-indulges in food and drink (cf. 1 Thess 5:7).

The master will return unannounced and unexpected. The master arrives unexpectedly, catches the evil slave in mid-debauch, and punishes him severely with dismemberment (cf. Luke 12:46).

assign him a place with the hypocrites. This is quite serious as hypocrisy is presented as the most heinous sin in Matthew (cf. 6:2ff; 7:5; 15:7; 22:18; 23:13ff).

weeping and gnashing of teeth. This is a graphic picture of the horror of eschatological doom (cf. 8:12; 13:42, 50; 21:41; 22:13; 25:30, 41, 46). To avoid such a terrifying fate, one must be constantly obedient to the master because one does not know when he will arrive (24:36, 39, 42, 44; 25:13). Compare the solemn exhortation of Luke 21:34-36.

COMMENTARY

In Matthew 24:36-51, Jesus continues the parabolic and paraenetic (or hortatory) emphasis that began in 24:32. This passage has three parts, the first stressing that the time of Jesus' return is unknowable (24:36-42), the second that disciples must be ready for an unexpected appearance of Jesus (24:43-44), and the third that disciples must faithfully obey their master until he returns (24:45-51). The first part draws an analogy between the days of Noah and the last days (cf. 2 Pet 3:3-7), warning against a preoccupation with daily life that does not take imminent divine judgment into account. Instead, alertness is necessary (24:42). The second part speaks parabolically of a homeowner who does not know that his home is about to be burglarized. The disciples are implicitly told not to emulate the homeowner but to be prepared for the unexpected return of Jesus (24:44). The third part continues the parabolic imagery with the master of a household entrusting his slave with a duty to perform during his absence. Two hypothetical scenarios are laid out, the first involving a good slave who is rewarded for his faithfulness (24:47), the second an evil slave whose profligate behavior warrants the master's wrath (24:50-51). This imagery warns disciples not to deceive themselves into a sinful lifestyle with the notion that Jesus will not return for a long time. All three parts of the passage stress the necessity of Jesus' followers being alert, prepared, and busy with their master's business until his return. Matthew 25 will continue with this parabolic and paraenetic emphasis.

The teaching that Jesus' return will be unexpected exposes the folly of those whose eschatological alertness rises and falls with the latest news from around the world. There are those "dispen-sensationalists," whose notion of prophecy leads them into a constant scrutiny of world events, especially the latest events in the Middle East, in a near frantic search of supposed prophetic fulfillments that signal the end of the world. Those of this ilk evidently are under the impression that thieves attempt to burglarize homes when the owners are at home with all the lights and the electronic alarm turned on. Their voices wax and wane in direct proportion to the degree of tension between Israel and the Palestinians. But according to Jesus, moments of increased world tensions would be less likely to portend Christ's return than moments of relative prosperity and tranquility (1 Thess 5:1-3). In any event, the disciples of Jesus must constantly be about the master's business, vigilantly awaiting his return. The correctness of one's eschatology is ultimately a matter of one's ethics, not one's speculation.

The Christology of Matthew 24:36.   It may be surprising for those who hold to the classical, orthodox doctrine of the Trinity and who, as a result, have a high view of Jesus to learn from this text that he claimed not to know the time of his return to earth. But this text, as well as its parallel in Mark 13:32 and Jesus' later comment to his disciples in Acts 1:7, all make the common point that the Father alone keeps this detail in his own inscrutable counsel. How this is possible, in light of the pre-existence and deity of Jesus, is not easily explained. However, it is clear that the incarnation of Jesus involved limitation of the use of his divine attributes (Phil 2:6-8; Gundry 1994:492). As a human being, Jesus became hungry and thirsty and tired (e.g., 4:2; 21:18; John 4:6; 19:28). He was empowered by the Spirit of God for his ministry and his miracles (3:16; 4:1; 12:18, 28; cf. Luke 3:22; 4:1, 14, 18; John 1:32; 3:34; Acts 10:38). After the temptation, he was in need of ministry from angels (4:11; cf. Luke 22:43). As he contemplated returning to the Father, he asked for the restoration of his glorious preincarnate prerogatives (John 17:1-5). Evangelical Christians are understandably concerned about this text, but they must recognize its emphasis of the genuine humanity of Jesus, whom Paul affirmed to be the *man* who was the sole mediator between God and humanity (1 Tim 2:5). For a helpful study of the ministry of the Holy Spirit in the life of Jesus, see Hawthorne (1991).

Eschatology. One detail of this passage has come in for extended discussion among evangelicals of a futurist bent. This is the language of separation—in which one is taken and another left at the coming of Jesus (24:40-42). Those who hold to the theory of a pre-tribulational rapture of the church, distinct from the return of Jesus to the earth after the tribulation (24:29), debate whether 24:40-42 speaks of the rapture taking believers from the earth and leaving unbelievers. The difficulty in coming to a conclusion on this matter is twofold. First, Jesus did not speak here in terms that approximate the distinction between a pre-tribulational rapture and a post-tribulational coming to the earth, as Paul arguably does (compare 1 Thess 4:13-18 with 2 Thess 1:6-10). Second, the language of one being taken and another left is ambiguous. On the analogy of the flood of Noah, those taken were swept away by the flood, and those who were left were protected in the ark (24:38-39; cf. 13:41). But the imagery of 24:31 seems to involve the taking or gathering of God's chosen ones, not those about to be judged (cf. 3:12). The better part of wisdom on this question is to regard it as an unanswerable diversion from the message of the passage, which is to stress alertness (24:42-44; Carson 1984:509). Ironically, it is possible in cases like this for exegesis to degenerate into a pedantry that distracts the student from the teaching of the passage. Intellectual debate over the intricacies of a text must not occur at the expense of obedience to its ethical directives.

◆   ## 6. The parable of the wise and foolish bridesmaids (25:1-13)

"Then the Kingdom of Heaven will be like ten bridesmaids* who took their lamps and went to meet the bridegroom. [2]Five of them were foolish, and five were wise. [3]The five who were foolish didn't take enough olive oil for their lamps, [4]but the other five were wise enough to take along extra oil. [5]When the bridegroom was delayed, they all became drowsy and fell asleep.

[6]"At midnight they were roused by the shout, 'Look, the bridegroom is coming! Come out and meet him!'

[7]"All the bridesmaids got up and prepared their lamps. [8]Then the five foolish ones asked the others, 'Please give us some of your oil because our lamps are going out.'

[9]"But the others replied, 'We don't have enough for all of us. Go to a shop and buy some for yourselves.'

[10]"But while they were gone to buy oil, the bridegroom came. Then those who were ready went in with him to the marriage feast, and the door was locked. [11]Later, when the other five bridesmaids returned, they stood outside, calling, 'Lord! Lord! Open the door for us!'

[12]"But he called back, 'Believe me, I don't know you!'

[13]"So you, too, must keep watch! For you do not know the day or hour of my return."

25:1 Or *virgins;* also in 25:7, 11.

14

NOTES

25:1 *The Kingdom of Heaven will be like.* This parable begins with the familiar comparison formula seen in 13:24, 31, 33, 44, 45, 47, 52; 18:23; 20:1. The reference to a wedding reminds the reader of the allusion to the same activity in the days of Noah (24:38).

bridesmaids. Lit., "virgins," young unmarried women who in the custom of that day attended the bride. It is not clear whether they waited with the bride at her father's house or waited at the groom's house for him to bring the bride to the wedding feast (Song 3:11; 1 Macc 9:37-42; Josephus *Antiquities* 13.20). The legal contract of betrothal or engagement would have already been executed, and the groom might take his bride at any time to celebrate their wedding and begin to live together (1:18).

25:2-5 *Five of them were foolish, and five were wise.* The wise and foolish bridesmaids are very similar to the faithful and evil servants in the previous parable (24:45, 48). The five foolish bridesmaids expect the groom to arrive rapidly, but the wise are prepared for a possible delay.

lamps. These may actually be torches, sticks with oil-soaked rags wrapped around one end.

extra oil. Lit., "oil in flasks."

the bridegroom. God's relationship with Israel is likened to a bridegroom's with a bride in the OT (e.g., Isa 54:4-6; 62:5; Jer 31:32; Ezek 16:7ff; Hos 2:16, 19), and in this parable Jesus portrays himself in an equivalent relationship with his disciples.

was delayed. As it happens, there is a delay (cf. 24:48), and the bridesmaids grow drowsy and fall asleep.

25:6 *Look, the bridegroom is coming!* In the middle of the night (24:43), a shout is heard announcing the bridegroom's imminent arrival (cf. the trumpet of 24:31). The bridesmaids are summoned to come out to meet him and join the procession to his house for the feast (22:2-14).

25:7-9 *prepared their lamps.* They prepared their lamps (perhaps torches) by trimming the wicks and adding oil. But the lamps of the foolish bridesmaids were going out for lack of oil (Job 18:5; Prov 13:9). The wise bridesmaids could not give them oil from their flasks because there would not be enough to go around and everyone would be in the dark. The foolish bridesmaids have no choice but to go out to buy more oil. Such a task takes time, especially in the middle of the night.

25:10 *while they were gone to buy oil, the bridegroom came.* Once he arrived, the procession to the wedding feast occurred. Once everyone arrived at the groom's house, the door was locked (cf. 24:33).

25:11-13 *Open the door for us!* The foolish bridesmaids arrived too late to be included in the wedding feast. Their appeal to the groom and his refusal to permit their entry contain language that ominously recalls 7:21-23 (cf. Ps 1:6; Luke 13:25). This seems unrealistically harsh, but compare 22:11-14 for similar treatment of wedding guests.

keep watch! For you do not know the day or hour of my return. The unmistakable lesson is clearly stated at the end of the story: constant alertness is necessary because the time of the bridegroom's coming is not known (24:3, 36, 39, 42-44, 50; Acts 1:6-7; 1 Thess 5:2-6). The problem is not that the bridesmaids slept, since the groom's arrival was delayed. The problem is that the foolish bridesmaids were not prepared when he did come. The NLT's words "of my return" are a correct interpretation of 25:13, but they are not present in the Gr. text.

COMMENTARY

The parable of the wise and foolish bridesmaids demonstrates for the last time in the discourse that the time of Jesus' return is unknowable (cf. 24:3, 36, 39, 42-44, 50; 25:13). This thesis has been stated propositionally (24:36) and then illustrated historically from the days of Noah (24:37-42). It is also presented in the parables about the unexpected burglar (24:43), good slave (24:45-47), and evil slave (24:48-51). As if these previous demonstrations of the point were not enough, the present parable illustrates it from yet another familiar event, a wedding. Expecting the immediate arrival of the groom to begin the wedding feast, five of the ten bridesmaids foolishly did not prepare for nightfall by bringing oil for their lamps. But the five others wisely prepared for a delay. The foolishness of the former group resulted in their missing the bridegroom and being banned from the wedding feast, but the wise preparations of the latter group led to their sharing in the joy of the wedding (cf. 9:15).

The interpretation of this parable has been unnecessarily complicated by excessive allegorizing. It is true that wedding feasts and lamps are used metaphorically elsewhere in Scripture (Rev 1:12-13; 19:7, 9). Jesus himself indicates that the features of certain parables have detailed correspondences with reality (13:18-23, 37-43, 49-50), but in the case of the present parable, Jesus supplied only a generalizing conclusion (25:13). It seems clear enough that Jesus is the bridegroom whose arrival is delayed, and that the wise and foolish bridesmaids are alert and lackadaisical disciples, respectively. The expectation of the bridegroom lends itself perfectly to the point of alert preparedness for the coming of Jesus, but one should not be concerned with whether the rapture of believers or the return of Jesus to the earth is in view (Walvoord 1974:196-197). Neither should one succumb to the common temptation to identify the oil in the parable with the Holy Spirit (Green 1988:240; Hendriksen 1973:879), or stress that salvation cannot be transferred from one person to another (Tasker:1961:234). Perhaps such speculations are pleasant intellectual exercises, but they divert attention from the ethical imperative found in 25:13 and thus function like the distracting activities which diverted Noah's generation from awareness of their imminent judgment (cf. 24:38-39).

The foolish bridesmaids' lack of prudence is similar to the foolishness of the man who built his house on the sand, a portrayal of one who did not obey the words of Jesus (7:24-27). A comparison of 24:48 and 25:5 shows that the lesson of this parable is the same as that of the evil slave. In both cases, some delay in the return of Jesus is postulated. But the two reactions to the delay are opposites, and in these opposite reactions there is a crucial lesson. In the first case, the evil slave irresponsibly overestimated the delay of the master's return and was unpleasantly surprised by the master's seemingly early arrival. In the second case, the foolish bridesmaids frivolously underestimated the delay in the groom's arrival and did not prepare for it. The evil slave's lackadaisical approach to the master's return is similar to the generation of Noah and the homeowner, neither of whom expected a problem (24:36-44). Neither were alert and ready. The foolish bridesmaids were not prepared to persevere to the end (cf. 10:22; 13:20-21; 24:13). From these opposite errors, the church learns that it can assume neither that Jesus will return immediately nor that he will return eventually. Christians must expect Jesus constantly, yet at the same time they must persevere and plan for future ministry in case his coming is delayed. These two duties must be held in dynamic tension if the church is to be faithful to the teaching of its master (Luke 12:35-36).

◆ 7. The parable of the three servants (25:14-30)

14"Again, the Kingdom of Heaven can be illustrated by the story of a man going on a long trip. He called together his servants and entrusted his money to them while he was gone. 15He gave five bags of silver* to one, two bags of silver to another, and one bag of silver to the last—dividing it in proportion to their abilities. He then left on his trip.

16"The servant who received the five bags of silver began to invest the money and earned five more. 17The servant with two bags of silver also went to work and earned two more. 18But the servant who received the one bag of silver dug a hole in the ground and hid the master's money.

19"After a long time their master returned from his trip and called them to give an account of how they had used his money. 20The servant to whom he had entrusted the five bags of silver came forward with five more and said, 'Master, you gave me five bags of silver to invest, and I have earned five more.'

21"The master was full of praise. 'Well done, my good and faithful servant. You have been faithful in handling this small amount, so now I will give you many more responsibilities. Let's celebrate together!*'

22"The servant who had received the two bags of silver came forward and said, 'Master, you gave me two bags of silver to invest, and I have earned two more.'

23"The master said, 'Well done, my good and faithful servant. You have been faithful in handling this small amount, so now I will give you many more responsibilities. Let's celebrate together!'

24"Then the servant with the one bag of silver came and said, 'Master, I knew you were a harsh man, harvesting crops you didn't plant and gathering crops you didn't cultivate. 25I was afraid I would lose your money, so I hid it in the earth. Look, here is your money back.'

26"But the master replied, 'You wicked and lazy servant! If you knew I harvested crops I didn't plant and gathered crops I didn't cultivate, 27why didn't you deposit my money in the bank? At least I could have gotten some interest on it.'

28"Then he ordered, 'Take the money from this servant, and give it to the one with the ten bags of silver. 29To those who use well what they are given, even more will be given, and they will have an abundance. But from those who do nothing, even what little they have will be taken away. 30Now throw this useless servant into outer darkness, where there will be weeping and gnashing of teeth.'

25:15 Greek *talents;* also throughout the story. A talent is equal to 75 pounds or 34 kilograms.   25:21 Greek *Enter into the joy of your master* [or *your Lord*]; also in 25:23.

NOTES

25:14-15 *Again, the Kingdom of Heaven can be illustrated by the story of.* This expansion comes from 25:1; this parable is lit. introduced only by the words "for it is like." This parable concerning an absentee master reminds the reader of two previous stories (21:33-39; 24:45-51). As the scene is set for this parable, three slaves are entrusted with the master's resources according to their individual abilities.

five bags of silver to one, two bags of silver to another, and one bag of silver to the last. The "bags of silver" are lit. "talents" (see NLT mg). The word translated "money" in 25:18 is lit. "silver," hence the NLT rendering. The talent (*talanton*) was originally a measure of weight and is variously estimated at 50 to 75 pounds. As a monetary term, its value varied, but it always connoted a very large sum, evidently around six thousand silver denarii (BDAG 988). This would be as much money as a day laborer could expect to earn over the span of nineteen years! Thus, the amount of money involved here is very high, perhaps to "imply the greatness of God's gifts to his people" (Davies and Allison 1997:405). For a similar parable, see Luke 19:11-27.

25:16-18 The use each slave makes of what was entrusted to him is explained here. The first two slaves each invest or do business with their talents and gain a one hundred percent profit, but the third slave only hides the master's money by burying it in the ground. Evidently, this was a common practice (cf. 13:44; *b. Bava Metzi'a* 42a).

25:19-22 *After a long time their master returned.* The matter of delay in the master's return occurs here for the third time in the context (cf. 24:48; 25:5). When the master finally returns, there must be an accounting of his resources (cf. 18:23); this portrays eschatological judgment. Each of the first two slaves demonstrate their one hundred percent profits.

25:23 *Well done, my good and faithful servant.* The master congratulates the first two slaves and heartily rewards them with additional responsibilities (cf. 24:47; 25:28-29; Luke 16:10; 19:17; *m. Avot* 4:2).

Let's celebrate together! Lit., "Enter into the joy of your Lord," which probably portrays entrance into the Kingdom and the joy of the eschatological banquet (cf. 8:11; 26:29). The greatest joy of a follower of Jesus is to share in Jesus' joy.

25:24-27 *here is your money back.* As the reader anticipates from 25:18, the situation with the third servant is totally different. Fearful of his master's reputation as a harsh man, he states that he has preserved the master's talent by hiding it in the ground (cf. 13:44), and then he returns it to him. He appears to believe his caution is commendable and attempts to persuade the master that it is so. Yet, despite his calling his master "Lord" (cf. 7:21-23) in his attempt at justifying himself, he earns nothing. The third slave's estimate of the master's harshness ironically proved to be correct. The master was angry that this slave, whom he described as wicked (cf. 7:11; 13:49; 22:10) and lazy, had earned no interest on the money. The slave's laziness was shown by the fact that far from doing business with his talent, he did not even put the money in a bank where it could earn some interest. Hiding the master's resources in the ground is as senseless and useless as hiding one's lamp under a basket (5:15).

25:28-29 *Take the money from this servant, and give it to the one with the ten bags of silver.* Furious with the third slave, the master orders that the single talent be taken from him and given to the first servant, who now has eleven talents. These verses serve as a further explanation for the master's seemingly harsh actions (see 8:29). The slaves who have resources due to their faithful stewardship will receive more and will have an abundance (13:12; cf. Prov 9:9; Luke 12:48; 19:26), but the slave who earned nothing with the master's talent has even that talent taken away.

25:30 *throw this useless servant into outer darkness.* Since he had earned nothing for the master, he was useless and received an extremely severe punishment (cf. 8:12; 13:42, 50; 22:13; 24:51). The first two slaves show that trustworthiness leads to greater blessing, but the third slave demonstrates that a lack of trustworthiness leads to the removal of the original blessing.

COMMENTARY

The structure of this parable is completely symmetrical, with each of the three scenes dealing with the three slaves in the same order:

1a. Five talents entrusted (25:15)
1b. Two talents entrusted (25:15)
1c. One talent entrusted (25:15)
2a. Five talents invested and five more earned (25:16)
2b. Two talents invested and two more earned (25:17)
2c. One talent hidden and nothing earned (25:18)
3a. Good and faithful slave rewarded (25:20-21)
3b. Good and faithful slave rewarded (25:22-23)
3c. Wicked and lazy servant punished (25:24-30)

Each of the successive three scenes is longer that the preceding one, with the most stress placed at the end on the punishment of the wicked slave. Thus the parable, despite its positive elements in 25:21, 23, is more of a warning against irresponsibility than an encouragement to faithfulness.

The preceding parables have been about alertness, and this one is particularly about the faithful stewardship which alertness produces. This time the issue is not whether the slaves will be surprised by the master's return but whether they will be dependable in the use of his resources. His gifts lead to their tasks. A key detail of this parable is that the master entrusted his resources to the slaves according to their individual abilities (25:15). The third slave received only one talent, so the master evidently realized that he had less ability than the other two slaves. Nonetheless, he ought to have earned something with the talent, and he did not. He was not given five talents, and he was not expected to earn five talents, but he was not permitted to earn nothing at all. Blomberg (1992:371) points out that whereas the foolish bridesmaids thought their task was easier than it turned out to be, the lazy slave thought his task was harder than it turned out to be. The point is that if the followers of Jesus are faithful to him during his absence, they will be good stewards of the opportunities and abilities he has entrusted to them (cf. Luke 12:42; Rom 12:6ff; 1 Cor 4:1-2; 7:7; 12:4ff; Eph 4:7-8; Titus 1:7; 1 Pet 4:10). Alertness requires effort and active participation in the work of the Kingdom. Perhaps the familiar proverb attributed to William Carey is appropriate here: "Attempt great things for God, expect great things from God." Disciples must not make, as it were, shaky investments with their Lord's resources, but neither can they excuse their laziness with the false excuse that they have incurred no losses. "When Christ returns, he will not ask if one had the date right but 'What have you been doing?'" (Garland 1993:241).

◆   8. The final judgment (25:31-46)

31"But when the Son of Man* comes in his glory, and all the angels with him, then he will sit upon his glorious throne. 32All the nations* will be gathered in his presence, and he will separate the people as a shepherd separates the sheep from the goats.

³³He will place the sheep at his right hand and the goats at his left.

³⁴"Then the King will say to those on his right, 'Come, you who are blessed by my Father, inherit the Kingdom prepared for you from the creation of the world. ³⁵For I was hungry, and you fed me. I was thirsty, and you gave me a drink. I was a stranger, and you invited me into your home. ³⁶I was naked, and you gave me clothing. I was sick, and you cared for me. I was in prison, and you visited me.'

³⁷"Then these righteous ones will reply, 'Lord, when did we ever see you hungry and feed you? Or thirsty and give you something to drink? ³⁸Or a stranger and show you hospitality? Or naked and give you clothing? ³⁹When did we ever see you sick or in prison and visit you?'

⁴⁰"And the King will say, 'I tell you the truth, when you did it to one of the least of these my brothers and sisters,* you were doing it to me!'

⁴¹"Then the King will turn to those on the left and say, 'Away with you, you cursed ones, into the eternal fire prepared for the devil and his demons.* ⁴²For I was hungry, and you didn't feed me. I was thirsty, and you didn't give me a drink. ⁴³I was a stranger, and you didn't invite me into your home. I was naked, and you didn't give me clothing. I was sick and in prison, and you didn't visit me.'

⁴⁴"Then they will reply, 'Lord, when did we ever see you hungry or thirsty or a stranger or naked or sick or in prison, and not help you?'

⁴⁵"And he will answer, 'I tell you the truth, when you refused to help the least of these my brothers and sisters, you were refusing to help me.'

⁴⁶"And they will go away into eternal punishment, but the righteous will go into eternal life."

25:31 "Son of Man" is a title Jesus used for himself.   **25:32** Or *peoples.*   **25:40** Greek *my brothers.*
25:41 Greek *his angels.*

NOTES

25:31 *when the Son of Man comes in his glory, and all the angels with him, then he will sit upon his glorious throne.* After the grim picture of the judgment of the lazy slave (25:30), the stage is set for this account of the return of Jesus as the glorious Son of Man with his angels to judge the nations (13:41; 16:27-28; 24:31; 26:64; cf. Dan 7:13-14; Zech 14:5; John 5:27; 2 Thess 1:7; *1 Enoch* 1:9; 61:8; 62:1-5; 69:27-29; 90:20-36). An added detail is the mention of his sitting on his glorious throne (19:28; cf. 5:34; 23:22; Luke 1:32; Rev 3:21).

25:32-33 *All the nations will be gathered in his presence, and he will separate [them].* All will be gathered before Jesus and separated (13:49) to his right and left as shepherds customarily separated sheep from goats (Ezek 34:17-20). In this context, unlike 20:23 where the right and left hands indicate second and third highest positions in the Kingdom, the right hand is the place of honor (22:44; 26:64) and the left hand is the place of shame (cf. 6:3; 27:38; 1 Kgs 2:19; 22:19). This "judgment" is not like a trial that involves suspense about the verdict but more like a hearing after the trial to pronounce the sentence. It is fitting, in view of other passages, for sheep to stand for genuine followers of Jesus (9:36; 10:6, 16; 15:24; 18:12; 26:31; cf. 2 Sam 24:1; Jer 23:3-4; Ezek 34:6; John 10:1-30; *1 Enoch* 90:6, 30, 32). Sheep were probably more valuable than goats because of the wool they produced. Some believe that "all the nations" means all the Gentile nations, excluding the Jews, but this is doubtful (cf. 24:9, 14; Davies and Allison 1997:422-423; Hagner 1995:742). It is not easy to correlate this scene with other judgment scenes in the NT because there is no reference to a resurrection (cf. Acts 17:31; Rom 14:10-12; 1 Cor 15:51-57; 2 Cor 5:10; Rev 20:11-15). Perhaps the resurrection is assumed.

25:34-40 Jesus has been described as Son of Man and his judgment of the nations has been likened to a shepherd's activity. But here he speaks as the king who determines who will enter his Kingdom. He speaks first to the sheep on his right hand and announces that they, whom the Father has blessed (5:3ff), will inherit (5:5; 19:29) the Kingdom due to their merciful ministry to him when he was hungry, thirsty (10:42), homeless (Job 31:32; 1 Tim 5:10; Heb 13:2), naked, and imprisoned (Heb 10:34; 13:3).

Lord, when did we ever see you hungry? When the righteous (10:41; 13:43, 49) professed surprise and ignorance of their sixfold, merciful ministry, Jesus announced that it was done for him when it was done for one of his little brothers. The amazement of those on the King's right hand is evidently due to their lack of recollection of ministering to Jesus when he was in need, but ministry to his people is regarded as ministry to him (10:40). This is the central principle of judgment in this passage (cf. Prov 19:17). The preparation of the Kingdom for the blessed ones in 25:34 should be contrasted with the preparation of eternal fire for the devil and his demons in 25:41. (See the following commentary for discussion of the identity of "the least of my brothers and sisters.")

25:41-45 *Away with you, you cursed ones, into the eternal fire prepared for the devil and his demons.* These verses are exactly symmetrical with 25:34-40, but those on the King's left are told to depart into eternal fire (cf. 7:23; 18:8) because they have not carried out the sixfold ministry to Jesus when he was in need. They too are amazed at the key principle of the judgment—that ministry to Jesus' little brothers amounts to ministry to him. Their judgment is due to a sin of omission, not commission. "Away with you" is similar to the strong language of 4:10 and 16:23. It is noteworthy that the eternal fire (3:12; 13:42, 50; 18:8-9) is not prepared for those on the king's left but for the devil and his demons (lit. "his angels"; cf. 2 Cor 12:7; Rev 12:7, 9). Unlike the Kingdom in 25:34, the place of eternal fire is not said to be prepared from the creation of the world.

25:46 *they will go away into eternal punishment, but the righteous will go into eternal life.* This summary recapitulates the treatment of those on the right and on the left, in inverted order. Those on the left go to eternal punishment, and those on the right go to eternal life (19:16, 29; cf. Dan 12:2; John 5:28-29). The unique gravity of this judgment is stressed by the repetition of the word "eternal." There is a clear parallel between the expressions used in this verse and those used earlier for the destinies of those on the right and left in 25:34 and 25:41.

COMMENTARY

Hagner (1995:740) rightly observes that "the final section of the eschatological discourse ends fittingly in a great judgment scene." This discourse began with the disciples' question about the coming of Jesus in 24:3, and it ends with his coming to judge all the nations in 25:31. But the disciples' question was primarily about the timing of Jesus' coming, and there is no chronology here. This passage deals with the significance of Jesus' coming, not its timing. It amounts to an exposition of 24:29-31.

Although some view Matthew 25:31-46 as a parable (e.g., Robinson 1928:208-209), its metaphorical elements (25:32b-33) are not extended throughout the discourse. One might describe it as a semi-parable, but it begins and concludes as a prose narrative of the judgment of the nations. The narrative appears to have four parts, which speak of the setting of the judgment (25:31-33), the invitation to the righteous to enter the Kingdom (25:34-40), the banishment of the wicked to eternal fire (25:41-45), and the chiastic conclusion (25:46). In general, this final section of the Olivet discourse adds the lesson of compassion to the lessons of alertness (24:32-25:13) and faithfulness (25:14-30), which have been inculcated as the proper ethical response to the coming of Jesus.

Jesus taught his disciples to love all people, even their enemies (5:43-47), but there must be a special love and concern for one's fellow disciples. Itinerant preachers would especially need the type of ministry mentioned in 25:35-36 (10:40; 3 John 5-8), but it is doubtful that they alone are in view here. Jesus is identified with his disciples and they with him. They are persecuted due to their connection with him (5:11; 10:18, 22, 25; 23:34). Thus, it is quite likely that the privation of Jesus' little brothers in 25:35-36 is due to their testimony for Jesus. When one shows mercy to a follower of Jesus, in a profound sense one is showing mercy to Jesus himself.

Interpretive Questions. The interpretation of this passage is earnestly debated (Gray 1989). Dispensationalists argue that the passage speaks not of a general judgment of resurrected mankind but of the judgment of living nations who are alive on earth at Christ's return. The standard of judgment is their treatment of the Jewish remnant during the tribulation (Toussaint 1980:288-289; Walvoord 1974:202). The context and language of the passage can lend themselves to this interpretation, but it is doubtful that Jesus was being as precise as the modern dispensational system is in regard to a series of judgments in the end times.

A more exegetically oriented issue is the identity of "the least of these my brothers and sisters" (lit. "these least of my brothers"). Some understand the nations assembled for this judgment as those who have never heard the gospel and who are judged on the basis of the light they had (Green 1988:243), but Jesus himself seems to discount this wishful thinking in 11:27. Those inclined to a socially-oriented gospel see the passage as stressing the necessity of deeds of mercy to anyone in need (Barclay 1975:2.325-326; Beare 1981:495; Davies and Allison 1997:429). No doubt, Jesus' disciples should perform deeds of mercy to those in need (9:13; 12:7), but it is doubtful that Jesus' little brothers are to be identified with the needy in general. The dispensationalist view that the passage speaks of the treatment of the Jewish remnant by Gentiles during the eschatological tribulation probably interprets it too narrowly but correctly understands the relationship between belief in Jesus and deeds of mercy to others. All these views, however, seem to miss or minimize the fact that in Matthew the "little ones" are the true family of Jesus (10:40-42; 12:46-50), and that Jesus' "brothers" are related to him spiritually (5:22-24, 47; 7:3-5; 12:48-50; 18:15, 21, 35; 23:8; 28:10; Hagner 1995:744-745). One dare not cause the spiritual ruin of these little ones (18:6), and one must genuinely forgive them when necessary (18:21, 35). In Jesus' community, the world's lust for status and prestige is out of place since all the disciples of Jesus are brothers (and sisters) in the same family (20:20-28; 23:8-10).

This passage also speaks to the awesome doctrine of eternal punishment. Although it seems that the doctrine of the annihilation of the lost is growing in popularity, the juxtaposition of eternal life and eternal punishment in 25:46 renders such a notion as wishful thinking. Matthew's descriptions of the destiny of the lost speak of "fire" (3:12; 13:40, 50; 18:8-9; 25:41, 46; cf. 2 Thess 1:8; 2 Pet 3:7; Jude 1:7; Rev 14:10; 19:20; 20:10, 14-15; 21:8) and/or "deep darkness" (8:12; 22:13; 25:30; cf. 2 Pet 2:4; Jude 1:6, 13). The dreadful horror of everlasting separation from God is vividly expressed by both metaphors.

Summary and Transition. The difficulties in interpreting Matthew 24–25 serve to remind us of our limitations as finite human beings. When Bible teachers of equal scholarship and devotion cannot agree on the particulars of a passage, one should shy away from dogmatism and keep an open mind toward further instruction. Matthew 24–25 shows that biblical prophecy is not mere prognostication or soothsaying. Only 24:4-31 directly responds to the disciples' question about the details of the future (24:3). Even this futuristic section of the discourse stresses the need for ethical obedience to Jesus (24:4, 13-14, 23, 26). The rest of the discourse (24:32–25:46) is paraenetic and parabolic, stressing how one should live in light of the future. In this second part of the discourse, future events are indeed mentioned (24:33, 36-37, 39-42, 44; 25:13, 31, 46), but only to support the ethical characteristics mandated for Jesus disciples—alertness (24:32–25:13), faithfulness (25:14-30), and compassion (25:31-46). Jesus never spoke of the future to merely satisfy curiosity or provoke speculation. Rather, he opened up the future to God's people for the sake of their present obedience to God's plan.

Since there is a focus on eschatology in each of Jesus' first four discourses, especially at or near their conclusions (7:22; 10:32, 39-42; 13:49; 18:35), it is not surprising that Jesus ends *all* his teaching in Matthew with eschatology (26:1). His teaching has equipped his disciples with ethics befitting his reign (chs 5–7), with warnings about the perils of ministry (ch 10), with awareness of the contrasting responses to the Kingdom message (ch 13), with values for the Kingdom family (ch 18), and with the proper perspective on the future (chs 24–25). This proper perspective takes into account both the unknown date of Jesus' return and the prospect of delay in that return. What is needed is a vigilance which does not veer into frivolous enthusiasm on one side or into cold apathy on the other (24:31–25:13). This vigilance is shown by faithful stewardship (25:14-30). This stewardship is exercised in helping those in need, especially one's brothers and sisters in Christ (25:31-46).

When Jesus concludes all his words, he has concluded the teaching that he commands his disciples to perpetuate and inculcate in his future followers from all the nations of the earth. With his magnificent body of teaching now concluded, events will now quickly move toward his being handed over to be crucified (26:2). He will give his life a ransom for many, to save his people from their sins and to inaugurate the new covenant in his blood (1:23; 20:28; 26:28).

◆ **VIII. Conclusion: Passion, Resurrection, and Commission (26:1–28:20)**
A. The Plot to Kill Jesus (26:1-5; cf. Mark 14:1-2;
Luke 21:37–22:1-2)

When Jesus had finished saying all these things, he said to his disciples, 2"As you know, Passover begins in two days, and the Son of Man* will be handed over to be crucified."

3At that same time the leading priests and elders were meeting at the residence of Caiaphas, the high priest, 4plotting how to capture Jesus secretly and kill him. 5"But not during the Passover celebration," they agreed, "or the people may riot."

26:2 "Son of Man" is a title Jesus used for himself.

NOTES

26:1-2 *When Jesus had finished saying all these things.* For the fifth and final time, Matthew concludes a section of Jesus' discourse with this formula (cf. 7:28; 11:1; 13:53; 19:1). Matthew portrays 26:1 not simply as the end of a discourse, but as the end of *all* (*pantas*) that Jesus has taught in this Gospel (28:20). His teaching about the rule of God, begun in 4:17, is completed.

Passover begins in two days. Evidently, Passover day (Nisan 14), when the lambs were killed, fell on a Thursday that year, and the following Feast of Unleavened Bread ran from Nisan 15–21 (Lev 23:5-6; Num 28:16-17). If so, the meal would have been held just after sundown on Thursday (Blomberg 1992:388; Davies and Allison 1997:437, although Hagner 1995:754 opts for Friday evening; but cf. 763, 767). In 26:2, Jesus was evidently speaking on Tuesday.

the Son of Man will be handed over to be crucified. His words serve to remind the disciples of all the previous passion predictions

26:3 *Caiaphas, the high priest.* In Second Temple times, the high priesthood had become a political appointment by Rome. Caiaphas, high priest from AD 18–36, was the instigator of the plot to kill Jesus (see John 11:49; 18:13-28).

COMMENTARY

Introduction to Matthew's Passion Narrative. The climactic events that have been repeatedly predicted since the Galilean ministry are now about to unfold (12:38-40; 16:4, 21; 17:12, 22-23; 20:17-19; 21:38-39; 23:32). Jesus was aware of the forces arrayed against him (26:2), yet he did not resist doing the will of the Father despite the suffering that would be involved (26:36-46). Ironically, the very religious leaders who opposed and sought to destroy Jesus were the unwitting instruments God used to fulfill his plan to exalt Jesus (Hagner 1995:755).

Jesus' last week in Jerusalem is given extended treatment in all four Gospels. This fact, along with the notable lack of material about Jesus' life before his public ministry, shows that the Gospels are not mere historical chronicles or biographies, but theologically motivated literary works. The Gospel narratives of events from Palm Sunday to the end of Jesus' earthly ministry take up Matthew 21–28, Mark 11–16; Luke 19–24, and John 12–21; the last week of Jesus' life occupies roughly one third of the total Gospel materials. It has been said that the Gospels are passion (suffering) narratives with extended introductions, and this is only a slight exaggeration.

Matthew's narrative of Jesus' suffering is prefaced with the stories of the Temple conflicts with the religious leaders (chs 21–23) and the Olivet or eschatological discourse (chs 24–25). In both of these sections, Matthew's material is more extensive than either Mark's or Luke's. When it comes to the passion narrative proper (chs 26–28), Matthew and Mark are parallel for the most part, with Luke and John, especially, contributing unique material. The general flow of Matthew's material is as follows:

1. Preparation of the disciples (26:1-46)
2. Arrest at Gethsemane (26:47-56)
3. Trial before Caiaphas (26:57-68)
4. Peter's three denials (26:69-75)
5. Trial before Pilate (27:1-2; 11-26) with interwoven account of Judas' suicide (27:3-10)
6. Jesus mocked and crucified (27:27-56)
7. Jesus buried by Joseph of Arimathea (27:57-61)
8. Jesus' resurrection and its denial (27:62–28:15)
9. The great commission (28:18-20)

There are several events and elements in Matthew's passion narrative (some form entire portions) that are unique to his Gospel among the Synoptics and that presumably indicate his special literary and theological emphases:

1. Jesus reminds the disciples of his impending death (26:1-2)
2. The amount of money paid Judas is specified as thirty pieces of silver (26:15; cf. Exod 21:32; Zech 11:12)
3. Judas asks Jesus if he is the betrayer (26:25)
4. Jesus' blood is presented as being poured out for the forgiveness of sins (26:28)
5. The second prayer in Gethsemane is presented as a direct quotation (26:42)
6. Jesus' words to Judas after the kiss (26:50)
7. Jesus' comments after the high priest's servant's ear is cut off about violence, the availability of angelic help, and scriptural fulfillment (26:52-54)
8. The high priest's demand before God that Jesus speak (26:63)
9. Sarcastic reference to Jesus as Messiah (26:68)
10. Jesus is described as a Galilean (26:69)
11. Peter's second denial includes an oath (26:72)
12. The purpose of the morning consultation is already decided: execute Jesus (27:1)
13. Pilate describes Jesus as the one who is called the Messiah (27:17, 22)
14. Pilate's wife recounts a dream and calls Jesus innocent (27:19)
15. Pilate washes his hands and the crowd took responsibility for Jesus' death (27:24-25)
16. The sign at the cross specifies the name of Jesus (27:37)
17. Emphasis on Jesus as the Son of God (27:40, 43)
18. Allusion to Psalm 22:8 (27:43)

19. Account of the earthquake and opening of the tombs (27:51-53)
20. Joseph of Arimathea is called a disciple (27:57)
21. The Jewish religious leaders get Pilate to guard Jesus' tomb (27:62-66)
22. Jesus meets the women after the resurrection (28:9-10)
23. The conspiracy to deny the resurrection (28:11-15).
24. Jesus has all authority, all nations are to be discipled, trinitarian baptismal formula, disciples are to be taught to obey all that Jesus commanded, promise to be with the disciples until the end of the age (28:18-20)

The magisterial work of Brown (1994) provides an extremely thorough discussion of the death of Jesus in all four Gospels. Brown's handling of Matthew's passion narrative begins with 26:30.

The Plot to Kill Jesus. Jesus told his disciples that he would be crucified during Passover. This is the first prediction that connects Jesus' death to the Passover (cf. 1 Cor 5:7). These words also showed that Jesus was not going to be surprised by the nefarious events which transpire in this chapter (26:21, 31, 45-46, 50, 54, 56). For discussion of the historical and synoptic questions, including whether Jesus was crucified in AD 30 or 33, see Blomberg (1987:175-180), Carson (1985:528-532), Hoehner (1976:65-114), and Keener (1999:607-611).

Matthew's mention of the leader's plot in 26:3-5 serves to confirm what Jesus said in 26:2. A plot against Jesus had been in place for some time (cf. 12:14; 22:15), but given the conflicts in the Temple, there was more reason than ever for the chief priests and elders to meet with the high priest Caiaphas (cf. John 11:49; 18:13-14, 24, 28; Josephus *Antiquities* 18.35) and plan to apprehend Jesus secretly and kill him. Secrecy was necessary because of Jesus' popularity with the multitudes of pilgrims who had arrived in Jerusalem for the Passover festival (21:26; 27:24). The leaders thought they would need to wait until after the Passover to arrest Jesus, but Judas' offer to betray Jesus would allow them to accomplish their goal more rapidly (26:14-16, 47ff).

◆ **B. The Anointing at Bethany (26:6-13; cf. Mark 14:3-9; John 12:2-11)**

⁶Meanwhile, Jesus was in Bethany at the home of Simon, a man who had previously had leprosy. ⁷While he was eating,* a woman came in with a beautiful alabaster jar of expensive perfume and poured it over his head.

⁸The disciples were indignant when they saw this. "What a waste!" they said. ⁹"It could have been sold for a high price and the money given to the poor."

¹⁰But Jesus, aware of this, replied, "Why criticize this woman for doing such a good thing to me? ¹¹You will always have the poor among you, but you will not always have me. ¹²She has poured this perfume on me to prepare my body for burial. ¹³I tell you the truth, wherever the Good News is preached throughout the world, this woman's deed will be remembered and discussed."

26:7 Or *reclining.*

NOTES

26:6 Jesus was in Bethany. Sandwiched between two sections of the betrayal story is the narrative of Jesus' anointing in Bethany (cf. Mark 14:3-9; John 12:2-11). Bethany was a village less than two miles east of Jerusalem on the Mount of Olives (21:17; John 11:1, 18).

Simon, a man who had previously had leprosy. Spending time in the home of Simon the leper, who is mentioned only here in the NT, would render Jesus ritually impure just before Passover (cf. 8:2). The NLT reflects the view of some that Simon was a former leper who had already been healed by Jesus. There may be four other Simons in this Gospel (4:18; 10:2, 4; 13:55; 16:16-17; 17:25; 27:32).

26:7 a woman came in with a beautiful alabaster jar of expensive perfume and poured it over his head. While Jesus was eating, an unnamed woman (but see John 12:3) surprisingly anointed his head with perfume.

26:8-9 What a waste! The disciples responded indignantly to what they perceived as an extravagance. They protested that the valuable perfume could have been sold and the money given to the poor (cf. 11:5; 19:21; cf. Luke 4:18; 21:1-4). But the next verses show that their apparent piety masked a serious lack of spiritual perception. The disciples were inexplicably oblivious to the absolutely exceptional nature of these days in Jerusalem.

26:10 Why criticize this woman? Jesus criticized the disciples for criticizing the woman. Her action might show her perception of the uniqueness of the hour (see note on 26:12), a perception the disciples lack.

26:11 You will always have the poor. Poor people will always be around (Deut 15:11), but Jesus' time on earth was short (26:2-3). Opportunities abound for helping the poor, but time was running out for honoring Jesus.

26:12 She has poured this perfume on me to prepare my body for burial. It is not clear how much the woman realized about Jesus' imminent betrayal, but Jesus interpreted her action as prophetic, a preparation for his burial (Davies and Allison 1997:447). In any event, Hagner (1995:758) goes too far in saying that the woman certainly did not intend to anoint Jesus for burial.

26:13 this woman's deed will be remembered. Her deed will be recounted and she will be remembered wherever the gospel is preached throughout the world (24:14; 28:19). The record of this story in Matthew, Mark, and John ensures that the act of the woman will continue to be remembered all over the world. Interestingly, Matthew does not mention that after the crucifixion Jesus' body was again anointed before it was placed in the tomb (27:59; cf. Mark 16:1; Luke 20:1; John 18:38-40).

COMMENTARY

In this passage one is struck by the fact that an obscure, unnamed woman seems to have greater recognition of the shortness of Jesus' remaining time on earth than Jesus' disciples had. Though the disciples had a legitimate point—one should care for the needy—the disciples' timing was all wrong. Despite their being at Jesus' side and hearing his repeated passion predictions, including one that should still be ringing in their ears (26:2), they acted as though it was time for business as usual. As the story of this chapter proceeds, this woman is portrayed sympathetically as serving Jesus while the disciples are corrected. Judas is the foil to the unnamed woman.

Jesus' words about the poor should not be misused as substantiation for a callous attitude about their needs. His comment that the poor are always present alludes to Deuteronomy 15:11, which speaks realistically about needy people in the context of the sabbatical year of remission when debts were to be forgiven (Deut 15:1-2). God commanded the Jews not to withhold a loan because the sabbatical year was near and the loan would be forgiven before it could be completely repaid (Deut 15:7-10). God's blessing will make up for what is lost when the loan is not repaid (Deut 15:4, 6, 10, 14, 18). Overall, Deuteronomy 15 is about helping the needy so that there will be no poor people in the land (Deut 15:4). Jesus' allusion to Deuteronomy 15:11 in 26:11 is a reminder of an ongoing responsibility, not a stoic comment about an inevitable situation. But the ongoing responsibility of caring for the poor paled in comparison with the urgency of caring for Jesus during his last days on earth (9:15).

◆   **C. Judas Agrees to Betray Jesus (26:14-16; cf. Mark 14:10-11; Luke 22:3-6)**

¹⁴Then Judas Iscariot, one of the twelve disciples, went to the leading priests ¹⁵and asked, "How much will you pay me to betray Jesus to you?" And they gave him thirty pieces of silver. ¹⁶From that time on, Judas began looking for an opportunity to betray Jesus.

NOTES
26:14-16 *How much will you pay me to betray Jesus to you?* This passage returns to the betrayal narrative of 26:1-5. It supplies the missing link to the leaders' plan (cf. Mark 14:10-11; Luke 22:3-6). Now they need not wait until after the Passover festival is concluded to arrest Jesus (26:47ff). With Judas's aid, they could apprehend him privately without inciting a riot among the people. Prior to this point, Judas was mentioned only in 10:4, where his name occurs last in the list of disciples with the qualifier "who later betrayed him." Matthew makes it clear that Judas initiated the betrayal by going to the chief priests seeking money. See John 12:6 on Judas's theft from the disciples' funds.

thirty pieces of silver. The price paid to Judas for the betrayal was thirty silver shekels. In Exod 21:32 this is the price to be paid to the owner of a slave gored by an ox. Zech 11:12-13 speaks sarcastically of this amount of money. Joseph was sold by his brothers to the Midianites for twenty shekels (Gen 37:28). A shekel was evidently worth four denarii, so thirty shekels would be around four months wages for a day laborer. This sum is not insignificant but is rather paltry compared with the value of the ointment used by the woman to anoint Jesus.

COMMENTARY
Judas was a pathetically and enigmatically evil person (26:24; John 17:12), and the motivation for his betraying Jesus is one of the more inscrutable matters in the Bible (Davies and Allison 1997:451-452). Some believe he took this action out of greed, since Judas asked how much the leaders would pay him (cf. 6:19-21, 24). He was disgusted at the waste of money when Jesus was anointed with the expensive perfume by the woman at Bethany (cf. John 12:4-6). Others theorize that Judas was looking for a military-political type of Messiah and had become disillusioned when Jesus' spiritually-oriented message was not widely received, especially by the leaders of Israel. Perhaps both greed and disillusionment were involved; greed

drove Judas to betray Jesus when he realized that Jesus was not a militaristic Messiah. Luke 22:3 and John 6:70; 13:2 cite satanic influence behind Judas' action. Blomberg (1992:387) is probably stretching things a bit in suggesting that Judas had perhaps committed the unpardonable sin (12:32), since there is no reason to suppose Judas attributed Jesus' miracles to the power of the devil. In any event, Judas sold out Jesus, later regretted doing so, and committed suicide (27:3-5).

The allusion to Zechariah 11:12-13 is subtle but important in that it connects Judas' betrayal to OT prophecy and thus supports the idea in Matthew 26 that God is in control of all the Passion week events, even the betrayal of Jesus (26:18, 31, 54, 56). This profound matter deserves reflection (cf. Acts 2:23; 4:27-28). Every follower of Jesus should also reflect on the monstrous treachery of Judas and grieve with the original disciples that one of the Twelve could betray the Lord (26:22).

◆   **D. The Last Supper (26:17-30; cf. Mark 14:12-25; Luke 22:7-20; John 13:21-30)**

[17]On the first day of the Festival of Unleavened Bread, the disciples came to Jesus and asked, "Where do you want us to prepare the Passover meal for you?" [18]"As you go into the city," he told them, "you will see a certain man. Tell him, 'The Teacher says: My time has come, and I will eat the Passover meal with my disciples at your house.' " [19]So the disciples did as Jesus told them and prepared the Passover meal there.

[20]When it was evening, Jesus sat down at the table* with the twelve disciples.* [21]While they were eating, he said, "I tell you the truth, one of you will betray me."

[22]Greatly distressed, each one asked in turn, "Am I the one, Lord?"

[23]He replied, "One of you who has just eaten from this bowl with me will betray me. [24]For the Son of Man must die, as the Scriptures declared long ago. But how terrible it will be for the one who betrays him. It would be far better for that man if he had never been born!"

[25]Judas, the one who would betray him, also asked, "Rabbi, am I the one?"

And Jesus told him, "You have said it."

[26]As they were eating, Jesus took some bread and blessed it. Then he broke it in pieces and gave it to the disciples, saying, "Take this and eat it, for this is my body."

[27]And he took a cup of wine and gave thanks to God for it. He gave it to them and said, "Each of you drink from it, [28]for this is my blood, which confirms the covenant* between God and his people. It is poured out as a sacrifice to forgive the sins of many. [29]Mark my words—I will not drink wine again until the day I drink it new with you in my Father's Kingdom."

[30]Then they sang a hymn and went out to the Mount of Olives.

26:20a Or *Jesus reclined.*   26:20b Some manuscripts read *the Twelve.*   26:28 Some manuscripts read *the new covenant.*

NOTES

26:17-19 Here the narrative returns to Jesus' last hours with the disciples (cf. Mark 14:12-25; Luke 22:7-20; John 13:21-30). He was about to move from Bethany (26:6) to Jerusalem (26:18).

Festival of Unleavened Bread. Due to the requirement for all leaven to be removed from Jewish homes, Passover was also known as the Festival of Unleavened Bread (Exod 12:1-20; Lev 23:4-8; Num 9:1-14; 28:17; Deut 16:1-8; *m. Pesahim;* Josephus *Antiquities* 18.29).

Where do you want us to prepare the Passover? On the first day of the eight-day feast, evidently Thursday (Exod 12:18-20; Gundry 1994:524), the disciples inquired as to where Jesus would eat the Passover meal. The way in which Jesus secured a room for the Passover celebration is similar to the way in which he had earlier secured a donkey for his entry into the city (cf. 21:2-3). A providential ordering of the circumstances mentioned in 26:18 is apparent.

My time has come. This is a cryptic reference to the impending arrest and crucifixion. It is quite difficult to reconcile the chronology implicit in this narrative with that of John 18:28, which implies that Jesus' trial before Pilate occurs before Passover (cf. Matt 27:11). For plausible explanations of this difference, see Carson 1984:528-532; Hoehner 1976:86-90; Ruckstuhl 1965:18-32.

26:20 *Jesus sat down at the table.* Lit., "he was reclining." The customary way to eat a formal meal in that day was to recline on cushions arranged in a U-shaped pattern (a triclinium) around food placed on a low table in the middle (9:10; 22:10; 26:7; BDAG 65).

the twelve disciples. The twelve disciples correspond to the twelve tribes of Israel in Exod 24:4.

26:21 *While they were eating.* After sundown on Thursday, the Passover meal was eaten. The Passover meal was celebrated at home, led by the head of the family, and Jesus would evidently serve as the head of the family of disciples in leading their meal. Thus, this passage illustrates Matt 12:46-50 in that those who do the will of the Father are Jesus' true family (Davies and Allison 1997:458).

one of you will betray me. At some point in the meal, likely near the beginning, Jesus made the arresting announcement that he would be betrayed by one of the Twelve. At this point, the disciples begin to learn what the reader of Matthew already knows from 26:14-16. Earlier comments had implied an act of betrayal (20:18; 26:2), but this statement is much more explicit. The reader is impressed that Jesus knew that his betrayal would be accomplished by Judas even though Judas had only recently agreed to do it.

26:22 *Am I the one, Lord?* The disciples had no inkling as to the identity of the betrayer, since they each began to ask Jesus whether they were the betrayer.

26:23-24 *One of you who has just eaten from this bowl with me.* Lit., "one who dipped his hand with me in the bowl," probably alluding to the custom of dipping food into *haroset,* a sweet sauce or relish (John 13:26; *m. Pesahim* 10:3).

as the Scriptures declared long ago. Lit., "as it is written concerning him."

It would be far better for that man if he had never been born! Jesus' comment on how terrible it will be for the betrayer is chilling (cf. 18:7; 1 *Enoch* 38:2).

26:25 *am I the one?* After waiting until all the others had spoken and following their example, Judas incredulously asked if he was the betrayer.

You have said it. Jesus responded with an ambiguous, qualified affirmation (cf. 26:64; 27:11) that stressed Judas's own words. A similar English idiom would be "You said it." This would let Judas know that Jesus was aware of his plot without alerting the other disciples to it.

26:26-30 As the meal proceeded after the dramatic announcement that the betrayer was present, Jesus attributed special significance to the unleavened bread and the wine (described as the cup in keeping with 20:22-23; 26:39). Evidently, the elements of the Passover meal were already viewed as symbolic (*m. Pesahim* 10:4-5), so Jesus' innovation relates to the symbolic referents, not to the use of symbolism itself. Although there is no explicit word of institution here, as in 1 Cor 11:24-25, Christians have universally viewed Jesus' implicit intent as establishing a practice which is to be repeated. Jesus instituted what Christians have come to call the Eucharist or Lord's Supper.

Take this and eat it, for this is my body. The broken bread (14:19; 15:36) represents his body.

Each of you drink from it, for this is my blood. The cup represents his blood.

blood, which confirms the covenant. Lit., "blood of the covenant." This phrase alludes to Exod 24:8 (cf. Zech 9:11; Heb 9:19-22; 10:29; 13:20). Some manuscripts (A C D W f.¹³ 𝔐) read "blood of the new covenant," but this is likely an interpolation from Luke 22:20 (cf. 1 Cor 11:25; Metzger 1994:54). The best manuscripts (𝔓37 𝔓45ᵛⁱᵈ ℵ B L Z) do not include the word "new." The newness is found in 26:29, where Jesus speaks prophetically of drinking new wine with his disciples in the future Kingdom. Thus, the institution of the Lord's supper is closely tied to the Passover, as well as to the new covenant (Jer 31:31-34). It also anticipates the ultimate eschatological feast in the future Kingdom (26:29; cf. 8:11; 22:2; 25:10; Rev 19:7ff).

It is poured out as a sacrifice to forgive the sins of many. See 1:21; 20:28; cf. Exod 12:21-27; Isa 53:4-12. The phrase "as a sacrifice" is not found in the Gr. text.

26:30 This is a hinge verse, connecting the private last supper to the ongoing story, which develops on the Mount of Olives.

they sang a hymn. At the end of the meal, they sang psalms (probably the Hallel, Pss 115–118; cf. *m. Pesahim* 10:6-7).

[they] went out to the Mount of Olives. Jesus and his disciples left the city for the Mount of Olives (cf. 21:17; 24:1-3). This shows that Jesus did not hide from his inevitable suffering. For additional discussions of the Passover meal in NT times and the relationship of the Lord's Supper to the Passover, see Chilton in Evans and Porter (2000:372-373, 376-377) and Stein in Green and McKnight (1992:444-450).

COMMENTARY

Matthew 26:17-30 contains four parts: (1) preparation for the Passover (26:17-19); (2) prediction of betrayal during the meal (27:20-25); (3) institution of the Lord's Supper (26:26-29); (4) transition back to the main plot (26:30).

Despite the confidence of some scholars, it is not clear at what point in the Passover meal Jesus predicted the betrayal and instituted his supper. Matthew's account does associate these events with a historical Passover meal, but he does not provide historical details which are extraneous to his theological purpose.

This Passover meal is both a beginning and an end. It was the last supper, Jesus' last meal with his disciples before his arrest, trials, and crucifixion. But it was also the first supper, the inauguration of the remembrance of Jesus by his new community. Jesus, in fulfillment of Old Testament pattern and prediction, was (as it were) bringing from his treasure things new and old (13:52). In this light, the Lord's Supper is not the Passover, but it is associated with the Passover (Stein in Green and McKnight 1992:446-447). In the future, when they reenact the last supper, as they eat the bread and drink the wine, the disciples will remember that Jesus did indeed shed his blood for them for the forgiveness of their sins. And they will remember his promise to share the table with them in the future Kingdom. As Paul put it, every time they eat the bread and drink the cup they will be announcing the Lord's death until he comes (1 Cor 11:26). The Lord's Supper is divinely ordained to remind Jesus' followers of what he has done and what he will do. Their present existence is framed by Jesus' past coming to redeem them and by his future coming to reign over the earth. These truths are powerfully impressed onto the hearts of his people when they participate in faith at the table. The sacrament of the Lord's Supper is neither an impotent memorial, an empty sign, nor an automatic source of saving grace. But when it is received in faith, it dynamically strengthens the people of God as it proclaims the central truth of the gospel of Jesus (Calvin 1960:2.1276-1303 [*Institutes* 4.14]; 1972:3.135-136). The early Christians probably observed the Lord's supper in the context of a regular fellowship meal or "love feast" (Acts 2:42; 20:7-12; 1 Cor 11:20-22; Jude 1:12; *Didache* 9-10; 14:1).

Despite the current popularity of "Passover Seder" celebrations in Christian churches at Easter, the order of the meal in New Testament times is not known with certainty. Attempts to read later Jewish Passover liturgy back into the New Testament and to invest it with Christian typological significance may be edifying, but the practice rests on a weak historical foundation. Mishnah *Pesahim* 10 is the earliest source for the seder liturgy, but the Mishnah was not compiled until around AD 200. Christians tend to identify the bread of the Lord's Supper with *m. Pesahim* 10:3 and the cup with the third cup, over which a benediction was said (*m. Pesahim* 10:7; *m. Berakhot* 6:1). But there is no mention of the roasted lamb, the four cups, or the traditional Jewish interpretation of these things. Also, it is not certain that the Mishnah preserves the same liturgy as that practiced by Jesus over one hundred and fifty years earlier (Davies and Allison 1997:469). It does seem clear that Jesus used the Passover meal as the context for the institution of his own supper, and one could say that for Matthew the Lord's Supper fulfilled the Passover, but the precise details of the correspondence are not known.

◆   ## E. Prediction of the Disciples' Desertion (26:31-35; cf. Mark 14:26-31; Luke 22:31-34; John 13:31-38)

[31] On the way, Jesus told them, "Tonight all of you will desert me. For the Scriptures say,

'God will strike* the Shepherd,
and the sheep of the flock will be scattered.'

[32] But after I have been raised from the dead, I will go ahead of you to Galilee and meet you there."

[33] Peter declared, "Even if everyone else deserts you, I will never desert you."

[34] Jesus replied, "I tell you the truth, Peter—this very night, before the rooster crows, you will deny three times that you even know me."

[35] "No!" Peter insisted. "Even if I have to die with you, I will never deny you!" And all the other disciples vowed the same.

26:31 Greek *I will strike.* Zech 13:7.

NOTES

26:31 *Tonight all of you will desert me.* Cf. Mark 14:26-31; Luke 22:39-40a; John 13:31-38. "Desert" is perhaps a weak rendering of a term which means "to be caused to stumble" or "to be led into sin" (*skandalisthēsesthe*; 5:29; 11:6; 13:21, 57; 15:12; 18:6, 8; 24:10; cf. BDAG 926). The image is that the disciples will seriously stumble in their faith.

the Scriptures say. Jesus cited this dire prediction by quoting Zech 13:7, which describes the scattering of the sheep that results when the shepherd is struck (cf. 9:36).

26:32 *after I have been raised from the dead, I will go ahead of you to Galilee and meet you there.* As serious as this desertion would be, it was not final, since Jesus promised to meet the disciples in Galilee after he was raised from the dead (cf. 28:7, 10, 16). Perhaps the picture of Jesus going ahead of the disciples to Galilee is intended to cause the reader to picture a shepherd going ahead of his sheep (cf. John 10:4). The resurrection of Jesus, previously mentioned several times (12:40; 16:21; 17:23; 20:19; 27:63-64; 28:6), would be a turning point in that Jesus would then bring the disciples as wandering sheep back into the fold.

26:33 *I will never desert you.* Peter has not been heard from for some time (19:27), but at this point he speaks up and becomes a prominent character throughout the rest of the chapter. Peter denied that he would deny the Lord (26:35; cf. 26:75). Peter put this very strongly, believing that he would be the last person to sin by deserting Jesus. Even if all the other disciples fell away, Peter believed he would remain faithful.

26:34-35 *you will deny three times that you even know me.* When Jesus told Peter that he would deny Jesus not once, but three times before a rooster crowed, Peter adamantly reaffirmed what he has just said, adding that he would die before denying Jesus. Peter's impetuous personality put him in the spotlight here (as in 14:28-31; 16:21-23), but in 26:35b it is added that all the disciples were saying the same thing Peter said.

COMMENTARY

This passage records another instance of Peter being against Jesus (cf. 16:22). Twice Jesus predicted Peter's future behavior (26:31, 34), and twice Peter strongly objected (26:33, 35). Told that all the disciples will scatter and be met by Jesus in Galilee, Peter insisted that he would never desert Jesus even if everyone else did. Told that he would do worse than desert Jesus, he would deny him three times, Peter affirmed that he would die first. The ensuing narrative shows just how wrong Peter was on both counts. But Peter had been wrong before, and had nevertheless overcome his momentary failing (16:22). The resurrection of Jesus would be the event that turned grief into joy, defeat into victory, and desertion into renewed allegiance (26:32; 28:7, 10, 16-20). At this point Peter did not know himself well enough to acknowledge his propensity to desert and deny Jesus. He would learn this bitter lesson (26:75) and be restored to fellowship with Jesus and ministry for Jesus (cf. John 21:15ff). According to tradition, Peter did eventually die a martyr's death rather than deny Jesus, though it was years after the crucifixion.

◆ **F. Jesus Prays in Gethsemane (26:36-46; cf. Mark 14:32-42; Luke 22:39-46)**

[36]Then Jesus went with them to the olive grove called Gethsemane, and he said, "Sit here while I go over there to pray." [37]He took Peter and Zebedee's two sons, James and John, and he became anguished and distressed. [38]He told them, "My soul is crushed with grief to the point of death. Stay here and keep watch with me."

[39]He went on a little farther and bowed with his face to the ground, praying, "My Father! If it is possible, let this cup of suffering be taken away from me. Yet I want your will to be done, not mine."

[40]Then he returned to the disciples and found them asleep. He said to Peter, "Couldn't you watch with me even one hour? [41]Keep watch and pray, so that you

will not give in to temptation. For the spirit is willing, but the body is weak!"

⁴²Then Jesus left them a second time and prayed, "My Father! If this cup cannot be taken away* unless I drink it, your will be done." ⁴³When he returned to them again, he found them sleeping, for they couldn't keep their eyes open.

26:42 Greek *If this cannot pass.*

⁴⁴So he went to pray a third time, saying the same things again. ⁴⁵Then he came to the disciples and said, "Go ahead and sleep. Have your rest. But look—the time has come. The Son of Man is betrayed into the hands of sinners. ⁴⁶Up, let's be going. Look, my betrayer is here!"

NOTES

26:36-38 Gethsemane. The name is evidently derived from two Heb. words meaning "oil press."

he took Peter and Zebedee's two sons, James and John. Jesus left the group and prayed semi-privately with Peter and the two sons of Zebedee (26:36-37; cf. Mark 14:32-42; Luke 22:40b-46; cf. Heb 5:7-9). The NLT goes beyond the Gr. text in spelling out the names of the sons of Zebedee.

My soul is crushed with grief to the point of death. Jesus' profound inner agony was like that of the psalmist in such Psalms as 3, 6, 31, 42.

26:39 *If it is possible, let this cup of suffering be taken away from me. Yet I want your will to be done, not mine.* Jesus' prayer (cf. 26:42, 44) honestly voiced his wish to avoid the suffering of the cross and, more importantly, his realization that his own wish might be overridden by the Father's. It is the Father's will that must be done (Matt 6:10; 26:53-54). Jesus spoke of his suffering as a cup (NLT's "cup of suffering" makes the metaphor explicit), which must be drunk (20:22-23; cf. Ps 11:6; 75:8; Isa 51:17, 22; Jer 25:15; 49:12; Rev 14:10; 16:19; 17:4; 18:6).

26:40 *found them asleep.* After praying Jesus returned to find the three disciples sleeping. A pathetic cycle is repeated three times as Jesus prays alone and then finds the disciples sleeping instead of staying alert with him (26:38-41, 42-43, 44). His anguish in the face of death is contrasted with their total lack of awareness of the hour and of concern for their master.

Peter is specifically addressed because he protested the loudest in 26:33-35 and he will deny the Lord in 26:69-75.

Couldn't you watch with me even one hour? Jesus' response to their lack of alertness is twofold: a rhetorical question about their insensitivity (26:40b), followed by an exhortation to alertness (26:41; cf. 24:42-43; 25:13). His mention of "one hour" in 26:40 may mean that he had been praying (and they have been sleeping) that long.

26:41 *the spirit is willing, but the body is weak!* Temptation due to the weakness of the "body" (lit. "flesh") will result if they do not remain alert. Their willingness of spirit (Ps 51:12) is evidenced by their protests in 26:35b, their weakness of flesh (Rom 6:19) by their seeming inability to remain alert with their master during his final and most difficult hours on earth (cf. Rom 8:4-17; Gal 5:16-24).

26:42-43 *If this cup cannot be taken away unless I drink it, your will be done.* Jesus' second prayer was expressed in a way that implies a deeper resignation to the Father's will. There are parallels here to the Lord's prayer in 6:9. This time there is no request for the cup to pass away, only agreement with the Father's plan that the cup can pass away only by being drunk by Jesus.

found them sleeping. After this prayer, Jesus discovered the disciples sleeping again. This time there is no question or exhortation, only the editorial explanation that they just couldn't keep their eyes open.

26:44-46 *to pray a third time.* Jesus left them to pray a third time and he again prayed as before (cf. 2 Cor 12:8). Returning to the disciples, he found them still asleep. It is interesting to compare this cycle of three lost opportunities to stay alert with Jesus to the cycle of Peter's three lost opportunities to confess Jesus in 26:69-75.

Go ahead and sleep. It is not clear if Jesus' first words to the disciples should be viewed as a statement (as in the NLT) or as a question ("Are you still sleeping and resting?"), similar to 26:40. It is perhaps a bit strange for Jesus to tell them to sleep one moment and rouse them the next.

the time has come. The Son of Man is betrayed. Jesus roused them with the announcement that the time of his betrayal, and indeed the betrayer himself, was at hand.

COMMENTARY

This passage contains three cycles of Jesus praying and the disciples sleeping. The repetition makes the points about Jesus and the disciples very clear. The solitary prayers of Jesus in Gethsemane are remarkable for several reasons. First, in these prayers Jesus put the Father's will before his own. He realistically anticipated the pain and suffering ahead of him (cf. 27:46) and wished that he did not have to endure it. At the same time, he was resigned to obeying the Father's plan. In this, he models the prayer he taught the disciples (6:9ff). His prayer also models his own exhortation to pray alertly and recognize the weakness of the flesh (26:41). The God-centeredness of the Gethsemane prayers of Jesus should be put alongside the temptation of Jesus in 4:1-11. Jesus lived on God's words whether or not he had bread. He would not test the Lord his God. He would worship only the Lord his God. He would do the will of the Lord his God, even if it led to suffering and death.

If it is thought that this understanding of Jesus' prayer does not do justice to his deity, one has only to consult the book of Hebrews, which stresses how Jesus' sufferings equipped him to be a sympathetic high priest for his followers (Heb 2:14-18; 4:14-16; 5:7-9). In no way should a high Christology deter us from appreciating the reality of Jesus' distress in the garden (26:37-39, 42, 44). The wonder of the incarnation of the Son of God is that Jesus was truly divine and truly human.

Jesus' Gethsemane experience reminds us of the weakness of his disciples (cf. 6:30; 8:26; 14:31; 16:8, 22; 17:20; 18:21; 19:13) as eloquently as it portrays his strength. Their lack of perception as to the significance of the anointing of Jesus at Bethany (26:10) shows that their minds were not focused on Jesus' reminder of the nearness of his death (26:2). Their unanimous denial that they would desert Jesus just after his prediction that they would do so amounts to outright unbelief caused by sinful self-confidence (26:31-35). One would think that such supposedly brave men would be able to keep watch with Jesus through the night, but even his inner circle of disciples failed him in his most vulnerable moment. The sons of Zebedee, James and John, who wanted the places of highest honor in the Kingdom, promised Jesus that they could drink his cup (20:22). But they couldn't even stay awake to share his grief. Given their performance in Gethsemane, their desertion when Jesus was arrested is not a surprise. The sleep of the disciples cannot help but remind the reader of the necessity for spiritual alertness in the face of moral testing (cf. 1 Cor

16:13; Eph 5:14; Col 4:2; 1 Thess 5:6-8; 1 Pet 5:8). The disciples' weakness reminds us of our own, yet the promises of our Lord sustain us as we serve him until he returns (e.g., 16:18; 19:28-29; 28:18, 20).

◆ **G. The Arrest of Jesus (26:47-56; cf. Mark 14:43-52; Luke 22:47-53; John 18:1-12)**

⁴⁷And even as Jesus said this, Judas, one of the twelve disciples, arrived with a crowd of men armed with swords and clubs. They had been sent by the leading priests and elders of the people. ⁴⁸The traitor, Judas, had given them a prearranged signal: "You will know which one to arrest when I greet him with a kiss." ⁴⁹So Judas came straight to Jesus. "Greetings, Rabbi!" he exclaimed and gave him the kiss.

⁵⁰Jesus said, "My friend, go ahead and do what you have come for."

Then the others grabbed Jesus and arrested him. ⁵¹But one of the men with Jesus pulled out his sword and struck the high priest's slave, slashing off his ear.

⁵²"Put away your sword," Jesus told him.

"Those who use the sword will die by the sword. ⁵³Don't you realize that I could ask my Father for thousands* of angels to protect us, and he would send them instantly? ⁵⁴But if I did, how would the Scriptures be fulfilled that describe what must happen now?"

⁵⁵Then Jesus said to the crowd, "Am I some dangerous revolutionary, that you come with swords and clubs to arrest me? Why didn't you arrest me in the Temple? I was there teaching every day. ⁵⁶But this is all happening to fulfill the words of the prophets as recorded in the Scriptures." At that point, all the disciples deserted him and fled.

26:53 Greek *twelve legions.*

N O T E S
26:47 Judas . . . arrived with a crowd of men armed with swords and clubs. This crowd was commissioned by the religious leaders to arrest Jesus (cf. Mark 14:43-52; Luke 22:47-53; John 18:2-12).

one of the twelve disciples. The treachery of Judas is emphasized all the more by the description that he was one of the twelve disciples (26:14, 21; cf. Ps 41:9; John 13:18).

26:48-49 "Rabbi!" he exclaimed and gave him the kiss. Judas had arranged with the leaders that the kiss would identify Jesus, evidently because Jesus was not known personally to them and it was dark. Judas is the only one to refer to Jesus as "rabbi" in Matthew (26:25, 49; cf. 23:7-8), and his betraying kiss is a despicable perversion of an action which would normally express brotherhood, affirmation, and honor (cf. Luke 7:45; Rom 16:16; 1 Pet 5:14).

26:50 My friend, go ahead and do what you have come for. Jesus' response to Judas is difficult to translate. It could be either a command telling Judas to do what he had come to do (cf. John 13:27) or a question asking him what he was doing. His referring to Judas as "friend" is ironic, but the word used here (*hetaire* [TG2083, ZG2279]) refers only to an acquaintance and does not imply a close relationship (as the word *philos* [TG5384A, ZG5813] would have; cf. 20:13; 22:12).

26:51 struck the high priest's slave. One of the disciples—identified as Peter in John 18:10—attempted to resist the arrest and managed only to cut off the ear of the high priest's slave.

26:52 Those who use the sword will die by the sword. Jesus commanded him to put his sword away with words that have since been used to support the view known as Christian pacifism or non-resistance (5:9, 39). In context, however, Jesus was speaking realistically about the ways of the fallen world (Gen 9:6; Jer 15:2; Rev 13:10). There is no mention of the arrest of the swordsman, evidently because the focus was on Jesus.

26:53 thousands of angels. Lit., "more than twelve legions of angels." A legion is a Roman military unit numbering six thousand soldiers (BDAG 587-588). The number twelve has obvious implications. Jesus had power available to him in the form of thousands of angels (cf. 4:6, 11; 13:41; 16:27; 25:31), but he would not oppose the plan ordained for him by the Father in the Scriptures (26:24, 56).

26:54 how would the Scriptures be fulfilled? The fulfillment of Scripture is a key motif in Matthew's theology (cf., e.g., 1:23 and the discussion of fulfillment under the heading "Major Themes" in the Introduction).

26:55-56 the crowd. In this context, this is the group that arrested him (26:47).

revolutionary. Gr. lēstēs. Given the context, this seems to be more likely than "bandit" (cf. 27:38; BDAG 594).

Why didn't you arrest me in the Temple? Jesus sarcastically told them that their stealth and use of force was unnecessary since he had been teaching publicly in the Temple every day (21:23). But the religous leaders could not arrest Jesus publicly in the Temple because of his popularity with the throngs of pilgrims who were in Jerusalem for the Passover (21:9-11, 15, 26; 26:5).

fulfill the words of the prophets. Their sinful plan mysteriously fulfilled the divinely ordained plan revealed in the prophetic Scriptures. As he uttered these words, they were immediately confirmed by the flight of the disciples in fulfillment of Jesus' words in 26:31, which cite Zech 13:7.

COMMENTARY

With 26:47 "the preliminaries are over" (Hagner 1995:787). Jesus had finished preparing his disciples for his inevitable suffering and death and their own failings. In the middle of the night Jesus was arrested by the religious leaders and deserted by his disciples, whose departure illustrates 16:25 (dissociating from Jesus might save the disciples' earthly lives but could also cost them their souls). Jesus would be subjected to a heavily biased trial. In the morning he would appear before Pilate and be handed over for crucifixion. By three in the afternoon he would be dead. But even in the midst of all of this, one gets the unmistakable impression that Jesus, or rather his Father in Heaven, was in charge (cf. John 10:18; Davies and Allison 1997:511).

These verses seem to show quite clearly that Jesus and his disciples were not subversives or "zealots," although that is the implication of the false charges soon to be brought against Jesus (26:61). Jesus was resigned to drinking the cup the Father's will placed before him, and he taught his disciples that violence only leads to more violence. Despite their boasts (26:35), the disciples offered minimal resistance to Jesus' arrest, and then they all ran away. The group sent to arrest Jesus was probably composed of Temple guards commanded by the high priest. One can rightly explain the bravery of Jesus, the treachery of Judas, the cowardice of the disciples, and the aggression of the arrest party as voluntary actions in character with each of the involved parties. But one must also notice the strong emphasis on God's predetermined plan in this passage (26:2, 18, 24, 31, 39, 42, 54, 56). Here is another example of the scriptural pattern of the compatibility of divine sovereignty and human responsibility.

◆ **H. Jesus Appears before the Sanhedrin (26:57-68; cf. Mark 14:53-65; Luke 22:54-55, 63-71)**

⁵⁷Then the people who had arrested Jesus led him to the home of Caiaphas, the high priest, where the teachers of religious law and the elders had gathered. ⁵⁸Meanwhile, Peter followed him at a distance and came to the high priest's courtyard. He went in and sat with the guards and waited to see how it would all end.

⁵⁹Inside, the leading priests and the entire high council* were trying to find witnesses who would lie about Jesus, so they could put him to death. ⁶⁰But even though they found many who agreed to give false witness, they could not use anyone's testimony. Finally, two men came forward ⁶¹who declared, "This man said, 'I am able to destroy the Temple of God and rebuild it in three days.'"

⁶²Then the high priest stood up and said to Jesus, "Well, aren't you going to answer these charges? What do you have to say for yourself?" ⁶³But Jesus remained silent. Then the high priest said to him, "I demand in the name of the living God— tell us if you are the Messiah, the Son of God."

⁶⁴Jesus replied, "You have said it. And in the future you will see the Son of Man seated in the place of power at God's right hand* and coming on the clouds of heaven."*

⁶⁵Then the high priest tore his clothing to show his horror and said, "Blasphemy! Why do we need other witnesses? You have all heard his blasphemy. ⁶⁶What is your verdict?"

"Guilty!" they shouted. "He deserves to die!"

⁶⁷Then they began to spit in Jesus' face and beat him with their fists. And some slapped him, ⁶⁸jeering, "Prophesy to us, you Messiah! Who hit you that time?"

26:59 Greek *the Sanhedrin.* 26:64a Greek *seated at the right hand of the power.* See Ps 110:1. 26:64b See Dan 7:13.

NOTES

26:57 *the home of Caiaphas, the high priest, where the teachers of religious law and the elders had gathered.* Cf. Mark 14:53-65; Luke 22:54-55; John 18:13-14, 19-24.

26:58 *Peter followed him at a distance.* It is briefly mentioned that Peter followed from a distance and sat down in the high priest's courtyard to see what would happen. This sets the scene for the story of Peter's three denials in 26:69-75.

26:59-61 *high council.* Lit., "Sanhedrin" (5:22; 10:17).

were trying to find witnesses. They had evidently been trying for some time to obtain false testimony against Jesus (9:3; 12:10, 24, 38; 16:1; 19:3), but nothing admissible was found despite the fact that many were willing to testify falsely. Eventually two men (18:16; cf. Deut 17:6; 19:15) came forward who testified that Jesus claimed to be *able to destroy the Temple of God and rebuild it in three days* (26:61). There is no previous record of anything resembling this in the synoptic Gospels, not even 24:2 (cf. 27:40), but the false charge evidently came from a misunderstanding (or a twisting) of Jesus' teaching recorded in John 2:18-22 (cf. Acts 6:13-14). Action against the Temple would be viewed as treason by many Jews and as sedition by the Roman authorities. Jesus' actions against the money changers and merchants in the Temple (21:12ff) were public knowledge and perhaps were viewed as corroborating the false testimony. The leaders of the Sanhedrin appear to have already decided that Jesus was a blasphemer, so it was easy for them to justify their actions. (For a fine summary discussion of the trial of Jesus, see Corley in Green and McKnight 1992:841-854.)

26:62-64 *Jesus remained silent.* When Caiaphas asked Jesus to respond to these charges, he initially kept silent (cf. 27:14; Isa 53:7; Acts 8:32).

I demand in the name of the living God—tell us whether you are the Messiah, the Son of God. This has the force of putting Jesus under oath. The title "Son of God" was interpreted messianically (2 Sam 7:14; Ps 2:7; 89:26-27). This question and Jesus' answer appear to have little relevance to the charge against Jesus, but the key Matthean motif of Jesus' divine sonship is raised.

You have said it. Jesus responded by ambiguously affirming the high priest's own words (cf. 26:25).

you will see the Son of Man seated in the place of power at God's right hand and coming on the clouds of heaven. Jesus continued by citing Dan 7:13, with introductory words from Ps 110:1, to the effect that he is indeed the glorious Son of Man who will come from the right hand of God (cf. 19:28; 24:30; 25:31; John 1:51; *1 Enoch* 62:5). The NLT's "sitting at God's right hand in the place of power" redundantly renders what is lit. "sitting at the right hand of the Power." Here "Power," an attribute uniquely associated with God, stands for God by metonymy. Blomberg (1992:403) is correct in pointing out that 26:64 is "the Christological climax of the Gospel thus far."

26:65-68 *tore his clothing to show his horror.* He showed his disgust by tearing his robes. This was a sign of extreme emotion, whether sorrow or anger (e.g., Gen 37:29; 2 Kgs 18:37-19:1; Job 1:20; Acts 14:14; *m. Sanhedrin* 7:5; Jdt 14:19; 1 Macc 11:71; Josephus *War* 2.316; but cf. Joel 2:13). The NLT brings this out by adding the words "to show his horror."

Blasphemy! The high priest regarded Jesus' speaking of himself in terms of Daniel's Son of Man as an outrageous blasphemy. He evidently viewed the Son of Man as a quasi-divine figure and believed that Jesus had arrogated divine prerogatives to himself. He asked why any more testimony was needed since he believed that Jesus' words in 26:64 were sufficient proof of his guilt. The Sanhedrin evidently agreed with his assessment that Jesus deserved to die (cf. Lev 24:16).

they began to spit in Jesus' face. See Isa 50:6.

beat him with their fists. Possibly some used whips or clubs (BDAG 903-904).

Prophesy to us, you Messiah! As they beat Jesus, they taunted him by sarcastically calling him the Messiah and asking him to prophecy to them about who was hitting him. Jesus exemplified his own teaching (5:38-42; cf. Isa 50:4-9).

C O M M E N T A R Y

This passage lays out the first of Jesus' two trials, although the term "trial" may be a misnomer here. The narrative of the trial before the high priest Caiaphas accomplishes two literary purposes. First, the sordid nature of the whole process is clearly exposed (26:59-61). Second, and more importantly, the claims of Christ to be Israel's Messiah are climactically pressed before the leaders of Israel. In a clear allusion to Daniel 7:13, Jesus acknowledges that he is the messianic Son of Man who will return to judge his false accusers and judges (26:64). Yet the leaders reject Jesus' testimony, accuse him of blasphemy, and treat him with sarcasm and utter contempt (26:65-68). It is Jesus' affirmation that he will return as the glorious Son of Man to judge his judges that seems to infuriate them. Such an eschatological reversal would be intolerable. Davies and Allison (1997:537) point out several aspects of the trial story that make irony its chief literary feature.

Christology.   The terse exchange between Jesus and Caiaphas in 26:62-64 contains one of the most explicit affirmations of Jesus' identity in all of Matthew. Jesus' citation of Dan 7:13 (and perhaps Ps 110:1) shows that he understood his identity and future mission in terms of the glorious, exalted Son of Man. Hagner (1995:799) rightly says, "Nowhere does Jesus reveal himself more than here."

The time frame implied by Jesus' words "in the future" in 26:64 is rather broad. Jesus will be installed as the glorious Son of Man at his resurrection, and Caiaphas himself will be confronted with this reality—the person Caiaphas judged unjustly will someday judge him justly. After the resurrection, Jesus would speak as the exalted Son of Man, prefacing his commission to the disciples with the words, "I have been given all authority" (28:18).

But the resurrection only inaugurates the glorious reign of Jesus (cf. John 7:39; 12:23, 32-33; 17:4-5; Acts 2:32-33; 13:33-37; Phil 2:9-11; Rev 5:5-10). That reign will be consummated by his return to judge and rule the earth (6:10; 13:41-43; 16:27; 19:28; 24:30; 25:31; cf. 2 Sam 7:12-16; Ps 2; Luke 1:32-33; Acts 17:30-31; 1 Cor 15:20-28; Rev 1:7; 2:26-27; 10:15; 19:11-16; 20:4-6). The resurrection vindicates Jesus' claims and seals the doom of his enemies. The return to earth realizes the final judgment, where all humanity will stand before the Son of Man. Unbelievers will be condemned, believers will be rewarded, and Jesus will reign in glory over his people in a new world from which the curse has been removed.

Anti-Semitism?   On the historical level it is clear that this trial was not carried out according to the just legal procedures that are found in *m. Sanhedrin* 4-7 (Brown 1994:357-363). According to this tractate, trials were not to be held at night, and capital cases could not be decided in one day. Several other details of Matthew's narrative are at odds with the Mishnaic laws for trials. One can explain this anomaly in different ways. One line of reasoning argues that the Mishnaic traditions were theoretical, not actual, and that they were written down over one hundred and fifty years after the trial of Jesus, but these traditions purport to be orally transmitted from earlier times. Non-evangelicals sometimes accuse Matthew of inventing much, or all, of the story for propaganda purposes (Beare 1981:519ff). In this view, Matthew's goal was to blame the Jews and exonerate the Romans in order to curry favor for Christianity with the Roman authorities.

But if Matthew and his community still identified themselves as Jews, this argument breaks down. Instead, Matthew preserves accurate historical information in his narrative in order to show that the religious leaders did not follow their own standards in dealing with Jesus (cf. the case of Stephen in Acts 6:11ff). It was expedient for them to break their own rules in order to quickly be rid of Jesus before the crowds became aware of what they were doing and before the Feast of Unleavened Bread went into full swing. Matthew did not want to indict Israel as a nation, not even all the Jews of his own day, let alone all Jews who have lived subsequently.

Rather, the trial narrative must be seen as part of Matthew's consistent negative portrayal of the Jerusalem establishment as corrupt leaders who left Israel like scattered sheep without a shepherd (9:36). These leaders did not interpret the law and the prophets in a manner that focused on the weightier matters. Instead, they sought to follow human traditions, which obscured the righteousness of the law (15:1-14). When Matthew, as a Jew writing to Jews, highlighted the corruption of the Jerusalem establishment, he was not being anti-Semitic, and Christians who take him that way make a serious error. Those who support their own anti-Semitic bias by appealing to Matthew should be roundly condemned in the strongest possible terms.

From Matthew's own theological standpoint, it was not ultimately the corrupt religious leaders or the weak Roman governor who were responsible for killing Jesus. Rather, it was God's plan being accomplished by the deeds of sinful men, Jews and Gentiles alike, so that sinners from every ethnic group might believe in Jesus the Messiah and be forgiven their sins by the shedding of his blood.

◆ **I. Peter's three denials (26:69-75; cf. Mark 14:66-72; Luke 22:55-62; John 18:25-27)**

⁶⁹Meanwhile, Peter was sitting outside in the courtyard. A servant girl came over and said to him, "You were one of those with Jesus the Galilean."

⁷⁰But Peter denied it in front of everyone. "I don't know what you're talking about," he said.

⁷¹Later, out by the gate, another servant girl noticed him and said to those standing around, "This man was with Jesus of Nazareth.*"

⁷²Again Peter denied it, this time with an oath. "I don't even know the man," he said.

⁷³A little later some of the other bystanders came over to Peter and said, "You must be one of them; we can tell by your Galilean accent."

⁷⁴Peter swore, "A curse on me if I'm lying—I don't know the man!" And immediately the rooster crowed.

⁷⁵Suddenly, Jesus' words flashed through Peter's mind: "Before the rooster crows, you will deny three times that you even know me." And he went away, weeping bitterly.

26:71 Or *Jesus the Nazarene.*

NOTES

26:69-70 The narrative now returns to Peter in the courtyard (26:58); it seems the reader is to view Peter's "trial" as more or less synonymous with Jesus' trial. As Jesus confesses, Peter denies. His three denials fulfill Jesus' prophecy (26:31-35), yet they raise many questions as comparisons are made with the other Gospels (cf. Mark 14:66-72; Luke 22:55-65; John 18:25-27).

You were one of those with Jesus the Galilean. As Peter sat outside the high priest's residence, he was accosted by a servant girl who accused him of being with Jesus the Galilean (cf. Luke 23:6), but he denied this before the crowd in the courtyard.

26:71-72 *This man was with Jesus of Nazareth.* As Peter was leaving the courtyard, another servant girl told the bystanders that Peter had been with Jesus of Nazareth (cf. 2:23).

Again Peter denied it, this time with an oath. Evidently Peter was falsely invoking God in some fashion (5:33-37; 14:7, 9; 23:16-22). The three accusations increasingly involve the bystanders. The first is made to Peter by a servant girl, and Peter denies it in the presence of bystanders. Another servant girl makes the second accusation to the bystanders, and the third accusation comes from the bystanders themselves (26:73).

26:73-75 The bystanders, a group more formidable than a servant girl, now charge Peter with being an associate of Jesus.

we can tell by your Galilean accent. His Galilean accent had given him away (cf. Acts 4:13).

A curse on me if I'm lying—I don't know the man! Peter was so upset that he punctuated his denial with vehement cursing and swearing, perhaps calling on God to curse him if he was lying. Davies and Allison (1997:548-549) argue plausibly that in a desperate attempt to prove he was not a disciple, Peter cursed Jesus.

immediately the rooster crowed. Suddenly, Jesus' words flashed through Peter's mind. At this third denial, a rooster crowed, and Peter was immediately and excruciatingly reminded of Jesus' prediction that he would deny him three times before a rooster crowed (26:34).

deny three times that you even know me. Lit., "deny me three times." Peter had claimed he would die before he denied Jesus, but he could not even respond truthfully to the question of a powerless servant girl. He wept bitterly as he went away, perhaps believing that the curse he had uttered would come upon him.

COMMENTARY

The Sanhedrin had mocked Jesus' prophetic insight, but now Peter's denials vindicate it. This passage clearly consists of three accusations that Peter was a follower of Jesus followed by three increasingly intense denials. It is striking that Peter was intimidated by a mere servant girl, and that his denials became increasingly punctuated with oaths and expletives (26:70, 72, 74). The denials became more emphatic as Peter moved further away from Jesus, from the courtyard (26:69) to the gateway (26:71) to his departure (26:74). The disciples who left all to follow Jesus had now deserted him (yet see John 18:15). One could easily sympathize with Peter denying the Lord once due to fear or embarrassment, but it is impossible to justify this threefold, increasingly vehement denial.

The Bible in many cases (e.g., Noah, Abraham, Moses, David, Solomon) presents it heroes "warts and all," as the saying goes. Matthew's Gospel is no exception, since he did not attempt to exclude the inconsistencies and failures of the disciples from his narrative. He did not even mention Jesus' subsequent rehabilitation of Peter (cf. John 21:15ff), so the reader is left with yet another blunt testimony to the weakness of the disciples. This is tempered somewhat when one is reminded of the forgiveness mentioned in 12:32 and the promise that Jesus will later meet the disciples in Galilee (26:32; 28:7, 10, 16). Peter's denial underlines the weakness of all the disciples (26:35), but it will not terminate their messianic mission if they are true to the resurrected Messiah and live by his power and presence (28:18-20).

It is instructive to compare Peter and Jesus. As Jesus confessed his divine, messianic identity before the supreme leader of Israel, Peter denied any knowledge of Jesus before a servant-girl (cf. 10:32-33; 1 Tim 6:13). Peter was immediately grief-stricken over his sin, but so was Judas (27:3). Therefore, it is also instructive to compare Peter and Judas. Judas betrayed the Lord, just as Jesus predicted. Afterwards he felt remorse, was rebuffed by the religious leaders, and committed suicide

(27:1-10). Peter also denied the Lord, just as Jesus predicted. Afterwards he felt remorse, was restored by Jesus, and resumed his role as the leader of the disciples (26:32; 28:10, 18-20). How can such opposite results come from such similar actions? In the case of Peter, human weakness led to momentary failure, but the pattern of Peter's life was one of discipleship. In all fairness to Peter, evidently he was the only disciple to follow Jesus to the High Priest's courtyard (yet see John 18:15). Granted, he failed miserably there, but the others did not go at all. On the other hand, Judas' remorse was not accompanied by deeds befitting true repentance.

In Matthew, Peter is first among the disciples of Jesus. He is singled out throughout the narrative as the representative disciple. He often speaks for the group (Turner 1989). His miserable failure in denying Jesus is a strong warning to all disciples. If Peter—of all people—could fall so low, so could anyone else. But if Peter—of all people—could be restored after falling so low, so could anyone else. All followers of Jesus should be horrified by Peter's denials and thrilled by his restoration.

Summary and Transition. As the plot to execute Jesus progressed (26:3-5, 14-16, 47-56), Jesus prepared his disciples for the end of his ministry on earth (26:6-13, 17-29). They still did not fully understand what was coming, and the inner circle of disciples could not even stay awake with Jesus during his agonizing struggle in Gethsemane (26:31-46). Judas then betrayed the Lord to the Jewish religious leaders (26:47-56), who led Jesus away for "trial" by Caiaphas the high priest (26:57-68). During this time Peter denied the Lord three times, just as Jesus predicted (26:69-75; cf. 26:33-35).

The plot of Matthew 26 interweaves Jesus' preparation of his disciples for his death and the Pharisees' scheme to hasten that death. As the events of the chapter rapidly unfold, Jesus remains in control as he repeatedly predicts his death (26:2, 12, 21, 23-24, 28, 32, 45, 54) and the trials it will bring to his disciples (26:31-35). Even his struggle in Gethsemane does not take away from the theme of his control, since he is always obedient to the will of the Father (26:39, 42, 44). Another strong theme is the sovereignty of God, especially as it relates to the fulfillment of the Old Testament (26:24, 31, 54, 56, 64). Thus, it appears that the monstrous treachery of Judas and the evil machinations of the religious leaders are both culpable acts (26:24, 64) and divine necessities that graciously provide forgiveness of sins (26:28; cf. 1:21; 3:6; 20:28). The chapter is therefore a profound testimony that the sovereignty of God and the responsible agency of people are compatible biblical truths, even though we may only articulate these truths feebly.

◆ J. The Suicide of Judas (27:1-10)

Very early in the morning the leading priests and the elders met again to lay plans for putting Jesus to death. ²Then they bound him, led him away, and took him to Pilate, the Roman governor. ³When Judas, who had betrayed him, realized that Jesus had been condemned to die, he was filled with remorse. So he took the thirty pieces of silver back to the leading priests and the elders. ⁴"I have sinned," he declared, "for I have betrayed an innocent man."

"What do we care?" they retorted. "That's your problem."

⁵Then Judas threw the silver coins down in the Temple and went out and hanged himself.

⁶The leading priests picked up the coins. "It wouldn't be right to put this money in the Temple treasury," they said, "since it was payment for murder."* ⁷After some discussion they finally decided to buy the potter's field, and they made it into a cemetery for foreigners. ⁸That is why the field is still called the Field of Blood. ⁹This fulfilled the prophecy of Jeremiah that says,

"They took* the thirty pieces
    of silver—
the price at which he was valued
    by the people of Israel,
¹⁰and purchased the potter's field,
    as the LORD directed.*"

27:6 Greek *since it is the price for blood.* 27:9 Or *I took.* 27:9-10 Greek *as the LORD directed me.* Zech 11:12-13; Jer 32:6-9.

NOTES

27:1-2 *met again to lay plans.* After the night hearing, the leaders "lay plans" (12:14; 22:15; 27:7; 28:12) in the morning (cf. 26:20) to transfer Jesus to the jurisdiction of Pilate (cf. Mark 15:1; Luke 22:66–23:1; John 18:28), evidently because only the Roman governor had authority to order executions (John 18:31; Brown 1994:363-372). The NLT's "met again" indicates that these events occurred later at a second meeting, but this is doubtful. Perhaps the reference to the formal decision in the morning should be viewed in light of *m. Sanhedrin* 4:1 which says that decisions in capital cases must be reached in the daytime (cf. Blomberg 1987:136-138).

took him to Pilate, the Roman governor. In 20:18-19, Jesus predicted that the religious leaders would hand him over to the Gentiles. This prediction is now fulfilled. Pilate served from AD 26–36 as one in a series of Roman governors (technically procurators or prefects) of Judea (cf. Luke 3:1;13:1; Acts 4:27; 1 Tim 6:13). He is viewed in a very bad light in extra-biblical sources, which portray him as insecure, insensitive to the Jews, and extremely harsh in the administration of justice (Josephus *Antiquities* 18.35, 55-62, 85-89; *War* 2.169-177; Philo *The Embassy to Gaius* 299-305; Tacitus *Annals* 15.44). (See Evans and Porter 2000:804 for a discussion of the inscription mentioning Pilate as prefect, which was discovered at Caesarea Maritima in 1961.)

27:3-4 Matthew inserts his unique narrative of Judas's suicide (cf. Acts 1:16-20; 2 Sam 17:23) between the Jewish (26:57-68; 27:1-2) and Roman (27:11-26) stages of Jesus' trial. It is difficult to establish the chronological relationship of Judas's remorse and suicide to the rest of the events in the chapter. The remorse was due to Jesus' being condemned, which may refer to Pilate's later decision. Or perhaps Judas was one of the bystanders in Caiaphas' courtyard and learned there that the Sanhedrin had condemned Jesus. In any event, the religious leaders in this passage had the time to receive Judas, which implies that they were no longer involved with Pilate (27:12, 20).

he was filled with remorse. It is difficult to understand why Judas felt remorse when Jesus had been condemned, since it seems obvious that this would be the result of the betrayal. Some commentators stress that the word used to express Judas's remorse is *metamelomai* [TG3338, ZG3564] (cf. 21:30, 32; 2 Cor 7:8; Heb 7:21), not *metanoeō* [TG3340, ZG3566] (cf. 3:2, 8, 11; 4:17; 11:20-21; 12:41), the word most often used for genuine repentance. Judas's subsequent actions, however, give us more insight into the state of his heart than the choice of Gr. vocabulary here.

he took the thirty pieces of silver back. Judas returned the thirty pieces of silver to the religious leaders and confessed his sin to them (Deut 27:25), but they harshly rebuffed him without care. They told him that his sin was his own problem (cf. 27:24), and they would have nothing to do with him.

27:5 *Judas threw the silver coins down in the Temple.* His action of throwing the money down in the Temple underlines his remorse and admission of guilt, but at this point it was too late to help Jesus.

hanged himself. Judas had found no peace of mind from his conversation with the religious leaders, so he chose suicide by hanging as a way of dealing with his guilt (cf. 2 Sam 17:23; *m. Sanhedrin* 10:2).

27:6-7 *It would be illegal to put this money in the Temple treasury.* The scrupulousness of the religious leaders regarding the disposal of Judas' money is amazing, given their indifference to such matters as seeking false witnesses against Jesus and even to Judas' personal anguish. While they were concerned about ritual purity, they were oblivious to their blatant violation of the fundamental ethics of the Torah. This is a blatant illustration of Jesus' point in 23:23—attention to trivial details has superseded the weightier matters of the law.

since it was payment for murder. This could make it sound like Judas was an assassin, not a traitor. The expression is lit. "it is the price of blood" (cf. NLT mg).

foreigners. This may refer to Jews who came to Jerusalem for religious festivals and died there.

27:8 *Field of Blood.* The field purchased by the priests was still called the Field of Blood when Matthew later wrote.

27:9-10 *This fulfilled the prophecy of Jeremiah.* The pathetic end of Judas and the purchase of the burial field was seen by Matthew as a fulfillment of Scripture. Matthew referred primarily to Zech 11:12-13, though the additional allusion to Jer 19:1-13 (and possibly Jer 18:2; 32:6-9) led him to refer the prophecy to Jeremiah. Blomberg (1992:409) and Gundry (1994:557-558) seem to be correct in pointing out that in addition to Zech 11:12-13, several features of Jer 19:1-13 are viewed by Matthew as typological, providing a pattern that is reenacted by the leading priests. It is not unusual for OT citations to be a combination of two or more texts (Davies and Allison 1997:568-569). This is the final "fulfillment formula" citation in Matthew. Some view this passage as having a redemptive meaning, in that the blood money goes for the burial of strangers or foreigners (cf. 25:35), signifying the extention of salvation to the Gentiles (Bruner 1990:1023). This, however, seems to read too much into the text. Others think that Matthew composed a non-historical story in 27:3-10 as a midrash (commentary) on Zech 11:12-13. If that were the case, one would have expected much closer correspondence between the story and Zechariah. It is better understood that Matthew noticed the similarities between his historical tradition and Zech 11 (Hagner 1995:811), and so he viewed Zechariah typologically. He saw in Jer 19 and Zech 11 "a pattern of apostasy and rejection that must find its ultimate fulfillment in the rejection of Jesus" (Carson 1984:566). And with this notion of prophetic fulfillment comes once again the implicit corollary of divine sovereignty.

COMMENTARY

Matthew 27:1-10 begins with the continuation of the trial story of 26:57-68, which was suspended by the story of Peter's denials (26:69-75). After 27:1-2, the subject changes to the story of Judas' suicide (27:3-8), which was viewed by Matthew as a fulfillment of prophecy (27:9-10). Matthew's pattern throughout the passion narrative has been to interweave stories about supporting characters and issues (26:6-13, 20-35; 27:3-10) into the main story of the sufferings of Jesus. In 27:9-10, Matthew's characteristic typological understanding of the Old Testament, expressed with a ful-fillment formula, occurs for the last time. Matthew apparently understood the shep-herd doomed to slaughter in Zechariah 13:7 as corresponding to Jesus and the thirty pieces of silver thrown to the potter in the Lord's house in Zechariah 11:13 as corresponding to the money Judas threw down in the Temple being used to buy potter's field. Matthew did not make up this story to fit Zechariah but read the prophets with a view to finding patterns in which an Old Testament person or event anticipated something in the life and ministry of Jesus.

Judas' Betrayal and Peter's Denial. As noted in the commentary on 26:69-75, it is instructive to compare and contrast the remorse of Peter after his temporary lapse with that of Judas after his act of ultimate treachery. Both acts were no doubt despi-cable, but Peter's denial pales in comparison with Judas's act. Peter returned to a life of following Jesus and was restored to his special office in the church (28:18-20; John 21:15-17). To mention his prominent ministry in the early church is to bela-bor the obvious. The remorse of Judas, however, does not amount to anything approaching genuine repentance unto salvation. This is clear not so much from the use of *metamelomai* [TG3338, ZG3564] in 27:3 (see notes above) as from the ensuing events. Granted, Judas acknowledged his sin and returned his blood money. Davies and Allison (1997:562, 565, 571) make much of this in their overly sympathetic portrayal of Judas, but he never attempted to seek Jesus' forgiveness or rejoin the disciples. His suicide is an indication of hopeless despair, not repentance. In Mat-thew repentance is shown by works, portrayed as fruit (3:8-10; 7:16-20; 13:38-40). Judas is remembered for his suicide, probably viewed as a violation of the sixth commandment (Exod 20:13; cf. *Genesis Rabbah* on 9:5; b. *Avodah Zarah* 18a; *Trac-tate Semahot* 2:1-2; but see Davies and Allison 1997:561-563). In view of such texts as Matthew 26:24 and John 6:70; 17:12, one may not hope that he was saved. Rather, one must be warned because he was lost.

◆   **K. Jesus' Trial before Pilate (27:11-26; cf. Mark 15:1-15; Luke 23:1-25; John 18:28-19:16)**

[11]Now Jesus was standing before Pilate, the Roman governor. "Are you the king of the Jews?" the governor asked him.

Jesus replied, "You have said it."

[12]But when the leading priests and the elders made their accusations against him, Jesus remained silent. [13]"Don't you hear all these charges they are bringing against you?" Pilate demanded. [14]But Jesus made no response to any of the charges, much to the governor's surprise.

[15]Now it was the governor's custom each year during the Passover celebration to release one prisoner to the crowd— anyone they wanted. [16]This year there was a notorious prisoner, a man named Bar-abbas.* [17]As the crowds gathered before Pilate's house that morning, he asked them, "Which one do you want me to re-lease to you—Barabbas, or Jesus who is called the Messiah?" [18](He knew very well that the religious leaders had arrested Jesus out of envy.)

[19]Just then, as Pilate was sitting on the judgment seat, his wife sent him this message: "Leave that innocent man alone. I suffered through a terrible nightmare about him last night."

²⁰Meanwhile, the leading priests and the elders persuaded the crowd to ask for Barabbas to be released and for Jesus to be put to death. ²¹So the governor asked again, "Which of these two do you want me to release to you?"

The crowd shouted back, "Barabbas!"

²²Pilate responded, "Then what should I do with Jesus who is called the Messiah?"

They shouted back, "Crucify him!"

²³"Why?" Pilate demanded. "What crime has he committed?"

But the mob roared even louder, "Crucify him!"

²⁴Pilate saw that he wasn't getting anywhere and that a riot was developing. So he sent for a bowl of water and washed his hands before the crowd, saying, "I am innocent of this man's blood. The responsibility is yours!"

²⁵And all the people yelled back, "We will take responsibility for his death—we and our children!"*

²⁶So Pilate released Barabbas to them. He ordered Jesus flogged with a lead-tipped whip, then turned him over to the Roman soldiers to be crucified.

27:16 Some manuscripts read *Jesus Barabbas;* also in 27:17.   27:25 Greek *"His blood be on us and on our children."*

NOTES

27:11 *Are you the king of the Jews?* Here the story of Jesus' trial resumes from 27:2. Pilate's examination of Jesus (cf. Mark 15:1-15; Luke 23:1-25; John 18:28–19:16) naturally begins with a concern about Jesus' kingship. Pilate's loyalty to Caesar would cause him to be concerned about any potential rivals (cf. John 18:36-37).

You have said it. In response, Jesus used the mild though enigmatic affirmation "you have said it" for the third time in the passion narrative (cf. 26:25, 64).

27:12-14 *Jesus remained silent.* Jesus did not say a word in response to the accusations of the Jewish religious leaders (26:60-66); this amazed Pilate, who urged him to defend himself. Although Jesus remained silent (cf. Isa 53:7), it was clear to Pilate that Jesus' kingship was no threat to Roman authority (27:17-18). The religious leaders persisted in hounding Jesus to death as they continued to accuse him, refused Pilate's offer of clemency for Jesus, and incited the crowd to pressure Pilate to execute him (27:12, 20).

27:15-17 *it was the governor's custom each year . . . to release one prisoner.* Matthew explains that it had become customary for the Romans to release a Jewish prisoner at Passover as a gesture of good will, and that they were currently holding "a notorious prisoner, a man named Barabbas." Pilate offered the crowd their choice of Barabbas or Jesus, probably thinking that the crowd would prefer the enigmatic Jesus to the notorious Barabbas. A fascinating feature of 27:17 is that a few ancient manuscripts have Barabbas' full name as "Jesus Barabbas" (Metzger 1994:56). This makes for an interesting contrast between Jesus Barabbas (which may mean "son of the father" or "son of the teacher") and Jesus who is called Messiah.

27:18 *the religious leaders had arrested Jesus out of envy.* Pilate had correctly perceived that there was nothing substantial in the charges against Jesus, and that the leaders were motivated by envy.

27:19 *Leave that innocent man alone.* Pilate's wife described Jesus as "innocent" (lit. "just, righteous"), and this no doubt contributed to Pilate's conclusion that Jesus was innocent.

a terrible nightmare about him. As Pilate learns of his wife's nightmare, another testimony to Jesus' innocence enters into the narrative. Dreams were often viewed as significant and prophetic in the ancient world, and the Bible contains many divine revelations in the form of dreams (1:20; 2:12, 13, 19).

27:20-23 the leading priests and the elders persuaded the crowds to ask for Barabbas. Matthew parenthetically notes the nefarious influence of the leaders on the crowd. When Pilate asked again which prisoner should be released, they called for Barabbas.

Crucify him! When he asked about Jesus' fate, they demanded he be crucified. When Pilate protested that Jesus was innocent, this only incited the crowd to shout more loudly for Jesus to be crucified. Jesus' former popularity with the crowd has evaporated (21:9, 11, 26; 26:5), but this is not surprising in that the crowd's expectations of a political-military Messiah were dashed when Jesus was arrested. Jesus' messianic credentials had been discredited in their view. It is also possible that this crowd is composed of Jerusalem residents instead of the Passover pilgrims who had praised Jesus when he entered Jerusalem (Blomberg 1992:412).

27:24 a riot was developing. Pilate could see that he had a near-riot on his hands, so he gave in to the crowd.

washed his hands. This was done to signify Pilate's non-participation in the decision to crucify Jesus (Deut 21:6-8; Ps 26:6; 73:13).

I am innocent of this man's blood. Pilate affirmed that the crowd, not he, would be responsible for Jesus' blood, and the crowd responded by accepting that responsibility for themselves and their children.

27:25 We will take responsibility for his death. Lit., "his blood be on us"—an expression which occurs elsewhere in both Testaments (Lev 20:9; Deut 19:10; Josh 2:19; 2 Sam 1:16; Jer 26:15; 51:35; Ezek 18:13; 33:4; Acts 5:28; 18:6; 20:26).

we and our children! The statement that their children will also be responsible for Jesus' death assumes the solidarity of the family (Josh 7:24; 2 Kgs 24:3-4; Jer 31:29; Lam 5:7; Ezek 18:2, 19-32). These awful incriminating words recall Jesus' prediction in 23:35-36 to the effect that the blood of all the righteous since Abel would come upon his contemporaries. It is likely that the destruction of the Temple in AD 70 was God's judgment upon the crowd and its children (Davies and Allison 1997:591-592). The view that this verse constitutes a blood libel for all Jews of every period of time is patently false. (See the commentary below for further discussion of this matter.)

27:26 Pilate released Barabbas. The notorious criminal Barabbas was preferred to the humble messiah Jesus.

He ordered Jesus flogged. This flogging was a horrible, flesh-ripping experience (Josephus *War* 2.306, 308; 5.449; 7.200-202) and would hasten Jesus' death once he was crucified.

COMMENTARY

Jesus' trial before Pilate involves two cycles of interrogation (27:11, 12-14), followed by an explanation of the customary Passover prisoner release and the availability of Barabbas (27:15-16). Then there are two cycles of Pilate asking the crowd whom they want to have released (27:17-20, 21), followed by two protests of Jesus' innocence (27:23; 27:24-25), followed by the delivery of Jesus for crucifixion (27:26). Besides Pilate and the crowd there are two other characters: Pilate's wife, who was for Jesus (27:19), and the leading priests and elders, who were against Jesus (27:12). Both the crowd and Pilate were influenced by the religious leaders; Pilate did not heed his wife.

Anti-Semitism? Matthew 27:20-25 takes its place alongside Matthew 23 as a passage frequently cited as being blatantly anti-Semitic (e.g., Sandmel 1978:66). Some conclude that Matthew portrays Pilate positively in order to exonerate or exculpate the Romans and indict or inculpate the Jews (e.g., Hill 1972:351), but Matthew's portrayal of Pilate is not really that positive; it coheres with the other ancient sources in presenting Pilate as insecure and unjust (See the notes on 27:1-2; Davies and Allison 1997:579). Pilate knew that Jesus was innocent, but he did not stop the miscarriage of justice. He knew that Jesus should be released instead of Barabbas, but he acceded to the wishes of the crowd because it was expedient to do so. His symbolic handwashing was pathetically inadequate and hypocritical, especially coming from one charged by the emperor with administering justice in Judea. The handwashing was meant to show that Pilate did not consent to the crowd's wish, but the shot was his to call, not the peoples'. If he did not consent, neither should he permit. Pilate comes across as a cowardly ruler who abdicated his responsibility. His only concern was with how all this impacted him. He lacked sufficient fortitude even to take his wife's advice and leave Jesus alone. "Pilate's title is ironic: the governor leaves the governing to others" (Davies and Allison 1997:583). Thus, Pilate must share in the guilt for Jesus' crucifixion.

But what of Matthew's famous "blood libel" text, 27:25? Is this intended to inculpate the Jews as a nation forever? In response to Pilate's washed hands and denial of responsibility for Jesus' death, the crowd clearly accepts that responsibility for themselves and their children. This passage has been frequently understood during the church's history as teaching that the Jews as a nation are to be viewed as despicable Christ-killers (as in Beare 1981:531). This interpretation is false, since all the founders of the church were Jewish and many Jews have believed in Jesus throughout the church's history. Matthew himself was a Christian Jew writing to Christian Jews in conflict with non-Christian Jews over the identity of Jesus the Jewish Messiah.

One way Christians have disavowed the blood libel view is to regard Matthew 27:25 as fiction (Beare 1981:531). But this merely adds a mistake about the historicity of the passage to the previous mistake about its meaning. On its surface the text is limited to those present before Pilate and their children, not the Jews as a nation at that time or at any other time (Saldarini 1994:32-33). The comment was made in the heat of the moment, not as a carefully reasoned theological position. There is no guarantee that a God of grace would hold the crowd to its rash statement any more than the twelve disciples would be held unforgivable for deserting Jesus and Peter for denying Jesus three times. Likewise, one should not expect that a God of justice would pardon Pilate for his diffidence and empty show of cleansing his hands.

If anything is clear in Matthew's Gospel, it is that Jesus came to save sinners—exemplified by such notorious people as tax collectors and harlots (9:13; 21:31). Sinners like these would likely be prevalent in the crowd that took responsibility for the blood of Jesus and there is no doubt that in Matthew's theology such sinners would be forgiven upon repentance. It is also clear in Matthew's Gospel that Jesus saved his most severe criticisms for the religious leaders whom he viewed as hypocrites. Perhaps this theme is an important part of the response to the "blood libel" view of Matthew 27:25. One notes in 27:20 that it was the leading priests and elders who persuaded the crowd to ask for Barabbas. If Jesus' Jewish contemporaries were an especially wicked generation (12:45; 23:36), it was largely because their leaders were especially wicked themselves. These corrupt leaders of Israel, then, are the ones to blame for the crowd's unfortunate statement in 27:25, and for Pilate's unprincipled acquiescence to the crowd's inflamed request (Davies and Allison 1997:593). This coheres perfectly with the Matthean theme of Jesus' conflicts with the leaders of Israel. So, in one sense, these leaders were responsible for the blood of Jesus, but in the most profound sense, all humans, Jews and Gentiles alike, are responsible for Jesus' pouring out his blood to forgive sins and inaugurate the new covenant. This was the plan of the heavenly Father, and Jesus drank the cup the Father gave him. Ultimately, then, it is those who do not believe in Jesus, Jews and Gentiles alike, who will be held responsible for the blood of Jesus (Hagner 1995:828).

◆ ## L. The Crucifixion of Jesus (27:27-44; cf. Mark 15:16-32; Luke 23:26-43; John 19:17-27)

[27]Some of the governor's soldiers took Jesus into their headquarters* and called out the entire regiment. [28]They stripped him and put a scarlet robe on him. [29]They wove thorn branches into a crown and put it on his head, and they placed a reed stick in his right hand as a scepter. Then they knelt before him in mockery and taunted, "Hail! King of the Jews!" [30]And they spit on him and grabbed the stick and struck him on the head with it. [31]When they were finally tired of mocking him, they took off the robe and put his own clothes on him again. Then they led him away to be crucified.

[32]Along the way, they came across a man named Simon, who was from Cyrene,* and the soldiers forced him to carry Jesus' cross. [33]And they went out to a place called Golgotha (which means "Place of the Skull"). [34]The soldiers gave him wine mixed with bitter gall, but when he had tasted it, he refused to drink it.

[35]After they had nailed him to the cross, the soldiers gambled for his clothes by throwing dice.* [36]Then they sat around and kept guard as he hung there. [37]A sign was fastened to the cross above Jesus' head, announcing the charge against him. It read: "This is Jesus, the King of the Jews." [38]Two revolutionaries* were crucified with him, one on his right and one on his left.

[39]The people passing by shouted abuse, shaking their heads in mockery. [40]"Look at you now!" they yelled at him. "You said you were going to destroy the Temple and rebuild it in three days. Well then, if you are the Son of God, save yourself and come down from the cross!"

[41]The leading priests, the teachers of religious law, and the elders also mocked Jesus. [42]"He saved others," they scoffed, "but he can't save himself! So he is the King of Israel, is he? Let him come down from the cross right now, and we will believe in him! [43]He trusted God, so let God rescue him now if he wants him! For he said, 'I am the Son of God.' " [44]Even the revolutionaries who were crucified with him ridiculed him in the same way.

27:27 Or into the Praetorium. 27:32 Cyrene was a city in northern Africa. 27:35 Greek by casting lots. A few late manuscripts add This fulfilled the word of the prophet: "They divided my garments among themselves and cast lots for my robe." See Ps 22:18. 27:38 Or criminals; also in 27:44.

NOTES

27:27 Events now lead relentlessly to the cross (cf. Mark 15:16-32; Luke 23:26-43; John 19:17-27), with 27:27-37 describing the actions of the soldiers.

took Jesus into their headquarters and called out the entire regiment. Before the execution detail took Jesus to Golgotha (27:31-32), they first mocked him before the entire regiment. NLT renders the word "praetorium" (see NLT mg) as the soldiers' headquarters, but more likely it is the governor's residence (BDAG 859). This was either at Herod's palace (just south of the present Jaffa Gate on the west side of the old city) or at the Antonia fortress bordering the northwest corner of the Temple enclosure. A "regiment" of soldiers was a cohort, one tenth of a legion or 600 men (*speira*, BDAG 936). The mockery of the Roman soldiers in Pilate's palace fulfills Jesus' prophecy in 20:19 (cf. Ps 22:8; Isa 50:6). This mockery recalls that of the religious leaders (26:67-68) and anticipates worse taunting to come (27:39-44).

27:28-30 *scarlet robe.* This robe, the crown of thorns, and the stick (Ps 2:9; 110:2; Jer 48:17) were all intended as a cruel parody of royal trappings. The Romans' derision is probably fueled by the fact that Jesus was purported to be the king of the despised Jews, a conquered people under Roman dominion.

they knelt before him in mockery. Ironically, some day these soldiers will join all humanity, not just the Jews, in rendering obeisance to the conquering Son of Man (Dan 7:13ff; Phil 2:9-11). Those of the regiment who were assigned to the burial detail will soon have reason to rethink their mockery of Jesus (27:54).

27:31 *they led him away to be crucified.* After this horrible charade, Jesus was led away to be crucified. Davies and Allison (1997:597) show that 27:27-31 has a chiastic structure.

27:32 *Simon, who was from Cyrene.* The mention of this man in passing is a striking historical allusion and may imply that Simon was or became a disciple of Jesus. Some speculate that he may be the same person as Simon called Niger in Acts 13:1. Cyrene was a north African city on the Mediterranean (cf. Acts 2:10; 6:9; 11:20; 13:1). It was the capital of the Roman province of *Cyrenaica*, roughly equivalent to modern Libya. Simon may have been a Jerusalem resident (Acts 6:9) or a religious pilgrim.

the soldiers forced him to carry Jesus' cross. The conscription of Simon to carry the cross bar of Jesus' cross probably indicates the degree of physical suffering already undergone by Jesus. Normally, the condemned criminal would be forced to carry his own cross (10:38; 16:24). The forced conscription of Simon reminds the reader of the teaching of Jesus in 5:41, to the effect that if one is forced (evidently by a soldier) to go one mile, one should go two.

27:33 *Golgotha (which means "Place of the Skull").* Ancient tradition identifies the site of the Church of the Holy Sepulchre with Golgotha, the Aramaic word for "skull." Perhaps a skull-like rock formation there gave rise to this name. The Latin word for skull is *calvaria*, from which the English word Calvary is derived. Crucifixions were used by conquerors as a public spectacle to humiliate rebels and quell resistance, so it is likely that Golgotha was near a well-traveled street, which would entail many observers (cf. 27:39; 3 Macc 5:21-24).

27:34 *wine mixed with bitter gall.* When they arrived at Golgotha, Jesus refused to drink the wine mixed with gall offered to him by the soldiers (but cf. 27:48 where he does drink the wine; also Ps 69:21; Prov 31:6). This was probably a sedative (*b. Sanhedrin* 43a) customarily offered to those about to experience the torture of crucifixion, but it may have been another act of mockery, since gall might have made the wine extremely bitter in taste (Davies and Allison 1997:612-613).

27:35 *After they had nailed him to the cross.* Matthew's narrative supplies few details of the actual crucifixion, stressing instead the actions of the people involved and the fulfillment of prophecy. See the commentary below for further details on crucifixion.

the soldiers gambled for his clothes. The soldiers of the execution detail would get the meager belongings of those who were crucified, and they determined who would get Jesus' garment by casting lots for it (Ps 22:18).

27:37 *A sign was fastened to the cross.* The sign was a *titulus* (a placard on which was written the charge against him).

This is Jesus, the King of the Jews. The charge or *titulus* against Jesus involves a profound irony. Jesus' kingship was rejected by the leaders of Israel, who worked to have him crucified. The Romans also mocked Jesus as king (27:29). Yet his very crucifixion was an enactment of his power to save his people from their sins, and his resurrection, ascension, and return progressively vindicate his claim to be the King of the Jews (cf. John 19:19-22; 1 Cor 1:18, 23-25).

27:38 *Two revolutionaries.* The criminals (cf. 26:55) on Jesus' right and left are mentioned here and later in 27:44 (cf. Isa 53:12). One cannot help but be reminded of 20:23.

27:39-40 *You said you were going to destroy the Temple and rebuild it in three days.* Jesus' alleged plans to destroy the Temple were brought up again here (cf. 26:61), as the passersby shook their heads (cf. Ps 22:7; 109:25; Jer 18:16; Lam 2:15) and mocked Jesus. The taunts capitalized on the incompatibility between Jesus' supposed high office and his actual low situation (cf. 4:3, 6).

if you are the Son of God, save yourself. If he could do something as miraculous as destroy the Temple, surely he could save his life. Certainly he could come down from the cross if he was the Son of God. The taunt to demonstrate his sonship by coming down from the cross (27:40, 42, 44) is particularly perverse since Jesus was willingly enduring the cross precisely because he was the obedient Son of God (cf. 26:39, 42, 44). Jesus knew that if he saved his life he would lose it and the lives of his people whom he came to save (1:21; 10:38-39; 16:24-26; 20:28; 26:28).

27:41-42 *he can't save himself!* The leading priests and elders had followed Jesus from Pilate's residence to the place of crucifixion (cf. 27:12). There the teachers of religious law, who had not appeared since they joined in the trial at Caiaphas' residence, rejoined them (26:57). Their taunts use the third person and they are not addressed directly to Jesus as are those of the passersby in 27:39-40, but if anything they are even more cutting. They scoffed that Jesus supposedly could save others but cannot save himself.

Let him come down . . . and we will believe. The leaders said they would believe that Jesus was the King of Israel if he would manifest his status by coming down from the cross. In their view, if Jesus really was God's trusting Son in whom God took pleasure (Ps 22:8-9; Wis 2:18-20; cf. Matt 3:17; 17:5; 26:63), God would rescue him from crucifixion. But it was God's will that Jesus drink the cup of crucifixion, pour out his own blood, and inaugurate the new covenant.

27:44 *the revolutionaries who were crucified with him ridiculed him in the same way.* These two added their voices to this barrage of taunts (but cf. Luke 23:39-43).

COMMENTARY

The narrative of Jesus' crucifixion is a story of the gruesome process of execution. The story begins with the action of the soldiers in mocking Jesus (27:27-31), conscribing Simon to carry the cross (27:32), arriving at Golgotha (27:33), offering Jesus wine with gall (27:34), crucifying Jesus (27:35a), gambling for his garments (27:35b), observing (27:36), and putting up the sign describing Jesus' identity

(27:37). The next section is an *inclusio* framed by the mention of the revolutionaries who were crucified on both sides of Jesus (27:38-44). The theme here is mockery, whether by the bystanders (27:39-40), the religious leaders (27:41-43), or the revolutionaries themselves (27:44). As Jesus was tempted three times (4:1-11), so he is mocked three times. Both the temptation and the mockery focus on Jesus' sonship. Both the devil and the various mockers confront Jesus with the alternative of reigning without suffering, but both times Jesus would have none of it.

The mockery of the passage is ironic, since Jesus really is the Son of God and the Temple would be destroyed within a generation. Jesus did in fact save others and will continue to do so. He is the King of Israel, who trusted in God, and God was supremely pleased with him. He did not come down from the cross but he did overcome death. Each point of sarcastic ridicule is, in fact, eventually shown to be true. The mockers were unwitting evangelists. The irony is never more pronounced than in the actions of the soldiers who dressed Jesus as a king and pretended to pay homage to him (27:27-31). What the soldiers acted out in cruel jest is prophetic of what really will happen some day. After his resurrection, Jesus was exalted as the glorious Son of Man and given all authority (28:18). His message of the rule of God continues to win willing subjects from all the nations of the earth. At the end of the age, he will return as the King and be seated on his glorious throne (25:31ff). Things are not always as they seem, and sometimes things are exactly the opposite of what they seem.

Old Testament 316. The crucifixion narrative is replete with Old Testament citations and allusions, the most prominent of which follow, listed in the order they appear:

27:34— Wine mixed with bitter gall (Ps 69:21; mercy or mockery?)
27:35— Garments divided by throwing dice (Ps 22:18)
27:36— Soldiers watch Jesus (Ps 22:17)
27:38— Counted among the rebels (Isa 53:12)
27:39— Shaking heads in mockery (Ps 22:7)
27:43— God will deliver if he trusts in him (Ps 22:8)
27:45— Darkness at noon (Amos 8:9)
27:46— "Why have you abandoned me?" (Ps 22:1)
27:57, 60— His grave with a rich man (Isa 53:9)

Anti-Semitism? It is also significant that perhaps the most vicious mockers of Jesus in the crucifixion narrative were Gentiles (27:27-31). This calls into question the tendency among Christians towards identifying Jews with rejection of Jesus and Gentiles with reception of Jesus, which is found in some treatments of Matthew's theology. There are examples in Matthew of Jews who love Jesus and of Gentiles who hate him. France (1985:397) goes too far in commenting on 27:44 when he says that "the totality of Jesus' rejection by his people is complete." Rather, not all of the mockers in the crucifixion narrative are Jews (27:27-31), and not all the Jews are mockers (27:55-57). Therefore, Matthew should not be charged with an unqualified negative view of the Jews nor a similarly unqualified positive view of the Gentiles.

Crucifixion. Crucifixion was cruel and unusual punishment, to say the least (Josephus *War* 1.97-98; 5.449-551; *Antiquities* 13.379-383; 18:63-64; Hengel 1977; Brown 1994:945-952). The Romans used it in the case of slaves, notorious criminals, and insurrectionists to make a political statement. Crucifixion asserted the dominion of Rome over conquered peoples by making a gruesome example of anyone who dared to upset the *pax Romana.* According to Josephus, it was frequently utilized during the siege of Jerusalem in AD 70. Although practices varied somewhat, crucifixion often involved driving a long nail (Luke 24:39; John 20:25; Col 2:14) through the victim's ankles into the vertical post of the cross and driving nails through the victim's outstretched hands or wrists into the horizontal beam of the cross. The precise medical cause of death by crucifixion is not clear. It is commonly thought that victims would die of asphyxia. They would eventually have difficulty supporting their own weight with their legs. Then it would become increasingly difficult to breathe when hanging by the arms. The process could take days, and at times the executors would break the legs of the victims to hasten their deaths, though in the case of Jesus this was not necessary (John 19:31-33). Another theory is that dehydration and loss of blood from the pre-crucifixion flogging and the nail wounds would cause death (Brown 1994:1088-1092).

The crucifixion narrative in Matthew is the culmination of the story of Jesus' rejection. It stresses the way in which various parties—the bystanders, the Jewish leaders, and the revolutionaries crucified with Jesus—taunt him. In their way of thinking, his crucifixion unmasked Jesus as an impotent pretender to messianic office. Jesus' ministry as Messiah, however, was never intended to involve the military leadership they expected to remove Rome's oppressive yoke. Jesus and John before him demanded individual Jewish repentance, not war against Rome. Jesus' messianic values are epitomized most clearly in 12:14-21. There the Pharisees were planning to kill Jesus because his healing on the Sabbath amounted to work in their view. In response, Jesus withdrew from conflict and counseled silence on the healing. The Kingdom is built not by the sword (26:52) but by one repentant disciple at a time. Such disciples acknowledge that following Jesus amounts to a transformation of fundamental values involving crucifixion of the old ego-centered life and renewal into a Kingdom-centered life of humble service (10:38-39; 16:24-26; 20:23, 26-28). In this messianic model, justice is achieved not by military prowess but by individual repentance and humble service to others, but the Jewish religious establishment of Jesus' day would have none of it.

In addition to modeling Kingdom values, Jesus' crucifixion accomplished redemption. Jesus saved his people from their sins (1:21) by giving his life as a ransom for them (20:28). This ransom entailed the sacrificial pouring out of his blood so that their sins could be forgiven (26:28). The Torah pronounces a curse on anyone who is hung on a tree (Deut 21:22-23; cf. Isa 53:3-6), and other New Testament authors develop this along the lines of vicarious sacrifice—on the cross Jesus bore the curse and penalty for the sins of his people so that they would not have to bear that curse themselves. There are subtle allusions to Deuteronomy 21:22-23

(Acts 5:30; 10:39; 13:29; 1 Pet 2:24) as well as an explicit citation of it in Galatians 3:13, both to the effect that Jesus took on himself the sin and guilt of his people and thereby achieved their forgiveness and redemption (Rom 3:24-26; 1 Cor 1:23-24; 2 Cor 5:21; 1 Tim 2:6). Paul develops the theology of crucifixion even further, teaching that the believer in Jesus has become identified with Jesus in death to the old life of sin and identified with Jesus in resurrection to a new life of holiness (Rom 5:12-6:11; 1 Cor 15:20-22; Gal 2:20; 6:14; Eph 2:1-6; 4:22-24; Col 2:8-15; 3:1-4). Paul's understanding of the redemptive effect of the cross also develops Matthew's stress on mission to Gentiles, since the new life in Christ is lived in community with all who believe in Jesus, whether Jew or Gentile (Rom 15:7-12; Eph 2:11-22; Col 3:9-11).

◆   **M. The Death of Jesus (27:45-56; cf. Mark 15:33-41; Luke 23:44-49; John 19:31-37)**

⁴⁵At noon, darkness fell across the whole land until three o'clock. ⁴⁶At about three o'clock, Jesus called out with a loud voice, *"Eli, Eli,** *lema sabachthani?"* which means "My God, my God, why have you abandoned me?"*

⁴⁷Some of the bystanders misunderstood and thought he was calling for the prophet Elijah. ⁴⁸One of them ran and filled a sponge with sour wine, holding it up to him on a reed stick so he could drink. ⁴⁹But the rest said, "Wait! Let's see whether Elijah comes to save him."*

⁵⁰Then Jesus shouted out again, and he released his spirit. ⁵¹At that moment the curtain in the sanctuary of the Temple was torn in two, from top to bottom. The earth shook, rocks split apart, ⁵²and tombs opened. The bodies of many godly men and women who had died were raised from the dead. ⁵³They left the cemetery after Jesus' resurrection, went into the holy city of Jerusalem, and appeared to many people.

⁵⁴The Roman officer* and the other soldiers at the crucifixion were terrified by the earthquake and all that had happened. They said, "This man truly was the Son of God!"

⁵⁵And many women who had come from Galilee with Jesus to care for him were watching from a distance. ⁵⁶Among them were Mary Magdalene, Mary (the mother of James and Joseph), and the mother of James and John, the sons of Zebedee.

27:46a Some manuscripts read *Eloi, Eloi.* 27:46b Ps 22:1. 27:49 Some manuscripts add *And another took a spear and pierced his side, and out flowed water and blood.* Compare John 19:34. 27:54 Greek *The centurion.*

NOTES

27:45 *At noon, darkness fell across the whole land until three o'clock.* Jesus had evidently been put on the cross around the middle of the morning. His death occurred at the end of a providential darkness that prevailed during what is normally the brightest part of the day, from noon to 3 p.m. (lit. "from the sixth to the ninth hour;" cf. Mark 15:33-41; Luke 23:44-49; John 19:28-37). This darkness (24:29) was appropriate, given the horrible suffering and divine abandonment (27:46) experienced by Jesus during these epochal hours (cf. Exod 10:22; Deut 28:29; Joel 2:2, 31; Amos 8:9).

27:46-47 *Jesus called out.* Jesus had evidently not spoken since his brief response to Pilate in 27:11, and when he broke his silence it was not to respond to his mockers but to cry out mournfully to God.

Eli, Eli, lema sabachthani. Jesus loudly cried these words from Ps 22:1 that expressed his deep awareness of and anguish over his loss of intimate communion with the Father: "Why have you abandoned me?"

thought he was calling for the prophet Elijah. In Heb. "my God" (transliterated in Gr. as *ēli* [TG2241, ZG2458]) sounds like the first two syllables of the name "Elijah," and some of the bystanders misunderstood, taking Jesus' quotation of Ps 22:1 as an attempt to summon Elijah. Preoccupation with Elijah was part of first-century Jewish eschatological speculation based on Mal 4:5-6 (cf. Matt 11:14; 16:14; 17:3, 10-13).

27:48 *sour wine.* Evidently the offer of sour wine (Ps 69:21; cf. Num 6:3; Ruth 2:14) was an act of kindness not appreciated by those who wished to see whether Elijah would come to rescue Jesus. Why the offer of wine was made after the misinterpreted cry of Jesus is not clear.

27:50 *Jesus shouted out again, and he released his spirit.* It seems surprising that one who had undergone the agonies experienced by Jesus would be able to muster a loud shout, but that is how Matthew reports Jesus died. The expression "released his spirit" is sometimes understood to mean that Jesus decided when he would die (Davies and Allison 1997:628; Hendriksen 1973:973), but this may be only an idiomatic expression for death (cf. Gen 35:18; 1 Esdr 4:21; Josephus *Antiquities* 1.218; 5.147; 12.430; 14.369).

27:51 *the curtain in the sanctuary of the Temple was torn in two.* The curtain that was torn was probably not the one between the Court of Israel and the Court of the Gentiles (Blomberg 1992:421) but either the inner one that separated the holy of holies from the holy place (Exod 26:31-35; Lev 16:2; 2 Chr 3:19) or the outer one in front of the holy place (Exod 26:37; 38:18; Num 3:26). The tearing of the curtain from top to bottom is taken by some scholars as symbolizing God's judgment on the Temple and its resulting obsolescence (e.g., Blomberg 1992:421; Hagner 1995:849, who seems to read too much of Hebrews into Matthew). But one wonders whether the AD 70 destruction necessarily requires the final obsolescence. Others view the tearing of the curtain as a vindication of Jesus as one who is greater than the Temple and its corrupt leaders (12:6; Gundry 1994:575). Davies and Allison (1997:632) point out that any judgment on the Temple, such as the tearing of the curtain, is first of all a judgment against the priests who were the custodians of the Temple. Since Matthew presents Jesus to his Christian Jewish community not as one who destroys but as one who fulfills the Torah (5:17ff), it is not likely that he thought in terms of the absolute end of the Temple, even though he had predicted its destruction in 24:2.

The earth shook, rocks split apart. The extraordinary phenomena accompanying Jesus' death were due to an earthquake (24:7; 28:2; cf. Isa 24:19; 29:6; Jer 10:10; Amos 8:8; Nah 1:5-6; Zech 14:4). The earthquake, like the darkening of the sun, was a providential event signifying God's epochal redemptive action.

27:52-53 *godly men and women who had died were raised from the dead.* Lit., "holy ones who had fallen asleep were raised."

They left the cemetery after Jesus' resurrection, went into the holy city of Jerusalem, and appeared to many people. The opening of the tombs (Ezek 37:13) is here associated with Jesus' death, but the appearance of the saints in the holy city evidently did not occur until after Jesus' resurrection (27:53). There are many questions as to the timing and nature of this rather bizarre event (Hagner 1995:849-852), but it is not ultimately helpful to view it as non-historical. As a preview of the ultimate resurrection of humanity (Gundry 1994:577), it is important that one recognize that this resurrection was as real as that of Jesus. Only then can this resurrection be appropriately contextualized as an effect of Jesus' resurrection and an augur of the final resurrection. Matthew said nothing about the ultimate end of those raised. One wonders whether their "resurrection" was a temporary resuscitation to physical life, after which they died. In this case, these saints would be like Lazarus in John 11. If the resurrection involved a transformation of the body like that of

Jesus, one wonders whether these saints ascended with Jesus to heaven. Matthew supplies no answers to such questions, and for this reason many scholars view 27:52-53 as more of a symbolic theological tale than an actual historical narrative.

27:54 Roman officer. Lit., "centurion," a commander of a hundred soldiers; cf. 8:5, 8, 13.

This man truly was the Son of God! The confession of the centurion and the other soldiers is crucial, not only as a foil to all the invectives hurled at Jesus since 27:27, but also as a cardinal example of Matthew's theme of mission to the Gentiles. These soldiers acknowledged what all the others refused to see, and Matthew used their words to echo a main theme in the first Gospel, that Jesus is the Son of God. What the soldiers themselves meant by "Son of God" probably does not approach Matthew's high Christology. They were probably terrified by the mid-day darkness and the earthquake accompanying Jesus' death and came to the conclusion that Jesus was in some sense a supernatural being.

27:55-56 many women . . . were watching from a distance. These women figure prominently in the narrative by standing closer to Jesus than the inner circle of his disciples (cf. 26:7; 27:61; 28:1, 5).

had come from Galilee. Some of these women had been disciples since the days of the Galilean ministry.

Mary Magdalene. Cf. Luke 8:2.

Mary (the mother of James and Joseph). This is the mother of Jesus; James and Joseph were his half-brothers.

the mother of James and John. Zebedee's wife had previously envisioned her sons sitting on both sides of Jesus' throne (20:20-21), but now she saw Jesus' cross with revolutionaries crucified on both sides of him. The two Marys mentioned here will appear again in 27:61; 28:1ff. Their presence forms the literary hinge between the burial and resurrection of Jesus.

COMMENTARY

The death of Jesus is the event that all of Matthew's narrative has been pointing to. There is a sense in which Matthew 1–25 is the introduction to the passion narrative in Matthew 26–28, and the centerpiece of the passion narrative is the death of Jesus. Matthew's narration of Jesus' death is much like his preceding material on the crucifixion. He spared the details of the event itself and stresses instead the actions of others, which are full of irony and Old Testament allusions. Jesus' death is attended by darkness and results in a rock-splitting earthquake. Nature itself thus testifies to the ominous, epochal significance of this event. The direct taunting of Jesus ceases at 27:46, and Jesus' desolate cry in 27:46 pierces the darkness with some of the most profound words in the entire Bible. How one who was uniquely God's Son in terms of such passages as 1:23; 3:17; 11:27; 16:16; and 17:5 could be forsaken by God "is one of the most impenetrable mysteries of the entire Gospel narrative" (Hagner 1995:845). This is not a loss of faith on Jesus' part but the expression of the deepest imaginable pain at being abandoned by his Father. Yet the abandonment sensed by Jesus was only temporary, and his vindication was coming soon.

Jesus' cry of dereliction was misunderstood by those watching to the very end (27:47-49). Unaware of the true significance of what had transpired, they imagined that Jesus was calling for Elijah. Although they had been mocking Jesus previously, some of them appeared half-seriously to expect Elijah to come miraculously to Jesus' rescue. But Jesus had to drink the dregs of the cup of suffering the Father had placed before him. His death amounts to the sacrificial pouring out of his blood as a ransom which saves his people from their sins (1:21; 20:28; 26:28).

The earthquake at Jesus' death (27:51ff) ripped the Temple veil and even the very rocks, so that tombs were opened and people are raised from the dead. The tearing of the veil vindicated Jesus, demonstrating that he was indeed one greater than the Temple (12:6). The splitting of the rocks and resulting opening of tombs was evidently a preview of the final resurrection, guaranteed by the imminent resurrection of Jesus (cf. 1 Cor 15:20, 23; Rev 1:5). Despite the rejection of Jesus by the leaders of Israel, and his abandonment, albeit temporary, by his own disciples, there were sympathetic witnesses to his death. The Roman soldiers who crucified Jesus were transformed into believers of a sort when they witnessed the manner of Jesus' death and its results. They may not have grasped all that Matthew conveys elsewhere in the title "Son of God," but their words indicate a positive response to the "light" they had and openness to further witness by Jesus' disciples. It is likely that some of them became disciples. Another largely unsung group watched the death of Jesus, no doubt in horror over the pain and taunting but in awe over the subsequent earthquake. These were the women mentioned in 27:55-56, who in days to come were the first to learn of the resurrection of Jesus, meet the resurrected Jesus himself, and, finally, tell the disciples about it. The preeminence of these faithful women in the account of the death of Jesus, taken alongside the shameful absence of the disciples, is a powerful warning against chauvinism in the community of Jesus' disciples (cf. 23:8-12; Gal 3:28). (For further reflection on the death of Jesus the Messiah, see the commentary on 27:27-44.)

◆   N. The Burial of Jesus (27:57-66; cf. Mark 15:42-47; Luke 23:50-56; John 19:38-42)

⁵⁷As evening approached, Joseph, a rich man from Arimathea who had become a follower of Jesus, ⁵⁸went to Pilate and asked for Jesus' body. And Pilate issued an order to release it to him. ⁵⁹Joseph took the body and wrapped it in a long sheet of clean linen cloth. ⁶⁰He placed it in his own new tomb, which had been carved out of the rock. Then he rolled a great stone across the entrance and left. ⁶¹Both Mary Magdalene and the other Mary were sitting across from the tomb and watching.

⁶²The next day, on the Sabbath,* the leading priests and Pharisees went to see Pilate. ⁶³They told him, "Sir, we remember what that deceiver once said while he was still alive: 'After three days I will rise from the dead.' ⁶⁴So we request that you seal the tomb until the third day. This will prevent his disciples from coming and stealing his body and then telling everyone he was raised from the dead! If that happens, we'll be worse off than we were at first."

⁶⁵Pilate replied, "Take guards and secure it the best you can." ⁶⁶So they sealed the tomb and posted guards to protect it.

27:62 Or *On the next day, which is after the Preparation.*

NOTES

27:57 The burial of Jesus unfolds as Friday afternoon gives way to evening (cf. Mark 15:42-47; Luke 23:50-56; John 19:31-42).

Joseph, a rich man from Arimathea. His appearance is unexpected. Very little is known about the obscure place of Arimathea (1 Macc 11:34; Josephus *Antiquities* 5.342; 13:127). The mention of Joseph's wealth may be an allusion to Isa 53:9.

had become a follower of Jesus. As both a rich man and a disciple (cf. Mark 15:43; John 19:38), Joseph is a unique person in Matthew's narrative, an example of God's power to do seemingly impossible things (cf. 19:23-26). Joseph, unlike the rich young ruler, did use his wealth to help the poor.

27:58-59 *went to Pilate and asked for Jesus' body.* Joseph obtained permission from Pilate to bury Jesus. Bodies were to be buried before sunset (Deut 21:22-23), and the burial of corpses was regarded as a righteous work (Acts 5:6, 10; 8:2; Josephus *War* 4.317; Tob 1:17-20). This would be all the more true on the eve of the Sabbath. But victims of crucifixion were often left on their crosses after their deaths to perpetuate the lesson of the futility of rebellion against Rome. When they were disposed of, this would often involve being unceremoniously thrown on a trash heap. Joseph's bold and reverential treatment of Jesus' body is a remarkable demonstration of his faith in the Messiah.

long sheet of clean linen cloth. Lit., "clean linen cloth."

27:60 *He placed it in his own new tomb.* This tomb was carved out of a rock escarpment, which was typical in those days. Visitors to Israel can see examples of such ancient tombs even today.

rolled a great stone across the entrance. The tomb was closed with a large stone, probably carved into a shape like a disc or millstone. The stone would roll in a groove carved into the ground across the front of the tomb. According to John 19:39-42, Nicodemus aided Joseph in burying Jesus.

27:61 *Mary Magdalene and the other Mary were sitting across from the tomb and watching.* The two Marys from 27:56 were still keeping watch over the body of Jesus; they would be the first to learn of the resurrection (28:5ff).

27:62 *on the Sabbath.* This correctly interprets an expression that speaks of the day after the day of preparation (for the Sabbath).

leading priests and Pharisees. The religious leaders continued to pursue Jesus even after his death. This time the Pharisees, last mentioned in Jesus' denunciations in Matt 23, joined the leading priests in asking Pilate to seal and guard the tomb. Here, two groups normally in tension with one another unite to accomplish a larger common purpose (cf. 21:45).

27:63-64 *that deceiver.* It is unclear how the chief priests and Pharisees became aware of Jesus' predictions concerning his resurrection. Jesus' repeated explicit predictions of his resurrection had been made only to his disciples (16:21; 17:22-23; 20:17-19). Perhaps the veiled predictions of the resurrection in terms of the sign of Jonah were understood by the Pharisees and Sadducees who heard it (12:38-40; 16:4). Calling Jesus a deceiver (Luke 23:14; John 7:12, 47), they feared the highly implausible event that his disciples would perpetrate further deception by stealing the body and then claiming that Jesus rose from the dead.

27:65 *Take guards.* Pilate's response should probably be taken as a command for the Jewish religious leaders to take a guard, evidently of Roman soldiers at Pilate's disposal, and secure the tomb, but possibly Pilate was permitting them to guard the tomb with their own resources—namely, the Temple police. However, the fact that these guards were called soldiers (28:12-13) and that they were accountable to Pilate (28:14) suggests that they were Roman soldiers.

27:66 they sealed the tomb and posted guards to protect it. If the former view is correct, these soldiers sealed the tomb and guarded it with the authority of Rome. The seal would likely be clay or wax pressed into the crack between the rolling stone and the tomb itself. The clay or wax would then have the imperial seal stamped on it (Dan 6:17), but this would not hinder the power of God at dawn the next morning.

COMMENTARY

This passage contains two sections, the first describes the burial of Jesus (27:57-61) and the second the fear of the Jewish religious leaders that the disciples would steal Jesus' body and make deceptive claims of his resurrection (27:62-66). Both sections involve a request being made to Pilate, and Pilate granting the request. This section sets up Matthew 28 because the burial of Jesus and guarding of his tomb are reversed by the resurrection and flight of the guards to the chief priests.

After all of the abuse Jesus had taken this day, the manner of his burial is surprising, to say the least. He is spared the ignominy of having his body hang on the cross after sundown, a sundown that led to the Sabbath during the Feast of Unleavened Bread. Leaving his body exposed would have added insult to injury, to say the least. But Joseph stepped in and brought the story of Jesus' horrible death to an end by giving him a decent burial. Fittingly, this was the kindest treatment Jesus received since the unnamed woman anointed him for his burial in 26:6-13.

The fear of the religious leaders that the disciples would steal Jesus' body and go on to deceive people with false resurrection claims seems to be irrational, even bordering on paranoia. The religious leaders thought too highly of the disciples, who were scattered, afraid, and hardly in a position to steal the body. But a far worse mistake is that the religious leaders thought so little of Jesus that they ruled out any possibility that God would make good on Jesus' promised resurrection. In any event, the post-resurrection appearances refute the stolen body theory of the resurrection (28:9, 17; cf. Acts 1:3-11; 1 Cor 15:5-8). The conspiracy that results after Jesus' resurrection shows the lengths to which unbelief will go in order to sustain its pretended autonomy (cf. 28:11-15; cf. Luke 16:31). The book of Acts portrays the ensuing confirmation of the worst fears of these religious leaders. Jesus whom they crucified had indeed risen from the dead and commissioned his followers to take this message to all the nations (Acts 2:24; 3:15; 10:40; 13:30; 17:31; 23:6-10; 24:15, 21; 25:19; 26:8, 23). And the last "deception" certainly does turn out to be "worse" than the first (27:64; cf. Acts 2:41-47; 6:7; 9:31; 21:20).

Summary and Transition. Matthew 27 carries the drama of Jesus' arrest and trial before the religious leaders to its awful conclusion, as Jesus is condemned by Pilate and crucified. After his death and burial, the Jewish religious leaders attempted to nullify any possibility of his predicted resurrection by guarding the tomb and sealing the stone. Certainly this is the low point of the Gospel for followers of Jesus the Messiah, but the seeming victory of Jesus' enemies was only temporary.

The chapter begins with the note that Jesus was sent to Pilate for condemnation (27:1-2) but interrupts this story line briefly with the pathetic account of Judas' remorse and suicide (27:3-10). Then Matthew returns to the trial of Jesus before Pilate and Pilate's somewhat reluctant deliverance of Jesus for crucifixion (27:11-26). Jesus was then cruelly mocked by the soldiers (27:27-31), led to Golgotha, crucified, and mocked even more (27:32-44). Matthew next features the circumstances of Jesus' death at the ninth hour (3 p.m.; 27:45-56), and the remarkable manner of his burial (27:57-61). The chapter concludes with yet another evidence of the hardness of the religious leaders' hearts as they did all in their power to prevent the disciples from stealing Jesus' body (27:62-66). This final section of the chapter sets the scene for the resurrection as the event that once for all exposes the folly and futility of those who would thwart the plan and purpose of God.

In this chapter, Matthew develops two contrasting themes in parallel fashion. On the one hand, the religious leaders continue their hard-hearted, cruel, mocking treatment of Jesus and admit their absolute responsibility for his execution (27:1, 4, 20, 41-43, 62). To the bitter end their amazing obstinacy in opposing Jesus continues. On the other hand, Jesus is repeatedly vindicated in the midst of this mockery by the officials of Israel and Rome. Judas remorsefully admitted that Jesus was innocent, and the religious leaders did not attempt to persuade him otherwise (27:4). Even Pilate was aware of the ulterior motives of the religious leaders and, along with his wife, regarded Jesus as innocent (27:18-19, 23-24). The Father provided meteorological phenomena, which befit the atrocity committed and provided a sort of vindication as well (27:51-53). A detachment of Roman soldiers was more perceptive than the Jewish religious leaders when they interpreted these phenomena as demonstrating that Jesus is the Son of God (27:54). While it is debatable how much the soldiers understood of Jesus' divine sonship, their sincere confession contrasts starkly with the taunts of the multitudes and the religious leaders (27:40, 43). This confession paves the way for the resurrected Jesus to send his disciples to all the nations, who must likewise confess in baptism the name of the Father, Son, and Holy Spirit (28:19).

◆ **O. The Resurrection of Jesus (28:1-10; cf. Mark 16:1-11; Luke 24:1-12; John 20:1-18)**

Early on Sunday morning,* as the new day was dawning, Mary Magdalene and the other Mary went out to visit the tomb. ²Suddenly there was a great earthquake! For an angel of the Lord came down from heaven, rolled aside the stone, and sat on it. ³His face shone like lightning, and his clothing was as white as snow. ⁴The guards shook with fear when they saw him, and they fell into a dead faint.

⁵Then the angel spoke to the women. "Don't be afraid!" he said. "I know you are looking for Jesus, who was crucified. ⁶He isn't here! He is risen from the dead, just as he said would happen. Come, see where his body was lying. ⁷And now, go quickly and tell his disciples that he has risen from the dead, and he is going ahead of you to Galilee. You will see him there. Remember what I have told you."

⁸The women ran quickly from the tomb. They were very frightened but also filled with great joy, and they rushed to give the disciples the angel's message. ⁹And as

they went, Jesus met them and greeted them. And they ran to him, grasped his feet, and worshiped him. ¹⁰Then Jesus said to them, "Don't be afraid! Go tell my brothers to leave for Galilee, and they will see me there."

28:1 Greek *After the Sabbath, on the first day of the week.*

NOTES

28:1 The comparison of Matthew's resurrection narrative with that of the other Gospels raises a number of questions regarding chronology and harmonization (cf. Mark 16:1-11; Luke 24:1-12; John 20:1-18; see the last paragraph of the commentary below for other resources on the resurrection).

Early on Sunday morning, as the new day was dawning. Lit., "after the Sabbath, as the first day of the week was dawning."

visit the tomb. Lit., "see the tomb." Their purpose in doing so is explained more clearly in Mark 16:1. It is significant that once again the female disciples were the closest to Jesus at a crucial juncture of the story (cf. 26:7; 27:56, 61). Evidently the disciples were still scattered (26:31-35).

28:2 *a great earthquake!* This severe earthquake reminds the reader of the earthquake which had occurred when Jesus died on Friday afternoon (27:51-53). It is possible to regard this as an aftershock of the previous earthquake (Blomberg 1992:427), which was accompanied by the epochal events that lead up to the resurrection of Jesus. Or, it may be better to see the quake as due to the angelic work mentioned in the next note. The sequence of the events in 28:2-3 is not clear. Either the earthquake had already occurred by the time the women arrived or it occurred as they viewed the tomb.

an angel . . . rolled aside the stone. The appearance of the angel to roll the stone aside evidently coincided with or caused the earthquake, but it is not clear whether this was visible to the women. Either way, the stone was rolled aside, not to let Jesus out, but to show the women that the tomb was empty because the resurrection had already occurred.

28:3 *His face shone like lightning.* The description of the awesome appearance of the angel is similar to other biblical accounts of angelic visitations (Dan 7:9; 10:6; Acts 1:10; Rev 10:1; 15:6). It is noteworthy that Matthew begins and ends with angelic activity; angels are involved with both the birth and resurrection of Jesus (1:20; 2:19).

28:4 *The guards shook with fear when they saw him, and they fell into a dead faint.* As it turns out, the detachment of guards and the imperial seal on the stone (27:65-66) were powerless to stop the removal of Jesus' body because it was not stolen by the disciples but raised by the Father. The glorious angel who rolled away the stone so astonished the guards that they fainted as if *they* were the dead ones.

28:5-6 *He is risen from the dead.* Lit., "he was raised from the dead"; this shows that the power of another, the Father, accomplished the miracle.

Come, see where his body was lying. After the angel told the women not to fear (cf. Luke 1:13, 30; 2:10), the angel coupled his announcement of the resurrection with an invitation for the women to look into the tomb and see for themselves. His words, "just as he said would happen," remind the women that Jesus had repeatedly predicted his resurrection (cf. 12:40; 16:21; 17:9, 23; 20:19; 26:32).

28:7 *he is going ahead of you to Galilee.* Jesus' earlier promise to meet the disciples in Galilee (26:32) is repeated here by the angel and later by Jesus himself (28:10). The promise was originally uttered in the context of Jesus' prediction that the disciples would desert him (26:31). It is the power of the resurrection that transforms the deserters back into disciples.

go . . . tell his disciples. . . . Remember what I have told you. Lit., "Behold, I have told you." This detail, which indicates that the women were the first witnesses of the empty tomb, is unusual and adds a ring of truth. Blomberg (1992:426) points out the high probability that if the story had been invented, male witnesses would have been fabricated.

28:8-9 *as they went, Jesus met them.* As the women hastened to report the news to the absentee apostles in obedience to the angel, they were met and greeted by none other than the risen Jesus himself.

grasped his feet, and worshiped him. Their worship of Jesus reminds the reader of similar actions by the Magi and others (2:2, 11; 8:2; 9:18; 14:33; 15:25; 18:26; 20:20; 28:9, 17). In view of Jesus reminding Satan that only God is to be worshiped (4:9-10), the women's worship is indicative of Matthew's high Christology. This first post-resurrection appearance of Jesus sets the tone for the proper response to him from now on—worship. The reader is evidently to picture them prostrated before Jesus, face to the ground, with arms outstretched and hands grasping Jesus' feet.

28:10 *Go tell my brothers to leave for Galilee.* Jesus himself reaffirmed the angel's promise (28:7), and referred to the disciples as his brothers (12:49-50; 23:8; 25:40; cf. Rom 8:29; Heb 2:11). This use of the family metaphor indicates great love and patience, since the disciples could be said to have "run away from home" in abandoning Jesus. Jesus welcomed the prodigals back home again.

C O M M E N T A R Y

In this section, the resurrection of Jesus is announced, not explained. The central focus of 28:1-10 is the empty tomb, revealed by an angel who rolled away the stone, causing an earthquake. He then showed the two women that their crucified master was no longer entombed. The glorious angel and the empty tomb caused the guards to faint. For the faithful women, the significance was that Jesus is indeed the Messiah and that they no longer needed to mourn him. They ran to tell his disciples the good news that he had risen. According to this passage, there were six witnesses to the resurrection:

1. The Father, whose miraculous activity is the presupposition of everything else and who is the implied agent of all the passive verbs that state that Jesus will be raised up (16:22; 28:6)
2. The glorious angel, who actually made the announcement (28:6a)
3. The empty tomb itself, which says nothing but signifies everything (28:6b)
4. The faithful women, who hurried to announce the resurrection to the disciples (28:8)
5. Jesus himself, who met the women on their way and reiterated that he would meet the disciples in Galilee (28:9-10)
6. The guards, who regained consciousness and told the leading priests what had happened (28:11)

In addition to these six witnesses, two other factors in the narrative provide additional testimony that Jesus was raised: the earthquake which accompanies the stone being rolled away marked the occurrence of an epochal event (28:2), and the religious leaders' conspiracy to deny the resurrection amounts to an indirect and ironic testimony that it did happen.

The Theological Significance of Jesus' Resurrection. Although often relegated to Easter Sunday, the resurrection of Jesus is the heart of the Christian gospel. Without the resurrection, the ministry of Jesus ends on a dismal note. But everything changes with the announcement: "He isn't here! He has risen from the dead, just as he said would happen" (28:6). The resurrection is not only the climax of Matthew's passion narrative, it is the heart of redemption itself. It may be helpful to remember that the resurrection of Jesus is the necessary prerequisite, the *sine qua non*, of several themes in Matthew's theology.

Without the resurrection of Jesus, there would be no Savior, since Jesus would have been a deluded liar instead of an exalted Lord. He had predicted several times that he would rise from the dead (12:40; 16:21; 17:9, 23; 20:19; 26:32). If he did not, he would be worthy only of pity, not faith and obedience (1 Cor 15:16-19).

Without the resurrection of Jesus, there would be no salvation, for Jesus' mission to save his people from their sins (1:21) would have come to the ignominious end of a cursed person who hung upon a tree (Deut 21:22-23; Gal 3:13). Jesus would not drink the new wine that represented his redeeming blood in the Father's Kingdom with his disciples. The blood of the new covenant would have been shed in vain (26:27-29).

Without the resurrection of Jesus, there would have been no apostolic foundation for the church, for it was the resurrection of Jesus that turned the deserters back into disciples (26:31-32). What could have brought the scattered disciples back into the fold except the message brought to them by the two women (28:7, 10)? What would Jesus have built his church upon (16:18) if Peter and his fellow disciples had remained deserters and deniers?

Without the resurrection of Jesus, there would be no model of sacrificial living instead of selfish living. Jesus taught his disciples the oxymoron of the crucified life, convincing them that the truly abundant life is the life dead to self-interest and that the truly miserable life is the life lived for self-interest. But this model would be incomplete if Jesus' suffering did not end in glory, and if his cross was never replaced with the crown (10:38-39; 16:24-26; 20:26-28; 23:12; Rom 6:1-11).

Without the resurrection of Jesus, there would be no rectification of all the wrongs done on earth since the fall of humanity in Genesis 3. The blood of the martyrs would cry out for all eternity without vindication (23:35; Rev 6:9-11). Those who did evil and violence to their fellow humans would never give account, and there would be no such thing as justice (13:37-42; cf. Dan 12:2). The resurrection guarantees the final judgment of all mankind (13:37-42; 16:27; 25:31; cf. Dan 12:2; Acts 17:31). Without the resurrection, Satan would win.

Without the resurrection of Jesus, there would be no resurrection and reward of his people (27:51-53). At the heart of Jesus' ethical teaching is the eschatological promise of the coming Kingdom (4:17). That Kingdom becomes the focus of the disciples' hope and values (6:10, 33), but how could it ever come to earth if its ruler remained in the grave? If Jesus remained in the grave he could not be exalted to sit on his throne, and with his throne unoccupied, what would become of the twelve thrones of his apostles, and of the rewards he promised to all who left what this world has to offer for the sake of his name (6:19-21; 13:43; 19:27-29; cf. Dan 12:3; Rev 2:26-27; 3:21)?

Without the resurrection of Jesus, there would be nothing. Therefore, those who want to communicate the good news of Jesus the Messiah must make sure that they stress the resurrection of Jesus as the essential explanation of the significance of his death. Attempts to communicate the gospel in ways that gain the attention and understanding of the lost are laudable, but not if such encapsulation amounts to truncation. Any so-called gospel which does not include focus on the resurrection of Jesus is not the authentic message of Jesus and the apostles (Acts 2:32; 3:15, 26; 4:2, 10, 33; 5:30; 10:40; 13:30ff; 17:18, 31; 23:6; 24:21; 25:19; 26:8, 23; Rom 1:4; 4:25; 6:4-5; 8:11; 10:9; 1 Cor 15; 2 Cor 4:10, 14; 13:4; Gal 1:1; Eph 1:20; 2:5; 4:10; Phil 2:8-9; Col 2:12; 3:1-4; 1 Thess 4:14; 1 Tim 3:16; Heb 1:3; 10:12; 12:3; 1 Pet 1:22; 3:18-22; Rev 5).

Studies of the resurrection are numerous. For a conservative attempt to answer the questions that arise when the four Gospel accounts are compared, see Wenham (1984). For the unique emphases of each Gospel, see Osborne (1984). Blomberg (1987:100-110) discusses historical matters. For an apologetic approach, see Craig in Wilkins and Moreland (1995:142-176).

◆ **P. Report of the Guard (28:11-15)**

¹¹As the women were on their way, some of the guards went into the city and told the leading priests what had happened. ¹²A meeting with the elders was called, and they decided to give the soldiers a large bribe. ¹³They told the soldiers, "You must say, 'Jesus' disciples came during the night while we were sleeping, and they stole his body.' ¹⁴If the governor hears about it, we'll stand up for you so you won't get in trouble." ¹⁵So the guards accepted the bribe and said what they were told to say. Their story spread widely among the Jews, and they still tell it today.

NOTES

28:11-12 *the guards.* These were probably Roman soldiers responsible to Pilate (see note on 27:65).

guards went into the city and told the leading priests what had happened. Just how much of the happenings at Jesus' tomb they saw is unclear, but the Gr. says that they told the priests "everything that happened." They had fainted when they saw the angel (28:4), but eventually regained consciousness and saw that the tomb was empty.

a large bribe. After the priests met with the elders, they bribed the guards and fabricated a story to explain the resurrection. Ironically, the very guards who were supposed to prevent a potential problem became an actual problem themselves. The story of the bribery of Judas to betray Jesus is near the beginning of the passion narrative, and this story of the bribery of the guards to lie about the resurrection is near the end of the passion narrative.

28:13-15 *they stole his body.* The story the guards were bribed and instructed to tell was also the premise that the leaders had used to get the guards to begin with—that is, they feared the theft of Jesus' body by the disciples (cf. John 20:1-2).

If the governor hears about it, we'll stand up for you. The religious leaders promised to protect them from Pilate, who would no doubt be enraged at their dereliction of duty. First

Judas was bribed, then the guards, and perhaps the leaders would need to bribe Pilate too. But their story is a patently false concoction—if the guards were asleep, how did they know that the disciples stole the body?

the guards accepted the bribe. The guards took the money and did as they were told.

Their story spread widely among the Jews, and they still tell it today. They spawned a hoax that continued to the time when the Gospel of Matthew was written. According to Justin Martyr, such stories were still in circulation during his lifetime (AD 100–165; cf. *Dialogue* 108.2).

COMMENTARY

In this passage the soldiers who were guarding Jesus' tomb became evangelists of Jesus' resurrection! Previously the leaders purported to need guards for fear that a resurrection hoax might occur, but those very guards later reported that a genuine resurrection had occurred. The leaders had outsmarted themselves: the very guards they secured to prevent a potential problem could now testify to an actual problem. So a "cover-up" had to be concocted, and money must change hands to ensure that everyone had the story straight.

The minds of the religious leaders were already made up about Jesus, and they did not want to be confused by the fact of his resurrection. This intensified their guilt. Perhaps they really believed that the disciples had used the occasion of an earthquake to steal the body, but most likely they made up the story with full knowledge that it was a lie. They had accused Jesus of being a deceiver (27:63-64), but now they were the ones willfully deceiving people about Jesus. They had refused to believe Jesus was the ultimate interpreter of Moses and the prophets, and they would not be persuaded even when someone was raised from the dead (Luke 16:31). However, one must never be pessimistic about the life-changing power of the gospel of Christ. The book of Acts speaks of thousands of converts in Jerusalem (Acts 2:41; 4:4), many of whom were priests (Acts 6:7).

None of the alternative explanations of the resurrection of Jesus satisfactorily explain what is recorded here. The explanation that the disciples stole the body is patently false, and other theories fare no better. Some have theorized that the women visited the wrong tomb, or that Jesus on the cross had merely swooned and later revived, or that there was so much wishful thinking on the part of the disciples that they had a collective hallucination and all thought that they saw Jesus. Only by *a priori*, worldview-driven assumptions that rule out supernatural events up front, can one dismiss this account outright.

◆   **Q. The Commission of the Risen Lord (28:16-20; cf. Mark 16:15-18)**

¹⁶Then the eleven disciples left for Galilee, going to the mountain where Jesus had told them to go. ¹⁷When they saw him, they worshiped him—but some of them doubted!

¹⁸Jesus came and told his disciples, "I have been given all authority in heaven and on earth. ¹⁹Therefore, go and make disciples of all the nations,* baptizing them in the name of the Father and the

Son and the Holy Spirit. ²⁰Teach these new   given you. And be sure of this: I am with
disciples to obey all the commands I have   you always, even to the end of the age."

28:19 Or *all peoples.*

N O T E S

28:16-17 *the eleven disciples left for Galilee.* The meeting in Galilee is fitting since the
disciples were native Galileans and would normally return home to Galilee after the
pilgrimage to Jerusalem for Passover and the Feast of Unleavened Bread. Given the previous association of Galilee with Gentiles (4:14-16; cf. Isa 9:1-2), it is fitting that a mandate
for mission to all the nations was given here. The disciples (only eleven in number now)
obeyed their Lord's instructions and traveled to a previously unmentioned, nameless
mountain that Jesus had evidently designated at some point (28:10).

going to the mountain. The name of the mountain is unimportant, but the fact that Jesus
met them on a mountain reminds the reader of the giving of the Torah from Mount Sinai
as well as previous mountain experiences in Matthew (4:8; 5:1; 14:23; 15:29; 17:1; 24:3;
Donaldson 1985).

28:17 *When they saw him, they worshiped him.* When the disciples first saw Jesus, like
the two faithful women, they worshiped him.

but some of them doubted! Lit., "some doubted." Most scholars agree with the NLT that
some of the disciples were less confident than the others, but others argue that all the
disciples doubted Jesus, or at least that they hesitated to worship him (e.g., Hagner
1995:884-85). The word translated "doubted" here occurs previously in 14:31 to describe
the little faith of Peter in doubting as he walked on the water and saw the wind. It can be
translated "hesitated" or "wavered" (*distazo,* BDAG 252), and Blomberg 1992:430 argues
that it does not refer to unbelief so much as to lack of spontaneous worship on the part
of some of the disciples. But this is far from clear, since the only other time the word is
used in Matthew (14:31) it is closely related to the familiar theme of "little faith" (cf.
6:30; 8:26; 16:8; 17:20). Whether one thinks of the disciples' response as hesitant or
doubting, it is surprising.

28:18 *I have been given all authority in heaven and on earth.* God's bestowal of
authority or power upon Jesus echoes Dan 7:13-14, 18, 22, 27 (cf. Eph 1:20-23; Phil 2:6-
11; Col 1:15-20; 1 Pet 3:18-22). Davies and Allison (1997:683) concisely explain the
similarities. In Daniel 7, the authority of the Son of Man passes from him to his community, and so it is in Matthew. Matthew has stressed repeatedly that Jesus is the king who
has authority to forgive sins and to save his people (Matt 1:1, 17, 21; 2:2; 7:29; 8:8-9;
9:6-8; 10:1; 11:27; 21:23; 24:14). Jesus demonstrated his authority by word and deed.
Hagner (1995:886) helpfully points out that the resurrection and exaltation of Jesus
result in a sort of permanent transfiguration (17:1-8). The glory that a few disciples saw
briefly at the transfiguration is now the permanent mode of Jesus' life as the exalted Son
of Man.

28:19 *Therefore, go and make disciples of all the nations.* It is crucial to note that this
verse begins with "therefore." The point is that Jesus, having been exalted, was now in a
position to send his disciples forth in mission. Their mission is possible because Jesus is
potent. Jesus had already commissioned his disciples to take the message of the Kingdom
to Israel alone (10:5-6; cf. 15:24ff), but now he commands them to take it to all the
nations (cf. Gen 12:3). Some take this as "all the Gentiles," and exclude the Jews from
the commission, but this is a mistake. No doubt the priority is on the Gentiles, but mission to the Gentiles is supplemental to mission to Israel, not a substitute for it. Ongoing
mission to Israel is assumed by 10:23 (Levine 1988). It is clear from Acts that the practice

of the apostolic church was to continue mission to the Jews. "Universal Lordship means universal mission" (Davies and Allison 1997:684). For a thorough discussion of this passage in the broader context of early Christian mission, see Schnabel 2004:1.348-367.

The central responsibility of the disciples is to reproduce themselves, to make more disciples. The other activities (go, baptize, teach) essentially describe how a disciple is made. "Disciple" originally designated one who followed an itinerant master, as Jesus' disciples had done. But since Jesus was about to depart this world, the term "disciple" took on a more metaphorical meaning. One now follows Jesus by understanding and obeying his teaching. If the message of Jesus is to reach all the nations, the disciples will obviously have to go to them.

baptizing them in the name of the Father and the Son and the Holy Spirit. Baptism will be the key, early step of new disciples that initiates them into the church. Their baptism is distinct from Jewish ritual washings because it is a single act. It differs from John's baptism because it is done with the triadic formula which invokes the Father, Son, and Holy Spirit (cf. *Didache* 7:1).

28:20 *Teach these new disciples to obey all the commands I have given you.* The mission mandate also involves teaching new disciples to obey all that Jesus commanded. One would expect that the major discourses of Jesus in Matthew would form the core of this teaching. Walvoord (1974:242) certainly errs by excluding Jesus' interpretation of the law of Moses from what is to be taught and by restricting the word "commands" to the new commandment of John 13:31-35. Since Jesus was a teacher, indeed the ultimate and definitive teacher of the Torah (4:23; 5:2, 17-48; 7:29; 9:35; 11:1; 13:34; 21:23; 26:55), it is not surprising that his disciples are to continue in this vein. This teaching is not merely to convey information but to change lives from disobedient to obedient behavior (5:17-20; 7:21-27).

I am with you always, even to the end of the age. The commission began with Jesus' announcement that he had received all authority; it is now concluded with Jesus' promise to be with his disciples constantly until the end of the age. The disciples' responsibilities are daunting, but they have amazing resources. They will need to drink deeply of both the power and the presence of Jesus if they are to fulfill his mandate. Jesus has already been called Immanuel, God's presence on earth (1:23; cf. Isa 7:14). His ministry demonstrated God's presence as the Spirit enabled him to be God's servant in compassionately serving the scattered sheep of Israel (9:36) and those oppressed by Satan (12:17-29). Now the disciples will experience Jesus' presence in a new way, evidently through the same Spirit that empowered him while he was ministering on earth. Even during the difficult times of dispute and discipline, they may be assured that Jesus' presence and authority will guide and confirm their decisions (18:18-20). This presence is permanent, lasting until "the end of the age." This expression has been used previously (13:39-40, 49; 24:3) and clearly refers to the time of eschatological judgment at the conclusion of the present order. Because the end of the age is in view, it seems clear that this commission is not merely for the original disciples but also for the disciples of the disciples of the disciples, in perpetuity until Jesus returns. All during this time there will never be a day when Jesus will not be present with his disciples as they are busy about the business of the Kingdom.

COMMENTARY

According to Luke and John, Jesus appeared to the disciples in Jerusalem after his resurrection (Luke 24:13-53; John 20:19–21:23; Acts 1:1-11). Then he met them in their native Galilee to charge them with a mission that would endure throughout the age. They worshiped him when they met him there, although some still doubted (cf. 14:31). The remedy for this doubt would be found in the disciples' growing realization of Jesus' power and presence, truths which bracket the responsibilities of the mission mandate.

One is immediately struck by the repetition of the word "all" in this passage:

1. Jesus has been given all authority (28:18).
2. Disciples are to be made of all nations (28:19).
3. Disciples are to obey all that Jesus commanded (28:20).
4. Jesus will be with the disciples always (lit. "all the days"; 28:20).

The universality of Jesus' power and perpetuity of his presence provide the dynamic for the universal discipleship mandate. The disciples will be able to disciple all the nations only as they recognize that Jesus has been given all authority and that he will be with them all the days until the end. The universal task is daunting, but it can be done because of the continuing power and presence of Jesus.

Matthew's story of Jesus concludes with a short chapter that describes the resurrection of Jesus (28:1-10), the cover-up perpetuated by the religious leaders (28:11-15), and the mandate of Jesus for discipling all the nations (28:16-20). The chapter covers the resurrection and postresurrection appearances rather concisely, stressing the religious leaders' opposition to the resurrection, and stressing the mission mandate of the exalted Messiah. Both of these themes, the former negative and the latter positive, are by now familiar to the attentive reader of Matthew.

There may be no better way to summarize the theology of Matthew than by following up on the themes found in the Great Commission. The setting of the commission finds the restored disciples worshiping Jesus, but not wholeheartedly. Throughout his Gospel, Matthew has presented the weaknesses of the disciples, but all the same, Jesus still promised to build his church on their foundational ministries. God's power can overcome their infirmities.

The commission itself is based in Christology, as Jesus describes his kingly authority in terms taken from Daniel 7:13ff. Here is Matthew's theology of the Kingdom in a nutshell. This Kingdom has both realized and unrealized elements, and the disciples are to long for and pray for its full manifestation on earth. The commission is concerned with making true disciples who obey Jesus—their Lord—not just casual hangers-on who may listen to his message without doing it. And these disciples are to be made not only from Israel, but from all the nations, where eager converts, reminiscent of the Roman officer and the Canaanite woman, will be found.

This universal mission also has cosmic implications. When people from all nations are discipled, a new humanity begins to be formed. Thus, obedience to the mission mandate turns out to fulfill (as a byproduct) the original creation mandate that God gave to humanity's first parents in the Garden of Eden.

As the disciples take Jesus' message to all nations and make disciples of them, they will experience the faithful Immanuel-presence of Jesus. Through the Spirit, Jesus will tell them what to say when they are under duress from outsiders, and he will be in their midst when they ask for wisdom in dealing with internal problems.

This presence of Jesus will end only when the age ends at his return. At that time the disciples' enemies will be judged and their sacrificial service rewarded. This will lead to nothing less than a regeneration of the world, and obedience to Jesus the exalted Messiah will no longer be merely partial. God's "will" will finally be done on earth as it is in heaven. *Soli Deo Gloria!*

BIBLIOGRAPHY

Aland, B. and J. Delobel
1994 *New Testament Exegesis, Textual Criticism, and Early Church History.* Kampen: Kok Pharos.

Allison, D. C.
1993 *The New Moses: A Matthean Typology.* Edinburgh: T & T Clark

Albright, W. and C. Mann.
1971 *Matthew.* Anchor Bible. New York: Doubleday.

Allen, W.
1912 *A Critical and Exegetical Commentary on the Gospel According to St. Matthew.* International Critical Commentary. Edinburgh: T & T Clark.

Bacon, B.
1930 *Studies in Matthew.* New York: Holt.

Balch, D., editor
1991 *The Social History of the Matthean Community.* Minneapolis: Fortress.

Barbieri, L. A. Jr.
1983 "Matthew," *Bible Knowledge Commentary.* ed. J. F. Walvoord and R. B. Zuck. Wheaton: Victor.

Barclay, W.
1975 *The Gospel of Matthew.* 2 vols. The Daily Study Bible. Philadelphia: Westminster.

Barnes, Albert
1868 *Notes, Explanatory and Practical, on the Gospels.* New York: Harper & Brothers.

Bauer, D.
1989 *The Structure of Matthew's Gospel.* Journal for the Study of the New Testament Supplement Series 31. Sheffield: Almond Press.

Baum, G.
1965 *Is the New Testament Anti-Semitic?* Glen Rock: Paulist.

Beare, F.
1981 *The Gospel According to Matthew.* New York: Harper.

Beasley-Murray, G.
1986 *Jesus and the Kingdom of God.* Grand Rapids: Eerdmans.
1993 *Jesus and the Last Days: The Interpretation of the Olivet Discourse.* Peabody, MA: Hendrikson.

Beck, Norman.
1985 *Mature Christianity: The Recognition and Repudiation of the Anti-Jewish Polemic in the New Testament.* Selinsgrove: Susquehanna University Press.

Berger, K. et al.
1995 *Hellenistic Commentary on the New Testament.* Nashville: Abingdon.

Blomberg, C.
1987 *The Historical Reliability of the Gospels.* Leicester: InterVarsity.
1990 *Introducing the Parables.* Downers Grove: InterVarsity.
1991 The Liberation of Illegitimacy: Women and Rulers in Matthew 1–2. *Biblical Theology Bulletin* 21:145-150.
1992 *Matthew.* The New American Commentary. Nashville: Broadman & Holman.

Boring, M. Eugene
1995 *The Gospel of Matthew.* Pp. 87-506 in *The New Interpreters Bible,* vol. 8. Editor, L. Keck. Nashville: Abingdon.

Bornkamm, G., G. Barth, and H. J. Held.
1963 *Tradition and Interpretation in Matthew.* Philadelphia: Westminster.

Brandon, S.
1951 *The Fall of Jerusalem and the Christian Church.* London: SPCK.

Broadus, J.
1886 *Commentary on the Gospel of Matthew.* American Commentary. Valley Forge: American Baptist Press.

Brooks, S.
1987 *Matthew's Community: The Evidence of his Special Sayings Material*. Journal for the Study of the New Testament Supplement Series 16. Sheffield: Sheffield Academic.

Brown, R.
1993 *The Birth of the Messiah*. New York: Doubleday.
1994 *The Death of the Messiah*. New York: Doubleday.

Brown, R., K. Donfried, and J. Reumann, editors
1973 *Peter in the New Testament*. Minneapolis: Augsburg/Paulist.

Bruce, F. F.
1988 *The Canon of Scripture*. Downers Grove: InterVarsity.

Bruner, F.
1987 *The Christbook* (Matthew 1–12). Waco: Word.
1990 *The Churchbook* (Matthew 13–28). Waco: Word.

Buchanan, G.
1996 *The Gospel of Matthew*. 2 vols. Lewiston, NY: Mellen.

Burgess, J.
1966 *A History of the Exegesis of Matthew 16:17-19 from 1781 to 1965*. Ann Arbor: Edwards Brothers.

Burnett, F.
1981 *The Testament of Jesus-Sophia: A Redaction-Critical Study of the Eschatological Discourse in Matthew*. Lanham: University Press of America.
1992 Exposing the Anti-Jewish Ideology of Matthew's Implied Author: The Characterization of God as Father. *Semeia* 59:155-192.

Butler, B.
1951 *The Originality of St. Matthew: A Critique of the Two-Document Hypothesis*. Cambridge: Cambridge University.

Calvin, John
1960 *Institutes of the Christian Religion*. Editor, J. McNeil. Translator, F. Battles. 2 vols. Philadelphia: Westminster. (Orig. Pub. c1559)
1972 *A Harmony of the Gospels Matthew, Mark, and Luke*. Editors, D. and T. Torrance. Translator, A. Morrison. 3 vols. Grand Rapids: Eerdmans. (Orig. Pub. c1555)

Campbell, K.
1978 The New Jerusalem in Matthew 5:14. *Scottish Journal of Theology* 31:335-363.

Cargal, T.
1991 "His blood be upon us and upon our children": A Matthean Double Entendre? *New Testament Studies* 37:101-112.

Carson, D.
1978 *The Sermon on the Mount*. Grand Rapids: Baker.
1984 *Matthew.*, in *The Expositor's Bible Commentary*. Editors, F. Gaebelein and J. Douglas. Grand Rapids: Zondervan, 8:1-599.
1987 *When Jesus Confronts the World*. Grand Rapids: Baker.

Carter, W.
1996 *Matthew: Storyteller, Interpreter, Evangelist*. Peabody, MA: Hendrickson.

Chilton, B.
1984 *A Galilean Rabbi and His Bible*. Wilmington: Glazier.

Comfort, P. W.
2007 *New Testament Text and Translation Commentary*. Carol Stream: Tyndale.

Comfort, P. W. and D. Barrett
2001 *The Text of the Earliest Greek New Testament Manuscripts*. Carol Stream: Tyndale.

Cook, M.
1983 Anti-Judaism in the New Testament. *Union Seminary Quarterly Review* 38:125-137.

Cope, O.
1976 *Matthew: A Scribe Trained for the Kingdom of Heaven*. Catholic Biblical Quarterly Monograph Series. Washington, D.C.: Catholic Biblical Association.

Cullmann, O.
1962 *Peter: Disciple, Apostle, Martyr.* 2nd ed. Translator, F. Filson. London: SCM.

Davies, A., editor
1979 *Anti-Semitism and the Foundation of Christianity.* New York: Paulist.

Davies, W. and D. Allison, Jr.
1988, 1991, 1997 *A Critical and Exegetical Commentary on the Gospel According to Saint Matthew.* 3 vols. International Critical Commentary. Edinburgh: T & T Clark.

Davis, C.
1973 The Fulfillment of Creation. A Study of Matthew's Genealogy. *Journal of the American Academy of Religion* 41:520-535.

Davison, J.
1985 Anomia and the Question of an Antinomian Polemic in Matthew. *Journal of Biblical Literature* 104:617-635.

Derrett, J.
1968 You build the tombs of the prophets. In *Studia Evangelica 4*, editor, F. Cross, 187-193. Berlin: Akademie Verlag.

Donaldson, T.
1985 *Jesus on the Mountain: A Study in Matthean Theology.* Journal of the Study of the New Testament Supplement Series 8. Sheffield: Sheffield Academic Press.

Dunn, J., editor
1992 *Jews and Christians: The Parting of the Ways AD 70-135.* Wissenschaftliche Untersuchungen zum Neuen Testament 66. Tübingen: Mohr (Siebeck).

Edwards, R.
1985 *Matthew's Story of Jesus.* Philadelphia: Fortress.

Elliott, M.
2000 *The Survivors of Israel.* Grand Rapids: Eerdmans.

Ellis, P.
1974 *Matthew: His Mind and His Message.* Collegeville, Minnesota: Liturgical.

Evans, C.
1989 Jesus' Action in the Temple: Cleansing or Portent of Destruction? *Catholic Biblical Quarterly* 51:237-270.
1995 *Jesus and His Contemporaries: Comparative Studies.* Leiden: Brill.

Evans, C. and S. Porter, editors
2000 *Dictionary of New Testament Background.* Downers Grove: InterVarsity.

Farmer, W.
1999 *Anti-Judaism and the Gospels.* Valley Forge: Trinity Press International.

Feldman, L.
1987 Is the New Testament Anti-Semitic? *Humanities* 21:1-14.

Fenton, J.
1963 *The Gospel of St. Matthew.* Pelican New Testament Commentaries. New York: Penguin.

Filson, F.
1960 *A Commentary on the Gospel According to St. Matthew.* Harper's New Testament Commentaries. New York: Harper.

Fitzmeyer, J.
1997 *The Semitic Background of the New Testament.* Grand Rapids: Eerdmans. This edition combines the previous works, *Essays on the Semitic Background of the New Testament* (Missoula: Scholars, 1974) and *A Wandering Aramean* (Missoula: Scholars, 1979).

Flusser, D.
1975 Two Anti-Jewish Montages in Matthew. *Immanuel* 5:37-45.

Fowler, H.
1968 *The Gospel of Matthew.* 4 vols. Joplin: College.

France, R.
1982 *Jesus and the Old Testament.* Grand Rapids: Baker.

1985 *Matthew.* Tyndale New Testament Commentary. Leicester: InterVarsity.

1989 *Matthew: Evangelist and Teacher.* Grand Rapids: Zondervan.

Freedman, D. N., editor

1992 *The Anchor Bible Dictionary.* 5 vols. New York: Doubleday.

Furnish, V.

1972 *The Love Command in the New Testament.* Nashville: Abingdon.

Gardner, R. B.

1991 *Matthew.* Believer's Church Bible Commentary. Scottdale: Herald Press.

Garland, D.

1979 *The Intention of Matthew 23.* Studien zum Neuen Testament 52. Leiden: Brill.

1993 *Reading Matthew.* New York: Crossroad.

Gaston, L.

1970 *No Stone on Another: Studies in the Significance of the Fall of Jerusalem.* Novum Testamentum Supplement Series 23. Leiden: Brill.

Gerhardsson, B.

1979 *The Mighty Acts of God according to Matthew.* Lund: Gleerup.

Goulder, M.

1974 *Midrash and Lection in Matthew.* London: SPCK.

Gray, S. W.

1989 *The Least of my Brothers; Matthew 25:31-46: A History of Interpretation.* Atlanta: Scholars Press.

Green, J. and S. McKnight, editors

1992 *Dictionary of Jesus and the Gospels.* Downers Grove: InterVarsity.

Green, M.

1988 *Matthew for Today.* Dallas: Word.

Guelich, R.

1976 The Matthean Beatitudes: "Entrance Requirements" or Eschatological Blessings? *Journal of Biblical Literature* 95:415-434.

1982 *The Sermon on the Mount.* Waco: Word.

1991 The Gospel Genre. In *The Gospel and the Gospels,* editor, P. Stuhlmacher, 173-208. Grand Rapids: Eerdmans.

Gundry, R.

1967 *The Use of the OT in St. Matthew's Gospel.* Studien zum Neuen Testament 18. Leiden: Brill.

1975 *Use of the Old Testament in St. Matthew's Gospel with Reference to Messianic Hope.* Leiden: Brill.

1982, 1994 *Matthew: A Commentary on His Literary and Theological Art.* Grand Rapids: Eerdmans.

Hagner, D.

1984 *The Jewish Reclamation of Jesus: An Analysis and Critique of Modern Jewish Study of Jesus.* Grand Rapids: Zondervan.

1993, 1995 *Matthew,* 2 vols. Word Biblical Commentary. Dallas: Word.

Hare, Douglas

1967 *The Theme of Jewish Persecution of Christians in the Gospel according to Matthew.* Society for New Testament Studies Monograph Series 6. Cambridge: Cambridge University Press.

1993 *Matthew.* Interpretation. Louisville: Knox.

Hare, D. and D. Harrington

1975 Make Disciples of All the Gentiles (Matthew 28:19). *Catholic Biblical Quarterly* 37:359-369.

Harrington, D.

1991 *The Gospel of Matthew.* Sacra Pagina. Collegeville, Minnesota: Liturgical.

Hartman, L.

1966 *Prophecy Interpreted: The Formation of Some Jewish Apocalyptic Texts and of the Eschatological Discourse of Mark 13.* Lund: Gleerup.

1972 Scriptural Exegesis in the Gospel of Matthew and the Problem of Communication. In *L'Evangile selon Matthieu: Rédaktion et Théologie,* editor, M. Didier, 31-52. Paris: Gembloux.

Hawthorne, G.
1991 *The Presence and the Power.* Dallas: Word.
Hay, D.
1973 *Glory at the Right Hand: Psalm 110 in Early Christian Literature.* Nashville: Abingdon.
Hendriksen, W.
1973 *The Gospel of Matthew.* Grand Rapids: Baker.
Hengel, M.
1977 *Crucifixion in the Ancient World.* Philadelphia: Fortress.
Heth, W. and G. Wenham
1984 *Jesus and Divorce.* London: Hodder.
Hiers, R.
1985 "Binding" and "Loosing": The Matthean Authorizations. *Journal of Biblical Literature* 104:233-250.
Hill, D.
1972 *The Gospel of Matthew.* New Century Bible Commentary. Grand Rapids: Eerdmans.
Hoch, C.
1995 *All Things New: The Significance of Newness for Biblical Theology.* Grand Rapids: Baker.
Hoehner, H.
1972 *Herod Antipas: A Contemporary of Jesus Christ.* Grand Rapids: Zondervan.
1976 *Chronological Aspects of the Life of Christ.* Grand Rapids: Zondervan.
Horsley, R. A.
1989 *The Liberation of Christmas: The Infancy Narratives in Social Context.* New York: Continuum.
Howard, G.
1987 *The Gospel of Matthew according to a Primitive Hebrew Text.* Macon: Mercer.
Howell, D.
1990 *Matthew's Inclusive Story.* Sheffield: Sheffield Academic Press.
Hultgren, A.
1979 *Jesus and His Adversaries: The Form and Function of the Conflict Stories in the Synoptic Tradition.* Minneapolis: Augsburg.
2000 *The Parables of Jesus: A Commentary.* Grand Rapids: Eerdmans.
Jeremias, J.
1955 *The Eucharistic Words of Jesus.* New York: Macmillan.
1967 *The Prayers of Jesus.* London: SCM.
Johnson, L.
1989 The New Testament's Anti-Jewish Slander and the Conventions of Ancient Rhetoric. *Journal of Biblical Literature* 108:419-441.
Kaiser, W.
1982 The Arrival of Elijah in Malachi and the Gospels. *Grace Theological Journal* 3:221-233.
Keener, C. S.
1999 *A Commentary on the Gospel of Matthew.* Grand Rapids: Eerdmans.
2000 *The NIV Application Commentary: Revelation.* Grand Rapids: Zondervan.
Kennard, J.
1950 *Render to God: A Study of the Tribute Passage.* New York: Oxford.
Kik, J.
1948 *Matthew Twenty-Four.* Philadelphia: Presbyterian and Reformed.
Kilpatrick, G.
1946 *The Origins of the Gospel according to Matthew.* Oxford: Clarendon.
Kingsbury, J.
1975 *Matthew: Structure, Christology, Kingdom.* Minneapolis: Fortress.
1979 The Figure of Peter in Matthew's Gospel as a Theological Problem. *Journal of Biblical Literature* 98:67-69.
1986 *Matthew.* Philadelphia: Fortress.

1987 The Developing Conflict between Jesus and the Jewish Leaders in Matthew's Gospel: A Literary-Critical Study. *Catholic Biblical Quarterly* 49:57-73.

1988 *Matthew as Story.* Philadelphia: Fortress.

1993 *Matthew.* Interpretation. Louisville: Knox.

Kissinger, W.

1975 *The Sermon on the Mount: A History of Interpretation and Bibliography.* Metuchen: Scarecrow.

Laansma, J.

1997 *I will give you rest: The 'Rest' Motif in the New Testament with Special Reference to Matthew 11 and Hebrews 3–4.* Tubingen: Mohr/Siebeck.

Lachs, S.

1987 *A Rabbinic Commentary on the New Testament: The Gospels of Matthew, Mark, and Luke.* Hoboken: KTAV.

Ladd, G.

1974 *The Presence of the Future.* Grand Rapids: Eerdmans.

Lampe, G. and K. Woollcombe

1957 *Essays on Typology.* Studies in Biblical Theology 22. Naperville: Allenson.

Lenski, R.

1961 *The Interpretation of St. Matthew's Gospel.* Minneapolis: Augsburg.

Levine, A.

1988 *The Social and Ethnic Dimensions of Matthean Salvation History: Go nowhere among the Gentiles.* Lewiston, NY: Mellen.

Lightfoot, J.

1997 *A Commentary on the New Testament from the Talmud and Hebraica.* 4 vols. Peabody, MA: Hendrickson (Orig. pub. c1675).

Linnemann, E.

1992 *Is There a Synoptic Problem?* Trans. R. Yarbrough. Grand Rapids: Baker.

Lloyd-Jones, D. M.

1981 *Studies in the Sermon on the Mount.* Grand Rapids: Eerdmans.

Loewe, H.

1940 *Render unto Caesar: Religious and Political Loyalty in Palestine.* Cambridge: Cambridge University Press.

Luz, U.

1989 *Matthew 1-7: A Commentary.* Trans., W. Linss. Minneapolis: Augsburg.

1994 *Matthew in History: Interpretation, Influence, and Effects.* Minneapolis: Augsburg.

1995 *The Theology of the Gospel of Matthew.* Cambridge: Cambridge University Press.

2001 *Matthew 8-20.* Trans., J. Crouch. Hermeneia. Minneapolis: Fortress.

Malina, B.

1990 Jewish Christianity or Christian Judaism: Toward a Hypothetical Definition. *Journal for the Study of Judaism* 7:46-57.

Malina, B. and J. Neyrey

1988 *Calling Jesus Names: The Social Value of Labels in Matthew.* Sonoma: Polebridge.

Mann, J.

1924 Rabbinic Studies in the Synoptic Gospels. *Hebrew Union College Annual* 1:323-355.

Marshall, I.

1978 *The Gospel of Luke.* Grand Rapids: Eerdmans.

1980 *Last Supper and Lord's Supper.* Grand Rapids: Eerdmans.

Massaux, Edouard

1990 The First Ecclesiastical Writers. Vol. 1 of *The Influence of the Gospel of Saint Matthew on Christian Literature before Saint Irenaeus.* Translators, N. Belval and S. Hecht. Macon: Mercer.

McCasland, S.

1961 Matthew Twists the Scripture. *Journal of Biblical Literature* 80:143-148.

McConnell, R.

1969 *Law and Prophecy in Matthew's Gospel.* Basel: Reinhardt.

McGuckin, J.
1986 *The Transfiguration of Christ in Scripture and Tradition.* Lewiston: Mellen.

McKnight, S.
1991 *A Light among the Gentiles: Jewish Missionary Activity in the Second Temple Period.* Minneapolis: Fortress.

1993 A Loyal Critic: Matthew's Polemic with Judaism in Theological Perspective. In *Anti-Semitism and Early Christianity: Issues of Polemic and Faith*, ed. C. Evans and D. Hagner, 55–79. Minneapolis: Fortress.

McNeile, A.
1949 *The Gospel according to St. Matthew.* London: Macmillan.

Meeks, W. and R. Wilken
1978 *Jews and Christians in Antioch in the First Four Centuries of the Common Era.* Society of Biblical Literature Sources for Biblical Study 13. Missoula: Scholars Press.

Meier, J.
1976 *Law and History in St. Matthew's Gospel: A Redactional Study of Matt 5:17–48.* Rome: Biblical Institute.

1978 *The Vision of Matthew: Christ, Church, and Morality in the First Gospel.* New York: Paulist.

1980 *Matthew.* Wilmington: Glazier.

Menninger, R.
1994 *Israel and the Church in the Gospel of Matthew.* New York: Peter Lang.

Metzger, B.
1951 The Formulas Introducing Quotations of Scripture in the New Testament and in the Mishnah. *Journal of Biblical Literature* 70:297–307.

1971 *A Textual Commentary on the Greek New Testament.* London: United Bible Societies.

1994 *A Textual Commentary on the Greek New Testament* (2nd edition). Stuttgart: Deutsche Bibelgesellschaft.

Miller, R.
1988 The Rejection of the Prophets in Q. *Journal of Biblical Literature* 107:225–240.

Montefiore, C. and H. Loewe
1974 *A Rabbinic Anthology.* New York: Schocken.

Morris, L.
1992 *The Gospel according to Matthew.* Grand Rapids: Eerdmans.

Moule, C.
1968 Fulfillment-Words in the New Testament: Use and Abuse. *New Testament Studies* 14:293–320.

Mounce, R.
1985 *Matthew.* Good News Commentary. San Francisco: Harper.

Neusner, J.
1973 *From Politics to Piety.* Englewood Cliffs: Doubleday.

Neusner, J. and E. Frerichs
1985 *To See Ourselves as Others See Us: Christians, Jews, "Others" in Late Antiquity.* Chico: Scholars Press.

Newport, K.
1995 *The Sources and Sitz im Leben of Matthew 23.* Journal for the Study of the New Testament Supplement Series 117. Sheffield: Sheffield Academic Press.

Niedner, F.
1989 Rereading Matthew on Jerusalem and Judaism. *Biblical Theology Bulletin* 19:43–47.

Nolland, J.
2005 *The Gospel According to Matthew.* New International Greek Testament Commentary. Grand Rapids: Eerdmans.

Orton, D.
1989 *The Understanding Scribe: Matthew and the Apocalyptic Ideal.* Sheffield: Sheffield Academic Press.

Osborne, G.
1984 *The Resurrection Narratives: A Redactional Study.* Grand Rapids: Baker.

Osborne, R.
1973 The Provenance of Matthew's Gospel. *Studies in Religion* 3:220-235.

Overman, J.
1990a Heroes and Villains in Palestinian Lore: Matthew's Use of Traditional Jewish Polemic in the Passion Narrative. In *Society of Biblical Literature 1990 Seminar Papers*, ed. D. J. Lull, 592-602. Atlanta: Scholars Press.

1990b *Matthew's Gospel and Formative Judaism*. Minneapolis: Fortress.

1996 *Church and Community in Crisis: The Gospel according to Matthew*. Valley Forge: Trinity.

Patte, D.
1987 *The Gospel according to Matthew: A Structural Commentary on Matthew's Faith*. Philadelphia: Fortress.

1988 Anti-Semitism in the New Testament: Confronting the Dark Side of Paul's and Matthew's Teaching. *Chicago Theological Seminary Register* 78:31-52.

1996 *Discipleship according to the Sermon on the Mount*. Valley Forge: Trinity.

Perlewitz, M.
1988 *The Gospel of Matthew*. Wilmington: Glazier.

Plummer, A.
1915 *An Exegetical Commentary on the Gospel According to St. Matthew*. London: R. Scott.

Plumptre, E.
1957 *The Gospel according to Matthew*. Grand Rapids: Zondervan. (Orig. Pub. c1902)

Powell, M.
1990 *What is Narrative Criticism?* Minneapolis: Fortress.

Pritz, R.
1988 *Nazarene Jewish Christianity: From the End of the New Testament until Its Disappearance in the Fourth Century*. Studia Postbiblica 37. Leiden: Brill.

Przybylski, B.
1980 *Righteousness in Matthew and in His World of Thought*. New York: Cambridge University Press.

1988 The Setting of Matthean Anti-Judaism. In *Anti-Judaism in Early Christianity*, ed. P. Richardson and O. Granskou, 181-200. Waterloo: Laurier.

Ridderbos, H. N.
1987 *Matthew*. Trans., R. Togtman. Grand Rapids: Zondervan.

Reinhartz, A.
1988 The New Testament and Anti-Judaism: A Literary-Critical Approach. *Journal of Ecumenical Studies* 25:524-537.

Rist, J.
1978 *On the Independence of Matthew and Mark*. Cambridge: Cambridge University.

Robinson, J.
1970 *Redating the New Testament*. London: SCM.

Robinson, T.
1928 *The Gospel of Matthew*. Moffatt New Testament Commentary. London: Hodder.

Ruckstuhl, E.
1965 *Chronology of the Last Days of Jesus*. New York: Desclee.

Russell, E.
1982 The Image of the Jew in Matthew's Gospel. *Studia Evangelica* 7:427-442.

1986 "Anti-Semitism" in the Gospel of Matthew. *Irish Biblical Studies* 8:183-196.

Ryken, L.
1984 *How to Read the Bible as Literature*. Grand Rapids: Zondervan

Saldarini, A.
1992a Delegitimation of Leaders in Matthew 23. *Catholic Biblical Quarterly* 54:659-680.

1992b The Gospel of Matthew and Jewish-Christian Conflict in the Galilee. In *The Galilee in Late Antiquity*, ed. L. Levine, 23-38. Cambridge, MA: Harvard.

1994 *Matthew's Christian-Jewish Community*. Chicago: University of Chicago.

Sanders, E. P.
1981 *Jewish and Christian Self-Definition.* Vol. 2 of *Aspects of Judaism in the Graeco-Roman Period.* London: SCM.

Sanders, J.
1992a Christians and Jews in the Roman Empire: A Conversation with Rodney Stark. *Sociological Analysis* 53:433-445.

1992b Jewish Christianity in Antioch before the Time of Hadrian: Where Does the Identity Lie? In *Society of Biblical Literature 1992 Seminar Papers,* ed. H. Lovering, Jr., 346-361. Atlanta: Scholars Press.

1993 *Schismatics, Sectarians, Dissidents, Deviants: The First Hundred Years of Jewish-Christian Relations.* Valley Forge: Trinity.

Sandmel, S.
1978 *Anti-Semitism in the New Testament?* Philadelphia: Fortress.

Schaberg, J.
1987 *The Illegitimacy of Jesus.* San Francisco: Harper.

Schiffman, L.
1981 Jewish Sectarianism in Second Temple Times. In *Great Schisms in Jewish History,* ed. R. Jospe and R. Wagner, 1-46. New York: KTAV.

Schnabel, E. J.
2004 *Early Christian Mission.* 2 vols. Downers Grove: InterVarsity.

Schweizer, E.
1975 *The Good News According to Matthew.* Atlanta: John Knox.

Senior, D.
1975 *The Passion Narrative according to St. Matthew.* Bibliotheca Ephemeridum Theologicarum Lovaniensium 39. Leuren: Leuren University.

1983 *What Are They Saying about Matthew?* New York: Paulist.

1985 *The Passion of Jesus in the Gospel of Matthew.* Wilmington: Glazier.

Shuler, P.
1982 *A Genre for the Gospels: The Biographical Character of Matthew.* Philadelphia: Fortress.

Sigal, P.
1986 *The Halakah of Jesus of Nazareth according to the Gospel of Matthew.* Lanham: University Press of America.

Sim, D.
1995 The Gospel of Matthew and the Gentiles. *Journal for the Study of the New Testament* 57:19-48.

1996a *Apocalyptic Eschatology in the Gospel of Matthew.* Society for New Testament Studies Monograph Series 88. Cambridge: Cambridge University Press.

1996b Christianity and Ethnicity in the Gospel of Matthew. In *Ethnicity and the Bible,* ed. Mark G. Brett, 171-195. Leiden: Brill.

1998 *The Gospel of Matthew and Christian Judaism.* Edinburgh: Clark.

Simonetti, M., editor
2001 *Matthew 1-13.* Ancient Christian Commentary on Scripture. Downers Grove: InterVarsity.

2002 *Matthew 14-28.* Ancient Christian Commentary on Scripture. Downers Grove: InterVarsity.

Slingerland, H.
1979 The Transjordanian Origin of Matthew's Gospel. *Journal for the Study of the New Testament* 3:18-28.

Smith, M.
1968 *Tannaitic Parallels to the Gospels.* Philadelphia: Society of Biblical Literature.

Smith, R.
1989 *Matthew.* Minneapolis: Augsburg.

Snodgrass, K.
1983 *The Parable of the Wicked Tenants.* Tübingen: Mohr (Siebeck).

Soarés-Prabhu, G.
1976 *The Formula Quotations in the Infancy Narratives of Saint Matthew's Gospel.* Anacleta Biblica 63. Rome: Biblical Institute.

Sproul, R. C.
1998 *The Last Days According to Jesus.* Grand Rapids: Baker.

Stanton, G.
1983 *The Interpretation of Matthew.* Philadelphia: Fortress.
1985 The Origin and Purpose of Matthew's Gospel: Matthean Scholarship from 1945-80. In *Aufstieg und Niedergang der römischen Welt* 2.25.3, ed. H. Temporini and W. Haase, 1891-1951. Berlin: De Gruyter.
1992 *A Gospel for a New People: Studies in Matthew.* Edinburgh: Clark.
1994 Revisiting Matthew's Communities. In *Society of Biblical Literature 1994 Seminar Papers,* ed. E. Lovering, 9-23. Atlanta: Scholars.

Stendahl, K.
1968 *The School of St. Matthew and Its Use of the Old Testament.* Philadelphia: Fortress.

Stoldt, H.
1980 *History and Criticism of the Marcan Hypothesis.* Trans. D. Niewyk. Macon: Mercer.

Stonehouse, N.
1979 *The Witness of the Synoptic Gospels to Christ.* Grand Rapids: Baker. (Orig. pub. as *The Witness of Matthew and Mark to Christ,* 1944; and *The Witness of Luke to Christ,* 1951.)

Stott, J. R. W.
1978 *Christian Counter-Culture.* Downers Grove: InterVarsity.

Suggs, M.
1970 *Wisdom, Christology, and Law in Matthew's Gospel.* Cambridge, MA: Harvard.

Talbert, C.
1977 *What is a Gospel? The Genre of the Canonical Gospels.* Philadelphia: Fortress.

Tasker, R.
1961 *The Gospel According to St. Matthew.* Tyndale New Testament Commentary. Grand Rapids: Eerdmans.

Taylor, J. E.
1997 *The Immerser: John the Baptist within Second Temple Judaism.* Grand Rapids: Eerdmans.

Telford, William
1980 *The Barren Temple and the Withered Fig Tree.* Journal for the Study of the New Testament Supplement Series 1. Sheffield: JSOT Press.

Thomas, R. L.
2002 *Three Views on the Origins of the Synoptic Gospels.* Grand Rapids: Kregel.

Toussaint, S.
1980 *Behold the King: A Study of Matthew.* Portland: Multnomah.

Trautman, D.
1966 *The Eunuch Logion of Matthew 19:12: Historical and Exegetical Dimensions as Related to Celibacy.* Rome: Catholic Book Agency.

Trevett, C.
1984 Approaching Matthew from the Second Century: The Under-Used Ignatian Correspondence. *Journal for the Study of the New Testament* 20:59-67.

Tuckett, C., editor
1983 *The Messianic Secret.* Philadelphia: Fortress.

Turner, D.
1989 The Structure and Sequence of Matthew 24:1—Interaction with Evangelical Treatments. *Grace Theological Journal* 10:3-27.
1991 *Primus inter Pares?* Peter in the Gospel of Matthew. In *New Testament Essays in Honor of Homer A. Kent Jr.,* ed. Gary T. Meadors, 179-201. Winona Lake: BMH.
1992a The New Jerusalem in Revelation 21:1—22:5: Consummation of a Biblical Continuum. In *Dispensationalism, Israel, and the Church: The Search for Definition,* ed. C. Blaising and D. Bock, 264-292. Grand Rapids: Zondervan.
1992b Whom Does God Approve? The Context, Structure, Purpose, and Exegesis of Matthew's Beatitudes. *Criswell Theological Review* 6:29-42.
2002 Matthew 21:43 and the Future of Israel. *Bibliotheca Sacra* 159:46-61.

Van Tilborg, S.
1972 *The Jewish Leaders in Matthew.* Leiden: Brill.

Verseput, D.
1986 *The Rejection of the Humble Messianic King: A Study of the Composition of Matthew 11–12.* Frankfurt: Peter Lang.

Viviano, B.
1979 Where Was the Gospel according to St. Matthew Written? *Catholic Biblical Quarterly* 41:533–546.

Walker, L.
2005 *Isaiah* in Cornerstone Biblical Commentary, vol. 11. Carol Stream: Tyndale House.

Walton, J. H.
1987 Isa 7:14: What's in a Name? Journal of the Evangelical Theological Society 30:289–306.

Walvoord, J. F.
974 *Matthew: thy kingdom come.* Chicago: Moody Press.

Weinfield, M.
1990 The Charge of Hypocrisy in Matthew 23 and in Jewish Sources. *Immanuel* 24/25:52–58.
1997 The Jewish Roots of Matthew's Vitriol. *Bible Review* 13:5.

Wenham, D.
1979 The Structure of Matthew 13. *New Testament Studies* 25:516–522.
1984a *Easter Enigm.* Exeter: Paternoster.
1984b *The Rediscovery of Jesus' Eschatological Discourse.* Sheffield: Sheffield Academic Press.

Wilkins, M.
1988 *The Concept of Disciple in Matthew's Gospel.* Leiden: Brill.

Wilkins, M. and J. Moreland, editors
1995 *Jesus under Fire.* Grand Rapids: Zondervan.

Willis, J. T.
1978 The Meaning of of Isaiah 7:14 and Its Application in Matthew 1:23. Restoration Quarterly 21:1–18.

Wilson, M.
1989 *Our Father Abraham.* Grand Rapids: Eerdmans.

Winkle, R.
1986 The Jeremiah Model for Jesus in the Temple. *Andrews University Seminary Studies* 24:155–172.

The Gospel of
Mark

DARRELL L. BOCK

INTRODUCTION TO
Mark

TODAY, THE GOSPEL OF MARK is generally regarded as the first Gospel to have been written (Stein 1987; Brown 1997:99-125; Guthrie 1990:136-208). Most of the church fathers of the first five centuries held that Matthew was the earliest Gospel, possibly because of its direct apostolic roots (see Irenaeus *Against Heresies* 3.1.1-2; Tertullian *Against Marcion* 4.2.1-5; Papias, as cited in Eusebius *Ecclesiastical History* 7.39.16; for evaluation, see Bock 2002a:163-165). However, the connection between Mark and the apostle Peter is also consistently affirmed by early church tradition, which helps to explain how a Gospel written by a non-apostolic figure became a part of the New Testament canon.

The belief that Mark is our earliest Gospel emerges from several factors: (1) Mark's outline seems to be fundamental to the basic structure of the three synoptic Gospels. In other words, when Matthew is not going his own way, he seems to be following Mark, and the same is true of Luke. This means that Mark is probably either our first written Gospel or the last of the Synoptics. (2) Mark says critical things about the disciples that are softened in the other Gospels. Textually, it seems more likely that later authors would remove or downplay such transparent failures (as Matthew and Luke do) than that a later author would add these accounts (thus, their presence in Mark argues against it being the third Gospel written). (3) Mark is the shortest Gospel, but in the accounts that are parallel to the other Gospels, it generally gives more detail. This makes it unlikely that Mark is a "summary" Gospel following Matthew and Mark. (4) Mark is an "action" Gospel, lacking much of the key discourse material found in the other Gospels. Again, if Mark were writing last and summarizing the other Gospels, it is hard to explain these omissions; there is no infancy account or evidence of a Sermon on the Mount or Plain. Since Mark was probably our first written Gospel, his outline has often been important in recent efforts to present the life of Christ, even though sections of it are probably not arranged chronologically but topically (e.g., the conflicts of Mark 2–3).

As with the other Gospels, discussions about authorship, date, and audience revolve around external testimony from witnesses in the later church and inferences based on internal features of the Gospel (for all the options discussed regarding these areas, see Guelich 1989: xxv-xxxii).

AUTHOR

As with the other Gospels, the author does not name himself in his work. We need to look to other sources to discover the author of this Gospel. Its association with Mark comes to us through early church testimony (Gundry 1993:1026-1045; Taylor 1966:1-8). According to Eusebius, Papias described Mark as Peter's interpreter (*Ecclesiastical History* 3.39.15). These remarks of Papias are often dated around AD 140, although some argue that they could actually be from as much as thirty years earlier, since Papias is associated with Polycarp, Ignatius, and Clement of Rome, and Eusebius's discussion precedes his mention of Emperor Trajan's persecution of around AD 110 (Gundry 1993:1027-1028). Papias claims that what he says goes back to John the elder (probably the apostle John), which moves the source of the information back one generation from his report. (Gundry, 1993:1032-1033, also discusses and rejects Eusebius's distinction between John the apostle and John the elder.) This remark places us at the end of the first century. Papias, as reported by Eusebius, claimed that

> Mark having become the interpreter of Peter, wrote down accurately, though not in order, whatsoever he remembered of the things said or done by Christ. For he neither heard the Lord nor followed him, but afterward, as I said, he followed Peter, who adapted his teaching to the needs of his hearers, but with no intention of giving a connected account of the Lord's discourses, so that Mark committed no error while he thus wrote some things as he remembered them. For he was careful of one thing, not to omit any of the things which he had heard, and not to state any of them falsely.

We have other sources beyond Papias. The Anti-Marcionite Prologue (about AD 180), Irenaeus (*Against Heresies* 3.1.1-2), and Clement of Alexandria (*Ecclesiastical History* 6.14.6) confirm this identification. Clement is reported to have said the following concerning Mark:

> The Gospel according to Mark had this occasion. As Peter had preached the word publicly at Rome, and declared the Gospel by the Spirit, many who were present requested that Mark, who had followed him for a long time and remembered his sayings, should write them out. And having composed the Gospel he gave it to those who had requested it.

Irenaeus wrote that "after their [Peter and Paul's] departure, Mark, the disciple and interpreter of Peter, did also hand down to us in writing what had been preached by Peter." The Prologue calls Mark "stump-fingered," giving us one of the most vivid and famous descriptions of any evangelist. Justin Martyr suggests that Mark was connected to Peter. In an allusion to Mark in Martyr's *Dialogue with Trypho* 106, he calls material from Mark 3:17 "the memoirs of him," referring to Peter. The superscriptions also confirm this connection (Hengel 1985:74-81). There is no external evidence for any other author. Taylor concludes, "There can be no doubt that the author of the Gospel was Mark, the attendant of Peter." The conclusion that the author was Mark "may be accepted as sound" (Taylor 1966:26).

Many people identify Mark as John Mark, a known assistant to Peter, Paul, and Barnabas (Acts 12:12, 25; 13:13; 15:37-39; Col 4:10; 2 Tim 4:11; Phlm 24; 1 Pet 5:13). Mark was a common name, so this conclusion is dependent to some degree on early church testimony and on the association of John Mark with both Peter and Paul. There are, however, no good alternatives to this conclusion (Blomberg 1997:124).

DATE

Determining Mark's date is somewhat difficult because the external testimony is not in agreement. Irenaeus, in *Against Heresies* 3.1.1-2, places the composition after the deaths of Peter and Paul around the late 60s, while Clement of Alexandria, as cited by Eusebius in *Ecclesiastical History* 2.15.2, dates it during Peter's and Paul's time in Rome, which could push the date back into the 50s. Most commentators opt for a date in the AD 65–70 range, while others place Mark just after AD 70. Those opting for the post-70 date argue unpersuasively that Mark 13, with its "prediction" of Jerusalem's destruction, must have a post-AD 70 perspective, since they view the account as "prophecy historicized." There is nothing in Mark 13 that points to such an "after the fact" prophecy. Rather, the chapter reflects the language of a covenantal judgment of God for covenantal unfaithfulness, something the exilic and post-exilic prophets taught (Gundry 1993:1042). However, if one accepts the testimony of Clement of Alexandria that Peter ratified Mark's work, then a date in the late 50s to mid-60s is possible. A mid- to late 60s date argues that although Mark got his material from Peter, he took some time to compile and compose his Gospel. A date in the late 50s or early 60s is a good possibility, but one in the mid- to late 60s is also possible, although the impact of that date is to push Matthew and Luke beyond AD 70, which may be too late for those gospels. (On how AD 70 relates to the date of the gospels, see my introduction to Luke in Bock 1994.) As with each Gospel, the discussion turns on what part of the external testimony one accepts, as well as on one's view of the order and date of composition among the Gospels.

AUDIENCE

The same text from Clement locates the Gospel's original audience in Rome. Later tradition claims a setting as far away as Egypt (John Chrysostom *Homilies on Matthew* 1.3). However, the Latinisms in the book suggest Rome as the most likely locale, and this also finds support in Mark's emphasis on suffering. The community in Rome experienced pressure both from Jews and from the empire (there was Roman pressure on the Jews in AD 49 and Nero persecuted Christians in AD 64). The Gospel of Mark indicates the tension that existed between the disciples and the Jews, especially those in charge of Judaism, realities that may well explain the Gospel's emphasis on suffering. The early Roman Christian community was being made aware that they could not follow Jesus without suffering just as the rejected Jesus himself suffered (10:35-45). They also were being shown that discipleship failures in their past could be overcome by the same power that enabled Jesus to endure the cross.

OCCASION AND PURPOSE OF WRITING

Given the emphasis on suffering in Mark, this Gospel was probably associated with a period of persecution, especially against the church in Rome (Lane 1974:24-25). The Gospel should, then, encourage Christians who suffer for their faith. The fact that Nero burned Christians, blaming them for the great fire in Rome, underscores the severity of the situation (Suetonius *Nero* 38). Christians were also disliked because they refused to share in the adulation and worship of the emperor that were part of Roman nationalism. They were seen as disloyal citizens.

For Mark, the Roman conflict was less important than the larger spiritual battle with Satan and the forces of evil, referred to as early as chapter 1 in the temptation scene and the exorcisms. The Gospel calls its followers to be loyal to the gospel and its message about Jesus. This requires a devoted and sacrificial discipleship (1:17, 20; 2:14; 10:28), one that is supported by the realization that Jesus is indeed all he showed himself to be in his earthly ministry. Jesus' vindication in resurrection is a precursor to his return.

Jesus' nature is revealed as his story is told, not as a secret, but as a gradual disclosure based on what Jesus did more than on what he said (Evans 2001:lxxi-lxxii). Titles for Jesus abound at the end of the Gospel when the disclosure is complete. When Jesus speaks of himself, most of his sayings refer to him as the suffering Son of Man and point to his rejection (Bock 2002b:602). Jesus knew he would suffer, faced this reality, and became the ransom for the world, knowing that God would vindicate him in the end. Those who embrace his Gospel will follow in the same victorious and triumphant way.

CANONICITY AND TEXTUAL HISTORY

The close connection of the Gospel of Mark to Peter explains its acceptance and circulation in the early church. Sometimes people argue that Matthew would never have used this Gospel as a basis for his own Gospel because Matthew was an eyewitness and Mark was not. However, Mark's strong association with Peter gives his Gospel credibility. It must have had apostolic links for the church to welcome it into the basic fourfold Gospel collection—a collection well established by the mid-second century—even though the church readily acknowledged that a non-apostle wrote it.

For solid summaries of the state of the ancient manuscripts of Mark, see Evans (2001:lix-lx). By way of summary, Mark is in only a few papyri: 𝔓45, 𝔓84, and 𝔓88. 𝔓45 (third century) contains Mark 4:36–9:31 and 11:27–12:28 (with lacunae); 𝔓84 (sixth century) preserves Mark 2:2-9 and 6:30-41 (with lacunae); 𝔓88 (fourth century) preserves Mark 2:1-26. Complete manuscripts appear in ℵ (to 16:8), A (to 16:20), B (to 16:8), D (to 16:20), and W (to 16:20). The Alexandrian manuscripts are 𝔓88, A, and B. A few witnesses have been identified as "Caesarean" in the Gospel of Mark. These manuscripts probably came from the text that Origen took with him from Alexandria to Caesarea and bear a mixture of the so-called "Western" and Alexandrian readings. These witnesses are 𝔓45 W (in 5:31–16:20) Θ 28 565 700 f1 f13 arm geo.

LITERARY STYLE

There is a large debate about the genre of "Gospel." Was it a new, unprecedented genre, or was it an extension of biography (Burridge 1992:107-274; Bauckham 1998)? The comparative study by Burridge argues that the closest ancient genre to the Gospels is ancient biography, because of how focused Mark is on describing the activity and teaching of a single figure. It has often been argued that biography is not appropriately compared with the Gospels, but the literary and semantic evidence Burridge brings forth indicates that Mark's form is closest to this category. This means that Mark was concerned to tell us about Jesus and the significance of his person and actions. This is not to say that this Gospel is neutral in its presentation; ancient biography had the goal of lifting up the importance of the figure being discussed, and Mark fits this description well. Unlike modern biography, ancient biography is more focused on a person's actions and teaching than on his psychology. Certain emphases make Mark's work unique and reflect a distinct sub-genre within ancient biography. One important detail about the term "gospel," as it came to be used in the church, is that the superscriptions to the Gospels are worded "the Gospel *according to* Mark," not the "Gospel *of* Mark" (Guelich 1989:xxvi; Hengel 1985:65-67). This implies that there is one gospel in many versions. The one gospel is "of God," and Mark gives but one representation of it, as the mediator of a much larger message. Although Mark's work was probably the first of its kind, it was seen as but one example of the story that emerged from the early church that eventually became known as the "fourfold" gospel—one gospel in four versions.

MAJOR THEMES

Mark begins with a note that what he is telling is "the Good News." As such, Mark's goal was clearly to tell his readers what Jesus was about as he brought the Good News to people and thereby revealed himself as the Christ, the Son of God. Jesus is the story and the point of the story.

To a lesser degree than Matthew or Luke, Mark also traces the Kingdom of God as a theme. For Mark, the Kingdom has elements that indicate its initial presence as immediate, while the bulk of the emphasis is that it will come in fullness one day in the future. Kingdom entry, available now, requires one to be like a child. The "mystery" of the Kingdom is that it starts out small, but will grow into a full harvest, accomplishing all that God has appointed it to. Part of Mark's goal is to explain what Jesus meant by the coming of God's rule and to specify how his coming both does and will fulfill God's plan. Jesus' rejection caused confusion, so Mark explains how a promised Messiah could meet with rejection as a part of God's plan (Guelich 1989:xlii). Mark corrects the danger that some would present the gospel in strictly triumphalist terms, since suffering rejection is also a part of the walk. For a community itself under duress, the cross marks the way ahead.

Mark is more a Gospel of action than of teaching. Things happen "immediately," which is one of Mark's favorite expressions. Mark has only two discourses, one on the parables of the Kingdom (4:1-33) and the eschatological discourse (13:1-37), but miracles abound—Mark includes twenty accounts. Combined with healing summaries, these units comprise a third of the Gospel and are nearly one-half of the first ten chapters (Twelftree 1999:57). These pictures of Jesus are important to Mark as he presents Jesus as one who displays authority both in his actions and his teachings. This authority underscores Jesus' identity as the Messiah (or Christ), the Son of God (1:1; 8:29). Mark's Christology presents Jesus as this promised figure. Jesus' claims of authority over sin, relationships, practices tied to purity, the Sabbath, and the Temple get him into trouble with the Jewish leaders, who soon determine that they must stop him. This conflict emerging from Jesus' claims is also a central feature of Mark's Gospel.

Jesus' authority was not based only on miraculous power. Mark highlights Jesus as the suffering Son of Man and Servant proportionately more than any other Gospel. In fact, nine of thirteen uses of the "Son of Man" title look to Jesus' suffering. Although Isaiah 53 is not cited, the descriptions of Jesus clearly parallel the portrait of the suffering servant, especially in the claim that his mission was to give his life as "a ransom for many" (10:45). The importance of understanding the suffering role probably explains Mark's record of the commands to silence given to those, including demons, who confessed Jesus as Messiah (1:44; 5:43; 9:9). Without an appreciation of his suffering, Jesus' messianic calling is misunderstood. Some have called this the messianic secret, but it was not that Jesus' identity as the Messiah was to be kept a secret but that it was not to be shared until it was more fully understood. Only as the cross drew near did the full scope of his divine promise and calling emerge. The disciples were not in a position to preach Jesus until they appreciated this aspect of his mission. The subsequent mission of the church makes this clear.

The servant Jesus is an example of how to walk with God in a world that rejects those sent by God. Here the pastoral demands of discipleship also appear (10:35-45). Mark is like Matthew in this respect. After suffering come glory and vindication. The same Son of Man will return one day to render judgment, as the eschatological discourse reveals. The need for discipleship and real listening to Jesus emerges clearly within Mark, since the evangelist unhesitatingly narrates the repeated failures of the disciples. Their instincts did not take them in the right direction; trust in God and his ways was required. Mark also notes the emotions of Jesus and the disciples more than any of the other Gospels.

Finally, Mark 6–14 shows that the experience of rejection and suffering challenged even the apostles' committment to discipleship. There is a great deal of discipleship failure in these chapters. The disciples have much to learn and one suspects that Mark wants his readers to identify with the difficulty as a way of gaining strength from the fact that these apostles did overcome their past failures. If

Mark is the John Mark of Acts 13:13, who abandoned Paul under pressure, then the theme may well be a reflection of his own experience and growth—in spite of the account of his failure in Acts, he persevered in discipleship as Colossians 4:10-11 bears witness.

In summary, Mark addresses a church under duress and suffering rejection as their Teacher had before them. The antidote to their stressful situation is to persevere and to look to Jesus as their example. The Gospel of Mark gives us one of the earliest glimpses as to how the church presented Jesus and his life to others who needed to be established in their walk with God.

OUTLINE

Many scholars today regard Mark as the first of the four canonical Gospels to be written. Its outline of Jesus' ministry has become the basic structure through which his life has been traced, even though sections of it are probably given in topical, not chronological, order (e.g., the conflicts of Mark 2–3).

The first major section of this Gospel is on Jesus' public ministry; Mark's account cycles through a consistent structure in each of its three sub-parts. There is a story about the disciples at the beginning (1:16-20; 3:13-19; 6:7-13) and a note about rejection or a summary at the end (3:7-12; 6:1-6; 8:22-26; Guelich 1992:516) of each of these sub-sections.

The turning point of Mark's Gospel is the confession that Jesus is the Christ (8:27-31). Before this confession, there is a miracle in which Jesus gives sight. After the confession comes the repeated information that he will suffer, a point the disciples struggle to grasp. Half of the Gospel treats the movement toward the final week of Jesus' ministry, while a full quarter of it is on the suffering of the last week. For Mark, these events are central to his story and to the theme of Jesus' sufferings.

I. Prologue on the Beginning of the Gospel (1:1-15)
   A. John the Baptist Prepares the Way (1:1-8; cf. Matt 3:1-12; Luke 3:1-14)
   B. The Baptism and Temptation of Jesus (1:9-15; cf. Matt 3:13-17; 4:1-11; Luke 3:21-23; 4:1-13)

II. Jesus' Public Ministry (1:16–8:26)
   A. Calling of Disciples and Beginning of Miracles (1:16–1:45)
      1. The first disciples (1:16-20; cf. Matt 4:18-22)
      2. Jesus casts out an evil spirit (1:21-28)
      3. Jesus' work continues in Capernaum and Galilee (1:29-45)
   B. Controversy Leading to Rejection (2:1–3:12)
      1. The first controversy: Jesus as Son of Man heals a paralytic and forgives sin (2:1-12; cf. Matt 9:1-8; Luke 5:17-26)
      2. The second controversy: Jesus calls Levi and eats with sinners (2:13-17; cf. Matt 9:9-13; Luke 5:27-32)

3. The third controversy: Jesus' disciples did not practice fasting
(2:18-22; cf. Matt 9:14-17; Luke 5:33-39)
4. The fourth controversy: Jesus' disciples violate the Sabbath
(2:23-28; cf. Matt 12:1-8; Luke 6:1-5)
5. The fifth controversy: Jesus heals on the Sabbath (3:1-6;
cf. Matt 12:9-14; Luke 6:6-11)
6. Summary of Jesus' early ministry (3:7-12; cf. Matt 12:15-21;
Luke 6:17-19)
C. Teaching on the Mystery-filled Kingdom and Miracles of Power Yield
Rejection (3:13-6:6a)
1. The choosing of the Twelve (3:13-19; cf. Luke 6:12-16)
2. The debate over Jesus' power: Is it from Satan or from God?
(3:20-30; cf. Matt 12:22-24)
3. Jesus' true family is those who do God's will (3:31-35;
cf. Matt 12:46-50)
4. Parable of the sower (4:1-20; cf. Matt 13:1-9)
5. Parable of the lamp (4:21-25)
6. Parable of the growing seed (4:26-29)
7. The mustard seed and a summary on parables (4:30-34;
cf. Matt 13:31-35)
8. Jesus calms a storm (4:35-41; Luke 8:22-25)
9. The healing of the Gerasene demoniac (5:1-20; cf. Luke 8:26-39)
10. The woman with the hemorrhage and Jairus's daughter (5:21-43;
cf. Luke 8:40-56)
11. Jesus faces rejection at Nazareth (6:1-6a; cf. Matt 13:53-58)
D. Challenge, Misunderstanding, and Confession (6:6b-8:26)
1. The Twelve are sent out (6:6b-13; cf. Luke 9:1-6)
2. The death of John the Baptist (6:14-29; cf. Matt 14:3-12;
Luke 9:7-10)
3. Jesus feeds five thousand (6:30-44; cf. Matt 14:13-21;
Luke 9:10-17; John 6:1-13)
4. Jesus walks on water (6:45-52; cf. Matt 14:22-33; John 6:14-21)
5. Healing of the sick in Gennesaret (6:53-56; cf. Matt 14:34-36)
6. Jesus' views on cleanliness and purity (7:1-23; cf. Matt 15:1-20)
7. The Syrophoenician woman's faith leads to healing (7:24-30;
cf. Matt 15:21-28)
8. Jesus heals a deaf and mute man (7:31-37; cf. Matt 15:29-31)
9. Jesus feeds four thousand (8:1-10; cf. Matt 15:32-39)
10. The Pharisees demand a sign (8:11-13; cf. Matt 16:1-4)
11. Dialogue about yeast among the Pharisees and Herod (8:14-21;
cf. Matt 16:5-12)
12. A blind man's healing at Bethsaida (8:22-26)

III. To Jerusalem, Passion and Vindication (8:27–16:8)
   A. Passion Predictions and Discipleship Teaching (8:27–10:52)
      1. Peter's confession at Caesarea Philippi (8:27-30; cf. Matt 16:13-20; Luke 9:18-21)
      2. Jesus begins to speak about his death and resurrection (8:31-33)
      3. Following Jesus (8:34–9:1; cf. Matt 16:21-28; Luke 9:22-27)
      4. Jesus' transfiguration (9:2-13; cf. Matt 17:1-13; Luke 9:28-36)
      5. Jesus performs an exorcism after the disciples' failure (9:14-29; cf. Matt 17:14-21; Luke 9:37-43)
      6. Jesus predicts his death again (9:30-32; cf. Matt 17:22-27; Luke 9:43-45)
      7. The greatest in the Kingdom (9:33-37; cf. Matt 18:1-14; Luke 9:46-48)
      8. Miscellaneous remarks about relationships and accountability (9:38-50)
      9. Jesus' remarks on divorce (10:1-12; cf. Matt 19:1-12)
      10. Jesus blesses the children (10:13-16; cf. Luke 18:15-17)
      11. Jesus encounters a rich man (10:17-31; cf. Matt 19:16-30; Luke 18:18-30)
      12. Jesus predicts his death again (10:32-34; cf. Matt 20:17-28; Luke 18:31-33)
      13. Jesus teaches about service (10:35-45)
      14. Jesus heals the blind man Bartimaeus (10:46-52; cf. Matt 20:29-33; Luke 18:35-43)
   B. Conflict in Jerusalem and Prediction of Judgment (11:1–13:37)
      1. Jesus' triumphal entry into Jerusalem (11:1-11; cf. Matt 21:1-11; Luke 19:29-44; John 12:12-19)
      2. Jesus curses the fig tree and clears the Temple (11:12-25; cf. Matt 21:12-22; Luke 19:45-48)
      3. Question about the source of Jesus' authority (11:27-33; cf. Matt 21:23-32; Luke 20:1-8)
      4. Parable of the evil tenants (12:1-12; cf. Matt 21:33-46; Luke 20:9-19)
      5. Question concerning paying taxes to Caesar (12:13-17; cf. Matt 22:15-22; Luke 20:20-26)
      6. Question about resurrection (12:18-27; cf. Matt 22:23-33; Luke 20:27-40)
      7. The most important commandment (12:28-34; cf. Matt 22:34-40)
      8. Question about the Messiah (12:35-37; cf. Matt 22:41-46; Luke 20:41-44)
      9. Contrasting the scribes and a widow (12:38-44; cf. Matt 23:1-12; Luke 20:45-47)

COMMENTARY ON
Mark

◆ I. Prologue on the Beginning of the Gospel (1:1-15)
   A. John the Baptist Prepares the Way (1:1-8; cf. Matt 3:1-12;
   Luke 3:1-14)

This is the Good News about Jesus the Messiah, the Son of God.* It began ²just as the prophet Isaiah had written:

"Look, I am sending my messenger
   ahead of you,
   and he will prepare your way.*
³ He is a voice shouting in the
   wilderness,
'Prepare the way for the LORD's
   coming!
Clear the road for him!'*"

⁴This messenger was John the Baptist. He was in the wilderness and preached that people should be baptized to show that they had repented of their sins and turned to God to be forgiven. ⁵All of Judea, including all the people of Jerusalem, went out to see and hear John. And when they confessed their sins, he baptized them in the Jordan River. ⁶His clothes were woven from coarse camel hair, and he wore a leather belt around his waist. For food he ate locusts and wild honey. ⁷John announced: "Someone is coming soon who is greater than I am—so much greater that I'm not even worthy to stoop down like a slave and untie the straps of his sandals. ⁸I baptize you with* water, but he will baptize you with the Holy Spirit!"

1:1 Some manuscripts do not include *the Son of God.*   1:2 Mal 3:1.   1:3 Isa 40:3 (Greek version).   1:8 Or *in;* also in 1:8b.

NOTES

1:1 *Good News.* We get our word "gospel" (BDAG 402-403) from this noun, *euangelion* [TG2098, ZG2295]. Mark narrates this special story of good news centered in the ministry of Jesus the Messiah (the Christ).

about Jesus the Messiah. The NLT correctly renders the objective genitive of the Gr. as "about." In the second century, this expression became a shorthand way of referring to narrative accounts that described Jesus' life and ministry, but it is probably not used in that technical way here. Mark is simply stating that this story is God's good news about how the power of God's coming kingdom and salvation manifested itself in and through Jesus the Christ, who is also the Son of God.

Son of God. There is debate as to whether or not this phrase is in the original text of Mark's gospel. The phrase is missing in some important early witnesses such as ℵ. It is likely that in these cases the phrase was accidentally omitted due to similar endings in the abbreviated forms of the sacred names: ΕΥΑΓΓΕΛΙΟΥ ΙΥ ΧΥ ΥΥ ΘΥ. The last four words look similar because each is written as a *nomen sacrum* (divine title). The first corrector of Codex Sinaiticus (a) added Y̅Y̅ Θ̅Y̅ before it left the scriptorium. However, not all ancient MSS wrote the word "Son" as the *nomen sacrum* Y̅Y̅, so this is not a conclusive argument (see Comfort 2007:[Mark 1:1]). It is more likely that "Son of God" was accidentally dropped than that a copyist expanded the introductory title, especially since the major MSS of B, D, and W support the reading (Metzger 1971:73). The title appears at a few key points in Mark (1:11; 15:39), pointing to the unique, intimate relationship the messianic Jesus had with the Father. Witherington (2001:69) compares this beginning of Mark to the Priene inscription about Caesar Octavian from 9 BC, which also uses the term "good news" and speaks of his birth as "the birthday of the god [that] was for the world the beginning of his good news." This is "the epiphany or advent of a deity" (Witherington 2001:70). Mark's gospel is about a person who makes a similar yet distinct claim to deity, a divine figure different from those Mark's Gentile audience may have been accustomed to hearing about.

1:2 *the prophet Isaiah.* The passage names Isaiah in the introductory formula and cites wording from Exod 23:20, Mal 3:1, and Isa 40:3. Malachi 3 speaks of a prophet to come like Elijah (also 4:5-6), while Exod 23 points to a messenger (lit., "angel") who leads the way. After the citation, Mark comments only on the portion from Isaiah that describes activity "in the wilderness," which explains his introductory formula. This is the only OT citation made by the narrator in this Gospel (Garland 1996:43; the other OT citations in this Gospel are made by Jesus). The point is that the preparation for God starts in the wilderness, as Mark 1:4 makes clear, not that John is a voice crying in the wilderness, as the text is often read (Witherington 2001:72).

1:5 *Jordan River.* The ministry of John the Baptist is traditionally associated with a location south of Jericho near the Wadi-el-Kelt (Guelich 1989:20). The lower Jordan valley was a wilderness and Elijah is also associated with this area (2 Kgs 2:6-14; also Elisha in 2 Kgs 5:8-14). Although Guelich is hesitant to make connections between John and Elijah, it appears that an overlap is likely at a few points in the text, as John's clothing also recalls Elijah's (2 Kgs 1:8, LXX).

1:7 *untie the straps of his sandals.* An important cultural detail; in later Judaism, untying the thong of someone's sandal was considered too menial a task for a Jewish slave to perform (*Mekilta Exodus* 21.2; *b. Ketubbot* 96a). If such an understanding goes back to John's time, then John was saying that the One to come is so great that John is not worthy even to perform the most menial of tasks for him. Thus, by comparison he is less than a slave. This kind of humility appears in John's Gospel (John 3:27-30). The NLT's addition of his not being worthy "even to stoop down like a slave" brings out this nuance.

1:8 *he will baptize you with the Holy Spirit.* This allusion to baptism is associated with the arrival of the eschaton in the OT (Isa 35:15; 44:3; Ezek 11:19; 36:26-27; 37:14; Joel 2:28-29 [3:1-2]). God's decisive act on behalf of humanity was announced as approaching in the baptizing ministry of the Messiah. This is why cleansing (water baptism) and repentance (what that cleansing represents) were part of John's ministry of preparation (1:4). Participation in John's baptism showed a readiness to receive the greater baptism that the coming One would bring. Preparation for forgiveness of sins leads to forgiveness when the greater One to whom John pointed is embraced. In OT thinking, when someone is cleansed and forgiven, God can indwell that person with the presence of his Spirit (Ezek 36:25-27). This summarizes Mark's gospel: cleansing, forgiveness, and the intimate divine presence all come through the Messiah to those who, in faith, embrace repentance and reorientation in their lives. Mark will mention the Spirit only a few more times in his gospel—in connection with Jesus' authority over demons (3:22, 29-30), the Spirit's work through a writer of Scripture (12:36), and the Spirit's speaking through persecuted believers (13:11).

COMMENTARY

The opening of Mark's Gospel contains a title, an appeal to Scripture, and the description of a prophetic figure, John the Baptist, whose calling was to announce the arrival of Jesus the Christ, the key figure in God's plan. Jesus is described as Messiah and Son of God, two major titles that highlight Jesus' uniqueness. "Messiah" signifies his role as the powerful deliverer who rules over the Kingdom and administers the hope, promise, and judgment of God (Cranfield 1959:35). "Son of God" underscores the unique relationship of this regal figure with God. Mark's Gospel will explain his identity as Son as it unfolds.

It is important to read a Gospel as a developing story. Some of what Mark means becomes clear as this theological narrative unfolds, from its beginning to its turning point in the passion and resurrection. Much as a mystery novel develops its various dimensions, the Gospel gains momentum as it portrays Jesus as the Messiah, Son of God. It is important to distinguish between what readers know with the help of Mark's prologue and what the characters within Mark's story knew (Witherington 2001:79). They must learn who Jesus is. Mark's narrative shows how this took place and the different reactions that revelation produced. This key point of the narrative is often lost on readers who have come to understand the whole story ahead of time. As Witherington (2001:79) says, "Seeing the narrative with the benefit of hindsight is a wonderful thing." Even so, keeping an eye on how the narrative develops through the experience of its characters is part of a careful reading. The Gospel narrative works upon its readers on more than one level at once.

Taking into account the verses immediately following this section, we see that in 1:1-13 Mark begins his narrative with a series of events orchestrated by God, foreshadowing for his readers where the whole story is headed (Garland 1996:42). God speaks about his plan from Scripture in 1:2-3. God speaks directly to Jesus from heaven to underscore Jesus' uniqueness in 1:11. The passage in 1:12-13 shows that Jesus was so important that an opponent from the spirit world would try to stop him, as Satan tested Jesus in the wilderness. This "behind the scenes" introduction to the cosmic dimensions of the story underscores Jesus' importance for Mark's readers. Only after this introduction does the story of Jesus' actual ministry begin, showing how people were confronted with who Jesus was. This heavenly vantage point dominates Mark's prologue in a way that is distinct from how most of the rest of the Gospel gradually unveils its story (Hooker 1991:31). Mark thus sets the stage with his prologue much as John's prologue does for his Gospel (John 1:1-18).

The story begins with God's plan as introduced in Scripture, especially in the prophets' predictions of a great day of deliverance, a new day that was being announced as present through a ministry taking place in the desert. Mark highlights Isaiah, but the citation he presents is actually a composite of Exodus 23:20; Malachi 3:1, with its messenger language; and the call for preparation from Isaiah 40:3. John's ministry prepared "the way" for the Lord's coming, like laying a red carpet as all creation was leveled for his entry and hearts were opened to watch for his arrival. The importance of John's ministry in the wilderness is affirmed in the citation and in Mark's exposition of the fulfillment of the passage in 1:4. Israel entered into the promise in the wilderness (Josh 1:11), and it was a destination for a person fleeing from sin (2 Macc 5:27; *Martyrdom of Isaiah* 2:7-11; 1QS 8:12-16; Garland 1996:52-53). Some anticipated that God would launch his great assault on evil from the wilderness (Isa 40:1-11, a "new exodus" deliverance; 1QM 1:2-3). The importance of the way of God is highlighted in the interplay between the "prepare your way" in 1:2 and "prepare the way for the Lord's coming" in 1:3. Preparing the way for the Lord's coming meant being ready to walk in the way he would announce, a way that had already been announced in Scripture.

John the Baptist appeared, just as God had said through Isaiah and others, in the wilderness. Israel came through the wilderness to enter the new land, and now, from the wilderness God announced a plan for another exodus to deliver his people. John was called to deliver a preparatory message; it involved active participation in a rite that signified acceptance and identification with this call. That rite was a cleansing baptism of repentance (the NLT says that the act showed that they had turned to God to "receive forgiveness of sins"). The cleansing rite was preparatory to their reception of forgiveness.

This sequence is made clear when Jesus is baptized and then the Spirit descends on him, so the point was not a "baptism of repentance on the basis of forgiveness of sins." This recognition of need constitutes the "turning" that is so basic to repentance and entrance into a faith relationship with God. (In the Old Testament, the Hebrew word meaning "to turn" was often used to signify repentance; Jer 4:28; 18:8; Jonah 3:9-10; TDNT 4:989-992). The real cleansing and forgiveness would be supplied by Jesus' future work. Forgiveness refers to release from sin, which is often understood as a debt incurred by an act, and here a debt that includes guilt and punishment (3:29; Acts 2:38; Eph 1:7; Heb 9:22). This release from debt was part of what God announced through John as preparatory "good news." Those who were ready for it participated in John's baptism, confessing their sins and thereby recognizing their need of the cleansing the baptism represented. This rite was so central to John's work that Mark literally calls him "John the baptizer" in 1:4, using a participle to make the point. He was the one "who is baptizing."

John attracted a great crowd from Judea and Jerusalem that journeyed out to the southern Jordan River area to hear him. John lived as an ascetic to show his total dependence on God. John was like Elijah at certain points of his ministry (2 Kgs 1:8), a connection that Jesus makes explicit in Mark 9:11-13. It was believed that Elijah would return before the Day of the Lord as a signal that God was about to deliver Israel (Mal 3:1-2; 4:5-6; Sir 48:10).

John's ministry was not just about the arrival of God's promised period of fresh activity, but also about the one who would be central to it. There was "someone . . . coming soon who is greater [mightier] than I." Despite all the prophetic airs surrounding John the Baptist, he was nothing in comparison to the one coming after him. The difference was so great that this prophet saw himself as more lowly than the most menial slave, not even worthy to untie the sandal thong of "the one to come." In *b. Ketubbot* 96a, R. Joshua b. Levi states that "all service that a slave must render to his master a student must render to his teacher, except untying his shoe" (Strack-Billerbeck 1922.1:121). John said that he was not worthy to perform this most humble of tasks for the One to come.

If John was a prophet, then how much greater was the One to come than a prophet? John explained that the coming One would not baptize with a mere symbol as he did. Rather, this greater One would bring the promised Spirit of God (Ezek 36:25-27; Isa 4:4, with an image of fire, which appears in the parallels of Matt 3:11 and Luke 3:16), the sign of God's presence and of the new day God would bring (1QS 4:20-21). What John could only represent in a rite, Jesus performed.

The Gospel is about the new life God gives through Jesus, who brought the divinely promised baptism of the Spirit. Jesus was clearly mightier than John and made the prophet pale by comparison. The cleansing of people's lives cleared the way for God's powerful presence in the Spirit. The good news of the One to come was about the forgiveness of sins that follows repentance and makes it possible to enter into fellowship and life with God by the presence of the promised Spirit within those who are cleansed.

◆ **B. The Baptism and Temptation of Jesus (1:9-15; cf. Matt 3:13-17; 4:1-11; Luke 3:21-23; 4:1-13)**

⁹One day Jesus came from Nazareth in Galilee, and John baptized him in the Jordan River. ¹⁰As Jesus came up out of the water, he saw the heavens splitting apart and the Holy Spirit descending on him* like a dove. ¹¹And a voice from heaven said, "You are my dearly loved Son, and you bring me great joy."

¹²The Spirit then compelled Jesus to go into the wilderness, ¹³where he was tempted by Satan for forty days. He was out among the wild animals, and angels took care of him.

¹⁴Later on, after John was arrested, Jesus went into Galilee, where he preached God's Good News.* ¹⁵"The time promised by God has come at last!" he announced. "The Kingdom of God is near! Repent of your sins and believe the Good News!"

1:10 Or *toward him*, or *into him.* 1:14 Some manuscripts read *the Good News of the Kingdom of God.*

NOTES

1:10 *he saw.* According to Mark, the descent of the Holy Spirit was seen only by Jesus. It was not a public event but God's private affirmation of Jesus.

the heavens splitting apart. Mark uses a very graphic term to describe how the Spirit came upon Jesus. First, he speaks of the heavens splitting apart (*schizomenous* [TG4977, ZG5387]), or being torn open as if God were coming in from outside the earth's sphere and invading its space (BDAG 981). The same verb is used to describe how the veil of the Temple was ripped during the crucifixion (15:38). Many find the background for this in Isa 64:1[63:19b] (TDNT 7:962). Isaiah appealed to God to tear the sky apart and come down to deliver his people. For Mark, the Spirit's descent upon Jesus began to answer that call. One of Mark's key terms, "immediately" (*euthus* [TG2117, ZG2317]), is not translated here in the NLT but should be noted as present in this verse. This is the first of

41 times that Mark uses this word (out of 51 NT uses). Mark notes that the splitting open of the sky happened as soon as Jesus emerged from the water during the baptism.

the Holy Spirit descending on him like a dove. The Spirit descended like the gentle flight of a dove. Mark's point is not that the Spirit looked like a dove but that the Spirit approached him as a dove would.

1:11 *a voice from heaven.* This is God's voice; Mark's prologue continues to emphasize actions from beyond this world. This is not the Jewish *bat qol*, or "daughter of the voice," which is understood as a heavenly substitute for God's voice (Strack-Billerbeck 1922:125-132). This is God directly speaking in the first person about his Son.

dearly loved Son. The citation fuses two OT texts: Ps 2:7 and Isa 42:1. The psalm portrays a king who has a unique relationship to God as his Son. Isaiah describes the Lord's servant as the chosen focus of God's special love. The Gr. word *agapētos* [TG627, ZG28] can have the force of "only" or "unique" (BDAG 7; Gen 22:2, 12, 16) and could mean "the one dear Son."

bring me great joy. God is especially pleased with this person. The remark is an endorsement and a call to be what Jesus is, a Servant-King.

1:12 *compelled.* This is strong language. The Spirit "compelled Jesus to go" to the wilderness, where he met Satan, another cosmic figure. The encounter was not accidental, but would show Jesus' superiority to Adam as a representative of humanity.

1:13 *Satan.* He is the great "adversary," as his name indicates. Satan does not play a major role in Mark, although demonic conflict does. After this scene, he is mentioned only in the dispute over the source of Jesus' healing power (3:23, 26), in the parable of the seed (4:15), and in the rebuke to Peter about Jesus suffering (8:33).

forty days. It is hard to establish whether this number is symbolic: The Israelite nation wandered for forty years (Num 14:34), and Elijah's fast (1 Kgs 19:8) and Moses's time on Mount Sinai (Exod 34:28) both lasted forty days.

among the wild animals. Once again, it is unclear if this detail is symbolic. In Judaism, wild animals were associated with threat or evil; their subjection could represent the defeat of evil and the arrival of the new era (Isa 13:21-22; Ezek 34:5, 8; *Testament of Issachar* 7:7; *Testament of Benjamin* 5:2; *Testament of Naphtali* 8:4; for animals as hostile to people, see *Apocalypse of Moses* 10:1–12:2). Alternatively, wild animals at peace picture an idyllic state (see discussion in France 2002:86) and could be part of a paradise motif (Isa 11:6; *2 Baruch [Syriac Apocalypse]* 73:6; Guelich 1989:38-39). Interestingly, animals are juxtaposed with angels in Ps 91:11-13 (Hooker 1991:50-51).

angels. The angels show God's support of Jesus during this time. Angels also provided sustenance for Elijah (1 Kgs 19:1-8) and, traditionally, for Adam and Eve (*b. Sanhedrin* 59b; cf. *Apocalypse of Moses* 29:1-6; *Life of Adam and Eve* 4:2). This divine care also hints that the new era of restored creation was present in Jesus.

1:14 *Good News.* The Gr. word *euangelion* [TG2098, ZG2295], repeated in 1:15, forms an inclusio with 1:1 and concludes the introduction.

1:15 *The time promised by God.* This phrase renders the idea of an appointed time being fulfilled. In 1:2, Scripture as written by Isaiah is fulfilled; here the appointed and predicted time described by that Scripture is realized. What was written had now come to pass. The conceptual connection forms another inclusio between the beginning and the end of the introduction.

has come at last. This rendering reflects a context in which the "time is fulfilled" and appears to indicate an event that had already been accomplished. The ambiguity of the

Gr. image of "is near" suggests that although the Kingdom had come, its power had not yet been fully manifested (Cranfield 1959:63-68).

Kingdom of God. This is the subject of Jesus' preaching and of the Gospel. It designates the rule of God in which he enacts his redeeming power and presence as he had promised (*basileia*, BAGD 134-135; Bock 2001:28-60). In Jesus, this reality has drawn so near as to be in the process of coming to pass (*engizō*, BAGD 213).

Repent of your sins and believe the Good News. Those who heard Jesus were called to turn from sin and embrace forgiveness as John prepared them to do. They must then believe that the Kingdom had approached and embrace it in faith. Sin could be dealt with because the Promised One of God had appeared in the person of Jesus.

COMMENTARY

Three short, significant scenes conclude the introduction to Mark's Gospel. John the Baptist's preparatory role in Mark concludes with his baptizing Jesus in the Jordan River. John makes only a cameo appearance here; the stars in the baptism are the voice of God and the astonishing appearance of his Spirit descending through the heavenly canopy to invade human space. The transcendent God gave the Spirit to his Son so he could fulfill his call. In a private experience between Father and Son that underscored Jesus' uniqueness, God called Jesus his beloved Son, one on whom his divine pleasure rested. The Spirit's coming marked Jesus as the one equipped for the task.

Mark's report gives his readers a glimpse of the previously hidden inner circle of divine interaction between Father, Son, and Spirit at the commencement of Jesus' ministry. As Son and Servant, Jesus would proclaim God's deliverance and bring it into reality. However, that deliverance would come in ways his audience did not anticipate and with much suffering. Mark will later highlight this unique aspect of Jesus' mission, but he is not to that point yet. Mark's point here is that the Father showed who the "greater" one to come was. The one who would baptize with the Spirit had been equipped by the Spirit. Jesus' submission to this baptism showed how he desired to identify with humanity and its desperate need for forgiveness and new life. Jesus' baptism thus reinforced John's preparatory message even as it set the stage for a decisive new act. The one who possessed God's Spirit would bring John's role to an end.

From this high moment of divine intimacy, Jesus was "compelled" to go into the wilderness to face the hostile forces of a fallen creation. Here he met another cosmic player—Satan, the great adversary. In a tantalizingly brief summary, we are told only that Satan tempted him for forty days, that he was among the wild animals, and that angels cared for him. It is left implicit that the temptations mentioned failed to bring down this new representative of humanity. It is often commented that Mark does not note Jesus' victory, but such a reading fails to penetrate the subtlety of Mark's text. If Satan had to pursue Jesus during forty days of temptation, the only reason the effort continued was because Satan failed. Nothing in the hostile environment overcame Jesus. Neither was he entirely alone, as the angels were continually caring for him (the Gr. is in the imperfect tense), indicating God's support. This is the only place in Mark where angels are said to help Jesus (Witherington 2001:81). Jesus emerged from the scene a victorious second Adam, succeeding where the first Adam had failed (a motif which Paul uses in Rom 5:12-19, and which John Milton chose as the theme of his second epic poem, *Paradise Regained*).

Mark then notes that John was arrested. Matthew and Luke tell us that the arrest came because John rebuked Herod Antipas for his divorce and remarriage to the divorced Herodias. After John's arrest, Jesus began to preach. The perfect tense used here (*peplērōtai* [TG4137A, ZG4444], "it has been fulfilled") points to a past act that continues to have effect at the time of writing (Guelich 1989:43). The appointed time was fulfilled! Jesus' message was also good news (*euangelion* [TG2098, ZG2295]) about what God was doing. The genitive "of God" in the Greek is probably plenary here: the message is *from* God, but it is also *about* his kingdom-rule that had come at its appointed time. Jesus' use of the idea of the appointed time makes it clear that he was referring to the rule God had promised he would bring to earth one day. As that kingdom-rule approached, two things were required as a response: repentance (a change of direction) and belief that the Kingdom had arrived. In a real sense, these two responses are really one. The new era of the Kingdom cannot be embraced without the need to share in it. Attachment to a previous way of life must be released to allow for participation in the new Kingdom and its benefits. Jesus would secure the means necessary for entrance into the forgiveness, life, and power of God's presence and rule. However, once again, this takes us ahead of Mark's story.

◆ **II. Jesus' Public Ministry (1:16–8:26)**
   A. Calling of Disciples and Beginning of Miracles (1:16–1:45)
   1. The first disciples (1:16–20; cf. Matt 4:18–22)

¹⁶One day as Jesus was walking along the shore of the Sea of Galilee, he saw Simon* and his brother Andrew throwing a net into the water, for they fished for a living. ¹⁷Jesus called out to them, "Come, follow me, and I will show you how to fish for people!" ¹⁸And they left their nets at once and followed him.

¹⁹A little farther up the shore Jesus saw Zebedee's sons, James and John, in a boat repairing their nets. ²⁰He called them at once, and they also followed him, leaving their father, Zebedee, in the boat with the hired men.

1:16 *Simon* is called "Peter" in 3:16 and thereafter.

NOTES
1:17-18 *followed him.* Gr. *akoloutheō* [TG190, ZG199]. This key verb referring to discipleship is an important term in Mark (BDAG 36-37; TDNT 2.210-216; Mark 1:18; 2:14-15; 8:34; 10:21, 28; 15:41). With one exception (Rev 14:4), the use of this term to refer to discipleship is limited to the Gospels. "Following" involves a commitment that makes all other ties secondary, which is why Jesus' followers often left other things behind (1:18, 20; 2:14; 10:21, 28; cf. Matt 8:22; Luke 9:61-62). Although Jesus' disciples are often compared to rabbinical students, this term is never used of a rabbi's student (Hengel 1981:50-57), so the

expression with this nuance appears to be of Christian origin. Here is radical discipleship. Jesus is put first, so family and vocation become secondary.

fish for people! This expression is also without solid precedent in the OT, inasmuch as similar examples are negative and point to being caught in *judgment* (Jer 16:16; Ezek 29:4-5; Amos 4:2; Hab 1:14-17; Cranfield 1959:70). The sense here is positive since, contextually, people are being caught for the Kingdom. Perhaps the need to catch involves a need to rescue, with its underlying assumption that those who are not caught will be judged (Witherington 2001:85-86) or that once the fish is caught his old life will be changed orever (Garland 1996:69).

C O M M E N T A R Y

The call of these four disciples seems abrupt. The first thing Jesus did after announcing the approach of the Kingdom was to gather disciples who would make following Jesus a priority over everything else, even their livelihood. They went from casting their nets at schools of fish to Jesus' school on catching people for the Kingdom. It is significant that Jesus called such people from everyday life, for God involves himself with everyday people, and that involvement then changes them. Rather than being students of the Law as rabbinical students were, the disciples were engaged with people (Guelich 1989:52-53). These men were willing to turn, believe the gospel, and redirect their lives accordingly.

Not everyone who responded to Jesus was called to follow him in such an absolute manner (5:18-20; Meier 2001:40-50). These would be special disciples, numbered among the Twelve. Their intimate proximity to Jesus would prepare them well to share Jesus' teaching with others. Their calling was in the tradition of previous callings, such as those of the prophets. Elisha followed Elijah, for example (1 Kgs 19:19-21). It should also be noted that Jesus initiated the call of these disciples, whereas in rabbinical circles it was more common for students to choose their teachers.

◆   2. Jesus casts out an evil spirit (1:21-28)

[21]Jesus and his companions went to the town of Capernaum. When the Sabbath day came, he went into the synagogue and began to teach. [22]The people were amazed at his teaching, for he taught with real authority—quite unlike the teachers of religious law.

[23]Suddenly, a man in the synagogue who was possessed by an evil* spirit began shouting, [24]"Why are you interfering with us, Jesus of Nazareth? Have you come to destroy us? I know who you are—the Holy One sent from God!"

[25]Jesus cut him short. "Be quiet! Come out of the man," he ordered. [26]At that, the evil spirit screamed, threw the man into a convulsion, and then came out of him.

[27]Amazement gripped the audience, and they began to discuss what had happened. "What sort of new teaching is this?" they asked excitedly. "It has such authority! Even evil spirits obey his orders!" [28]The news about Jesus spread quickly throughout the entire region of Galilee.

1:23 Greek *unclean;* also in 1:26, 27.

NOTES

1:21 *synagogue*. This was the Jewish meeting place where the law was read and studied; it was also a place for prayer, the education of children, and other community events (TDNT 7:821-828). Most significant communities had a Jewish synagogue, and larger cities may have had more than one. Jesus often ministered in synagogues because any competent male (as regulated by synagogue elders; Hooker 1991:62-63; Mark 1:22, 39; 6:2) could comment on the Scriptures. The synagogue mentioned here was in Capernaum, now often identified with *Tell Hum* on the northwest shore of the Sea of Galilee, about two miles west of where the Jordan River enters the lake (Cranfield 1959:71). Capernaum was a fishing village. The synagogue that has been excavated there is from after the time of Jesus, but it may be the site of this earlier synagogue. Witherington (2001:88-89) defends the idea that such buildings did exist in the first century.

1:22 *amazed*. Mark uses seven different verbs to describe amazement (Cranfield 1959:73); this verb (*ekplēssomai* [TG1605, ZG1742]) also appears in 6:2; 7:37; 11:18. The concept of amazement is ambiguous in that it could either be a first step toward faith or be motivated by offense at what Jesus was doing. In this scene, the amazement simply led to discussion about what was going on. The ambiguity is left there for Mark's readers to contemplate against the backdrop of his introduction to the Gospel about who Jesus is. No doubt Mark used the concept to portray Jesus as different from all other teachers; those who heard him sensed this even though they could not explain it.

authority. See also 1:27. This term summarizes a dominating characteristic of Jesus' teaching that will become an issue later in his ministry. Authority can mean (1) the power or ability to act or (2) the right to take certain action. Here the former is intended, for the words Jesus taught were accompanied by authoritative acts, as the exorcism in 1:23-28 shows.

quite unlike the teachers of religious law. Jesus taught with a power distinct from that of the scribes ("teachers of religious law" in the NLT), who made judgments for various Jewish sects about the meaning and application of the law, and made their living copying Torah texts (EDNT 1:259-260). Meier (2001:549-260) emphasizes that "scribe" refers to the function of copying sacred texts, not to a particular party of Jews or to their role in adjudicating the law (i.e., scribes could belong to any sect within Judaism, as indicated by the phrase "the teachers of religious law who were Pharisees" in 2:16). Later in Mark, the issue will be Jesus' right to speak and act as he did. In Mark, when Jesus speaks with authority, the scribes are always noted in contrast (1:21-27; 2:5-12; 11:27-33). Only one text in Mark commends a scribe (12:28-34), and the scribes are often seen in opposition to Jesus (3:22; 7:1, 5; 8:31; 10:33; 14:1, 43, 53; 15:1, 31; Guelich 1989:56). Jesus' independence from such authority disturbed the Jewish leaders. Mark also makes the important point that people noticed Jesus' distinctive character. Jesus' authority was not derivative; it was more direct than that of the other religious leaders.

1:23 *evil spirit*. The Gr. refers to an unclean spirit that would have been regarded by Jews as malevolent or evil (*Jubilees* 10:1; *Testament of Benjamin* 5:2; 1QM 13:5). Mark refers to such spirits eleven times, with six of the references occurring in two scenes (1:23, 26-27; 3:11, 30; 5:2, 8, 13; 6:7; 7:25; 9:25). They are clearly described as destructive beings (5:2-13; 9:17-27). It is no accident that Jesus encountered demons early in his ministry, for there was a cosmic dimension to his work. The spirits' remarks also make it clear that they were aware of Jesus' authority, which extended far beyond what he said to what he was able to do (1:27).

1:24 *Why are you interfering with us?* It was unusual for a man possessed by an evil spirit to be in the synagogue, but perhaps his condition was not entirely evident until Jesus' presence forced the spirit in the man to react and ask, lit., "What do you want with us?" This phrase, also found in Judg 11:12 and 1 Kgs 17:18, is an idiom for, "Why are you interfering with us?" or "What have we to do with each other?" The phrase is used by an inferior to a superior (Guelich 1989:56-57)—the spirit sensed that Jesus' holy presence was a threat. So Jesus and the spirit are engaged in a type of spiritual combat.

Holy One sent from God! The remark contrasts the unclean spirit that was speaking with Jesus, the Holy One (Hooker 1991:64), as purity met the impure. A destructive force encountered a power of deliverance. The title suggests a close association with the Holy God (cf. Aaron, Ps 106:16; Elisha, 2 Kgs 4:9; the saints of God, Dan 7:18-27; see also Isa 40:25; 57:15). The title clearly points to Jesus' superior cosmic authority since the demons wondered if he might destroy them. The remark is a clue to how Jesus' heavenly opponents viewed him and gives insight into his true identity. It was often the case in exorcisms that naming the opponent was a key to control (Bock 2002b:101-102); this instance of naming was likely such an attempt on the part of the demons.

1:25 *Be quiet!* This call to silence occurs only twice in Mark, once here and once in Jesus' rebuke to the wind and sea in 4:39 (a similar idea appears in 3:12). The expression shows Jesus' authority and precedes his exorcism of the demon from the man. It was a common way to exert control in an exorcism (PGM IX.4, 9; PGM IV.1243, 1245, 3013; Witherington 2001:91). There is no magic here, no incantation or other type of help. Jesus' word alone was good enough.

1:26 *threw the man into a convulsion.* Violence accompanied the demon's departure. The man was violently shaken by the exorcism. The verb behind this expression (*sparassō* [TG4682, ZG5057]) is used only three times in the NT, and always of a demon trying to harm a person (9:26; Luke 9:39). The term in classical Gr. refers to animals such as dogs shaking or ripping up a victim (LSJ, 1624). That the foundation of the heavens "shook" reflects usage in the Gr. OT (2 Sam 22:8). In Josephus, the term describes Ezra as reacting to the marrying of wives outside the faith by rending his garments and casting himself down on the ground in grief (*Antiquities* 11.141).

1:27 *Amazement.* This is a different term for amazement (*ethambēthēsan* [TG2284, ZG2501]) than in the reference to astonishment in 1:22 (see note). Only Mark uses this verb in the NT. In 10:24 the verb describes the disciples' amazement at Jesus' comment about the rich. The NT uses of the term all suggest perplexity with the sense of being caught off guard in "sudden bewilderment and total shock" (BDAG 442; EDNT 2.128). They were trying to sort out the things they had seen and heard (see also 10:32).

COMMENTARY

Jesus' story begins in Mark with his miraculous activity against the cosmic forces that oppose humanity. Mark, like Luke, presents an exorcism as Jesus' first miracle (Matthew shows Jesus cleansing a leper, and John tells about Jesus' changing water into wine). Of thirteen miracles in Mark, four are exorcisms, more than any other type of miracle narrated by Mark. In contrast, John's Gospel has no exorcisms. Most of Mark's miracles occur in the first half of his Gospel and comprise almost half of that material (Witherington 2001:92). The miracles were not automatically persuasive, for the Pharisees still opposed him (3:6), the scribes considered him demon possessed (3:22), those in his hometown did not respond (6:2-3), and Herod thought of him as John the Baptist returned from the dead (6:14-16). Even the disciples repeatedly misunderstood him (6:52; 8:17-21; Witherington 2001:94).

The function of Jesus' exorcisms was to underscore Jesus' authority and the cosmic scope of his work. Jesus had come to set all creation right. This miracle took place in the synagogue, a holy place, and Jesus' word of rebuke was authoritative enough to accomplish the exorcism. In this event, Jesus is portrayed as the regal Son-Servant who is God's Holy One. The exact meaning of the demons' confessions would not automatically be clear to Jesus' audience. Their remarks indicated that Jesus' authority threatened them because of his close connection with divine power. Mark makes the case from the very beginning that Jesus was not an average prophet or servant of God. There was something unique in his teaching that initiated a special time of fulfillment (Guelich 1989:58).

Mark finishes his presentation of this event with the perplexity all of this was producing in the crowd. Jesus had a new and special type of authority. He was not merely discussing law, ethics, or even theology as the scribes might have done. Rather, demons were being confronted face-to-face and defeated. Needless to say, such news spread around the region because people were not accustomed to such events.

◆   3. Jesus' work continues in Capernaum and Galilee (1:29-45)

²⁹After Jesus left the synagogue with James and John, they went to Simon and Andrew's home. ³⁰Now Simon's mother-in-law was sick in bed with a high fever. They told Jesus about her right away. ³¹So he went to her bedside, took her by the hand, and helped her sit up. Then the fever left her, and she prepared a meal for them.

³²That evening after sunset, many sick and demon-possessed people were brought to Jesus. ³³The whole town gathered at the door to watch. ³⁴So Jesus healed many people who were sick with various diseases, and he cast out many demons. But because the demons knew who he was, he did not allow them to speak.

³⁵Before daybreak the next morning, Jesus got up and went out to an isolated place to pray. ³⁶Later Simon and the others went out to find him. ³⁷When they found him, they said, "Everyone is looking for you."

³⁸But Jesus replied, "We must go on to other towns as well, and I will preach to them, too. That is why I came." ³⁹So he traveled throughout the region of Galilee, preaching in the synagogues and casting out demons.

⁴⁰A man with leprosy came and knelt in front of Jesus, begging to be healed. "If you are willing, you can heal me and make me clean," he said.

⁴¹Moved with compassion,* Jesus reached out and touched him. "I am willing," he said. "Be healed!" ⁴²Instantly the leprosy disappeared, and the man was healed. ⁴³Then Jesus sent him on his way with a stern warning: ⁴⁴"Don't tell anyone about this. Instead, go to the priest and let him examine you. Take along the offering required in the law of Moses for those who have been healed of leprosy.* This will be a public testimony that you have been cleansed."

⁴⁵But the man went and spread the word, proclaiming to everyone what had happened. As a result, large crowds soon surrounded Jesus, and he couldn't publicly enter a town anywhere. He had to stay out in the secluded places, but people from everywhere kept coming to him.

1:41 Some manuscripts read *Moved with anger.*   1:44 See Lev 14:2-32.

NOTES

1:31 *the fever left her, and she prepared a meal for them.* This is Jesus' first healing in Mark. It is unusual in that it involved a man healing a woman who was not a family member, and it was done on the Sabbath if the later Jewish text of *b. Berakhot* 5a is a guide to earlier Jewish practice (Witherington 2001:98; the late date of the text may reflect later Jewish practice). That it was the Sabbath was potentially controversial, but this seems to have been the private healing of a relative of a key disciple, Peter, who apparently was married (1 Cor 9:5). The healing led immediately to her serving them. Mark uses the verb *diakoneō* [TG1247, ZG1354] to describe her preparation of a meal for them. This is the normal use of this verb from which we get our word "deacon" (EDNT 1:302; Luke 17:8). Her immediate service indicated that her healing was quick and complete, and illustrates the service that receiving God's grace should produce (note the theological use of the "deacon" idea in 9:33-37 and 10:43-45).

1:34 *he did not allow them to speak.* After the healing, Jesus continued to perform exorcisms but prevented the demons from giving their testimony. This remark continues the theme of Jesus' authority from the first exorcism.

1:35 *went out to an isolated place to pray.* In Mark, Jesus goes alone to pray three times: here, in 6:46 (before the miracle of walking on the water), and in 14:35-39 (at Gethsemane). In the midst of a demanding period of ministry, Jesus sought communion with God. Jesus' private prayer contrasts with what he said about the scribes and their public prayers (12:38-40).

1:36 *went out to find him.* The verb used in this description (*katediōxen* [TG2614, ZG2870]) is quite vivid. It means "to hunt someone down" and is often used in a hostile sense (cf. Marcus 2000:202; Ps 17:38 [LXX]; *Psalms of Solomon* 15:8; and BDAG 516). Marcus suggests that whereas Jesus had called the disciples to be fishers of people, here they were hunting him down or pursuing him. Jesus will instruct them on the requirements of his ministry.

1:38 *We must go on to other towns.* The Gr. is softer in tone, reading "Let us go in another direction to neighboring towns." This is a mission statement, indicating that Jesus came to preach to a larger region, and not just to Capernaum (1:24; 2:17; 10:45; Witherington 2001:102).

came. Lit., "came out," an expression we do not use much in English. It has the nuance of being sent by God in a calling (Amos 7:14-15; Josephus *Antiquities* 3.400; Marcus 2000:204). In 1:24 and here, two reasons are given for Jesus' coming: to confront evil forces and to preach. These two ideas are repeated in 1:39. The term for "preach" (*kērussō* [TG2784, ZG3062]) both here and in 1:39 is not the term for instruction but for missionary proclamation (Guelich 1989:43). It probably refers to preaching the gospel as previously mentioned (1:14-15).

1:39 *preaching in the synagogues and casting out demons.* Jesus' cosmic battle continued to be a part of his ministry so that his actions matched his words. What he did in Capernaum (1:21-28), he also did elsewhere.

1:40 *leprosy.* This word refers to an array of skin diseases that rendered a Jewish person unclean and required a life of isolation from society (Lev 13–14; *m. Nega'im*). Lepers were to announce their presence and the danger of contamination by crying out, "Unclean, unclean!" (Lev 13:45-46; Cranfield 1959:90). The leper's approach to Jesus violated this legal tradition, but it expressed the confidence that Jesus was capable of reversing his condition. Sometimes such diseases were regarded as divine judgments (2 Kgs 5:7). Other texts discussing the disease are Num 12:9-12, Job 18:13, and 11QTemple^a 45:17-18.

If you are willing. In Gr., this is a third class condition, so the request is made without any presumption—i.e., "If you are willing, and I am not saying whether you are or not." The leper knew that Jesus could make him clean, but he was not certain whether he would or not, although his willingness to risk approaching Jesus meant that he came in the hope that his request would be graciously granted.

1:41 *Moved with compassion.* A few MSS, of which D and some Old Latin renderings are the most important, read "moved with anger" (cf. NLT mg). Some argue that this is the harder reading, because it is more difficult to explain a copyist's move from compassion to anger. If it were original, then Jesus' anger would be set against the man's condition, not his request (Luke 13:16; Marcus 2000:206; Hooker 1991:79). But compassion is slightly more likely to be the original sense, given the overwhelming external spread of the MSS (Metzger 1971:76-77 also notes that Mark's use of anger is clearly attested in other verses: 3:5; 10:14). Mark loved to note Jesus' emotions; here, Jesus acted graciously out of compassion for the man's plight (on compassion, see 6:34; 8:2; 9:22). The healing would be extended with a symbolic touch, since Jesus' power to cleanse was greater than leprosy's power to stain (contrast 2 Kgs 5:1-14; Num 12:9-15). The significance of this is more clear in other Gospel texts (Matt 11:5; Luke 7:22).

1:43 *a stern warning.* The Gr. verb *embrimaomai* [TG1690, ZG1839] lit. means "to snort" or "be indignant" (BDAG 322; Mark 14:5; John 11:33, 38). Jesus sternly restricted the public announcement of what had taken place while urging the leper to follow the law by showing himself to the priest so he could be declared clean (1:44; Lev 14:1-20). Mark notes such calls to silence with respect to demons (1:34; 3:12), those healed (1:43-44; 5:43; 7:36), and the disciples (8:30; 9:9). It appears that a major concern was to avoid the excessive publicity that this aspect of Jesus' work could generate (Guelich 1989:76).

1:44 *testimony that you have been cleansed.* This public testimony was a liturgical recognition before God alone of God's gracious work of healing through Jesus. The Gr. also allows for the interpretation, "a testimony against them." In other spots where this expression appears, it is negative, meaning "against them" (6:11; 13:9; TDNT 4:502-503). The meaning appears to be that the evidence of God's acting through Jesus (when the healed man offered a sacrifice) would stand as a testimony against the priests when they came to reject the reality that God was working through Jesus.

1:45 *But the man went and spread the word.* The cleansed leper did not obey Jesus and Jesus got the publicity he had hoped to avoid.

proclaiming. Interestingly, the man "preached" (*kērussō* [TG2784, ZG3062]) his testimony.

COMMENTARY

Mark portrays these early scenes of Jesus' ministry almost like a battle between Jesus and the cosmic forces of evil, with humans as both the victims and the prize in the battle. Jesus fought demons and overcame disease as he preached the good news of God's deliverance. What he claimed about God's promise of deliverance, he backed up with action. So Peter's mother-in-law was healed of fever and her healing led her into serving them. Meanwhile, the entire village began to seek him out for healing and exorcism. Jesus healed graciously, but he commanded the demons not to say who he was.

This command of silence suggests that Jesus was not interested in drawing too much attention to this testimony. Possible reasons for his hesitation are that (1) it might be misread, as the view of the scribes in 3:22 suggests; (2) Jesus preferred that the awareness of who he was should emerge intrinsically from the nature of his ministry and teaching; (3) Jesus wanted to prevent the wrong kind of attention from being drawn to the miracles themselves and what could accompany them; and (4) the crowd could not yet appreciate exactly what such a confession really meant for God's plan. This last reason explains why Jesus gradually taught the disciples who he was and also explains how Mark gradually unfurls his story. The concern that miracles would overshadow what they represented is evident from the development of the scene. One exorcism in a synagogue led to Jesus' being overwhelmed with requests to heal and to exorcise. He performed them graciously, but it is clear, as Mark's story proceeds, that Jesus was concerned that the miracles not detract from his message.

Jesus withdrew from the public clamor to pray, to be alone with God. When the disciples sought him out to return, Jesus responded with a different plan. He would move on throughout Galilee doing what he had done in Capernaum, teaching and exorcising demons. The message must be taken elsewhere.

Nothing pictures Jesus' ability to offer cleansing so clearly as his healing of a leper. This disease isolated those afflicted from the rest of society out of fear that they would render others unclean. Even the law required such isolation, but Jesus' presence was stronger than the contagion. The leper wanted the cleansing Jesus offered. Jesus extended his compassion and healed the man, and then explained that the only testimony the man should give was what was required by the law. Jesus was still concerned that the proper features of his ministry be emphasized. Unfortunately, the man did not heed the restriction. This was not the only time that Jesus' command would be ignored. As a result, Jesus was overwhelmed by the crowds and could not find relief even by withdrawing to the desert.

One other point is important. Mark develops the idea of Jesus' increasing popularity, from "spread throughout" in verse 28 to "whole town gathered" in verse 34 to "everyone is looking" in verse 37 to "he couldn't publicly enter a town" in verse 45. This radical popularity with the crowds stands in contrast with the radical rejection by the leaders in 2:1–3:6 that comes next. This juxtaposition of crowd reception versus leadership rejection is a theme Mark develops throughout his gospel.

◆ **B. Controversy Leading to Rejection (2:1–3:12)**

1. The first controversy: Jesus as Son of Man heals a paralytic and forgives sin (2:1-12; cf. Matt 9:1-8; Luke 5:17-26)

When Jesus returned to Capernaum several days later, the news spread quickly that he was back home. ²Soon the house where he was staying was so packed with visitors that there was no more room, even outside the door. While he was preaching God's word to them, ³four men arrived carrying a paralyzed man on a mat. ⁴They couldn't bring him to Jesus because of the crowd, so they dug a hole through the roof above his head. Then they lowered the man on his mat, right down in front of Jesus. ⁵Seeing their faith, Jesus said to the paralyzed man, "My child, your sins are forgiven."

⁶But some of the teachers of religious

law who were sitting there thought to themselves, ⁷"What is he saying? This is blasphemy! Only God can forgive sins!"

⁸Jesus knew immediately what they were thinking, so he asked them, "Why do you question this in your hearts? ⁹Is it easier to say to the paralyzed man 'Your sins are forgiven,' or 'Stand up, pick up your mat, and walk'? ¹⁰So I will prove to you

that the Son of Man* has the authority on earth to forgive sins." Then Jesus turned to the paralyzed man and said, ¹¹"Stand up, pick up your mat, and go home!"

¹²And the man jumped up, grabbed his mat, and walked out through the stunned onlookers. They were all amazed and praised God, exclaiming, "We've never seen anything like this before!"

2:10 "Son of Man" is a title Jesus used for himself.

NOTES

2:1 *Jesus returned to Capernaum.* The return suggests two things: (1) that Jesus' initial tour through Galilee was completed, and (2) that Capernaum was the headquarters for his ministry.

2:2 *visitors.* According to Mark, there was a large audience for this event; the NLT translates "many" as "visitors." In 2:4, they are called a crowd. In 2:6, it is also noted that scribes (NLT, "teachers of religious law") are present. Matthew notes scribes (Matt 9:3) and crowds (Matt 9:8), and Luke specifies that the crowds included scribes and Pharisees (Luke 5:17, 21). The point is that Jesus' activities were now beginning to draw a variety of people to see what Jesus was doing and saying.

preaching God's word. Lit., "speaking the word," an idiom for preaching God's message. In Mark "the word" often refers to something Jesus teaches (2:2; 4:14-20, 33; 8:32; Guelich 1989:84). The expression also creates a link back to 1:45 with its use of "word."

2:3 *paralyzed man.* This is the only event involving a paralytic in Mark and Luke. Matthew reports the healing of paralysis two other times as well (Matt 4:24; 8:6). Acts also has two such events (Acts 8:7; 9:33).

2:4 *dug a hole through the roof.* The literal phrase here is "unroofed the roof." They created an opening so they could lower the mat on which the man lay. The mat could have been like many wood and cloth pallets one sees today in the Middle East. The house would have been a flat-roofed home with a staircase up the back.

2:5 *their faith.* Mark likes to use both the noun and the verb for faith (1:15; 4:40; 5:34-36; 9:19, 23-24, 42; 10:52; 11:22-24). The inner conviction and trust of the paralytic and his friends in Jesus' power is evident in the effort they made to get to Jesus. Mark commends their faith as it was manifest in their action. In Mark, faith is expressed concretely as it overcomes obstacles placed in its way (Guelich 1989:85).

your sins are forgiven. This remark got Jesus into trouble with the theologians. In spite of the fact that it is expressed as a divine passive that attributes forgiveness to God (see Lev 4:26, 31; 2 Sam 12:13; or Qumran's *Prayer of Nabonidus* [4Q242]).

2:6 *teachers of religious law.* The Gr. refers to "the scribes," whose fundamental task was to copy the sacred text, not just to render judgment about it. The great amount of time they spent with the sacred texts helped to qualify them for making judgments about the law.

2:7 *blasphemy! Only God can forgive sins!* Something about the way Jesus expressed this forgiveness made it clear to them that he was claiming to be more than a healer or prophet. In their view, Jesus was not honoring God, but slandering him by making such claims. Blasphemy is dishonoring or slandering someone, usually through arrogant or disrespectful speech against them (BDAG 178). In Jewish culture it could also spill over into disrespectful acts (Bock 1998:30-112). Jesus traded charges of blasphemy with the teachers of religious law later (3:22); he was convicted of blasphemy at his examination (14:63-64), and the people blasphemed Jesus while he was on the cross (15:29-30).

2:8 *Jesus knew immediately what they were thinking.* Jesus had insight into the minds of those who were criticizing him. Such a perception might reflect his unique role as Son of Man, but could also reflect revelatory insight that God can give to others. The Gr. has, "and Jesus perceiving in his spirit." The NLT renders the sense of the remark well.

2:9 Jesus' question presents a dilemma. It appears to be easier to offer forgiveness, for this cannot immediately be seen and evaluated, whereas telling the man to walk requires that he do so. So in one sense it is easier to speak of forgiveness than to give healing. However, to really be able to forgive sin is hard because one must have the authority to actually do it. The question sets up a connection that Jesus makes in 2:10. Jesus did not back off from the dispute; he wished to engage them on this controversial point and affirm his authority to do these things.

2:10 *I will prove to you that the Son of Man has the authority on earth to forgive sins.* Although some argue that these verses are Mark's narrative commentary, it is better to see this verse as part of the scene in which Jesus affirms his authority. Healing can be seen, but forgiveness cannot be seen. Jesus said that his healing of the paralytic would make evident the truth of his claims about forgiveness. If God worked through him in healing, then these claims would be vindicated. The Gr. reads, "that you might know that the Son of Man has authority." The NLT rendering, "I will prove" emphasizes the vindication that the healing represents.

2:12 *We've never seen anything like this.* The crowd's reaction indicates that something unusual had taken place. In effect, their reaction was, "What's going on here?" This scene has an open ending that invites the reader to contemplate what is being described.

C O M M E N T A R Y

This first of five controversy scenes indicates that one of the issues over which Jesus and the religious authorities battled was his claim to forgive sin. The scribes wondered how Jesus could know that God was willing to forgive the sins of the paralytic. Many ancient Jews connected sin and sickness, as indicated in Jewish texts such as *b. Nedarim* 41a, which says "No one gets up from his sick bed until all his sins are forgiven" (Hooker 1991:85). But no one could forgive these sins except God, as the *Midrash Psalms* 17:3 reads, "No one can forgive transgressions but you [God]" (Marcus 2000:217). So Jesus assumed a divine prerogative here, or at least knowledge of divine preferences (Exod 34:6-7; Isa 43:25; 44:22).

Furthermore, Jesus affirmed his authority as the Son of Man, and the scribes viewed this as blasphemy. At this point in Mark, the source of this title for Jesus is not clear. Later in the Gospel, the title will be associated with Daniel 7:13-14, where a person is described who rides the clouds, approaches the Ancient of Days (God) in heaven, and receives authority to judge. Its use in Judaism in *1 Enoch* 39–71 and *4 Ezra* 13 also points to a figure with such authority (Garland 1996:95-96). "Son of Man" is Jesus' favorite way of referring to himself; in Mark, the title appears fourteen times. It will be important to trace what the Son of Man does in Mark. Forgiving sins is one of his abilities. In 2:10, Jesus emphasizes his authority by referring to himself in this way. In other contexts, Jesus used the term to foretell his suffering or the authority he would have on his return.

The conflict presented in Mark 2 and the judgment that circulated around this first controversy would remain the same when Jesus was examined by the Sanhedrin (Mark 14). He claimed authority as the Son of Man, and they claimed that this was blasphemy (Bock 1998:188). However, the problem for the leaders was that Jesus gave signs that backed up his claims; his healings validated those claims that were otherwise unobservable. This is a passage in which word and deed work together to make a theological point. The form of the account is a mixture of a pronouncement (2:10) and a miracle story, another illustration of word and deed explaining each other.

◆ ### 2. The second controversy: Jesus calls Levi and eats with sinners (2:13-17; cf. Matt 9:9-13; Luke 5:27-32)

¹³Then Jesus went out to the lakeshore again and taught the crowds that were coming to him. ¹⁴As he walked along, he saw Levi son of Alphaeus sitting at his tax collector's booth. "Follow me and be my disciple," Jesus said to him. So Levi got up and followed him.

¹⁵Later, Levi invited Jesus and his disciples to his home as dinner guests, along with many tax collectors and other disreputable sinners. (There were many people of this kind among Jesus' followers.) ¹⁶But when the teachers of religious law who were Pharisees* saw him eating with tax collectors and other sinners, they asked his disciples, "Why does he eat with such scum?*"

¹⁷When Jesus heard this, he told them, "Healthy people don't need a doctor—sick people do. I have come to call not those who think they are righteous, but those who know they are sinners."

2:16a Greek *the scribes of the Pharisees.* 2:16b Greek *with tax collectors and sinners?*

NOTES

2:14 *Levi*. This may be the same person as Matthew, with Levi as his second name, as was common in Jewish contexts (Lane 1974:100-101). Others reject this identification (Guelich 1989:99-100).

***tax collector's booth*.** This booth would have been in the jurisdiction of Herod Antipas and was probably located in Capernaum (Sherwin-White 1963:125-126). Tax collectors were disliked by Jews because they reminded people of Roman authority by collecting taxes for them, spent much of their time in contact with Gentiles, and were often dishonest (Donahue 1971:39-61). Later mishnaic and talmudic texts compare them to murderers and robbers (*m. Nedarim* 3:4; *b. Bava Qamma* 113a). It is perhaps better to speak of them as "toll collectors" because Levi was collecting usage taxes, or indirect taxes based on use and consumption. Levi would have had to bid for the right to collect taxes and to add a surcharge for his efforts (Luke 3:13; 19:8; Marcus 2000:225). Great opportunity for abuse existed in setting the amount of the surcharge.

***Levi got up and followed him*.** As with Peter and the three others in 1:16-20, the call to follow Jesus was a call to discipleship.

2:15 *sinners*. Toll collectors were not the only disreputable people Jesus drew. Mark uses the general category of "sinners" for other social outcasts that were drawn to Jesus.

2:16 *teachers of religious law who were Pharisees*. These scribes were also Pharisees; they regarded table fellowship with such people as implying acceptance of them and their sins.

such scum. This rendering attempts to convey the emotive force of the lit. expression, "toll collectors and sinners." These were two groups of disreputable people that the Pharisees thought Jesus should not be so friendly with. Their objection could be that their food was not properly tithed (Deut 14:22; Matt 23:23) or prepared with proper attention to purity (7:1-8), or there may have been other issues related to cleanliness (*m. Hagigah* 2:7; Hooker 1991:96; Marcus 2000:227). They also feared that such association would lead to sharing in sinful practices (so the later text, *b. Berakhot* 43b).

COMMENTARY

Hooker (1991:94) perceptively suggests that this story about Jesus' eating with sinners and tax collectors illustrates the theme of forgiveness introduced in 2:1-12. This account also presents a controversy in the form of a pronouncement, where every-thing in the passage drives towards Jesus' concluding utterance; whatever offense the religious officials took at Jesus' associations, he was justified in seeking out sinners— this was his calling. Thus, one finds Jesus wherever there is disease that needs to be healed. Jesus did not wait for sinners to approach him, as the calling of Levi shows. Rather, he made it clear that he and the God he represented sought out such people for entry into fresh relationship with God. This account shows God's absolute commit-ment to reach people as Jesus associates with sinners in order to bring them to God.

Jesus said, "Healthy people don't need a doctor—sick people do. I have come to call not those who think they are righteous, but those who know they are sinners." This is Jesus' mission statement. The only other such statement in Mark is in 10:45. His divine task was not to treat the righteous but to heal the spiritually ill. Jesus had come to help sinners (Cranfield 1959:106) and his ability to heal, cleanse, and for-give revealed his divine power (cf. Exod 15:26).

◆   ## 3. The third controversy: Jesus' disciples did not practice fasting (2:18-22; cf. Matt 9:14-17; Luke 5:33-39)

[18]Once when John's disciples and the Pharisees were fasting, some people came to Jesus and asked, "Why don't your disci-ples fast like John's disciples and the Pharisees do?"

[19]Jesus replied, "Do wedding guests fast while celebrating with the groom? Of course not. They can't fast while the groom is with them. [20]But someday the groom will be taken away from them, and then they will fast.

[21]"Besides, who would patch old cloth-ing with new cloth? For the new patch would shrink and rip away from the old cloth, leaving an even bigger tear than before.

[22]"And no one puts new wine into old wineskins. For the wine would burst the wineskins, and the wine and the skins would both be lost. New wine calls for new wineskins."

NOTES

2:18 *Why don't your disciples fast?* The question concerns an important religious practice that John's disciples and the Pharisees thought the pious should observe. As an ascetic, John probably made a point of fasting. Mark does not specify who asked the question here. It was a cultural expectation that Jesus, as a pious religious figure, should be fasting like other pious figures. Luke 18:12 reports that the Pharisees fasted twice a week. This was on the second and fifth days of the week as noted in *Didache* 8:1 (our Monday and Thursday). Some speculate that this scene was really only about John and Jesus and reflected a concern of the early church, but this is highly unlikely since the dispute does not really fit the later setting (Guelich 1989:103).

2:19 *celebrating with the groom*. The NLT rendering again captures the force of the Gr., which reads, "while the groom is with them." The celebration of the banquet table was an image of the special relationship between God and Israel (TDNT 4:1103). It recalled a special time when God was especially active on behalf of his people and their salvation (Isa 54:4-8; 62:5; Ezek 16:7-14; Hos 2). Jesus' presence was a special indication of divine presence and activity; this called for celebration and feasting, and fasting was not appropriate. Later Jewish practice indicates that some religious obligations were not required of wedding celebrants (Marcus 2000:233; *b. Sukkah* 25b; living in booths was not required for celebrants of a wedding that took place during this feast). Such an idea seems to be operative in Jesus' example.

2:20 *the groom will be taken away*. Jesus is not specific here, other than to indicate that things would change in the future when the groom was no longer present. Lane (1974:111) speaks of the language here as "cryptic," with no definite allusion to a violent death. The narrative as a whole makes clear that this imagery alludes to Jesus' death, at which point fasting will again be appropriate.

2:21 *new patch would shrink*. New cloth was not preshrunk, and the process of washing and drying the garment would cause it to shrink.

2:22 *burst the wineskins*. New wine had yet to ferment, and wine fermenting in a closed container puts pressure on that container. New wineskins would stretch during fermentation, but the brittle leather of old wineskins would crack and rupture.

C O M M E N T A R Y

Jesus took a question about fasting and broadened it to show how his practice was distinct. One explanation was in the nature of the current time. His presence was a time of celebration, so fasting was not appropriate. There would come a time when he would no longer be present, and fasting would then be appropriate again. The second explanation is more comprehensive. Something really fresh and new had come in Jesus.

Jesus' two illustrations (concerning the new patch and the new wine) show that one could not simply fuse the message and person of Jesus to everything that Judaism had been. To do so would cause damage, as when a new patch of cloth was washed, since it would shrink and pull on the old cloth, which was worn thin and had no more give to it. Jesus asserted that something new and fresh had come, which would also require new ways.

The two illustrations basically make the same point. If there is a difference, it is that the first is written from the standpoint of the old material, while the second takes up the perspective of the new. An old garment does not take a new patch, for it would tear the garment. New wine does not go into old wineskins. The old skins have stretched as far as they can. When the new wine ferments, it will burst the old worn skins and both the wine and the skins will be lost. The wine of the new era needs fresh containers and new ways. Jesus noted that both the old and the new are damaged when they are wrongly combined.

The new wine needs new wineskins and new cloth can only be attached to new cloth. Jesus' ways would be different. His coming did not merely change the cover on Judaism. It was a new era that called for new ways of relating to God.

◆ ## 4. The fourth controversy: Jesus' disciples violate the Sabbath (2:23-28; cf. Matt 12:1-8; Luke 6:1-5)

²³One Sabbath day as Jesus was walking through some grainfields, his disciples began breaking off heads of grain to eat. ²⁴But the Pharisees said to Jesus, "Look, why are they breaking the law by harvesting grain on the Sabbath?"

²⁵Jesus said to them, "Haven't you ever read in the Scriptures what David did when he and his companions were hungry? ²⁶He went into the house of God (during the days when Abiathar was high priest) and broke the law by eating the sacred loaves of bread that only the priests are allowed to eat. He also gave some to his companions."

²⁷Then Jesus said to them, "The Sabbath was made to meet the needs of people, and not people to meet the requirements of the Sabbath. ²⁸So the Son of Man is Lord, even over the Sabbath!"

NOTES

2:23 *Sabbath.* In Judaism, the last day of the week (our Friday night to Saturday night) is set aside as a day of rest (Exod 20:8-11; Lev 23:1-3). Jews mark the day from sunset to sunset.

began breaking off heads of grain to eat. Certain areas of a field were reserved for travelers or foreigners (Deut 23:25), so taking the grain was not a problem. Those who were very careful about the law believed that on the Sabbath, grain should not be plucked or threshed (*m. Shabbat* 7:2; Lane 1974:114-115). This act would have been viewed by some as a violation of Sabbath rest, which was one of the Ten Commandments (Exod 20:10; 34:21; Deut 5:12-15; for other examples of strict Sabbath laws, see CD 10:14-11:18. *Jubilees*, esp. in 2:17-33 and 50:1-13, discusses the importance of Sabbath practice; cf. Guelich 1989:121). Since Jesus was responsible for the behavior of his followers in religious matters, the issue was raised for his explanation. Marcus (2000:240) cites Seneca *Troades* 290 here: "He who forbids not sin when in control commands it." Since the grain was ready for harvesting, it was probably April or May (Hooker 1991:102).

2:24 *breaking the law by harvesting grain on the Sabbath.* The Pharisees' charge was that the Sabbath had been violated. This scene may be compressed since the Pharisees were probably not following them around looking for violations. Rather, the Pharisees happened to hear of it and so the charge was raised (Witherington 2001:129).

2:25-26 *David . . . and his companions . . . [ate] the sacred loaves of bread.* Jesus referred to the incident in which David and his men ate the sacred loaves of bread that were reserved for priests (1 Sam 21:1-6; see Lev 24:5-9; Exod 25:30). God did not judge David for this act, so by implication, this exceptional situation did not violate the law. This did not happen on the Sabbath, but it is a parallel example in which the letter of the law was violated but the act was still permitted. Later Jews believed that this event took place on the Sabbath (*b. Menahot* 95b; *Yalqut Shim'oni* 2.130; Witherington 2001:130; Hooker 1991:103-104 takes this as the time when the bread was removed to be consumed if *Midrash Rabbah Lev* 32.3 is a correct guide).

during the days when Abiathar was high priest. This remark is in tension with 1 Sam 21:1, 2, 8, where Ahimelech, Abiathar's father, was named as high priest. Matthew and Luke omit this reference. Some argue that it is a vague literary reference indicating the general section of 1 Samuel containing the account. (The issue is discussed in Lane 1974:116.) Witherington (2001:130) suggests the reference may have been to a general time and meant "in the day of Abiathar," but that a translation issue obscured it.

2:27 to meet the needs of people. Jesus stated the priority and purpose of the Sabbath. The day of rest was to serve and benefit people, not become an obstacle to them. For Jewish views of the Sabbath, see *Jubilees* 2:17, where the Sabbath is called a "great sign." The Jews took a Sabbath (i.e., rested) from all work on the seventh day. It was seen as a gift to be enjoyed. Interestingly, the later Jewish text *Mekilta Exodus* [109b] on 31:13-14 reads, "The Sabbath was delivered to you, not you to the Sabbath," though the point is that Israel received the day to be observed as a matter of privilege (Guelich 1989:124). The day was designed to be refreshing (Exod 23:12; Deut 5:14); Jesus' point was that taking basic nourishment on this day did not violate it.

COMMENTARY

Jesus and his disciples' practices were unusual. One of the more disputed areas was Jesus' observance of the Sabbath. In an incident that involved taking grain on the Sabbath, Jesus defended his disciples with two arguments. First, the Sabbath was never intended to create a situation in which basic human needs went unmet. Jesus made this point with the example of David, who also "broke" the law to obtain food. The second, more fundamental point was that Jesus, as Son of Man, had authority over the Sabbath.

Whatever the exact nature of the analogy with David, Jesus' final argument was his primary one. The Son of Man has authority, even over something as important as the Sabbath, for he is Lord. Some try to apply this reference to the Son of Man to humans and their authority, but that is probably not intended here. Nowhere in Judaism was it thought that humans had authority over the Sabbath. The appeal here is to a special and limited authority that resided uniquely in Jesus (Witherington 2001:132). He had the right to make the call about what could and could not be done. Jesus' authority thus applied not only to forgiveness, relationships, and religious practice, but also to the most sacred day of the Jewish week. Mark is delineating the extent of Jesus' claims and authority. The Sabbath was made for people, but only one man has authority over it.

♦ ### 5. The fifth controversy: Jesus heals on the Sabbath (3:1-6; cf. Matt 12:9-14; Luke 6:6-11)

Jesus went into the synagogue again and noticed a man with a deformed hand. ²Since it was the Sabbath, Jesus' enemies watched him closely. If he healed the man's hand, they planned to accuse him of working on the Sabbath.

³Jesus said to the man with the deformed hand, "Come and stand in front of everyone." ⁴Then he turned to his critics and asked, "Does the law permit good deeds on the Sabbath, or is it a day for doing evil? Is this a day to save life or to destroy it?" But they wouldn't answer him.

⁵He looked around at them angrily and was deeply saddened by their hard hearts. Then he said to the man, "Hold out your hand." So the man held out his hand, and it was restored! ⁶At once the Pharisees went away and met with the supporters of Herod to plot how to kill Jesus.

NOTES

3:1 deformed. The man's hand was withered (*exērammenēn* [TG3583A, ZG3830]), like a plant desiccated by drought (BDAG 684). The result was paralysis.

3:2 If he healed. This remark suggests that Jesus' "enemies" (in Gr., a vague "they") fully expected him to heal the man with the deformed hand. They had the sense that Jesus would respond compassionately to the man in this way.

3:4 to save life or to destroy it? Jesus posed the ironic dilemma of the scene. Those who accused Jesus of violating the Sabbath were faulting him for doing something good and were trying to destroy him. Mark 3:2 makes it clear that they were searching for such an opening. Their hope was that he would discredit himself as a divine agent. Meanwhile, by healing, Jesus was doing good and improving the quality of someone's life. Jesus raised the question of who was really honoring God and blessing his creation—the point of the Sabbath rest—by what they were doing.

3:5 angrily and was deeply saddened by their hard hearts. Mark often notes Jesus' emotions. He does so here by showing the mixture of anger and sadness Jesus experienced at their refusal to understand what he had been saying to them. A hard heart meant that their perception had become rigid and stubborn (Hooker 1991:107). The term for "hard" (*pōrōsei* [TG4457, ZG4801]) refers to something hardened or dulled (BDAG 900). One might refer to a callous understanding that both angered and saddened Jesus. His only Sabbath work was a command for the man to stretch out his hand. The man's obedience made the healing evident.

3:6 plot how to kill Jesus. Pharisees and Herodians joined in a commitment to stop Jesus. The Herodians were Jewish supporters of Herod, so religious (Pharisees) and political (Herodians) Jews were united in wanting to kill Jesus. Jesus' challenge to a variety of practices and sacred days motivated their decision. The rest of the Gospel explains how the plot was carried out. Note the contrast between this and the positive response to Jesus' ministry in 1:45.

COMMENTARY

This unit rounds out and concludes the controversy section of Mark. Cases of paralysis bookend the unit. Jesus' ministry caused controversy because of his unique authority to offer forgiveness, his association with sinners, his disciples' not fasting, and his Sabbath activities. In each case, a pronouncement by Jesus makes the case for his action. In each case, he claims to have the authority to determine the most appropriate action and to perform it. Each step accelerated the opposition's reaction against Jesus. By the time he acted to "save life" and "do good" on the Sabbath, his opponents, while trying to defend the sacred day, ironically ended up doing evil and being destructive on the Sabbath. Jesus' actions turned everything upside down. In their defense of the law, they violated it by plotting murder against one who understood that the law existed to serve people, not to unduly confine them.

◆   **6. Summary of Jesus' early ministry (3:7-12; cf. Matt 12:15-21; Luke 6:17-19)**

⁷Jesus went out to the lake with his disciples, and a large crowd followed him. They came from all over Galilee, Judea, ⁸Jerusalem, Idumea, from east of the Jordan River, and even from as far north as Tyre and Sidon. The news about his miracles had spread far and wide, and vast numbers of people came to see him.

9Jesus instructed his disciples to have a boat ready so the crowd would not crush him. 10He had healed many people that day, so all the sick people eagerly pushed forward to touch him. 11And whenever those possessed by evil* spirits caught sight of him, the spirits would throw them to the ground in front of him shrieking, "You are the Son of God!" 12But Jesus sternly commanded the spirits not to reveal who he was.

3:11 Greek *unclean;* also in 3:30.

NOTES

3:7 *Jesus went.* Some suggest that Jesus' withdrawal in 3:7 is really a "fleeing" from the plot, because the term for "withdraw" (*anechōrēsen* [TG402, ZG432]) used here can have that meaning (Matt 2:12-14, 22; John 6:15; Marcus 2000:257). However, Jesus' move did not put him in less contact with people or restrict his access to them.

3:8 *as far north as Tyre and Sidon.* These towns were not part of Israel. They indicate that Jesus' popularity had extended beyond the nation, although many Jews lived in these regions. The locales in Idumea and east of the Jordan make a similar point. The only areas not mentioned are Samaria and the Decapolis, which were predominantly Gentile. The point of popular attention was Jesus' miraculous activity, a focus Jesus had tried to prevent (1:44).

3:9 *crowd would not crush him.* So many were present that the disciples had to work to prevent Jesus from being crushed (*thlibō* [TG2346, ZG2567]; BDAG 457) by the crowd. Jesus worked from a boat at the edge of the shore so that people could approach without crushing him.

3:10 *eagerly pushed forward.* The NLT has translated the force of the verb *epipiptō* [TG1968, ZG2158] ("to press upon"; BDAG 377) very well here. People were eagerly approaching Jesus to be healed of their various tormenting conditions (*mastigas* [TG3148, ZG3465]; BDAG 620). This term for "disease" referred to a whip or a lash, but metaphorically had come to also refer to tormenting illnesses. Their desire to touch Jesus reflects cultural ideas shared with the OT (1 Kgs 17:21; 2 Kgs 4:34; 13:21; Guelich 1989:148). They believed that bodily contact would put them in touch with Jesus' healing power.

3:11-12 *the Son of God! . . . commanded the spirits not to reveal who he was.* Jesus commanded them to be silent. The Gr. *epitimaō* [TG2008, ZG2203] often translates a Heb. term denoting rebuke (Job 26:11; Ps 80:16; 104:7; 106:9; Zech 3:2; Lane 1974:130). Jesus refused such disclosure from the world of spirits. He preferred for his identity to emerge from his words and deeds. This silence is part of the "messianic secret" theme in Mark (see the "Major Themes" section in the Introduction).

COMMENTARY

Despite the rise of opposition, Jesus' popularity and ministry continued as before, except that now the crowds were growing, as they came in from virtually everywhere in the region. Healings and exorcisms continued as the crowds pressed upon Jesus to gain access to the physical deliverance he provided.

Jesus also continued to exercise authority over demons and to silence their confessions of him as the "Son of God." This title is rare in Mark, appearing only here, in 1:1 (in the introductory heading of the Gospel), and in 15:39 (in the climactic moment of the centurion's confession). A variation of the expression appears at 1:11 (the voice of God at Jesus' baptism calling Jesus the beloved son), 5:7 (also at an exorcism), and 14:61 (in the question at Jesus' examination). Jesus did not use this title of himself in Mark. Jesus had silenced a demon making a similar confession in 1:24-25 ("the Holy One sent from God"). As discussed there and in 1:34, the silencing had to do with the source of the confession as well as with a concern for timing and for potential confusion about what such a confession might mean. The consistency of the demons' confessions stand in contrast to the various opinions expressed by humans in Mark (1:27; 2:6-7; 4:41; 6:2-3, 14-16; 8:27-28).

From a literary perspective, this unit is a bridge to the next phase of Mark's Gospel. The section ends with Jesus' ministry gaining wide attention, even as it surfaced opposition. The next unit will detail the nature of his teaching and further trace his impact.

◆   ## C. Teaching on the Mystery-filled Kingdom and Miracles of Power Yield Rejection (3:13–6:6a)
1. The choosing of the Twelve (3:13-19; cf. Luke 6:12-16)

¹³Afterward Jesus went up on a mountain and called out the ones he wanted to go with him. And they came to him. ¹⁴Then he appointed twelve of them and called them his apostles.* They were to accompany him, and he would send them out to preach, ¹⁵giving them authority to cast out demons. ¹⁶These are the twelve he chose:
Simon (whom he named Peter),
¹⁷James and John (the sons of Zebedee, but Jesus nicknamed them "Sons of Thunder"*),
¹⁸Andrew,
Philip,
Bartholomew,
Matthew,
Thomas,
James (son of Alphaeus),
Thaddaeus,
Simon (the zealot*),
¹⁹Judas Iscariot (who later betrayed him).

3:14 Some manuscripts do not include *and called them his apostles.*   3:17 Greek *whom he named Boanerges, which means Sons of Thunder.*   3:18 Greek *the Cananean,* an Aramaic term for Jewish nationalists.

NOTES

3:13 *Jesus went up on a mountain.* Though the area was likely what we would consider a "hillside," Mark's use of "mountain" may allude to the mountain as the site where God acts and reveals, as he did with Moses at Sinai. The phrase Mark uses is *anabainei eis to oros* [TG3735, ZG4001] (mountain), which recalls a frequent expression in the Pentateuch that describes Moses' activity (Exod 19:3; 24:1-4; Num 27:12ff; Deut 9:7-10:11; Marcus 2000:266). If this allusion is intended, then Jesus' selection of the Twelve was a moment not unlike Israel's formation as a structured theocracy (Guelich 1989:156-157 argues against the allusion).

3:14 *twelve.* This number adds to the sense of an intentional typology between the disciples and Israel. Like the twelve tribes, the twelve apostles were chosen to preach the new message of the approaching Kingdom (TDNT 2:325-328). The setting of the selection is important. As the nation's leaders moved to reject Jesus, the emissary of God selected his own twelve leaders to make a claim for the nation (Hooker 1991:111). Their names are listed in 3:16-19. We know very little about most of the Twelve and in fact, the only four mentioned in Mark after this list is given are Peter, James, John, and Judas Iscariot.

called them his apostles. The presence of this phrase in the Gr. original of Mark is disputed, but the earliest MSS have it, including ℵ and B. Those who argue against its inclusion think the phrase is more likely to have been added to conform with Luke 6:13 and treat its omission as the harder reading (Marcus 2000:263). However, the use of similar terms for "send" in 3:14 might have led to an error of sight and a skipping of the initial phrase. By calling the twelve the "apostles," Jesus designated them as his commissioned representatives with authority to proclaim his message.

3:15 *authority to cast out demons.* Jesus extended their authority to include the conflict with demons that had been part of his own ministry to this point (1:39). Their parallel activity underscored their connection with Jesus.

3:16 *Simon (whom he named Peter).* For Peter to have two names was not unusual; this was a common practice at that time. His second name, Peter, means "rock." We first meet him in Mark at 1:16-20, where he left his nets and, with Andrew and the sons of Zebedee (James and John), joined Jesus.

3:17 *Sons of Thunder.* These brothers also received a second name, "Sons of Thunder." We are not told why they were given this name (see Guelich 1989:162).

3:18 *Matthew . . . Simon.* See the commentary below.

Thaddaeus. In Luke's list (Luke 6:14-16; Acts 1:13), this position is occupied by Judas, son of James, but the possibility of two names for the same person may be at work here.

3:19 *Judas Iscariot (who later betrayed him).* Whenever Judas is named, his betrayal is always noted. He is also last in the list.

COMMENTARY

Jesus was planning his moves even as opposition was rising. By naming twelve to serve in a special role, he made it clear that he was making a claim on Israel. That the Twelve were rooted in the historical ministry of Jesus becomes clear in Acts 1:21-26, when Judas has to be replaced to complete the group of twelve again. As to the historical character of the group, the early church would never have created a story in which Jesus selected his betrayer. This is not a story that one makes up about a leader's ability to select people or about his key followers.

The selection of the Twelve shows that Jesus planned to work with others alongside him. They would represent him and help to declare the message of the Kingdom. As Mark also made abundantly clear, they had much to learn about how that program would work.

The first listed among the Twelve is Peter. He was clearly the leader of the entire group, and he made a key confession at Caesarea Philippi (8:27-30). James and John are named second and third because they, with Peter, formed an inner group of three disciples that saw Jesus raise a little girl from the dead (Luke 8:51), witnessed Jesus on the mount of Transfiguration (9:2-8), and were asked to pray with Jesus during his time of trial (14:33).

Two other notable disciples are Simon the zealot and Matthew. The title "zealot" suggests that Simon was a nationalist, willing to fight to free Israel from Roman rule, before he became a disciple. Although the zealots did not appear as a formal party until the sixties in the first century, some were committed to this political position before then. Then there is Matthew, who collected taxes for Rome (2:13-14;

Matt 9:9), a position in direct opposition to Simon's. Thus there is evidence within the Twelve of the very reconciliation Jesus sought to give to people, not only with God but also with one another.

◆ ## 2. The debate over Jesus' power: Is it from Satan or from God? (3:20-30; cf. Matt 12:22-24)

20One time Jesus entered a house, and the crowds began to gather again. Soon he and his disciples couldn't even find time to eat. 21When his family heard what was happening, they tried to take him away. "He's out of his mind," they said.

22But the teachers of religious law who had arrived from Jerusalem said, "He's possessed by Satan,* the prince of demons. That's where he gets the power to cast out demons."

23Jesus called them over and responded with an illustration. "How can Satan cast out Satan?" he asked. 24"A kingdom divided by civil war will collapse. 25Similarly, a family splintered by feuding will fall apart. 26And if Satan is divided and fights against himself, how can he stand? He would never survive. 27Let me illustrate this further. Who is powerful enough to enter the house of a strong man like Satan and plunder his goods? Only someone even stronger—someone who could tie him up and then plunder his house.

28"I tell you the truth, all sin and blasphemy can be forgiven, 29but anyone who blasphemes the Holy Spirit will never be forgiven. This is a sin with eternal consequences." 30He told them this because they were saying, "He's possessed by an evil spirit."

3:22 Greek *Beelzeboul;* other manuscripts read *Beezeboul;* Latin version reads *Beelzebub.*

NOTES

3:20 *couldn't even find time to eat.* The crowds continued to grow. In 3:9, Jesus had to get in a boat to handle the crowds; now the presence of the crowds had become constant. Mark is carefully tracing the growth of Jesus' ministry.

3:21 *to take him away.* This often refers to arresting someone, so the idea was for his family to place him in their own custody (6:17; 12:12).

"He's out of his mind," they said. The syntax of this verse is not entirely clear. Who was making the judgment that Jesus had gone too far in his claims and had lost his senses? The most natural reading is that some of his own family members shared this concern, since until now the crowds had been drawn to Jesus and the only opponents were members of religious parties such as the Pharisees. That would leave the nearest antecedent as *hoi par autou,* which is a reference to family members (BDAG 756-757; Prov 31:21; Susanna 33; Josephus *Antiquities* 1.193). This is confirmed in 3:31 as Jesus' brothers and mother seek his attention after this exchange. We know from John 7:5 that Jesus' brothers did not believe in him during a portion of his ministry and here the concern seems to be for Jesus' well being. Since official opposition to his extensive claims was rising, perhaps they desired to come and get him to prevent his being harmed. It was a well-intentioned but misguided attempt to protect Jesus (Lane [1974:138] calls it a "gross misjudgment"). Their view was that Jesus was "beside himself" and operating outside of normal boundaries. Thus the NLT's "out of his mind" conveys the sense well. Later Christians were viewed similarly (Acts 26:24-26; 1 Cor 14:23; 2 Cor 5:13; Marcus 2000:271).

3:22 *teachers of religious law.* This is a reference to the scribes (see 1:22 and note).

He's possessed by Satan, the prince of demons. As the NLT mg indicates, *Beelzeboul* [TG954, ZG1015] is named in the Gr. This name originally referred to a Canaanite god (Marcus 2000:272); it became an alternate way of referring to Satan as head of the demons and stands parallel to the "prince of demons" in this verse. For the hierarchy of demons in Jewish thinking, see 1QS 3:20-21 and *Testament of Solomon* 2:9; 3:5; 6:1. Jews had many names for Satan, including Beliar/Belial (*Jubilees* 1:20; 2 Cor 6:15), Asmodeus (Tobit 3:8), and Mastema (*Jubilees* 10:8; 11:5; 17:16). The charge was important as recognition that supernatural power was at work through Jesus. There was no doubt that he was performing unusual works. The debate was over the source of his power. Later Jewish teachers also charged Jesus with practicing sorcery (*b. Sanhedrin* 43a; 107b; Lane 1974:142). Jesus' response to such charges follows.

3:23 *illustration.* The Gr. is plural and refers to the proverbial maxims that Jesus quoted; they are followed by a key parabolic image in 3:27 (Lane 1974:142).

How can Satan cast out Satan? Jesus' fundamental argument was that if Satan was casting out demons, he was undoing his own work; Jesus was asking if that really made sense.

3:24 *divided by civil war.* The NLT renders the sense of the phrase "if a kingdom is divided against itself." Jesus' point was that such internal division made a kingdom weaker and more susceptible to defeat. Satan would never follow such a strategy. "Satan has more sense than to destroy his own kingdom" (Hooker 1991:116). So that explanation for Jesus' authority was not credible. Jesus makes essentially the same point in 3:25, referring to a "family," which could refer to a dynasty of rulers, something also suggested by the idea of a kingdom or dominion.

3:26 *He would never survive.* Here the NLT renders the force of "is coming to an end." Jesus' point is still that Satan would not seek to destroy his own authority in this subversive way, which would bring his rule to an end of his own accord. Preservation, not self-destruction, is Satan's goal.

3:27 *Let me illustrate this further.* This phrase is not found in Mark. The NLT creates a transition to a fresh example that Jesus sets forth.

tie him up. This refers to "binding the strong man," who represents Satan. Jesus maintained that his miracles made it evident that one stronger than Satan had entered Satan's home and would plunder the power and possessions that Satan once controlled. In short, Jesus' presence meant Satan's defeat, and the miracles demonstrated this. Jesus' miracles were not evidence of power being exercised through Satan but the exact opposite. The judgment that Jesus casts out demons by Satan's power could not be more wrong. The remark shows that Jesus' battle was taking place on a cosmic, supernatural stage, since Satan was a chief enemy.

3:28 *I tell you the truth.* This introductory remark using *amēn* [TG281, ZG297] is the first of thirteen uses of this term in Mark (excluding the occurrence after 16:8 in the shorter ending). The expression is only used with sayings of Jesus as it signifies extremely significant announcements. Jesus "solemnly guarantees the truth of what he is about to say" (Cranfield 1959:140), so this warning against blaspheming the Spirit is marked out as serious.

3:29 *anyone who blasphemes the Holy Spirit.* In the context of Mark, the sin was attributing to Satan work that the Spirit had done. It was the refusal to see Jesus' work and ministry as being rooted in the activity of God's Spirit. This is clear from 3:30, where Jesus refuted the charge that he was possessed by evil spirits and warned against slandering (i.e., blaspheming) the work of the Spirit. In Mark, this decisive and firm refusal to understand who Jesus is constitutes an unpardonable sin.

eternal consequences. The NLT brings out the effect of being guilty of an "eternal sin" by this rendering, which combines the idea of a sin that cannot be forgiven (lit., "does not have forgiveness unto the age") with that of an act having eternal duration.

3:30 *possessed by an evil spirit.* To say that Jesus "has an unclean spirit" is to suggest that a destructive spirit controlled the acts Jesus performed. The NLT rendering conveys this. In the Gr., there is an important juxtaposition here. Jesus acted by the Holy Spirit (3:29) despite the leaders' false claim that he had an unclean spirit. The verb used in the charge is in the imperfect ("they were saying"), so this charge was regularly leveled against Jesus.

COMMENTARY

This unit summarizes Mark's story to this point in his Gospel. Various opinions were gathering around Jesus' ability to heal. Only three options could explain what was taking place: (1) He had lost his mind and was thinking too highly of himself, as at least some in his family feared; (2) He was operating under the direction of a sinister power, as the scribes claimed; or (3) He was working by the power of the Spirit of God, the position Jesus defended by excluding the satanic option. The same idea is expressed in C. S. Lewis' famous "Liar, Lunatic, or Lord" options for who Jesus is, which are taken from the options Mark raises in this passage. Either Jesus lied about his authority (it was really from Satan, or was only a delusion; see 3:21), or he is Lord and his authority is from God, as affirmed by the Spirit (see 3:29).

Jesus' argument against the scribes was that if healings and exorcisms were taking place under Satan's power, then Satan was undoing his own work. It was not plausible for Satan to be consciously engaged in self-destruction. The leaders risked being guilty of an unforgivable sin if they persisted in their erroneous judgment, since they were slandering the work of God's Spirit as operative in Jesus. So the lines were drawn.

Jesus' opponents never questioned that Jesus was performing unusual deeds. The debate concerned their origin, not their existence. Mark describes the lines of the debate and warns about the eternal consequences of making the wrong choice. The blasphemy was serious, for it was "the conscious and deliberate rejection of the saving power and grace of God released through Jesus' word and act" (Lane 1974:145).

◆ **3. Jesus' true family is those who do God's will (3:31-35; cf. Matt 12:46-50)**

³¹Then Jesus' mother and brothers came to see him. They stood outside and sent word for him to come out and talk with them. ³²There was a crowd sitting around Jesus, and someone said, "Your mother and your brothers* are outside asking for you." ³³Jesus replied, "Who is my mother? Who are my brothers?" ³⁴Then he looked at those around him and said, "Look, these are my mother and brothers. ³⁵Anyone who does God's will is my brother and sister and mother."

3:32 Some manuscripts add *and sisters.*

NOTES

3:32 *Your mother and your brothers.* This text makes it clear that Mary had other children besides Jesus. It appears that they were seeking Jesus' attention in 3:21 as well. After "brothers," some manuscripts (AD 700) add "and your sisters." The note with this verse indicates some uncertainty about the inclusion of this phrase from the Gr. version of Mark. It was probably not original to Mark and there is good testimony against its inclusion (ℵ B C L W). Culturally, it is unlikely that sisters would be included in seeking Jesus out in this manner (Metzger 1971:82). It also makes the remarks more parallel to 3:35, which does mention "sister." Thus, it is more likely to have been added than omitted, though an error of sight leading to omission is also possible (by skipping one phrase due to repeated mentions of *sou* [TG4771, ZG5148]).

COMMENTARY

This short unit underscores how Jesus' presence was drawing new lines of community. The new demarcation emerges through the significance of Jesus' presence. Those who do God's will respond positively to him and become part of a new community whose shared loyalty to God might well transcend even the bond of family.

Jesus affirmed that his true family is not his biological family, but those who follow the will of God (Luke 11:27-28). Placed in this context and followed by the parables of the Kingdom, the point is to be responsive to Jesus' message about God and his plan, a message his mother and brothers were apparently struggling to accept. The account might be especially poignant if others who were responding to Jesus were facing the same lack of acceptance from family members (Marcus 2000:285-286). In effect, Jesus affirmed a new family and a new community. Since the family was the most significant of ancient relationships, this point was important. Even the most fundamental human relationships are not as central a defining point for identity and action as is loyalty to God.

◆   ## 4. Parable of the sower (4:1-20; cf. Matt 13:1-9)

Once again Jesus began teaching by the lakeshore. A very large crowd soon gathered around him, so he got into a boat. Then he sat in the boat while all the people remained on the shore. ²He taught them by telling many stories in the form of parables, such as this one:

³"Listen! A farmer went out to plant some seed. ⁴As he scattered it across his field, some of the seed fell on a footpath, and the birds came and ate it. ⁵Other seed fell on shallow soil with underlying rock. The seed sprouted quickly because the soil was shallow. ⁶But the plant soon wilted under the hot sun, and since it didn't have deep roots, it died. ⁷Other seed fell among thorns that grew up and choked out the tender plants so they produced no grain. ⁸Still other seeds fell on fertile soil, and they sprouted, grew, and produced a crop that was thirty, sixty, and even a hundred times as much as had been planted!"

⁹Then he said, "Anyone with ears to hear should listen and understand."

¹⁰Later, when Jesus was alone with the twelve disciples and with the others who were gathered around, they asked him what the parables meant.

¹¹He replied, "You are permitted to understand the secret* of the Kingdom of God. But I use parables for everything I say to outsiders, ¹²so that the Scriptures might be fulfilled:

'When they see what I do,
    they will learn nothing.
When they hear what I say,
    they will not understand.
Otherwise, they will turn to me
    and be forgiven.'*"

¹³Then Jesus said to them, "If you can't understand the meaning of this parable,

how will you understand all the other parables? ¹⁴The farmer plants seed by taking God's word to others. ¹⁵The seed that fell on the footpath represents those who hear the message, only to have Satan come at once and take it away. ¹⁶The seed on the rocky soil represents those who hear the message and immediately receive it with joy. ¹⁷But since they don't have deep roots, they don't last long. They fall away as soon as they have problems or are persecuted for believing God's word. ¹⁸The seed that fell among the thorns represents others who hear God's word, ¹⁹but all too quickly the message is crowded out by the worries of this life, the lure of wealth, and the desire for other things, so no fruit is produced. ²⁰And the seed that fell on good soil represents those who hear and accept God's word and produce a harvest of thirty, sixty, or even a hundred times as much as had been planted.

4:11 Greek *mystery.* 4:12 Isa 6:9-10 (Greek version).

NOTES

4:1 *by the lakeshore.* This refers to the Sea of Galilee, which is about eight by fourteen miles in size.

large crowd. This is the largest gathering in the Gospel of Mark thus far. Jesus was still out in the open teaching people as in 3:9 (see also 2:13).

boat. This is the first of several boat scenes in Mark 4–8, others of which include the stilling of the storm (4:35-41), Jesus' walk on the water (6:45-52), and a discussion about leaven (8:14-21). Each of these scenes involves a criticism of the disciples, but in this first boat scene they were instructed. An ancient first-century BC–AD boat was found in Galilee in 1986. It measured 26.5 feet long by 7.5 feet wide by 4.5 feet deep (Hanson and Oakman 1998:110). It was probably typical of boats at this time.

4:2 *parables.* This term covers a wide array of teaching tools from short examples, maxims, or proverbial figures known in Heb. as *mashal* [TH4912, ZH5442], to longer stories developed as theological illustrations (Lane 1974:150-51). The shorter ones are found in 3:23-27. Here we have a longer one.

4:3 *Listen!* The parable begins with a call to hear that marks out its importance.

farmer. In the Gr., this refers to a sower of seed, who was probably also a farmer, which explains the NLT rendering.

4:4 *footpath.* Alongside a field, there would often be a footpath where those traveling could walk without ruining the crops. The ground there would be packed down from all the foot travel, so seed would sit exposed on its surface where birds could get it. In Palestine, farmers sowed first and then plowed.

4:8 *thirty, sixty, and even a hundred times as much.* The seed that fell in the good soil stands in contrast to the three other seed groups that fell on the path, on shallow soil, and among the thorns. It did what seed is supposed to do, which is to bear fruit. Some seeds were more productive than others.

4:9 *should listen and understand.* This NLT rendering develops one of Jesus' common expressions—"the one with ears to hear, let him hear." The point is not merely for the sound to be perceived but for the message to be heeded, so the NLT rendering is a good one. Jesus was revealing a divine mystery (4:11), and he wanted people to pay attention to it.

4:11 *the secret of the Kingdom of God.* "Secret" renders the Gr. word for "mystery" (*mustērion* [TG3466, ZG3696]); Jesus' point was that the parables contained revelation about the Kingdom. This is the term's only occurence in Mark. In Mark's perspective, there are insiders and outsiders to understanding what God is doing—the disciples are privileged to know what is going on.

4:12 *learn nothing . . . not understand. Otherwise, they will turn.* This verse is a short-ened citation from Isa 6:9-10. The key differences are that third person verbs open the first clause (rather than second person) and the concluding reference is to being forgiven rather than healed. These differences are like the targum of Isaiah (Marcus 2000:300). The differ-ences so strongly paralleled in the Aramaic setting may indicate that the age of the tradition reaches back into Jesus' time. Unlike the other texts, the Gospel of Mark reverses the order of perception to seeing/hearing. Marcus (2000:300) suggests that this is because Mark liked to highlight the role of vision (8:22-26; 10:46-52; numerous times in ch 13; 15:32, 36, 39). In context, the statement explains that Isaiah's ministry was one of hardening.

so that . . . Otherwise. A huge debate swirls around the use of *hina* [TG2443, ZG2671] at the beginning of the verse and *mēpote* [TG3379, ZG3607] toward its end. Does *hina* (in order that) mean that the purpose of the parables was to obscure belief (so Marcus 2000:299-300)? This takes the *hina* as a final clause and stresses the Gr. Mark uses to introduce the quota-tion. Or does *mēpote* (lest) introduce an indirect question and *hina* stand as epexegetical (so Guelich 1989:211-12), so that the passage describes the effect of their failure to embrace the parables? This latter interpretation relies on the force of the commonly assumed Aramaic behind the saying (viz., "that is, seeing they learn nothing . . . if they had turned and been forgiven"). The decision here is not an easy one, especially granted that Matthew and Luke have softer renderings in Gr. (more like the proposed underlying Aramaic option—and it is likely the original saying was given in Aramaic), so that the Gr. differences are translational issues in the tradition. This Aramaic-based reading is less harsh than the way Mark's Gr. can be read. The NLT leaves the text somewhat ambiguous on this point by using "when" at the beginning of the citation and "otherwise" near the end. The OT idea of repentance is alluded to in the idea of turning (*shub* [TH7725, ZH8740]). In other words, parables are judg-ments that prevent outsiders from becoming responsive. The debate is whether that preven-tion is by previous divine design or the effect of an earlier lack of responsiveness. Either way, the use of parables meant that judgment was taking place.

4:14 *God's word.* Jesus begins by noting that the seed is "the word." In 4:11, the topic of this word is the message of the Kingdom, the key content of these parables. So this parable is about different ways that people respond to the word that comes from God about the Kingdom. Mark uses "the word" in this way to speak of the Gospel (1:14; 2:2; 4:33; cf. Acts 6:4; 10:36-37, 44; Col 4:3).

4:15 *The seed that fell.* This phrase is repeated with all four soils (4:16, 18, 20); it lit. reads, "these are those." The sowing imagery used in Judaism was flexible (*4 Ezra* 8:41; 9:31; Marcus 2000:308). In other words, the parable sometimes speaks of seed as the word that is sown (4:14), but elsewhere the seed is the different types of people with different kinds of heart attitudes into whom the word is sown (4:15, 16, 18, 20). The parable is not about the word as an abstract, isolated concept, but about the ways that the word is received and responded to once it is "taken in."

Satan. Some seed never has a chance to produce fruit (the goal within the imagery) because Satan snatches it from the surface of the path. In Judaism, Satan is sometimes com-pared to a bird (*Apocalypse of Abraham* 13:3-8). Despite being bound by having lost his bat-tle with Jesus (3:27), Satan is portrayed as still being active (Hooker 1991:131).

4:16 *with joy.* The seed on the rocky soil initially reacts with openness, which sadly does not last (4:17).

4:17 *they don't have deep roots.* In Judaism, the wicked are commonly identified as root-less (Sir 23:25; 40:15; Wis 4:3; cf. Marcus 2000:309). Their temporary faith exposes them as lacking the genuine faith that brings forth fruit.

fall away. Gr. *skandalizontai* [TG4624A, ZG4997]. The noun *skandalon* [TG4625, ZG4998] refers to someone who views the message of the cross as an offense, a barrier to belief (1 Cor 1:23). To fall away is to trip over this obstacle. Jesus' point is that in these cases, the shame of persecution is greater than a person's embrace of the message, so they stumble over the message in times of trouble. This term denotes apostasy, or lack of real faith (TDNT 7:349).

have problems. Rootless believers fall away when tribulation or persecution arises on account of the word.

4:19 *worries of this life, the lure of wealth, and the desire for other things.* The seed among thorns pictures those who get so encumbered with the basic enticements of this world that they produce no fruit. The seed again fails to accomplish its purpose. The terms used here do not appear frequently in the Synoptics. "Worries" is used elsewhere only in Luke 21:34; "lure" appears only here and in its parallel, Matt 13:22; and "desire" has no parallel akin to its use here, although it is used positively in Luke 22:15. The theme of riches and the problems of the rich are a concern (Matt 6:24-25; 19:23-24; Mark 10:25; Luke 1:53; 12:21). In this case, the failure lies with the distractions that prevent the person from benefiting from the word. The one thing the first three groups share is that none of them are fruitful. In the terms of the parable, they are all failures.

4:20 *hear and accept God's word and produce a harvest.* Here the seed reaches its goal. The word is heard, accepted, and has a yield. The idea behind the word for "accepting" is that of welcoming the word, of openly taking it in (Jas 1:21; Cranfield 1959:163).

thirty, sixty, or even a hundred times. These varying yields indicate that disciples have different levels of productivity. When the word reaches a prepared heart, it flourishes.

COMMENTARY

Mark 4, with its teaching on the Kingdom, is the first of two major teaching blocks in Mark, the other being the Olivet discourse in Mark 13. The opening section of Mark 4 indicates the importance of the Kingdom message to Jesus' preaching and to the hurdles he faced. Jesus began with the parable of a sower. By definition, parables teach by making a comparison and paint a picture through that comparison. What the parable of the sower depicts—the preaching of the word about the Kingdom—is not noted until 4:11, 14. This parable and those that follow, as a group, tell us important things about Jesus' message concerning the Kingdom and the plan that goes with it.

Jesus' main point is that the parables reveal the Kingdom of God. Those who get the point understand "the mystery of the Kingdom." The Greek term for mystery (*mustērion* [TG3466, ZG3696]) has roots in the Old Testament idea of raz [TA10661, ZA10661], where God discloses something that requires a gifted person to interpret what is said (someone like Daniel) or that is made clear with the coming of what was promised (Dan 2:18-19; 12:8-10; TDNT 4:814-821; the term also shows up at Qumran in CD 3:18; 1QH 13[5]:36; cf. Marcus 2000:298). The term is singular here, but probably operates as a collective idea. Thus, the "secret" (the "mystery") has many parts that as a whole comprise the mystery of the Kingdom. The key features of mystery in Mark 4 are tied to God's sovereign plan and to the various responses to the Kingdom, such as the great fruitfulness of those who respond, the availability of the Kingdom, the almost hidden way in which it grows, and the fact that it starts out small but ends up covering the whole earth. The disciples had access to the mystery, since the text says that it had been given to them to understand. Others did not understand, and these remained outside the Kingdom.

One of the functions of parables, as the citation from Isaiah 6:9-10 shows, is that they also judge those who are unresponsive, since they contain "concealed revelation." Those outside of Jesus' community would not understand the parables on their own. This failure to respond to what was seen and heard is a consistent theme in Mark (2:16; 3:2; 7:2-5; 11:18; 14:58, 64). Jesus compared the lack of response in Israel and his subsequent use of parables to the earlier ministry of Isaiah. In fact, Jesus' ministry, especially his use of parables, bears out the fulfillment of Isaiah 6:9-10: the judgment on a people already hardened meant that they would not be responding, for although something was put before them that they could see and hear, they did not respond with an understanding that would turn them toward forgiveness.

In 4:13, Jesus suggests that the parable of the sower is crucial to understanding the other parables, so he explains it to his disciples, thus unveiling the mystery. His explanation also relieves a tension that might suggest that 4:11 meant that the disciples should instinctively comprehend the parables without such an explanation. The advantage the disciples had over outsiders was that they had Jesus' interpretation of the parables.

The message of the parable is that there are varying degrees of receptivity to the word of God. Some people never grasp the word because Satan interferes before they even have a chance to interact with it. Others are distracted by the pressures of a world that does not welcome the message, or by the cares, concerns, and enticements of life. Many never yield fruit even when they are initially attracted to the word. By contrast, when the seed of the word encounters a receptive heart, it produces fruit in varying degrees. All disciples are urged to be receptive and fruitful, not allowing the rejection of the world to get in their way.

For these people, neither Satan, persecutions, nor the cares of this world distract them from embracing the word of the Kingdom. They will be the fruitful ones. Fruitfulness, including the imagery of large yields, was a common Old Testament metaphor portraying the blessings and products of the new age (Jer 31:12; Hos 2:21-22; Joel 2:22; Amos 9:13; Zech 8:12; Marcus 2000:295). The extraordinary sizes of the yields (a normal harvest would be about ten times the amount sown) point to the great success of the harvest (Witherington 2001:165-166).

◆   5. Parable of the lamp (4:21-25)

21Then Jesus asked them, "Would anyone light a lamp and then put it under a basket or under a bed? Of course not! A lamp is placed on a stand, where its light will shine. 22For everything that is hidden will eventually be brought into the open, and every secret will be brought to light. 23Anyone with ears to hear should listen and understand."

24Then he added, "Pay close attention to

what you hear. The closer you listen, the more understanding you will be given*— and you will receive even more. ²⁵To those who listen to my teaching, more under- standing will be given. But for those who are not listening, even what little under- standing they have will be taken away from them."

4:24 Or *The measure you give will be the measure you get back.*

NOTES

4:21 *basket.* This was probably a two-gallon measure (Hooker 1991:133).

Of course not! The NLT accurately brings out the force of the rhetorical question. The structure of the initial question in Gr. expects a negative answer, just as the second expects a positive reply. The NLT breaks up the question into two clear parts with this exclamation as a transition between them. A lamp goes on a stand where it can give light.

4:22 *everything that is hidden will eventually be brought into the open.* Jesus brings a message with a note of accountability. This will accompany judgment when the Kingdom and its comprehensive character are completely revealed and the light is fully manifest in the end. Until then, the Kingdom seems like a hidden secret.

4:23 *should listen and understand.* See note on 4:9.

4:24 *The closer you listen, the more understanding you will be given.* This NLT rendering explains "the measure you give will be the measure you get back" (cf. NLT mg). The passage assumes that one will pay attention to the light and notes that such attention will be rewarded with more positive exposure to the light.

4:25 *even what little understanding they have will be taken away.* This is a warning that those who do not pay attention to the light will end up with nothing, even losing what little understanding they once had.

COMMENTARY

The main point of this parable is that the word of the Kingdom is like a light that God has set on a stand to guide people on their way and to expose what is really going on (4:22). The implication is that people should heed the light (4:23). But this parable is also enigmatic in its juxtaposition of light with that which is hidden. The Kingdom appears to be both: its character is light, but it is also hidden in that people are not seeing it for the light that it is. The Kingdom will not remain hidden forever. It is seemingly hidden now in that its full power is not evident, but even in its concealed form it will do an exposing work, and rejection of the Kingdom will one day be shown for what it is. In other words, what seems hidden now about the Kingdom's presence will one day be fully displayed and at the same time will expose all things. Jesus here notes that one of the functions of light is to expose (so Ps 119:105; Marcus 2000:318). Such exposure will take place one day in conjunc- tion with the exercise of Kingdom authority. Even though the seed of the word gets various responses, as the previous parable showed, it will ultimately still achieve its goal of exposing what is present within people. The exhortation is to pay careful attention to the light, to hear and heed the Kingdom message. Those who do heed the message will be blessed with more revelation and blessing. Those who do not heed it will end up with nothing.

◆ 6. Parable of the growing seed (4:26-29)

²⁶Jesus also said, "The Kingdom of God is like a farmer who scatters seed on the ground. ²⁷Night and day, while he's asleep or awake, the seed sprouts and grows, but he does not understand how it happens. ²⁸The earth produces the crops on its own. First a leaf blade pushes through, then the heads of wheat are formed, and finally the grain ripens. ²⁹And as soon as the grain is ready, the farmer comes and harvests it with a sickle, for the harvest time has come."

NOTES

4:28 *on its own.* The earth produces its yield automatically (*automatē* [ᵀᴳ844, ᶻᴳ897]), by a process the farmer does not understand.

COMMENTARY

This parable is unique to Mark. The growth of the Kingdom is like the growth of seed. The humans who work the land do not fully understand how this growth takes place. There is something mysterious and inevitable about the Kingdom's development. God is responsible for how the crop will come to maturity.

In the end, the time will come to reap what has been sown. Harvest is an image of judgment, as Joel 3:13 indicates—a time when evil is judged and righteousness is vindicated. The seed of the Kingdom will grow, and judgment will come, even though the exact process is not clearly understood by the one who sows the seed.

◆ 7. The mustard seed and a summary on parables (4:30-34; cf. Matt 13:31-35)

³⁰Jesus said, "How can I describe the Kingdom of God? What story should I use to illustrate it? ³¹It is like a mustard seed planted in the ground. It is the smallest of all seeds, ³²but it becomes the largest of all garden plants; it grows long branches, and birds can make nests in its shade." ³³Jesus used many similar stories and illustrations to teach the people as much as they could understand. ³⁴In fact, in his public ministry he never taught without using parables; but afterward, when he was alone with his disciples, he explained everything to them.

NOTES

4:31 *smallest of all seeds.* The mustard seed is proverbially called the smallest seed (TDNT 7:288).

4:32 *largest of all garden plants . . . birds can make nests in its shade.* The background to the birds nesting is probably Ezek 17:23. The small seed produces an unusually large plant that is eight to ten feet tall and one that birds can nest in. The backdrop is the replanting of the Davidic house that results in shelter (for the image of birds in the nest, see Ezek 31:6; Dan 4:12, 14, 21).

COMMENTARY

This final parable emphasizes the shelter that the Kingdom brings. There is some discussion as to whether the birds depict Gentiles, but in Mark's version of this parable that point is not clear. The summary in 4:33-34 simply reiterates that Jesus taught with parables and then explained everything to his disciples. This unit concludes one of two major discourses in Mark, the other being the Olivet discourse.

The Kingdom is the theme of Jesus' teaching. God is at work in the sowing of seed, but the seed's effectiveness is tied to the nature of its reception. The kingdom grows in mysterious ways. As light, it will expose all things and bring judgment. It will start small but grow to be a place of shelter (4:32). The kingdom may not have come in an expected way, but its coming and success are inevitable.

◆   ## 8. Jesus calms a storm (4:35-41; cf. Luke 8:22-25)

³⁵As evening came, Jesus said to his disciples, "Let's cross to the other side of the lake." ³⁶So they took Jesus in the boat and started out, leaving the crowds behind (although other boats followed). ³⁷But soon a fierce storm came up. High waves were breaking into the boat, and it began to fill with water.

³⁸Jesus was sleeping at the back of the boat with his head on a cushion. The disciples woke him up, shouting, "Teacher, don't you care that we're going to drown?"

³⁹When Jesus woke up, he rebuked the wind and said to the waves, "Silence! Be still!" Suddenly the wind stopped, and there was a great calm. ⁴⁰Then he asked them, "Why are you afraid? Do you still have no faith?"

⁴¹The disciples were absolutely terrified. "Who is this man?" they asked each other. "Even the wind and waves obey him!"

NOTES

4:37 a fierce storm came up. The Sea of Galilee is surrounded by hills except in the southern area, where the Jordan River exits. With certain wind patterns, air can funnel up into the lake and get trapped, creating quick and violent storms. That apparently happened in this case. Key biblical scenes involving storms and seas include Exod 14:21-31; Ps 107:23-32; Jonah 1:1-16; Acts 27.

4:38 Jesus was sleeping. Jesus was probably sleeping in the stern of the boat at the helmsman's station where there was some protection from getting wet. The cushion may have been a sandbag used for ballast (Marcus 2000:333). His sleeping may indicate his calm trust in God (Ps 4:8). Here is Mark's first description of discipleship failure (see the Major Themes section in the introduction).

Teacher, don't you care that we're going to drown? This question uses the negative particle *ou* [TG3756, ZG4024] and is asked in a way that makes it clear that the disciples knew that Jesus cared about their well-being despite the tone of their question. The conflict shows their panic.

4:39 he rebuked the wind and said to the waves. This language is similar to that of an exorcism (1:25). Jesus' authority extended over creation and provoked the reflective question of 4:41. In some parts of the ancient world, the waters were associated with evil.

Be still! This command is lit. "Be muzzled" (Deut 25:4, LXX; 1 Tim 5:18), but the NLT picks up the effects of the muzzling: silence and peace (BDAG 1060; Luke 4:35).

4:40 Why are you afraid? Jesus questions their timidity; *deiloi* [TG1169, ZG1264] indicates cowardice or lack of courage (Deut 20:8; Judg 7:3; 1 Macc 3:56). For Mark, fear is the opposite of faith (5:15-17, 36; 6:49-52; 10:32; 11:18; 16:8). Jesus' remark is a call to trust him.

Do you still have no faith? Jesus' final question uses the interrogative adverb *oupō* [TG3768, ZG4037], which means "not yet" (BDAG 737). Jesus pressed the matter: "Do you still have no faith?"

4:41 *absolutely terrified.* The NLT very clearly translates the Semitic idiom retained in the Gr. "feared with great fear" (Jonah 1:10, LXX). Jesus' great authority left them in awe.

Even *the wind and waves obey him!* The remark points to Ps 107:29 and Ps 89:8-9. Jesus' actions revealed that he had divine control over creation. That such authority resided in a person left the disciples stunned. It raised the question of who Jesus was. By stopping the scene here (creating an "open ending"), Mark leaves the reader to ponder the answer to this question.

COMMENTARY

The storm must have been quite serious, since the experienced fishermen on board were terrified. Their fear of dying was much like that recorded in Jonah 1. Things were clearly beyond their control, so they asked Jesus to help. His help far exceeded their expectations; he didn't rescue them from the storm but stilled the storm itself.

This miracle begins a sequence of four miracles (see 5:1-43) that show Jesus' comprehensive authority. To begin with, creation is significant as a clearly divine domain. In ancient everyday life, perhaps no force was more powerful and omnipresent than nature. Coping with the elements was a factor of daily life, so Jesus' ability to calm the storm and his exhortation to the disciples to have faith and not be afraid was a basic lesson in their discipleship. But beyond the significance of their immediate deliverance was what this act suggested about Jesus' divine enablement. What kind of man could have power like that possessed by God? No man on his own can tame nature. The incident ends with a question about who Jesus really is. The rest of the Gospel answers that question.

In an interesting twist, 2 Maccabees 9:8 tells a story about the evil king Antiochus Epiphanes trying to calm a storm and failing. When he died, it was in part God's retribution for his trying to do something that only God had the right to do (Marcus 2000:333-334). At Qumran, such authority was said to reside in the Messiah (4Q521 2 ii 1).

◆ ### 9. The healing of the Gerasene demoniac (5:1-20; cf. Luke 8:26-39)

So they arrived at the other side of the lake, in the region of the Gerasenes.* ²When Jesus climbed out of the boat, a man possessed by an evil* spirit came out from a cemetery to meet him. ³This man lived among the burial caves and could no longer be restrained, even with a chain. ⁴Whenever he was put into chains and shackles—as he often was—he snapped the chains from his wrists and smashed the shackles. No one was strong enough to subdue him. ⁵Day and night he wandered among the burial caves and in the hills, howling and cutting himself with sharp stones.

⁶When Jesus was still some distance away, the man saw him, ran to meet him, and bowed low before him. ⁷With a shriek, he screamed, "Why are you interfering with me, Jesus, Son of the Most High

God? In the name of God, I beg you, don't torture me!" [8]For Jesus had already said to the spirit, "Come out of the man, you evil spirit."

[9]Then Jesus demanded, "What is your name?"

And he replied, "My name is Legion, because there are many of us inside this man." [10]Then the evil spirits begged him again and again not to send them to some distant place.

[11]There happened to be a large herd of pigs feeding on the hillside nearby. [12]"Send us into those pigs," the spirits begged. "Let us enter them."

[13]So Jesus gave them permission. The evil spirits came out of the man and entered the pigs, and the entire herd of 2,000 pigs plunged down the steep hillside into the lake and drowned in the water.

[14]The herdsmen fled to the nearby town and the surrounding countryside, spreading the news as they ran. People rushed out to see what had happened. [15]A crowd soon gathered around Jesus, and they saw the man who had been possessed by the legion of demons. He was sitting there fully clothed and perfectly sane, and they were all afraid. [16]Then those who had seen what happened told the others about the demon-possessed man and the pigs. [17]And the crowd began pleading with Jesus to go away and leave them alone.

[18]As Jesus was getting into the boat, the man who had been demon possessed begged to go with him. [19]But Jesus said, "No, go home to your family, and tell them everything the Lord has done for you and how merciful he has been." [20]So the man started off to visit the Ten Towns* of that region and began to proclaim the great things Jesus had done for him; and everyone was amazed at what he told them.

5:1 Other manuscripts read *Gadarenes;* still others read *Gergesenes.* See Matt 8:28; Luke 8:26.   5:2 Greek *unclean;* also in 5:8, 13.   5:20 Greek *Decapolis.*

NOTES

5:1 *Gerasenes.* This is the reading in ℵ* B D. Other manuscripts read "Gadarene" (A C 𝔐) or "Gergesene" (ℵ² L). The last reading is too poorly attested to be the likely original. Matthew's parallel reads "Gadarene," which possibly explains this textual variation as an effort to bring the two texts into tighter agreement. The better manuscripts of Mark have "Gerasenes" and Luke's reading is parallel to Mark. Gerasa (modern Jerash, Jordan) is about thirty-seven miles from the Sea of Galilee, while Gadara (modern Umm Qais, Jordan) is about six miles from it. In either case, the location was a predominantly Gentile area in what was known as the Decapolis region, so the tradition surrounding this miracle appears to be regional. Perhaps the better-known locale was cited rather than the actual one. Another possibility is that a lesser-known "Gerasa" on the eastern shore of Galilee was intended (so Cranfield 1959:176; Lane 1974:181).

5:2 *evil spirit.* This same expression appears in 1:23. For details, see that discussion.

5:3 *lived among the burial caves.* The tombs of the cemetery in an area outside the city were associated with death and ritual uncleanness. In later Judaism, spending the night on a grave was taken as a sign that one had gone mad (*b. Hagigah* 3b; Marcus 2000:343). People would want a cemetery cleansed so they could visit the graves of their loved ones (Gundry 1993:258, who also explains why an allusion to Isa 65:1-7, 11 LXX and its association of demons with tombs is not present, although the text from the prophet does show that such a connection was sometimes made).

could no longer be restrained, even with a chain. The attempt to fetter the man suggests that he was demon possessed and needed controlling. That the bonds could not hold him only reinforced that perception. The man's state was particularly dire; he was isolated and destructive, even self-destructive (5:5).

5:4 *he snapped the chains . . . smashed the shackles.* In Gr., the verbs are passive ("had been torn apart by him . . . had been smashed"). This unusual use of the passive may suggest that the man was not acting alone.

No one was strong enough to subdue him. The description reminds one of the strong man who was overcome by someone even stronger in 3:27. This man needed such a confrontation.

5:6 *bowed low before him.* The expression here is "worshiped" him, which often involved bowing before the one being honored. The only other place Mark uses this verb is at the mocking of Jesus (15:19).

5:7 *Why are you interfering with me?* Lit., "What do you have to do with me?" (see 1:24). The demon was trying to put Jesus off.

Son of the Most High God. The title "Most High God" is common in the LXX; Gentiles used it to refer to God (Gen 14:18-20; Num 24:16; Isa 14:14; Dan 3:26; 4:2 [3:32, LXX]; cf. 1 Esdras 2:3; 6:31; 8:19, 21; 2 Macc 3:31; 3 Macc 7:9; Acts 16:17). The title acknowledges God's residence in heaven and his sovereignty (Deut 32:8; Dan 4:17). For the title "Son of God," see the discussion of 1:1. Once again, supernatural forces make this confession (1:24).

don't torture me! Jesus' authority was recognized in the demons' request not to be punished. They used a term that often refers to the punishment of prisoners (BDAG 168; MM 104; NIDNTT 3:856). This is ironic since the man was already in torment, as is often the case with demon possession (1:26; 5:2-5; 9:17-18, 20-22, 26).

5:9 *Legion.* The demon has the name of the largest unit in the Roman army, consisting of 3,000–6,000 soldiers (Marcus 2000:345). The point of the name is to indicate that this man was a victim of multiple possessions. He was a severe case. It also shows that the battle Jesus faces here is one against a large number, not merely a one-on-one battle.

5:10 *begged.* The Gr. for this word is in the imperfect, so the pleading is vividly portrayed as ongoing, not as just a momentary request. Such pleas were not unprecedented in Judaism (*Testament of Solomon* 2:6).

send them to some distant place. The demons' request was that Jesus not remove them "outside the region" (as the Gr. reads). The NLT has rendered this as "some distant place." Perhaps they feared being judged and sent immediately to the abyss (see 5:7b). They may also have wanted to remain in the region where they were used to working (Guelich 1989:281).

5:11 *pigs.* The pigs indicate that this was a Gentile region; Jews would not work with these ceremonially unclean animals (*m. Bava Qamma* 7:7).

5:12 *Send us into those pigs.* The symbolism is important here. The unclean demons requested residence in the unclean pigs rather than experience judgment.

5:13 *the entire herd of 2,000 pigs plunged down . . . into the lake and drowned.* This herd was large by ancient standards, as most were of about 150 animals (Gundry 1993:252). Many discuss the property damage that occurred here and raise a moral issue about what Jesus permitted. However, the damage was slight compared to what would have happened if such cosmic forces had been allowed to run around freely.

5:15 *saw the man who had been possessed . . . sitting . . . and perfectly sane.* This verse shows the evidence of the healing rather dramatically—the demoniac had a sound mind and was behaving calmly. This was quite a contrast after the people's inability to restrain him (5:4). His demon possession is expressed with a present participle ("the one who is demon possessed"). He was marked by who he had been. In 5:18, the participle switches to an aorist that describes "the one who had been demon possessed."

they were all afraid. In several passages in Mark, such fear is not respect for God, but a debilitating and paralyzing dread (5:36; 6:50; 9:32; 10:32; 11:18, 32; 12:12; 16:8).

5:17 *pleading with Jesus to go away.* It is not entirely clear what motivated this request for Jesus to leave. Two suggestions are that (1) the damage the healing had done to the local economy and religion was a concern. Pigs were used for food and for sacrifices in this region. How unpredictable it would be to have Jesus around! (2) More likely, however, this direct encounter with supernatural power made them uneasy. Despite the healing Jesus brought, he was not welcome. This stranger had "bound the strong man"—now who would restrain him?

5:18 *begged to go with him.* The former demoniac wanted to become a disciple who traveled with Jesus (lit., "that he might be with him"; see 3:14). In contrast to the townspeople of 5:17, this man appreciated what Jesus had done. Jesus refused the request for reasons that are not made clear.

5:19 *how merciful he has been.* Jesus told the man to stay at home and testify to what God had done for him. He was to emphasize God's mercy because divine benevolence had healed him.

5:20 *Jesus.* The man began to tell what Jesus had done. There was no way that the man could do this without including Jesus' part in the healing (Guelich 1989:286).

COMMENTARY

This miracle shows the extent of Jesus' authority over demons. Here he exorcised an entire legion of demons. The detail of the miracle is unprecedented. Much space is occupied in describing the man's helpless condition under demonic influence, including his self-destructive behavior and the devastating effects of demon possession. The unusual form of the exorcism only reinforces this impression. The journey of the pigs to their death in the sea enhances the sense of the destructiveness of Satan and his minions. The account affirms the danger of allowing evil to roam the earth unchecked, but Jesus is stronger than evil, and the demons cowered at his power. Jesus transformed the formerly possessed man and gave him new life.

As exciting as this should have been, however, those in the Decapolis wanted nothing to do with such an unpredictable divine presence or its consequences, so they asked Jesus to leave. The Gentile region was no more open to Jesus than the Jewish area was. They rejected the mercy of God.

The man who had been possessed was different. He accepted God's mercy and desired to be among those who traveled with Jesus. Denied that opportunity, he was told by Jesus to remain at home and witness to his neighbors. His call was to explain what God had done for him. Instead of being asked to keep silent as others had been, this man was encouraged to tell his story, possibly because the messianic mission (in Jewish terms) was less likely to be misunderstood in this Gentile area (for remarks that commentators on Mark overstate the theme of secrecy, see Hooker 1991:145). In fact, the man told what Jesus had done for him, or better, he "proclaimed" it (*kērussō* [TG2784, ZG3062]).

◆   10. The woman with the hemorrhage and Jairus's daughter (5:21-43; cf. Luke 8:40-56)

²¹Jesus got into the boat again and went back to the other side of the lake, where a large crowd gathered around him on the shore. ²²Then a leader of the local synagogue, whose name was Jairus, arrived. When he saw Jesus, he fell at his feet, ²³pleading fervently with him. "My little daughter is dying," he said. "Please come and lay your hands on her; heal her so she can live."

²⁴Jesus went with him, and all the people followed, crowding around him. ²⁵A woman in the crowd had suffered for twelve years with constant bleeding. ²⁶She had suffered a great deal from many doctors, and over the years she had spent everything she had to pay them, but she had gotten no better. In fact, she had gotten worse. ²⁷She had heard about Jesus, so she came up behind him through the crowd and touched his robe. ²⁸For she thought to herself, "If I can just touch his robe, I will be healed." ²⁹Immediately the bleeding stopped, and she could feel in her body that she had been healed of her terrible condition.

³⁰Jesus realized at once that healing power had gone out from him, so he turned around in the crowd and asked, "Who touched my robe?"

³¹His disciples said to him, "Look at this crowd pressing around you. How can you ask, 'Who touched me?'"

³²But he kept on looking around to see who had done it. ³³Then the frightened woman, trembling at the realization of what had happened to her, came and fell to her knees in front of him and told him what she had done. ³⁴And he said to her, "Daughter, your faith has made you well. Go in peace. Your suffering is over."

³⁵While he was still speaking to her, messengers arrived from the home of Jairus, the leader of the synagogue. They told him, "Your daughter is dead. There's no use troubling the Teacher now."

³⁶But Jesus overheard* them and said to Jairus, "Don't be afraid. Just have faith."

³⁷Then Jesus stopped the crowd and wouldn't let anyone go with him except Peter, James, and John (the brother of James). ³⁸When they came to the home of the synagogue leader, Jesus saw much commotion and weeping and wailing. ³⁹He went inside and asked, "Why all this commotion and weeping? The child isn't dead; she's only asleep."

⁴⁰The crowd laughed at him. But he made them all leave, and he took the girl's father and mother and his three disciples into the room where the girl was lying. ⁴¹Holding her hand, he said to her, *"Talitha koum,"* which means "Little girl, get up!" ⁴²And the girl, who was twelve years old, immediately stood up and walked around! They were overwhelmed and totally amazed. ⁴³Jesus gave them strict orders not to tell anyone what had happened, and then he told them to give her something to eat.

5:36 Or *ignored.*

NOTES

5:22 *leader of the local synagogue.* Jairus was a key figure at the synagogue who helped to direct the worship services and operate the building. A local synagogue could have more than one leader (Acts 13:15). He would have been a "lay leader." This is one of the few scenes in Mark in which a Jewish leader was responsive to Jesus.

fell at his feet. This prostration (*piptō* [ᵀᴳ4098, ᶻᴳ4406]) indicated his respect for Jesus; the Syro-Phoenician woman will later do the same (7:25).

5:23 *is dying.* Lit., "has the last" or "has [it] terminally"; our idiom might be "is on her last leg." The leader understood that Jesus could heal her.

lay your hands on her. In the Heb. OT, there is no example of a healing that involved the laying on of hands. In the LXX, the idea is found in 2 Kgs 5:11 (Guelich 1989:295).

5:25 *constant bleeding.* This is lit. "a flow of blood," a euphemistic reference to vaginal bleeding. It made the woman ceremonially unclean (the language matches Lev 15:25-30) and a source of uncleanness, thus prohibiting her from marital relations and to some degree restricting a normal social life. Key Jewish texts for this condition include 11QTemple 45:7-17, 46:16-18, 48:14-17; Josephus *Antiquities* 3.261; and *m. Niddah.* Marcus (2000:357-358) surveys the issues involved in the Jewish background of this scene. The unclean woman's social position and status were exactly opposite to those of Jairus. Jesus ministered to the whole gamut of society.

5:26 *had gotten worse.* In Judaism, doctors were viewed on a spectrum between esteem (Sir 38:1-5) and contempt (*m. Qiddushin* 4.14; Tob 2:10; Geulich 1989:297).

5:27 *touched his robe.* There was an ancient belief that a person's power could be conducted by his or her clothes (see 3:10; 6:56; Acts 19:12).

5:28 *If I can just touch his robe.* This is expressed as a Gr. third class condition, expressed as a pure hope with no presumption as to its likelihood. However, her willingness to violate the rules governing uncleanness showed her determination.

5:29 *the bleeding stopped.* Lit., "the well of her blood was dried up." The language reflects Lev 12:7, LXX, where the rite of cleanliness is described. The woman was restored.

her terrible condition. Her condition is described very graphically in Gr. as an affliction or "whipping" that had been removed (BDAG 620).

5:30 *healing power had gone out from him.* Jesus knew that someone had touched him. As one who possessed healing power and transcended any defilement that normally would result from such contact, Jesus now made public what the woman had naturally hoped would remain private.

5:31 *'Who touched me?'* The disciples were amazed that Jesus would ask such a question. The crowd was so tight around him that numerous people were touching him. Jesus, however, knew the difference between casual contact and what had taken place. God had acted graciously in healing this woman (Lane 1974:192-193) and she needed to understand that.

5:32 *who had done it.* This expression is feminine ("the woman who had done this"), indicating that either Jesus or the narrator knew that this was a woman. A narrative comment to that effect seems superfluous as the story makes this clear, so there is a hint here that Jesus was aware of who it was. Jesus sought her out for her sake, not his own.

5:33 *came and fell . . . and told him what she had done.* Jesus' question elicited the woman's public testimony. She was trembling because she had not been able to be healed anonymously. Would he be angry that she had made him unclean? She told "the whole truth" (so the Gr.) of what she had done and Jesus reassured her that all was well. She learned that what had taken place was not simply an ancient form of magic. While all of this went on, Jairus waited. One can only imagine how he felt about the delay in treating his daughter.

5:35 *Your daughter is dead.* The delay caused by the woman's healing was apparently devastating for Jairus and his daughter. In the messengers' view, she had died and it was too late to help her now. Jesus should be sent on his way.

5:36 *Jesus overheard them.* Jesus heard the message but continued as though nothing had been said. The NLT mg has "ignored" because the word *parakouō* [TG3878, ZG4159] (overheard) can also mean "ignored," as it consistently does in the LXX. This is, in effect, what Jesus did (BDAG 767); he heard what the messengers said but continued on his mission to help Jairus. Having just commended the woman's faith, Jesus issued a call to recognize and trust what God could do through him. The present imperative call to faith means "keep on believing."

5:37 *except Peter, James, and John.* This is one of a handful of events, such as the Transfiguration, the Olivet discourse, and Gethsemane, where only the inner circle of the Twelve observed what took place (Taylor 1966:294). Crowds and mourners (5:40) were excluded. Luke 8:51 notes that the parents were also there.

5:38 *saw much commotion and weeping and wailing.* This is one of the clear indications that the girl had died. Mourners were customary in Judaism, although whether these were professional mourners or just friends and neighbors is not clear in Mark.

5:39 *only asleep.* This is a frequent euphemism that indicates that death is not permanent. It appears elsewhere in the NT with this meaning (see 1 Thess 5:10, with the same verb, *katheudō* [TG2518, ZG2761]; see also Dan 12:7, LXX and Ps 87:6, LXX; Taylor 1966:295). *Genesis Rabbah* 17.5 associates sleep with incomplete death. Jesus may be alluding to such an idea as he declares her not to be dead. Jesus knew that the girl would not remain dead; rather, her situation was more like a person taking a nap.

5:40 *laughed.* The crowd viewed Jesus' claim that the girl was not permanently dead as ridiculous. In their view, Jesus either misunderstood the tragic situation or he was being silly. *kategelōn* [TG2606, ZG2860], the verb the NLT translates as "laughed," has a nuance of ridicule and is used only in this scene in the NT (Matt 9:24; Luke 8:53).

5:41 *Talitha koum.* Mark often uses Aramaic expressions directly and then explains them (3:17; 7:11, 34; 11:9-10; 14:36; 15:22, 34; Taylor 1966:296). Here it is Jesus' call for the girl to come back to life. As 5:42 indicates, she "arose" (aorist tense in Gr.) and "continued walking" (imperfect tense in Gr.). This miraculous resuscitation had precedent (cf. Elijah in 1 Kgs 17:17-23 and Elisha in 2 Kgs 4:18-37).

5:42 *totally amazed.* This term (*ekstasis* [TG1611, ZG1749]) is rare in the synoptic Gospels, appearing only here, in Mark 16:8, and in Luke 5:26. It is used only in the context of miracles.

5:43 *strict orders not to tell anyone.* Once again, Jesus restricted the discussion of this miracle. The possible reasons for this are considered in the note on Mark 1:34 (see also 1:25, 43; 3:11).

COMMENTARY

This double miracle completes a sequence of four consecutive miracles in Mark. Luke's Gospel keeps this tight sequence, while Matthew spreads these miracles across four chapters. The difference suggests that the unit is an anthology of Jesus' miraculous activities, with incidents placed side by side that show Jesus' authority over creation, demons, disease (and uncleanness), and death. His ministry had certainly taken on an unusual scope for a human. His display of power was divine. The power of the new era was overcoming the law of the old. The instantaneous nature of the woman's healing and of Jesus' immediate response indicates that something unusual had occurred. In the Greek it is clear that the power went out "from" him (*ek* [TG1537, ZG1666]), not "through" him (Cranfield 1959:185). Jesus was not the mere conduit of this power but its source.

The woman touched this source and was healed by her faith in that power. Jesus commended the faith of the woman who sought him out and explained that her faith had made her well (2:5; 10:52). Her willingness to recognize God's work through Jesus and to receive what God offered had restored her health. She could now go on in life knowing that she had been restored to peace (Heb., *shalom* [TH7965, ZH8934]; Judg 18:6; 1 Sam 1:17) from the "whipping" of her disease.

Jesus' divine power was also manifest in raising Jairus's daughter after her death, but Jesus did not want to draw excessive attention to such healing. Although it underscored God's work through him, it also pictured a greater authority and deliverance that were crucial parts of his message. The danger was that people would be drawn to the miracles and remain oblivious to what they depicted—that God was uniquely working through Jesus to show his authority over creation, cosmic forces, disease, and life itself. This is the most important knowledge to grasp about Jesus.

All this activity continued despite opposition and the hesitation of some to accept what Jesus was doing. Mark wanted his readers to appreciate just how powerfully God was expressing his presence in and through Jesus.

◆ ## 11. Jesus faces rejection at Nazareth (6:1-6a; cf. Matt 13:53-58)

Jesus left that part of the country and returned with his disciples to Nazareth, his hometown. ²The next Sabbath he began teaching in the synagogue, and many who heard him were amazed. They asked, "Where did he get all this wisdom and the power to perform such miracles?" ³Then they scoffed, "He's just a carpenter, the son of Mary* and the brother of James, Joseph,* Judas, and Simon. And his sisters live right here among us." They were deeply offended and refused to believe in him.

⁴Then Jesus told them, "A prophet is honored everywhere except in his own hometown and among his relatives and his own family." ⁵And because of their unbelief, he couldn't do any miracles among them except to place his hands on a few sick people and heal them. ⁶And he was amazed at their unbelief.

6:3a Some manuscripts read *He's just the son of the carpenter and of Mary.*   6:3b Most manuscripts read *Joses;* see Matt 13:55.

NOTES

6:2 amazed. Mark frequently uses this term to express the crowd's reaction to Jesus (*exeplēssonto* [TG1605, ZG1742]). In 1:22 and 11:18, the amazement is over Jesus' teaching in general. In 7:37, it is in reaction to his healing work. In 10:26, it is the reaction to his teaching about the difficulty of the wealthy entering the Kingdom. The term need not indicate belief, but simply astonishment.

6:3 He's just a carpenter. This is actually a question in Gr. that expects a positive reply. The NLT captures the point of the objection, which is that no common person living in Nazareth could be a major figure used by God. He worked as a "craftsman," a term often rendered "carpenter," because woodworking is the most likely referent (supported by widespread tradition in the early church associating Joseph with carpentry, though in 1 Kgs 13:19, LXX, the term refers to a stone craftsman; BDAG 995; MM 628-629). The passage then lists members of Jesus' family. These remarks about Jesus show how efforts by the apocryphal gospels to attribute miracles to a young Jesus are misguided and wrong. Nothing in these remarks indicates Jesus had done unusual acts earlier in his life. It was with the beginning of his public ministry that this kind of activity began.

the son of Mary. This reference is unusual because normally the son's father would be named, in this case, Joseph. It may allude to Jesus' unusual birth and show an awareness that Mary was Jesus' mother in a way that Joseph was not his father (Hurtado 1989:92). It also might simply indicate that Joseph was then deceased.

were deeply offended. This term (*eskandalizonto* [TG4624A, ZG4997]) is important in the NT; it refers to someone "tripping over" or "stumbling over" an idea so as to fall in rejecting it (see 4:17). Figuratively, it means being offended at something. It connotes a lack of belief, so the NLT reference to their refusal to believe brings out that implication.

6:4 *A prophet is honored everywhere except in his own hometown.* This proverb appears in all the synoptic versions of this scene (Matt 13:57; Luke 4:24). There is evidence of its wide use (Taylor 1966:301).

6:5 *he couldn't do any miracles.* Jesus did not perform many miracles in Nazareth because the people were not in a frame of mind to appreciate their significance, and might attribute them to the wrong source, as 3:22 suggests.

6:6 *he was amazed.* Jesus was amazed by the Nazarenes' unbelief (on unbelief, see EDNT 1:121-123).

COMMENTARY

The people were amazed at Jesus' wisdom and miraculous power (see 5:30). Part of their amazement was that such power resided in this "hometown boy" (6:1, 3) whose family background was well known to them. Their familiar knowledge of him kept them from seeing Jesus' identity. Jesus said that "a prophet is honored everywhere except in his own hometown." Jesus affirmed himself as a prophet, but the people of Nazareth were hesitant to accept him at this revelatory level. If they rejected him even as a prophet, they would never entertain the thought that he was at the center of God's work for the Kingdom.

The failure of Jesus' hometown to accept even his prophetic status shows the difficulty Jesus faced in having his message received. His background was not what was expected for a major figure sent by God, so Jesus' work was restricted in Nazareth. The rising tone of Jesus' rejection took on a poignant note as it extended even into his home and family. Only the resurrection would reverse this for his brothers.

◆   **D. Challenge, Misunderstanding, and Confession (6:6b–8:26)**
      1. The Twelve are sent out (6:6b–13; cf. Luke 9:1–6)

Then Jesus went from village to village, teaching the people. ⁷And he called his twelve disciples together and began sending them out two by two, giving them authority to cast out evil* spirits. ⁸He told them to take nothing for their journey except a walking stick—no food, no traveler's bag, no money.* ⁹He allowed them to wear sandals but not to take a change of clothes. ¹⁰"Wherever you go," he said, "stay in the same house until you leave town. ¹¹But if any place refuses to welcome you or listen to you, shake its dust from your feet as you leave to show that you have abandoned those people to their fate."

¹²So the disciples went out, telling everyone they met to repent of their sins and turn to God. ¹³And they cast out many demons and healed many sick people, anointing them with olive oil.

6:7 Greek *unclean.*   6:8 Greek *no copper coins in their money belts.*

NOTES

6:7 *authority to cast out evil spirits.* Now Jesus extended his authority over demons to the Twelve. Despite opposition, the mission expanded awareness of the message. The issue of authority is important to Mark (1:22, 27; 2:10; 11:27-33). Traveling in pairs was common in Judaism (Luke 7:18; John 1:37).

6:8 *take nothing.* Jesus urged them to travel in a way that expressed both the urgency and the itinerant nature of their work.

no traveler's bag. Beggars and itinerant philosophers who sought donations often used this bag to collect money (*Diogenes Laertius* 6.13, 22; Gundry 1993:309 works through the background in detail and notes Jesus' action is distinct). Jesus forbade its use on this trip.

no money. This money was in copper coins.

6:9 *change of clothes.* This is lit. "two tunics," representing the luxury of a change of clothes (Taylor 1966:305). This explains the NLT rendering. The outer garment often functioned as a bedroll for poor people (Hurtado 1989:93, 97), so the point is that they were to trust God for every aspect of their care.

6:11 *shake its dust from your feet.* Culturally, this act meant that the "unclean" state of the town (for rejecting those whom God had sent) was no longer attached to the feet of the messengers (Matt 10:14; Mark 6:11; Acts 13:51; 18:6; cf. Neh 5:13).

to show that you have abandoned those people to their fate. This expanded rendering of the more ambiguous Gr. ("as a testimony against them") gives the symbolic meaning of the act. It also symbolized dissociation from someone.

6:12 *repent.* This key term for response to the Gospel is used in many synoptic texts (Matt 3:2; 4:17; 11:20-21; 12:41; Mark 1:15; Luke 13:3, 5; 15:7, 10).

6:13 *cast out many demons and healed many.* This summary looks like one that could be about Jesus, and that is the point. The ministry of the Twelve would replicate his ministry.

COMMENTARY

Jesus expanded the coverage of his message by sending the Twelve out in pairs. They also had the authenticating authority over demons and disease that underscored the credibility of their message that the new era of God's rule had appeared. These messengers traveled in a way that showed their dependence upon God. Their commission was to enter a city and preach. If those in the city or town responded, then the pair of missionaries remained. If not, their departure was to make clear the city's accountability to God for rejecting the offer of the Gospel. They did this by shaking the dust off their feet. This was an act that pious Jews normally performed in leaving a Gentile city (Lane 1974:209; *m. Ohalot* 2.3; *m. Teharot* 4.5; *t. Bava Qamma* I.5). As a result, the town was responsible for their decision to act like pagans. Guelich (1989:322-323) is right to say that the idea of the pagan act of the town and their culpability are both alluded to by this rebuke of the Jewish community.

The context for this passage is rejection, as the Nazareth scene precedes it and the John the Baptist scene follows. Both the forerunner and the promised One were experiencing rejection, but the word was still going forth.

◆ 2. The death of John the Baptist (6:14-29; cf. Matt 14:3-12; Luke 9:7-10)

¹⁴Herod Antipas, the king, soon heard about Jesus, because everyone was talking about him. Some were saying,* "This must be John the Baptist raised from the dead. That is why he can do such miracles." ¹⁵Others said, "He's the prophet Elijah." Still others said, "He's a prophet like the other great prophets of the past."

¹⁶When Herod heard about Jesus, he said, "John, the man I beheaded, has come back from the dead."

¹⁷For Herod had sent soldiers to arrest and imprison John as a favor to Herodias. She had been his brother Philip's wife, but Herod had married her. ¹⁸John had been telling Herod, "It is against God's law for you to marry your brother's wife." ¹⁹So Herodias bore a grudge against John and wanted to kill him. But without Herod's approval she was powerless, ²⁰for Herod respected John; and knowing that he was a good and holy man, he protected him. Herod was greatly disturbed whenever he talked with John, but even so, he liked to listen to him.

²¹Herodias's chance finally came on Herod's birthday. He gave a party for his high government officials, army officers, and the leading citizens of Galilee. ²²Then his daughter, also named Herodias,* came in and performed a dance that greatly pleased Herod and his guests. "Ask me for anything you like," the king said to the girl, "and I will give it to you." ²³He even vowed, "I will give you whatever you ask, up to half my kingdom!"

²⁴She went out and asked her mother, "What should I ask for?"

Her mother told her, "Ask for the head of John the Baptist!"

²⁵So the girl hurried back to the king and told him, "I want the head of John the Baptist, right now, on a tray!"

²⁶Then the king deeply regretted what he had said; but because of the vows he had made in front of his guests, he couldn't refuse her. ²⁷So he immediately sent an executioner to the prison to cut off John's head and bring it to him. The soldier beheaded John in the prison, ²⁸brought his head on a tray, and gave it to the girl, who took it to her mother. ²⁹When John's disciples heard what had happened, they came to get his body and buried it in a tomb.

6:14 Some manuscripts read *He was saying.* 6:22 Some manuscripts read *the daughter of Herodias herself.*

NOTES

6:14 *Herod Antipas.* He was one of the client-kings of Rome, the son of Herod the Great, and of Idumean descent. He had authority over the neighboring regions of Galilee and Perea from 4 BC to AD 39.

the king. Officially, Herod Antipas was a "tetrarch," of lesser status than a king. However, he was popularly referred to as a king.

6:15 *Elijah.* Many regarded Jesus as some type of prophetic figure. He was called Elijah either because of his miraculous work (see 6:14) or because of Elijah's association with the end times (Mal 4:5-6).

6:16 *John, the man I beheaded, has come back from the dead.* He probably meant that the spirit of John inhabited Jesus, as Jews did not believe in an immediate individual bodily resurrection apart from the resurrection at the end times. In Acts 2 and at the close of the Gospels, Jesus' immediate bodily resurrection as himself is declared, *apart* from the final resurrection.

6:17 *Philip's.* Some argue that Mark erred here in referring to Philip the tetrarch, but Mark probably referred to another Herod, adding the second name Philip to make his identity clear (Guelich 1989:331).

6:19 *bore a grudge.* This rare term (*enechō* [TG1758, ZG1923]) is used only here and in Luke 11:53 in the Gospels. It refers to someone who opposes someone or something. In Luke, it is used of the scribes and Pharisees who opposed Jesus after he rebuked them.

without Herod's approval she was powerless. The NLT renders the Gr. expression, "but she could not" with this explanatory detail. Without Herod's approval she could not have John killed.

6:20 *respected.* According to the Gr., Herod feared (*phobeomai* [TG5399, ZG5828]) John.

he protected him. Herod was captivated by John and respected his piety even in the face of criticism. The literal Gr. is that Herod "kept him safe."

greatly disturbed. The Gr. term means to be at a loss about something (*aporeō* [TG639, ZG679]). It describes the disciples' reaction when Jesus initially announced that he would be betrayed by one of them (John 13:22). It was the women's first reaction when they discovered the empty tomb (Luke 24:4).

6:22 *his daughter, also named Herodias.* This reading is supported by א B D L. It is generally agreed that Salome is referred to here, so some speak of an error by Mark. However, it is possible that she also bore her mother's name. Another possibility is that the text follows the alternate textual reading in which she is simply identified as Herodias' daughter. That reading, found in the Textus Receptus, is not as well attested externally, but for a defense of its originality, see Gundry 1993:320. If this was Salome, she was in her middle teens.

performed a dance. Two options must be noted here. Either this dance was not as sexually suggestive as modern renderings tend to suggest, or Herod's family was not scrupulous as to the discretion of women in the family (Hooker 1991:161). It is hard to be sure which cultural scenario was at work here. The early church fathers describe such regal parties as similar to pagan rites (Origen *Commentary on Matthew* 10.22; Marcus 2000:395. On Herod's lack of concern for Jewish sensibilities, see Josephus *Antiquities* 18.38 or *War* 2.2.5, where dancing in the family is noted). It may be that Herod was indifferent to the public behavior of his daughter.

pleased. The term here is *areskō* [TG700, ZG743], which in the LXX often means being pleased by being aroused (Gen 19:8; Esth 2:4, 9; Job 31:10; cf. Jdt 12:14). The language is similar to that of Esth 2:9.

6:23 *up to half my kingdom!* This may be hyperbolic, but the point is that she was free to ask for whatever she wanted and Herod had bound himself by a public vow to honor her request. The language recalls Esth 5:3.

6:26 *he couldn't refuse her.* More lit., "he did not wish to break his word to her." The vow Herod made gave him no honorable alternatives. The culture was very much rooted in issues of honor and shame, so John had to be killed, much to Herod's regret. The term *perilupos* [TG4036, ZG4337] means to be very sorrowful.

6:27 *executioner.* The term here is *spekoulatōr* [TG4688, ZG5063], which refers to a body guard who does whatever the king requires. He could also perform executions (Marcus 2000:397; Tacitus *History* 1.24-25; 2.11). As a client-king, Herod apparently had the authority to execute people.

6:28 *his head on a tray.* In the *Midrash on Esther* 1:19-21, the head of Vashti is brought to the king on a platter (Guelich 1989:333).

6:29 *buried it in a tomb.* John's disciples were allowed to give his body an appropriate burial.

This verse also marks the end of an A-B-A pattern in ch 6 where the focus is first on rejection (1–6), then mission (7–13), and finally rejection and death (14–29). John the Baptist's fate before Herod pictures the kind of suffering those who affirm Jesus may face.

COMMENTARY

This passage explains how Herod killed John. The implication that Jesus ministered as though he were John the Baptist returned from the dead indicates that the injustice and guilt for executing John were being exacted in the continuation of his power despite John's death. Thus, the details about the death underscore Herod's sense of responsibility for what was continuing to take place (6:17 begins with an explanatory use of "for").

John the Baptist was arrested because he spoke out against the unlawful marriage of Herod and Herodias, who had both gotten divorced to marry each other. This was probably not the only point of contention with the law, as they had also married within the family (Lev 18:16; 20:21). One was not to marry a brother unless levirate marriage was invoked. Josephus also notes this event (*Antiquities* 18.5.2.116-119) and speaks of John's call to repentance as being of concern to the leader. He does not mention the marriage explicitly, although the previous section does mention the turmoil the marriage produced with King Aretas, the father of Herod's original bride.

This event is important because it shows the opposition to John's call for righteousness. Mark makes it clear that the stakes in this calling are high. One can lose one's life by speaking truth that those in power do not want to hear. The portrayal of such ruthlessness in Herod's house fits the history of his family, which often held power with an iron grip, going all the way back to Herod the Great, who even killed family members and a wife when he felt his grasp on power slipping. Mark was setting up his theme of suffering for following in God's way. John the Baptist was a forerunner to Jesus, not only in announcing his approach, but also in the pattern of obedience he represented—an obedience that cost him his life.

◆   ## 3. Jesus feeds five thousand (6:30-44; cf. Matt 14:13-21; Luke 9:10-17; John 6:1-13)

[30]The apostles returned to Jesus from their ministry tour and told him all they had done and taught. [31]Then Jesus said, "Let's go off by ourselves to a quiet place and rest awhile." He said this because there were so many people coming and going that Jesus and his apostles didn't even have time to eat.

[32]So they left by boat for a quiet place, where they could be alone. [33]But many people recognized them and saw them leaving, and people from many towns ran ahead along the shore and got there ahead of them. [34]Jesus saw the huge crowd as he stepped from the boat, and he had compassion on them because they were like sheep without a shepherd. So he began teaching them many things.

[35]Late in the afternoon his disciples came to him and said, "This is a remote place, and it's already getting late. [36]Send the crowds away so they can go to the nearby farms and villages and buy something to eat."

[37]But Jesus said, "You feed them."

"With what?" they asked. "We'd have to work for months to earn enough money* to buy food for all these people!"

[38]"How much bread do you have?" he asked. "Go and find out."

They came back and reported, "We have five loaves of bread and two fish."

³⁹Then Jesus told the disciples to have the people sit down in groups on the green grass. ⁴⁰So they sat down in groups of fifty or a hundred.

⁴¹Jesus took the five loaves and two fish, looked up toward heaven, and blessed them. Then, breaking the loaves into pieces, he kept giving the bread to the dis-ciples so they could distribute it to the people. He also divided the fish for everyone to share. ⁴²They all ate as much as they wanted, ⁴³and afterward, the disciples picked up twelve baskets of leftover bread and fish. ⁴⁴A total of 5,000 men and their families were fed from those loaves!

6:37 Greek *It would take 200 denarii.* A denarius was equivalent to a laborer's full day's wage.

NOTES

6:31 *to a quiet place.* This refers to a place in the wilderness (*erēmos* [ᵀᴳ2048A, ᶻᴳ2245]), which 6:39 makes clear was not a wasteland but an isolated location. In 1:35, Jesus sought such a place to pray. By 1:45, he had to seek such space in order to handle the crowds, which were now so great that he needed a lonely place away from where he was minister-ing. In the midst of opposition, Jesus was still drawing crowds, and this continued to make him a threat. In John 6, this miracle is parallel to the provision of manna in the wilderness of the Exodus. It may be that the wilderness locale evoked such symbolism. The exact loca-tion of this event is not known. If Jesus was ministering in his normal setting, he could have been anywhere on the northern half of the Sea of Galilee.

6:34 *had compassion on them.* The leaderless condition of the people moved Jesus to compassion and he taught them despite his need for quiet time. Jesus was often moved to act out of his compassion (1:41; 6:34; 8:2; 9:22; Matt 9:36; 14:14; 15:32; 20:34; Luke 7:13).

6:37 *You feed them.* The disciples urged Jesus to let the people go get a meal since it was late and they had no food. Instead, Jesus challenged the disciples to feed the crowd.

We'd have to work for months. The Gr. indicates wages of 200 denarii (so NLT mg). This was almost a half-year's labor. The disciples were shocked that Jesus would expect them to buy and haul such provisions to this locale. There is almost a note of rebuke in their response that Jesus would make such a crazy suggestion. The disciples are totally clueless as to Jesus' real intent in making such a provision. This stark portrayal of them is softened in the parallel Gospels.

6:39 *green grass.* This is a particularly vivid detail. The scene has a serene, pastoral feel (cf. Ps 23:1-2), even though it was not yet clear where all the food would come from. The mood contrasts with the dilemma.

6:40 *fifty or a hundred.* Such groupings would facilitate distribution.

6:41 *He also divided the fish for everyone to share.* The Gr. explicitly says that two fish were divided among the vast crowd. Although some associate this scene with the Last Sup-per (see 14:23), the way Jesus gives thanks here is generic to all such scenes. The point is that all had their needs met and were satisfied by what Jesus provided (6:42). The miracle of Jesus' creative power also affirmed his ability to give sustenance.

6:43 *twelve baskets.* Jesus provided even more resources than were needed. The baskets in which the excess was collected were large enough to hold a human (Acts 9:25; Taylor 1966:325). The "twelve" may point to meeting the needs of the twelve tribes of Israel.

6:44 *5,000 men.* The crowd was significantly large. Since there were 5,000 men, the crowd was actually larger.

COMMENTARY

In this section, we see Jesus as provider and protector. In this scene, he compassion-ately feeds a people in need. The idea of people lacking a shepherd has rich Old Tes-tament roots. In Numbers 27:17, Moses appointed Joshua to such a role in view of his own impending death, so that the people would not be sheep without a shep-herd. In Ezekiel 34, God rebuked the Jewish leaders for not being the shepherds he had called them to be (see Ezek 34:4). God said that he would be their shepherd, and that he would give them a shepherd from the house of David (Ezek 34:24). Mark portrays Jesus as stepping into that role, a depiction shared by Johns' Gospel (esp. John 10). Jesus was a leader-shepherd like Moses and Joshua, but greater than them because Jesus, through his creative power, provided a crowd of 5,000 men with an abundance of food. He not only met their need, but he did so to overflow-ing, as twelve huge baskets were filled with leftovers. Jesus was more than able to meet their basic needs.

All of this happened through the disciples that Jesus urged to make provision for the crowd. Incredulous at first, the disciples followed Jesus' instructions and met the people's need. Though real food was given, the scene is symbolic of how the dis-ciples would be able to provide life-giving nourishment to those they served. A pic-ture of their future ministry emerges here, although subsequent events show that they did not yet grasp the point.

A note on structure is also helpful here. We have two miracles that mention feed-ing (6:37, 52) connected to the disciple's failure framing a section which centers first on the connection between the disciples' failure and the Pharisees (also called "hardened" in 3:5 and 10:5 as the disciples are in 6:52) and then on the "little peo-ple" who do well. Failure is not a given. Some get it.

◆   ## 4. Jesus walks on water (6:45-52; cf. Matt 14:22-33; John 6:14-21)

[45]Immediately after this, Jesus insisted that his disciples get back into the boat and head across the lake to Bethsaida, while he sent the people home. [46]After telling everyone good-bye, he went up into the hills by himself to pray.

[47]Late that night, the disciples were in their boat in the middle of the lake, and Jesus was alone on land. [48]He saw that they were in serious trouble, rowing hard and struggling against the wind and waves. About three o'clock in the morn-ing* Jesus came toward them, walking on the water. He intended to go past them, [49]but when they saw him walking on the water, they cried out in terror, thinking he was a ghost. [50]They were all terrified when they saw him.

But Jesus spoke to them at once. "Don't be afraid," he said. "Take courage! I am here!*" [51]Then he climbed into the boat, and the wind stopped. They were totally amazed, [52]for they still didn't understand the significance of the miracle of the loaves. Their hearts were too hard to take it in.

6:48 Greek *About the fourth watch of the night.*   6:50 Or *The 'I AM' is here;* Greek reads *I am.* See Exod 3:14.

NOTES

6:45 *Bethsaida.* This village was located at the northern tip of the Sea of Galilee at the mouth of the Jordan River. In 8:22, it is the setting for the healing of a blind man. In Matt 11:21 (cf. Luke 10:13), it is one of the villages over which Jesus pronounced a woe.

6:46 *he went up into the hills by himself to pray.* Jesus again sought solitude with God (see 6:31). This is the last mention of Jesus praying until Gethsemane in ch 14.

6:48 *they were in serious trouble.* The imagery in the Gr. is of "being tormented in [their] rowing." They were not making progress, and rowing was a struggle. The wind was against them, and it was very late (the "fourth watch," or "three o'clock in the morning" as the NLT puts it). The fourth watch (*phulakē*) in Roman reckoning actually indicated a time somewhere between three and six in the morning (BDAG 1067). Thus, they had been rowing in rough water for up to nine hours, assuming they left at dusk.

walking on the water. Here is another miracle showing Jesus' control over creation. Hurtado (1989:103) notes this as the second sea miracle in Mark (4:35-41; cf. Job 9:8; Ps 77:19, which speak of God possessing such power). Jesus was crossing the lake more easily on foot than the men were by using the oars.

6:50 *I am here!* It is hard to be certain of the Gr. meaning here, which reads *egō eimi* and can be rendered as "I am" or "it is I." The NLT has rendered it as Jesus' simple declaration of his presence. Some suggest that it echoes the self-identification of God (Isa 43:25; 48:12; 51:12) with a force like that in Exod 3:14. If this is the idea, it is subtly expressed.

6:51 *totally amazed.* This is the last time in Mark that people react in amazement at what Jesus has done (the paralytic, 2:12; raising of Jairus's daughter, 5:42). In each case a divine act caused the amazement (forgiving sins, raising from the dead, walking on water, halting the wind).

6:52 *didn't understand . . . Their hearts were too hard to take it in.* This remark makes it clear that there was more to these miracles than merely feeding people or calming nature. They pointed to who Jesus was, but even the disciples missed this (at least initially). Matthew 14:33 seems to indicate they did eventually get the point and understood the act pointed to Jesus' identity as the Son of God. Mark's comment here fits his thematic pattern of noting how the disciples often failed. Of the evangelists, only Mark ties the disciples' failure to hardened hearts. When they reacted instinctively to Jesus, rather than with a dependent faith, they reacted in a wrong way; they eventually outgrow this pattern, as Acts shows.

COMMENTARY

Once again Jesus showed his power over creation and astounded the disciples who were still trying to grasp Jesus' identity. Jesus' walk on the water startled them and caught them unprepared, as it would most anyone. The disciples thought he was an apparition or spirit (*phantasma* [TG5326, ZG5753]). In Jewish thought, such a being might be perceived as a demon, often associated with the sea and chaos (Hurtado 1989:106). Even more mysterious, the text says that Jesus' initial intent was simply to walk past the boat over to the other side. Only the disciples' reaction stopped him. Some scholars understand Jesus' wanting to pass them by as being like God's "passing by" Moses (Exod 33:17-34:8; Marcus 2000:426). This idea of divine revelation can be affirmed by Jesus' statement in 6:50—*egō eimi* (see note). Jesus responded to the disciples' cry and revealed himself to them. He had placed himself in a position to encourage them if they sought his aid and could understand his power. Two Old Testament figures, Moses and Elijah, are associated with miraculous events concerning water (Exod 14:21-22; 2 Kgs 2:8). However, both of these were partings of the water; Jesus' act was without precedent.

For a second time, Jesus miraculously calmed the weather and thereby revealed his divine power, but the disciples' hearts were hardened and they did not yet understand (6:52). Mark indicates that the disciples did not yet appreciate the creative, life-giving, divine power at work in Jesus. They had failed to learn the lesson of the feeding of the multitudes. (Mark will say this again of the disciples in 8:17.) This ending differs from Matthew's positive conclusion in which the disciples bow before Jesus and declare him to be the Son of God. However, in Matthew's context, it may be that they recognized Jesus' messianic authority but still without appreciating fully who they were confessing. In short, Matthew saw the glass of the disciples' understanding as half full, while Mark saw it as half empty.

◆   **5. Healing of the sick in Gennesaret (6:53-56; cf. Matt 14:34-36)**

⁵³After they had crossed the lake, they landed at Gennesaret. They brought the boat to shore ⁵⁴and climbed out. The people recognized Jesus at once, ⁵⁵and they ran throughout the whole area, carrying sick people on mats to wherever they heard he was. ⁵⁶Wherever he went—in villages, cities, or the countryside—they brought the sick out to the marketplaces. They begged him to let the sick touch at least the fringe of his robe, and all who touched him were healed.

NOTES

6:53 *Gennesaret.* The exact location is not certain. It is either a small plain on the northwestern shore of the Sea of Galilee south of Capernaum or a town on that plain (Lane 1974:239).

6:56 *to let the sick touch at least the fringe of his robe.* The attitude here is like that of the woman in 5:25-28 (see note on 3:10 about touching; see also Acts 5:15; 19:11-12 for healing through touch).

the fringe of his robe. The reference is probably to the tassels on the fringe of Jewish garments that signified dedication to God (Hurtado 1989:91; Marcus 2000:437; Num 15:38-40; Deut 22:12; Matt 23:5).

COMMENTARY

This summary shows that Jesus was continuing his ministry of compassion (see 3:7-12) even though the crowds did not really understand his work. Jesus' comprehensive power attested to his divine identity, but the people continued to see him as a wonder-worker. For Mark, this was an unfortunate attitude, because Jesus was so much more than this.

◆   **6. Jesus' views on cleanliness and purity (7:1-23; cf. Matt 15:1-20)**

One day some Pharisees and teachers of religious law arrived from Jerusalem to see Jesus. ²They noticed that some of his disciples failed to follow the Jewish ritual of hand washing before eating. ³(The Jews, especially the Pharisees, do not eat until they have poured water over their cupped hands,* as required by their ancient traditions. 4Similarly, they don't eat anything from the market until they immerse their hands* in water. This is but one of many traditions they have clung to—such as their ceremonial washing of cups, pitchers, and kettles.*)

5So the Pharisees and teachers of religious law asked him, "Why don't your disciples follow our age-old tradition? They eat without first performing the handwashing ceremony."

6Jesus replied, "You hypocrites! Isaiah was right when he prophesied about you, for he wrote,

These people honor me with their lips,
    but their hearts are far from me.
7Their worship is a farce,
    for they teach man-made ideas as
    commands from God.'*

8For you ignore God's law and substitute your own tradition."

9Then he said, "You skillfully sidestep God's law in order to hold on to your own tradition. 10For instance, Moses gave you this law from God: 'Honor your father and mother,'* and 'Anyone who speaks disrespectfully of father or mother must be put to death.'* 11But you say it is all right for people to say to their parents, 'Sorry, I can't help you. For I have vowed to give to God what I would have given to you.'* 12In this way, you let them disregard their needy parents. 13And so you cancel the word of God in order to hand down your own tradition. And this is only one example among many others."

14Then Jesus called to the crowd to come and hear. "All of you listen," he said, "and try to understand. 15It's not what goes into your body that defiles you; you are defiled by what comes from your heart.*"

17Then Jesus went into a house to get away from the crowd, and his disciples asked him what he meant by the parable he had just used. 18"Don't you understand either?" he asked. "Can't you see that the food you put into your body cannot defile you? 19Food doesn't go into your heart, but only passes through the stomach and then goes into the sewer." (By saying this, he declared that every kind of food is acceptable in God's eyes.)

20And then he added, "It is what comes from inside that defiles you. 21For from within, out of a person's heart, come evil thoughts, sexual immorality, theft, murder, 22adultery, greed, wickedness, deceit, lustful desires, envy, slander, pride, and foolishness. 23All these vile things come from within; they are what defile you."

7:3 Greek have washed with the fist.   7:4a Some manuscripts read sprinkle themselves.   7:4b Some manuscripts add and dining couches.   7:7 Isa 29:13 (Greek version).   7:10a Exod 20:12; Deut 5:16.   7:10b Exod 21:17 (Greek version); Lev 20:9 (Greek version).   7:11 Greek 'What I would have given to you is Corban' (that is, a gift).   7:15 Some manuscripts add verse 16, Anyone with ears to hear should listen and understand. Compare 4:9, 23.

NOTES

7:2 *hand washing before eating.* Mark explains this practice in 7:3. This is one indication that his audience was not primarily Jewish.

7:3 *poured water over their cupped hands.* The practice was to wash "the fist" (cf. NLT mg), but the exact meaning of this term is disputed. Did it mean one washed up to the wrist? Did it indicate the amount of water to be poured? Did one pour with a cupped hand? The full details are not clear, but it seems that only a small amount of water was needed to meet the requirement. Hooker notes that the instruction from the Mishnah (*m. Yadayim* 1.1; 2.3) was to use an amount of water equivalent to the size of one and a half eggs. Observance of this custom was especially important after coming from the marketplace, where uncleanness might easily be contracted (cf. *y. Shevi'it* 6.1, 36c; Marcus 2000:442).

required by their ancient traditions. Lit., "the tradition of the elders" (for discussion on this, see Josephus *Antiquities* 13.297, 408). According to the law, priests were to wash their hands before offering a sacrifice (Num 18:8-13), something that kept them from becoming "common" or unclean (Lev 15:11, LXX). This instruction was then extended to lay people in the first century, especially by the Pharisees and Essenes (Guelich 1989:363-364; Hooker 1991:174-175; *b. Hullin* 105a, 106a-b; *b. Shabbat* 13b-14b). The Pharisees appear to be pressing Jesus on this matter.

7:4 *ceremonial washing of cups, pitchers, and kettles.* Commands regarding washings and issues of cleanliness covering all kinds of situations can be found in Lev 11–15. Jewish tradition came to expand this practice to discuss the specific objects washed in detail so as to protect a person from uncleanliness. This raised issues of *teharot* (cleannesses) for the Jews, something an entire order of the Mishnah discusses in twelve tractates, one of which (*m. Yadayim*) is entirely on the subject of hands (Guelich 1989:364; also Jdt 12:7; *Epistle of Aristeas* 305; *Sibylline Oracles* 3:591-593).

7:5 *follow our age-old tradition.* Lit., "walk according to the tradition of the elders." To "walk" in Judaism is to "live" in a certain way. Jewish halakha (from the verb for "go" or "walk") taught about the walk of actual religious life and practice. The expression "tradition of the elders" refers back to 7:3.

7:6-7 *You hypocrites!* This phrase is far more common in Matthew (thirteen times) than in Mark, where this is its only use. Luke uses it three times. A hypocrite is really an "actor" (LSJ 1886), and not the person he or she appears to be.

their hearts are far from me. . . . Their worship is a farce for they teach man-made ideas as commands from God. The citation is from Isa 29:13, especially as it appears in the LXX.

7:8 *substitute your own tradition.* Lit., "hold fast the tradition of men." By saying this, Jesus demoted the "elders" (Gundry 1993:351). If they did not act in accord with God's will, then their authority was worthless. The point is important. Religious authority is derived from God and from following him; it is not a matter of appointment or appearances.

7:9 *skillfully sidestep God's law.* The language here is actually a little stronger than the NLT suggests. The Gr. reads, "You reject the command of God well." Jesus argued that they were in complete disobedience. The adverb "well" adds a touch of sarcasm, because they did this so "beautifully" (*kalōs* [TG2573, ZG2822]).

in order to hold on to your own tradition. Their rejection was to "establish" or "validate" their tradition. God's voice was muted by their tradition. The next few verses illustrate how this worked.

7:10 *Honor your father and mother.* Jesus' example was not an obscure law but one of the Ten Commandments. In Judaism, honoring one's parents was one of the most important duties a person could undertake (Exod 20:12; Deut 5:16; cf. Exod 21:17; Lev 20:9).

Anyone who speaks disrespectfully of father or mother must be put to death. The death penalty shows the seriousness of the violation of cursing one's parents.

7:11 *But you say.* What Moses said (see 7:10) stood in contrast to what "you say." It was commandment versus tradition, and tradition had won.

vowed to give to God. Jesus was discussing the "Corban" (cf. NLT mg), a vow that cancelled other obligations. The term "corban" means "gift" and the associated vow designated something one owned as belonging to God and thus rendered it unusable for any other purpose (Lev 2:1, 4, 12-13; Josephus *Antiquities* 4.73; *Against Apion* 1.167; *m. Nedarim* 5.6). Taking this religious vow either prevented a person from using his resources to help care for his parents or became such a focal point that he simply disregarded their needs. Jesus saw the act as a violation of the divine command to honor one's parents. An ancient ossuary has this inscription over it to protect the contents, "All that a man may find to his profit in this ossuary is an offering (*qorban* [TH7133, ZH7933]) to God from him who is within it" (Hooker 1991:177). By the third century, this practice was rejected in Judaism but apparently only after some debate (*m. Nedarim* 9.1; Marcus 2000:445; Guelich 1989:369-370). Jesus may not be rebuking all Pharisees here, but those among them who were so strict about such vows and traditions.

7:12 *disregard their needy parents.* They no longer did anything on behalf of their parents because the vow to God released them from their obligations.

7:13 *you cancel.* They cancelled or set aside God's word by giving such a controlling status to tradition. This verb (*akuroō* [TG208, ZG218]) is used only three times in the NT (in the parallel Matt 15:6 and in Gal 3:17).

7:14 *the crowd.* Jesus broadened his remarks beyond the Pharisees and scribes; he called on the crowd to really comprehend what he was saying.

7:15 *you are defiled by what comes from your heart.* Lit., "the things that come out of a person are the common [or defiled] things of a person." The NLT rendering anticipates the detailed explanation Jesus gives to the disciples in 7:21, where the heart is prominent.

7:16 This verse is not in the earlier MSS of Mark (א B L 0274) and thus it is absent in many recent translations. It restates the call to hear already given in 7:14.

7:18 *Can't you see?* This question expects a positive reply. They should be able to make this observation.

cannot defile you. Jesus turned his attention from hand washing to food. He explained why food is not an ultimate concern, since it both enters and exits the body (7:19). In this, Jesus was in continuity with the OT prophets (Isa 1:10-20; Amos 5:21-27; Hurtado 1989:111).

7:19 *goes into the sewer.* The NLT renders the imagery as graphically as the Gr. does.

By saying this, he declared that every kind of food is acceptable in God's eyes. The Gr. is a participial phrase, "cleaning all foods." As he often does, Mark treats this as a narrative aside, indicating that this was his own remark about what Jesus said (3:30; 5:8; 7:3-4; 13:14). The disciples probably did not realize this implication at the time, but they came to appreciate the saying later. Peter's vision of the sheet with all kinds of food on it in Acts 10 shows that it was several years before the disciples realized how God viewed this issue of food. The NT relates ongoing discussion about appropriate diet (Rom 14; Gal 2:1-21). In making such remarks, Jesus showed his authority over the law, which discussed clean and unclean foods.

7:20 *what comes from inside . . . defiles you.* The key principle for Jesus is that it is what proceeds from within, from the heart (7:21)—actions and thoughts that impact relationships—that defiles a person.

7:21 *evil thoughts, sexual immorality, theft, murder.* This list of vices resembles the "deeds of the flesh" in Gal 5:19-21 (cf. Wis 14:25-26; 1QS 4:9-11; Rom 1:29-31; 1 Pet 4:13). Such lists were common, and some were very long (Philo, *Sacrifices of Cain and Abel* 32 has 150 items; Marcus 2000:459). These destructive behaviors damage relationships. The "evil thoughts" almost have the force of "evil devising" because the term for "thoughts" includes the idea of "pondering" (Taylor 1966:345). How one handles the sexuality of the body, possessions, and life completes the list in 7:21. Completing the list in 7:22 are marital infidelity, an unhealthy desire for possessions, a misleading lack of integrity, general lack of decency, jealousy of others (lit., "an evil eye"), false accusation, arrogance, and a flippant lack of judgment. On the evil eye, see Deut 15:9; Prov 28:22; Sir 14:8-10; 35:8-10.

COMMENTARY

This passage is significant because it presents Jesus' handling of traditional Jewish issues and his attitude about certain laws. Part of Jesus' defense of his disciples' not washing their hands before the meal to prevent ritual uncleanness was to accuse the Pharisees of majoring on minors and adding to the law, while hypocritically honoring God with their lips but not with their hearts. Furthermore, they nullified God's commands for the sake of their tradition (7:6-8). In light of this, Jesus cited Isaiah's identical complaint against Israel centuries earlier. The age-old tradition was met by an appeal to age-old prophecy. Isaiah's rebuke comprehensively addressed hearts distant from God, empty worship, and commands to follow man-made teachings. For words and inner actions to be estranged constituted a serious offense by a people who were to honor God with heart, mind, and strength as the key Jewish confession of Deuteronomy 6:4-5 urged. This confession was affirmed regularly, but Jesus said that their practices violated it. Jesus complained that their worship was empty (*matēn* [TG3155, ZG3472]), an expression that the NLT renders as a farce, thus communicating the emotional force of the idea. The LXX makes the point about empty worship more explicitly than the Hebrew, but the idea is implied in what the Hebrew says (Guelich 1989:366-367).

Jesus then illustrated their hypocrisy with the example of the Corban (see notes on 7:9-13). The "handed down" tradition passed on from generation to generation got more attention and was valued more than God's word. The Corban example was but one among many. In a few verses, Jesus said that they had neglected and nullified God's word (Guelich 1989:370).

Jesus then exposed their whole notion of ritual purity. His statement is potent: "It's not what goes into your body that defiles you; you are defiled by what comes from your heart." He then said that the things that really damage our lives are not those things that come from creation, but the ways in which we treat one another. A series of vices that are mostly relational or tied to thought processes are specified in 7:21-22. Mark calls this remark a "parable" in 7:17, where that term takes on the meaning of a "wise saying." The remark in its original Jewish setting did not reject the food laws, as it seems clear from Acts that the early church in Jerusalem continued such practices. Jesus was not challenging or rejecting purity and food laws, but stating the priority of relationships, much as the prophets challenged sacrifices by saying that God wanted true hearts (Hos 6:6; Hooker 1991:179). The effect of the remark, however, was to relativize the importance of such practices. Gundry (1993:354) notes that Isaiah's distinction between lips and heart may have motivated the remark. Jesus was criticizing the idea that unwashed hands transmitted the uncleanness of common food to the eater (Marcus 2000:446). The point is not about hygiene but about ritual purity and spirituality. In the Mishnah (*m. Eduyyot* 5.6), there is an account of a rabbi who questioned such cleansing practices and was put under a ban (a call to separate that ended with a stone being placed on his coffin to show the rejection of his teaching). Such an account shows how serious Jesus' remarks were.

Here Jesus pronounced an authoritative ruling: what defiles is not what goes into a person only to be biologically eliminated, but what comes forth from the heart. This makes the food law relative without explicitly annulling it. It states that what God is most concerned about is the heart and relationships. Numerous passages about Jesus show him making this point, whether in the texts from Matthew in which Jesus cites Hosea 6:6 (Matt 9:13; 12:7) or in his complaining that the leaders tithed but neglected major things such as justice and love (Matt 23:23; Luke 11:42). That such a saying came to be seen as removing distinctions between clean and unclean foods is not surprising, given Jesus' focus on issues tied to behavior over those about the condition of food.

Two key concerns emerge from this text. The first has to do with Jesus' definition of spirituality in terms of heart actions, thought, and interaction with others. This is an extension of Jesus' emphasis on the law of loving God and loving one's neighbor, where the focus is on right relationship. The second is the implication that Jesus' remarks had for his own authority. Who had the right to make pronouncements about issues tied to Jewish tradition and to the law? Jesus' apparent comfort in speaking on matters pertaining to the law and with making judgments about them suggests a self-understanding that he could speak for God in his divine role and call.

♦   ## 7. The Syrophoenician woman's faith leads to healing (7:24-30; cf. Matt 15:21-28)

24Then Jesus left Galilee and went north to the region of Tyre.* He didn't want anyone to know which house he was staying in, but he couldn't keep it a secret. 25Right away a woman who had heard about him came and fell at his feet. Her little girl was possessed by an evil* spirit, 26and she begged him to cast out the demon from her daughter.

Since she was a Gentile, born in Syrian Phoenicia, 27Jesus told her, "First I should feed the children—my own family, the Jews.* It isn't right to take food from the children and throw it to the dogs."

28She replied, "That's true, Lord, but even the dogs under the table are allowed to eat the scraps from the children's plates."

29"Good answer!" he said. "Now go home, for the demon has left your daughter." 30And when she arrived home, she found her little girl lying quietly in bed, and the demon was gone.

7:24 Some manuscripts add *and Sidon.*   7:25 Greek *unclean.*   7:27 Greek *Let the children eat first.*

NOTES

7:24 *Tyre.* Relations were strained between Galilee and Tyre since agricultural resources often migrated from Galilee to Tyre, leaving some Jewish folks in Galilee with little to eat (Josephus *Against Apion* 1.13).

7:25 *fell at his feet.* This act of respect shows that the woman saw Jesus as superior to herself. The only other one to do this in Mark is Jairus (5:22).

evil spirit. Lit., "unclean spirit," (see 1:23 and note); the description sets up yet another exorcism. This miracle deals with another kind of uncleanness from that just discussed in 7:1-23. Jesus was battling for people against the unclean spirits.

7:26 born in Syrian Phoenicia. This description gives the woman's specific nationality. She was from an area north of Israel in the Roman province of Syria (which includes modern day Lebanon), rather than from Libya.

7:29 the demon has left. Jesus proclaimed that the healing was complete as a result of the woman's response of faith, a fact confirmed in 7:30. Like the centurion of Luke 7, this Gentile appreciated Jesus' authority.

COMMENTARY

Once again, Jesus was trying to gain some time away from the crowds. This time he went to a Gentile region in the hope that leaving Israel would give him a break. The effort was not successful. Right away he encountered a Syrophoenician woman who begged him to heal her demon-possessed daughter.

The verbal exchange between Jesus and the woman is remarkable. He told her, "It isn't right to take food from the children and throw it to the dogs." This proverbial statement compared Israelites to children (Exod 4:22; Deut 32:6; Hos 11:1) and people of other nations to dogs. Both are a part of the home but caring for the family comes before caring for pets. The dogs in this image are not scavengers or wild dogs, so the image is not as derogatory of Gentiles as it could be. It is a way of picturing Israel's priority as covenant recipients at this time. Many claim that the Gospels reflect a later church attitude, but this saying is clearly rooted in Jesus' ministry, given the way Gentiles are placed second to Israelites (Hurtado 1989:115).

The woman's response is remarkable: "That's true, Lord, but even the dogs under the table are allowed to eat the scraps from the children's plates." The woman accepted Jesus' point but added that even pets get some of the leftovers. Since the imagery has the pet dogs under the table and accepting what fell to them, her reply showed a humility and persistence that Jesus honored as exemplary faith. She clearly believed that Jesus could heal her child even though she was a Gentile.

This passage shows Jesus acting on behalf of a Gentile; it also highlights a Gentile that was more responsive to Jesus than most Israelites. The text shows Jesus' initial focus on Israel, but his compassion extended to anyone who recognized his or her need and Jesus' ability to meet it. Mark has now given us one exemplary male and one exemplary female Gentile, showing the balance in Jesus' ministry (the demoniac of Mark 5 likely was a Gentile since he lived in a region where pigs were raised). However, there is another important contrast: that between the failure of the disciples in this section of Mark and the faith and response of both the deaf mute (a male) and the Syro-Phoenician woman. Once again, common people do well.

◆   8. Jesus heals a deaf and mute man (7:31-37; cf. Matt 15:29-31)

[31]Jesus left Tyre and went up to Sidon before going back to the Sea of Galilee and the region of the Ten Towns.* [32]A deaf man with a speech impediment was brought to him, and the people begged Jesus to lay his hands on the man to heal him.

[33]Jesus led him away from the crowd so they could be alone. He put his fingers

into the man's ears. Then, spitting on his own fingers, he touched the man's tongue. [34]Looking up to heaven, he sighed and said, *"Ephphatha,"* which means, "Be opened!" [35]Instantly the man could hear perfectly, and his tongue was freed so he could speak plainly!

7:31 Greek *Decapolis.*

[36]Jesus told the crowd not to tell anyone, but the more he told them not to, the more they spread the news. [37]They were completely amazed and said again and again, "Everything he does is wonderful. He even makes the deaf to hear and gives speech to those who cannot speak."

NOTES

7:31 *Ten Towns.* This was the Decapolis, a predominantly Gentile region consisting of ten towns east of the Jordan River. Jesus is now moving outside of Israel, a hint of where the church will go.

7:32 *man with a speech impediment.* The Gr. term *mogilalos* [TG3424A, ZG3652] is used only here in the NT and only at Isa 35:6 in the LXX (see commentary).

7:33 *touched the man's tongue.* In this verse, either Jesus was making clear by his actions what he intended to do or these actions reflected other healings of this type in the ancient world (cf. Hurtado 1989:117; Mark 8:23; John 9:6; and the healings alleged of Vespasian, an emperor who came after Jesus—Tacitus *Histories* 4.81; Suetonius *Vespasian* 7; Taylor 1966:354).

7:34 *Looking up to heaven.* Jesus showed his connection with heaven.

Ephphatha. Mark again simply repeats the Aramaic (see 3:17 NLT mg; 5:41; 11:9-10 NLT mg; 14:36; 15:22, 34), then translates it into Gr. as "be opened."

7:35 *his tongue was freed.* The Gr. metaphor is hard to render in English. It says, "The bonds of his tongue were loosed." His tongue was "unshackled" (Marcus 2000:475).

7:36 *told the crowd not to tell anyone.* Since 1:25, Jesus has attempted to silence efforts to promote his healings (1:34, 44-45; 3:12; 8:26; see comments on the "messianic secret" in the Major Themes section of the introduction). The crowds that gathered for the healings were becoming very large, and people continued to speak even more openly. The verbs here are imperfect, so Jesus was continually making such efforts, and the people were continually declaring his work.

COMMENTARY

Yet another miracle focuses on what God was doing through Jesus. As he looked to heaven, Jesus healed a deaf and dumb man. The entire act evoked the hope of Isaiah 35, an important prediction of a future time when God would heal the blind, deaf, lame, and mute. The last statement of the passage ("He even makes the deaf to hear and gives speech to those who cannot speak") echoes Isaiah 35:6 and its prediction that at a special time, God would work to heal his people. The statement may allude to the entire context of Isaiah 35:1-10.

God was working through Jesus in a special way to deliver his people. All kinds of astonishing miracles were coming through the hands of one special person. The crowds were "completely amazed" at the scope and consistency of Jesus' healings (this is the only place where Mark expresses this degree of astonishment). They knew that God had to be at work, but what did it all mean? A further round of miracles in Mark 8 will further explain what was happening.

◆   9. Jesus feeds four thousand (8:1-10; cf. Matt 15:32-39)

About this time another large crowd had gathered, and the people ran out of food again. Jesus called his disciples and told them, ²"I feel sorry for these people. They have been here with me for three days, and they have nothing left to eat. ³If I send them home hungry, they will faint along the way. For some of them have come a long distance."

⁴His disciples replied, "How are we supposed to find enough food to feed them out here in the wilderness?"

⁵Jesus asked, "How much bread do you have?"

"Seven loaves," they replied.

⁶So Jesus told all the people to sit down on the ground. Then he took the seven loaves, thanked God for them, and broke them into pieces. He gave them to his disciples, who distributed the bread to the crowd. ⁷A few small fish were found, too, so Jesus also blessed these and told the disciples to distribute them.

⁸They ate as much as they wanted. Afterward, the disciples picked up seven large baskets of leftover food. ⁹There were about 4,000 people in the crowd that day, and Jesus sent them home after they had eaten. ¹⁰Immediately after this, he got into a boat with his disciples and crossed over to the region of Dalmanutha.

NOTES

8:2 *I feel sorry for these people.* This note of compassion for the hungry crowds that had been with Jesus for three days opens this miracle account. Mark often notes Jesus' compassion (e.g., 1:41; 6:34).

8:4 *How are we supposed to find enough food?* The disciples responded in this way when Jesus said that the crowd was too tired to be sent home for food. Despite the earlier feeding of the 5,000 (6:35-44), the disciples were incredulous about how they could feed such a large group. For a defense that this event is distinct from Mark 6 and is not a doublet of the same event, see France (2002:306-307). Presumably, Jesus was still in the Decapolis region, so this was probably a Gentile crowd. If so, Jesus' divine provision extended beyond Israel.

8:5 *Seven loaves.* This compares to the five loaves and two fish of the earlier feeding. If there is symbolism in the number, it is no longer clear (Guelich 1989:405; cf. Marcus 2000:488-489, who says it simply suggests fullness).

8:6 *took . . . broke . . . gave . . . distributed.* The description almost matches the earlier miracle, with three differences: (1) There is no mention here of Jesus' looking up to heaven; (2) Jesus gave thanks instead of a blessing; and (3) there is no mention of dividing the crowd up into groups.

8:7 *A few small fish.* Unlike the earlier account, the fish are noted almost as an afterthought. However, their presence shows that the passage does not intend Eucharistic symbolism.

8:8 *as much as they wanted.* There was more than enough, as the seven baskets full of leftovers show. In the earlier miracle, there were twelve baskets left over, though Mark uses a different term for basket here (*spuris* [TG4711, ZG5083] versus the earlier *kophinos* [TG2894, ZG3186]—see note on 6:43). Such baskets could be large enough to hold a person (Acts 9:25), although some were only the size of a lunch pail. While the distinct term may suggest smaller baskets, these were probably of the larger sort.

8:9 *4,000 people.* There were 5,000 men at the earlier feeding miracle (6:44). Here the entire crowd was 4,000 people.

8:10 *Dalmanutha.* This is the best reading among variants of the verse, as most of the major uncial MSS (א A B C L 0274) have it. Dalmanutha is unknown today, but the parallel in Matt 15:39 reads "Magadan," while variants for Mark read "Mageda" (Dᶜ) or

"Magdala" (Θ). Lane suggests that this is an alternate name for Magdala (Lane 1974:275). Others have placed the event in the Gerasa region (Taylor [1966:361] mentions Eusebius and Jerome for this view, while suggesting that the locale was near Tiberias and that the obscure name shows that the tradition was primitive).

COMMENTARY

The second feeding miracle continues the theme of Jesus' special activity in light of Isaiah 35. God supplying manna to the Israelites is the Old Testament parallel to Jesus providing food for people in the wilderness. Jesus was demonstrating that a new era of God's deliverance had come, a period that fulfilled Isaiah 35. In this case, Gentiles were the beneficiaries.

Jesus' work replicated what he had done elsewhere and underscored his ability to provide for life through his disciples. The miracle also replicated what God had done in the wilderness for the nation of Israel during the Exodus, so this act had multifaceted significance. This miracle sequence makes the impending rejection even harder to understand. Mark's point is that only people with closed eyes and hearts could fail to appreciate that Jesus was working by the power of God.

◆   ## 10. The Pharisees demand a sign (8:11-13; cf. Matt 16:1-4)

¹¹When the Pharisees heard that Jesus had arrived, they came and started to argue with him. Testing him, they demanded that he show them a miraculous sign from heaven to prove his authority. ¹²When he heard this, he sighed deeply in his spirit and said, "Why do these people keep demanding a miraculous sign? I tell you the truth, I will not give this generation any such sign." ¹³So he got back into the boat and left them, and he crossed to the other side of the lake.

NOTES

8:11 *Testing him, they demanded that he show them a miraculous sign from heaven to prove his authority.* The NLT adds the explanatory phrase "to prove his authority" to the request for a heavenly sign, a request that was also a test. The addition makes explicit what such a sign would indicate. The mention of testing points to the dispute that has been a constant part of Mark's account (2:6-12, 16-17, 18-22, 23-28; 3:1-5; 7:1-23; Hurtado 1989:130).

8:12 *he sighed deeply.* Mark again notes Jesus' emotions (1:41; 3:5; 6:6; 10:14; 14:34). This term appears in the LXX (Sir 25:18; 2 Macc 6:30).

Why do these people keep demanding a miraculous sign? Only the blind could fail to see what God was doing through Jesus and thereby ask for more proof. Mark rarely refers to a sign; he views such requests negatively, since they reflected a lack of belief (as here) or a readiness to be deceived (as in 13:4, 22).

I will not give this generation any such sign. In Gr., the unusual construction used to express this refusal makes the remark emphatic (Taylor [1966:362] calls the refusal "absolute"). Mark omits the appeal to the sign of Jonah that is included in Matthew and Luke. Mark's version is curt and brusque.

8:13 *to the other side.* Jesus again crossed the lake that was at the center of his activity. Only this general description of the setting is given.

COMMENTARY

Jesus refused the demand for a specific sign. In all likelihood, the request was for some apocalyptic, Elijah-like sign that would definitively point to the arrival of the end time. Perhaps the request was for something that would make Jesus distinct from others who healed and exorcised. Since Jesus had done nothing but give signs, the request for a very specific sign ignored the great variety of evidence Jesus had already provided concerning his authority from God.

Jesus was already showing them who he was and that God was working through him. Therefore, Jesus refused their request for a sign and noted that they were placing inappropriate demands on God's work, dictating what it should look like by seeking a specific indicator. The generation that saw Jesus had enough evidence to believe in him as the Messiah, the Son of God. To ask for more evidence was to manifest their unbelief.

◆   ## 11. Dialogue about yeast among the Pharisees and Herod (8:14-21; cf. Matt 16:5-12)

14But the disciples had forgotten to bring any food. They had only one loaf of bread with them in the boat. 15As they were crossing the lake, Jesus warned them, "Watch out! Beware of the yeast of the Pharisees and of Herod."

16At this they began to argue with each other because they hadn't brought any bread. 17Jesus knew what they were saying, so he said, "Why are you arguing about having no bread? Don't you know or understand even yet? Are your hearts too hard to take it in? 18'You have eyes—

can't you see? You have ears—can't you hear?'* Don't you remember anything at all? 19When I fed the 5,000 with five loaves of bread, how many baskets of leftovers did you pick up afterward?"

"Twelve," they said.

20"And when I fed the 4,000 with seven loaves, how many large baskets of leftovers did you pick up?"

"Seven," they said.

21"Don't you understand yet?" he asked them.

8:18 Jer 5:21.

NOTES

8:14 *only one loaf of bread.* Mark's reader is now conditioned to expect that the absence of provisions will lead to some form of teaching from Jesus. Although some have seen the one loaf as referring either to Jesus or to the Lord's Table, these seem distant from the point. Jesus turned the circumstance of the single loaf into a symbol about his opponents, not himself.

8:15 *Beware of the yeast of the Pharisees and of Herod.* Jesus made a symbol of the bread, although the disciples were slow to realize it. The Gr. mentions "leaven" (*zumēs* [TG2219, ZG2434]), which technically is distinct from yeast (Marcus 2000:506; BDAG 429). However, "yeast" is the closest common equivalent in our experience. This was an apt symbol for the spreading of evil by the Pharisees because in making bread, a little leaven would spread through all the dough. Matthew's version mentions the Sadducees, not Herod (Matt 16:6; also 15:12), and ties the image to their teachings, while Luke 12:1 notes only the Pharisees and their hypocrisy.

8:16 *began to argue.* Still thinking on the material plane of literal food, the disciples argued, probably about who was responsible for the omission (8:17). The reference to not bringing any bread meant, in context, that not enough bread had been brought to take care of everyone.

8:17-18 *Don't you know or understand even yet? . . . hearts . . . eyes . . . ears? . . . Don't you remember anything at all?* Jesus asked a series of five questions that pointed to the disciples' failure to understand or appreciate the meaning of what he had just done with the bread. This is the fourth such text in Mark (4:13, 40; 6:52—again, *hard hearts*). The first question echoes a question in Isa 40:21, a call to embrace God's sovereignty and power. The references to eyes and ears recall Jer 5:21, where the nation's lack of understanding led her into exile. The rebuke was a serious call (Ps 95:8; Isa 6:9-10; 63:17; Ezek 12:2), a call to understand, to open their hearts, to see, and to hear (see Deut 29:2-4, LXX; Marcus 2000:513). This rebuke is placed between two scenes in which Jesus demonstrated that he could heal physical blindness (8:22-26) and deafness (7:31-37); these picture his ability to heal at a deeper level and bring the messianic era such healing suggests.

8:19 *how many baskets of leftovers?* Maintaining the distinction in the terminology for baskets in these events, Jesus reviewed how many leftovers the feedings of the 5,000 and the 4,000 had produced. These two questions make a total of seven questions, the same number as the number of baskets of leftovers at the end of this event.

8:21 *Don't you understand yet?* The concluding question to ponder gives this passage an "open" literary ending. Jesus asked if the disciples did not yet understand the meaning of his work of provision. This concludes his rebuke and sets up the confession at Caesarea Philippi, where Peter will step forward with a reply.

C O M M E N T A R Y

The disciples were still processing the significance of Jesus' work and they were slow to get the point. This incident in which the disciples were preoccupied with not having brought enough bread triggered Jesus' warning to the disciples about an evil inclination in Herod and in the teaching of the Pharisees. Jesus warned that their reactions corrupted spiritual sustenance.

The background for this was the prohibition of yeast or leaven at Passover (Exod 12:14-20). In Judaism, such leaven signified evil inclinations (Taylor 1966:365; *Genesis Rabbah* 34.10; 1 Cor 5:6-8). That the Jewish leaders sought signs while refusing to believe indicated their corrupt hearts, as 7:1-23 has already suggested. Those who reject a sign such as that given to Israel during the Exodus (i.e., manna from heaven) will miss out on blessing and stand condemned.

Jesus drew the disciples' attention to his ability to provide physical sustenance; he also said that the provision of food was a picture of what he could provide spiritually. This "picture in kind" was not unusual in Jesus' teaching. In Luke 5:1-11, the miraculous catch of fish stood for how Jesus would make the disciples fishers of people. After an exorcism, Jesus noted that this demonstrated his overtaking the house of Satan, the strong man. However, the disciples did not understand. The numbers of twelve and seven indicate God's care for his people and the fullness of that provision. A new era of provision, like that of the Exodus, had come.

◆ 12. A blind man's healing at Bethsaida (8:22-26)

²²When they arrived at Bethsaida, some people brought a blind man to Jesus, and they begged him to touch the man and heal him. ²³Jesus took the blind man by the hand and led him out of the village. Then, spitting on the man's eyes, he laid his hands on him and asked, "Can you see anything now?"

²⁴The man looked around. "Yes," he said, "I see people, but I can't see them very clearly. They look like trees walking around."

²⁵Then Jesus placed his hands on the man's eyes again, and his eyes were opened. His sight was completely restored, and he could see everything clearly. ²⁶Jesus sent him away, saying, "Don't go back into the village on your way home."

NOTES

8:22 *Bethsaida*. This town of a few thousand was located on the northern shore of the Sea of Galilee.

they begged him to touch the man and heal him. The crowd interceded for the blind man.

8:23 *led him out of the village*. One unusual feature of the healing was that Jesus took the man away to heal him. This was probably to keep from drawing excessive attention to the event.

spitting on the man's eyes. Jesus also did something like this in 7:33. Its significance is discussed in the commentary to that passage. This narrative is very parallel to 7:32-37 (see Taylor 1966:368-369, who concludes that two events are in view, not a doublet).

8:24 *looked around*. The verb here can mean "regained his sight" (Matt 11:5; Mark 10:51-52; Luke 18:41-43; John 9:11; Acts 9:17-18). That is probably its significance here, but to report on his seeing, he would have had to look around.

They look like trees walking around. Since the man knew what trees looked like, he was probably not born blind. There is a Gr. parallel somewhat similar to this account in which the god Asclepius heals a man in his temple at Epidauros and the man first sees trees in the temple (Johnson 1960:145; *Inscriptiones Graecae*, IV².1.121-122, entry 18).

8:25 *His sight was completely restored*. Jesus completed the two-stage healing. This miracle, not included in Matthew and Luke, is one of the few Marcan texts that does not show up in another Gospel. It may have been omitted elsewhere because of the stages involved in the healing.

8:26 *Don't go back into the village*. Once again, Jesus tried to limit the attention given to his healing work.

COMMENTARY

Jesus was sought to bring sight to the blind. This further allusion to Isaiah 35:5-6 recalls the earlier rebuke in which the disciples were said to have eyes that did not see (8:18). In one sense, full restoration to spiritual health is a process. Jesus' healing the blind man in stages illustrated the disciples' gradual move toward clarity of understanding. Peter's following confession that Jesus was the Messiah represented a major advance in their understanding.

◆ III. To Jerusalem, Passion, and Vindication (8:27–16:8)
  A. Passion Predictions and Discipleship Teaching (8:27–10:52)
    1. Peter's confession at Caesarea Philippi (8:27-30;
      cf. Matt 16:13-20; Luke 9:18-21)

²⁷Jesus and his disciples left Galilee and went up to the villages near Caesarea Philippi. As they were walking along, he asked them, "Who do people say I am?"
²⁸"Well," they replied, "some say John the Baptist, some say Elijah, and others say you are one of the other prophets."

²⁹Then he asked them, "But who do you say I am?"
Peter replied, "You are the Messiah.*"
³⁰But Jesus warned them not to tell anyone about him.

8:29 Or *the Christ*. *Messiah* (a Hebrew term) and *Christ* (a Greek term) both mean "the anointed one."

NOTES
8:27 *Caesarea Philippi.* This town was north of the Sea of Galilee at the source of the Jordan River, southwest of Mount Hermon. It was a predominantly non-Jewish area ruled by Herod Philip. It was named after Caesar and Philip and was known for its beauty.

As they were walking along. The theme of "the way" appears frequently in Mark 8–10 (8:3, 27; 9:33-34; 10:17, 32, 46, 52). Jesus was on a divinely directed journey.

Who do people say I am? This question introduces the turning point in Mark's Gospel.

COMMENTARY
This crucial passage in Mark concerns the disciples' understanding of Jesus' identity. Peter took the lead in confessing that Jesus was the Messiah. Once this confession was made, the discussion turned to the kind of Messiah Jesus would be, namely, one who suffered. But first, Jesus asked who other people thought he was. The point of the passage is the contrast between the crowd's perceptions and that of the disciples.

The crowds thought that Jesus was either "John the Baptist . . . Elijah . . . [or] one of the other prophets." The crowds respected Jesus as one through whom God was working, in contrast to the rejection from the Jewish leaders. The answer was significant in communicating the crowd's regard for Jesus, but it was still inadequate. The reference to John the Baptist probably suggested that the spirit of John the Baptist was present in Jesus. Elijah pointed to the nearness of the eschatological age (Mal 4:5).

Jesus turned the question to the disciples, who had been with him for some time. Had their familiarity with him helped them understand who he was? Peter answered for the group by confessing, "You are the Christ." Although there is some difference in this answer in each synoptic (Matthew has "Christ, Son of the Living God" and Luke has "the Christ of God"), the gist they affirm is that Jesus is the Christ. Peter affirmed that Jesus was the unique, promised, anointed one of God. The reply evokes 1:1, while 14:61-62 shows the title as a key point of dispute with the Jewish leaders. The point of the answer was in the contrast between Jesus as merely a prophet and as the promised, chosen One of God. If Jesus was the Messiah, then he stood at the center of God's plan and there was no other like him. The disciples understood this much, but they had much more to learn about the Messiah. They had expected a powerful conquering figure, probably very much like the militaristic victor pictured in the *Psalms of Solomon* 17–18.

After the confession, Jesus commanded the disciples not to say this to anyone else. The type of Messiah they expected and the type of Messiah he would be were very different, as the next few passages will show. Until they understood who Jesus was as the Messiah, they were to remember the confession but not proclaim it. This feature shows the authenticity of the passage, for the early church openly proclaimed Jesus as the Messiah. This restriction applied only until the disciples appreciated who Jesus was in his suffering. Until they appreciated that dimension of his work, they were not ready to explain Jesus' role within the Kingdom. The rest of the Gospel is dedicated to making that role clear and to showing its impact on Jesus' disciples, who must walk the same path. Taylor (1966:377) also argues that proclaiming Jesus as Messiah would have had political overtones that had to be avoided until Jesus' use of the term was really understood.

◆ ## 2. Jesus begins to speak about his death and resurrection (8:31-33)

³¹Then Jesus began to tell them that the Son of Man* must suffer many terrible things and be rejected by the elders, the leading priests, and the teachers of religious law. He would be killed, but three days later he would rise from the dead. ³²As he talked about this openly with his disciples, Peter took him aside and began to reprimand him for saying such things.* ³³Jesus turned around and looked at his disciples, then reprimanded Peter. "Get away from me, Satan!" he said. "You are seeing things merely from a human point of view, not from God's."

8:31 "Son of Man" is a title Jesus used for himself. 8:32 Or *began to correct him.*

NOTES

8:31 *the Son of Man must suffer many terrible things . . . be killed, but three days later he would rise from the dead.* Here in a nutshell is the first prediction of what lay ahead (cf. 9:30-32; 10:32-34). Jesus now described himself with his favorite self-designation, "Son of Man." As a representative of humanity and one who would one day be their judge, he first must suffer judgment himself. The use of the term about necessity (*dei* [TG1163, ZG1256]) underscores the divine nature of the plan. These things must occur.

8:32 *talked about this openly.* The passage indicates that Jesus spoke of these things in an open and direct way. He said them plainly. It was almost too clear and too much for them to accept. The powerful Messiah would die! The disciples never grasped these predictions prior to Jesus' death and resurrection.

Peter . . . began to reprimand him. One of the wordplays of this passage occurs when Jesus and Peter exchange rebukes in 8:32-33, as the verb *epitimaō* [TG2008, ZG2203] appears in both passages (see also 8:30).

8:33 *looked at his disciples, then reprimanded Peter. "Get away from me, Satan!"* The verb that the NLT translates as "reprimand" means "to rebuke," matching the verb in 8:32. Jesus looked at his disciples as he spoke to Peter, showing that the remark was intended for all of them. The rebuke could not be stronger. Peter was addressed as Satan's proxy, having expressed a satanic idea, namely, that Jesus would never suffer (France 2002:338).

You are seeing things merely from a human point of view, not from God's. This explains the rebuke. A human perspective argues that Jesus should exercise his messianic prerogatives as an expression of raw power with no suffering. However, God's plan was that by suffering, Jesus would identify with the fallen condition of people and take care of sin on their behalf. The rejection and suffering were an integral part of the plan, and now with this introduced, Jesus can fully address the nature of discipleship (8:34–9:1).

COMMENTARY

The exchange between Jesus and Peter after Peter's great confession of Jesus as the Messiah shows that the disciples still had much to learn. They had no clue as to the importance or necessity of Jesus' suffering. This strong rebuke sends the first of many signals in the next few passages that these disciples (as well as Mark's readers) need to understand the path that Jesus would take, one the disciples would also have to follow. The passage indicates how aware Jesus was of his mission and of the suffering he would face as well as his resolve to face it. Jesus interpreted suggestions that such suffering should not be undertaken as the thoughts of Satan, even when they came from the lips of a major disciple like Peter. Jesus had a calling, and he would answer that call.

Jesus would be rejected by the religious leaders, be put to death, and then be raised from the dead. The passive verbs used to express these realities show that Jesus was part of a plan in which he was the key object. The leaders would reject and kill him, as 12:10 also shows, and God would bring him back to life. The disciples did not want to include this prediction as part of the plan, but Jesus' response showed that it was at its very center. The disciples had much to learn about how God would work through Jesus. Some questioned the prediction of this text, but anyone who had seen what happened to John the Baptist could understand the risk Jesus faced. Jesus' understanding of his ultimate vindication simply showed how clearly he understood his mission and his appreciation that God would not abandon him or it.

By contrast, the disciples did not grasp that Jesus was not only the Son of Man and the Messiah, but also the suffering servant. So surprising was this that Peter, who had just acknowledged Jesus as the unique Messiah, took Jesus aside to reprimand him. The rebuke was surely because Jesus did not highlight himself as a conquering hero. Peter conducted his own private theological class for Jesus, but it was Peter who had to learn the lesson.

◆   3. Following Jesus (8:34–9:1; cf. Matt 16:21–28; Luke 9:22–27)

34Then, calling the crowd to join his disciples, he said, "If any of you wants to be my follower, you must turn from your selfish ways, take up your cross, and follow me. 35If you try to hang on to your life, you will lose it. But if you give up your life for my sake and for the sake of the Good News, you will save it. 36And what do you benefit if you gain the whole world but lose your own soul?* 37Is anything worth more than your soul? 38If anyone is ashamed of me and my message in these adulterous and sinful days, the Son of Man will be ashamed of that person when he returns in the glory of his Father with the holy angels."

8:36 Or *your self?* also in 8:37.

CHAPTER 9

Jesus went on to say, "I tell you the truth, some standing here right now will not die before they see the Kingdom of God arrive in great power!"

NOTES

8:34 *be my follower.* The NLT is paraphrasing here, as the Gr. reads, "come after me." Of course, what is intended is following in Jesus' path as a disciple, so the NLT brings out the force of the metaphor of "coming after" Jesus.

turn from your selfish ways. Once again, the NLT is bringing out the force of the Gr., which translates as, "must deny oneself." The essence of this denial is not asceticism, but turning from a selfish focus in life to doing things God's way (Cranfield 1959:281-282; Hooker 1991:208). The imperative is in the aorist tense, so this "turn" is urged as a basic reorientation of priorities.

take up your cross. This instruction is also an aorist imperative. Since Jesus had not yet spoken of his crucifixion, this metaphor alluding to his coming crucifixion is proleptic. The picture will become a reality.

follow me. This command is in the present imperative. Unlike the previous two commands that look at a basic reorientation, the following of Jesus is a constant, ongoing call, a sustained pursuit of Jesus' way (Taylor 1966:381). Following is not an act accomplished in one moment, but the constant practice of one who embraces Jesus. This means that following Jesus is the greatest vocation in life, regardless of what others think or do to one as a result.

8:35 *If you try to hang on to your life.* Lit., "whoever would save his life." There is a wordplay with the key term, *psuchē* [TG5590, ZG6034], which can be translated "life" or "soul," and refers to "real life" or "inner life"—that which is truly central (see BDAG 1098-1099; France 2002:340-341). The play is on preserving the earthly life (seen as preserving the life that includes a soul), only to lose the opportunity to possess the "real life" in the end.

But if you give up your life. This renders the phrase "whoever loses his life." It is opposite to the previous scenario and the result is opposite as well. Paradoxically, to lose one's earthly life is to save one's inner life for the life to come.

for my sake and for the sake of the Good News. The text shows that a disciple's allegiance is to the person Jesus and to God's Gospel, his Good News, at the same time (10:29). They are interrelated.

8:36 *And what do you benefit if you gain the whole world but lose your own soul?* The key term for life (*psuchē* [TG5590, ZG6034]) is still being used here. Jesus makes clear what is at stake, echoing the language of Ps 49:7-8. The reference to "soul" is a way of discussing one's life and eternal wellbeing; the "saving" and "losing" look back to the saving and losing of 8:35; issues of eternal life and the life beyond are in view in the earlier wordplay.

8:37 *Is anything worth more than your soul?* The NLT again brings out the force of the Gr., "What might a man give in exchange for his soul?" with a paraphrase. The wordplay with *psuchē* [TG5590, ZG6034] (soul) continues. The term for "exchange" appears only here in the NT. The expected answer is that nothing is as valuable as preserving the soul, because nothing is worth more than the soul. As BDAG (86) notes, "nothing would compensate for such a loss."

8:38 *me and my message.* Jesus and the message of the Kingdom are again linked (8:35).

these adulterous and sinful days. This renders the phrase "in this sinful and adulterous generation," in which "generation" has a moral overtone about the people of that time. The phrase "sinful and adulterous" appears only here, but the idea of people adulterating their relationship with God is common in the OT (Isa 1:4, 21; Hos 2).

the Son of Man will be ashamed of that person. The Son of Man is here viewed as a judge at the end times. Those who had paid attention to Jesus' use of the phrase "Son of Man" would recognize this indirect reference to himself as that coming authority. (The parallel in Matt 10:33 simply says "I.") This remark indicates the key issue of the Gospel. Will one identify with Jesus, the Son of Man to whom one's soul is ultimately accountable? To shun the Son is to face the prospect of being shunned by him when he returns with the angels to exercise judgment in the power and glory of the Father (14:62). That is, to lose one's soul. This is the first clear reference to a return in Mark, though 4:21-22, 30-32 have suggested it (France 2002:342 dissents, seeing it as about the Son of Man's entry into authority, an unlikely reading, given the "shame" concept and the language of "coming in glory").

9:1 *some standing here right now will not die before they see.* These words of Jesus have been debated, but the most likely meaning is that some of the disciples would get a glimpse of the Kingdom's full glory in the Transfiguration that follows. For seven interpretive options, see Cranfield (1959:286-289). Peter, James, and John get the glimpse of Jesus transformed and all it implied about his authority. Peter's commentary appears in 2 Pet 1:16-18.

COMMENTARY

These words weren't just addressed to the twelve disciples. Jesus spoke to the crowd, making it clear that he wanted those who followed him to appreciate the significance of responding to him (Lane 1974:306). Since life and death are mentioned here, the passage does not treat discipleship as a distinct step in responding to Jesus. The teaching is not for an elite but for all, so Jesus presents the entire package of what faith means when one embraces Jesus. It means believing Jesus on his own terms.

To follow Jesus means to turn from a selfish orientation, pick up "the cross," and take on the rejection that is part of associating with Jesus in a world that does not appreciate him. The cross pictures the rejection and humiliation that was associated with crucifixion. A disciple must understand that this rejection that comes with following Jesus may even lead to death, for the disciple's experience may well be like the teacher's.

Since Jesus suffered, his disciples would do the same. Some people will consider this and want to be spared persecution and rejection rather than to identify with Jesus and his message. One can choose to hold onto life and acceptance in the world at the expense of one's soul and one's life with God. The prospective disciple that protects the earthly life will not face rejection by others in the world, but will lose the life of the world to come.

Jesus urges would-be disciples to experience the rejection of this world and thus gain spiritual well-being. More than the loss of physical life is being discussed here, for what is lost is something thought to be protected and retained through the preservation of physical life. The choice to gain the world but lose one's soul ends in emptiness as the self is obliterated in the process of rejecting God's way.

Those who reject Jesus in this lifetime are ashamed of the Son of Man. In the last day, when the Judge comes in power and glory, he will be ashamed of those who have rejected him. The implication is that identification with the Son of Man preserves one's spiritual well-being, both now and in the judgment to come.

◆   **4. Jesus' transfiguration (9:2-13; cf. Matt 17:1-13; Luke 9:28-36)**

²Six days later Jesus took Peter, James, and John, and led them up a high mountain to be alone. As the men watched, Jesus' appearance was transformed, ³and his clothes became dazzling white, far whiter than any earthly bleach could ever make them. ⁴Then Elijah and Moses appeared and began talking with Jesus.

⁵Peter exclaimed, "Rabbi, it's wonderful for us to be here! Let's make three shelters as memorials*—one for you, one for Moses, and one for Elijah." ⁶He said this because he didn't really know what else to say, for they were all terrified.

⁷Then a cloud overshadowed them, and a voice from the cloud said, "This is my dearly loved Son. Listen to him." ⁸Suddenly, when they looked around, Moses and Elijah were gone, and they saw only Jesus with them.

⁹As they went back down the mountain, he told them not to tell anyone what they had seen until the Son of Man* had risen from the dead. ¹⁰So they kept it to themselves, but they often asked each other what he meant by "rising from the dead."

¹¹Then they asked him, "Why do the teachers of religious law insist that Elijah must return before the Messiah comes?*"

¹²Jesus responded, "Elijah is indeed coming first to get everything ready. Yet why do the Scriptures say that the Son of Man must suffer greatly and be treated with utter contempt? ¹³But I tell you, Elijah has already come, and they chose to abuse him, just as the Scriptures predicted."

9:5 Greek *three tabernacles.* 9:9 "Son of Man" is a title Jesus used for himself. 9:11 Greek *that Elijah must come first?*

NOTES

9:2 *Six days.* Outside of the Passion week, no other statement of timing is this exact. There may be an allusion to Exod 24:16-17 (Lane 1974:317).

Peter, James, and John. At a few points, Jesus gives this inner circle of disciples a unique experience (5:37; 14:33; cf. 13:3 with Andrew).

mountain. The mountain where this took place is unknown, but among the suggestions are Mount Tabor, Mount Hermon, or a site to the southeast of Caesarea Philippi such as Mount Meron (France 2002:350).

Jesus' appearance was transformed. Jesus was "metamorphosed"; his appearance blazed in bright light with the glory of his heavenly origin (Dan 12:3; 2 Baruch 51:3, 5, 10, 12; 1 Enoch 38:4; 104:2; another conceptual parallel could be the transfiguration of Moses's face at Sinai).

9:3 *his clothes became dazzling white.* This glorious brightness indicated Jesus' cosmic character. Dazzling white clothes are a sign of supernatural existence, as seen with angels or other images of God (Dan 7:9; Matt 28:3; Mark 16:5; John 20:12; 1 Enoch 14:10; 2 Enoch 22:8-9; France 2002:351 notes that this term for "shining" is often used of shining stars). No effort to bleach the garments could have made them whiter.

9:4 *Elijah and Moses.* These major OT saints add importance to the moment.

9:5 make three shelters as memorials. Peter wanted to celebrate something like the Festival of Shelters (Lev 23:39-43) to honor Moses, Elijah, and Jesus. This feast recalled the Exodus and God's provision during their travel in the wilderness. There was an idea that in the end, Israel might return to life in tents as at the beginning of their national journey (Hooker 1991:217). That expectation may be at play here. Israel's history was represented, so in Peter's view the moment should be celebrated with the three great men as guests of honor. It appears that Peter expected the three disciples to serve and honor the three guests.

9:6 didn't really know what else to say. Peter really did not understand the scene; he spoke without knowledge and out of fear (for fearing, see 1:22). A voice from heaven would set the scene right and make Jesus' uniqueness clear.

9:7 a cloud overshadowed them. This is the imagery of the Shekinah presence of God, like the cloud at Mount Sinai when Moses received the law (Exod 19:9, 16; 24:15-16; 40:35). It means that God was present and about to speak, and it was his voice that came from the cloud.

This is my dearly loved Son. Listen to him. The divine utterance at Jesus' baptism (1:11) is repeated, with three differences: (1) God says "this" is my beloved Son, not "you are" my beloved son; (2) there is no mention of "in whom I am well pleased"; and (3) the phrase "listen to him" from Deut 18:15 is added. The first difference identifies Jesus as the royal Son in the language of Ps 2 for the sake of the disciples, unlike the more private experience of the voice at the baptism. The connection with the baptism reminds Mark's reader that this Son is also a Servant. The switch from "well pleased" to "listen to him" is a call to follow this prophet, who like Moses reveals God's will and way. The point is that Jesus is greater than Moses or Elijah.

9:8 Moses and Elijah were gone. The Gr. reads, "they no longer saw anyone," which the NLT renders in an explanatory way. With Jesus revealed and his uniqueness declared, there was no other need to have Moses or Elijah present. As the verse ends, "only Jesus" was necessary.

9:9 not to tell anyone what they had seen until the Son of Man had risen from the dead. The disciples were not yet ready to preach Jesus because they didn't yet appreciate precisely how he fit into God's plan. Jesus told them to remain silent until the Son of Man (that is, Jesus) had risen, a remark that echoes 8:31. The "silence" motif reaches from 1:25 to as recently as 8:29. This strong injunction uses the verb *diesteilato* [TG1291, ZG1403] that appears elsewhere in similar contexts (5:43; 7:36; 8:15).

9:10 they kept it to themselves. The disciples kept their experience private, as the verb *krateō* [TG2902, ZG3195] means "to guard, keep, or hold onto something" (Cranfield 1959:297). Other scholars (Hooker 1991:219) take the phrase to mean, "they seized on this saying," but this does not readily follow the thought of 9:9.

asked each other what he meant by "rising from the dead." The Gr. here could be rendered, "questioning what the rising of the dead meant." The disciples still did not understand how to fit Jesus' declaration about rising from the dead into a messianic portrait. They were hearing Jesus' words but did not grasp them because Judaism only recognized a general resurrection at the end of time, not an individual resurrection separate from the end.

9:11 Elijah must return. The disciples could not figure out the resurrection, but from Jewish teaching about the end times, they did know that Elijah must return before the Messiah would come. The roots of this promise are in Mal 3:1 and 4:5-6; Sir 48:10 also says that the Messiah will participate in the restoration of the nation. Elijah's presence with Jesus seems to have sparked the question.

9:12 Elijah is indeed coming first to get everything ready for the Messiah. Jesus affirmed the promise of Elijah's coming but did not immediately give details. In referring to the

Messiah, the NLT explains a major feature of what is implied in the Gr. The Gr. text speaks of the "restoration of all things." This promise throughout the prophets that God would bring the nation of Israel into a golden era came to include messianic expectations (Jer 15:19; 16:15; 24:6-7; 31:31-34; 50:19-20 [27:19-20 LXX]; Ezek 34–37; Hos 11:8-11; Amos 9:11-15). The question implies an era of power and glory.

why do the Scriptures say that the Son of Man must suffer . . . and be treated with utter contempt? Jesus returned to the theme of the Son of Man's suffering, for the disciples had to grasp this as well as the images of glory.

9:13 *Elijah has already come.* This describes John the Baptist, who had "found his Jezebel in Herodias" (Taylor 1966:395, citing Swete).

they chose to abuse him, just as the Scriptures predicted. John the Baptist is a type of Elijah. Both suffered rejection during bleak times of spiritual defection in Israel's history (1 Kgs 19:2, 10). Implied is that the Son of Man will also experience what John experienced. The disciples should be prepared.

COMMENTARY

The transfiguration was a crucial event in Jesus' career in that his unique status was again confirmed. This confirmation did not come from just anyone. God spoke from heaven on behalf of Jesus, his Son, who was completely transfigured in the presence of three disciples. These disciples were told not to speak of the event until after the Son of Man was raised, because affirmation of Jesus as God's beloved Son also came with the call to listen to him. John alludes to this experience of seeing Jesus' glory in John 1:14 and 1 John 1:1-3. Peter speaks of it explicitly in 2 Peter 1:16-18.

Two significant figures, Moses and Elijah, appeared alongside Jesus. Moses, who received the law, looked back to the formation of Israel. Here he is important as one who predicted that a prophet like himself would come (Deut 18:15-19), while Elijah was regarded as the prophet who pointed to the new era (Mal 3:1; 4:5-6). There is also a tradition linking Moses to Elijah as one who did not experience death (2 Kgs 2:1-12, for Elijah; for Jewish tradition on Moses, see Josephus *Antiquities* 4.48; cf. Deut 32:50-51).

The wording from Deuteronomy 18:15 ("listen to him") presents Jesus as a second prophet like Moses, one who issued a new instruction from God as Moses did. Since the disciples' understanding of God's program was flawed, thinking only of glory and not of suffering, they needed instruction on what Jesus would do. That class began almost immediately, as they were reluctant to speak of Jesus' resurrection and asked about Elijah instead. In 9:13, Jesus makes it clear that Elijah had come, was abused, and suffered—a reference to the ministry of John the Baptist. In Matthew 17:11, there is a hint that Elijah was still to come, despite John's coming, which seems to mean that he will reappear at the end. Thus, Jesus turned Elijah into a type. He is John the Baptist, who suffered as Elijah did and as the Son of Man would.

The great era the disciples expected would not come without pain; the Son of Man must suffer. It appears that Jesus combined references to the Son of Man with imagery of the servant (Isa 52:13–53:12) and of the righteous sufferer of the Psalter

(Pss 22; 69, among others) to make this point. Jesus wanted the disciples to see that the mission of the Messiah was not glory and triumph alone. There was a painful mission that he must first carry out. Hurtado (1989:147) says that "intelligent talk of the glory of Jesus cannot be done apart from emphasis upon his death and resurrection, and that any Christian preaching and devotion that is not centered on the meaning of these events is shallow and confused."

◆   ## 5. Jesus performs an exorcism after the disciples' failure (9:14-29; cf. Matt 17:14-21; Luke 9:37-43)

14When they returned to the other disciples, they saw a large crowd surrounding them, and some teachers of religious law were arguing with them. 15When the crowd saw Jesus, they were overwhelmed with awe, and they ran to greet him.

16"What is all this arguing about?" Jesus asked.

17One of the men in the crowd spoke up and said, "Teacher, I brought my son so you could heal him. He is possessed by an evil spirit that won't let him talk. 18And whenever this spirit seizes him, it throws him violently to the ground. Then he foams at the mouth and grinds his teeth and becomes rigid.* So I asked your disciples to cast out the evil spirit, but they couldn't do it."

19Jesus said to them,* "You faithless people! How long must I be with you? How long must I put up with you? Bring the boy to me."

20So they brought the boy. But when the evil spirit saw Jesus, it threw the child into a violent convulsion, and he fell to the ground, writhing and foaming at the mouth.

21"How long has this been happening?" Jesus asked the boy's father.

He replied, "Since he was a little boy. 22The spirit often throws him into the fire or into water, trying to kill him. Have mercy on us and help us, if you can."

23"What do you mean, 'If I can'?" Jesus asked. "Anything is possible if a person believes."

24The father instantly cried out, "I do believe, but help me overcome my unbelief!"

25When Jesus saw that the crowd of onlookers was growing, he rebuked the evil* spirit. "Listen, you spirit that makes this boy unable to hear and speak," he said. "I command you to come out of this child and never enter him again!"

26Then the spirit screamed and threw the boy into another violent convulsion and left him. The boy appeared to be dead. A murmur ran through the crowd as people said, "He's dead." 27But Jesus took him by the hand and helped him to his feet, and he stood up.

28Afterward, when Jesus was alone in the house with his disciples, they asked him, "Why couldn't we cast out that evil spirit?"

29Jesus replied, "This kind can be cast out only by prayer.*"

9:18 Or becomes weak.   9:19 Or said to his disciples.   9:25 Greek unclean.   9:29 Some manuscripts read by prayer and fasting.

NOTES

9:15 overwhelmed with awe. The use of xethambēthēsan [TG1568, ZG1701] here is the first of four uses of this verb in Mark (14:33; 16:5-6), the only NT writer to use the word. It refers to great surprise or perplexity (BDAG 303). In this context, the term could indicate surprise and excitement.

9:17 *an evil spirit that won't let him talk.* The possessed boy was also unable to speak. This is one of several similar scenes in Mark (cf. 1:25-26, 34; 5:8, 12-13; 7:29, 35, 37).

9:18 *it throws him violently to the ground.* This demon was particularly vicious in his treatment of the boy, which added to his father's concern. These details of hostile treatment in vv. 18, 20, 22, and 26 are lacking in Matthew.

becomes rigid. After the seizures, the boy was left wasted and spent. The verb (*xērainetai* [TG3583A, ZG3830]) means "to dry up." The boy was immobilized by the seizures.

they couldn't do it. The disciples' failure probably motivated the debate that becomes the hub of the passage. Once again the disciples fail and will need to learn from Jesus as v. 19 suggests.

9:20 *violent convulsion.* The demon seized the boy just as described in 9:18. The situation was desperate and dangerous.

9:21 *Since he was a little boy.* Jesus asked how long this had been going on and was told that the boy had suffered from this terrible condition for some time—ever since he was a small child.

9:22 *trying to kill him.* As with the Gerasene demoniac, this demon's presence had a destructive effect on the person it possessed, which is what demons always seek to do.

Have mercy on us and help us. The request for Jesus' aid and compassion was made with the understanding that this could not be demanded, but only received as Jesus' kind work of mercy. The mention of compassion ("have mercy") is the last of four passages where this verb (*splanchnizomai* [TG4697, ZG5072]) appears in Mark (1:41; 6:34; 8:2). However, this is the only place in Mark where Jesus' compassion is requested. Other texts simply note that he exercised it. The request for help will be renewed in 9:24 with respect to faith. These are the only two verses where Mark uses the verb *boētheō* [TG997, ZG1070], often used in appeals for God' help (Taylor 1966:399).

9:24 *help me overcome my unbelief!* The man was of two minds. With one mind, he believed; with the other, he did not believe. The man asked for help in overcoming his doubt, so Jesus acted on his behalf. The term used for "help" is the same one used in 9:22. Jesus met the man's doubt with affirming action. Here is another common person seeking Jesus and being aided by him.

9:25 *come out of this child and never enter him again!* Jesus rebuked the spirit and ordered him out. In this verse, we are told for the first time that the boy was both deaf and mute; he had been imprisoned in a world of silence. Jesus' miracle changed that.

9:26 *the spirit screamed and threw the boy into another violent convulsion.* The spirit departed quite visibly with one last attempt to damage the boy. The mention of the convulsion recalls 9:18, 20, 22.

He's dead. The crowd reacted to the danger of the convulsion out of their lack of appreciation for Jesus' power and authority. They soon discovered they were wrong.

9:27 *helped him to his feet.* Jesus helped the boy get up to show that he had been healed. There is a wordplay in Gr. with the phrase, "raised him up." Mark 5:41-42 describes a similar proof of healing.

9:28 *Why couldn't we cast out that evil spirit?* The disciples were still questioning and learning. Apparently they viewed their healing gift as automatic. Jesus corrected this impression with his reply.

9:29 *only by prayer.* This is one of two passages in Mark that mention prayer using *proseuchē* [TG4335, ZG4666] (cf. 11:17), and this is the only term he uses for the practice. The term refers to prayer in a general and comprehensive sense and not so much to daily requests as other terms for prayer that mean "to ask" (*aiteō*) or "to request" (*deomai*; Balz and Schneider 1993:3.166). Some MSS add "and fasting" here, but it is more likely that these words were added than that they were dropped from the original text of Mark (Cranfield 1959:304-305).

COMMENTARY

When Jesus returned from the mountain of Transfiguration with James, John, and Peter, there was a dispute going on among the other disciples, the crowd, and the scribes. As the transfiguration was taking place on the mountain, the remaining disciples had gotten themselves into a disagreement about how to handle a demon-possessed boy. Apparently, since the disciples were unable to heal him, the scribes were challenging the validity of their ministry. Jesus intervened and performed another exorcism, one of four in the book of Mark (1:21-28; 5:1-20; 7:24-30). In this case, the focus was less on the miracle than on the attitudes of those around it.

Jesus rebuked all the people for their lack of faith, calling them a "faithless generation" (so the Gr.). This is the only place in Mark that this phrase appears (Matt 17:17 and Luke 9:41 are parallel accounts). Jesus' rebuke suggests that the people's rejection and lack of faith had a role in what failed to occur. The Greek term for "generation" (*genea* [TG1074, ZG1155]) is used in a negative ethical sense in 8:12, 38. The conceptual roots of this expression may go back to Deuteronomy 32:5, which refers to a twisted and deceitful generation. Jesus' rebuke, "How long must I be with you? How long must I put up with you?" implied that he would not remain with them long and that the disciples, therefore, needed to develop their faith. The people's lack of faith was a painful reality with which Jesus had to cope. Yet despite their failure, Jesus compassionately healed the boy.

The man seeking healing for his boy also needed encouragement to believe, so Jesus said, "Anything is possible if a person believes." Jesus underscored the importance of faith (1:15; 5:36; 11:23-24) in his call for the man to believe and trust in his ability to overcome the destructive forces dwelling in the child. Jesus did not promise a magic mantra, but underscored that anything could be accomplished through faith within the context of God's will. He affirmed faith and submission.

The disciples needed to understand that their ministry was not an automatic exercise of giftedness. They needed to depend on the Father, looking to him in prayer and relying on his presence and power. Their failure was not in their giftedness but in how they used their gifts. The prayer in question was not formulaic, and Jesus never used such prayer to heal. Rather, he turned to God, asking him to exercise his authority and power.

◆   ## 6. Jesus predicts his death again (9:30-32; cf. Matt 17:22-23; Luke 9:43-45)

[30]Leaving that region, they traveled through Galilee. Jesus didn't want anyone to know he was there, [31]for he wanted to spend more time with his disciples and teach them. He said to them, "The Son of Man is going to be betrayed into the

hands of his enemies. He will be killed, but three days later he will rise from the dead." ³²They didn't understand what he was saying, however, and they were afraid to ask him what he meant.

NOTES

9:31 *The Son of Man is going to be betrayed. . . . He will be killed, but . . . he will rise.* This is the second of three predictions in this central unit of Mark (8:31; 10:32-34). There is also mention of the Son of Man's rising from the dead in 9:9, which (according to 9:10) the disciples did not understand. This is the briefest of the three predictive passages. The note of betrayal may echo Isa 53:6, 12, LXX (Lane 1974:337; also in Paul, Rom 4:25; 8:32). The betrayal is presented proleptically (as already accomplished) in the present tense: The Son of Man "is being betrayed" (Taylor 1966:403). The verse begins with Jesus teaching and saying these things to the disciples; expressed in Gr. by the imperfect tense, the point is that Jesus was telling them these things regularly.

9:32 *They didn't understand . . . they were afraid to ask.* As in 9:10, the disciples did not comprehend the remarks about the resurrection. Their fear about asking him also parallels the earlier remarks.

COMMENTARY

Jesus again sought to withdraw from the crowds for a moment (cf. 6:46). He wanted to concentrate on teaching his disciples, whose need for instruction was made obvious by the previous scenes. For the second time, he told them that the Son of Man was going to be betrayed, killed, and raised from the dead. Significantly, it is the "Son of Man" who experiences death and resurrection in all three predictions, although Mark 10 is more detailed. According to the Greek, the Son of Man was betrayed into the hands of men; this is ironic because the one who represented humanity was given over to humanity to meet his death (France 2002:372).

The disciples still did not understand what Jesus was talking about. It is not clear why they were reluctant to ask, as they often did make queries (4:10; 7:17; 9:11, 28; 10:10; 13:3; France 2002:372). Perhaps they understood just enough of the situation, especially in light of Jesus' rebuke of Peter, that they thought the details were best left undisclosed. They may have feared the answer. For those who expected a glorious redeemer, such remarks would have been surprising and disturbing. Only the resurrection would make matters clear. The contrast between Jesus' selfless perspective and the selfish focus of the disciples is still another example of discipleship failure and indicates what they must learn.

◆   ## 7. The greatest in the Kingdom (9:33-37; cf. Matt 18:1-14; Luke 9:46-48)

³³After they arrived at Capernaum and settled in a house, Jesus asked his disciples, "What were you discussing out on the road?" ³⁴But they didn't answer, because they had been arguing about which of them was the greatest. ³⁵He sat down, called the twelve disciples over to him, and said, "Whoever wants to be first must take last place and be the servant of everyone else."

³⁶Then he put a little child among them. Taking the child in his arms, he said to

them, 37"Anyone who welcomes a little
child like this on my behalf* welcomes
me, and anyone who welcomes me wel-

comes not only me but also my Father
who sent me."

9:37 Greek *in my name.*

NOTES

9:33 *Capernaum.* Jesus traveled back to his ministry headquarters.

What were you discussing? The verb for "discuss" (*dialogizomai* [TG1260, ZG1368]) often means "to reason"; here it suggests that sides have been taken and the issue has been discussed in detail (BDAG 232; Luke 9:46, where the related noun is present). Perhaps the question about who was greatest was sparked by the fact that only Peter, James, and John were taken up the mountain with Jesus (9:2-8).

9:35 *Whoever wants to be first must take last place and be the servant of everyone else.* Jesus' reply went in the exact opposite direction as the debate; he stressed that those who took the last place and served others stood in first place, as far as he was concerned. The term "servant" (*diakonos* [TG1249, ZG1356]) stands for one engaged in everyday service, such as Elisha was for Elijah (Josephus *Antiquities* 8.354), or like government officials, table attendants, and couriers (Rom 13:4; Col 4:7).

9:36 *little child.* Mark uses the general term for a child (*paidion* [TG3813, ZG4086]), so it is not clear just how old he was. Since Jesus took the child into his arms, he was probably small. Children were largely ignored in the ancient world, so they are good examples of people lacking status.

9:37 *Anyone who welcomes a little child like this on my behalf welcomes me . . . not only me but also my Father who sent me.* In bringing up a "little child" (*paidion*), Jesus illustrated his point about service (Luke 9:48) in a natural way, since the word for "child" in Gr. (*pais*) could also be used to mean "servant" (Hurtado 1989:153). The expression "on my behalf" is more lit. "in my name," and could indicate that the "child" was a follower of Jesus.

COMMENTARY

The juxtaposition of Jesus announcing his approaching suffering and the disciples debating who was the greatest is ironic, for it shows how little they understood God's way. The sense of embarrassment suggested in the text underscores their sense that something was wrong with their debate.

This passage discloses Jesus' values. Humanity is of value and so is service. Concern about rank should not be an issue for disciples. An apparently insignificant child provided an example. The one who welcomed this child of no status was actually welcoming Jesus and the Father. In this remark, Jesus elevated "nobodies" to a position of great significance, so that status became meaningless. If you are a person, you are important. Another point is more subtle. Given the rejection Jesus had faced, welcoming him was commendable, just as welcoming someone else of seeming insignificance was.

The tone of this text is similar to that of Matthew 25:31-46. To act kindly on someone's behalf was to perform this act for Jesus. If everyone is important, then the status question the disciples were debating was meaningless. This reversal of the world's values is the major lesson of this text.

◆   8. Miscellaneous remarks about relationships and accountability
       (9:38-50)

³⁸John said to Jesus, "Teacher, we saw someone using your name to cast out demons, but we told him to stop because he wasn't in our group."

³⁹"Don't stop him!" Jesus said. "No one who performs a miracle in my name will soon be able to speak evil of me. ⁴⁰Anyone who is not against us is for us. ⁴¹If anyone gives you even a cup of water because you belong to the Messiah, I tell you the truth, that person will surely be rewarded.

⁴²"But if you cause one of these little ones who trusts in me to fall into sin, it would be better for you to be thrown into the sea with a large millstone hung around your neck. ⁴³If your hand causes you to sin, cut it off. It's better to enter eternal life with only one hand than to go into the unquenchable fires of hell* with two hands.* ⁴⁵If your foot causes you to sin, cut it off. It's better to enter eternal life with only one foot than to be thrown into hell with two feet.* ⁴⁷And if your eye causes you to sin, gouge it out. It's better to enter the Kingdom of God with only one eye than to have two eyes and be thrown into hell, ⁴⁸'where the maggots never die and the fire never goes out.'*

⁴⁹"For everyone will be tested with fire.* ⁵⁰Salt is good for seasoning. But if it loses its flavor, how do you make it salty again? You must have the qualities of salt among yourselves and live in peace with each other."

9:43a Greek *Gehenna;* also in 9:45, 47.   9:43b Some manuscripts add verse 44, *'where the maggots never die and the fire never goes out.'* See 9:48.   9:45 Some manuscripts add verse 46, *'where the maggots never die and the fire never goes out.'* See 9:48.   9:48 Isa 66:24.   9:49 Greek *salted with fire;* other manuscripts add *and every sacrifice will be salted with salt.*

NOTES

9:41 *that person will surely be rewarded.* The one who gives a cup of water to a person who bears the name of Christ will be rewarded. The scorching sun of the area made the simple offer of a cup of water an act of hospitality.

9:42 *if you cause one of these little ones who trusts in me to fall into sin.* The warning is probably directed toward a serious sin such as defection. The verb *skandalizō* [TG4624, ZG4997] refers to stumbling over an obstacle (Cranfield 1959:313).

it would be better . . . to be thrown into the sea. To lead someone to reject Christ is to face serious consequences. A cruel demise such as being drowned by the weight of a millstone would be a better fate. Even the least of those who belong to Jesus means this much to him. We must avoid being a conduit for sin.

9:43 *If your hand causes you to sin, cut it off.* Jesus now follows with three illustrations that take the same form. If a hand, foot, or eye is a cause of sin, one should "cut it off" or "gouge it out." The remark is rhetorical, for if the command were followed literally, only two violations would be permitted (on the debate as to whether these remarks are literal or rhetorical, see France 2002:382, who notes that Deut 14:1 prohibits self-mutilation)! On tracing sin to different body parts, see Job 31:1, 5, 7; Prov 6:16-19; Rom 3:1-18.

the unquenchable fires of hell. The Gr. term for "hell" is *geenna* [TG1067, ZG1147]. In 9:48, Jesus states that in Gehenna, the "maggots never die and the fire never goes out." Jdt 16:17 gives a Jewish view of judgment as endless conscious torment, since the condemned weep forever. See also Sir 7:17, where fire and worms await the dead. Hooker (1991:232) argues that Mark's image is of a fire that burns endlessly, not of a body that burns endlessly. Judith does not read that way. See also *1 Enoch* 27:2; 54:1-6; 90:26-27; *4 Ezra* 7:36-44, which do appear to teach annihilation; see *4 Ezra* 7:61, where the dead are extinguished by fire, so also *2 Baruch* 85:13-15. In contrast, *Sibylline Oracles* 2:283-312 foresees eternal torment.

9:44, 46, 48 *where the maggots never die and the fire never goes out.* Mark 9:44 and 9:46 are part of a textual problem, since many key MSS (א B C L W) do not include them. The parallelism with the end of v. 48 that vv. 44 and 46 reflect might suggest that the verses belong to Mark, as then all three illustrations would be virtually parallel in wording. It is harder to explain how the verses dropped out, if they were original (Metzger 1971:102), so it is likely that 9:44, 46 were not originally part of Mark. However, 9:48 is original to Mark.

9:49 *tested with fire.* The Gr. reads "salted with fire," which the NLT has rendered in a way that makes the figure clear. In addition, some MSS add, "and every sacrifice will be salted with salt." This makes each sacrifice accountable as well. This reading, which comes with variations in the Gr., is not in the best MSS and is probably not original to Mark. The first remark shows the "word stitch" character of this section as it connects with the mention of the fire of Gehenna in the earlier verse. There is no contextual carryover of subject, merely a linking of texts using fire or salt. This verse underscores that everyone has ongoing account-ability to Jesus for their actions. Testing through persecution should keep each person fresh (Lane 1974:349; 1 Pet 1:7; 4:12). The root of the image is in OT sacrifices that contained salt (Lev 2:13; Ezek 43:24).

9:50 *if it loses its flavor.* Jesus used the figure of salt, again on the word stitch basis, to call for effectiveness from his disciple. Salt is for seasoning, but if it loses its taste, it is worthless.

You must have the qualities of salt among yourselves and live in peace with each other. The exhortation is to "remain salty"—to exercise distinctive behavior that leads to peace and unity with others. This is one way the disciples would mark themselves out as different from the world.

COMMENTARY

John of Zebedee, of the inner circle of the disciples, saw someone performing an exorcism in Jesus' name. John thought this person should be stopped because he was not one of the Twelve. Jesus said the issue was not whether he belonged in the group, but whether God was working through him in such a way as to affirm God's presence in Jesus. Thus Jesus said, "No one who performs a miracle in my name will soon be able to speak evil of me" (9:39). Jesus affirmed that ministry in his name was not limited to an elite few and that a person who was a vessel of God's power was not an enemy, but an ally in ministry. This was yet another blow to the disci-ples' impression that they had special status (France 2002:376).

Jesus said, "Anyone who is not against us is for us." In the context of rejection sur-rounding Jesus, those who supported him or who did not oppose him should be appreciated (see Num 11:26-29). Those who were responsive to him should be seen as allies with the potential to be more fully responsive. The new community Jesus was building was not an exclusive club. Those who appreciated Jesus or were open to him were welcome. France (2002:378-379) says that in all of these exam-ples, "disciples are called on to be cautious in drawing lines of demarcation. They are to be a church, not a sect."

Jesus then addressed the serious issue of upsetting another person's faith. Jesus warned: "if you cause one of these little ones who trust in me to fall into sin, it would be better for you to be thrown into the sea with a large millstone hung around your neck." Then Jesus spoke of avoiding anything that would cause a per-son to sin. Better to destroy one's hand, foot, or eye than to go to hell. The point is that the hand, foot, or eye should not be used as instruments for sin and should be severed from such a use. "Whatever in one's life tempts one to be untrue to God must be discarded, promptly and decisively, even as a surgeon amputates a hand or a leg in order to save a life" (Lane 1974:348).

The second of the three illustrations has only a slight variation in form in that the Greek changes from referring to entry into "the life" (eternal life) to entry into the Kingdom of God. The shift shows that the "what" (the life) takes place in the context of the "where," through entry and membership in the Kingdom. "It's better to enter eternal life/the Kingdom of God... than ... be thrown into hell." It is far better to deal with sin and to handicap the agent of sin than to leave sin unaddressed and find oneself condemned to hell (*geenna* [TG1067, ZG1147]). This is the only place that Mark refers to Gehenna, whose name comes from the place where Jerusalem endlessly burned its garbage (2 Kgs 23:10). Jesus very graphically called his disciples to deal seriously with sin, removing it at its root.

Gehenna (hell) is a place of endless destruction and torment where maggots do not die and the consuming fire always burns. The NLT image of the maggot is a modern expression for the idea expressed in Greek that the "worm" never dies. That image comes from Isaiah 66:24, where the damned are tormented by a never-dying worm that signifies the permanence of judgment. The image is intended to be gruesome. Gehenna is a place to avoid at all costs.

By way of summary, this unit is a collection of sayings about relational responsibilities. The disciples were not to be elitists. Ministry in Jesus' name by those who were responsive to him should be respected. However, disciples should be intolerant of their own sin, knowing that they are accountable before God. Leading a disciple to defect from God is worse than criminal and deserves a punishment worse than drowning. Disciples should separate themselves from those dynamics within themselves that lead to sin. Correcting the sin that limits our "freedoms" is better than experiencing judgment in Gehenna. Finally, we need to be salt, recognizing that each act is weighed by God to keep us fresh, even through suffering. The call to be salt also means that disciples should be at peace with each other. Disciples should not be concerned with rank or with trying to control who can minister in God's name.

◆   ### 9. Jesus' remarks on divorce (10:1-12; cf. Matt 19:1-12)

Then Jesus left Capernaum and went down to the region of Judea and into the area east of the Jordan River. Once again crowds gathered around him, and as usual he was teaching them.

²Some Pharisees came and tried to trap him with this question: "Should a man be allowed to divorce his wife?"

³Jesus answered them with a question: "What did Moses say in the law about divorce?"

⁴"Well, he permitted it," they replied. "He said a man can give his wife a written notice of divorce and send her away."*

⁵But Jesus responded, "He wrote this commandment only as a concession to your hard hearts. ⁶But 'God made them male and female'* from the beginning of

creation. ⁷'This explains why a man leaves his father and mother and is joined to his wife,* ⁸and the two are united into one.'* Since they are no longer two but one, ⁹let no one split apart what God has joined together."

¹⁰Later, when he was alone with his disciples in the house, they brought up the subject again. ¹¹He told them, "Whoever divorces his wife and marries someone else commits adultery against her. ¹²And if a woman divorces her husband and marries someone else, she commits adultery."

10:4 See Deut 24:1.   10:6 Gen 1:27; 5:2.   10:7 Some manuscripts do not include *and is joined to his wife.*
10:7-8 Gen 2:24.

NOTES

10:1 *Judea.* Jesus left the region of Galilee, where most of his ministry had taken place, and moved in the direction of Jerusalem. This placed him in an area where John the Baptist had also worked.

crowds gathered . . . he was teaching them. Jesus' remarks were made in a public setting, in contrast to his earlier teaching of the disciples. The parallel passage in Matt 19:1-12 is more detailed.

10:2 *tried to trap him.* The narrative remark makes it clear that these Pharisees were not interested in the answer for its informational value. They were hoping to use it against Jesus. Perhaps they could catch Jesus in a remark that would get him in trouble with Herod Antipas, as John the Baptist had been (Hurtado 1989:160).

Should a man be allowed to divorce his wife? The question was a source of dispute in Judaism. Some argued that a man could divorce a woman for any act, even one as trivial as a badly cooked meal. Others held the view that immorality was the only legitimate cause for divorce (*m. Gittin* 9.1-3, 10 gives examples of writs of divorce). In ancient Judaism, only a man could get a divorce, while in the Gentile world, either party could seek one. Divorce was important, for it allowed a woman to retain her dowry when leaving the marriage unless she had been sexually unfaithful (Hurtado 1989:167; Hanson and Oakman 1998:37-43). The dowry was in part intended to be passed to any children of the couple. Divorce also gave a woman the right to seek a new husband.

10:3 *What did Moses say in the law about divorce?* Jesus drew the discussion back to Scripture, working behind the tradition to the sacred text.

10:4 *he permitted it. . . . He said a man could give his wife a written notice of divorce and send her away.* The reply, which is discussed in detail in the Jewish tradition of the Mishnah in *m. Gittin,* addresses the right to divorce but is silent as to the situations that permit it. Jewish writs of divorce broke the marriage bond and came with the right to remarry. The reply looks back to Deut 24:1-4, where a writ is permitted upon having discovered "something wrong with her." The meaning of this phrase was debated among the rabbis.

10:5 *as a concession to your hard hearts.* In the Gr., the phrase about hard hearts is moved forward, so that it is emphasized ("for your hard hearts Moses wrote this command"). It refers to human stubbornness (Deut 10:16; Jer 4:4; Sir 16:10) and sin as the cause of divorce. In Deuteronomy, the context is to love God with a whole heart, not in stubbornness.

10:6 *God made them male and female.* Jesus cites Gen 1:27 and makes the point that at the creation, man and woman were intended to work side by side.

10:8 *the two are united into one.* Genesis 2:24 makes it clear that God's design was for marriage to be a relationship of oneness, with husband and wife forming a unit. The NLT brings out this sense by its rendering of the literal "the two shall become one flesh."

Although some might read Jesus' refusal to engage Deut 24 as a rejection of the law, the use of Genesis shows his respect for the law alongside a recognition that some laws exist because people fall short of righteousness.

Since they are no longer two but one. Here is the key idea. Marriage makes a unit put together before God and by God (see 10:9—God has joined them together).

10:9 let no one split apart what God has joined together. This order is reversed in the Gr.: "what God has joined together no man should split apart." The verb for God's "yoking [the two] together" makes the union a sacred act, not one of merely human choice (*suzeugnumi* [TG4801, ZG5183]; BDAG 954).

10:10 he was alone with his disciples. The final remarks about marriage belong to an elaboration the disciples had requested. His attention to adultery shows how seriously Jesus took the marriage commitment and union. Such comments for the sake of the disciples are common in Mark (4:1-12, 33-34; 7:17-23; 9:28-29).

10:12 And if a woman divorces her husband and marries someone else, she commits adultery. Textual variants make the issue one of a woman's desertion and remarriage, but they are less well supported by the manuscript evidence.

C O M M E N T A R Y

In these verses, Jesus shows little patience with the view that one could get a divorce for just about any reason. In fact, Jesus noted that divorce, even on the narrow grounds allowed by Moses, was only tolerated, not recommended. Jesus never gave acceptable grounds for divorce. Rather, he said that God's intent was that the marriage union should make a new kind of unit that would remain together. Even the exceptions given in Matthew on the basis of sexual immorality do not contradict the desire that marriage be maintained, although they recognize that this may not always be possible.

Marriage was designed to be permanent. God is responsible for the union, and those in the union are accountable to God for their commitment to it. Relational commitments to God and to each other govern ethics, not figuring out what a person can get by with. The effect of Jesus' remarks was that women, who tended to be treated as property in marriage, should be seen as equal partners, since marriage is a male-female unit with no special preference given to men (Hurtado 1989:160-161).

Jesus said, "Whoever divorces his wife and marries someone else commits adultery against her" (10:11). He thereby applied the standard that the marriage commitment was to be permanent. Thus, divorce that leads to remarriage is adultery, for the first bond is still in place. Mark presents the remark without qualification, while Matthew notes sexual immorality as an exception. The remark is in the context of marriage as a divine design, as an ideal that should especially be followed in a community that says it honors God. The act violates the seventh commandment (Exod 20:14). Another key point is that the violation is against the spouse, giving the woman an ethical right in the marriage. The same is true in the next verse about the man. In Judaism, adultery was understood as a violation against the other husband, not against one's wife (Cranfield 1959:321; Hooker 1991:236). Relational sensitivity to the bond between the partners is the key point here, not the statement of the law.

Jesus then added, "and if a woman divorces her husband and marries someone else, she commits adultery" (10:12). The key to this statement is that what is true for the man is also true for the woman. Since only Mark has this, some scholars suggest that Mark added it to address a Gentile reality that did not apply in Judaism. However, this assumes that Jesus was not aware of or concerned about Gentile practice and that he would limit himself to dominant Jewish concerns on such a question, not to mention the recent public example of Herodias, in which a prominent Jewish woman did undertake such an initiative (Evans 2001:85-86). Jesus' independent handling of several issues in Judaism makes such assumptions questionable. Jesus made it clear that the same ethical standard applied to both genders. In a Jewish culture that normally saw divorce as a right controlled and determined only by men, this was a significant recognition of the woman's ethical responsibility (for evidence that Jewish women could act in limited circumstances, see *m. Ketubbot* 7.10; Evans 2001:85).

This passage has had a significant impact on the discussion of marriage in the church. Jesus states clearly that by divine design, marriage is to be for life; he affirms reluctance to divorce because of its ethical consequences. It was permitted by Moses as a concession to hardheartedness, not as a right to be pursued. The relational equality of the man and woman and their shared ethical responsibility show that Jesus' concern was not to issue a new law, but to affirm the integrity of the relational bond and the mutual responsibility of the divinely designed oneness that marriage forms. As to the contemporary application of such standards in a culture where divorce and remarriage are common, the words of France (2002:394) state the balance well:

> The practical application of this teaching in a society in which both adultery and divorce are common and legally permissible cannot be straightforward. But Mark's Jesus offers no direct guidance on the problem, simply a clear, unequivocal, and utterly uncompromising principle that marriage is permanent and divorce (together with the resultant remarriage) is wrong. Whatever the other considerations which pastoral concern may bring to bear, some of them no doubt on values drawn from Jesus' teaching on other subjects, no approach can claim his support which does not take as its guiding principle the understanding of marriage set forth in vv. 9 and 11-12.

◆   10. Jesus blesses the children (10:13-16; cf. Luke 18:15-17)

[13]One day some parents brought their children to Jesus so he could touch and bless them. But the disciples scolded the parents for bothering him.

[14]When Jesus saw what was happening, he was angry with his disciples. He said to them, "Let the children come to me. Don't stop them! For the Kingdom of God belongs to those who are like these children. [15]I tell you the truth, anyone who doesn't receive the Kingdom of God like a child will never enter it." [16]Then he took the children in his arms and placed his hands on their heads and blessed them.

NOTES

10:13 *the disciples scolded the parents for bothering him.* The Gr. simply says, "The disciples rebuked them." They wanted to stop people from bringing children to Jesus for his blessing.

10:14 *he was angry with his disciples.* Jesus rejected the disciples' response and their devaluing of these children. Once again in Mark, the disciples have much to learn, and only Mark notes Jesus' emotion at this event. They had forgotten the point of Jesus' teaching in 9:37.

COMMENTARY

That the disciples desired to prevent Jesus from taking time with children reflected a cultural view of children as unimportant. Lane (1974:361) cites a papyrus in which a husband writes to tell his wife that if an expectant child is a boy she should let it live, but if it is a girl, she should cast it out (*Oxyrhynchus Papyri* 4.744, lines 9-10). In a culture in which children were devalued, they could be callously exposed to death.

Jesus reversed the cultural attitudes by saying that "the Kingdom of God belongs to those who are like these children" (10:14). The Kingdom is made up of people who are as simple and devalued as they are. If children are important to the Kingdom, everyone is important to the Kingdom, and it is "to those who are like these" that the Kingdom belongs (Matt 5:3; Luke 12:32). Children are symbols of what believers are like.

Jesus then added, "Anyone who doesn't receive the Kingdom of God like a child will never enter it" (10:15). Jesus made an example of the childlike qualities of low social status and dependence. As children have no inherent credentials to make them acceptable, disciples also bring no resume of merited status that will commend them to God ("he is utterly helpless in his relationship to the Kingdom," Lane 1974:360). Disciples before God are like children who are dependent on adults to make their way in the world. To receive the Kingdom is to welcome it on the terms on which it is offered, which here means realizing that no one has a right to possess it. It is a gift of divine grace.

Jesus thus elevated the stature of all people of any background by welcoming these children. They represent every member of the Kingdom; those who come to God are dependent on him and no stature of their own gives them kingdom rights. The kingdom is to be received as children receive things in their lives.

◆   **11. Jesus encounters a rich man (10:17-31; cf. Matt 19:16-30; Luke 18:18-30)**

¹⁷As Jesus was starting out on his way to Jerusalem, a man came running up to him, knelt down, and asked, "Good Teacher, what must I do to inherit eternal life?"

¹⁸"Why do you call me good?" Jesus asked. "Only God is truly good. ¹⁹But to answer your question, you know the commandments: 'You must not murder. You must not commit adultery. You must not steal. You must not testify falsely. You

must not cheat anyone. Honor your father and mother.'*"

²⁰"Teacher," the man replied, "I've obeyed all these commandments since I was young."

²¹Looking at the man, Jesus felt genuine love for him. "There is still one thing you haven't done," he told him. "Go and sell all your possessions and give the money to the poor, and you will have treasure in heaven. Then come, follow me."

²²At this the man's face fell, and he went away sad, for he had many possessions.

²³Jesus looked around and said to his disciples, "How hard it is for the rich to enter the Kingdom of God!" ²⁴This amazed them. But Jesus said again, "Dear children, it is very hard* to enter the Kingdom of God. ²⁵In fact, it is easier for a camel to go through the eye of a needle than for a rich person to enter the Kingdom of God!"

²⁶The disciples were astounded. "Then who in the world can be saved?" they asked.

²⁷Jesus looked at them intently and said, "Humanly speaking, it is impossible. But not with God. Everything is possible with God."

²⁸Then Peter began to speak up. "We've given up everything to follow you," he said.

²⁹"Yes," Jesus replied, "and I assure you that everyone who has given up house or brothers or sisters or mother or father or children or property, for my sake and for the Good News, ³⁰will receive now in return a hundred times as many houses, brothers, sisters, mothers, children, and property—along with persecution. And in the world to come that person will have eternal life. ³¹But many who are the greatest now will be least important then, and those who seem least important now will be the greatest then.*"

10:19 Exod 20:12-16; Deut 5:16-20.   10:24 Some manuscripts read *very hard for those who trust in riches.*
10:31 Greek *But many who are first will be last; and the last, first.*

NOTES

10:17 on his way to Jerusalem. The NLT rendering is more specific than the Gr., which has only "setting out on the way." The destination of the journey is made explicit in 10:32, so by adding "to Jerusalem," the NLT anticipates that later clarification.

what must I do to inherit eternal life? This question is really about how the man can be sure to participate in the resurrection of the righteous (Dan 12:1-2), as 10:23-30 makes clear. Mark 9:42-48 equates this to entering the Kingdom. The question presupposes that salvation is the product of human effort (Lane 1974:365). This is the only place that Mark uses the verb "inherit."

10:18 Why do you call me good? Jesus rejected the "good teacher" greeting of the questioner, probably to avoid condescension by the rich man. The man's remark was not insincere, just misdirected. Jesus would answer as required, and not because he was complimented. Jesus' saying that "only God is truly good" puts the man on notice that he would get a direct reply and that his only concern was with God's honor (Evans 2001:96). It is too subtle to see Jesus as affirming his own deity or as making any statement concerning himself and sin (France 2002:402).

10:19 you know the commandments. Jesus responded by noting the second part of the Ten Commandments, which deals with human relationships (Exod 20:12-16; Deut 5:16-20), thus showing his commitment to the relational aspect of spiritual life. God desires a response that pursues righteousness. The reference to defrauding replaces the idea of coveting, and possibly concretizes that commandment. The fifth commandment comes last in this list, the only commandment listed that isn't expressed negatively.

10:20 I've obeyed all these commandments since I was young. The rich man had no sense of lack, for he said that his record of obedience was unblemished. He had kept (lit., "guarded") the commandments from his youth. He possibly anticipated affirmation, but Jesus had not finished with him yet.

10:21 Jesus felt genuine love for him. The text makes it clear that Jesus' demand was rooted in his love for the man and in his awareness that he needed to redirect his life priorities.

sell all . . . follow me. The call to go and sell is expressed as an aorist imperative, which calls for a single decisive act.

10:22 he went away sad, for he had many possessions. The man's departure answers the questions. This is the first place in Mark's narrative that we are told that the man was wealthy. He left because he could not respond positively to Jesus' instruction. There is some question as to whether the man departed with sadness or anger, as the term *stugnazō* [ᵀᴳ4768, ᶻᴳ5145] speaks of a face that falls and can refer to anger (Ezek 26:16; Dan 2:12; Wis 17:5), to being gloomy (BDAG 949), or to being appalled (Ezek 27:35; 32:10), which may fit best here. His possessions meant more to him than serving others with what he owned and more than following Jesus to gain eternal life. The passage echoes 4:19 and 8:35-37. Affluence can be a real barrier to knowing God (France 2002:400-401).

10:23 How hard it is for the rich to enter the Kingdom of God! Jesus used the rich man's reaction to typify the problem the rich have in responding to Jesus and his teaching on the Kingdom. The illustration that follows argues that such entry is impossible without God's help. The idea is repeated in 10:24 to emphasize the point. The word used for "hard" (*duskolōs* [ᵀᴳ1423, ᶻᴳ1552]) usually pictures someone who is hard to please (France 2002:404), but here it pertains to something that is difficult to accomplish (BDAG 265).

10:24 This amazed them. The remarks amazed (*ethambounto* [ᵀᴳ2284, ᶻᴳ2501]) the disciples; the term used suggests that they were surprised and could not entirely process what Jesus was saying (1:27; 10:32; Acts 3:11; BDAG 442).

10:25 it is easier for a camel to go through the eye of a needle. Despite efforts to argue otherwise by differently interpreting the eye of the needle, Jesus' point is that in human terms, entry into the Kingdom by the rich is impossible, as 10:27 makes clear (Cranfield 1959:332; France 2002:405). The rhetorical point is that it is harder for a rich person to enter the Kingdom on his or her own than for a camel to pass through the eye of a needle. Rabbis used the illustration of an elephant going through the eye of a needle (*b. Bava Metzi'a* 38b).

10:26 Then who in the world can be saved? The disciples' reaction came from their understanding that the rich were blessed by God (Job 1:10; 42:10; Isa 3:10; Lane 1974:369). If the rich could not enter into the Kingdom, who could? In this verse, the disciples have moved from the amazement of 10:24 to exceeding astonishment. The verb *exeplēssonto* [ᵀᴳ1605, ᶻᴳ1742] means being amazed to the extent of being overwhelmed (1:22; 6:2; 7:37; 11:18; BDAG 308).

10:27 Everything is possible with God. Jesus' reply makes it clear that God is able to do what man cannot do (on this idea, see Gen 18:14; Job 10:13, LXX; 42:2; Zech 8:6, LXX). A heart changed by God *can* embrace Jesus and his call.

10:28 We've given up everything to follow you. Now Peter wanted reassurance that the disciples had responded to Jesus' call. He asked with some uncertainty and anxiety (Lane 1974:37), hoping that Jesus would affirm the disciples' commitment, which he did. The verb for "leaving" is in the aorist tense, denoting a renunciation that took place in the past, while the perfect tense of "following" looks to the ongoing effects of choosing to follow Jesus (Cranfield 1959:333).

10:30 will receive now in return a hundred times as many . . . along with persecution. Jesus promised that a new family and home—those of the church—would await the follower who made this sacrifice, but they would also experience persecution. The term for persecution (*diōgmos* [TG1375, ZG1501]) always refers to religious persecution in the NT (Acts 8:1; 13:50; 2 Cor 12:10; 2 Thess 1:4; BDAG 253).

And in the world to come that person will have eternal life. Now the passage comes full circle back to the rich man's question in 10:17. People who align themselves with Jesus and the Gospel will gain eternal life in the world to come. A person is not saved by something he or she does, but by the one with whom they establish a relationship. In other parts of the NT, this means exercising faith in God and in the one he sent, Jesus Christ.

10:31 *many who are the greatest now will be the least important then . . . least important now will be the greatest.* There is some discussion as to whether the remark affirms the disciples' choice or is a rebuke in light of Peter's outburst in 10:28, but the reaffirmation of their commitment in 10:29-30 favors an affirmation here. When Jesus issues a rebuke, especially in Mark, he usually does not confront so subtly (but see France 2002:409, who sees a subtle rebuke of any sense of superiority as Peter's outburst might imply).

COMMENTARY

Jesus' request of the rich man is the keynote of this passage: "Go and sell all your possessions and give the money to the poor, and you will have treasure in heaven. Then come, follow me" (10:21). Jesus challenged the man to exchange the blessings of this life for those of the life to come (see Matt 6:19-21; *Psalms of Solomon* 9:5; *2 Baruch* 24:1; Sir 29:10-12; cf. Evans 2001:99). The instruction to sell all, give to the poor, and follow Jesus exposed the man's priorities. Jesus explicitly answered the man's question about attaining eternal life by calling him to leave his earthly attachments behind and follow. This is not a universal reply to every situation, as others who are said to be part of the Kingdom were not asked to sell all (Cranfield 1959:330; cf. Zacchaeus in Luke 19:1-10). Jesus tested whether the man's possessions on earth were of more value to him than what the "Good Teacher" valued and taught. The entire passage is very important, for in it Jesus clarified what commitment to him entailed and what it would take to receive eternal life—namely, an alliance with him and with the gospel. This seems to run counter to the idea that salvation is by grace, but this impression reflects a superficial understanding of Jesus' point. Alliance to Jesus means being rejected by those who reject him. It also means that preferring acceptance by the world and what it offers will prevent one from embracing Jesus and his call. The rich man refused Jesus because the treasure of earth meant more to him than the treasure of heaven.

It was different for the disciples. Jesus affirmed what the disciples had done and what they would receive for choosing to follow him. He noted that their sacrifice was for Jesus' sake and for the gospel, as the two are closely intertwined in God's plan. God acknowledges the gifts of family, material benefits, and property when they are relinquished for the sake of the gospel.

Jesus affirmed that Peter and the disciples would receive rich blessings in this life—a new family and new types of possessions—and eternal life in the world to come. The rich man missed the eternal life he requested and wished to earn his own salvation; the disciples received it by coming to Jesus in the gracious way that he asked, allowing the things of earth to matter less to them than Jesus and the gospel.

To conclude this section, Jesus touched on the theme of eschatological reversal that would be part of the judgment. Many who were presently in power would not be in power then. Many of the neglected and persecuted would then be exalted. God's standards are not those of the world. To sacrifice now will bring later abundance. The remark probably reminded the disciples that those who chose riches in this life would be lacking later.

◆   12. Jesus predicts his death again (10:32-34; cf. Matt 20:17-19; Luke 18:31-33)

³²They were now on the way up to Jerusalem, and Jesus was walking ahead of them. The disciples were filled with awe, and the people following behind were overwhelmed with fear. Taking the twelve disciples aside, Jesus once more began to describe everything that was about to happen to him. ³³"Listen," he said, "we're going up to Jerusalem, where the Son of Man* will be betrayed to the leading priests and the teachers of religious law. They will sentence him to die and hand him over to the Romans.* ³⁴They will mock him, spit on him, flog him with a whip, and kill him, but after three days he will rise again."

10:33a "Son of Man" is a title Jesus used for himself.   10:33b Greek *the Gentiles*.

NOTES

10:32 *to Jerusalem*. As in Luke 9:51–19:44, Jesus is portrayed as being on a journey to Jerusalem, where his suffering awaited. This is the first time in Mark that Jerusalem is clearly noted as Jesus' destination.

***awe . . . fear*.** These notes about the emotions of the disciples and the crowds add an air of drama to the journey. There is a sense that this will not be a normal trip to Jerusalem; it is possible that the people even sensed the divine presence with Jesus (Evans 2001:108).

10:33 *hand him over to the Romans*. Lit., "hand him over to the Gentiles" (cf. NLT mg). This is the one prediction that notes a handing over to the Gentiles.

COMMENTARY

This is the third major section in which Jesus predicts what will happen to him in Jerusalem (8:31-33; 9:30-32). This prediction highlights both the Jewish and the Roman involvement, including the mocking, spitting, and beating Jesus will suffer (Lane 1974:375; for their fulfillment in Mark 14–16, see Evans 2001:106). These details are unique to this prediction; only his death and resurrection are noted in the earlier versions. The account of the disciples' and crowds' emotion during Jesus' journey to Jerusalem is followed by details that prepare us for the monumental events that will take place there, the significance of which his audience did not yet appreciate.

First, Jesus stated that the Son of Man would be handed over to the chief priests and scribes. The Jewish leaders would decide his fate by sentencing him to death and delivering him to the "Gentiles," which in this context refers to the Roman leadership of Pilate. Then, Jesus predicted the details of his suffering: "They will mock him, spit on him, flog him with a whip, and kill him." He followed this with a prediction of his resurrection: "but after three days he will rise again." Jesus would be dishonored, beaten, and put to death. France (2002:413) notes the Isaianic roots of this language (Isa 50:6; 53:3, 5, 8-9, 12; also Ps 22:7). This death would not be the end, however; there would be a resurrection. No one reacted to Jesus' prediction at this time. As with Jesus' earlier predictions, the disciples still did not understand these remarks about his death and resurrection. Their reaction to his arrest, death, and burial would continue to display their confusion over this issue, but Jesus' resurrection would finally open their ears.

◆ 13. Jesus teaches about service (10:35-45)

³⁵Then James and John, the sons of Zebedee, came over and spoke to him. "Teacher," they said, "we want you to do us a favor."

³⁶"What is your request?" he asked.

³⁷They replied, "When you sit on your glorious throne, we want to sit in places of honor next to you, one on your right and the other on your left."

³⁸But Jesus said to them, "You don't know what you are asking! Are you able to drink from the bitter cup of suffering I am about to drink? Are you able to be baptized with the baptism of suffering I must be baptized with?"

³⁹"Oh yes," they replied, "we are able!"

Then Jesus told them, "You will indeed drink from my bitter cup and be baptized with my baptism of suffering. ⁴⁰But I have no right to say who will sit on my right or my left. God has prepared those places for the ones he has chosen."

⁴¹When the ten other disciples heard what James and John had asked, they were indignant. ⁴²So Jesus called them together and said, "You know that the rulers in this world lord it over their people, and officials flaunt their authority over those under them. ⁴³But among you it will be different. Whoever wants to be a leader among you must be your servant, ⁴⁴and whoever wants to be first among you must be the slave of everyone else. ⁴⁵For even the Son of Man came not to be served but to serve others and to give his life as a ransom for many."

NOTES

10:35 *do us a favor.* The NLT renders the Gr., "do for us whatever we ask," into idiomatic English.

10:36 *What is your request?* The NLT renders the Gr., "what do you want me to do?" idiomatically.

10:37 *we want to sit in places of honor.* The Gr. reads, "we want to sit in your glory," which the NLT renders concretely by mentioning places of honor.

10:38 *Are you able to drink from the bitter cup of suffering . . . to be baptized with the baptism of suffering?* The cup refers to the judgment Jesus would experience for others and the rejection it would entail (Ps 23:5; 116:13; 75:8; Isa 51:17-22; Jer 25:15-28; 49:12; 51:7; Ezek 23:31-34; Taylor 1966:440-41). The NLT refers to the cup and baptism of suffering to make the implied point explicit.

10:40 *But I have no right to say.* Jesus said that he was not in a position to decide who would sit where in his Kingdom. God has chosen certain people to have these roles, and he knows "those for whom it is prepared." The NLT renders this as ***God has prepared those places for the ones he has chosen.***

10:41 *indignant.* This verb is used only two other times in Mark. One is in 10:14, where Jesus was angered by the disciples' refusal to let the children see him. The other is in 14:4, where the disciples were angry with the woman who anointed Jesus with the expensive perfume.

10:42 *Jesus called them together.* Jesus called the disciples over to hear the instructions in these verses, thus underscoring the importance of his pronouncement (3:23; 7:14; 8:34; 12:43; France 2002:418).

10:43 *among you it will be different.* Jesus made it clear that it would not be so among his disciples. They must lead in a different way.

servant. Jesus used this term to describe a leader that is different from the world. It is an everyday term (*diakonos* [TG1249, ZG1356]) describing one who serves others (TDNT 2:82-85, 88). It referred to various types of attendants, such as those who serve a king (Matt 22:13; John 2:5).

10:44 *the slave of everyone else.* Jesus intensifies the imagery by referring to a slave or bondservant, a position most would wish to avoid. To be great or to be first means being a servant or a slave of all. There is a sense of obligation about a slave's work that is important to the description (BDAG 260; TDNT 2:261; Rom 6:17-20).

10:45 *the Son of Man came not to be served but to serve others and to give his life as a ransom for many.* This verse is one of the most important in Mark (for a detailed but succinct treatment, see Evans 2001:119-125). It is Jesus' mission statement that the one with authority, the Son of Man, came to serve (on such mission statements by Jesus, see 2:17; Matt 5:17; 10:34-35; Luke 5:31-32; 12:49; 19:10; John 9:39; 10:10). *diakonēsai* [TG1247, ZG1354] is the verb form of the noun "servant." That service extended to Jesus giving his life (his soul, *psuchē* [TG5590, ZG6034]) for (*anti* [TG473, ZG505], "on behalf of, in the place of") many (NIDNTT 3:1179-1180). The expression has roots in Isa 53:10, 12 and expresses the way that Jesus would serve by paying the debt of sin (see the linking of giving, ransom, and life in Exod 21:30, LXX; Sir 29:15; 1 Macc 2:50; note also Isa 43:3-4; Mark 14:24). The idea of ransom also appears in 1 Tim 2:6 (NIDNTT 3:189-200; TDNT 4:340). It looks to the release of prisoners and other captives (Josephus *Antiquities* 14.107). Roots for such atoning ideas already existed in Judaism (2 Macc 7:37-38; 4 Macc 1:11; 11QtgJob 38:2-3; *Prayer of Azariah* 3:15-17 [English]; *Life of Adam and Eve* 3:1; Evans 2001:122).

COMMENTARY

The sons of Zebedee looked forward to the day when Jesus would rule with power and authority from his throne. They wanted a major share in his power, with seats that would rank them right next to Jesus in importance (being seated on the right and the left meant having the seats of greatest power; cf. 1 Kgs 2:19; Ps 45:9; 110:1; Mark 12:36; 14:62). Once again, the disciples missed a major aspect of Jesus' teaching, so Jesus corrected them. This repeats a similar kind of failure, seen in 9:32-33.

Jesus reminded them of the one thing they had been slow to accept—that he would suffer greatly. Jesus had told them repeatedly that associating with him was not about power. To sit with him in glory required them to undergo what he would go through. After the sons of Zebedee said that they could drink this cup, Jesus promised that they would share in it. Indeed, James was martyred for his faith (Acts 12:2).

When the other disciples heard the request of James and John, they were indignant (see note on 10:41). Probably their indignation was not righteous, but fueled by the same ambition that led the sons of Zebedee to ask their question. Evans (2001:118) notes the suggestion that James and John were related to Jesus as cousins. If so, their request had a touch of nepotism in it. The other disciples did not appreciate their request, and Jesus rejected it.

Jesus corrected their error by pointing out how the nations equated leadership with giving orders and authority with lording it over others. The significance of this instruction is seen in the exhortation to elders in 1 Peter 5:3. Unlike the world, leadership in the Kingdom is not defined by power or the way in which leaders direct others. Rather, leadership means service and caring to the point of being a slave of those served.

Jesus said, "The Son of Man came not to be served but to serve others and to give his life as a ransom for many." As such, he provided the ultimate example of servanthood and drew many to himself (see extensive note on 10:45). To rank before God, one should forget about rank. Leadership is not about having a high position but about how one cares for others.

◆   14. Jesus heals the blind man Bartimaeus (10:46-52; cf. Matt 20:29-33; Luke 18:35-43)

46Then they reached Jericho, and as Jesus and his disciples left town, a large crowd followed him. A blind beggar named Bartimaeus (son of Timaeus) was sitting beside the road. 47When Bartimaeus heard that Jesus of Nazareth was nearby, he began to shout, "Jesus, Son of David, have mercy on me!"

48"Be quiet!" many of the people yelled at him.

But he only shouted louder, "Son of David, have mercy on me!"

49When Jesus heard him, he stopped and said, "Tell him to come here."

So they called the blind man. "Cheer up," they said. "Come on, he's calling you!" 50Bartimaeus threw aside his coat, jumped up, and came to Jesus.

51"What do you want me to do for you?" Jesus asked.

"My rabbi,*" the blind man said, "I want to see!"

52And Jesus said to him, "Go, for your faith has healed you." Instantly the man could see, and he followed Jesus down the road.*

10:51 Greek uses the Hebrew term *Rabboni.*   10:52 Or *on the way.*

NOTES

10:46 *Jericho.* At this point, Jesus was only fifteen miles northeast of Jerusalem and five miles west of the Jordan River.

10:48 *Be quiet! . . . But he only shouted louder.* The crowd thought that Bartimaeus was not worthy to call out to Jesus, impose demands upon him, or take his time, so they told him to be quiet. The blind man did not back off, but continued to cry out to Jesus. This is expressed in the imperfect tense (*ekrazen* [TG2896, ZG3189]), emphasizing that his call was ongoing.

10:50 *threw aside his coat.* The blind man had laid his cloak on the ground to collect alms from compassionate people. He now tossed it aside.

10:51 *My rabbi.* The blind man addressed Jesus respectfully in a way that may indicate that he saw Jesus as his Lord. The term means "my master" as well as "my teacher" (Evans 2001:134).

I want to see! The blind man clearly trusted Jesus' power to heal and he had the courage to call out to him despite the crowd's opposition. This is a picture of persistent faith.

10:52 *your faith has healed you.* Jesus commended the man's faith as the means by which he was healed (5:34; Luke 7:50; 17:19). Once he was healed, the man became Jesus' follower.

COMMENTARY

The opening description of Bartimaeus as a "blind beggar" indicates that he had no social rank or importance. Since he was blind, he had to beg for his basic needs. The crowds' rejection of his pleas (10:48) showed his lack of status, but this did not matter to Jesus.

Though Bartimaeus was blind, he understood a great deal about Jesus; he called out to him as "Son of David" and asked him to heal him out of his mercy (cf. *Psalms of Solomon* 17:21). The idea that the Son of David could heal might seem strange, but in Judaism there was a tradition that Solomon, as David's son, was specially enabled by God to heal (Josephus *Antiquities* 8.41-47; cf. 4Q521). Jesus never discouraged the use of this title. As Jesus drew near to Jerusalem, his previous hesitation to allow people to name him as the Messiah was lifted (France 2002:424).

Bartimaeus's healing highlights Jesus' continued work of compassion and his ability to bring sight to those in darkness. It also dramatizes an example of faith. Unlike the rich man a few scenes earlier who had everything except spiritual insight, the blind man had nothing but saw clearly. He understood that Jesus, as Son of David, could heal, and that he had the power of God to bring renewal of life. Jesus commended the faith by which he spoke up in the midst of a crowd that wanted to silence him. The man was healed; he came to full sight and followed Jesus to Jerusalem. This last healing in Mark exemplifies how Jesus brought sight to those who could not see. This is also the last section of Jesus' training of the disciples.

◆   **B. Conflict in Jerusalem and Prediction of Judgment (11:1–13:37)**
     1. Jesus' triumphal entry into Jerusalem (11:1–11;
        cf. Matt 21:1–11; Luke 19:29–44; John 12:12–19)

As Jesus and his disciples approached Jerusalem, they came to the towns of Bethphage and Bethany on the Mount of Olives. Jesus sent two of them on ahead. ²"Go into that village over there," he told them. "As soon as you enter it, you will see a young donkey tied there that no one has ever ridden. Untie it and bring it here. ³If anyone asks, 'What are you doing?' just say, 'The Lord needs it and will return it soon.'"

⁴The two disciples left and found the colt standing in the street, tied outside the front door. ⁵As they were untying it, some bystanders demanded, "What are you doing, untying that colt?" ⁶They said what Jesus had told them to say, and they were permitted to take it. ⁷Then they brought the colt to Jesus and threw their garments over it, and he sat on it.

⁸Many in the crowd spread their garments on the road ahead of him, and others spread leafy branches they had cut in the fields. ⁹Jesus was in the center of the procession, and the people all around him were shouting,

"Praise God!*
  Blessings on the one who comes in
    the name of the LORD!
10 Blessings on the coming Kingdom of
    our ancestor David!
  Praise God in highest heaven!"*

11So Jesus came to Jerusalem and went into the Temple. After looking around carefully at everything, he left because it was late in the afternoon. Then he returned to Bethany with the twelve disciples.

11:9 Greek *Hosanna*, an exclamation of praise that literally means "save now"; also in 11:10.   11:9-10 Pss 118:25-26; 148:1.

NOTES

11:1 *Bethphage and Bethany.* Jesus was now very close to Jerusalem. Bethany is located two miles from the city, with Bethphage about a half mile away. The Mount of Olives, with its peak of over 2,600 feet, was just to the east of Jerusalem.

11:2 *young donkey.* The Gr. word *pōlos* [TG4454, ZG4798] describes the colt of a horse or an ass (BDAG 900; TDNT 6.959-961). Since it had not been ridden, it was suitable for a king (*m. Sanhedrin* 2.5), since no one but a king was to ride a king's horse (note also the sacred use of animals in Num 19:2; Deut 21:3; 1 Sam 6:7; Lane 1974:395).

11:3 *The Lord needs it.* This declaration invokes a custom known as *angaria* (from *angareuw* [TG29, ZG30]; cf. Matt 5:41; 27:32), in which a person of significance (most commonly an officer of the Roman government) could take possession of someone else's property or require them to perform a task. Since Jesus was such a respected figure, this remark was sufficient for the disciples to secure the animal.

11:6 *they were permitted to take it.* The animal was found and taken just as Jesus had indicated. As often happened toward the end of his ministry, Jesus was very aware of what would take place.

11:7 *threw their garments over it.* This act recalls a coronation (1 Kgs 1:38-40; 2 Kgs 9:13; Evans 2001:143).

11:8 *spread their garments . . . spread leafy branches.* Clothes laid on the road made a "red carpet" for someone of significance (2 Kgs 9:13). The Greeks also did this (Plutarch, *Cato Minor* 7; Evans 2001:144). The laying of palms and other materials took place at the Feast of Tabernacles (2 Macc 10:7, the welcome of Judas Maccabaeus; *m. Sukkah* 3–4; France 2002:433).

11:9 *Praise God!* This is the NLT's rendering of the Gr. *hōsanna* [TG5614, ZG6057], which means "save now!" It was used as a call to praise, which explains the NLT's wording (*m. Sukkah* 4.5). "Hosanna" shows up again at the end of the cry of praise in 11:10b. The expression can express praise or be the cry of a prayer as the Psalter shows.

who comes in the name of the LORD! This allusion to Ps 118:26 welcomes a leader who approaches the Temple.

11:10 *kingdom of our father David.* This remark shows the praise involves the promise of God to David and the hope for a delivering king (2 Sam 7:6-16, the Davidic covenant; Ps 132). In other words, the praise is for the arrival of messianic promise.

11:11 *went into the Temple.* Jesus went directly to the Temple but did not stay because it was late. Pilgrims often stayed just outside of Jerusalem; Jesus returned to Bethany for the night.

COMMENTARY

In this scene, Jesus entered the city as a humble dignitary in a way that recalls the Zechariah 9:9 prediction that the Messiah-King would come into Jerusalem (Zion) riding on a donkey. Jesus rode into the city, whereas pilgrims were supposed to walk. This shows that Jesus intended to be noticed (France 2002:428-29)—his riding a donkey was a sign of his kingship.

The disciples and the crowds began to praise him in the words of Psalm 118, acclaiming Jesus as "the one who comes in the name of the Lord." They shouted, "Blessings on the coming Kingdom of our ancestor David." Their praise was motivated by the promise of a future Davidic rule. Jesus presented himself as a king and was acknowledged as such. He did nothing to prevent this perception of him. This is the second connection of Jesus with David, as Bartimaeus had called out to the Son of David for healing (10:47).

The crowd, of course, did not fully understand what they were acclaiming, as their reaction to Jesus later in the week would show. Nonetheless, the entry was important; it shows Jesus accepting such praise, since he was the one who arranged for the animal he rode into the city. He seems to have intentionally evoked the fulfillment of Zechariah 9:9. This was Jerusalem's chance to receive Jesus as one sent from God. It seemed that they were going to do so, but the drama quickly took a dark turn. The one who was welcomed as the Messiah-King would be killed within the week.

◆   2. Jesus curses the fig tree and clears the Temple (11:12-25;
       cf. Matt 21:12-22; Luke 19:45-48)

¹²The next morning as they were leaving Bethany, Jesus was hungry. ¹³He noticed a fig tree in full leaf a little way off, so he went over to see if he could find any figs. But there were only leaves because it was too early in the season for fruit. ¹⁴Then Jesus said to the tree, "May no one ever eat your fruit again!" And the disciples heard him say it.

¹⁵When they arrived back in Jerusalem, Jesus entered the Temple and began to drive out the people buying and selling animals for sacrifices. He knocked over the tables of the money changers and the chairs of those selling doves, ¹⁶and he stopped everyone from using the Temple as a marketplace.* ¹⁷He said to them, "The Scriptures declare, 'My Temple will be called a house of prayer for all nations,' but you have turned it into a den of thieves.'"*

¹⁸When the leading priests and teachers of religious law heard what Jesus had done, they began planning how to kill him.

But they were afraid of him because the people were so amazed at his teaching.

¹⁹That evening Jesus and the disciples left* the city.

²⁰The next morning as they passed by the fig tree he had cursed, the disciples noticed it had withered from the roots up. ²¹Peter remembered what Jesus had said to the tree on the previous day and exclaimed, "Look, Rabbi! The fig tree you cursed has withered and died!"

²²Then Jesus said to the disciples, "Have faith in God. ²³I tell you the truth, you can say to this mountain, 'May you be lifted up and thrown into the sea,' and it will happen. But you must really believe it will happen and have no doubt in your heart. ²⁴I tell you, you can pray for anything, and if you believe that you've received it, it will be yours. ²⁵But when you are praying, first forgive anyone you are holding a grudge against, so that your Father in heaven will forgive your sins, too.*"

11:16 Or from carrying merchandise through the Temple.   11:17 Isa 56:7; Jer 7:11.   11:19 Greek they left; other manuscripts read he left.   11:25 Some manuscripts add verse 26, But if you refuse to forgive, your Father in heaven will not forgive your sins. Compare Matt 6:15.

NOTES

11:12 *Jesus was hungry.* This brief remark sets the context for the cursing of the fig tree, a rare case in which Jesus used his power to judge.

11:13 *fig tree.* Often associated with the vine and having a rich and varied symbolic role in the OT, this tree and its fruit frequently represent the people of God (TDNT 7:752; Isa 28:4; Jer 8:13; 24:1-10; 29:17; Hos 9:10; France 2002:439-440).

it was too early in the season for fruit. Jesus sought figs from a tree whose fruit was not yet ripe. It was early to mid-April. Early figs ripened in May and June, while later figs came in August to October. The remark may indicate something about the timing for Israel, or better, the lack of timing for her. It is not yet her time. It was "too early" for her.

11:15 *Jesus . . . began to drive out the people buying and selling animals for sacrifices. He knocked over the tables of the money changers.* The key point of background for this scene is the likelihood that over the objections of the Sanhedrin, Caiaphas had just relocated the place where sacrifices could be purchased. He had moved it closer to the central Temple area (France 2002:444), so what used to take place at the Mount of Olives was now located in the outer court of the Gentiles. This setup only lasted for a two to three week period during Passover (Hooker 1991:268).

11:16 *he stopped everyone from using the Temple as a marketplace.* The NLT's rendering is very interpretive. The Gr. says that Jesus did not allow anyone to carry anything through the Temple, which the NLT renders as a judgment against using the Temple as a "marketplace." This was perhaps the case. Such activity was necessary because of the legal requirements that certain currency be used (Tyrian "shekels"; Exod 30:11-16) and the need for unblemished sacrifices (*m. Sheqalim* 1.1, 3; Lane 1974:405). Questions would have been about the location of such activity and how it was being done.

11:20 *The next morning . . . the disciples noticed it had withered from the roots up.* The curse had taken effect overnight. Matthew 21:19 simply notes that the tree withered at once.

11:21 *The fig tree you cursed has withered and died!* Peter noted that Jesus' words had resulted in the fig tree's death. The remark invited a comment from Jesus, which he supplied.

11:22 *Have faith in God.* Jesus began by noting that the unusual things they saw resulted from faith in God. His exhortation to have faith was also an observation that faith had a role in this event.

11:23 *you can say to this mountain, 'May you be lifted up and thrown into the sea,' and it will happen.* Jesus used the rhetorical illustration of a particular mountain uprooting itself and being tossed into the sea. His point was that faith can accomplish things that would otherwise be impossible. "It will happen" renders "it will be done," with the passive verbal suggesting that God will do it. It should be noted that the prayer in v. 24 is a corporate one; the text is not focused on private prayer (France 2002:448). The Mount of Olives or the Temple mount may be the particular mountain in view here. Evans (2001:188-89) opts for an eschatological reading rather than a proverbial one. His point is that Jesus was picturing a mountain's removal, not mountain moving activity. God was bringing a transforming salvation to the earth (others, such as Hooker 1991:270, suggest that Mark is referring to the judgment of Israel, pictured as the Temple Mount in Jerusalem). This salvation is prayed for and the answer is about salvation. This could be the meaning of the passage. However, the generic reference to "all prayer" in 11:24 makes this view less likely, as it appears to look at prayer in principle, but it is possible that 11:24 expands as a principle that which the specific prayer of 11:23 addresses (Lane 1974:410).

But you must really believe it will happen and have no doubt in your heart. Here the NLT renders "does not doubt in his heart, but believes that what he says will come to pass" (see Jas 1:6). Jesus emphasized that believing in God's capacity to act was a significant part of the request.

11:25 *first forgive anyone you are holding a grudge against, so that your Father in heaven will forgive your sins, too.* As Jesus noted, an unwillingness to forgive impedes prayer. Jesus mentions this theme elsewhere and it also shows up in the epistles (as the principle behind the request for forgiveness in the Lord's prayer, Matt 5:21-26; with reference to worship, Matt 18:21-35; and with reference to forgiving, 1 Pet 3:7). The Father will hesitate to answer the prayer of an unforgiving spirit.

[11:26] See NLT mg on 11:25. This verse, which is not attested in the older MSS of Mark, makes the point that the Father will not forgive those who do not forgive; it is paralleled in Matt 6:15. The verse is present in A C D 𝔐, but is absent in the key witnesses ℵ B L W.

COMMENTARY

The judgment miracle of the withered fig tree is the last miracle in Mark. The unfruitful tree is cast aside. Most commentators see this as a sign that Israel would be judged because they were not ready for Jesus' coming (e.g. Hooker, 1991:261). Evans (2001:158) argues that nothing in Mark points in this direction. Rather, because of its juxtaposition with the following scene, he sees this as a picture of the destruction of the Temple. As such, it is another case of Mark sandwiching episodes together so that one helps explain another. As the fig tree was dead, so was Israel and her Temple worship. The scene ends with Jesus' comment to the disciples. The fig tree will reemerge for attention in 11:20. The fact that the scene of Jesus clearing the Temple is embedded in that of the cursing of the fig tree is important, because the Temple scene helps to explain why the fig tree was cursed. The question is whether the imagery points to the Temple or to those who were in charge of it at that time.

As for the Temple clearing, Jesus was not opposed to the selling of sacrifices per se. The Temple worshippers needed sacrifices, but the way in which these sales were taking place was desecrating the sacred space (see note on 11:15). More important was the authority this symbolic act presupposed. Evans (2001:166) calls the action a "demonstration" in the Temple precincts—a prophetic protest, not a takeover. The act declared that Jesus had the right to assess the way the Temple was being operated, apart from the opinions of the Temple leadership; thus the act was a direct attack on the validity of the Temple's Jewish leaders.

Jesus made the bold declaration, "My Temple will be called a house of prayer for all nations, but you have turned it into a den of thieves" (11:17). In so doing, he cited Isaiah 56:7 and Jeremiah 7:11, contrasting what the Temple should be (a house of prayer for the nations) with what it had become (a den of thieves). Jeremiah 7 is a particularly significant critique of the Temple; it did not guarantee the protection of Jerusalem because its worship was corrupt (Evans 2001:173-179 has a full discussion). If its worship was a sham, there is a sense in which the people were "brigands," robbing God and the Temple of its honor by their insincere worship (Hooker 1991:264). This was open and public robbery (NIDNTT 3.377-379; John 12:6; Luke 10:30). There is also a potential parallel to 1 Kings 8:41-43, in which Solomon looked to the day when all nations would worship at the Temple. Jesus portrayed himself as understanding God's will and intentions for the Temple, and he stood up for the honor of God that the leaders had failed to uphold. He also defended the Temple as a place for Gentiles, something that Caiaphas had undercut in allowing the sales to take place there. Mark's emphasis, however, is on the compromise of the whole Temple as a sacred site.

Jesus could not have challenged the Jews' leadership more directly, and he did this in the most sacred, public locale possible. Jesus was not alone in his criticism of the Jewish leaders, as Qumran and other texts show (1QpHab 1:13; 8:9; 9:9; 11:4; *Testament of Moses* 7:6-10; *Antiquities* 20.179-81, 207; *2 Baruch* 10:18; Evans 2001:168). What may have been unique was that he made his protest about the Temple on the sacred site (for other Temple-related protests in Judaism that were not about the Temple per se but which met with strong official reaction, see Evans 2001:170; Josephus *Antiquities* 13.292, 13.372-373, 17.149-167). The chief priests and scribes decided that Jesus had to be stopped. His challenge to them through his actions in the sacred holy place would spell his demise, but they were afraid of him because the people were so amazed at Jesus' teaching. Jesus' popularity was the major obstacle to their murderous plan. They had to figure out how to arrest Jesus without inciting the crowd.

In summary, the Temple cleansing and the cursing of the fig tree are key events in Mark. They show Jesus as exercising authority at the sacred center of Judaism. Whether his actions predicted the destruction of the Temple or were a call to reform it, Jesus made an important claim to speak for God about the most holy location in Judaism. It was probably an act of reform, as he proclaimed that the Temple should be a "house of prayer for all nations." However, his use of Jeremiah with its exilic context may imply that the Temple was subject to judgment.

Did Jesus act as a prophet or as a messianic figure? At the least, his actions were prophetic, but in his entry into Jerusalem, the people invoked the Davidic hope by hailing him as a king. They expected, as seen in the fourteenth blessing of the Eighteen Benedictions, that the coming of the king and the purging of Jerusalem would come at the end. (Bock 2002b:373 discusses this specific benediction, which prays for Jerusalem's restoration, the building of a Temple and the raising up of David's throne; also Schürer 1979:2.458 discusses the entire prayer.) Jesus' actions in the Temple were regal.

Jesus actions' also directly challenged the leaders' authority and reinforced their commitment to stopping him so that they could remain in control. This set up the backdrop for the cursing of the fig tree, which most likely alluded to Israel's status as the people of God. Jesus cursed the tree as a picture of imminent judgment, because the nation was about to reject him.

Jesus' act of judgment through a miraculous declaration got the disciples' attention. Jesus turned this into a call to believe in God. He was at work, even in unusual ways; therefore, the possibility that God will continue to work in surprising and seemingly impossible ways continues for those who believe that God can do this. Jesus issued a call to pray with faith: "You can pray for anything, and if you believe that you've received it, it will be yours" (11:24). God can and will do great things, if they are requested in faith. This remark is stated in absolute and unqualified terms, probably for rhetorical impact. Jesus was not giving a blank check, promising that anything we want that we believe God can supply will be ours. Rather, he was calling for prayer of faith. In the end, God determines how prayers are answered.

◆   ## 3. Question about the source of Jesus' authority (11:27-33; cf. Matt 21:23-32; Luke 20:1-8)

²⁷Again they entered Jerusalem. As Jesus was walking through the Temple area, the leading priests, the teachers of religious law, and the elders came up to him. ²⁸They demanded, "By what authority are you doing all these things? Who gave you the right to do them?"

²⁹"I'll tell you by what authority I do these things if you answer one question," Jesus replied. ³⁰"Did John's authority to baptize come from heaven, or was it merely human? Answer me!"

³¹They talked it over among themselves. "If we say it was from heaven, he will ask why we didn't believe John. ³²But do we dare say it was merely human?" For they were afraid of what the people would do, because everyone believed that John was a prophet. ³³So they finally replied, "We don't know."

And Jesus responded, "Then I won't tell you by what authority I do these things."

NOTES

11:27 *the leading priests, the teachers of religious law, and the elders.* The chief priests, scribes, and elders plotted against Jesus (11:18; 12:12; 14:1, 10-11; 14:43, 53; 15:1). The elders were the lay members of the council (TDNT 6.658-59; Josephus *Life* 194).

11:28 *They demanded.* The NLT's translation assumes a tone of challenge in the question, as the Gr. simply has, "they said to him." The question was raised in a context in which Jesus' action left them displeased, so the NLT's sense is not unlikely.

11:29 *if you answer one question.* Responding to a question with a question was common in rabbinic debate (Lane 1974:413; Mark 10:2-3).

11:30 *Did John's authority to baptize come from heaven, or was it merely human?* Jesus set up an analogy between John's work (and the source of the Baptist's authority) and his own. The parallel is that John's ministry was not authorized by the leaders, but if it came from God, then it should have been heeded. The same was true of Jesus' ministry.

11:31 *If we say it was from heaven, he will ask why we didn't believe John.* The Gr. grammatical structure here is a third class condition, so the "if" premise is simply set forth without indicating whether it was accepted or not. It is a simple hypothetical.

11:32 *But do we dare say it was merely human?* This rendering reflects a deliberative sense in the Gr.: "should we say it was human?" The NLT renders the fear expressed later in Gr. as "dare say." The leaders stopped considering this reply before completing the thought, for it was obvious that the public would not swallow such an answer (France 2002:455 says they stopped expressing what would be seen as a "diplomatic gaffe").

because everyone believed that John was a prophet. The leaders feared the crowd because the people regarded John as one truly sent from God.

COMMENTARY

This is the first of several controversies during Jesus' final week. The major Jewish leaders raised a question about Jesus' religious authority, since his actions in the Temple directly challenged their authority. The text introduces the chief priests, scribes, and elders as the ones who plotted against Jesus. They asked him, "By what authority are you doing all these things? Who gave you the right to do them?" These questions set the tone for what would remain an issue throughout the final section of Mark. Who was speaking for God—the Jewish leaders, or Jesus? Their question implied that Jesus had no authority since he did not get it from them.

Jesus replied with a question of his own, raising the possibility that God might act through someone they had not authorized. By asking his question about John the Baptist, Jesus effectively gave his answer. Just as God blessed John without the leaders' approval, so God blessed Jesus. If John's ministry was from heaven, then the leaders should have responded to it, but they did not. They knew that Jesus would ask them why they had not listened to John if they answered that his ministry came from heaven. The leaders also knew that if they said John's ministry was from earth ("merely human"), the people would not respect them, because the people believed that John was a true prophet.

The leaders contemplated the options in terms of how they would play out publicly. Popular opinion prevented them from expressing their own thoughts, so they refused to give Jesus a straight answer, saying, "We don't know." It is not to their credit that those leaders who should have been able to recognize God's work in John "did not know" what God was doing. The leaders were blind and disingenuous in failing to answer the question.

Consequently, Jesus responded, "Then I won't tell you by what authority I do these things." Jesus refused to explain the source of his authority, although anyone reading Mark knows the answer. He also was not only saying that he was a prophet like John. His ride into Jerusalem on the donkey made it clear that he saw himself in other, greater terms. He was the Messiah-King who had come to deliver Jerusalem, but the leaders of Israel rejected him as such.

◆   ### 4. Parable of the evil tenants (12:1-12; cf. Matt 21:33-46; Luke 20:9-19)

Then Jesus began teaching them with stories: "A man planted a vineyard. He built a wall around it, dug a pit for pressing out the grape juice, and built a lookout tower. Then he leased the vineyard to tenant farmers and moved to another country. ²At the time of the grape harvest, he sent one of his servants to collect his share of the crop. ³But the farmers grabbed the servant, beat him up, and sent him back empty-handed. ⁴The owner then sent another servant, but they insulted him and beat him over the head. ⁵The next servant he sent was killed. Others he sent were either beaten or killed, ⁶until there was only one left—his son whom he loved dearly. The owner finally sent him, thinking, 'Surely they will respect my son.'

⁷"But the tenant farmers said to one another, 'Here comes the heir to this

estate. Let's kill him and get the estate for ourselves!' ⁸So they grabbed him and murdered him and threw his body out of the vineyard.

⁹"What do you suppose the owner of the vineyard will do?" Jesus asked. "I'll tell you—he will come and kill those farmers and lease the vineyard to others. ¹⁰Didn't you ever read this in the Scriptures?

'The stone that the builders rejected has now become the cornerstone. ¹¹This is the Lord's doing, and it is wonderful to see.'*"

¹²The religious leaders* wanted to arrest Jesus because they realized he was telling the story against them—they were the wicked farmers. But they were afraid of the crowd, so they left him and went away.

12:10-11 Ps 118:22-23.   12:12 Greek *They.*

NOTES

12:1 *vineyard.* This is a traditional way to refer to Israel, as Isa 5:1-7 makes clear. The vineyard wall provided protection, and the tower made it possible to watch for danger. God planted this vineyard.

tenant farmers. These were the Jewish leaders (see 12:12). The backdrop is the common first-century Galilean and Judean pattern of an owner's renting out a farm to tenant farmers (Hurtado 1989:197). France (2002:459) notes that perhaps the leaders in Jerusalem were themselves land owners, thereby creating an ironic contrast.

12:2 *sent one of his servants to collect his share of the crop.* The image now shifts to a portrayal of the prophets who sought spiritual fruit in Israel. Prophets were often called servants in the OT (Jer 7:25; Amos 3:7; Zech 1:6).

12:3 *beat him up.* The prophets were persecuted and rejected. No fruit was given over to God, and his messenger was rejected.

12:4 *they insulted him and beat him over the head.* This rejection of a prophet was not an isolated incident. Other prophets had been sent and rejected. This fits the teaching of the OT (2 Sam 10:2-5 speaks of David's servants being treated in a similar way; 2 Kgs 17:7-20; 2 Chr 24:20-22; 36:15-16; Jer 25:3-7; 26:20-23; cf. France 2002:460). The next servants were beaten or killed. The treatment experienced by John the Baptist and what the leaders were about to do to Jesus had been going on for a long time; the resistance had grown stronger with time.

12:6 *his son whom he loved dearly.* Finally, the owner sent his beloved son (*agapētos* [ᵀᴳ27, ᶻᴳ28]) as his last and most important representative. This represents Jesus and recalls how God addressed him at his baptism and transfiguration (Mark 1:11; 9:7).

12:10 *The stone that the builders rejected has now become the cornerstone.* There is debate as to whether a cornerstone or a capstone is intended, but a cornerstone is likely, especially given the application of the image in Eph 2:20-22 and 1 Pet 2:6-7, and the fact that it is linked with Isa 28:16 and the idea that one can stumble over the stone, as Luke 20:18 suggests (so the NLT rendering and NIDNTT 3.388-390). See Evans 2001:238 for the view that a capstone is meant. The psalm also appears in Acts 4:11; 1 Pet 2:4, 7; Rom 9:32-33.

12:12 *The religious leaders wanted to arrest Jesus.* They were seeking to arrest him; the Gr. uses an imperfect tense, so their effort to apprehend Jesus was ongoing.

they realized he was telling the story against them. The Gr. is slightly more ambiguous as to who knew that the parable was told against the leaders (either the leaders or the crowd are "they"), but it is likely that the leaders were intended, since the verse then gives their reactions (France 2002:464).

But they were afraid of the crowd. For the second time in just a few verses, their fear of the crowd is noted (11:31). If they grabbed him, a riot might result, so they waited.

COMMENTARY

Jesus' parable makes it clear that the Judean leaders were part of the historical pattern of the nation. God had long sought fruit from them without finding it. The prophets he sent were consistently abused and persecuted. One servant after another was mistreated. The rejection remained intense and repetitive, so God finally sent his Son. Logic suggests that the son would meet with respect, not abuse, and the owner sent his son with the expectation that they would identify him and treat him accordingly.

But the land tenants said, "Here comes the heir. . . . Let's kill him and get the estate for ourselves!" The statement is revealing. The tenants identified the Son but decided to remove him, expecting that they would then get the farm since they had worked it. The premise was that if owned land lacked an heir, those who worked the land would get it (Lane 1974:416-419). This, of course, presupposes that the lack of an heir is not due to the murderous actions of the tenants! The lack of logic shows the blindness of sin. Their action shows no respect for the Father or the Son. They did not respect God's messenger, so they did not respect God.

The text says, "They grabbed him and murdered him and threw his body out of the vineyard" (12:8). Thus, the parable anticipates Jesus' rejection and execution by the leaders. The Son's being cast outside looks to Jesus' suffering "outside the city gates" (Heb 13:12). In the story, the Son was even dishonored by being left unburied. Of course, from the way that the story is told, a listener would wonder how anyone could do all that to the son. Jesus' point was that the leaders would do this to him.

But God, the Lord and master, would judge the tenant farmers for their wickedness. The owner of the vineyard is called the Lord (*kurios* [TG2962, ZG3261]), a common title for God. As 12:9 says, "he will come and kill those farmers and lease the vineyard to others." As Jesus predicted, the farmers would be destroyed and others would thereby have a chance to make the vineyard fruitful. In context, the remarks mean that the Jewish leaders would be judged, and the community led by the Twelve and Jesus' other disciples would be given the opportunity to bring forth fruit.

After telling the story, Jesus cited Psalm 118:22, which describes builders who rejected a stone that would become the key to what God was constructing. In the original Psalm, the stone, the king and leader of the nation, was rejected by others. The Jewish leaders would have seen themselves as supporting such a king, but Jesus' reading subverted their understanding, showing them to be enemies of the king because they did not recognize the one God had sent. By focusing on the tenants as enemies, Jesus made it clear that his complaint was not about Israel as a whole, but about the Jewish leaders. This part of the story stands in contrast to Isaiah 5:5-6.

Jesus then quoted Psalm 118:23 "This is the Lord's doing, and it is wonderful to see." This declaration about God's will emphasizes that although rejection was part of the situation, this had not caught God by surprise. Rather, it was part of God's amazing design.

Ironically, the leaders who heard the parable and knew that it was about them determined to arrest Jesus and kill him, thereby fulfilling the parable. Their question about Jesus' authority from the previous passage was not turned against them. The leaders had abused their authority, and God would take it from them. The dominant question of who was speaking for God continues in scene after scene of this chapter.

◆   ## 5. Question concerning paying taxes to Caesar (12:13-17; cf. Matt 22:15-22; Luke 20:20-26)

¹³Later the leaders sent some Pharisees and supporters of Herod to trap Jesus into saying something for which he could be arrested. ¹⁴"Teacher," they said, "we know how honest you are. You are impartial and don't play favorites. You teach the way of God truthfully. Now tell us—is it right to pay taxes to Caesar or not? ¹⁵Should we pay them, or shouldn't we?"

Jesus saw through their hypocrisy and said, "Why are you trying to trap me? Show me a Roman coin,* and I'll tell you." ¹⁶When they handed it to him, he asked, "Whose picture and title are stamped on it?"

"Caesar's," they replied.

¹⁷"Well, then," Jesus said, "give to Caesar what belongs to Caesar, and give to God what belongs to God."

His reply completely amazed them.

12:15 Greek *a denarius.*

NOTES

12:13 *to trap Jesus.* The Gr. word for "trap" (*agreuō* [TG64, ZG65]) means to snare, as one does an animal or an unsuspecting person (Job 10:16, LXX; Prov 5:22; 6:25; BDAG 15).

12:14 *we know how honest you are. You are impartial. . . . You teach the way of God truthfully.* The way that the passage is introduced makes it clear that this three-fold compliment was less than honest in intention, despite its being true. The impartiality referred to is of not being a "respecter of faces" (TDNT 6:779-780).

is it right to pay taxes to Caesar or not? The political question was whether Jews had an obligation to pay the poll tax of the foreign power that occupied their land. Judas the Galilean had led a revolt against such a tax in AD 6 (Hurtado 1989:198; Josephus *War* 2.118; *Antiquities* 17.308; 18.1-10; 20.102). The poll tax was a second tax for Jews, since they also supported the Temple; the Roman tax was especially disliked because it imposed this burden on the people in addition to indicating their subservience to Rome.

12:15 *saw through their hypocrisy.* Jesus was well aware of why the question had been asked, and he explicitly noted his awareness: "Why are you trying to trap me?"

12:17 *give to Caesar what belongs to Caesar, and give to God what belongs to God.* The verb used here is often used of paying a debt (*apodidōmi* [TG591, ZG625]; Matt 5:26; 18:25-26, 28-30, 34; Luke 7:42; 12:59).

His reply completely amazed them. Their amazement means that they were processing the answer, even though they recognized that Jesus had eluded their trap.

COMMENTARY

The introductory verse in this scene makes it clear that the leaders' question ("Is it right to pay taxes to Caesar or not?") was not asked innocently but with the intention of obtaining a political charge against Jesus that they could take to the Roman officials. If the Romans would deal with Jesus, then the leaders would not be responsible for his demise. They might accomplish this by a question that could coax a statement against paying taxes to Rome. However, if Jesus said that Jews should pay taxes to Rome, then the Jews who longed for a messianic challenge to Rome would be discouraged from identifying with Jesus' mission. It was no surprise to find Pharisees and allies of Herod asking the question. The Herodians would be interested to see if Jesus would challenge their leader.

The political question was whether or not Jews were obligated to pay the poll tax of the foreign power that occupied their country. Because it underscored Israel's subjection to pagan Rome, the tax was unpopular. Jesus knew that they were trying to trap him, so he asked them to show him a Roman coin. Jesus was specifically asking for a denarius, the basic Roman coin, and his approach was to show that the Jewish leaders already participated in the Roman economy. They used Roman coins in their daily lives. So he asked them to show him a coin stamped with Caesar's name and image.

So Jesus asked the obvious: "Whose picture and title are stamped on it?" Caesar distributed these coins and they were marked accordingly, as his questioners acknowledged. The inscription on some Roman coins described Tiberius as "Son of the Divine Augustus," which pious Jews regarded as blasphemous. However, the leaders did not object so much that they refused to use the coins to meet their daily expenses.

Then Jesus answered, "Give to Caesar what belongs to Caesar, and give to God what belongs to God." Jesus' reply recognized that Caesar had a sphere of responsibility and that God had one as well. Those coins belonged to Caesar and ran the economy he oversaw, so they should give him his due. However, they should also be sure that God was given what was owed to him. The previous parable (12:1-12) had already warned that the leaders failed to do exactly that.

In conclusion, the Jewish leaders tried to construe Jesus as a political revolutionary, but they failed to catch him speaking against Rome. All modern readings that make Jesus into a political figure fail to note that Jesus passed up the opportunity to feature this in his teaching. This passage is also often used to speak of two spheres of authority to justify the separation of the state from God. That is not the point of this text, which simply says that the state has its responsibility in running society and that people also have to give God the loyalty due to him (see Rom 13:7; 1 Pet 2:13-14).

◆   ### 6. Question about resurrection (12:18-27; cf. Matt 22:23-33; Luke 20:27-40)

18Then Jesus was approached by some Sadducees—religious leaders who say there is no resurrection from the dead. They posed this question: 19"Teacher, Moses gave us a law that if a man dies, leaving a wife without children, his brother should marry the widow and have a child who will carry on the brother's name.* ²⁰Well, suppose there were seven brothers. The oldest one married and then died without children. ²¹So the second brother married the widow, but he also died without children. Then the third brother married her. ²²This continued with all seven of them, and still there were no children. Last of all, the woman also died. ²³So tell us, whose wife will she be in the resurrection? For all seven were married to her."

²⁴Jesus replied, "Your mistake is that you don't know the Scriptures, and you don't know the power of God. ²⁵For when the dead rise, they will neither marry nor be given in marriage. In this respect they will be like the angels in heaven.

²⁶"But now, as to whether the dead will be raised—haven't you ever read about this in the writings of Moses, in the story of the burning bush? Long after Abraham, Isaac, and Jacob had died, God said to Moses,* 'I am the God of Abraham, the God of Isaac, and the God of Jacob.'* ²⁷So he is the God of the living, not the dead. You have made a serious error."

12:19 See Deut 25:5-6.   12:26a Greek *in the story of the bush? God said to him.*   12:26b Exod 3:6.

NOTES

12:18 *Sadducees.* This group held the bulk of political power in Israel because they came from the upper classes that had compromised with Rome in order to share power (Josephus *Antiquities* 18.16-17; *War* 2.164-166). France (2002:470) and Lane (1974:426) describe them as an aristocratic body. Their name probably derives from the name Zadok, high priest from the time of David (2 Sam 8:17; 19:11). This is the only place Mark mentions them. They also have a prominent role in the book of Acts (Acts 4:1-4; 5:17-18). As philosophical naturalists, they rejected the idea of a resurrection, much like many Greeks did.

12:19 *Moses gave us a law.* The Sadducees cited the levirate law that required a brother to marry the widow of another brother if the couple were childless (Deut 25:5-10 and the mishnaic tractate of *m. Yevamot*; Gen 38:8 is an example; see also Josephus *Antiquities* 4.254-255). The purpose of the law was to preserve the name and property of the dead brother.

12:20-23 *seven brothers . . . married and then died without children . . . This continued with all seven of them . . . Last of all, the woman also died. . . . whose wife will she be in the resurrection?* The scenario is of a woman who goes into the afterlife having had seven husbands and no children. Tobit 3–7 tells a story of a woman with seven husbands who had no children, but the book does not raise this problem (though Levirate marriage is noted in Tobit 4:12; 6:9-12; 7:11; Lane 1974:427).

12:24 *Your mistake is that you don't know the Scriptures.* In a rhetorical question that expects a positive reply, he asked, "Is this not why you err?" The NLT is correct in rendering this as "your mistake is that . . ." The imagery of the verb for err (*planaomai* [TG4105A, ZG4414]) is of leading someone astray by taking them off the right path (Deut 22:1; Ps 119:176 [118:176 LXX]; Isa 53:6; Ezek 34:4, 16; Matt 18:12-13; Mark 13:5-6; 2 Tim 3:13; 1 Pet 2:25; 1 John 2:26).

12:26 *I am the God of Abraham, the God of Isaac, and the God of Jacob.* The point of the explanation is not the grammar or the present tense of the supplied verbs for Exod 3 but the theology of God's still being addressed as the God of the patriarchs (see Commentary).

12:27 *he is the God of the living, not the dead.* The Jews had a group of prayers called the 'Amidah (also known as the Eighteen Benedictions), a portion of which read, "You quicken the dead with great mercy . . . and keep your faith with those who sleep in the dust" (Lane 1974:428).

COMMENTARY

The Sadducees did not believe in the resurrection, as the opening verse (12:18) notes; they also doubted the existence of angels and focused on the Torah at the expense of the rest of the Hebrew Scriptures. They intended to show that the resurrection was ludicrous by posing a situation in which a woman shared seven husbands (who were also brothers) after the resurrection. If the woman was married to seven men, how could she possibly take care of them all? The Sadducees assumed that this was an affront to monogamy, and that the afterlife is like this life.

Jesus began his reply to them by pointing out a double error in their question. They did not know what Scripture teaches, and they underestimated the power of God. Jesus did not play Scripture against an understanding of God here, but suggested that Scripture points to God, who in turn has the power to accomplish what Scripture declares about him. These points about Scripture and God's character are important, because people sometimes suggest that Scripture teaches cold abstract doctrine at the expense of a relationship with God. Jesus used Scripture as a lens that gives a focused glimpse of who God is and of what his power can accomplish. The doctrine of resurrection shows that Scripture points to God's character and activity, for in order for there to be a resurrection, God must exercise his creative power.

As Jesus continued his response, he dealt with the Sadducees' theology. It was wrong of them to assume that the afterlife is like this life. Jesus said, "they will neither marry nor be given in marriage . . . they will be like the angels in heaven" (12:25). Life in eternity will not involve marriage; it will be the kind of existence that the angels presently enjoy, of being in direct fellowship with God (1 Enoch 15:5-7 indicates that there is no need for angels to marry and give birth because they are immortal, spiritual beings). Thus Jesus took care of the "polygamy problem."

He then asked the Sadducees, "Haven't you ever read about this in the writings of Moses . . . 'I am the God of Abraham, the God of Isaac, and the God of Jacob'?" Jesus was citing the Torah, the part of the Hebrew Scripture that the Sadducees respected most. From Exodus 3:6, he noted that after the death of the patriarchs, God was still addressed as their God. Many Jews also believed this (see 4 Macc 7:19 and 16:25, where the patriarchs are said not to have died, but to live unto God; see Evans 2001:257). The assumption was that they are still alive, and that God was still their God after their death. God is also still keeping promises that he made to them. A great liturgical phrase of Judaism refers to God as "the God of Abraham, Isaac, and Jacob." This is a way of saying that God is the God of promise. God is still their God, as explained in the next statement, "So he is the God of the living, not the dead."

God is a God of the living, not of those who have perished. For God to be called the God of Abraham after Abraham has died means that Abraham is still alive, which presupposes resurrection. Failure to see this was a major error. In the end, Jesus agreed with the Pharisees that the Scripture teaches resurrection.

Resurrection is at the heart of our future hope. Its reality means ultimate accountability to God, whereas its denial reduces religious faith to this life, to a materialistic view of salvation with no future or heavenly kingdom. With no heavenly hope, justice would also function only in the context of this life, and religion would be reduced to mere ethics. For Jesus, religious faith was more than that; it was a belief in God's restorative work and in his rule over creation. For these reasons, Jesus said that a doctrine denying resurrection was a serious error that cut off the hope God gives us for the restoration of creation. Jesus defended resurrection, while emphasizing that the afterlife is different from this life.

◆   ### 7. The most important commandment (12:28-34; cf. Matt 22:34-40)

28One of the teachers of religious law was standing there listening to the debate. He realized that Jesus had answered well, so he asked, "Of all the commandments, which is the most important?"

29Jesus replied, "The most important commandment is this: 'Listen, O Israel! The LORD our God is the one and only LORD. 30And you must love the LORD your God with all your heart, all your soul, all your mind, and all your strength.'* 31The second is equally important: 'Love your neighbor as yourself.'* No other commandment is greater than these."

32The teacher of religious law replied, "Well said, Teacher. You have spoken the truth by saying that there is only one God and no other. 33And I know it is important to love him with all my heart and all my understanding and all my strength, and to love my neighbor as myself. This is more important than to offer all of the burnt offerings and sacrifices required in the law."

34Realizing how much the man understood, Jesus said to him, "You are not far from the Kingdom of God." And after that, no one dared to ask him any more questions.

12:29-30 Deut 6:4-5.   12:31 Lev 19:18.

NOTES

12:28 *Of all the commandments, which is the most important?* This text introduces the significant theological issue of whether the commandments can be prioritized. This was often discussed among the rabbis (Hooker 1991:287).

12:31 *The second . . . 'Love your neighbor as yourself.' No other commandment is greater than these.* Judaism also taught this (Akiba in *Sifra* 89a [on Lev 19:15-20]; Hillel in *b. Shabbat* 31a says that "What is hateful to you, do not do to your neighbor" is the whole of the law; *Testament of Issachar* 5:2; Philo *Decalogue* 109-110; Hooker 1991:288; also Rom 13:8; Gal 5:14; Jas 2:8). Other Jewish texts take another direction. Simeon the Just (c. 200 BC) taught, "The world rests on three things: the Law, the sacrificial worship, and expressions of love" (*m. Avot* 1.2; Lane 1974:434).

12:32 *You have spoken the truth by saying that there is only one God and no other.* The scribe commended Jesus' reply, and especially his focus on the one God.

12:33 *This is more important than to offer all of the burnt offerings and sacrifices required in the law.* After reaffirming the two commands, the scribe added his own commentary of prioritization. He noted that the two foci on love are more important than any liturgical requirements calling for offerings or sacrifices. The NLT renders as "more important" a phrase that in the Gr. simply states that love is "much more" than offerings and sacrifices. The NLT makes the force of the remark clear. In a sense, these priorities were already implied by the argument that the commandments to love were the greatest commandments. The scribe's remark made this explicit.

12:34 *Realizing how much the man understood.* The NLT renders well the sense of the Gr., which says that "Jesus saw that the man answered wisely."

no one dared to ask him any more questions. Jesus' answers in these controversies were so effective that the questions stopped. Jesus had demonstated his competency.

COMMENTARY

This passage is significant because it brings the controversies to an end while revealing how Jesus prioritized the law. In saying, "Listen, O Israel! The LORD our God is the one and only LORD," Jesus was quoting the *Shema'*, a Scripture beginning in Deuteronomy 6:4 that Jews recited twice daily to declare the uniqueness of the LORD God in a world of many gods. (The word *shema'* [TH8085, ZH9048], "to hear," is the first word in the Hebrew text of Deut 6:4—a call for Israel to listen.) Jesus used the unique character of God to launch a discussion of the great commandments (so also Josephus *Against Apion* 2.190, who says that the first commandment concerns God). God's personal nature and his desire for relationship are underscored by the declaration that he is "our" God; he is also the Lord who rules the universe. Jesus continued by saying, "You must love the Lord your God with all your heart, all your soul, all your mind, and all your strength." God's existence as the Lord who is our God carries a corollary: our love for him must involve the entire person. Everything we do radiates from this theological core. Life and theology begin at the same place, from a love relationship with the living God to whom we submit as to the one and only Lord. Thus, this is the first commandment in priority.

Jesus then cited Leviticus 19:18 ("Love your neighbor as yourself"), thereby completing his focus on relational commands about love as the greatest commandments. Being properly related to God entails being properly related to others. The scribe appreciated Jesus' answer and said that expressing love far outweighs offering sacrifices. Other Old Testament texts say that God desires mercy, not sacrifice (1 Sam 15:22; Isa 1:11; Hos 6:6; Jer 6:20; 7:22-23; Mic 6:6-8; Evans 2001:265-266).

Jesus told the scribe, "You are not far from the Kingdom of God" (12:34). The Kingdom concerns more than a love ethic, but love is fundamental to the Kingdom. Jesus affirmed this man's insight here in the one scene in Mark in which Jesus and a Jewish questioner agree. All the man needed for access to God's promise was allegiance to Jesus, God's sent One.

In summary, the two foremost commands are to love God completely and to love one's neighbor as oneself. Jesus affirmed that these commandments were of greater importance than offerings and sacrifices. However, the text also makes it clear that although an ethical orientation toward God and others is central, it does not bring one into the Kingdom. When Jesus addresses the Messiah's status in the next passage, he puts the last piece of the puzzle in place. Participation in the Kingdom is not possible without understanding who the Messiah is. To love God is to love the One sent to bring God's promise.

◆   ## 8. Question about the Messiah (12:35-37; cf. Matt 22:41-46; Luke 20:41-44)

35Later, as Jesus was teaching the people in the Temple, he asked, "Why do the teachers of religious law claim that the Messiah is the son of David? 36For David himself, speaking under the inspiration of the Holy Spirit, said,

'The LORD said to my Lord,
Sit in the place of honor at my right hand

until I humble your enemies
beneath your feet.'*

37Since David himself called the Messiah 'my Lord,' how can the Messiah be his son?" The large crowd listened to him with great delight.

12:36 Ps 110:1.

NOTES

12:35 *Jesus was teaching the people in the Temple.* In Mark's account, Jesus is often depicted as teaching near the end of his ministry (11:15-16, 27; 13:1; 14:49; cf. Luke 21:37).

the Messiah is the son of David. The roots of this understanding extend back to texts such as 2 Sam 7:12-16; Isa 9:2-7; 11:1-9; Jer 23:5-6, 33:15; Zech 3:8; 6:12; Amos 9:11. The *Psalms of Solomon* 17-18 also give this presentation of the Messiah. The NT acknowledges this relationship of David to Jesus (Rom 1:2-4; 2 Tim 2:8; Matt 1:20; Luke 1:27, 32, 69; 2:4, 11; Rev 5:5; 22:16).

12:36 *the LORD said to my Lord.* This citation from Psalm 110:1 introduces perhaps the most important Old Testament text used in the NT to explain Jesus. It declares three key points: (1) that the one who God addresses is a descendant of David who also is his Lord despite being younger, a reversal of form that points to the uniqueness of the figure; (2) It stresses and explains where Jesus will go on his resurrection, at the side of the Father sharing authority from his right hand, and (3) that total victory will come one day to this figure as all will be set at his feet.

12:37 *with great delight.* Jesus' remarks pleased the crowd because he had bested "the experts" in ways that led people to ponder. The term for delight (*hēdeōs* [TG2234, ZG2452]) means that they enjoyed what took place (BDAG 434; Mark 6:20).

COMMENTARY

Jesus again took the initiative, as he did with the parable of the tenants. Jesus' remark here deals with a central expectation about the Messiah, that he would be a royal descendant of David (see note on 12:35). Jesus adjusted this understanding with his interpretation of Psalm 110:1, in which David addressed the issue of the Messiah under the inspiration of the Spirit. It was common knowledge in Judaism that David was an inspired writer (2 Sam 23:2; 11QPs^a 27:2-4, 11; Evans 2001:273). Jesus then focused on David's words, "the LORD said to my Lord." David addressed the Messiah to come as one to whom God (the LORD, Yahweh) spoke directly and as being David's Lord (*'adonay* [TH136, ZH151], "my Lord"). Since David the king had as high a rank as was humanly possible, how could David have a Lord beyond the LORD?

The psalm continues, "Sit in the place of honor at my right hand until I humble your enemies beneath your feet," which underscores the authority God gave to the Messiah by giving him a seat at his right hand. This text answers the question of authority raised in Mark 11:28 by saying that the one that David called his LORD had a seat at God's side and that God would give him victory over his enemies. Jesus did not elaborate on this point by connecting it to his exaltation, or by saying that he was this figure. Mark's readers, remembering 8:29, should know that this discussion is about Jesus. The key to understanding the Messiah is not that he is David's son, but that he is the exalted "Lord." This One was authorized to sit at God's side.

Jesus' final question is poignant. "Since David himself called the Messiah 'my Lord,' how can the Messiah be his son?" (12:37). Jesus' question did not deny that the Messiah was David's son. Rather, the question was like a rabbinic antinomy, in which two points of unequal significance are juxtaposed. Jesus' point was that his being Lord to a grand figure like David was more important than his being David's son. In this patriarchal culture, an ancestor had the higher rank. Reversing this for a king's descendant so that a child ranked higher than the greatest king suggested the Messiah's unique status. This understanding would deepen when Jesus was exalted after his resurrection. Then it would become even clearer that Jesus meant that "Lord" was his key title, showing the sovereign position he had at God's side. France (2002:488) prefers to point to a title such as "Son of God" in contrast to "son of David" and in light of Mark's focus on the title from Mark 1:1, but this works only if one already appreciates that "Son of God" is enhanced beyond its normal Jewish usage. The position and function of Jesus' sovereign role are key here; the idea of "Lord" works fine by itself, if not as an appeal to the exalted "Son of Man," then as a title Jesus used of himself.

◆ ## 9. Contrasting the scribes and a widow (12:38-44; cf. Matt 23:1-12; Luke 20:45-47)

38Jesus also taught: "Beware of these teachers of religious law! For they like to parade around in flowing robes and receive respectful greetings as they walk in the marketplaces. 39And how they love the seats of honor in the synagogues and the head table at banquets. 40Yet they shamelessly cheat widows out of their property and then pretend to be pious by making long prayers in public. Because of this, they will be more severely punished."

41Jesus sat down near the collection box in the Temple and watched as the crowds dropped in their money. Many rich people put in large amounts. 42Then a poor widow came and dropped in two small coins.*

43Jesus called his disciples to him and said, "I tell you the truth, this poor widow has given more than all the others who are making contributions. 44For they gave a tiny part of their surplus, but she, poor as she is, has given everything she had to live on."

12:42 Greek two lepta, which is a kodrantes [i.e., a quadrans].

NOTES

12:38 *Beware of these teachers of religious law!* Jesus warned the crowd about people whose authority was misdirected. These drew attention to themselves and not to God. The tense of the verb means that the people were to be on constant watch to avoid following the example of such people (see Mark 8:15).

respectful greetings. In Judaism, religious authorities were to be given a special greeting in the market place (Matt 23:7). Jesus condemned this type of self-directed attention, along with the "flowing robes" that also drew attention to their status. These leaders also had attention-getting cloaks known as *tallith*. The *stolē* [TG4749, ZG5124] refers to such a ceremonial robe (Esth 6:8; Josephus *Antiquities* 3.151; 11.80).

12:39 *seats of honor.* These seats, whether at the synagogue or at banquets, also show how these religious figures loved to draw attention to themselves (Josephus *Antiquities* 15.21; according to *t. Megillah* 3.21, the leaders sat facing the people with their backs to the sanctuary; Evans 2001:278).

12:40 *they shamelessly cheat widows.* The NLT renders the Gr. figure of those who "devour widow's houses" more concretely here (*Testament of Moses* 7:6-10). What is specifically meant is not clear. The range of options runs from cheating widows out of their estates for services rendered, to taking houses as pledges for debt they could not repay, to charging for intercessory prayer. Evans (2001:279) notes six options.

pretend to be pious by making long prayers. The next complaint is that their piety had nothing to do with sincerity before God. It was a public show, even when prayers were made. The term *prophasis* [TG4392, ZG4733] means to do something by pretext or for mere appearance (BDAG 889; Matt 6:5; Phil 1:18). Matthew has a much longer condemnation at this point in his gospel (Matt 23).

12:41 *the collection box.* The location of this box is uncertain. The temple had thirteen receptacles for such contributions; they were designed like trumpets and were located on the wall in the Court of Women (*m. Sheqalim* 6.5). Another possibility is the treasury itself, which would have had a place for gifts. However, given the presence of the widow, one of the thirteen receptacles is more likely.

12:42 *two small coins.* In Gr., this phrase refers to two lepta or quadrans, as Mark explains (BDAG 550). These were the smallest coins in the currency, and a lepton was only worth 1/128 of a denarius. That worked out to about six minutes' wage at a basic worker's daily pay level. In other words, it was next to nothing in contrast to the large amounts that the wealthy put in.

12:43 *this poor widow has given more than all the others.* Jesus commended the widow's contribution as greater than those of the rich. Jesus may have known that the woman was a widow by the way she was dressed. The next verse will explain the point.

12:44 *For . . . she . . . has given everything she had to live on.* In contrast to others who contributed out of their abundance, this widow gave "out of her want . . . the whole of her life." The Gr. makes the point in two distinct phrases, making it very clear that her gift was of the resources she applied to the basic necessities of life. The NLT has combined these into a single expression.

COMMENTARY

The narcissistic and ostentatious religious leaders took advantage of widows, the most vulnerable members of ancient Middle Eastern society. Jesus condemned this lack of love for people in need, which led right into another contrast between the religious leaders and a widow. The widow was extolled and some of Jesus' most fundamental values were promoted. Sacrificial giving is something that deeply delights God in general, as it does in the case of this widow. He does not look at the size of the gift but at the dimensions of the sacrifice behind it (cf. 1 Sam 16:7; God looks on the heart of the giver). Some have greater resources than others, and some who give next to nothing, give all. The widow is contrasted with the rich and even more so with the religious leaders whose example was altogether to be avoided, for they did not give. Rather, they took advantage of others and sought praise to their own glory. Jesus warned that they would "be more severely punished" (12:40). Their misleading behavior made them more culpable before God.

◆ ## 10. The destruction of the Temple and return of the Son of Man (13:1-37; cf. Matt 24:1-36; Luke 21:5-36)

As Jesus was leaving the Temple that day, one of his disciples said, "Teacher, look at these magnificent buildings! Look at the impressive stones in the walls."

²Jesus replied, "Yes, look at these great buildings. But they will be completely demolished. Not one stone will be left on top of another!"

³Later, Jesus sat on the Mount of Olives across the valley from the Temple. Peter, James, John, and Andrew came to him privately and asked him, ⁴"Tell us, when will all this happen? What sign will show us that these things are about to be fulfilled?"

⁵Jesus replied, "Don't let anyone mislead you, ⁶for many will come in my name, claiming, 'I am the Messiah.'* They will deceive many. ⁷And you will hear of wars and threats of wars, but don't panic. Yes, these things must take place, but the end won't follow immediately. ⁸Nation will go to war against nation, and kingdom against kingdom. There will be earthquakes in many parts of the world, as well as famines. But this is only the first of the birth pains, with more to come.

⁹"When these things begin to happen, watch out! You will be handed over to the local councils and beaten in the synagogues. You will stand trial before governors and kings because you are my followers. But this will be your opportunity to tell them about me.* ¹⁰For the Good News must first be preached to all nations.* ¹¹But when you are arrested and stand trial, don't worry in advance about what to say. Just say what God tells you at that time, for it is not you who will be speaking, but the Holy Spirit.

¹²"A brother will betray his brother to death, a father will betray his own child, and children will rebel against their parents and cause them to be killed. ¹³And everyone will hate you because you are my followers.* But the one who endures to the end will be saved.

¹⁴"The day is coming when you will see the sacrilegious object that causes desecration* standing where he* should not be." (Reader, pay attention!) "Then those in Judea must flee to the hills. ¹⁵A person out on the deck of a roof must not go down into the house to pack. ¹⁶A person out in the field must not return even to get a coat. ¹⁷How terrible it will be for pregnant women and for nursing mothers in those days. ¹⁸And pray that your flight will not be in winter. ¹⁹For there will be greater anguish in those days than at any time since God created the world. And it will never be so great again. ²⁰In fact, unless the Lord shortens that time of calamity, not a single person will survive. But for the sake of his chosen ones he has shortened those days.

²¹"Then if anyone tells you, 'Look, here is the Messiah,' or 'There he is,' don't believe it. ²²For false messiahs and false prophets

will rise up and perform signs and wonders so as to deceive, if possible, even God's chosen ones. ²³Watch out! I have warned you about this ahead of time!

²⁴"At that time, after the anguish of those days,

the sun will be darkened,
    the moon will give no light,
²⁵the stars will fall from the sky,
    and the powers in the heavens will
    be shaken.*

²⁶Then everyone will see the Son of Man* coming on the clouds with great power and glory.* ²⁷And he will send out his angels to gather his chosen ones from all over the world*—from the farthest ends of the earth and heaven.

²⁸"Now learn a lesson from the fig tree. When its branches bud and its leaves begin to sprout, you know that summer is near. ²⁹In the same way, when you see all these things taking place, you can know that his return is very near, right at the door. ³⁰I tell you the truth, this generation* will not pass from the scene before all these things take place. ³¹Heaven and earth will disappear, but my words will never disappear.

³²"However, no one knows the day or hour when these things will happen, not even the angels in heaven or the Son himself. Only the Father knows. ³³And since you don't know when that time will come, be on guard! Stay alert*!

³⁴"The coming of the Son of Man can be illustrated by the story of a man going on a long trip. When he left home, he gave each of his slaves instructions about the work they were to do, and he told the gatekeeper to watch for his return. ³⁵You, too, must keep watch! For you don't know when the master of the household will return—in the evening, at midnight, before dawn, or at daybreak. ³⁶Don't let him find you sleeping when he arrives without warning. ³⁷I say to you what I say to everyone: Watch for him!"

13:6 Greek *claiming, 'I am.'*   13:9 Or *But this will be your testimony against them.*   13:10 Or *all peoples.*
13:13 Greek *on account of my name.*   13:14a Greek *the abomination of desolation.* See Dan 9:27; 11:31;
12:11.   13:14b Or *it.*   13:24-25 See Isa 13:10; 34:4; Joel 2:10.   13:26a "Son of Man" is a title Jesus used
for himself.   13:26b See Dan 7:13.   13:27 Greek *from the four winds.*   13:30 Or *this age,* or *this nation.*
13:33 Some manuscripts add *and pray.*

NOTES

13:1 *look at these magnificent buildings!* The Temple, which was being enhanced by Herod, was impressive. Josephus said that it looked like a snow-capped mountain rising up in the midst of Jerusalem (Josephus *War* 5.184-226, esp. 222-223). Stones found there are fifteen meters long and two and a half meters wide; they weighed 420 to 600 tons (Evans 2001:299). It is the temple and its future that triggers the discourse. The temple was destroyed in AD 70, which has led to interpretive debates about what Jesus meant in the whole of the discourse (for this debate and views, see the discussion in the commentary below).

13:2 *they will be completely demolished. Not one stone will be left on top of another!* The NLT clearly brings out Jesus' imagery in referring to the building's being completely demolished. The Gr. reads, "There will not be one stone left on another that will not be thrown down."

13:3 *Mount of Olives.* This was often the setting for discussing judgment (Ezek 11:23; 43:2; Zech 14:3-4; Evans 2001:304).

Peter, James, John, and Andrew. Four "inner circle" disciples were part of this discussion, not the usual three (Peter, James, John). The difference gives evidence of careful historical detail and recollection. In Mark, the discussion known as the Olivet discourse is triggered by a private question of some of the key disciples.

13:4 *when will all this happen? What sign will show us that these things are about to be fulfilled?* The questions recognize that Jesus had predicted an event of great significance for

Jerusalem. The Temple would not be destroyed unless God was engaged in a serious work. So they asked about the timing and about whether there would be any special indicator or warning signal, a sign (*sēmeion* [TG4592, ZG4956]) that these things were about to happen (on this concept, see Exod 3:12; Isa 7:11; 4 Ezra 4:52; Evans 2001:305). In Gr., the questions center twice around "these things" (*tauta* [TG3778A, ZG4047]; note the plural) happening. Jesus' reply confirms that his remarks dealt with more than the Temple.

13:5 Don't let anyone mislead you. The verb *planaō* [TG4105, ZG4414] means not being deceived or led into error (12:24; Gal 6:7; Rev 2:20). The NLT obscures the verbal idea of "taking heed" (*blepete* [TG991, ZG1063]). This idea and variations on it also appear in 13:9, 23, 33, 35, and 37.

13:6 claiming, 'I am the Messiah.' They will deceive many. The error to avoid is the idea that anyone else could be the Christ. Taylor (1966:503-504) argues that the meaning here is a messianic or quasi-messianic claim.

13:7 you will hear of wars and threats of wars. Another feature of the period will be rampant rumors of war. This is seen in Jewish texts on the end times (1 Enoch 99:4; 2 Baruch 27:5; 4 Ezra 13:31; 15:15; note also Isa 8:21; 13:13; 14:30; 19:2; Jer 23:19; 51:46; Ezek 5:12; Hag 2:6; Zech 14:4; Taylor 1966:505). In other words, this is a prophetic theme. The Temple will be destroyed in a period of chaos.

but the end won't follow immediately. Jesus said that such chaos would still not indicate the end. This is Mark's first direct mention of "the end." The Temple's destruction suggests that the end was also related to its demise. How that relationship was to work was not yet detailed, except that the events that pointed to the Temple's destruction would not indicate the end. This remark made it clear that there were many events to come before the return of the Son of Man, which was Jesus' indirect way to refer to himself.

13:8 will go to war . . . earthquakes . . . famines. Jesus continued to describe a period of intense political and natural chaos.

first of the birth pains, with more to come. Picturing the end as the travail of a woman giving birth (also an OT theme; see Isa 26:17; Jer 4:31; 6:24; 22:23; Hos 13:13; Mic 4:9-10, sometimes about the nations and other times about Israel), Jesus said that these events were but the first part of the delivery of the end times.

13:12 will betray . . . will rebel. Alluding to Mic 7:6, Jesus made it clear that the persecution and division would touch families, as brothers betrayed brothers, fathers turned against children, and children turned against parents. The pain would be great because the conflict would involve those so near. Matthew 10:21 is similar in force. This idea also has parallels in Judaism (1 Enoch 100:1-2; Jubilees 23:19; 4 Ezra 6:24; 3 Baruch 4:17; Evans 2001:312).

13:13 And everyone will hate you because you are my followers. The NLT speaks of allegiance to Jesus; the Gr. says "on account of my name." The rendering is a good one, as the point is that their association with Jesus will bring their arrest and persecution.

But the one who endures to the end will be saved. This reference to "the end" is not to the final point on the eschatological calendar; it refers to the end of an individual's journey.

13:14 the sacrilegious object that causes desecration standing where he should not be. This is a very explanatory rendering of the Greek: "the abomination of desolation set up where it [the abomination] ought not be." The language comes from Dan 12:11, and the historical example at the root of the image is Daniel's prophetic prediction of Antiochus Epiphanes and his desecration of the Temple in 167 BC (see 1 Macc 1:54; 2 Macc 6:2; other passages in Daniel note the theme; Dan 8:13; 9:27; 11:31). What is described is the desecration of the Holy of Holies.

Reader, pay attention! This parenthetical remark calls the reader to appreciate the significance of what is taking place.

Then those in Judea must flee to the hills. The call is to appreciate the danger of this time, when no one should remain in Jerusalem or its environs. All of Judea will be at risk in this time of severe judgment. Hills were regarded as a refuge in the OT (Gen 14:10; Jer 16:16; Ezek 7:16).

13:15 *must not go down into the house to pack.* The tribulation will be so intense that there will be no time to gather things in an organized withdrawal. The quicker one can get away, the better.

13:16 *A person out in the field must not return even to get a coat.* Again, the intensity and suddenness of the judgment means there will be no time even to gather a small item.

13:17 *How terrible it will be for pregnant women.* The tribulation will be so severe that it will be a dreadful time for pregnant women and for mothers with nursing children. What normally is a blessing will become a bad situation. This is noted in Jewish texts (*4 Ezra* 16:40-46) and in the OT as a problem at times of judgment (Jer 44:7; Lam 2:11; 4:4). The expression "how terrible" renders the force of the Gr. idea of "woe" that Jesus pronounces here for those who are pregnant at this time. It is a lament over their suffering.

13:18 *And pray that your flight will not be in winter.* If the time to flee comes in winter, then the escape will be even more difficult. Everything that Jesus said here pointed to the terribly difficult nature of the time. In winter, streams would swell from the rain, making movement next to impossible (Lane 1974:470).

13:19 *For there will be greater anguish in those days than at any time since God created the world. And it will never be so great again.* The "tribulation" of these days will be unprecedented. It will be necessary to flee, but this may be difficult. There has never been a time like it nor will there be in the future. The key term is *thlipsis* [TG2347, ZG2568], referring to a time of disturbance (Rev 1:9; 7:14). The description points to the decisive time of world rebellion described in Dan 12:1. As such, it appears to speak to events at the very end of the speech's timeframe.

13:20 *unless the Lord shortens that time of calamity, not a single person will survive. But for the sake of his chosen ones he has shortened those days.* This period of unprecedented tribulation will be so intense that were it not cut short for the sake of believers, no one would survive (an idea expressed in Jewish discussion of the end to show its severity, Dan 12:7; *1 Enoch* 80:2, 4; *4 Ezra* 4:26; *3 Baruch* 9; 4Q385 3:3-5 [a.k.a. *Pseudo-Ezekiel*]; Evans 2001:323 suggests the influence of Isa 60:21-22).

13:24 *after the anguish of those days.* The NLT renders the Gr., "after that tribulation," with this phrase.

the sun will be darkened, the moon will give no light. One reason why no one will need to look for the return of the Son of Man and the vindication he brings is that there will be cosmic signs to signal his arrival. The picture is of a creation in alteration; the language is from Isa 13:10 (see also Ezek 32:7; Joel 2:10; 2:31; 3:15; Amos 8:9; Lane 1974:475).

13:25 *the stars will fall from the sky, and the powers in the heavens will be shaken.* Isaiah 34:4 is cited here. This OT theme carried over into Judaism (Judg 5:5; Ps 18:7; 114:7; Amos 9:5; Mic 1:4; Nah 1:5; Hab 3:6; *Testament of Moses* 10:1-5; *1 Enoch* 57:2; Evans 2001:328). As with the entire speech, these themes were common in texts about the coming judgment.

13:27 *he will send out his angels to gather his chosen ones from all over the world.* The major point of his coming, his parousia, will be to vindicate the elect. Angels will gather believers from all the corners of the earth (Deut 30:3-4; Ps 50:3-5; Isa 43:6; 66:8; Jer 32:37; Zech 2:6, 10; Tob 14:10; *1 Enoch* 62:13-14; *Psalms of Solomon* 8:28; 11:1-4; 17:28). With this note of gathering those present at his return, Jesus ended the discussion of the signs and began to summarize.

13:28 *learn a lesson from the fig tree. When its branches bud and its leaves begin to sprout, you know that summer is near.* Jesus used the picture of a budding plant to illustrate how one can sense the approaching judgment. Since these events occurred at the time of Passover, the trees were in the very condition Jesus was describing. Jesus said that when one saw the things he had been describing beginning to happen, it would be evident that the end was approaching, just as budding figs in March/April presage the fully blooming trees of May/June (see the commentary for the significance of the metaphor).

13:30 *this generation will not pass from the scene before all these things take place.* The note in the NLT mg indicates the difficulty with the verse; see the commentary for the various views.

13:31 *Heaven and earth will disappear, but my words will never disappear.* Jesus emphatically states that what he has prophetically declared will come to pass. His word is more permanent than the creation (Isa 40:7-8).

13:32 *However, no one knows the day or hour . . . not even the angels in heaven or the Son himself. Only the Father knows.* Jesus declared that the timing was strictly limited to the Father's knowledge. This remark of Jesus is so unusual in claiming ignorance on this important point that it apparently caused a measure of controversy in the early church. There is evidence that it was so controversial that a few later copyists of the text omitted it. Jesus knew that these things would certainly happen, but that only the Father knows the timing. France (2002:544) discusses the theological perspective of the remark in terms of Jesus' use of his divine attributes or, better, his lack of reliance upon them during his incarnation. Lane (1974:482) speaks of God not delegating this knowledge to the Son. Mark 13:33 and 35 reinforce the point that the time is unknown except to God.

13:33 *be on guard! Stay alert!* Once again Jesus told the disciples to watch and be observant (see 13:9). The double command with these synonyms is emphatic. The first verb was also used in 13:9; the second is a term from wisdom literature (Job 21:32; Prov 8:34; Wis 6:15; Sir 36:16). This theme of watching runs through the entire speech. The point is not to try and figure out all of the timing, for Jesus has just said it cannot be known. However, one can keep an eye on these things as they are unfolding, like watching the fig tree bud. That is what Jesus urges here.

13:34 *The coming of the Son of Man can be illustrated by the story of a man going on a long trip. . . . he told the gatekeeper to watch for his return.* A parable concludes the discourse. Disciples are like servants looking for their master to return home from a trip. They are to watch (see the next verse) and be ready for him to return at any hour.

13:35 *You, too, must keep watch! For you don't know when the master of the household will return.* This verb for watching (*grēgoreō* [TG1127, ZG1213]) means to stay awake or alert (BDAG 207-208). It appears in 13:34, 35, and 37. Jesus' call is to pay attention, since the exact time of the return is not known. The timing is expressed in terms of the usual four Roman watches: evening, midnight, dawn (Gr., "at cock's crow"), daybreak. He could come at any time.

13:36 *Don't let him find you sleeping when he arrives without warning.* The warning is to be awake when he suddenly returns (NLT, "without warning"). Disciples should be walking with God and alert to his return. Until then, they should be faithful stewards; there should be no dereliction of duty (Evans 2001:341).

13:37 *I say to you what I say to everyone: Watch for him!* The NLT expands on the command to watch and makes it specific by making clear who is anticipated. The discourse closes with an exhortation to everyone, not just to the four disciples present (13:3).

COMMENTARY

The passage begins with the disciples admiring the Temple's excellent workmanship. Their remark implied that this glorious building would be around for a long time. Perhaps they were also looking forward to taking it over as Jesus' assistants. As great and massive and magnificent as the Temple was, however, it was doomed to destruction (Josephus describes the Temple's destruction and the fire that accompanied it in *War* 6.249-266; 7.1-3). Jesus' remark about the Temple's destruction also presupposed a terrible catastrophe for Jerusalem (Jer 7:11; 26:17-19; Amos 9:1; Mic 3:12). Later, the disciples asked about this.

Jesus' first warning, "Don't let anyone mislead you," deals with claims of messianic presence. Given Jesus' suffering, others might come along claiming to be the real and powerful Messiah. Jesus told the disciples not to be fooled. When such claims occurred, they would deceive many. Josephus notes some of these troublesome figures in Jewish history: (1) Simon of Perea, who assumed the diadem and plundered royal palaces (*Antiquities* 17.10.6.273-276); (2) Athronges, the shepherd of Judea, who wore a diadem (*Antiquities* 17.10.7.278-284); (3) Theudas (*Antiquities* 20.5.1.97-99); (4) sons of Judas of Galilee (*Antiquities* 20.5.2.102); (5) the Egyptian (*Antiquities* 20.8.6.169-172); (6) an imposter (*Antiquities* 20.8.10.188); (7) Sicarii (*War* 2.13.3.254); (8) Judas the Galilean (*War* 2.8.1.118); (9) Simon bar-Giora (*War* 4.9.3-8.503-544); (10) a false prophet (*War* 6.5.2.285); (11) Eleazar of the Sicarii, who fought at Masada (*War* 7.8.1.253; 7.8.2.275). Although Josephus never said that they made messianic claims, France (2002:510-511) and Evans (2001:306) regard some mentioned by Josephus as regal claimants. The explicit claim to be the Messiah did not appear until Bar Kochba made it around AD 132.

Jesus then told the disciples that certain signs would mark the onset of the end times (see notes on 13:7-8). He explicitly told them that "when these things begin to happen, watch out! You will be handed over to the local councils. . . . You will stand trial before governors and kings because you are my followers" (13:9). Disciples should pay attention to such signs; they indicate that persecution will come for those who follow Jesus. Disciples appear before Jewish councils in Acts 4, while others testify before governors in Acts 23–24. Jesus told them that this persecution would lead to witness that could sometimes make a big impression, as in the example of Stephen's effect on Paul (cf. Acts 7 with Acts 22:4-5, 20-21). Jesus indicated that the gospel would get out into the world as a result of such persecution, a point made in Acts, Romans (1:5, 8; 10:18; 15:18-24), and Colossians (1:5-6, 23).

With respect to their witness and gospel preaching, Jesus said, "Don't worry in advance about what to say. Just say what God tells you at that time, for it is not you who will be speaking, but the Holy Spirit" (13:11). Jesus therein made a promise. The Spirit would enable disciples who were persecuted to speak about their faith. They need have no anxiety because God would be with them through the Spirit. The Spirit is poured out in the messianic age (Isa 11:1-2; Joel 2:28-29), and one of the Spirit's roles is to testify for God through his disciples. As God did through Moses, he will enable his servants to speak (Exod 4:10-17). The book of Acts shows how this was realized.

The first section of this speech ends with a call to persevere: "The one who endures to the end will be saved." Salvation stands at the end of a hard road. This call
is equivalent to Revelation's "one who overcomes." God will see and honor such
faithfulness.

Jesus' speech then shifts to a specific event that will trigger the end times. He told
the disciples they would see "the abomination of desolation set up where it ought
not be" (13:14, Gr.). The language comes from Daniel 12:11 and the historical example behind the image is Antiochus Epiphanes and his desecration of the Temple
in 167 BC (1 Macc 1:54; 2 Macc 6:2; other passages in Daniel note the theme: Dan
11:31; cf. Dan 8:13; 9:27). The term "abomination" concerns shameful acts associated with a place of sacrifice or idolatry (Deut 7:25-26; 1 Kgs 14:24; 2 Kgs 23:13;
2 Chr 15:8; Jer 16:18; Ezek 5:11; TDNT 1:598-600). Jesus indicated that when the
Temple was invaded and a Gentile stood in the holy place, the prediction about the
Temple was about to occur (2 Thess 2:3-4 also appears to refer to this, in relation to
the end time event of the Antichrist). Though some raise the issue of events in Judea
in Jesus' time as being fulfilled here (Lane 1974:467-469), it is more likely that
those events picture what the decisive desecration will be like in the end times,
given that this discourse ends with the return of the Son of Man. Among the early
precedents are zealot victories that led to Roman occupation (Josephus War 2.20.1;
4.3.7; 4.3.10), Caligula's effort to place images in the Temple (Philo Legatio ad
Gaium; Josephus Antiquities 18.8.2-9), Pilate's attempt to place standards in the city
(Josephus Antiquities 18.3.1), and Titus's entry into Jerusalem and the Temple (Josephus War 6.4.7). Evans (2001:318-319) discusses these four first-century options
but notes that none of them is a good fit. Pilate and Caligula never carried out their
plan and the Zealots do not fit the description. Titus visited the Temple after it was
destroyed, so there was no altar to desecrate.

The abomination that causes desolation will bring about great tribulation. Mark
13:14-27 points to the decisive time of world rebellion described in Daniel 12:1. This
unprecedented period is also called the "great tribulation" because it is uniquely
disruptive. Other Old Testament and Jewish texts also make claims to unprecedented
calamity (Exod 10:14; 11:6; Joel 2:2; Jer 30:7; Bar 2:2; 1 Macc 9:27; 1QM 1.11-12; Testament of Moses 8:1), but the context in relation to the Son of Man's return means that
this time is decisively tied to the vindication of the saints. Yet the remark in 13:19 that
this tribulation is unique to any that precedes or succeeds it suggests that this event
will not occur at the very end of history, but sometime before then.

During this period, some will claim to know where the Messiah is, but such declarations are not to be believed. As 13:24-27 makes clear, when the Son of Man returns, it
will be obvious. Jesus said, "false messiahs . . . will rise up and perform signs and wonders so as to deceive, if possible, even God's chosen ones" (13:22). Such claims might
be persuasive and capable of deceiving even believers because miraculous activity will
accompany the claims (2 Thess 2:9). Thus, Jesus told his disciples, "Watch out! I have
warned you!" (13:23). Nothing should catch them by surprise because they had been
warned about the false claimants and the other difficulties that lay ahead.

After these difficult days, worse things will come: "The sun will be darkened, the moon will give no light, the stars will fall from the sky, and the powers in the heavens will be shaken" (13:24-25). The language shows that the "lights are going out" on the current world order. However, in reading the text this way, one should be careful not to reduce the imagery strictly to metaphor, because the return of the Son of Man will bring about a change in the world order even at its most basic, physical level.

Following these cosmic catastrophes, "everyone will see the Son of Man coming on the clouds with great power and glory" (13:26). Jesus used imagery from Daniel 7:13 to describe the coming of the Son of Man. In that passage, one "like a son of man" receives the authority to judge from the Ancient One and rides the clouds, a figure reserved for God or the gods in the Old Testament. Daniel 7 pictures the Son of Man receiving authority from God to execute judgment; in this passage, he is coming to earth to exercise that power. France (2002:535-536) argues that the language is not about a physical return but depicts Jesus and the church as being given heavenly power and authority. For France, the gathering of the chosen ones (13:27) is not an event in which the saints are gathered, but a realization that the nations are included in the people of God. But in this interpretation, it is not clear how the gathering at the Son of Man's coming constitutes the kind of vindication anticipated in the Old Testament. The view is also undercut by the idea that this event follows a period of unprecedented tribulation (see the remarks by Evans 2001:328-329).

Following his discussion of the end times, Jesus said, "Learn a lesson from the fig tree. When its branches bud and its leaves begin to sprout, you know that summer is near" (13:28). Jesus used the picture of a budding plant to declare that one can sense when judgment comes. These events occurred at the time of Passover, when the trees were in the very condition Jesus described. At the end of this speech, Jesus was not discussing the destruction of the Temple, but the return of the Son of Man to vindicate the saints. Thus there is a suggestion that the return is separate from the destruction of the Temple. This interpretation counters that of France (2002:501-502, 530-533), who argues that almost everything in the passage before 13:32 is about AD 70. However, there was no gathering of the saints in AD 70, so his interpretation fails. Jesus' statement about the budding fig tree uses a theme commonly associated with judgment when the Day of the Lord is discussed in the Old Testament. A judgment that will happen soon (in this case the destruction of the Temple) is like the decisive judgment (the return of the Son of Man), so that one event anticipates the other. This kind of "pattern" prophecy is what we observe here, even though that pattern was not clear to the listeners. So Jesus said that when these things begin to happen (as with budding figs in March/April), the end is approaching (just as the tree fully blooms in May/June).

Jesus then said, "When you see all these things taking place, you can know that his return is very near, right at the door" (13:29). Jesus thus completed the comparison. It is less than clear whether "these things" refer to the beginning of the discourse and the false claimants or to the things that complete it, such as the abomination and especially the cosmic signs. Probably the latter events are included, which also explains why the NLT has added the reference to "all" these things. The rationale for this choice is that the appearing of the Son of Man at the end is portrayed as obvious, as signaled by cosmic indicators. In addition, the emphasis is on the signs that let one know the end is near, not on the timing of the end. So the nearness is related especially to those events coming before the end. The NLT also renders "it" as a reference to the return. Possibly "it" means "he" and refers to the Son of Man, but this does not really change the basic meaning of the passage.

Following this, Jesus made the bold assertion that "this generation will not pass from the scene before all these things take place." The Greek term for "generation" (*genea* [TG1074, ZG1155]) can refer to (1) a given generation, which might extend forty years or so, (2) a given age, speaking of a broader period, or (3) a given group of people (ethnic or ethical) such as a nation or a righteous or wicked generation (see BDAG 191-192, where the "wicked" generation is discussed in point 2). If the term is temporal and refers to the generation Jesus addressed, then the return did not happen for that group (unless one reads the verse as heavily symbolic of the destruction of Jerusalem as France 2002:501-502 and Lane 1974:480 do). Other suggestions are also made: (1) The generation referred to is the one that sees the abomination of desolation. Once that event occurs, things happen very quickly. "Generation" does not refer to a given temporal group or to the generation of the disciples addressed, but it is the group that sees the "great tribulation" events that are just before the end. (2) The generation may be a positive ethical reference, so that it is the "righteous" generation that will not pass away before all this takes place. In this case, the point is that the righteous will ultimately be vindicated. The problem with this option is that this is a very rare use of the term. (3) The term could refer to the "wicked" generation, in which case the point is that wickedness will remain until the judgment comes. This is the more common ethical use of the term, but it seems to state the obvious (Evans 2001:335 apparently takes this view). (4) A few take the term as referring to a race and to Israel on the basis of usage such as that in Luke 16:8. However, this ethnic use of the term for Israel is not common. (5) "All these things" refers to the signs Jesus has listed that point to the end rather than the events of the end. Thus, the current generation would see all the signs pointing to the end (the events of AD 70) as a guarantee that the events of the end will occur as Jesus predicts, though the end itself would come after the current generation.

Of these five readings, the first three and the last are all possible, with the first being slightly more likely than the second or third, since this temporal use of the term is more common and fits contextually with the call to understand when the abomination occurs. The fifth view underscores the logic of why Jesus would point to "all these things," not to describe end time events, but to reveal how quickly the signs pointing to the end would come. I think that views one and five are the most likely, and it is hard to choose between them. According to view one, once the abomination (such as that done by Antiochus, not the Temple's destruction in AD 70) takes place, the vindication of the saints in the return of the Son of Man to earth is not far away. In view five, the events point to the end as signs; they connect with the Temple's destruction in AD 70 and therefore take place within a generation.

In summary, this discourse indicates that Israel will be judged; it will be a hard time for those present because of persecution, and the Temple will be destroyed. But this discourse, subject to so much discussion, does not merely deal with the destruction of the Temple. It also pictures a time when the Temple will be desecrated by one standing in the Holy Place; there will be a period of unprecedented persecution, and then the Son of Man will return to judge the world. Because of its typological or pattern-acts structure, it can be hard to tell if the nearer destruction or the more distant return is in view. Various scenarios have been considered as possible chronologies for the events. Some argue that the passage only treats AD 70, or at least substantially so. However, this does not address the Son of Man's return, and to argue that only 13:32-37 deal with that future theme makes the discourse too disjointed. It is better to recognize the "pattern" in the discourse. "Pattern prophecy" is typical of Old Testament discussions of the Day of the Lord (more clearly seen now than when originally given). In this type of utterance, a judgment in the short term pictures or patterns a greater judgment to come at the end. The way that things happen in AD 70 anticipates how they will happen at the end. So to talk about one period is to also mirror or pattern the other. Jesus wove the two together here because their nature will be similar. (Matthew's version of the speech makes this somewhat clearer by separating the question of the Temple's destruction from that of the Lord's return. Luke does the same. What is clear in Matthew and Luke is that the events covered by the entire speech stretch from the time of Jesus' disciples through the destruction of the Temple until the return. It is not a discourse strictly about the period just before Jesus' return.) In this context, the unprecedented level of persecution and the return to gather the elect make sense because the passage ultimately looks at the vindication of the elect and at God's promise to judge the earth, predictions whose promises go back into the Old Testament (which is why I have noted the numerous thematic connections to OT and Jewish expression).

Jesus portrayed the events of the end as completing the hopes of the law and the prophets. Some call this period the "great tribulation," which reflects the unprecedented chaos of the period. Some connect this period to Daniel's seventieth week, making the most intense period seven years long. This is likely, though less certain. Other interpreters simply speak of an unprecedented time of chaos ending in Jesus' return. Either way, the point is the decisive vindication of the elect that emerges at the return. The key point of the text is that disciples need to remain faithful until Jesus' return, keeping watch for indications that the Son of Man is coming.

◆ **C. King of the Jews Executed for Blasphemy, Confessed as God's Son, and Vindicated by God (14:1-16:8)**
   1. The plot to arrest Jesus (14:1-2; cf. Matt 26:1-5; Luke 21:37-22:1-2)

It was now two days before Passover and the Festival of Unleavened Bread. The leading priests and the teachers of religious law were still looking for an opportunity to capture Jesus secretly and kill him. ²"But not during the Passover celebration," they agreed, "or the people may riot."

NOTES

14:1 *two days before Passover.* The 12th or 13th of Nisan (depending on whether Mark is including Passover day in his count or not), which fell in April/May of the Roman calendar. Passover and Unleavened Bread occurred together (Nisan 14–21; for Passover, see Exod 12:1-14, 21-51; Lev 23:4-5; Num 9:1-14; 28:16; Deut 16:1-7; for Unleavened Bread, see Exod 12:15-20; 13:6-10; 34:18; Lev 23:6-8; Num 28:16-25; Deut 16:3-4, 8).

were still looking for an opportunity to capture Jesus secretly and kill him. Jesus' remarks and actions in Jerusalem had led to the leadership's decision to stop Jesus (on the leadership's role, see 8:31; 10:33; 11:18, 27; 14:43, 53; 15:1). The only question was how and when, given how many people were in the city. They hoped to get him by stealth (*dolō* [TG1388, ZG1515]), and Passover was a difficult time to do this.

14:2 *the people may riot.* This riot could have been like the one Josephus notes in *Antiquities* 17.213-215 in 4 BC, or like the scene in Acts 21:34, which is also called by the term Mark uses here, *thorubos* [TG2351, ZG2573].

COMMENTARY

The timing of these events is given specifically. We are in the middle of the last week of Jesus' life, very shortly before Passover (see note on 14:1). These holidays celebrated the deliverance of the nation. According to some estimates, the population of Jerusalem quadrupled during this time. France suggests some 180,000 present, but for others the likely number is 125,000 (France 2002:548; Lane 1974:490 speaks of 50,000-250,000). The religious leaders decided that they could not arrest Jesus during the Passover. Jesus was too popular with the people and a riot might bring in the Romans and make the situation too volatile.

These two short verses set the stage for the passion events. They show the leaders as plotting but still at a loss. They thought that the Passover was not the right time to arrest Jesus. However, soon Judas would cause them to think differently and act quickly.

Here we again observe Mark structuring another sandwiched sequence, with the anointing placed between the two halves of Judas's betrayal to contrast the two. The anointing by the woman shows Jesus being honored in the midst of a move to reject Jesus.

◆   ## 2. The anointing at Bethany (14:3-9; cf. Matt 26:6-13; John 12:2-11)

³Meanwhile, Jesus was in Bethany at the home of Simon, a man who had previously had leprosy. While he was eating,* a woman came in with a beautiful alabaster jar of expensive perfume made from essence of nard. She broke open the jar and poured the perfume over his head.

⁴Some of those at the table were indignant. "Why waste such expensive perfume?" they asked. ⁵"It could have been sold for a year's wages* and the money given to the poor!" So they scolded her harshly.

⁶But Jesus replied, "Leave her alone. Why criticize her for doing such a good thing to me? ⁷You will always have the poor among you, and you can help them whenever you want to. But you will not always have me. ⁸She has done what she could and has anointed my body for burial ahead of time. ⁹I tell you the truth, wherever the Good News is preached throughout the world, this woman's deed will be remembered and discussed."

14:3 Or *reclining.*   14:5 Greek *for 300 denarii.* A denarius was equivalent to a laborer's full day's wage.

NOTES

14:3 *Simon, a man who had previously had leprosy.* This detail makes this event distinct from Luke 7:36-50, where Pharisees were present. They would never have been with a leper and would have been slow to associate with one whose main association had been with leprosy (on a lack of clarity as to Simon the leper's state at the time of this meal, see Gundry 1993:812). It is possible the home was associated with him and yet he was not present at the meal. If so, Pharisees would not seek out a home where leprosy was or perhaps had been recently present. The NLT rendering assumes a cure has already taken place, which also is possible. What is important to Mark is the association of the locale with one known as a leper. The detail shows that Jesus continued to socialize with those on the fringes of society.

14:5 *"sold for a year's wages . . . given to the poor!" So they scolded her harshly.* The Gr. refers to "three hundred denarii," which was about a year's wage. The poor were especially remembered at Passover time (John 13:27-29; Lane 1974:493). Those complaining did not appreciate the woman's action and told her so.

14:6 *Leave her alone. Why criticize her for doing such a good thing to me?* Jesus came to her defense. He described her act as a good thing (Gr., "good work").

14:7 *You will always have the poor among you.* Jesus' remark on the poor comes from Deut 15:11 (Hurtado 1989:232).

14:8 *She has . . . anointed my body for burial ahead of time.* The verb for anointing here is *murizō* [TG3462, ZG3690], its only use in the NT; it speaks of anointing a corpse according to Jewish custom (*m. Shabbat* 23:5; BDAG 661). This verb is related to the noun for myrrh and points to anointing with perfume.

COMMENTARY

This event seems to parallel John 12:1-8, although John places this event six days before Passover. It may be that Mark moved the event into the last week sequence because its outcome, Judas' betrayal, came in the time frame of the final few days.

While Jesus was eating, "a woman came in with a beautiful alabaster jar of expensive perfume" (14:3). The woman's alabaster jar and perfume, which Mark names as nard (Lane 1974:492), were worth a great deal of money, up to a year's wages (14:5). The woman poured it out on Jesus to anoint and honor him (2 Kgs 9:6 has an event like this involving Jehu). The reaction to this act tells us this was no common anointing. The woman broke the flask and emptied it—her offering was total, sparing nothing.

Some observers of this event were furious and said that the nard had been wasted, as it could have been sold and the money given to the poor. Jesus responded, "You will always have the poor among you. . . . But you will not always have me." They could take care of the poor later, as the poor would always be around.

The woman was more sensitive than anyone around her, whether she intended this as an anointing for Jesus' death or whether Jesus assigned this significance to her act (Hurtado 1989:229-230). Jesus said, "This woman's deed will be remembered" and thereby memorialized it. He noted that her act would be recalled as an appropriate way to have honored Jesus by all who preach the gospel. It was appropriate to sacrifice this perfume worth a year's wage because Jesus was worthy of such honor.

◆   ### 3. Judas betrays Jesus (14:10-11; cf. Matt 26:14-16; Luke 22:3-6)

¹⁰Then Judas Iscariot, one of the twelve disciples, went to the leading priests to arrange to betray Jesus to them. ¹¹They were delighted when they heard why he had come, and they promised to give him money. So he began looking for an opportunity to betray Jesus.

NOTES
14:10 to betray Jesus to them. Judas decided to hand Jesus over to the leading priests. The Gr. verb for "betray" (*paradidōmi* [ᵀᴳ3860, ᶻᴳ4140]) appears here and in 14:11, 18, 21, 41, 42, 44. Thus, betrayal is a major feature of the description of Judas' action. It is the same verb used by Jesus in his predictions (9:31; 10:33).

14:11 they promised to give him money. Matthew 26:15 notes that the reward was thirty pieces of silver.

COMMENTARY
The religious leaders who wanted to arrest Jesus had thought that they could not do it during Passover because the people might riot. Their plans changed when Judas entered the picture. They were delighted that Judas approached them, because they could claim that Jesus' activities had been exposed by one of his own. They could say, "We were just doing our duty." They also had a chance to seize him away from the crowd.

In all of this, Jesus is depicted as the righteous sufferer (Ps 41:9; Lane 1974:495), for his death is triggered by one of his own. The doors were now open for Jesus' arrest. Mark sets the Last Supper in the context of this betrayal. None of this caught Jesus by surprise, for he knew what was about to happen.

◆ ## 4. The Last Supper (14:12-26; cf. Matt 26:17-30; Luke 22:7-20; John 13:21-30)

¹²On the first day of the Festival of Unleavened Bread, when the Passover lamb is sacrificed, Jesus' disciples asked him, "Where do you want us to go to prepare the Passover meal for you?"

¹³So Jesus sent two of them into Jerusalem with these instructions: "As you go into the city, a man carrying a pitcher of water will meet you. Follow him. ¹⁴At the house he enters, say to the owner, 'The Teacher asks: Where is the guest room where I can eat the Passover meal with my disciples?' ¹⁵He will take you upstairs to a large room that is already set up. That is where you should prepare our meal." ¹⁶So the two disciples went into the city and found everything just as Jesus had said, and they prepared the Passover meal there.

¹⁷In the evening Jesus arrived with the twelve disciples.* ¹⁸As they were at the table* eating, Jesus said, "I tell you the truth, one of you eating with me here will betray me."

¹⁹Greatly distressed, each one asked in turn, "Am I the one?"

²⁰He replied, "It is one of you twelve who is eating from this bowl with me. ²¹For the Son of Man* must die, as the Scriptures declared long ago. But how terrible it will be for the one who betrays him. It would be far better for that man if he had never been born!"

²²As they were eating, Jesus took some bread and blessed it. Then he broke it in pieces and gave it to the disciples, saying, "Take it, for this is my body."

²³And he took a cup of wine and gave thanks to God for it. He gave it to them, and they all drank from it. ²⁴And he said to them, "This is my blood, which confirms the covenant* between God and his people. It is poured out as a sacrifice for many. ²⁵I tell you the truth, I will not drink wine again until the day I drink it new in the Kingdom of God."

²⁶Then they sang a hymn and went out to the Mount of Olives.

14:17 Greek *the Twelve.* 14:18 Or *As they reclined.* 14:21 "Son of Man" is a title Jesus used for himself. 14:24 Some manuscripts read *the new covenant.*

NOTES

14:12 *Where do you want us to go to prepare the Passover meal?* Mark notes that this conversation took place on the first day of the Festival of Unleavened Bread. This description reflects the fact that Passover and Unleavened Bread (which followed it immediately) were treated as one holiday season (so Josephus *War* 5.99). So the day is Passover night-day, when the Passover lamb was sacrificed. For the details of a Passover meal, see *m. Pesahim* 10:1-7; other elements of procuring the sacrifice are in *m. Pesahim* 1:1-3.

14:13 *a man carrying a pitcher of water will meet you.* This key instruction communicated Jesus' awareness of events. He knew where the meal would be held and how the disciples could meet the person who would arrange it.

14:14 *The Teacher asks.* The second key instruction was about the owner of the room. All that would be needed was to indicate that "the Teacher" had a need and the room would be provided. It was there that they would eat the Passover meal.

14:15 *to a large room.* Since this "large upper room" was already prepared for the meal, it appears that Jesus had already planned for the meal to be in this place.

14:16 *So the two disciples went . . . and found everything just as Jesus had said.* Jesus was very aware of what was taking place. The disciples prepared the meal in this room.

14:17 *In the evening.* Mark makes it clear that this was an evening meal like a Passover meal (Exod 12:8). Normal meals started earlier. If this was a Passover meal, it would have four courses/cups and last until almost midnight (see *m. Pesahim* 10:1-6, 9; Lane 1974:501-502). The four cups occur (1) with the preliminary course to bless the Passover day, (2) after an explaination of Passover and the singing of some of the Hallel psalms [Pss 113–118], (3) following the meal of lamb, unleavened bread, and bitter herbs, and (4) following the concluding portion of the Hallel (Bock 1996:1722-1723). It is not clear which cup exactly is meant given that only one cup is mentioned in Matthew and Mark (while Luke mentions two). However, an early cup is likely with the bread being a part of the third course.

14:19 *Greatly distressed, each one asked in turn, "Am I the one?"* The disciples understood; in distress, each inquired if it might be he. A narrative gap that the reading urges us to fill is what it must have been like for Judas, as each one around the room asked the question. The question is asked in Gr. with an interrogative that expects a negative reply. Each of them was seeking assurance that he was not the one.

14:20 *It is one of you twelve who is eating from this bowl with me.* Jesus indicated that the candidate was one of those around him, sharing his bowl. The Passover meal had a common bowl, probably the one in which the sauce for the bitter herbs was placed (Cranfield 1959:424).

14:21 *For the Son of Man must die, as the Scriptures declared long ago. But how terrible it will be for the one who betrays him.* Divine design and human accountability come together here. The Gr. says that the Son of Man "goes as it is written of him," a theme introduced earlier in Mark (8:31; 9:12). The NLT's "how terrible" concretely conveys the meaning of the "woe" Jesus uttered about the fate of his betrayer (on "woe," see EDNT 540). The mention of Scripture in connection with Jesus' inevitable death echoes texts like Luke 24:43-47 and 1 Cor 15:1-3.

14:23 *he took a cup of wine.* It is not clear which cup of the meal this was, but the purpose of the third cup was to praise God for bringing salvation to his people, so it is a possible candidate according to Lane (1974:506). Others argue that it was an earlier cup, assuming that the bread was a part of the meal after the second cup. Both views assume that a Passover meal was being celebrated. It is hard to know which cup is meant. Luke indicates that Jesus had multiple cups but refused to drink after this cup was taken, leaving his final cup of the meal untouched. France (2002:569) sees this as possible.

14:24 *This is my blood, which confirms the covenant between God and his people. It is poured out as a sacrifice for many.* The NLT has a good explanatory rendering of the Gr., which reads, "This is my blood of the covenant, which is poured out for the many." "The many" are those who believe in Jesus. Evans (2001:386-387) suggests precedent for such thinking in Judaism from 4 Macc 1:11b; 17:21b-22; 18:3-4; 2 Macc 7:33, 37-38; *Testament of Moses* 9:6b–10:1; *Liber antiquitatum biblicarum* 18:5; and other Jewish texts. He also notes (2001:390-391) how the breaking of the bread could suggest the hope of the Messiah; a portion of the unleavened bread eaten at Passover was known as the *afikomen* in reference to "the one who comes" (i.e. the Messiah). This symbolism, if it has such a background, would soften the image of eating the body and drinking the blood.

14:26 *they sang a hymn.* The Hallel psalms (Pss 113–118; Lane 1974:501-502) were sung at the Passover meal. As Jesus and his disciples proceeded to the Mount of Olives, they were singing these praises to God. Jesus' death would be painful, but God could be praised for what was about to occur.

COMMENTARY

There is a problem of chronology between the Synoptic Gospels and John's Gospel. Mark is clear that this was a Passover meal, while John suggests that the Passover lambs were sacrificed the next afternoon when Jesus was crucified (John 13:1; 18:28; 19:14, 31, 42). Various solutions to the problem have been proposed. (1) It is possible that John was discussing the sacrifices of the Passover season that were offered during the week (so argues Lane 1974:497-498). If this is correct, then both Gospels are right but are referring to different sacrifices of that holiday season. (2) Evans (2001:370-372) favors Jesus eating a solemn meal that still had a Passover feel by its being proximate to the Passover, while opting for John's chronology. (3) France (2002:559-562) argues that Mark and John are both correct in that Jesus presented the meal as if it were a Passover meal and that Mark was calculating days in a sunset to sunset mode, so that the sacrifice was made after sunset on the same night it was consumed and on the same day as the bulk of sacrifices for the Passover from the next afternoon. It is hard to be sure which view is correct, although France's view may have the most merit.

As the meal begins, a powerful juxtaposition emerges. One of his own would betray Jesus, in an act of treachery designed to derail him. Jesus bluntly said, "One of you eating with me here will betray me" (14:18). Jesus knew what was taking place. The announcement adds a somber tone to the meal, making it clear to the disciples later that Jesus was not caught off guard and that he hadn't made any attempt to stop what was taking place. Thus Jesus said, "For the Son of Man must die, as the Scripture declared long ago. But how terrible it will be for the one who betrays him" (14:21). Divine design and human accountability come together here. There was a divine plan that the chosen judge must suffer first, but the one who betrayed him was responsible for his actions. Jesus said, "It would be far better for that man if he had never been born!" Here is a declaration of judgment. Judas had met the Lord, ministered at his side, and made a decision that Jesus was not who he claimed to be. To betray the Son of Man to whom God gives authority is the most calamitous error.

The scene then shifts to what is known as the "Last Supper." "Jesus took some bread and blessed it . . . broke it . . . and gave it to the disciples, saying, 'Take it, for this is my body' " (14:22). Jesus made the meal into something about himself, which shows his personal authority. Especially if this is the Passover meal, it shows that Jesus could associate himself with the most sacred liturgical parts of Judaism and transform them. Even if the meal only evoked the Passover, the same point is implied (Hooker 1991:341). In the Passover meal, this would be the bread of affliction (Hooker 1991:340; but see discussion of 14:24 for another possible option for Passover background). Placed in a Passover context, this imagery would be very explicit. Jesus pointed to another time of suffering.

Jesus took the unleavened bread and symbolically associated it with his body. What had referred to the deliverance from Egypt now referred to a new deliverance (*m. Pesahim* 10:5). Their partaking of the bread identified them with Jesus and with what Jesus was about to do for them in his death. The idea here is not very different from John's image of Jesus as the "bread of life" (John 6:16-59).

Then Jesus "took a cup of wine . . . gave thanks . . . gave it to them, and they all drank from it. And he said to them, 'This is my blood, which confirms the covenant between God and his people. It is poured out as a sacrifice for many' " (14:23-24). Drinking the cup signified this relationship and associated it with the "pouring out" of Jesus' very life as a sacrifice that established fresh covenantal grounds for relationship to God. The symbolic drinking of blood was a shocking image that indicated the unusual nature of the sacrifice. The "blood of the covenant" evokes Exodus 24:6 in a fresh way. The parallel in Luke 22:20 names this as the "new" covenant, with its provision of forgiveness and the law written "on their hearts," the inner work of God through the Spirit (Jer 31:31-33). "Many" indicates that the work is not applied to all, but only to those who associate themselves with Jesus' work by faith (evoking Isa 53:11-12; Mark 10:45).

At the end of the meal Jesus said, "I will not drink wine again until the day I drink it new in the Kingdom of God" (14:25). Here Jesus looked to the consummation that his death would provide. There would be a banquet celebration to recreate this meal in the Kingdom (Isa 25:6; Matt 8:11; Luke 14:15; Rev 19:9) and he looked forward to that day. The church's celebration at the Lord's Table also looks forward to that day, as we proclaim "the Lord's death until he comes again" (1 Cor 11:26). There will be a period of great celebration when Jesus' work is complete.

The Last Supper portrays the disciples' connection with Jesus' death. By partaking of bread and drinking the wine, the participants identified with Jesus' death to the core of their being. Passover yields to Calvary as deliverance comes again. Those who realize it are born again into a relationship of divine forgiveness and enablement though the gift of the Spirit to indwell and empower the person to righteousness. That is what Jesus saw in the meal. As the book of Hebrews later puts it, it was for the joy set before him that he endured the shame of the cross (Heb 12:2). The meal celebrates the pain he took to get to the joy.

The church has debated how the symbolism of this sacred meal works. Do the bread and wine actually become the body and blood of Jesus in a mysterious transformation, as Roman Catholicism teaches (known as transubstanitiation)? Or, is the presence of Jesus somehow all around the elements without physically changing them as Luther argued (consubstantiation)? Or is the meal merely a symbolic memorial, with the language and ritual intended to picture Jesus' work, as many other movements of the Reformation, such as that of Zwingli, argued (memorial view)? The text of this scene does not answer such questions but a view close to the second seems most likely: Both of the first two views argue that when Jesus said the bread and wine were his body and blood, he was using the language of liturgical mystery rather than mere symbolism, yet the idea of the elements becoming Christ seems too crass. It is clear that something makes this meal very sacred, yet the Old Testament prescribes acts that are rich in significant symbolism. What can be affirmed, regardless of the view taken, is that Jesus changed the liturgy of events tied to the Exodus and reimaged them to apply to himself. His presence at this sacred meal as the church regularly observes it is certain.

◆ **5. Peter's denials predicted (14:27-31; cf. Matt 26:31-35; Luke 22:31-38; John 13:31-38)**

²⁷On the way, Jesus told them, "All of you will desert me. For the Scriptures say,

'God will strike* the Shepherd,
    and the sheep will be scattered.'

²⁸But after I am raised from the dead, I will go ahead of you to Galilee and meet you there."

²⁹Peter said to him, "Even if everyone else deserts you, I never will."

³⁰Jesus replied, "I tell you the truth, Peter—this very night, before the rooster crows twice, you will deny three times that you even know me."

³¹"No!" Peter declared emphatically. "Even if I have to die with you, I will never deny you!" And all the others vowed the same.

14:27 Greek *I will strike.* Zech 13:7.

NOTES

14:27 *All of you will desert me.* Jesus predicted that in his death he would go to the cross alone. The disciples stumbled by taking offense over him. The verb is *skandalizomai* [ᵀᴳ4624A, ᶻᴳ4997]. It was used of those who took offense or fell away (4:17; 9:42, 43, 45, 47; 14:29).

For the Scriptures say, 'God will strike the Shepherd, and the sheep will be scattered.' Jesus cited Zech 13:7, which looks to Israel's apostasy; this is a strong condemnation. The NLT renders the Gr., "I will strike," with "God will strike," making the speaker clear (see NLT mg).

14:29 *Even if everyone else deserts you, I never will.* In this remark, Peter claimed that he would not run away out of fear. This showed that he did not know himself or the situation as well as Jesus did. This is the third time Peter has misspoken in Mark (8:31-33; 9:5-7).

14:30 *this very night, before the rooster crows twice, you will deny three times that you even know me.* Jesus knew Peter well in general, and he was specifically aware of what he would do and when. Before the early morning cock crowing was complete, Peter would deny Jesus three times. The NLT explains the term correctly by noting that Peter would deny knowing Jesus (Evans 2001:402). It was the opposite of confessing someone (Luke 12:8-9). The entire scene shows that Jesus was quite aware of what was happening.

14:31 *Even if I have to die with you, I will never deny you!* Once again, Peter claimed that he would stand with Jesus even to the death. This time he said it more emphatically, using a double negative (*ou mē* [ᵀᴳ3364, ᶻᴳ4024 + 3590]) to make the point. As he commonly did, Mark not only noted the remark, but also the emphatic manner in which it was given. The others joined in support of his claim.

COMMENTARY

This section begins with Jesus telling his disciples that he will die alone—bereft of their support. Citing Zechariah 13:7, Jesus predicted, "God will strike the Shepherd, and the sheep will be scattered." In the crucifixion, God chose to offer his son, the shepherd, for sacrifice. The Zechariah text focuses on the cleansing of God's people that results from the striking of the shepherd. At the moment that the Shepherd suffers, the sheep scatter, sensing that they are not protected. In fact, Jesus' death is the very protection that they need, as suggested by the mention of the resurrection in the next verse.

Jesus then promised them, "After I am raised from the dead, I will go ahead of you to Galilee and meet you there" (14:28). Jesus reassured the disciples that their scattering would be temporary. After his resurrection, he would meet them in Galilee, the very place where his ministry began. It is sometimes said that Mark has no resurrection appearances. However, in its prediction about Jesus, this text indicates that Mark was aware of such events even though his short ending does not narrate a specific appearance (see also 16:7).

When Jesus predicted that the disciples would desert him, Peter affirmed that he would never desert Jesus. Peter did not understand himself or what was coming. The other disciples also affirmed their loyalty, but Jesus knew what would happen, for he understood how weak people can be. Peter's bold assertions and subsequent failure make him look very weak and foolish. That this failure is recorded in the Gospels shows that this is authentic history; the early church would not make up such a story about its leaders.

◆   ## 6. Jesus at Gethsemane (14:32-42; cf. Matt 26:36-46; Luke 22:39-46)

³²They went to the olive grove called Gethsemane, and Jesus said, "Sit here while I go and pray." ³³He took Peter, James, and John with him, and he became deeply troubled and distressed. ³⁴He told them, "My soul is crushed with grief to the point of death. Stay here and keep watch with me."

³⁵He went on a little farther and fell to the ground. He prayed that, if it were possible, the awful hour awaiting him might pass him by. ³⁶"Abba, Father,"* he cried out, "everything is possible for you. Please take this cup of suffering away from me. Yet I want your will to be done, not mine."

³⁷Then he returned and found the disciples asleep. He said to Peter, "Simon, are you asleep? Couldn't you watch with me even one hour? ³⁸Keep watch and pray, so that you will not give in to temptation. For the spirit is willing, but the body is weak."

³⁹Then Jesus left them again and prayed the same prayer as before. ⁴⁰When he returned to them again, he found them sleeping, for they couldn't keep their eyes open. And they didn't know what to say.

⁴¹When he returned to them the third time, he said, "Go ahead and sleep. Have your rest. But no—the time has come. The Son of Man is betrayed into the hands of sinners. ⁴²Up, let's be going. Look, my betrayer is here!"

14:36 Abba is an Aramaic term for "father."

NOTES

14:32 *Gethsemane.* Gethsemane was located in an orchard of olive trees in the Kidron Valley outside the eastern wall of Jerusalem below the Mount of Olives. The name means "oil press."

Sit here while I go and pray. Mark often shows Jesus praying or teaching about prayer (1:35; 6:46; 9:29; 11:17; 11:24-25; 13:18).

14:33 *took Peter, James, and John.* This inner circle was included once again (5:37; 9:2; 13:3).

deeply troubled and distressed. Mark again notes Jesus' emotions. The two verbs are quite vivid; the first (*ekthambeisthai* [TG1568, ZG1701]) speaks of intense perplexity or excitement (BDAG 303), and only Mark uses the term (9:15; 16:5-6). The related, less intense verb *thambeō* [TG2284, ZG2501] also appears only in Mark (1:27; 10:24, 32). The second verb in the verse (*adēmoneō* [TG85, ZG86]) refers to distress or anxiety (BDAG 19) and also appears rarely in the NT (Matt 26:37; Phil 2:26).

14:34 *My soul is crushed with grief.* The key term is *perilupos* [TG4036, ZG4337], which refers to intense grief or sorrow (6:26; Luke 18:23; BDAG 802). Jesus acknowledged his emotion as he began to pray. Scripture is forthright about Jesus' human reactions to what he was about to face.

to the point of death. This conceptually alludes to Ps 42:5-6, 9, 12, which looks to a deliverance from God and calls for waiting on God (cf. Sir 37:2).

keep watch with me. Jesus asked the disciples to be alert, much as he had told them to be watchful about future events (13:37).

14:35 *He prayed that, if it were possible, the awful hour awaiting him might pass him by.* Jesus' initial request was that the upcoming "hour" might not take place but pass him by. The NLT adds an adjective describing the hour as an "awful" one, since a painful crucifixion and death awaited him.

14:36 *Abba, Father.* The opening of the prayer is intense, as indicated by the double reference to the Father, first in Aramaic and then in Gr. (Rom 8:15-16; Gal 4:6).

everything is possible for you. Jesus began by acknowledging God's sovereignty and power as the basis for his request.

Please take this cup of suffering away from me. Jesus requests that "this cup" be removed. The NLT defines it as a cup of suffering, since death was in view. However, the specific reference might have been to the judgment and wrath Jesus would experience on behalf of others, since a cup often represents God's judgment (10:38-39; Isa 51:17, 22; Ezek 23:32-34; Lam 4:21; Ps 11:6 [10:6 LXX]; *Martyrdom of the Ascension of Isaiah* 5:13; *Martyrdom of Polycarp* 14:2; TDNT 6:152-153).

14:39 *Jesus left them again and prayed the same prayer.* The Gr. says that Jesus "said the same word."

14:41 *But no—the time has come. The Son of Man is betrayed into the hands of sinners.* The verb for betrayal is the one Mark has used throughout (*paradidōmi* [TG3860, ZG4140]). The NLT phrase "but no" translates an enigmatic use of *apechei* [TG566, ZG600]. Many translations render the term with "it is enough," according to one of its less common uses. This would express Jesus' sense that his time to pray and urge them to pray had run out. The verb more often refers to things that are settled, such as bank accounts, but even this use is rare (France 2002:589). Evans (2001:416-417) suggests an ambiguous "Is it far off?" with the referent left unclear (sleep, or more probably, betrayal). Regardless, the "hour" (so the Gr. *hōra* [TG5610, ZG6052]) had come, and it was time for the betrayer to act.

COMMENTARY

No passage shows the human side of Jesus more vividly than this text. He openly came to grips with death, asked to bypass it, and then expressed his submission to the Father's will. He first asked that the cup of suffering—even the cup of God's wrath—pass from him. Jesus knew that drinking the cup meant taking God's judgment and wrath upon himself on behalf of others (see note on 14:36). Knowing that he could not escape this, he told the Father, "I want your will to be done, not mine" (14:36). The spirit and example of this prayer express Jesus' submission to the Father's will. This attitude is reflected in the prayer Jesus gave to the disciples, "Your will be done on earth as in heaven."

As Jesus prayed to bring himself into submission to the Father's will, the disciples fell asleep. He came to them and asked, "Couldn't you watch with me even one hour?" (14:37). That Peter and the others failed to stay awake suggests their lack of preparation for what was to come. Jesus told them, "Keep watch and pray, so you will not give in to temptation" (14:38). The disciples needed to prepare for the important spiritual battle ahead, and even at this late point in the Gospel, the disciples still had much to learn. Temptation to sin must be met with prayer. Jesus told them, "The spirit is willing, but the body is weak" (14:38). This saying expresses well the status of Peter and the others. They may have desired to be faithful and stand with Jesus, but fear would overtake them as they sought to preserve their lives. Jesus came to the disciples three times, and all three times they had failed to stay awake. Peter will fail three more times with his three denials. Jesus stood alone at the time of trial. On behalf of others, Jesus would drink the cup of suffering and punishment that God would send his way. He was ready as the betrayer approached.

◆   **7. Jesus is betrayed and arrested (14:43-52; cf. Matt 26:47-56; Luke 22:47-53; John 18:2-12)**

⁴³And immediately, even as Jesus said this, Judas, one of the twelve disciples, arrived with a crowd of men armed with swords and clubs. They had been sent by the leading priests, the teachers of religious law, and the elders. ⁴⁴The traitor, Judas, had given them a prearranged signal: "You will know which one to arrest when I greet him with a kiss. Then you can take him away under guard." ⁴⁵As soon as they arrived, Judas walked up to Jesus. "Rabbi!" he exclaimed, and gave him the kiss.

⁴⁶Then the others grabbed Jesus and arrested him. ⁴⁷But one of the men with Jesus pulled out his sword and struck the high priest's slave, slashing off his ear.

⁴⁸Jesus asked them, "Am I some dangerous revolutionary, that you come with swords and clubs to arrest me? ⁴⁹Why didn't you arrest me in the Temple? I was there among you teaching every day. But these things are happening to fulfill what the Scriptures say about me."

⁵⁰Then all his disciples deserted him and ran away. ⁵¹One young man following behind was clothed only in a long linen shirt. When the mob tried to grab him, ⁵²he slipped out of his shirt and ran away naked.

NOTES

14:43 *Judas, one of the twelve disciples, arrived with a crowd of men armed with swords and clubs. They had been sent by the leading priests, the teachers of religious law, and the elders.* In his betrayal, Judas was supported by a host of armed men sent by the Jewish leaders. Mark gives no specifics as to who they were, making them sound like rabble rousers (Hooker 1991:351; Taylor 1966:558 speaks of hired rabble, but Luke 22:52 and John 18:3, 12 make it clear that some law and order officials from the Temple and from the Romans were present). The temple guards were probably Levites, but they may have employed others who wished to help (Lane 1974:524 speaks of accompanying court attendants). Josephus notes that such a group appeared later to help the priests quell a disturbance (*Antiquities* 20.181, 206–207; see Evans 2001:423). Short swords (*machairōn* [TG3162, ZG3479]) and clubs were the weapons of choice.

14:46 *grabbed Jesus and arrested him.* They "grabbed" him and "arrested" him. Jesus now submitted to the hands of sinners (14:41).

14:47 *slashing off his ear.* One of the disciples (identified in John 18:10 as Simon Peter) fought. Luke tells us that Jesus healed the servant's ear. Unlike the other Gospels, Mark does not record any rebuke of the disciples here.

14:49 *Why didn't you arrest me in the Temple?* Jesus points out that this arrest could have been made publicly, but they chose to do it by stealth. This was a very "undercover" arrest.

But these things are happening to fulfill what the Scriptures say about me. Jesus noted that these events came as no surprise, but were part of a plan to fulfill Scripture. The Gr. lacks an opening clause to introduce the *hina* [TG2443, ZG2671] phrase, but rhetorically it is a declaration like the NLT rendering (France 2002:595).

14:52 *ran away naked.* Some suggest an allusion to the naked man fleeing in Amos 2:16, where the judgment was so great that the mighty could only flee naked (Lane 1974:527). Evans (2001:428) argues that the LXX speaks of the naked man as being pursued, not fleeing, and that it is not clear that the naked man was among the mighty. France (2002:596) also doubts an allusion to Amos; the matter is not at all clear.

COMMENTARY

Judas' presence allowed the religious leaders to meet Jesus away from the crowd. However, they were not sure how the disciples might respond, so they came prepared for battle. When Judas approached, he betrayed Jesus with a kiss, ironically twisting a sign of friendship and devotion into an act of denial. The kiss ensured that the right person would be arrested by the armed men who did not know Jesus or could not recognize him in the dark. To make matters worse, Judas called him "Rabbi!" This title means "teacher" (9:5; 10:51; 11:21), but what Judas did here, he did not learn from Jesus.

Jesus asked those who came to arrest him, "Am I some dangerous revolutionary?" (*lēstēs* [TG3027, ZG3334]; 14:48). Jesus asked if he had shown any indications of being an insurgent or robber who was worthy of an arrest with swords and clubs. This is ironic in light of Jesus' charge of 11:17. The robbers of the Temple arrested the deliverer as though he were a robber. After his arrest, "all his disciples deserted him and ran away" (14:50). Just as Jesus predicted in 14:27, the sheep scattered when the shepherd was struck.

The passage ends with one curious detail: "One young man following behind was clothed only in a long linen shirt. When the mob tried to grab him, he slipped out of his shirt and ran away naked" (14:51-52). The identity of this figure has been repeatedly discussed, especially given the vividness of the detail and its seeming unrelatedness to the main line of the story. Was this one showing courage in trying not to flee or was he coming to warn Jesus? Tradition has suggested that this might be Mark, a witness to the events described, but the young man is not identified. Taylor (1966:652) speaks only of an eyewitness known to Mark. It is clear, nonetheless, that the event made an impression on Mark. With this disciple's naked flight, all the disciples had abandoned Jesus and left him alone.

◆   8. The Jewish leaders examine Jesus (14:53-65; cf. Matt 26:57-68;
     Luke 22:54)

⁵³They took Jesus to the high priest's home where the leading priests, the elders, and the teachers of religious law had gathered. ⁵⁴Meanwhile, Peter followed him at a distance and went right into the high priest's courtyard. There he sat with the guards, warming himself by the fire.

⁵⁵Inside, the leading priests and the entire high council* were trying to find evidence against Jesus, so they could put him to death. But they couldn't find any. ⁵⁶Many false witnesses spoke against him, but they contradicted each other. ⁵⁷Finally, some men stood up and gave this false testimony: ⁵⁸"We heard him say, 'I will destroy this Temple made with human hands, and in three days I will build another, made without human hands.' " ⁵⁹But even then they didn't get their stories straight!

⁶⁰Then the high priest stood up before the others and asked Jesus, "Well, aren't you going to answer these charges? What do you have to say for yourself?" ⁶¹But Jesus was silent and made no reply. Then the high priest asked him, "Are you the Messiah, the Son of the Blessed One?"

⁶²Jesus said, "I AM.* And you will see the Son of Man seated in the place of power at God's right hand* and coming on the clouds of heaven.*"

⁶³Then the high priest tore his clothing to show his horror and said, "Why do we need other witnesses? ⁶⁴You have all heard his blasphemy. What is your verdict?"

"Guilty!" they all cried. "He deserves to die!"

⁶⁵Then some of them began to spit at him, and they blindfolded him and beat him with their fists. "Prophesy to us," they jeered. And the guards slapped him as they took him away.

14:55 Greek the Sanhedrin. 14:62a Or The 'I AM' is here; or I am the LORD. See Exod 3:14. 14:62b Greek at the right hand of the power. See Ps 110:1. 14:62c See Dan 7:13.

NOTES

14:53 *the leading priests, the elders, and the teachers of religious law had gathered.* The Jewish leaders that had made the arrest (14:43) gathered in the residence of the high priest Caiaphas to examine Jesus. Mark never names this high priest in his Gospel. He is named in John's Gospel (18:24). This event took place at night because, in part, the leadership wanted to deal with Jesus as quickly as possible. The event was really not a trial in the sense of seeking a verdict to determine a proper resolution. It was more like a grand jury investigation to gather facts that would allow the leadership to ask Rome to execute Jesus, something only Rome could legally do (for full background to this and a full defense of its historicity, see Bock 1998).

14:54 *Peter followed him at a distance.* Peter was trying to maintain his vow to stand with Jesus, but from a distance. He ended up by a fire in the courtyard of the high priest's home.

14:55 *the leading priests and the entire high council were trying to find evidence against Jesus, so they could put him to death. But they couldn't find any.* This was not a trial but more like a grand jury investigation, since the authority to put Jesus to death belonged to Rome. If the investigation worked like a legal scene, then *m. Sanhedrin* 4.3-4 gives the configuration: the members present sat in a semicircle, while minutes were taken by two clerks on each end. The witnesses and the accused sat in the middle (Lane 1974:532).

14:58 *Temple made with human hands.* "Made with human hands" often suggests something inadequate or less than holy (Lev 26:1, 30; Isa 2:18; 10:11; 19:1; 21:9; 31:7; Hurtado 1989:253). Only Mark has descriptions of the Temples made with and without hands.

Mark also uses a term (*naos* [TG3485, ZG3724]) that designates the sanctuary as the part of the Temple being discussed (France 2002:606).

14:60 *Well, aren't you going to answer these charges? What do you have to say for yourself?* The NLT's somewhat paraphrastic rendering brings out the emotional force of the high priest's query. After asking whether Jesus had anything to say in answer to the charges, he asked, "What is it these men testify against you?" The NLT rendering gives Jesus the opportunity to speak in his own defense.

14:61 *But Jesus was silent and made no reply.* Jesus made no reply to this process that had already determined what was going to happen. The situation recalls Isa 53:7.

Then the high priest asked him, "Are you the Messiah, the Son of the Blessed One?" The high priest asked Jesus if he were the Messiah, for this is what they needed to take before Pilate. If he made this confession, they could say he was claiming to be King of the Jews. For most Jews, the figure of the Son of Man would refer to a judge. Since that judgment would include the nations, it implied Jesus' kingship (Dan 7:9-27; *1 Enoch* 62:1-16; *Psalms of Solomon* 17–18). The final deliverer would be the Messiah, King of the Jews. Out of respect, the phrase "Son of the Blessed One," is used instead of naming God. Calling God blessed alluded to his uniqueness (*m. Berakhot* 7.3; *1 Enoch* 77:2).

14:62 *Jesus said, "I AM. And you will see the Son of Man seated in the place of power at God's right hand and coming on the clouds of heaven."* This reply is highly significant, for Jesus thus supplied the testimony that sent him to the cross, while laying out a choice before the council as to who he was. The Gr. is, "You will see the Son of Man sitting at the right hand of power." The NLT rendering obscures Jesus' choice to replace the high priest's euphemism with one of his own in order to communicate his own respect for God's name. To refer to God as "the power" invoked the kind of divine authority and power God exercised at the Exodus (*1 Enoch* 62:7; esp. *Sifre Numbers* §12 [on 15:31]; *b. Eruvin* 54b; *b. Yevamot* 105b).

14:63 *the high priest tore his clothing to show his horror.* This act showed that the high priest regarded Jesus' remarks as blasphemous. The NLT adds "show his horror." The Gr. does not have the phrase, but that emotion would have accompanied this act.

Why do we need other witnesses? The priest noted that Jesus had given them all they needed as testimony to take to Rome. Ironically, Jesus had provided the testimony the Jews could not supply themselves, and this testimony would send him to the cross. Jesus' reply—that he was their judge and would come with authority—identified him as the final deliverer, the Messiah, King of the Jews.

14:64 *You have all heard his blasphemy.* The priest specified that in their view, Jesus' crime was the slanderous dishonoring of God.

"What is your verdict?" "Guilty," they all cried. "He deserves to die." The leaders rendered their judgment—they would take Jesus to Pilate.

14:65 *Then some of them began to spit at him, and they blindfolded him and beat him with their fists. "Prophesy to us," they jeered. And the guards slapped him as they took him away.* Jesus was mocked by the soldiers and was treated with disrespect as they took him away.

COMMENTARY

The sources for this scene are often questioned, since Jesus was present without any of his disciples. But numerous sources could have supplied this information. Some of the council or some tied closely to it eventually supported Jesus (Joseph of Arimathea, Nicodemus, Paul). In addition, the public debate over Jesus' death would have surfaced the Jewish rationale for his death. Since this would have become public knowledge, sources existed beyond Jesus.

The Jewish leaders were seeking a charge that would yield a guilty verdict from the Romans. This was a gathering of the highest Jewish leaders, comprised of the chief priests and the Sanhedrin, the chief council of the Jews (*m. Sanhedrin* 1.6). Whether all seventy members were present, considering how fast the trial was assembled, is not clear (France 2002:603; Evans [2001:444] speaks of several members convening here). Surely a quorum was present; as a group, they sought charges against Jesus.

They were initially unable to find a charge that would stick because their witnesses did not agree. The leaders knew that if they took a charge to Rome, their testimony would have to be coherent. What they were gathering did not meet that standard and they knew it. They were violating the law they sought to defend (Exod 20:16). Though Mark's portrayal has the feel of a railroaded judgment, the leaders were trying to determine what might work and what was futile (see France 2002:604-605, who notes how Jeremiah barely escaped with his life when he spoke against the Temple as a precedent for the reaction; Jer 26:7-24).

Finally, some men stood up and gave this false testimony: "We heard him say, 'I will destroy this Temple made with human hands, and in three days I will build another, made without human hands'" (14:58). This focused attention on the volatile topic of the Temple. If Jesus could be shown to have disturbed the sacred site, then the Romans would have to prevent a public riot. Their accusation that Jesus was destroying the Temple (note the first person—"*I* will destroy") was false. According to John 2:19, Jesus said, "Destroy this temple and in three days I will raise it up." Jesus did not say he would destroy the Temple, and in any case, Jesus was speaking of his body rather than the Temple. Thus, the testimony was false, although Jesus' remarks established a contrast between the Jerusalem Temple built with people's hands that he would destroy in covenantal judgment, and the temple God would rebuild by resurrection (his body, probably both physical and spiritual in terms of the community his resurrection would form).

All told, the testimonies about Jesus destroying the Temple did not jive. The leaders recognized that this charge was not well supported by the current testimony as they needed for two or three witnesses to agree (Num 35:30; Deut 17:6; 19:15). Mark does not say whether the disagreement was in the timing of the statement or in its interpretation, but the leaders knew that the differences, whatever they were, would be exposed. So the Temple charge came to a dead end.

Eventually, however, Jesus gave them a direct reply about his identity by telling them that he was the Messiah. He did this by combining allusions to Psalm 110:1 and Daniel 7:13. He said that he was able to go directly into God's presence to sit with him in heaven, thereby sharing authority at his side. He would also return as the eschatological judge that Daniel describes as the Son of Man riding the clouds (Exod 14:19-20; 34:5; Num 10:34; Ps 104:3; Isa 19:1; only God or the gods ride the clouds in the OT). In other words, Jesus was not just the Messiah, but also the eschatological judge who was about to sit in God's presence to pass judgement on the process now underway. The Jewish leadership may have thought that Jesus was on trial, but one day he would be their judge. To these leaders, Jesus' claim was worse than if he had said that he would sit in the Holy Place in the Temple; Jesus was claiming to be able to sit directly in God's presence in heaven, something that was not regarded as possible except in a few exceptional and controversial cases (Bock 1998:113-183; of the Son of Man in *1 Enoch* and figuratively of Moses in the *Exagoge of Ezekiel*). Jesus claimed to be more than the Messiah and his exaltation would demonstrate the validity of the claim. The Jews heard it as blasphemy and sent Jesus on to the Romans.

This confrontation included the fundamental choices that still exist concerning Jesus. Either Jesus is the Messiah and the Son of God who sits at God's side, or he was a blasphemer. Jesus claimed to have direct access to God and to have the authority to judge humanity. The Jewish leaders viewed this as blasphemy and wanted him stopped, and the confrontation led to the cross. The irony is that Jesus himself supplied the testimony to take to Pilate that the Jewish leaders could not get by their own efforts. He chose to go to the cross and provide the deliverance his suffering would make possible. Jesus knew that his story would not end on a cross, but at the right hand of God, with the authority to judge and to ride the clouds as only someone of his stature can do.

◆ ## 9. Peter's denials (14:66-72; cf. Matt 26:69-75; Luke 22:55-65; John 18:25-27)

⁶⁶Meanwhile, Peter was in the courtyard below. One of the servant girls who worked for the high priest came by ⁶⁷and noticed Peter warming himself at the fire. She looked at him closely and said, "You were one of those with Jesus of Nazareth.*"

⁶⁸But Peter denied it. "I don't know what you're talking about," he said, and he went out into the entryway. Just then, a rooster crowed.*

⁶⁹When the servant girl saw him standing there, she began telling the others, "This man is definitely one of them!" ⁷⁰But Peter denied it again.

A little later some of the other bystanders confronted Peter and said, "You must be one of them, because you are a Galilean."

⁷¹Peter swore, "A curse on me if I'm lying—I don't know this man you're talking about!" ⁷²And immediately the rooster crowed the second time.

Suddenly, Jesus' words flashed through Peter's mind: "Before the rooster crows twice, you will deny three times that you even know me." And he broke down and wept.

14:67 Or *Jesus the Nazarene.*   14:68 Some manuscripts do not include *Just then, a rooster crowed.*

NOTES

14:66 *Peter was in the courtyard below.* Roman houses typically had a courtyard in the central area of the house.

14:68 *Just then, a rooster crowed.* This passage is absent in some very important MSS (א B L W); it may have been added in anticipation of the second crowing mentioned in 14:72.

14:71 Peter swore, "A curse on me if I am lying—I don't know this man you're talking about!" The NLT turns the narrative of Peter's invoking a curse on himself into part of the response. His third denial is the most emphatic.

14:72 And immediately the rooster crowed the second time. Jesus' prediction had come true. The time was between midnight and 3:00 AM (Hurtado 1989:256).

COMMENTARY

Of Peter's three denials, two came when he was confronted by a servant girl. She said, "You were one of those with Jesus of Nazareth" and Peter responded, "I don't know what you're talking about" (14:67-68). The Greek is emphatic, as Peter said that he neither knew Jesus nor understood what the girl meant. He protested a little too much in this denial—a cock crowed shortly. He moved to the entryway to avoid the pressure, but the servant girl persisted. "This man is definitely one of them," she told others (14:69), but Peter denied it again (14:70). After this, "Some of the other bystanders confronted Peter and said, 'You must be one of them; because you are a Galilean'" (14:70). The other Gospels indicate that Peter's accent gave him away (Matt 26:73). Peter put a curse on himself, vowing that he wasn't lying when he said, "I don't know this man you're talking about!" (14:71). As soon as he said this, the rooster crowed a second time. Jesus' prediction had come true. The text then says, "Suddenly Jesus' words flashed through Peter's mind: 'Before the rooster crows twice, you will deny three times that you even know me.' And he broke down and wept" (14:72). Recalling Jesus' remarks, Peter cried in pain and disappointment. He also had abandoned Jesus.

So as Jesus predicted, Peter denied Jesus three times, and the other disciples had completely abandoned Jesus. That this unflattering story about the most prominent disciple is included in Mark supports the veracity of the entire account.

◆   10. Jesus' trial before Pilate (15:1-15; cf. Matt 27:11-26;
        Luke 23:1-25; John 18:28-19:16)

Very early in the morning the leading priests, the elders, and the teachers of religious law—the entire high council*—met to discuss their next step. They bound Jesus, led him away, and took him to Pilate, the Roman governor.

²Pilate asked Jesus, "Are you the king of the Jews?"

Jesus replied, "You have said it."

³Then the leading priests kept accusing him of many crimes, ⁴and Pilate asked him, "Aren't you going to answer them? What about all these charges they are bringing against you?" ⁵But Jesus said nothing, much to Pilate's surprise.

⁶Now it was the governor's custom each year during the Passover celebration to release one prisoner—anyone the people requested. ⁷One of the prisoners at that time was Barabbas, a revolutionary who had committed murder in an uprising. ⁸The crowd went to Pilate and asked him to release a prisoner as usual.

⁹"Would you like me to release to you this 'King of the Jews'?" Pilate asked. ¹⁰(For he realized by now that the leading priests had arrested Jesus out of envy.) ¹¹But at this point the leading priests stirred up the crowd to demand the release of Barabbas instead of Jesus. ¹²Pilate asked them, "Then what should I do with this man you call the king of the Jews?"

¹³They shouted back, "Crucify him!"

¹⁴"Why?" Pilate demanded. "What crime has he committed?"

But the mob roared even louder, "Crucify him!"

¹⁵So to pacify the crowd, Pilate released Barabbas to them. He ordered Jesus flogged with a lead-tipped whip, then turned him over to the Roman soldiers to be crucified.

15:1 Greek *the Sanhedrin;* also in 15:43.

NOTES

15:1 *took him to Pilate.* The actual Gr. is "handed him over" (*paredōkan* [TG3860, ZG4140]). This verb appears frequently for the "giving over" of Jesus (9:31; 10:33; 14:10, 11, 18, 21, 41-44). As the Roman governor, Pilate collected the taxes for Rome, kept the peace, selected the high priest, and protected Rome's interests in Israel.

15:2 *Pilate asked Jesus, "Are you the king of the Jews?" Jesus replied, "You have said it."* Jesus responded by acknowledging that Pilate had made the remark. This was a roundabout way of saying, "Yes, I am, but not in the sense you intend." This was Jesus' qualified acceptance that he was (and is) the Messiah (on the grammar, see BDF §441; cf. Matt 26:25, 64; 27:11; Luke 22:70; 23:3; John 18:37; Lane 1974:551). Ironically, Pilate gave recognition to who Jesus was.

15:3 *Then the leading priests kept accusing him of many crimes.* Mark gives no details, but Luke 23:2 speaks of leading the people astray, not paying taxes to Rome, and claiming to be a king. The last charge was already on the table, as 15:2 makes clear.

15:4 *Pilate asked him, "Aren't you going to answer them? What about all these charges they are bringing against you?"* Pilate gave Jesus the opportunity to respond. The structure of the Gr. indicates that Pilate fully expected a reply.

15:5 *But Jesus said nothing, much to Pilate's surprise.* Pilate was amazed that Jesus remained silent. The scene again evokes Isa 53:7. Jesus' silence suggested that something was not right about the charges.

15:6 *Now it was the governor's custom each year during the Passover celebration to release one prisoner—anyone the people requested.* We have no outside corroboration of this custom, but that is because we know very little about what Pilate did except when he upset the Jews or was involved with Jesus. Lane (1974:553) notes a singular amnesty enacted in AD 85 by the governor of Egypt as a parallel.

15:7 *Barabbas, a revolutionary.* Pilate allowed the crowd a choice between Barabbas and Jesus. Barabbas is described as a participant in a disturbance (*stasei* [TG4714, ZG5087]) who commited a murder during the incident. He is described in the Gr. as part of a group of insurrectionists—a "revolutionary" (*stasiastōn* [TG4955A, ZG5086]; see BDAG 940). There is precedent for similar use of this term and related words in Jewish literature (Jdt 7:15; 2 Macc 4:30; 14:6; Josephus *War* 6.2.8). Ironically, Barabbas's name means "son of the father" in Aramaic, though Mark does not note that. Barabbas's freedom at Jesus' expense highlights the substitutionary nature of Jesus' death.

15:11 *the leading priests stirred up the crowd.* Mark holds the chief priests responsible as the major force behind Jesus' demise. The verb *anaseiō* [TG383, ZG411] means to "shake up," so "stirring up the crowd" is a good English rendering (Luke 23:5; BDAG 71; Cranfield 1959:450).

15:15 *flogged.* On ancient descriptions, see Josephus *War* 2.306, 308; 5.449; Livy *History* 33.36. Mark says that Jesus was scourged, and the NLT has noted the kind of whipping this was likely to be.

turned him over. The NLT explains that when Jesus was "delivered over" (*paredōken* [TG3860, ZG4140]), he was given to Roman soldiers (for this key term in Mark for being "delivered over," see 15:1). These soldiers were most likely mercenaries—legionaries from surrounding areas. Luke 23:2 and John 19:12 tell us that if Pilate did not deal with Jesus, the charge could be made he was not doing his job, since it related to keeping the peace in the region and the possibility of a king other than Caesar.

crucified. On crucifixion, see TDNT 7:573-574; it is regarded as the cruelest form of execution and as "servile punishment" (Evans 2001:482, citing Valerius Maximus 2.7.12; Tacitus *Histories* 2.72; 4.11; for details, see Hengel 1977). Mark gives no details about it when he narrates Jesus' death.

COMMENTARY

The section begins with "the leading priests, the elders, and the teachers of religious law" (the entire high council) taking Jesus to Pilate. This is the same group that had been driving events since Jesus was arrested (14:43). Since Pilate was in Jerusalem for the feast, it was seen as wise to get this resolved while Pilate was present. So they went to him "very early in the morning" (15:1).

For Pilate, the political dimensions of Jesus' claims were important. Was he claiming to be another king in competition with Caesar? If he was, it was Pilate's duty to eliminate this threat. In Mark, "King of the Jews" is a description attributed to Jesus exclusively by those who were responsible for his execution—namely, Pilate, the hostile crowd, the soldiers, the chief priests, and the scribes (15:2, 9, 12, 18, 26, 32).

According to Mark, it was the crowd that sought the customary amnesty for a prisoner this Passover. Cranfield (1959:450) suggests that the crowd might have been filled with Barabbas's supporters, just in case amnesty were offered. The crowd, stirred up by the leading priests, asked for the release of Barabbas, a revolutionary (see note on 15:7). Pilate turned Jesus' destiny over to the crowd: "Would you like me to release this 'King of the Jews'?" (15:9). As Pilate asked if Jesus should be given his freedom, he mockingly described Jesus as king. To Pilate, Jesus was an insignificant figure from Galilee, but Pilate "realized by now that the leading priests had arrested Jesus out of envy" (15:10). Pilate recognized that the battle between Jesus and the leaders was a power struggle. The leaders were jealous of the things Jesus could do and were protecting their own power (12:12, 37b).

After hearing that the crowd wanted Barabbas, he turned to them and asked, "Then what should I do with this man you call the king of the Jews?" (15:12). This is the third use of "king of the Jews" in this chapter, with two more instances to follow (15:18, 26). The response from the crowd was startling. "They shouted back, 'Crucify him!'" (15:13). Although the leaders had driven the movement to have Jesus killed, the crowd supported it. Incredulous, Pilate asked the crowd, "Why? . . . What crime has he committed?" (15:14). Pilate still viewed Jesus as innocent (see also 15:10) and as not deserving death. But as the crowd continued to ask for Jesus' crucifixion, Pilate was faced with a public disturbance, so he decided to pacify the crowd by acting in a way that would preserve his popularity rather than serve justice. His alternative plan had failed and he released Barabbas to them. If this move did not go well, Pilate could say that he had simply listened to the locals.

Pilate "ordered Jesus flogged with a lead-tipped whip, then turned him over to the Roman soldiers to be crucified" (15:15). In preparation for crucifixion, those who were to be executed were flogged with whips tipped with lead or animal bone chips, often with the prisoners attached to a pillar (Taylor 1966:584). The idea was to get the victim bleeding so that death would come more quickly.

In this section, Pilate's examination of Jesus shows the pressure that the Jewish leaders placed on the governor. The leaders brought Jesus to him, got the crowd worked up over Jesus, and pressed for the death penalty. Although he tried to get Jesus released, Pilate found the public pressure, and the resulting political threat, to be too great. He knew that Jesus was innocent, but sent him to death anyway. The crowd opted for Barabbas instead of Jesus when they had a chance to free a prisoner, and Jesus was substituted for a state criminal. Jesus died for another, who was freed by his death. In that exchange, Mark pictures the substitutionary death of Jesus (10:45).

◆   11. The soldiers mock Jesus (15:16-20; cf. Matt 27:27-31)

16The soldiers took Jesus into the courtyard of the governor's headquarters (called the Praetorium) and called out the entire regiment. 17They dressed him in a purple robe, and they wove thorn branches into a crown and put it on his head. 18Then they saluted him and taunted, "Hail! King of the Jews!" 19And they struck him on the head with a reed stick, spit on him, and dropped to their knees in mock worship. 20When they were finally tired of mocking him, they took off the purple robe and put his own clothes on him again. Then they led him away to be crucified.

NOTES

15:16 *governor's headquarters.* This was probably Herod's palace (France 2002:637). Pilate would have been Herod's guest, or else have had a room at the Roman fortress, the Antonia. The courtyard suggests Herod's palace; some ancient traditions identify a location on the western slope of the Tyropeon Valley (noted by Evans 2001:489).

entire regiment. If this was a *cohort*, it was a unit of 600 men. If the term is being used in a less technical sense, then it was probably a *maniple*, or about 200 men.

15:18 *taunted, "Hail! King of the Jews!"* Such mockery of a prisoner was quite common. Evans (2001:488) notes a scene involving a street person in Philo (*Flaccus* 6.36-39) and an incident involving the deposed Vitellius in AD 69 from Dio Cassius (64.20-21; so also Eleazar, according to 4 Macc 6:1-30).

15:20 *When they were finally tired of mocking him . . . they led him away to be crucified.* Having had their fun, the soldiers took back the purple robe, clothed him, and sent him to his death. The word for mock (*empaizō* [TG1702, ZG1850]) can mean "to treat cruelly" (2 Macc 7:7, 10; TDNT 5:63).

put his own clothes on him. This suggests that as a concession to Jewish sensibilities (*m. Sanhedrin* 6.3), Jesus was not crucified in the nude. If the soldiers later took his garments prior to the crucifixion, they may have left his undergarment, while soldiers cast lots for his tunic.

COMMENTARY

The soldiers began mocking Jesus by dressing him in a robe the color of wealth and royalty (Luke 16:19; Rev 18:12; 1 Macc 10:20, 62, 69; 11:58; 14:43-44) and giving him a mock crown of thorns (1 Macc 5:20; 2 Macc 14:4). Some suggest that this crown was made of the long spines of the date palm (Hooker 1991:370), but France (2002:638) questions this.

The soldiers continued to mock and taunt Jesus, thereby showing their complete disrespect for him. The soldiers dropping to their knees imitated the worship of Caesar (Taylor 1966:586). The title they taunted him with ("King of the Jews") shows the political-regal issue that swirled around his person. He was executed as a messianic pretender. When the accounts refer to Jesus as "King of the Jews" (see 15:9), they show that Jesus was executed for more than being a prophet.

Jesus was treated with contempt by the soldiers, all in fulfillment of what he had predicted in 10:34. That Jesus should suffer so much, even as he was about to die on behalf of many (10:45), indicates just how serious the condition of humanity is with regard to the things of God. Jesus went to the cross as a rejected King of the Jews, but God did not share man's rejection of Jesus, and would soon vindicate him through the resurrection.

◆   12. Jesus' crucifixion and death (15:21-39; cf. Matt 27:32-56; Luke 23:26-49; John 19:17-37)

²¹A passerby named Simon, who was from Cyrene,* was coming in from the countryside just then, and the soldiers forced him to carry Jesus' cross. (Simon was the father of Alexander and Rufus.) ²²And they brought Jesus to a place called Golgotha (which means "Place of the Skull"). ²³They offered him wine drugged with myrrh, but he refused it.

²⁴Then the soldiers nailed him to the cross. They divided his clothes and threw dice* to decide who would get each piece. ²⁵It was nine o'clock in the morning when they crucified him. ²⁶A sign was fastened to the cross, announcing the charge against him. It read, "The King of the Jews." ²⁷Two revolutionaries* were crucified with him, one on his right and one on his left.*

²⁹The people passing by shouted abuse, shaking their heads in mockery. "Ha! Look at you now!" they yelled at him. "You said you were going to destroy the Temple and rebuild it in three days. ³⁰Well then, save yourself and come down from the cross!"

³¹The leading priests and teachers of religious law also mocked Jesus. "He saved others," they scoffed, "but he can't save himself! ³²Let this Messiah, this King of Israel, come down from the cross so we can see it and believe him!" Even the men who were crucified with Jesus ridiculed him.

³³At noon, darkness fell across the whole land until three o'clock. ³⁴Then at three o'clock Jesus called out with a loud voice, "Eloi, Eloi, lema sabachthani?" which means "My God, my God, why have you abandoned me?"*

³⁵Some of the bystanders misunderstood and thought he was calling for the prophet Elijah. ³⁶One of them ran and filled a sponge with sour wine, holding it up to him on a reed stick so he could drink. "Wait!" he said. "Let's see whether Elijah comes to take him down!"

³⁷Then Jesus uttered another loud cry and breathed his last. ³⁸And the curtain in the sanctuary of the Temple was torn in two, from top to bottom.

³⁹When the Roman officer* who stood facing him* saw how he had died, he exclaimed, "This man truly was the Son of God!"

15:21 *Cyrene* was a city in northern Africa.   **15:24** Greek *cast lots.* See Ps 22:18.   **15:27a** Or *Two criminals.*
15:27b Some manuscripts add verse 28, *And the Scripture was fulfilled that said, "He was counted among those who were rebels."* See Isa 53:12; also compare Luke 22:37.   **15:34** Ps 22:1.   **15:39a** Greek *the centurion;* similarly in 15:44, 45.   **15:39b** Some manuscripts add *heard his cry and.*

NOTES

15:21 *Rufus.* This figure could well be one who later became a leader in Rome (Rom 16:13). As one of those who helped bear the cross, he would have been carrying the cross beam, not the main pole which would already be at the crucifixion site. It is also debated whether the shape of the cross would have been more like a capital T or a lowercase t, or like the Russian cross with more of an X shape. The fact that there is room for a charge above Jesus' head means that the lowercase t type of cross is most likely (Brown 1997:948).

15:22 *Golgotha.* This site has traditionally been associated with the present location of the Church of the Holy Sepulchre, some 300 meters from Herod's palace (France 2002:642 and Brown 1997:937-940, who argues for it over the site in the Garden Tomb area). Hooker (1991:372) notes the association of the locale with the burial place of Adam's skull in Jewish thinking.

15:23 *They offered him wine drugged with myrrh, but he refused it.* The offer of such a drink was not unusual (Prov 31:6; *b. Sanhedrin* 43a; see Mark 14:25, where Jesus said he would not drink again until the consummation; Cranfield 1959:455). The wine may have come from the sympathetic women who were present (France 2002:643). The addition of myrrh made the wine a kind of delicacy and was intended to ease his suffering (Pliny *Natural History* 14.15, 92-93).

15:24 *Then the soldiers nailed him to the cross.* In 1968, the remains of a crucified man nailed to a cross were discovered at Giv'at ha-Mivtar (Lane 1974:564-565). His feet were nailed together at the heels, which would have made it difficult for him to bear his weight and breathe while crucified. Those crucified could be nailed or tied to the cross, but this text indicates nailing as do the appearances where Jesus invites his disciples to touch his wounds (John 20:27).

They divided his clothes and threw dice to decide who would get each piece. The soldiers gambled for his clothes, and lots were cast to see who would get each piece (see Ps 22:18). Tacitus (*Annals* 6.29) notes that those sentenced to death lost their property rights.

15:25 *It was nine o'clock in the morning when they crucified him.* The Gr. refers to the "third hour," which on a sunrise to sunrise schedule would mean 9:00 AM. John 19:14 mentions the sixth hour. Of course, the death took time (note 15:33-34). John was probably highlighting the overlap of the crucifixion with the time of sacrifice later in the day.

15:27 *Two revolutionaries were crucified with him, one on his right and one on his left.* The NLT describes the criminals as revolutionaries, which reflects the use of *lēstēs* [TG3027, ZG3334]. This term is often used of a person who acts against the state, but it can also refer to a mere robber (BDAG 594). In his typical brevity, Mark tells us little else about these two except that they contributed to the ridicule (15:32).

15:28 The NLT mg to 15:27 reads, "Some MSS add verse 28, *And the Scripture was fulfilled that said, 'He was counted among those who were rebels.'*" This verse was probably not a part of the original text of Mark's Gospel, since the manuscript evidence for its inclusion is basically a Byzantine reading. Alexandrian and Western witnesses (such as ℵ A B C D) exclude it. It was borrowed from Luke 22:37, a parallel text, which cites Isa 53:12.

15:29 *The people passing by shouted abuse.* The term for "shouting abuse" here is *blasphēmeō* [TG987, ZG1059], which indicates slander. It could suggest blasphemy, especially for a writer like Mark who respected Jesus.

15:31 *mocked Jesus.* The verb for mock (*empaizō* [TG1702, ZG1850]) is the same one used of the Roman soldiers in 15:20. Jews and Gentiles mocked him and rejected him. Evans (2001:505) notes how the mocking of Jesus resembles the portrayal of Isaiah's experience in the Jewish text *Martyrdom and Ascension of Isaiah* 5:2-3. There is irony and a kind of unwitting prophecy here as Jesus will, in fact, come down from the cross and live again (for a similar unwitting prophecy, see Caiaphas in John 11:51).

15:33 *At noon, darkness fell across the whole land until three o'clock.* In the Gr., the time period is from the sixth hour until the ninth hour. Creation manifested an apocalyptic darkness that pointed to judgment (Exod 10:21-22; Deut 28:29; Isa 13:10; Amos 8:9-10). Philo (*Providence* 2.50) spoke of such darkness as indicating the death of a king or the destruction of a city (Lane 1974:571). Here it could portend either.

15:35 *bystanders . . . thought he was calling for the prophet Elijah.* Some observers thought that Jesus might finally be reacting to his taunters by calling on God to send Elijah to his rescue. Elijah was seen as a protector of the innocent (Sir 48:10; TDNT 2:930-935; Evans 2001:507-508; France 202:654 mentions the later Jewish story in *b. Avodah Zarah* 17b where Elijah rescues Rabbi Eleazar from a Roman trial).

15:36 *filled a sponge with sour wine.* This was probably "wine vinegar" (the term here is *oxos* [TG3690, ZG3954], BDAG 715, a "favorite beverage of the lower ranks of society"). Someone hoped that perhaps the wine would strengthen Jesus to await Elijah's arrival. It appears to have been offered by one of the Jews who thought Jesus was calling for deliverance. See Ps 69:21, which places the act in the context of a righteous sufferer.

15:38 *And the curtain . . . of the Temple was torn in two, from top to bottom.* This detail shows another way in which creation responded to Jesus' death. This curtain may have governed entry into the Holy Place (Exod 26:37) or into the Holy of Holies (Exod 26:31). These curtains were at least 55 cubits high (France 2002:656). The curtain by the Holy of Holies that pictured the heavens would have been most visible to the public (Evans 2001:509). The symbolic meaning of the act is debated. Was it to signal the Temple's destruction, as France (2002:657), Evans (2001:509), and some of the Fathers argue (see Lane 1974:575; Tertullian *Against Marcion* 4.42)? Or was it a sign that access to God had been opened up, since the curtain prevented entrance to some (see Nolland 1993:1157-1158 discussing Luke, which has parallel imagery)? Or might it be both (Bock 1996:1861 also discussing Luke)? The event is uncorroborated, but there is a curious later tradition in Judaism that during the last forty years before the Temple's demise, the sanctuary doors would open by themselves (*b. Yoma* 39b).

COMMENTARY

Jesus, who had just been flogged, was apparently too weak to carry the crossbeam for his crucifixion to the site of execution, though this was expected of each condemned person (Plutarch *Moralia* 554 A: "Each of the condemned carried his own cross"). So Simon from Cyrene (in North Africa) was selected to bear the cross for Jesus (15:21). Mark identifies him as father to Alexander and Rufus; this suggests that the man became a Christian and was known to Mark's audience (Cranfield 1959:454). At the time, he was probably a diaspora Jew.

The execution took place at Golgotha, which in Aramaic means "Place of the Skull" (15:22). The site was either associated with a skull because it looked like one, or because many had "lost their heads" there. The alternative name, "Calvary," comes from the Latin and shares the meaning "skull." Before the soldiers nailed Jesus to the crossbeam, they offered him drugged wine (see note on 15:23), but Jesus refused to take anything to dull the pain and suffering. The crossbeam was laid on the ground, and then Jesus was nailed to the cross and lifted up to hang on the main beam already in the ground. There he was left to die.

Mark tells us that "a sign was fastened to the cross, announcing the charge against him. It read, 'The King of the Jews'" (15:26). With a crucifixion, a charge accompanied the sentenced person. Here it is clear that the Romans viewed Jesus' death as politically motivated. Jesus was mocked as "King of the Jews" (15:18), and he was executed for the same charge (see also 15:2). Cranfield (1959:456) says that the "governor unwittingly proclaimed the truth of Jesus' messianic kingship." All four Gospels note "King of the Jews" as a part of the charge, while differing in other details (Matt 27:37; Luke 23:38; John 19:19 has the fullest statement). Evans (2001:503-504) notes that the expression does not originate with Mark, but with the Romans. Jews would have called such a figure "our King" or "our Messiah." The expression "King of the Jews" suggests a viewpoint outside of Judaism, which contributes to the scene's authenticity. Mark's point is that the real blasphemy was with the people, not in the one being crucified for blasphemy (14:64).

As Jesus was dying on the cross, people passed by, shouting words of abuse. As Mark describes it, they were "shaking their heads in mockery" (15:29), in the tone of Psalm 22:7 and 69:20 (also Jer 18:16). Jesus is portrayed as the righteous sufferer. The people yelled at him, "Ha! Look at you now! . . . you were going to destroy the Temple and rebuild it in three days" (15:29). The issue of the Temple came up again, as it did at the trial (14:58). The point of their remarks is that Jesus had failed—he would not meet his third-day claim. Though they could not conceive it, he would meet the claim in his resurrected body (see John 2:19-22). The mocking and abuse continued, as the people shouted out, "Well then, save yourself and come down from the cross!" (15:30). The irony reaches its height here. Those who mocked Jesus thought he had failed. In fact, he would not only be rescued from the death of the cross, but would also save many others in the process.

The narrative continues with more mocking. "The leading priests and teachers of religious law also mocked Jesus. 'He saved others,' they scoffed, 'but he can't save himself!'" (15:31). The irony kicks up one more level. The Jewish leaders spoke of Jesus' deliverance of others (probably an allusion to his miracles), regarding it as a sign of Jesus' impotence that he could not deliver himself. What kind of a Christ-King deliverer could be hanging on a cross? With the resurrection, God, the ultimate deliverer, would save Jesus and thereby provide salvation for others. This verse also echoes Psalm 22:7-8. The scoffing is expressed in an imperfect tense, indicating ongoing derision. Taylor (1966:592) argues that the scene rings true, as "it is hard to believe that this speech is a product of creative imagination." Skeptics sometimes suggest that the leaders would not have been present (as Hooker 1991:374), but they had too much invested not to see the execution through to its end.

They continued their abuse by shouting out, "Let this Messiah, this King of Israel, come down from the cross so we can see it and believe in him!" (15:32). They taunted the King that if he would come down from the cross and survive crucifixion, they would believe. Of course, the reader knows that their faith did not follow when Jesus was raised from death. To call Jesus "King of Israel" adds a nationalist note to the taunt. The call to do something that they could see and respond to may be a slight against Jesus' reply in 14:62. Wisdom of Solomon 2:17-18 teaches that God helps the righteous man and Jesus was failing that test. As France (2002:649) notes, Jesus was losing his soul in order to help others attain theirs, a variation on the theme of 8:35. The taunting was so bad that even the two men crucified with Jesus joined in the derision (15:32).

In the midst of all this mockery, Jesus called out with a loud voice, "Eloi, Eloi, lema sabachthani?" which means, "My God, my God, why have you abandoned me?" (15:34). He was not calling out to Elijah (see notes on 15:35-36). In the darkness of judgment, Jesus suffered the anguish of judgment. In Aramaic, he cried out the lament of Psalm 22:1 (the third place in Mark where Aramaic is used; 5:41; 14:36 NLT mg; Matt 27:46 transliterates Heb. here). In the anguish of separation from God, Jesus reached out to the Father, as the psalm declares the sufferer's trust in God (Ps 22:22, 24, 30-31). However, there is no such note of hope here; Mark simply leaves us with the agony of the cross. Jesus was bearing sin for others (10:45).

Then Mark tells us, "Jesus uttered another loud cry and breathed his last" (15:37). Now it was finished. Elijah had not come, only death. But in three days, life would come. As Lane (1974:574) says, "The meaning of his death becomes clear only from the perspective of the triumph of resurrection which marked his vindication and demonstrated that death had no claim on him." Only then did Jesus "come down" from the cross by being taken up to the Father.

After his resurrection, many would come to realize that Jesus was and is the Son of God. A Roman officer realized this by seeing how Jesus died. The text says, "When the Roman officer who stood facing him saw how he had died, he exclaimed, 'This man truly was the Son of God!' " (15:39). This is the climactic confession of the crucifixion and of the book. It matches 1:1 (and 1:11). This soldier, neutral or even initially hostile in his view of Jesus, saw all that transpired and recognized Jesus' unique relationship to God. The soldier was probably the centurion in charge of the execution. Mark uses a Latin loan word to describe the solider—(*kēnturiōn* [TG2760, ZG3035], meaning "centurion." In contrast to all the mockery by the Jewish leaders and others, this Gentile saw what was going on. Apparently the final words, the darkness, and Jesus' shout were what convinced him that they had killed one who was what he claimed to be. For Jesus to be strong enough to shout at the end of a crucifixion was unusual. How much the centurion actually understood of what he confessed is debated (note Evans 2001:510), as he would not have had the background to know much more than that Jesus was a divinely enabled, commissioned King. Still, his confession was more than a contradiction to the death sentence Jesus received, and the fuller meaning of the title "Son of God" was clear to Mark's readers (1:1, 11; 3:11; 5:7; 9:7; 12:6; 13:32; 14:61-62). On this note, the crucifixion scene ends.

By way of summary, the reader sees the swirl of reactions produced by Jesus' crucifixion. People passing by, the Jewish leaders, most of the soldiers, and those who were hanged with him all mocked him. The descriptions allude to a righteous sufferer meeting unjust rejection, recalling Psalms 22 and 69. The creation went dark in judgment. The temple veil was rent, also pointing to judgment and the opening up of heaven; Jesus went to the Father, having provided the way to God. Finally, a single solider recognized that Jesus, slain as King of the Jews and mocked for not being able to save himself, was indeed the Son of God. The one executed was seen by one of his executioners as executing the will of God. Despite Jesus' death, he was still God's Son, as events three days later would dramatically confirm.

◆   13. Jesus' burial (15:40-47; cf. Matt 27:57-66; Luke 23:50-56; John 19:31-42)

⁴⁰Some women were there, watching from a distance, including Mary Magdalene, Mary (the mother of James the younger and of Joseph*), and Salome. ⁴¹They had been followers of Jesus and had cared for him while he was in Galilee. Many other women who had come with him to Jerusalem were also there.

⁴²This all happened on Friday, the day of preparation,* the day before the Sabbath. As evening approached, ⁴³Joseph of Arimathea took a risk and went to Pilate and asked for Jesus' body. (Joseph was an honored member of the high council, and

he was waiting for the Kingdom of God to come.) ⁴⁴Pilate couldn't believe that Jesus was already dead, so he called for the Roman officer and asked if he had died yet. ⁴⁵The officer confirmed that Jesus was dead, so Pilate told Joseph he could have the body. ⁴⁶Joseph bought a long sheet of linen cloth. Then he took Jesus' body down from the cross, wrapped it in the cloth, and laid it in a tomb that had been carved out of the rock. Then he rolled a stone in front of the entrance. ⁴⁷Mary Magdalene and Mary the mother of Joseph saw where Jesus' body was laid.

15:40 Greek *Joses;* also in 15:47. See Matt 27:56.   15:42 Greek *It was the day of preparation.*

NOTES

15:43 *Joseph of Arimathea took a risk and went to Pilate and asked for Jesus' body. (Joseph was an honored member of the high council, and he was waiting for the Kingdom of God to come.)* Joseph is noted in all four Gospels (Matt 27:57; Luke 23:51; John 19:38). In Mark, the Gr. speaks of Joseph's "taking courage" or "being bold" (*tolmēsas* [ᵀᴳ5111, ᶻᴳ5528]), which suggests the note of risk the NLT translation highlights.

15:44 *Pilate couldn't believe that Jesus was already dead, so he called for the Roman officer and asked if he had died yet.* The NLT strengthens the Gr., which says that "Pilate wondered if he were already dead" to indicate amazement that the body was already being requested. Death by crucifixion could take hours or days longer than Jesus had been on the cross (Evans 2001:520; Hengel 1977:29-31), so Pilate called the centurion to verify his death. There is some discussion as to whether Pilate asked if he had been dead long or asked if he were already dead, since there is a textual problem. Some of the earliest MSS have "already dead" (B D W), but this looks like an easier reading than the more difficult *ei palai* [TG3819, ZG4093], which means "if [he had been dead] long," in most other MSS (including ℵ A C L).

15:45 *The officer confirmed that Jesus was dead, so Pilate told Joseph he could have the body.* Upon confirming the death, Pilate gave the body to Joseph to do with as he wished. This lit. reads that Pilate "gifted Joseph with the corpse." The word *ptōma* [TG4430, ZG4773] always refers to a corpse in the NT (Matt 14:12; 24:28; Rev 11:8-9; TDNT 6:166-167). Mark's only other use of the word concerns John the Baptist's body (6:29).

COMMENTARY

This section begins with a transition between the crucifixion scene and the burial scene by noting that certain women who witnessed Jesus' crucifixion (15:40-41) also saw where and how Jesus was buried (15:42-47). The section begins with the statement, "Some women were there, watching from a distance, including Mary Magdalene, Mary (the mother of James the younger and of Joseph), and Salome." Witnesses were present who knew Jesus and were aware of all that had taken place. They had seen the crucifixion and the burial. They are witnesses despite the fact that the witness of women was often prohibited as having no legal value at that time (Tacitus *Annals* 6.29; Josephus *Antiquities* 4.219). This supports the historical character of the details, because if someone were trying to invent witnesses to prove a point, they would not use women.

All three women are mentioned here for the first time in Mark. Mary Magdalene has a key role in the resurrection accounts in all the Gospels (see also Luke 8:2). Salome is also involved in Mark's resurrection account (16:1). She may be the mother of the sons of Zebedee noted in Matthew 27:56, but the name was a common one, making this less than certain. The other Mary could be the same person as Mary, the wife of Clopas (John 19:25), and/or the same as the mother of James and Joseph in Matthew 27:56 (one of the sons was also known as Joses, the name Mark uses in the Gr. here). She was probably not Mary, the mother of Jesus, as she is listed second and the connection is made to others, not to Jesus.

Mark tells the reader that these women "had been followers of Jesus and had cared for him while he was in Galilee. Many other women who had come with him to Jerusalem were also there" (15:40). These three women (Mary Magdalene, Mary, and Salome) were the most prominent among a larger group of pilgrims traveling with Jesus. They had cared for Jesus, as Luke 8:1-3 reports.

Having noted which women were present at the crucifixion, Mark says, "This all happened on Friday, the day of preparation, the day before the Sabbath" (15:42). Mark locates the day specifically as the day of preparation before the day of Sabbath rest. Everything for the Sabbath was prepared that day, so the Sabbath could be a day of rest. To fulfill Jewish law, a person's body had to be buried on the day of their death. This meant that preparations for burial had to happen quickly, in the three hours between Jesus' death and the sun's setting that ended the day (Deut 21:23; 2 Sam 21:12-14; Tob 1:17-19; 2:3-7, where burying the dead is an act of piety).

Joseph of Arimathea came to Pilate and asked for Jesus' body. His request challenged the opinion of those who sought Jesus' death by requesting a decent burial for Jesus. As a member of the Sanhedrin (or high council), he was a major Jewish leader (Evans 2001:518-519 defends the historicity of his presence in the account). Not everyone rejected Jesus. Joseph's description as one who awaited the Kingdom also suggests that he was not hostile to Jesus. Either he was not present at the hearing where "all" condemned Jesus (14:64), or the earlier verse was hyperbolic in referring to the overwhelming majority with no dissenting voice heard. He asked to have Jesus' body, which the Romans would otherwise have left to rot on the cross or be eaten by birds (Lane 1974:578). Jews were more inclined to at least dispose of the body, but Joseph wanted Jesus to have an appropriate tomb.

Mark slows down his account to note a few details of Joseph's care of Jesus' body in five distinct actions: "Joseph bought a long sheet of linen . . . took Jesus' body down . . . wrapped it . . . laid it in a tomb that had been carved out of the rock. Then he rolled a stone in front of the entrance" (15:46). The major items omitted from the account are the washing of the body, a detail important to Jews (*m. Sanhedrin* 23.5), and any note about spices (see John 19:40), which would also have been likely. The rock tomb was probably a family burial place. Joseph probably acted with others, because rolling the stone would have been a major task for just one person (Lane 1974:580). John's Gospel tells us that Nicodemus helped to give Jesus an honorable burial (John 19:39-40).

Mark concludes this section by telling his readers that "Mary Magdalene and Mary the mother of Joseph saw where Jesus' body was laid" (15:47). Two of the women noted in 15:40 watched Joseph inter Jesus' body, so the burial was witnessed by two people, the minimum number required in another context to verify evidence demanding a death sentence (Deut 17:6; 19:15). That women were the key witnesses is unusual, but again this points to the account's trustworthiness (see comments above).

This section tells us that Jesus was buried with dignity by Joseph, a Jewish leader, verifying that not every prominent Jew was against Jesus. This section also informs us that Jesus was definitely dead. He was buried in a tomb known to his followers, and his body was not left to rot or to remain dishonorably exposed overnight. Pilate permitted all of this. Two witnesses saw his dead body being buried. The scene was set for Jesus' resurrection from the dead.

◆   ## 14. The resurrection of Jesus (16:1-8; cf. Matt 28:1-10; Luke 24:1-12; John 20:1-18)

Saturday evening, when the Sabbath ended, Mary Magdalene, Mary the mother of James, and Salome went out and purchased burial spices so they could anoint Jesus' body. ²Very early on Sunday morning,* just at sunrise, they went to the tomb. ³On the way they were asking each other, "Who will roll away the stone for us from the entrance to the tomb?" ⁴But as they arrived, they looked up and saw that the stone, which was very large, had already been rolled aside.

⁵When they entered the tomb, they saw a young man clothed in a white robe sit-

ting on the right side. The women were shocked, ⁶but the angel said, "Don't be alarmed. You are looking for Jesus of Nazareth,* who was crucified. He isn't here! He is risen from the dead! Look, this is where they laid his body. ⁷Now go and tell his disciples, including Peter, that Jesus is going ahead of you to Galilee. You will see him there, just as he told you before he died."

⁸The women fled from the tomb, trembling and bewildered, and they said nothing to anyone because they were too frightened.*

16:2 Greek *on the first day of the week*; also in 16:9.   16:6 Or *Jesus the Nazarene.*   16:8 The most reliable early manuscripts of the Gospel of Mark end at verse 8. Other manuscripts include various endings to the Gospel. A few include both the "shorter ending" and the "longer ending." The majority of manuscripts include the "longer ending" immediately after verse 8.

NOTES

16:1 *purchased burial spices.* This term for spices is used only in this scene in the NT (Luke 23:56; 24:1; John 19:40).

16:2 *Very early on Sunday morning, just at sunrise.* The unusual double reference to the time as very early in the morning at sunrise emphasizes that the women went as soon as they could, as night became morning.

16:3 *Who will roll away the stone for us?* The women were concerned about how they would get into the tomb. These stones were anywhere from five to six feet in diameter, so they weighed hundreds of pounds (Evans 2001:535). Such stones were set into a groove in front of the entrance, making their removal difficult.

16:5 *saw a young man.* In Judaism, angels were described as young men (2 Macc 3:26, 33; Josephus *Antiquities* 5.277; France 2002:679).

shocked. exethambēthēsan [^{TG}1568, ^{ZG}1701]; cf. 14:33.

16:8 *The women fled from the tomb, trembling and bewildered, and they said nothing to anyone because they were too frightened.* At this point we must address the fact that among the various manuscripts, five endings to Mark have been preserved: (1) The Gospel could end at 16:8, per the evidence of ℵ B 304 syr^s cop^{sa} (one MS) arm geo (two MSS) Hesychius Eusebius and MSS according to Eusebius, Jerome, and Severus. (2) The NLT's "shorter ending", per the evidence of it^k. (3) The NLT's "longer ending" of 16:9-20, per the evidence of A C D 037 038 f¹³ 33 𝔐 Irenaeus, Augustine, and MSS according to Eusebius, Jerome, and Severus. (4) There is an alternate longer ending with an addition after 16:14 ("And they excused themselves, saying, 'This age of lawlessness and unbelief is under Satan, who does not allow the truth and power of God to prevail over the unclean things of the spirits. Therefore reveal your righteousness now'—thus they spoke to Christ. And Christ replied to them, 'The term of years of Satan's power has been fulfilled, but other terrible things draw near. And for those who have sinned I was handed over to death, that they may return to the truth and sin no more, that they may inherit the spiritual and imperishable glory of righteousness that is in heaven'"; see the NRSV mg and the NLT mg), per the evidence of W and MSS according to Jerome. (5) Including both the shorter ending and the traditional longer ending is also possible, per the evidence of L 044 083 099 274^{mg} 579 syr^{h (mg)} cop^{sa} (MSS) cop^{bo} (MSS).

The manuscript evidence suggests that 16:8 is the original ending of Mark (Lane 1974:591-592); the two earliest extant MSS (ℵ and B) end there. Certain church fathers, such as Clement and Origen, did not know of the longer ending, while Eusebius, Jerome, and Severus noted its absence in most of the Gr. MSS they knew. It is also lacking in the Eusebian canons on the Gospels from the third century. This is important evidence for its non-originality, for if it existed there is no good explanation for their not using it (France 2002:685-687).

However, many find the ending at 16:8 so abrupt that they suggest that the original ending of Mark has been lost or that this ending was not Mark's original intention (France 2002: 684; Evans 2001:539). Even if 16:8 did not originally conclude this Gospel, there still is no clear support for a longer ending other than these factors: (1) the stylistic oddity of *gar* [TG1063, ZG1142] (for) in the final phrase of the book, and (2) the post-resurrection appearances of Jesus in Matthew and Luke suggesting an appearance in the original Mark.

The history of the alternate endings of Mark is discussed in the commentary. The existence of several longer versions strongly suggests that they are later additions to the abrupt ending of 16:8. That the traditional longer version (16:9-20) contains a combination of the other Gospels' endings also suggests its secondary character, as does its distinct vocabulary. There are numerous points of contact with the other Gospels—three with Luke, two with Matthew, two with John, and five with Acts. These are noted below (for further discussion on the endings to Mark, see Comfort 2007:[Matt 16:8]).

COMMENTARY

The women mentioned at the beginning of this chapter witnessed Jesus' crucifixion and/or burial (see Commentary on 15:40-47). The first thing they did after the Sabbath was purchase spices (*arōmata* [TG759, ZG808]) to anoint Jesus as a shield for the decaying body odor. Mark does not note that Joseph anointed Jesus with spices, so this is the only anointing mentioned in Mark. However, John says that Nicodemus brought spices and anointed Jesus' body (John 19:39-40). The Synoptic Gospels note Joseph's involvement in the burial, keeping the story simple. These women came to Jesus' tomb early Sunday morning to anoint his body. This was their own way of honoring Jesus, so if they did see Joseph anointing Jesus (15:47), this did not preclude them from doing so as well.

On the way to the tomb, they wondered who would roll the stone away for them. When the women arrived, "they looked up and saw that the stone, which was very large, had already been rolled aside" (16:4). Their problem was solved. The very large stone was now off to the side so they could enter the tomb. When they passed through the entry tunnel and into the chamber, "they saw a young man clothed in a white robe sitting on the right side" (16:5). This person should probably be regarded as a heavenly figure, such as an angel (see note on 16:5; see also Matt 28:2-3; Mark 9:2-3; John 20:12; Acts 1:10; 10:30; Rev 6:11; 7:9, 13). He told them, "Don't be alarmed. You are looking for Jesus of Nazareth, who was crucified. He isn't here! He is risen from the dead! Look, this is where they laid his body." His revelatory message announced that the resurrection had taken place. The tomb was empty; Jesus' body was no longer among the dead. This could be a scene of discipleship failure at one level, since the women, like their male compatriots, did not take Jesus' resurrection announcements to heart. However, the remark does not really come across as a rebuke. It is more an encouragement to really believe the resurrection has taken place. So the failure is less explicitly presented than earlier in Mark. The ending, if Mark ends at 16:8, leaves the reader hanging. What will he or she do? The opportunity for faith exists—the reader must not be left paralyzed by fear, but take advantage of this opportunity.

The resurrection was a fundamental declaration of the early church (Acts 2:29;

1 Cor 15:3-8, 11). The women were the first to get the message of Jesus' resurrection. Again, this detail would be odd if someone had fabricated Jesus' resurrection, because in that culture it was the witness of men that mattered, not that of women. Hence, the historicity of the account is confirmed (see commentary on 15:40-47).

The angel told the women, "Now go and tell his disciples, including Peter, that Jesus is going ahead of you to Galilee. You will see him there, just as he told you before he died" (16:7). The disciples were instructed to meet Jesus in Galilee, including Peter, who had been restored to the group after his denials. Jesus would do as he had predicted (14:27-28). This remark makes it clear that although Mark did not give details of Jesus' appearances after his resurrection (according to the short ending of Mark; see note on 16:8), Jesus did appear to his disciples. Verse 7 also makes it clear that the story did not end with fear and silence. Jesus did appear to his disciples and someone had to have reported the empty tomb and the message to go to Galilee for that appearance.

If the book ends at 16:8, then the experience of the resurrection is portrayed as an initially overwhelming experience, inciting fear and initial silence in the women. I say "initial silence" because the disciples did get to Galilee and did see Jesus, as Matthew narrates (Matt 28:16-20; Cranfield 1959:469), indicating that the women did eventually speak. John 20:18 has Mary report Jesus' appearance, but does so in a way that may suggest Mary hung around the tomb for a while, finding it hard to believe initially.

Why would Mark end his gospel this way—if, indeed, this is the end of the gospel? It would create an open ending that would allow readers to contemplate these unusual events and make a response of faith to God's unexpected, unusual, and powerful work, a theme in Mark's Gospel (4:41; 5:15, 33, 36; 6:50; 9:6, 32). The declaration of resurrection leaves no alternatives but to remain in fear or to believe. The tomb was empty and Jesus would appear to the disciples (16:5-7). It was time to respond.

The gospel ends with Jesus' resurrection declared as an event to be believed, even though it was almost too much to believe. The women were not prepared to see an empty tomb. Everything about the scene caught them off guard and left them numb, but clearly, it took place. The Gospel's record of the women's experience shows that they eventually talked, for where else would the testimony have come from?

◆ IV. The Added Endings to Mark (post-16:8)
A. The Shorter Ending (post-16:8)

Then they briefly reported all this to Peter and his companions. Afterward Jesus himself sent them out from east to west with the sacred and unfailing message of salvation that gives eternal life. Amen.

NOTES

[Shorter Ending of Mark] This ending appears by itself after 16:8 in it^k, and with the traditional longer ending (16:9-20) in L 044 083 099 274^mg 579 syr^h mg cop^sa, bo mss (see note on 16:8).

COMMENTARY

This short ending does two things. First, it notes that the women did report to Peter (see 16:7) and others. Second, it says that Jesus sent them out to preach the sacred and unfailing message of eternal salvation. Then, with a solemn and unprecedented use of "amen," it closes.

◆   B. The Longer Ending (16:9-20)

⁹After Jesus rose from the dead early on Sunday morning, the first person who saw him was Mary Magdalene, the woman from whom he had cast out seven demons. ¹⁰She went to the disciples, who were grieving and weeping, and told them what had happened. ¹¹But when she told them that Jesus was alive and she had seen him, they didn't believe her.

¹²Afterward he appeared in a different form to two of his followers who were walking from Jerusalem into the country. ¹³They rushed back to tell the others, but no one believed them.

¹⁴Still later he appeared to the eleven disciples as they were eating together. He rebuked them for their stubborn unbelief because they refused to believe those who had seen him after he had been raised from the dead.*

¹⁵And then he told them, "Go into all the world and preach the Good News to everyone. ¹⁶Anyone who believes and is baptized will be saved. But anyone who refuses to believe will be condemned. ¹⁷These miraculous signs will accompany those who believe: They will cast out demons in my name, and they will speak in new languages.* ¹⁸They will be able to handle snakes with safety, and if they drink anything poisonous, it won't hurt them. They will be able to place their hands on the sick, and they will be healed."

¹⁹When the Lord Jesus had finished talking with them, he was taken up into heaven and sat down in the place of honor at God's right hand. ²⁰And the disciples went everywhere and preached, and the Lord worked through them, confirming what they said by many miraculous signs.

16:14 Some early manuscripts add: *And they excused themselves, saying, "This age of lawlessness and unbelief is under Satan, who does not permit God's truth and power to conquer the evil [unclean] spirits. Therefore, reveal your justice now." This is what they said to Christ. And Christ replied to them, "The period of years of Satan's power has been fulfilled, but other dreadful things will happen soon. And I was handed over to death for those who have sinned, so that they may return to the truth and sin no more, and so they may inherit the spiritual, incorruptible, and righteous glory in heaven."* 16:17 Or *new tongues;* some manuscripts omit *new.*

NOTES

16:9 *the first person who saw him was Mary Magdalene, the woman from whom he cast out seven demons.* This description of Mary recalls Luke 8:2.

16:14 As the note at 16:8 indicates, Codex W has a long addition, which involves a defense by the disciples of their doubting response: "This age of lawlessness and unbelief is under Satan, who does not permit God's truth and power to conquer the evil spirits. Therefore reveal your justice now." In response, Jesus declared the end of Satan's power as a time fulfilled, and predicted that dreadful things would happen. He noted that he was handed over to death for those who sinned, to prevent them from sinning as they returned to the truth. The result is that they will inherit spiritual, incorruptible, and righteous glory in heaven. This terminology is uniquely distinct from the Gospels.

16:15 *Go into all the world and preach the Good News to everyone.* The expression "to everyone" in the NLT is "all the creation" in Gr., so the rendering clarifies the common meaning of the figure. "Going" is a dependent participle in the Gr., so the believers were commanded primarily to preach but that by means of their going into all the world.

16:17 *speak in new languages.* The NLT renders "tongues" as "new languages," highlighting the fresh linguistic enablement that is the gift.

16:18 *They will be able to handle snakes with safety, and if they drink anything poisonous, it won't hurt them.* Second century Jewish texts also speak of not being overcome by poison (*Testament of Joseph* 6:2; *Testament of Benjamin* 3:5; 5:2). Cf. Acts 28:3-6.

16:19 *he was taken up into heaven and sat down in the place of honor at God's right hand.* The NLT adds a reference to the right hand of God as a "place of honor," which simply explains its importance.

16:20 *the Lord worked through them.* Lit., "the Lord working with them." The Gr. term *sunergountos* [TG4903, ZG5300] means to "work together" with someone.

COMMENTARY

The traditional longer ending to Mark was composed by someone (perhaps in the second century) who drew from the other Gospels and Acts. The writer's mention that Jesus first appeared to Mary Magdalene (16:9) parallels John 20:11-18. However, the writer then goes on to say that Mary went to the disciples and told them that she had seen the risen Christ (16:10-11). This doesn't concur with John 20:1-2 or any of the other Gospels, where Mary first went to tell the disciples only that the tomb was empty. Jesus had not yet appeared. The writer then tells us that the disciples did not believe Mary (16:11). This note of a lack of faith parallels Luke 24:11, but in Luke, the angelic appearance and the empty tomb are not believed.

Following this, the writer of the longer ending wrote, "Afterward he appeared in a different form to two of his followers who were walking from Jerusalem into the country" (16:12). The Emmaus Road appearance is recorded in Luke 24:13-35. The idea that Jesus had "another form" comes from the fact that initially the two disciples on the way to Emmaus did not recognize him. The writer then says, "They rushed back to tell the others, but no one believed them" (16:13). This summarizes Luke 24:33-35, but the note of unbelief is distinct and may come from 24:34, because in Luke, the Emmaus report is trumped by the report of an appearance to Peter. There is no indication in Luke that the report was not believed.

In 16:14, the writer says, "still later he [Jesus] appeared to the eleven disciples as they were eating together." This apparently alludes to Luke 24:38-41. The text continues, "He rebuked them for their stubborn unbelief because they refused to believe those who had seen him after he had been raised from the dead." This does not allude to a specific text, but it is similar to Luke 24:11 and resembles the doubting Thomas scene (John 20:24-29). After this, Jesus told the disciples to "go into all the world and preach the Good News to everyone" (16:15). This is the longer reading's equivalent of the Great Commission recorded in Matthew 28:18-20. In the longer ending, however, Jesus says, "Anyone who believes and is baptized will be saved. But anyone who refuses to believe will be condemned" (16:16). The remark is very similar to John 3:18, 36. The text, probably a second century addition, indicates the importance of baptism in the early church.

The writer then moves to a number of items pertaining to miraculous signs. Jesus says, "These miraculous signs will accompany those who believe: They will cast out demons in my name, and they will speak in new languages" (16:17). The passage underscores the miraculous signs believers would employ in support of the gospel message. Texts such as John 14:12 and Acts 5:12 may be in view, as well as the accounts of Acts 2:3-4; 10:46; 16:18; 19:6. Some curious words follow: "They will be able to handle snakes with safety, and if they drink anything poisonous, it won't hurt them. They will be able to place their hands on the sick, and they will be healed" (16:18). The reference to snakes reflects the language of Acts 28:3-6 and Luke 10:19. The events of Acts 3:7 and 9:12, 17 point to the laying on of hands for healing.

The writer of the longer ending then records the ascension, based on Luke 24:50-53 and Acts 1:2, 9-11. He concludes with the words, "And the disciples went everywhere and preached, and the Lord worked through them, confirming what they said by many miraculous signs" (16:20). This final verse of the long ending notes the fulfillment of the commission, in that the disciples obeyed the call of 16:15 by preaching the gospel. Furthermore, what Jesus predicted would happen (16:17-18) was now happening—the Lord was confirming the disciples' work with many miraculous signs.

BIBLIOGRAPHY

Bauckham, Richard, editor
1988 *The Gospels for All Christians: Rethinking Gospel Audiences.* Grand Rapids: Eerdmans.

Blomberg, Craig
1997 *Jesus and the Gospels.* Nashville: Broadman & Holman.

Bock, Darrell L.
1994 *Luke 1:1–9:50.* Baker's Exegetical Commentary on the New Testament 3a. Grand Rapids: Baker.

1996 *Luke 9:51–24:53.* Baker's Exegetical Commentary on the New Testament 3b. Grand Rapids: Baker.

1998 *Blasphemy and Exaltation in Judaism and the Final Examination of Jesus.* Tübingen: Mohr Siebeck.

2001 "The Kingdom of God in New Testament Theology," Pp. 28-60 in *Looking into the Future: Evangelical Studies in Eschatology.* Editor, David W. Baker. Grand Rapids: Baker.

2002a *Studying the Historical Jesus.* Grand Rapids: Baker.

2002b *Jesus According to Scripture.* Grand Rapids: Baker.

Brown, Raymond E.
1997 *An Introduction to the New Testament.* The Anchor Bible Reference Library. New York: Doubleday.

Burridge, Richard A.
1992 *What Are the Gospels? A Comparison with Greco-Roman Biography.* Society for New Testament Studies Monograph Series 70. Cambridge: Cambridge University Press.

Comfort, Philip
2007 *New Testament Text and Translation Commentary.* Carol Stream: Tyndale.

Cranfield, C. E. B.
1959 *The Gospel according to Saint Mark.* The Cambridge Greek Commentary. Cambridge: Cambridge University Press.

Donahue, J. R.
1971 "Tax Collectors and Sinners: An Attempt at Identification," *Catholic Biblical Quarterly* 33:39-61.

Evans, Craig A.
2001 *Mark 8:27–16:20.* Word Biblical Commentary. Dallas: Word.

France, R. T.
2002 *The Gospel of Mark.* The New International Greek Testament Commentary. Grand Rapids: Eerdmans.

Garland, David E.
1996 *The NIV Application Commentary: Mark.* Grand Rapids: Zondervan.

Guelich, R. A.
1989 *Mark 1–8:26.* Word Biblical Commentary. Dallas: Word.

1992 "Mark." Pp. 512-525 in *Dictionary of Jesus and the Gospels.* Editors, Joel Green, Scot McKnight, and I. Howard Marshall. Downers Grove, Illinois: InterVarsity.

Gundry, Robert H.
1993 *Mark: A Commentary on His Apology for the Cross.* Grand Rapids: Eerdmans.

Guthrie, Donald
1990 *New Testament Introduction.* Rev. ed. Downers Grove: InterVarsity.

Hanson, K. C. and Douglas E. Oakman
1998 *Palestine in the Time of Jesus: Social Structures and Social Conflicts.* Minneapolis: Fortress.

Hengel, Martin
1977 *Crucifixion in the Ancient World and the Folly of the Message of the Cross.* Philadelphia: Fortress.

1981 *The Charismatic Leader and His Followers.* Translator, James C. G. Greig; editor, John Riches. Edinburgh: T & T Clark.

1985 *Studies in the Gospel of Mark.* Translator, John Bowden. London: SCM.

Hooker, Morna D.
1991 *The Gospel According to Saint Mark.* Black's New Testament Commentaries. London: A & C Black.

Hurtado, Larry
1989 *Mark.* New International Biblical Commentary. Peabody, MA: Hendrickson.

Johnson, S. E.
1960 *The Gospel according to St. Mark.* Harper's New Testament Commentaries. New York: Harpers.

Lane, William L.
1974 *The Gospel according to Mark.* New International Commentary on the New Testament. Grand Rapids: Eerdmans.

Marcus, Joel
2000 *Mark 1-8.* The Anchor Bible. New York: Doubleday.

Meier, John P.
2001 *A Marginal Jew: Rethinking the Historical Jesus.* Vol. 3, *Companions and Competitors.* The Anchor Bible Reference Library. New York: Doubleday.

Metzger, Bruce M.
1971 *A Textual Commentary on the Greek New Testament.* New York: United Bible Societies.

Nolland, John.
1993 *Luke 18:35–24:53.* Word Biblical Commentary. Dallas: Word.

Schürer, E. (G. Vermes, F. Millar, M. Black, editors)
1979 *The History of the Jewish People in the Age of Jesus Christ.* Vol. 2. Rev ed. Edinburgh: T & T Clark.

Sherwin-White, A. N.
1963 *Roman Society and Roman Law in the New Testament.* Oxford: Clarendon.

Stein, Robert H.
1987 *The Synoptic Problem.* Grand Rapids: Baker.

Strack, Herman, and Paul Billerbeck
1922–1961 *Kommentar zum Neuen Testament aus Talmud und Midrasch.* 6 vols. Munich: Beck.

Taylor, Vincent
1966 *The Gospel according to St Mark.* 2nd ed. New York: Macmillan.

Twelftree, Graham H.
1999 *Jesus the Miracle Worker: A Historical and Theological Study.* Downers Grove: InterVarsity.

Witherington III, Ben
2001 *The Gospel of Mark: A Socio-Rhetorical Commentary.* Grand Rapids: Eerdmans.